The SAGE Handbook of
Current Developments in Grounded Theory

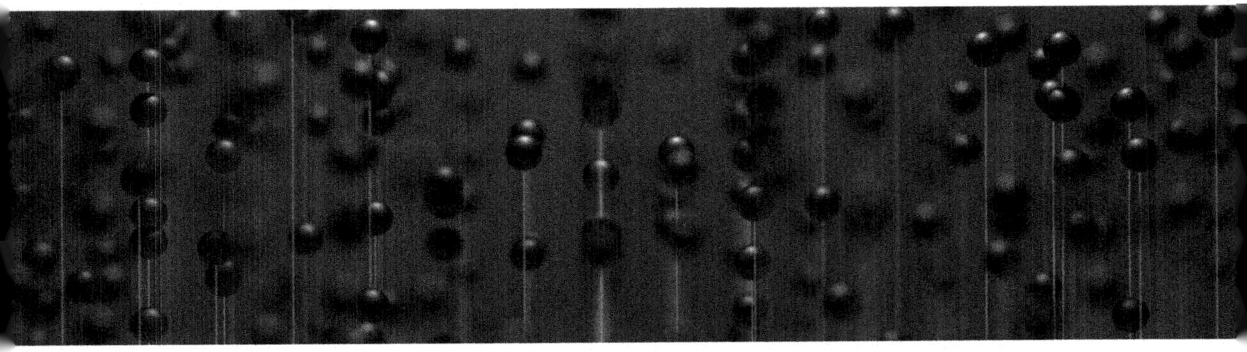

The SAGE Handbook of Current Developments in Grounded Theory

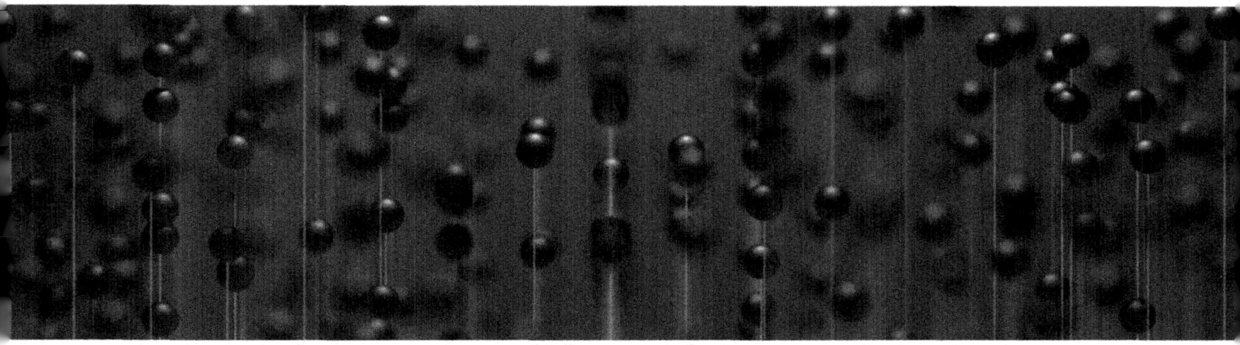

Edited by
Antony Bryant and
Kathy Charmaz

SAGE reference
Los Angeles | London | New Delhi | Singapore | Washington DC | Melbourne

SAGE

Los Angeles | London | New Delhi
Singapore | Washington DC | Melbourne

SAGE Publications Ltd
1 Oliver's Yard
55 City Road
London EC1Y 1SP

SAGE Publications Inc.
2455 Teller Road
Thousand Oaks, California 91320

SAGE Publications India Pvt Ltd
B 1/I 1 Mohan Cooperative Industrial Area
Mathura Road
New Delhi 110 044

SAGE Publications Asia-Pacific Pte Ltd
3 Church Street
#10-04 Samsung Hub
Singapore 049483

Editor: Jai Seaman
Editorial Assistant: Umeeka Raichura
Production Editor: Sushant Nailwal
Copyeditor: Sarah Bury
Proofreader: Sharon Cawood
Indexer: Caroline Eley
Marketing Manager: Ben Griffin-Sherwood
Cover Design: Bhairvi Gudka
Typeset by Cenveo Publisher Services
Printed in the UK

Library of Congress Control Number: 2018948215

British Library Cataloguing in Publication data

A catalogue record for this book is available from the British Library

978-1-4739-7095-3

Contents

List of Figures

List of Tables

Notes on the Editors and Contributors

THE EDITORS

Antony Bryant is Professor of Informatics at Leeds Beckett University. He has published widely on aspects of Information Management and Digital Technology and is a senior member on the editorial board of several major journals. He has worked with Kathy Charmaz for many years, writing on GTM and encouraging researchers in their use of constructivist/Pragmatist forms of the method. Professor Bryant has supervised or examined more than 50 PhDs, many of them using GTM in one form or another. His most recent publications on GTM include *Grounded Theory and Grounded Theorizing* (Oxford University Press, 2017) and *The Varieties of Grounded Theory* (SAGE, 2019), published as part of the *Swifts* series. He is Senior Editor of both *The SAGE Handbook of Grounded Theory* (2007) and *The SAGE Handbook of Current Developments in Grounded Theory.*

Kathy Charmaz is Professor Emerita of Sociology and the former Director of the Faculty Writing Program at Sonoma State University. She received her doctoral degree from the University of California, San Francisco, where she studied with Anselm Strauss and Barney Glaser. She has written, co-authored, or co-edited 14 books, including two award-winning works: *Good Days, Bad Days: The Self in Illness and Time* and *Constructing Grounded Theory*. Professor Charmaz has also written or co-authored over 50 articles and chapters about qualitative research. She received the George Herbert Mead award for Lifetime Achievement from the Society for the Study of Symbolic Interaction, the Leo G. Reeder award for distinguished contributions from the Medical Sociology Section of the American Sociological Association and the Lifetime Achievement award from the International Congress of Qualitative Inquiry. Professor Charmaz gives workshops on qualitative methods, grounded theory, symbolic interactionism, medical sociology, and scholarly writing around the globe.

THE CONTRIBUTORS

Roxanne Bainbridge is from the Gungarri/Kunja nations of South Western Queensland. She is a Professorial Research Fellow in Indigenous Health and Director of the Centre for Indigenous Health Equity Research at Central Queensland University Australia where she is responsible for the Centre's strategic and operational leadership. She is also a global Atlantic Fellow for Social Equity; and Associate Editor for the Health Promotion

Journal of Australia. Roxanne holds a National Health and Medical Research Council Career Development Fellowship that focusses on mental health for Aboriginal and Torres Strait Islander adolescents. Her discipline is Medical Anthropology, and, her methodological expertise is in community-driven, high-impact applied research conducted in participatory action-oriented research approaches and systems sciences. She uses her research expertise to contribute to raising the health and prosperity of Aboriginal and Torres Strait nations in Australia. Roxanne is a strong advocate for Aboriginal community-controlled health and committed to improving the integrity and quality of research to maximise its impact and benefit to society. Her specific proficiencies are in research impact assessment and evaluation; integrated quality improvement; grounded theory; evidence reviews; and auto/ethnographic approaches.

Linda Liska Belgrave is an Associate Professor of Sociology in the Department of Sociology at the University of Miami. Her scholarly interests include grounded theory, medical sociology, social psychology, and social justice. She has pursued research on the daily lives of African-American caregivers of families with Alzheimer's disease, the conceptualization of successful aging, and academic freedom. Most recently, she has explored the social meanings of infectious disease.

Melanie Birks is Professor and Head of Nursing and Midwifery at James Cook University. She has extensive experience and expertise in educational administration, teaching and curriculum development in local, international, military, and civilian environments. Her research interests are in the areas of health professional education and workforce issues. Melanie is passionate about producing graduates who make a positive contribution to the healthcare system. Her track record in research, grant success, and consultancies demonstrates her determination to advance scholarship. This commitment is reflected in her extensive publication record, which includes over 100 peer-reviewed publications. Melanie is internationally recognized as an expert in grounded theory methodology. She is co-author with Jane Mills of a number of textbooks, including *Grounded Theory: A Practical Guide* (2011 and 2015) and *Qualitative Methodology: A Practical Guide* (2014).

Stacy M. Carter is Professor and Director of the Australian Centre for Health Engagement, Evidence and Values (ACHEEV) in the School of Health and Society at the University of Wollongong, Australia. ACHEEV focuses on developing new approaches to address contentious health problems, including vaccine refusal, screening, anti-microbial resistance, and especially overdiagnosis. She is a member of the Wiser Healthcare Collaboration (wiserhealthcare.org.au), is Associate Editor for the journals Public Health Ethics and BMC Medical Ethics, and tweets sporadically @stacymcarter.

Lauren Clark is Professor of Nursing at the University of Utah with a background in medical anthropology and community health nursing. She studies the cultural dimensions of health behavior using ethnography and grounded theory. Her previously published research addresses disability/disabling chronic conditions and healthy lifestyle behaviors among health disparity groups.

Adele E. Clarke is Professor Emerita of Sociology and History of Health Sciences at UC, San Francisco. She completed her PhD with Anselm Strauss, has used grounded theory since 1980, and developed situational analysis as an extension of it. Her book *Situational Analysis: Grounded Theory after the Postmodern Turn* (Sage, 2005) won the Cooley Distinguished Book Award, Society for the Study of Symbolic Interaction. A second edition was published in 2018 with Carrie Friese and Rachel Washburn as co-authors. They also co-edited a reader, *Situational Analysis in Practice* (Routledge, 2015). Clarke received the 2013 Bernal Prize for Outstanding Contributions from the Society for Social Studies of Science and the 2015 Reeder Award for Distinguished Contributions to Medical Sociology. Her research centered on social, cultural, and historical studies of science, technology, and medicine, especially biomedicalization and technologies for women. She continues to publish on situational analysis and reproductive politics.

Joanna Crossman is an Adjunct Associate Professor at the Business School, University of South Australia and Pro Vice Chancellor: Scholarship & Innovation at ICMS in Sydney. Joanna is a member of the Centre for Workplace Excellence at the University of South Australia and the recipient of a number of awards for internationalisation, teaching and learning and research. Her international career in Scandinavia, the UAE, Malaysia, the UK and Australia has included the general management of an international company, various directorships, the management of a successful accreditation consultancy, educational management and a range of academic positions. She has authored 58 peer reviewed publications in the form of journal papers (*The Journal of Business Ethics, Higher Education, Higher Education Research & Development and The Oxford Review of Education*), book chapters, and research and teaching texts, largely concerned with business ethics and workplace spirituality, internationalisation, communication, interculturality and experiential education. Joanna is also the co-editor of the Emerald journal, Journal of International Education in Business.

Norman K. Denzin is Distinguished Professor of Communications, College of Communications Scholar, and Research Professor of Communications, Sociology, and Humanities at the University of Illinois, Urbana-Champaign. He is the author or editor of more than two dozen books, including *The Qualitative Manifesto* (Routledge, 2010); *Qualitative Inquiry Under Fire* (Routledge, 2009); *Reading Race* (Sage, 2002); *Interpretive Autoethnography* (Sage, 2014); *The Cinematic Society: The Voyeur's Gaze* (Sage, 1995); and four books on the American West. He is past editor of *The Sociological Quarterly*, co-editor (with Yvonna S. Lincoln) of five editions of the *SAGE Handbook of Qualitative Research*, co-editor (with Lincoln) of the methods journal *Qualitative Inquiry*, founding editor of *Cultural Studies*, *Critical Methodologies* and *International Review of Qualitative Research*, and founding director of the International Congress of Qualitative Inquiry.

Joyce M. Duckles is an Assistant Professor of Human Development at the Warner School of Education and Human Development, Dr. Joyce Duckles specializes in family studies, community development, informal learning, and participatory research practices. She conducts research on family engagement and community development through critical grounded theory inquiry and community-based participatory research practices. Her recent scholarship interests include a seven-year ethnographic collaborative project on urban transformation in the Beechwood community, the Growing a Healthy Community project supporting the sustainable development of locally grown food, businesses and community spaces, and developing and researching the ENGOAL program, a collaborative endeavor with colleagues from the Warner School and the School of Nursing to train and support older adults as health researchers. She has presented widely on the relational strategies and models of transformation emerging from these projects, on supporting neighborhood and family well-being, and on addressing the inequalities and disparities across community and health through re-framing notions of collaborative research and publicly engaged scholarship.

Ciarán Dunne is an Assistant Professor in Dublin City University, Ireland, where he lectures across several disciplines, including Sociology, Social Entrepreneurship, Research Methods, Creative Thinking, Spanish language, and Intercultural Studies. He has a strong interest in building meaningful connections between academia and broader society, with the specific aim of tackling social issues. He collaborates with multiple organisations in the field of social innovation, where he promotes qualitative research as a key component in identifying and understanding the challenges, needs and opportunities facing individuals and groups.

Uwe Flick is Professor of Qualitative Research in Social Science and Education at the Freie Universität Berlin, Germany. His main research interests are qualitative methods, social representations in the fields of individual and public health, vulnerable groups such as homeless adolescents, or migrants and refugees, and technological change in everyday life. He is the author of *Introducing Research Methodology: A Beginner's Guide to Doing a Research Project* (2nd ed., Sage, 2015) and editor of *A Companion to Qualitative Research* (Sage, 2004), *The SAGE Handbook of Qualitative Data Analysis* (Sage, 2014), and the *Psychology of the Social* (Cambridge University Press, 1998). Most recently, he wrote *Designing Qualitative Research* (2nd ed., Sage, 2018), *Doing Grounded Theory* (Sage, 2018), *Doing Triangulation and Mixed Methods* (Sage, 2018), *Managing Quality in Qualitative Research* (2nd ed., Sage, 2018), and *An Introduction to Qualitive Research* (6th ed., Sage, 2018), and he has edited *The SAGE Qualitative Research Kit* (2nd ed., Sage) and the *The SAGE Handbook of Qualitative Data Collection* (Sage, 2018).

Hilary Flowers is a doctoral candidate in the Department of Sociology, University of California, Los Angeles. Her research interests include the subfields of gender, social demography, and the family.

Susanne Friese started working with computer software for qualitative data analysis in 1992. Her initial contact with CAQDAS tools was from 1992 to 1994, as she was employed at Qualis Research in the USA. In following years, she worked with the CAQDAS Project in England (1994–1996), where she taught classes on The Ethnograph and Nud*ist (today NVivo). Two additional software programs, MAXQDA and ATLAS.ti, followed shortly. Susanne has accompanied numerous projects around the world in a consulting capacity, authored didactic materials, and is the author of the ATLAS.ti User's Manual, sample projects and other documentations. The third edition of her book *Qualitative Data Analysis with ATLAS.ti* will be published in 2019 with SAGE. Susanne's academic home is the Max Planck Institute for the Study of Religious and Ethnic Diversity in Göttingen (Germany), where she pursues her methodological interest, especially with regard to computer-assisted qualitative data analysis.

Jane F. Gilgun is a Professor at the School of Social Work, University of Minnesota, Twin Cities, USA. She has done qualitative research since her graduate school days in the early 1980s. She has published many articles on qualitative methods as well as research articles and books based on qualitative methods. She has lectured and consulted locally, nationally, and internationally on qualitative methods. She has specialized in grounded theory, deductive qualitative analysis, and descriptive research associated with the Chicago School of Sociology. This research seeks to understand the experiences and the meanings persons give to their experiences. Researchers can move to theory-testing and theory-generation once they have developed descriptive material organized by categories, or they can conclude their research with descriptions. Professor Gilgun is past president of the International Association of Qualitative Inquiry (2012–2015). She is the founding director of Social Work Day, which has taken place each May for eight years at the International Congress on Qualitative Inquiry, held in Urbana-Champaign, IL. She is the editor of *Qualitative Inquiry in Social Work*, a publication of Social Work Day, and is editor of a special collection of articles from Social Work Day to be published in *Qualitative Social Work: Research and Practice.* Her areas of research are resilience or how people overcome adversities, factors associated with good outcomes when children have experienced complex trauma, the development of violent behaviors, the meanings of violence to perpetrators, and an oral history of a progressive Christian church. Professor Gilgun has a PhD in Child and Family Studies from Syracuse University, a master's in social work from the University of Chicago, a licentiate in family studies and human sexuality from the Catholic University of Louvain, Louvain, Belgium, and a bachelor's and master's degree in British and American Literature from the Catholic University of American in Washington, DC, and the University of Rhode Island, Kingston, RI, respectively.

Barney Glaser received his BA degree at Stanford University in 1952. He studied contemporary literature for a year at the Sorbonne, University of Paris, and spent 2 years in the US Army, one of which was in Freiburg, Germany. Here, he became fluent in German and also studied literature at the University of Freiburg during off hours. Dr. Glaser received his PhD from Columbia University in 1961, following which he joined Anselm Strauss at the University of California San Francisco. He and Strauss collaborated in doing the dying in hospitals study and in teaching methods and analysis to PhD and DNS students. Glaser's dissertation was published as a book, *Organizational Scientists: Their Professional Careers* (Bobbs-Merrill, 1964). In 1968, he published *Organizational Careers: A Sourcebook for Theory* (Aldine, 1968). His work with Anselm Strauss resulted in the 1965 publication of *Awareness of Dying* (Aldine) and was immediately a resounding success. Based on the tremendous interest in the study of the dying, Glaser and Strauss were asked to write *The Discovery of Grounded Theory* (1967) to show how the research had been done. This was another big success and as the seminal guide to grounded theory methodology is still in demand 40 years later. Glaser and Strauss followed the publication of *Discovery* with two more books on dying: *Time for Dying* (1968) and *Anguish* (1970) followed by *Status Passage* (1971) and *Chronic Illness and the Quality of Life* (1975). For the past 30 years, Dr. Glaser has written extensively on classic grounded theory producing a further thirteen books. His works are read throughout the world. Most are now published by Sociology Press. In addition to his books, Glaser has written countless articles and has become the source of guidance and inspiration for a global network of researchers seeking to study the methodology and undertake classic grounded theory research. To respond to the need and demand for methodological guidance, Glaser continues to offer annual grounded theory troubleshooting seminars that attract both novice and experienced researchers from around the world. In recognition of his contribution to the research community, Dr. Glaser received an honorary doctorate from Stockholm University, Sweden in 1998.

Andrea Gorra received her PhD in 2008 from Leeds Metropolitan University, using the grounded theory methodology to research the ethical implications of mobile phone location tracking, under the supervision of Professors Tony Bryant and Edward Halpin. Born in Germany, she holds a degree in Business-Computing (Dortmund, Germany) and an MSc E-commerce (Leeds, UK). She worked at Leeds Beckett University as a Researcher for the Centre for Excellence in Teaching and Learning - Active Learning in Computing, UK (2006-2009) and as Principal Lecturer at Leeds Business School (2010-2017), teaching, developing and managing a range of courses and programs on-campus and online. Andrea has published in the areas of pedagogy and e-learning, and co-edited the book 'Disabled Students in Education: Technology, Transition and Inclusivity' (2011). She is an experienced PhD supervisor and has contributed to the following books by sharing her grounded theory coding strategies:

- Bryant, Antony (2017) The Grounded Theory Method: Pragmatism in Research Practice. New York, NY Oxford University Press.
- Birks, Melanie & Mills, Jane (2015). Grounded theory: a practical guide. London, SAGE.

Andrea has recently moved to Ottawa, Canada, where she currently works for Carleton University.

Gregory Hadley is a Professor of Applied Linguistics and Western Cultural Studies at Niigata University, Japan, and a Visiting Fellow at The University of Oxford (Kellogg). He has written a number of works on grounded theory, including *Grounded Theory in Applied Linguistics Research: A Practical Guide* (Routledge, 2017) and *English for Academic Purposes in Neoliberal Universities: A Critical Grounded Theory* (Springer, 2015). His professional website can be found at http://www2.human.niigata-u.ac.jp/~ghadley/main/

Sharlene Hesse-Biber is a Professor of Sociology and Director of the Women's & Gender Studies Program at Boston College in Chestnut Hill, Massachusetts. Dr. Hesse-Biber has written widely on methods issues, including a particular interest in the role of technology and emergent methods in social research. To name just a few, she has authored *Mixed Methods Research: Merging Theory with Practice* (Guilford, 2010), contributed to both *Handbook of Grounded Theory* (Sage, 2008) and *Handbook of Mixed Methods Research* (Sage second edition, 2010), and edited *Handbook of Feminist Research: Theory and Praxis* (Sage, 2007; 2012). Most recently, Dr. Hesse-Biber has co-edited *The Oxford Handbook of Multi and Mixed Methods Research* (Oxford, 2015) as well as released her monograph on women and genetic testing, *Waiting for Cancer to Come: Genetic Testing and Women's Medical Decision Making for Hereditary Breast and Ovarian Cancer,* (2014) with The University of Michigan Press. In addition to this, she has co-developed the software program HyperRESEARCH, a computer-assisted program for analyzing qualitative data, and the new transcription tool HyperTRANSCRIBE.

Judith A. Holton is an Associate Professor of Management with the Ron Joyce Centre for Business Studies at Mount Allison University, Sackville, NB, Canada, where she teaches courses in leadership and strategy. Dr Holton has worked closely with Barney Glaser as co-author and as grounded theory seminar leader. She has led several seminars, including seminars in Canada, the UK, Sweden, and Hong Kong. She has written a number of methodological papers and books about classic grounded theory and is author (with Isabelle Walsh) of *Classic Grounded Theory: Applications with Qualitative and Quantitative Data* (Sage, 2017). As the founding editor of *The Grounded Theory Review* (2004–2011), a research journal dedicated to classic grounded theory research, Dr Holton was instrumental in furthering the advancement of classic grounded theory and encouraging and mentoring emerging grounded theorists throughout the world to publish their research.

Mitsuyuki Inaba is a Professor at the College of Policy Science, Ritsumeikan University in Osaka, Japan. His research interests include Computational Linguistics, Digital Humanities, and Digital Forensics. He has published many article and research papers applying Text Mining and Computer-Assisted Qualitative Data Analysis Software (CAQDAS) to the fields of forensic science and learning science. He is an executive board member of Japan Society of Mixed Methods Research (JSMMR), ADHO (Alliance of Digital Humanities Organizations) centerNet international committee, and ADHO Multi-Lingual and Multi-Cultural committee. He is also a member of the Association for Computing Machinery (ACM), Japanese Society of Artificial Intelligence (JSAI), Japanese Cognitive Science Society (JCSS), and other academic associations.

Katherine Irwin is a Professor of Sociology at the University of Hawai'i, Manoa. Her research areas include gender, race, and class inequalities, youth culture, women and drug use, youth violence, girls in the juvenile justice system, and delinquency prevention programming. She is the co-author, with Meda Chesney-Lind, of *Beyond Bad Girls: Gender, Violence, and Hype*. Her most recent book with Karen Umemoto is titled *Jacked Up and Unjust: Pacific Islander Teens Confront Violent Legacies* and is the 2018 winner of ASA's Asian America outstanding book award.

R. Burke Johnson is a Professor in the Department of Counseling and Instructional Sciences, University of South Alabama, USA. He is a research methodologist who has written extensively in the areas of mixed methods and multimethod research. He is co-author or co-editor of multiple books, three of which are *The Oxford Handbook of Multimethod and Mixed Methods Research Inquiry* (Oxford University Press, 2015), *Educational Research: Quantitative, Qualitative, and Mixed Approaches* (6th ed., Sage, 2014), and *Research Methods, Design, and Analysis* (12th ed., Pearson, 2014). Burke has Master's degrees in psychology, sociology, and public administration, and a PhD in an interdisciplinary methodology program. This training has enabled Burke to bring an interdisciplinary perspective to methods, methodology, paradigms, and philosophy of social science. For more information, see www.southalabama.edu/colleges/ceps/faculty/johnson.html

Hisako Kakai is a Professor of International Communication in School of International Politics, Economics, and Communication at Aoyama Gakuin University in Tokyo. Her research interests include research methodology and culture's influence on cancer communication and medical decision making. In her research, Hisako has been using both qualitative and quantitative approaches. She has published numerous journal articles and books in both English and Japanese. She co-translated into Japanese *Constructing Grounded Theory: A practical guide through qualitative analysis* by Kathy Charmaz (2006). Hisako is an editorial board member for the *Journal of Mixed Methods Research*. From 2015 to 2017, she served as the founding President of the Japan Society for Mixed Methods Research (JSMMR), the first and sole mixed methods academic association in Japan.

Udo Kelle is a Professor for Social Research Methods and Statistics at the Helmut-Schmidt-University in Hamburg, Germany. He received his doctoral degree 1992 at the Special Collaborative Center 186 of the German National Science Foundation about life course research and his venia legendi in sociology at the University of Bremen in 2005. From 1996 until 2005 he was Lecturer in Research Methods at the University of Vechta, and between 2005 and 2010 Professor for Social Research Methods at Philipps University, Marburg. His research interests cover the fields of social research methodology and their epistemological underpinnings, the relation between qualitative and quantitative methods ('Mixed Methods'), life course research, and the sociology of religion.

Krzysztof T. Konecki is a Full Professor and Vice Dean for Research at the Faculty of Economics and Sociology, University of Lodz. He is also the head of the Sociology of Organization and Management Department. His interests lie in qualitative sociology, symbolic interactionism, grounded theory, the methodology of social sciences, visual sociology, communication and intercultural management, organizational culture and management, phenomenological research, and contemplative studies. He is the editor-in-chief of *Qualitative Sociology Review* and he holds the position of President of Polish Sociological Association and is a member of Board of European Society for Study of Symbolic Interaction. Professor Krzysztof T. Konecki is a hatha-yoga instructor and published the book *Is the Body the Temple of the Soul? Modern Yoga Practice as a Psychosocial Phenomenon (2015)*. Most recently he wrote *Advances in Contemplative Social Research (2018)*.

Vivian B. Martin is Professor and Chair of Journalism, Central Connecticut State University. A former newspaper reporter and magazine writer, she developed a theory on *purposive news-attending* for her doctoral work. Her current interest is formal grounded theory. She is a fellow of the Grounded Theory Institute. Along with Astrid Gynnild, she co-edited *Grounded Theory: The Philosophy, Method, and Work of Barney Glaser*.

Janya McCalman is a National Health and Medical Research Fellow at Central Queensland University. She has methodological expertise in participatory and action-oriented research for improving the quality of services and environments that support Indigenous resilience and empowerment. She has utilised situational maps, social worlds analysis and constructivist grounded theory methods to identify improvement pathways in collaboration with Indigenous health services, schools and other organisations, and in response to their priority issues. She has also applied grounded theory methods to systematic reviews of the literature.

Günter Mey is a Professor for Developmental Psychology at the University Magdeburg-Stendal and Director of the Berlin Institute for Qualitative Research. He is responsible for the annual 'Berlin Meeting on Qualitative Research' and editor of *Forum Qualitative Sozialforschung / Forum: Qualitative Social Research* (*FQS*). His main research areas are childhood studies, youth culture, and generational ordering. His methodological focus is grounded theory methodology (GTM), and he is especially interested in linking GTM and visual methods as well as GTM and narrative psychology. Together with Katja Mruck, he co-edited *The Grounded Theory Reader* and *The German Handbook on Qualitative Research in Psychology* (both published by Springer). For further information see: www.humanwissenschaften.hs-magdeburg.de/l/~xmey or www.institut.qualitative-forschung.de.

Jane Mills is the Pro Vice Chancellor, College of Health at Massey University, New Zealand. Considered one of Australia's foremost primary healthcare academics, with extensive experience leading and managing teams in both government and tertiary sectors, her research portfolio focuses on rural and public health, the health workforce, and health system strengthening. With a career vision to improve the health and wellbeing of individuals, families, and communities, Professor Mills believes education and research are powerful vehicles for change that makes a positive difference. She is an internationally recognized grounded theorist who, along with Professor Melanie Birks, wrote the popular text *Grounded Theory: A Practical Guide*. This work has furthered the development of the fundamental grounded theory methods of theoretical coding and storyline analysis. The original text has over 1,500 citations and has been reprinted several times since its publication in 2011. A second edition was released in February 2015.

Janice M. Morse (RN, PhD(Nurs), PhD (Anthro) FAAN) is a professor and the Barnes Presidential Endowed Chair at the College of Nursing, University of Utah. She was previously a professor and the Founder, Director and Scientific Director of the International Institute for Qualitative Methodology at the University of Alberta, Canada, and Professor at The Pennsylvania State University. She serves as editor of *Qualitative Health Research* (Sage) and has authored many books on qualitative methods.

George Moses is an experienced community-based activist, researcher and executive who understands the need to balance scholarly research with the practical application needed for positive transformation in challenged communities. As Executive Director of a North East Area Development (a local CBO), George brings to the organization over 20 years of experience in grass roots community development and many years of experience in neighborhood organizing and empowerment. He is developer and spokesperson for the "Smart Choices" Anti-Drug Dealer Initiative, a collaborative between the Rochester Police Department and the Neighborhood Empowerment Team. He is the key liaison for the establishment of the 1st Western New York Children's Defense Fund Freedom Schools and a spokesperson for the Children's Defense Fund "Dismantling the Cradle to Prison Pipeline" initiative. He is recognized for his ability to build consensus among diverse constituencies and to consistently bring to fruition neighborhood initiatives. He has presented nationally and internationally and published widely on CBPR practices, housing and neighborhood development practices and policies, and creating sustainable initiatives to support families and youth.

Robert Moses is the Director of Economic Development for North East Area Development, Inc., Robert Moses embraces the principles of cooperative economics and self-determination as he studies and constructs pathways to entrepreneurship and employment for local youth and adults. Rob has collaborated for seven years as a community-university activist, co-researcher, co-implementer and co-author on multiple community-based participatory research projects. His scholarship includes a critical ethnographic study of urban transformation, a study on food insecurity and food access, and research on supporting transformational pathways and spaces for collective community engagement. He has presented on CBPR practices and entrepreneurship at academic and policy conferences and has co-authored multiple book chapters and journal articles on creating and sustaining interdependent hubs and transformational pathways in urban communities.

Katja Mruck has a PhD in Psychology and is an expert both for qualitative methods and for open-access publishing. She is the main editor of the journal *Forum Qualitative Sozialforschung / Forum: Qualitative Social Research (FQS),* director of the Berlin Institute for Qualitative Research, and part of the e-publishing/open access team at Freie Universität Berlin. Together with Günter Mey, she co-edited *The Grounded Theory Reader* and *The German Handbook on Qualitative Research in Psychology* (both published by Springer). For further information see www.qualitative-research.net/ and www.qualitative-forschung.de.

Hiroko Noma is an Associate Professor at Faculty of Foreign Studies, Bunkyo Gakuin University in Tokyo, where she teaches undergraduate and postgraduate courses primarily in management and intercultural communication. Her research interests are in interculturality, interpersonal communication, trust and emotions in organisational settings. She has published a number of articles on intercultural communication in Japanese multinationals and interpersonal trust in the workplace. Her areas of expertise also include industrial counselling, and her current research projects focus on the role and influence of emotions in the trust process at work, and emotional labour of primary and secondary school teachers in Japan.

Kumar Ravi Priya has been serving as a Professor of Psychology at the Department of Humanities and Social Sciences at the Indian Institute of Technology Kanpur, India, since November 2018. He is a Fulbright-Nehru Academic and Professional Fellowship Awardee, 2017–2018 at Connecticut College, USA. Utilizing ethnography and grounded theory methodologies, he has studied mental health from interdisciplinary perspectives (that focuses on experiences of social suffering and healing) among the survivors of communal and political violence and natural disasters in India. Dr Priya has published in journals, such as *Theory and Psychology*, *Culture, Medicine and Psychiatry*, *Qualitative Research*, *Qualitative Health Research*, *Qualitative Research in Psychology*, *Economic and Political Weekly*, *Journal of Health Management*, *Psychology and Developing Societies*, *Psychological Studies*, and *Eastern Anthropologist*. He has co-edited *Qualitative Research on Illness, Wellbeing and Self-Growth: Contemporary Indian Perspective* (Routledge, Taylor & Francis, 2015).

Michelle Redman-MacLaren is a public health researcher known for her ability to facilitate action-oriented research for positive health outcomes. She achieves this through participatory, decolonising health research with Pacific Islander and Indigenous Australian peoples sensitive to culture, spirituality and gender. For her PhD research, Michelle innovated a critical grounded theory methodology. Transformational grounded theory encompasses ontological offerings of critical realism informed by participatory action research and decolonising research methodologies. This approach to grounded theory was used to identify the implications of male circumcision practices with women in PNG, including women's risk of HIV transmission.

Jo Reichertz, born in 1949, is a Professor of Communication Science and Sociology. He has studied mathematics, sociology and communication science at the Universities of Bonn, Essen, and Hagen. He held a professorship at the University of Essen from 1992 until 2015. His focus of research covers the sociology of communication, sociology of science, sociology of knowledge, sociology of culture, qualitative research, and hermeneutics. His publications include *The power of words and the media.* (VS Verlag 3rd ed. 2014), *Power of communication. What is communication and what is it capable of? And why can it do that?* (VS Verlag, 2009), *The significance of abduction in social research. About the discovery of the new.* (Springer 2nd ed., 2013), *Interpret together. The group interpretation as a communicative process.*(Springer, 2013), *Qualitative and interpretative social research. An invitation* (Springer, 2016). He has held several guest professorships in Austria at the University of Vienna (Sociology) and in Switzerland at the University of St Gallen (Sociology). Since 2015 he has held a Senior Fellowship and is a member of the Board of Directors of the Institute for Advanced Study in the Humanities, Essen, and is the head of the research area Culture of Communication.

Kapriskie Seide is a doctoral student in the Department of Sociology at the University of Miami. Her scholarly work lies in two programmatic areas, medical sociology and race/ethnic relations. She is interested in exploring the ways in which social contexts at micro and macro levels (e.g. epidemics, natural disasters, and migration) affect health outcomes, particularly for racial/ethnic minorities and people living with disabilities in the US, the Caribbean and Latin America.

Jörg Strübing is a Professor of sociology at the Department of Sociology University of Tübingen, Germany. He served at University of Kassel, both Free and Technical University of Berlin and at the University of Illinois, Urbana Champaign. His research is on qualitative methods and methodologies, the theoretical link between pragmatism and practice theories, and on practices of digital self-tracking. Recent publications include: *Anselm Strauss* (Universitätsverlag Konstanz, 2007), *Qualitative Social Research: A Textbook* (*Qualitative Sozialforschung*, 2nd ed., de Gruyter/Oldenbourg 2018), *Grounded Theory* (3rd ed., 2014), *Where is the Meat/d? Pragmatism and Practice Theory* (Campus, 2017), *Living on Numbers* (Leben nach Zahlen, transcript, 2016; co-edited); *Criteria for Qualitative Research: A Stimulus for Discussion* (Zeitschrift für Soziologie, 47: 83-100, 2018; co-authored).

Massimiliano Tarozzi is currently Co-director of the Development Education Research Centre at UCL – Institute of Education. He is also associate professor at the Department for Life Quality Studies, University of Bologna, where he completed a PhD in Education.

He has taught qualitative research methods for years and is also regularly invited to lead seminars on GTM in doctoral programmes in Italy and in several universities worldwide, including the US, Brazil, Argentina, and China. He has been the editor of *Encyclopaideia: Journal of Phenomenology and Education* for more than 10 years (now co-editor) and is a member of the editorial board of several qualitative research journals. He has intensively written on GTM. Among his publications is *Che cos'è la grounded theory* (2008, six reprints and translated into Portuguese) and he has translated into Italian Glaser & Strauss, *The Discovery of Grounded Theory* (2009), with a conversation with B. Glaser, which was also translated into English and German. One of his articles about translating GTM has been re-published in A. Clarke & K. Charmaz *Grounded Theory and Situational Analysis* (Sage, 2014). A new book, *What is Grounded Theory*, is currently in press for Bloomsbury.

Iddo Tavory is an Associate Professor of Sociology at NYU. A sociologist of culture and an ethnographer, he is interested in the interactional patterns through which people come to construct and understand their lives across situations. His book *Abductive Analysis: Theorizing Qualitative Research* (with Stefan Timmermans, Chicago University Press, 2014) provides a pragmatist account that allows researchers to make the most of the surprises that emerge in the process of research. His second book, *Summoned* (Chicago University Press, 2016), is an ethnography of a Jewish neighborhood in Los Angeles as well as a treatise on the co-constitution of interaction, identity, and social worlds. He is currently working on an ethnography of an advertising agency in New York and co-authoring a book on pro bono work and notions of worth in the advertising world. Among other awards, Iddo has been awarded the Lewis Coser Award for theoretical agenda setting in sociology.

Robert Thornberg is Professor of Education in the Department of Behavioural Sciences and Learning at Linköping University. He is also a Board member of the Nordic Educational Research Association (NERA). His current research is on school bullying, especially with a focus on social and moral processes involved in bullying, bystander rationales, reactions and actions, and students' perspectives, experiences and explanations. His second line of research is on values education including morals, norms, and student participation in everyday school life. A third line of research is on teacher education, especially student teachers' motives to become a teacher and their experiences of distressed situations during teacher training. Professor Thornberg uses a range of research methods such as qualitative interviewing, focus groups, questionnaires, and ethnographic fieldwork but has a particular expertise in GTM. He has published numerous articles in a range of peer-reviewed journals and written and co-authored book chapters on GTM in various method books.

Stefan Timmermans is Professor of Sociology at UCLA. His research interests include medical sociology and science studies. He has conducted research on medical technologies, health professions, death and dying, and population health. He is the author, most recently, of *Postmortem: How Medical Examiners Explain Suspicious Deaths* (Chicago University Press, 2006), *Saving Babies? The Consequences of Newborn Genetic Screening* (Chicago University Press, 2013, with Mara Buchbinder) and *Abductive Analysis: Theorizing Qualitative Research* (Chicago University Press, 2014, with Iddo Tavory).

Cathy Urquhart is Professor of Digital Business at Manchester Metropolitan University Business School. Her research interests include grounded theory and qualitative research methods, and also the use of digital innovation for societal good. She has written extensively on grounded theory in the discipline of information systems since 2001, and has an international reputation for her application of grounded theory. She is the author of *Grounded Theory for Qualitative Research*, published by Sage in 2013. Details of the book can be found at: www.uk.sagepub.com/books/Book232280. Her website can be found here https://www2.mmu.ac.uk/business-school/about-us/our-staff/otehm/profile/index.php?id=899 and her email address is c.urquhart@mmu.ac.uk

Isabelle Walsh is a Distinguished Professor of Management, Associate Dean of the Digitalization Academy in SKEMA Business School – Université Côte d'Azur, France, and a Fellow of Barney Glaser's Grounded Theory Institute. Her research themes include methodological issues, Information Systems usage, quality in higher education, knowledge sharing, and change management. Her research has been published in several international top-tier outlets. She is the author of over 60 articles, books, and book chapters, several of which have won awards. Beyond her research achievements, she has extensive corporate and consultancy experience. Her teaching is aligned with her research themes. For more information, please see http://walshisabelle.com/

Mary Whiteside is a senior lecturer in Social Work and Social Policy at La Trobe University. Her research expertise lies in exploring and intervening in complex social issues, often the consequences of intergenerational trauma, using qualitative, participatory and mixed methods approaches. Her research has contributed to significant changes for individuals and communities in relation to empowerment and wellbeing at individual, family, organisation and community levels; and changes in professional practice. Mary's PhD research involved the development of grounded theory of empowerment in the context of Aboriginal Australia and made an important contribution to understanding how secondary data can be used in grounded theory studies.

Senior Editor's Introduction

In 2007 Kathy Charmaz and I edited *The Sage Handbook of Grounded Theory*, marking 40 years since Barney Glaser and Anselm Strauss published *The Discovery of Grounded Theory: Strategies for Qualitative Research*. The method has continued to advance in the interim, while retaining its challenging and innovative characteristics. Correspondingly, the chapters in the 2007 edition are still highly relevant, while the chapters in this companion volume engage with more recent developments, complementing and supplementing the earlier one, and also providing additional discussion and clarification.

One feature of GTM (the Grounded Theory Method) has been the way in which the method has grown into differing variants, not always existing happily side by side. Strauss and Corbin already saw this in the 1990s, noting that

> no inventor has permanent possession of the invention—certainly not even its name—and furthermore we would not wish to do so. No doubt we will always prefer the later versions of grounded theory that are closest to or elaborate our own, but a child once launched is very much subject to a combination of its origins and the evolving contingencies of life. Can it be otherwise with a methodology? (Strauss & Corbin, 1994: 283)

Yet in the twenty-first century, GTM continues to perplex the world of research methods. Although it is now well over 50 years since its first appearance in a series of journal articles and the publication of *Awareness of Dying* in the early to mid-1960s, it is still something of a perpetual teenager or adolescent – highly popular, challenging, and misunderstood. At the recent conference hosted by the European Society for Studies in Symbolic Interaction (EU SSI), I gave a keynote with the title 'The Really Very Curious Incident of the Grounded Theory Method: Continual Permutations of Misunderstanding'. I argued that it is quite bizarre that GTM continues to be a target of criticism, misunderstanding, and ill-judgement such a long time after its first appearance. It is simultaneously enormously popular and widely misunderstood.

The chapters that follow reflect this complex heritage. They are not intended to establish an orthodoxy for GTM; that would be to misconstrue and betray the initial motivation of Glaser and Strauss. Rather they offer readers the opportunity to understand some of the wealth of resources that now constitute the GTM body of work, with all the richness that has been building since the 1960s.

In my recent book (Bryant, 2017) I argued that GTM now needs to be seen as comprising a number of 'essences' and a number of 'accidents'. The latter largely arise from the context – social, cultural, and political – from which the method arose, and these now need to be clearly dismantled and then jettisoned. Unfortunately, such aspects often only come into focus years or decades later, and in many cases prove to be the source of much confusion and misunderstanding on all sides.

My view of the 'essences' of GTM can be stated as follows:[1]

> Coding-cum-analysis-cum-memoing – the form and strategy for coding in GTM was and remains innovative in many ways, including its starting point, and its iterative aspect; also, the link to memoing, which was absent from the earliest writings, but is now a key aspect.

Substantive and formal theory generation – this developed in part from Merton's idea that research should aim to provide theories of the middle range. In contrast to mid-twentieth-century preoccupations with hypothetical structural explanations of whole societies, Merton (1957) advocated constructing theories to explain empirical problems – both Substantive Grounded Theories and Formal Grounded Theories are examples of this.[2]

Purposive/convenience sampling followed by theoretical sampling – qualitative sampling was and still is misunderstood, particularly by those whose research experience and expertise is derived largely or wholly from a quantitative background; GTM offers a basis for clarifying sampling issues for qualitative research in general.

Theoretical saturation – often seen as a weakness of GTM, but, used correctly, it is in fact a strength of the method, since unlike many methods, it offers the rationale for claiming to have reached an interim end-point for a research endeavour.

Use of the literature – initially to establish the basis for the research, but far more importantly, to refer to and engage with the relevant literature as an additional and critical form of data against which interim or later analyses can be positioned – this is what is referred to as theoretical coding.

Criteria – fit, grab, work, modifiability; and also Charmaz's credibility, originality, resonance, usefulness

Openness to serendipity

Pragmatism – particularly the ways in which GTM now has to be understood as a method for what I have termed 'enacting abstraction and abduction'.

Some of these are important for many other, if not all other, methods, but several are specific to GTM, and their combination is certainly unique to the method. More critically, taken together they embody a distinctively persuasive, coherent, rigorous, and effective method for undertaking qualitative research.

I do not expect all the contributors to this volume to concur with this concise account, nor with all the chapters that follow; indeed, I would be amazed if that was the case. Glaser and Strauss, particularly in *Discovery*, were keen to throw down a challenge to their peers, and stir up controversy and debate. Those of us wishing to follow in their footsteps need to do likewise, but we must take care to understand the important distinction made by Albert Camus (2000 [1951]) between the *historical rebel* and *metaphysical rebel*. The former aims at perfection and some set of 'absolute values'; the latter accepts the absurdity of the drama of social existence and the 'unreasonable silence of the world', recognizing social existence and any attempts to encapsulate it as uncertain, complex, and chaotic. GTM is the research method for metaphysical rebels *par excellence*, so it is no wonder that it remains beset by controversy and discord, both from within and without; yet it continues to provide an inimitable spur and support for challenging and innovative research and conceptualization.

The initial plan for this volume was for Kathy and me to provide an editors' introduction, discussing some of the issues arising from the chapters and also considering GTM in a wider context as it has developed since 2007. As it transpired, I more than exceeded this brief and produced my own extended discussion running to over 40,000 words. Kathy offered some key critical insights as the work progressed, but decided that the best strategy was for me to publish the account under my own name. At first, I proposed it as the opening chapter for this volume, but in discussion with Jai Seaman, we decided that it would be more appropriate if it appeared as a separate but related publication (Bryant, 2019); a solution that Kathy had also suggested. Consequently, it was revised and has now been published as *The Varieties of Grounded Theory* in the SAGE Swifts series of monographs. It has retained clear references to the chapters that follow, albeit taking up a wide range of issues relating to GTM.

Notes

1 Most of the key terms are included in the *Discursive Glossary*; a more detailed account of these 'essences' can be found in Bryant (2019), the section on 'Core Characteristics of GTM'.
2 Herbert Blumer, a close colleague of Strauss in Chicago, similarly criticized 'grand theory' in his essay 'What is wrong with social theory?' (1954).

REFERENCES

Blumer, H. (1954). What is wrong with social theory? *American Sociological Review*, 19: 3–10.
Bryant, A. (2017). *Grounded Theory and Grounded Theorizing: Pragmatism in Research Practice*. Oxford: Oxford University Press.
Bryant, A. (2019). *The Varieties of Grounded Theory*. London: Sage.
Camus, A. (2000 [1951]). *The Rebel*. Harmondsworth: Penguin.
Glaser, B., & Strauss, A. (1965). *Awareness of Dying*. Chicago,IL: Aldine
Glaser, B., & Strauss, A. (1967). *Discovery of Grounded Theory: Strategies for Qualitative Research*. Chicago, IL: Aldine.
Merton, R. K. (1957). *Social Theory and Social Structure*. New York: Free Press.
Strauss, A. L., & Corbin, J. (1994). Grounded theory methodology – an overview. In N. K. Denzin & Y. S. Lincoln (Eds.), *Handbook of Qualitative Research* (1st ed.) (pp. 273–285). Thousand Oaks, CA: Sage.

Editors' Introduction

In 2007 we published *The Handbook of Grounded Theory* (Bryant & Charmaz, 2007a), comprising 27 chapters from a range of contributors that included Barney Glaser, several of the earliest cohort of students on the UCSF[1] Doctoral Programme, and representatives from the German-speaking GTM (Grounded Theory Method) tradition, whose instruction had largely come from Anselm Strauss. Taken as a whole, the volume offered a key resource for those interested in learning more about GTM, including how it could be located within the qualitative methods domain, both in terms of comparison and complementarity with other methods.

Some of the key features of that collection included discussions on GTM and pragmatism, abduction, and the relationship of GTM to critical theory, action research, and ethnography; also the ways in which GTM needed to engage with reflexivity, feminism, and racial/ethnic diversity. Since 2007 these and other issues have developed in importance for methods in general, as well as for GTM in particular. Yet the chapters from 2007 retain their significance and relevance for anyone seeking further understanding of the method and its use by experienced GT researchers. Consequently, in planning this collection we have always envisaged it as *an extension and companion volume*, rather than an updated version of its predecessor. As such we did not want simply to invite contributors to the 2007 edition to provide revised and updated chapters based on their earlier work, instead we asked them to consider significantly different submissions. In addition, we approached people who had not contributed to the 2007 edition, in many cases asking them to cover topics that had not previously been addressed specifically. We also deliberately sought contributions from those outside the English-speaking and German-speaking GT traditions.

The result is this companion volume consisting of 31 chapters grouped into six sections, although in many cases individual chapters address issues across many and varied aspects; their inclusion in one section rather than another being something of a compromise. Taken as a whole, the chapters themselves demonstrate the ways in which discussion and articulation of methods issues has developed, both with regard to GTM and across the research spectrum in general.

Our introduction and opening chapter to the 2007 volume offered an overview of the method (Bryant & Charmaz, 2007b), and discussed the historical development of GTM that also encompassed an epistemological account of the method's origins and later variants (Bryant & Charmaz, 2007c). Part I builds on this with a chapter by Adele Clarke.[2]

Clarke Clarke situates GTM in the history of qualitative inquiry since WWII, and relates its developments vis-à-vis the interpretive turn since the 1990s. Her chapter includes discussion of the ways in which GTM was marked from the start by its origins – via Strauss – in the Chicago School. She situates GTM and contrasts it with other research traditions, drawing on the ideas of a number of key social and cultural writers, including Marcuse, Habermas, Dewey, Bourdieu, Hoggart, Hall, and indirectly, Gramsci.

Part II consists of four chapters each addressing the concept of theories and theory building. Jörg Strübing focuses on Anselm Strauss and the ways in which Strauss can and should be regarded as a key figure in the social sciences, not only for his work on GTM, but also for his efforts to re-invigorate and revive Pragmatism, combined with his writings on social action, including his efforts to reconcile the macro, meso, and micro levels of sociological analysis. Strübing argues persuasively that Strauss's concept of 'trajectory' is crucial in his work, relating to all three facets of his contribution to social theory. Udo Kelle is also at pains to stress the importance of Strauss's work on action and interaction, and Kelle argues that this orientation is one key to understanding the paradigm model proposed by Strauss and Corbin in the 1990s. Kelle also provides an important and ameliorative perspective on the differences that developed between Glaser and Strauss in the 1990s. Cathy Urquhart highlights the theory-building aspects of GTM, discussing the meaning of the term 'theory' itself, as well as the ways in which substantive grounded theories (SGTs) can and might be developed into formal ones (FGTs). Finally, Jane Gilgun takes up the ways in which Glaser and Strauss's position with regards to prior knowledge, deduction, and hypotheses needs to be tempered by an understanding of the ways in which theories can be generated using deductive qualitative analysis (DQA), which she situates within the tradition of the Chicago School, and also relates to GTM.

Part III includes a wide range of chapters on GTM in practice. Uwe Flick takes up the issue of research design in the context of GTM. In common with many other contributors, he stresses the importance of the Chicago School studies undertaken by Strauss and his colleagues in the 1950s and early 1960s in the development of GTM. Flick argues that although the concept of triangulation was not specifically present in GTM, the method is readily and fruitfully open to use of triangulation, particularly as developed from Denzin's work.

Chapters 7–9 focus on two key processes in GTM: sampling and coding. Janice Morse and Lauren Clark discuss sampling, a topic that continues to provide problems for GTM researchers confronted with colleagues and others whose understanding of the term is derived from quantitative research. Morse and Clark centre their chapter on the different ways in which 'data adequacy' is established in different methods contexts. In so doing they provide a clear and coherent basis for GTM researchers in their publications. Linda Belgrave and Kapriskie Seide set themselves the task of clarifying the concept of coding in the context of GTM. They are keen to stress that although GTM incorporates a highly specific and distinctive form of coding, the early texts were somewhat ambiguous on the details of process itself, while later texts used confused and confusing terminology for key aspects, sometimes at odds with earlier statements. This confusion was then further compounded by the variants of GTM, which themselves incorporated distinctive and potentially confusing advice on coding. A further challenge in coding comes about when the data are largely or entirely in one language, but the analysis and findings need to be presented in another – in most cases English. Massimiliano Tarozzi argues that researchers in general need to take far more account of this problem, and that in discussing the issue of translating from one language to another, researchers can and should become aware of the ways in which the move from data in any language to codes and later stages of analysis involves similar forms of 'translation' even if the source and target languages are the same.

The topic of the literature review remains a contentious one for GTM, although there have been numerous clarifications over the years. Robert Thornberg and Ciarán Dunne offer their account of the ways in which literature can and should be used in GTM research, distinguishing between initial, ongoing, and final phases in referring to and engaging with relevant sources and materials. Moreover, they stress that engaging with literature as GTM research progresses is particularly important given the developing awareness of the role of abduction in GTM research.

Vivian Martin develops the theme of the role of the literature, and also echoes Thornberg and Dunne in relating abduction to the use of the literature. She establishes her argument around the development of Formal Grounded Theories (FGTs), which necessarily have to range across disciplinary boundaries and so involve engagement with a variety of sources and materials.

Melanie Birks and Jane Mills then look at the way in which the GTM process of analysis can be enhanced or facilitated by taking a storyline approach – something that was referred to by Strauss and Corbin, in the context of guiding students in their selective coding, aimed at developing credible conceptualizations. Birks and Mills argue that used effectively and imaginatively, storyline can assist researchers as they move from their initial codes towards higher levels of abstraction and related sets of concepts.

Jo Reichertz contributed a key chapter on abduction to the 2007 *Handbook*, and he has been influential in articulating the importance of abduction in the context of GTM. His new chapter updates and extends his position, offering a clear statement affirming the abductive nature of GTM, and the ways in which developments in the method from the 1990s onwards have emphasized and enhanced this aspect. On the other hand, he also offers a set of criticisms of abduction, pointing to the ways in which the term has been misconstrued and misused, particularly by those in the artificial intelligence (AI) community.

CAQDAS – Computer Aided/Assisted Qualitative Data Analysis Software – was already in widespread use when we were preparing the 2007 *Handbook*, but it is now far more prevalent and accessible, and the generation of young researchers who have come of age since 2000 take many digital tools for granted. Chapters 14 and 15 take up the topic in different but complementary ways. Suzanne Friese draws on her extensive experience with a wide variety of forms of CAQDAS, posing the question whether using GTM and CAQDAS is a 'happy pairing' or a 'remodeling' of GTM. She comes down clearly in favour of the former, although with clear warnings regarding how CAQDAS is actually used. Her chapter uses an example of GTM from Strauss and Corbin's work in the 1990s, implementing it in three well-known packages – Atlas.ti, NVivo, and MAXQDA. Andrea Gorra adds to this with her study of how a small group of current GTM researchers use digital technology, not only CAQDAS packages, but more generally. Echoing some of the points made by Friese, Gorra found that students were insightful in their use of technology, taking up and dropping various tools on the basis of how useful or distracting they proved to be, with an overall issue being the amount of time that was required to learn and become adept in tool use balanced against the potential time-saving that might result.

Mitsuyuki Inaba and Hisako Kakai take up some of the concerns of Friese and Gorra in their respective chapters, seeking to demonstrate how GTM can be used in an era of Big Data. This leads them to look at the ways in which technologies in this era provide new approaches to data analysis, using text mining, together with various forms of analytics that can help in the creation of visualizations of the data.

Krzysztof Konecki enhances Glaser's dictum 'All is data' with his discussion of visual data, albeit pointing out that for many researchers visual data are not taken seriously, when in fact they can provide a rich resource for GTM researchers. He introduces the term 'multi-slice imagining', derived from Glaser and Strauss's term 'slices of data'. But he also cautions against too simplistic an approach to visual sources, which need to be treated differently from non-visual ones. He argues that Clarke's 'situational analysis' offers a starting point, being derived from GTM while making use of visual materials in developing 'situational maps'.

The last two chapters in this section locate GTM against specific contexts, seeking in both cases to augment the conceptual reach and intensity of the method. Katherine Irwin reports on her development as a grounded theorist, having eschewed the search for a single social process in her work, while adhering to a constructivist orientation. Irwin's account demonstrates the ways in which a researcher 'un-learns' her presuppositions in the wake of her investigations but confirms her in her aspirations to develop insights that empower disempowered groups and use her work in the constant struggle for social justice. Kumar Ravi Priya reinforces many of these points, also arguing that taking a constructivist stance necessarily involves relating to social actors in the research context as co-creators. He is particularly concerned to demonstrate the ways in which this orientation – specifically eschewing disinterestedness in favour of encompassing empathy and compassion – has a positive impact on GTM research.

The two chapters in Part IV deal with some reflections on using and teaching GTM. This is an important topic, and had there been the space, it would have been useful to include several different contributions. At this stage we can only point this out and leave it to others to address in future publications. Judith Holton makes the case for what is required for a GTM researcher, and then considers the ways in which mentors and supervisors should and should not intervene in their students' projects. She reports both on her own experience and that of the many people who have attended Barney Glaser's seminars and workshops. Barney Glaser himself takes up some of these issues, accentuating the importance for GTM researchers to move from what he terms 'grounded description' to conceptualizations and grounded theories.

Part V encompasses chapters that locate GTM against qualitative research practice more generally. Norm Denzin, a key figure in the development of qualitative research since the 1970s, offers an account of GTM set against a background in which research is seen as a performance, and GTM is re-characterized as Grounded Interpretation. Denzin takes this further, being adamant that researchers must be cognizant of critical issues such as race and indigeneity, eventually advocating what he terms Grounded Indigenous Inquiry, combined with performance ethnography.

Katja Mruck and Günther Mey revisit the topic of self-reflexivity, locating GTM against a variety of other methods, such as auto-ethnography. They offer a critical analysis of a wide range of literature on reflexivity, and the ways in which different GTM writers have sought to incorporate this key process.

Sharlene Hesse-Biber and Hilary Flowers also advocate re-characterizing GTM, arguing that for feminist researchers GTM cannot evade the reality of women's lived experiences, and that this has repercussions, for example, on the generic and open-ended questions that GTM researchers should consider at the outset of their studies, and also on aspects such as sampling. They refer to this move as mixed methods research, and the next chapter by Burke Johnson and Isabelle Walsh takes up the topic. A specific concern with mixed methods is a relatively recent phenomenon, and the terminology can be confusing. Johnson and Walsh, however, offer their clarification and discussion, using the term Mixed Grounded Theory, aiming to combine GTM with some of the key features of mixed methods.

Iddo Tavory and Stefan Timmermans offer a discussion on GTM and abduction, arguing that the two are distinct approaches, each asking different questions and looking for different outcomes – although both require researchers to develop their theorizing skills, which cannot be taken for granted.

Stacy Carter, writing from the standpoint of an ethicist, and taking her lead from Kathy Charmaz' work on social justice and GTM, argues for the ways in which GTM can be enhanced with an encounter with empirical ethics, also pointing out how the latter can benefit from engaging with GTM. Whereas some have argued that GTM leaves things as they are, because it takes existing data and appears simply to let the data speak for itself without taking any critical stance, others have emphatically countered this and deliberately re-oriented GTM to put social justice and other concerns at the centre. Carter takes this one step further, arguing that the received wisdom that sees a stark distinction or dichotomy between the descriptive and the normative – i.e. the 'is' and the 'ought' – needs to be jettisoned and replaced by an interweaving and incorporating of the two. Gregory Hadley takes a similar position, arguing that GTM needs to take a critical turn through some form of engagement with critical social theory (CST). On the other hand, he also recognizes that in so doing GTM researchers may be forcing their investigations to fit preconceived categories, running counter to one of the key characteristics of the method. His discussion encompasses both the common points, complementarities, and the incompatibilities of GTM and CST.

Part VI consists of three chapters that look at GTM from a global perspective, in some regards developing themes and ideas present in some of the chapters in the earlier sections. Joanna Crossman and Hiroko Noma discuss the implications of internationalization, highlighting the issues that have arisen from the export of GTM to parts of the world where the faculty, researchers, and students are largely non-American and non-European, and where cultural and linguistic issues – largely taken for granted in North America and Western Europe – loom large. Their discussion takes up the challenge posed by Kathy Charmaz, who has pointed out the almost complete disregard by grounded theorists of the cultural assumptions that underlie the method. Roxanne Bainbridge, Janya McCalman, Michelle Redman-MacLaren, and Mary Whiteside develop this line of thought, outlining their work, which is based on their decolonizing variation of GTM. They draw on their research in Indigenous Australian and Pacific contexts, showing how GTM as a decolonizing tool can provide fresh perspectives on globalization and indigeneity. Joyce M. Duckles, George Moses, and Robert Moses enhance these ideas, derived from their longitudinal urban ethnographic study, focusing their chapter on the ways in which GTM, clearly drawing on its roots in Symbolic Interactionism and Pragmatism, has a place in both community-based participatory research and practices of community development.

The volume finally includes a *Discursive Glossary* covering GTM terminology, it is largely derived from Charmaz's *Constructing* (2014), but also includes extracts from the chapters in this volume and the *Handbook* from 2007.

In introducing the chapters we also note the sad passing of three contributors to the 2007 volume, Susan Leigh Star, Phyllis Stern, and Carolyn Wiener.

Notes

1 University of California, San Francisco
2 Originally, Part I included a chapter by Bryant discussing the other contributions and the issues raised against a wider view of GTM and qualitative research in general. This has now been published as *The Varieties of Grounded Theory*, part of the *Swifts Series* (Bryant, 2019).

REFERENCES

Bryant, A. (2019). *The Varieties of Grounded Theory*. London: Sage.

Bryant, A., & Charmaz, K. (Eds.) (2007a). *The SAGE Handbook of Grounded Theory*. London: Sage.

Bryant, A., & Charmaz, K. (2007b). 'Grounded theory research: Method and practices pre-eminent qualitative research method, Editors' Introduction'. In A. Bryant & K. Charmaz (Eds.), *Sage Handbook of Grounded Theory* (pp. 1–28). London: Sage.

Bryant, A., & Charmaz, K. (2007c). 'Grounded theory in historical perspective: An epistemological account'. In A. Bryant & K. Charmaz (Eds.), *The Sage Handbook of Grounded Theory* (pp. 31–57). London: Sage.

Charmaz, K. (2014). *Constructing Grounded Theory*. London: Sage.

PART I

The Grounded Theory Method: 50 Years On

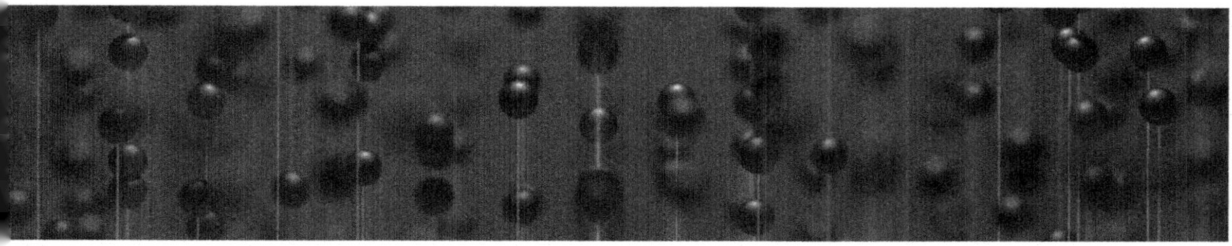

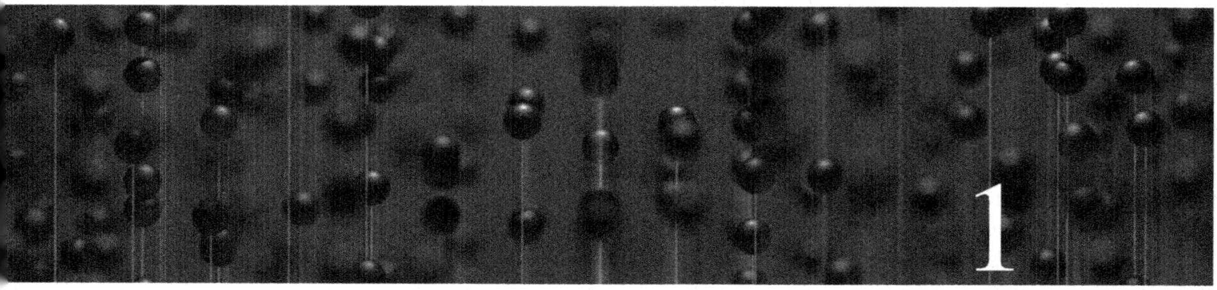

Situating Grounded Theory and Situational Analysis in Interpretive Qualitative Inquiry

Adele E. Clarke

This chapter engages the common question, 'How do grounded theory and situational analysis fit into the contemporary research methods scene?'[1] Reviewing the development of qualitative inquiry since World War II, this chapter first details the modernist phase c1950-1970 including the 1960s constructionist turn. Created in 1967, grounded theory constituted the first "manifesto" in the long qualitative renaissance, posing many challenges to positivist orthodoxies. I next elaborate the era of 'turns' in qualitative inquiry c1970-2000, including narrative, postmodern, poststructural, etc., along with feminist, critical and other critiques integral to the interpretive turn. *The Handbook of Qualitative Inquiry* was another manifesto in the long qualitative renaissance, highlighting the uneven reception of the poststructural/interpretive turn in qualitative inquiry. All these developments led to the tremendous growth of qualitative methods as transdisciplinary, the wide array of approaches practiced today, and their increasing transnationalization.[2]

I then sketch a current genealogy of grounded theory as divergent grounded theory approaches have elaborated over the past 50 years, including the emergence of situational analysis within the grounded theory tradition. I conclude by discussing changes in qualitative inquiry in the 21st century, including the shift from distinguishing "qual vs quant" to "positivist vs interpretivist" approaches, and various pressing problems confronting interpretive methods. I end with pragmatist-inspired hopes for the future of research.[3]

A NOTE ON THE TRADITIONAL ERA C. 1900–1950

Ethnography, the name under which most early qualitative inquiry was pursued, has a deep history, extending back centuries.[4] Early contributions, often Western travelers' accounts of non-Western locales and their peoples (e.g., Pratt 1992), were described by Said (1978) as stories of 'the Other,' often exoticizing or 'orientalizing' them. Since the late 19th century, in both anthropology and sociology, (more or less) naive realist ethnographies professionalized such accounts, the first of which was W.E.B. DuBois' (1899) *The Philadelphia Negro* (Erickson 2018: 39).

Called 'the traditional period' of qualitative inquiry by Denzin and Lincoln (1994: 7), initial anthropological scholarship centered largely on 'primitive' groups in the South Seas (Malinowski 1922) and Native Americans (Kroeber 1902–1907).[5] In contrast, American sociologists focused largely on the city and 'civic others' (Vidich & Lyman 1994: 31): minority communities (W.E.B. DuBois 1899; Frazier 1939), immigrants (Thomas & Znaniecki 1918–1920), deviants (Thrasher 1926), the poor (Sutherland & Locke 1936), and various subcultures (Cressey 1932). Such studies of 'outsiders' (Becker 1963), in which the Other continues to be othered, have been aptly described as 'the ethnography of assimilation' (Vidich & Lyman 2000). Much of this sociological work emerged from the University of Chicago and became known as the Chicago School.[6]

This early anthropological and sociological work, while justifiably critiqued, especially for routinely 'studying down' (e.g., Geertz 1973; Morris 2015), nevertheless pioneered qualitative inquiry. Moreover, it raised important civic issues of concern to democracy, including how marginalities and race and class differences 'matter' when racial and ethnic segregation were the norm if not the law.

While the Great Depression and World War II slowed developments, qualitative inquiry expanded in subject matter, including criminology (e.g., Sutherland 1949) and community studies (Vidich & Bensman 1958). Meanwhile, *quantitative* social science research was on the rise, especially at Harvard, Columbia and (surprisingly) the University of Chicago (Fine 1995; Bulmer 1997; Abbott 1999; Rawls 2018).

THE MODERNIST PHASE C. 1950–1970

Post-World War II, a new scientific era flourished and research became 'the name of the game' in academia and beyond – requisite not only across both the natural and social sciences but also in the professions, humanities and industry. Initially in the West but expanding transnationally, schools of education, nursing, medicine, social work, business, management, organizations and emerging specialties/disciplines in universities, such as communications, race and ethic studies, cultural studies, and women's and gender studies, each and all viewed research capacities as requisite for faculty and graduate students, as well as for disciplinary and specialty advancement.

During the Cold War, scientism and quantitative approaches held sway, especially via survey research and demography in the social sciences, and epidemiology in the health sciences. Quantitative functionalist sociology, dominated by survey research, had taken deep hold by the late 1930s and dramatically expanded post-World War II (Ross 1990; Harding 2015). However, Manicas (2007: 7) subtitled his article on this era 'The Rise and Fall of Scientism,' noting that several enduring if marginal strands of anti-scientism kept interpretive alternatives alive.

One important strand, deriving from Chicago School sociology and American pragmatist philosophy, was *symbolic interactionism*, a name originally coined by Blumer in 1937 (1969: 1 fn). Blumer's book was a lively defense of interpretive research, largely against structural functionalism. Interactionism sustained Chicago School engagements with diversity, marginality and racism (e.g., Reynolds & Herman-Kinney 2003), and some works are considered prescient of postmodernism and poststructuralism.[7] This century, a new strand called critical interactionism is coalescing.[8]

The second enduring strand of anti-scientism in Cold War American social science that nurtured interpretation was C. Wright Mills' (1959) more critical approach in *The Sociological Imagination*, also with deep roots in American pragmatist philosophy. The third and last enduring strand of anti-scientism was ethnomethodology (e.g., Garfinkel 1967), although some conversational analysts may view their approaches as doing better positivist science.

The Constructionist Turn

Fundamental to the coming qualitative renaissance, explicit social constructionism was triggered in 1966 by Berger and Luckmann's classic *The Social Construction of Reality: A Treatise in the Sociology of Knowledge*, and very widely taken up. Constructionism (or constructivism) assumes that people (*including* researchers) construct or interpret the realities in which they participate *through their own situated perspectives*.[9] For contructionists, there is no one 'true' reality. Partial accounts of perceived realities understood 'through the eyes of the beholder' are the goal. Constructivism became the epistemological and ontological grounding of much if not most qualitative inquiry transnationally by the end of the century (e.g., Pascale 2011).

Constructivism can be viewed as an early formulation of what Keller (2012) calls 'the interpretive paradigm.' Knoblauch, Flick and Maeder (2005: 5, emphasis added), in an article on 'Qualitative Methods in Europe,' stated that this paradigm is:[10]

> ...based on theories like symbolic interactionism, phenomenology, hermeneutics, ethnomethodology etc.—positions that stress the importance of investigating action and the social world *from the point of view of the actors themselves*. In a Kuhnian sense, this interpretive paradigm was supposed to substitute for the 'normative paradigm', represented by structural functionalism or Rational Choice theories. Qualitative research, as it exists nowadays, is supported by and dependent upon a line of thought that is orientated towards meaning, context, interpretation, understanding and reflexivity.

In the US, Blumer's (1969) *Symbolic Interactionism* was an early sociological 'manifesto' for constructionism and the interpretive turn, advocating 'intimate familiarity' with the studied world to enable the researcher to understand and portray participants' interpretations more accurately than quantitative methods could. In anthropology, Geertz's (1973) *The Interpretation of Cultures* provoked similar debates and directly called into question the reflexivity of the researcher in constructing accounts.

The importance of the constructivist turn for the future of interpretive qualitative inquiry cannot be overstated. In the words of St. Pierre, 'We really do have to rethink almost everything [in order] to [fully come around a] "turn"' (quoted in Denzin & Giardina 2015: 452). Its uptake was transdisciplinary, transnational (Holstein & Gubrium 2007) and enduring (Weinberg 2015; Holstein 2018).[11]

The Birth of Grounded Theory and Challenges to Positivist Orthodoxies

Then, in 1967 from a tiny medical sociology setting at UC San Francisco, a new manifesto explicitly advocating qualitative inquiry appeared: Barney Glaser and Anselm Strauss's *Discovery of Grounded Theory: Strategies for Qualitative Research.*[12] Charmaz (2014: 1080; see also 2008) asserts that it is difficult to over-estimate the power of this intervention as a fresh and contemporary defense of and rallying cry for qualitative inquiry: 'Their book made a cutting-edge statement because it punctured notions of methodological consensus *and* offered systematic strategies for qualitative research practice.' It was a crucial turning point in the 'qualitative revolution' still unfolding today (Denzin & Lincoln 1994: ix).

Over the next half-century, GT became the most popular form of qualitative analysis on the planet with literally thousands of dissertations, articles and books using GT and on GT as method.[13] Its popularity was due in large part to its profoundly *empirical* orientation. Rather than being theory-driven, GT is based in abductively moving back and forth between empirical materials and efforts to conceptualize them via increasingly robust and sophisticated theorizing and sampling.[14] It quickly grabbed the imaginations of scholars with interpretive orientations.

GT also reanimated older qualitative approaches and provoked the generation of new ones. Denzin and Lincoln (1994: 8) aptly call the years c. 1950–1970 'the modernist phase' including ethnography, field research, interview and related studies, including GT ethnographies.[15] Numerous qualitative textbooks were published in the US, including Schatzman and Strauss's (1973) *Field Research: Strategies for a Natural Sociology* (see also Bogdan & Taylor 1975).

By the 1970s in the US, normative functionalist and related positivist approaches were under siege. Goffman wholly dismissed the scientistic claims of positivist (especially quantitative) sociology in 1971, asserting: 'A sort of sympathetic magic seems to be involved, … being that if you go through the motions attributable to science then science will result. But it hasn't' (quoted in Vidich & Lyman 1994: 40). In anthropology, Geertz's (1973) *The Interpretation of Cultures* argued for 'thick description.' Geertz applauded that 'the old functionalist, positivist, behavioral totalizing approaches to the human disciplines were giving way to a more pluralist, interpretive, open-ended perspective,' while boundaries between social sciences and humanities were blurring as well (Denzin & Lincoln 1994: 9).

At least in the US, UK and Germany, Berger and Luckmann's (1966) *The Social Construction of Reality* provided key theoretical/philosophical grounding for GT and many other modes of qualitative inquiry. Important to the later transnational renaissance of interpretive qualitative research, at about this time, papers by Blumer, Garfinkel, Cicourel and others were translated and published in German as a two-volume reader titled *Everyday Knowledge, Interaction and Social Reality* (Arbeitsgruppe Bielefelder Soziologen 1973). This and other translations constituted the first big post-war push for the revival of qualitative research in Germany.[16] In one key paper, Wilson (1970: 701) wrote, '…in the interpretive view of social interaction, in contrast with the normative paradigm, … the meanings of situations and actions are interpretations formulated on particular occasions and … subject to reformulation.'[17]

In 1983, German sociologist Hans-Georg Soeffner (1983, 2004a, 2004b), a close colleague of Strauss, made a very significant distinction regarding approaches to research.

He asserted that the fundamental distinction among *all approaches to research, both qualitative and quantitative*, was between Cartesian (positivist) and hermeneutic (interpretive) perspectives. He further asserted that *this* distinction, rather than that between quantitative versus qualitative approaches, was the more important and enduring distinction regarding approaches to research.[18] As we shall see, this was quite prescient of 21st-century developments.

In sum, the initially modernist qualitative revival gained momentum until there was a full-fledged 'renaissance of qualitative research' (Gobo 2005) involving an interesting series of intellectual 'turns,' discussed next.

THE ERA OF 'TURNS' IN QUALITATIVE INQUIRY C. 1970–2000

The Interpretive Turn/The Interpretive Paradigm

The next thirty or so years, c. 1970–2000, was an era of considerable change characterized by the coalescence of constructionism, the 'interpretive turn,' and a tsunami of critiques of traditional approaches to qualitative inquiry. Conceptually, the 'interpretive turn' has its European historical roots in Kant, Nietzche, Marx, Freud, Dilthey, and Weberian *verstehen*. In the US, American pragmatist philosophy and interactionist sociology contributed Mead's (1927/1964, 1934/1962; Cefaï 2016) work on perspective, and the Thomas's (1923/1978; Thomas & Thomas 1928/1970) theorem. This proto-constructionist 'theorem' had asserted in the 1920s that if things are believed or *interpreted* as real, they are real in their consequences. Berger and Luckman's (1966) *The Social Construction of Reality* significantly deepened the grasp and reach of constructionism.

The interpretive turn became a cultural force with several foundational assumptions:[19]

- Meaning is re-located from 'reality out there' to 'reality as experienced by the perceiver;'
- An observer is assumed to inevitably be a *participant* in what is observed, more or less reflexive;
- Interpretations are *not* universal but must be located and situated in space and time;
- Cultures are best understood as unevenly changing assemblages of distinctive symbols and signifying practices;
- Interpretation *per se* is conditioned by historic geopolitical and cultural perspectives mediated by symbols and practices.

Today the 'interpretive turn' has become the broader, more inclusive term for such assumptions and practices, also often construed as featuring aspects of critical, poststructural, and postmodern approaches, discussed next.

Feminist, Critical and Other Critiques and Responses

Participants in the interpretive turn in qualitative inquiry also took critiques generated by civil rights, anti-racism, anti-war, feminist, LGBT and other social movements in the 1960s and 1970s very seriously. Critiques are attempts to retheorize a problematic and have their own methodological implications. Both Dewey (1939) and Blumer (1969) had vividly asserted the nonfungibility of theory and method and most of the critical projects discussed here grasped this point. Theoretical approaches imply methodological approaches, and *vice versa*. Feminist interactionist Leigh Star (1989) further developed this insight as the concept of 'theory/methods packages,' detailing how aspects of ontology, epistemology, and practice are integral – co-constitutive.[20] Thus the critiques of the 1960s generated methodological innovations *along with* new approaches to theorizing.

Significantly, critiques of *both* qualitative and quantitative research were mounted in the US on the grounds that such research commonly had sexist, racist, classist, elitist, homophobic and/or voyeuristic colonialist tendencies.[21] Some critiques generated new interpretive approaches that specifically attempt to address those problematics. Here I briefly discuss critical and feminist approaches, and engage postcolonial and decolonizing/indigenous research innovations later.

Critical theory and research often emphasize interpretive approaches and are commonly traced not only to Marx and Marxists such as Gramsci, but also to the Frankfurt School of Critical Theory, including Adorno, Horkheimer, Marcuse and Habermas both pre- and post-World War II and varyingly located. Early critical theorists engaged Marxism and its historical applications, and also sought to reinterpret Freud, synthesizing Marxism and psychoanalysis. Post-World War II work took up the materialist conditions of life and problems posed by fascism in Europe. More recently, critical social scientists have documented patterns of injustice, subjugation, the reproduction of inequalities, and the changing nature of capitalism and its consequences in an ongoing research and praxis agenda (e.g., Kincheloe & McLaren 1994; Schwalbe 2008; Kincheloe, McLaren & Steinberg 2011, 2018; Steinberg & Cannella 2012; Cannella 2015).

Neo-Marxist and other critical approaches expanded dramatically after the 1960s, due in part to social movement activism which highlighted the persistence of profound inequalities in the US despite the post-war boom. For example, Herbert Marcuse became 'the philosophical voice of the New Left' in the 1960s, concerned with political emancipation (Kincheloe & McLaren 1994: 139). Jürgen Habermas's (e.g., 1967) work integrated critical theory and pragmatism in Deweyan efforts to link communicative rationality and the public sphere.[22] Pierre Bourdieu, through his *Outline of a Theory of Practice* (1972/1977) and field theory (1975), founded a major research institute in Paris that elaborates his approaches transnationally (discussed below).

In the UK, the Centre for Contemporary Cultural Studies (CCCS) at the University of Birmingham, founded by Richard Hoggart in 1964, became a driving transnational and transdisciplinary force for the interpretive study of subcultures, marginalities, popular culture and media. Its researchers included Stuart Hall, Maureen McNeil, Hazel Carby, Celia Lury and Sarah Franklin, known for combining Gramscian, critical, feminist, poststructural and critical race theorizing. They founded cultural studies as a disciplinary field, often in competition with sociology and other social sciences (e.g., Grossberg, Nelson & Treichler 1992). They also renovated qualitative sociology, especially ethnography (e.g., Lury & Wakeford 2012), and subculture studies (e.g., Gelder 2005) in the UK and beyond. The influence of the Centre, especially the critical and innovatively Gramscian work of Stuart Hall on race, identity and community, still echoes loudly despite its tragic closure in 2002 under neoliberalism (Webster 2004).

Despite deep differences both within and among various critical communities of practice, there was general accord by the 1970s that 'mainstream research practices [both quantitative and qualitative] were generally, although often unwittingly, implicated in the reproduction of systems of class, race and gender oppression' (Kincheloe & McClaren 1994: 140). Insights from these critiques have generated new critical approaches to research by feminist, anti-racist, LGTBQ, disability studies and other scholars now extending across almost half a century (e.g., Alexander 2018; Donnor & Ladson-Billings 2018).

The tremendous growth of feminist research was supported by the growth of women's and later gender studies in the academy. The feminist adage that 'the personal is political,' or 'lived experience matters,' was a key early generator of research issues as well as the central tenet of consciousness-raising. *Signs: A Journal of Women in Culture and Society* (f. 1975) published many 'feminist state of the discipline' assessments, clarifying disciplinary and transdisciplinary feminist research concerns. Major debates, research texts and readers soon emerged (e.g., Cook & Fonow 1986; Harding 1987).

While there were – and are – many significant pioneers in feminist research, two are of particular note. Sociologist Dorothy Smith (1987) believed power relations blind us, and wrote a searing critique of the discipline calling for a new feminist sociology using 'experience as data' (e.g., Campbell & Monicom 1995), and critiquing 'ruling knowledges.' Smith's (1990) theoretical sociology of knowledge approach seeks to grasp 'the conceptual politics of power' dwelling in discourses particularly oppressive to females. Congruent with the precepts of theory and methods as co-constitutive – forming a 'package' – Smith and collaborators then developed the institutional ethnography method, especially useful for organizational and policy-oriented research.[23]

Second, sociologist Patricia Hill Collins (1990) published perhaps the major anti-racist feminist statement as *Black Feminist Thought: Knowledge, Consciousness, and the Politics of Empowerment*, still echoing loudly across the social sciences and humanities. Her theoretically astute work was soon combined with that of legal scholar Kimberle Crenshaw (1989, 1991; Crenshaw et al. 1996) in the concept of *intersectionality*, asserting that race, class, gender and other major identities (such as sexuality, disability, etc.) are simultaneous and embodied. They are non-fungible, co-constitutive, and generative of *distinctive lived experiences* that should be understood as such through research on intersectionalities.[24]

In anthropology, major debates about what constituted 'good' *interpretive* ethnographic work included Geertz (1973) *The Interpretation of Cultures*, Clifford and Marcus's (1986) *Writing Culture: The Poetics and Politics of Ethnography*, and Rosaldo's (1989) *Culture and Truth: The Remaking of Social Analysis*, which questioned 'distanced normalizing description.' The almost complete absence of women's voices in Clifford and Marcus's (1986) edited volume provoked a strong feminist response, *Women Writing Culture*, edited by Behar and Gordon (1995).[25] Visweswaran's (1994) brilliant *Fictions of Feminist Ethnography* also brought feminist research issues together with postcolonial, cultural and discourse concerns in anthropology and beyond. *Feminist Dilemmas in Fieldwork* (Wolf 1996) attended to distinctively gendered ethnographic challenges.

In education, Lather's (1991) *Getting Smart: Feminist Research and Pedagogy With/In the Postmodern* and related work (e.g., Lather 1993) broke new ground in feminist poststructural research that became transdisciplinarily influential. Lather established a key center of gravity that seeded American education research and has also been transnationally taken up.[26]

Gradually, the array of readers and handbooks on feminist research has grown increasingly transdisciplinary in seeking to 'liberate method,' also reflecting the strong transdisciplinarity of women's and gender studies (e.g., DeVault 1999; Hesse-Biber 2006a, 2006b, 2013a, 2013b).[27] Further, in feminist research, *both* qualitative and quantitative approaches can be legitimate (e.g., Sprague 2005). Stanley (1990) even had a section on 'Demolishing the "Quantitative" v. "Qualitative" Divide,' later echoed by Haraway's (1999) assertion that counting for feminist purposes (such as documenting infant mortality where such deaths were not being recorded for political reasons) mattered immensely.

In sum, the various critical and feminist turns have developed over time, often but certainly not only contributing to the interpretive paradigm.

Postmodernisms, Poststructuralisms and the Handbook of Qualitative Inquiry

> For those who have moved out from under a narrow scientificity, other practices are being rehearsed toward changing the social imaginary about research. Moving beyond the normalized apparatuses of our own training, a social science more answerable to the complications of our knowing is beginning to take place. (Patti Lather 2007: 19)

At the same time that critical and feminist approaches were thriving, postmodernisms and poststructuralisms continued to inform interpretive projects. Postmodern scholars 'questioned the entire Enlightenment project of authoritative academic discourse concerning human activity, whether this manifested in the arts, in history, or in the social sciences' (Erickson 2018: 50). Across the disciplines in the West and beyond, the work of Foucault, Derrida, Deleuze and other theorists began traveling widely and rupturing many taken-for-granted assumptions – not only about theory but also about method. That is, changes in qualitative inquiry are often provoked through infusions of new theoretical insights.

A further series of often overlapping 'turns' then continued to choreograph emergent scholarship beyond the critical and feminist turns. These included the linguistic (e.g., Rorty 1967), deconstructive (e.g., Derrida 1978), participatory action (Greenwood & Levin 1998), cultural (e.g., Clifford & Marcus 1986), narrative (e.g., Riessman 1993; Holstein & Gubrium 2012; Chase 2018), practice (e.g., Schatzki, Knorr Cetina & von Savigny 2001), postmodern (e.g., Denzin 1991), and poststructural (Lather 1993) turns (see also Lather 2007: 1–3, 2013).

By the late 1980s, the term 'human sciences' indicated the continued turning away from scientistic and behavioral approaches toward more contextualized (I would say situated) approaches to the centrality of meaning and interpretation to understanding social life.[28] '[I]t suggests a critical and historical approach which transcends [social science disciplines] and links their interests with those of philosophy, literary criticism, aesthetics, law and politics' (Editorial for first issue of *History of the Human Sciences* 1988: 1). At issue here is that 'a "social" science emphasizing "prediction" and "control" can too easily use the veil of "objectivity" to hide a dehumanizing impulse' (Yanow & Schwartz-Shea 2006: 388).

Additional critical challenges of this era were posed by crises of representation and reflexivity. Anthropologists took the lead in articulating the significance of *researcher* reflexivity and how gender, class, race and other attributes are manifest within *all* research processes, including relations between researchers and those being studied, as well as research products. Rosaldo's (1989) remarkable *Culture and Truth: The Remaking of Cultural Analysis* called for a new ethnographic candor (see also Clifford & Marcus 1986). Anthropologist Geertz's (1973) call for 'thick description' was echoed by sociologist Denzin's (1989: 52) call for 'thick interpretation' in *Interpretive Interactionism*, which interweaves interactionism and poststructuralisms (see also Fontana 2005). Clough's (1998) *The End(s) of Ethnography: From Realism to Social Criticism* questioned the very possibility of qualitative inquiry amid the many 'turns.'

In education and far beyond, Lather's (1993) 'Fertile Obsession: Validity after Poststructuralism' challenged the non-reflexive core of positivism and became iconic (see also Lather 1991). Morse (1989) placed 'sticky issues' on the table, recruiting qualitative nurse researchers to create 'a contemporary dialogue.' And Michelle Fine's (1994) still remarkable paper, 'Working the Hyphens: Reinventing Self and Other in Qualitative Research,' laid out both the need for and means of addressing the crisis of representation and reflexivity as accounting for the relentless presence of the researcher at *all* stages of the research process (see also Pascale 2008; von Unger 2016). Reiterating pragmatist George Herbert Mead, political scientists Yanow and Schwartz-Shea (2006: 385) reflexively note that 'data are generated, not "given."'[29] The title of a recent book on 'big data' captures this wonderfully: *'Raw Data' is an Oxymoron* (Gitelman 2013).

The first edition of Denzin and Lincoln's huge and hugely successful *Handbook of Qualitative Research* in 1994 announced that the renaissance in qualitative inquiry had arrived. Precisely because it brought together a very wide array of older and newer approaches to qualitative inquiry across multiple disciplines, the *Handbook* drew many interpretive and revisioned qualitative approaches under a broad umbrella, placing once 'distant cousins' in direct conversation.

This *Handbook* was *the second manifesto of the qualitative revolution* – urging engagement to both broaden interpretive approaches and strengthen them globally. It forever changed the face of qualitative inquiry and the teaching of qualitative methods in the US and beyond. It was no longer possible to wholly ignore the postmodern/poststructural/interpretive turns, though some continue to try, sustaining the 'contested' character of the field.

The emergent sensibility of this era had at its core the poststructuralist 'doubt that any discourse has privileged place, any method or theory a universal and general claim to authoritative knowledge' (Richardson, quoted in Denzin & Lincoln 1994: 2). Today interpretive scholars make that doubt generative by rethinking the work that doubt can do in research processes *per se* (Locke, Golden-Biddle & Feldman 2008). The moral and ethical issues involved in understanding and acknowledging that representing *is* intervening (e.g., Hacking 1983) are complex and continue to demand attentive engagement. These issues are at the very heart of contemporary interpretive efforts, especially work that engages indigenous concerns.[30]

Reception of the Poststructural/Interpretive Turns

Interpretations of the poststructural/interpretive turn range(d) very very widely from grave skepticism about the very possibility of further research (e.g., Clough 1998) to viewing its possibilities for thinking usefully outside of modern paradigms as strong encouragement to reexamine methods and their assumptions (e.g., Lather 1991, 1993). According to Spencer (2001), in Anglophone anthropology this turn was 'an accident waiting to happen.' The confrontation was already over-determined by critiques dating back to the 1970s, especially those posed by feminisms and Said's *Orientalism* (1978), both of which addressed highly problematic anthropological representational practices of othering and exoticization.

In parallel, I would assert that in the US, Denzin and Lincoln's (1994) *Handbook of Qualitative Research* was the 'revolution waiting to happen' in US qualitative sociology, communications, cultural studies, education, nursing, etc. As Spencer (2001: 444) noted, 'The models of phlegmatic orthodoxy which had dominated … had somehow ceased to carry conviction,' and 'much of the volume's early impact was heavily polarized, along more or less generational lines.'

Some interactionists have taken this turn (myself included, initially via science and technology studies, about which more below). For example, Virginia Olesen (2001: 267–268) described being 'literally swept away' by a panel Norm Denzin organized: 'From the podium began to flow words, ideas, revelations and emotions so daring, so stimulating, so divergent from the usual desiccated presentations that I feel intellectual jubilation. … I fly home, a phoenix risen from the ashes of a sociology that seems out of step, out of tune and strangely old fashioned.' Such energies have now fueled decades of fresh scholarship.

Other Anglophone researchers remain more wedded to traditional ethnographic approaches, creating serious schisms across qualitative worlds.[31] Prus (1996: 17), for example, derided the nihilistic relativism of postmodernism.[32] Atkinson and Delamont (2006) described the debate about poststructuralism as located 'in the roiling smoke' of the battlefield, while Hammersley (2008: 11) claimed that 'the future of qualitative research is endangered.' Denzin (2009) replied by writing a play titled 'Apocalypse Now,' accusing them, per Foucault, of attempting to 'discipline qualitative research' (Denzin, Lincoln & Giardina 2006). In some places, such debates continue to haunt qualitative inquiry, but not everywhere nor consistently.[33]

Interpretation, poststructuralism and postmodernism, however contested, became keywords. Overall, US scholars were rather late to incorporate this largely European scholarship (Manicas 2007: 17), and the work of Foucault was especially rupturing for certain disciplines (e.g., sociology). But by 2011, there was sufficient momentum for a remarkable conference in California on 'Foucault across the Disciplines' (Koopman 2011b), and a special issue of Foucault Studies on Foucault and Pragmatism (e.g., Koopman 2011a).[34] The Atlantic Ocean is finally intellectually becoming what the British have long called it – 'the pond' – and much more wading back and forth is occurring.

At the turn of this century, Charmaz (1995, 2000) argued explicitly for a more constructivist interpretive GT. Yet even constructionism, which had interactionist roots that date to the 1920s[35] and fostered many qualitative approaches, was still too provocative for some traditional researchers such as Glaser (e.g., 2002b). Constructionism had itself entered US public discourse via the bitter 'culture wars' of the 1980s and 1990s (e.g., Hilgartner 1997) that again echo very loudly today.[36]

Yet we were far from alone in appreciating the Denzin and Lincoln (1994) *Handbook*. Gubrium and Holstein (1997; see also 2003) viewed postmodernism as one of several 'new languages of qualitative method' deserving of serious attention,[37] and tried mediating by seeking renewed attention to 'methods talk.' They (1997: 80) further asserted that sociologists were 'lagging considerably behind their anthropologist kin,' and cited works in science and technology studies (e.g., Latour & Woolgar 1979; Latour 1987) as 'empirical projects that retain sociological orientations and objectives within more-or-less postmodernist frameworks.'[38] I heartily agree!

Some critical researchers also welcomed poststructuralist interventions: 'In our view, postmodern criticism does not so much weaken the Marxist tradition as help to expand the Marxian critique of capitalist social relations by addressing the ambiguity currently surrounding the reconstituted nature of classes and class consciousness and by interrogating "the cultural logic of late capitalism"' (Kincheloe & McLaren 1994: 142; Steinberg & Cannella 2012).

Meanwhile, the renaissance in qualitative inquiry has continued to manifest elsewhere in the academy including 'recent scholarly "movements" seeking diversity in methodology, such as "Perestroika" in US political science' and parallel developments in European economics (Yanow & Schwartz-Shea 2006: 388).[39] Since the 1990s, a qualitative revolution in psychology has led to a qualitative section with its own journal and strong contributions in applied, feminist, and multicultural areas (Wertz et al. 2011: 78).

FROM GROUNDED THEORY TO GROUNDED THEORIES C. 1990–2015

Interestingly, after their *Discovery of Grounded Theory* appeared in 1967, Glaser and Strauss ceased writing publications focused on methods together.[40] Each subsequently published single-authored methods articles and his own important methods book: Glaser's (1978) *Theoretical Sensitivity* and Strauss's (1987) *Qualitative Analysis for Social Scientists.*[41] I and many others have argued that Glaser has remained faithful to the more positivist functionalist sociology of Merton and Lazarsfeld at Columbia, with whom he originally trained.[42] The positivist character of Glaserian GT is vividly realist and naively empiricist. In sometimes sharp contrast, and reflecting his own philosophical pragmatism, Strauss became increasingly constructionist in his thinking (Strauss 1987, 1991b, 1993) and remained an interpretive symbolic interactionist all his life, at least as devoted to developing interactionist theory as he was methods.[43]

The Elaboration of Grounded Theories

In 1990, Anselm Strauss and Juliet Corbin published the first edition of *The Basics of Qualitative Research: Grounded Theory Procedures and Techniques*, essentially a 'how to' textbook largely in the constructionist interactionist tradition, which became extremely popular. Later editions (1998; Corbin & Strauss 2008, 2015) were completed after Strauss's death in 1996. *The Basics* added to the extant GT research tool box, including axial coding and a more procedural orientation.

Strauss and Corbin's (1990) *Basics* book provoked very serious rebuttals by Glaser (1992, 2002b, 2006; Glaser with Holton 2004), who then began his sustained campaign for the purity of *his* version of the original – now called objectivist or Glaserian GT (e.g., Stern 2009; Martin & Gynnild 2011; Holton & Walsh 2016) used in both qualitative and quantitative research. Others too were critical of the *Basics* books as overly procedural – but from different perspectives.[44]

During the first decade of this century, GT was greatly elaborated transnationally. Kathy Charmaz (2006, 2014) produced her fully interpretivist constructivist text *Constructing Grounded Theory*, already in its second edition. In fact, Bryant (2009: 14) credits Kathy Charmaz's (1995, 2000, 2006, 2007, 2009) push for a more fully constructivist GT with resurrecting a method characterized by many as 'naively inductivist.' Also key in that rejuvenation was the ambitious first *Handbook of Grounded Theory* which appeared in 2007, co-edited by Tony Bryant and Charmaz, it had contributions from Australia, Canada, Germany, the UK, the US, and New Zealand.[45] This second edition further sustains GT's transnational orientation.

Additional GT texts have appeared as well. Dey's (1999) is especially sensitive to policy concerns. Locke's (2001) specially attends to management and organizations issues. Corbin and Strauss's later editions (2008, 2015) include health and nursing concerns, as does Birks and Mills's (2011). Through his information science background, Bryant's (2017) book emphasizes the centrality of pragmatist philosophy to grounded theorizing, including abduction. He also takes up current research challenges such as 'big data.' Charmaz (2005, 2011, 2016b; Charmaz, Thornberg & Keane 2018) and others have thoughtfully extended GT as a critical social justice methodology.

Many of the theoretical and methodological developments discussed here as part of the interpretive turn have contributed to the various elaborations of GT over the nearly five decades of its use and to the recent development of SA (discussed below). By the new millennium, then, several different emphases in GT were in active circulation: *Glaserian* (1978, 1992, 2006) as positivist and objectivist, *Straussian* (1987; Strauss & Corbin 1990, 1998) as constructionist, interactionist and interpretivist, and *Constructivist* in Charmaz's (1995, 2000, 2006) interpretivist innovations. SA soon joined them.

The Emergence of Situational Analysis

Situational analysis (SA), an extension of Straussian GT and Constructivist GT, emerged at the turn of this century and reflects the altered landscapes of social theory and qualitative inquiry since the interpretive turn (Clarke 2003, 2005; Clarke & Charmaz 2014; Clarke, Friese & Washburn 2015, 2018). Appropriately, the theoretical bases of SA begin from those of Straussian GT: Chicago School ecologies and symbolic interactionism, placing special emphasis on Strauss's social worlds/arenas theory.[46] Like Charmaz's (2000, 2006, 2014) constructivist GT, SA views the processes of data analysis as abductive as well as inductive, and relies on theoretical sampling for theoretical enrichment and analyzing conundrums.[47]

In extending SA to include poststructural concerns, I also braided several recent theoretic innovations into the groundings of SA. First was Foucault's work, especially on discourses, fields of practice and conditions of possibility. From my science and technology studies (STS) background, I knew that taking the nonhuman in the situation – things of all kinds – explicitly into account was essential. So, drawing on pragmatist philosopher Mead (1938, 1972; McCarthy 1984) and science studies, I argued that *nonhuman things* (living and not) are wholly worthy of our analytic attention for posthumanist analysis, especially in situational maps.[48] Nonhuman is very broadly construed to include natural and built environments, technologies, plants and animals, etc. – whatever is empirically there in the situation.

I was also deeply inspired by Deleuze and Guattari's (1987: 21) rhizomic analytics which undergird situational maps: '[T]he rhizome pertains to a map that must be produced, constructed, a map that is always detachable, connectable, reversible, modifiable, and has multiple entryways and exits and its own lines of flight. It is tracings that must be put on the map, not the opposite.' All of these theoretical insights helped open up SA's empirical attentiveness and deepened its analytic capacities.

SA is also very much part of what I term 'the (re)turn to the social' or the *reconfiguration of relationality* across the social sciences and humanities, manifest in both quantitative and qualitative methods. This distributed 'turn' has involved heterogeneous and sorely needed theoretical and methodological reconceptualizations of the social *per se*. Historically, research data and analysis were conceptualized as centered on the micro (interpersonal), meso (social/organizational/institutional) or macro (broad historical patterning such as urbanization, industrialization) 'levels.' Qualitative inquiry was thought to hold sway largely over the micro and (perhaps) meso levels.[49]

Poststructural theories by and large abjure this tripartite framework, seeing it as failing to grasp the fundamental poststructural assumption of relationality – that social phenomena are *co-constituted*, produced through the relations of entities at *all* levels of organizational complexity (e.g., Jasanoff 2004). That is, social phenomena are *non-fungibly* 'all of the above.' Therefore, analytic focus should be on complexities, relationalities and ecologies explicitly situated in space and time, including geopolitically.[50]

The '(re)turn toward the social' has coalesced around a number of often overlapping or hybrid approaches. In qualitative inquiry across the disciplines these currently include: Bourdieusian field theory,[51] Foucauldian discourse analysis,[52] Foucauldian *dispositif* or apparatus,[53] actor-network theory (ANT),[54] assemblage theory,[55] rhizomic analytics,[56] and the hybrid method of SA. All have earlier roots but have been varyingly renovated to take recent developments into fuller account.

SA also relies on the inherent strength of constructivist GT in closely attending to context by 'turning away from acontextual description' (Charmaz 2006: 271). In fact, in SA, I explicitly drew upon the concept of *situation* instead of context (Clarke 2005: 71–72):

> *The conditions* ***of*** *the situation are* ***in*** *the situation.* There is no such thing as 'context.' The conditional elements of the situation need to be specified in the analysis of the situation itself as *they are constitutive of it*, not merely surrounding it or framing it or contributing to it. They *are* it. Regardless of whether some might construe them as local or global, internal or external, close-in or far away or whatever, the fundamental question is *'How do these conditions appear—make themselves felt as consequential—****inside*** *the empirical situation under examination?'* At least some answers to that question can be found through doing situational analyses.

In SA, a situation is broadly conceived ecologically (Dewey 1938: Chapter 4; Star 1995; Clarke & Star 2008). Focus is on generating understandings of the *relationalities* among all the elements empirically found in the situation of interest through mapping them in various ways. These elements are understood as co-constitutive – they help to make each other up and together constitute the situation as a whole. As Dewey (1938: 66–68) argued, things have meaning only in relation to the situations in which they are found or occur.[57]

Doing a situational analysis involves making three different kinds of maps to describe and analyze various facets of the situation of inquiry. The method is empirically wide open to using all kinds of materials to generate these maps. Materials can be gathered through interviewing, ethnographic strategies, and the analysis of documents. Moreover, SA deeply encourages the inclusion of extant discourse materials found in the situation of interest, including narrative, visual and/or historical materials. All of the maps are developed, revisited and revised across the life of the project.

First are **situational maps** that focus on *empirically detailing precisely what elements are in the broader situation*. The elements may include human, nonhuman things, animals, technologies, organizations, institutions, natural resources, political economic elements, social and cultural traditions, particular visuals, cultural phenomena, spatial and temporal issues, popular and other discourses pertinent to the situation, symbolic elements, contested elements, discursive constructions of actors in the situation, etc. The relevance of various elements to particular questions remains to be analyzed later through the empirical materials. That is, specifying *how* they matter, their relative power, implicated actors, etc., happens downstream in the research process, including through other maps.

SA concerns with 'the (re)turn to the social' are especially manifest in the **social worlds/arenas maps** which frames the social worlds, organizational and institutional structures and their interrelations in the broader situation of inquiry. These are based on Strauss's social worlds/arenas theory which he developed separately though in tandem with his constructionist grounded theory.[58] Here collectivities are called social worlds and are committed to social action in one or more arenas of concern in the situation. The goal is to map all the major social worlds, organizations, and institutions and their arenas of action. The analyst(s) usually generates one social worlds/arenas map for the project, refining it through analyzing new data. While many qualitative research strategies simply do not attend to collective social, organizational and institutional elements, as a student of Strauss, I was much attuned to them in developing SA.

The third and last kind of map done as part of SA is **positional maps**. In any situation, there are generally a number of contested or debated issues, and positional maps analyze them. By focusing on two elements in a debate at a time, a positional map can lay out the full range of positions articulated in the data about them. Moreover, positional maps also allow the analyst to specify *positions not taken* in the discursive materials to determine whether there are *implicated actors* in the situation (an analysis of power discussed below). Researchers commonly do a number of positional maps in an SA project.

Precisely because SA mapping involves *empirically specifying the elements* of the situation *per se*, it can be used to analyze many highly heterogeneous situations. Unlike Glaserian GT, SA *promotes* analysis of differences and range of variation. Glaser and Strauss (1967) wrote about difference as 'negative' cases and largely sought a singular basic social process. SA resists such oversimplification, focusing instead on analyzing *relationalities* both within and across the three kinds of maps. It seeks processes and contingencies by analyzing difference(s) and complexities.

Another major change from earlier GT is that SA takes the turn to discourse analysis very seriously (e.g., Keller 2013). Urging analysis of extant narrative, visual and historical discourse materials in the situation, SA also provides resources for this (Clarke 2005: Chapters 4–7; Clarke, Friese & Washburn 2018: Chapters 10–13). In constructivist GT, Charmaz (2014: 45–54) urges this as well.

Like constructivist GT, SA provides tools for analyzing 'how power, oppression, and iniquities differentially affect, individuals, groups and categories of people' (Charmaz 2011: 361–362). Analyzing power is especially important in SA as an explicitly feminist and anti-racist method, and is pursued through several strategies. First, social worlds/arenas maps facilitate analysis of their relative power, providing a 'big picture' of the 'conditions of possibility.' Such structural portraits that limit the potential for change remain rare in qualitative inquiry.

Second, SA analyses seek to specify whether there are *implicated actors* in the situation under study. Implicated actors can be physically present but silenced, or wholly absent. Regardless, they are discursively constructed by other actors with greater power in the situation for their (the other actors') own purposes. Neither category of implicated actors is actively involved in self-representation, nor are they consulted. The capacity to analyze the presence of implicated actors, precisely *how and for what purposes* they are constructed by others, and the *consequences of those constructions*, provide SA with distinctively critical tools. That is, SA allows explicit analysis of subtle as well as more blatant uses of power and their consequences.[59]

Third, SA mapping enhances visibility of *epistemic diversity* via the explicit recognition that different 'ways of knowing' or 'local epistemologies' may be lively in the situation.[60] SA seeks to represent *all the actors and discourses in the situation regardless of their power*, rupturing taken-for-granted hierarchies. This thorough representational work is a key feature of SA as a poststructuralist and interpretive approach with a strong critical edge.[61]

Last, SA not only tolerates the messy complexities of life but relishes engaging them. In *After Method: Mess in Social Science Research*, Law (2004: 14, emphasis in original) argued '(social) science should also be trying to make and know realities that are vague and indefinite *because much of the world is enacted in that way*.' Law (2007) objects to the tidying up of real life performed in most research, calling it inappropriately 'hygienic.' SA explicitly seeks to address these problems directly (e.g., Clarke with Keller 2014). Each kind of map pushes analysts to engage and explicate different forms of complexities in the situation.

In the current qualitative landscape, SA contributes to the overall interpretive project both transdisciplinarily and transnationally.[62] These include feminist research (see also Clarke 2006, 2012b), postcolonial and decolonizing approaches (Clarke In prep.b), science and technology studies, critical inquiry, education studies, environmental studies, food studies, organizations studies, psychology, addiction studies, social work, health and medicine studies, communications, library and information sciences, ethnic studies, aging studies, LGBTQ studies, disaster studies, design, and transportation studies.[63]

A Genealogy of Grounded Theory and Situational Analysis

Particularly important for GT and SA today is the likelihood of confusion among the different grounded theory approaches now in circulation. To clarify, a few years ago, Jan Morse organized a 'grounded theory bash' which produced *Developing Grounded Theory: The Second Generation* (Morse et al. 2009).[64] It includes chapters on each GT emphasis lively today: the late Phyllis Stern represented *Glaserian GT*, Barbara Bowers *dimensional analysis*,[65] Juliet Corbin *Straussian GT*, Kathy Charmaz *constructivist GT*, and Adele Clarke *situationist* GT or SA. Productive conversations among the book's contributors aimed at clarifying similarities and persistent differences and provocative conversations across them were included in the book, demonstrating a generosity of spirit which Anselm would have applauded. Figure 1.1 delineates relations among the different approaches historically.[66]

Looking at Figure 1.1, the almost immediate separation of the methodological paths of Strauss and Glaser is vivid. Glaser published his own GT methods book a decade post *Discovery*, and others especially after 1990. In contrast, in 1973, Strauss co-authored *Field Research: Strategies for a Natural Sociology* with Schatzman. Focusing instead on medical sociology for some years, Strauss did not publish his own methods book until 1987, but subsequently turned emphatically (but not solely)

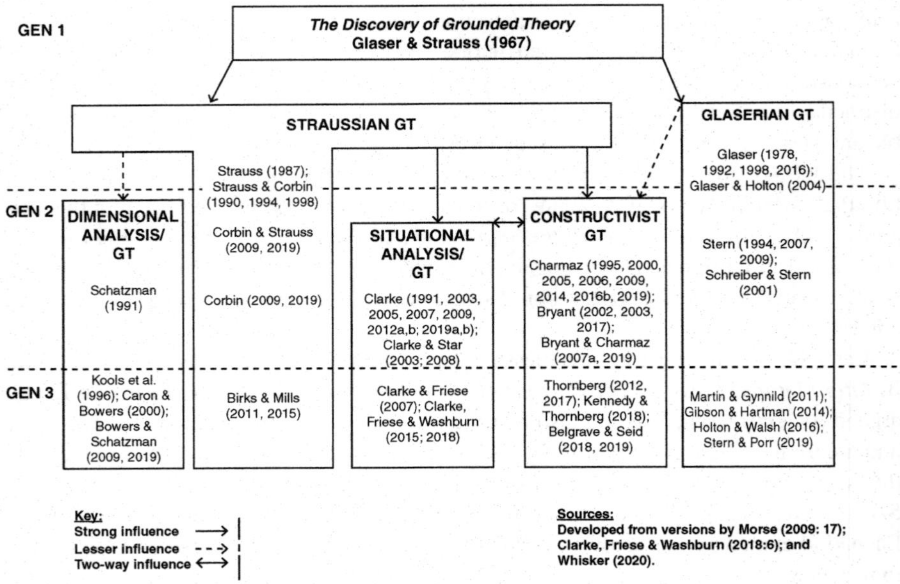

Figure 1.1 A Genealogy of Grounded Theory and Situational Analysis

towards methods for the remainder of his life. Today, constructivist GT and SA are the more common approaches in use.

QUALITATIVE INQUIRY IN THE 21ST CENTURY: 2000–2017

In a millennial review, two main themes in current qualitative inquiry in Europe were discerned by Knoblauch, Flick and Maeder (2005: Abstract): diversity in new approaches, and unity in sharing the interpretive paradigm. They also remind us that qualitative inquiries are 'imprinted by cultures ... their surrounding institutions, traditions and political as well as economic contexts,' the historical situatedness of our work on the planet. The new century has also seen changes in the broader landscape of social research.

There is today 'a new geography of knowledge' (Outhwaite & Turner 2007: 2). In the twenty plus years since the first edition of the *Handbook of Qualitative Research* (Denzin & Lincoln 1994), new ways of configuring *both* qualitative and quantitative research have crystallized in terms of positivisms, constructionisms, interpretation, etc., both across disciplines and transnationally. On the one hand, despite prolonged and varied refutations of positivisms, it is amazingly easy to track their 'uncanny persistence' across the human sciences (Steinmetz 2005: 2). Yet there are also major changes since the mid/late 20th century, 'when positivist epistemology, quantitative methodology, and conservative political ideology seemed always to go hand in hand' (Wyly 2009: 310). Of course, as Wyly also notes, this neat alignment was always contingent and contextual. But still, many of us use(d) it as shorthand, assuming that liberatory feminist, queer, social justice, postcolonial, indigenous and related commitments are more common in contemporary *qualitative* inquiry.

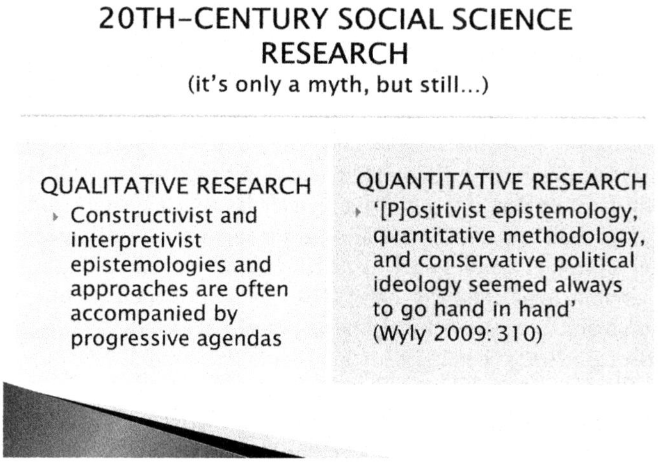

Figure 1.2 20th-century Social Science Research: 'Qual vs Quant' Approaches

But today this 'qual versus quant' shorthand is no longer apt (if it ever really was). For diverse reasons, the political alignments of a research project must now be interrogated rather than assumed by its methodology. One reason, Wyly (2009: 310) argues, is that 'Right-wing political operatives have coopted many of the epistemologies and methods traditionally associated with the postpositivist academic left.' But also, and significant here, progressive researchers are *themselves* pursuing *both* quantitative and mixed

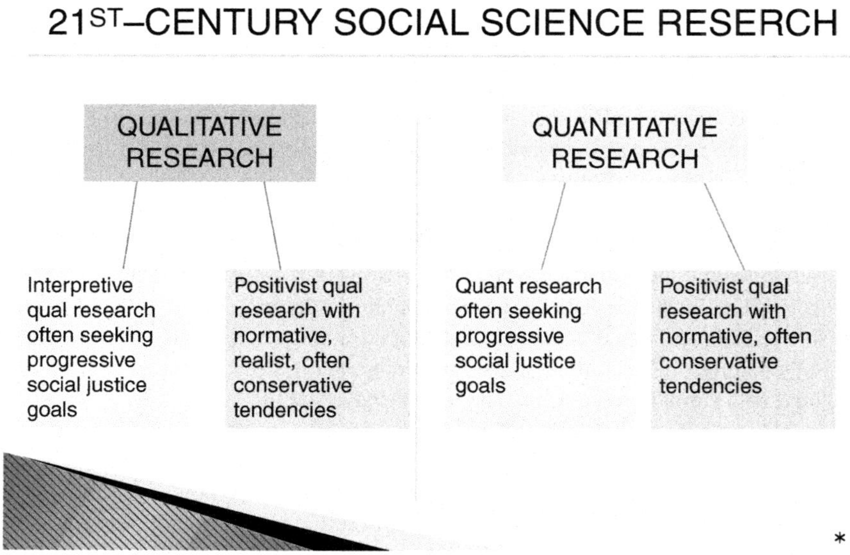

Figure 1.3 21st-century Social Science Research: Positivist vs Interpretive Approaches

methods research for various reasons, certainly including hoping to 'make a difference' in terms of public policy around issues such as race, gender, class, etc.

For example, progressive epidemiologists have led the way in *quantitative* health inequalities research (e.g., Krieger 2013). And critical geographers have recently adopted a 'strategic positivism' to revitalize policy relevance and build emancipatory geographies (e.g., Wyly 2009). Feminist sociologists pursue quantitative biosocial studies, asserting that feminists must participate to have gender issues adequately addressed in such domains (e.g., Springer et al. 2012). In addition, quantitative research *per se* has long been requisite in revealing inequalities such as racism and sexism and assessing the effectiveness of interventions (e.g., Haraway 1999; Williams & Mohammed 2013). And the very groundings of quantitative research have been expanded, including *Indigenous Statistics* (Walter & Anderson 2013), which asks 'what should be counted?'

Moreover, there are also important reconfigurings *within qualitative methods worlds* across disciplines and transnationally. Due to several 'triggering' factors, *positivist qualitative* methods and *interpretive qualitative* methods have now crystallized under two separate umbrellas. Ironically, the first trigger of this separation was the remarkable success of qualitative inquiry transnationally (if unevenly) as it has increasingly institutionalized in research curricula across the social sciences, humanities, professional education and beyond – even in computer and information science, the military, science education, food services and applied linguistics![67] The wide array of new national and international qualitative organizations, annual conferences, journals, etc., allows greater distinctions to be made *within* qualitative inquiry.[68]

Second, there has been a conservative tendency toward standardization and formalization of qualitative approaches which Knoblauch (2013) asserts places the 'interpretivist project' (Keller 2012) *intrinsically at risk*. Analytical openness is requisite for interpretation, but standards instead promote formalism and premature closure, especially in the hands of anxious beginners.[69] A third related factor 'dividing' the *qualitative world* into distinctive positivist and interpretivist camps has been neoliberal attempts to 'scientize' qualitative inquiry, often called 'evidence-based' research (EBR) or 'scientifically-based' research (SBR) movements, particular forms of standardization. Lather (2013: 635; see also 2010) wonderfully called such initiatives efforts to 'discipline and punish,' reminding us that research methods are always already historically situated.

In the US, extensive neoliberal attempts to 'scientize' or 'repositivize' in a 'rage for accountability' (Lather 2006: 783–784) have occurred, especially in education[70] and the health professions.[71] Many other disciplines and specialties have been similarly if less intensely affected, including sociology.[72] In both the UK (Henwood & Lang 2005) and Germany (Flick 2005: 15), national research organizations have urged 'integrative curricular formations' of 'proven' methods for doctoral training and beyond. 'Proven' methods generally manifest realist ontological orientations and objectivist epistemologies; 'mixed methods' with similar problematics may also be advocated.[73]

Moreover, EBR efforts often seek to marginalize innovative interpretive approaches, and lively debates have ensued (e.g., Yanow & Schwartz-Shea 2006, 2013; Becker 2010). Sadly, neoliberal guidelines often control access to funding and tend to support more positivist *qualitative* efforts. If universities are 'teaching machines,' as Spivak (1993) asserted, they are also increasingly 'research machines.' Colleagues in 'soft money careers,' doing research for a living and living from grant to grant, have described the EBR movement as no less than the 'bastardizing' of qualitative inquiry.

One researcher described what she was asked to do as 'drive-by ethnography' (Erickson 2018: 56). Software analyses of one-shot interview transcripts dominate, focused on frequencies for content 'analyses,' generating an 'anybody can do it' qualitative sham. (I do not mean that recent software developments are not incredibly useful – they assuredly can be[74] – but software should not replace serious scholarly analysis, merely assist in doing it.)

At the same time (but largely regardless of funding), other qualitative communities have also coalesced into an array of distinctive and *non*-overlapping configurations. For example, there is today a strong transnational critical Bourdieusian ethnographic tradition with major centers of gravity in France, the US, the UK and Germany, and many publications in the journal *Ethnography*, among others. This work often empirically examines various forms and structures of inequality interpreted via Bourdieu's theoretical frames. Some Bourdieusians claim the high ground for their approaches over all others.[75] Others engage more widely, with issues such as the adequacy of interviews in the contemporary moment.[76] Interpretive scholars not within the Bourdieusian fold also draw on his concepts such as cultural capital (e.g., Shim 2010).

Some other qualitative communities of practice have largely eschewed the constructionist/interpretive turn and refused engagements with poststructural, feminist or postcolonial social theories. They rely largely on neo-positivist or post-positivist traditional ethnographic approaches with different historical roots. In the social sciences, for example, there is an annual Qualitative Analysis Conference in Canada, books such as *Ethnographies Revisited: Constructing Theory in the Field* (Puddephatt, Shaffir & Kleinecht 2009), and journals that more or less maintain traditional approaches.[77]

While Glaserian GT[78] fits comfortably under this loosely neo-positivist qualitative umbrella, this community of practice, much like Bourdieusians, remains largely aloof from all others, including other approaches to GT.[79] Both qualitative *and quantitative* forms of Glaserian GT are pursued, and all other GT approaches strongly criticized, including SA (e.g., Martin & Gynnild 2011; Holton & Walsh 2016; Apramian et al. 2017).

In sharp contrast, the very broad interpretive qualitative methods umbrella has been zestfully held up against positivist and neo-positivist deluges by many and diverse willing arms. A remarkably wide range of approaches dwells here from autoethnography and phenomenology with emphases on lived experience to conversational analysis and ethnomethodology,[80] arrays of feminist, critical and cultural studies approaches, Foucauldian and other modes of discourse analysis (widely taken up in Europe).[81] Interpretive and critical interactionism (Denzin 1989, 2001; Jacobsen forthcoming 2019), constructivist GT (Charmaz 2000, 2014) and SA (Clarke 2005; Clarke, Friese & Washburn 2015, 2018) all dwell very comfortably here.

This broad interpretive umbrella was initially generated especially but not only by the Denzin and Lincoln *Handbooks of Qualitative Research* (1994, 2000, 2005, 2011, 2018) and the International Institute of Qualitative Inquiry. Since 2005, the Institute has hosted annual Congresses every May in Urbana, Illinois, of about 1600 people from around 80 countries with pre-conferences in different languages (Portuguese, Turkish, Spanish, etc.) and 'special interest groups' focused on various issues (e.g., indigenous research, critical research).[82] These conferences and many others are effective organizing devices for the transnational social movement now globalizing the legitimacy of interpretive qualitative research across the disciplines (Wertz et al. 2011).[83] There are related readers,[84] and new interpretive journals, including *Qualitative Inquiry*, the *International Review of*

Qualitative Research and *Cultural Studies/Critical Methodologies*, as well as many long-established journals which welcome diverse interpretive approaches.

The 21st century has also brought renewed energy to critical, feminist, anti-racist and, most recently, to LGBTQ research, which today are increasingly hybrid traditions (Kincheloe, McLaren & Steinberg 2011). Recent critical readers (e.g., Steinberg & Cannella 2012; Denzin & Giardina 2015) include attention to 'all of the above.' An edited volume on *Researching Non-Heterosexual Sexualities* (Phellas 2012) is distinctively transdisciplinary as well as addressing *both* qualitative and quantitative concerns. Contemporary texts combining critical and feminist work also attend to *both* qualitative and quantitative approaches (e.g., Sprague 2005; Hesse-Biber 2006a, 2006b, 2013a, 2013b) and explicitly activist research (e.g., Naples 2003; DeVault 2018). Feminist research has also been ambitiously assessed.[85]

Flyvberg's (2001) call for 'a social science that matters' captured some of the motivations for recent changes, promoting more democratic and inclusive approaches, less polemical and more dialogical forms of engagement. Emerging from the 'qualitative wars' of the late 20th century, scholars have called for less focus on universals and prediction and more on context, practice and putting experience to work. Flyvberg nicely framed this juncture where critical practice traditions (e.g., Bourdieu and others) began blurring with pragmatist philosophical attention to practice (e.g., Dewey) and poststructural framings (e.g., Foucault 1980, 2004; Dreyfus & Rabinow 1983), generating productive syntheses that continue to proliferate and hybridize.

Perhaps the greatest push in democratizing directions has been the rapid growth of participatory action, indigenous/decolonizing and (post)colonial research approaches, all typically involving strategies for fuller participation by those studied. Again, these are also often hybrid approaches. Action research, participatory action research and cooperative inquiry (multiple terms are used) have roots in various critical traditions, including Bateson's holism, Friere's liberationist educational strategies and Habermasian communicative strategies (e.g., Reason 1994; Torre et al. 2018). Such approaches have also been fueled by the turn toward reflexivity, especially *vis-à-vis* power (e.g., Reason & Bradbury-Huang 2008). They have been extensively used in education (e.g., Noffke & Somekh 2009) and health (e.g., Minkler & Wallerstein 2008). In the guest editor's assessment of a Special Issue on Ten Years of Critical Qualitative Research at the International Congress of Qualitative Inquiry, Gomez and Zapata-Sepulveda (2016) further asserted that the elaboration of approaches enhancing social justice, indigenous and postcolonial research was the major development of the decade.[86]

Relations of power between researchers and those studied have historically been particularly fraught in colonial and (post)colonial sites and with indigenous populations. Over recent decades, an array of new 'decolonizing' practices, strategies for participation and innovative approaches in such sites have appeared (e.g., Tuhiwai Smith 1999, 2007, 2012; Denzin, Lincoln & Tuhiwai Smith 2008; Denzin & Giardina 2013). This is due in no small part to the fact that indigenous people are now scholars themselves, seeking to undertake research differently, including understanding and legitimating radically different local epistemologies and ontologies toward enhanced epistemic diversity in research (e.g., Rains, Archibald & Deyhle 2000; Battiste 2007; Chilisa 2011; Pascale 2011; Bainbridge, Whiteside & McCalman 2013; Mertens, Cram & Chilisa 2014; TallBear 2014).

Engaging epistemic diversity requires explicit recognition in *all* research processes and products that there are many and diverse 'ways of knowing' or 'local epistemologies.'[87] These may include distinctive communities of practice, different paradigms within the same discipline or across the sciences and/or within and across cultures and subcultures. Decolonizing and indigenous approaches are particularly attentive to such issues. But the implications are considerably broader in that a wide array of non-indigenous communities may also share quite different epistemologies from dominant cultures in which they dwell, nicely captured in Deleuze and Guattari's (1983b) concept of 'minor literatures.' Some may be (post)colonials in diaspora for whom issues of hybridity are particularly vivid.[88] Others may share ethnic/cultural heritages or commitments to distinctive worldviews. Most have been ignored. Recognizing and representing epistemic diversity is also deeply integral to enhancing social justice.[89] Notably, such strategies offer some promise for qualitative inquiry to recover from its still too often voyeuristic and colonizing origins and routine patterns of 'studying down' rather than 'studying up' – or better still, 'studying across' various divides.[90]

Flowing from feminist poststructural implications for qualitative inquiry (e.g., Lather 1991, 2007), another dense yet intriguing set of recent debates centers on 'post-qualitative research.' Here critiques of 'mainstream qualitative research' are, of necessity, (re)mounted, including its inherent voyeurism, lack of reflexivity and power analytics, and subtly reinvented forms of scientism and neo-positivism (e.g., St. Pierre 2011, 2013; Lather 2013; Lather & St. Pierre 2013). In addition, non-foundationalist 'new materialisms' are also engaged (e.g., Maclure 2011, 2015), with an ontological insistence on the weight of the material and serious attention to relationalities.

Under the banner of '(post)qualitative research,' Lather, St. Pierre, MacLure and others have problematized various research processes, such as collecting 'data' and 'coding,' among the most provocative current interventions.[91] Highly transdisciplinary, these debates also 'rematch' earlier critical versus poststructural confrontations, now differently inflected (e.g., Dimitriadis 2016). These debates also engage many of the concerns and forms of analysis I intentionally 'built-in' to SA as a hybrid interactionist *and* poststructuralist extension of GT.[92] While continuing to value and learn from 'post-qualitative' explorations, with Keller (2017) and others, I argue that critical research remains necessary and informative, however challenging and partial.

Last, a major feature of the new millennium is how widely both quantitative and qualitative approaches *and* innovative theorizing are traveling (e.g., Flick 2014b; Denzin & Lincoln 2018), and how widely research is valued (Appadurai 2006). There are today more intentionally transnational venues for publication about research, such as the new *International Review of Qualitative Research* and *International Journal of Social Research Methodology*, as well as established journals publishing work from many countries.[93] The online journal *FQS: Forum: Qualitative Social Research/Sozialforschung* innovatively offers abstracts of everything in English (now the lingua franca of academia), while articles may be in many other languages, allowing broader access.[94] And transnational qualitative organizations continue to proliferate.[95] While qualitative inquiry may be a minority tradition in terms of research overall, it is also robust, enduring and thriving transdisciplinarily and transnationally.

Pressing Problems and Pragmatist Hopes for the Future of Qualitative Inquiry

> We have deliberately constructed our framework to respect all ways of working because this protects our ability to argue for our own way of working.

> The alternative, seen too often in the literature, is a vicious circle of contempt between opposing positions
>
> – Carter & Little (2007: 1327)

As we move into the 21st century, we confront some pressing problems briefly noted here,[96] along with my pragmatist hopes and strategies for engaging them – and unanticipated others. As difficult as it is to communicate the profound impact that *The Discovery of Grounded Theory* (1967) had in the 1960s and 1970s, it is equally if not more difficult to communicate the profound impacts postmodernisms and poststructuralisms have had in qualitative inquiry since the 1980s. Significantly, rejections of them often also dismissed or displaced other critiques of 'mainstream' qualitative research, including those of feminist, anti-racist, postcolonial, LGBTQ, indigenous, participatory and other scholars. However, communities of practice deeply committed to these agendas have ably rallied, are flourishing in various niches, and increasingly influence research concerns more broadly.

A primary domain of their influence is increasing concern with 'epistemic diversity' (e.g., Battiste 2007) and 'epistemic modernization' (Hess 2007) – enhancing the legitimacy of diverse 'ways of knowing' on an increasingly connected planet characterized by knowledge societies. With Harding (2015), I would argue that these moves are desperately needed to nourish the future of research of all kinds – not only qualitative inquiry. They are part of re-linking scientific research to projects of democratizing social movements around the globe.[97]

Another problem area is that polarizations such as the schisms in qualitative worlds often involve particularly pernicious forms of 'dumbing down' qualitative inquiry, such as EBR. A major antidote is explicit engagement with complexities and relationalities, and serious efforts to represent them clearly – not only acknowledging but seriously engaging the very very messy nature of life itself, as Law (2004, 2007) has vividly urged. Both constructivist GT and SA address problems obscured on the 'battlefield' (Atkinson & Delamont 2006) between modernist/traditional and more poststructural approaches to qualitative inquiry (Charmaz 2005, 2011; Clarke with Keller 2014; Charmaz, Thornberg & Keane 2018). With many others, we are committed to 'advancing qualitative inquiry as a way of being and a way of knowing' (Denzin & Giardina 2015: 444; Star 2007).

Another major challenge 'in these times' for all qualitative inquiry and research in general are the pernicious consequences of neoliberalism for the academy, especially public higher education. These include massive structural changes in universities, the near collapse of public funding of higher education (down c. 18% per student in the US since 2008) and tremendous preferences for 'hard' sciences, and the growth of 'audit cultures' in the academy.[98] All have huge implications for how we do our work, who may fund it, what kinds of research get funded, etc.

The proliferation of approaches to qualitative inquiry also poses challenges (Knoblauch 2013), and some practitioners lament this profusion (e.g., Adler & Adler 2008; Hammersley 2008: 181). In contrast, I agree with Yanow and Schwartz-Shea (2006: 390): 'If knowledge is power, then methodological pluralism disperses that power, whereas "one best way" concentrates it. Reembracing interpretive approaches as a legitimate scientific undertaking, then, strengthens both the human sciences and democracy.' Happily, Dewey's pragmatism still echoes loudly.

To sustain Gubrium and Holstein's (1997) efforts to create 'new languages of qualitative method' and Preissle's (2006: 687) vision of qualitative inquiry as multiple communities of practice operating as a 'confederacy,' the concept of 'agonistic pluralism' can be usefully – pragmatically – put to work. My goal here is to promote methodological *pluralism* against methodological *tribalism*, and to also facilitate inter-and trans-disciplinarity.[99] Political theorist Chantal Mouffe (2000: 102–103, original emphasis) wrote:

> *Antagonism* is struggle between enemies, while *agonism* is struggle between adversaries. ... [E]nvisaged from the perspective of 'agonistic pluralism,' the aim of democratic politics is to transform *antagonism* into *agonism* ... providing channels through which collective passions will be given ways to express themselves over issues which ... will not construct the opponent as an enemy but as an adversary. ... [F]or 'agonistic pluralism', the prime task of democratic politics is not to eliminate passions from the sphere of the public, in order to render a rational consensus possible, but to mobilize those passions towards democratic designs.

Agonistic pluralism not only does *not* deny differences of perspective, it also legitimates conflicts arising from different interests, values and perspectives (Moss 2007: 235). It promotes the generative tensions of pluralism (Wertz et al. 2011: 82). It promotes engagement without domination by one camp or phony consensus, echoing Strauss's (1993) idea of negotiations as including 'cooperation without consensus.'[100] Erickson (2018: 59) further asserts that it will be useful to adopt 'a certain degree of humility as we consider what any of our work is capable of accomplishing, whatever our particular approach and commitments might be.'

Engagement without domination, cooperation without consensus, and such humility will all become increasingly important as the transnationalization of qualitative inquiry – and most everything else – continues. We will face many challenges of translation – linguistic, cultural, perspectival, epistemological, and even ontological – wherein cooperation will be of inestimable value in sharing and enhancing the interpretive paradigm. A passionate pluralism without contempt seems a worthy strategy for negotiating more democratizing futures in qualitative inquiry.

Notes

1 An earlier version appeared in Clarke, Friese & Washburn (2015: 22–49). I thank Reiner Keller, Jörg Strübing, Monica Casper, Kathy Charmaz, Antony Bryant, Carrie Friese, Rachel Washburn, Hella von Unger, and Virginia Olesen for generous comments.

2 On the history of qualitative inquiry, see e.g., Gobo (2005), Manicas (2007), Denzin & Lincoln's 'Introductions' (1994, 2000, 2005, 2011, 2018), Bryant & Charmaz (2007b), Vidich & Lyman (1994), Platt (1996), Rosaldo (1989), Flick (2014a), Knoblauch (2013), Atkinson et al. (2001), Preissle (2006), Clark & Scheurich (2008), Seale et al. (2004), Outhwaite & Turner (2007), Lincoln (2010), Teddlie & Tashakkori (2011), Wertz et al. (2011), Bassi Follari (2014), Erickson (2018), Westbrook (2018), and Denzin & Giardina (2015: esp. Chapter 1 and Epilogue. See also the 2015 Special Issue: Qualitative Research at 20 of *Qualitative Inquiry* 21(7); and the Special Issue edited by Aitor Gomez and Pamela Zapata-Sepulveda (2016) on Ten Years of Critical Qualitative Research at the International Congress of Qualitative Inquiry in the *International Review of Qualitative Research* 9(2): 137–227. My own transnational understanding remains very partial. On transnationalization, see e.g., Knoblauch

(2013) and the 2014 Special Issue: Challenges for Qualitative Inquiry as a Global Endeavor guest edited by Uwe Fleck of *Qualitative Inquiry* 20(9). The Special Issue on The State of the Art of Qualitative Research in Europe in *FQS* [6(3): 2005] reviews developments nation by nation. See: www.qualitative-research.net/index.php/fqs/issue/view/1. On the slow but sure growth in Italy, see also Bruni and Gobo (2005). Reiner Keller and Angelika Poferl (forthcoming, 2019) are doing histories of qualitative inquiry in Germany and France; see also Mey & Mruck (2007) and Schütze (2008).

3 For histories of GT method in practice, see Bryant & Charmaz (2007b), Editors' Introductions (this volume), Morse et al. (2009, forthcoming 2019), and Clarke, Friese & Washburn 2018: esp. 1-8).

4 Other terms used include life and case history analysis and field research.

5 I find Denzin and Lincoln's (1994) periodizations apt until the late 20th century when, to me, heterogeneity and hybridity largely defy overarching labels. Knoblauch (2013) makes a similar point regarding Europe.

6 See e.g., Bowden & Low (2013), Bulmer (1984) and Fine (1995). On later areas of focus at Chicago, see e.g., Fine (1995), Bulmer (1997) and Abbott (1999, 2009).

7 See e.g., Ferguson et al. (1990). Stonequist's (1937/1961) *The Marginal Man*, and Hughes' early work (1971a, 1971b) were exemplary. In the US, Simmel's *The Stranger* (1908/1971) and other work inspired the Chicago theoretical heritage, though not in Germany. Chicago interactionists Everett Hughes and Nils Anderson both spent time in Germany post-World War II both doing and advising on research.

8 On critical interactionism, see e.g., Sandstrom & Fine (2003), Schwalbe (2008), Clarke (forthcoming, 2019b) and Jacobsen (forthcoming, 2019).

9 In practice, these terms are often used interchangeably today. However, I agree with Charmaz's (2014) historical distinction which uses 'constructionist' to characterize earlier usage (1970s–1990s) which assumed that research participants' accounts were constructions but often or largely tacitly exempted researchers themselves from such processes. Realist ethnographers such as Robert Prus, David Snow and others fall into this camp. By the late 1990s, the turn toward reflexivity (e.g., Fine 1994; Fine et al. 2000), often spearheaded by feminists, engendered use of the term 'constructivist', which includes researchers as constructing their accounts as well. See Clarke (2005: Chapter 1) and Clarke, Friese & Washburn (2018: Chapter 2) for discussions of reflexivity *vis-à-vis* GT and SA. See also Charmaz (2000, 2007, 2008, 2009, 2016b).

10 See also Rabinow & Sullivan (1987) and Keller (2012). T.P. Wilson (1970) originated this term.

11 Ethnomethodologist Lynch (1998) offers a genealogy focused on qualitative methods (see also Velody & Williams 1998; Lincoln & Guba 2013; and Weinberg 2015).

12 Dean Helen Nahm of the University of California, San Francisco School of Nursing hired Anselm Strauss c. 1960 to initiate research training for nursing faculty toward enhanced professionalization of nursing. Initially through grants, Strauss then hired Fred Davis, Virginia Olesen, Leonard Schatzman and Barney Glaser. Related Doctoral Programs were soon established in Nursing (DNS in 1968, PhD in 1982) and Sociology (PhD in 1968). Glaser left UCSF in the late 1970s. Strauss was Clarke's faculty advisor when she was a UCSF doctoral student, and upon his retirement she was hired by that department in 1989.

13 A Google search (8/22/16) yielded 3,350,000 results – many likely duplicates.

14 On GT theoretical sampling, see Charmaz (2014: Chapter 8). On GT, SA and abduction, see Clarke, Friese & Washburn (2018: Chapter 2). On abduction, see also note 39.

15 See Spradley (1980), Van Maanen (1995) and Atkinson et al. (2001). On GT ethnography, see Charmaz & Mitchell (2001). Here the researcher focuses less on 'thick description' and more on analysis of particular social processes (Charmaz, personal communication, 2014).

16 Special thanks to Jürg Strübing for telling me of this development and Wilson's (1970) highly significant paper. A number of later well-known German scholars of interpretive methods, such as Fritz Schütze (2008), translated the texts.

17 I quote from the original English article. Reiner Keller titled his 2012 book *Das interpretative Paradigma* following from Thomas' 1970 intervention; Keller's book won the 2014 German Sociological

Association prize for the best sociology book of the past two years. Keller and Strübing also note that the German situation *vis-à-vis* qualitative research was complex in ways that go far beyond the purview of this brief historical overview.

18 He relied in part on the translation of Wilson's (1970) paper for this assertion.

19 On the interpretive turn, see especially Rabinow & Sullivan (1987), Hiley, Bowman, & Schusterman (1991), and Outhwaite & Turner (2007: 359–457).

20 Star (1989) demonstrated the materiality and consequentiality of 'theory/methods packages' in brain research (see also Star 1991, 1995, 2007). On co-constitution, see Jasanoff (2004). On the uptake of 'theory-methods packages,' see e.g., Clarke & Star (2007), Hekman (2007) and Jensen (2014). In GT, see Charmaz (2014: Chapters 9 & 10); in SA, see Clarke (2005: 2–5) and Clarke, Friese & Washburn (2015: 87, 2018: Chapter 2). On Star's work, see Bowker, Timmermans, Clarke, & Balka (2015).

21 See e.g., Behar & Gordon (1995), Denzin & Lincoln (1994), Naples (2003), Hesse-Biber (2006a, 2006b), Tuhiwai Smith (1999) and Dillard (2008).

22 Habermas discussed the work of Mead, Garfinkel, Cicourel, Strauss and Goffmann. After Thomas Luckmann returned to Germany, Alfred Schütz, Mead and symbolic interaction also received greater attention there. Habermas's Western universalist assumptions were highly problematic, as were Flyvbjerg's (2001).

23 On 'theory/methods packages,' see note 20. On institutional ethnography, see e.g., Campbell & Monicom (1995), Campbell & Gregor (2002), Smith (2005) and Smith & Turner (2014).

24 On intersectionality, see e.g., Schulz & Mullings (2006) and Grzanka (2014). Early contributors included Alice Walker and Audrey Lorde. *Signs: A Journal of Women in Culture and Society* had a special issue on 'Intersectionality: Theorizing Power, Empowering Theory' (Summer 2013, vol. 38, no. 4).

25 Mary Louise Pratt was the only woman contributor.

26 US scholars here include St. Pierre & Pillow (2002) and Jackson & Mazzei (2012). See also Lather (2017).

27 Institutionally in the US, this reflects the success both of women's and gender studies and of doctoral 'special emphases' in feminist research which enroll students from many disciplines, legitimating scholars *vis-à-vis* future teaching in women's and gender studies, as well as their home disciplines.

28 See Yanow & Schwartz-Shea (2006: xii), who also (2006: 389–390) note that 'human sciences' is often considered a better translation of a common German term for interpretive work – 'Geisteswissenschaften' – in contrast with 'Naturwissenschaften' or natural sciences. Of course, this reenacts the Enlightenment split between 'man' and nature challenged by science and technology studies (e.g., Latour & Woolgar 1979), posthumanism (e.g., Braidotti 2013) and the nonhuman turn (e.g., Grusin 2015) from different angles.

29 Philosopher Mead (1938: 98) brilliantly wrote: '…facts are not there to be picked up. They have to be dissected out, and the data are the most difficult of abstractions in any field. More particularly, their very form is dependent upon the problem within which they lie.'

30 On indigenous research, see e.g., Rains, Archibald, & Deyhle (2000), Battiste (2007), Bainbridge, Whiteside, & McCalman (2013), Chilisa (2011), Mertens, Cram, & Chilisa (2014), and Tuhiwai Smith (1999, 2007, 2012).

31 These debates and rifts have occurred both in symbolic interactionism and in other qualitative research worlds. For examples, see Denzin & Lincoln (1994, 1995, 2000, 2005, 2011: 10), Snow & Morrill (1995), Denzin (2010), Atkinson & Delamont (2006), Hammersley (2008), and Adler & Adler (2008).

32 On kinds of relativisms, see Hollis & Lukes (1982). On pragmatist philosophy-inflected relativism and its important links to pluralism and cooperation without consensus, see Strauss (1993) and Star (1995: 9–12); on 'Why I Am Not a Nazi,' see Star (2015: 19–22) and Becker (1967/1970).

33 The contestation seems especially strong in English-speaking qualitative domains. On 'jockeying for position,' see Erickson (2018: 53). Lynch (2012: 452) discusses how, when approaches travel, there

tends to be 'drift and slippage from one node to another, with relatively weak and decentralized policing.'

34 See e.g., http://humweb.ucsc.edu/foucaultacrossthedisciplines/foucault.htm. See also Koopman (2009). Baiocchi, Graizbord, & Rodríguez-Muñiz (2013) have even explored Foucault-influenced actor-network theory and the 'ethnographic imagination.'

35 See Thomas (1923/1978) and Thomas & Thomas's (1928/1970) proto-constructionist 'theorem.'

36 One echoing consists in climate change deniers defending their position by attempting to appropriate the social construction of scientific facts as framed in the specialty of science and technology studies (STS) (e.g., Latour & Woolgar 1979; Latour 1987), but without an adequate grasp of Kuhn or the history of science, rendering their refutations absurdist.

37 The others were naturalism, ethnography and emotionalism.

38 Silverman & Marvasti (2008: 18) deliberately misrepresent the moderate position taken by Gubrium and Holstein, asserting that their critique, taken wholly out of context, is best represented by 'ominous words.'

39 The American Political Science Association established an Organized Section on Qualitative and Multi-Method Research in 2003 (Collier & Elman 2008). Robert Adcock, the section's Newsletter editor (personal communication, 7/7/14), noted that over time it became a 'broad, pluralistic section that includes, but is far from limited to, a self-consciously "interpretive" sub-group.' See www1.maxwell.syr.edu/moynihan/cqrm/APSA_s_Qualitative_and_Multi-Method_Research_Section/

40 There were two prior joint methods publications, Glaser & Strauss (1965) on the 'Discovery of Substantive Theory: A Basic Strategy Underlying Qualitative Research,' and Glaser & Strauss (1966) on 'The Purpose and Credibility of Qualitative Research.' After *Discovery* was published in 1967, they briefly continued publishing together on their collaborative substantive projects, including reflections on their methods use in the project (e.g., Glaser & Strauss 1968, 1971; Strauss & Glaser 1970). But they did not co-author any further books or articles focused solely on method.

41 For their subsequent individual methods articles, see e.g., Glaser (1965, 1969, 1992, 2002a,b) and Strauss (1970, 1978, 1982a, 1982b, 1984, 1991b, 1995).

42 See e.g., Atkinson, Coffey, & Delamont (2003: 150), Bryant (2002), Charmaz (2000, 2006, 2014), and Strübing (2007, 2017, 2018). Glaser's (1965, reprinted 1969) earliest publication on GT was 'The Constant Comparative Method of Qualitative Analysis,' which cited and thanked both Merton and Lazarsfeld for their comments.

43 See e.g., Maines (1991), Hildenbrand (2004), Charmaz (2008), Clarke (2007, 2008a, 2008b), Charmaz & Clarke (2020), Schütze (2008) and Strübing (2007, 2017, 2018). See Strauss's website for a list of his many publications on Chicago sociology/interactionism: http://dne2.ucsf.edu/public/anselmstrauss/index.html. Bryant (2009) found it oddly curious that despite his deep pragmatist philosophical roots, Strauss did *not* publish on the many linkages of Straussian GT with pragmatism. I suspect Strauss thought those linkages were clarified through his more theoretical, especially interactionist, writings. Strauss's career was considerably more sociological, rather than more strictly methodological (like Glaser's).

44 See e.g., Charmaz (1995, 2000), Bryant (2009), Clarke (2005: Chapter 2).

45 Like Susan Leigh Star (2007), Antony Bryant was initially trained as a sociologist (he by Giddens, she by Strauss) and later went into informatics.

46 Strauss developed both the 'negotiated order framework' stressing *social processes* (e.g., Strauss 1979, 1982a; Strauss et al. 1964; Clarke In prep. a) and the social worlds framework stressing *social structuring* (e.g., Strauss 1978, 1979, 1982b, 1984, 1991a, 1993; Strauss et al. 1964; Clarke 2005; Clarke & Star 2008). These are flip sides of the same theoretical project in his pragmatist/interactionist action-oriented sociology which also generated the useful concept 'cooperation without consensus' (e.g., Strauss 1993; Star 1993; Clarke & Star 2008).

47 On abduction, see also Hildenbrand (2004), Reichertz (2007), Richardson & Kramer (2006), Strübing (2007) and Tavory & Timmermans (2014).

48 Thanks to Daniel Cefaï (2016) for drawing my attention to Mead's lovely work on the farmer, the fig tree and the wasp. The term 'nonhuman' is from actor-network theory (ANT) (Latour & Woolgar

1979; Latour 1987; Law & Hassard 1999); and material semiotics (Law's version of ANT) (Law 2009 @ www.google.de/#q=material+semiotics+law). ANT is an analytic approach with its origins in French and British science and technology studies. It is known for its executive orientation because, if successful, a particular node on an actor-network becomes an 'obligatory point of passage' for many if not most other actors/nodes. Like SA, Law emphasizes relationality.

49 See Seale et al. (2004: 3) for the Parsonian version.

50 See e.g., Lather (2007), Law (2004, 2007), Law & Hassard (1999), Star (1995) and Clarke with Keller (2014). Gubrium & Holstein (1997: 77) note 'postmodern sociologists allow for the possibility of relational patterning.' See related arguments by Burawoy (1998, 2000).

51 See e.g., Bourdieu (1972/1977, 1975). 'The field' (*le champ*) is one of French critical sociologist Pierre Bourdieu's main concepts. A field is a setting in which agents are positioned as the result of interactions among the rules of the specific field which vary, and the agent's own habitus and social, economic and cultural capital. Fields are hierarchical and interactive with one another, though for Bourdieu, largely subordinate to class and power relations. There are strong parallels with Strauss's social worlds/arenas theory developed at about the same time, but with interactionist rather than Marxist roots. Both are conflict orientations, but quite differently inflected.

52 See e.g., Foucault (1973), Simon (1996), Keller (2013) and Kendall & Wickham (1999, 2004).

53 A *dispositif* is a web of connections among seemingly disparate concepts, discourses, technologies, infrastructures, practices, and institutions (e.g., Foucault 1980: 194–228; Bussolini 2010).

54 On ANT, see note 48.

55 For Deleuze and Guattari (1987: 3–4, 8, 1983a), an assemblage brings together heterogeneous entities in dynamic, fluid relations. It can expand, contract, etc., and is an inherently unstable phenomenon. See also, e.g., Delanda (2006), Marcus & Sakka (2006), McLeod (2014), Suchman (2012) and Coleman & Ringrose (2013).

56 Deleuze & Guattari (1987: 21) summarize the characteristics of a rhizome: 'unlike trees or their roots, the rhizome connects any point to any other point, and its traits are not necessarily linked to traits of the same nature. … It has neither beginning nor end, but always a middle (milieu) from which it grows and which it overspills. … [T]he rhizome … is always detachable, connectable, reversible, modifiable, and has multiple entryways and exits and its own lines of flight.' See also Jensen & Rodje (2010).

57 See also Clarke, Friese, & Washburn (2018: 47–49, 68–71).

58 On Strauss's social worlds/arenas theory, see note 46.

59 See Clarke (2005: 45–51) and Clarke, Friese, & Washburn (2018: 76–77) for further discussion. For the original development of the concept, see Clarke & Montini (1993).

60 On epistemic diversity, see Battiste (2007), Dillard (2008) and Meyer (2008), as well as related transdisciplinary moves toward social justice (e.g., Charmaz 2005, 2011; Charmaz, Thornberg, & Keane 2018). See also Geertz (1983) on 'local knowledge.'

61 I use the terms pluralist and relativist distinctively as a pluralism of representation and a relativism of relationality, assuredly *NOT* as an equal valuation of what is represented. See Star (1995: 9–12, 2015: 19–22). This form of representation does *not* seek a consensus that erases positionality, but rather one that preserves it by operating as 'cooperation without consensus' (Star 1993).

62 The German translation of the SA text (Clarke 2012a) was sponsored by Reiner Keller (e.g., 2013) whose own method of discourse analysis, the Sociology of Knowledge Approach to Discourse (SKAD) similarly relies on social constructionism and the sociology of knowledge.

63 For SA exemplars from these areas, see Appendices B and C in Clarke, Friese, & Washburn (2015, 2017).

64 A second edition is underway, due out in 2019.

65 Dimensional analysis, a variant of GT, was developed by Leonard Schatzman (now deceased), former student and colleague of Strauss and sociology faculty at UCSF, and further developed by Barbara Bowers and Susan Kools. See, e.g., Schatzman (1991), Kools, McCarthy, Durham, & Robrecht (1996) and Bowers & Schatzman (2009, forthcoming 2019).

66 The first such genealogy was developed by Jan Morse (2009: 17). I updated and extended it elsewhere (Clarke, Friese & Washburn 2018:6), and again in Figure 1.1 here, with appreciation to Craig Whisker (forthcoming, 2020) for noting a 3rd generation. Special thanks to Jan Morse for organizing the conference on which *Developing Grounded Theory: The Second Generation* was based, and both its first (Morse et al. 2009) and second (Morse et al. forthcoming 2019) editions. Her attention to and appreciation of the broad GT tradition are distinctively discerning and sophisticated.

67 Thanks to Kathy Charmaz for helping to expand this extraordinary list.

68 For Europe, see e.g., the Special Issue on The State of the Art of Qualitative Research in Europe in *FQS* 6(3): 2005: www.qualitative-research.net/index.php/fqs/issue/view/1. See also note 2.

69 However unwittingly, due in part to efforts to teach the method more clearly, the Strauss & Corbin (1990, 1998) *Basics* books made it seem that GT both could and should be routinized and standardized. On standardization and its problems, see Bowker & Star (1999), Lampland & Star (2009) and Timmermans & Epstein (2010).

70 In education, see e.g., Lather (2006, 2010, 2013), Teddlie & Tashakkori (2011), focused issues of *Qualitative* Inquiry 10, Nos 1 and 2 (2004), and of the *International Journal of Qualitative Studies in Education* 19, No. 6 (2006).

71 In health care, see e.g., Daly (2005), Timmermans & Berg (2003) and Knaapen (2013). In nursing, one website offers a menu of other sites each offering different standards! See www.nursingworld.org/research-toolkit/appraising-the-evidence.

72 In sociology, see on NSF Reports, e.g., Becker (2010), Lamont & White (2005) and Ragin, Nagel, & White (2004).

73 For an amusing and agonizing intervention in evidence-based debates, see Denzin (2018). I cannot engage mixed methods here, but for entrée to that history, see Denzin (2010) and the 2010 Special Issue of *Qualitative Inquiry* 16(6). See also Denzin & Lincoln (2011: 2, 716), cf. Morse & Niehaus (2016).

74 On recent developments, see Davidson, Paulus, & Jackson (2016) and Denzin & Lincoln (2018).

75 See Wacquant (2002) and Burawoy (1998, 2000); for responses to their parochialism, see Dunier (2002), Anderson (2002), Newman (2002) and Adler & Adler (2005). See also Anderson, Brooks, Gunnn & Jones (2004).

76 See e.g., Savage & Burrows (2007) and Lamont & Swidler (2014).

77 See www.qualitatives.ca/past-programs.

78 See e.g., Glaser (1965, 1969, 1978, 1992, 2006, 2016) and Glaser & Holton (2004).

79 It has its own Grounded Theory Institute, Sociology Press, *The Grounded Theory Review* journal, and edited volumes. See www.groundedtheory.com/what-is-gt.aspx. Recent exceptions to this isolationism include Apramian et al. (2017) and reflections such as Nelson (2015), Locke (2015) and the 2015 Special Issue of *Organizational Research Methods* 18(4), offering discussion of Glaserian and other forms of GT.

80 Ethnomethodologists often dwell apart from other qualitative communities of practice. See Lynch (1998) and Pascale (2011: 105–138).

81 For a review of European discourse analysis, see Keller (2013).

82 See www.iiqi.org/. Information about the Special Interest Groups can be found in the IAQI Newsletter: see http://icqi.org/qi-newsletters/.

83 Other regular conferences in English include the Canadian Qualitatives (see www.qualitatives.ca/Home), the International Institute for Qualitative Methodology (see www.iiqm.ualberta.ca/), and the Summer Institute in Qualitative Research: Putting Theory to Work, held at the Education and Social Research Institute, Manchester Metropolitan University (see www2.mmu.ac.uk/esri/). The Newsletter of *The Qualitative Sociology Review* lists upcoming conferences internationally (see www.qualitativesociologyreview.org/ENG/journal_news_eng.php). There is also a new European Congress of Qualitative Inquiry (ECQI) which first met in 2017; see https://kuleuvencongres.be/ecfi2019.

84 For example, the ICQI produces conference-based thematic books (e.g., Denzin & Giardina 2009, 2013, 2015).

85 See e.g., Olesen (2007, 2011, 2018), Kitzinger (2004), Fonow & Cook (2005), Hekman (2007), Sprague (2016) and DeVault (2018).

86 See the 2016 Special Issue of the *International Review of Qualitative Research* 9(2).

87 Local is meant in Geertz's (1983) sense that local practices always transform ideas and methods that have traveled, also a core argument of science and technology studies (e. a., Star 1995).

88 On significant differences between (post)colonial and decolonizing/indigenous issues and approaches, see Donald (2012) and the special issue of *Feminist Studies* (43 (3), 2017) on Decolonial Postcolonial Approaches: A Dialogue. See www.feministstudies.org/issues/ vol–40–49/43–3. html.

89 See also Battiste (2007), Charmaz (2005, 2011, 2016a; Charmaz, Thornberg, & Keane 2018), Dillard (2008) and Meyer (2008).

90 On studying 'up', see Hertz & Imber (1995) and Reid (2001). See also Bassi Follari (2014).

91 In the UK, see Maclure (2011, 2015). On rethinking 'data,' see Benozza, Bell, & Koro-Ljungberg (2013). See also *International Journal of Qualitative Studies in Education* 26(6), 2013. Erickson (2018: 54–55) makes the significant point that problematics with the 'knowing subject' (underscored in post-qualitative inquiry) were not *initially* raised by Foucault and others, but much earlier by Boas, Mead, Dewey, Marx and Althusser.

92 See Clarke (2005: Chapters 1–2, 2012b), Clarke with Keller (2014), Clarke, Friese, & Washburn (2015, 2018: Part I).

93 Both *Qualitative Inquiry* and *Qualitative Research*, for example, are quite transnational.

94 I agree with Knoblauch's (2013: para. 11) lament that demands to publish in English contribute to the standardization of qualitative methods. *FQS*'s approach offers a counter-balancing strategy.

95 On transnational qualitative groups, see note 83.

96 On pressing problems, see also the 2015 Special Issue: *Qualitative Inquiry* at 20, *Qualitative Inquiry* 21(7), especially articles by Cannella, Flick, and Lester & O'Reilly.

97 Harding (2015) argues more specifically that such democratization of knowledge projects was the spirit behind the Enlightenment, which has been largely displaced as research domains have been profoundly colonized by military and capitalist interests. She argues for a 'strong objectivity' most deeply informed by the needs of those who have the least.

98 See e.g., Leonhardt (2017: SR2), Newfield (2016) and Westbrook (2018). David Theo Goldberg's insightful 'The Afterlife of the Humanities' goes far beyond the humanities in explaining this situation: http://humafterlife.uchri.org/. On audit cultures, see Spooner (2018).

99 On interdisciplinarity, see Barry & Born (2013).

100 See also Star (1993) and Clarke & Star (2007).

REFERENCES

Abbott, A. (1999). *Department and Discipline: Chicago Sociology at One Hundred*. Chicago, IL: University of Chicago Press.

Abbott, A. (2009). Organizations and the Chicago School. In P. Adler (Ed.), *Oxford Handbook of Sociology and Organization Studies: Classical Foundations*. [Online.] Oxford: Oxford University Press.

Adler, P.A. & P. Adler (2005). Review Essay: Lost in Translation? Review of Wacquant's *Body and Soul*. *Symbolic Interaction 28*(3): 433–435.

Adler, P.A. & P. Adler (2008). The Four Faces of Ethnography. *Sociological Quarterly 49*(4): 1–30.

Alexander, B. (2018). Queer/Quare Theory: Worldmaking and Methodologies. In N.K. Denzin & Y.S. Lincoln (Eds.), *Sage Handbook of Qualitative Research* (5th ed., pp. 275–308). Thousand Oaks, CA: Sage.

Anderson, E. (2002). The Ideologically Driven Critique. *American Journal of Sociology* 107(6): 1533–1550.

Anderson, E., S.N. Brooks, R. Gunn & N. Jones (Guest Eds.) (2004). Special Issue on Being Here and Being There: Fieldwork Encounters and Ethnographic Discoveries. *The Annals of the American Academy of Political and Social Sciences 595*: 6–326.

Appadurai, Arjun (2006). The Right to Research. *Globalization, Societies and Education 4*(2): 167–177.

Apramian, T., S. Cristancho, C. Watling & L. Lingard (2017). (Re)Grounding Grounded Theory: A Close Reading of Theory in Four Schools. *Qualitative Research 17*(4): 359–376.

Arbeitsgruppe Bielefelder Soziologen (Eds.) (1973). *Alltagswissen. Interaktion und gesellschaftliche Wirklichkeit*. Hamburg: Rowohlt.

Atkinson, P., A. Coffey, & S. Delamont. (2003). *Key Themes in Qualitative Research: Continuities and Change*. Walnut Creek, CA: Alta Mira Press.

Atkinson, P., A. Coffey, S. Delamont, J. Lofland, & L. Lofland (Eds.) (2001). *Handbook of Ethnography*. London: Sage.

Atkinson, P. & S. Delamont (2006). In the Roiling Smoke: Qualitative Inquiry and Contested Fields. *International Journal of Qualitative Studies in Education 19*(6): 747–755.

Bainbridge, R., M. Whiteside, & J. McCalman (2013). Being, Knowing and Doing: A Phronetic Approach to Constructing Grounded Theory with Aboriginal Australian Partners. *Qualitative Health Research* 23(2): 275–288.

Baiocchi, G., D. Graizbord, & M. Rodríguez-Muñiz. (2013). Actor-Network Theory and the Ethnographic Imagination: An Exercise in Translation. *Qualitative Sociology 36*: 323-341.

Barry, A., & G. Born (Eds.). (2013). Interdisciplinarity: Reconfigurations of the Social and Natural Sciences. London: Routledge.

Bassi Follari, J. (2014). Quantitative/Qualitative: The Paleozoic Debate. *Forum: Qualitative Social Research 15*(2) online.

Battiste, M. (2007). Research Ethics for Protecting Indigenous Knowledge and Heritage: Institutional and Researcher Responsibilities. In N.K. Denzin & M.D. Giardina (Eds.), *Ethical Futures in Qualitative Research: Decolonizing the Politics of Knowledge*. London: Routledge.

Becker, H.S. (1963). *Outsiders: Studies in the Sociology of Deviance*. New York: Free Press.

Becker, H.S. (1967/1970). Whose Side Are We On? In H.S. Becker (Ed.), *Sociological Work: Method and Substance* (pp. 123–134). New Brunswick, NJ: Transaction Books.

Becker, H.S. (2010). *How to Find out How to do Qualitative Research*. [Comment on the National Science Foundation Report on Qualitative Research]: http://home.earthlink.net/~hsbecker/articles/NSF.html

Behar, R. & D.A. Gordon (Eds.) (1995). *Women Writing Culture*. Berkeley, CA: University of California Press.

Belgrave, L.L., & Seide, K. (2018) Grounded Theory Methodology: Principles and Practices. In P. Liamputtong (Ed.) *Handbook of Research Methods in Health Social Sciences* (pp.1–18). Singapore: Springer.

Belgrave L.L., & Seide K. (2019). Coding in Grounded Theory. In A. Bryant & K. Charmaz (Eds.) *SAGE Handbook of Current Developments in Grounded Theory* (pp. 167–185). London: Sage.

Benozza, A., H. Bell, & M. Koro-Ljungberg (2013). Moving between Nuisance, Secrets, and Splinters as Data. *Cultural Studies <-> Critical Methdologies 13*(4): 309–315.

Berger, P. & Luckman, T. (1966). *The Social Construction of Reality: A Treatise in the Sociology of Knowledge*. Garden City, NY: Doubleday.

Birks, M. & J. Mills (2011). *Grounded Theory: A Practical Guide* (1st ed). London: Sage.

Birks, M. & J. Mills (2015). *Grounded Theory: A Practical Guide* (2nd ed). London: Sage.

Blumer, H. (1969). *Symbolic Interactionism: Perspective and Method.* Englewood Cliffs, NJ: Prentice-Hall.

Bogdan, R. & S.J. Taylor (1975). *Introduction to Qualitative Research Methods: A Phenomenological Approach to the Social Sciences*. New York: John Wiley.

Bourdieu, P. (1972/1977). *Outline of a Theory of Practice*. Cambridge, UK: Cambridge University Press.

Bourdieu, P. (1975). The Specificity of the Scientific Field and the Social Conditions of the Progress of Reason. *Social Science Information 14*(6): 19–47.

Bowden, G. & J. Low (2013). The Chicago School as Symbol and Enactment. In J. Low & G. Bowden (Eds.), *The Chicago School Diaspora: Epistemology and Substance* (pp. 3–28). Montreal: McGill-Queen's University Press.

Bowers, B. & L. Schatzman (2009). Leonard Schatzman and Dimensional Analysis. In J. M. Morse, P. N. Stern, J. M. Corbin, K. C. Charmaz, B. Bowers, & A. E. Clarke (Eds.), *Developing Grounded Theory: The Second Generation* (pp. 86–126). London: Routledge (1st ed.).

Bowers, B., & Schatzman, L. (Forthcoming, 2019). Dimensional Analysis. In J. M. Morse, P. N. Stern, J. Corbin, B. Bowers, K. Charmaz, A. E. Clarke, & C. Porrs. *Grounded theory: The second generation.* London: Routledge (2nd ed.).

Bowker, G. & S.L. Star (1999). *Sorting Things Out: Classification and Its Consequences*. Cambridge, MA: MIT Press.

Bowker, G., S. Timmermans, A.E. Clarke, & E. Balka (Eds.) (2015). *Boundary Objects and Beyond: Working with Susan Leigh Star*. Cambridge, MA: MIT Press.

Braidotti, R. (2013). *The Posthuman.* Cambridge, UK: Polity Press.

Bruni, A. & G. Gobo (2005). Qualitative Research in Italy. *FQS: Forum: Qualitative Social Research* 6(3): Article 41.

Bryant, A. (2002). Re-grounding Grounded Theory. *Journal of Information Technology Theory and Application 4*(1): 25–42.

Bryant, A. (2003). A Constructive/ist Response to Glaser. *FQS: Forum: Qualitative Social Research 4*(1).

Bryant, A. (2009). Grounded Theory and Pragmatism: The Curious Case of Anselm Strauss. *FQS: Forum: Qualitative Social Research 4*(1).

Bryant, A. (2017). *Grounded Theory and Grounded Theorizing: Pragmatism in Research Practice*. Oxford, UK: Oxford University Press.

Bryant, A. & K. Charmaz (Eds.) (2007a). *Sage Handbook of Grounded Theory* (1st & 2nd eds.). London: Sage.

Bryant, A. & K. Charmaz (2007b). Grounded Theory in Historical Perspective: An Epistemological Account. In A. Bryant & K. Charmaz (Eds.), *Sage Handbook of Grounded Theory* (pp. 31–57). London: Sage.

Bryant, A., & K. Charmaz (Eds.). (2019). *SAGE Handbook of Current Developments in Grounded Theory*. London: Sage, 2nd ed.

Bulmer, M. (1984). *The Chicago School of Sociology: Institutionalization, Diversity and the Rise of Sociological Research*. Chicago, IL: University of Chicago Press.

Bulmer, M. (1997). Quantification and Chicago Social Science in the 1920s: A Neglected Tradition. In K. Plummer (Ed.), *The Chicago School: Critical Assessments. Volume 4: Methodology and Experience* (Vol. 4, pp. 5–31). London: Routledge.

Burawoy, M. (1998). The Extended Case Method. *Sociological Theory 16*(1): 4–33.

Burawoy, M. (2000). Introduction. In Michael Burawoy et al. (Eds.), *Global Ethnography: Forces, Connections and Imaginations in a Postmodern World* (pp. 1–40). Berkeley, CA: University of California Press.

Bussolini, J. (2010). What is a Dispositif? *Foucault Studies 10*: 85–107.

Campbell, M. & F. Gregor (2002). *Mapping Social Relations: A Primer in Doing Institutional Ethnography*. Aurora, Canada: Garamond.

Campbell, M. & A. Monicom (Eds.) (1995). *Knowledge, Experience and Ruling: Studies in the Social Organization of Knowledge*. Toronto: University of Toronto Press.

Cannella, G. (2015). Qualitative Research as Living Within/Transforming Complex Power Relations. *Qualitative Inquiry 21*(7): 594–598.

Caron, C.D. & B.J. Bowers (2000). Methods and Application of Dimensional Analysis: A Contribution to Concept and Knowledge Development in Nursing. In B.L. Rogers & K.A. Knafl (Eds.), *Concept and Knowledge Development in Nursing* (2nd ed., pp. 285–320). Philadelphia, PA: Saunders.

Carter, S.M. & M. Little (2007). Justifying Knowledge, Justifying Method, Taking Action: Epistemologies, Methodologies, and Methods in Qualitative Research. *Qualitative Health Research 17*(10): 1316–1328.

Cefaï, D. (2016). Social Worlds: The Legacy of Mead's Social Ecology in Chicago Sociology. In H. Joas & D. Huebner (Eds.), *The Timeliness of G.H. Mead* (pp. 164–184). Chicago, IL: University of Chicago Press.

Charmaz, K. (1995). Between Positivism and Postmodernism: Implications for Methods. *Studies in Symbolic Interaction 17*: 43–72.

Charmaz, K. (2000). Grounded Theory: Objectivist and Constructivist Methods. In N. Denzin & Y. Lincoln (Eds.), *Handbook of Qualitative Research* (2nd ed., pp. 509–536). Thousand Oaks, CA: Sage.

Charmaz, K. (2005). Grounded Theory in the 21st Century: A Qualitative Method for Advancing Social Justice Research. In N. Denzin & Y. Lincoln (Eds.), *The SAGE Handbook of Qualitative Research* (3rd ed., pp. 507–536). Thousand Oaks, CA: Sage.

Charmaz, K. (2006, 2014). *Constructing Grounded Theory: A Practical Guide through Qualitative Analysis* (1st & 2nd eds.). London: Sage.

Charmaz, K. (2007). Constructionism and Grounded Theory. In J.A. Holstein & J.F. Gubrium (Eds.), *Handbook of Constructionist Research* (pp. 397–412). New York: Guilford Press.

Charmaz, K. (2008). The Legacy of Anselm Strauss in Constructivist Grounded Theory. In N. Denzin (Ed.), *Studies in Symbolic Interaction 32*: 127–142.

Charmaz, K. (2009). Shifting the Grounds: Constructivist Grounded Theory Methods. In J.M. Morse, P.N. Stern, J.M. Corbin, K.C. Charmaz, B. Bowers, & A.E. Clarke, *Developing Grounded Theory: The Second Generation* (pp. 127–155). London: Routledge.

Charmaz, K. (2011). Grounded Theory Methods in Social Justice Research. In N.L. Denzin & Y. Lincoln (Eds.), *The Sage Handbook of Qualitative Research* (4th ed., pp. 359–380). Thousand Oaks, CA: Sage.

Charmaz, K. (2014). Grounded Theory in Global Perspective: Reviews by International Researchers. *Qualitative Inquiry 20*(9): 1074–1084.

Charmaz, K. (2016a). The Power of Stories and the Potential of Theorizing for Social Justice Studies. In N. Denzin & M. Guardino (Eds.), *Qualitative Inquiry through a Critical Lens* (pp. 41–56). London: Routledge.

Charmaz, K. (2016b). The Power of Constructivist Grounded Theory for Critical Inquiry. *Qualitative Inquiry 23*(1): 34–45.

Charmaz, K. (Forthcoming 2019). The Genesis, Grounds, and Growth of Constructivist Grounded Theory. In J. M. Morse, P. N. Stern, J. Corbin, B. Bowers, K. Charmaz, A. E. Clarke, & C. Porrs. *Grounded theory: The second generation*. London: Routledge, 2nd ed.

Charmaz, K. & A.E. Clarke (2020). Anselm Strauss: Game Changer. In P. Atkinson, S. Delamont, M. Hardy & M. Williams (Eds.) *SAGE Research Methods Foundations*. London: Sage.

Charmaz, K. & R. Mitchell. (2001). Grounded Theory in Ethnography. In P. Atkinson, A. Coffey, S. Delamont, L. Lofland, & J. Lofland (Eds.) *Handbook of Ethnography* (pp. 160-174). London: Sage.

Charmaz, K., R. Thornberg, & E. Keane (2018). Evolving Grounded Theory and Social Justice Inquiry. In N. Denzin & Y. Lincoln (Eds.), *The Sage Handbook of Qualitative Research* (5th ed.). Thousand Oaks, CA: Sage.

Chase, S. (2018). Narrative Inquiry: Toward Theoretical and Methodological Maturity. In N.K. Denzin & Y.S. Lincoln (Eds.), *The Sage Handbook of Qualitative Research* (5th ed., pp. 546–560). Thousand Oaks, CA: Sage.

Chilisa, Bagele (2011). *Indigenous Research Methodologies*. London: Sage.

Clark, M.C. & J.J. Scheurich (2008). Editorial: The State of Qualitative Research in the Early 21st Century – Take 2. *International Journal of Qualitative Studies in Education 21*: 313.

Clarke, A.E. (1991). Social Worlds Theory as Organisation*al* Theory. In D. Maines (Ed.), *Social Organization and Social Process: Essays in Honor of Anselm Strauss* (pp. 17-42). Hawthorne, NY: Aldine de Gruyter.

Clarke, A.E. (2003). Situational Analyses: Grounded Theory Mapping after the Postmodern Turn. *Symbolic Interaction*, *26*(4): 553–576.

Clarke, A.E. (2005). *Situational Analysis: Grounded Theory after the Postmodern Turn*. Thousand Oaks, CA: Sage.

Clarke, A.E. (2006). Feminisms, Grounded Theory and Situational Analysis. In S. Hesse-Biber (Ed.), *Handbook of Feminist Research: Theory and Praxis* (pp. 345–370). Thousand Oaks, CA: Sage.

Clarke, A.E. (2007). Grounded Theory: Conflicts, Debates and Situational Analysis. In W. Outhwaite & S.P. Turner (Eds.), *Handbook of Social Science Methodology* (pp. 838–885). Thousand Oaks, CA: Sage.

Clarke, A. E. (2008a). Introduction. In N. Denzin (Ed.), Special Section: Celebrating Anselm Strauss and Forty Years of Grounded Theory. *Studies in Symbolic Interaction 32*:61–69.

Clarke, A.E. (2008b). Sex/Gender and Race/Ethnicity in the Legacy of Anselm Strauss. In Special Section: Celebrating Anselm Strauss and Forty Years of Grounded Theory, in N. Denzin (Ed.), *Studies in Symbolic Interaction 32*: 161–176.

Clarke, A.E. (2009). From Grounded Theory to Situational Analysis: What's New? Why? How? In J. Morse, P. Stern, J. Corbin, B. Bowers, K. Charmaz, & A. Clarke, *Developing Grounded Theory: The Second Generation* (pp. 194–235). London: Routledge.

Clarke, A.E. (2012a). *Situationsanalyse: Grounded Theory nach dem Postmodern Turn*. Hrsg. Einleitung von Reiner Keller. Wiesbaden: VS-Verlag für Sozialwissenschaften. German Translation of *Situational Analysis* (1st ed.).

Clarke, A.E. (2012b, 2015). Feminisms, Grounded Theory and Situational Analysis Revisited. In S. Hesse-Biber (Ed.), *Handbook of Feminist Research: Theory and Praxis* (2nd ed., pp. 388–412). Thousand Oaks, CA: Sage. Reprinted in Clarke, A. E., Friese, C. & Washburn, R. (Eds.). (2015). *Situational analysis in practice: Mapping research with grounded theory* (pp. 119–154). London: Routledge.

Clarke, A.E. (Forthcoming 2019a). From Grounded Theory to Situational Analysis: What's New? Why? How? In J. Morse, P. Stern, J. Corbin, B. Bowers, K. Charmaz, A. E. Clarke, & C. Porr. *Grounded Theory: The Second Generation*. London: Routledge, 2nd ed.

Clarke, A.E. (forthcoming, 2019b). Situational Analysis: A Critical Interactionist Method of Qualitative Inquiry. In M.H. Jacobsen (Ed.), *Critical and Cultural Interactionism*. London: Routledge.

Clarke, A.E. (In prep. a). 'Everyone was Negotiating about Something': Forty Years of Straussian Negotiated Order Research. To appear in D. Vom Lehn, N, Ruiz-Juno, & W. Gibson (Eds.), *Handbook of Interactionism*. London: Routledge.

Clarke, A.E. (In prep. b). Situational Analysis as a Participatory, Decolonizing and (Post)colonial Approach. Paper presented at the International Congress of Qualitative Inquiry, Urbana/Champaign IL, May 20, 2016. To be submitted to *Qualitative Inquiry*.

Clarke, A.E. & K. Charmaz (Eds.) (2014). *Grounded Theory and Situational Analysis*. Sage Benchmarks in Social Research Series (4 vols). London: Sage.

Clarke, A.E. & C. Friese (2007). Situational Analysis: Going Beyond Traditional Grounded Theory. In A. Bryant & K. Charmaz (Eds.), *The Handbook of Grounded Theory* (pp. 694–743). London: Sage.

Clarke, A.E., C. Friese, & R. Washburn (Eds.) (2015). *Situational Analysis in Practice: Mapping Research with Grounded Theory*. London: Routledge.

Clarke, A.E., C. Friese & R. Washburn (2018). *Situational Analysis: Grounded Theory after the Interpretive Turn*. Thousand Oaks, CA: Sage.

Clarke, A.E. with R. Keller (2014). Engaging Complexities: Working against Simplification as an Agenda for Qualitative Research Today. *FQS: Forum: Qualitative Social Research* 15(2) [online].

Clarke, A.E., & T. Montini. (1993). The Many Faces of RU486: Tales of Situated Knowledges and Technological Contestations. *Science, Technology and Human Values 18*(1): 42-78.

Clarke, A. E., & Star, S. L. (2003). Studies of Science, Technology and Medicine. In L. Reynolds & N. Herman (Eds.), *Handbook of Symbolic Interactionism* (pp. 539-574). London: Routledge.

Clarke, A. E., & Star, S. L. (2007). The Social Worlds/Arenas/Discourse Framework as a Theory-Methods Package. In M. Lynch, O. Amsterdamska and E. Hackett (Eds.) *The New Handbook of Science and Technology Studies*. Cambridge, MA: MIT Press.

Clarke, A.E. & Star, S. L. (2008). Social Worlds/Arenas as a Theory-Methods Package. In E. Hackett, O. Amsterdamska, M. Lynch, & J. Wacjman (Eds.), *Handbook of Science and Technology Studies* (3rd ed., pp. 113–137). Cambridge, MA: MIT Press.

Clifford, J. & Marcus, G. (1986). *Writing Culture: The Poetics and Politics of Ethnography*. Berkeley, CA: University of California Press.

Clough, Patricia (1998). *The End(s) of Ethnography: From Realism to Social Criticism*. New York: Peter Lang.

Coleman, R. & J. Ringrose (Eds.) (2013). *Deleuze and Research Methodologies*. Edinburgh: University of Edinburgh Press.

Collier, D., & C. Elman. (2008). Qualitative and Multi-Method Research: Organizations, Publication, and Reflections on Integration. In *Oxford Handbook of Political Methodology*, pp. 780-795. Available at: https://ssrn.com/abstract=1750525 (accessed 10/19/18).

Collins, P.H. (1990). *Black Feminist Thought: Knowledge, Consciousness, and the Politics of Empowerment*. Boston, MA: Unwin Hyman.

Cook, J.A. & M.M. Fonow. (1986). Knowledge and Women's Interests: Issues of Epistemology and Methodology in Feminist Sociological Research. *Sociological Inquiry* 56(1): 2-29.

Corbin, J. (2009). Taking an Analytic Journey. In J. M. Morse, P. N. Stern, J. Corbin, B. Bowers, K. Charmaz, & A. E. Clarke (Eds.), *Developing grounded theory: The second generation* (pp.35-53). Walnut Creek, CA: Left Coast Press.

Corbin, J. (Forthcoming 2019). Strauss's Grounded Theory. In J. Morse, P. Stern, J. Corbin, B. Bowers, K. Charmaz, A. E. Clarke, & C. Porr. *Grounded theory: The second generation*. London: Routledge, 2nd ed.

Corbin, J. & A. Strauss (2008, 2015). *Basics of Qualitative Research: Grounded Theory Procedures and Techniques* (3rd & 4th eds.). Thousand Oaks, CA: Sage.

Crenshaw, K. (1989). Demarginalizing the Intersection of Race and Sex: A Black Feminist Critique of Antidiscrimination Doctrine, Feminist Theory and Antiracist Politics. *University of Chicago Legal Forum* 140: 139–167.

Crenshaw, K. (1991). Mapping the Margins: Identity Politics, Intersectionality, and Violence Against Women. *Stanford Law Review* 43(6): 1241–1299.

Crenshaw, K., N. Gotanda, G. Peller, & K. Thomas (Eds.) (1996). *Critical Race Theory: The Key Writings that Formed the Movement*. New York: The New Press.

Cressey, P.G. (1932). *The Taxi-Dance Hall: A Sociological Study*. Chicago, IL: University of Chicago Press.

Daly, J. (2005). *Evidence-based Medicine and the Search for a Science of Clinical Care*. Berkeley, CA: University of California Press.

Davidson, J., T. Paulus, & K. Jackson (2016). Speculating on the Future of Digital Tools for Qualitative Research. *Qualitative Inquiry* 22(7): 606–610.

Delanda, M. (2006). *A New Philosophy of Society: Assemblage Theory and Social Complexity*. London: Continuum.

Deleuze, G. & F. Guattari (1983a). *Anti-Oedipus: Capitalism and Schizophrenia I*. Minneapolis, MN: University of Minnesota Press.

Deleuze, G. & F. Guattari (1983b). What is a Minor Literature? (edited by R. Brinkley). *Mississippi Review 11*(3): 13–33.

Deleuze, G. & F. Guattari (1987). Introduction: Rhizome. In *A Thousand Plateaus: Capitalism and Schizophrenia II* (pp. 3–25). Minneapolis, MN: University of Minnesota Press.

Denzin, N. (1989, 2001). *Interpretive Interactionism* (1st & 2nd eds.). Newbury Park, CA: Sage.

Denzin, N. (1991). *Images of Postmodern Society: Social Theory and Contemporary Cinema*. Newbury Park, CA: Sage

Denzin, N. (2009). Apocalypse Now: overcoming resistances to qualitative inquiry. *International Review of Qualitative Research* 2(3): 331–343.

Denzin, N. (2010). Moments, Mixed Methods, and Paradigm Dialogs. *Qualitative Inquiry* 16(6): 419–427.

Denzin, N. (2018). The Elephant in the Living Room, or Extending the Conversation about the Politics of Evidence. *The Sage Handbook of Qualitative Research* (5th ed.). Thousand Oaks, CA: Sage.

Denzin, N.K. & M.D. Giardina (Eds.) (2009). *Qualitative Inquiry and Social Justice*. London: Routledge.

Denzin, N.K. & M.D. Giardina (Eds.) (2013). *Global Dimensions of Qualitative Inquiry*. London: Routledge.

Denzin, N.K. & M.D. Giardina (Eds.) (2015). *Qualitative Inquiry—Past, Present, and Future: A Critical Reader*. London: Routledge.

Denzin, N.K. & Y.S. Lincoln (Eds.) (1994, 2000, 2005, 2011, 2018). *The Sage Handbook of Qualitative Research* (1st, 2nd, 3rd, 4th & 5th eds.). Thousand Oaks, CA: Sage.

Denzin, N.K. & Y.S. Lincoln (1995). Transforming Qualitative Research Methods: Is it a Revolution? *Journal of Contemporary Ethnography* 24(3): 349–358.

Denzin, N.K., Y.S. Lincoln, & M.D. Giardina. (2006). Disciplining Qualitative Research. *International Journal of Qualitative Studies in Education* 19(6):769–782.

Denzin, N.K., Y.S. Lincoln, & L. Tuhiwai Smith (Eds.) (2008). *Handbook of Critical and Indigenous Methodologies*. Thousand Oaks, CA: Sage.

Derrida, J. (1978). *Writing and Difference* (A. Bass, Trans.). Chicago: University of Chicago Press.

DeVault, M.L. (1999). *Liberating Method: Feminism and Social Research*. Philadelphia, PA: Temple University Press.

DeVault, M.L. (2018). Feminist Qualitative Research in the Millenium's Second Decade. In N.K. Denzin & Y.S. Lincoln (Eds.), *The Sage Handbook of Qualitative Research* (5th ed., pp. 176–194). Thousand Oaks, CA: Sage.

Dewey, J. (1938). *Logic: The Theory of Inquiry*. New York: H. Holt and Co.

Dewey, J. (1939). Experience, Knowledge and Value: A Rejoinder. In J.A. Boydston (Ed.), *The Later Works (1925–1953): 1939–1941/Essays, Reviews, and Miscellany* (Vol. 14). Carbondale, IL: Southern Illinois University Press.

Dey, I. (1999). *Grounding Grounded Theory: Guidelines for Qualitative Inquiry*. San Diego, CA: Academic Press.

Dillard, C.B. (2008). When the Ground is Black the Ground is Fertile: Exploring Endarkened Feminist Epistemology and Healing Methodologies of the Spirit. In N.K. Denzin, Y.S. Lincoln, & L. Tuhiwai Smith (Eds.), *Handbook of Critical and Indigenous Methodologies* (pp. 277–293). Thousand Oaks, CA: Sage.

Dimitriadis, G. (2016). Reading Qualitative Inquiry through Critical Pedagogy: Some Reflections. *International Review of Qualitative Research* 9(2): 140–146.

Donald, D. (2012). Indigenous Métissage: A Decolonizing Research Sensibility. *International Journal of Qualitative Studies in Education* 25(5): 533–555.

Donnor, J. & G. Ladson-Billings (2018). Critical Race Theory Scholarship and the Post-Racial Imaginary. In N.K. Denzin & Y.S. Lincoln (Eds.), *The Sage Handbook of Qualitative Research* (5th ed., pp. 195–213). Thousand Oaks, CA: Sage.

Dreyfus, H.L. & P. Rabinow (1983). *Michel Foucault: Beyond Structuralism and Hermeneutics* (2nd ed.). Chicago, IL: University of Chicago Press.

DuBois, W.E.B. (1899) *The Philadelphia Negro: A Social Study*. Philadelphia, PA: [published for] The University of Pennsylvania.

Dunier, M. (2002). What Kind of Combat Sport is Sociology? *American Journal of Sociology* 107(6): 1551–1576.

Erickson, F. (2018). Qualitative Methods: Histories in Social and Educational Research. In N.K. Denzin & Y.S. Lincoln (Eds.), *The Sage Handbook of Qualitative Research* (5th ed., pp. 36–65). Thousand Oaks, CA: Sage.

Ferguson, R., M. Gever, T.T. Minh-ha, & C. West (Eds.) (1990). *Out There: Marginalization and Contemporary Culture*. Cambridge, MA: MIT Press.

Fine, G.A. (Ed.) (1995). *A Second Chicago School? The Development of a Postwar American Sociology*. Chicago, IL: University of Chicago Press.

Fine, M. (1994). Working the Hyphens: Reinventing Self and Other in Qualitative Research. In N. Denzin & Y. Lincoln (Eds.), *Handbook of Qualitative Research* (pp. 70–82). Thousand Oaks, CA: Sage.

Fine, M., L. Weis, S. Weseen, & L. Mun Wong (2000). For Whom? Qualitative Research, Representations, and Social Responsibilities. In N. Denzin & Y. Lincoln (Eds.), *Handbook of Qualitative Research* (2nd ed., pp. 107–132). Thousand Oaks, CA: Sage.

Flick, U. (2005). Qualitative Research in Sociology in Germany and the US—State of the Art, Differences and Developments. *FQS: Forum: Qualitative Social Research* 6(3): Article 23. www.qualitative-research.net/index.php/fqs/article/view/17/38

Flick, U. (2014a). A Brief History of Qualitative Research. In U. Flick, *An Introduction to Qualitative Research*. London: Sage.

Flick, U. (2014b). Challenges for Qualitative Inquiry as a Global Endeavor. *Qualitative Inquiry* 20(9): 1059–1063.

Flyvberg, B. (2001). *Making Social Science Matter: Why Social Inquiry Fails and How it Can Succeed Again*. New York: Cambridge University Press.
Fonow, M.M. & J.A. Cook (2005). Feminist Methodology: New Applications in the Academy and Public Policy. *Signs: Journal of Women in Culture and Society* 30(4): 211–236.
Fontana, A. (2005). The Postmodern Turn in Interactionism. *Studies in Symbolic Interaction* 28: 239–254.
Foucault, M. (1973). *The Order of Things: An Archeology of the Human Sciences*. New York: Vintage/Random House.
Foucault, M. (1980). *Power/Knowledge: Selected Interviews and Other Writings 1972–1977*. (C. Gordon, Ed.). New York: Pantheon.
Foucault, M. (2004). *Sécurité, Territoire, Population: Cours au Collège de France, 1977–1978*. Paris: Gallimard.
Frazier, E.F. (1939). *The Negro Family in the United States*. Chicago, IL: University of Chicago Press.
Garfinkel, H. (1967). *Studies in Ethnomethodology*. Englewood Cliffs, NJ: Prentice-Hall.
Geertz, C. (1973). *The Interpretation of Cultures: Selected Essays*. New York: Basic Books.
Geertz, C. (1983). *Local Knowledge: Further Essays in Interpretive Anthropology*. New York: Basic Books.
Gelder, K. (2005). *The Subcultures Reader* (2nd ed.). London: Routledge.
Gibson, B., & J. Hartman. (2014). *Rediscovering Grounded Theory*. London: Sage.
Gitelman, L. (Ed.) (2013). *Raw Data is an Oxymoron*. Cambridge, MA: MIT Press.
Glaser, B.G. (1965, 1969). The Constant Comparative Method of Qualitative Analysis. *Social Problems* 12(4): 436–445. Reprinted in G.J. McCall & J.L. Simmons (Eds.), *Issues in Participant Observation* (pp. 216–228). Reading, MA: Addison-Wesley.
Glaser, B.G. (1978). *Theoretical Sensitivity: Advances in the Methodology of Grounded Theory*. Mill Valley, CA: Sociology Press.
Glaser, B.G. (1992). *Emergence versus Forcing: Basics of Grounded Theory Analysis*. Mill Valley, CA: Sociology Press.
Glaser, B.G. (1998). *Doing Grounded Theory: Issues and Discussions*. Mill Valley, CA: Sociology Press.
Glaser, B.G. (2002a). Grounded Theory and Gender Relevance. *Health Care for Women International* 23(8): 786–793.
Glaser, B.G. (2002b). Constructivist Grounded Theory? *FQS: Forum: Qualitative Social Research* 3(3). Retrieved from www.qualitative-research.net/fqs.
Glaser, B.G. (2006). *Doing Formal Grounded Theory: A Proposal*. Mill Valley, CA: Sociology Press.
Glaser, B.G. (2016). Grounded Theory Perspective: Its Origin and Growth. *Grounded Theory Review: An International Journal*, 15(1).
Glaser, B.G., with J. Holton (2004). Remodeling Grounded Theory. *FSQ: Forum for Qualitative Social Research* 5(2).
Glaser, B.G. & A.L. Strauss (1965). Discovery of Substantive Theory: A Basic Strategy Underlying Qualitative Research. *American Behavioral Sciences* 8: 5–12.
Glaser, B.G. & A.L. Strauss (1966). The Purpose and Credibility of Qualitative Research. *Nursing Research* 15: 56–61.
Glaser, B.G. & A.L. Strauss (1967). *The Discovery of Grounded Theory: Strategies for Qualitative Research*. New York: Aldine.
Glaser, B.G. & A.L. Strauss (1968). *Time for Dying*. Chicago, IL: Aldine.
Glaser, B.G. & A.L. Strauss (1971). *Status Passage: A Formal Theory*. Chicago, IL: Aldine Atherton.
Gobo, G. (2005). The Renaissance of Qualitative Methods. *FQS: Forum: Qualitative Social Research* 6(3), www.qualitative-research.net/index.php/fqs/article/view/5
Gomez, A. & P. Zapata-Sepulveda (2016). Ten Years of Critical Qualitative Research at the International Congress of Qualitative Inquiry. *International Review of Qualitative Research* 9(2): 137–139.
Greenwood, D.J., & M. Levin. (1998). Action Research, Science, And The Co-Optation of Social Research. *Studies in Cultures, Organizations and Societies* 4:237–261.
Grossberg, L., C. Nelson, & P. Treichler (Eds.) (1992). *Cultural Studies*. New York: Routledge.

Grusin, R.A. (2015). *The Nonhuman Turn*. Minneapolis, MN: University of Minnesota Press.
Grzanka, P.R. (Ed.) (2014). *Intersectionality: A Foundations and Frontiers Reader*. Boulder, CO: Westview Press.
Gubrium, J., & J.A. Holstein (Eds.) (1997). *The New Language of Qualitative Method.* London: Oxford University Press.
Gubrium, J., & J.A. Holstein (Eds.) (2003). *PostModern Interviewing.* Thousand Oaks, CA: Sage,
Habermas, J. (1967). *On the Logics of the Social Sciences*. Cambridge, MA: MIT Press.
Hacking, I. (1983). *Representing and Intervening: Introductory Topics in the Philosophy of Natural Science*. Cambridge, UK: Cambridge University Press.
Hammersley, M. (2008). *Questioning Qualitative Inquiry: Critical Essays*. London: Sage.
Haraway, D.J. (1999). The Virtual Speculum in the New World Order. In A.E. Clarke & V.L. Olesen (Eds.), *Revisioning Women, Health, and Healing: Feminist, Cultural, and Technoscience Perspectives* (pp. 49–96). New York: Routledge.
Harding, S. (Ed.) (1987). *Feminism and Methodology: Social Science Issues*. Bloomington, IN: Indiana University Press.
Harding, S. (2015). *Objectivity and Diversity: Another Logic of Scientific Research*. Chicago, IL: University of Chicago Press.
Hekman, S. (2007). Feminist Methodology. In W. Outhwaite & S.P. Turner (Eds.), *Handbook of Social Science Methodology* (pp. 534–546). Thousand Oaks, CA: Sage.
Henwood, K. & I. Lang (2005). Qualitative Social Science in the UK: Commentary of the 'State of the Art'. *FQS: Forum: Qualitative Social Research/Sozialforschung* 6(2): Article 48.
Hertz, R. & J.B. Imber (Eds.) (1995). *Studying Elites Using Qualitative Methods*. London: Sage.
Hess, D. (2007). *Alternative Pathways in Science and Industry: Activism, Innovation, and the Environment in an Era of Globalization*. Cambridge, MA: MIT Press.
Hesse-Biber, S.N. (Ed.) (2006a, 2013a). *Handbook of Feminist Research: Theory and Praxis* (1st & 2nd eds.). Thousand Oaks, CA: Sage.
Hesse-Biber, S.N. (Ed.). (2006b, 2013b). *Feminist Research Practice: A Primer* (1st & 2nd eds.). Thousand Oaks, CA: Sage.
Hildenbrand, B. (2004). Anselm Strauss. In U. Flick, E. von Kardorff, & I. Steinke (Eds.), *A Companion to Qualitative Research* (pp. 17–23). London: Sage.
Hiley, D.R., J.F. Bowman, & R. Schusterman (Eds.) (1991). *The Interpretive Turn: Philosophy, Science, Culture*. Ithaca, NY: Cornell University Press.
Hilgartner, S. (1997). The Sokal Affair in Context. *Science, Technology and Human Values* 22(4):506–522.
Hollis, M. & S. Lukes (Eds.) (1982). *Rationality and Relativism.* Cambridge, MA: MIT Press.
Holstein, J.A. (2018). Advancing a Constructionist Analytics. In N.K. Denzin & Y.S. Lincoln (Eds.), *Sage Handbook of Qualitative Research* (5th ed., pp. 395–410). Thousand Oaks, CA: Sage.
Holstein, J.A. & J.F. Gubrium (Eds.) (2007). *Handbook of Constructionist Research*. Thousand Oaks, CA: Sage.
Holstein, J.A. & J.F. Gubrium (Eds.) (2012). *Varieties of Narrative Analysis*. Thousand Oaks, CA: Sage.
Holton, J.A. & I. Walsh (2016). *Classic Grounded Theory: Applications with Qualitative and Quantitative Data.* Thousand Oaks, CA: Sage.
Hughes, E.C. (1971a, 1971b). *The Sociological Eye: Vol. 1 Selected Papers on Institutions and Race* (pp. 5–278), Vol. 2 *Selected Papers on Work, Self and the Study of Society* (pp. 283–584). Chicago, IL: Aldine Atherton.
Jackson, A.Y. & L.A. Mazzei. (2012). *Thinking with Theory in Qualitative Research: Viewing Data across Multiple Perspectives*. New York: Routledge.
Jacobsen, M.H. (Ed.) (forthcoming, 2019). *Critical and Cultural Interactionism*. London: Routledge.
Jasanoff, S. (Ed.) (2004). *States of Knowledge: The Co-Production of Science and Social Order*. London: Routledge.
Jensen, C.B. (2014). Continuous Variations: The Conceptual and Empirical in STS. *Science, Technology & Human Values* 39(2): 192–213.

Jensen, C.B. & K. Rodje (Eds.) (2010). *Deleuzian Intersections: Science, Technology, Anthropology*. New York: Berghahn Books.

Keller, R. (2012). *Das interpretative Paradigma. Eine Einführung*. Wiesbaden: VS-Verlag für Sozialwissenschaften. English translation: *The Interpretive Paradigm*. London: Sage, 2018.

Keller, R. (2013). *Doing Discourse Research: An Introduction for Social Scientists*. Translated by Bryan Jenner. Thousand Oaks, CA: Sage.

Keller, R. (2017). Has Critique Run Out of Steam? – On Discourse Research as Critical Inquiry. *Qualitative Inquiry* 23(1): 58–68.

Keller, R. & A. Poferl. (Forthcoming 2019). Epistemic Cultures in Sociology Between Individual Inspiration and Legitimization by Procedure: Developments of Qualitative and Interpretive Research in German and French Sociology Since the 1960s. *Forum: Qualitative Sozialforschung / Forum: Qualitative Social Research —FQS* (Online journal).

Kendall, G. & G. Wickham (1999). *Using Foucault's Methods*. London: Sage.

Kendall, G. & G. Wickham (2004). The Foucaultian Framework. In C. Seale, G. Gobo, J.F. Gubrium, & D. Silverman (Eds.), *Qualitative Research Practice* (pp. 141–150). London: Sage.

Kennedy, B. L. & R. Thornberg.(2018). Deduction, Induction, and Abduction. In Flick, U.(Ed.) *The SAGE Handbook of Qualitative Data Collection* (pp. 40-64). London: Sage.

Kincheloe, J. & P. McLaren (1994). Rethinking Critical Theory and Qualitative Research. In N. Denzin & Y. Lincoln (Eds.), *Handbook of Qualitative Research* (1st ed., pp. 138–157). Thousand Oaks, CA: Sage.

Kincheloe, J.L., P. McLaren, & S.R. Steinberg (2011, 2018). Critical Pedagogy and Qualitative Research: Moving to the Bricolage. In N. Denzin & Y. Lincoln (Eds.), *Handbook of Qualitative Research* (4th ed., pp. 163–178; 5th ed., pp. 236–260). Thousand Oaks, CA: Sage.

Kitzinger, C. (2004). Feminist Approaches. In C. Seale, G. Gobo, J.F. Gubrium, & D. Silverman (Eds.), *Qualitative Research Practice* (pp. 125–140). London: Sage.

Knaapen, L. (2013). Being 'Evidence-based' in the Absence of Evidence: The Management of Non-evidence in Guideline Development. *Social Studies of Science* 43(5): 681–706.

Knoblauch, H. (2013). Qualitative Methods at the Crossroads: Recent Developments in Interpretive Social Research. *FSQ: Forum Qualitative Sozialforschung/Forum: Qualitative Social Research* 14(3), Article 12, http://nbn-resolving.de/urn:nbn:de:0114-fqs1303128.

Knoblauch, H., U. Flick, & C. Maeder (2005). Qualitative Methods in Europe: The Variety of Social Research. *FQS: Forum: Qualitative Social Research* 6(3): Article 34, www.qualitative-research.net/index.php/fqs/article/view/3/8

Kools, S., M. McCarthy, R. Durham, & L. Robrecht (1996). Dimensional Analysis: Broadening the Conception of Grounded Theory. *Qualitative Health Research* 6(3): 312–330.

Koopman, C. (2009). *Pragmatism as Transition: Historicity and Hopein James, Dewey & Rorty*. New York: Columbia University Press.

Koopman, C. (2011a). Foucault and Pragmatism: Introductory Notes on Metaphilosophical Methodology. *Foucault Studies* 11:3–10.

Koopman, C. (2011b). Foucault Across the Disciplines: Introductory Notes on Contingency in Critical Inquiry. *History of the Human Science* 24(4):1–12.

Krieger, N. (2013). *Epidemiology and the People's Health: Theory and Context*. Oxford, UK: Oxford University Press.

Kroeber, A.L. (1902–1907). *The Arapaho*. Lincoln, NB: University of Nebraska Press.

Lamont, M. & A. Swidler (2014). Methodological Pluralism and the Possibilities and Limits of Interviewing. *Qualitative Sociology* 37: 153–171.

Lamont, M. & P. White (2005). *Workshop on Interdisciplinary Standards for Systematic Qualitative Research*. Washington, DC: National Science Foundation.

Lampland, M. & S.L. Star (Eds.) (2009). *Standards and their Stories: How Quantifying, Classifying and Formalizing Practices Shape Everyday Life*. Ithaca, NY: Cornell University Press.

Lather, P. (1991). *Getting Smart: Feminist Research and Pedagogy with/in the Postmodern*. New York: Routledge.

Lather, P. (1993). Fertile Obsession: Validity after Poststructuralism. *Sociological Quarterly* 34(4): 673–693.

Lather, P. (2006). Foucauldian Scientificity: Rethinking the Nexus of Qualitative Research and Educational Policy Analysis. *International Journal of Qualitative Studies in Education* 19(6): 783–791.

Lather, P. (2007). *Getting Lost: Feminist Efforts Toward a Double(d) Science*. Albany, NY: State University of New York (SUNY) Press.

Lather, P. (2010). *Engaging Science Policy: From the Side of the Messy*. New York: Peter Lang.

Lather, P. (2013). Methodology-21: What Do We Do in the Afterward? *International Journal of Qualitative Studies in Education* 26(6): 634–645.

Lather, P. (2017). *(Post)Critical Methodologies: The Science Possible after the Critiques: The Selected Works of Patti Lather*. New York: Routledge.

Lather, P. & E. St. Pierre (2013). Post-Qualitative Research. *International Journal of Qualitative Studies in Education 26*(6): 629–633.

Latour, B. (1987). *Science in Action: How to Follow Scientists and Engineers through Society*. Cambridge, MA: Harvard University Press.

Latour, B. & S. Woolgar (1979). *Laboratory Life: The Social Construction of Scientific Facts*. Beverley Hills, CA: Sage.

Law, J. (2004). *After Method: Mess in Social Science Research*. London: Routledge.

Law, J. (2007). Making a Mess with Method. In W. Outhwaite & S.P. Turner (Eds.), *Handbook of Social Science Methodology* (pp. 595–606). Thousand Oaks, CA: Sage.

Law, J. (2009). Actor Network Theory and Material Semiotics. In B.S. Turner (Ed.), *The New Blackwell Companion to Social Theory* (pp. 141–158). Oxford, UK: Blackwell.

Law, J. & J. Hassard (Eds.) (1999). *Actor Network Theory and After*. Oxford, UK: Blackwell.

Leonhardt, D. (2017). America's Great Working-Class Colleges. *The New York Times*, January 22: Sunday Review 2.

Lincoln, Y.S. (2010). 'What a Long, Strange Trip It's Been…': Twenty-five Years of Qualitative and New Paradigm Research. *Qualitative Inquiry* 16(1): 3–9.

Lincoln, Y.S. & E.G. Guba (2013). *The Constructivist Credo*. London: Routledge.

Locke, K. (2001). *Grounded Theory in Management Research*. London: Sage.

Locke, K. (2015). Pragmatic Reflections on a Conversation about Grounded Theory in Management and Organization Studies. *Organizational Research Methods* 18(4): 612–619.

Locke, K., K. Golden-Biddle, & M. S. Feldman. (2008). Making Doubt Generative: Rethinking the Role of Doubt in the Research Process. *Organization Science* 19(6):907-918.

Lury, C. & N. Wakeford (Eds.) (2012). *Inventive Methods: The Happening of the Social*. London: Routledge.

Lynch, M. (1998). Towards a Constructivist Genealogy of Social Constructivism. In I. Velody & R. Williams (Eds.), *The Politics of Constructionism* (pp. 13–32). London: Sage.

Lynch, M. (2012). Self-Exemplifying Revolutions: Notes on Kuhn and Latour. *Social Studies of Science* 42(3): 449–455.

Maclure, M. (2011). Qualitative Inquiry: Where are the Ruins? *Qualitative Inquiry* 17(10): 997–1005.

Maclure, M. (2015). The 'New Materialisms': A Thorn in the Flesh of Critical Qualitative Inquiry? In G.S. Cannella, M. Salazar Perez, & P.A. Pasque (Eds.), *Critical Qualitative Inquiry: Foundations and Futures*. London: Routledge.

Maines, D. (Ed.) (1991). *Social Organization and Social Process: Essays in Honor of Anselm Strauss*. Hawthorne, NY: Aldine de Gruyter.

Malinowski, B. (1922). *Argonauts of the Western Pacific*. New York: Dutton.

Manicas, P. (2007). The Social Sciences since World War II: The Rise and Fall of Scientism. In W. Outhwaite & S.P. Turner (Eds.), *Handbook of Social Science Methodology* (pp. 7–31). Thousand Oaks, CA: Sage.

Marcus, G.E. & E. Saka (2006). Assemblage. *Theory, Culture and Society* 23(2–3): 101–109.

Martin, V. & A. Gynnild (Eds.) (2011). *Grounded Theory: The Philosophy, Method, and Work of Barney Glaser*. Boca Raton, FL: Brown Walker Press.

McCarthy, D. (1984). Towards a Sociology of the Physical World: George Herbert Mead on Physical Objects. *Studies in Symbolic Interaction* 5: 105–121.

McLeod, K. (2014). Orientating to Assembling: Qualitative Inquiry for More-than-Human Worlds. *International Journal of Qualitative Methods* 13. Open access journal.

Mead, G.H. (1927/1964). The Objective Reality of Perspectives. In A.J. Reck (Ed.), *Selected Writings of George Herbert Mead* (pp. 306–319). Chicago, IL: University of Chicago Press.

Mead, G.H. (1934/1962). *Mind, Self and Society*. Ed. C.W. Morris. Chicago, IL: University of Chicago Press.

Mead, G.H. (1938, 1972). *The Philosophy of the Act*. Chicago, IL: University of Chicago Press.

Mertens, D.M., F. Cram, & B. Chilisa (Eds.) (2014). *Indigenous Pathways into Social Research: Voices of a New Generation*. London: Routledge.

Mey, G. & K. Mruck (2007). Qualitative Research in Germany: A Short Cartography. *International Sociology* 22(2): 138–154.

Meyer, M.A. (2008). Indigenous and Authentic: Hawaiian Epistemology and the Triangulation of Meaning. In N. Denzin, Y. Lincoln, & L. Tuhiwai Smith (Eds.), *Handbook of Critical and Indigenous Methodologies* (pp. 217–233). Thousand Oaks, CA: Sage.

Mills, C.W. (1959). *The Sociological Imagination*. New York: Oxford University Press.

Minkler, M. & N. Wallerstein (Eds.) (2008). *Community-based Participatory Research for Health: From Process to Outcomes* (2nd ed.). San Francisco, CA: Jossey-Bass.

Morris, A. (2015). *The Scholar Denied: W.E.B. Du Bois and the Birth of Modern Sociology.* Berkeley, CA: University of California Press.

Morse, J. (Ed.) 1989. *Qualitative Nursing Research: A Contemporary Dialogue*. Newbury Park, CA: Sage.

Morse, J. (2009). Tussles, Tensions, and Resolutions. In J. Morse, P.N. Stern, J. Corbin, B. Bowers, K. Charmaz, & A.E. Clarke. *Developing Grounded Theory: The Second Generation* (pp. 13-22). London: Routledge.

Morse, J. & L. Niehaus (2016). *Mixed Method Design: Principles and Procedures* (2nd ed.). London: Routledge.

Morse, J., P.N. Stern, J. Corbin, B. Bowers, K. Charmaz, & A.E. Clarke (2009). *Developing Grounded Theory: The Second Generation*. London: Routledge.

Morse, J. M., Stern, P. N., Corbin, J., Bowers, B., Charmaz, K., Clarke, A. E., & Porr, C. (Forthcoming 2019). *Grounded Theory: The Second Generation* (2nd ed.). London: Routledge.

Moss, P. (2007). Meetings across the Paradigmatic Divide. *Educational Philosophy and Theory* 39(3): 229–245.

Mouffe, C. (2000). *The Democratic Paradox*. London: Verso.

Naples, N.A. (2003). *Feminism and Method: Ethnography, Discourse Analysis and Activist Research*. New York: Routledge.

Nelson, J. (2015). Navigating Grounded Theory: A Critical and Reflective Response to the Challenges of Using Grounded Theory in an Education PhD. *Critical and Reflective Practice in Education* 4 [online journal].

Newfield, C. (2016). *The Great Mistake: How We Wrecked Public Universities and How We Can Fix Them*. Baltimore, MD: The Johns Hopkins University Press.

Newman, K. (2002). No Shame: The View from the Left Bank. *American Journal of Sociology* 107(6): 1577–1599.

Noffke, S.E. & B. Somekh (Eds.) (2009). *The Sage Handbook of Educational Action Research*. Thousand Oaks, CA: Sage.

Olesen, V.L. (2001). 'Do Whatever You Want': Audiences Created, Creating, Recreating. *Qualitative Inquiry* 7(3): 267–273.

Olesen, V.L. (2007). Feminist Qualitative Research and Grounded Theory: Complexities, Criticisms and Opportunities. In A. Bryant & K. Charmaz (Eds.), *Handbook of Grounded Theory* (pp. 417–35). London: Sage.

Olesen, V.L. (2011, 2018). Feminist Qualitative Research in the Millenium's First Decade: Developments, Challenges, Prospects. In N.K. Denzin & Y.S. Lincoln (Eds.), *Handbook of Qualitative Research* (4th ed., pp. 129–146; 5th ed., pp. 151–175). Thousand Oaks, CA: Sage.

Outhwaite, W. & S.P. Turner (Eds.) (2007). *Handbook of Social Science Methodology.* Thousand Oaks, CA: Sage.

Pascale, C.M. (2008). Talking about Race: Shifting the Analytical Paradigm. *Qualitative Inquiry*: 14(5): 723–741.

Pascale, C.M. (2011). *Cartographies of Knowledge: Exploring Qualitative Epistemologies*. Los Angeles, CA: Sage.

Phellas, C.N. (Ed.) (2012). *Researching Non-Heterosexual Sexualities*. Farnham, UK: Ashgate.

Platt, J. (1996). *A History of Sociological Research Methods in America, 1920-1960*. Cambridge, UK: Cambridge University Press.

Pratt, M.L. (1992). *Imperial Eyes: Travel Writing and Transculturation*. London: Routledge.

Preissle, J. (2006). Envisioning Qualitative Inquiry. *International Journal of Qualitative Studies in Education* 19(6): 685–695.

Prus, R. (1996). *Symbolic Interaction and Ethnographic Research*. Albany, NY: State University of New York (SUNY) Press.

Puddephatt, A., W. Shaffir, & S.W. Kleinecht (Eds.) (2009). *Ethnographies Revisited: Constructing Theory in the Field*. New York: Routledge.

Rabinow, P. & W.M. Sullivan (Eds.) (1987). The Interpretive Turn: A Second Look. In P. Rabinow & W.M. Sullivan (Eds.), *Interpretive Social Science: A Second Look* (pp. 1–30). Berkeley, CA: University of California Press.

Ragin, C.C., J. Nahgel, & P. White (2004). *Workshop on Scientific Foundations of Qualitative Research*. Washington, DC: National Science Foundation. See www.nsf.gov/pubs/2004/nsf04219/nsf04219.pdf

Rains, F.V., J.A. Archibald, & D. Deyhle (2000). Through Our Eyes and in Our Words – The Voices of Indigenous Scholars. Special Issue. *International Journal of Qualitative Studies in Education* 13(4): 337–342.

Rawls, A.W. (2018). The Wartime Narrative in US Sociology, 1940-1947: Stigmatizing Qualitative Sociology in the Name of 'Science.' *European Journal of Social Theory* 21(4):526-546.

Reason, P. (1994). Three Approaches to Participative Inquiry. In N.K. Denzin & Y.S. Lincoln (Eds.), *Handbook of Qualitative Research* (pp. 324–339). Thousand Oaks, CA: Sage.

Reason, P. & H. Bradbury-Huang (Eds.) (2008). *The Sage Handbook of Action Research: Participative Inquiry and Practice* (2nd ed.). Thousand Oaks, CA: Sage.

Reichertz, J. (2007). Abduction: The Logic of Discovery of Grounded Theory. In A. Bryant & K. Charmaz (Eds.), *Handbook of Grounded Theory* (pp. 214–228). London: Sage.

Reid, R. (2001). Researcher or Smoker? Or, When the Other isn't Other Enough in Studying 'across' Tobacco Control. In R. Reid & S. Traweek (Eds.), *Doing Science and Culture* (pp. 119–150). New York: Routledge.

Reynolds, L. & N. Herman-Kinney (Eds.) (2003). *Handbook of Symbolic Interactionism*. Walnut Creek, CA: AltaMira Press.

Richardson, R. & E.H. Kramer (2006). Abduction as the Type of Inference that Characterizes the Development of a Grounded Theory. *Qualitative Research* 6(4): 497–513.

Riessman, C. K. (1993). *Narrative Analysis*. Newbury Park, CA: Sage.

Rorty, R. (1967). *The Linguistic Turn: Recent Essays in Philosophical Method*. Chicago: University of Chicago Press.

Rosaldo, R. (1989). *Culture and Truth: The Remaking of Social Analysis*. Boston, MA: Beacon.

Ross, D. (1990). *The Origins of American Social Science*. Cambridge, UK: Cambridge University Press.

Said, E. (1978). *Orientalism*. New York: Random House.

Sandstrom, K.L. & G.A. Fine (2003). Triumphs, Emerging Voices, and the Future. In L.T. Reynolds & N.J. Herman-Kinney (Eds.), *Handbook of Symbolic Interactionism* (pp. 1041–1057). Walnut Creek, CA: AltaMira Press.

Savage, M. & R. Burrows (2007). The Coming Crisis of Empirical Sociology. *Sociology* 41(5): 885–899.

Schatzki, T.R., K. Knorr Cetina, & E. von Savigny (Eds.) (2001). *The Practice Turn in Contemporary Theory*. London: Routledge.

Schatzman, L. (1991). Dimensional Analysis: Notes on an Alternative Approach to the Grounding of Theory in Qualitative Research. In D. Maines (Ed.), *Social Organization and Social Process: Essays in Honor of Anselm Strauss* (pp. 303–314). Hawthorne, NY: Aldine de Gruyter.

Schatzman, L. & A. Strauss (1973). *Field Research: Strategies for a Natural Sociology*. Englewood Cliffs, NJ: Prentice-Hall.

Schreiber, R.S. & P.N. Stern (Eds.) (2001). *Using Grounded Theory in Nursing*. New York: Springer.

Schulz, A.J. & L. Mullings (Eds.) (2006). *Gender, Race, Class, and Health: Intersectional Approaches*. San Francisco, CA: Jossey-Bass.

Schütze, F. (2008). The Legacy in Germany Today of Anselm Strauss's Vision and Practice of Sociology. In N. Denzin (Ed.), *Studies in Symbolic Interaction* 32: 103–126.

Schwalbe, Michael L. (2008). *Rigging the Game: How Inequality is Reproduced in Everyday Life*. New York: Oxford University Press.

Seale, C., G. Gobo, J.F. Gubrium, & D. Silverman (Eds.) (2004). *Qualitative Research Practice*. London: Sage.

Shim, J.K. (2010). Cultural Health Capital: A Theoretical Approach to Understanding Health Care Interactions and the Dynamics of Unequal Treatment. *Journal of Health and Social Behavior* 51(1): 1–15.

Silverman, D. & A. Marvasti (2008). *Doing Qualitative Research: A Comprehensive Guide*. London: Sage.

Simmel, G. (1908/1971). The Stranger. In *Georg Simmel on Individuality and Social Forms: Selected Writings*. Ed. D.N. Levine (pp. 143–149). Chicago, IL: University of Chicago Press.

Simon, J. (1996). Discipline and Punish: The Birth of a Middle-Range Research Strategy. *Contemporary Sociology—A Journal of Reviews* 25(3): 316–319.

Smith, D.E. (1987). *The Everyday World as Problematic: A Feminist Sociology*. Boston, MA: Northeastern University Press.

Smith, D.E. (1990). *The Conceptual Politics of Power*. Boston, MA: Northeastern University Press.

Smith, D.E. (2005). *Institutional Ethnography: A Sociology for People*. Lanham, DE: Rowman and Littlefield.

Smith, D.E. & S.M. Turner (Eds.) (2014). *Incorporating Texts into Institutional Ethnographies*. Toronto: University of Toronto Press.

Snow, D.A. & C. Morrill (1995). A Revolutionary Handbook or a Handbook for Revolution? *Journal of Contemporary Ethnography* 24(3): 341–362.

Soeffner, H.-G. (1983, 2004a). Anmerkungen zu gemeinsamen Standards standardisierter und nicht-standardisierter Verfahren in der Sozialforschung. In H.-G. Soeffner, *Auslegung des Alltags – Der Alltag der Auslegung. Zur wissenssoziologischen Konzeption einer sozialwissenschaftlichen Hermeneutik* (1st and 2nd eds., pp. 61–77). Konstanz, Germany: UVK/UTB.

Soeffner, H.-G. (2004b). Social Science Hermeneutics. In U. Flick, E. Kardoff, & I. Steinke (Eds.), *A Companion to Qualitative Research* (pp. 95–100). London: Sage.

Spencer, J. (2001). Ethnography After Post-modernism. In P. Atkinson, A. Coffey, S. Delamont, J. Lofland, & L. Lofland (Eds.) *Handbook of Ethnography* (pp. 443–452). London: Sage..

Spivak, G.C. (1993). *Outside in the Teaching Machine*. London: Routledge.

Spooner, M. (2018). Qualitative Research and Global Audit Culture. In N.K. Denzin & Y.S. Lincoln (Eds.), *Sage Handbook of Qualitative Research* (5th ed., pp. 894–914). Thousand Oaks, CA: Sage.

Spradley, J.P. (1980). *Participant Observation*. New York: Holt, Rinehart & Winston.

Sprague, J. (2005). *Feminist Methodologies for Critical Researchers: Bridging Differences* (1st ed). Lanham, MD: Rowman & Littlefield.

Sprague, J. (2016). *Feminist Methodologies for Critical Researchers: Bridging Differences* (2nd ed). Lanham, MD: Rowman & Littlefield.

Springer, K.W., J.M. Stellman, & R. Jordan-Young (2012). Beyond a Catalogue of Differences: A Theoretical Frame and Good Practice Guidelines for Researching Sex/Gender in Human Health. *Social Science & Medicine* 74(11): 1817–1824.

St. Pierre, E.A. (2011). Post Qualitative Research: The Critique and the Coming After. In N. Denzin & Y. Lincoln (Eds.), *The Sage Handbook of Qualitative Inquiry* (pp. 611–626). Thousand Oaks, CA: Sage.

St. Pierre, E.A. (2013). The Posts Continue: Becoming. *International Journal of Qualitative Studies in Education 26*(6): 646–657.

St. Pierre, E.A. & W.S. Pillow (Eds.) (2002). *Working the Ruins: Feminist Poststructural Theory and Methods in Education*. New York: Routledge.

Stanley, L. (Ed.) (1990). *Feminist Praxis: Research, Theory and Epistemology in Feminist Sociology*. London: Routledge.

Star, S.L. (1989). *Regions of the Mind: Brain Research and the Quest for Scientific Certainty*. Stanford, CA: Stanford University Press.

Star, S.L. (1991). The Sociology of the Invisible: The Primacy of Work in the Writings of Anselm Strauss. In D.R. Maines (Ed.), *Social Organization and Social Processes: Essays in Honor of Anselm Strauss* (pp. 265–283). Hawthorne, NY: Aldine de Gruyter.

Star, S.L. (1993). Cooperation without Consensus in Scientific Problem Solving: Dynamics of Closure in Open Systems. In S. Easterbrook (Ed.), *CSCW: Cooperation or Conflict?* (pp. 93–105). London: Springer.

Star, S.L. (Ed.) (1995). *Ecologies of Knowledge: New Directions in the Sociology of Science and Technology*. Albany, NY: State University of New York Press. Introduction reprinted in G. Bowker, S. Timmermans, A.E. Clarke, & E. Balka (Eds.), *Boundary Objects and Beyond: Working with Susan Leigh Star* (pp. 13–46). Cambridge, MA: MIT Press.

Star, S.L. (2007). Living Grounded Theory: Cognitive and Emotional Forms of Pragmatism. In A. Bryant & K. Charmaz (Eds.), *The Sage Handbook of Grounded Theory* (pp. 75–94). Thousand Oaks, CA: Sage.

Star, S.L. (2015). Revisiting *Ecologies of Knowledge: Work and Politics in Science and Technology*. In G. Bowker, S. Timmermans, A.E. Clarke, & E. Balka (Eds.) *Boundary Objects and Beyond: Working with Susan Leigh Star* (pp. 13–46). Cambridge, MA: MIT Press.

Steinberg, S.R. & G.S. Cannella (Eds.) (2012). *Critical Qualitative Research Reader*. New York: Peter Lang.

Steinmetz, G. (Ed.) (2005). *The Politics of Method in the Human Sciences: Positivism and Its Epistemological Others*. Durham, NC: Duke University Press.

Stern, P.N. (1994). Eroding Grounded Theory. In J. Morse (Ed.), *Critical Issues in Qualitative Research Methods* (pp. 212–223). Thousand Oaks, CA: Sage.

Stern, P.N. (2007). On Solid Ground: Essential Properties for Growing Grounded Theory. In A. Bryant & K. Charmaz (Eds.), *Handbook of Grounded Theory* (pp. 114–126). London: Sage.

Stern, P.N. (2009). In the Beginning Glaser and Strauss Created Grounded Theory. In J.M. Morse, P.N. Stern, J.M. Corbin, K. Charmaz, B. Bowers, & A.E. Clarke, *Developing Grounded Theory: The Second Generation* (pp. 24–29). London: Routledge.

Stern, P. N. & Porr, C. (Forthcoming 2019). Glaserian grounded theory. In J. Morse, P.N. Stern, J. Corbin, B. Bowers, K. Charmaz, A.E. Clarke, & C. Porr. *Grounded theory: The second generation*. London: Routledge, 2nd ed.

Stonequist, E.V. (1937/1961). *The Marginal Man: A Study in Personality and Culture*. New York: Russell & Russell.

Strauss, A.L. (1970). Discovering New Theory from Previous Theory. In T. Shibutani (Ed.), *Human Nature and Collective Behavior: Papers in Honor of Herbert Blumer* (pp. 46–53). Englewood Cliffs, NJ: Prentice-Hall.

Strauss, A.L. (1978). A Social Worlds Perspective. *Studies in Symbolic Interaction* 1: 119–128.

Strauss, A.L. (1979). *Negotiations: Varieties, Contexts, Processes and Social Order*. San Francisco, CA: Jossey-Bass.

Strauss, A.L. (1982a). Interorganizational Negotiation. *Urban Life 11*(3): 350–367.

Strauss, A.L. (1982b). Social Worlds and Legitimation Processes. In N. Denzin (Ed.), *Studies in Symbolic Interaction* (*Vol. 4*, pp. 171–190). Greenwich, CT: JAI Press.

Strauss, A.L. (1984). Social Worlds and Their Segmentation Processes. *Studies in Symbolic Interaction* 5: 123–139.

Strauss, A.L. (1987). *Qualitative Analysis for Social Scientists.* Cambridge, UK: Cambridge University Press.

Strauss, A.L. (1991a). *Creating Sociological Awareness: Collective Images and Symbolic Representation*. New Brunswick, NJ: Transaction.

Strauss, A.L. (1991b). A Personal History of the Development of Grounded Theory. *Qualitative Family Research: A Newsletter of the Qualitative Family Research Network* 5(2), http://dne2.ucsf.edu/public/anselmstrauss/groundedtheory.html (accessed 12/29/16).

Strauss, A.L. (1993). *Continual Permutations of Action*. New York: Aldine de Gruyter.

Strauss, A.L. (1995). Notes on the Nature and Development of General Theories. *Qualitative Inquiry 1*(1): 7–18.

Strauss, A.L. & J. Corbin (1990, 1998). *The Basics of Qualitative Analysis: Grounded Theory Procedures and Techniques* (1st & 2nd eds.). Newbury Park, CA: Sage.

Strauss, A. L., & J. Corbin. (1994). Grounded Theory Methodology: An Overview. In N. Denzin & Y. Lincoln (Eds.), *Handbook of Qualitative Research* (pp. 273-285). Thousand Oaks, CA: Sage (1st ed.).

Strauss, A.L. & B.G. Glaser (1970). *Anguish: The Case History of a Dying Trajectory*. San Francisco, CA: Sociology Press.

Strauss, A.L., L. Schatzman, R. Bucher, D. Ehrlich, & M. Sabshin (1964). *Psychiatric Ideologies and Institutions*. Glencoe, IL: Free Press.

Strübing, J. (2007). Research as Pragmatic Problem-Solving: The Pragmatist Roots of Empirically-Grounded Theorizing. In A. Bryant & K. Charmaz (Eds.), *Handbook of Grounded Theory* (pp. 580–602). London: Sage.

Strübing, J. (2017). Anselm L. Strauss: Action/Work as Process and Perspective. In M.H. Jacobsen (Ed.), *The Interactionist Imagination: Meaning, Situation and Micro-Social Order* (pp. 263–289). London: Palgrave/Macmillan.

Strübing, J. (2018). Anselm L. Strauss: Action as Process in Grounded Theory. In A. Bryant & K. Charmaz (Eds.), *Handbook of Grounded Theory* (2nd ed.). London: Sage.

Suchman, L. (2012). Configuration. In C. Lury & N. Wakeford (Eds.), *Inventive Methods: The Happening of the Social* (pp. 49–60). London: Routledge.

Sutherland, E. & H. Locke (1936). *Twenty Thousand Homeless Men*. Chicago, IL: J.B. Lippincott.

Sutherland, E.H. (1949). *White Collar Crime*. New York: Dryden Press.

TallBear, K. (2014). Standing with and Speaking as Faith: A Feminist-Indigenous Approach to Inquiry. *Journal of Research Practice 10*(2): 1–7.

Tavory, I. & S. Timmermans (2014). *Abductive Analysis: Theorizing Qualitative Research*. Chicago, IL: University of Chicago Press.

Teddlie, C. & A. Tashakkori. (2011). Mixed Methods Research: Contemporary Issues in an Emerging Field. In N. Denzin & Y. Lincoln (Eds.) *The Sage Handbook of Qualitative Research* (pp. 285–300). Thousand Oak, CA: Sage.

Thomas, W.I. (1923/1978). The Definition of the Situation. In R. Farrell & V. Swigert (Eds.), *Social Deviance* (pp. 54–57). Philadelphia, PA: Lippincott.

Thomas, W.I. & D.S. Thomas (1928/1970). Situations Defined as Real Are Real in Their Consequences. In G.P. Stone & H.A. Farberman (Eds.), *Social Psychology through Symbolic Interaction* (pp. 154–155). Waltham, MA: Xerox College Publishing.

Thomas, W.I. & F. Znaniecki (1918–1920). *The Polish Peasant in Europe and America*. Boston, MA: Brager.

Thornberg, R. (2012). Informed Grounded Theory. *Scandinavian Journal of Educational Research 56*(3):243–259.

Thornberg, R. (2017). Grounded Theory. In D. Wyse, N. Welwyn, E. Smith, & L. E. Suter (Eds.) *The BERA/SAGE Handbook of Educational Research* (*Vol. 1*, pp. 355–375). London: Sage.

Thrasher, F.M. (1926). *The Gang: A Study of 1,313 Gangs in Chicago*. Chicago, IL: University of Chicago Press.

Timmermans, S. & M. Berg (2003). *The Gold Standard: The Challenge of Evidence-Based Medicine and Standardization in Health Care*. Philadelphia, PA: Temple University Press.

Timmermans, S. & S. Epstein (2010). A World of Standards but not a Standard World: Toward a Sociology and Standards and Standardization. *Annual Review of Sociology* 36: 69–89.

Torre, M.E., B. Stoudt, E. Manoff, & M. Fine (2018). Critical Participatory Action Research on State Violence: Bearing Wit(h)ness across Fault Lines of Power, Privilege and Dispossession. In N.K. Denzin & Y.S. Lincoln (Eds.), *Sage Handbook of Qualitative Research* (5th ed., pp. 492–516). Thousand Oaks, CA: Sage.

Tuhiwai Smith, L. (1999, 2012). *Decolonizing Methodologies: Research and Indigenous People* (1st & 2nd eds.). London: Zed Books.

Tuhiwai Smith, L. (2007). On Tricky Ground: Researching the Native in the Age of Uncertainty. In N. Denzin & Y. Lincoln (Eds.), *The Sage Handbook of Qualitative Research* (3rd ed., pp. 85–108). Thousand Oaks, CA: Sage.

Van Maanen, J. (1995). An End to Innocence: The Ethnography of Ethnography. In J. Van Maanen (Ed.), *Representation in Ethnography* (pp. 1–35). Thousand Oaks, CA: Sage.

Velody, I. & R. Williams (Eds.) (1998). *The Politics of Constructionism*. London: Sage.

Vidich, A.J. & J. Bensman (1958). *Small Town in Mass Society: Class, Power and Religion in a Rural Community*. Chicago, IL: University of Illinois Press.

Vidich, A.J. & S.M. Lyman (1994, 2000). Qualitative Methods: Their History in Sociology and Anthropology. In N.K. Denzin & Y.S. Lincoln (Eds.), *Handbook of Qualitative Research* (1st ed., pp. 23–59; 2nd ed., pp. 37–84). Thousand Oaks, CA: Sage.

Visweswaran, K. (1994). *Fictions of Feminist Ethnography*. Minneapolis, MN: University of Minnesota Press.

Von Unger, H. (2016). Reflexivity Beyond Regulations: Teaching Research Ethics and Qualitative Methods in Germany. *Qualitative Inquiry 22*(2): 87–98.

Wacquant, L. (2002). Scrutinizing the Street: Poverty, Morality, and the Pitfalls of Urban Ethnography. *American Journal of Sociology* 107: 1468–1532.

Walter, M. & C. Anderson (2013). *Indigenous Statistics: A Quantitative Methodology*. London: Routledge.

Webster, F. (2004). Cultural Studies and Sociology at, and after, the Closure of the Birmingham School. *Cultural Studies 18*(6): 848.

Weinberg, D. (2015). *Contemporary Social Constructionism: Key Themes*. Philadelphia, PA: Temple University Press.

Wertz, F.J., K. Charmaz, L.M. McMullen, R. Josselson, R. Anderson, & E. McSpadden (2011). *Five Ways of Doing Qualitative Analysis: Phenomenological Psychology, Grounded Theory, Discourse Analysis, Narrative Analysis & Intuitive Inquiry*. New York: Guilford Press.

Westbrook, D. (2018). Critical Issues for Qualitative Research. In N.K. Denzin & Y.S. Lincoln (Eds.), *The Sage Handbook of Qualitative Research* (5th ed., pp. 915–922). Thousand Oaks, CA: Sage.

Whisker, C. (Forthcoming 2020). A genealogy of grounded theory and situational analysis [Figure]. *A Situational Analysis of Family Therapy in Aotearoa New Zealand, 1990-1995* [working title]. Doctoral dissertation in progress. La Trobe University, Melbourne, Australia.

Williams, D.R. & S.A. Mohammed (2013). Racism and Health II: A Needed Research Agenda for Effective Interventions. *American Behavioral Scientist 5*(8): 1200–1226.

Wilson, T.P. (1970). Conceptions of Interaction and Forms of Sociological Explanation. *American Sociological Review 35*(4): 697–710.

Wolf, D. L. (1996). *Feminist Dilemmas in Fieldwork.* Boulder, CO: Westview.

Wyly, E. (2009). Strategic Positivism. *The Professional Geographer 61*(3): 310–322.

Yanow, D. & P. Schwartz-Shea (2006, 2013). *Interpretation and Method: Empirical Research Methods and the Interpretive Turn* (1st & 2nd eds.). New York: Routledge.

PART II

Theories and Theorizing in Grounded Theory

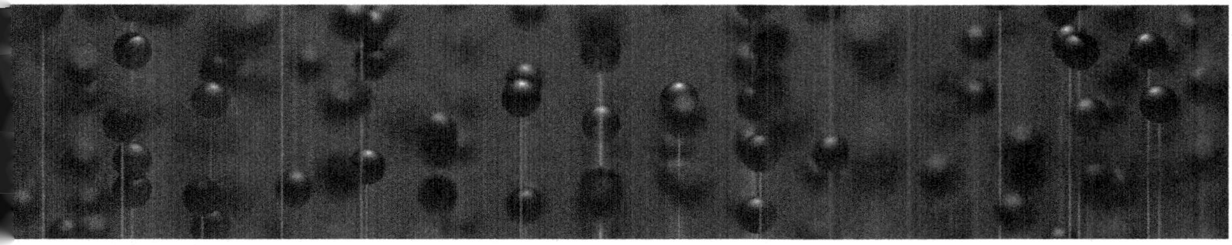

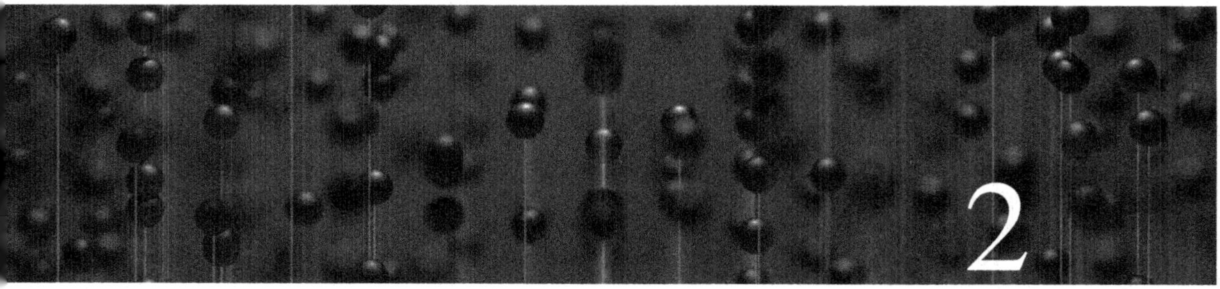

The Pragmatism of Anselm L. Strauss: Linking Theory and Method

Jörg Strübing

INTRODUCTION[1]

This chapter will shed some light on the life and the theoretical works of the American sociologist Anselm Strauss (1916–1996). Already well-known as one of the founding fathers of Grounded Theory, his achievements in social theory, and especially his firm re-grounding of the interactionist project in its pragmatist roots, often remain underestimated. There are several reasons for this. The most obvious is the great success of the grounded theory research style established by Glaser and Strauss (1967), a success which sadly seems to have largely outshined Strauss's theoretical works. Another reason is that Strauss did not fit into the established division of labor in sociology between, on the one hand, empirical researchers and, on the other, social theorists and philosophers. He did both and built one on the grounds of the other. In addition, Strauss neither built his social theory from scratch nor did he center it on one key idea. His theorizing has been a lifelong step-by-step iteration of theoretical concepts derived from working on empirical problems and driven by a basic philosophical compass inherited from early American pragmatism. In a way he lived and practiced what Clarke and Star (2007) called a 'Theory-Methods Package', that is, a co-development of theory and methods in the course of ongoing research. His later theoretical writings, thoroughly grounded in decades of empirical studies on illness and healthcare, are structured by two core categories, process and perspective, which are both approached with a focus on action and work. In shifting the Blumerian emphasis from *symbolic* interaction towards a more material view of sociality as situated activity, and thereby blurring the somewhat artificial separation of action from structure, Strauss both established a strictly anti-dualistic view of the social and showed the dynamic tension between doubt and belief to be the mover of human activity.

An interesting point regarding Strauss is that although his early academic education brought him in close contact with pragmatism, especially with Dewey's epistemology and philosophy of science, he entered American academic sociology at a point in history where interactionism in the then prevailing Blumerian variant of symbolic interactionism was close to losing contact with some key pragmatist elements, such as the critical stance towards dichotomies, the emphasis on processes instead of objects or the pivotal role of creative abductions in scientific problem-solving processes. Although prominent in the works of its founder George Herbert Mead and other early figures in Chicago School sociology, only a faint afterglow of pragmatist thinking in Blumer's interpretation of Mead's works remained. In developing his own theoretical stance, Strauss not only regenerated pragmatism, but also combined it with the ecological approach proposed by Robert Park and Ernest Burgess (1921) and further developed by Everett C. Hughes (1957/1971). Resulting from these theoretical influences, empirical experiences, and creative problem-solvings, the conceptual groundwork laid by Strauss allows for pragmatist interactionism to adequately deal with postmodern challenges such as the participation of nonhuman entities in social activity or the importance of discourse in shaping situated action and at the same time being shaped in these situations.

THINGS FALLING INTO PLACES: THE LIFE OF A PRAGMATIST

Born on December 18, 1916, in New York, Anselm Leonard Strauss grew up in Mount Vernon, a typical middle-class suburb in Westchester County. He was the eldest of three children, and his father Julius Strauss taught sports at a high school in New York while his mother, Minnie Rothschild Strauss, fulfilled her role as a housewife. Although his family origins lie in Germany and his grandparents migrated from there between 1860 and 1870, Strauss rather saw himself as the child of a typical American family than a migrant. Jewish by birth, according to him these cultural and religious roots had no deep impact on his life (Legewie & Schervier-Legewie 2004).

We cannot fully understand Strauss's biography without considering the grave health problems from which he started to suffer in his youth. Due to severe breathing problems, his doctors advised him to choose a dry and warm south-west state such as Arizona for his undergraduate studies. However, in 1935, he finally ended up studying at the University of Virginia in Richmond. He never shook off his fragile health status, which later escalated to a micro heart attack in 1972 and a severe heart attack eight years later. His chronic heart disease made it difficult for Strauss in his later years, to live the normal life of a social scientist including travelling, conferences and public debates.

His health problems even influenced the subject of his undergraduate studies: Strauss began by studying sciences because after all the medical treatments he endured during his youth he wanted to become a surgeon (Legewie & Schervier-Legewie 2004). However, bored after his first year of studies he added courses in humanities, sociology and psychology to his schedule (Baszanger 1998: 355). While in Virginia he got involved with Chicago-style social science and philosophy through his first teacher Floyd House, a former student of Robert E. Park in Chicago. House introduced Park's and Mead's perspectives as self-evident and Strauss 'absorbed this general sociological orientation much as goldfish accept their environment' (Strauss 1996: 6). It was also through Floyd House that the young Strauss came to read the classical pragmatists, namely Dewey and his philosophy of science. Despite his serious stake in the social sciences, Strauss graduated from the University of Virginia with a BA in biology.

Due to his fragile health state, Strauss was spared the fate of many men of his generation. Instead of fighting in World War II, he was able to continue his studies from 1939 until 1944 at the University of Chicago, where he studied sociology, social psychology and anthropology under the auspices of Herbert Blumer. Blumer convinced Strauss to devote his master's thesis to a critical review of the concept of 'attitude' in social science research. However, because Blumer's never-ending critical comments compelled him to rewrite his thesis again and again, Strauss finished the manuscript of his dissertation on marital choice (Strauss 1945) under Ernest Burgess before his master's thesis had been accepted (Strauss 1996: 5). This episode nicely characterizes how Strauss experienced his relation to Blumer, who taught him a lot, but with his strict criticisms also discouraged curiosity and creativity (ibid.).

Having finished his PhD, Strauss left Chicago for a two-year teaching job at Lawrence College in Wisconsin before he became an assistant professor at the University of Indiana. There he met Alfred R. Lindesmith, who had become known for his empirical research on opiate addiction in the research style of Znaniecki's analytic induction. Lindesmith and Strauss became life-long friends, and together published the classic interactionist textbook *Social Psychology* (1949). It was through the joint writing of this book that Strauss gained a critical distance from his former mentor Blumer. He found Blumer excellent in pointing out wishful social theoretical goals, but not equally gifted in developing these theories or suitable empirical paths in their direction (Strauss 1996: 7).

In his early years as a professional sociologist, Strauss did not have his own method either. That changed when, in 1952, he went back to the University of Chicago as an assistant professor and began to work with Everett C. Hughes. During his graduate studies, he had avoided Hughes' readings, which he deemed mere story-telling. Then when working with him, he found in Hughes' fieldwork practices a clue to his own methods problems (Baszanger 1998: 356). In Hughes, a descendant of Parks' famous research group, Strauss became connected to a very practical empirical strand of sociological research, which he blended with the theoretical depths of the Dewey-Mead-Blumer line of pragmatist-interactionism. Moreover, and no less important, in working with Hughes, Strauss became acquainted with Erving Goffman, Fred Davis, Tomatsu Shibutani, Eliot Freidson and Howard S. Becker, who would become his life-long close colleagues and friends.

A second impact the collaboration with Hughes had on Strauss's development lies in a higher regard for organizational and processual aspects of the social (Corbin 1991: 24). Hughes' ecological approach, with its understanding of organizations as processes organized by their commitment to goals enacted in dealing with different environments (Hughes 1957/1971), would become a core inspiration for Strauss's later sociology of work and organization. The influence of this perspective can first be seen in Strauss's monograph *Mirrors and Masks* (Strauss 1959).

Together with Hughes, Becker and Blanche Geer, Strauss then took part in the fieldwork study *Boys in White* (Becker et al. 1961) on the professional socialization of medical students conducted at the University of Kansas in the late 1950s. Although Hughes and Strauss were mainly responsible for the conceptual and analytic work, Strauss did spend about three months on fieldwork at the medical school and started to develop his own style of comparative analytic work with empirical cases. Directly following this first fieldwork experience, Strauss initiated another team ethnographic research project at both Chicago State Hospital and Michael Reese Hospital, where from 1958 to 1960 he also served as research director. The study he conducted together with Leonard Schatzman, Rue Bucher, Danuta Ehrlich and Melvin Sabshin, resulted in the monograph *Psychiatric Ideologies and Institutions* (Strauss et al. 1964). Here, Strauss presented his first and most important empirically-derived theoretical concept, the 'negotiated order approach'. Strauss and his colleagues showed that decisions about psychiatric treatments, rather than being based on solid and unquestionable professional knowledge, were in fact more often than not the result of a constant stream of negotiations involving professionals, nurses and even patients. This understanding of social order as a 'processual ordering', as he later phrased it more adequately (Strauss 1993), became the core of his theoretical work.

In 1960, Strauss was awarded a full professorship at University of California in San Francisco. Very fittingly, given the subject matter of his previous research in professional medical work, his new position was located in the UC San Francisco School of Nursing, a position he accepted with the understanding that he would later be able to found a PhD program in Sociology and that it would become a department in a proposed school of social sciences. Though delayed, the program began in 1968. It was in San Francisco that Strauss finally left his professional career in social psychology behind and became a full-fledged sociologist. Key to the research program Strauss established at UCSF was a large research grant offered to him by the US National Institutes of Mental Health (NIMH). Strauss intended to follow in depth a trace that was already highlighted in *Boys in White*: While medical students at that time learned a lot about saving their patients' lives, they did not, however, learn to deal with dying patients and their relatives (Glaser & Strauss 1965: 4).

Together with Barney Glaser, a Columbia PhD in sociology who had studied with Robert K. Merton and Paul Lazarsfeld, and Jeanne Quint Benoliel, a trained nurse and nursing scientist, Strauss investigated how the process of dying in the organizational and professional setting of hospitals is socially constructed and performed. It was through their studies that the idea of death and dying as socially constructed knowledge issues was established in both sociology and medical practice. With their key concepts of the 'awareness context' and the 'dying trajectory', Strauss and his collaborators were among the founders of the sociology of medicine. After years of fieldwork, the project resulted in three important monographs, two of them regarding the above-mentioned key concepts, while the third became one of the most influential books on qualitative research methodology: *The Discovery of Grounded Theory* (Glaser & Strauss 1967).

A series of empirical studies on varied topics of medical work and care ensued across the following decades. In *The Social Organization of Medical Work* (Strauss et al. 1985), Strauss broadened his view on hospitals by investigating in general how organized medical work is done. At this point, work became the centering perspective through which Strauss approached his fields of research. In pursuit of this perspective, he published a series of articles explicitly addressing the interactive organizing of work. Here he developed both the core of his social worlds theory (Strauss 1978) and a sound sociological theory of organization (Strauss 1985, 1988). Yet all these more general concepts remained embedded in his empirical research on medical topics.

In 1987, aged 71, Strauss formally retired. Yet despite his fragile health after a severe heart attack in 1980, with his retirement he began another very productive phase of his work. He not only published his first methods textbook on grounded theory (Strauss 1987), but more importantly, he started to complete his theoretical works. Apart from some theoretical and reflexive papers, for example on Mead's conception of time and evolution (Strauss 1991), it was largely in his last monograph *Continual Permutations of Action* (1993) that Strauss drew together the different lines of his theoretical thinking based on the vast amount of empirical work he had done.

No longer able to do much travelling, Strauss and his wife Fran made their home an open house for his students, friends and colleagues from abroad. The kitchen table became an informal office and the place for vivid debates as well as of scholarly guidance.[2] Still engaged not only in writing but also in some empirical fieldwork, Anselm Strauss died of another heart attack on September 5, 1996.

THEORY OF IDENTITY: FROM SOCIAL PSYCHOLOGY TO SOCIOLOGY

In his first important monograph *Mirrors and Masks* (1959), Strauss highlights an issue that is core to the interactionist project and that was addressed by a considerable number of scholars at that time (namely Goffman and Shibutani, or, for that matter, Erickson): the issue of identity. However, he gives focusing on identity a different twist: Instead of defining identity and identity formation in ways used by contemporary psychologists, Strauss turns the notion of identity into an instrument to investigate those *social* processes in which identity is – at least in parts – formed (1959/1997: 15). That is, he digs deeper into the symbolic and cultural foundations out of which identity results. Leaving topics of personal identity aside, Strauss concentrates on the social dimensions of identity, in other words, 'how persons become implicated with other persons and are affected and affect each other through these implications' (ibid.).

Initially, *Mirrors and Masks* was meant to be a short essay on identification. However, it ended up integrating organizational and institutional elements to generate a full-fledged social theory of identity formation (Baszanger 1998: 356). Here, Strauss demonstrated a sophisticated understanding of how language and process shape people's dynamic relationships between their perception of identity and actions concerning it. The impact of this book cannot be overestimated. Maines and Charlton (1985), for instance, identified *Mirrors and Masks* as a general 'turning point' for symbolic interactionism in overcoming the self-limitations of social psychology to become fully sociological.

Retrospectively, *Mirrors and Masks* appears to be the agenda-setting paper for Strauss's life-long research program. It addresses topics such as the role of social worlds in establishing and maintaining social order, the fluidity of both social formations and identities, and the importance of perspectives in the constitution of social reality. Alas, none of these topics appeared in a saturated form. The notion of social worlds, for example, is adopted from Shibutani, while it took Strauss another twenty years until he developed his own theoretical stance on this subject matter. He then criticized Shibutani for both limiting his understanding of social worlds to symbolic exchange and neglecting the material dimension of social activity and its constitutive role in maintaining social order. Still, with *Mirrors and Masks* Strauss managed to integrate topics of identity and identity formation as core issues into an interactionist sociology and at the same time adding an organizational and structural view to it. Through this, he steered interactionism into the position of a full-fledged empirically-oriented sociology encompassing micro, meso, and macro level issues.

ACTION/WORK AS CREATOR OF REALITY

As Isabelle Baszanger (1998: 1) put it, '(t)he concept of action can be seen as Ariadne's thread that weaves the work of Anselm Strauss together'. However, in order to understand the specifics of the Straussian perspective on social processes it is important to have a closer look at the specific phrasings Strauss gave his notion of action. First, although the word 'action' may evoke images of an isolated, atomized act as it is typical for Weberian approaches or rational choice theories, this is not at all what Strauss had in mind. For him, action 'though expressed in English language as a noun is actually a verb – "to act"' (Strauss 1993: 22). He wrote this in the initial section of the first chapter of *Continual Permutations of Action*, indicating right from the start that his theoretical exposition centers on a *processual perspective* on the social. A second phrasing is action as *interaction.* Actions are embedded in interactions. That is, rather than recognizing actions as existing on their own, as single entities, they are only analytically definable units within a larger stream of action. 'Yet the rare theorists who write about action, *per se* (such as Weber, Schütz, and Parsons) tend to begin with the *act*, with a separate island of action; not with the assumption that interaction is the prior central concept, nor the assumption that to separate action from interaction is an analytic artifact' (Strauss 1993: 25). Third, Strauss not only treats acting as synonymous with working, but his complete analytic perspective focuses on the social process of working together. More than his choice of research fields (most often larger organizations such as hospitals), it is his special curiosity about work-related issues that signifies Strauss's approach to action-as-work. He used to ask questions such as 'How do they accomplish it?', a more specific variant of Geertz's 'What the hell is going on?' (Geertz as quoted by Olson 1991: 248).

A fourth dimension that enriches and specifies Strauss's notion of action is the *body*: 'No action is possible without the body' (Strauss 1993: 23). It sounds trivial at first but in the light of the strong emphasis that interactionists such as Blumer and Shibutani placed on the dimension of *symbolic* communication as the mover of interaction, Strauss's statement and the fact that he positioned it as the first of his 19 basic assumptions in *Continual Permutations of Action* indicates that this is a pivotal issue for him. Long before the 'body turn' appeared on the social science stage, Strauss took on the task of detailing what the body as a necessary condition for action means and what consequences a developed concept of body has for sociological analysis. Rather than being a mere tool for performing mentally pre-designed actions, the acting self is conceptualized as a bodily self: 'the dualism of distinguishing between mind and body is rejected' (Strauss 1993: 23). By the same token, body is not thought of as a limited physical entity, but rather as 'multifaceted' (ibid.), including multiple body processes that represent layers of relations between the acting self and its environments. While Goffman defines interaction as bound to the physically present selves and others, Strauss points out the preconditions and the consequences of this boundedness of symbolic interaction to physical/material processes.

PROCESS AND PERSPECTIVE INSTEAD OF STRUCTURE AND ACTION

One of the core issues of social theory is the relation between structure and action. Often treated in chicken-and-egg fashion, social theorists try to decide which comes first: action or structure. Strauss, however, with his pragmatist background, did not bother much with unfruitful dichotomies. Instead, he follows Hughes' stance: '... not change but the dynamics of remaining the same is the miracle which social science must explain' (Hughes 1955: 6). The way Strauss tackled the issue can best be seen in his concept of 'processual ordering' (Strauss 1993: 245 *et passim*). Social order, instead of being either the stable Parsonian frame within which action takes place, or the result of accumulated individual acts, in Strauss's conception appears as a continuous process evoked by ongoing interactions. These, in turn, both rely on and are shaped by what actors from their respective points of view perceive as given resources and constraints. Interaction is always situated. It takes place in the view of and dedicated towards the specific conditions experienced in the processes of interacting. Strauss maintains that these conditions are far more than just other humans and their activities in face-to-face contact. Rather they consist literally of any issue occurring in the perspectives of actors as relevant: established divisions of labor, the material resistance of the built environment, the actual perception of time constraints or a growing feeling of uneasiness and despair in light of an upcoming risky surgery, for example. (Inter)action responds – consciously or not – to the whole range of these conditions. Moreover, it does so in various ways, thereby re-establishing or modifying them in acts of practical confirmation, denial, manipulation, and so on.

By referring to Dewey, Strauss states that the permanence of seemingly stable structures is nothing but a function of these entities in respect to other elements of the lived environment that are experienced as relatively quick, rapidly changing, or irregular (Strauss 1993: 246). Not surprisingly, both Dewey and Strauss (along with most interactionists) reject the concept of structural determination. Instead, they insist that even the most difficult constraints, although they must be taken into account, are still conditions to which actors may respond in different ways. This is, at the same time, the source of creativity.

'Processual ordering' or, in its earlier variant, the 'negotiated order approach', represents a more advanced version of Thomas and Thomas's (1928) 'definition of the situation' in spelling out the basic dialectics of human activity. As Dewey put it: 'Whatever influences the changes of other things is itself changed' (1929: 73). This perspective fosters the idea of human actors literally being constituted in relation to other entities, be they human, other biological entities, or material substance, rather than reifying the Cartesian divide between the individual and its environment.

SOCIAL ORDER BY COMMITMENT: SOCIAL WORLDS, ARENAS, AND ORGANIZATIONS

By the same token, Strauss conceptualized arenas and social worlds, the other key concepts of his theory, as open and fluid processes, risky and unpredictable. Based on a pragmatist understanding, in his theory of social worlds and arenas (Strauss 1978, 1993: 209pp) he combines various theoretical and empirical influences, namely Meads notion of 'universes of discourse' (Mead 1934: 89), Shibutani's reference group theory (Shibutani 1955), Hughes' ecological approach and his own empirical experiences in the field of medical and care work.[3] Instead of regarding it as given, Strauss sees social order as an issue that has to continuously be solved and solved again. Moreover, conflict is more likely than consensus in such processes. For him, '[t]he generic social process is assumed to be intergroup conflict unless and until the data prove otherwise' (Clarke 1991: 129).

That is, *social worlds*, as the basic formations of social order and temporary results of social processes, have to be explained in empirical analysis. For Strauss, social worlds are, as Clarke wrote, 'groups with shared commitments to certain activities, sharing resources of many kinds to achieve their goals, and building shared ideologies about how to go about their business' (Clarke 1991: 131). The key point in Strauss's analytic concept of social worlds is the notion of 'activities'. While Mead and especially Shibutani regard social worlds as based on communication and discourse, Strauss brings the argument down to earth: Social order results from doing things together, which in turn involves 'palpable matter' (Strauss 1978: 121) and not just communication.

> There are sites where activities occur: hence space and a shaped landscape are relevant. *Technology* (inherited or innovative modes of carrying out the social world's activities) is always involved. … In social worlds at the outset, there may be only temporary divisions of labor, but once under way, *organizations* inevitably evolve to further one aspect or another of the world's activities. (Strauss 1978: 122)

Thus, social worlds are formed by a practical, situated commitment to similar activities. People do not belong to social worlds by formal or explicit memberships. Instead, it is the amount of commitment to the core activities of the social world that makes them more or less a member of this world. Strauss notes: 'Perhaps it would be better to discard the concept here of boundaries and substitute something like peripheries, and thus avoid arousing irrelevant imagery' (Strauss 1993: 214). In fact, he did not go as far as that. However, in his concept of membership of social worlds, he demonstrates this idea practically: While an individual's level of belonging to a social world might vary between peripheral or central, at the same time 'we all have multiple memberships' (Strauss 1993: 213). A member of the profession of engineers might simultaneously be a mother, an amateur golf player, and a devoted supporter of a local basketball team. Thus, different commitments might every now and again enter into conflict with each other.

Strauss's role models for social worlds are professions, at least they were at the outset of Strauss's work on these concepts. The empirical findings of the collaborative psychiatric ideologies study clearly indicated that social worlds such as professions (e.g., psychiatry) might consist of social subworlds like psychoanalysts and behavioral therapists. Another suitable example for this argument is scientific communities. At the same time, organizations might host particular representatives of a large number of different social worlds, for example, nurses, medical practitioners, administrators, and physiotherapists. The structure of social worlds, their shape and their relations to other social worlds are, for Strauss, an ongoing and continual process. There are segmentation processes (Strauss 1984), within which new social subworlds might splinter off into autonomous movers while others might vanish completely (if people cease to show practical commitments to its activities).

The second core concept of Strauss's social worlds theory is that of *arenas*. Here he refers to 'interaction by social worlds around issues—where actions concerning these are being debated, fought out, negotiated, manipulated, and even coerced within and among the social worlds' (Strauss 1993: 226). Arenas are where social worlds meet. That is, if social order has to be explained and if interaction is seen as the obligatory point of passage through which every change of social order has to be processed, then the arena stands for those analytically reconstructed units in which a certain issue or sets of issues are fought out. 'As whirlpools of argumentative action, they lie at the very heart of permanence and change of each social world' (Strauss 1993: 227). Arena is a concept for cooperation without agreement, disagreement that cannot be solved instantaneously and thus results at least for some time in a more or less stable social form (ibid).

We tend to think of arenas as large-scale political fields of debate that exist around topics such as 'the' refugee problem, or TTIP (Transatlantic Trade and Investment Partnership). However, a striking and analytically most useful feature of Strauss's theoretical concepts is what I call 'scalability': Social worlds can be fairly small and more local (e.g., a community initiative for a sustainable energy project) or large and stretched out over societies (e.g., people around the worldwide engaged against). The same is true for arenas, they 'exist at every level of organizational action, from the most microscopic to the most macroscopic' (Strauss 1993: 227). There are arenas regarding how societies should organize care for the elderly, with state health agencies, stakeholders in social policy, health insurance companies, representatives of employers and unions, as well as those of older citizens who negotiate in various sites (e.g., in talk shows, parliaments, on the street, and in newspapers). At the same time, arenas might be as small as the ongoing debate in a progressive housing project over how to behave in shared bathrooms.

There are two key points that signify arenas, regardless of how far-reaching or limited they might be: 'First, arenas ... involve questions of policy about directions of action. Second, the source of issues and debate can be both internal and external to the participating social worlds-subworlds' (Strauss 1993: 227). Thus, arenas do not merely manage the relations between social worlds or subworlds. Instead, arenas constitute their general mode of noting and engaging issues of joint concern to the different social worlds. At the same time, Strauss does *not* conceive of arenas as formal sites of negotiations such as committees, parliaments or group meetings that convene on a regular basis (although such organizational forms are often a part of arenas). As an analytic tool, the concept of arena helps to identify all sorts of interactive contributions to solve an issue between an open number of affected social worlds/subworlds. When viewed in this way, it is often a surprise how large the number of social worlds involved is and how intricately interwoven the various sites, modes and organizational forms of a particular arena are.

Just as formally constituted elements might become part of an arena, *organizations* more generally speaking exist in a delicate interplay with social worlds and arenas. Based on Hughes' notion of organizations as 'going concerns' (Hughes 1957/1971), for Strauss, an organization is built around an organizational goal, to which its members are committed in various ways. However similar this sounds to Strauss's definition of social worlds, both concepts differ in important properties: While for social worlds the notion of boundaries proves to be largely meaningless, organizations are generally used to having formal, legally (and often physically) secured boundaries, materialized in membership cards, labor contracts, fences, and lawyers. Alas, in terms of social processes of ordering, these formal boundaries are just another resource and may in fact be quite permeable. The commitment of formal members varies largely within organizations. For Strauss, this is because organizations are usually populated by representatives of different social worlds or subworlds. These representatives' commitments to organizational going concerns are thus deeply impregnated by their professions, status groups, factions or religious movements they belong or adhere to. For example, both car designers and assembly-line workers are committed to building cars for their employing company. 'So, whom does this complex, multi-world organization represent?' (Strauss 1993: 228). That is, negotiations about representation and authenticity are core both to organizational processes and to ongoing arenas.

The combined package of these three concepts of social worlds, arenas and organizations allows not only for powerful analytical reconstructions of existing social worlds, but, moreover, for re-solving them into their generic processes. Society, understood in terms of social worlds and arenas is, as Strauss put it,

> A universe marked by tremendous fluidity; it won't and can't stand still. It is a universe where fragmentation, splintering, and disappearance are the mirror images of appearance, emergence and coalescence. This is a universe when nothing is strictly determined. (Strauss 1978: 123)

When Strauss wrote these lines in the late 1970s, the dominant sociological discourse was still driven by structural functionalists and neo-Marxist scholars, who were attacking symbolic interactionism in the 1960–1980s, claiming the pre-eminence of structural categories like race, class, and gender for social processes. Later, however, still referring to these struggles, Strauss underscored the special achievement of social worlds/arenas theory by stating: 'I shall argue that if the concept of social worlds is made central to the conceptualization of society, then a radically different view of society emerges' (Strauss 1993: 211).

A NEW ANALYTIC PERSPECTIVE FOR RESEARCHING INTERACTION: ARCS OF WORK AND TRAJECTORIES

When core activities, issues, and going concerns are at the heart of what constitutes a social world, an arena, or an organization, a detailed analysis of work is of pivotal interest to any social world analysis. Following the empirical study *The Social Organization of Medical Work* (Strauss et al. 1985), Strauss published two theoretical articles where he outlined his analytic perspective on work processes (Strauss 1985, 1988). Here, his central concepts were the interplay between *lines of work* and *arcs of work*. Instead of regarding the analysis of work as a specialized task of a certain fraction of sociology, Strauss and his colleagues were convinced that a work-and-occupation perspective would be far too limiting. As his long-time collaborator in San Francisco Elihu Gerson put it: 'rather, we should be thinking of work as all the activities in which people engage in order to accomplish their ends' (Gerson 1983).

Thus, analytic attention is drawn to the practical organizing of processes in which things are produced, achieved, brought forth, or accomplished. An important advantage of this perspective is that it regards all kinds of activities as work regardless of whether they are part of formal work organizations, unpaid household work, or any other practical activity of achieving something. Here again, Strauss's emphasis is on processes and how they are continuously organized. He maintains that organizing work, instead of being a separate task of work organizations, rather happens 'on the fly', within the performative work process. 'Articulation work', as he terms it (Strauss 1985: 2), is a mode of working that distributes tasks among actors, articulates the different practical contributions, and makes them mutually accountable. Where formal work organization results in plans about how work should be performed, leaving what Garfinkel called a 'hiatus' between rule and practice, Strauss maintains that in an interactionist perspective, the factual organizing is done practically in work-asinteraction. Plans and rules are resources, then, employed in interactions in various interpretations by participating actors.

Consequently, work processes do not exist *per se* but offer a *Gestalt* only in analytic retrospect. Empirical reconstructions are a suitable means to uncover to which 'end' or 'going concern' a certain activity is what kind of contribution. Strauss shows that in 'working' at least three things happen at the same time: people follow their sequence of tasks, thereby contributing to one or another going concern, and, in doing so, they articulate their various activities by way of 'interactional alignment' (Strauss 1988: 168). Two analytic perspectives can be employed. One would be to reconstruct 'lines of work', that is, in Gerson's phrasing 'all the activities which go into carrying out a particular kind of work, without reference to a particular work situation' (Gerson 1983: 4). We can think of this as what a carpenter, an architect, or a bank clerk, for example, does in pursuing his or her professional activities. In contrast, an 'arc of work … consists of the totality of tasks arrayed both sequentially and simultaneously along the course of the trajectory or project' (Strauss 1985: 4). Different from analyzing pre-designed divisions of labor, reconstructing arcs of work also accounts for how the actors involved jointly go about the contingencies and obstacles that lurk along their path to their respective going concern. In reconstructing arcs of work, the analyst looks back from the results to all the contributions that made it happen. That way, a certain result, situation, a state of being, or a product becomes visible as the outcome of numerous contributions of actors involved, be it active or passive, consciously or not, purposefully or accidentally. Each contribution is regarded in light of how it changed the development of the outcome under scrutiny.

While the concept 'arc of work' is dedicated to the analysis of work processes, its structure can be generalized into a basic sociological concept. Strauss did that in his notion of 'trajectory'. He uses this term nearly synonymously with the term 'project' in the above quoted definition of arcs of work. In fact, the concept of trajectory is much older and stems from a different generative question. Strauss and Glaser had already coined the term 'dying trajectory' in the 1960s in the course of their investigation of death and dying in hospitals and it became the core concept of their monograph *Time for Dying* (1968). They wrote: 'The major dimensions of a dying trajectory … are … [f]irst, dying is almost always *unscheduled*; second, the sequence of steps is *not institutionally prescribed*; and third, the actions of the various participants are only *partly regulated*' (Glaser & Strauss 1968: 247). Twenty-five years later, Strauss noted in retrospect that the more and more 'elaborated conceptualization of trajectory was the central concept in my sociological, interactionist theory of action' (Strauss 1993: 53). Its centrality for Strauss is due to the fact that, in his opinion, trajectory links up nicely with the 'Pragmatist theoretical action scheme [that is; J.S.] work is entailed in the process of unblocking the blocked action, and moving along into the future' (Strauss 1993: 52). Trajectory is a specific concept used to generally analyze all types of work in the wider sense of problem-solving activities that Dewey (1938) had in mind when he conceptualized how actors deal practically with those 'inhibitions of action' that Mead (1932/1959: 172) made central in his theory of action. In this respect, trajectory is not only most central to Strauss's theory, but at the same time it is an excellent example of how he translated the kernel of a pragmatist philosophy of the social into his interactionist sociological theory.

There are two modes in which Strauss employs his trajectory concept: '(1) the course of any experienced phenomenon as it evolves over time ... And (2) the actions and interactions to its evolution' (Strauss 1993: 53–54). It is similar to a figure-ground *Gestalt* switch that allows us to see a phenomenon on its way and, in the next moment, the contributions that made it happen that way. For Strauss, the centrality of the trajectory concept lies in its account of both phenomena as processes and the delicate relation between purposeful acting on something and unforeseen events. Social phenomena regarded as unfolding trajectories consist of activities directed towards them intentionally or inadvertently, consciously or not knowingly. Yet, at the same time, these events shape the course of a phenomenon that – from the perspective of participants – is just happening and cannot fully be taken into account in advance.

The dying trajectory is a good example of a type of trajectories of suffering. It has been studied not only by Strauss and Glaser, but also in Germany by Riemann and Schütze (1991). An uncountable number of events affect the course of individual biographies and although these do not strictly determine the life course of a person, they are not under control of this person either. He or she has to react to these events (say, the death of a parent, an upcoming war) and even ignoring them would exert some kind of impact on the individual's biography. Thus, trajectories prove to be 'not entirely manageable' (Strauss 1993: 53) and at the same time are still the unique product of serious of actions and interactions.

Interestingly, although Strauss died too soon to realize that link, the concept of trajectory has a lot in common with the concept of 'practices', as vividly discussed in recent praxeological debates (Schatzki, Knorr Cetina, & von Savigny 2001; Reckwitz 2002). Trajectories like practices have an existence independent of single actors, who, in the end, are just participants in the course of events.

ENHANCING GROUNDED THEORY TO A THEORY-METHODS PACKAGE

While this is not a chapter about the methodological achievements of Strauss as part of a handbook on grounded theory, it would nonetheless remain somewhat incomplete without relating his methodological position to his theoretical development. More recently, Clarke and Star (2007), two of his former doctoral students, proposed the notion of 'theory-methods-packages' as a concept to overcome the common framing of empirical methods as mere (neutral and innocent) tools, utilized for limited purposes of dealing with 'the empirical'. The case of Strauss is a striking example for how delicately theoretical and methodological development depend on each other. In his early career, Strauss, disillusioned by his mentor Blumer, had been searching for systematic, yet creative ways to derive his theoretical ideas from empirical findings.[4] Therefore, inspired by

Hughes, Strauss started to dig deeper into comparative heuristics. This path came to fruition when he started to work empirically with his colleague Barney Glaser, who as a Columbia School alumnus had a markedly different methodological training. In their research practice, they developed a set of systematically articulated heuristics, altogether a research style that allowed scientists to turn their empirical results theoretical by elaborating their meaning *vis-à-vis* respective practical or theoretical problems. Grounded Theory, as they termed it (Glaser & Strauss 1967), turned out to become one of the most influential research styles within the interpretive paradigm of empirical social research. More importantly for our argument here, it proved to be the core of Strauss's *modus operandi* for bringing forth new theoretical insights. At the same time, his empirical research was firmly based not only on the ontological beliefs he gained from a pragmatist philosophy of science (Strübing 2007b), but as his career progressed, more and more on those empirically grounded concepts derived from his previous empirical studies. Social worlds and arenas, negotiated order, trajectories, articulation work: All these theory figures are as much an outcome of Strauss's empirical research as they are theoretical sensitivities for his later studies. On a second level, the strong ties between Strauss's pragmatist predisposition and his methodological perspective show up in the operational mode of Grounded Theory as a research style: The iterative-cyclical process mode he proposes (Strauss & Corbin 1994) mirrors Dewey's model of problem-solving – as does his notion of theory as a 'never-ending process' (Glaser & Strauss 1967: 40). Also, the idea of theoretical sensitivity resonates with Mead's concept of perspective (Mead 1932/1959).

SUMMARY AND CONCLUSION

Anselm Strauss was undoubtedly a child of his time, living at the edge of late western modernity, struggling with the predominance of both structuralist and functionalist approaches in social theory, and deductive, positivist methodologies in empirical research. His emphasis on process and perspective can be read as his response not only to unbalanced structure/action constructions (structuralism, subjectivism), but at the same time to more recent approaches that tried to 'compromise towards the middle' (such as Bourdieu and Giddens). His solution is radical, in that it resolves the dualism of structure/action, subject/object, individual/society, and mind/body into a continuum of perspectival processing differences with interactive problem-solving as its *modus operandi*. He clearly formulated his conception from American pragmatism, namely from Dewey and Mead. It is striking, though, how late in his career, despite his early contact with pragmatist thinking, he explicitly addressed this perspective. In Strauss's early methodological writings, we find only cursory references to pragmatism. The same is true for most of those papers in which he introduced new theoretical concepts drawn from his empirical research. Although in these papers he did not neglect his pragmatist roots, neither did he argue with them systematically. This changed only from the late 1980s on, when he started to refer in depth, especially to Dewey and Mead. Only in 1993 with his last monograph *Continual Permutations of Action* did he outline in more detail an encompassing pragmatist social theory. Only in this book, he brought together all his important theoretical concepts. Moreover, he did so not in the conventional way of reprinting a collection of older articles in one edited volume. Instead, in *Continual Permutations* he organized all these concepts in ways that showed them to be part of a larger, overarching theoretical perspective, that is, pragmatism.

Beside Dewey and Mead, Everett C. Hughes was clearly the other important source of inspiration for Strauss. Not just in terms of the practicalities of conducting empirical research, but also theoretically, Strauss benefited greatly from Hughes and his ecological approach. Although the Park–Hughes line of human ecology is itself deeply rooted in pragmatist philosophy, the notion of conflict and the insight that on a regular base it works to result in more stable states of being, is a feature of Strauss's theory that is clearly a legacy of Hughes – which can be seen most clearly in his studies of work. For Strauss, this idea is missing in pragmatism so far: 'curiously the pragmatists did not build those insights and positions into their theory of action, thereby leaving it incomplete…' (Strauss 1993: 225). In his social theory, Strauss succeeded in integrating these two important influences into a coherent theoretical perspective.

He did not, however, embrace postmodern poststructural theoretical thinking all too enthusiastically. His understanding has been that already with *Mirrors and Masks*, he had set a pragmatist interactionist tone that, as he puts it in a foreword to the Transaction Edition of that book, 'runs as a ground base in virtually all of my writings' (Strauss 1959, 1997: 2). He hoped this to be a 'less ideological voice to that (postmodern; J.S.) current din' (ibid.). Although not alien to his approach, discourse theory and analysis did not become part of his approach. The same holds true for the notion of nonhuman actants – ironically despite the fact that in the 1980s Bruno Latour during a sabbatical spent some time in San Francisco and worked with some of Strauss's close colleagues.[5] Also, Strauss's notion of action, while critical to the Weberian and Schützian tradition, does not fully elaborate praxeological ideas of social processes being organized largely by practices, rendering 'acting' as an always already shared endeavor between participating entities of all sorts. In addition, while Strauss and his wife and life-long companion Fran were politically engaged citizens, not much of this engagement appeared in explicit form in his theoretical works – in stark contrast to how some of his successors linked their research agenda to political issues.[6] While in all these aspects Strauss remained a classic late modern liberal academic, with his theory, though, he prepared the ground for further developments at the junction of pragmatism and practice theories (Strübing 2017).

Thus, what does Anselm Strauss's life and work mean for the interactionist project in sociology? Where, apart from his methodological heritage, are the marks he left in current social sciences? A number of his PhD students and later colleagues (like Adele Clarke, who followed him in his position at UCSF, Susan Leigh Star, or Joan Fujimura) picked up not only his research style, but also stepped into his theoretical shoes. Beginning in the early 1980s, they started to broaden Strauss's research agenda on health and medicine and shifted it more to the then prospering new fields of STS and gender studies. This move went hand in hand with further developments of both his methodology (Clarke 2005; Corbin & Strauss, 2008, 2015; Charmaz 2014), and the theoretical and ontological perspective of the pragmatist-interactionist project (Strübing 2007b; Timmermans & Tavory, 2012). In empirical studies on fields such as reproduction sciences (Clarke 1998), the organizing of cancer research (Fujimura 1987), or forms of cooperation in brain research (Star 1983), these scholars developed important new theoretical concepts. Most influential among those were, for eample, the notion of 'boundary objects' to account for the issue of heterogeneous cooperation in science (Star & Griesemer 1989; Bowker et al. 2016), or a new definition of the concept of 'situation' to better account for discourse, practices, and positionalities (Clarke 2005).

This chapter addressed the theoretical contributions of Anselm Strauss and deliberately left out his methodological works. However, it is exactly this kind of false dichotomies that were at the heart of Strauss's criticism in both theory and methods. Clarke and Star (2007) turned this critical stance into a conceptual frame and proposed in an ontological argument that social research needs to be done in 'theory-methods packages' to overcome problems of both deductive and inductive research. Not surprisingly, they suggested the package of grounded theory and Strauss's social worlds/arenas theory as specifically well-suited for the study of organized social activities.

As a pragmatist, Strauss himself would not take his theory as complete or final but as 'just a pause in the never-ending process of generating theory' (Glaser & Strauss 1967: 40) – a very humble statement for a remarkable contribution to pragmatist interactionist theory and interpretive research practice.

Notes

1 I am indebted both to Louise-Alice Härtig for making this paper readable to native speakers of English and to my dear colleague Adele Clarke for numerous invaluable comments on an earlier version of this text.

2 Among them were a considerable number of German scholars. Most of them made contact with Strauss on the occasion of two conferences near Konstanz, Germany, in 1974. The network established through these meetings and some follow-ups might account for the extraordinary resonance Strauss's works had and still have in German sociology (Schütze 2008; Strübing 2007a).

3 For a more detailed account on how the social world concepts of Mead, Shibutani and Strauss relate, see Cefaï (2016).

4 In a retrospective interview, Strauss noted: 'Blumer didn't have a method at all. He just said: Do with your data whatever you want' (Legewie & Schervier-Legewie 2004).

5 Leigh Star even revised parts of *Science in Action* for Latour (personal communication with Leigh Star 1998) (Latour 1987).

6 For a more detailed account on how Strauss handled the tension between reform and science see Baszanger (1998: 373) and Clarke (2008).

REFERENCES

Baszanger, Isabelle (1998) The Work Sites of an American Interactionist: Anselm L. Strauss, 1917–1996. *Symbolic Interaction*, *21*(4): 353–377.

Becker, Howard S. et al. (1961) *Boys in White: Student Culture in Medical School*. Chicago, IL: University of Chicago Press.

Bowker, Geoffrey C. et al. (Eds.) (2016) *Boundary Objects and Beyond: Working with Susan Leigh Star*. Cambridge, MA: MIT Press.

Cefaï, Daniel (2016) Social Worlds: The Legacy of Mead's Social Ecology in Chicago Sociology. In Hans Joas & Daniel R. Huebner (Eds.), *George Herbert Mead at 150*. Cambridge, MA: MIT Press. pp. 164–184.

Charmaz, Kathy (2014) *Constructing Grounded Theory* (2nd Edition). Los Angeles, CA: Sage.

Clarke, Adele E. (1991) Social Worlds/Arenas Theory as Organizational Theory. In David R. Maines (Ed.), *Social Organization and Social Process: Essays in Honor of Anselm Strauss*. New York: Aldine de Gruyter. pp. 119–158.

Clarke, Adele E. (1998) *Disciplining Reproduction: Modernity, American Life Sciences, and 'the Problem of Sex'*. Berkeley, CA: University of California Press.

Clarke, Adele E. (2005) *Situational Analysis: Grounded Theory after the Postmodern Turn*. Thousand Oaks, CA: Sage.

Clarke, Adele E. (2008) Sex/Gender and Race/Ethnicity in the Legacy of Anselm Strauss. *Studies in Symbolic Interaction (Special Issue Celebrating Anselm Strauss and Forty Years of Grounded Theory), 32*: 159–174.

Clarke, Adele E. & Star, Susan Leigh (2007) The Social Worlds Framework as a Theory-Methods Package. In Edward Hackett, Olga Amsterdamska, Michael Lynch, & Judy Wacjman (Eds.), *Handbook of Science and Technology Studies*. Cambridge, MA: MIT Press. pp. 113–137.

Corbin, Juliet (1991) Anselm Strauss: An Intellectual Biography. In David R. Maines (Ed.), *Social Organizations and Sozial Processes: Essays in Honour of Anselm Strauss*. New York: Aldine de Gruyter. pp. 17–42.

Corbin, Juliet & Strauss, Anselm L. (2008, 2015) *Basics of Qualitative Research: Techniques and Procedures for Developing Grounded Theory*. Los Angeles, CA: Sage.

Dewey, John (1929) *Experience and Nature*. Chicago, IL: Open Court Publishing Co.

Dewey, John (1938) *Logic, the Theory of Inquiry*. New York: Holt, Rinehart and Winston.

Fujimura, Joan H. (1987) Constructing 'do-able' Problems in Cancer Research: Articulating Alignment. *Social Studies of Science*, *17*: 257–293.

Gerson, Elihu M. (1983) Work and Going Concerns: Some Implications of Hughes' Work. Tremont Research Institute, San Francisco (unpublished manuscript).

Glaser, Barney G. & Strauss, Anselm L. (1965) *Awareness of Dying*. Chicago, IL: Aldine.

Glaser, Barney G. & Strauss, Anselm L. (1967) *The Discovery of Grounded Theory: Strategies for Qualitative Research*. Chicago, IL: Aldine.

Glaser, Barney G. & Strauss, Anselm L. (1968) *Time for Dying*. Chicago, IL: Aldine.

Hughes, Everett C. (1955) Introduction. In Robert E. Park & Everett C. Hughes (Eds.), *The Collected Papers of Robert Ezra Park. Selected Papers, Bd. 3: Society. Collective Behavior; News and Opinion; Sociology and Modern Society*. Glencoe, IL: Free Press. pp. 3–58.

Hughes, Everett C. (1957/1971) Going concerns: The Study of American Institutions. In Everett C. Hughes (Ed.), *The sociological Eye*. Chicago, IL: Aldine. pp. 52–64.

Latour, Bruno (1987) *Science in Action: How to Follow Scientists and Engineers through Society*. Cambridge, MA: Harvard University Press.

Legewie, Heiner & Schervier-Legewie, Barbara (2004) Anselm Strauss: Research is Hard Work, it's Always a bit Suffering. Therefore, on the Other Side Research Should be Fun. *Forum Qualitative Sozialforschung / Forum: Qualitative Social Research*, *5*(3), *Special Issue: FQS Interviews* I: 90 paragraphs.

Lindesmith, Alfred R. & Strauss, Anselm L. (1949) *Social Psychology*. New York: The Dryden Press.

Maines, David R. & Charlton, Jay (1985) The Negotiated Order Approach to the Study of Social Organization. *Studies in Symbolic Interaction* (*Supplement 1*): 271–308.

Mead, George Herbert (1934) *Mind, Self & Society from the Standpoint of a Social Behaviorist*. Chicago, IL: University of Chicago Press.

Mead, George Herbert (1932/1959) *The Philosophy of the Present*. La Salle, IL: Open Court Publishing Co.

Olson, Gary A. (1991) The Social Scientist as Author: Clifford Geertz on Ethnography and Social Construction. *Journal of Advanced Composition*, *11*(2): 245–268.

Park, Robert E. & Burgess, Ernest W. (1921) *Introduction to the Science of Sociology*. Chicago, IL: University of Chicago Press.

Reckwitz, Andreas (2002) Toward a Theory of Social Practices: A Development in Culturalist Theorizing. *European Journal of Social Theory*, *5*(2): 245–265.

Riemann, Gerhard & Schütze, Fritz (1991) 'Trajectory' as a Basic Theoretical Concept for Analyzing Suffering and Disorderly Social Processes. In David R. Maines (Ed.), *Social Organizations and Sozial Processes: Essays in Honour of Anselm Strauss*. New York: Aldine. pp. 333–357.

Schatzki, Theodore R., Knorr-Cetina, Karin, & von Savigny, Eike (Eds.) (2001) *The Practice Turn in Contemporary Theory*. London: Routledge.

Schütze, Fritz (2008) The Legacy in Germany today of Anselm Strauss' Vision and Practice of Sociology. In Norman K. Denzin (Ed.), *Studies in Symbolic Interaction*. pp. 103–126.

Shibutani, Tomatsu (1955) Reference Groups as Perspectives. *American Journal of Sociology*, *60*: 562–569.

Star, Susan Leigh (1983) *Scientific Theories as Going Concerns: The Development of the Localizationist Perspective in Neurophysiology, 1870–1906*. San Francisco, CA: University of California San Francisco.

Star, Susan Leigh & Griesemer, James R. (1989) Institutional Ecology, 'Translations' and Boundary Objects: Amateurs and Professionals in Berkeley's Museum of Vertebrate Zoology, 1907–1939. *Social Studies of Science*, *19*: 387–420.

Strauss, Anselm L. (1945) A Study of three Psychological Factors Affecting Choice of Mate in a College-Metropolitan Population. PhD Disseration. Chicago, Il: University of Chicago.

Strauss, Anselm L. (1959) *Mirrors and Masks: The Search for Identity*. Glencoe, IL: Free Press.

Strauss, Anselm L. (1978) A Social World Perspective. *Studies in Symbolic Interaction*, *1*: 119–128.

Strauss, Anselm L. (1984) Social Worlds and their Segmentation Process. *Studies in Symbolic Interaction*, *5*: 123–139.

Strauss, Anselm L. (1985) Work and the Division of Labor. *Sociological Quarterly*, *26*(1): 1–19.

Strauss, Anselm L. (1987) *Qualitative Analysis for Social Scientists*. New York: Cambridge University Press.

Strauss, Anselm L. (1988) The Articulation of Project Work: An Organizational Process. *Sociological Quarterly*, *29*(2): 163–178.

Strauss, Anselm L. (1991) Mead's Multiple Conceptions of Time and Evolution: Their Contexts and their Consequences. *International sociology*, *6*: 411–426.

Strauss, Anselm L. (1993) *Continual Permutations of Action*. New York: W. de Gruyter.

Strauss, Anselm L. (1996) A Partial Line of Descent: Blumer and I. *Studies in Symbolic Interaction*, *20*: 3–22.

Strauss, Anselm L. (1959/1997) *Mirrors and Masks: The Search for Identity*. New Brunswick, NJ: Transaction.

Strauss, Anselm L. & Corbin, Juliet (1994) Grounded Theory Methodology: An Overview. In Norman K. Denzin (Ed.), *Handbook of Qualitative Research*. London and New York: Sage. pp. 273–285.

Strauss, Anselm L. et al. (1964) *Psychiatric Ideologies and Institutions*. London and Glencoe, IL: Free Press.

Strauss, Anselm L. et al. (1985) *The Social Organization of Medical Work*. Chicago, IL: University of Chicago Press.

Strübing, Jörg (2007a) *Anselm Strauss*. Konstanz: UVK.

Strübing, Jörg (2007b) Research as Pragmatic Problem-Solving: The Pragmatist Roots of empirically-grounded Theorizing. In Antony Bryant & Kathy Charmaz (Eds.), *The Sage Handbook of Grounded Theory*. London: Sage. pp. 581–601.

Strübing, Jörg (2017) Where is the Meat/d? Pragmatismus und Praxistheorien als reziprokes Ergänzungsverhältnis. In Hella Dietz, Frithjof Nungesser, & Andreas Pettenkofer (Eds.), *Pragmatismus und Theorie sozialer Praktiken: Vom Nutzen einer Theoriedifferenz*. Frankfurt a. M and New York: Campus. pp. 41–75

Thomas, William I. & Thomas, Dorothy Swaine (1928) *The Child in America: Behavior Problems and Programs*. New York: Alfred A. Knopf.

Timmermans, Stefan & Tavory, Iddo (2012) Theory Construction in Qualitative Research: From Grounded Theory to Abductive Analysis. *Sociological Theory*, *30*: 167–186.

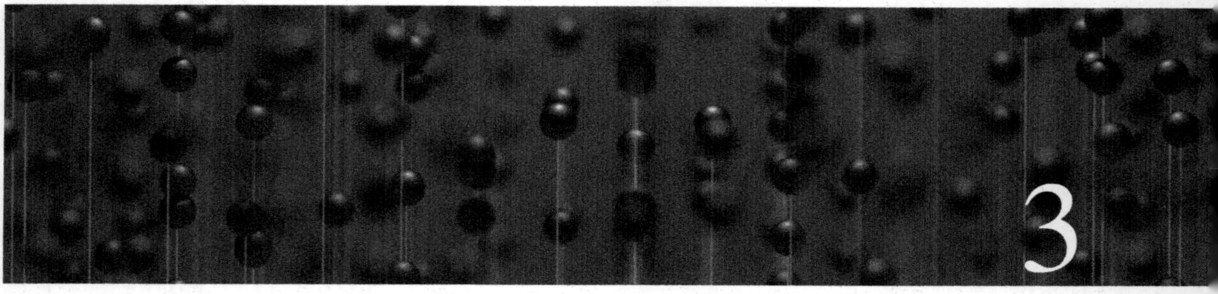

The Status of Theories and Models in Grounded Theory

Udo Kelle

INTRODUCTION

Glaser and Strauss's first ground-breaking methodological writing, *The Discovery of Grounded Theory* (1967) was meant to propose an alternative to classical hypothetico-deductive research: theoretical categories and hypotheses should not be developed without any contact to the research field and then tested with the help of empirical observations, but 'emerge' from empirical data instead. This metaphor was often understood in such a way that researchers should abandon their previous theoretical knowledge before analyzing their data. However, contrary to such a naïve inductivist understanding, Glaser and Strauss already maintained that researchers would need 'theoretical sensitivity' – the ability to conceptualize relevant data in theoretical terms, which can be achieved only by drawing on already existing theories and models. The development of Grounded Theory Methodology (GTM) was characterized by different attempts to elaborate the concept of 'theoretical sensitivity' and to describe modes of a non-deductive use of theories and models in the process of empirically grounded theory building. Thereby a variety of new and complex concepts were proposed like 'theoretical coding', 'coding families', 'axial coding', 'coding paradigm' and many others.

The chapter will give an overview about this debate and its history and will explain the different concepts by drawing on practical examples. In the first section the concept of category building through theoretically sensitive 'constant comparisons' will be briefly outlined. It will be shown that this process cannot adequately be understood if the role of previous theoretical knowledge is not explicitly taken into account. One of the most important challenges in GTM is that one has to reconcile the claim to let categories emerge (instead of forcing preconceived theoretical terms on the data) with the impossibility to abandon previous theoretical knowledge. In the second section I will discuss the different approaches Glaser and Strauss developed to solve this problem and which led to the divide between 'Glaserian' and 'Straussian' GTM, as the two strands are nowadays often called (Thornberg 2012, p. 244): Glaser's notions of 'theoretical coding' and 'coding families' and the concept of 'coding paradigm' put forward by Strauss and Corbin. The pros and cons of both modes to include theories and models into GTM will be treated and it will be discussed under which conditions and for which research questions these different approaches are best suited.

In the third section of the chapter I will discuss certain basic methodological questions surrounding the role of theories and models in GTM: the function of different types of logical inferences, 'induction', 'deduction' and 'retroduction' in theory building and theory testing will be discussed. Furthermore, it will be shown that an adequate reflection about the role of theories and models in GTM requires a thorough differentiation between different types of theoretical categories. Thereby different aspects of theoretical statements have to be taken into account, such as their scope, their source (universal statements vs middle and small range theories), their degree of explicitness (theoretical knowledge consisting of explicit statements vs implicit, 'incorporated' knowledge), as well as their empirical content (falsifiable vs non-falsifiable statements).

THEORY BUILDING THROUGH CONSTANT COMPARISON – BASIC RULES FROM THE '*DISCOVERY*-BOOK'

Glaser and Strauss started the *Discovery*-book by criticizing the '*overemphasis in current sociology on the verification of theory, and a resultant de-emphasis on the prior step of discovering what concepts and hypotheses are relevant for the area that one wishes to research*' (Glaser & Strauss 1967, pp. 1f.). Contrary to the idea that the main purpose of empirical research is the testing of explicit theoretical assumptions, they favoured a method for the 'initial, systematic discovery of the theory from the data of social research' (p. 3). In Glaser and Strauss's understanding of what a theory is and what it consists of, the concept of 'category' played a crucial role: categories are not only the building blocks and basic elements of theories, they are also important tools used throughout the whole research process to develop fully-fledged theories. Theoretical statements (or in other words, 'hypotheses') are basically formed by connecting categories. Thus, the first and most important question for non-deductive, data-based construction of theories would be: how can researchers ensure the 'grounding' of categories in empirical data? In the *Discovery*-book, two basic rules are given:

- Categories must not be forced on data; they should 'emerge' instead in an ongoing process of data collection and analysis.
- While developing categories the sociologist should employ 'theoretical sensitivity', which means the ability to 'see relevant data' and to reflect upon empirical data material with the help of theoretical terms.

The Emergence of Categories and their Properties from the Data

The basic operations in the long process of category building are '*coding*' and the *constant comparison* of data, codes and the emerging categories. The term 'coding' obviously reflected the experiences of Barney Glaser as a research assistant in Paul Lazarsfeld's institute in the 1950s, since it is adopted from quantitative social research, or, more precisely, from quantitative content analysis: there it means to describe attributes of certain bits of data (e.g., paragraphs of a certain newspaper article in a research project about mass media, or an answer to an open-ended question in a survey) with the help of certain codes. These can, for instance, refer to an opinion or attitude expressed in a newspaper article. Thereby codes represent values of certain variables (e.g., the values 'affirmation' or 'disapproval' of a variable called 'Evaluation of political events'). In this way every unit of analysis can be investigated to find out whether a certain value of a variable applies to it. The purpose of the whole (hypothetico-deductive) process, which requires a predefined coding scheme before coding starts, is to count code frequencies for all relevant data.

In 1960 Howard Becker and Blanche Geer adopted the term 'coding' for qualitative research by using it for the process of relating text passages in field protocols to predefined codes. The main purpose of qualitative coding *sensu* Becker and Geer was not to count codes but to be able to collect different text passages which (in the researcher's opinion) refer to a certain topic (Becker & Geer 1960, p. 280f.) However, since an important aim of this process was to '*constitute proof for a given proposition*', this procedure (at least partially) still represented a hypothetico-deductive strategy. The approach put forward in *The Discovery of Grounded Theory*, however, was not part of a process of hypotheses testing, but '*concerned with generating and plausibly suggesting many categories, properties and hypotheses about general problems*' (Glaser & Strauss 1967, p. 104). Therefore, coding should be done without a predefined coding scheme. Coding categories should rather 'emerge' from the data if the analyst '*starts by coding each incident in his data into as many categories as possible*' (ibid., p. 105). This emergence of categories should be supported by the '*constant comparative method*': while coding the analyst constantly compares the already coded incidents (which usually means text segments in field notes or interviews which relate to the incidents) with each other and with incidents not yet coded. '*This constant comparison of the incidents very soon starts to generate theoretical properties of the category*' (ibid., p. 106).

From the early days of grounded theory many users of the method found it difficult to understand the notions 'category' and 'property' and to utilize them in research practice, since these terms were only vaguely defined in the *Discovery*-book. Glaser and Strauss gave the following example: In their research project about the interaction between hospital workers and their moribund patients they found the category 'social loss' – nurses tend to think about their dying patients in terms of the loss which their death would mean for their social environment (e.g., '*What will the children and the husband do without her*', p. 106). By constantly comparing incidents relevant for (and coded with) that category they found various '*theoretical properties*' of the category, for instance '*... we realized that some patients are perceived as a high social loss and others as a low social loss, and that patient care tends to vary positively with degree of social loss*' (ibid.). Whereas the notion 'category' can refer to any noun which researchers find relevant for their research area, the term 'property' is more difficult to grasp: are both the concepts '*high social loss*' and '*patient care*' theoretical properties of the category '*social loss*' and what does that exactly mean?

It is helpful here to draw on the terminology of basic mathematical set or type theory to gain a better understanding of the relation between incidents, categories and their properties: *objects* (i.e., *incidents* like text passages describing utterances of nurses) can be assigned to a certain *class* or *type* or *category* (e.g., '*utterances about social loss*'). Classes or types or categories (these three notions can be treated as equivalent) can be divided in *subclasses*, *subtypes* or *subcategories*. Subclasses or subcategories can themselves be divided into further subcategories. A basic idea of grounded theory is that the whole structure or system of categories should not be exclusively developed in a top-down manner by deriving subcategories from major categories. Instead, researchers are encouraged to find major categories by comparing the initially found categories which may later become subcategories of a higher order category. Thereby a hierarchically ordered structure of subcategories can develop (see Figure 3.1): thus, it becomes possible to differentiate incidents in the data or text passages classified as dealing with social loss according to the subcategory '*degree of social loss*' by forming further subcategories '*high social loss*', '*medium social loss*' and '*low social loss*'. The whole range or set of these three subcategories then represents a 'theoretical property' of the category 'social loss'.

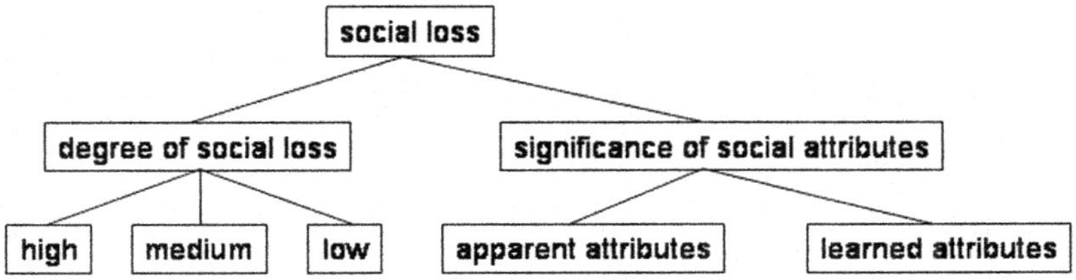

Figure 3.1 A hierarchically ordered structure of subcategories

Thereby it is important to note that classes can always be divided into subclasses according to *different* criteria. Nurses, for instance, use *social attributes* to calculate social loss, some of which are *perceived immediately* (like age, gender…), while others are *learned after some time* (like social class, educational status…). Thus '*significance of social attributes*' could form a further subcategory of 'social loss' with the two subcategories '*apparent attributes*' and '*learned attributes*'.

There are sets of (sub)categories which are mutually exclusive, while others are not. The subcategories '*high social loss*', '*medium social loss*' and '*low social loss*' form such a range of mutually exclusive (non-overlapping) classes: there should be no incident which can be assigned to more than one of the three subcategories (which means that a certain utterance about a social loss cannot express simultaneously 'high social loss' and 'low social loss'). There are other categories or classes to which objects can be assigned simultaneously. Figure 3.2 demonstrates a very simple geometrical example for that.

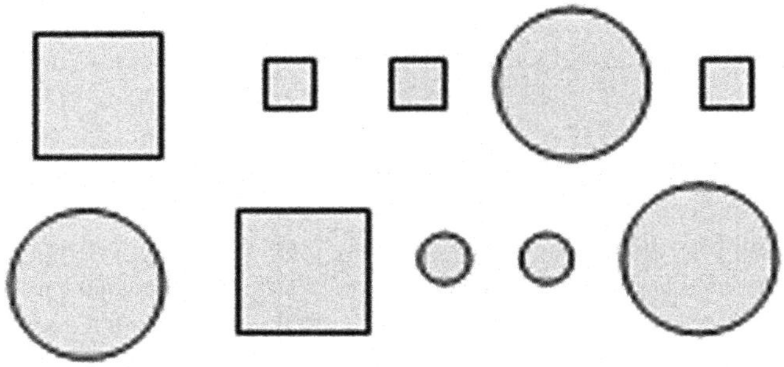

Figure 3.2 A geometric example of categories assigned simultaneously

The 10 objects can be classified according to the category 'size' (with the subcategories 'small' and 'big') and according to the category 'shape' (with the subcategories 'rectangular' and 'circular').

In grounded theory, incidents and text segments can be also assigned to several categories in a similar (albeit more complicated) fashion: by carefully comparing text segments dealing with 'social loss' one may find out that many of them can be also attributed to a category one names '*patient care*' (since they contain nurses' utterances about how to care for dying patients) and to the subcategories '*intense patient care*' or '*cursory patient care*'. One may even find out that text segments relating to 'high social loss' can often be assigned to 'intense patient care', which shows a possible relation between the two categories. This relation can be regarded as a *theoretical property* of the category 'social loss' likewise.

By looking for commonalities and differences between incidents, the constant comparative method can thus reveal two different kinds of theoretical properties: possible *sets of subcategories* of a given category, on the one hand, and *relations* to other categories, on the other hand. The decisive question of constant comparison is thus: *According to which criteria do the incidents vary?* These criteria of variation form the categories or subcategories the analyst looks for, or they are at least suggestive of such categories. Thereby the analyst always has to obtain the rule: *do not force preconceived categories on the data, but let the categories emerge.*

Theoretical Sensitivity as a Prerequisite for Theory Building

Similar to the concepts 'category' and 'properties of categories', many beginners in Grounded Theory may also find the idea of 'emergence' difficult to apply. In particular, Glaser and Strauss's request '*literally to ignore the literature of theory and fact on the area under study, in order to assure that the emergence of categories will not be contaminated ...*' (Glaser & Strauss 1967, p. 37) can make the search for categories extremely tedious, in particular, if the instruction to let categories emerge is understood as the demand to transform every idea into a category which comes into the mind when inspecting the data. A group of junior researchers I supported in their research described this problem as follows:

> Especially the application of an open coding strategy recommended by Glaser and Strauss—the text is read line by line and coded ad hoc—proved to be unexpectedly awkward and time consuming. ... [I]n the beginning we had the understanding that 'everything counts' and 'everything is important'—every yet marginal incident and phenomenon was coded, recorded in numerous memos and extensively discussed. This led to an unsurmountable mass of data.... (cf. Kelle et al. 2002, translated from German to English by Udo Kelle)

These researchers did not use line-by-line coding as a device for an initial 'breaking down' of the data (as proposed by Glaser and Strauss), but as a tedious task of tracking down their 'complete and true meaning'. Although this certainly goes against Glaser and Strauss's intentions, the experience of these researchers underlines an important issue: it is impossible to use codes in order to describe or summarize data in a neutral way so that an exclusive or sole meaning of these data can be found. Different perspectives researchers carry with themselves necessarily lead to different accounts of the same data and, consequently, to different codes. These different perspectives are constituted, among other things, by the researchers' theoretical background knowledge. This mirrors the insight from modern philosophy of science that scientific observations are always 'theory laden' (cf. Hanson 1965). The idea that theoretical categories can be derived by simple ('inductive') generalization from observable data if researchers free their minds from any theoretical preconceptions whatsoever manifests a rather outmoded view of scientific inquiry (often called 'naïve empiricism' or 'naïve inductivism', cf. Chalmers 1999) – nowadays it is a widely accepted insight in philosophy of science and cognitive psychology that '*there are and can be no sensations unimpregnated by expectations*' (Lakatos 1978, p. 15) and that the construction of theoretical categories, whether empirically grounded or not, cannot start *ab ovo*, but must draw on existing knowledge: '*the world is always perceived through the "lenses" of some conceptual network or other and that such networks and the languages in which they are embedded may, for all we know, provide an ineliminable "tint" to what we perceive*' (Laudan 1977, p. 15). Empirical researchers would need such 'lenses' or conceptual networks, otherwise they would not be able to observe and describe meaningful events.

Glaser and Strauss did not overlook this problem, as one can see if one reads the *Discovery*-book with care. Already on page 3 they emphasize: '*Of course, the researcher does not approach reality as a tabula rasa. He [sic] must have a perspective that will help him see relevant data and abstract significant categories from his scrutiny of the data*' (Glaser & Strauss 1967, p. 3). Later on, a more detailed account is given about what is meant by the ability to 'see relevant data'. To discover grounded theories, one needs '*theoretical sensitivity*', an '*ability to have theoretical insight into (one's) area of research, combined with an ability to make something of (one's) insights*' (p. 46). But how can this ability be achieved? The *Discovery*-book contains only a few pages addressing this issue, containing two advices about how theoretical sensitivity can be achieved and improved:

1. The sociologist should harbour '*an armamentarium of categories and hypotheses on substantive and formal levels. This theory that exists within a sociologist can be used in generating his [sic] specific theory...*' (ibid.). Thus, existing theories and models can be helpful in category building and fruitful insights shall be drawn from them. And Glaser and Strauss maintain that an empirically grounded theory usually combines categories and hypotheses which have emerged from the data with concepts from already existing theories and models.
2. Thereby a strong commitment to '*one specific preconceived theory*' (ibid.) must be avoided to get around the danger that categories of a 'pet theory' are forced on the data.

'*Indeed the trick is to line up what one takes as theoretically possible or probable with what one is finding in the field*' (p. 253). This trick, however, is difficult to learn. Since the concept of 'emergence' is so highly esteemed in the *Discovery*-book and readers are advised elsewhere to abstain from reading literature about one's research field some readers may be easily drawn towards the idea that theoretical concepts emerge from the data only if one approaches the field with no preconceived theories whatsoever. Others who wish to demonstrate 'theoretical sensitivity' may be worried that they will force inappropriate categories on the data when applying a specific sociological theory. It is obviously a challenging task not to approach the empirical field with a predefined set of categories but to hold various different theories in abeyance in order to use theoretical concepts only if they fit the data. Unfortunately, the *Discovery*-book neither gave clear methodological rules nor practical examples about how previous theoretical knowledge can be fruitfully introduced in empirically grounded theory building. Thus, the two basic rules already mentioned (first, to abstain from forcing preconceived concepts, and, second, to utilize theoretical sensitivity in this process) are obviously difficult to reconcile.

THE 'GLASERIAN' VS THE 'STRAUSSIAN APPROACH' – TWO WAYS OF INCLUDING EXISTING THEORIES AND MODELS IN GROUNDED THEORY BUILDING

It clearly has a liberating and stimulating effect especially on junior researchers or doctoral students if they are invited to allow their data to inspire new ideas and insights instead of applying previously formulated theories and models on the field or restricting empirical work on the 'testing' of 'hypotheses'. However, in the years following the *Discovery*-book the antagonism between 'emergence' and 'theoretical sensitivity' remained a major problem. Thereby Glaser and Strauss undertook a variety of efforts to clarify the idea of theoretical sensitivity: in his monograph about 'Theoretical Sensitivity', Glaser invented the terms 'theoretical codes', 'theoretical coding' and 'coding families' to show how researchers may draw on existing theories to structure their developing grounded theories. Strauss proposed the use of a 'coding paradigm' which can be used to develop and relate categories of the emerging grounded theory to each other.

Glaser's Model of 'Theoretical Coding'

Since the discussion of theoretical sensitivity turned out to be '*a major gap in the Discovery book*' (Glaser 1978, p. 1), Glaser tried to unfold the technical or 'how-to-do' aspects of theoretical sensitivity in his monograph with this title. There he invented the differentiation between 'theoretical coding' and 'substantive coding' and between 'substantive codes' and 'theoretical codes'. (The word 'codes' was used as synonymous with the terms 'categories and their properties' invented in the *Discovery*-book.)

Substantive codes, which shall relate to the empirical substance of the research domain are developed during 'open coding' (the first stage of the coding process). It could be either words informed by the language use of actors in the field (so-called 'in vivo codes') or notions drawn from sociological terminology (called 'sociological constructs'). To establish relations between substantive codes *theoretical codes* are needed which '*conceptualize how the substantive codes may relate to each other as hypotheses to be integrated into a theory*' (Glaser 1978, p. 72). Theoretical codes, in other words, are terms which describe possible relations between substantive codes and thereby help to form theoretical models. Glaser drew on a variety of formal and abstract concepts from epistemology and sociological 'grand theory' which make basic claims about the ordering of the (social) world to give examples for such theoretical codes. Terms like *causes*, *contexts*, *consequences* and *conditions*, for instance, may be used to integrate previously found substantive codes into a *causal model* by calling certain events (which were coded with the help of substantive codes) *causes* and others *effects*. Glaser presented a list of theoretical 'coding families' merging concepts, which come from various (sociological, philosophical or everyday) contexts, as, for example,

- terms, which relate to the degree of an attribute or property ('*degree family*'), like 'limit', 'range', 'extent', 'amount', etc.,
- terms, which refer to the relation between a whole and its elements ('*dimension family*'), like 'element', 'part', 'facet', 'slice', 'sector', 'aspect', 'segment', etc.,
- terms, which refer to cultural phenomena ('*cultural family*') like 'social norms', 'social values', 'social beliefs', etc.,

and 14 further coding families containing notions from diverse theoretical backgrounds. Thereby, many of these terms can be subsumed under different coding families: the term *goal*, for instance, belongs to a coding family referring to action strategies ('*strategies family*') as well as to a coding family referring to the relation between means and ends ('*means-goal family*').

Coding families may thus serve as a pool of concepts which guides researchers in developing their ability to think about empirical observations in theoretical terms. However, researchers can make sense of Glaser's unsorted list of coding families only if they are clear about their inner relations and their embeddedness into greater conceptual networks. Let's take as an example the coding family 'six Cs' ('Causes, Contexts, Contingencies, Consequences, Covariances, Conditions', p. 74), which is, according to Glaser, the 'bread and butter' theoretical code of sociology: terms denoting causal relations (like 'cause', 'condition', 'consequence', etc.) are in themselves not sufficient for developing causal models. To construct causal models about relations between *specific* events one would need *substantial* (i.e., sociological, psychological…) categories which define those *types of events* generally considered as causes and those usually seen as effects. By using merely formal terms like 'cause' or 'consequence' without referring to substantial categories, all kinds of events in the research field could be seen (arbitrarily) as causes and effects: employing the concept of causality while studying youth delinquency could similarly lead to seeing deviant behaviour either as a cause or as an effect of negative sanctions. To choose between these two possibilities one does not primarily need formal terms (like 'cause' and 'effect') but a theoretical code from sociology or social psychology which either explains sanctions as a result of behaviour (like, for instance, classical learning theory or role theory) or which describes deviant behaviour as a result of sanctions (like labelling theory). *Formal* or *logical categories* (like 'causality') have to be differentiated from *substantial sociological concepts* (like 'social roles', 'identity', 'culture'), and codes from both types must always be combined to develop empirically grounded categories and theories. Unfortunately, the *Theoretical Sensitivity* book does not address this issue, which makes it particularly difficult for junior researchers to adequately use the concept of theoretical coding, since this concept does not entail practical advice about how to structure the emerging categories with the help of the various theoretical notions listed there (Glaser 1978). The whole range of coding families presented may clearly help in discovering possible theoretical relations between incidents in the data or between substantial categories. However, the use of this unordered list for constructing 'grounded theories' remains difficult for researchers without a broad background knowledge about the different theoretical perspectives entailed in the coding family list.

Anselm Strauss's Concept of a 'Coding Paradigm'

In his book '*Qualitative Analysis for Social Scientists*', which evolved in 1987 from a series of research seminars set up to train students in Grounded Theory (Strauss,

Schervier-Legewie 2004), Anselm Strauss explicates in a more concrete manner how researchers may develop empirically grounded categories in a theoretically informed way. Like Glaser before him (who had for his book *Theoretical Sensitivity* drawn on experiences from the same seminar which he had run between 1968 and the late 1970s), Strauss had realized the difficulties novices '*have in generating genuine categories. The common tendency is simply to take a bit of the data (a phrase or sentence or paragraph) and translate that into a précis of it*' (Strauss 1987, p. 29). Many users of Grounded Theory procedures, novices in particular, often did not come to terms with developing true theoretical categories. Instead, the categories which emerged from the data frequently remained mere summaries or descriptions.

When Strauss wrote his own new methodological monograph, he and Barney Glaser had not worked together on joint research projects for quite a long time. Although pages of the introduction were filled with extensive quotes from Glaser's *Theoretical Sensitivity* and some of the terms Glaser had invented were mentioned (for instance, 'open coding', 'in vivo codes' or 'sociological constructs'), Strauss paid absolutely no heed to two concepts pivotal to Glaser's view on theoretical sensitivity: 'theoretical coding' and 'coding families'. Furthermore, Strauss invented the new term 'coding paradigm' which should be used to structure data and to clarify relations between categories.

> *It is central to the coding procedures. Although especially helpful to beginning analysts, in a short time this paradigm quite literally becomes part and parcel of the analyst's thought processes. Whether explicit or implicit, it functions as a reminder to code data for relevance to whatever phenomena are referenced by a given category...* (Strauss 1987, p. 27)

The coding paradigm comes into play during 'axial coding', an advanced stage of open coding. Whereas open coding starts by '*scrutinizing the fieldnote, interview, or other document very closely; line by line, or even word by word. The aim is to produce concepts that seem to fit the data*' (ibid., p. 28), axial coding '*consists of intense analysis done around one category at time in terms of the paradigm items*' (p. 32). This category forms the 'axis' around which further coding and category building is done and may eventually become the core category of the emerging theory.

Strauss elaborates further on the concepts 'coding paradigm' and 'axial coding' in *Basics of Qualitative Research*, published together with a new co-author, Juliet Corbin (Strauss & Corbin 1990), which attempted to describe grounded theory procedures in a didactic step-by-step mode. The coding paradigm, as one could see there, fulfils the same function as a Glaserian coding family – it represents a group of abstract theoretical terms which are used to develop categories from the data and to find relations between them. Similar to Glaser's coding families, the coding paradigm takes into account that the development of categories requires the possibility to draw on some kind of theoretical framework if one wants to avoid being flooded by the data.

But, whereas Glaser had proposed a long and loosely ordered list of more or less related groups of sociological and formal terms, Strauss and Corbin advised researchers to use one general model of action rooted in pragmatist and interactionist social theory (cf. Strauss 1990, p. 7; Corbin 1991, p. 36) to build a skeleton or 'axis' for the developing categories and their relations. Thereby, a general '*paradigm model*' (Strauss & Corbin 1990, p. 99) shall support the analysis of action and interaction strategies of the actors in the field, whereby special emphasis is laid on their intentions and goals. For this purpose, categories developed during open coding shall be investigated whether they relate to (1) *phenomena* at which the actions and interactions in the domain under study are directed, (2) *causal conditions* which lead to the occurrence of these phenomena, (3) attributes of the *context* of the investigated phenomena, (4) additional *intervening conditions* by which the investigated phenomena are influenced, (5) *action and interactional strategies* actors use to handle the phenomena and (6) the *consequences* of their actions and interactions. In order to develop an 'axis' for the developing grounded theory types of phenomena, contexts, causal and intervening conditions and consequences relevant for the most important category or categories shall be identified. If, for instance, social aspects of chronic pain are investigated, the researcher shall try to determine action contexts in the data which are typical for patients with chronic pain as well as characteristic patterns of pain management. Thereafter it can be examined which pain management strategies are used by persons with chronic pain under certain conditions and in varying action contexts. This may lead to the construction of models of action as a basis for a theory about action strategies generally pursued under conditions of chronic pain. In this concept we also find a resonance of the emphasis on analyzing processes put forward in early Grounded Theory, which led Barney Glaser to further develop his own idea of 'Basic Social Processes' (Glaser 1978, p. 93ff.)

Pros and Cons of the Two Approaches

With regard to the role of previous theoretical knowledge in developing grounded theories, there are now two different versions of grounded theory methodology available. The split between Glaser and Strauss was even widened when Glaser condemned Strauss's and Corbin's work in a (in some parts hostile and even offensive) polemic attack (Glaser 1992) (which was never publicly answered by Strauss and Corbin): by applying the concepts of axial coding and coding paradigms, researchers would force categories on data instead of allowing them to emerge. However, there still remains a lot of common ground between the two approaches – both represent attempts to solve a fundamental methodological problem arising from the claim to let categories 'emerge' from the data: empirical research which starts from scratch without any theoretical preconceptions whatsoever simply cannot work – such a method would yield a plethora of incoherent observations and descriptions rather than empirically grounded categories or hypotheses. The emergence of theoretical codes or categories from the data is dependent on the ability to grasp empirical phenomena in theoretical terms, or, in other words, on 'theoretical sensitivity', a competence that demands training and background in sociological theory (which Glaser also still conceded, see Glaser 1992, p. 28). If the Glaserian approach is used, researchers would even need a rather advanced understanding of different schools of thought, of their terminology and their possible relations to choose useful coding families for certain data and to combine them in meaningful ways. Nevertheless, research novices will have difficulties to handle a more or less unsystematic compilation of theoretical terms from various (sociological and epistemological) backgrounds bundled in the list of coding families. And researchers with a broad theoretical background knowledge and a longstanding experience in the application of theoretical terms will certainly not need such a list.

Strauss's and Corbin's 'coding paradigm', which describes the construction of a framework for developing grounded categories in an explicit manner, may be much more helpful for researchers with limited experience in conceptualizing empirical data in theoretical terms. However, the specific theoretical perspective embedded in the coding paradigm also firmly ties users to a specific theoretical tradition – philosophical and sociological pragmatism originating from the works of Peirce, Dewey and Mead. Therefore, Glaser's critique that the coding paradigm may lead to the forcing of categories on the data cannot be dismissed. However, Strauss's and Corbin's coding paradigm is connected to a broad and general understanding of action compatible with a wide variety of sociological theories (ranging, for example, from sociological phenomenology to Rational Choice Theory and even to functionalist role theory). Thus, the model of 'purposeful, goal oriented' action entailed in the coding paradigm is also pivotal for Rational Choice approaches like, for instance, Ajzen's 'Theory of planned behaviour' (Ajzen 1991). 'Subjective norms' and 'perceived behavioural control', which – according to that approach – motivate action, could then be considered as part of 'intervening conditions' in terms of the coding paradigm. Or, if one adopts a perspective coming from functionalist role theory and wishes to stress the significant influence of the social environment's role expectancies on the actor's intentions, one would include this aspect in the part of the coding paradigm Strauss and Corbin called 'context'. Thus, it would be easy to adapt the coding paradigm to different theories of action.

Such a general understanding of action is also entailed in several of Glaser's coding families – there it could be regarded as a combination of aspects dispersed among different coding families, since it blends parts of the first coding family ('the six Cs, comprising causes, contexts, contingencies, consequences, covariances and conditions') with the 'strategy family' and the 'means-goal family'. Especially in its earliest version (Strauss & Corbin 1990), the coding paradigm is linked to a micro-sociological approach emphasizing the role of human action and agency in social life, a perspective which is also shared by Glaser: in *Theoretical Sensitivity*, he himself asserts that coding has to be related to *actions* of the actors in the empirical domain. Furthermore, the concept of 'Basic Social Processes', patterns of behaviour which are 'relevant and problematic for those involved' (Glaser 1978, p. 92), which is crucial for Glaserian grounded theory, shows strong associations to sociological pragmatism by reminding us of Dewey's concept of 'habits as social functions' (Dewey 1922). Human action and interaction, according to Dewey, consist of ongoing streams of acts which are structured as socially mediated, routinized and habitualized process patterns and which follow each other in continuing sequences of stages. The analysis of such successive stages forming basic social processes is of utmost importance for the Glaserian approach, whereby 'critical junctures' play an important role (Glaser & Holton 2005), periods of time 'between stages when the occurrence or non-occurrence of a particular critical event will determine whether a new stage is entered' (Glaser & Holton 2005). This resonates with Dewey's concept of social action, where routinized patterns of actions are challenged by the occurrence of unforeseen problems leading to creative processes of the invention of new process patterns.

However, an interesting question would be whether theoretical coding *sensu* Glaser was meant to encourage a pluralistic use of theoretical codes, including concepts from macro-sociology as well (although it certainly could be expanded in that direction). The substantial sociological coding families (e.g., the 'identity self family' or the 'mainline family'), as compared to formal and logical coding families (like the 'six Cs', the 'process family' or the 'degree family') listed in *Theoretical Sensitivity* (Glaser 1978, p. 74ff.) are overwhelmingly related to a micro-sociological perspective which centres around actors and their actions (with categories like 'strategies', 'tactics', 'maneuverings', 'identity', 'goals', 'anticipated consequences', and others). Glaser does not present a coding family referring to system theory (with terms like 'integration', 'differentiation' or 'emergent properties').

Social researchers with a strong background in macro-sociology and system theory may thus feel uncomfortable with both strategies developed to explicate the use of previous theoretical knowledge in grounded theory building – coding families and coding paradigm – since these strategies are (at least in their initial form) biased towards a micro-sociological and action-oriented approach. To employ grounded theory methodology without adopting this (meta)theoretical orientation would require – if one follows the Glaserian route – that one finds suitable theoretical codes and coding families in literature stemming from one's own theoretical approach. If one prefers to draw on the Straussian approach, one would have to construct one's own coding paradigm connected to another theoretical tradition. Grounded Theory Methodology is certainly flexible enough for theoretical pluralism: in a study about the process of caregiving for frail relatives, for instance, one may use theoretical codes derived from decision theory (focusing on the intentions of the actors, as well as their perceived 'costs' and 'benefits' of caregiving) or codes based on role theory (focusing on the expectations of the social environment). However, one has to keep in mind that theoretical codes must not be 'forced' on the data (which means that the data material itself has to suggest their use: one may only apply an approach based on utility theory, for instance, if the research subjects did refer to something which can be considered as 'costs' or 'benefits' of caregiving). This makes such a strategy much more challenging for novices than the use of a ready-made conceptual framework or coding paradigm, but gives them more flexibility at the same time.

With regard to the role of previous theoretical knowledge, the most important difference between Glaserian and Straussian grounded theory building is that Strauss suggests the utilization of a specific theoretical framework based on pragmatist theory of action, whereas with the Glaserian approach coding and category building has to be conducted on the basis of a broad theoretical background knowledge which cannot be made fully explicit in the beginning of analysis. Unfortunately, Glaser tends to overdraw these differences and resorts to an inductivist rhetoric by asking the grounded theory user to approach the research field without any precise research questions or research problems ('*He moves in with the abstract wonderment of what is going on that is an issue and how it is handled*', Glaser 1992, p. 22), and thereby burdens his method with unrealistic truth claims: '*In grounded theory ... when the analyst sorts by theoretical codes everything fits, as the world is socially integrated and grounded theory simply catches this integration through emergence*' (ibid., p. 84). '*Grounded theory looks for what is, not what might be, and therefore needs no test*' (ibid, p. 67). Such assertions carry the (positivistic) idea that, by using an inductive method, researchers may gain the ability to conceive 'mere facts' and 'see things as they are'. However, Glaser has made clear elsewhere, especially by inventing the concept of 'theoretical coding' (Glaser 1978, p. 72), that theoretical concepts do not simply arise from the data alone but require 'theoretical coding' (categorizing of data with the help of previous theoretical knowledge). Thus the suspicion arises that his 'emergence talk' does not describe a methodological strategy but simply offers a way to rhetorically immunize the 'grounded' theories researchers develop from their data, by employing Glaser's method, from being criticized; claiming that categories or statements which have emerged from the data with the help of the one and only 'true path' of GTM cannot be wrong and would never need further corroboration – this would indeed represent an epistemological self-authorization to consider oneself infallible.

Current Developments

The divide between 'Glaserian' and 'Straussian' GTM has persisted ever since. With regard to previous theoretical knowledge in GTM, Glaser and his followers claim to represent 'classical' grounded theory and argue from an inductivist point of view: the basic purpose of empirical research is 'to produce a clear, accurate understanding of what is' (Simmons 2011, p. 18). That can only be obtained if researchers do not bring any 'preconceived questions or categories' (2011, p. 24) with them. Contrary to that, advocates of the Straussian approach stress that 'theories, professional knowledge that we carry within our heads, inform our research in multiple ways' (Corbin & Strauss 2008, p. 32), and that researchers' theoretical sensitivity may increase with the theoretical background knowledge at hand. The use of concepts from the literature is thus encouraged, as long as they do not block the researchers' creativity. However, in the current edition of *Basics of Qualitative Research* (Corbin & Strauss 2015), the notions of 'axial coding' and the 'coding paradigm' are put more into the background. Here Juliet Corbin expresses concerns that by sticking to the coding paradigm too formally, researchers may 'rigidify' the analytic process (Corbin & Strauss 2015). The use of one particular coding paradigm seems indeed to be a certain risk – that the respective theoretical (micro-sociological) perspective may be used to 'force' data.

In the past decades, further varieties of GTM have emerged, the most prominent among them being Kathy Charmaz's 'constructivist' GTM. Charmaz tries to strengthen and accentuate the interpretivist and constructivist elements in GTM: theories are not so much 'discovered' or 'emerge' from the data but constructed by researchers through their 'past and present involvements and interactions with people, perspectives, and research practices' (Charmaz 2006, p. 10). In other respects, Charmaz is closer to the Glaserian approach, by drawing on the general concept of coding families (while she criticizes the concrete list of coding families Glaser had proposed in his early book *Theoretical Sensitivity* and never reworked and reviewed in his later writings).

Contrary to the view of strict Glaserians, many proponents of differing schools of GTM agree on not to 'dismiss extant theoretical and research literature nor apply it mechanically to empirical cases. … Instead these researchers use the literature as a possible source of inspiration, ideas, "aha!" experiences, creative associations, critical reflections, and multiple lenses' (Thornberg 2012, p. 249). Thornberg called this supplementation of GTM techniques with explicit literature review 'Informed GT'.

USING THEORIES AND MODELS IN BUILDING EMPIRICALLY GROUNDED THEORIES: METHODOLOGICAL FOUNDATIONS

The important role of previous theoretical knowledge is now widely acknowledged in the GTM community, but the logical and methodological basis of theoretically informed *and* empirically grounded theory building often remains obscure: is this a deductive or inductive process? If one does not engage in the 'testing' of ready-made hypotheses, what is the role of previous theories and models in such a process of non-deductive theory building? What kinds of theories may be used for this purpose and how are they used properly (e.g., without 'forcing' categories on the data)? In the following we will discuss these questions in detail.

Deduction, Induction and Abduction

According to a classical standard view in the philosophy of science, theories are interrelated sets of statements claiming to establish 'general principles' by means of which a variety of empirical phenomena can be described or explained (Hempel 1952, p. 1). Some of these statements can be directly linked to empirical observations. Following a famous metaphor of Hempel, a theory is a network of terms (following our terminology we would say 'categories') which 'floats, as it were, above the plane of observation and is anchored to it by rules of interpretation'. These rule of interpretation link certain points of the network 'with specific places in the plane of observation…: From certain observational data, we may ascend, via an interpretive string, to some point in the theoretical network, thence proceed, via definitions and hypotheses to other points, from which another interpretive string permits a descent to the plane of observation' (Hempel 1952, p. 36).

In the philosophical debate 'ascent' and 'descent' from and into this network are traditionally related to two modes of inference, called 'deduction' and 'induction'. With deductions, one descends from the theoretical level to the level of empirical observation: social researchers employing theories of class conflict, for instance, may deduce that such conflicts occur in the research field. By making this deduction, they draw a link from a general theory to an empirical hypothesis: 'If A (a theoretical statement) is true then we would expect the empirical phenomenon C to happen.' This expectation represents an 'empirical hypothesis' (in contrast to the 'theoretical hypothesis' A on the 'plane of theory'). By induction, one 'ascends' to the level of theoretical statements by generalizing empirical observation statements: a social researcher frequently hearing from migratory workers about conflicts with police may come to the conclusion that migratory workers often have such problems. However, such an inductive generalization is not category or theory building, since theories are not merely *summaries*, but *explanations* of data. An inference which links an empirical observation to a theoretical explanation is neither a deduction nor an induction, but a third kind of inference described by the pragmatist philosopher Charles Peirce under the name 'hypothesis' or 'abduction' (see also Reichertz, in this volume), nowadays often called 'retroduction' or 'inference to the best explanation' (Hanson 1965; Lipton 2004). Such an inference starts with an empirical observation, for instance 'A migratory worker reports about trouble with the police' and thus is similar to an induction. But contrary to induction, one does not collect further observations to generalize the statement, but draws on a theoretical statement to explain it, for example by claiming that 'members of deviant social groups are stigmatized by agencies of social control'. Contrary to a deduction, a retroduction does not follow with necessity from premises: even if we accept the explanation, it still begs the question whether a single migratory worker was stigmatized because he or she was regarded as a member of a deviant group or whether the trouble with the police occurred due to a real misdemeanour. Furthermore, a retroduction does not exclude alternative explanations; it only serves to find possible hypotheses explaining empirical findings – therefore Peirce also used the term 'hypothesis' to account for this kind of inference.

In the works of Peirce one can distinguish between two types of hypothetical inference depending on whether the explanatory theoretical statement was already at hand or not. If a researcher explains a phenomenon by subsuming it under already known theoretical concepts, Peirce has (especially in his later writings) used the term 'induction by characters' or 'qualitative induction'. In this way social researchers may identify certain events as instances of deviant behaviour, of stigmatization through institutions of social control, and so forth.

However, if a surprising event cannot be explained by previous theoretical knowledge, a second form of hypothetical reasoning comes into play called 'abduction' (Peirce 1974, 5.189). Abductions lead to possible explanations for surprising facts by generating new categories. This is a creative act which sometimes 'comes to us like a flash' (ibid., 5.182), but the researcher's creativity is limited: abductions must be related to previous knowledge – 'different elements of the hypothesis were in our minds before' (ibid., 5.181): new experiences are connected to previous knowledge so that (often longstanding, well-accepted) elements of that knowledge must be abandoned and modified, making them consistent with the surprising observation. In both types of hypothetical inference previous theoretical knowledge is needed: one either applies this knowledge (by subsuming an incident under a general term through qualitative induction) or modifies and transforms it (by finding new categories through abductive inferences).

Different kinds of empirical research draw on deductive, inductive and retroductive inferences in different ways, thereby constituting distinct strategies of reasoning: in quantitative (especially, experimental) 'hypothetico-deductive' research, singular statements are deduced from general theories in order to formulate empirically testable propositions. By (enumerative) induction, empirical observation statements are collected which are suited to provide evidence or counter-evidence to a certain statement. This can be done both in quantitative research ('inductive statistics') and in qualitative research (e.g., when 'minimizing' differences in theoretical sampling). Retroduction comes into play when empirical data obtained by quantitative or qualitative methods are explained with the help of well-known categories and theories (qualitative induction *sensu* Peirce), or if surprising empirical findings are explained by theoretical innovations, for example, with the help of a newly found category.

Different Types of Theories and Models and their Role in Grounded Theory Building

Theoretical propositions are developed, built and modified through chains of inferences. To obtain a deeper understanding of this process it is important to differentiate between different kinds of theoretical statements with regard to their *scope*, *source*, *degree of explicitness* and *empirical content*.

- If one looks at the *scope* of theoretical statements, one can distinguish between statements from 'grand theories' and from 'middle-range theories': *grand theories* relate to all social phenomena regardless of time and space and make universal claims applicable to all societies at all times (like Durkheim's types of 'social integration' or Cooley's and Mead's concept of the 'self'), 'Middle-range theories' (Merton 1968, p. 39) have limited scope and refer to certain societies, cultures or specific social groups, for example Weber's thesis about the relation between the Protestant ethic and capitalism (which refers to a certain period in European history) or Glaser and Strauss's model about interactions between patients, their relatives and hospital staff (Glaser & Strauss 1965).
- With regard to *source*, one may differentiate between *theoretical concepts from an academic background*, on the one hand, and *common sense concepts*, on the other hand: Common sense concepts are used by researchers and research subjects alike, they may be as abstract and complicated as many academic theories and they often form an amalgam of categories from various backgrounds – from local sense knowledge, passed orally within a particular culture, information coming from the media, ideas stemming from political and religious contexts, as well as scientific terms.

- Researchers may draw both on *explicit* and *implicit* theoretical categories. Course books in social theory usually attempt to describe theoretical categories as explicitly as possible, but experienced sociologists may be able to categorize and understand social events almost instantly after having observed them as exemplars of a certain theoretical category. Their theoretical training may have provided them with a conceptual lens that allows them to immediately 'see' instances of social inequality, norm conflicts, stigmatization, identity formation or whatever else, without the necessity to make all these stocks of theoretical knowledge explicit in advance.
- With regard to the degree of *empirical content*, theoretical terms and statements may either be *easily falsifiable* (= have high empirical content) or be *difficult to falsify* (= have low empirical content). A statement like '*All young adults from middle-class background (defined in terms of income and educational status of their parents) attend university*' is a good example for a statement with high empirical content: it can be easily falsified (by finding just one middle-class person without university education). To make such a statement more realistic, a probabilistic element has to be included: '*Young adults from middle-class background have better chances of attending university than young people from a working-class background.*' Although this statement contains less empirical content, it is still contentful, since it could be disproved by investigating a great sample of young adults with different class backgrounds. Contrary to that, theoretical categories from many 'grand theories' – like 'identity', 'status', 'roles', 'systems', 'structure', and the like – usually lack empirical content: their broadness and abstractness make it difficult, if not impossible, to directly disprove them. As an example, take the statement: 'A social role defines the expected behaviour connected to a given social status.' An empirical test disproving this sentence is hard to imagine – a person who tries to find a counter-example (that means a social role not defining behaviour connected to a certain status) would even demonstrate thereby that they do not understand the statement, which is not meant for being empirically tested but defines the category 'social role'. Each theory entails or at least refers to categories and assumptions of that kind. To derive empirical statements from such basic categories or assumptions, one would need additional information and auxiliary assumptions which describe, for instance, expectations regarding a certain role in a given organization.

Types of Theories and Types of Reasoning

The types of logical inference described above – deduction, induction and retroduction – can be combined with types of theoretical knowledge in different ways, leading to distinct strategies to connect theory and data:

- deductive theory testing,
- retroductive theory building applying categories with low empirical content either by drawing on implicit theoretical knowledge or by constructing an explicit heuristic-analytic framework,
- retroductive theory application and theory building using categories with high empirical content.

Deductive theory testing

This is a basic strategy in most of experimental and non-experimental quantitative psychological and social research. Theoretical categories and hypotheses with high empirical content and high falsifiability (like the hypothesis mentioned above about the educational achievements of young adults with middle-class background) are formulated and then 'operationalized' (e.g., by defining 'young adults' as '*men and women aged between 18 years and 25 years*' or defining 'educational status' as '*level of school leaving exam*'). Based on these operational definitions, measurement instruments (e.g., questionnaires) are constructed and (mostly standardized) data are collected and analyzed with statistical methods. This is clearly not a strategy feasible in the context of GTM.

Retroductive theory building using categories with low empirical content

Since categories cannot emerge from data on their own, the construction of empirically grounded theories always requires some sort of previous theoretical knowledge.

Retroduction means connecting empirical observations with theory either by subsuming the observations under already known categories (qualitative induction) or by finding new categories (abduction). In GTM, such categories, which do not force data but which can serve as heuristic devices for the discovery of previously unknown phenomena, are appreciated. Theoretical categories with low empirical content drawn from grand theories are often ideally suited for this purpose since they may sensitize researchers for theoretically relevant phenomena in the field. Herbert Blumer had proposed the term '*sensitizing concepts*' to denote abstract notions like 'institution' or 'personality' which '*lack precise reference and have no bench marks which allow a clean-cut identification of a specific instance* (but) *merely suggest directions along which to look*' (Blumer 1954, p. 7). Sensitizing concepts usually lack empirical content so that they can be applied to a wide array of phenomena (and thus cannot be 'verified' or 'falsified' in any sense) and they can serve as *heuristic devices* for the construction of empirically grounded categories. A category like 'identity' is much more difficult to operationalize than 'educational status of parents' and it may be difficult to derive falsifiable propositions from this category without further empirical information – the assertion that individuals develop a certain identity in a given social domain does not contain a lot of empirical content by itself. Such a concept could be, however, extremely useful if one wants to formulate empirical research questions for a given substantive field: Does identity formation play an important role in the empirical domain under study? What processes of identity formation take place? Is the identity of certain actors challenged by others? Which strategies do actors employ to defend and to maintain their identity if it is challenged? etc. Such heuristic categories do not force the data, since they lack empirical content. This is their strength in the context of exploratory, interpretive research. They fit various kinds of social reality and it will not be necessary to know concrete facts about the investigated domain before data collection takes place.

In principle, there are two ways to introduce heuristic concepts with low empirical content into the process of empirically grounded theory building:

- One way would be to have a great stock of theoretical concepts ('coding families') available, which stay implicit in the researcher's mind most of the time and from which the most suitable for a given research field may suddenly 'emerge' (not from the data alone, but from a sudden connection the analyst discovers between an empirical incident and a concept he or she had in mind for a long time without thinking about it). This may take the form of the 'sudden flash' of abduction that Peirce described. It is a creative act that still has strong presuppositions, since this creativity is dependent on a very broad implicit background knowledge about theoretical concepts.
- A less challenging strategy would be to build an explicit conceptual frame ('coding paradigm') in advance. This would require an explicit, thorough examination of the different elements of certain theories, thereby keeping in mind the risk that some of the used concepts may 'force the data'.

The use of a predefined coding paradigm to subsume empirical observation under certain categories represents qualitative induction *sensu* Peirce. Thereby the use of a single 'pet theory' may easily lead to the neglect of heuristic concepts better suited for the investigated domain. Even rather abstract concepts with low empirical content that capture a broad variety of different processes and events may still exclude certain phenomena from being analyzed: thus, the extended use of concepts from micro-sociological action theory (e.g., 'actors', 'goals', 'strategies'…) can preclude a system theory and macro-perspective on the research domain.

Consequently, drawing on different and even competing theoretical perspectives may often be a better strategy than staying with a limited number of favourite concepts, but it would also require considerable training and background knowledge in social theory. This knowledge would pay off, however, since a huge variety of concepts coming from differing theoretical approaches in sociology and social psychology can be used as heuristic devices. This even relates to schools of thought which are normally remote from qualitative research, like rational choice theory. The core assumption of rational choice theories is that human actors will choose the action from a given set of alternatives which seems the most adequate for achieving a desired goal. However, without specifying *which* goals the actors pursue and *which* actions they consider to be adequate, the theory is like an '*empty sack*' (cf. Simon 1985). Consequently, rational choice concepts can serve as typical examples for categories with low empirical content which can be applied as heuristic devices: one may, for instance, code incidents in the data which refer to the potential *costs* and *benefits* certain actions have for the actors, or one may code data which relate to the *intentions* and *goals* of the research subjects or to the *means* they use to reach their goals. Thus, a wide array of categories from different theoretical traditions can be used in GTM.

A further type of heuristic categories suitable for GTM may be called 'topic-oriented codes': these may either (like 'school', 'work' or 'family') relate to general common-sense knowledge or to local knowledge of the investigated field. In the latter case, such codes are often found in the material itself during open coding ('*in vivo codes*'). Both topic-oriented codes and heuristic theoretical concepts must not force data – furthermore, one should always ask whether a category may lead to the exclusion of certain phenomena from being analyzed (like the category 'young adults' would exclude older persons), since this would show that the category contains too much empirical content and thus only refers to a limited set of phenomena.

The use of categories with high empirical content in grounded theory

In grounded theory building the analyst does not start by constructing categories with high empirical content, but by applying abstract theoretical categories with general scope (which refer to various kinds of phenomena) but limited empirical content (like 'identity' or 'social role') as heuristic devices and with topic-oriented codes (like 'work' or 'school'). The aim is to develop empirically grounded categories with a limited scope and high empirical content (like 'identity formation of juveniles taken away from their parents and living in care homes in Great Britain').

However, in some situations it may be fruitful to employ categories and assertions with *high* empirical content. A researcher investigating the process of caregiving to frail elderly people, for instance, may discover that Arlie Hochschild's category '*emotional labour*' (Hochschild 1983) is helpful for understanding social interactions in this field. This category, initially developed to describe typical patterns of interaction between flight attendants and air passengers, can thus adopt a heuristic function in the investigation of another research domain, although it comprises more empirical content than terms like 'identity' or 'intentions': not all kinds of social interactions demand emotional labour, and compared to other heuristic categories or propositions the assumption that certain professionals provide emotional labour can be falsified.

However, the concept can still be helpful for the analysis of social phenomena in a certain field. Consequently, it can also be sensible in grounded theory research to use distinct and well-defined categories and propositions which contain enough empirical content to be empirically tested. This strategy, named 'analytic induction' by researchers and methodologists from the 'Chicago School' in the 1930s, was used in numerous well-known qualitative studies and later on fell into undeserved oblivion: initial hypotheses are examined and modified with the help of empirical evidence provided by so-called 'crucial cases' (cf. Lindesmith 1946/1968; Cressey 1953/1971, pp. 104f). This mode of analysis clearly carries a certain risk to force categories on the data which are not suited for the research field. We have already discussed this danger in relation to Strauss's and Corbin's coding paradigm, which is useful for the description of a wide array of social phenomena but may draw researchers towards a micro-sociological orientation they do not necessarily share. The advice, however, to use only abstract categories with great scope and low empirical content may constrict especially inexperienced researchers, since not each heuristic concept can draw the attention to sociologically relevant phenomena. Novices, in particular, may be overstrained by the task to select the heuristic category most suited for their research field among a vast selection of coding families.

Which kinds of theory may we generate by employing the types of reasoning described: induction, deduction and retroduction? As must have become clear from preceding sections, induction will never generate theory, it only helps with the generalization of already existing theoretical statements. Likewise, the mere process of deductive theory testing would not lead to a new theory in itself – it merely helps to corroborate or disprove existing theoretical statements (given that, in the first place, these statements contain enough empirical content to be tested). However, by using a hypothetico-deductive research design, researchers confronted with empirical evidence falsifying their initial theoretical assumptions may develop a new hypothesis in a creative act of insight. One would call this an abduction. To allow for the development of data-based ('grounded') theoretical categories and statements is the great promise offered by GTM. This is ideally pursued by using retroductive inferences whereby categories with low empirical content are applied in a certain field of investigation. However, according to the underlying philosophy of GTM, this process would fail if researchers end up with general, abstract and broad categories carrying little or no empirical content. Categories developed in a GTM study must not be as abstract as the concepts one finds in course books about Social Theory. A category or theory really 'grounded' in the data should have enough empirical content to provide readers with meaningful information about previously unknown or poorly understood domains of social life.

CONCLUDING REMARKS

One of the most important challenges in GTM is to reconcile the need of letting categories emerge from the data (instead of forcing preconceived theoretical terms on them) with the impossibility to abandon previous theoretical knowledge. Consequently, when working with GTM one must avoid the temptation to force theoretical 'pet concepts' on the data and naïve inductivism likewise. Existing theories and models are indispensable tools in building empirically grounded theories, but they have to be used in an epistemologically informed and sophisticated way. First, it is helpful to fully understand the logical foundations of empirically grounded theory building: it is not (enumerative) induction (which means the generalization of statements about single events) which leads to new categories, but retroduction, a kind of inference in which a new category 'emerges' through a creative combination of empirical data with previous theoretical knowledge. Researchers with a large stock of theoretical categories at their disposition and a deep-reaching knowledge about their interrelations may easily start coding without a predefined category scheme, thereby permanently drawing on their implicit theoretical knowledge. But, if one has difficulties to select and combine appropriate theoretical categories for one's research domain, one would be well advised to draw on existing coding paradigms (like that proposed by Strauss and Corbin) or even to construct a heuristic theoretical framework for one's project. In doing so, one should be very careful to utilize concepts which enhance theoretical sensitivity and serve as heuristic devices and which do not force the data.

For this purpose, it is also helpful to know and understand the methodological differences between various kinds of theoretical concepts and categories, as well as to be informed about their use in research practice: hypothetico-deductive, experimental and quantitative research requires clear-cut and empirically contentful categories and hypotheses (which in GTM are usually only formulated at fairly advanced stages of the process), whereas broad and abstract theoretical notions with a large scope are helpful for the empirically grounded generation of categories, since their lack of empirical content gives them flexibility to describe a great variety of empirical phenomena. Due to their lack of empirical content, they do not force the data and fit various kinds of social reality. Heuristic categories play the role of a theoretical axis or a 'skeleton' to which the 'flesh' of empirically contentful information from the research domain is added. The goal is to develop empirically grounded categories and propositions about relations between these categories. Category building of that kind starts by using heuristic concepts and proceeds to the construction of categories and propositions with growing empirical content. Thereby, the decisive question which helps to distinguish between empirically contentful and heuristic theoretical categories must always be: Does the category exclude interesting and relevant phenomena in the empirical field from being analyzed?

REFERENCES

Ajzen, Icek (1991). The Theory of Planned Behavior. *Organizational Behavior and Human Decision Processes*, *50*, 179–211.

Becker, Howard & Geer, Blanche (1960). Participant Observation: The Analysis of Qualitative Field Data. In Richard N. Adams & Jack J. Preiss (Eds.), *Human Organization Research: Field Relations and Techniques*. Homewood, IL: The Dorsey Press. pp. 267–289.

Blumer, Herbert (1954). What is Wrong with Social Theory? *American Sociological Review*, *19*, 3–10.

Chalmers, Alan F. (1999). *What is this Thing Called Science?* Maidenhead: Open University Press.

Charmaz, Kathy (2006). *Constructing Grounded Theory: A Practical Guide through Qualitative Analysis*. London: Sage.

Corbin, Juliet (1991). Anselm Strauss: An Intellectual Biography. In David R. Maines (Ed.), *Social Organization and Social Process: Essays in Honor of Anselm Strauss*. New York: Aldine de Gruyter. pp. 17–44.

Corbin, Juliet & Strauss, Anselm (2008, 2015) *Basics of Qualitative Research: Techniques and Procedures for Developing Grounded Theory* (3rd & 4th edition). Thousand Oaks, CA: Sage.

Cressey, Donald R. (1953/1971). *Other People's Money: A Study in the Social Psychology of Embezzlement*. Belmont, CA: Wadsworth.

Dewey, J. (1922). *Human Nature and Conduct*. New York: Holt.

Glaser, Barney (1978). *Theoretical Sensitivity: Advances in the Methodology of Grounded Theory.* Mill Valley, CA: The Sociology Press.

Glaser, Barney (1992). *Emergence vs. Forcing: Basics of Grounded Theory Analysis*. Mill Valley, CA: Sociology Press.

Glaser, Barney & Holton, Judith (2005). Basic Social Processes. *Grounded Theory Review*, *3*(4), www. http://groundedtheoryreview.com/2005/06/22/1533/

Glaser, Barney & Strauss, Anselm (1965). *Awareness of Dying.* Chicago, IL: Aldine.

Glaser, Barney & Strauss, Anselm (1967). *The Discovery of Grounded Theory: Strategies for Qualitative Research*. New York: Aldine de Gruyter

Hanson, Norwood R. (1965). *Patterns of Discovery: An Inquiry into the Conceptual Foundations of Science*. Cambridge: Cambridge University Press.

Hempel, Carl G. (1952). *Fundamentals of Concept Formation in Empirical Science.* Chicago, IL: University of Chicago Press.

Hochschild, Arlie (1983). *The Managed Heart: Commercialization of Human Feeling*. Berkeley, CA: University of California Press.

Kelle, Udo, Marx, Janine, Pengel, Sandra, Uhlhorn, Kai, & Witt, Ingmar (2002). Die Rolle theoretischer Heuristiken im qualitativen Forschungsprozeß – ein Werkstattbericht. In Hans-Uwe Otto, Gertrud Oelerich, & Heinz-Günter Micheel (Eds.), *Empirische Forschung und Soziale Arbeit. Ein Lehr- und Arbeitsbuch*. Neuwied und Kriftel: Luchterhand. pp. 11–130.

Lakatos, Imre (1978). *The Methodology of Scientific Research Programmes*. Cambridge: Cambridge University Press.

Laudan, Larry (1977). *Progress and its Problems: Towards a Theory of Scientific Growth*. London and Henley: Routledge & Kegan Paul.

Lindesmith, Alfred R. (1946/1968). *Addiction and Opiates*. Chicago, IL: Aldine.

Lipton, Peter (2004). *Inference to the Best Explanation*. London: Routledge.

Merton, Robert (1968). *Social Theory and Social Structure*. New York: Free Press.

Peirce, Charles S. (1974). *Collected Papers*. Ed. C. Hartshore et al. Cambridge, MA: The Belknap Press of Harvard University Press.

Simmons, Odis E. (2011). Why Classic Grounded Theory? In Vivian B. Martin & Astrid Gynnild (Eds.), *Grounded Theory: The Philosophy, Method and Work of Barney Glaser*. Boca Raton, FL: Brown Walker. pp. 15–30.

Simon, Herbert A. (1985). Human Nature in Politics: The Dialogue of Psychology with Political Science. *The American Political Science Review*, *79*, 293–304.

Strauss, Anselm L. (1987). *Qualitative Analysis for Social Scientists*. Cambridge and New York: Cambridge University Press.

Strauss, Anselm L. (1990). *Creating Sociological Awareness*. New Brunswick, NJ: Transaction.

Strauss, Anselm L. & Corbin, Juliet (1990). *Basics of Qualitative Research: Grounded Theory Procedures and Techniques*. Newbury Park, CA: Sage.

Strauss, Anselm L. & Schervier-Legewie, Barbara (2004). Anselm Strauss: Research is Hard Work, it's Always a bit Suffering. Therefore, on the Other Side Research Should be Fun. *Forum Qualitative Social Research*, *5*. [http://dx.doi.org/10.17169/fqs-5.3.562]

Thornberg, Robert (2012). Informed Grounded Theory. *Scandinavian Journal of Educational Research*, *56*(3), 243–259.

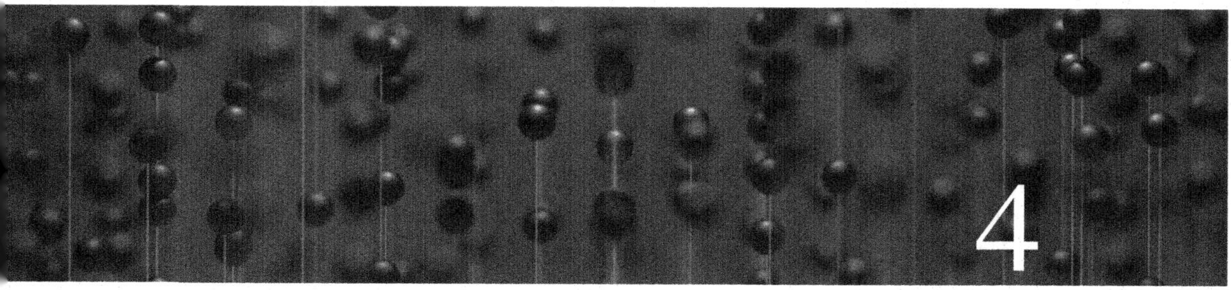

Grounded Theory's Best Kept Secret: The Ability to Build Theory

Cathy Urquhart

INTRODUCTION

As a lifelong passionate adherent of grounded theory method (GTM), and having watched GTM become more and more popular, and relevant, in a range of academic disciplines, I have one outstanding question. Why is it that the recommendations of Glaser and Strauss (1967) for moving from substantive to formal theory are not more widely discussed? If we take as our starting point Glaser and Strauss's definition of substantive theory, which is one developed for a substantive, or empirical area of inquiry, it is clear that the majority of theories generated using GTM fall into this definition. Why is it that we do not then attempt to build formal theory, which Glaser and Strauss define as one developed for a formal, or conceptual area of inquiry? Especially as Glaser and Strauss point out that substantive and formal theories exist on distinguishable levels of generality, and that each type can shade at points into the other?

Given an ongoing concern about theory building in many newer academic disciplines (Weber 2003; Lester 2005; Oswick, Fleming and Hanlon 2011; Johnson, Eksted and Jacobson, 2012), which centre on those disciplines' ability to build formal theory, it seems timely to examine this question in more detail, and to explore GTM's undoubted contribution to a larger theory building effort in academic disciplines. While some social sciences have a long history of abstract theorizing (e.g., Stinchcombe 1991), many newer disciplines do not. Even in those disciplines, the advice of Glaser and Strauss (1967) with regard to theoretical sampling, looking at dissimilar and similar groups with unsaturated and saturated categories, seems rarely acted upon, presumably because of some difficulties operationalizing the advice. I remain convinced that this advice gives us valuable guidance when building theory, because it gives us advice on extending the scope and generality of a theory, which in turn can lead us to building bigger, more formal theories.

The rest of this chapter looks at theory building debates in the newer academic disciplines and considers GTMs contribution to the idea of theory. I then look at Glaser and Strauss's (1967) recommendations about theory building in detail, with special reference to minimizing and maximizing group differences. What might those recommendations tell us in 2017? What might we learn when we apply those recommendations?

THEORY AND GROUNDED THEORY

Glaser and Strauss (1967) set out the role of theory in sociology as both enabling prediction and explanation of behaviour, and also as 'being readily understandable to sociologists of any viewpoint, to students and to significant laymen'. They also state that the theory needs to be clear enough to be operationalized in quantitative studies where appropriate. They were also concerned with issues of fit of the theory, by which they meant that the theory must be able to explain the phenomena, and not be forced on to the phenomena as an explanation. Above all, they pointed out that enduring theories are based on data, are grounded in that data, and cannot easily be refuted (Glaser and Strauss 1967). They also made the important point that how theories are assessed is also dependent on how the theory was generated.

If we fast forward to recent debates about theory in management, and in information systems, we see some similar themes. For instance, Corley and Gioia (2011) are as concerned with the utility of a management theory as its originality. Oswick, Fleming and Hanlon (2011) wonder if theory borrowing from other disciplines constrains the development of new and indigenous theories. This also raises issues of fit of those borrowed theories, and whether those theories are adequately grounded in data from their home discipline. In software engineering, the question has been raised about the absence of theories in the discipline (Johnson et al. 2012), and the utility of theories to the discipline.

In information systems, a lively debate about the importance of theory to the discipline occurred in 2014. Avison and Malaurent (2014) railed against what they saw as a fetishing of theory in the discipline, the fact that various theories fell in and out of favour, and again, raised questions about the fit of borrowed theories. Their piece was accompanied by several commentaries from Lee (2014), Markus (2014), and Gregor (2014). One striking agreement among the commentaries was that there was indeed a lack of consensus about what a theory is.

Overall then, we see in these debates a lack of consensus about what theory is, and also a concern about the fit of theories imported from older reference disciplines. While the first is probably attributable to the newness of some of these disciplines, it is interesting to note that there are also concerns about fit and groundedness of theories, whether imported from outside the discipline (fit) or within the discipline (groundedness).

Gregor (2006) is quoted in a number of these debates, and her definition of theory bears repeating here because it is both broad and helpful. She defines theories as '*abstract entities that aim to describe, explain, and enhance understanding of the world and in some cases, to provide predictions of what will happen in the future and to give a basis for intervention and action*' (p. 616). She further categorizes theories into those that analyze and describe (but do not contain causal relationships), theories for explanation (but with no testable propositions), theories for prediction (testable propositions but no causal explanations), and theories for both explanation and prediction. She also adds theories for design and action, which can be seen as more specific to information systems and software engineering.

Gregor also defines the components of all theories as containing a means of representation, constructs, statements of relationship, and scope. It is useful to consider how these conventional components compare to the grounded theory process of theory building, simply because it seems rarely that grounded theory is discussed in the same way as theory in general – yet the components are the same, as Table 4.1 comparing Gregor's components to GTM indicates.

A few points in the above table bear further discussion. First, and most importantly, the constructs in a grounded theory are *grounded* in data. Second, the founding fathers of grounded theory knew that a parsimonious theory was important – hence the recommendation that one or two 'core' categories (or constructs) should make up a grounded theory. This recommendation helps to raise the level of the theory and widen its potential scope. Third, grounded theories rarely have relationships described in mathematical terms, because they are grounded (usually)[1] in qualitative data. That said, it is entirely possible to generate propositions about causal relationships in a grounded theory. If we look at the range of academic theories available to us, there are many different relationships represented in theories. For instance, in structuration theory, Giddens (1984) posits that social systems are created and reproduced by an inseparable duality of structure and agency. Theories like structuration theory are of course precisely the sort of 'grand' armchair theories that Glaser and Strauss (1967) felt did not provide sufficient theory for new areas, or simply did not work. Interestingly, Giddens did not think that his theory should be used for guiding the practice of research, but rather as a sensitizing device, which is entirely reasonable, as it can be seen as a 'grand' or formal theory.[2]

This brings us to the final point in Table 4.1, which is the issue of scope. The inevitable consequence of a grounded theory is that it tends to be a substantive theory, pertaining to the area being investigated, because if the theory needs to be grounded in data, it will naturally limit the scope of the theory to what can be observed in a single study. It is this issue of scope – and the associated boundary conditions and context – that seem to be less discussed in the literature. While in the physical sciences, boundary conditions are typically solutions expressed as equations, in the social sciences, these conditions are more likely to be boundaries of race, gender and class – and the truly universal theories might transcend these boundaries (Spatz and Kardas 2008). Davison and Martinsons (2016) have discussed the issue of theory scope in information systems, asking to what extent are the findings of a study strictly limited to the original context, and the importance of boundary conditions. Within grounded theory, there is a degree of clarity around the issue of scope, because it is clear that the scope of the theory can be extended by following the advice on theoretical sampling. The next sections look at Glaser and Strauss's definitions of substantive and formal theory, then examine their recommendations on moving substantive theory to formal theory, using theoretical sampling.

DEFINING SUBSTANTIVE AND FORMAL THEORY

Glaser and Strauss (1967) define substantive theory as 'that developed for a substantive, or empirical area of sociological inquiry' (p. 32). They define formal theory 'that developed for a formal, or conceptual area of sociological inquiry' (p. 32). They are careful to

Table 4.1 Comparing Gregor (2006) components to grounded theory building (Urquhart, 2013)

Theory Component	*Definition*	*In Grounded Theory*
Means of representation	The theory must be represented physically in some way: in words, mathematical terms, symbolic logic, diagrams, tables or graphically.	Theories in GTM are often represented by a narrative framework, diagrams or statements of hypotheses.
Constructs	These refer to the phenomena of interest in the theory (Dubin's 'units'). All of the primary constructs in the theory should be well defined. Many different types of constructs are possible: for example, observational (real) terms, theoretical (nominal) terms and collective terms.	In GTM, the aim is to get to one to two core categories or constructs. This makes for a more parsimonious and coherent theory. All the constructs in a grounded theory are grounded in data, which can be equated to observational (real) terms.
Statements of relationship	These show relationships among the constructs. Again, these may be of many types: associative, compositional, unidirectional, bidirectional, conditional, or causal. The nature of the relationship specified depends on the purpose of the theory. Very simple relationships can be specified: for example, 'x is a member of class A.'	In GTM, because the theory is often (but not always) based on qualitative data, relationships are not often described in mathematical terms. There is a lot of guidance in GTM about the sort of relationships that are possible between constructs, in the form of coding families (Glaser 1978) and a coding paradigm (Corbin and Strauss 2008)
Scope	The scope is specified by the degree of generality of the statements of relationships (signified by modal qualifiers such as 'some', 'many', 'all' and 'never') and statements of boundaries showing the limits of generalizations.	GTM aims to produce substantive theories which pertain to the area being investigated. The scope and generalizability can be extended by theoretical sampling (Glaser 1978). The substantive theory can and should be engaged with existing theories – in grounded theory, existing theories can also be seen as slices of data which help build the theory.

say that both types of theory can be considered middle-range and are not all-inclusive 'grand theories'. Glaser and Strauss point out that substantive and formal theories only differ in terms of the degree of generality – that is, the *scope* of the theory. Formal theory is created by comparative analysis among different kinds of substantive cases. So, gradually the scope is increased, by different contexts and boundary conditions, represented by different substantive cases.

They suggest that, for substantive theory, the theorist can select groups from the same substantive class, regardless of where they are found (p. 53). They give the example of comparing an 'emergency ward' to all kinds of medical wards, in all kinds of hospitals, in all countries. If, however, one was to progress towards a formal theory, they suggest that it would be useful to see the emergency ward as a subclass of emergency organizations.

So let us look more deeply at the definitions of substantive and formal theory. One key difference is that formal theory categories are not underpinned by high empirical content,[3] despite the fact that they have their origin in empirical data. For the purpose of Table 4.2, categories can also be seen as constructs, as defined by Gregor (2006). In grounded theory, the aim is to get to one or two core categories for a parsimonious theory (Glaser 1978; Strauss 1987). This helps the researcher to get to a reasonable level of abstraction, and mitigates against having too many low-level categories, sometimes an inevitable consequence of detailed line-by-line coding. Importantly, it helps the researcher to pull together and integrate the theory around one central concern. In

Table 4.2 Considering the differences between substantive and formal theory

	Substantive Theory	*Formal Theory*
Categories	One or two core categories, underpinned by many instances in the data (high empirical content).	Underpinned by very few instances in the data. The categories that help build those formal categories, however, are underpinned by data. The formal theory category or construct is usually abstract, e.g., structure, process, role, identity, network, social capital.
Relationships (Theoretical Codes)	Ideas for the relationships come from coding families or other theories, in line with theoretical sensitivity. Those relationships are 'grounded' in the data, to the extent that they are evidenced in theoretical memos and write-ups of the research.	Often the relationships or underlying mechanisms are unique – this is what distinguishes a formal theory. Again, the relationships or mechanisms will often be underpinned by empirics at the lower level.
Scope	Scope is limited to the substantive (empirical) area of inquiry and pertains to the area being investigated.	Scope is extended by comparative analysis between different types of substantive cases.

turn, those core categories are underpinned by lower level categories that are firmly grounded in the data.

As the scope of a substantive theory is extended towards a formal one, category or construct names by necessity become simpler, and more abstract, because that construct has to apply to a large number of substantive cases.

Relationships between constructs or categories in grounded theory are named 'theoretical codes' by Glaser (1978) in his famed book *Theoretical Sensitivity*. The idea of theoretical sensitivity, articulated in the 1967 book, is that the grounded theorist has to be sufficiently aware of theories, and how they are constructed, in order to be able to construct their own. Glaser proposed 18 'coding families' in *Theoretical Sensitivity* that give inspiration for relationships between categories. These families (now totalling 41, with the families proposed in Glaser (2005)) are themselves often inspired by how other theories conceptualize phenomena. A few examples of theoretical families are given in Table 4.3.

Of course, there is also guidance on relating categories in the Straussian version of grounded theory. Strauss in 1987 proposed a coding paradigm of conditions, consequences, interactions, strategies and consequences, using a procedure he named 'axial coding'. He says the purpose of this element of axial coding is to 'hypothesize about conditions, consequences, interactions, strategies and consequences', that is, to think about how the categories relate. Later, Strauss and Corbin (1990) published a further coding paradigm, which prompted the now famous dispute between Glaser and Strauss. It is interesting to note, however, that the strictures about this paradigm moved from mandatory to optional, over time. Table 4.4 explains the evolution of the coding paradigm.

Moving to the question of scope, Glaser and Strauss (1967) distinguish between scope of the population covered by the theory and the conceptual level of the theory (p. 52). So for a substantive theory, different groups would be selected of exactly the same substantive type – they give the example of federal bookkeeping departments. However, if the aim is to progress to formal theory, increasingly dissimilar – and larger – groups need to be selected. The key sentences in the 1967 book are as follows:

> when the sociologist's purpose is to discover formal theory, he [sic] will definitely select dissimilar, substantive groups from the larger class, while increasing his theory's scope. *And he will also find himself comparing groups that seem to be non-comparable on the substantive level, but that on the formal level are conceptually comparable.* ... For example, while fire departments and emergency wards are substantially dissimilar, their conceptual comparability is still readily apparent ... it must be explained on a higher conceptual level.' (p. 54) (author's emphasis)

Clearly, Glaser and Strauss considered in great detail, from the beginning, the differences between substantive and formal theory, and how to move from one to the other, from a practical point of view. The next section discusses their recommendations for theoretical sampling, which are rarely discussed in the grounded theory literature, despite the undoubted insights they give us for the theory-building process.

GLASER AND STRAUSS'S RECOMMENDATIONS FOR BUILDING THEORY USING THEORETICAL SAMPLING

It is very clear that Glaser and Strauss were engaged from the outset with practical considerations for building theory – for them, the key issue of what data to collect next

Table 4.3 Examples of Theoretical Families from Glaser (1978, 2005), adapted from Urquhart (2013)

Family	*Comment*
The 6 Cs – Causes, Contexts, Contingencies, Consequences, Covariances and Conditions	This basic coding family, together with family 5, the Strategy Family, was adapted by (Strauss and Corbin 1990) as their coding paradigm of 'Causal Conditions, Context, Intervening Conditions, Action/Interaction Strategies and Consequences'.
Process – Stages, staging, phases, phasing, progresssions, passages, gradations, transititions, steps, ranks, careers, ordering, trajectories, chains, sequencings, etc.	Glaser remarks that a process should have at least two stages.
The Dimension Family – Dimensions, elements, division, piece of, properties of, facet, slice, sector, portion, segment, part, aspect, section	As Glaser says, the more we learn of a category, the more we see of its dimensions. Of all theoretical codes, this is one that all researchers are likely to use. It is also important to realize that, when theorizing, that we can privilege one dimension over another – it can become a full-blown category.
The Type Family – Type, form, kinds, styles, classes, genre	Glaser says while dimensions divide up the whole, types show variation in the whole. So, for instance, you might have a number of styles of introducing a problem in a conversation.
The Strategy Family – Strategies, tactics, mechanisms, managed, way, manipulation, manoeuvrings, dealing with, handling, techniques, ploys, means, goals, arrangements, dominating, positioning	The Strauss and Corbin (1990) coding paradigm seems to be a mixture of this family and the first family.
Moment capture, when a quick intervention is critical to causing an optimal outcome, e.g., closing a deal	This is a new theoretical code introduced in the 2005 book.
Frames, which are excavated through discourse patterns and are socio-cultural in nature	Also in the 2005 book, and based on communication theory.

(Continued)

Table 4.3 Examples of Theoretical Families from Glaser (1978, 2005), adapted from Urquhart (2013) (Continued)

Family	*Comment*
Causal family, a relative of the 6Cs family. This includes several aspects: (1) Bias random walk, (2) Amplifying causal looping, (3) Conjectural causation, (4) Repetitive causal reproductions, (5) Equifinality, (6) Reciprocal causation, (7) Triggers, (8) Causal paths, (9) Perpetual causal looping	(Glaser 2005) gives some interesting nuances of causation in this theoretical code. Bias random walk is where all variables are in a flux, 'then on the introduction of a crucial variable … then of a sudden all of the variables fall into organization' Amplifying causal looping, 'where consequences become causes, and one sees either worsening or improving progressions or escalating severity' Conjectural causation, where it is not always easy to identify decisive causal combinations Repetitive causal reproductions, when a repeated action keeps producing the same consequences Equifinality, where no matter what the causes and paths, the same consequence will occur Reciprocal causation, where there is a similar interaction of effects or amplified causal looping Triggers, which are sudden causes that set off a consequence or set of consequences Causal paths, used to intervene in changing or stopping a consequence Perpetual causal looping, a mathematical model, an ordered calculated growth of increased size based on a set temporal path

Table 4.4 The evolving nature of the Straussian coding paradigm (adapted from Urquhart 2013)

Coding Paradigm	*Comment on evolving use of paradigm*
Conditions, consequences, interactions, strategies and consequences (Strauss 1987)	In the 1987 book, it is clear that the coding paradigm is not an optional part of coding. Researchers are told to 'follow the coding paradigm' p. 81.
Causal Conditions, Context, Intervening Conditions, Action/Interaction, Strategies and Consequences (Strauss and Corbin 1990)	In the 1990 book the paradigm is modified to include different types of conditions and actions.
Conditions (causal, intervening, and contextual), Actions/Interactions (strategic or routine tactics), Consequences (immediate, cumulative, reversible, foreseen or unseen) (Strauss and Corbin 1998)	In the 1998 book, conditions are clustered together, strategies are clustered under actions and consequences elaborated on.
Conditions, interactions and emotions, consequences (Corbin and Strauss 2008)	In the 2008 book, the paradigm loses its prominence and is presented as an optional analytic tool for novice researchers. That said, the conditional/consequence matrix, used in previous editions to think about relationships between micro and macro conditions, now has a more central place in coding.

was always controlled by the emerging theory. The great contribution of their chapter on theoretical sampling in the 1967 book was their assertion that the selection of comparison groups gave control over two aspects of the developing theory – first, conceptual level, and second, population scope. This is expressed in a table on p. 58 of the book, reproduced in this section as Table 4.5, that shows the consequences of minimizing and maximizing differences in groups, and considering the variations *within the data* of those groups. Obviously, variations in the data are expressed by variations in categories.

For Glaser and Strauss, the purpose of selecting groups is not about comparisons between and inside substantive groups, useful though that may be. Their criteria are 'theoretical purpose and relevance – not of structural circumstance' (p. 48).

Glaser and Strauss also lay great stress on either maximizing or minimizing differences between groups to control 'theoretical relevance' (p. 55) of data collection. They also point out that this then has a bearing on categories. For instance, if a similar group is chosen, many more instances of a category will be collected, while important differences might be spotted that were not noticed in earlier data collection. This is important for establishing the properties of a particular category, and Glaser and Strauss suggest that these properties are established *before* differences in groups are maximized.

When maximizing differences between groups, data in a particular category will vary. This allows the researcher to think about the 'strategic similarities' between groups,

Table 4.5 Consequences of minimizing and maximizing differences in comparison groups for generation of theory (Glaser and Strauss, 1967, p. 58)

Group Differences	*Data on Category*	
	Similar	*Diverse*
Minimized	Maximum similarity in data leads to: Verifying usefulness of category; Generating basic properties; Establishing a set of conditions for a degree of category. These can be used for prediction.	Identifying/developing fundamental differences under which category and hypothesis vary.
Maximized	Identifying/developing fundamental uniformities of greatest scope.	Maximum diversity in data quickly forces: Dense developing of properties of categories; integrating of categories and properties; delimiting scope of theory.

which give the uniformities of scope within the theory. They state that maximizing '*brings out the widest possible coverage on ranges, continua, degrees, types, uniformities, variations, causes, conditions, consequences, probabilities of relationships, strategies, process, structural mechanisms, and so forth, all necessary for elaboration of the theory*' (p. 57). We can see here too an early reference to theoretical coding (Glaser 1978) and a recognition that a widening of scope means that relationships between constructs have to be reconsidered. They summarize their recommendations in the table that is reproduced here (Table 4.5).

Another way of thinking about this table is that its key contribution falls into two areas. First, it helps us see that *maximizing differences between groups helps us extend the scope of the theory* we are working on. Second, *we can raise the conceptual level of our substantive theory by considering the categories themselves*. In particular, we can consider the unsaturated categories in our analysis as a promising avenue to raise the conceptual level of the theory, by guiding us to more interesting groups. The fascinating thing about this table is that it draws attention not only to issues of scope, but issues of the data, as expressed by the categories themselves, and how considering categories can improve the quality and conceptual level of the theory.

While Eisenhardt (1989) popularized theoretical sampling for group differences, she did not consider theoretical sampling of concepts in the same way as suggested above. However, she talked about within-case comparison based on categories, which can be seen as a variation of sampling for concepts in the data. The differences in strategy between grounded theorists and mainstream qualitative researchers can perhaps be seen as a consequence of different methodologies for theory building – Eisenhardt (1989) used cases, while grounded theory methodology relies upon slices of data. So, how might these recommendations for theoretical sampling, as suggested by Glaser and Strauss, be carried out? What happens if we try to follow what Table 4.5 suggests?

ENACTING THE RECOMMENDATIONS FOR THEORETICAL SAMPLING

In Vaast and Urquhart (2017), I briefly discuss what Glaser and Strauss's advice on theoretical sampling might mean in practice for the generation of social media theory, and use the example of Facebook statuses. In this section, I expand in detail on that example, and the steps of theory building that I believe are implied by Table 4.5, in order for us to explore what can be learned from those recommendations.

Glaser and Strauss state that, at the beginning of generating a substantive theory, differences should be minimized in comparative groups. We can choose to minimize or maximize differences in groups along several dimensions, such as age, country, language, political affiliation, and so on. Maximizing those differences helps use theorize on relationships, conditions, patterns and mechanisms (Glaser and Strauss 1967, p. 57). In our Facebook example explained below, we may wish to look at slices of data from other online sources, such as personal blogs, Twitter feeds, or how a person responds to other comments from people below the line (BTL) when commenting on a news article. The theoretical sampling and choice of data slices depends on how the theory develops. It is important to realize that the motivations for theoretical sampling are theoretically motivated; it is not a question of simply verifying the category in various populations. How might we operationalize the advice from Glaser and Strauss on theoretical sampling, and how does it help the development of a theory? Each step in the example is cross referenced to Table 4.6 below.

Step 0

Let us imagine we are trying to understand how people use Facebook. Suppose we start with a group of individuals aged 18–25, based in the UK, who use Facebook. By coding their Facebook statuses, we can see that there are many instances of people actively managing their Facebook statuses. Those statuses are chosen, or curated, to give the best possible impression of that person's life and circumstances. We draw this conclusion from the data because there are very few statuses that do not portray the status owner as someone who is successful, surrounded by friends, and enjoying travel. We decide to call this concept or code 'curating'. At the same time, we notice another interesting, minority use of Facebook status – a very personalized status that seems to be aimed at only a few people who might understand it. This concept we choose to call 'personalizing'. At this point, then, we have a choice whether to pursue the theory development via saturated or unsaturated concepts (Lehmann 2010). What should we do next?

We can base our theoretical sampling on either 'curation' – what we could call maximum similarity in data, or 'personalizing', what we could call a fundamental difference in the data as to how people approach their Facebook statuses. In this example, we first choose to pursue the unsaturated concept 'personalizing', in order to learn more about the category, and proceed to Step 1.

Step 1

We would then sample a new Facebook group, of the same age, 18–25, in the same country, for the unsaturated concept of Personalizing. Thus group differences are minimized (it is a similar group) but we are pursuing diverse concepts in the data.

Table 4.6 Example of theory building using Glaser and Strauss's recommendations for comparison groups

Group Differences	*Concepts in the Data*	
	Similar	*Diverse*
Minimized	Maximum similarity in data leads to: Verifying usefulness of category; Generating basic properties; Establishing a set of conditions for a degree of category. These can be used for prediction.	Identifying/developing fundamental differences under which category and hypothesis vary
Example – Sampling Facebook population of similar age and in same country	**Self-presentation through status message. ('Curating') First stage of theory building STEP 0 Improve the theory by theoretical sampling for unsaturated concepts in similar populations →**	**Communicating to a few people through highly personal status message ('Personalizing') Self-presentation through status message. ('Curating')**
		STEP 1 These identified as aspects of a broader category called 'Impression Management' Extend the scope of the theory further by sampling a different group for 'Impression Management'
Maximized	Identifying/developing fundamental uniformities of greatest scope	Maximum diversity in data quickly forces: Dense developing of properties of categories; integrating of categories and properties; delimiting scope of theory
Example – Sampling diverse Facebook population – different ages, different countries	**Managing of Facebook Status. ('Impression Management' consisting of 'Curating', 'Personalizing', and other properties discovered) STEP 2 Extend the scope of the theory further by considering new unsaturated concepts that emerge →**	**Sample for unsaturated concepts discovered in previous phase, to further extend the theory scope and deepen the category of Impression Management STEP 3**

Our slices of data would actively seek out statuses that are Personalizing, for the purpose of learning more about this particular category. This will quickly fill out the category and help us understand how it might vary in different circumstances. Obviously, both 'Curating' and 'Personalizing' could be subsumed into a higher level concept of, say, 'Impression Management' as the theory increases in scope, and we could probably expect new categories to emerge, which can be aspects of 'Impression Management'.

Step 2

We could then proceed to maximize group differences by sampling different age groups, and different countries, in order to deepen the theory and 'identify the fundamental uniformities of greatest scope'. In this stage, we will be paying attention to the saturated concepts of curating, and possibly personalizing. This will further fill out the category 'Impression Management', which consists, at present of curating and personalizing, and perhaps other types of Impression Management discovered in Step 1. So, depending on how the theory is developing and the different properties of 'Impression Management', it might be apposite to sample a Facebook group that is older, or the same age range in a different country, so see if the categories hold true in a different culture. We could also consider whether membership of various Facebook groups has any sway on Impression Management. Thus, the theory is increasing in depth in this stage. Impression Management is also a category that is quite abstract, which in future, may help us towards a formal theory.

Step 3

Again, we would be sampling a different group to maximize group differences, but also considering further unsaturated concepts that have been discovered in Step 2, to delimit the theory and densify the theory. At this stage, one could consider sampling slices of data not from Facebook but other online sources, such as Twitter, or extending the age range further, or sampling more slices from people from various Facebook groups. Obviously, how those differences are maximized has a direct bearing on the theory development, and may also suggest new relationships between concepts. How the category of Impression Management is being filled out will suggest new avenues of theoretical sampling, until the theory is suitably densified and has adequate (theoretical) scope for the research purpose.

Note that this example gives but one route through the table, and it is a matter of judgement of how one might proceed through the table – the choice is to maximize group differences immediately, or pay attention to unsaturated concepts and deepening of the category while minimizing group differences. My own preference is for the latter, as this seems to me the best way to deepen the theory by ensuring it is grounded in lots of instances from a similar group. It's also important to note how, as we might proceed to a formal theory, the category becomes more abstract (in this example, 'Impression Management') and not underpinned by empirical data, as this job is done by the lower-level categories that underpin that more abstract category (in this example, 'Curating' and 'Personalizing', and no doubt many other categories). To me, the contribution of this table is not only understanding that we can extend the scope of a theory by paying attention to like and unlike groups, but that our theoretical sampling can be guided by our categories.

LEVELS AND SCOPE OF THEORY

The previous section discussed, in detail, the guidance available from Glaser and Strauss for theory building using similar and dissimilar groups. It is helpful guidance, so, why is it not more known in the mainstream of qualitative research, and considered in numerous qualitative research textbooks consulted by graduate students? To me, the answer to this question resides in two places. First, in comparatively new disciplines, such as information systems and management, we are still unfamiliar with the process of theory building, and lack theoretical sensitivity, hence the debates on and lack of consensus on theory building in those two disciplines. Grounded theory is unique in how it encourages us to build theory systematically by use of constant comparison and theoretical sampling of groups. It also helps us understand, in detail, how theories shade into another from the substantive to the formal. So many of the newer disciplines lack a deep appreciation for the structures of theories, conveyed in grounded theory by theoretical families and the coding paradigm, and by the idea of theory mechanisms in the social sciences.

Second, by contrast, in the social sciences, there has been indeed a great deal of debate about the nature of theory, largely focused on mechanisms. However, a lot of current discussion on mechanisms tend to focus on opening up the black box, and work from higher levels of theory to lower ones[4] to provide explanations. Davison and Martinsons (2016) complain about a rush to universalism in the information systems discipline, where theories borrowed from other reference disciplines are applied, regardless of the context of that application. They make a plea for the understanding and clear explication of boundary conditions when using theories, lest the context of the study be ignored. My commentary on that article (Urquhart 2016) suggested that particularism versus universalism is a false dichotomy. Grounded theorists know that Glaser (1978) states that levels of theory shade into one another as a theory becomes more and more abstracted, from substantive to formal. Stinchcombe (1991) was keenly aware of the issue of levels of theory when writing about theory mechanisms in social science. His proposition was that paying attention to lower-level mechanisms would result in a more 'supple' theory at the higher level. His definition of mechanisms is:

> (1) a piece of scientific reasoning which is independently verifiable and gives rise to theoretical reasoning, (2) gives knowledge about a component process (generally one with units of analysis at a lower level) of another theory (ordinarily a theory with units at a different 'higher' level) thereby (3) increasing the suppleness, complexity, elegance or believability of the theory at a higher level without excessive multiplication of entities in that higher level theory (4) without doing too much violence (in the necessary simplification at the lower level to make the higher level go) to what we know as the main facts at the lower level. (p. 367)

This description will be immediately be recognizable to grounded theorists as a description of theoretical coding, and the need to ground those theoretical codes at the lower level, while at the same time making sure that the level of abstraction holds.

Figure 4.1 is offered as a summary of Glaser and Strauss's vision of theory building, without compromising the original vision. For me, the key insight of their approach is not that we extend the scope of the theory by sampling different groups, but that we are theoretically guided by category development as we do so.

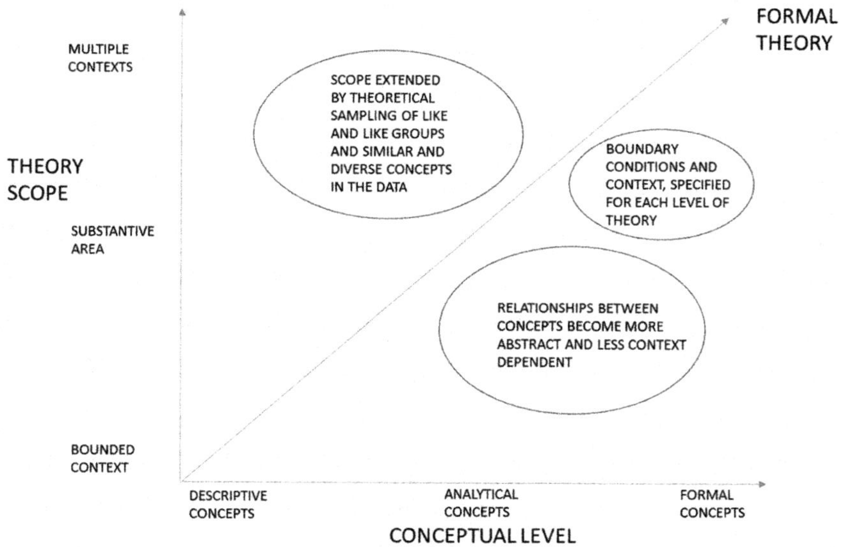

Figure 4.1 Theory Scope and Conceptual Level

The *x* axis represents Conceptual Level, and the *y* axis Theory Scope. These are the two dimensions that are acted upon by following Glaser and Strauss's guidance on theoretical sampling. The process of sampling similar or dissimilar groups extends the scope, but it is by paying attention to saturated and unsaturated concepts that the conceptual level of the theory, and its direction, is considered and worked on.

Theory Scope

The starting point for theory building is a bounded context, where seed concepts are generated. These seed concepts might not even be empirically grounded, and little more than hunches (Urquhart, Lehmann and Myers 2010). Substantive theories, which grounded theorists are very familiar with, pertain to the specific area being investigated, but the concepts generated in that theory exist independently of that data. Formal theories focus on conceptual entities. The scope of a theory is extended by sampling like and unlike groups, guided by concepts in the data. The suggestion here too is that boundary conditions are specified for each level of theory. In grounded theory terms, these boundary conditions are represented by theoretical codes and the categories. The suggestion of Figure 4.1 (and Davison and Martinsons (2016)) is that these conditions and contexts should be clearly specified when a theory is published.

Conceptual Level

When we first begin to code data, we inevitably code descriptively as it is necessary to explain the data to ourselves. As we begin to theorize about the data, and write theoretical memos, our concepts become more analytic and less context dependent. The same applies to the relationships between concepts, where we have the challenge described by

Stinchcombe (1991) of making sure the relationships we posit between concepts at the lower level also reside at the higher level.

DISCUSSION AND CONCLUSION

It is clear from the discussion that Glaser and Strauss did indeed have clear and systematic recommendations for theory building from 1967 onwards. One problem seems to be that, because grounded theory is seen as producing rich, qualitative theories that are about micro phenomena, these recommendations seem not have permeated into the wider academic disciplines in which we work. Layder's critique (Layder 1998) about the hopelessly detailed nature of a grounded theory, it seems, has not been fully put to rest. It is easy to see why – the very nature of the grounded theory process means we start with a very detailed and inimate relationship with the data. This is both the strength and weakness of grounded theory. The scale of the task of building a grounded theory means that we often leave it to others to then take our theories and either apply them to other contexts or test them. One possible route is to take our substantive theories and widen their scope, but the emphasis on novelty, at least in my own discipline, seems to mean that once a substantive theory is published, it cannot be elaborated upon.

That said, my observation of the newer disciplines I work with – management, information systems (IS) and software engineering – is that these disciplines often struggle with theory building and the nature of theory. Unlike my sociologist colleagues, we are largely unfamiliar with the notion of mechanisms or how formal theories are used. Grounded theory offers clear and practical guidelines on how a theory that applies to one area can be extended to another area, and also how the conceptual level of a theory can be pushed to levels of further abstraction. I would contend that newer disciplines can learn from the clarity and systematic nature of Glaser and Strauss's recommendations, because, for those disciplines, advancing new and larger theories are important. There seems to be very little discussion of levels of theory in the newer disciplines – theory is either treated as universal, generally coming from other reference disciplines, and grounded theories are not considered as contributions to the overall theory building effort. Worse, we seem to lack the language to discuss theory and theoretical contribution. In information systems, Burton-Jones, McLean andMonod (2014) make an excellent contribution to the IS theory debate when they suggests moving away from ideas of process/variance theories that are prominent in the discipline towards conceptual latitude and fit, and focusing on constructs and relationships. As Davison and Martinsons (2016) suggest, it would also be helpful if people using and advancing theories considered the context in which they were created, and the context in which they are subsequently applied. Categorizing the type of theoretical contribution could also be fruitful; for instance, Colquitt and Zapata-Phelan (2007) suggest that contributions can be categorized from those which introduce significant new concepts, and examine new relationships and processes, to those that attempt to replicate theories. They then consider to what extent that contribution is grounded, empirically or theoretically (Colquitt and Zapata-Phelan 2007).

The division between grounded theorists and their colleagues will hopefully fade as the division between qualitative and quantitative research recedes. Often, the phenomenon itself will demand a combination of quantitative and qualitative research. We need to change policies via quantitative evidence, but before we do that, we need qualitative research into what people do. The advent of Big Data and the ubiquity of social media calls for both qualitative and quantitative research – understanding patterns in data requires a qualitative understanding of why people do what they do. For too long, in my opinion, Glaser and Strauss's stellar contribution to understanding how we build theory, and how we scale up that theory, have been ignored by the mainstream of many of our academic disciplines. It is my sincere hope that this chapter contributes to interpreting the intentions of Glaser and Strauss's advice on theoretical sampling. Glaser and Strauss represent a huge intellectual contribution to theory building in the twentieth and twenty-first centuries, and these ideas can and should help theory builders everywhere.

Notes

1 Glaser and Strauss (1967) and Glaser's monograph on quantitative GT (Glaser 2008) state that grounded theories can be built from quantitative data. Walsh (2014) gives an interesting illustration of using quantitative GT in a grounded theory building process by means of cluster analysis in a mixed method study.
2 That said, Giddens' view of his own theory has been challenged by proponents of 'strong' structuration theory, in, for example, Stones (2005).
3 I am indebted to Udo Kelle for this insight, and for his very helpful comments on this chapter.
4 I am indebted to my colleague Olga Volkoff for this insight.

ACKNOWLEDGEMENTS

I am very grateful to Udo Kelle, Stefan Seidel, Olga Volkoff and Hamid Pousti, all of whom gave extremely helpful comments on an earlier draft of this chapter.

REFERENCES

Avison, D. and J. Malaurent (2014). Is Theory King? Questioning the Theory Fetish in Information Systems. *Journal of Information Technology 29*: 327–336.

Burton-Jones, A., McLean E. & Monod. E (2014). Theoretical Perspectives on IS Research: From Variance and Process to Conceptual Latitude and Fit. *European Journal of Information Systems 24*(6): 401–419.

Colquitt, J. A. and C. P. Zapata-Phelan (2007). Trends in Theory Building and Theory Testing: A Five-Decade Study of the *Academy of Management Journal*. *Academy of Management Journal 50*(6): 1281–1303.

Corbin, J. and A. L. Strauss (2008). *Basics of Qualitative Research: Techniques and Procedures for Developing Grounded Theory*. Thousand Oaks, CA: Sage.

Corley, K. and D. Gioia (2011). Building Theory about Theory Building: What Consititutes a Theoretical Contribution? *Academy of Management Review 36*(1): 12–32.

Davison, R. M. and M. G. Martinsons (2016). Context is King! Considering Particularism in Research Design and Reporting. *Journal of Information Technology 31*(3): 241–249.

Eisenhardt, K. M. (1989). Building Theories from Case Study Research. *Academy of Management Review 14*: 532–550.

Giddens, A. (1984). *The constitution of society: Outline of the theory of structuration*. Cambridge: Polity Press.

Glaser, B. G. (1978). *Theoretical Sensitivity: Advances in the Methodology of Grounded Theory*. Mill Valley, CA: Sociology Press.

Glaser, B. G. (2005). *The Grounded Theory Perspective III: Theoretical Coding*. Mill Valley, CA: Sociology Press.

Glaser, B. G. (2008). *Doing Quantitative Grounded Theory*. Mill Valley, CA: Sociology Press.

Glaser, B. G. and A. L. Strauss (1967). *The Discovery of Grounded Theory: Strategies for Qualitative Research*. New York: Aldine.

Gregor, S. (2006). The Nature of Theory in Information Systems. *MIS Quarterly 30*(3): 611–642.

Gregor, S. (2014). Theory – Still King but Needing a Revolution! *Journal of Information Technology 29*: 337–340.

Johnson, P., Ekstedt, M and Jacobson I (2012). Where's the Theory for Software Engineering? *IEEE Software* (September/October).

Layder, D. (1998). *Sociological Practice: Linking Theory and Research*. London: Sage.

Lee, A. S. (2014). Theory is King? But First, What is Theory? *Journal of Information Technology 29*: 350–352.

Lehmann, H. (2010). *The Dynamics of International Information Systems: Anatomy of a Grounded Theory Investigation*. New York: Springerlink.

Lester, F. K. (2005). On the Theoretical, Conceptual, and Philosophical Foundations for Research in Mathematics Education. *ZDM 37*(6): 457–467.

Markus, L. M. (2014). Maybe not the King, but an Invaluable Subordinate: A Commentary on Avison and Malaurent's Advocacy of 'Theory Light' IS Research. *Journal of Information Technology 29*: 341–345.

Oswick, C., P. Fleming and G. Hanlon (2011). From Borrowing to Blending: Rethinking the Processes of Organizational Theory Building. *Academy of Management Review 36*(2): 318–337.

Spatz, C. and E. P. Kardas (2008). *Research Methods in Psychology: Ideas, Techniques, and Reports*. New York: McGraw-Hill.

Stinchcombe, A. L. (1991). The Conditions of Fruitfulness of Theorizing about Mechanisms in Social Science. *Philosophy of the Social Sciences 21*(3): 367–388.

Stones, R. (2005). *Structuration Theory*. London: Palgrave.

Strauss, A. L. (1987). *Qualitative Analysis for Social Scientists*. Cambridge, UK: University of Cambridge Press.

Strauss, A. and J. Corbin (1990). *Basics of Qualitative Research: Grounded Theory Procedures and Techniques*. Newbury Park, CA: Sage.

Strauss, A. L. and J. Corbin (1998). *Basics of Qualitative Research: Techniques and Procedures for Developing Grounded Theory*. London: Sage.

Urquhart, C. (2016). Response to Davison and Martinsons: Context is King! Yes and No – It's Still All about Theory (Building). *Journal of Information Technology 31*(3): 254–256.

Urquhart, C. (2013). *Grounded Theory for Qualitative Research: A Practical Guide*. London: Sage.

Urquhart, C., H. Lehmann and M. Myers (2010). Putting the Theory Back into Grounded Theory: Guidelines for Grounded Theory Studies in Information Systems. *Information Systems Journal 20*(4): 357–381.

Vaast E and Urquhart C (2017) Building Grounded Theory with Social Media Data, in: Raza Mir and Sanjay Jain (Eds) *Routledge Companion to Qualitative Research in Organization Studies*, Taylor and Francis: London, pp 408–422.

Walsh, I. (2014). Using Quantitative Data in Mixed-Design Grounded Theory Studies: An Enhanced Path to Formal Grounded Theory in Information Systems. *European Journal of Information Systems 24*(5) pp 531–557.

Weber, R. (2003). Editor's Comments: Theoretically Speaking. *MIS Quarterly 27*(3): iii–xii.

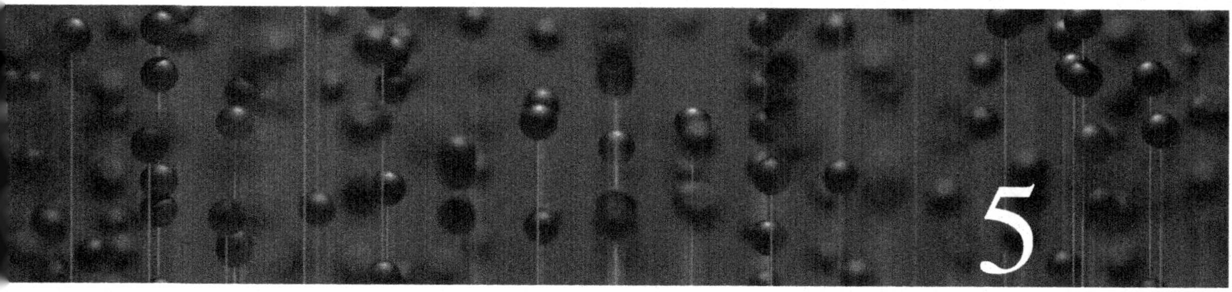

5

Deductive Qualitative Analysis and Grounded Theory: Sensitizing Concepts and Hypothesis-Testing

Jane F. Gilgun

Glaser and Strauss (1967) were clear about the dangers of imposing prior concepts on data, and they also warned against logico-deductive methods that begin with hypotheses that researchers cannot change but either accept or reject them when the analysis is concluded. They also wrote that they hoped their emphasis on theory generation stimulated other researchers 'to codify and publish their own methods of generating theory' (p. 8). Whether they imagined that one day someone would propose an approach to theory development that used both prior concepts and deductive methods I do not know. That, however, is what I propose in this chapter. I also propose the use of positive case analysis, also known as negative case analysis, as a procedure for seeking to undermine, refute, and reformulate emerging findings, thus steering researchers away from imposing prior concepts on data and toward hypothesis-testing that allows for the modification of hypotheses during analysis.

The purposes of this chapter are to describe a method of generating theory – as well as the development of descriptive research such as ethnographies and narratives – that I call deductive qualitative analysis (DQA), to show how DQA responds to Glaser's and Strauss's concerns about deductive research and imposition of concepts on data, and to situate DQA within the traditions of the Chicago School of Sociology. In addition, I will show that deductive processes have a place in Grounded Theory (GT) and that researchers gradually realized this, although Glaser continues to state that GT is based on inductive processes. This chapter is methodological in nature. I provide some guidelines for the conduct of DQA, but I do not intend this chapter to be a how-to-do DQA.

Deductive qualitative analysis is one of three approaches to research associated with the Chicago School of Sociology. The other two are GT and field research, which is descriptive in nature, and sometimes referred to as ethnographic research or field research.

DQA is an updating of analytic induction (AI), which is an approach older than GT and that is also associated with the Chicago School. Deductive qualitative analysis and its predecessor AI allows for qualitative hypothesis-testing as well as concept-guided descriptive research, which is research that begins with sensitizing concepts. The use of sensitizing concepts is traditional in the Chicago School for decades before Blumer (1969) gave them a name (Gilgun 1999b, 2005, 2016). Each of these three types produce findings that are grounded in data on which findings are based. The defining characteristics of DQA are: (1) the use of concepts and/or hypotheses from the onset of the research, (2) positive case analysis that involves the search for data whose meanings might lead to modifications, refutations, and reformulations of concepts and hypotheses, both the initial material and the material that researchers develop over the course of research, and (3) embeddedness in the perspectives of the Chicago School of Sociology.

The Chicago School goes back to the early part of the twentieth century (Bulmer 1984; Deegan 1990; Faris 1967; Fine 1995; Forte 2004; Gilgun 1999b; Low & Bowden 2013). The School, however, in the words of Becker (1999), is 'open to various ways of doing sociology' (p. 10). The ideas underlying DQA are not representative of the entire tradition. Furthermore, sociologists are among my intended audiences but so are members of other disciplines, such as the applied fields of social work, psychology, psychotherapy, family therapy, management, nursing, and other health sciences.

DEDUCTIVE QUALITATIVE ANALYSIS

In this section, I show that:

- DQA is an updating of analytic induction that went into eclipse in the mid-twentieth century;
- DQA, like other approaches to research associated with the Chicago School, is a way of thinking that is consistent with the scientific method;
- deductive reasoning and thinking have at least three forms;
- the Chicago School's ideas about 'complete thinking,' which includes retroduction (abduction), induction, and deduction, are responses to concerns about deductive qualitative research; and
- GT itself has many elements of the Chicago School style of deductive thinking, elements it shares with DQA.

The Evolution of Deductive Qualitative Analysis

Deductive qualitative analysis is an updating of AI, whose procedures guided the work of many Chicago School researchers, including Thomas and Znaniecki (1918–1920), Angell (1936), Becker (1953), Becker, Geer, Hughes, and Strauss (1961), Cressey (1950, 1953), Lindesmith (1947), and Sutherland (1937, 1949). Even Strauss may have used one of the two signature procedures of analytic induction without naming them. For example, Schatzman reported in an interview that Strauss and colleagues (Strauss, Schaztman, Bucher, Ehrlich, & Sabshin 1964) used concepts from organizational theory in their study of interactions in psychiatric hospitals (Gilgun 1993). Both organizational theory and the notion of interactions were present from the onset of their study, which would make the study an example of analytic induction because of its use of sensitizing concepts. Schatzman described how he, Strauss and colleagues did prolonged observations, had long discussions that included disagreements, and continual analysis of data to identify and then to document the theory of negotiated order that they built from the analysis and from their initial sensitizing concepts.

By the mid-1950s, analytic induction fell into disrepute after a series of articles pointed out deficits. The deficits were not in its core procedures, which are use of stand-alone concepts and hypotheses from the onset of inquiries and negative case analysis, but for its purported claims to being able to produce causal, universal hypotheses (Glaser & Strauss 1967; Goldenberg 1993; Manning 1982; Robinson 1951; Vidich & Lyman 2000). Some researchers made these claims, but, as discussed earlier, other researchers stated that findings are provisional and subject to revision, in other words, indeterminate.

Claims of causality were typical. Becker (1953), for instance, discussed his theory of marijuana use as if he had captured causal processes. Both Cressey (1953) in his study of embezzling and Lindesmith (1947) in his study of opium addiction assumed that their hypotheses are causal, although they never clearly stated what they meant by this term. Lindesmith reflected on whether, in order to establish causal relationships, effects are 'necessary' or simply 'understandable' when they come after alleged causes (p. 98). This suggests that he may have been thinking of cause as associational and not determinate.

Cressey (1953) also briefly discussed cause, basing his views on Mill's (1843) method of logic, but he also viewed his findings as provisional, as discussed earlier. Sutherland (1949) was so adamant about the causal nature of hypotheses related to the origins of crime that he may have provoked a backlash against analytic induction, for which he was a powerful advocate. Laub and Sampson (1991) provided detail on the controversies that Sutherland stirred. Analytic induction attained a 'spoiled identity.'

Researchers who used analytic induction argued that they must state their hypotheses in universal terms in order for them to be testable. Lindesmith (1947) drew upon Braithwaite (1960), Lewin (1935), and Znaniecki (1934) to make this argument. He pointed out that because a hypothesis stated in universal terms 'claims much, it is easily disproved if it is indeed false' (p. 19). Within the spirit of falsifiability, Becker (1953) stated he wrote his hypotheses in universal language so as to permit testing. Hammersley (2011) wrote one of a few recent articles on analytic induction, and he affirmed the claims of some researchers that analytic induction produces causal, universal hypotheses. He cites no research using analytic induction since the mid-twentieth-century work of Becker, Cressey, and Lindesmith. A search for articles using the term 'analytic induction' show only a few articles in the last half century, including one I wrote (Gilgun 1995) more than 20 years ago. How researchers who used analytic induction defined cause and universality is open to interpretation, but I suspect that all but Sutherland viewed both as indeterminate. Their critics defined these terms for them and rejected their claims. This appears to have caused lasting damage to all of the tenets of analytic induction.

I believe the term *analytic induction* is so deeply linked to deterministic notions of causality and universality that it has a spoiled identity. The term may best be left as part of a history that researchers have overlooked for decades. In response to these issues, I coined the term *deductive qualitative analysis*. Deductive qualitative analysis moves away from problematic issues connected to analytic induction and preserves and updates procedures and principles that have much to offer, as I will show in this chapter.

I also sought to re-work AI because I wanted to promote the development and testing of theory qualitatively. As a graduate student in family studies, I was imbued with the importance of theory development, although how to do so was unclear. Cressey's (1950) account of how he tested and revised theory qualitatively showed a way to do this. Even Glaser and Strauss (1967) thought testing grounded theory was vital. They wrote:

> When the vital job of testing a newly generated theory begins, the evidence from which it was generated is quite likely to be forgotten or ignored. Now, the focus is on the new evidence that will be used for verifying only part of the theory. Furthermore, sociologists will find it worthwhile to risk a period in their careers in order to test grounded theories, since these theories are certain to be highly applicable to areas under study. (pp. 28–29)

They, however, did not offer suggestions about how to do this. While there may be other ways to test theories qualitatively, the procedures I discuss in this chapter show one viable way. I wrote many other published and non-published papers to arrive at the formulations present in the current chapter (Gilgun 2001, 2004, 2005, 2007, 2008, 2010, 2012a, 2012b, 2014, 2015).

Other reasons to re-introduce deductive procedures into qualitative research is that most researchers are trained in deductive approaches, meaning we are trained to do literature reviews, define terms, and develop research questions and hypotheses. We are primed to begin research with conceptual material. With the procedures of DQA, we can avoid a concern of Glaser and Strauss (1967), which was the imposition of theory on data regardless of fit. They advocated for theories that were linked or grounded to data. They also advocated for concepts and theories that earned their way into the analysis because of their fit with data. The procedures of DQA pay heed to these concerns. Positive case analysis ensures links between concepts and data and shows how to reject concepts and theories that do not fit.

Gatekeepers will not approve proposals for funding and for dissertation research without literature reviews and the other usual components of research plans. Deductive qualitative analysis clarifies confusion about proposal writing when research is supposed to be about constructing something new in the process of doing the research. Research can begin with tightly constructed literature reviews, clearly defined concepts, and research questions and hypotheses. Strauss (1987) recommended that students who are preparing to write proposals do preliminary fieldwork to identify a focus and a literature review to add to their understandings. They could still implement the procedures of grounded theory if they entered the field with minds as open as possible. From my point of view, the principles of positive case analysis positions researchers to challenge their presuppositions and emerging findings. The procedures of DQA provide guidance for doing research as Glaser and Strauss (1967) envisioned it, as well as how other researchers in the Chicago tradition envisioned it. A contribution of DQA is clarity about the use of existing research and theory.

A Way of Thinking

The idea that DQA is a way of thinking is important to the case I make in this chapter. In making the case, I am following in the footsteps of researchers associated with the Chicago School of Sociology. Bob Bogdan (Bogdan & Biklen 2007), who through his teaching and writing has guided many researchers in how they do fieldwork, or descriptive qualitative research, pointed out that qualitative research is about thinking conceptually. He said about his training in fieldwork, also sometimes called ethnography, with Blanche Geer (Becker, Geer, & Hughes 1968; Becker et al. 1961): 'Blanche modeled how to think conceptually. What I got out of her seminar was not the content. She was teaching a way of thinking' (Gilgun 1992, p. 9). Geer earned a PhD in sociology from the University of Chicago and is a researcher in the tradition of the Chicago School of Sociology. Glaser (1978) emphasized the centrality of ideas in qualitative research and for sociology in general: 'Good ideas contribute the most to the science of sociology' (p. 8). Also, Strauss (1992) wrote, grounded theory 'is a general way of thinking about analysis' (p. 2).

DQA and the Scientific Method

In DQA, researchers begin their studies with concepts and hypotheses with the hope that the conceptual material will aid their thinking in terms of the insights they provide and the directions of inquiry they suggest. In brief, concepts and hypotheses in DQA serve sensitizing purposes in the spirit of Blumer's (1969) ideas about sensitizing concepts. Researchers using DQA are curious and not doctrinaire about the helpfulness of initial conceptual material. I, for example, begin my research with the hope that the initial material will help me see what I might otherwise not have seen and that the analysis in which I engage will led to refutation and reformulation of the initial material and thus to a closer fit between the resulting conceptual material and the data that are the foundation of my theorizing. One of the clearest examples of research that begins with hypotheses and that involves the modification of hypotheses during data collection and analysis is the study of Cressey (1950, 1953) of embezzlers. Cressey began with a hypothesis that he developed from research by Sutherland (1937, 1949) on white-collar crime that posited that embezzlers consider embezzlement a technical violation and ended with the hypothesis that embezzlers consider embezzlement to be illegal and to be a violation of financial trust that arises from seeking solutions to non-shareable problems.

At their core, the procedures of DQA compose a form of scientific method, with scientific method involving hypotheses, tests of hypotheses, and revisions (Anderson & Hepburn 2015; Osbeck 2014; Yuan 2005), or conjectures, refutations, and reformulations (Popper 1969). In DQA, the initial conceptual material composes the conjectures, and positive case analysis and related procedures of analysis are the vehicles for refutations. Researchers refute and reformulate part or all of the conceptual material when their interpretations of data provide the evidence to do so.

Blumer (1969), who used the term *sensitizing concepts* to describe initial material, described them as notions that help researchers to focus their inquiries and to notice and name aspects of phenomena they might otherwise have overlooked. Blumer's understanding of sensitizing concepts is a principle upon which I base DQA. Along with Waller (1934) and others from the Chicago School, Blumer also pointed out that, as helpful as initial concepts and theory are, they also may blind researchers to other aspects of phenomena that might be significant to their understandings. Such a consequence of the use of initial theory led researchers to purposefully think about and search for exceptions to their emerging findings. They gave the search for exceptions the name *negative case analysis* (Becker 1953; Cressey 1950; Gilgun 1995, 2001, 2007, 2008, 2014, 2015; Znaniecki 1934). Researchers sought negative cases in order to revise emerging findings so that their thinking accounts for exceptions and contradictions, and thus account more fully for possible diversity in findings.

In DQA, the term *positive case analysis* takes the place of the term *negative case analysis* because the search for exceptions and the desire for diversity of findings are positive goals. Positive case analysis guides researchers to construct theory and descriptions that account for patterns and exceptions to general patterns over the course of the research. Consistent with notions of indeterminacy (Charmaz 2014), the findings of DQA are provisional, subject to revision when researchers have evidence to do so.

Recognition of the provisional nature of research findings has a long history in the Chicago School. For instance, Thomas and Znaniecki (1927), early contributors to the Chicago School, stated that, although they sought to develop 'generally applicable conclusions,' they did not consider their work on Polish immigrants in Europe and the United States as giving 'any definitive and universally valid sociological truths' (pp. 340–341). Rather, they said that their work is suggestive and prepares the ground for further research. Cressey (1950), at the end of his account of the multiple times that he changed his theory of embezzlement during data collection and analysis, wrote about his final hypothesis: 'the fact that it was revised several times probably means that future revisions will be necessary' (p. 743).

Sources of Initial Material

In DQA, sources of initial concepts and hypotheses can be from anywhere, including indigenous knowledge, experiences of disempowered persons, hunches, researcher personal and professional experiences, published research and theory, and conceptual frameworks that others have constructed (Cressey 1950, 1953; Gilgun 1995, 2012a, 2015; Lindesmith 1947). Researchers do not judge the viability of initial material according to its source; what is at issue is whether and how initial material illuminates aspects of phenomena of interest and how the initial material is tested and elaborated upon. Unlike quantitative deductive analysis, the tenets of DQA guide researchers to modify hypotheses and concepts during the course of research as they have evidence to do so. The quality of the testing, refutations, and reformulations is what counts. Even Glaser and Strauss (1971) used a conceptual framework in the development of a formal theory of status passage. They defined formal theory as a general theory related to a 'formal or conceptual area of sociological inquiry, such as stigma, deviation behavior' and others (p. v).

Using the codes and frameworks of others is a viable way of applying and developing theory. For example, I used the codes of Roland Barthes in my analysis of a case of family murder (Gilgun 1999a) and the concepts of justice and care from the work of Gilligan (Brown & Gilligan 1992; Gilligan 1982; Gilligan, Ward, Taylor, & Bardige 1988) in an analysis of the moral discourse of incest perpetrators (Gilgun 1995). The family murder project was descriptive, and the family incest study involved hypothesis test and modification. I found that these pre-established codes helped me to see what I until then had overlooked. Not only was I the interviewer for the life histories upon which both articles were based, but I had read the transcripts many times. It wasn't until I chose Barthes' and Gilligan's concepts out of a hunch that they might be helpful that I saw new dimensions in the accounts of research participants.

These ideas did not activate themselves in my mind when I did earlier analyses of these cases. I was theoretically insensitive to these ideas. Rather, the ideas came from an external source. I was curious about their usefulness in my research on violence. It would not have occurred to me to ask questions of the data that their ideas stimulated. These prior ideas increased my theoretical sensitivity. In turn, they become provisional codes subject to testing, revision, rejection, and replacement as I analyzed transcripts, fieldnotes, and other data.

Deduction

There are at least three different versions of deduction in the social sciences. One is the logico-deductive approach that troubled Glaser and Strauss (1967). A second is syllogistic logic, and the third is deduction as Chicago School of Sociology methodologists understood it. Peirce (1998), an originator of American pragmatism, discussed the concept of retroduction, which he also called abduction, as part of scientific research that begins with retroduction and involves deduction and induction.

Hypothetico-deductive processes

Hypothetico-deductive research is usually quantitative in nature and is the type of research that is most commonly taught in higher education in the United States. Researchers construct hypotheses from existing research and theory, and they test the hypotheses in a series of clearly specified steps. They do not change hypotheses during the course of data collection and analysis. The analysis ends when researchers have evidence that the hypotheses were not refuted or that they were. If the hypotheses were refuted, then researchers reformulate them. Researchers then can test the reformulated and the unrefuted hypotheses in other projects.

Logico-deductive research procedures may underlie the concerns of Glaser and Strauss (1967) when they said logico-deductive research obstructs 'scientific intelligence.' Some contemporary researchers, such as Corley (2015) and Walsh et al. (2015), object to deduction on the grounds that researchers cannot modify findings in the course of the research. Glaser is the last author of the Walsh et al. article, and so we can assume that he continues to view deduction in terms of logico-deductive research and possibly deductive logic. Glaser and colleagues apparently are unaware of thinking about deduction as a flexible process within the Chicago School of Sociology. Bryant (2017) also raised concerns about the immutability of hypotheses in 'hypothesis-based research' where the hypotheses are 'fixed, definitive statements for all time' (p. 109). He called upon Glaser and Strauss's (1967) criterion of modifiability as a guideline for the development of grounded theories. Modifiability does not fit quantitative logico-deductive research, but it does fit DQA, as I discussed earlier and discuss in more detail below.

Syllogistic logic

Another type of deduction is syllogistic logic. Syllogisms have a major premise, a minor premise, and a conclusion. Perhaps the most famous is All men are mortal (major premise), Socrates is a man (minor premise), and therefore Socrates is mortal (conclusion). The conclusion is the deduction, drawn from the logic of the major and minor premises (Langerlund 2016). Although syllogisms appear to be fixed and determinate, concrete instances can force changes in major premises.

Syllogistic logic could also be part of objections to hypothesis-testing among grounded theorists because of its inflexibility in movement from major to minor premise and then to the conclusion. However, with the DQA approach, researchers pose hypotheses with the expectation that analysis will lead to changing them. In fact, I do DQA in order the change the initial material because I expect new data sets will contain information that I did not have previously. When there is no evidence for modification, then researchers do not change them. This is unlikely, but open-minded researchers would see such an outcome as possible.

The Chicago School's 'complete thinking'

In the Chicago School of Sociology, deduction involves movement from the general to the particular and is inseparable from inductive reasoning (Gilgun 2016). Znaniecki (1934) stated that this ongoing movement between concepts and the empirical world is the basis for knowledge development. Dewey (1933) called this movement 'complete thinking' (p. 82) and 'a complete act of thought' (p. 73). For Dewey (1910), deduction is a process of testing hypotheses for the purposes of 'confirming, refuting, and modifying' them (p. 82), while induction guides researchers to attempt to be open-minded and set aside their preconceptions and biases to the extent possible in order to see concrete instances in new ways. Dewey acknowledged the impossibility of purging the self of presuppositions, but he recommended the attempt. Researchers like me, who have done qualitative research within the Chicago tradition for decades, have applied these ideas uncountable numbers of times.

Retroduction

Peirce, an American pragmatist and one of Dewey's teachers (Burch 2014), may have influenced Dewey's thinking on the relationship between induction and deduction. Peirce had an interest not only in relationships between deduction and induction, but also how researchers arrive at the initial hypotheses to test, a process he called *retroduction* or *abduction* (Burch 2014; Daniel 2008; Mcauliffe 2015; Peirce 1998). (I prefer the term *retroduction* because *abduction* has negative connotations derived from my research on violence.) Abduction or retroduction is a way of thinking that starts with surprising, puzzling, unexpected observations that Peirce called 'fallible insights' (p. 532) that stimulate scientists to come up with what he calls guesses, inferences, of fallible hypotheses about what might have preceded the observation. This is a kind of retrospective or retroductive reasoning, from C back to A, as Peirce described the process.

Retroduction in practice involves the generation of hypotheses to explain the puzzling event and then choosing the most plausible. Researchers choose plausible hypotheses not by testing them empirically but by reasoning and doing a kind of thought experiment. The next step is to subject the most plausible hypotheses to syllogistic logic in order to formulate hypotheses that researchers test. The hypotheses scientists deduce are then subjected to empirical testing. In Peirce's (1998) words, plausible explanations become hypotheses whose 'deductive consequences may be experimentally tested' (p. 532). Peirce's views on abduction, deduction, and induction are similar to Popper's (1969) notions of conjectures, refutations, and reformulations. Conjectures for Peirce, however, are composed of at least two process: retroduction (abduction) and then the deducing of testable hypotheses.

First comes the unexpected, surprising finding and then comes the retrospective search for theory that might aid to understanding, or reasoning from C back to A or several As. Abduction occurs at the beginning of an investigation, as I found in my reading of Peirce (1998), and that my reading of Mcauliffe (2015) confirmed.

Retroductive Logic, DQA, and GT

Retroductive logic provides a rationale for the use of initial conceptual material in the conduct of research in that it assumes that researchers begin their inquiries with hypotheses and also explains how researchers identify and develop the hypotheses in the first place. Two of the three defining characteristics of DQA are related to this description of retroduction: the use of initial conceptual material and the fact that these ideas are part of Chicago School perspectives. The third defining characteristic, positive case analysis, also is part of Chicago School perspectives, and this procedure is a component of the scientific method, not only as Peirce understood it, but as the scientific method is generally understood. To my knowledge, Peirce did not advocate for purposefully seeking cases that would support the modification of hypotheses but I cannot imagine that he would oppose it.

Methodologists see a place for retroduction, which they call abduction, in the procedures of GT. More than 40 years after Glaser and Strauss (1967) originated GT, methodologists began to recognize that retroduction, which they call abduction, may fit some analytic procedures such as where researchers consider many plausible theories to explain unexpected findings they identify in the course of data collection and analysis (Bryant 2009; Charmaz 2014, 2017; Morgan 2007; Reichertz 2007). They recognized that this is not an inductive process, but is abductive (retroductive) in nature, where researchers search for theory that might enlighten the ongoing analysis. An emerging consensus is that abduction is both an initial process and a process that occurs during data collection and analysis (Bryant 2009; Charmaz 2017). For instance, Bryant said one understanding of abduction is akin to Popper's conjecture, and the second involved processes that occur during analysis. Charmaz described Peirce's (1998) initial processes of abduction as I did earlier. She then moved to describe abduction as a kind of problem-solving that takes places as researchers considered plausible theoretical explanations for the emerging findings and move back and forth between examinations of data and theories that might aid in the analysis.

If GT involves both initial and within-analysis abduction, then grounded theorists have legitimized beginning research with conceptual material, which, as discussed, is a defining characteristic of DQA. It is no leap to move from GT methodologists' notions of initial abductive processes and the use of many kinds of initial conceptual material, as is the practice in DQA. Logically, the processes would be the same. Once in the field, DQA researchers operate like those who do GT: they put aside the initial material to the extent possible and attempt to be open-minded about what they notice in data; in other words, to engage in the second type of abductive reasoning.

Deductive qualitative analysis positions researchers to be theoretically sensitive in ways that GT may not. Doing literature reviews before entering the field not only alerts researchers to what is known and what could do with further investigation, but also sensitizes researchers to what might be significant in their areas of interest. As Covan (2007) reported, not being theoretically sensitive is an issue for newer researchers. I have found theoretical sensitivity to be a continuing issue even after my 35-year research career. Researchers overlook what might be significant if we are not familiar with a range of theories. Bryant (2009) made a case for abductive reasoning as contributing to theoretical sensitivity. Using initial conceptual material also contributes to theoretical sensitivity.

Positive case analysis is a pro-active procedure of DQA that guides the researcher to purposefully seek data whose meanings can add to and challenge any emerging concepts and working hypotheses. Theoretical sampling, a term that originated with GT, may at some points serve similar purposes, especially since some grounded theorists also suggest that researchers search for negative cases in addition to doing theoretical sampling. For instance, Glaser and Strauss (1967), Corbin and Strauss (2015), and Charmaz (2014) recommended that researchers look for negative cases, which they describe as cases that are exceptions to emerging findings and that add dimensions to findings.

The search for negative cases is a deductive process in that it requires researchers to have concepts in mind in order to recognize a case as different from others. Selective, axial, and theoretical coding also are deductive processes. They require that researchers apply concepts to data while also seeking establish connections between concepts, sometimes called categories. (See Glaser & Holton 2004; Corbin & Strauss 2015.) Constant comparison is also deductive because researchers must have concepts constructed from the concrete instances they are comparing.

In conclusion, abductive and deductive processes are part of GT. One of the two meanings of abduction acknowledges the importance of conjectures, turning conjectures into hypotheses, and then testing hypotheses. The second meaning is a description of processes involved in analysis. In addition, there are deductive as well as inductive processes in GT, as GT methodologists have pointed out. If this assessment is accurate, then GT methodologists have opened the door for DQA which is as clear as possible about the use of initial conceptual material and the importance of deductive thinking and procedures as well as the importance of induction. DQA also has procedures that deal with the threats that some types of deductive reasoning pose to the integrity of theory-generating and theory-guided research.

Other Deductive Aspects of GT

There are other deductive aspects of GT that support my assertion that it makes sense to begin research with explicit conceptual material. For instance, Glaser and Strauss (1967) and other methodologists (Charmaz 2014; Corbin & Strauss 2015; Glaser & Holton 2004) noted the importance of researchers' insights and perspectives, which involve deductive thinking in the style of the Chicago School. These discussions contain elements of retroduction (abduction).

Insight

According to Glaser and Strauss (1967), the generation of theory from data requires insight. From their points of view, insight has three sources: reflections on personal experience, on related research and theory, and on the meanings of data. They said, 'The root source of all significant theorizing is the sensitive insights of the observer himself [sic]' (p. 251). Insights that contribute to theory, however, must be systematically and adequately investigated and developed so that they can move beyond anecdote, an idea that is consistent with Peirce's (1998) notion of abduction. Strauss (1987) continued to discuss the role of insight in generating questions as well as how insight is connected to experience and induction. Charmaz (2014) mentioned insight 72 times in her most recent text on constructivist GT, such as her statement: 'A pivotal insight or realization of analytic connections can happen any time during the research process' (location 918). The most recent edition of Corbin and Strauss (2015) had 107 mentions, such as insight gives GT its 'dynamic edge' (location 522).

Insight is part of the tradition of the Chicago School of Sociology. Waller (1934) maintained that qualitative insight is the basis of knowledge and is the 'touchstone of scientific method' (p. 288). Waller extended this idea to include a central place for non-observables such as imagination in scientific methods and processes. He wrote:

> The application of insight as the touchstone of method enables us to evaluate properly the role of imagination in scientific method. The scientific process is akin to the artistic process; it is a process of selecting out those elements of experience which fit together and recombining them in the mind. Much of this kind of research is simply ceaseless mulling over, and even the physical scientist has considerable need of an armchair. (p. 290)

Insight and imagination, then, are long-standing components of Chicago School of Sociology knowledge-building and are part of both GT and DQA.

Researchers' perspectives

Researchers' perspectives also have a role in Glaser and Strauss's (1967) thinking about theory generation. In a footnote, they said that researchers are not *tabula rasa* and therefore they have perspectives that help them 'see relevant data and abstract significant categories from his [sic] scrutiny of the data' (p. 3). This is a description of theoretical sensitivity (Glaser 1978) that involves researchers' general stores of knowledge, including personal and professional experience, that is characterized by movement from theory to data to theory, or the kind of inductive-deductive reasoning that Dewey (1933) and Znaniecki (1934) discussed and that GT methodologists increasingly acknowledge, as discussed earlier. Researchers' experiences and the theories with which they are familiar sensitize researchers to aspects of the phenomena of interest that they might otherwise overlook. This is the deductive dimension of the deduction-induction process. Perspectives provide researchers with frameworks that sensitize them to what might be operative in data. Covan (2007), as a student, wrote she was in awe of her teacher Glaser's knowledge of theory and thus of his theoretical sensitivity, but as a student, she noted that she had a way to go to have in-depth knowledge of theory, despite her already considerable exposure to sociological theories.

Charmaz and Strauss also addressed issues related to researchers' perspectives. Charmaz (2014), who revised procedures and methodological principles of GT to be responsive to contemporary thought about constructivism, sees researchers' perspectives as pivotal. This makes sense, since perspectives are foundational to constructivism. Strauss also wrote about the social constructions of our understandings of reality (Corbin & Strauss 2015; Strauss 1987), although he comes across in some of this writings as a positivist (Charmaz 2014). Researchers' perspectives as influencing what they notice and how they interpret what they notice are well-established in social research (Kelle 2005).

To conclude, hopefully it is clear that deduction comes in several varieties and in doing qualitative analysis, induction, deduction, and retroduction are in continual interplay, along with researchers' insights and perspectives. These processes in combination fit with Dewey's concept of complete thinking and are foundational for understanding ways of thinking in the doing of DQA and GT.

DQA, GT, and Descriptive Research

Glaser (1992, 2016) appears to be the only GT methodologist who opposes using procedures associated with GT to develop descriptive research. Those who affirm the possibility have ties to the Chicago School of Sociology and its tradition of field research which is descriptive in nature. For Glaser, using procedures associated with GT results in the downgrading and eroding of the goal of the development of grounded theory, while he also stated that descriptive research is 'quite worthy, respectable and acceptable' (Glaser & Holton 2004, n.p.). Other GT methodologists, such as Corbin and Strauss (2015) and Charmaz (2014) accept description as an outcome of research using procedures they associate with GT. They want researchers to be clear whether their goal is the development of theory or of descriptions. Charmaz (2014) wrote that researchers can adapt procedures associated with GT to do various types of research without having a goal of theory development. Some of the confusion may be a result of the conflation of the two on the part of some GT methodologists. For instance, in their various writings together, Strauss and Corbin have blended the two, rather than making them distinct, for example, as is shown in the titles of the various editions of their text: *Basics of Qualitative Research*, with *Techniques and Procedures for Developing Grounded Theory* as the subtitle. I have never understood these titles. In the main title, the claim is that they are showing readers how to do qualitative research, and in the subtitle they are showing readers how to develop grounded theory.

Field studies, often called ethnographies, are intrinsic to Chicago School traditions (Bogdan & Biklen 2007; Lofland, Snow, Anderson, & Lofland 2006). Most of the early Chicago School monographs are descriptive. Anderson's (1923) ethnography of homeless men, one of the many Chicago School urban ethnographies, made light of theory in research when he noted that 'the book contained not a single sociological concept' (p. 403). His book contains concepts, of course, but not highly abstract concepts and hypotheses; rather, his book uses concepts that organize and bring order to his descriptive findings.

The procedures of DQA and GT guide researchers to identify concepts as well as theories, and thus they both are useful for descriptive research. Furthermore, if researchers are going to theorize, they first need descriptive material on which to base their theorizing. A grounded theory typically presents itself with the theory and the data on which the theory is based. The data are descriptive in nature. Glaser, however, does not present the descriptive material on which he bases his theory, as the perusal of his research reports shows. He also does not recommend recording and transcribing interviews; instead he relies on memos (Glaser 1992). Glaser's brand of theory development does not rely on the careful assembly of supporting material. Furthermore, Glaser appears to be unfamiliar with the Chicago School of Sociology in general and ethnographic research in particular, which could also contribute to his rejection of descriptive research that methods associated with GT might generate.

While much more can be said about descriptive qualitative research, I will make three general observations in response to Glaser's (2016) 'No No' about GT and descriptive research. One, the procedures associated with GT, such as theoretical sensitivity, comparison, and coding, are not original to GT but are generic procedures in qualitative research that are part of Chicago School traditions and other traditions in qualitative research. Researchers can and do use them to develop descriptions. Two, descriptions require concepts because something has to organize descriptive findings. Concepts do this. If researchers want to build theories, which in the Chicago tradition, are abstract statements of relationships from descriptive material (Gilgun 2005), that can be a good thing, but not essential. Three, in order to build a case for the trustworthiness of theories, researchers provide sufficient descriptive material that allows readers to come to their own conclusions which might differ from the conclusions of the researchers. This is a principle associated with the Chicago School, a principle that Becker et al. (1961) stated in their field study of medical school education.

DISCUSSION

Deductive qualitative analysis is one of three types of research associated with the Chicago School of Sociology. The other two are GT and fieldwork, which is descriptive in nature. The three defining characteristics of DQA are not only compatible with descriptive research and GT, but GT methodologists provide some basis for these defining characteristics, such as their notion of abduction and the search for negative cases. Recently, GT methodologist have explored GT's roots in the Chicago School (Bryant 2009, 2017; Charmaz 2014, 2017; Corbin & Strauss 2015), cross-validating my attempts to show DQA's roots in the Chicago School.

Deductive qualitative analysis is clear about the place of initial research and theory and also has procedures for avoiding the pitfalls that Glaser and Strauss (1967) and more contemporary methodologists have about deduction in qualitative research. Besides clarity, other reasons for making a place for explicit deductive procedures in qualitative research is that most researchers are trained in deductive approaches, meaning we are trained to do literature reviews, define terms, and develop research questions and hypotheses. We are primed to begin research with conceptual material. Researchers can avoid a concern of Glaser and Strauss (1967), which was the imposition of theory on data regardless of fit, through positive case analysis, the continual testing of concepts and theories for fit, and the notions of conjectures, refutations, and reformulation, which are procedures of the scientific method. Positive case analysis ensures the identification and construction of links between concepts and data and shows how to reject or modify representations of concepts and theories that do not fit.

In conclusion, DQA is a way of doing research that builds on skills and expectations that most researchers already have, while it also fulfills the goals that Glaser and Strauss (1967) had for GT. Deductive qualitative analysis is a response to Glaser and Strauss's invitation to researchers to develop other ways of developing theory. As I have shown, DQA and GT have much in common, owing not only to their common roots but also to what I have come to see as common-sense processes that are encoded in the scientific method.

REFERENCES

Anderson, H. & Hepburn, B. (2015). Scientific method. *Stanford Encyclopedia of Philosophy*. http://plato.stanford.edu/entries/scientific-method/

Anderson, N. (1923). *The hobo: The sociology of the homeless man*. Chicago, IL: University of Chicago Press.

Angell, Robert C. (1936). *The family encounters the depression*. New York: Scribner.

Becker, H. (1953). Becoming a marihuana user. *American Journal of Sociology*, *59*, 235–242.

Becker, H. S. (1999). The Chicago School, so-called. *Qualitative Sociology*, *22*(1), 3–12.

Becker, H. S., Geer, B., & Hughes, E. (1968). *Making the grade*. New York: Wiley.

Becker, H. S., Geer, B., Hughes, E. C., & Strauss, A. L. (1961). *Boys in white: Student culture in medical school*. Chicago, IL: University of Chicago Press.

Blumer, H. (1969). What is wrong with social theory? In Herbert Blumer (1969/1986), *Symbolic interactionism* (pp. 140–152). Berkeley, CA: University of California Press. Originally published in *Vol. XIX* in *The American Sociological Review*.

Bogdan, R. C. & Biklen, S. K. (2007). *Qualitative research for education* (5th ed.). Boston, MA: Allyn & Bacon.

Braithwaite, R. B. (1960). *Scientific explanation: A study of the function of theory, probability, and law in science*. New York: Harper.

Brown, L. M. & Gilligan, C. (1992). *Meeting at the crossroads: Women's psychology and girls' development*. Cambridge, MA: Harvard University Press.

Bryant, A. (2009). Grounded theory and pragmatism: The curious case of Anselm Strauss [113 paragraphs]. *Forum Qualitative Sozialforschung / Forum: Qualitative Social Research*, *10*(3), Article 2, http://nbn-resolving.de/urn:nbn:de:0114-fqs090325.

Bryant, A. (2017). Grounded theory and grounded theorizing: Pragmatism in research practice. Oxford: Oxford University Press.

Bulmer, M. (1984). The Chicago School of Sociology: Institutionalization, diversity, and the rise of sociological research. Chicago, IL: University of Chicago Press.

Burch, R. (2014). Charles Sanders Pierce. *Stanford Encyclopedia of Philosophy* (Winter 2014 Edition). Ed. Edward N. Zalta, https://plato.stanford.edu/archives/win2014/entries/peirce/.

Charmaz, K. (2014). Constructing grounded theory: A practical guide through qualitative analysis (2nd ed.). London: Sage.

Charmaz, K. (2017). The power of constructivist grounded theory for critical inquiry. *Qualitative Inquiry*, *23*(1), 34–45.

Corbin, J. & Strauss, A. (2015). Basics of qualitative research: Techniques and procedures for developing grounded theory (4th ed.). Beverly Hills, CA: Sage.

Corley, K. G. (2015). A commentary on 'What grounded theory is…' Engaging a phenomenon from the perspective of those living it. *Organizational Research Methods*, *18*(4), 600–605.

Covan, E. K. (2007). The discovery of grounded theory in practice: The legacy of multiple methods mentors. In A. Bryant & K. Charmaz (Eds.), *The Sage handbook of grounded theory* (pp. 58–93). Thousand Oaks, CA: Sage.

Cressey, D. R. (1950). Criminal violation of financial trust. *American Sociological Review*, *15*(6), 738–743.

Cressey, D. R. (1953). *Other people's money*. Glencoe, IL: Free Press.

Daniel, J. (2008). From ugly duckling to swan: C. S. Peirce, abduction, and the pursuit of scientific theories. *Transactions of the Charles S. Peirce Society*, *44*(3), 446–468.

Deegan, M. J. (1990). Jane Addams and the men of the Chicago School, 1892–1918. New Brunswick, NJ: Transaction.

Dewey, J. (1910). *How we think*. Amherst, NY: Prometheus.

Dewey, J. (1933). *How we think* (2nd ed.). New York: D.C. Heath.

Faris, R. E. L. (1967). *Chicago sociology: 1920–1932*. Chicago, IL: University of Chicago Press.

Fine, G. A. (Ed.) (1995). *A second Chicago School?* Chicago, IL: University of Chicago Press.

Forte, J. A. (2004). Symbolic interactionism and social work: A forgotten legacy. Part 1. *Families in Society*, *85*(3), 391–400.

Gilgun, J. F. (1992). Field methods training in the Chicago School traditions: The early career of Bob Bogdan. *Qualitative Family Research*, *6*(1), 8–11.

Gilgun, J. F. (1993). Dimensional analysis and grounded theory: Interviews with Leonard Schatzman. *Qualitative Family Research*, *7*(1–2), 4–7.

Gilgun, J. F. (1995). We shared something special: The moral discourse of incest perpetrators. *Journal of Marriage and the Family*, *57*, 265–281.

Gilgun, J. F. (1999a). Fingernails painted red: A feminist, semiotic analysis of 'hot' text. *Qualitative Inquiry*, *5*, 181–207.

Gilgun, J. F. (1999b). Methodological pluralism and qualitative family research. In Suzanne K. Steinmetz, Marvin B. Sussman, & Gary W. Peterson (Eds.), *Handbook of marriage and the family* (2nd ed., pp. 219–261). New York: Plenum.

Gilgun J. F. (2001). Case study research, analytic induction, and theory development: The future and the past. Paper presented at the Preconference Workshop on Theory Construction and Research Methodology, National Conference on Family Relations, Rochester, NY, November 16.

Gilgun, J. F. (2004). Deductive qualitative analysis and family theory-building. In V. Bengston, P. D. Anderson, K. Allen, A. Acock, & D. Klein (Eds.), *Sourcebook of family theory and methods* (pp. 83–84). Thousand Oaks, CA: Sage.

Gilgun, J. F. (2005). Qualitative research and family psychology. *Journal of Family Psychology*, *19*(1), 40–50.

Gilgun, J. F. (2007). The legacy of the Chicago School of sociology for family theory-building. Paper presented at Pre-Conference Workshop on Theory Construction and Research Methodology, National Council on Family Relation, Pittsburgh, PA, November 13.

Gilgun, J. F. (2008). Deductive qualitative analysis as middle ground. Paper presented at the Midwest Conference on Qualitative Research, St. Paul, MN, April 12.

Gilgun, J. F. (2010). Methods for enhancing theory and knowledge about problems, policies, and practice. In Katherine Briar, Joan Orme, Roy Ruckdeschel, & Ian Shaw (Eds.), *The Sage handbook of social work research* (pp. 281–297). Thousand Oaks, CA: Sage.

Gilgun, J. F. (2012a). Enduring themes in qualitative family research. *Journal of Family Theory and Review*, *4*, 80–95.

Gilgun, J. F. (2012b) Hand into glove: Grounded theory, deductive qualitative analysis and social work research and practice. In Anne E. Fortune, William Reid, & Robert Miller (Eds.), *Qualitative methods in social work* (2nd ed., pp. 107–134). New York: Columbia University Press.

Gilgun, J. F. (2014). Chicago School traditions: Deductive qualitative analysis and grounded theory. Amazon.

Gilgun, J. F. (2015). Research and theory building in social work. In William Nichols (Ed.), *Encyclopedia of social and behavioral sciences* (2nd ed., pp. 502–507). New York: Elselvier.

Gilgun, J. F. (2016). Deductive qualitative analysis and the search for black swans. Paper presented at the Pre-conference Workshop on Theory Construction and Research Methodology, National Council on Family Relations, Minneapolis, MN, November 1.

Gilligan, C. (1982). In a different voice: Psychological theory and women's development. Cambridge, MA: Harvard University Press.

Gilligan, C. Ward, J., Taylor, J. M., & Bardige, B. (Eds.) (1988). *Mapping the moral domain: A contribution of women's thinking to psychological theory and education*. Cambridge, MA: Harvard University Press.

Glaser, B. (1978). *Theoretical sensitivity.* Mill Valley, CA: Sociology Press.

Glaser, B. (1992). *Basics of grounded theory analysis*. Mill Valley, CA: Sociology Press.

Glaser, B. (2016). Grounded description: No No. *The Grounded Theory Review*, *15*(2), 3–7.

Glaser, B. & Holton, J. (2004). Remodeling grounded theory. *Forum: Qualitative Social Research*, *5*(2). www.qualitative-research.net/index.php/fqs/article/view/607/1315

Glaser, B. & Strauss, A. (1967). *The discovery of grounded theory.* Chicago, IL: Aldine.

Glaser, B. & Strauss, A. L. (1971). *Status passage*. New Brunswick, NJ: Transaction.

Goldenberg, S. (1993). Analytic induction revisited. *Canadian Journal of Sociology*, *18*(*2*), 161–176.

Hammersley, M, (2011). On Becker's studies of marijuana use as an example of analytic induction. *Philosophy of the Social Sciences 41*(*4*), 535–566.

Kelle, U. (2005). 'Emergence' vs. 'Forcing' of empirical data? A crucial problem of 'grounded theory' reconsidered. *Forum: Qualitative Social Research*, *6*(2), Article 27, paragraphs 49 & 50.

Langerlund, H. (2016). Medieval theories of the syllogism. *Stanford Encyclopedia of Philosophy*. http://plato.stanford.edu/entries/medieval-syllogism/

Laub, J. H., & Sampson, R. J. (1991). The Sutherland-Glueck debate: On the sociology of criminological knowledge. *American Journal of Sociology*, *96*(*6*), 1402–1440.

Lewin, K. (1935). *A dynamic theory of personality*. New York: McGraw-Hill.

Lindesmith, A. R. (1947). *Opiate addiction.* Bloomington, IN: Principia.

Lofland, J., Snow, D. A., Anderson, L., & Lofland, L. (2006). *Analyzing social settings* (4th ed.). Australia: Thomson Wadsworth.

Low, J. & Bowden, G. (Eds.) (2013). *The Chicago School diaspora: Epistemology and substance*. Montreal: McGill-Queen's University Press.

Mcauliffe, W. H. B. (2015). How did abduction get confused with inference to the best explanation? *Transactions of the Charles S. Peirce Society: A Quarterly Journal in American Philosophy*, *51*(3), 300–319.

Manning, P. K. (1982). Analytic induction. In R. B. Smith & P. K. Manning (Eds.), *Qualitative methods, Vol. II, of Handbook of Social Sciences* (pp. 273–302). Cambridge, MA: Ballinger.

Mill, J. S. (1843). *A system of logic*. New York: Harper.

Morgan, D. L. (2007). Paradigms lost and pragmatism regained: Methodological implications of combining qualitative and quantitative methods. *Journal of Mixed Methods Research*, *1*(1), 48–76.

Peirce, C. S. (1998). *The essential Peirce: Selected philosophical writings (1893–1913)*. Peirce Edition Project. Bloomington, IN: Indiana University Press.

Popper K. R. (1969). *The logic of scientific discovery*. New York: Basic Books.

Osbeck, L. (2014) Scientific reasoning as sense-making: Implications for qualitative inquiry. *Qualitative Psychology*, *1*(1), 34–46.

Reichertz, J. (2007). Abduction: The logic of discovery in grounded theory. In A. Bryant & K. Charmaz (Eds.), *The Sage handbook of grounded theory* (pp. 214–228). London: Sage.

Strauss, A. (1987). *Qualitative analysis for social scientists*. New York: Cambridge University Press.

Robinson, W. S. (1951). The logical structure of analytic induction. *American Sociological Review*, *16*, 812–818.

Strauss, A. (1992). A personal history of grounded theory. *Qualitative Family Research*, *5*(2), 1–2.

Strauss, A., Schatzman, L., Bucher, R., Ehrlich, D.& Sabshin, M. (1964). *Psychiatric ideologies and institutions.* New York: Free Press.

Sutherland, E. H. (1937). *The professional thief*. Chicago, IL: University of Chicago Press.

Sutherland, E. H. (1949) *White collar crime*. New York: Holt, Rinehart & Winston.

Thomas, W. I., & Znaniecki, F. (1918–1920). *The Polish peasant in Europe and America* (*Vols 1–2*). New York: Knopf.

Thomas, W.I., & Znaniecki, F. (1927). *The Polish peasant in Europe and America* (2nd ed.). Oxford, England: Knopf.

Vidich, A. J. & Lyman, S. M. (2000). Qualitative methods: Their history in sociology and anthropology. In N. K. Denzin & Y. S. Lincoln (Eds.), *Handbook of qualitative research* (2nd ed.). (37–84). Thousand Oaks, CA: Sage.

Waller, W. (1934). Insight and the scientific method. *American Journal of Sociology*, *XL*, 285–297.

Walsh, I., Holton, J. A., Bailyn, L., Fernandez, W., Levina, N., & Glaser, B. (2015). What grounded theory is…a critically reflective conversation among scholars. *Organizational Research Methods*, *18*(*4*), 581–599.

Yuan, Y. H. (2005). *On the scientific method learned from Albert Einstein in 2005 – the World Year of Physics*. Ithaca, NY: Cornell University Library. https://arxiv.org/abs/physics/0510124

Znaniecki, F. (1934). *The method of sociology*. New York: Farrar & Rinehart.

PART III

Grounded Theory in Practice

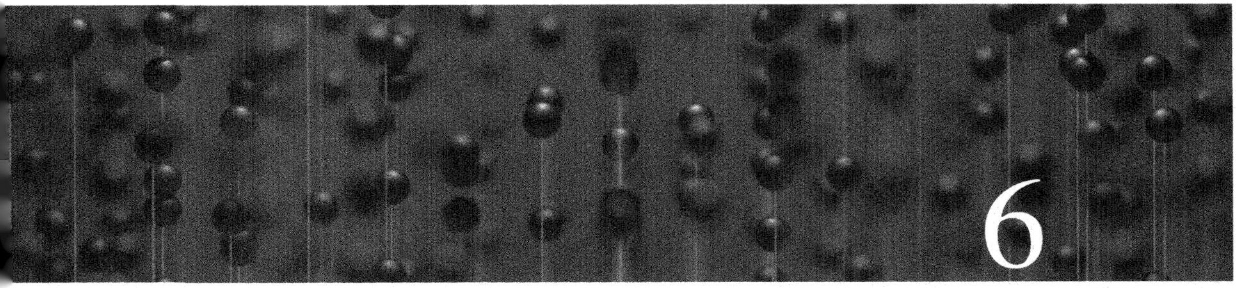

From Intuition to Reflexive Construction: Research Design and Triangulation in Grounded Theory Research

Uwe Flick

INTRODUCTION: REFLEXIVE CONSTRUCTION OF GROUNDED THEORIES

The main topics of this chapter are largely absent in the grounded theory literature as the first edition of this *Handbook* (Bryant and Charmaz 2007) and the textbooks by Charmaz (2014), Holton and Walsh (2017), Bryant (2017) and others reveal. The term 'research design' has been long associated with controlling bias in quantitative research and therefore it is neither that widespread in qualitative research in general nor part of the grounded theory lexicon. 'Triangulation' has been long (mis-) understood as simple confirmation of results with other results or with results from using other methods for studying the same phenomenon. Again, this may look like something not very relevant as a principle for methodological discussions in grounded theory. However, if both terms are understood in less narrow ways, they address issues that are relevant for grounded theory research and have always been. The use of the ideas in the background of these concepts has been more or less implicit in grounded theory practice without explicitly using or discussing the terms as principles. One example of an implicit use of these ideas is the early statement of Glaser and Strauss (1967) that grounded theory research should work with various 'slices of data'. This is similar to the concept of 'data triangulation' (Denzin 1970; Flick 2018c) without spelling it out in a methodological way. Another example is the notion of Becker, Geer, Hughes, and Strauss (1961) that a research design in research similar to what was called later 'grounded theory research' emerges in the end rather than in the beginning of a study. In this chapter, research design and triangulation will be discussed for their contribution to spelling out the planning and doing of research in grounded theory more explicitly. It shall be discussed how far they can make explicit and transparent, what is often done implicitly in (successful) grounded theory research.

Vague Intuitionalism in Grounded Theory Methodology

The aim of this chapter is to take both terms and discuss them in a way that makes their relevance for grounded theory more explicit. The idea behind this chapter is that methodological discussions in grounded theory sometimes have been based since the beginning on some kinds of *vague intuitionalism*, which makes it a bit difficult to transfer these discussions into future use – teaching grounded theory to novices, planning and conducting new projects. This vague intuitionalism includes (1) the claim of intuition in the field, which makes the research work ('just do it!' – Glaser 1992); (2) the uniqueness of the founding fathers as researchers, personalities, and teachers – which shall not be questioned, but is difficult to implement in new research or learning. This vague intuitionalism also includes (3) the idea of flexibility in the field – to develop and choose methodological approaches, kinds of data and cases in the process (according to the idea of emergent methods) and to finish when saturation has been reached. Again, these principles shall not be questioned, but are challenging when applied in new research with novices to qualitative research or grounded theory. This vague intuitionalism finally includes (4) the emphasis on abduction as the principle of inference and reasoning and (5) the idea of discovering theories in the field. Again, these ideas should be less questioned than taking into account that they are difficult to transfer to new research(ers). We will begin with the last two aspects, which in some ways have increased this vague intuitionalism in recent developments.

Abduction as a Principle of Discovery in Grounded Theory Research

The idea of abduction has become quite prominent in the recent grounded theory discourse as a main principle of reasoning (see Strauss 1987; Reichertz 2007; Charmaz 2014; Thornberg and Charmaz 2014; Kennedy and Thornberg 2018). Charmaz explains why this is so:

> Why is grounded theory an abductive method? Because grounded theory involves *reasoning* about experience for making theoretical conjectures – inferences – and then checking them through further experience – empirical data. In this sense, grounded theory methods are abductive.... In short, grounded theory relies on *reasoning – making inferences* – about empirical experience. Thus a major strength of the grounded theory method is that these budding conceptualizations can lead researchers in the most useful, emergent and often unanticipated theoretical direction to understand their data. (2014, p. 201)

Abduction was originally introduced by pragmatist Charles Sanders Peirce (1878/1958) as a third principle of reasoning in addition to induction and deduction. Given the debates in grounded theory between the Glaserian approach (which is strongly emphasizing a more or less pure inductivism as a feature of grounded theory) and the Strauss and Corbin approach (suggesting a combination of induction and deduction once their second step of axial coding has been reached – see Kelle 2005), the appeal of abduction may also be to open up a way out of this debate. However, the price for this way out is the stronger emphasis on creativity and intuition in proceeding along this path of inquiry:

> In abduction, qualitative researchers use a selective and creative process to examine how the data support existing theories or hypotheses as well as how the data may call for modifications in existing understandings.... They go beyond the data and pre-existing theoretical knowledge by modifying, elaborating upon, or rejecting theory if needed, or putting old ideas together in new ways to examine, understand, and explain the data. Like the fictional detective Sherlock Holmes, they constantly move back and forth between data and theories, and make comparisons and interpretations in searching for patterns and the best possible explanations. (Kennedy and Thornberg 2018, p. 52)

We cannot go deeper into this debate here, but for the issue of vague intuitionalism it is relevant to see that younger researchers, in doing a PhD, often lack the expertise of Glaser, Strauss, Charmaz or Bryant and are left alone to make creativity, abduction and discovery work in their research.

Constructing Grounded Theories

A second turn led from seeing grounded theory research less as a process of intuitive discovery by using methods to understanding such research as a process of constructing theories and taking specific decisions for methods, for fields, and for selecting people, events, materials as data (see Charmaz 2014). This is a major step towards 'grounding' the research in grounded theory in the researchers' activities and choices in the field.

From Sacred Data to Unearthing Hidden Meanings

In the development of grounded theory research as a field, the original understanding of the concept of data has been challenged. Statements such as 'all is data' (Glaser 2002) highlight this original understanding. Glaser and Strauss (1967) already have a rather pragmatic approach to the concept of data, when they outline:

> a way that sociologists can greatly extend the range of qualitative data serviceable for generating theory, and with relatively little expenditure of time, money, and effort. Principally what is required are some imagination, some ingenuity and, most of all, a considerable shift in attitude toward qualitative materials themselves. (1967, p. 161)

Clarke (2005) formulates a skepticism about this understanding of the role of data in grounded theory research:

> I am directly challenging the ways in which Glaser and Strauss originally talked about 'the data', which often had a magical quality predicated on their being separate from the researcher and somehow sacred. The phrase 'letting the data speak for themselves' captures this 'autonomous' quality they imputed to 'the data'. (2005, p. 75)

Clarke here is taking up an essential aspect of the intuitionalism mentioned above: In the original versions of grounded theory research, theoretical insights in general and categories in a technical sense 'emerge' from the data if the researchers are only open enough in the field (and not 'disoriented' by taking existing theories into account). Her response to this idea is:

> Yes, but you also need, then, to be sure to collect data that can explicitly address the salience or lack of salience of any of these issues for the situation at hand. Awaiting 'emergence' from the data is not enough. (2005, pp. 75–76)

In these considerations, Clarke makes a point for going beyond this basic concept of grounded theory – a (more or less experienced) researcher turns to an interesting field in a very open manner and discovers what is going on there by letting the data and categories emerge. Clarke emphasizes that once the research starts less from such a general interest or curiosity but more from an existing inequality (as in feminist or social problems-oriented research), researchers should invest more in planning the research and in systematizing the data collection. This brings us to the concepts that are the main topics of this chapter.

Stages of Expertise

The wider backgrounds for the following considerations are based on the (interrelated) five-stage models of (developing) expertise in areas of nursing (Benner 1982) and of artificial intelligence (Dreyfus and Dreyfus 1986). It would go beyond this chapter to discuss these models in detail. They reach from *novice* (stage 1) over *advanced beginner* (2), *competent* (3), *proficient* (4) and (5) *expert* (see also Bryant 2017, chapter 13). The interesting point in our context is that the first stages of expertise are strongly based on rules that are applied to concrete situations and explicit knowledge. Only the fifth stage (expert) is more and more based on intuition and tacit knowledge, and operates without constant or regular references to rules and explicit knowledge. Applied to our context, much of the methodological literature on how to do grounded theory starts from examples of expertise that work with intuition and tacit knowledge and less with explication of rules, steps, and methods.

DESIGNING GROUNDED THEORY RESEARCH

What is linked to the term 'research design' in social research? In the next step, several understandings of this term will be discussed in a comparative way. In quantitative research, 'research design' is strongly linked to controlling and standardization of research situations for increasing or assuring the validity and reliability of the research and its outcomes, neither of which are objectives of grounded theory (research). Beyond these aspects of standardization and control, designing a study includes a wider range of aspects. A more general definition comes from Charles Ragin, who defines the term 'research design':

> Research design is a plan for collecting and analyzing evidence that will make it possible for the investigator to answer whatever questions he or she has posed. The design of an investigation touches almost all aspects of the research, from the minute details of data collection to the selection of the techniques of data analysis. (1994, p. 191)

Design in the Process

That the interest in research design is not very prominent in grounded theory may have several reasons. A first reason may be the current understanding of grounded theory as an emergent method, as outlined by Charmaz (2008, p. 155), starting from

> a working definition of an emergent method as inductive, indeterminate, and open-ended. An emergent method begins with the empirical world and builds an inductive understanding of it as events unfold and knowledge accrues. Social scientists who use emergent methods can study research problems that arise in the empirical world and can pursue unanticipated directions of inquiry in this world. Emergent methods are particularly well suited for studying uncharted, contingent, or dynamic phenomena.

In the general discussion about emergent methods (see Hesse-Biber and Leavy 2008), ideas of planning a research project by outlining a research design are also not very prominent (although exceptions such as Wright (2009) exist). In linking the discourses of grounded theory and emergent methods, the role of emergence in grounded theory research becomes a double one: Not only the 'findings' of grounded theory research (i.e., the categories developed and used, and also the resulting theory) are understood as emerging (in particular in classic grounded theory, see Glaser 1992; or Holton and Walsh 2017; as well as Kelle 2014) but also the use of methods. This may be a good perspective for describing the process and use of methodological tools in a successful study in retrospect by expert researchers. However, the question here is, again, whether this is a helpful orientation for a grounded study still to be undertaken, and also for novices in the field.

Second, that the interest in research design has not played a big role in the grounded theory lexicon can be traced back to the very early studies and maybe finds its reasons in them. Becker, Geer, Hughes, and Strauss (1961) show in some sense a quite typical understanding of the term 'research design' in grounded theory research. Although the book about their study (*Boys in White*) has a chapter on 'research design', they begin it with the statement:

> In one sense, our study had no design. That is, we had no well-worked-out set of hypotheses to be tested, no data-gathering instruments, purposely designed to secure information relevant to these hypotheses, no set of analytic procedures specified in advance. Insofar as the term 'design' implies these features of elaborate prior planning, our study had none. If we take the idea of design in a larger and looser sense, using it to identify those elements of order, system, and consistency our procedures did exhibit, our study had a design. We can say what this was by describing our original view of our problem, our theoretical and methodological commitments, and the way these affected our research and were affected by it as we proceeded. (1961, p. 17)

In a similar way, Hammersley and Atkinson (1995, p. 24) argue in the context of ethnography that 'research design should be a reflexive process which operates throughout every stage of a project'. Such a flexible understanding of the term 'research design' opens a perspective for using it in the context of grounded theory as an emergent method (Charmaz 2008).

Thus, we may state at this point that there seems to be (at least in comparison to quantitative research) a less concrete concept of research design in qualitative and grounded theory research. However, we can outline the focus of this concept: First, a research design here is not something set up at one point in the preparation of a project and then just applied in the field. It rather is developed (or emerging) in the process of the project and in the conditions of the field that is studied. It has more to do with reflecting the research and field in this process by the researchers and less with defining the design at the desk of the methodologist beforehand. Second, research design refers to more than validity issues.

Approaches as Research Designs

In some cases, 'research design' is used in a different way, referring to grounded theory research: Creswell (2013) discusses five major approaches (or traditions) of qualitative research, with grounded theory research being among them. He then describes the characteristics of the approaches and sees doing research according to these characteristics as selecting a research design, such as grounded theory, for example.

> A key idea is that this theory development does not come 'off the shelf,' but rather is generated or 'grounded' in data from participants who have experienced the process (Strauss & Corbin 1998). Thus, grounded theory is a qualitative research design in which the inquirer generates a general explanation (a theory) of a process, an action, or an interaction shaped by the views of a large number of participants. (Creswell 2013, p. 83)

Taking up such an approach is then the main aspect of designing qualitative research for Creswell. How far this understanding – grounded theory as one major research design in qualitative research – takes into account that there are several versions of how to understand and do grounded theory now, remains open. Creswell refers both to Corbin and Strauss (2007) and Charmaz (2006) when describing the procedures of doing grounded theory. At the same time, the more concrete issues of how to use grounded theory in a concrete field, the decisions to be taken in this process and project remain secondary, too. At least this concept of research design enforces researchers to reflect and account as to why they selected grounded theory as the approach for their study. Creswell's argumentations about research design (also in Creswell 2014) continuously moves between designing how to do the study (in the above sense) and designing writings about it (proposals in the beginning or reports in the end).

Approaches to Research Design in Grounded Theory Research

In her reflections about the need for stronger planning of grounded theory, Clarke (2005, p. 77) points out that the issue of research design leads right away into the contested areas of the disputes between Strauss and Glaser. She also discusses their differing approaches and her own (situational analysis) as some kind of basic design in grounded theory without going into details. However, she outlines her view on research design:

> Atkinson and Coffey [2001] … assert that, while not emphasizing design in an a priori sense, traditional grounded theory actually "bootlegs' design into itself via theoretical sampling across the duration of the project. While also relying on traditional theoretical sampling, I am arguing that we also need to *design* our research from the outset in order to explicitly gather data about theoretically and substantively underdeveloped areas that may lie in our situations of inquiry. (Clarke 2005, p. 76)

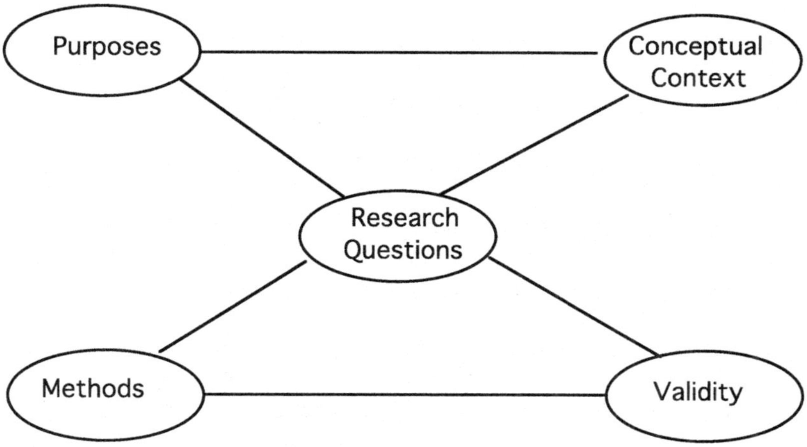

Figure 6.1 An interactive model of research design (Maxwell, 2013, p. 5)

Components of Research Designs and their Relevance for Grounded Theory Research

In other cases, research design is described as including several components. Maxwell (2013, p. 5) sees purposes, conceptual context, methods and validity as such components grouped around the central one (the research question). In his 'interactive model of research design', the term 'design' itself is not visible (see Figure 6.1).

This again has a process approach to designing qualitative research in general and includes some kind of interaction or negotiation between the components that are included. This understanding of design is open for adapting the research to the conditions in the field and of the issue that is studied, and thus comes closer to grounded theory research – even when understood as emerging method – than other concepts of research design. Maxwell sees aspects such as the purposes of a study, the conceptual context, methods, validity and research question as interdependent. Seeing these components in an interactive model, this concept allows changes in the methods used in the field, and the (further) development of the conceptual context, as in a grounded theory study. Maxwell's model also is based on rejecting the dominance of one of its components, for example, the research questions, which is often supposed to define the other components mentioned in the model. Bryman (2007) has studied empirically how researchers deal with the issue of research questions. He made a distinction between a *universalistic* model and a *particularistic* model. In the particularistic model, the research question has a particular role for designing the research in detail, which includes that the question drives the decision for a specific approach or research program, for example, for taking a grounded theory approach. In the universalistic model, the dominance of the research question becomes relative to the adherence to a specific understanding of research – the researcher who has always used grounded theory will tend to use it also in a new study and adapt the research question so that this approach will work. However, it can be discussed whether the components in Maxwell's model are the only ones relevant in designing qualitative research in a concrete way. This question becomes even more important if we take grounded theory as a point of reference.

In my own works about qualitative research designs (see Flick 2018i, 2018a), I mentioned several components of research design in a qualitative study, which can be summarized in four major areas:

a. The *aims of the study* include its *general goals* and its *generalization goals*: What is the intention behind doing the study? In our context, a major aim can be to develop a theory about a specific phenomenon in the field under study or to provide detailed descriptions of the field and phenomenon. Other aims can be the evaluation of a process or service. Generalization goals can, on the one hand, refer to making statements about the phenomenon in the field (or case) that was studied or more general statements beyond it. In the case of grounded theory, this distinction is taken up in the difference between substantive theories (referring to a phenomenon in a field) and formal theory (referring to a phenomenon in several fields). For Glaser (2002), such a generalization seems to be a major goal. For constructivist grounded theorists, it may be a product of their research but being attentive to positionality precedes generalizing. Thus, generalizations can be a major part of an understanding of grounded theory as an emergent method (Charmaz 2008).
b. *Aspects brought to the field* include the *theoretical framework* and the concrete *research questions* to be answered. The theoretical framework can become concrete in the sensitizing concepts that are used for disclosing a field or phenomenon under study. It can also refer to several levels such as theories about the issue under study and the more methodological assumptions of the research program that is pursued. The first aspect may be surprising in the context of grounded theory research where the theories are supposed to be discovered in the field. But the recent discussions about the use of the literature in grounded theory research (see Dunne 2011; Thornberg and Dunne, this volume) demonstrate that existing theoretical and empirical knowledge plays an increasingly important role in grounded theory research as well and if only as a challenge to deal with. The second level in the theoretical framework, that is, the methodological assumptions of the research program used as orientation, is becoming more and more relevant the more the field of grounded theory research proliferates – in Glaser's approach, Strauss and Corbin's approach, Charmaz's approach and Clarke's approach. This is further proliferated by the versions of grounded theory research developed in nursing (see Morse et al. 2009) and in management research (see Fendt and Sachs 2008), for example. The version and its understanding of research and of grounded theory practices will influence what the researcher adopting it will do in the concrete study and field and thus influence the design of the study.
c. *Methods and methodology* includes three aspects: the *selection of empirical material*, the *methodological procedures* that are applied, and the *degree of standardization and control* in the way the research is done. In the first aspect, the differentiation of Morse (2007 and this volume) shows that grounded theory research is not limited to using theoretical sampling, which only becomes relevant in later stages of the analysis and theory development. In the early stages of the research other forms of sampling are applied, such as convenience sampling and purposeful sampling (Morse 2007, pp. 235–237). Which forms of selecting cases, materials and so on are used has a strong influence on the design of the concrete study. The methodological procedures, on the one hand, include strategies of data collection or, in case of naturally occurring data (see Toerien 2014; Charmaz 2017; Potter and Shaw 2018), the use of existing data (photos, recordings, documents). Which of these to use should be decided according to which phenomenon and field are supposed to be studied. On the other hand, the methodological procedures include the ways these data are analyzed. Here again, the term 'using grounded theory coding' has been proliferated according to the versions of grounded theory mentioned above. Which one is selected and applied (or taken as an orientation) is a major decision in constructing a research design in grounded theory research. The third aspect, standardization and control, mostly plays a minor role in the openness characterizing methodological approaches in grounded theory. However, once research teams work in a project and develop some degree of sharing the work,

a consensus about how to proceed in the field and with the data seems necessary (see Cornish, Gillespie and Zittoun 2014), and in a grounded theory project also.

d. *Practical framework conditions* of doing a study include the *temporal, personal, and material resources* that are available. These aspects are often underestimated in planning a study. They not only refer to financial resources that can be used or the time-scale of a project (e.g., in the context of a thesis), but also the research experience and skills of the researchers that are involved. Although grounded theory is often seen as easy to do, as it does not seem to involve highly developed methodological skills, for example, resources become a design issue when the research proves to be more complicated than expected. Enough experience in the field and with research seems important for taking the right decisions in sampling, analyzing the data, and stopping the research.

Basic Designs in Qualitative Research and their Relevance for Grounded Theory Research

At the beginning of this section we have discussed the idea of equating research designs with approaches as in the case of the distinctions Creswell (2013) has suggested. This idea might not contribute much to using the concept of research design for improving or advancing grounded theory research as it basically sees the latter as a research design. As we saw in the preceding section of the chapter, there are a lot of design issues inside a grounded theory approach, which are neglected if grounded theory itself is declared a design. In what follows a different perspective is taken, when we discuss the basic designs I have identified elsewhere (see Flick 2018i, 2018a) for their relevance for grounded theory research (see Figure 6.2).

For a more systematic approach to these basic research designs I take two perspectives: One focusing on the dimension of (a) comparison and the other (b) on the dimension of development and process over time.

a. Comparison is a major principle and feature of grounded theory research as Glaser and Strauss (1967) and in particular Glaser (1969) already have clarified in the principle of constant comparative method, which includes four elements: '(1) comparing incidents applicable to each category, (2) integrating categories and their properties, (3) delimiting the theory, and (4) writing the theory' (1969, p. 220). For Glaser, the systematic circularity of this process is an essential feature:

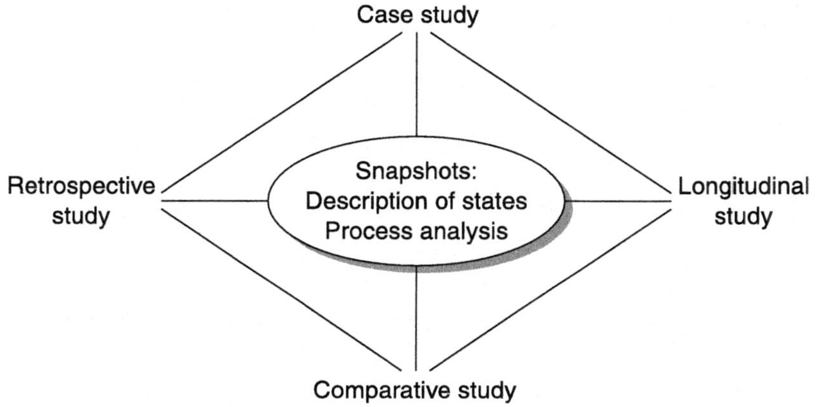

Figure 6.2 Basic designs in qualitative research

> Although this method is a continuous growth process—each stage after a time transforms itself into the next—previous stages remain in operation throughout the analysis and provide continuous development to the following stage until the analysis is terminated. (1969, p. 220)

Comparison as an organizing principle in designing qualitative research covers two main alternatives: *case studies* and *comparative studies.* Again, the difference lies in the degree of explicitness. A comparative study in most examples is defined by a number of cases (e.g., people, institutions, settings, etc.) that are in the focus of the research right away. Often these cases are not analyzed in a holistic manner, but one or several dimensions of comparison are defined. These dimensions can be relevant in selecting the cases, in juxtaposing elements or excerpts and the like. Defining these dimensions right away makes the comparison in the project explicit and the project a comparative study. For grounded theory research, such a comparative study on several cases can be a starting point for developing first concepts based on the expected differences between the cases. A case study takes a more holistic approach to the single case (field, institution, person, setting). Of course, a case study includes comparison as well – between members of an institution, between incidents in the field, for example. Dimensions of such comparison may develop along the way. That is why comparison is more implicit here if seen from a research design angle. It is also implicit because the selection of the single case is often the result of an implicit comparison with other possible cases, which then defines why this case and no other one is studied. For a grounded theory study, this implicit comparison becomes relevant in selecting the field to study, in developing the constant comparison and in selecting the next case(s) to continue with. A case study design can also comprise a series of cases that are studied one after the other.

b. *Time and process* is another essential dimension in grounded theory research, as studies such as Corbin and Strauss (1988) may demonstrate. As a design principle in qualitative research and grounded theory, we can distinguish three basic research designs along this dimension – retrospective research, snapshots, and longitudinal studies. The first design is focusing on a given state at a specific moment – what is the way of dealing with the knowledge about someone dying in a specific period, perhaps in several settings and what kind of grounded theory can be developed from empirical research? The second setting is adopting the idea of longitudinal research – and to focus the empirical research and theory development on process and change over time by collecting data repeatedly and comparing the several field contacts and data (for longitudinal qualitative research see Henwood, Shirani and Groves 2018). The third basic research design is more often used in qualitative research for covering process and development. Here the approach is retrospective, for example, by using biographical or narrative data for reconstructing the process that leads to a current state. In our example, the focus here would be about the changes in dealing with death, the dying of a person, and knowledge and communication about this over the last twenty years, for example.

These basic designs can in some ways be combined, in a retrospective case study or a longitudinal comparative study, for instance. They can also be triangulated. For example, a snapshot (e.g., observations in the here and now of the participants' practices) can be complemented by a more retrospective approach (e.g., the participants' migration histories).

The suggestions for how to design qualitative research made so far can be used for making what is done in grounded theory research a bit more systematic. Without going into further details or suggestions, this need is stated also in general by Clarke (2005, p. 76):

> Dealing with research design and data gathering as active practices, as part of the theory/methods package of grounded theory/symbolic interactionism is requisite. These have been lacunae in grounded theory.

Spelling out design issues in grounded theory will not only make the research more systematic, but also make it easier to plan new projects and to teach the approach to novices in the beginning with less intuitionalism as a basic principle. Whether this systematization can be advanced by a more explicit use of triangulation in grounded theory will be discussed in the next step.

TRIANGULATION IN GROUNDED THEORY RESEARCH

If we take again the first edition of this *Handbook* (Bryant and Charmaz 2007) as a reference, it looks like triangulation is also a concept which is not too prominent in grounded theory discussions about methodology. However, the ideas behind triangulation are not too far away from what is done in grounded theory research. The main idea of triangulation is to extend the research by using several methods, differing theories or multiple researchers. The resulting extension of data and interpretations in the process is seen as a contribution to make the research and results more credible and fruitful.

Background of the Concept

For developing the relation between triangulation and grounded theory a bit further, we should first have a look at the background of the concept. It has a longer history in social sciences (see Flick 2018b), but in our context it became prominent with Denzin's suggestions (1970), in which he distinguished four forms: *Data* triangulation combines various sorts of data (e.g., verbal data coming from interviews and observational data coming from ethnography). *Investigator* triangulation builds on including several researchers and their perspectives on the issue. *Theoretical* triangulation combines various theoretical approaches and applies them to what is studied. Most prominent is *methodological* triangulation, which focuses on combining several methodological approaches in one method (*within methods* triangulation) or in several independent methods (*between methods* triangulation). In the beginning, the use of triangulation was oriented on confirming results from one method with those coming from a second approach, but the discussion has since developed further.

Development of the Concept

Thus, it makes sense to distinguish several phases in the development of the concept (see Flick 2018b, 2018d): 'Triangulation 1.0' can be used for characterizing the original concept suggested by Denzin (1970), which aimed at validation by playing off methods against each other. This concept was heavily criticized in the following years (see Flick 1992 for an overview). However, it is still the one referred to in discussions about mixed methods (e.g., in Mark (2015) or by Creswell (2014, p. 201)).

In later publications (e.g., Denzin 1989, p. 246) and in responding to the critiques mentioned above, Denzin sees triangulation in a more differentiated way. Now it is conceived as a strategy on the road to a deeper understanding of an issue under study. The aim is to advance a step to more knowledge and is less toward validity and objectivity in interpretations. Now, triangulation is also no longer seen as a strategy for confirming findings from one approach with findings from using a second approach. Triangulation is now rather aiming at broader, deeper, more comprehensive understandings of what is studied. That often includes or heads at discrepancies and contradictions in the findings. For highlighting this shift in the concept, Denzin uses the term 'triangulation 2.0' (Denzin 2012), which is also relevant in his distinction of triangulation from mixed methods.

Further elaborating this reformulation of triangulation includes a number of suggestions for spelling out the concept in a more differentiated way (Flick 2018b): A *weak program* of triangulation focuses on confirming results (as mentioned above) or uses it as a criterion for assessing the quality of qualitative research (as in Lincoln and Guba's (1985) criterion of credibility, which builds upon triangulation). Combinations of methods remain rather pragmatic. In a *strong program* of triangulation, the emphasis is on collecting new insights rather than on confirming the ones already obtained. Triangulation then becomes a strategy towards extra knowledge and an extension of a research program, which includes the systematic selection of various methods and the combination of research perspectives linked to these methods. In such a combination, a systematic triangulation of perspectives (see Flick 1992) should be included – different kinds of knowledge, or knowledge and practices, or experiences from various actors in the field. Finally, this strong program of triangulation is based on the idea of a *comprehensive* triangulation: For Denzin (1970), data and investigator, theoretical and methodological triangulation were alternatives, of which researchers should select one. In a *comprehensive* triangulation, several investigators collaborate (investigator triangulation) and bring their different theoretical perspectives (disciplinary backgrounds, for example – theoretical triangulation) into the research. This may lead to the combination of several methods (methodological triangulation), which provide several forms of data to be combined (data triangulation). For summarizing these more recent developments, the term 'triangulation 3.0' (see Flick 2018b) is used.

In times when the concept of 'data' has become an issue of discussion (see Flick 2018f) and criticism (see Denzin 2018 and Flick 2018e), triangulation becomes relevant again in a particular way for challenging a rather naïve (e.g., all is data – Glaser 1992) or sacred understanding of data (for this aspect, see above and Clarke 2005). The idea of challenging data by using several types of data, however, is not aiming at confirming views (as in Denzin's original understanding of playing methods off against each other – see above) but at unfolding the diversity in the data, showing the limits of a single data approach. This challenging, critical approach of triangulation to data can be seen as 'triangulation 4.0' (Flick 2018d). It is more focused on contradiction and complementarity in the data than confirmation and corroboration. This use of triangulation can be a fruitful way of intensifying the diversity in a grounded theory study by making the use of data more systematic at the same time.

THE RELEVANCE OF TRIANGULATION FOR GROUNDED THEORY

The details of triangulation discussed so far are not specific for grounded theory research but are relevant for qualitative research in general. Denzin had linked his concept of triangulation to a better grounding of theory development in general, but there are a number of closer links between triangulation and grounded theory in the literature.

Data Triangulation: Slices of Data

As there are only few explicit references linking triangulation and grounded theory, we will work out this connection a bit more using both implicit and explicit links between both. If we go back to Glaser and Strauss (1967), we find their ideas about using 'slices of data' (p. 65) in the context of theoretical sampling:

> In theoretical sampling, no one kind of data on a category nor technique for data collection is necessarily appropriate. Different kinds of data give the analyst different views or vantage points from which to understand a category and to develop its properties; these different views we have called slices of data. (1967, p. 65)

This idea comes very close to what Denzin later (1970) developed as 'data triangulation', in particular, when the latter is not used for validating but for extending the knowledge that is developed. Glaser and Strauss see the multiplicity of perspectives as an aim of collecting the slices of data:

> As everyone knows, different people in different positions may offer as 'the facts' very different information about the same subject, and they vary that information considerably when talking to different people. Furthermore, the information itself may be continuously changing as the group changes, and different documents on the same subject can be quite contradictory. (1967, p. 67)

The differences in perspective will not lead to relativism if they are subjected to a comparative analysis (p. 68), but they will make the developed theory more comprehensive: 'The theory based on diverse data has taken into consideration more aspects of the substantial or formal area, and therefore can cope with more diversity in conditions and exceptions to hypotheses' (1967, p. 68).

If we turn these suggestions into some kind of advice for planning future research projects using grounded theory, the suggestion is to plan systematically the use of several kinds of data, to pursue their production systematically for being able to compare them for their differences and commonalities. For example, in a study about homeless adolescents and chronic illness, adolescents were interviewed about their perceptions of their diseases, of their symptoms and about their experiences with seeking and using professional treatment. People were interviewed who are working with this target group or who could be addressed by the adolescents in case of problems (service providers). They were asked about their perceptions of homeless adolescents and about what they see as reasons why the adolescents turn to professional help or don't. It became evident that the adolescents' perceptions and those of the service providers about dealing with chronic illness on the street in some parts only gradually differ and in other parts they differ completely. The latter is the case for how the relevance of alcohol and drugs is evaluated as problem solver (as seen by the adolescents) or as problem intensifier (as seen by the service providers). At the same time, the adolescents and service providers differ in their perception of their health-related need for help. The adolescents see a rather limited need for such a help, while the physicians and social workers see a very strong need (see Flick 2011). This allows taking diverse perspectives on the issue and field under study and then triangulating them in a systematic way.

Investigator Triangulation: Diversity in Teamwork

Qualitative research in general is often based on collaborative teamwork (see Cornish et al. 2014). In particular, if we look at the writings of Strauss (1987) and Glaser and Strauss (1967), the role of teamwork in grounded theory also becomes clear. Wiener (2007) has described this in more detail for the example of a research project led by Strauss, and emphasized the diversity in the team members' backgrounds – theoretically, professionally, in their interests and in their experience with the issue under study (2007, p. 294 and p. 297). However, this account of the research highlights that the people involved had these backgrounds and how fruitful this was. The outcome of this process is very much 'grounded' in the personality of the project's leader and how he managed the process. For planning further grounded theory projects, the idea of systematically integrating researchers with different (methodological or theoretical) backgrounds into a research team can be seen as an application of investigator triangulation.

Theoretical Triangulation as Confrontation of Research Perspectives

Theoretical triangulation usually refers to combining (or juxtaposing) several substantial theories of the issue under study. In the context of grounded theory research, theoretical triangulation is discussed for combining grounded theory with other research approaches or perspectives. This can refer to methodological programs – such as combining grounded theory and discourse analysis (as in Clarke 2005) – but it also refers to taking a theoretical perspective into the analysis of data in a grounded theory study. A number of examples can be found in which a grounded theory approach has been triangulated with a different theoretical research perspective. The methodologically relevant question, however, concerns the function of this different theoretical perspective for developing a grounded theory. Wilson and Hutchinson (1991), for example, have triangulated Heideggerian hermeneutics and grounded theory as two 'qualitative methods':

> Triangulation of these two qualitative methods in one study can illuminate clinical realities that elude alternative approaches. Hermeneutics reveals the uniqueness of shared meanings and common practices that can inform the way we think about our practice; grounded theory provides a conceptual framework useful for planning interventions and further quantitative research. (1991, p. 263)

This means that the one approach – hermeneutics – is seen as the perspective that provides the insights (into meanings and practices), and grounded theory is located around the implementation of these insights into further research and interventions.

For Annells (2006), this article was a starting point for developing the triangulation of Heideggerian hermeneutics and grounded theory into using them in two distinct phases of a research project, 'which can be complementary for gaining vital, but different types of understanding that can be useful for best practice about a phenomenon central to a problem or a curiosity' (2006, p. 58). Here, the role of both approaches is seen on a comparable level – both are complementary in producing insights. Rennie (2000) has developed this kind of triangulation into a more integrative approach seeing grounded theory as 'methodical hermeneutics'.

Kushner and Morrow (2003) have used the term 'theoretical triangulation' for merging grounded theory, feminist and critical theory: 'We propose a third path that focuses on the interplay between grounded, feminist, and critical theories, as a strategy that provides a more comprehensive account of the relations between agency, structure, and critique' (2003, p. 30). They understand theoretical triangulation as a 'constant grounding process at the level of data gathering and analysis, coupled with internal checks (constant comparisons in the terminology of grounded theory) on theoretical arguments based on back and forth movement between questions posed with both feminist and critical theories' (2003, p. 38). This example raises the question about how far the feminist and critical theories delimit what can be developed from empirical material into a grounded theory. Gibson (2007, p. 443) criticizes Kushner and Morrow's suggestion (2003) as being rather unclear in the details of what the authors suggest they are doing and what the meaning of this is. However, it can be seen as another example of taking other (theoretical) approaches into account for advancing the process of grounded theory development in the tradition of (theoretical) triangulation.

In their book, Wertz et al. (2011) provide the results of a more practical triangulation of several theoretical approaches with grounded theory in the step of analyzing empirical material. They take one interview and analyze it from five different research perspectives (among them grounded theory, discourse analysis and narrative research). They also provide some detailed comparison of what pairs of approaches produced as differences and similarities in analyzing the text. It also becomes evident that not only the procedure of how the text is analyzed varies across the five approaches, but also which aspects are put in the foreground: We find 'constructing a grounded theory of loss and regaining a valued self' (Charmaz 2011) as the approach and result of the grounded theory approach, whereas the discourse analysis of the same material focuses on 'enhancing oneself, diminishing others' (McMullen 2011). This book offers interesting insights into the differences and commonalities of various empirical approaches to the same material.

Methodological Triangulation between and within Methods in Grounded Theory Research

For the research practice in the context of grounded theory, methodological triangulation may be the most relevant aspect. Similar to ethnography, we can distinguish between implicit triangulation (see Flick 2018c, Chapter 4, for this) and an explicit use of the concept. Implicit triangulation uses and combines several methods and data in an ad-hoc manner. Sometimes the methods are applied less systematically than flexibly reacting to the challenges and offers from the field. A more explicit triangulation combines ethnography either as an approach focusing on observations with a specific interview method for example, which is applied in a more systematic way (see Flick 2018c), or as several methods (such as observation and interviewing) that are triangulated in a systematic way again within an ethnography: A specific form of interviewing is part of the overall design and is combined with observation and document analysis, and both are applied systematically again. This distinction can be applied to grounded theory research as well.

Either a grounded theory study combines several approaches in an ad-hoc manner and thus the triangulation remains implicit, or a grounded theory approach is triangulated with other methodological approaches or several methods are triangulated in a grounded theory study in a more systematic way. Both can be understood as explicit triangulation. In Denzin's (1970) terminology, these forms of combinations are called 'between-methods' triangulation.

Within-methods triangulation refers to combining several approaches in one method. If grounded theory is understood as a *method*, this can again include several strategies of collecting data (observation, talking to people, analyzing documents, etc.), but it can be discussed whether it is helpful to see this approach as a method. An example may illustrate the idea of within-methods triangulation a bit more in detail. The idea is that several methodological approaches with differing backgrounds are combined in one method for accessing a phenomenon in a more comprehensive way. The episodic interview (see Flick 2000, 2018c) starts from the notion that people have various forms of knowledge about an issue. These forms should be addressed in different ways. Episodic knowledge refers to concrete situations in which certain experiences have been made (My first day in school…). Semantic knowledge refers to more general concepts (A good teacher is ….). The first form of knowledge can be accessed best in narratives, when asking interviewees to recount specific situations ('Can you please recall your first experience with school and tell me about this situation?'). The second form can be accessed by asking questions ('What is a good teacher for you?'). The combination of both forms of data (small-scale narratives with statements such as definitions, etc.) can give a broader understanding of the issue under study, in particular if it is a phenomenon we do not know much about. This will make such a form of interviewing more relevant for grounded theory research than other forms. Such an interview, which is based on with-in methods triangulation, can be integrated in a research design based on between-methods triangulation.

AN EXAMPLE OF USING THESE STRATEGIES: MIGRATION AND LONG-TERM UNEMPLOYMENT

In this example of a recent study (see Flick, Hans, Hirseland, Rasch, and Röhnsch 2017), the focus of research is on understanding the experiences and problems of migrants to Germany from the former Soviet Union and Turkey with being long-term unemployed, and with the institutions that are supposed to help them find work again (called 'job-centers') and provide basic social support. The latter is linked to the condition that the recipients are actively seeking regular employment. The design of this research is a comparative study linking a retrospective approach with a snapshot. Several methods are triangulated – episodic interviews and go-alongs (Kusenbach 2018) with the migrants complemented by focus groups with them and expert interviews with job center staff. The intention behind using these methods is to take different perspectives on the phenomenon of migrants' long-term unemployment.

The episodic interviews in this study address both episodic knowledge (referring to concrete situations and circumstance – e.g., when I first lost my job…) and semantic knowledge (referring to concepts and connections between them – e.g., what work means to them? What is the relevance of unemployment?). In technical terms, the episodic interview aims at combining small-scale situation narratives with question/answer sequences. Interviewees are invited to recount situations relevant to them in the context of the study's topic – e.g., about how they came to Germany, how they tried and found access (or failed to find access) to regular work, to professional support or experiences with job-centers and service providers, or how they develop or maintain social networks in their 'new' environment. Questions beyond that invitation to recount situations and experiences refer to the interviewees' representations of work or of unemployment, for example. The main areas covered in the interviews are work- and/or unemployment-related experiences and practices, help-seeking behavior experiences with the social support system and expectations about help. The interviews were conducted in German, or consecutively interpreted, or completely done and transcribed in Russian (or Turkish) and then verbatim translated to German. For extending our understanding of how our participants live with being unemployed and of the support and control offered by the institutions, we used 'go-alongs' (Kusenbach 2018) as a second methodological approach. This method aimed at gaining insights into the local life-worlds of the study participants, getting closer to their own everyday relevancies and being able to analyze socio-spatial integration. Participants were asked to suggest the spatial center of their everyday life as meeting points, from which places of major importance for them should be accessible within walking distance. Then participants were asked to describe spots of great importance to them – the places they liked, disliked or just used regularly – with the help of a street map and then walked us to some of these places. The choice of the places shown and the route taken was left to the participants. While walking around, they explained particular meanings and talked about activities associated with these places. This approach goes beyond regular interviews in two respects: First, the go-along takes the research into the localized life-worlds of our participants. This allows us to analyze perceptions of participants' everyday spaces. Second, it allows us to analyze life-worlds and spaces in the participants' perspectives and to complement these views with the researchers' perspectives. In this sense, the methodological approaches allow a systematic triangulation of perspectives. Data are analyzed by using thematic coding and the study can be seen as a first step in the longer process of constructing a grounded theory of the phenomenon under study.

CONCLUSION

As we saw earlier in this chapter, grounded theory studies often rely on a rather intuitionalist approach, in which they end up in having developed some kind of research design along the way. At the same time, using several methods, combining data, or investigators, often is part of doing the study. If we take models of expertise as a background for transferring skills of doing grounded theory to novices, it will be helpful to spell out these implicit practices of designing and triangulating in grounded theory in a more explicit way. This will then allow us to use the potential of triangulation in grounded theory for applying a systematic triangulation of perspectives (of several actors in the field, for example) on the issue under study. This chapter aims at contributing to the stronger consideration of research design and triangulation issues in grounded theory research.

ACKNOWLEDGEMENTS

I would like to thank Kathy Charmaz and Tony Bryant for their helpful comments and both editors for their patience. This chapter builds on parts of Flick (2018g).

REFERENCES

Annells, M. (2006) Triangulation of qualitative approaches: Hermeneutical phenomenology and grounded theory. *Journal of Advanced Nursing*, *56*, 55–61.

Atkinson, P. and Coffey, A. (2001) Revisiting the relationship between participant observation and interviewing. In Gubrium, J. F. and Holstein, J. A. (Eds.), *Handbook of interview research.* Thousand Oaks: SAGE. pp. 801–814.

Becker, H. S., Geer, B., Hughes, E. C., and Strauss, A. L. (1961) *Boys in White: Student Culture in Medical School*. Chicago, IL: University of Chicago Press.

Benner, P. (1982) From novice to expert. *American Journal of Nursing*, *82*, 402–407.

Bryant, A. (2017) *Grounded Theory and Grounded Theorizing: Pragmatism in Research Practice*. Oxford: Oxford University Press.

Bryant, A. and Charmaz, K. (Eds.) (2007) *The SAGE Handbook of Grounded Theory*. London: Sage.

Bryman, A. (2007) The research question in social research: What is its role? *International Journal of Social Research Methodology*, *10*, 5–20.

Charmaz, K. (2006) *Constructing Grounded Theory: A Practical Guide Through Qualitative Analysis*. Thousand Oaks, CA: Sage.

Charmaz, K. (2008) Grounded theory as an emergent method. In S. N. Hesse-Biber and P. Leavy (Eds.), *The Handbook of Emergent Methods*. New York: Guilford Press. pp. 155–170.

Charmaz, K. (2011) A constructivist grounded theory analysis of losing and regaining a valued Self. In F. J. Wertz, K. Charmaz, L. M. McMullen, R. Josselson, R. Anderson, and E. McSpadden, *Five Ways of Doing Qualitative Analysis*. New York: Guilford Press. pp. 165–204.

Charmaz, K. (2014) *Constructing Grounded Theory: A Practical Guide Through Qualitative Analysis* (2nd edn). Thousand Oaks, CA: Sage.

Charmaz, K. (2017) The power of constructivist grounded theory for critical inquiry. *Qualitative Inquiry*, *23*(1), 34–45. Online first as doi:10.1177/1077800416657105.

Clarke, A. (2005) *Situational Analysis: Grounded Theory after the Postmodern Turn*. Thousand Oaks, CA: Sage.

Corbin, J. and Strauss, A. (1988) *Unending Work and Care: Managing Chronic Illness at Home*. San Francisco, CA: Jossey-Bass.

Corbin, J. and Strauss, A. (2007) *Basics of Qualitative Research* (2nd edn). London: Sage.

Cornish, F., Gillespie, A., and Zittoun, T. (2014) Collaborative data analysis. In U. Flick (Ed.), *The SAGE Handbook of Qualitative Data Analysis*. London: Sage. pp. 79–93.

Creswell, J. W. (2013) *Research Design: Qualitative, Quantitative and Mixed Methods Approaches* (3rd edn). Thousand Oaks, CA: Sage.

Creswell, J. W. (2014) *Qualitative Inquiry and Research Design: Choosing among Five Traditions* (2nd edn). Thousand Oaks, CA: Sage.

Denzin, N. K. (1970) Strategies of multiple triangulation. In N. Denzin, *The Research Act in Sociology: A Theoretical Introduction to Sociological Method*. New York: McGraw-Hill, pp. 297–313.

Denzin, N. K. (1989) *The Research Act* (3rd edn). Englewood Cliffs, NJ: Prentice-Hall (1st edn 1970).

Denzin, N. K. (2012) Triangulation 2.0. *Journal of Mixed Methods Research*, *6*(2), 80–88.

Denzin, N. K. (2018) Performance, hermeneutics, interpretation. In U. Flick (Ed.), *The SAGE Handbook of Qualitative Data Collection*. London: Sage. pp. 200–216.

Dreyfus, H. L. and Dreyfus, S. E. (1986) *Mind over Machine: The Power of Human Intuition and Expertise in the Era of the Computer*. New York: The Free Press.

Dunne, C. (2011) The place of the literature review in grounded theory research. *International Journal of Social Research Methodology*, *14*, 111–124.

Fendt, J. and Sachs, W. (2008) Grounded theory method in management research: Users' perspectives. *Organizational Research Methods*, *11*, 430–455.

Flick, U. (1992) Triangulation revisited: Strategy of or alternative to validation of qualitative data. *Journal for the Theory of Social Behavior*, *22*, 175–197.

Flick U. (2000) Episodic interviewing. In M. Bauer and G. Gaskell (Eds.), *Qualitative Researching with Text, Image and Sound: A Handbook*. London: Sage. pp. 75–92.
Flick, U. (2011) Mixing methods, triangulation and integrated research: Challenges for qualitative research in a world of crisis. In N. Denzin and M. Giardina (Eds.), *Qualitative Inquiry and Global Crisis*. Walnut Creek, CA: Left Coast Press. pp. 132–152.
Flick U. (2018i) *An Introduction to Qualitative Research* (5th edn). London: Sage.
Flick, U. (2018a) *Designing Qualitative Research* (Book 1 of *The SAGE Qualitative Research Kit*, 2nd edn) London: Sage.
Flick U. (2018b) Triangulation. In N. K. Denzin and Y. S. Lincoln (Eds.), *The SAGE Handbook of Qualitative Research* (5th edn). London: Sage. pp. 444–461.
Flick, U. (2018c) *Doing Triangulation and Mixed Methods* (Book 9 of *The SAGE Qualitative Research Kit*, 2nd edn). London: Sage.
Flick, U. (2018d) Triangulation. In U. Flick (Ed.), *The SAGE Handbook of Qualitative Data Collection*. London: Sage. pp. 527–544.
Flick, U. (2018e) Doing qualitative data collection: Charting the routes. In U. Flick (Ed.) *The SAGE Handbook of Qualitative Data Collection*. London: Sage. pp. 3–16.
Flick, U. (Ed.) (2018f) *The SAGE Handbook of Qualitative Data Collection*. London: Sage.
Flick, U. (2018g) *Doing Grounded Theory* (Book 8 of *The SAGE Qualitative Research Kit*, 2nd edn). London: Sage.
Flick, U., Hans, B., Hirseland, A., Rasche, S., and Röhnsch, G. (2017) Migration, unemployment, and lifeworld: Challenges for a new critical qualitative inquiry in migration. *Qualitative Inquiry*, *23*(1), 77–88. doi: 10.1177/1077800416655828.
Gibson, B. (2007) Accommodating critical theory. In A. Bryant and K. Charmaz (Eds.), *The SAGE Handbook of Grounded Theory*. London: Sage. pp. 436–453.
Glaser, B. G. (1969) The constant comparative method of qualitative analysis. In G. J. McCall and J. L. Simmons (Eds.), *Issues in Participant Observation*. Reading, MA: Addison-Wesley. pp. 216–228.
Glaser, B. G. (1992) *Basics of Grounded Theory Analysis*. Mill Valley, CA: Sociology Press.
Glaser, B. G. (2002) Conceptualization: On theory and theorizing using grounded theory. *International Journal of Qualitative Methods*, *1*(2), 23–38. doi: 10.1177/160940690200100203.
Glaser, B. G. and Strauss, A. L. (1967) *The Discovery of Grounded Theory: Strategies for Qualitative Research*. New York: Aldine.
Hammersley, M. and Atkinson. P. (1995) *Ethnography: Principles in Practice* (2nd edn). London: Routledge.
Henwood, K., Shirani, F., and Groves, C. (2018) Using photographs in interviews: When we lack the words to say what practice means. In U. Flick (Ed.), *The SAGE Handbook of Qualitative Data Collection*. London: Sage, pp. 599–614.
Hesse-Biber, S. N. and Leavy, P. (Eds.) (2008) *The Handbook of Emergent Methods*. New York: Guilford Press.
Holton, J. A. and Walsh, I. (2017) *Classic Grounded Theory: Applications with Qualitative and Quantitative Data*. London: Sage.
Kelle, U. (2005) Emergence vs. forcing of empirical data? A crucial problem of 'grounded theory' reconsidered. *Forum Qualitative Sozialforschung / Forum: Qualitative Social Research*, *6*(2), Art. 27. Available at www.qualitative-research.net/fqs-texte/2–05/05–2–27–e.htm.
Kelle, U. (2014) 'Theorization from data', in U. Flick (Ed.), *The SAGE Handbook of Qualitative Data Analysis*. London: Sage, pp. 554–568.
Kennedy, B. and Thornberg, R. (2018) Deduction, induction, and abduction. In U. Flick (Ed.), *The SAGE Handbook of Qualitative Data Collection*. London: Sage. pp. 49–64.
Kusenbach, M. (2018) Go-alongs. In U. Flick (Ed.), *The SAGE Handbook of Qualitative Data Collection*. London: Sage. pp. 344–361.
Kushner, K. E. and Morrow, R. (2003) Grounded theory, feminist theory, critical theory: Toward theoretical triangulation. *Advances in Nursing Science*, *26*(1), 30–43.
Lincoln, Y. S. and Guba, E. G. (1985) *Naturalistic Inquiry*. London: Sage.

Mark, M. (2015) Quantitatively driven approaches to multi- and mixed-methods research. In S. Hesse-Biber and R. B. Johnson (Eds.), *The Oxford Handbook of Multi and Mixed Methods Research Inquiry*. Oxford: Oxford University Press. pp. 21–41.

Maxwell, J. A. (2013) *Qualitative Research Design: An Interactive Approach* (3rd edn). Thousand Oaks, CA: Sage.

McMullen, L. (2011) A discursive analysis of Teresa's protocol: Enhancing oneself, diminishing others. In F. J. Wertz, K. Charmaz, L. M. McMullen, R. Josselson, R. Anderson, and E. McSpadden, *Five Ways of Doing Qualitative Analysis*. New York: Guilford Press. pp. 205–223.

Morse, J. M. (2007) Sampling in grounded theory. In A. Bryant and K. Charmaz (Eds.), *The SAGE Handbook of Grounded Theory*. London: Sage. pp. 229–244.

Morse, J. M., Stern, P. N., Corbin, J., Bowers, B., Charmaz, K., and Clarke, A. E. (Eds.) (2009). *Developing Grounded Theory: The Second Generation*. Walnut Creek, CA: Left Coast Press.

Peirce, C. S. (1878/1958) *Collected Papers*. Cambridge, MA: Harvard University Press.

Potter, J. and Shaw, C. (2018) Naturally occurring data. In U. Flick (Ed.), *The SAGE Handbook of Qualitative Data Collection*. London: Sage. pp. 182–199.

Ragin, C. C. (1994) *Constructing Social Research*. Thousand Oaks, CA: Pine Forge Press.

Reichertz, J. (2007) 'Abduction: The logic of discovery of grounded theory', in A. Bryant and K. Charmaz (Eds.), *The Sage Handbook of Grounded Theory*. London: Sage. pp. 214–228.

Rennie, D. (2000) Grounded theory methodology as methodological hermeneutics: Reconciling realism and relativism. *Theory and Psychology*, *10*, 481–502.

Strauss, A. L. (1987) *Qualitative Analysis for Social Scientists*. Cambridge: Cambridge University Press.

Strauss, A. L. and Corbin, J. (1998) *Basics of Qualitative Research* (2nd edn). London: Sage.

Thornberg, R. and Charmaz, K. (2014) 'Grounded theory and theoretical coding,' in U. Flick (ed.), *The SAGE Handbook of Qualitative Data Analysis*. London: SAGE, pp. 153–169.

Toerien, M. (2014) Conversations and conversation analysis. In U. Flick (Ed.), *The SAGE Handbook of Qualitative Data Analysis*. London: Sage. pp. 327–340.

Wertz, F. J., Charmaz, K., McMullen, L. M., Josselson, R., Anderson, R., and McSpadden, E. (2011) *Five Ways of Doing Qualitative Analysis*. New York: Guilford Press.

Wiener, C. (2007) Making teams work in conducting grounded theory. In A. Bryant and K. Charmaz (Eds.), *The SAGE Handbook of Grounded Theory*. London: Sage. pp. 293–310.

Wilson, H. S. and Hutchinson, S. A. (1991) Triangulation of methods: Heideggerian hermeneutics and grounded theory. *Qualitative Health Research*, *1*, 263–276.

Wright, H. (2009) Using an 'emergent design' to study adult education. *Educate-Special Issue*, December, 62–73.

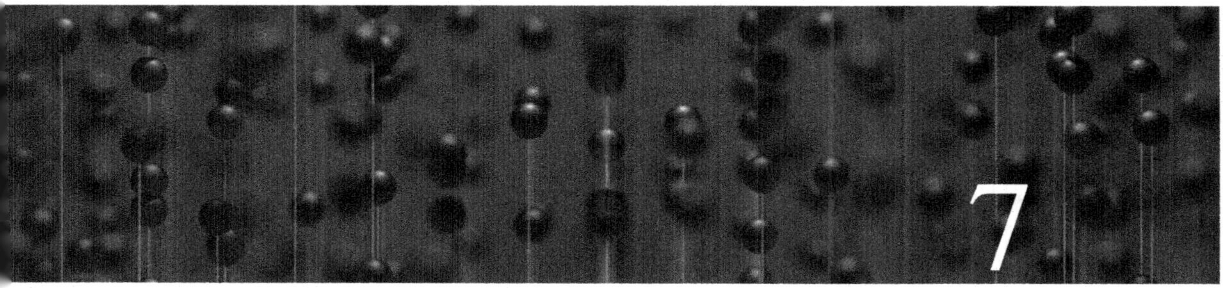

The Nuances of Grounded Theory Sampling and the Pivotal Role of Theoretical Sampling

Janice M. Morse and Lauren Clark

In this chapter, we provide an overview of sampling as it contributes to the development of robust grounded theory. We argue that sampling is not a procedure that is delegated for locating subjects who represent the population at the beginning of the study, as it is in quantitative inquiry. Rather, in qualitative inquiry, the goal of sampling is to represent the phenomenon. In grounded theory, it is a procedural tool that is integral to the entire research process, with the goal of attaining excellent data that enables the development and verification of an abstract and generalizable theory. Here, we first explicate the different types of sampling and the utilization of the knowledge attained from sampling at various points of the development of your grounded theory. Initial purposeful samples ensure targeted coalescence of data, and other strategies scope the domain; theoretical sampling solidifies the theoretical development. In the final section, we discuss how we overcome problems that may occur while sampling. We also discuss how to represent your sample when writing a final manuscript, particularly the section for demographic description of participants and when illustrating your results.

QUALITATIVE SAMPLING

Sampling is the key to rigorous research. Yet there are extraordinary differences between sampling strategies for quantitative and for qualitative research. In *quantitative* research, the sampling strategy goal is to represent the population. In *qualitative* inquiry, the goal of sampling is to represent the phenomenon of interest, that is, the topic of whatever you are studying, primarily through interviewing and, to a lesser extent, by observation or the use of other documents. In *quantitative* research, sampling is based on principles of randomization, so that everyone in this population has an equal chance of being selected for the study. In qualitative inquiry, sampling enables access to new dimensions of the topic that arise during reflexive inquiry. These two different research goals (the population or the topic) give us two different methodological perspectives and provide us with two different approaches to sampling.

In qualitative inquiry, first sampling is based on the researcher's need to understand the phenomenon. The researcher's understanding builds incrementally as the study progresses: who is invited to participate in the study (i.e., the sample) is determined by *what they know* about the topic: that is, what they may contribute – their experience, role, and so forth. As this requisite knowledge changes throughout the study, so does the *type of participant* who is invited to participate change. In this light, the second difference between quantitative and qualitative sampling is the *pacing of the sample*. Quantitative samples are generally determined at one time, at the beginning of the study by setting parameters of inclusion/exclusion criteria. Additional subjects must meet the original study selection criteria, even if they are invited to participate later in the study 'for replacement' if the original pool of sampled participants is depleted.

Qualitative samples are usually initially selected by 'convenience' and expertise. That is, the researcher identifies participants who are likely to have had (or be knowledgeable about) the experience of the research topic, have time to participate, be willing to reflect and talk about the experience (Spradley, 1979). You may find a convenience sample by asking for volunteers, by advertising in newspapers, by asking for referrals from friends and other contacts, or by using a snowball sample. You may also start your work with community stakeholders with expert knowledge, then look for people living the day-to-day experience, as we did in a study of falls among older adults in a rural region of the US (Clark, Thorseon, Goss, Zimmer, & DiGuiseppi, 2013). Care is taken that the scope of the domain is included. Later, as the researcher's understanding about the phenomenon increases, participants are selected according to the 'needs of the study' or, in grounded theory, the 'needs of the developing theory', particularly in developing the concepts and the theoretical properties of the category. This sampling procedure in grounded theory, known as 'theoretical sampling' (Glaser, 1978; Strauss, 1987), enables the researcher to purposefully select the sample (according to what data are needed to be explicated or confirmed).

The most critical difference between quantitative and qualitative sampling is the concept of the *adequacy*. In quantitative research, *data adequacy* is usually determined statistically and is described numerically, usually based on the number of subjects needed to establish the power to detect differences by group. In qualitative inquiry, *data adequacy* is determined by the amount of data obtained from participants who are able to describe the phenomenon and the identified concepts (i.e., an appropriate sample). If the participants are experiential experts about the topic, they will be able to provide copious amounts of pertinent descriptive data. Thus, the size (i.e., the number of participants) of the qualitative sample is dependent on two dimensions: the amount of excellent data obtained (data adequacy) and participant appropriateness.

Both of these dimensions are unknown until the researcher understands more about what is being studied, partway through the data collection. The number also varies according to the scope and complexity of the study aims (what we call the 'messiness' of the phenomenon). Thus, the required number of participants cannot be estimated at the beginning of the study. The more obscure and complex the phenomenon, the larger the sample required to achieve adequacy of data. Similarly, the less expert or articulate the participants are in describing the experience, the greater the number of participants in the sample.

Another consideration for qualitative researchers is the study method and the type of data collected. That is, the amount of data required for the specific method and the type of analysis, the degree to which the research area is developed – meaning what is already known about it – and the nature of rigor, verification and confirmation that will be used. For instance, grounded theory requires a 'moderate' sample size for a qualitative study (and the exact size depends on the scope and abstractness of your study), what is known (the amount of prior research on this topic), and adequate data necessary for confirmation by saturation.

GROUNDED THEORY SAMPLING

Grounded theory involves an emergent design, which means that sampling strategies must be flexible, and be used for developing the concepts, as well as constructing and confirming the theory. Sampling strategies must facilitate the development of abstract, generalizable mid-range theory, one that will be confirmed in the process of development, that will be transferable other settings, and has practical applications.

In other words, who is invited to participate in your grounded theory study is crucial for the attainment of excellent data, and for the ultimate quality of the grounded theory. By astute sampling and ongoing analysis of data obtained, the researcher will be able to determine the boundaries of the phenomenon, the depth of description needed, identify relevant concepts and their interactions, recognize the range of variation and the degree of generality, effectively, purposefully, and efficiently. But one of the most frustrating aspects of sampling for new researchers is that the samples required later in the analysis cannot be predicted by size (how many) nor by type of participants (who); therefore, this aspect of the sample cannot be planned completely at the proposal stage, nor can the researcher determine how large the sample will be. This is frustrating for the researcher, for ethical review (from the institutional review board [IRB]) for project extensions, or, at the proposal stage, for estimating your budget and how long the project will take. Our advice is to overestimate on all of these dimensions, so that you do not have to continually reapply to the IRB to amend the sampling procedure or expand sample size, or to respond to the question 'When will you be finished?'

In grounded theory, sampling is integrated into the process of inquiry. Sampling occurs throughout the analytic process, simultaneously with data analysis, thus making sampling the most complex and important component of the study. The strategies for sample selection change throughout; as the analysis matures, the selection of participants becomes more purposeful and theoretically driven, and the analytic procedures change. As the researcher gains analytic understanding, new and often more specific questions arise. To answer those questions, the purpose of the sampling strategy changes, and the criteria for participant inclusion in the sample may shift. For instance, if you are studying the process parents experience in making sense of the unexpected Down syndrome diagnosis for their newborn, you would start by interviewing parents of newborns with Down syndrome, as we did (Clark, Canary, McDougle, in review). Later we reached a point in our inquiry where we needed to include parents who received a prenatal diagnosis, rather than a neonatal diagnosis, to explore how they received the news and began to make sense of it. Since parents typically shared the news first with their own parents, we also included grandparents to gain a perspective of how telling the news and hearing the news was part of the process for both parents and grandparents.

In order to develop the concepts as they emerge, the focus of sampling changes from the population or group, to deliberately selecting those participants with specific characteristics to including a contrast group to verify or extend the theory. Further, sampling from the library and including research on the topic conducted by others in your analysis expands your theory beyond the specific context. This increases the abstraction of your theory and enables its generalizability to other concepts, by linking to other theories, experiences and populations. Once concepts are understood, through notions of equivalences, this process moves the theory beyond the first context, making it relevant for other contexts, linking it to practice, and allows the researcher to recognize and expand contexts for application or intervention.

THE TYPE OF SAMPLING VARIES ACCORDING TO THE ANALYTIC USES

Grounded theory sampling continues throughout all stages of the study. But the type of sampling changes as the process is described and theory develops. The grounded theory research design must be described at the proposal stage and decisions made. Consider if you want to:

1. Follow the participants through the experience, sampling according to pre-selected timeframes during the experience as it unfolds?
2. Sample different participants cross-sectionally at pre-identified milestones that occur within the experience? Or
3. Conduct retrospective interviews, asking participants who have had the experience, to tell their story.

1. Following Participants through the Experience

This is a common approach to grounded theory data collection. But certain characteristics about the experience must be present before it can be used. For instance, the experience that the researcher is investigating must be patterned or perhaps even predictable. That is, the participant's experience must be relatively defined, so that the researcher may contact participants and obtain their permission to interview them about, or to observe them, when the event that is to be studied occurs. This means that, for the purposes of obtaining informed consent, the experience must have a clear beginning and end point, and the researcher can negotiate his or her research involvement with the participant.

When negotiating the research relationship, the researcher must be reasonably certain at the outset about what he or she wants to know, how involved they will be with the participant, the anticipated endpoint of their research relationship, and so forth. Without such clarity the amount of data collected rapidly becomes unwieldly, and the researcher overwhelmed. On the other hand, the researcher must be flexible, accommodating the emerging (and often unanticipated) findings. Further, if there is no pre-defined endpoint (for instance, if the researcher is studying dying, and the participant lingers), the researcher may take much longer than he or she expects, and research funds may become strained. Besides, it is always useful to know when you are finished.

The researcher must also consider if close contact with the participants will provide the type of data needed. Does the research question require details of everyday events? If the changes in daily living occur slowly, they may even be more difficult to record, particularly if the researcher had less frequent contact. On the other hand, if contact is less frequent, as any parent of a toddler will report, changes may occur between data collections points, and be missed.

Therefore, remember about the armchair walkthrough (Morse, 1999; Richards & Morse, 2012). This means contemplating the various segments of your research at the proposal stage, and anticipating how it may evolve. Make your sampling frame plans carefully and thoughtfully. If circumstances change, then remember that you have the flexibility to change your plans accordingly.

2. Sampling by Pre-identified Milestones

This sampling frame is determined by the researcher's interpretation of the literature, as applied to the research problem and the participants.[1] For instance, if you are studying fatigue in farmers, you may wish to observe and interview at certain points in the daily or annual cycle in the life of the farmer (milking time, planting crops, harvesting, or whatever fits your research problem). The trick is to be certain that you are not missing a significant event, and that the milestones you have identified are the ones that are important. If you are studying nurses' work when a patient codes, for instance, it is problematic if you arrive for data collection only to be told 'Oh, you should have been here yesterday, we had a code at shift change!'

3. Sampling Using Retrospective Interviews

Who do you interview? Regardless of the type of interview you use, it is important to select 'experts' to interview. These are individuals who have experienced the phenomenon or who have observed those who have experience it. The type of interview you select depends on the amount of information known about the topic and the amount of structure in the interview.

Unstructured interviews

Unstructured retrospective interviews are our preferred way for beginning grounded theory data collection. Basically, participants who have already gone through the experience are identified and invited to 'tell their story'. This approach has several advantages: People tend to tell their story sequentially, so these data are the ideal form for the grounded theorist to code and organize the trajectories and the core variable; the significant events remain vivid and easily explained and examined; the participant may have had time to process the events, and therefore not only to be able to describe the event, but also explain the significance of the event (Corbin & Morse, 2003). The fears of psychologists that people tend to forget significant features of the experience by the time they are interviewed are unfounded. People remember details of important events, and the less important details are simply not reported. As the participant's story unfolds, the participant's emotions will reflect those emotions that were experienced during the actual event.

Thus, if the story is distressing, the participant will re-experience the distress. This emotional re-enactment (Morse, 2002) is one of the indices of a valid interview.[2]

4. Other Types of Interviews and Samples

Some interviewing techniques facilitate the development of grounded theory better (and easier) than others. That said, 'all is [sic] data' (Glaser, 2007), meaning that data from different kinds of interviews may contribute to the developing theory. Listed below are interview techniques that form the backbone of grounded theory participation.

Guided interviews

Guided interviews are 6–8 questions that take the participants through the experience, ordering the experience. Guided interviews therefore provide minimal structure to the interview stories, while at the same time providing freedom for the researcher to ask supplemental questions. Guided interviews are useful for new researchers, who many not have the confidence to conduct unstructured interviews.

Semi-structured interviews

These are open-ended questions that guide the participant through the entire scenario. The question stems are prepared (and often the prompts), and all questions are asked of all participants in the same order (McIntosh & Morse, 2015). However, because data are analyzed all at once at the end of data collection, much of the reflexivity required for the sampling strategies necessary for excellent grounded theory (and discussed herein) is lost. These interviews are often used in grounded theory, yet one serious limitation is that much of the reflexivity needed in grounded theory may be unavailable if this format is used.

Focus groups interviews

Interviewing in focus groups consist of general questions asked by a facilitator of 6 to 10 participants. The facilitator's role is to foster general balanced conversion around the topic. If used in grounded theory, once the basic understanding has been gained, then subsequent focus groups may address more specific aspects of the topic. However, this form of interviewing does not provide interview data in the form required for grounded theory analysis. Data are public, rather than intimate conversation; and the conversational format does not allow for in-depth discussion. Most problematic is the way focus groups erase the contours and variations of individual experience, arriving at the most common, generic process explanations. Nuances individuals report are often important and shared, but if they are too private or embarrassing or unique, focus groups steamroll over nuance and variation to arrive at group-endorsed macro-level generalities. There is little left for the grounded theorist to work with due to the group conversational format. Focus group interviews are therefore not recommended as a stand-alone data collection strategy for grounded theory, but they may be used to supplement other data collection strategies in a study.

Observations

When grounded theory was first developed, an observational component was also included (Benoliel, 1996). More recently, interviews comprise the primary data source in grounded theory research. After an interview it may be opportune to negotiate with the participant what you would like to observe, how long you would like to observe, and when you might arrive to observe an event or day-to-day process germane to the research topic. The researcher will also select the style of observation, from complete observer to complete participant. The researcher records observations in the form of field notes, and any queries directed to the participants during that time become informal interview data inserted into the written field notes.

SAMPLING VARIES WITH THE ANALYTIC STAGE OF DEVELOPMENT OF THE GROUNDED THEORY

In grounded theory, the strategies of sampling used are according to the level of development of the grounded theory. A summary of these tasks follows:

The first task is *Grasping the phenomenon*, or obtaining a broad overview of the phenomenon, and for this, a convenience sample of experts is usually used. These are generally participants who have lived through the experience and are asked to retrospectively 'tell their story'. Next, *the trajectory of the theory is identified*, and the theory developed further using negative cases, and confirmed. You will begin theoretical sampling, deliberately selecting participants who have had a particular experience or a different type of experience. Now the *theory is constructed*, by linking concepts. Data collection continues by building any thin areas. Finally, in the *phase of confirmation, translation and application*, the theory is recontextualized and implemented.

The analytic stages and the types of sampling techniques for each stage are shown on Table 7.1. Two things are important about this table. First, as the study develops analytically, the researcher may select different groups of participants (or settings, or documents, etc.) at different times, for different reasons. The analytic purpose for the sample is listed in the left column; the type of sample is labelled on the top row; and the level of theory development is shown on the right column. Second, as the analytic purpose of the study changes, the researcher may return to data already collected (i.e., the first sample) and re-examine those data for a different purpose. For instance, initially, the purpose of gathering those data using a convenience sample may be to grasp the phenomenon, but later in the analysis, the researcher may return to the same interviews, examining the interviews for information to determine boundaries or about negative cases, and so forth. *If* the necessary information is not available in the first data collected, then the researcher will have to pull an additional sample for that specific purpose.

The greatest limitation in grounded theory (and unfortunately the most common error) is drawing an inadequate sample, and consequently not having enough data. Worst of all is not recognizing that one's data are insufficient. Sample inadequacy may arise because the researcher has too few participants available to invite into the study. Alternatively, as previously discussed, the researcher may delimit the amount of data obtained from each person, by using an interview strategy that restricts and circumscribed responses from participants (such as semi-structured interviews or focus group interviews) and therefore limits the amount of data obtained from each participant.

Table 7.1 Analytic sampling and types of samples required for developing grounded theory

Purpose	*Types of theoretical samples*						**Level of theoretical development on completion of sample**
	Purposeful/ Retrospective interviews with experts	*Purposeful/ Theoretical: Expanding variety of 'cases'*	*Purposeful/ Theoretical: Sampling for depth and range of experiences within stages*	*Library search for similar processes, concepts and theory*	*Purposeful/ Theoretical: Seeking negative cases*	*Purposeful/ Theoretical: Group interviews*	
1. Grasping the phenomenon							
a. Sampling to obtain an initial understanding	x						Recognizing 'what is going on': concepts, preliminary trajectory
b. Sampling for process	x	x					
c. Sampling for maximum variation –conceptual –demographic	x	x					Knowing what to look for, now recognizing it in context
d. Sampling to chase important leads	x	x					No gaps
2. Identifying theoretical components							
a. Sampling to locate and create concepts	x	x					Complete set of concepts
b. Sampling for Identifying trajectory(ies)	x	x	x				Learning to recognize stages/phases

c. Sampling for pattern identification (& change)	x	x	x				Identifying causes, conditions and consequences between stages
d. Sampling for confirmation	x	x	x				Integrating negative cases
e. Sampling for negative cases	x	x	x				
3. Constructing the theory							
a. Sampling to link concepts	x	x	x	x			Developing theoretical statements
b. Obtaining certainty: –confirmation	x	x	x	x	x		Filling in the gaps
c. Sampling for saturation	x	x	x	x	x	x	Ensuring comprehensiveness
d. Sampling for verification	x	x	x	x	x	x	Supports emerging ideas
4. Sampling for theory development							
a. Sampling to determineequivalency in concepts across contexts	x	x	x	x	x		Making it generalizable (data from Library)
b. Sampling for theoretical group interviews	x	x	x	x	x	x	Theoretical/conceptual completion
c. Sampling to Recontextualize –sampling for application	x	x	x	x	x	x	Finalizing theory

1. Grasping the Phenomenon

How does the researcher learn 'what is going on' about the phenomenon? Grounded theory always commences, as do most other qualitative methods, by using a *convenience* sample. This sample is basically inviting those who are available to participate in your study. The purpose of this sample is to find out as much as one can about the topic of interest, inviting participants to be interviewed who have already experienced the event in its most extreme form (a 'retrospective' sample), to provide us with a broad overview, and therefore giving the researcher a 'feel for' the topic. We do not invite those who are in the midst of the experience, because they know only a part of the story (for them, it is still unresolved), and they have not yet processed the experience cognitively by constructing meaning around the experience and its influence on their day-to-day life. Identify the sample of those who have the condition and retrospectively describe it (column 1). By using theoretical cells, you may be able to saturate your theory by choosing those who are both positive and negative cases. However, it is insufficient to simply do the retrospective interviews with experts all at one time and use them as a static dataset.

a. Sampling to obtain an initial understanding

How do you 'obtain an initial understanding?' The initial overview of the phenomenon is obtained by using interviews that give the participants the freedom to express themselves; this is, of course, a validity issue. *Unstructured interviews* work best (as previously described) because participants can have time to tell their stories, without interruption, Participants tells their story from start to finish, so that the sequential process, later needed for the development of the BSP (basic social process) (Glaser, 1978) or core variable (Strauss, 1987), may be easily identified. Sometimes a participant tells only a 'slice' of the story, the part that the participant *thinks* that the researcher wants to hear. For instance, in nursing we may get the disease story rooted in medical care – visits to the doctors, medications and treatments ordered – that is, not the experience of the illness, but concrete disease-based information that we could have obtained from the patient's chart. If this happens, do not interrupt. But once the person has told that storyline, take them back to the beginning and ask: 'Tell me how you felt during that experience' and you will then be told the illness story.[3]

By selecting a sample of participants who have had the experience within the last six months, you may be accused by others of selecting a biased sample. Perhaps, but our purpose is to obtain an excellent overall description of the event, so that the characteristics and concepts within the phenomenon involved are clearly described. To do this you must use the most obvious, clearest, and best example of the experience. We are using the term 'biased sample' intentionally as a positive concept because you as the researcher are deliberately biasing your sample to get the best exemplars through purposeful sampling. Once you understand the phenomenon of interest and the characteristics (attributes) involved, you will be able to recognize the phenomenon in other settings, and in average experiences that may co-occur with other experiences, or in 'weaker' instances in which other concepts to do with co-occurring experiences may be present.

b. Sampling for process

Grounded theorists are interested in discovering meaning within a *process*. The major methods for eliciting such data are:

1. To follow participants through the experience, sampling at regular intervals or when certain pre-identified milestones occur. From your knowledge about the phenomenon, identify milestones. For a person describing an illness, these milestones may be such events as getting a diagnosis, entering the hospital, having surgery, being discharged, getting well. Interviews are scheduled at each of these points.
2. To interview different participants, who are experiencing each pre-identified milestone. If you feel the experience is reasonably the same for all participants, another model may be to identify the milestones above and interview different participants at those pre-identified milestones. This, of course, is less time-consuming than waiting for a cohort to enter each phase.
3. To conduct 'retrospective' interviews from those who have recently gone through the entire experience, as discussed earlier. Once these narratives are collected from several participants, you may begin to notice patterns in the experiences that they are interviewing about. These patterns may be 'turning points' that are the transitions in the trajectory. They may be point of divergence or decisions that participants must make. They may be instances of self-realization or recognition about what is happening.

At this time, you begin working with abstract categories and must *transition* to *theoretical sampling*. Once the main storyline of the narrative has been identified, and the major transitions, the researcher can, at that time, go back to other participants who are in the midst of living through these transitions, and sample for more data at those points in time. Transitioning to theoretical sampling marks entry into ambiguous territory, as grounded theorists begin simultaneous data analysis along with recursive data collection from carefully chosen participants. Ultimately, theoretical sampling to solidify categories and elaborate the depiction of the overall phenomenon is what builds the grounded theory. Some experts may suggest theoretical sampling sets grounded theory apart as the sole means of iterative theory development, but we disagree. Theoretical sampling represents the strategic process used to craft the richly saturated categorical components in the theory, order those components, and describe the transition points and properties of the grounded theory. We propose the hallmark of grounded theory is an iterative and increasingly elegant elaboration of middle-range theory based on data from participants chosen by theoretical sampling procedures.

Considering sample size: how many participants are sampled at this stage? Minimally 10 (but preferably more), for you need to have enough stories to see some regularity or commonalities between the participants' experiences. By regularity, we do not mean standard calendar events that may be involved in their stories, but similarities in responses to the events. And, of course, the broader or noisier the topic of your study, the more interviews you will need to reach this stage. If you select your participants carefully – people who are 'good to talk to' – you will reach your milestones of 'getting a feel for what is going on' more quickly. Your data are only as good as your participants. And of course, as good as your skills as an analyst.

c. Sampling for maximum variation

There are two types of variations of consider: *diversity contextual variation* and diversity/ demographic variation.

First, diversity contextual variation. At this point, we realize that your data may be specifically homogeneous: everyone appears to have had the same experience.[4] Yet you know that the experience may occur in different forms, according to different settings, situations or circumstances. It is a mistake to declare "the sample is saturated" and stop there. Therefore, you must deliberately sample to get information about these 'other forms' of the concept. For example, if you are studying *hope*, you know that hope is a relatively high-level concept that is used in various forms (for examples, see Morse & Doberneck, 1995). Therefore, you must scope your participants to ensure you obtain data about all of these forms of the concept, and do not have any gaps. Those researchers who do not sample for variation, often report that they have 'reached saturation'. But their claim is premature, and their completed studies are not likely to contain new insights.

Second, sampling for diversity/demographic variation. Look at your sample: Do you have adequate data from both males and females? From professionals and from lower socioeconomic class? From 'insiders' and 'outsiders'? From other cultural/ethnic groups? Are there various characteristics of your participants that are important to your topic? Your coded demographic data will provide this information. Run the search to see if there is any bias in the categories by gender or other demographic variables – anything missing or very deficient?

The next consideration requires judgement: Ethnicity, for example, is tricky. You must determine if your sample should be cohesive culturally/ethnically. If you believe that cultural perception is different, and that is important in your study, then you must saturate each cultural group in your sample (Morse, 1995). Your demographic coding will help you to answer these questions reasonably quickly. If not, then the ethnicity of your sample it will not affect your results. Of course, the ability to communicate is crucial, so be certain to ask if your participants can speak English.

d. Sampling to chase important leads

One of the crucial differences in qualitative and quantitative samples is that in the *qualitative* sample, each participant is speaking for themselves AND also giving you information about others. In the *quantitative* sample, the person is usually only giving you data about him- or herself.

This fact has important implications for sample size. In *qualitative* research, counting *how many* people in your study does not represent your dataset at all. Participants in your study may speak in generalities about their family and compare it with other families they have known, children speak about others in their classroom, and at school. How many others? We do not know. Sometimes participants speak of themselves as a group: 'We, mothers with these children, ____'. Participants may say: 'some people do this____, and some people do that____.' Such cues in the interviews are crucial for your subsequent sampling frames. As the participants sort their world for you, they are telling how you can organize your data, and where to go for further information. But you do not have any information about your sample size and how many people they are representing when they make such statements.

By this stage in your study, you feel you are starting to get somewhere. You are feeling excitement, beginning to understand your topic, and beginning to build an interesting dataset, and have data with which to work. You are coding daily, and data are being sorted into categories or themes. You are memo-ing as fast as you can, and recording ideas. You can recognize an important lead when you are given one, and are gaining confidence in chasing these leads. But you are still only beginning. As you move forward with this analysis, do not forget the library as a resource. Keep searching the literature as new articles are released.

Where do you look for this information? Some information will be included in your first group of interviews; some you will obtain from the literature; some from your every-day knowledge. Yet sometimes you will have to select additional participants with the experiences you need to include in your data. This we call *theoretical sampling*, and it will be addressed shortly.

2. Identifying the Theoretical Components

Now that you have a handle on the topic, some knowledge of the scope and limits of your topic, it is time to begin the theoretical analysis.

a. Sampling to locate and create concepts

This occurs through the processes of coding and building categories. As you code you are developing a sense of what is important to your participants. These perceptions accrue in your categories, and may, as data builds and your thinking about these data (in memos) increases, be separated into smaller perspectives or subcategories. Importantly, these concepts are about the *topic*. Each has all of the information about a certain topic – things that were there at the beginning of the process and things that appeared at the end are all in the same category. These categories do not tell the researcher very much about the ordering according to time and maturation of the concepts; this must be done in a second data sort (or re-sort).

b. Sampling for identifying trajectories

One of the significant aspects of grounded theory that is not accessible to phenomenology or ethnography is the 'process' lens of the grounded theorist (Charmaz, 2014; Corbin & Strauss, 2015). Grounded theorists are fascinated by changing phenomena, by trajectories, by transitions, by causes and consequences (Corbin & Strauss, 2015). The grounded theorist's language of theory is in the use of gerunds and keeping the perspective of the theory *action-oriented* with the use of gerunds (Charmaz, 2014, 2015).

c. Sampling for pattern identification

Now we know what we have, and recognize the trajectory, we must reorder our data according to the way these data mature. To do this we must return to the original interviews and look to see where in the story each data piece appears, according to our understanding of the emerging trajectories, in a sampling strategy called 'intra project sampling' (Morse, 2007). Within each category, sort the data accordingly.

d. Sampling for confirmation

Confirming one's data is an extremely important step, and it may take several forms. First, you must have adequate data, so that the composition of the concepts is derived from several participants – not just one person. It is not necessary that you record the number of participants, just that you know that the category contains several different perspectives about the same event or occurrence, and the descriptions are detailed. This is what is meant by *rich data*. One account supports the other – they will not be exactly the same, of course, but each account adds to the description of the others.

e. Sampling for negative cases

Negative cases are those accounts that contradict or that do not support the other data. Such data must be carefully examined, as negative data may simply be the fact that something was omitted or missing from an account, and the researcher has to go back and verify that this negative instance was something that, in this case, did not happen.

If the negative case was a contrary example, then the researcher must try to find others who have the same characteristics, and sample for more cases. Negative cases are as important to the developing theory as supporting cases, and these cases should also be sampled until saturation is reached.

3. Constructing Theory

a. Sampling to link concepts

In your emerging theory, the concepts may change or link to new concepts at the transitions. However, concepts that are nestled together within a stage of your theory, may also be considered allied concepts, and share attributes. The concepts may interact, be dependent on one another, or simply coexist.

b. Sampling to obtain certainty

There is some discussion about 'knowing' in qualitative inquiry, because the researcher cannot validly use counting, statistics and p values to provide 'concrete' data about the association of characteristics. This must be done by 'opening' and examining the concepts in order to examine their shared characteristics (see Morse & Penrod, 1999).

c. Sampling for saturation

Saturation generally refers to the continuance of sampling and data collection until data overlap within the categories. It is to ensure that thin data have been expanded to the level of appropriateness. That is, some data *approximate* other data collected for other participants, and even in other situations. A single example does not 'sit' by itself in a category.

d. Sampling for verification

Sampling for verification is the deliberate seeking of data that supports an emerging idea. The researcher seeks independent participants and asks: 'Some people have told me _____. Is this how it is for you?' Usually data that are being verified are more detailed than the theoretical confirmation and expansion, as is sought in theoretical groups' interviews, discussed later.

4. Sampling for Theory Development

Theory development is the process of organizing your concepts according to the way they link into your emerging theory.

Ask: Which concepts are to do with the initial part of the process? How do they interact together? Are some of the concepts pieces (or smaller concepts) that are embedded in the larger concepts?

Ask: What leads to the transition? What changes? Does the concept change? Transform into something else? Or drop out in the next stage? Do all concepts link to the next stage?

Ordering the concepts is rather like putting puzzle pieces together. *Diagramming* facilitates this process. As your theory develops, the first task is to ensure that your concepts are placed in the correct position among other concepts – both horizontally and vertically. Diagramming at this phase is essential – it assists with clarifying conceptual boundaries, ensures that the conceptual attributes are correctly placed, and your definitions are solid. It also ensures that your trajectories are 'alive,' and the conditions for moving from one stage to another are strong. Select many examples and scrutinize the conditions and consequences in each transition.

Identify the core category (Strauss, 1987) (or the basic social psychological process [Glaser, 1978]). This is the most important component of the grounded theory. It is really 'what the study is about'. A core category goes right through the whole process: it is 'what holds the grounded theory together' and is 'central to the integration of the theory' (Strauss, 1987, p. 21). It may change or alter its form as it goes through the process, but the other concepts are probably involved and linked to the core category.

a. Sampling to determine equivalency across contexts

This is sampling in the 'library,' to link to other's concepts and theories. At this phase, it is time to return to the library and locate the work of others who have described similar processes. Such searching is difficult, as the similar work may not have been conducted in the same contexts, with the same groups or populations and even be working in another discipline. Furthermore, the other investigators may have used qualitatively different terms for their concepts and theories. Sometimes you are provided links at conferences: 'Oh, Joe is interested in that process – he is working on ____ (thus and so)'. Nevertheless, by searching you will find something that will be important: explore it, compare it, explore its concepts. If you are lucky, and there are concepts or processes that will help you, cite it. Consider such work as evidence that you are on the right trail. Because you are still working the results, bring this literature in as data and as evidence supporting your ideas.

b. Sampling for theoretical group interviews

Critical examination of your concepts and theory may reveal that while you have much data about common aspects, some more crucial aspects are thin and not well developed. At this time, your theoretical sampling takes yet another form, as theoretical group interviews. Theoretical groups interviews are a form of specialized focus group. They are small: two or three of your most eloquent participants are invited to share experiences[5] and to assist with the analysis. In preparation for the meeting, participants are sent the preliminary findings, and have time to think about how the results have been developed from the earlier stage of the research. Once they are comfortable with the other members of the group, the researcher begins the session by asking questions about the categories and transitions about which we have little data, and that are considered 'thin'. They are asked to tell examples from their experience (or others' experiences) that can help the researcher understand what is happening at particular points. Record the conversation as data. Thus, theoretical group interviews provide additional participant data that confirms, refutes, or makes adjustments to one's model at an abstract level.[6] It is therefore a crucial verification strategy that strengthens or modifies your theory.

c. Sampling to Recontextualize

The final sampling strategy is to place your theory back into the context from which it was developed, for the purposes of *implementing* the new theoretical model, and as a process of *translation* to identify other contexts that would benefit from these insights. Alternatively, the researcher may deliberately select a site that is different from the original site, but which has important characteristics in common. This, in essence, is not only testing the efficacy of the results, but also the generalizability of the theory itself.

The researcher may also identify interventions that extend from their theory. These theoretically-based interventions may be tested at this time, or as supplementary evidence-based projects. For instance, over a number of years, Wuest and her colleagues developed a grounded theory of women who left abusing marital relationships (Wuest, Ford-Gilboe, Merritt-Gray, & Berman, 2003). The central problem was *Strengthening Capacity to Limit Intrusion (SCLI)*, with the four processes of providing, rebutting, renewing self, and regenerating family. To identify primary healthcare interventions to reduce the impact of intrusion after leaving a spouse, the researchers searched for interventions and developed a program, iHEAL (Interventions for Health Enhancement After Leaving) (Ford-Gilboe, Merritt-Gray, Varcoe, & Wuest 2011). However, the research team quickly realized that the fit between the grounded theory and the interventions available was poor, and investigation (*and sampling*) had to continue to modify and improve the fit between the theory and the available interventions (Wuest, Ford-Gilboe, Merritt-Gray & Varcoe, 2013). This was an essential reciprocal process continuing the grounded theory processes of emergent fit, including constant comparative analysis, and the sampling for the collection of new data for theoretical refinement and the modification of interventions. In this way, the theory becomes recontextualized and generalized.

NOTIONS OF EQUIVALENCE

The goal of an abstract theory is to ensure that the theory is generalizable, for a theory, no matter how insightful, is of limited use if it has no application to other settings or situations.

Therefore, the researcher deliberately seeks equivalence in other contexts. The researcher must seek commonalities with attributes by comparing it with allied concepts and looks for commonalities with associated concepts and theories. Note that we have suggested 'commonalities.' In the social sciences, we look for resemblance – nothing is *exactly* the same.

Where do we look for these commonalities? This is quite a difficult question, because the 'competitors' are using different terms for their concepts and theories. Concepts that are important in one discipline may have quite a different term for the same concept in another discipline. Therefore, it may be necessary to talk and read widely, to locate the relevant research.

Consider this example: A theory of privacy maintenance was developed in a nursing home (Applegate & Morse, 1994). It showed that the types of interaction between the resident and the nurse was based on the perception of the other as a friend, acquaintance or an object. This theory has broad implications for any setting that is hierarchal and where dependent relationships occur – in prisons, boarding schools, hospital settings – so that anyone searching for the concept 'privacy' should not delimit the search by setting, nor discount this study because it was conducted in a nursing home. Similarly, I have described the concept of enduring of patients in a trauma setting (Morse, 2017), but enduring may be seen is other settings in which emotions must be suppressed in order for the person to maintain control of self.

Equivalence in Other Concepts and Theories

Theoretical congestion

A quite serious problem in qualitative inquiry is the notion, held by doctoral students and others, that grounded theory has to be original. Your grounded theory must make a contribution that is unique, has not been previously described, and that such an original contribution is essential for attaining a doctoral degree.

Unfortunately, (or fortunately) qualitatively-derived theory is becoming quite a crowded field (Charmaz, 2015; Morse, 2000). This means that we should be able to synthesize similar theories and create a very powerful theory. But it does not quite work that way (see Thorne, 2017). Therefore, new investigators try to ensure that their theory is unique in two ways. The first is by neglecting to sample in the library (i.e., search the literature) for similar concepts and theories. To ensure that their theory is unique, and to determine how their theory is linked to other theories in the area, researchers should search in the library for similar concepts and theories, and then compare and contrast the concepts or theories. This last comparison is difficult, as it must be clear to you by now that the researcher must search beyond the boundaries of the context and population of his or her study. Often allied concepts may be located, and in this case the researcher then has the task of determining the similarities of the concepts, and how the theories are so much alike, but different in essential ways. But this step is essential if the claim of originality of one's work is to hold. Without this step, we have many similar/same weaker theories with different labels, a problem called 'theoretical congestion' (Morse, 2000). Note that we are still working in the results, theoretically building our own theory, so these citations of similar comparative work occur in the literature. Some disciplines do this routinely throughout their results (e.g., anthropology) while still maintaining an inductive thrust.

The second way to ensure uniqueness of the theory is for the researcher to label the concepts, processes, and core categories using lexemes.[7] This is a double-edged sword. First, the lexemes may not be very descriptive concept labels and may have a very distinctive local meaning. This keeps the theoretical work localized and works against your goal of generalizability. But it also inhibits your project from being merged into the larger stream of concepts and theories that are developing around your phenomenon. From the outsider's perspective, those who are using search terms to locate similar work, will not find your work – it will be excluded from literature reviews and meta-analyses, and will die quietly in the library.

THE PRACTICALITIES OF SAMPLING

In this section, we address special problems that may occur when sampling for grounded theory: how to manage difficulties that naturally occur during the course of the project. How do you overcome data insufficiency? How does one supplement 'scant' samples that yield thin data? How might a hypothetical case be used in analysis? And what should researchers do if the sample is limited and even when using a total sample, saturation cannot be reached?

Data Insufficiency

Of course, data may be insufficient in one or both adequacy and appropriateness dimensions. Inadequacy may occur because the phenomenon you are studying is relatively rare, and even using a total sample (i.e., all of the participants available) your data will still be *thin* in some aspect. Your study may be exploring an uncommon event, the phenomenon may be considered private so that you cannot gain permission to access participants, you may not have access for more participants, or you may simply be out of time. And money. And enthusiasm.

There are a number of ways you may supplement your sample, and the strategy you choose depends on the stage you are at in the analysis, or what you may need to know.

a. Hypothetical data

If you are studying relatively rare or uncommon events, one way to obtain some understanding of the event is to ask participants to show you what they would do if____. The acting or demonstrating may be reasonable data for your purposes. Supposing, for instance, you are studying lay midwives and birthing, and your study relies on observing an actual birth to view their techniques of delivery. Of course, when you are studying something it never happens. An alternative may be to ask the birth attendants to *show you* what you want to know: the birth position, the herbs used, the sounds of birthing, and how they manage distressed mothers. Discuss data you already have and ask question: if these are *normal births*, what other kinds of births are there?

b. Shadowed data

Use *shadowed data* to ask: 'Is this the way other midwives do ________?', 'Are there other kinds of practices?' When these participants tell you 'some do this ___, and some do that ____', you get a notion about how *representative* your data are of these phenomena under study. Shadowed data are therefore an excellent technique to use if you are studying something that may be embarrassing to participants. They will tell you what others may do ('not *me*, of course'), and therefore shadowed data provide access to knowledge that would otherwise be inaccessible.

c. Supplement using other data types

Corbin and Strauss (2015) provide an excellent example of seeking data in autobiographies, when Corbin was not able to locate participants. She found excellent information in autobiographical and biographical literature, which she incorporated into her study as data.[8]

d. Hypothetical cases

When using Glaserian techniques of sorting participants into groups according to certain characteristics (2×2s) (Glaser, 1978), researchers may sort participants to recognize the type of individual that would have those characteristics if they had the resources to theoretically sample and locate them. If the researchers are conducting a master's thesis and have conducted excellent theoretical work on the sample they have, they may stop the sampling at this point and present their results, providing a description of the hypothetical sample (for examples, see Morse & Johnson, 1991).[9]

e. Limited total sample

Often when researchers have permission to collect data at a single institution (such as a hospital) and are collecting data on a relatively rare condition, even using *all* cases available over a certain timeframe, does not give enough data to ensure saturation of all categories. Other forms of sampling – advertising, approaching groups, using saturated data are all exhausted or not feasible. In this case, the researcher may be forced to close the study and note the limitations for sampling – of data insufficiency and inadequacy in the discussion.

When Do You Cease Sampling?

When your study is finished? When do you stop, and when do you close the door? Some researchers make the decision that their study is compete when they run out of time, research funds, or energy. Your theory may have some holes or gaps – the important thing is to know where these gaps are, and not to dodge these issues in your Discussion section.

Ideally, when the study is completed, your theory is comprehensive, defensible, rich in its explanatory power, insightful, useful, and broad in scope. When presenting your theory, you are able to answer questions *competently*. This means, with additional examples, you capably discuss the unique contribution your theory makes, and how it is similar to, and different from, allied theories that may be used in different situations and contexts.

The final criterion for finishing the grounded theory the *theoretical transference*. Well-developed qualitative concepts and theories must have application beyond the context and situation in which they were first identified. The common belief of qualitative researchers, that qualitative research is not generalizable, is incorrect. The onus is on the researcher to illustrate the application of the concept or theory in multiple situations. Qualitative researchers present the practice of limiting generalization by referring to their sample using demographics is false and misleading.[10] We forget the quantifiable demographics used in quantitative research are simply proxies for sociological cultural groups. Because qualitative research moves beyond the concrete descriptors to levels of abstraction that transcend the particular, the abstract findings may be applied to other situations with similar characteristics.

SUMMARY

Sampling is literally the foundation of good grounded theory. Whomever the researcher selects as a participant to interview or observe provides the core of your inquiry – the story, descriptions, examples, and illustrations – that will enable you to identify, interpret or build categories, themes, concepts, and theory. The qualitative researcher is not passive in the selection of participants, nor is sampling a process delegated to chance. The sample must be deliberately selected, first by carefully selecting a convenience sample of *appropriate* participants, and, second, by selecting appropriate participants based on certain characteristics. Data obtained from the original convenience sample may be re-examined for the data needed later in the study *or* from participants who have been selected for the information that is necessary. In grounded theory, data are synthesized in categories apart from (separated from) the participants themselves – but later, once the theory is understood, participants may be used as illustrative exemplars in the emerging and abstract theory to further recontextualize the results. The final type of sampling – *sampling for application* – is to determine and select an appropriate fit for the application of the results and ultimate evidenced-based testing/utilization of the theory.

What is achieved when the careful grounded theorist has completed successive waves of sampling using a progression of theoretically-selected participants? The researcher codes the interviews as a first step in understanding what is happening. But then, in subsequent analytic phases, they must return to the original interviews to elicit information that they did not realize or recognize they needed until the theory began to fall into place. Nevertheless, these initial interviews are supplemented with theoretical sampling of subsequent participants. These processes, along with astute theorizing, confirmation, and linkages to the literature, will produce solid, rigorous, and useful grounded theory.

Notes

1 Glaser (1978) suggests this step is unnecessary and the student should avoid the literature. Our approach is the reverse – to know the literature and to use it as a mental 'sounding board' to reflect and compare to what you are seeing in your analysis.
2 There is a classroom demonstration for those students who do not appreciate this phenomenon: ask students who are married and select a volunteer. Ask the student to tell you about how she/he met his/her husband. The student will pause to reflect and his/her face will glow. At his point interrupt the student. Say 'I don't need the story, I just wanted to see your face when you revisited that time'.
3 Some researchers use a *guided interview*. As previously described, this method consists of asking 6–10 open-ended questions that provide a loose structure or framework for the interview. This is a strategy that is between the unstructured open-ended interview (an 'innocent' perspective) and the structure

of a semi-structured or focus group interview (in which you are supposed have some knowledge about the topic). This is useful for new researchers who may find that unstructured format intimidating ('Supposing they don't talk?'), but always ensure that you have asked 'Is there anything else you would like to tell me?' at the end of the interview. May (1991) notes that the real interview may begin at the doorway, when the researcher is leaving, and advises researchers not to turn their recorders off.

4 Unfortunately, new researchers confuse this 'homogeneity' for saturation, and consider their study complete. Of course, it is far from completed.

5 Because the researcher is no longer maintaining confidentiality and anonymity, IRB and separate participant consents for theoretical group members are required for this portion. We give them lunch to make such sharing less formal.

6 Participants need to be warned that they may not see any quotations that they recognize as their 'own', but rather should be able to recognize the theory.

7 Lexemes are local terms, often slang. Often researchers use a phrase or short quote as a descriptor, and this is equally problematic, as it also keeps the research close to the context and works against generalizability.

8 Morse (2011) also used autobiographical accounts when seeking to understand what patients actually heard when being given 'bad' diagnostic news.

9 Morse argues that the difference between a master's thesis and a doctoral dissertation is the more limited scope of the master's thesis and the use of hypothetical groups.

10 Qualitative researchers are their own worst enemy, delimiting their own research using inappropriate criteria.

REFERENCES

Applegate, M. & Morse, J. M. (1994). Personal privacy and interaction patterns in a nursing home. *Journal of Aging Studies*, *8*(4), 413–434.

Benoliel, Jeanne Quint. (1996). Grounded theory and nursing knowledge. *Qualitative Health Research*, *6*(3), 406–428.

Charmaz, Kathy. (2014). *Constructing Grounded Theory* (2nd ed.). Thousand Oaks, CA: Sage.

Charmaz, Kathy. (2015). Teaching theory construction with initial grounded theory tools: A reflection on lessons and learning. *Qualitative Health Research*, *25*(12), 1501–1622.

Clark, Lauren, Canary, Heather, & McDougle, K. (in review). The family sense-making process after a Down syndrome diagnose.

Clark, Lauren, Thoreson, Sallie, Goss, Cynthia, Zimmer, Lorena M., & DiGuiseppi, Carolyn. (2013). Understanding fall meaning and context in marketing balance classes to older adults. *Journal of Applied Gerontology*, *32*(1), 96–110. DOI: 10.1177/0733464811399896

Corbin, Juliet & Morse, Janice M. (2003). The unstructured interactive interview: Issues of reciprocity and risks. *Qualitative Inquiry*, *9*(3), 335–354.

Corbin, Juliet & Strauss, Anselm. (2015). *Basics of Qualitative Research* (4th ed.). Thousand Oaks, CA: Sage.

Ford-Gilboe, Marilyn, Merritt-Gray, M., Varcoe, Colleen, & Wuest, Judith. (2011). A theory-based primary health care intervention for women who have left abusive partners. *Advances in Nursing Science*, *34*(3), 198–214. DOI: 10.1097/ANS.0b013e3182228cdc.

Glaser, Barney G. (1978). *Theoretical Sensitivity*. Mill Valley, CA: Sociology Press.

Glaser, Barney G. (2007). All is data. *Grounded Theory Review: An International Journal.* Online http://groundedtheoryreview.com/2007/03/30/1194/

May, Katharyn A. (1991). Interview techniques in qualitative research: Concerns and challenges. In J. M. Morse (Ed.), *Qualitative Nursing Research: A Contemporary Dialogue* (pp. 188–201). Newbury Park, CA: Sage.

McIntosh, Michele J. & Morse, Janice M. (2015). Situating and constructing diversity in semi-structured interviews. *Global Qualitative Nursing Research*, *2*, 1–12. DOI: 10.1177/2333393615597674

Morse, Janice M. (1995). NIH and the methodological melting pot. *Qualitative Health Research*, *5*(1), 4–6.

Morse, Janice M. (1999). The armchair walkthrough. *Qualitative Health Research*, *9*(4), 435–436.

Morse, Janice M. (2000). Theoretical congestion. *Qualitative Health Research*, *10*(6) 715–716.

Morse, Janice M. (2002). Emotional reenactment. *Qualitative Health Research*, *12*(2), 147–147. DOI: 10.1177/104973230201200201.

Morse, Janice M. (2006). Strategies of intraproject sampling. In P. Munhall (Ed.), *Nursing Research: A Qualitative Perspective* (4th ed., pp. 529–540). Boston, MA: Jones & Bartlett.

Morse, Janice M. (2007). Sampling in grounded theory research. In A. Bryant & K. Charmaz (Eds.), *The SAGE Handbook of grounded theory* (pp. 229–244). London: Sage.

Morse, Janice M. (2011). Hearing bad news. *Journal of Humanistic Medicine*, *32*, 187–211. DOI: 10.1007/s10912-011-9138-4.

Morse, Janice M. (2017). *Analyzing and Conceptualizing the Theoretical Foundations of Nursing*. New York: Springer.

Morse, Janice M. & Doberneck, B. M. (1995). Delineating the concept of hope. *Image: Journal of Nursing Scholarship*, *27*(4), 277–285.

Morse, Janice M. & Johnson, Joy L. (1991). *The Illness Experience: Dimensions of Suffering*. Newbury Park, CA: Sage.

Morse, Janice M. & Penrod, J. (1999). Linking concepts of enduring, suffering, and hope. *Image: Journal of Nursing Scholarship*, *31*(2), 145–150.

Richards, Lyn & Morse, Janice M. (2012). *Readme First for a Students Guide to Qualitative Research* (3rd ed.). Thousand Oaks, CA: Sage.

Spradley, James P. (1979). *The Ethnographic Interview*. New York: Holt, Rinehart & Winston.

Strauss, Anselm, L. (1987). *Qualitative Analysis for Social Scientists*. Cambridge, UK: Cambridge University Press.

Thorne, Sally. (2017). Metasynthetic madness: What kind of monster have we created? *Qualitative Health Research*, *27*(1), 3–12. DOI: 10.1177/1049732316679370

Wuest, J., Ford-Gilboe, M., Merritt-Gray, M., & Berman, H. (2003). Intrusion: The central problem for family health promotion among children and single mothers after leaving an abusive partner. *Qualitative Health Research*, *13*(5), 597–622. DOI: 10.1177/1049732303251231

Wuest, J., Ford-Gilboe, M., Merritt-Gray, M., & Varcoe, C. (2013). Building on 'grab', attending to 'fit', and being prepared to 'modify': How grounded theory 'works' to guide interventions for abused women. In Cheryl T. Beck (Ed.), *Routledge International Handbook of Qualitative Nursing Research* (pp. 32–46). London and New York: Routledge, Taylor Francis.

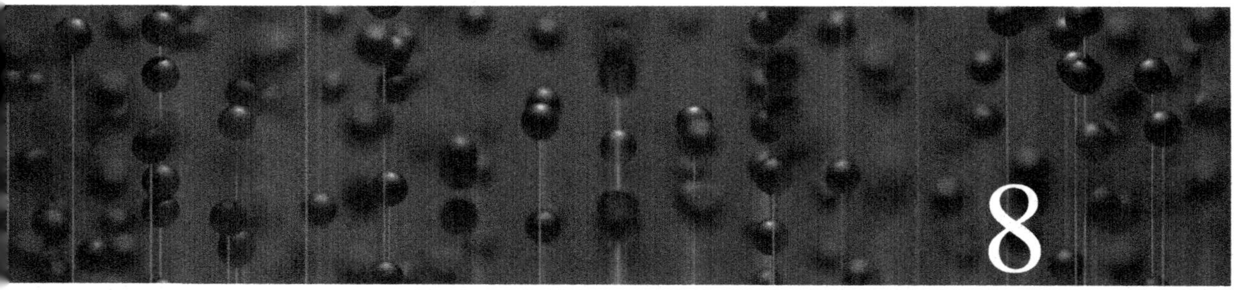

8

Coding for Grounded Theory

Linda Liska Belgrave and Kapriskie Seide

With the ground-breaking publication of *The Discovery of Grounded Theory* (1967), Barney G. Glaser and Anselm L. Strauss not only provided qualitative researchers with a systematic approach to analyzing qualitative data and using them to inductively generate useful theory, but also strong arguments for why we should do so (though not all users of the methodology have theory as a goal: Bryant 2002; Charmaz & Belgrave 2012). Since that publication, a number of grounded theorists, working from varied research paradigms, have further explicated the methodology, proposed analytic tools to use with it, and/or proposed alternative approaches or extensions to the methodology. The result is a wide range of choices for those who would use grounded theory methodology (GTM). Of course, one person's garden of riches is another's tangled forest, waiting to trap the unwary. This might be especially true for novice researchers and those attempting GTM for the first time. Daniel A. Nagel et al. (2015, p. 366) argue that difficulties flowing from the wide diversity of approaches to GTM are compounded by 'tensions between positivism/post-positivism and constructivism' and a general failure among researchers to distinguish between GTM as methodology or analytic framework.

Antony Bryant and Kathy Charmaz (2007a) argue that GTM can be seen as a somewhat turbulent family of methods, with a variety of interpretations, modifications, and conflicting claims regarding validity, authenticity, and varying views of key features. Regardless of research paradigm and whether one views grounded theory as a complete methodology (GTM) or simply as an approach to the analysis of qualitative data, coding of one sort or another is an integral element of analysis for virtually all approaches. That said, contrary to some understandings, GTM is much more than coding (Bryant 2017). Our goals in this chapter are to sort through the major branches of the GTM family. We compare their approaches to coding, providing examples of coding using Glaserian GTM and Constructivist GTM, as well as a note on Computer Assisted Qualitative Data Analysis (CAQDA). We do this in a spirit of celebrating what we see as a rich garden of methodological possibilities, suited to diverse research paradigms. This is not to deny our differences, but to value our pluralism. In this, we see ourselves in tune with authors such as Phyllis Noerager Stern (2007), Adele Clarke (2009) and Frederick J. Wertz et al. (2011).

APPROACHES TO CODING

It is difficult to separate coding from other elements of analysis in GTM, much less order these elements sequentially because the various elements of analysis are not only integrated but also used concurrently. In fact, when using full GTM, analysis is integrated and conducted simultaneously/iteratively/abductively with data collection, as one moves back and forth between levels of analysis and between analysis and further data collection (e.g., Bryant 2017; Charmaz 2006, 2014; Corbin & Strauss 2015; Glaser & Strauss 1965, 1967; Strauss & Corbin 1990). Nonetheless, there must be a starting point and some organizational scheme, so we present elements of coding approaches as steps in a process, emphasizing that this process is not linear.

What is Coding?

The inseparability of coding from other elements of data analysis is dramatically illustrated by Glaser and Strauss (1967), who weave their discussion of coding into a chapter on 'The Constant Comparative Method of Qualitative Analysis'. In what appears, in hindsight, to be somewhat ironic, they explain that 'The purpose of the constant comparative method of joint coding and analysis is to generate theory more systematically than allowed by [coding data first and then analyzing them], *by using explicit coding and analytic procedures*' (1967, p. 102, emphasis in original). In fact, they never define, much less explain, coding beyond telling us that 'Coding need consist only of noting categories on margins, but can be done more elaborately (e.g., on cards)' (1967, p. 106) and, reflecting their realist research paradigm, assuring us that categories and their properties will emerge.

Fortunately, more recent writings offer further guidance (see Table 8.1), possibly reflecting authors' having had to answer questions such as 'What's a code?' and 'How do categories emerge?' In the first edition of this *Handbook*, Bryant and Charmaz offer perhaps the most straightforward definition of coding: 'the process of defining what the data is about' (2007b: 605). They also take on emergence, incorporating their constructivist approach, by explaining that 'codes are emergent,' developing as researchers study their data; codes are not in the data but are developed through researchers' work. Anselm Strauss and Juliet Corbin point to the centrality of coding when they define it as 'the process of analyzing data' (1990, p. 61); a clearer definition is offered in Corbin and Strauss (2015, p. 57): 'denoting concepts to stand for meaning.' Note that Strauss and Corbin (1990) provide additional definitions of coding for each element of their approach. Similarly, Charmaz tells us that 'coding means that we attach labels to segments of data that depict what each segment is about' (2006, p. 3) and that 'through coding, we raise analytic questions about our data from the very beginning of data collection' (2014, p. 5). Note that these latter definitions make clear that codes, even modest or in-vivo codes, are *conceptual*, not simple labels.

In the Beginning – Glaser and Strauss

With *Discovery*, Glaser and Strauss (1967) broke away from the dominant research paradigm of the time – not only positivist, but deductive, heavily quantitative and with an

Table 8.1 Five major approaches to coding

	Glaser & Strauss	*Glaser*	*Strauss & Corbin*	*Charmaz/ Bryant*	*Clarke*
Research Paradigm	Objectivist Realist	Objectivist Realist Positivist	Objectivist Realist Interpretive[1]	Constructivist Interpretivist	Interpretive Situationist, Constructionist
Approach to Coding	Comparisons: Incidents; Incidents to properties; Delimit theory	Substantive coding: Open coding Selective coding Theoretical coding	Open coding Axial coding Selective coding	Initial coding Open coding Focused coding Varied coding strategies[2] Axial coding[3] Theoretical coding[3]	Open coding[4] Axial coding[4] Situational mapping Social Worlds/ Arenas mapping Positional mapping
Analytic Tools		Coding families	Conditional matrix	Coding families[3]	
Early Coding	Incidents	Line-by-line	Paragraph-by-paragraph; Phrase-by-phrase; Line-by-line Micro coding (specific strategic words)	Line-by-line Incident-by-incident; Word-by-word	Word-by-word Segment-by-segment

[1] Interpreted variously, from post-positivist to constructivist.

[2] Bryant provides varied examples of strategies for moving forward from open codes.

[3] Discussed by both; neither advocated nor discouraged.

[4] Overview presented, not instructional *per se*.

increasing divide between theory and research. Importantly, they 'essentially joined epistemological critique with practical guidelines for action' (Charmaz 2014, p. 7). They not only challenged the 'quantitative orthodoxy' but also offered 'a foundation for rendering the processes and procedures of qualitative investigation visible, comprehensible, and replicable' (Bryant and Charmaz 2007c, p. 33), providing a way to present qualitative research as rigorous and valid.

Glaser and Strauss (1967, p. 102) do not provide the sort of 'explicit coding and analytic procedures' we expect and use today. In fact, they do not write of various stages or levels of coding, *per se*, though they do write of codes, categories, and properties, which appear to emerge at different points during the constant comparative analysis. For this approach to coding, the researcher begins by coding incidents, coding each into as many categories as possible, constantly comparing every incident labeled with a particular code to other incidents carrying the same code. This process of constant comparison will 'start to generate theoretical properties of the category' and the analyst will begin to think in terms of ranges of types, dimensions of categories, conditions influencing categories, consequences of categories and relationships between categories. One writes memos throughout this process. Coding is a process of taking apart the story, so that one can rearrange it, can see categories and their properties. This, all of this, is the first step. The second step involves integrating categories and properties. Here the researcher moves from comparing incident to incident to comparing incidents with properties of categories. This process 'causes the accumulated knowledge pertaining to a property of the category to readily start to become integrated,' 'the diverse properties themselves start to become integrated' (p. 109) and categories to become integrated with each other. The third stage, delimiting the theory, involves '[discovering] underlying uniformities in the original set of categories or their properties' (p. 110), which enables the researcher to reduce the number of categories with which he or she is working while moving to higher-level concepts. At the same time, the categories become theoretically saturated. The final stage is writing theory. At this point, one has a theory, as well as coded data and memos, with which to work.

We rely on rather extensive quotations (here and below) partly because the work of Glaser and Strauss is the basis for more recent developments, but also to make a few points. First, the impossibility of separating coding from other elements of analysis, even writing, is clear. Second, the descriptions of what, concretely, to do at each stage are rather vague, reflecting assumptions of shared knowledge that might not be warranted. Third, Glaser and Strauss's use of labels for what one does at each stage, rather than names of categories, emphasizes the processual and complex nature of coding and moving between levels of coding. While codes themselves might be labels, coding is more than labeling. Finally, the language used clearly reflects the objectivist/realist orientation of this original version of GTM. The researcher makes seemingly endless comparisons, but this is to allow the codes, categories, properties and, indeed, the theory to emerge.

Classical GTM – Glaser

In *Theoretical Sensitivity* (1978), Glaser provides considerable methodological detail, pinning down what was so abstract in *Discovery*. He introduces coding by emphasizing its key position between data and theory and its conceptual nature: 'The essential relationship between data and theory is a conceptual code' (p. 55), then explains that codes conceptualize 'the underlying pattern of a set of empirical indicators.' In coding, one fractures (breaks apart) the data, organizing it into codes. This moves the researcher from the empirical to the abstract level. Glaser discusses multiple types of coding, specifically: substantive coding (with two sub-types – open coding and selective coding) and theoretical coding. Substantive codes conceptualize the empirical field, while theoretical codes conceptualize relationships between substantive codes.

Substantive coding begins with line-by-line, open coding, in which one codes each line or sentence of his or her data in 'every way possible' (p. 57), similar to the advice in *Discovery*. This is the point in the research to take chances, to run with one's theoretical sensitivity. This is a process of discovery, a chance to step back from the empirical data and see the potentials that they contain. Despite this emphasis on openness and possibilities, Glaser provides a number of rules for the process, the first of which is to ask questions of the data, a technique carried forward in other explications of GTM, albeit with somewhat different questions for some (e.g., Bryant 2017; Charmaz 2006, 2014; Corbin & Strauss 2015; Strauss & Corbin 1990). The three most fundamental questions are:

'What is this data a study of?... What category does this incident indicate?... [and] What is actually happening in the data?' (Glaser 1978, p. 57). Other rules include admonitions to write memos as one codes, to stay within one's substantive field at this point and to avoid assuming that demographics (e.g., age, race, gender) are relevant; everything to be included in the theory must earn its way in. Finally, Glaser cautions against moving to selective coding prematurely. With selective coding, one begins to focus his or her work. Here the researcher focuses on one core 'variable,' and those 'variables' that relate to it in ways that are meaningful for the emerging theory. This core 'variable' then guides ongoing data collection and theoretical sampling. Consistent with his positivist/objectivist/realist approach Glaser is working with a concept-indicator model, as shown by the quote above and the extensive advice he provides on constructing typologies.

Theoretical coding 'weave[s] the fractured story back together again' (1978, p. 72). Here one conceptualizes relationships among substantive codes. For Glaser, these relationships are hypotheses, to be integrated into the theory. For Stern (2007, pp. 120–121), theoretical codes help us to look 'at a variable in an abstract rather than a substantive way.' Glaser introduces 18 coding families, an analytic tool that can be used to stimulate, broaden and strengthen the theoretical sensitivity the researcher brings to theoretical coding. For instance, The Six Cs, 'the bread and butter theoretical code of sociology' (Glaser 1978, p. 74) consist of causes, contexts, contingencies, consequences, covariates and conditions. Process constitutes another family, containing concepts such as stages, phases, transitions, careers, and the like. Glaser discusses potential pitfalls of depending on some of these 'families,' rather than grounding them and notes that his coding families are not exhaustive, that other authors will introduce additional families. He also notes that basic social processes are typically named with gerunds, though this can be overdone. Charmaz (2006, 2014) argues that some of Glaser's coding families reflect positivist concepts, that important families are missing (e.g., agency, power and narrative), while others, such as inequality, are either buried or presented in a conceptually biased way. We see that coding approaches and conceptual tools reflect research paradigms, but can be helpful if used thoughtfully, always remembering that concepts must earn their way into one's theory. Again, coding is more than simply applying labels to pieces of data.

Box 8.1 Glaserian GTM Coding in Practice

We provide examples of Glaserian substantive coding and theoretical coding drawn from the work of Dr. Caroline Jane Porr (Porr, 2009; Porr, Drummond and Olson 2012; Stern and Porr, 2016) in which she employed a Glaserian GT methodology. The interaction between helping professionals and their clients is vital to the wellbeing of the clients and impinges on the latter's health and self. In her work, Porr lays out a theoretical and practical foundation for professionals to create and fortify a bridge between them and vulnerable and potentially stigmatized clients. Specifically, she explored the ways in which public health nurses can develop an interpersonal relationship with these clients in their practice as part of a holistic approach to maternal/child health. Initially, in her dissertation, Porr (2009) formulated a theoretical model, named *Targeting Essence: Pragmatic Variation of the Therapeutic Relationship*, comprised of essential elements that elucidate the processes of building the said relationship between public health nurses (PHN) and lower income single mothers. We have adapted tables from Stern and Porr (2016) to illustrate Porr's use of Glaserian coding, shortening them to focus on the elements discussed here. Note that Porr's first step in substantive coding was to define codeable data segments (see Table 8.2). As she coded, she identified which numbered line connected to which piece of her coding label, enabling her to move back and forth between codes and data. The bottom section of the table illustrates a step up in abstraction, with the selection of codes that fit together, and their labeling as a conceptual category.

Table 8.2 Stern and Porr's (2016, pp. 82–83) substantive coding example

	Substantive Coding	
Procedure	*Data*	*Examples*
Identify data	**Transcript: Public Health Nurse**	Line 1 – 3
segments.	1. well you know I think often people	Comprise a
Assign	2. think that if these moms would just	Data segment:
labelled	3. get a job. If they would just work	*1 'Well you*
codes.	4. harder. Now I realized how complex	*Know I think*
	5. it is; it's not a single issue. It's not	*Often 2 people*
	6. any one factor. You look at lone-	*Think that if*
	7. parent families, some of the mothers	*Moms 3 would*
	8. might be dealing with mental health	*Just get a job.'*
	9. issues. Or they might have grown	The labeled
	10. up in a family that never knew any	Code is
	11. different than living on a low-income.	Designated by
	12. How do you get beyond and how do	Italics:
	13. you get a job when your housing is a	
	14. problem? Mothers will visit me and	*'people think*
	15. tell me they don't have food today.	*That if moms*
	16. They have to go to the foodbank and	*Would just get*
	17. that will take them all day. They have	*A job'*
	18. to organize housing and try to get	[Note.
	19. government assistance.	Caroline
	20. And they look at me, 'Oh you mean	labels her segments
	21. welfare.' You know, public assistance	with long
	22. requires that mothers find a place	verbatim
	23. before mothers are given that first	titles at first,
	24. check. And then mothers have little	during early analysis,
	25. children. Who is going to take care	to provide context.]
	26. of them? There are so many things	
	27. that are required of moms from each	
	28. of these government agencies. Wow!	
	29. I'm not the person trying to put it all	
	30. Together.	

Group Labeled Codes into Conceptual Categories	**Labeled Codes Selected from Transcripts** 1. PHNs follow mother's agenda/priorities 2. Mothers not sure they can trust PHNs 3. Threatening are personal questions versus generic questions 4. PHN's gut feelings 5. PHN know the mother's history 6. PHN conscious of tone, cries 'to sound up but not disgustingly up'	Labeled Codes 1, 3, 5, 7, 8, 17, 18, 19, 21, can be grouped into a conceptual category, temporarily named: CLIENT FOCUSED

Porr's complete model includes six stages: projecting optimism, child as mediating presence, ascertaining motives, exercising social facility, concerted intentionality, and redrawing professional boundaries. Based on her findings, Public Health Nurses (PHNs) can start building a rapport with a client through the first two stages: projecting optimism and child as mediating presence. These stages entail exhibiting a friendly demeanor, giving verbal praise, and focusing on the client's child. In Table 8.3, Porr illustrates the use of coding families to pin down relationships and flesh out her theory.

Table 8.3 Stern and Porr's (2016, pp. 89–91) theoretical coding example

	Theoretical Coding	
Procedure	*Data*	*Example*
Once a. the problem and resolving basic social psychological process are apparent, b. a list of relevant conceptual categories and labeled codes have been selected, and c. theoretical sampling is underway, use coding families to further densify, to establish relationships, and to assist formulating a theoretical structure	**[Sample]** **Conceptual Categories Related to the Basic Social Psychological Process, 'Targeting Essence'** PROJECTIING OPTIMISM: • PHN is 'upbeat', 'peppy' • PHN's Verbal Praise • PHN's STRENGHTS-BASED APPROACH • POSITIVE ENGAGEMENT • Mother's MISTRUST • Mother's DEFENSIVENESS CHILD AS MEDIATING PRESENCE: • PHN focuses on child • Mother evaluates PHN's level of interest in her child • New baby, new LEASE ON LIFE REDRAWING PROFESSIONAL BOUDARIES: • PHN fills SOCIAL SUPPORT • PHN is CONFIDANTE, FRIEND, SURROGATE MOTHER, SISTER, COACH ADVOCATE and PSEUDO-COUNSELOR • *PHN revisits professional boundaries*	Two of the Six Cs: Causes (Sources, reasons, explanations, accounting or anticipated consequences), Context or Ambiance Using the first C (Causes) Why would the conceptual category, Projecting Optimism be of benefit to building relationship? Using the second C (Context) When is Projecting Optimism beneficial to relationship building?

She shows that 'Redrawing professional boundaries' represents the last stage of this process where the line between professional and personal boundaries could blur. At this final stage, the PHNs had assumed a variety of other roles (confidante, friend, surrogate mother, sister, coach advocate, and pseudo counselor) for the client as duties of PHNs could lead them to assume other roles aside from that of a helping professional. In the course of getting professional help, clients could seek to fill a social support void that is normally filled by a network of kith and/or kin. PHNs could find themselves filling this void, which leads them to revisit and redraw their professional boundaries. She proposed a framework for practice based on her formulated theoretical model that could serve as a repertoire for helping professionals serving stigmatized vulnerable populations.

A Procedural Approach – Strauss and Corbin

Strauss and Corbin (1990; Corbin & Strauss 2015) present a detailed, technique and procedure-oriented approach to coding for GTM – open coding, axial coding, and selective coding – as well as a conceptual tool – the conditional matrix. While they write of 'data collection, analysis and theory [standing] in a reciprocal relationship with each other' (1990, p. 23), the emphasis in their work is on data analysis. Given the vagueness with which this is treated in earlier work, it is no wonder that researchers have gravitated to their approach. It offers relief from some of the ambiguity of actually doing GTM, an ambiguity that can be difficult and unnerving.

Strauss and Corbin free up open coding (their starting point) by acknowledging that researchers might code paragraph-by-paragraph, line-by-line, phrase-by-phrase or even focus on single words that stand out as significant (micro-analysis). Open coding is 'the process of breaking down, examining, comparing, conceptualizing, and categorizing data' (1990, p. 61). While others have indicated that the first coding step is to fracture or break apart the data into discrete, meaningful pieces and label these with conceptual codes (which can be myriad in number), this is perhaps clearer as stated succinctly by these authors. One then groups into categories concepts that seem to go with the same phenomenon. In their early work, Strauss and Corbin suggest two ways one might go about grouping concepts together. One can examine a concept, ask what phenomenon it reflects and then look back at one's data to see if this concept is similar to or different from others. Or one can look at the observation as a whole and ask 'What does this seem to be about?' They claim that either way 'we should reach the same conclusion' (1990, p. 66). This stance, which is not made in the later work, strongly suggests an objectivist, realist research paradigm. Once concepts are grouped into categories, one looks for their properties/attributes and dimensions.

Axial coding, the next step, is used to pull one's data back together by relating categories to subcategories, using a coding paradigm. While the 'terminology used in the paradigm is borrowed from standard scientific terms scientists used in relationship to theory' (Corbin & Strauss 2015, p. 157), the terms are subtly changed in the later work, compared to the first. 'Causal conditions' become simply 'conditions' and the model is pared down from '(A) CAUSAL CONDITIONS → (B) PHENOMENON → (C) CONTEXT → (D) INTERVENING CONDITIONS → (E) ACTION/INTERACTION STRATEGIES → (F) CONSEQUENCES' (Strauss & Corbin 1990, p. 99) to conditions, actions/interactions and consequences, with no model, and introduced as an analytic tool (Corbin & Strauss 2015).

In both versions, the paradigm is a tool used to ask questions of one's data, but in the newer discussion it is both simpler and a move away from a model that feels post-positivist to an approach more open to an interpretive attitude. For instance, when one looks for explanations given in the data, these 'may be implicit or explicit in field notes' (2015, p. 158). While she does not use Strauss and Corbin's axial coding herself, Charmaz (2006, 2014) argues that the availability of this framework will be valuable to some, helping them to extend their analytic reach, but at the risk of being limited or restricted if it is applied mechanically.

Selective coding, the third procedural step, involves settling on one's core category, relating it to other categories, validating these relationships and fleshing out any categories that are incomplete. This is a parallel process to axial coding but at a higher level of abstraction. Again, one proposes relationships and then goes back to the data to validate them. In the 2015 edition of *Basics*, selective coding does not appear as a separate step (or in the index at all), but is part of Theoretical Integration, illustrating the fine line between coding, *per se*, and other elements of analysis.

In addition to coding steps, Strauss and Corbin provide the 'conditional matrix' as an analytic tool. The conditional matrix is '...a diagram, useful for considering the wide range of conditions and consequences related to the phenomenon under study. [It] enables the analyst to both distinguish and link levels of conditions and consequences' (1990, p. 158). The goal is to increase the analyst's theoretical sensitivity and apply that sensitivity to the conditions, actions/interactions, and consequences, as laid out in the coding paradigm.

It is difficult to identify Strauss and Corbin's research paradigm. They have been variously categorized as post-positivist (Charmaz 2011, p. 168), objectivist (Charmaz & Belgrave 2012, p. 349), interpretive (Bryant & Charmaz 2007c and procedural, post-positivist/constructivist (Clarke 2015). This seems to flow from different strands in their joint work, their use of language, and changes in *Basics* over time, particularly between early versions of the text and the third and fourth editions, which are largely Corbin's work. For instance, after explaining that 'theories are constructions, Corbin and Strauss (2015, p. 26) use confirmatory language to argue that 'conscientious analysts attempt to validate their interpretations by comparing one piece of data against another, always looking for contradictions to their interpretations as well as validation' (pp. 382–383).

Constructivist GTM – Charmaz, Bryant

With the first publication of *Constructing Grounded Theory* (2006, 2014), Charmaz offered a solution to those wanting to use GTM but put off by the positivist and post-positivist assumptions of the dominant approaches. Here was an approach that moved GTM away from 'outdated modernist epistemology' and resonated with researchers who rejected assumptions of 'an objective external reality, a passive, neutral observer or a detached, narrow empiricism' and recognized that research, itself, is constructed (2006: 13). We address the coding approaches of Charmaz (2006, 2014) and Bryant (2017) in this discussion, even though they differ somewhat, because of their joint analysis of, and influence on, GTM, particularly with the first *Handbook of Grounded Theory* (2007), a key text in the field (Bryant 2017: 86). Charmaz presents two coding stages, initial and focused, while discussing the axial and focused coding of Strauss and Corbin and Glaser, respectively. Bryant (2017) advocates beginning with open coding (sometimes using the term 'initial coding') and then leaves later stages of coding strategies open, providing multiple examples of work following differing strategies. Both advocate coding with gerunds, to capture and preserve action, though Bryant warns against forcing gerunds on the data.

When using Charmaz's initial coding, one sticks close to the data, codes for action (when possible) and remains open to all theoretical possibilities. As with other forms of early coding, one asks questions of the data, beginning with: 'What is this a study of?' (Glaser, 1978, p. 57), but also 'What does the data suggest? Pronounce? From whose point of view?' (Charmaz 2006, p. 47, 2014, p. 116) and 'What theoretical category does this specific datum indicate?' (Glaser, 1978). What is different when using constructivist GTM is the explicit acknowledgment that: 'We construct codes ... we define what we see as significant in the data and describe what we think is happening [and] interpret participants' tacit meanings' (Charmaz 2014, pp. 114–116). Charmaz advocates line-by-line coding to fracture the data. This stimulates ideas that might not appear if coding for larger themes and lets the researcher see detail and patterns that otherwise might not be noticed. It backs one out of the participant's worldview. Questions to ask include 'What process(es) is at issue here? How can I define it? How does this process develop? What are the consequences of the process?' (2014, p. 127). While Charmaz works with line-by-line coding, she notes that word-for-word coding might be preferable for those working with documents or internet blogs or for those interested in phenomenology. Similarly, incident-by-incident coding might be more useful with observational data, which have already been subject to selection and interpretation in their recording. Regardless of the level at which one is coding, constant comparative methods are at the heart of coding. Bryant (2017, p. 176) reminds the reader that the whole purpose of open (or initial) coding is 'to produce useable and useful abstractions.' He emphasizes openness, staying close to the data, constant comparison, preserving action, comparing data with data and moving quickly through the data.

Focused coding is done at a higher level of abstraction than initial coding. It is used to synthesize large segments of data. Here one compares initial codes in order to select those that have the most analytic power or determine a new code that captures a number of initial codes. Focused coding directs the ongoing research. Here again, Charmaz offers useful questions, such as 'Which of these codes best account for the data? What do your comparisons between codes indicate? Do your focused codes reveal gaps in the data?' and 'What kinds of theoretical categories do these codes indicate?' (2014, pp. 140–141, 144).

Charmaz also discusses Strauss and Corbin's axial coding for bringing fractured data back together by specifying properties and dimensions of a category and relating categories to subcategories (see above). In the second edition of her book, Charmaz (2014) reviews praise and criticism of this approach. She herself prefers a more emergent approach to developing subcategories and relating them to each other over a procedural one. Charmaz is concerned with the 'extent to which theoretical coding is an application or emergent process' (2014, p. 150). She distinguishes between the wise use of theoretical codes, such as Glaser's (1978) coding families, to add precision and clarity and simple application of them, which can impose a poorly fitting framework for the analysis, providing advice for how to use theoretical coding effectively.

Bryant (2017) presents a number of strategies for advancing analysis beyond initial, open coding, noting selective, focused and theoretical coding as higher levels of coding, without advocating for any one or set of these. Rather, he provides detailed examples of creative combinations of strategies used by his students. He reminds the reader that research plans are not the same as research in the world, suggesting that understanding multiple strategies gives one the tools to move forward, despite it all.

It is noteworthy that both Charmaz (2006, 2014) and Bryant (2017) introduce and explain multiple coding strategies, whether or not they use these themselves. While other GTM authors state that their offerings are recommendations, rather than rules, Charmaz and Bryant show this by discussing other frameworks, their pros and cons, and the circumstances in which they might be useful.

Box 8.2 Constructivist GTM Coding in Practice

This following example is drawn from the second author's research into the everyday lives of Haitians during the cholera epidemic in Haiti. After a brief introduction of her study (Seide, 2016), we present Kapriskie's GTM story.

While studies investigating the cholera epidemic guided public health responses to control its spread, questions pertaining to its social dimension became glaring as the number of cholera cases in Haiti vacillated over the years. Given the importance of understanding people's behaviors in the transmission of cholera (Whiteford, 2004), I argued for the investigation of individuals' social reality when analyzing the impact of this multifaceted public health issue. I traveled to Haiti during the summer of 2016 to examine how the cholera epidemic changed the lives of Haitians in Port-au-Prince with a focus on the social context in which they live (Seide, 2016). I used symbolic interactionism and the social construction of reality for the theoretical framework of my study, and a constructivist GTM. The emergent theoretical model *The Process of Adaptation Amidst the Ongoing Cholera Epidemic* explains how Haitians utilized two major resources (financial means and social networks) as means of adaptation to the changing conjuncture of the epidemic. For people with limited or no access to these means, cholera is an afterthought as they are more preoccupied by the trials of their everyday lives. This harsh reality is translated by the adage *mikrob pa touye Ayisyen* [microbes don't kill Haitians] which is a critique, rather than a description, of the stagnant grueling living conditions in the country endured by many.

Coding in Data Analysis

For this study, I conducted thirty (30) in-depth interviews and manually analyzed them in Haitian Creole. Infrastructural limitations such as frequent power outages prevented me from using NVIVO. Analyses were done in Creole and findings translated as needed for English-speaking audiences. The coding and data analysis for this study followed Charmaz's process of coding using Constructivist GTM (Charmaz 2014). Here, I provide a detailed example of my demarche for two final concepts 'Making adjustments to protect self and health' and 'Living in fear'.

I coded interview transcripts line-by-line using gerund verbs (see Table 8.4) with the words of the participants when possible. In Haitian Creole, there are no gerund forms. With the guidance of my thesis chair (Linda Belgrave) and that of different Creole speakers, I used the infinitive form of verbs as a conjugational alternative. In the Creole linguistic context, the infinitive seemed the most appropriate verb form that fulfilled the purpose of gerunds in the coding process in English. I also coded some field notes about pertinent observations which often helped situate individual experiences within a wider context.

Table 8.4 Kapriskie's examples of line-by-line Initial codes translated from Creole transcripts

Words of Participants by Line	*Initial Codes*
The situation changed in Port-au-Prince and people did not eat like before	Noting changes in people's eating habits in the capital
… a lot of people did not eat in restaurants, they did not eat out	avoiding restaurants or carryout
… there is a group (or class) of people it [fish] is reserved for.	Distinguishing class based differences in fish/food consumption.
Cholera could've, and still can, I think, blemish the prestige that comes with my positions.	Identifying effects of illness on occupational status;
People would avoid me. I would have less contracts.	Laying out potential cost of illness on interactions
Why do you think people from the higher classes go through such length to hide the fact that they had cholera?	Explaining (closeted) behavioral differences by social class.
If it is not bottled, I don't drink it.	Drinking bottled water
I avoid the *baiser de paix* [kiss of peace] at church. I can't help it.	Avoiding kiss of peace at church
I brush my teeth with *Culligan* water only now and I'd shower with it too if it wouldn't ruin me.	Brushing with *Culligan*/preferring *Culligan* water
My boss wanted me to use Clorox in everything: dishes, water, cleaning.	Using Clorox in everything
I prefer waving hands to hugging since the outbreak	Being more inclined to wave hands than hug
I used to *kore* [fist bump] everyone when things were worst, I still do it now but I hug occasionally	Being more inclined to *kore* (fist bump) with occasional hugs

Source: Kapriskie MA thesis

Initially, I had two temporary categories: 'avoiding consumption of seafood' and 'eating/consuming seafood.' During the peak of the cholera epidemic, many people avoided consuming food prone to cholera contamination – especially seafood. Accordingly, I focused on the former category and discarded the latter. In one of my memos I wrote: 'How can people stay away from fish AND eat fish at the same time? This makes no sense.' After my twelfth interview, I realized that 'avoiding consumption of seafood' was a relevant property of the descriptive category 'eating habits.' By constantly comparing incidents, and interviewing participants with more diverse backgrounds, my data became nuanced. In addition, I coded my observations of local marketplaces where I inquired about product prices and trends from vendors. As a result, I found that within the context of the epidemic, eating habits did not change in the same fashion. For example, while some people avoided consuming seafood, others incorporated these products in their *dietary preferences*, not habits (see Table 8.5). At the peak of the epidemic, many foods susceptible to contamination (i.e., seafood, street food, crudité, etc.) became unpopular. This decrease in demand drove down the price of certain food items that are otherwise costly and coveted on the Haitian

Table 8.5 Kapriskie's excerpt of the line-by-line open coding, the subsequent selective coding, and the final concepts

Data	*Initial Coding*	*Focused Coding*	*Final Concepts*
'The situation changed in Port-au-Prince and people ate differently… a lot of people did not eat in restaurants, they did not eat out, they did not buy beverages on the streets when cholera was at its worst. When you look at the people who have cholera, it was very sad.' (Abdias)	Noting changes in people's eating habits in the capital; avoiding restaurants or carryout; bypassing purchase of beverage on the streets during peak of cholera; Being marked by state of cholera sufferers.	Changing eating habits	Making Adjustments to Protect Self and Health:
'The cost of fish dropped when cholera started. Although many people avoided fish, many other people seized the occasion to eat it because fish, like I explained to you, people consider fish…there is a group (or class) of people it is reserved for…' (Nadia)	Linking fish price drop to cholera; Observing differences in fish consumptions; Observing patterns of fish consumption by social groups; Distinguishing class based differences in fish/food consumption.		
'Cholera came and created a distance between members of this society…People no longer kissed or hugged. You either *kore* or you waved. It was like that for a while.' (Ben)	Noticing distance between people in society due to cholera; Listing changes in direct interactions.	Changing Interactions	
'My neighbors threatened to burn me alive and chop me up with a machete if I got out of the house. They thought that they would get sick from the air I breathe. I stayed inside and only went out at night when people slept…' (Romain)	Receiving death threats from neighbors [for having cholera]; Remarking that disease believed to be airborne by neighbors; being sequestered from people.		

(Continued)

Table 8.5 (*Continued*)

Data	*Initial Coding*	*Focused Coding*	*Final Concepts*
'When the epidemic was out of control, like many people, I avoided touching other people. Now, I consider shaking hands at times but I have this overpowering need to wash my hands right after…I hug and kiss my kid only. I don't give a shit! The heck with anyone who thinks I'm being odd if I don't want to cajole them.' (Varice)	Avoiding touching other people at peak of epidemic; Shaking hands at times post-peak of epidemic; Feeling compulsion to wash hands right after hand shake post-peak of epidemic; limiting hug and kiss to close relative (kid); Disregarding people's opinion or critique of 'minimal contact' behavior		
'There are people who treat cholera sufferers as deviants. They even see them as perpetrators at time to protect yourself from' (Rasta)	Seeing cholera sufferers as deviants; Seeing themselves as potential victims of cholera	Creating distance from illness	Living in fear
'No one likes to be associated with cholera to this day. That is why people avoided you when you tried recruiting them. It is not as bad as it used to be, but cholera is not something that you will hear in talks.' (Bob)	Avoiding being associated with cholera; Avoiding being recruited for study on cholera; Delineating gravity of epidemic over time (not as bad); Noticing avoidance of cholera topic in talks.		

Source: Kapriskie MA thesis

market – the most notable being fresh fish. Reviewing my initial coding of earlier interviews directed my attention toward the importance of marketplaces to make sense of certain local practices which tended to be taken for granted. Some participants admitted never giving much thoughts about marketplaces until the interview. At a later stage in the analysis, with the use of a more focused code 'changing eating habits,' the descriptive categories 'avoiding consumption of seafood' and 'eating/consuming seafood' grew into substantive categories that provided more contextual clarity. I found that people who normally could not afford fish seized the occasion to consume it. The price drops opened access to resources usually inaccessible to the poor. Note that I had to work between early and later interviews and observations and between initial and focused codes and categories in order to make sense of these changes in fish consumption.

Changes in daily interactions, on the other hand, were more homogeneous and all participants reported changes in daily routines and habits as time passed by. In general, cholera represented a threat to people's health as well as their self, for the illness is constructed as a threat to sufferers' identity and social status. The pathology of the illness (stemming from ingesting a bacteria found in feces) exacerbated negative perceptions of cholera suffers who are often blamed for their conditions and labeled as 'dirty,' 'lacking hygiene,' or 'uneducated.' These perceptions gave impetus to a myriad of changes in daily interactions to the detriment of cholera sufferers and individuals suspected of having cholera. These individuals experienced cholera related stigma and discrimination. Once I identified a group of categories, I would select the most relevant ones to my research questions through further inquiry (i.e., theoretical sampling). I constructed different categories and laid out their meanings, interconnections, and properties with memos. The line-by-line codes provided hinges to connect related responses from other participants. Following the Constructivist GTM guidelines, as I progressed and begun to focus code, core categories evolved into conceptual categories. At that stage, I found more unexpected patterns and ideas that led me to be more selective throughout the coding process. I proceeded in this fashion by linking pertinent categories, verifying their relationships, and fleshing them out. Their constant comparison allowed me to elaborate and integrate them to explain a process. 'Making Adjustments to Protect Self and Health' and 'Living in fear' (Table 8.5) are two of the six core/final concepts that tie together the more detailed levels of codes and categories. The protection of self and health is manifested through a series of changes – not all of them in accordance with biomedical guidelines. While fish was avoided by those who followed strict health and safety guidelines, others saw an opportunity to have access to a coveted item (otherwise unaffordable) to have 'a taste' of the lifestyle of the others (in this context, those who can afford it) or make up for lost time. Living in fear of cholera was manifested by the adoption of exclusionary practices as a way of creating a safe haven free of cholera. Each core concept allowed me to synthesize the whats, the hows and the whys of people's experiences and realities amid the epidemic.

As a novice user of grounded theory, I admit taking a martinet approach to the guidelines of constructivist GTM (Charmaz 2014; Charmaz & Belgrave 2012). Over the course of the analysis, with the guidance of my advisor, I gained more confidence in the analysis process and held the GTM guidelines with a gentler grip. One of the most challenging aspects of this process for me was 'seeing' then rendering the contested realities of the participants which were either parallel to my social reality (hence close to my assumptions) or completely outside of my frame of reference. Coding the interviews line-by-line with the words of the participants was a tedious tears-inducing yet indispensable labor for three major reasons: (1) it prevented me from intellectualizing the lived experienced of the participants during the epidemic, (2) it helped me construct very detailed concepts, and (3) it facilitated the flow of the translation process.

Situational Analysis – Clarke

Adele Clarke presents situational analysis (SA) as an approach that extends and goes beyond GTM, putting situational complexity front and center in a symbolic interactionist grounded theory/methods package, pushing the envelope on 'postmodernization of the social' (Clarke & Friese 2007, p. 364; Clarke, Friese, & Washburn 2015). SA extends GTM beyond the usual use of interview and/or observational data to discursive data (Clarke et al. 2015). SA goes beyond conventional GTM by shifting the focus from human action to collective action; '*the situation of inquiry itself broadly conceived is the key unit of analysis*' (2015, p. 133, emphasis in original) and taking both non-human and implicated actors into account (Clarke 2009). One hope/promise is that SA, with historical materials, can be used to theorize 'long-term politico-economic and related change' (Clarke et al. 2015, p. 141).

While Clarke does not present mapping as a coding strategy *per se*, we include it in Table 8.1 and discuss it here because (a) mapping is the SA method of fracturing or taking apart data and (b) we see it as a parallel to the advanced levels of coding in more conventional GTM, all of which go well beyond applying abstract labels to pieces of data. There are three types of mapping – situational, social worlds/arenas and positional – supplemental to traditional GTM. These 'center on elucidating the key elements, discourses, structures, and conditions of possibility that characterize the situation of inquiry' (Clarke 2009, p. 211). As with other approaches to GTM coding and analysis, various mapping techniques might be particularly useful in different situations.

Situational mapping 'lay[s] out the major human, non-human, discursive, and other elements in the research situation of inquiry and provoke[s] analysis of relations among them' (Clarke 2009, p. 210). Note the parallels here to comparing incidents/initial/open coding, which identify and analytically label pieces of data, and comparing incidents to properties/selective/axial coding/focused coding, all of which move toward discovering or constructing relationships between the elements or categories that will make up one's theory. Situational maps are created in two versions, messy and ordered. Messy maps are working versions. Here one works to capture complexity, rather than simplifying (not unlike early, very open coding). For ordered mapping, Clarke (2009) provides potential categories, such as individual human elements/actors, collective human elements/actors, political/economic elements, spatial elements, and the like to jog one's thinking. One is absolutely not to try to fill all of these categories, but only those that actually appear in one's data. To use other language, categories must earn their way into situational maps, as must elements of any theory discovered or constructed using GTM. Situational mapping can be used to plan a research project and then, later, to analyze data.

Social worlds/arena mapping works with meso-level interpretations of situations. Here one focuses on collective actors and their arenas of discourse and commitment. In this step, the analyst focuses on social organizational, institutional and discursive dimensions from an explicitly postmodern stance. Boundaries might be open and discourses contradictory (Clarke et al. 2015, pp. 133–134).

Positional mapping attends to 'major positions taken, and *not* taken, in the data' (Clarke 2009, p. 210, emphasis in the original), regarding differences, concerns, and controversies, in the situation of interest. The goal is to represent positions taken whether individually or collectively. Here one works at multiple levels, from individual to organizational (Clarke et al. 2015, p. 134). Note that here one explicitly attends to silences.

A BRIEF NOTE ON COMPUTER ASSISTED QUALITATIVE DATA ANALYSIS

We want to speak briefly to our experience with Computer Assisted Qualitative Data Analysis (CAQDA), using NVivo. (See the chapters on GTM and CAQDAS by Andrea Gorra and Susanne Friese in this volume for a fuller explication of these tools and their use – Chapter 14 and 15.) Computer packages can be tremendously helpful in manipulating large amounts of data, pulling together all instances of a code we want to examine, whether for constant comparison or consideration as a core category. Changing codes, grouping codes into a category at a higher level of abstraction, and modeling can be done more quickly and easily than by hand, perhaps enhanced by the ability to try various versions, to see what makes the most sense. At the same time, how we use these tools to manipulate our data matters (Konopásek 2007). For one thing, the *ability* to code and manipulate everything in our data can become the *demand* to code and manipulate everything, in which case we lose the promise of GTM that comes with focusing our analysis and data collection. Also, and more troubling, the ability to manipulate codes at various levels, can become an act of playing with codes. In working with Brenda Frie, who is very adept with NVivo, on her analysis, the first author realized that something was wrong, but could not put her finger on it. Suddenly, everything was very abstract and somehow empty. We realized that we were looking at and discussing only codes, not data. The process had become very seductive, as NVivo encouraged working codes to codes as we moved from one level to the next. This pulled us away from her data, which threatened to undermine the groundedness of her theory (Frie 2017). Neither of these are impossible hurdles, but possibilities of which researchers, especially those who use computers as naturally as some of us use pen and paper, should be aware. CAQDA can be a wonderful resource but has pitfalls, as does any tool or approach to data analysis.

CONCLUSIONS

A first, and obvious, conclusion is that we come to GTM from a variety of research paradigms and epistemological stances. Certainly, these influence how we interpret our tasks and our goals. We might aim for a generalizable theory that can explain and predict, based on a social reality that exists outside human action, much less outside a researcher/theorist. Alternatively, we might see ourselves developing a somewhat indeterminate theory intended to provide an understanding of some phenomenon, using interpretations of data that reflect multiple realities and meanings. Finally, we might reflexively construct a theory using data that we, as researchers, jointly construct with participants, knowing that researchers coming from other perspectives would likely produce different theories. In constructing theory, we might focus on social action or social situations/worlds at various levels of collectivity and analysis. The point here is that GTM is a large family, including researchers moving in diverse directions. We might each have a preferred research paradigm or even argue amongst ourselves, but our work grows from a shared base and, like members of any family, we can't deny our kinship. That said, we want to be aware of the assumptions underlying our research paradigms. While 'researchers can use basic grounded theory guidelines such as coding, memo-writing, and sampling for theory development, and comparative methods are, in many ways, neutral ... *how* we use these guidelines is not neutral; nor are the assumptions they bring to our research' (Charmaz 2006, p. 9, emphasis in the original).

Second, the term 'coding' and its common understanding are deceptively simple. Even the most preliminary/open/initial coding is analysis. It involves abstracting something we see in our data and defining it with a label that is conceptual, whether we create it or use the language of study participants. More advanced levels of coding, whether we use selective coding, theoretical coding, axial coding, focused coding or mapping, are quite complex, certainly more so than the term 'coding' implies. Moreover, coding cannot be separated from other elements of analysis, such as memo writing and theoretical sampling. It is no wonder that novice researchers or those new to GTM are sometimes intimidated or confused. It would behoove us to appreciate this explicitly and teach it as such.

Finally, we have multiple and varied approaches to coding in GTM. Each is based on certain assumptions, often implicit, offers specific advantages and contains related drawbacks, again, often implicit. Most developers of GTM present their coding approach as a set of guidelines, rather than rules written in stone. Yet, they can be read as the latter, so that researchers can find themselves forcing analyses that perhaps are not best suited to their own assumptions and goals. It is good to remind ourselves and our students that, while GTM is not a free-for-all, 'methodological statements need to be presented, treated, and understood as heuristics and not algorithms' (Bryant 2017, p. 60). GTM is a robust methodology. It is possible to draw from the works of multiple methodologists, bringing awareness of underlying assumptions, benefits and potential problems to one's specific project. Or, to put it more simply and to paraphrase Barbossa, 'the code [ing approach] is more what you'd call "guidelines" than actual rules. Welcome aboard [GTM]!' (Bruckheimer & Vabinski 2003).

REFERENCES

Bruckheimer, J. & Vabinski, G. (2003). *Pirates of the Caribbean: The Curse of the Black Pearl*. USA: Walt Disney Pictures.

Bryant, A. (2002). Re-grounding Grounded Theory. *Journal of Information Technology Theory & Applications*, *4*(1), 25–42.

Bryant, A. (2017). *Grounded Theory and Grounded Theorizing: Pragmatism in Research Practice*. New York: Oxford University Press.

Bryant, A. & Charmaz, K. (2007a). Introduction: Grounded Theory Research: Methods & Practices. In A. Bryant & K. Charmaz (Eds.), *The Sage Handbook of Grounded Theory*. London: Sage. pp. 1–28.

Bryant, A. & Charmaz, K. (Eds.) (2007b). *The Sage Handbook of Grounded Theory*. London: Sage.

Bryant, A. & Charmaz, K. (2007c). Grounded Theory in Historical Perspective: An Epistemological Account. In A. Bryant & K. Charmaz (Eds.), *The Sage Handbook of Grounded Theory*. London: Sage. pp. 31–57.

Charmaz, K. (2006). *Constructing Grounded Theory: A Practical Guide Through Qualitative Analysis*. London: Sage.

Charmaz, K. (2011). A Constructivist Grounded Theory Analysis of Losing and Regaining a Valued Self. In F. J. Wertz, K. Charmaz, L. M. McMullen, R. Josselson, R. Anderson, & E. McSpadden, *Five Ways of Doing Qualitative Analysis*. New York: Guilford Press. pp. 165–204.

Charmaz, K. (2014). *Constructing Grounded Theory* (2nd ed.). Los Angeles, CA: Sage.

Charmaz, K. & Belgrave, L. L. (2012). Qualitative Interviewing and Grounded Theory Analysis. In J. F. Gubrium, J. A. Holstein, A. B. Marvasti, & K. D. McKinney (Eds.), *The Sage Handbook of Interview Research: The Complexity of the Craft*. Los Angeles, CA: Sage. pp. 347–365.

Clarke, A. (2009). From Grounded Theory to Situational Analysis: What's New? Why? How? In J. M. Morse, P. N. Stern, J. Corbin, B. Bowers, K. Charmaz, & A. E. Clarke (Eds.), *Developing Grounded Theory: The Second Generation*. Walnut Creek, CA: Left Coast Press. pp. 194–233.

Clarke, A. (2015). Feminisms, Grounded Theory, and Situational Analysis Revisited. In A. E. Clarke, C. Friese, & R. Washburn (Eds.), *Situational Analysis in Practice: Mapping Research with Grounded Theory.* Walnut Creek, CA: Left Coast Press. pp. 84–154.

Clarke, A. & Friese, C. (2007). Grounded Theory Using Situational Analysis. In A. Bryant & K. Charmaz (Eds.), *The Sage Handbook of Grounded Theory*. London: Sage. pp. 363–397.

Clarke, A., Friese, C., & Washburn, R. (Eds.) (2015). *Situational Analysis in Practice: Mapping Research with Grounded Theory*. Walnut Creek, CA: Left Coast Press.

Corbin, J. & Strauss, A. (2015). *Basics of Qualitative Research: Techniques and Procedures for Developing Grounded Theory*. Los Angeles, CA: Sage.

Frie, B. (2017). Personal communication regarding: How Healthcare Students Decide to Participate in Honors: A Grounded Theory. Unpublished Dissertation, St Cloud State University.

Glaser, B. G. (1978). *Theoretical Sensitivity*. Mill Valley, CA: Sociology Press.

Glaser, B. G. & Strauss, A. L. (1965). *Awareness of Dying*. Chicago, IL: Aldine Pub.

Glaser, B. G. & Strauss, A. L. (1967). *The Discovery of Grounded Theory: Strategies for Qualitative Research*. New York: Aldine de Gruyter.

Konopásek, Z. (2007). Making Thinking Visible with ATLAS.ti: Computer Assisted Qualitative Analysis as Textual Practices. *Historical Social Research* (Suppl. 19), 276–298.

Nagel, D. A., Burns, V. F., Tilley, C., & Aubin, D. (2015). When Novice Researchers Adopt Constructivist Grounded Theory: Navigating Less Travelled Paradigmatic and Methodological Paths in PhD Dissertation Work. *International Journal of Doctoral Studies*, *10*, 365–383.

Porr, C. J. (2009). Establishing Therapeutic Relationships in the Context of Public Health Nursing Practice. Doctoral Dissertation, University of Alberta.

Porr, C. J., Drummond J., & Olson K. (2012). Establishing Therapeutic Relationships with Vulnerable and Potentially Stigmatized Clients. *Qualitative Health Research*, *22*(3), 384–396.

Seide, K. (2016). In the Midst of It All: A Qualitative Study of the Everyday Life of Haitians during an Ongoing Cholera Epidemic. Unpublished Master's Thesis, University of Miami.

Stern, P. N. (2007). On Solid Ground: Essential Properties for Growing Grounded Theory. In A. Bryant & K. Charmaz (Eds.), *The Sage Handbook of Grounded Theory.* London: Sage. pp. 114–126.

Stern, P. N. & Porr C. J. (2016). *Essentials of Accessible Grounded Theory*. New York: Routledge.

Strauss, A. & Corbin, J. (1990). *Grounded Theory Procedures and Techniques*. Newbury Park, CA: Sage.

Wertz, F. J., Charmaz, K., McMullen, L. M., Josselson, R., Anderson, R., & McSpadden, E. (2011). *Five Ways of Doing Qualitative Analysis*. New York: Guilford Press.

Whiteford, L. M. (2004). Cholera and Other Water-Borne Diseases. In C. R. Embers & M. Embers (Eds.), *Encyclopedia of Medical Anthropology: Health and Illness in the World's Cultures*. New York: Springer. pp. 305–311.

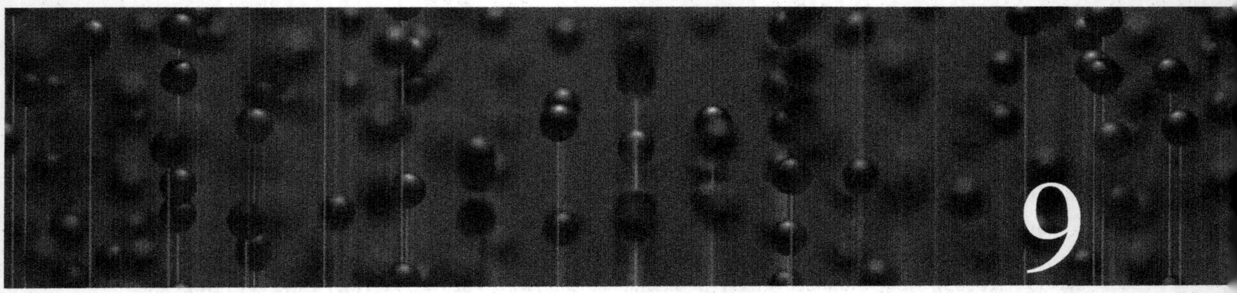

Coding and Translating: Language as a Heuristic Apparatus

Massimiliano Tarozzi

> La lingua italiana, che in ciò chiamo unica fra le vive, può nel tradurre conservare il carattere di ciascun autore in modo che sia tutto insieme forestiero e italiano ... Ma ciò non lo consegue con la minuta esattezza del tedesco ... bensì colla infinta pieghevolezza e versatilità della sua indole e che costituisce la sua indole. (Giacomo Leopardi)[1]

INTRODUCTION

Translation is the endeavour to cross borders, to build bridges across cultural barriers, seeking and offering linguistic hospitality, an effort which seems to be vital in these times of building walls to repel foreigners, immigrants or refugees. However, this endeavour is not merely an action rooted in compassionate and human commitment, but also a device, or an 'apparatus' (Agamben 2009) to better know the world.

This is particularly evident in doing qualitative research, which is constitutively sensitive to cultural diversity; the researcher is a culturally defined subject and analysis is embedded in processes of mutual meaning-making (Denzin & Lincoln 2005). In Grounded Theory Method (GTM), the role played by translation in the conceptualization process can be even more crucial. The issue of English translation assumes a particular and relevant importance within the GTM and reveals how epistemological and theoretical assumptions cannot be taken for granted. These assumptions are shaped by language, which subsequently frames the research. Therefore, completing and following a translation using the GTM involves more than using the method only in a merely functional and instrumental way, as the language in the research is definitely a heuristic device. Even if translation requires the grounded theorist to engage in a sophisticated critical reading of a text in the early stage of coding, it also allows for greater analytical detail, because it helps the researcher to conceptualize, and thus favours the inductive process and the logical synthesis of the translation.

To summarize my argument, the question of translation in doing the GTM cannot be taken for granted. This is especially evident in different fields related to the practice of research in general and of the GTM in particular, namely: (1) using the GTM in cultures and countries in which researchers would be using the translation, (2) issues arising when international researchers are using the original GTM sources in English but conducting their studies in their native languages, and (3) presenting research results in English of data collected and analyzed in other languages.

Following certain theories of translation, which I briefly summarize below, the use of another language could be a gain for the grounded theorist. In fact, coding in another language requires continuous acts of interlinguistic translation that increase our capability to comprehend our data, and offer sophisticated interpretive instruments, helping to refine analysis. Every translation is the result of elaborate acts of de-coding, in the source language, and re-encoding in the target language, which occur at several levels: semantic, syntactic, and pragmatic. Therefore, these continuous processes of de-coding and re-encoding support and make more effective the various coding phases that the GTM requires for data analysis.

In this chapter, I argue that if one posits the translation process as a non-neutral tool, collecting, analyzing and presenting GTM research in a foreign language could be a powerful analytical tool and not merely an interpretive resource. The rationale of my argument is rooted in Umberto Eco's theoretical perspective on translation. In contrast with deconstructionism in translation, Eco claims that one can say *almost* the same thing in another language. 'Almost' can be considered the propositional content of a phenomenon resulting from complex acts of cultural negotiation.

According to this perspective, translation is a process of understanding meanings, which requires the translator to exert interpretive and analytical acts in the source language as well as in elaboration and writing in the target language. Translation is a process that has many similarities with the coding process in the GTM. Every interlinguistic translation entails interconnected and multiple processes of de-coding, in the source language, and re-encoding in the target language. Therefore, the processes of de-coding and re-encoding can support and increase effectiveness of the three GTM coding phases. In other words, coding in another language implies interlinguistic translation which increases our facility to comprehend, and offers sophisticated interpretive instruments, helping in the refinement of our analysis, as is demonstrated by those who work multilingually using the various opportunities in coding provided from different languages.

Over the last 20 years, several issues regarding translation in qualitative research have arisen that merit further discussion beyond this chapter, such as the use of interpreters in qualitative research (Davidson 2000; Kapborg & Berterö 2002), the problems of cross-cultural interviewing (De Figueiredo 1980; Ryen 2001; Larking et al. 2007), the incorporation of diversity issues in the GTM (O'Neil Green et al. 2007) or the gathering and interpretation of language-dependent qualitative data (Esposito 2001). Although each of these issues merits further attention, they are beyond the scope of this chapter.

Instead, in this chapter I would like to focus on the translation process rather than the outcome; on the methodological implications, especially evident in the GTM, of translating as a semantic and cognitive process that researchers outside the Anglo-American context are forced to make. In fact, the number of GTM users in the world has grown exponentially over the last 10 years in diverse disciplines and professions (Charmaz 2014a, 2014b). The use of the GTM has spread far beyond the North American context where it originated, especially since the 2000s.

English has been adopted as the global research lingua franca: the language most frequently used to communicate research findings across national borders among native speakers of many different languages (Santos et al. 2014). Consequently, non-Anglo-American scholars are forced into confrontation with this language that, like Latin in the Middle Ages and modern times, is recognized as the language of the international scientific community, when dealing with one's research data and publishing research results.

Therefore, in this chapter, after a necessary premise about the hegemonic role of the English language within the international scientific community of qualitative researchers, I will focus on the advantages that this cultural hegemony offers to non-native English speakers.

After having briefly developed my theoretical framework in dealing with translation, I will develop my argument along two main lines. First, I will argue that translation can play a key role not only in the interpretation of data but also in the analytic process. This is possible when one considers the very nature of translation, which has some similarities with the GTM analytic process. Second, I will highlight the benefits of coding in different languages. A few concrete examples are provided to illustrate some practical coding strategies that can be practised to benefit from the use of a language other than the researcher's mother tongue. Before this, however, a couple of historical examples are provided below, as introductive vignettes illustrating the broader role of translation in building new knowledge by bridging cultural gaps. Kumarajiva and the Toledo School in the 4th and 12th centuries respectively, are paradigmatic examples of transforming the marginal role of minorities into creators of new knowledge thanks to translation activities.

TRANSLATION AS AN INTERCULTURAL PROCESS CREATING NEW KNOWLEDGE: TWO HISTORICAL EXAMPLES

The following examples show that translation is an intercultural endeavour, embodying not only the transfer of content from one linguistic code to another, but also creating new knowledge and an intercultural ethos of welcoming diversity. Both these aspects – new knowledge and intercultural ethos – are essential resources for qualitative researchers, including grounded theorists, and which so far have not been taken into due consideration within methodological and, above all, epistemological reflection. Since the translation brings with it both these aspects, translation can be a valuable resource for those who do qualitative research.

The first is the case of Kumarajiva (344–413), the great translator of Buddhist sutras from Sanskrit to Chinese, who played a key role in the spread of Mahayana Buddhist philosophy across Asia (Tizzano 2011). In the 4th century it was not easy to imagine that the Buddhist philosophy could cross the natural and impassable watershed represented by the Himalayas. Yet Buddhist teaching has developed mainly in China, gradually losing contact with its Indian birthplace where it rapidly disappeared. A transition occurred which was not without trauma. The civilization of the ancient Chinese Empire had traditionally been closed to foreign influences, so Kumarajiva's translation work was greatly favoured. Kumarajiva was half Turkish, half Indian, and spent most of his life in China. He could therefore play this role of intercultural mediator thanks to his plural identity; and this was the case for the foremost translators in the history of humanity. Referring to a Kumarajiva translation printed in the 8th century, Amartya Sen wrote that his story, involving China, India and Turkey in a cultural and linguistic hybridization, was a model of a non-Western globalized effort with positive, lasting influence and value for the whole world (Sen 2002).

A second emblematical example of the cultural and knowledge advantage and gain stimulated by translation is that of the translation school in Toledo in the 12th and 13th centuries. Here, in the heart of Spain, thanks to tolerant religious policies, a number of faiths coexisted peacefully, namely *Mozarabes* (Arabized Christians), Muslims, Jews and Catholics. This exceptional intercultural melting-pot, then favoured by the enlightened policies of Alfonso X of Castile, created the conditions for the emergence of a translation movement from Arabic into Latin (using Castilian as an intermediate language), and then from Arabic directly into Castilian. Due to this translation work Greek–Latin classical texts (preserved only in Arabic translation), scientific texts of astronomy by Arabic scholars, and Jewish, Persian and Arabic literature became available to all European scholars. Over time, the school attracted translators from all over Europe, such as, to name only a few, Gerard of Cremona (Italy), Rudolf of Bruges (Flemish), Michael Scot (Scotland) and Hermannus Alemannus (Germany). Thanks to this group of scholars and writers, the knowledge acquired from the Arab, Greek and Hebrew texts found its way into the heart of the universities in Europe. Another side effect of this linguistic enterprise was the promotion of a revised version of the Castilian language that not only incorporated the technical terms of Arab origin, but also reformed its Castilian syntactic structure, thus laying the foundations for modern Spanish as a global language.

That same Europe which today closes its borders to Arabs can trace the roots of its civilization to the lively cross-cultural context of Toledo.

RESEARCH-RELATED TRANSLATION ISSUES

International, globalized scholars, non-native speakers of English, including myself, deal with translation in a number of fields today. The globalization of research has created a parallel process of textual transformation from a domestic source language into English. For academic purposes, researchers worldwide must translate the contents related to their research practice into English as a second language in a number of ways: they translate data collected in different languages, present and write up research results in English, but also read and constantly cite academic literature written in English (both field-related and methodological literature), and sometimes translate it into other languages (as I did for my translation into Italian of Glaser & Strauss's *Discovery*, [Glaser & Strauss 2009]), and finally teach research methods, in English, to international students.

In all these cases, the failure of researchers to recognize the role of translation on data and its subsequent analysis, has been noted, which might ultimately have consequences for the final outcome of the study (Temple 1997; Birbili 2000; Temple & Young 2004).

It is particularly worrisome that even in qualitative research, which should be rooted in a different theoretical horizon from the conventional objectivist science, there is often an a-critical assumption that methods are context-free, research is language free, and the same meaning in the source language can be found in all target languages regardless of cultural contexts. Consequently, this disregards a fundamental assumption for qualitative research, namely that different languages somehow construct different ways of seeing social contexts, and this poses methodological and epistemological challenges for the researcher.

Therefore, there is a growing tendency by some to give serious consideration to the issues of translation and their intertwining analytical practices, acknowledging that researchers 'have accepted to varying degrees the view that meaning is constructed in rather than expressed by language' (Barrett 1992, p. 203) and that this is not a neutral exercise (see also Bradby 2002; Duranti 2003). As for the GTM, Kathy Charmaz has rightly and long pointed out that methods develop within specific contexts rather than being context-free (Charmaz 2014b), and it is worth recalling here that GMT has arisen in the particular North American social and cultural context.

Therefore, doing research in a multi-language context, which constantly implies translation acts, might be a valuable resource which prevents what every qualitative researcher should always bear in mind, namely that neither language nor the epistemological premises in which cross-cultural issues are rooted should ever be taken for granted. Bilingual researchers in a monolingual globalized world, are somehow forced to consider the use of language as a 'non-neutral' research tool, while English native scholars are allowed to take it for granted. This concerns mainly those who speak minor languages. It is no coincidence that in the history of translation it is precisely these people who have come to depend upon translation for their commercial, political, and cultural livelihood, and that have demonstrated a deeper knowledge about translation and a better ability to adapt themselves to situations and conflicts (Gentzler 1993, p. 75). However, this condition of belonging to a minority language group is obviously not only beneficial or costless.

TOWARDS A POST-COLONIAL GTM

Doing research in a monolingual globalized word reveals that linguistic difference is often linked to a power differential, even in the scientific community. There is a risk of academic colonialism, and research-related translation issues can unveil the question of the hegemonic power of English within the global social scientific community.

Following Foucault, not only knowledge but also language is *power* (Foucault 1980). Non-native English-speaking researchers are experiencing the double hegemony of both the Anglo-Saxon culture of social science and the current dominance of the English language in the scientific community. Among the first to report phenomena of academic colonialism, built and reinforced also through the use of the English language, was the Finnish scholar Pertti Alasuutari (2004), who pointed out that the United States and the United Kingdom dominated both the logic and the form of qualitative research methods. He was then followed by numerous global scholars who began to question both the dominance of the Anglo-American core and the current divide between qualitative research in the core and in the periphery (Mruck et al. 2005; Cisneros Puebla et al. 2006; Hsiung 2012).

Against this coloniality of knowledge some have claimed the need of post-colonial methodologies and of preserving local languages against the hegemony of English, in particular by working qualitatively with multicultural populations that can contribute to making contemporary research methods 'culturally flexible' (Gobo 2011).

In the GTM, the question of power differential and the hegemony of English, which definitively influences the analysis, can be actively transformed in further sources of data. Power inequalities and injustice can be analyzed in the GTM (Charmaz 2011; Levy 2015). In particular, the GTM rooted in the social justice perspective can critically examine the social structures that create the unequal distribution of power. Power issues and colonial hegemony risk remaining unseen in the GTM, because they are 'extant concepts' (Glaser 1978), and not developed within the GTM analysis, and therefore they cannot be imported into the analysis. However, according to Charmaz, they can be scrutinized as *sensitizing concepts*. In this way, 'we can define if, when, how, to what extent, and under which conditions these concepts become relevant to the study' (Charmaz 2005, p. 512). This can also easily be applied to power differential in translation issues. This perspective recalls the post-colonial Gayatri Spivak's theory of translation. In her fine essay on the politics of translation (1992), Spivak criticizes the 'hegemonic monolinguistic culture' in which both writers and readers are immersed. Monolingualism, which also pervades the methodological thinking of social research, is dominant in the translation policies studied by Spivak and this reinforces the marginalization of subaltern and oppressed minorities. Hence the risk of domesticating plurilinguism in the mainstream English culture and language could certainly be an important issue (social, political but also methodological), that working straddling more than one language reveals.

In this vein, more than Derrida's idea, which invites us to develop something like a postmodern and non-Eurocentric approach to translation, following Boaventura de Sousa Santos, in the GTM analytical process we need a theory of translation to transfer some concepts from one social and theoretical discourse to another (Garavito & Santos 2005), by keeping the attention to 'foreignizing' the other culture's text. As I noted elsewhere (Tarozzi 2013), whenever one deals with the translation of a text that is rooted in a different culture, there is always a choice between *domesticating* and *foreignizing* (rendering foreign) the translation (Venuti 1995). In 'domesticating' a translation, the translator (and the editor) decide to play down cultural differences as much as possible by bringing the original text within the philological parameters of the target culture, smoothing every rough edge (and thereby the translator's subjectivity vanishes). It is a kind of cultural assimilation work, ethnocentric to some extent, in which the dominant culture prevails. 'Foreignizing' the translation means purposely maintaining some 'estranging' elements of the parlance of the culture of origin, which, though they may undermine the overall fluency of the text, serves to remind the reader of its difference and distance from the host culture.

In sum, translation plays a crucial role in many aspects of qualitative research and in the GTM it assumes some special features. Over the past few decades, researchers who faced these translation problems, have found some pragmatic solutions, such as back-translation (Brislin 1970; Chapman & Carter 1979),[2] in managing sources of data collected in different languages. Here I will focus on a different aspect that is closely related to the special features of the GTM: namely, on the impact of translation processes on the analytical process. Here, translation embodies a way to allow concepts to emerge that, on the surface, seem less tied to the contexts and languages for expressing them. But above all, I will show how the translation process can offer extra tools precisely to abstract concepts from the data.

TRANSLATION'S RATIONALE

To create post-colonial qualitative methods, and in particular post-colonial GTM, theories of translation play a critical role and can provide a theoretical background for methodological thinking. Translation studies or translation theory, which, to some extent, can only be considered to have been a separate discipline since the 1980s (Gentzler 1993), can provide a meaningful theoretical framework to understand the implications of the methodological work straddling more than one language. But not all theories of translation go in the direction in which I am interested for the purpose of this chapter.

In short, my position is placed along a third way between a neo-positivist, 'scientific' approach to the translation that seeks an objective correspondence based on the existence of universal rules of grammar and universal lexical forms, and a totally subjective hermeneutic perspective, which aims to rebuild a new content in the target language.

The radical subjectivist perspective of deconstructionism, which has given so much to the theory of contemporary translation, does not seem to offer enlightening elements in the relationship between translation and analytical processes. Indeed, deconstructionists do not provide a proper theory of translation but use translation to raise questions on language, such as that 'in the process of translating texts, one can come as close as possible to that elusive notion or experience of *différance*,[3] which underlies the approach' (Gentzler 1993, p. 145).

Moreover, according to the provoking position of Derrida, who views translation as a place that significantly opens to philosophical reflection on reality, 'The origin of philosophy is translation or the thesis of translatability' (Derrida 1985, p. 120). Again, following Derrida, the same impossibility of translation reveals the ontological relationship between things and the ways to signify them: 'In the limits to which it is possible or at least *appears* possible translation practice is the difference between signified and signifier' (Derrida 1981, p. 21). This statement is full of consequences and implications for the processes of data collection and analysis, but is beyond the scope of this chapter.

Although it is hard to ignore the key role of language in constructing, rather than simply conveying, meanings, as I claimed elsewhere (Tarozzi 2012), I do not believe that the problems raised by the translation process should force one to resort to a radical relativism and deem it impossible to say the same thing in two languages. Derrida's deconstructionism in translation, based on the Foucauldian perspective that nothing exists behind language, denies the possibility of the equivalent meaning of a word in one language and its correspondent in another, leaving the translator as the suspect author of an autonomous work, far from the original.

While in translation an objectivist correspondence based on 'scientific' rules is simply incompatible with the basic assumption of qualitative research, and for the same reasons an objectivist grounded theory has been criticized (Charmaz 2000), I also disagree with the radical subjectivism of Derrida claiming that 'translation is another name of the impossible' (1998 [1996], p. 74). In the same vein, a moderate constructivism seems to be Kathy Charmaz's perspective of constructivist GTM, where she wrote 'my form of constructivism, however, does not subscribe to the radical subjectivism and individual reductionism assumed by some advocates of constructivism' (Morse 2009, p. 134). I agree instead with Umberto Eco's (2003) perspective, maintaining that translators are inclined to the generic possibility of equivalence (fidelity), but limited as to its 'propositional content'. Eco affirms that any literal translation is impossible. However, in translating, he believes one can say *almost* the same thing. This 'almost' is a propositional content and the result of linguistic and, above all, cultural negotiation (Eco 2003). This 'almost' is what also directs the analytical process of the GTM in transforming or translating empirical data into concepts. The propositional content is the conceptual quota that can legitimately and reasonably be abstracted from the data. The GTM researcher can account for only a very limited portion of the conceptual richness embedded in the data, but it is still relevant and meaningful to theoretically reconstruct a social process.

To do so, it is certainly necessary to renounce the myth of the Absolute Translation, and instead settle for what Ricoeur called 'an equivalence without adequacy' (Ricoeur 2006 [1998]) or sameness, where we are forced to accept the roughness of the source language where we feel uncomfortable. In this discomfort, the analytical process typical of the GTM takes place; from here one can abstract concepts, topics and categories that can give theoretical meaning to the data.

Besides, by saying almost the same thing within a negotiated dialogic horizon, according to Ricoeur, the translator also experiences an ethical follow-up or consequence: the condition of 'linguistic hospitality' of the participant as 'foreigner' in our own language. This is a powerful tool for deepening the relationship between the researcher and the researched, to fill the gap with the other, and allows the collection of rich and meaningful data. Linguistic hospitality, made possible by translation, is a methodological plus, a hunch that brings the researcher deeper into the data, and, in the GTM, an extra resource for constant comparison. In such a theoretical sense, translation could become a gain for the researcher, instead of a loss, or a mere waste of time.

DEALING WITH LANGUAGES AS A RESOURCE FOR THE GTM

Doing research across multiple languages can be an asset rather than a loss for grounded theorists and theory-building qualitative approaches, and more than descriptive or interpretive analysis. The enduring and uncertain tension of transferring something from the source language to the target one can offer an analytical advantage in terms of a more accurate understanding of the text, which offers new possibilities to generate theory.

Writers and refined translators such as Italo Calvino and Jorge Luis Borges agreed that translating is the most authentic and direct way to read a text. Along the same lines, George Steiner claimed that 'understanding is translation' (Steiner 2004 [1975], p. 32), and more recently Spivak wrote that 'Translation is the most intimate act of reading' (Spivak 1992). In the practice of GTM research dealing with data expressed in text form, a GT-translator that feels discomfort goes deeper than the GT-reader who feels at ease with the text. Where the latter tends to establish a simple coding relationship between text and concepts, the former combines two texts, and thus is forced to take into account the two cultural and linguistic encyclopaedias in which each text is rooted (Steiner 2004 [1975]). This means that translating becomes a sophisticated analytical device for abstracting concepts from data, both if one translates data originally collected in another language into English, and if one codes or writes a report in English of data originally collected in a different language.

I am aware that considering two cultural and linguistic encyclopaedias can be confusing and distracting in the actual research practice, as it raises the level of interpretation and obscures conceptual abstraction. Novices, in particular, may face difficulties in an excessive attention to linguistic nuances that such a meticulous translation imposes. Hence, they risk getting lost in translation and do not succeed in distilling the data to bring out the concepts. It is no coincidence that some authors suggest using translation at a later stage in a study, and only of concepts and categories that had been developed from data in a source language (Chen & Boore 2010). Nevertheless, their argument is based on the fact that the process of translation and back-translation of all the data collected in a study would be remarkably expensive in both time and cost. Conversely, it is my argument that translation is a key analytic resource. This means that even if it requires a sophisticated critical reading of a text in the early stage of coding, it also allows for greater analytical detail, because it helps the researcher to conceptualize, and thus favours the inductive process and its logic synthesis, as I illustrate in the following section where a correspondence between the conceptualization process in GMT and the sematic itinerary in the translation is elaborated.

Below, I will develop my argument by outlining the implications of translating in relation to the coding strategies applied in the GTM (Tarozzi 2013) in two main areas. First, I will compare Jakobson's threefold theory of translation with the analytical processes of the GTM. Although the two processes of translation and coding are of a different nature, and aim at different objectives, the practice of translation offers strategies that help coding. Second, on this ground, I will underline the benefits of using multiple languages in coding.

Translation and Coding Processes

Translating is not only a linguistic exercise. Roman Jakobson (1959) has broadened the process of translating to the semantic sphere, highlighting its pragmatic, historical, semiotic, as well as cultural dimensions. In the conceptual analysis of a text, according to the theoretical framework and rationale presented in the above section, assigning meaning to words or propositions cannot be narrowed to a linguistic construction. Therefore, his approach offers meaningful stimuli to GTM researchers, in particular by comparing steps of the translation process and those of GTM analysis.

The contribution of Jakobson, a milestone in contemporary translation theory, at least until the deconstructionist revolution, is relevant here because it went beyond the traditional distinction between a formal translation (i.e., a translation that is consistent with the form of the original text) and a free translation (i.e., a translation that uses innovative forms) (Gentzler 1993). Jakobson reframed the question of translation by posing it at a different level, taking it out of the boundaries of linguistics and comparing it to other disciplines, such as cultural anthropology, narrative studies and of course semiology, understood as the study of the signs in the linguistic context then included in the semiotics. In his 1959 essay, Roman Jakobson distinguished three well-known types of translation:

1. *Endolinguistic* (or intralinguistic): The interpretation of signs by means of other signs of the same language. It is the translation within the same linguistic system, by means of reformulation (e.g., bachelor = an unmarried man), the paraphrasis of a poem, by recasting it in prose, but also the transcription of an oral message in its written form (called *rewording*) is included in this type.
2. *Interlinguistic:* It is the *translation proper*, the interpretation of signs through the signs of another language or the transposition of signs by means of different linguistic systems. For example, bachelor = 'scapolo' (in Italian).

3. *Intersemiotic*: The transfer, or 'transmutation', of verbal signs to non-verbal sign systems (or vice versa). For example, from language into art, music or into a movie. A good contemporary case of this is the detailed description of the famous picture *Las meniñas* by Velasquez in the introduction of Foucault's (1966) book *Les mots et les choses*.

Jakobson's three types of translation reinforce the resemblance between the steps of the translation process and those of GTM analysis, thus revealing that translation is a powerful analytic resource, as summarized in Table 9.1.

From the three types of comparison proposed by Jakobson descend a number of suggestions not only for the practice of GTM coding more broadly, but for qualitative data collection and analysis.

First, initial/open coding is concerned with both endolinguistic and interlingusitic translation.

For endolinguistic translation, initial coding should label the original text using similar words, to recast ideas, events, incidents, personal accounts, etc. communicated through a written text by the participants, in fewer words, by necessarily using different terms. It requires the researcher to transform segments of text into summarizing codes using low conceptual, mostly descriptive codes or labels. Labelling is definitively a linguistic reformulation procedure of significant segments of text in a different code expressed through labels that are easy to store, combine and manipulate.

While it is undeniable that coding means a set of procedures to conceptualize data, in a constructivist GTM the analytical process of conceptualization is not done in an objective way. Coding is not the application of a series of mechanical procedures that can objectively be applied to produce well-ordered occurrences hidden behind the multiplicity of data. Coding work does not reveal working models of phenomena, nor guarantee access to the thing themselves, nor 'discovers' structural latent patterns of a substantive theory. Codes are not there, enclosed in the data, but it is up to the researcher of the task to co-construct them. Thus, coding is closely linked to naming processes and labelling phenomena and is inextricably involved in the dimension of language. Through coding, the researcher constructs the interpretive categories, which are still grounded in the phenomena that generated them. In this perspective, to bring out as much meaning as possible

Table 9.1 Comparing Jakobson's three types of translation and the steps in the GTM coding process

Type	*Translation process*	*Similar actions in coding*
Endolinguistic	Translation within the same linguistic system **Reformulation**	Transcription, initial word-by-word coding Textual analysis
Interlinguistic	Transposition of signs by means of different linguistic systems **Translation proper**	Coding and de-coding: Transcription 3 levels of coding Writing
Intersemiotic	Interpretation of verbal signs throughout non-verbal sign systems **Trasmutation**	Writing observations Take notes (transforming actions into written text)

incorporated in a particularly rich and evocative word, researchers require a close proximity to the text, at least in the early stages of coding, to bring out just what the participants wanted to express, without adding arbitrary interpretations, or being aware of their own prejudiced perspective. To this purpose, the GTM proposes, among other strategies, word-by-word coding, which is effective with particular types of texts or in some coding steps. In dealing with certain types of documents, one may have to approach a text as if it were a literary text. Not by chance did Glaser write that he learned to do initial coding when studying French literature at the Sorbonne, where he was trained in the skill of 'explication de text' (Glaser 1998, p. 24): reading closely line by line to ascertain what exactly the author is saying, to generate concepts that closely fit without imputation. Glaser used a tool of literary criticism in initial coding to transform a text in its linguistic declinations, recasting data using a sophisticated linguistic tool.

Second, interlinguistic translation occurs every time we use a different language as a research instrument in three different GTM endeavours, namely (1) by collecting data, mostly interviewing in a language different from the one of analysis or presentation; (2) by coding, in the same language of the data or in another; and (3) by writing in a language different from (1) and/or (2). I contend that in all these situations, while there are evident difficulties in transposing data and thoughts into another linguistic-cultural context, there are also remarkable benefits and extra resources that need to come with some warnings. Based on historical examples, a counter-hegemonic perspective, and theoretical assumptions on translation studies, I have argued that translation thinking and practices at every level of GTM procedures can be an analytical resource and a further source of data, can produce new knowledge and facilitate intercultural understanding, can prevent taking language issues for granted, and can be an extra resource of constant comparison.

Third, the transformation-into-text of data taken from facts, events and phenomena can be understood as an operation of intersemiotic translation, that is, a translation of signs and symbols across different contexts not only within a linguistic/textual context. The observation as an instrument of data collection transmutes contextualized events, places, time and subjects' actions into a unique text that can be further elaborated and analyzed. Therefore, field notes taken from observations are a similar exercise to the *ekphrasis*; the detailed (the Greek verb *ekphrazein* means 'describe in detail') written translation of a visual work of art, popular in ancient literature. Being a verbal representation of a visual representation *ekphrasis* is an illuminating form of translation of a sign of a sign, which recalls the role of the observer in collecting data or in combining visual and verbal data. Moreover, the transcription of an interview is always a translation act. While some claim that the transposition of an oral message in its written form is a 'transcription' or a 'notation' (Mounin 1965 [1963]), when it comes to the transcription of interviews aimed at an analysis within a GTM, I believe that every transcription is also a translation. There is nothing automatic about transcription. It is the first analytical level, since it is an interpretive effort that reduces complex verbal and non-verbal communication to a unique, textual dimension (Tarozzi 2015 [2008], p. 86). This is why I maintain that interviews should be recorded and carefully transcribed. This effort facilitates conceptualization, since transcription, as intersemiotic translation, is a further level of coding.

In general, one can observe that these three types of translation and analytic processes share the same characteristic: a full equivalence between the cultural and linguistic systems of the source and target text is impossible, as is clear for those who collect data in a language other than their own. I remember, for example, during research on teacher education programmes in multicultural contexts that I carried out in Southern California, when some participants mentioned to me the untranslatable concept of 'urban schools' or 'urban area'. It was a key notion for the purpose of the study but it was impossible to find an equivalent meaning in Italian. Back-translation, evoked for decades by some researchers (Brislin 1970; Chapman & Carter 1979), does not completely resolve this problem. It advances understanding just a little further and has the undeniable merit of stimulating the participation of the participants, but it does not dissolve the theoretical knot behind the impossibility of a direct correspondence, on the sole linguistic plan, between the source and target language. However, since they nevertheless attempt to say almost the same thing, the translator has to use criteria that transcend the purely linguistic and to apply continuous processes of decoding and re-encoding from the source to the target language. While the two processes – translating and coding – are constitutively different in their aims, it is not chance that one echoes the other. The interpretive process, which is always a decoding and re-encoding process, implicit in the action of translation according to a sociolinguistic approach (Nida 1979; Nida & Taber 1982), which inspired Chomsky's generative transformational grammar, encompasses a fluctuating semantic itinerary seeking a functional equivalence lying in the core, the kernel, the deep structure, or the essence, of the original text. In other words, translation, according to this theoretical perspective, is a cognitive process seeking in the target-language an equivalence with the original term in the source language. This equivalence, which can be only functional, is found in the semantic core, in the essence, that requires a process of abstraction to capture the kernel of a word or an expression. This process is very similar to conceptualization in the GTM, where the fluctuating analytical itinerary looks to produce concepts from data, through coding procedures. These threefold coding procedures – initial, focused, theoretical – are in fact de-coding and re-encoding acts. The constructivist grounded theorist not only applies functional analytic procedures to unveil concepts and processes that are enclosed in the data, but also interpretively deconstructs possible meanings in the data (de-encoding) in order to conceptually elaborate them (en-coding) to construct a theory. In Table 9.2, the two similar itineraries are portrayed to highlight some functional commonalities.

Nonetheless, the translation process, as well as the analytical one, always takes place in specific contexts, which are entangled by mutual relationships, and require the fusion of horizons. According to the theories of translation in the 1990s, translation is seen not only as a linguistic phenomenon, but also as a cultural one. Because of the close relationship between language and identity, translation is always an intercultural process which requires non-technical negotiation skills that bring to mind the characteristics of

Table 9.2 Two similar fluctuating itineraries

Translation process	GTM process
Source language	*Data*
Reading (the source text)	Data collection and open coding
(Semiotic) analysis of the source text	Focused/axial coding
Interpretation	Theoretical coding
Elaboration in the target text	Integrating theory
Writing in the target text	Writing the report
Target language	**Theory**

theoretical sensitivity (Glaser 1978) that have to do with momentum, insight, and seeing possibilities.

In this sense, in carrying out cross-cultural research, approaching a source text is an encounter with the other, the foreigner, who, in qualitative research, plays the role of the participant (and the texts he or she produced). If such an encounter does not take place in the reassuring mother tongue, but in the inadequacy, inaccuracy, dissatisfaction, and within the continuous processes of adjustment required by the use of another language (Derrida 1998 [1996]) in the GTM investigative process, this need not be solely a difficulty but can instead be turned into a powerful analytical tool.

Coding in Different Languages

Another area in which working between two or more languages can be a benefit for the GTM is coding procedure. As Charmaz observed, the 'characteristics of specific languages matter, as do the characteristics of cultural traditions and norms' (Charmaz 2014b, p. 1078). National languages have a huge impact, not only on data collection, but also in data analysis, especially in methodologies such as the GTM, which pay so much attention to the conceptualizing power of the language. Charmaz further observes that 'grounded theorists have given scant attention to how the structure and content of specific languages can affect inquiry'. The language is undoubtedly an analysis tool, as in the GTM coding operations, which are operated through a language like a trawler's net, which can catch different types of fish depending on its size and the type of rope from which it is made. So the functions and syntactic and especially morphological features of the various languages allow us to conceptualize textual data differently during the various stages of coding.

In my experience, I have noticed that Italian is extremely appropriate for supplying careful, rich, and refined descriptions. My native language has several declensions to express grammatical relations, relational categories such as gender and number for nouns, and numerous variations in verb conjugations that enlarge the possibility of precise description. Thanks to its characteristics, Italian is more suitable than English for the first phases of coding and for early memos. On the other hand, English is a more conceptualizing language than Italian, and has greater propositional power. Therefore, it seems more suitable for making propositional statements, binding concepts, expressing complex, and tricky categories with synthetic nomenclature. My argument is that in the GTM we are not forced to choose one language over another while we are coding. The advantage of a plurilinguistic coding is that working through more languages is not only possible but, to some extent, even beneficial when this allows the researcher to label concepts in a more sophisticated way and then capture phenomena in the analysis. Untranslatable words, such as the Danish *Hygge* (a state of coziness and comfort describing an ambience or mood); the Italian *Commuovere* (to be moved emotionally, usually relating to a moving story); the Norwegian *Utepils* (the feeling of sitting outside on a sunny day enjoying a beer); the Japanese *Kyoikumama* (a mother who continuously pushes her child into academic achievements), all these words are a meaningful way to code in few words complex phenomena and situations, not to mention very long German words which are practically long sentences in any other language.

After all, according to Derrida, translation puts us in contact with the plurality of languages and meanings. One never writes in just one language but is always already writing in multiple languages. This is even more evident in the coding operations where the multiplicity of languages allows us to collect, capture and express different concepts with more variety and possibilities. For example, in a piece of cross-cultural research, some Canadian colleagues describing an oncological patient's experience of fatigue, used the code 'spaghetti legs', translating an original expression used *in vivo* by Italian participants.

Languages, in the GTM are sophisticated heuristic devices for collecting and analyzing data and their function must not be underestimated or taken for granted. The characteristics of these devices depend on the very nature of each language, which opens different access routes to the data and especially to the conceptualization.

Contemporary linguistics has identified different and refined morphological types, which group languages according to their common morphological structures. In short, some languages, called 'isolating' or analytical, have a greater analytical power as they provide a closer correspondence between words and the morphemes that express them, with no particular variations. To take an example from the Latin language, which is not a pure isolating one, the expression 'cogito ergo sum', with few morphological variations and simple, not composed words, conceptually captures in three words a broad philosophical argument. In other languages, called synthetic languages, words are formed by combining different morphemes according to different morphological types. Basically, in this second type of languages, words have a large variability (gender, number, case, etc.) and a wide array of combinations of various morphemes within a single word. For example, the English pronouns 'he' (or accusative him), in Italian has a number of different declensions: 'egli' (masculine singular) or 'esso'. But also 'gli' (= to him; dative), 'lo' (= him accusative), and again 'lui' (to be used with a proposition, with an accusative value). All these morphemes can be enclosed in the same word as pronominal particles. For example, 'restituir-glie-la' = to give him it back (the thing is something feminine).

More synthetic languages are suitable for a detailed description, for the labelling of phenomena that remain fitting to the text of the participants, without proceeding with excessive jumps in the categorization. Unlike others (Charmaz 2014a), I argue that in the GTM it is crucial that in the early stages of research, the researcher remains very close to the data, multiplying the number and variety of codes, showing even the slightest nuances in the text. It is undoubtedly a more difficult task and more time-consuming, but it guarantees that the emerging theory is well rooted and grounded in the data. Otherwise, the rational, neatly-designed and systematic conceptual model emerging from the analysis risks, as often happens, being detached from the data and being more an exercise of abstraction and theorization rather than an empirical product.

In this vein, most isolating languages allow researchers to capture evanescent and centrifugal meanings in a short, highly evocative expression and conceptualizing, such as the synthetic 'being overpowered', which neatly conceptualizes a set of actions into an essential one. They help the analysis to rise up from the text, to prevent the emerging theory from remaining with a low conceptual power and therefore being irrelevant. In particular, in focused and theoretical coding phases, when the summarizing ability to immediately capture the essence of a text or a set of codes through understandable micro-texts is critical, isolating languages are extremely helpful. This is particularly evident when it is necessary to summarize as much as possible, as in naming core categories. To translate into Italian the perfectly constructed core category 'supernormalizing' used by Charmaz in her research on chronic illness, would require three lines of text. The difference between these two kinds of languages, when used as a device for GTM analysis, has a great impact in being able to express (or construct) the concrete and the abstract, or in their descriptive or conceptualizing power.

While purely analytic or purely synthetic languages do not exist in reality (Chinese and Esquimese come close), English is commonly regarded as an 'isolating' (or analytic) language (even though it is not purely isolating, but weakly fusional), whereas Italian is more 'inflectional' (or synthetic) from the morphological point of view (Comrie 1989 [1983]). As I have said, English is not precisely an isolating language but, being a mixed language, more closely resembles an isolating one and definitively has its advantages in terms of analytical ability, synthetizing and conceptual power. In the above-mentioned research in Southern California, I used the summarizing code 'LA segregated' to conceptualize in focus coding a number of more detailed codes and related themes. To express the same concept in Italian, I would have needed to have written three lines of text.

That is why in the early stages of analysis (open and initial coding), regardless of the language of the data, Italian is particularly suitable because it closely fits the original data. Many other languages, most Indo-European and especially neo-Latin ones, can better describe meaningful segments of text with long and accurate codes than English or other isolating languages. The more the analysis proceeds into selective and theoretical coding, the more English becomes appropriate for sorting and conceptualization, when it is necessary to label concepts.

To make an example of a long descriptive early code, well expressed in Italian, consider this: 'bambino presentato come problematico per fatiche familiari' (which more or less means 'child presented as problematic for family hardships'). The profile of a 'problematic' child is a representation of an early-years school teacher and this nuance should be present in the code. Moreover, the word 'problematico' is a rich and dense concept encompassing considerable meaning regarding the existential condition but also the social definition of the child. And, finally, the noun 'fatiche' (plural, feminine), embraces a number of diverse nuances of existential (self-) representation and also behaviours: difficulties, efforts, suffering, labour, discomfort, deprivation, etc.

Here I have limited myself to considering the languages with which I work most. It sometimes occurs to me to code also using Latin because by using its syntactic characteristics, more than morphological ones, it allows me to conceptualize better than in other languages. For example, the Latin construct 'ablative absolute' is extremely efficacious in expressing in a synthetic and implicit form a full subordinate clause. To give an example which can still be found in modern languages, basically for its synthetic ability, consider the expressions: '*mutatis mutandis*', with the things that need to be changed (*mutandis*) having been changed (*mutatis*), or '*cuius regio, eius religio*' (which in English can be translated with the same amount of words: whose realm, his religion), which means a more complex concept, namely that the religion of the sovereign was to dictate the religion of those ruled.

Each language has different morphological characteristics, and thus it represents a different analytical device. I can only imagine what it might be like coding in a polysynthetic or incorporating language, such as Chinese or the Vietnamese, that can condense into a single word information that in other languages would require the construction of a whole sentence.

In the GTM, the coding process is not only a descriptive or interpretive process, where the ability of linguistic expression in the language of research is essential, but is also mainly a conceptualizing, analytical and abstracting process. Here language primarily has an instrumental function to foster the emergence of concepts, categories and themes. Therefore, it is less important what language one uses to this purpose. The GTM researcher working across languages will be able to use all the tools and language skills at his disposal effectively. Of course, such skills are not necessarily required, but if a researcher possesses refined competences of textual analysis, they will certainly be able to code more effectively. We are referring here especially to open or initial coding, where codes are labelled phenomena, and where the smallest textual fragments can contribute to building future concepts. When early concepts will develop into categories and themes, then the way in which they will be named (and defined) is crucial. Giving categories a proper name, fitting data, regardless of the language we use, is a key factor for theoretically elaborating the process under analysis.

A further example of the implications of typical features of a language, in this case syntactic, in the process of coding with regard to research in practice, is the use of the '–ing form' that is emblematic of the GTM. First Glaser (1978) and then Charmaz (2006) have invited its use as a form to express categories in coding and in writing memos. Gerunds helps in detecting processes and actions. According to Charmaz, a gerund 'fosters theoretical sensitivity because these words nudge us out of static topics and into enacted processes' (Charmaz 2006, p. 136). In the latest edition of her *Constructing Grounded Theory* (Charmaz 2014a), she invites readers to compare gerunds with their noun forms (describing vs description; stating vs statement). While gerunds express a strong sense of action and sequence, nouns 'turn these actions into topics' (Charmaz 2014a, p. 120). These two forms –gerunds and their noun forms – therefore respond to different coding questions and highlight different data characteristics. The problem is that the gerund does not exist in all languages, and certainly not in Italian, at least not with the same function which it has in the English language.

A gerund (or –ing form) is a verbal form which can be used as a noun implying action (in this sense, it is very similar to the basic use of a gerund in classical Latin). This verbal form, with this function, does not exist in Italian or in many other neo-Latin languages (i.e., Spanish and French), where the gerund exists but with other linguistic functions (support in building periphrastic propositions and serving as an adverbial subordinate). In its place, in Italian, we use the infinitive form that freezes our conceptual labels into rather icy and fixed descriptions. While coding in Italian, we must make do with these more static grammatical forms, which, like nouns, neither connote the dynamic movement of a concept nor disclose the action's power.

For this reason, very often, while I am working in Italian, it occurs to me to code in English (or sometimes even in Latin), using –ing forms, exactly because of the flexibility of the language in expressing synthetically dense concepts and to better emphasize action and processes. Otherwise, in Italian, we have to resort to nouns that are more flexible or expressions that lack grammatical accuracy, but these, in turn, allow us to preserve the intensity and evocative power of a code.

In sum, to limit the comparison solely between the two languages that I more often practise, English is more synthetic than Italian and condenses meanings with fewer words. It is therefore perfect for creating conceptual codes and categories, or for expressing action through its –ing forms. On the other hand, these syntheses are less accurate and less fitting for the data than in Italian, which gives the researcher more linguistic options to denote a concept or a category with greater clarity and expressive power.

CONCLUSION

I disagree with those who argue that the GTM can be used as a neutral tool, regardless of the epistemology in which it is rooted, because it does not fit any established research paradigm (Holton 2007). On the contrary, as the theoretical demand of translation shows, an epistemological study to not take translation for granted seems necessary. If one abandons a monolinguistic conception of the GTM and starts thinking of it globally, it can definitely be seen that the very language is not a mere tool but creates meanings and diverse functionalities.

The implications of translation reveal how the GTM cannot be applied anywhere with varied epistemologies or at least that several theoretical frameworks lead to different applications of the method and produce different outcomes, of which one should at least be informed and responsible.

Applying the GTM across languages and collecting and analyzing data in a language other than one's mother tongue are intercultural mediation acts between a source and a target text, but also between data and its conceptualizations. This (finite) interpretive effort is a fruitful exercise that leads to a better understanding of and how to apply the GTM. Obviously, the translator/researcher plays an extremely uncomfortable role in which he or she tries to adapt imprecise language tools to the foreignness of the text through which data are expressed. This discomfort, which the researcher always experiences, is further compounded by the use of more linguistic codes: the mother language and the lingua franca of global research. However, this uncomfortable epistemic role may, to some extent, also be a desirable and necessary methodological exercise for positioning ourselves as researchers and for making explicit our own philosophical stance in which a GTM is embedded.

Notes

1 Giacomo Leopardi (1976). *Zibaldone*, a cura di Binni-Ghidetti (Vol. II, pp. 1949–1950). Firenze: Sansoni.

2 Back-translation is translating from the target language (e.g., English) back to the source language (e.g., Chinese) and the equivalence between source and target versions can be evaluated (Brislin 1970; Chapman & Carter 1979).

3 'Différance', a deliberate misspelling of the term *difference*, is a key notion in Derrida's philosophy, defining the relationship between text and meaning in a radical non-essentialist way at the very basis of deconstructionism (Derrida 1982).

REFERENCES

Agamben, G. (2009). *What is an Apparatus? And Other Essays*. Stanford, CA: Stanford University Press.

Alasuutari, P. (2004). The globalization of qualitative research. In C. Seale, G. Gobo, J. F. Gubrium, & D. Silverman (Eds.), *Qualitative Research Practice* (pp. 595–608). London: Sage.

Barrett, M. (1992). Words and things: Materialism and method in contemporary feminist analysis. In M. Barrett & A. Phillips (Eds.), *Destabilizing Theory: Contemporary Feminist Debates* (pp. 201–219). Cambridge: Polity Press.

Birbili, M. (2000). Translating from one language to another. *Social Research Update*, *31*. Retrieved 24 October 2016 from www.soc.surrey.ac.uk/sru/html.

Bradby, H. (2002). Translating culture and language: A research note on multilingual settings. *Sociology of Health & Illness*, *24*(6), 842–855.

Brislin, R. (1970). Back-translation for cross-cultural research. *Journal of Cross-Cultural Psychology*, *1*, 185–216.

Chapman, D. W. & Carter, J. F. (1979). Translation procedures for the cross-cultural use of measurement. *Educational Evaluation and Policy Analysis*, *1*, 71–76.

Charmaz, K. (2000). Grounded theory: Objectivist and constructivist methods. In Norman K. Denzin & Yvonna S. Lincoln (Eds.), *Handbook of qualitative research* (2nd ed., pp.509–535). Thousand Oaks, CA: Sage.

Charmaz, K. (2005). Grounded theory in the 21st century: Applications for advancing social justice studies. In N. K. Denzin & Y. S Lincoln (Eds.), *The Sage Handbook of Qualitative Research* (3rd ed., pp. 507–535). Thousand Oaks, CA: Sage.

Charmaz, K. (2006). *Constructing Grounded Theory: A Practical Guide Through Qualitative Analysis*. London: Sage.

Charmaz, K. (2011). Grounded theory methods in social justice research. In N. K. Denzin & Y. S. Lincoln (Eds.), *The Sage Handbook of Qualitative Research* (4th ed., pp. 359–380). Thousand Oaks, CA: Sage.

Charmaz, K. (2014a). *Constructing Grounded Theory* (2nd ed.). Thousand Oaks, CA: Sage.

Charmaz, K. (2014b). Grounded theory in global perspective: Reviews by international researchers. *Qualitative Inquiry*, *20*(9), 1074–1084.

Chen, H. Y. & Boore, J. R. (2010). Translation and back-translation in qualitative nursing research: Methodological review. *Journal of Clinical Nursing*, *19*, 234–239.

Cisneros Puebla, C. A., Domínguez Figaredo, Daniel, Faux, Robert, Kölbl, Carlos, & Packer, Martin (2006). Editorial: About qualitative research epistemologies and peripheries. *Forum Qualitative Sozialforschung / Forum: Qualitative Social Research*, *7*(4), Art. 4. Retrieved 25 October 2016 from http://nbn-resolving.de/urn:nbn:de:0114-fqs060444.

Comrie, B. (1989 [1983]). *Language Universals and Linguistic Typology* (2nd ed.). Oxford: Blackwell.

Davidson, B. (2000). The interpreter as institutional gatekeeper. *Journal of Sociolinguistics*, *4*(3), 379–405.

De Figueiredo, J. M. (1980). Some methodological remarks on transcultural interviewing. *International Journal of Social Psychiatry*, *4*(26), 280–292.

Denzin, N. K. & Lincoln, Y. S. (2005). Introduction: The discipline and practice of qualitative research. In N. K. Denzin & Y. S. Lincoln (Eds.), *The Sage Handbook of Qualitative Research* (pp. 1–32). Thousand Oaks, CA: SAGE.

Derrida, J. (1981). *Positions*. Chicago, IL: University of Chicago Press.

Derrida, J. (1982). *Margins of Philosophy*. Chicago, IL: University of Chicago Press.

Derrida, J. (1985). *The Ear of the Other: Otobiography, Transference, Translation*. New York: Schocken Books.

Derrida, J. (1998 [1996]). *Monolingualism of the Other, or, The Prosthesis of Origin*. Stanford, CA: Stanford University Press.

Duranti, A. (2003). Language as culture in U.S. anthropology, *Current Anthropology*, *44*(3), 323–347.

Eco, U. (2003). *Mouse or Rat? Translation as Negotiation*. London: Weidenfeld & Nicolson.

Esposito, N. (2001). From meaning to meaning. *Qualitative Health Research*, *11*, 568–579.

Foucault, Michel (1966). *Les mots et les choses: Une archéologie des sciences humaines* [*The Order of Things An Archaeology of the Human Sciences*]. Paris: Gallimard.

Foucault, M. (1980). *Power/Knowledge: Selected Interviews and Other Writings, 1972–1977*. New York: Pantheon Books.

Garavito, R. C. A. & Santos, B. S. (2005). *Law and Globalization from Below: Towards a Cosmopolitan Legality*. Cambridge, UK: Cambridge University Press.

Gentzler, E. (1993). *Contemporary Translation Theories*. London: Routledge.

Glaser, B. G. (1978). *Theoretical Sensitivity: Advances in the Methodology of Grounded Theory*. Mill Valley, CA: Sociology Press.

Glaser, B. G. (1998). *Doing Grounded Theory: Issues and Discussions*. Mill Valley, CA: Sociology Press.

Glaser B. & Strauss A. (2009). *La scoperta della Grounded Theory. Strategie per la ricerca qualitativa*. (Massimiliano Tarozzi, Trans.). Roma: Armando.

Gobo, G. (2011). Glocalizing methodology? The encounter between local methodologies. *International Journal of Social Research Methodology*, *14*(6), 417–437.

Holton, J. (2007). The coding process and its challenges. In A. Bryant & K. Charmaz (Eds.), *The Sage handbook of grounded theory* (pp. 265–289). London: Sage.

Hsiung, Ping-Chun (2012). The globalization of qualitative research: Challenging Anglo-American domination and local hegemonic discourse. *Forum Qualitative Sozialforschung / Forum: Qualitative Social Research*, *13*(1), Art. 21. Retrieved 25 October 2016.

Jakobson, R. (1959). On linguistic aspects of translation. In Reuben A. Brower (Ed.), *On Translation* (pp. 232–239). Cambridge, MA: Harvard University Press.

Kapborg, I. & Berterö, C. (2002). Using an interpreter in qualitative interviews: Does it threaten validity? *Nursing Inquiry*, *9*(1), 52–56.

Larkin, P. J., Dierckx, C. B., & Schotsmans, P. (2007). Multilingual translation issues in qualitative research: Reflections on a metaphorical process. *Qualitative Health Research*, *17*(4), 468–476.

Levy, D. L. (2015). Discovering grounded theories for social justice. In C. W. Johnson & D. C. Parry (Eds.), *Fostering Social Justice through Qualitative Inquiry: A Methodological Guide*. (pp. 71–99). Walnut Creek, CA: Left Coast Press.

Morse, J. M. (2009). *Developing grounded theory: The second generation*. San Francisco: Left Coast Press. Now London: Routledge.

Mounin, G. (1965 [1963]). *Teoria e storia della traduzione [Les problèmes théoriques de la traduction*. Torino: Einaudi [Paris: Gallimard].

Mruck, K., Cisneros Puebla, C. A., & Faux, R. (2005). Editorial: About qualitative research centers and peripheries. *Forum Qualitative Sozialforschung / Forum: Qualitative Social Research*, *6*(3), Art. 49. Retrieved 25 October 2016 http://nbn-resolving.de/urn:nbn:de:0114-fqs0503491.

Nida, E. A. (1979). Translating means communicating: A sociolinguistic theory of translation I. *The Bible Translator*, *30*(1), 101–107; and *II*, *30*(3) (7/1979), 318–325.

Nida, E. A. & Taber, C. (1982). *The Theory and Practice of Translation*. Leiden, NL: E. J. Brill.

O'Neil Green, D., Creswell, J., Shope, R., & Plano Clark, V. (2007). Grounded theory and racial/ethnic diversity. In A. Bryant & K. Charmaz (Eds.), *The Sage Handbook of Grounded Theory* (pp. 472–492). London: Sage.

Ricoeur, P. (2006 [1998]). Translation as challenge and source of happiness. In Paul Ricoeur, *On Translation* (pp. 3–10). New York: Routledge.

Ryen, A. (2001). Cross-cultural interviewing. In J. F. Gubrium & J. A. Holstein (Eds.), *Handbook of Interview Research: Context and Method* (pp. 335–354). Thousand Oaks, CA: Sage.

Santos, H. P. O., Black, A. M., & Sandelowski, M. (2014). Timing of translation in cross-language qualitative research. *Qualitative Health Research*, *25*(1), 134–144.

Sen, A. (2002). How to judge globalism. *The American Prospect*, 4 January.

Spivak, G. (1992). The politics of translation. In M. Barrett & A. Phillips (Eds.), *Destabilizing Theory: Contemporary Feminist Debates* (pp. 177–200). Cambridge, UK: Polity Press.

Steiner, G. (2004 [1975]). *After Babel: Aspects of Language and Translation*. New York: Oxford University Press.

Tarozzi, M. (2012). Translating grounded theory into another language: When translating is doing. In V. Martin & A. Gynnild (Eds.), *Grounded Theory: Philosophy, Method, and the Work of Barney Glaser* (pp. 161–175). Boca Raton, FL: Brown Walker Press.

Tarozzi, M. (2013). Translating and doing grounded theory methodology: Intercultural mediation as an analytic resource. *Forum Qualitative Sozialforschung / Forum: Qualitative Social Research*, *14*(2), Art. 6.

Tarozzi, M. (2015[2008]). *Che cos'è la grounded theory* (5th reprint). Roma: Carocci.

Temple, B. (1997). Watch your tongue: Issues in translation and cross-cultural research. *Sociology*, *31*, 607–618.

Temple, B. & Young, A. (2004). Qualitative research and translation dilemmas. *Qualitative Research*, *4*, 161–178.

Tizzano, P. (2011). Kumarajiva's visibility: Proposals for research in Translation Studies, in *International Seminar 'Kumarajiva: Philosopher and Seer'*, New Delhi: Indira Gandhi National Centre for the Arts.

Venuti, L. (1995). *The Translator's Invisibility*. London: Routledge.

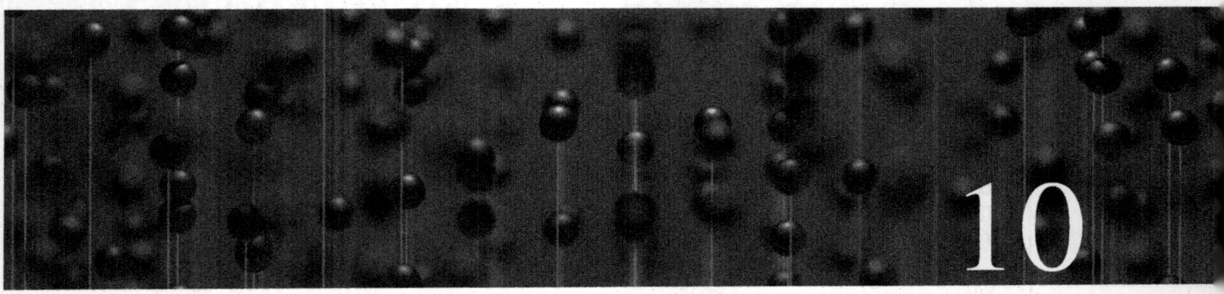

Literature Review in Grounded Theory

Robert Thornberg and Ciarán Dunne

> 'This is indeed a mystery,' I remarked. 'What do you imagine that it means?'
>
> 'I have no data yet. It is a capital mistake to theorise before one has data. Insensibly one begins to twist facts to suit theories, instead of theories to suit facts.' (Dr Watson describes a dialogue between himself and Sherlock Holmes in 'A Scandal in Bohemia', Conan Doyle, 1891: 63)

In 1967, Glaser and Strauss acknowledged the influence of the sociologist Robert K. Merton and his work on middle-range theory. At the same time, however, they criticized Merton's idea that theory can be generated through speculation and then assumed to be valid and relevant until disproven by quantitative methods. Like the fictive detective Sherlock Holmes in the excerpt above, Glaser and Strauss argued, 'His reasoning necessarily leads to the position *that data should fit the theory*, in contrast to our position that *the theory should fit the data*' (1967: 261). With reference to the sociologist and symbolic interactionist Herbert Blumer, Glaser and Strauss (1967) claimed that social scientists need to theorize from the data rather than from the armchair, a position with which we agree. Qualitative researchers who simply deduce from pre-existing theories risk running into problems such as overlooking aspects of the social life and data that are outside the scope of the specific theory which they are using as an analytical lens. This problem, in turn, can involve over-interpreting and distorting certain data, shoehorning ideas into the findings, or remaining uncritical towards a theory without examining its empirical validity, culminating in a process of circular reasoning (for a discussion about the problems of merely relying on theory deduction in qualitative research, see Kennedy-Lewis and Thornberg, 2018). If researchers uncritically treat a certain theory as true, right or superior, they will become 'data resistant', disregarding or overlooking data that do not support that particular theory, and their research will act as a self-fulfilling prophecy. As Tavory and Timmermans (2014: 1–2) state:

> These researchers are so wedded to a conceptual framework that all they do is repeat or add a minor nuance to their preferred theory ... they push us to ignore many of the surprises that emerge during fieldwork, to dismiss as noise any observation that does not fit predetermined conceptual categories. ... Sometimes we wonder why the authors even took the trouble to do the empirical work; it seems they knew what they would find, and the theory seems to have said it all before.

More importantly, and related to the criticism of forcing data by preconception, Glaser and Strauss (1967) stressed that the use and verification of 'grand theories' by quantitative methods, which dominated the field of social research of the 1960s, lacked the ambition and methods to discover and generate new theories. They pointed to the need for theory generation in social science, and offered grounded theory method (GTM) as an inductive, iterative, and systematic research approach designed to explore and analyze data in order to generate theories on the studied phenomena. They concisely defined GTM as 'the discovery of theory from data' (Glaser and Strauss, 1967: 1). At least three reasons account for why GTM is necessary: (1) the literature does not provide enough theories to cover all aspects or areas of the social life; (2) due to their lack of grounding in data, extant theories seldom fit or work, nor are relevant or sufficiently understandable to use in research which aspires to be sensitive to the empirical field and its participants (Glaser and Strauss, 1967); and (3) our reality is dynamic, continuously shaped by diverse, subjective lived experiences and innovations. As Blumer (1969: 23) contends, 'the history of empirical science shows that the reality of the empirical world appears in the "here and now" and is continuously recast with the achievement of new discoveries. The danger of the belief that the reality of the empirical world exists in a perpetually fixed form comes in the natural disposition to take existing knowledge of that reality as constituting the perpetual fixed form.' For example, 20 years ago there was no need for theories relating to phenomena such as how individuals consume online content through mobile devices, construct and communicate online identities, or engage in and respond to online bullying on social media. However, these concerns are of great importance in contemporary society and, as such, it is valuable to have theories grounded in empirical data which explore and explain such behaviours.

THE AMBIVALENT DICTUM OF NO PRECONCEPTION

Since its introduction by Glaser and Strauss in 1967, an ongoing discussion has ensued about how and when to engage with extant literature when using GTM. The original dictum directed researchers to delay the literature review until the end of analysis. This dictum has prompted much debate over the years and still represents one of the most polemical and contentious aspects of GTM at both an ideological and practical level (e.g., Dunne, 2011; Giles et al., 2013; Glaser, 2013; Heath, 2006; Martin, 2006; McCallin, 2006; McGhee et al., 2007; Ramalho et al., 2015; Thistoll et al., 2016; Thornberg, 2012). Indeed, according to Urquhart (2007: 350–351), the 'injunction that no literature that relates to the phenomena should be studied before coding the data is one of the most widespread reasons for the lack of use of grounded theory'.

In their original version of GTM, Glaser and Strauss stated that an effective strategy to remain sensitive to the data was 'literally to ignore the literature of theory and fact on the area under study, in order to assure that the emergence of categories will not be contaminated by concepts more suited to different areas' (1967: 37). They argued that similarities and convergences with the literature could then be established *after* the analytical categories have emerged. However, as will be discussed, the practical espousal of this dictum is highly problematic. Furthermore, they posited that theoretical sensitivity encompasses the researcher's 'ability to have theoretical insights into his area of research, combined with an ability to make something of his insights' (1967: 46), while cautioning that theoretical sensitivity will, however, be lost if the researcher 'commits himself exclusively to one specific preconceived theory … for then he becomes doctrinaire and can no longer "see around" either his pet theory or any other' (1967: 47). Thus, the problem here seems not to be about knowing pre-existing theories, but how to relate and integrate them into the study in a way which does not undermine or devalue the actual data.

This problem emerges when a certain theory is privileged in a rather uncritical manner as being true, right, relevant and superior, instead of considering it as one among many, which are fallible, provisional, and of potential, but not *a priori*, relevance to the data. In the final chapter of their book, Glaser and Strauss concluded that researchers cannot erase all their theoretical knowledge from their mind before starting the study, but 'the trick is to line up what one takes as theoretically possible or probable with what one is finding in the field' (1967: 253), and to 'cultivate' existing sources of theoretical insights by focusing on the data. As such, from the outset there has been an ongoing discussion about how and when to engage with extant literature when using GTM.

THE PLACE OF LITERATURE REVIEW IN VARIOUS GTMS

Since 1967, GTM has been further developed in different versions, and the three most widespread versions today are *Glaserian* GTM (Glaser, 1978, 1998, 2005), *Straussian* GTM (Corbin and Strauss, 2015; Strauss, 1987; Strauss and Corbin, 1990, 1998), and *constructivist* GTM (Bryant, 2002; Charmaz, 2000, 2006, 2014; Thornberg and Charmaz, 2014). Here we will describe the place of the literature review in these major versions of GTM.

Glaserian GTM

In contrast to the two later versions, Glaser (1978, 1998, 2001, 2013) has continued to argue that the literature should not be reviewed prior to data collection. His main arguments for this position is to keep the grounded theorist as free and open as possible to discover, and to avoid contamination in terms of forcing data into pre-existing concepts that do not fit with data, or have no relevance to the substantive area and the participants. In addition, Glaser (1998) argues that the grounded theorists cannot know which literature may be relevant to review until the end of the analysis. By delaying the literature review until the end of the study, time is therefore saved from reading literature which ultimately does not contribute to the study or theory development.

Glaser's position reflects the positivist ideal of an unbiased *tabula rasa* researcher who without preconception discovers theory from the data by just doing GT with trust in its process and letting the data 'speak for itself' (e.g., Glaser, 1992, 1998). He claims that 'data is rendered objective to a high degree by most research methods and GT in particular by looking at many cases on the same phenomenon, when jointly collecting and coding data, to correct for bias and make the data objective' (Glaser, 2003: 173). In sum, the main rationale for postponing the literature review in Glaserian GTM is that the theory has to be discovered within the data, rather than being imposed on it from pre-existing literature.

At the same time, Glaser (1978, 1998, 2005) recommends that in order to enhance theoretical sensitivity, grounded theorists have to read literature in other unrelated fields. By studying and knowing many scientific theories, they can identify several logics for relating and integrating concepts (that is, theoretical codes) embedded in these theories, and thus develop a rich repertoire of theoretical codes:

> One reads theories in any field and tries to figure out the theoretical models being used. ... It is a challenge to penetrate the patterns of latent logic in other's [*sic*] writings. It makes the researcher sensitive to many codes and how they are used. He or she should take the time it takes to understand as many theoretical codes as possible by reading the research literature. This is a very important part of developing theoretical sensitivity. (Glaser, 1998: 164–165)

Glaser (2005: 11) argues that the more theoretical codes the grounded theorists learn, the more they have 'the variability of seeing them emerge and fitting them to the theory'.

Nevertheless, as pointed out by Thornberg (2012), Glaser's strategy causes problems. If researchers at the outset avoid reading literature in the actual field of study, but instead read literature from various other unrelated fields to learn theoretical codes, before finally undertaking a literature review in the specific field at the end of the analysis, 'they will soon drive themselves into a corner during their research career because of the accumulative reduction of possible research fields, which they still have not read literature about' (Thornberg, 2012: 244). Furthermore, if researchers have a fear of contamination from reading literature relating to the substantive area, would it not be a risk of contamination and 'carry-over effects' even when reading literature from other fields? As such, notwithstanding the accepted view the data should be privileged above extant theories, the logic of avoiding engagement with literature in the specific domain of research appears highly problematic. Indeed, even among Glaserian grounded theorists, there is an ongoing discussion towards a less strict dictum of delaying the literature review (see Martin, Chapter 11, this volume).

Straussian GTM

Although Strauss, as a co-author with Glaser, initially advocated delaying the literature review, Charmaz (2014: 306) claims that, for Strauss, his stance was rhetorical. 'I base this point on many conversations and interviews I had with Strauss, who assumed that grounded theorists had prior lives and knowledge before embarking their research'. Similarly, Strauss and Corbin (1990: 48) state that 'we all bring to the inquiry a considerable background in professional and disciplinary literature' and that one source of theoretical sensitivity is literature, including readings on theory, research, and documents. 'By having some familiarity with these publications, you have a rich background of information that "sensitizes" you to what is going on with the phenomenon you are studying' (1990: 42). Thus, in contrast to the Glaserian GTM, Strauss and Corbin (1990, 1998;

Corbin and Strauss, 2015) adopt a more liberal stance, arguing that literature can be used more actively in GT research as long as the researcher does not allow it to block creativity and obstruct discovery.

According to the Straussian GTM, familiarity with relevant literature can enhance one's sensitivity to subtle nuances in data, provide a source of useful concepts for comparing data, stimulate questions during the analytical process, such as when there is a discrepancy between a researcher's data and the findings reported in the literature, and suggest areas for theoretical sampling. Using the literature enriches the analysis, while simultaneously encouraging the grounded theorists to take a critical stance and challenge 'emergent' concepts and ideas. At the same time, Strauss and Corbin (1990) stress that we do not need to review all the literature beforehand given that discovery is our purpose and therefore we cannot know in advance all categories relevant to the emerging and evolving theory. This is similar to the point made by Glaser. Early reading in the field, therefore, does not eliminate a need to return to the literature both during and at the end of the analysis.

Constructivist GTM

Constructivist GTM offers a different perspective to both the Straussian and, most notably, the Glaserian approach, in its rejection of claims of objectivity and the ideal of an unbiased *tabula rasa* researcher. Instead, this position explicitly argues that neither data nor theories are discovered, but rather are constructed by the researchers as a result of their interactions with the participants and the field. They co-construct data together with the participants, while their social, cultural and historical settings, academic training and personal worldviews inevitably influence these data, the analysis thereof, and the 'emergent' theory (Charmaz, 2006, 2009, 2014; Mills et al., 2006; Thornberg and Charmaz, 2014). As Charmaz (2014: 239) puts it, the constructed 'theory *depends* on the researcher's view; it does not and cannot stand outside of it'.

Rather than trying to erase their preconceptions or pretend that their privileges and preconceptions do not influence the research process, grounded theorists have to engage in reflexivity and explicate their preconceptions and positions during every phase of data gathering and analysis (Charmaz, 2014; Charmaz et al., 2018). 'Arguments for delaying the literature review often assume that researchers remain uncritical of what they read and are easily persuaded by it' (Charmaz, 2014: 307). It underestimates their abilities to engage in reflexivity (Dunne, 2011), and to consider and compare pre-existing theories and research findings without imposing them on data (Urquhart, 2007). Strauss and Corbin (1998: 47), as well as Charmaz (2014: 117), quote Dey (1993(63), who states, 'In short, there is a difference between an open mind and an empty head. To analyze data, we need to use accumulated knowledge, not dispense with it. The issue is not whether to use existing knowledge, but how'. According to Charmaz (2014), grounded theorists have to engage the literature in their field critically and comparatively in relation to the actual project. Like Strauss and Corbin, she recommends that the researcher starts with a preliminary literature review and uses it 'without letting it stifle your creativity or strangle your theory' (Charmaz, 2014: 308). Charmaz emphasizes, and we agree, that the initial literature review is not the same as the final version of the literature review. The latter has to be written to fit the specific aim, to present the grounded theory and arguments of the research report, and is also dependent on the specific journal or task.

Different Phases of Literature Review in GTM

Keeping in mind the guidelines of the Straussian and, more so, the Constructivist versions of grounded theory, the implication is that the researcher maintains an ongoing relationship with the extant literature throughout the research process. However, like many relationships, this one responds and adjusts to the ongoing analysis of data and therefore evolves over time. As such, we can identify at least three main phases of literature review in GTM.

The first phase is an *initial literature review* which takes place in the early stage of the research process, prior to the commencement of data collection. Despite Glaser's explicit advice against engaging with literature at this stage, numerous benefits result from such engagement, which are examined in detail in a later section. Among these is the argument that an initial literature review helps establish *if, how, when, where, why* and *by whom* a given topic has been studied (or not) to date. The primary interest at this point is to become broadly familiar with the geography of a subject and locate oneself within this research terrain by understanding existing empirical findings, rather than simply seeking out and clinging to theoretical frameworks used in such studies. Indeed, we agree that researchers using grounded theory should adopt a sceptical stance to any theoretical framework employed in similar studies (Strauss and Corbin 1990), and thus, remain non-committed to the literature and aware of its limitations to maintain openness to the field (Martin, 2006). In essence, rather than constrain and contaminate the researcher, this initial literature review should be both empowering and enriching, imbuing the researcher with the confidence to move forward with the study.

The second phase is an *ongoing literature review* which takes place during the data collection and, unlike the first phase, is heavily informed by the raw data (e.g., qualitative interview data) which the researcher gathers. During this phase the researcher may seek to identify empirical studies which relate to findings (e.g., themes, ideas, hypotheses) emerging from the iterative process between data collection and analysis. For example, consider a study exploring pressures faced by students in higher education. If perchance, family responsibilities such as childcare were to emerge as a factor linked with programme incompletion for 'mature students', the researcher may engage with the literature on mature students in higher education to establish whether other evidence supports or contradicts this finding. Also, during this phase, as the data collection progresses and the construction of the grounded theory shifts from being tentative to increasingly focused and robust, the researcher seeks to identify existing theories and concepts which help to elevate the grounded theory to a more abstract level.

Finally, the third phase is the *final literature review* which takes place towards the end of the study, as the researcher seeks to contextualize the constructed grounded theory in relation to established theoretical ideas and identify theoretical reference points against which to compare and contrast the data. This review is crucial in terms of locating the study within or across disciplines. Indeed, some of the theories which strongly resonate with a constructed grounded theory may be new to a given field or discipline. In the case of Dunne (2008), for example, his grounded theory study indicated that 'utility' – the subjectively perceived value interacting with 'the other' – was a powerful mediator of intercultural relations among international and local students. This finding found strong resonance with 'social exchange theory' (Thibaut and Kelley, 1959), which until then had been a theory that received very little attention in intercultural studies, but offers significant value to the field. As such, this third phase of the literature review is a vital step in demonstrating the researcher's ability to situate the constructed grounded theory within extant theoretical ideas and propositions, as well as highlighting its contribution to the field. In sum, each of the three phases is targeted and purposeful, yet each one fulfils a discrete and important function in the overall research process.

PROBLEMS WITH PURE INDUCTION AND THE LEGACY OF PEIRCE'S ABDUCTION

The main assumption behind the original dictum to delay the literature review is the idea of *pure induction*, in which researchers gather and analyze theory-free data without any prior theoretical knowledge and preconception. This position is, however, severely criticized and has to be considered as a 'dead' position within the field of philosophy of science (e.g., Chalmers, 1999; Hanson, 1965; Popper, 1959). It is a position that Chalmers (1999) has labelled *naïve inductivism* because it fails to recognize that researchers are situated within an historical, ideological, and sociocultural context.

Empirical observation is never free from preconceptions, but inevitably a 'theory-laden' undertaking shaped by prior knowledge (Bendassolli, 2013; Hanson, 1965; Kelle, 1995). The early positivists made the claim that 'it's all there in the data' (Kelle, 2014), but we can no longer retreat behind their claim (Bryant, 2009), which makes trouble for the position of pure induction. However, when induction is adopted in an interpretative or constructivist qualitative research tradition, such as Straussian GTM (Corbin and Strauss, 2008, 2015) and constructivist GTM (Charmaz, 2006, 2014), the empirical cases are always considered as *interpreted and constructed data* rather than raw data (Kennedy-Lewis and Thornberg, 2018), and therefore not independent and free from the researchers' lenses and prior knowledge. Thus, in accordance with their underlying epistemology, researchers do not claim to offer an exact picture, but rather an interpretative portrayal of the phenomenon studied (Charmaz, 2014).

Although GTM is often described as an inductive method, many grounded theorists recognize GTM to be based on an interplay between induction and abduction (e.g., Bryant, 2009; Kelle, 2005; Reichertz, 2007; Richardson and Kramer, 2006; Thornberg and Charmaz, 2014). The scientist, philosopher and one of the earliest proponents of pragmatism, Charles S. Peirce (1960, 1979), developed *abduction* as a third mode of inference to add beside induction and deduction. Because he used different terms when writing about abduction (i.e., abduction, retroduction, presumption, and hypothesis) and developed the meaning of abduction over time, there continues to be a debate among scholars on how to define abduction (e.g., Anderson, 1987; De Waal, 2013; Kachab, 2013; McKaughan, 2008; Paavola, 2004; Reichertz, 2007; Schurz, 2008; Tavory and Timmermans, 2014).

We understand abduction as a selective and creative process in which the researcher carefully examines which hypothesis explains a particular case or segment of data better than any other candidate hypotheses for further investigation (Douven, 2011; Kennedy-Lewis and Thornberg, 2018; Peirce, 1960, 1979). It is a creative process with an unorthodox, critical and sceptical attitude towards theory (including one's own developed concepts), in which every new insight is a result of modifying, elaborating, expanding or rejecting prior knowledge and putting old ideas together in new ways to explore, understand and explain the data. Indeed, central to creativity is the process of drawing on apparently unrelated knowledge sets and making connections between them in order to produce novel and useful outputs (Cheng et al., 2008; Kurtzberg 2005).

Like a detective, researchers constantly move back and forth between data and pre-existing knowledge or theories, and make comparisons and interpretations in searching for patterns and the best possible explanations (Bryant, 2009; Carson, 2009; Eco, 1981; Thornberg, 2012; Truzzi, 1976). According to Kelle (1995), researchers' ability to draw good abductive inferences is dependent on their previous knowledge, rejection of dogmatic beliefs, and the development of open-mindedness. The literature is therefore a vital resource when conducting abduction in GTM.

THE ADVANTAGES OF A LITERATURE REVIEW

In presenting both the Straussian and constructivist perspectives, a number of arguments in favour of engaging with literature at an early stage in the research process have been alluded to. However, it is useful to consider these in a more formal manner. As has been discussed, the Glaserian dictum against engaging with literature at an early stage is based on the premise that the literature could 'contaminate' the data collection, analysis and theory development through the imposition of extant theoretical frameworks, ideas or hypotheses. Thus, the early literature review could ultimately stifle and compromise the authenticity, quality and originality of the study.

However, coupled with the aforementioned fallacy of pure induction upon which Glaser's dictum is predicated, the merits of his approach can be challenged on the pragmatic grounds that postponing a literature review until data collection is in progress is simply impractical. For many researchers, in particular doctoral students, a rigorous literature review is demanded at an early stage to secure funding or ethical approval. Rather than simply critiquing the dictum of avoiding early engagement with the literature, however, it is perhaps more useful to reflect on the potential benefits derived from undertaking an early literature review when using the GTM.

In the first instance, such a review often assists in establishing a defensible rationale for a given study, including the selection of a specific research approach (Coyne and Cowley, 2006; McGhee et al., 2007). Secondly, by reviewing extant literature the researcher can identify relevant knowledge gaps which merit investigation (Creswell, 1998), while simultaneously confirming that the proposed study has not previously been conducted (Chiovitti and Piran, 2003). Thirdly, a literature review indicates precisely how a phenomenon has been studied to date (McMenamin, 2006), facilitates the contextualization of the study (McCann and Clark, 2003a), and 'can help the researcher develop "sensitising concepts" (McCann and Clark, 2003a; Coffey and Atkinson, 1996), gain theoretical sensitivity (McGhee et al., 2007; McCann and Clark, 2003b; Strauss and Corbin, 1998), avoid conceptual and methodological pitfalls (McGhee et al., 2007), and actually become aware of, rather than numb to, possible unhelpful preconceptions (Maijala, Paavilainen, and Astedt-Kurki, 2003)' (Dunne 2011: 116). In addition to these benefits, it should be noted that opting to remain 'unencumbered' by extant literature during the early stage of a study can expose the researcher to criticism, as articulated by Coffey and Atkinson (1996: 157):

> The open-mindedness of the researcher should not be mistaken for the empty mindedness of the researcher who is not adequately steeped in the research traditions of a discipline. It is after all, not very clever to rediscover the wheel, and the student or researcher who is ignorant of the relevant literature is always in danger of doing the equivalent.

Whether from a practical or epistemological perspective, the collective arguments in favour of conducting a literature review in the substantive area prior to formal data collection and analysis are compelling. Furthermore, as already alluded to, the very notion that a researcher engages in research and data collection without some level of prior knowledge of the substantive area is unrealistic. This point is acknowledged by numerous scholars such as Charmaz (2006), Dey (1993), Dunne (2011) and Keane (2015). Indeed, Eisenhardt (2002: 12) contends that 'it is impossible to achieve this idea of a clean theoretical slate'. As such, rather than deny the reality of the situation, it is preferable to acknowledge it and employ mechanisms, such as reflexivity, which may assuage the potential risks associated with prior or early engagement with the substantive area. Indeed, to forfeit the benefits derived from an early literature review in an attempt to eliminate a perceived threat to the research process which is (a) an unsubstantiated threat, and (b) in any event largely inescapable, amounts to a disproportionate response which could culminate in a Pyrrhic victory for those purists who staunchly espouse the original dictum.

A PRAGMATIC AND GROUNDED THEORETICAL STANCE TOWARDS LITERATURE

Corbin and Strauss (2015) as well as Charmaz (2014) state that GTM is rooted in the American pragmatist tradition developed at the University of Chicago. The most important thinkers and founding fathers of pragmatism were Charles S. Peirce (1839–1914), William James (1842–1910), and John Dewey (1859–1952), but George Herbert Mead (1863–1931) was also a major figure in this tradition (Biesta and Burbules, 2003). In this section, we will argue that both a pragmatist stance towards pre-existing theories, as well as applying specific GTM techniques during the literature review, can help grounded theorists harness the advantages of conducting an initial, ongoing and final literature review without 'forcing' it on data.

Theoretical Agnosticism: Knowledge as Provisional and Fallible

With his transactional approach to epistemology, Dewey (1929) rejected both objectivism and subjectivism. Although his position 'does assert that knowledge is a construction, it is not a construction of the human mind, but a construction that is located in the organism–environment transaction itself. What is constructed – over and over again – is the dynamic balance of organism and environment, which manifests itself both in specific changes in the environment and specific changes in the patterns of action of the organism' (Biesta and Burbules, 2003: 11). Thus, knowledge is simultaneously a construction and based on reality. As a culturally embedded social process, it is tentative and fallible (Biesta and Burbules, 2003; Thayer-Bacon, 2001, 2003a, 2003b). *Fallibilism* means that we can never attain knowledge that is certain because we are fallible, limited and contextual beings. Our knowledge and our criteria of its justification or plausibility are situated and socially constructed, and therefore corrigible and continually in need of critique and reconstruction (Thayer-Bacon, 2001, 2003a, 2003b). In addition, we are living 'in an ever-changing world in which each new situation is in some respect unique' (Biesta and Burbules, 2003: 13). Although a certain theory might have been shown to be highly relevant and useful in a particular sociocultural context or historical time, it may be found to be inadequate or less relevant and useful in another context or time.

Thus, one implication of pragmatism is to view pre-existing theories and research findings, as well as the findings, concepts and theory that we are developing in an actual study, as provisional and fallible, and therefore in continually need of re/adjustment, correction and re/construction (Thayer-Bacon, 2001; Thornberg, 2012). If we take a look at GTM, Glaser (1978, 1998), for instance, emphasizes that a grounded theory and its concepts have to be understood as modifiable. Modification is seen as a part of theory generation, which also includes a critical attitude towards pre-existing or already generated theories. 'We soon learned that generation is an ever modifying process and nothing is sacred if the analyst is dedicated to giving priority attention to the data. Doctrinarism and excess loyalty to pet ideas defeat this priority' (Glaser, 1978: 5).

From a pragmatist view of knowledge, grounded theorists have to avoid subscribing to any of the theories they might know or have reviewed before or during data gathering and analysis (Timmermans and Tavory, 2007). In accordance with its emphasis on fallibalism, any ideas have to be open to doubt (see Bryant, 2009), reflecting what Chenitz (1986: 44) refers to as 'a cautious and sceptical attitude about the literature throughout the study'. For this, Henwood and Pidgeon (2003) use the term *theoretical agnosticism*, which we understand as an open-minded and critical stance towards pre-existing theories and research findings throughout the research project (also see Charmaz, 2014; Thornberg, 2012).

This pragmatist stance towards literature *might* help draw the attention of grounded theorists to potentially relevant or significant features of data and provide useful analytical tools without forcing, thereby avoiding the risk of 'contamination' which underpins Glaser's stance. 'Although there is no guarantee that "old" knowledge will be successful for the solution of the problem at hand, it can at least suggest a variety of different approaches for understanding the situation, interpreting observations, and possible action' (Biesta and Burbules, 2003: 61). As such, the literature review has to be understood as an open, non-committal, critical and pluralistic dialogue between the grounded theorist, the literature, the data and the 'emerging' theory and its concepts and relationships.

Theoretical Pluralism and Playfulness

In contrast to deduction and in line with abduction, good detectives as well as good grounded theorists are not uncritically committed and limited to one theory or hypothesis – being stuck with a 'pet code' leading to 'forcing' and 'distorting data' in Glaser's terms – but 'are confronted with thousands of possible explanatory conjectures (or conclusions) – everyone in the village might be the murderer' (Schurz, 2008: 203). Therefore, they need to remain open to using several possible theories or hypotheses as lenses and analytical tools in the search for the best possible explanations and understandings.

When the Swedish Prime Minister Olof Palme was murdered in Stockholm 1986, a special investigation unit on the assassination was set up with a chief investigator who had never led such investigation in the past. The 'theory' that Palme had been murdered by members of the left-wing Kurdish Workers' Party (PKK) quickly became popular and, despite significant data to the contrary, remained the 'main trail' for the special investigation unit, into which all available resources were directed, leaving other possible trails or hypotheses unexplored or overlooked. This 'deductive inquiry' tried to 'force' the 'theory' to the data and was ultimately found to be fruitless, with the chief of the special investigation unit removed from the case after one year. An abductive inquiry would have instead seriously considered and scrutinized several possible 'theories' or 'hypotheses' by constantly comparing them to each other and with data.

Influenced by Peirce and pragmatism, Thayer-Bacon (2001) refers to the Indian allegory of the six blind men around an elephant to approach the diversity within social and educational research. In this tale, six blind men examine an elephant from various positions and describe it as either a rope, a tree, a fan, a snake, a wall, or a spear, depending upon which part of the elephant that each man has touched. The metaphor does not only illustrate how situated, limited, fallible and provisional knowledge is, but also the need for dialogue between different positions, perspectives, hypotheses, or theories. 'Peirce would advise the six blind men to start talking to each other and share the information each of them has. Only by acting as a community of inquirers can they hope to gather a more complete understanding of elephants, one they can all agree upon' (Thayer-Bacon, 2001: 401). According to Kelle (2005), using different and even competing theoretical perspectives in the research process is helpful to deal with the risk of otherwise forcing pre-existing theories and concepts onto the data and neglecting other pre-existing theories and concepts that would suit the data even better. It is a way of keeping an open mind (Dey, 1993), and thus avoiding getting stuck in a blinkered and myopic position exemplified by the 'PKK trail' and the tale of the elephant. Thornberg (2012: 250) argues that such *theoretical pluralism* initiates a critical, creative and sensitive conversation between various and even conflicting theoretical perspectives in order to examine and make sense of data, helping the grounded theorist 'to take a critical stance toward each of them and thus remain theoretically agnostic during the analysis' (2012: 250).

Creativity is essential in abduction (Anderson, 1987) and, according to Strauss and Corbin (1990: 27), a vital component in GTM in order to break through assumptions, create new order out of the old, to aptly name categories, and 'to let the mind wander and make the free associations that are necessary for generating stimulating questions and for coming up with the comparisons that lead to discovery'. Charmaz (2006, 2014) states that constructing theory is not a purely mechanical process, but rather includes a creative *theoretical playfulness*. Thornberg (2012) recommends that grounded theorists expand Charmaz's notion of theoretical playfulness by also inviting pre-existing theories and concepts into this playfulness. In other words, to play with and consider them in novel, useful and unorthodox ways during the constant comparison process. As in all qualitative inquiry, an interplay between critical and creative thinking generates new possibilities and original connections through exposure to diverse knowledge sets. Theoretical agnosticism, pluralism and playfulness follow a pragmatist stance towards pre-existing theories, previous research findings, actual data and ongoing analysis and theorizing. As such, we argue that by espousing these values, grounded theorists can consciously harness the potential value of extant knowledge, without being unwittingly and unquestionably harnessed to it.

Adopting GTM Techniques in the Literature Review

The tool box of GTM offers researchers effective techniques to conduct a literature review which remains open-minded and sensitive to data. For example, Thornberg (2012) suggests that grounded theorists should apply the logic of *theoretical sampling* in relation to the ongoing literature review during the study. In order words, in particular during the second phase of the literature review, they search and read literature guided by the codes, concepts, questions and ideas that they develop during data gathering and analysis. In this iterative process, coding and questions take grounded theorists to some of the literature, which in turn sends them back to the empirical field and to their provisional codes and concepts with new lenses and questions, and so on. In his GT study on values education in everyday school life, for example, Thornberg (2007, 2008a, 2008b, 2009) moved back and forth between a range of theoretical frameworks in his search for plausible hypotheses and explanations.

Early in his fieldwork, Thornberg found that teachers' main concern in everyday values education was their efforts to get students to understand and comply with various rules in school. Through theoretically sampling the literature on school rules, Thornberg examined what other scholars had done in this field, and continued to constantly compare his data and concepts with the literature in an iterative process. The analysis and its emerging patterns and concepts guided his ongoing literature review. For instance, when Thornberg examined and began to conceptualize how students value and make meanings of various school rules, data and codes were constantly compared with a range of theories on how children reason about rules. In these constant comparisons, Thornberg identified striking similarities but also substantial differences between (a) his data and emerging concepts, and (b) social domain theory and research (e.g., Nucci, 2001), which was helpful in the theorizing process. Thus, social domain theory earned its way into the analysis. Although his grounded theory of schoolchildren's reasoning about school rules was in part informed by this pre-existing theory, as a result of abductive inference, constant comparisons and theoretical sampling of literature, Thornberg (2008b) also came to challenge and suggest further elaboration of the social domain theory based on his grounded theory. His work reflects an interplay between induction (in which he never was *tabula rasa*) and abduction (in which he always was open to re-think, modify, challenge and reject the theory or hypothesis in his interaction with data) that created powerful iterative processes between data collection and analysis, and between data and theory.

The *constant comparative method* is another powerful GTM technique to adopt in the ongoing and final literature review (Giles et al., 2013). Ramalho et al. (2015) claim that this technique is helpful in order to integrate literature with the constructed codes, concepts and, finally, the theory, by comparing the literature with the data, codes, categories and memos written during the study. Such constant comparison 'validates or rejects the literature as useful for the research. During this process, the data should be constantly and actively put first over any literature' (2015: § 20). Furthermore, *memo-writing* represents another important technique which promotes critical and creative thinking, connection-making and reflexivity, and therefore helps the grounded theorists compare literature with, and relate it to, the data, the developed categories, and the emerging grounded theory (Ramalho et al., 2015; Thornberg, 2012). 'Memos can aid the researcher to use the literature as a tool towards the engagement of a theoretical dialogue with the data, without allowing such literature to define the research' (Ramalho et al., 2015: §21). This analytical and creative process facilitates abductive reasoning and theoretical agnosticism, pluralism and playfulness, at the same time as it documents the grounded theorist's thinking process and the theorizing from data in a manner which is sensitive, creative and critical to existing literature.

CONCLUSION

While disagreeing with Glaser and Strauss's (1967) dictum against early engagement with literature, it should be recognized that this injunction has served an important purpose in stimulating debate on the role of a literature review in grounded theory. Indeed, it has highlighted the potential risks associated with researchers' unquestioning acquiescence to dominant theoretical frameworks. In keeping with a constructivist epistemological perspective, in this chapter we have argued that rather than positivist researchers 'discovering' a theory hidden within data, grounded theory involves the organic construction of a theory, the nature of which will be inevitably informed by the interplay between the researcher, the environment, the participants and the literature. As such, rather than avoiding early engagement with extant literature in a futile attempt to prevent so-called 'contamination', researchers opting to employ GTM should adopt a deliberate, informed and conscious stance on this topic. That is, they should recognize that early engagement with existing literature offers benefits which far outweigh the drawbacks, while not dismissing the potential for such drawbacks. Importantly, existing theoretical constructs and frameworks should 'earn their way into your narrative' (Charmaz 2006: 126) by fulfilling criteria set by the researcher. Through the espousal of values such as theoretical agnosticism, pluralism, and playfulness, which are enacted through specific techniques like theoretical sampling, constant comparison, reflexivity and memo-writing, early and ongoing engagement with existing literature can be harnessed to produce creative, insightful, robust theories which are firmly grounded in the specific research environment and derived from privileging empirical data rather than extant theories. Was this not the fundamental objective at the genesis of grounded theory?

REFERENCES

Anderson, D. R. (1987) *Creativity and the Philosophy of C.S.* Peirce. Dordrecht: Martinus Nijhoff.

Bendassolli, P. F. (2013) 'Theory building in qualitative research: Reconsidering the problem of induction', *Forum: Qualitative Social Research*, *14*(1): Art. 25. Retrieved March 20, 2014, from www.qualitativeresearch.net/index.php/fqs/article/view/1851

Biesta, G. J. J. and Burbules, N. C. (2003) *Pragmatism and Educational Research*. Oxford: Rowman & Littlefield.

Blumer, H. (1969) *Symbolic Interactionism*. Berkeley, CA: University of California Press.

Bryant, A. (2002) 'Re-grounding grounded theory', *The Journal of Information Technology Theory and Application*, *4*: 25–42.

Bryant, A. (2009) 'Grounded theory and pragmatism: The curious case of Anselm Strauss', *Forum: Qualitative Social Research*, *10*(3): Art. 2. Retrieved July 4, 2011, from www.qualitative-research.net/index.php/fqs/article/viewArticle/1358/2850

Carson, D. (2009) 'The abduction of Sherlock Holmes', *International Journal of Police Science & Management*, *11*: 193–202.

Chalmers, A. F. (1999) *What Is This Thing Called Science?* (3rd edn). New York: Open University Press.

Charmaz, K. (2000) 'Grounded theory: Objectivist and constructivist methods', in N. K. Denzin and Y. S. Lincoln (eds.), *Handbook of Qualitative Research* (2nd edn). Thousand Oaks, CA: Sage. pp. 509–535.

Charmaz, K. (2006) *Constructing Grounded Theory*. London: Sage.

Charmaz, K. (2009) 'Shifting the grounds: Constructivist grounded theory methods for the twenty-first century', in J. M. Morse, P. N. Stern, J. Corbin, B. Bowers, K. Charmaz and A. E. Clarke (eds.), *Developing Grounded Theory: The Second Generation*. Walnut Creek, CA: Left Coast Press. pp. 127–154.

Charmaz, K. (2014) *Constructing Grounded Theory* (2nd edn). Thousand Oaks, CA: Sage.

Charmaz, K., Thornberg, R. and Keane, E. (2018) 'Evolving grounded theory and social justice inquiry', in N. K. Denzin and Y. S. Lincoln (eds.), *The SAGE Handbook of Qualitative Research* (5th edn). Thousand Oaks, CA: Sage. pp. 411–443.

Cheng, C. Y., Sanchez-Burks, J. and Lee, F. (2008) 'Connecting the dots within creative performance and identity integration', *Psychological Science*, *19*(11): 1178–1184.

Chenitz, W. C. (1986) 'Getting started: The research proposal for a grounded theory study', in W. C. Chenitz and J. M. Swanson (eds.), *From Practice to Grounded Theory: Qualitative Research in Nursing*. Menlo Park, CA: Addison-Wesley. pp. 39–47.

Chiovitti, R. F. and Piran, N. (2003) 'Rigour and grounded theory research', *Journal of Advanced Nursing*, *44*(4): 427–435.

Coffey, A. and Aktinson, P. (1996) *Making Sense of Qualitative Data: Complementary Research Strategies*. Thousand Oaks, CA: Sage.

Corbin, J. and Strauss, A. (2008) *Basics of Qualitative Research* (3rd edn). Thousand Oaks, CA: Sage

Corbin, J. and Strauss, A. (2015) *Basics of Qualitative Research* (4th edn). Thousand Oaks, CA: Sage.

Coyne, I. and Cowley, S. (2006) 'Using grounded theory to research parent participation', *Journal of Research in Nursing*, *11*(6): 501–515.

Creswell, J. (1998) *Qualitative Inquiry and Research Design: Choosing Among Five Traditions*. Thousand Oaks, CA: Sage.

De Waal, C. (2013) *Peirce: A Guide for the Perplexed*. London: Bloomsbury.

Dewey, J. (1929) 'The quest for certainty', in *The Later Works (1925–1953)* (*Vol. 4*). Edited by A. Boydston. Carbondale, IL: Southern Illinois University Press.

Dey I. (1993) Qualitative data analysis:A user-friendly guide for social scientists. Routledge, London.

Douven, I. (2011) 'Peirce on abduction', in E. N. Zalta (principal ed.), *Stanford Encyclopedia of Philosophy*. Retrieved July 4, 2011, http://plato.stanford.edu/entries/abduction/

Doyle, A. C. (1891) 'Adventures of Sherlock Holmes: A scandal in Bohemia', *Strand Magazine*, *2* (July to December): 61–75.

Dunne, C. (2008). *'We know them, but we don't know them': a grounded theory approach to exploring host students' perspectives on intercultural contact in an Irish university* (Doctoral dissertation, Dublin City University).

Dunne, C. (2011) 'The place of literature review in grounded theory research', *International Journal of Social Research Methodology*, *14*: 111–124.

Eco, U. (1981) 'Guessing: From Aristotle to Sherlock Holmes', *Versus*, *30*: 3–19.

Eisenhardt, K. M. (2002). Building theories from case study research in Huberman, AM & Miles, MB (eds) The qualitative researcher's companion. Thousand Oaks: Sage. pp. 5–36.

Giles, T., King, L. and de Lacey, S. (2013) 'The timing of the literature review in grounded theory research: An open mind versus an empty head', *Advances in Nursing Science*, *36*(2): E29–E40.

Glaser, B. G. (1978) *Theoretical Sensitivity*. Mill Valley, CA: Sociology Press.

Glaser, B. G. (1992) *Basics of Grounded Theory Analysis*. Mill Valley, CA: Sociology Press.

Glaser, B. G. (1998) *Doing Grounded Theory: Issues and Discussions*. Mill Valley, CA: Sociology Press.

Glaser, B. G. (2001) *The Grounded Theory Perspective I: Conceptualization Contrasted with Description*. Mill Valley, CA: Sociology Press.

Glaser, B. G. (2003) *The Grounded Theory Perspective II: Description's Remodeling of Grounded Theory Methodology.* Mill Valley, CA: Sociology Press.

Glaser, B. G. (2005) *The Grounded Theory Perspective III: Theoretical Coding*. Mill Valley, CA: Sociology Press.

Glaser, B. G. (2013) *No Preconceptions: The Grounded Theory Dictum*. Mill Valley, CA: Sociology Press.

Glaser, B. G. and Strauss, A. L. (1967) *The Discovery of Grounded Theory*. Chicago, IL: Aldine.

Hanson, N. R. (1965) *Patterns of Discovery: An Inquiry into the Conceptual Foundations of Science*. Cambridge: Cambridge University Press.

Heath, H. (2006) 'Exploring the influences and use of the literature during a grounded theory study', *Journal of Research in Nursing*, *11*: 519–528.

Henwood, K. and Pidgeon, N. (2003) 'Grounded theory in psychological research', in P. M. Camic, J. E. Rhodes and L. Yardley (eds.), *Qualitative Research in Psychology: Expanding Perspectives in Methodology and Design*. Washington, DC: American Psychological Association. pp. 131–155.

Keane, E. (2015) 'Considering the practical implementation of constructivist grounded theory in a study of widening participation in Irish higher education', *International Journal of Social Research Methodology*, *18*(4): 415–431.

Kelle, U. (1995) 'Theories as heuristic tools in qualitative research', in I. Maso, P. A. Atkinson, S. Delamont and J. C. Verhoeven (eds.), *Openness in Research: The Tension between Self and Other*. Assen: van Gorcum. pp. 33–50.

Kelle, U. (2005) '"Emergence" vs. "forcing" of empirical data? A crucial problem of "grounded theory" reconsidered', *Forum: Qualitative Social Research*, *6*(2): Art. 27. Retrieved July 4, 2011, from www.qualitative-research.net/index.php/fqs/article/viewArticle/467/1000

Kelle, U. (2014) 'Theorization from data', in U. Flick (ed.), *The SAGE Handbook of Qualitative Data Analysis*. London: Sage. pp. 554–568.

Kennedy-Lewis, B. L. and Thornberg, R. (2018) 'Deduction, induction, abduction', in U. Flick (ed.), *The SAGE Handbook of Qualitative Data Collection*. London: Sage. pp. 49–64.

Khachab, C. E. (2013) 'The logical goodness of abduction in C. S. Peirce's thought', *Transactions of the Charles S. Peirce Society*, *49*(2): 157–177.

Kurtzberg, T. R. (2005) 'Feeling creative, being creative: An empirical study of diversity and creativity in teams', *Creativity Research Journal*, *17*(1): 51–65.

Maijala H., Paavilainen E. and Astedt-Kurki, P. (2003) 'The use of grounded theory to study interaction', *Nurse Researcher*, *11*(2): 40–57.

Martin, V. B. (2006) 'The relationship between an emerging grounded theory and the existing literature: Four phases for consideration', *Grounded Theory Review*, *5*: 47–57.

McCallin, A. M. (2006) 'Grappling with the literature in a grounded theory study', *Grounded Theory Review*, *5*: 11–27.

McCann, T. and Clark, E. (2003a) Grounded Theory in Nursing Research: Part 1 – Methodology. *Nurse Researcher*, *11*(2): 7–18.

McCann, T. and Clark, E. (2003b) Grounded Theory in Nursing Research: Part 2 – Critique. *Nurse Researcher*, *11*(2): 19–28.

McGhee, G., Marland, G. R. and Atkinson, J. (2007) 'Grounded theory research: Literature reviewing and reflexivity', *Journal of Advanced Nursing*, *60*: 334–342.

McKaughan, D. J. (2008) 'From ugly ducking to Swan: C. S. Peirce, abduction, and the pursuit of scientific theories', *Transactions of the Charles S. Peirce Society*, *44*(3): 446–468.

McMenamin, I. (2006) 'Process and text: Teaching students to review the literature', *PS: Political Science and Politics*, *39*(1): 132–146.

Mills, J., Bonner, A. and Francis, K. (2006) 'Adopting a constructivist approach to grounded theory: Implications for research design', *International Journal of Nursing Practice*, *12*(1): 8–13.

Nucci, L. P. (2001) *Education in the Moral Domain*. Cambridge: Cambridge University Press.

Paavola, S. (2004) 'Abduction as a logic and methodology of discovery: The importance of strategies', *Foundation of Science*, *9*: 267–283.

Peirce, C. S. (1960) *Collected Papers of Charles Sanders Peirce. Vol. I: Principle of Philosophy; Vol. II: Elements of Logic*. Edited by A. W. Burks. Cambridge, MA: Harvard University Press.
Peirce, C. S. (1979) *Collected Paper of Charles Sanders Peirce. Vol. III: Science and Philosophy*. Edited by A. W. Burks. Cambridge, MA: Harvard University Press.
Popper, K. (1959) *The Logic of Scientific Discovery*. London: Hutchison.
Ramalho, R., Adams, P., Huggard, P. and Hoare, K. (2015) 'Literature review and constructivist grounded theory methodology', *Forum: Qualitative Social Research*, *16*(3): Art. 19, http://nbn-resolving.de/urn:nbn:de:0114-fqs1503199
Reichertz, J. (2007) 'Abduction: The logic of discovery of grounded theory', in A. Bryant and K. Charmaz (eds.), *The SAGE Handbook of Grounded Theory*. London: Sage. pp. 214–228.
Richardson, R. and Kramer, E. H. (2006) 'Abduction as the type of inference that characterizes the development of a grounded theory', *Qualitative Research*, *6*(4): 245–249.
Schurz, G. (2008) 'Patterns of abduction', *Synthese*, *164*(2): 201–234.
Strauss, A. L. (1987) *Qualitative Analysis for Social Scientists*. New York: Cambridge University Press.
Strauss, A. L. and Corbin, J. (1990) *Basics of Qualitative Research*. Newbury Park, CA: Sage.
Strauss, A. L. and Corbin, J. (1998) *Basics of Qualitative Research: Grounded Theory Procedures and Techniques* (2nd edn). Thousand Oaks, CA: Sage.
Tavory, I. and Timmermans, S. (2014) *Abductive Analysis: Theorizing Qualitative Research*. Chicago, IL: The University of Chicago Press.
Thayer-Bacon, B. J. (2001) 'An examination and redescription of epistemology', J. L. Kincheloe and D. K. Well (eds.), *Standards and Schooling in the United States: An Encyclopedia*. Santa Barbara, CA: ABC-CLIO. pp. 397–418.
Thayer-Bacon, B. J. (2003a) 'Pragmatism and feminism as qualified relativism', *Studies in Philosophy and Education*, *22*: 417–438.
Thayer-Bacon, B. J. (2003b) *Relational (e)pistemologies*. New York: Peter Lang.
Thibaut, J.W. and Kelley, H.H. (1959). The Social Psychology of Groups. New York: Wiley.
Thistoll, T., Hooper, V. and Pauleen, D. J. (2016) 'Acquiring and developing theoretical sensitivity through undertaking a grounded preliminary literature review', *Quality & Quantity*, *50*: 619–636.
Thornberg, R. (2007) 'Inconsistences in everyday patterns of school rules', *Ethnography and Education*, *2*: 401–416.
Thornberg, R. (2008a) 'A categorisation of school rules', *Educational Studies*, *34*: 25–33.
Thornberg, R. (2008b) 'School children's reasoning about school rules', *Research Papers in Education*, *23*: 37–52.
Thornberg, R. (2009) 'The moral construction of the good pupil embedded in school rules', *Education, Citizenship and Social Justice*, *4*: 245–261.
Thornberg, R. (2012) 'Informed grounded theory', *Scandinavian Journal of Educational Research*, *56*(3): 243–259.
Thornberg, R. and Charmaz, K. (2014) 'Grounded theory and theoretical coding', in U. Flick (ed.), *The SAGE Handbook of Qualitative Data Analysis*. London: Sage. pp. 153–169.
Timmermans, S. and Tavory, I. (2007) 'Advancing ethnographic research through grounded theory practice', in A. Bryant and K. Charmaz (eds.), *The SAGE Handbook of Grounded Theory*. Los Angeles, CA: Sage. pp. 493–512.
Truzzi, M. (1976) 'Selective attention: Sherlock Holmes: Applied social psychologist', in W.B. Sanders (ed.), *The Sociologist as Detective* (2nd edn). New York: Praeger. pp. 50–86.
Urquhart, C. (2007) 'The evolving nature of grounded theory method: The case of the information systems discipline', in A. Bryant and K. Charmaz (eds.), *The SAGE Handbook of Grounded Theory*. Los Angeles, CA: Sage. pp. 339–360.

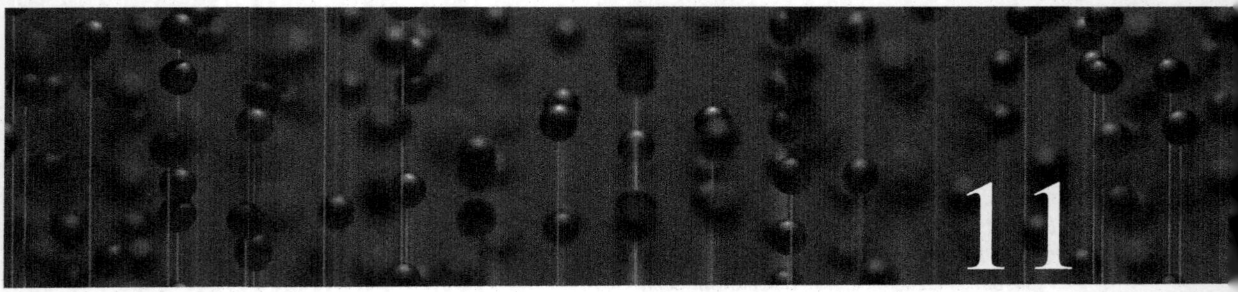

Using Popular and Academic Literature as Data for Formal Grounded Theory

Vivian B. Martin

Formal grounded theory, which extends the core concept of a theory in one substantive area to explain a range of phenomena from other spheres of activity, is the great unfulfilled promise of grounded theory methodology. The originators of grounded theory did some early work, such as a theory on status passage (Glaser & Strauss, 1971), suggesting that their vision was realistic. There are any number of reasons for the dearth of formal grounded theories – researcher interest, skill, or disciplinary priorities – but this chapter argues that aspects of the method are in need of greater explication if its potential is to be realized. Toward that end, this chapter focuses on the use of extant literature, both academic and popular, for theory-building. After situating current interest in formal grounded theory within qualitative inquiry, I address the challenges of using literature as data, which continues to be an underdeveloped component of theory development in grounded theory methodology. I will provide some discussion on the need for a more explicit understanding of abduction, the inference process through which theorists link data, existing literature, and other insights to explain phenomena they encounter in the field.

My view, and those of others I will discuss, is that abduction is implicated throughout grounded theory's protocols, in particular theoretical sampling, constant comparison, and in the concept of theoretical sensitivity. Many grounded theorists, however, do not work with an understanding of those implications. The use of literature as data to develop formal theory makes the connection more explicit due to the navigation of many different ideas and disciplines. To illustrate, I draw on my development of the concept of *discounting awareness*, which examines how people interact with uncomfortable phenomena, people, ideas, and situations, and is the core concept in a formal grounded theory of defensive disattending. Using academic and popular literature, I examine discounting awareness across many spheres of everyday life, from interpersonal reactions to political discourse.

I discuss the methodological issues pertaining to the use of literature as data and explicate four phases of using literature – scoping the literature, sampling the literature, bridging the literature, and confirming the theory – that guide researchers as they move a concept from substantive to formal theory.

The argument presented here is one of optimism for theorizing with grounded theory. However, I also acknowledge that some forms of metasyntheses, the integration of multiple qualitative theories on a similar or related topic, may have bypassed formal grounded theory as a more practical goal, especially in nursing and health research. In these modified formal theories, theorists use a set of studies, either all grounded theory or a mix of qualitative studies, around one topic. These are not formal grounded theories in the original sense but may carry that label. The projects can be found in several areas, among them marriage theory (Chenail, George, Wulff, Duffy, Scott, & Tomm, 2012), addiction recovery and domestic violence (Kearney, 1998a, 2001), and workplace violence (Ventura-Madangeng & Wilson, 2009). Kearney (1998b) coined the term 'ready to wear' formal theories to capture the practice of building theories from existing related grounded theories and/or qualitative studies in nursing. In scaling back the ambition for formal grounded theories, theorists may have found a fit that better serves knowledge-building in their fields. One could visualize metasyntheses having an impact on the evolution of formal grounded theory in those, usually mature, disciplines, and others they influence.

My use of 'mature' is a way to think about the diffusion of grounded theory in various fields, and hence, the likelihood of influence within and outside of a discipline. Nursing research arguably has a sustained use of grounded theory, which is in keeping with grounded theory's origins at the University of California San Francisco's School of Nursing. If we were to conceptualize the adoption of grounded theory on a spectrum of diffusion, nursing research would be a mature entry, its researchers providing a steady arena of theory development, methodological discussions, and practitioner-scholars whose works reach beyond the discipline and inform grounded theory methodology. Grounded theorists in other vastly different fields cannot ignore grounded theory in nursing if they are serious about the methodology.

Despite its status in qualitative research, grounded theory does not have an established methodological leader in most disciplines. Education, information systems, and some of the management/organizational-related disciplines make up the small group that do. Urquhart (2007) wrote that grounded theory was introduced in information systems in the 1980s but characterized the presence of grounded theory as still small. Nevertheless, information systems has a methodological discourse aimed at making grounded theory more robust in the discipline (Bryant, 2002; Bryant, Hughes, Myers, Trauth, & Urquhart, 2004; Urquhart, Lehmann, & Myers, 2010; Seidel & Urquhart, 2013; Urquhart & Fernandez, 2013). The state of grounded theory is more advanced than in other fields, including my own of communication and media studies, where editors and reviewers equate the method with highly descriptive qualitative studies. The disciplines that produce more thoroughly scrutinized grounded theories are in a better position to adopt ready-to-wear formal grounded theories. However, meta-analyses have attracted critics who argue that such studies are superficial and strip innovative studies of their original context-bound insights. Thorne (2017) is an example of the rising criticism of metasyntheses, particularly in health studies. For those interested in formal grounded theory, there is still space to work toward its potential.

QUALITATIVE INQUIRY: OLD AND NEW CHALLENGES

The prospects for formal grounded theory are hampered by some of the challenges facing qualitative inquiry in general. Qualitative inquiry has won a robust space for itself within academic research; it is the subject of an array of journals in traditional disciplines, such as anthropology and sociology, and applied areas, such as marketing, nursing, and health studies. The adoption of qualitative methods has not removed the hesitancy with which disciplines accept such work, however. The long-held concerns about rigor, the size of samples, and generalizability remain. In updating an earlier essay, Hammersley (2008), both a qualitative practitioner and methodologist, wrote of what he argued are the failed promises of qualitative research. In his view, qualitative work lacks the diversity of voices he claims it promised. He argued that qualitative work has privileged the voice of the marginalized over those in power. This is a curious concern given the opportunities those in dominant positions have to be heard. It also moves against the sustained discourse of qualitative inquiry as a space for social justice work (Denzin, 2010). Hammersley has also criticized qualitative studies for their reliance on interviews and limited use of other types of data.

Reviewing the first 20 years of the journal *Qualitative Inquiry*, Flick (2015) observed that many of the challenges that faced qualitative research in the 1980s and 1990s, including concerns with rigor and quality, remain. He also summarized a number of emerging concerns internationally. He identified trends such as evidence-based research and the rise of big social science projects, with collaborators across departments and institutions, as a threat to small, individual qualitative studies. Flick cited new ethical issues around utilizing qualitative methods with migrant populations as challenges for researchers and Institutional Review Boards (IRBs). Further, he discussed metasyntheses, which are growing to meet the need of evidence-based practice. These studies, which I cited earlier as possibly supplanting formal grounded theories in some fields, seek the type of authority or sense of cumulative knowledge associated with quantitative meta-analyses. Flick suggested that qualitative metasyntheses could marginalize qualitative work such as observational ethnography and others based on methods not as easily incorporated as interview studies. Further, mixed-method studies, which at one time seemed to offer increased rigor and credibility, have marginalized qualitative research; the model for working with such studies has been limited (Flick, 2015, p. 606).

FROM INDUCTION TO ABDUCTION

Arguably, the challenge of building theory from empirical observation, often described as the induction problem (Bryant & Charmaz, 2007; Reichertz, 2007; Bendassoli, 2013), is the most critical concern for qualitative inquiry. Tavory and Timmermans (2014) have argued that the interplay of observation, method, and theory 'remains one of the key dilemmas facing any qualitative researcher' (p. 2). They argued that inductive and deductive approaches cannot produce creative theories; the researcher is boxed in between the two mindsets without recourse when stumped by unsurprising findings. Their counter-strategy is a more explicit use of abduction to broaden theorists' repertoire. Qualitative theorists and researchers increasingly describe their process of inference as abductive, but abduction is very layered and not always so easily held still for examination.

Shank (1998), for instance, cited six modes that have emerged in the literature, from the type of everyday cognition people utilize to solve problems to empirical research. They are: '(a) reasoning to the reason or hunch; (b) reasoning to the clue; (c) reasoning to the metaphor or analogy; (d) reasoning to the symptom; (e) reasoning to the pattern; (f) reasoning to the explanation' (Shank, 1998, pp. 848–849). The variety of abductive reasoning modes suggests that a qualitative researcher or grounded theorist might come to adopt different modes at different points in a project, depending on its phase and type of content.

In building their argument for abductive analysis as a method in its own right, Tavory and Timmermans (2014) train their criticism on grounded theory, noting its place as the dominant form of theorizing in qualitative data analysis. This strategy is unfortunate. Grounded theory becomes a strawman even as Tavory and Timmermans acknowledged that much of what is labeled as grounded theory is mislabeled and does not follow the protocols of any of the leading versions of grounded theory methodology (GTM). By using a broad brush, the critique failed to engage with the abductive aspects of GTM. Moreover, the authors ignored the history of grounded theory and the increasing explication of abduction as part of the method. 'Although shifting the focus to abduction is welcome news, we do not think rebranding the core of grounded theory solves its epistemological problems,' they wrote (Tavory & Timmermans, 2014, p. 16).

Although, as Bruscaglioni (2016) noted, grounded theorists have yet to explicate a full understanding of how abduction works in grounded theory, grounded theory is not a newcomer to abduction. Recognizing the abductive traces in grounded theory, Haig (1995) defended grounded theory from those who criticized it for simple induction. Haig wrote that the method could be 'suitably reconstructed' as an exemplary scientific method and discussed how tending to its abductive implications would accomplish that. Charmaz (2014), a student of both Glaser and Strauss in San Francisco, has written that Strauss understood the abductive elements of grounded theory methodology from its earliest days.

Reichertz (2007), though noting that Strauss never wrote about abduction or the philosopher Charles Peirce beyond a footnote, traced the presence of abduction in Strauss's early conceptions and later years. His verdict was that later GT contains the logic of both abductive reasoning and qualitative induction. 'The logic of later GT thus permits abductive reasoning, counts on it, enables it, grants it place. More is not necessary,' he wrote (Reichertz, 2007, p. 225). Reichertz's analysis included work Strauss did with Corbin (Strauss & Corbin, 1990) and proposed that it is the abductive aspect of the work that drove the disagreement between Glaser and Strauss (Glaser, 1992).

One needs some caution here. Glaser has invoked GTM's abductive nature in his troubleshooting seminars as a way to explain misconceptions of GT as purely inductive. He has not elaborated on the abductive process, however. Glaser does differ from Strauss on the role of extant theory in grounded theory, but it may not be accurate to say Glaser rejects abduction as a property of GTM.

Tavory and Timmermans have proposed what they call a 'pragmatist theory of meaning and inference in qualitative research' (2014, p. 120). They have linked note-taking, memo-writing, and the examination of transcripts to a process in which theorists 'defamiliarize' data in such a way that they start to see it differently. The other part of the abductive process – a defining aspect of it for the authors – is the employment of a broad knowledge of theory coming at the data from different angles. Serious students of grounded theory will recognize these prescriptions as how grounded theory should ideally work. Tavory and Timmermans, however, sidestepped discussions of how abductive processes interpolate grounded theory techniques, from data comparison through memo-writing and theoretical sampling and the write-up. Their project in effect is positioned as a counter to the weaknesses they have perceived as intrinsic to grounded theory.

To be fair, recovering grounded theory was not the goal Tavory and Timmermans assigned themselves. Yet Thornberg and Dunne, in Chapter 10 of this Handbook, address the deep interplay of abduction, theoretical sensitivity, and literature in grounded theory. As others have written, abduction is already assumed in the method. In their failure to engage with the abductive aspects of grounded theory, Tavory and Timmermans missed the opportunity to meet many qualitative researchers where they are: struggling with grounded theory. The authors' discussion of the need to approach theory development with a wide theoretical repertoire is an example of this evasion.

The early grounded theory writings, even while calling for distance from extant literature at the start of a project, envisioned theoretical sensitivity, which is necessarily abductive, guiding the theorist. Theoretical sensitivity in both the 1967 codification of the method and Glaser's *Theoretical Sensitivity* (1978) included the researcher's experiences and evolving awareness of the issues in the subject area, as well as an appreciation for the broader realm of theory. Glaser and Strauss, as trained sociologists, assumed a higher engagement with theory than is the case for many novices who come to grounded theory from applied fields that are often atheoretical. Glaser's *Theoretical Sensitivity* (1978), for example, presents the theoretical codes and coding families out of the sociological context from which they were originally conceived (Gibson & Hartman, 2014). The decontextualizing can result in a naïve application of the codes. Although the list of coding families is a handy way to launch thinking about the shape of theories, the list, or crib sheet in some instances, is not an adequate replacement for actual knowledge of sociological theorizing as it pertains to social processes. I concur with Gibson and Hartman's (2014) observation that the lack of engagement with sociology hampers grounded theories.

Importantly, theoretical sensitivity in grounded theory has also envisioned a theorist who, though schooled in the broader enterprise of theory, begins research with an openness unhampered by extant theory. The need to straddle the gap between knowledge and openness is a tension in the abductive process and grounded theory. Tavory and Timmermans are skeptical of theorists who move into the field with a predetermined theory to which they add little new knowledge. They have also criticized grounded theorists, especially those associated with Glaser's model of grounded theory, who reject the use of extant literature at the start of a project. Theoretical sensitivity in grounded theory is stalled in part by unresolved debates about the role of extant literature in grounded theory. Further, the tension makes the abductive reasoning processes in grounded theory less explicit. As I argue, the lack of a cohesive approach to literature hinders substantive and formal theory. I address that unresolved debate briefly before extending the discussion into using literature as data.

The Role of Literature in Grounded Theory

The role of literature in grounded theory is contested space, but in many ways the issue is a red herring. Early in the codification of the method, Glaser and Strauss (1967) wrote:

> an effective strategy is, at first, literally to ignore the literature of theory and fact of the area under study, in order to ensure the emergence of categories will not be contaminated by concepts more suited to different areas. Similarities and convergences with the literature can be established after the analytic core of categories have been established. (p. 37)

Their recommendation was never a call to ignore literature completely; the early work also acknowledged that grounded theorists as people with experiences do not enter the field as a blank slate. The myth of the *tabula rasa* is among those Urquhart and Fernandez (2013) seek to discredit, noting its misinterpretation in literature in information management and elsewhere. Glaser's model differs from other versions of GTM in his view that grounded theorists should not read the existing literature in their area of study at the start of the project. He has argued for this strategy as a way to lessen preconceptions; he has further argued that the initial literature often turns out not to be the relevant literature, causing grounded theorists to waste time pursuing it.

Coming to grounded theory after a career in journalism, I could never imagine plunging into a project without some preparation. 'Check the clips' before proceeding is one of the maxims in the newsroom. Although I agree with Glaser's view that new literature will suggest itself in the field, having no knowledge of the literature against which to compare observations in the field can result in wasted time and opportunities. Academics work in silos, often pursuing theories on similar topics but with different lines of research that never intersect. Grounded theory is a method that can link the dead ends or seemingly disparate lines of inquiry through conceptualizing and linking concepts. Spending some time with the known literature at the start of a project can expedite the conceptual integration needed for theoretical saturation.

Other grounded theorists whose work is identified with Glaser's model have expressed a preference for some preliminary review of pertinent literature. McCallin (2006) wrote that in a world where researchers are expected to be up to date with issues in their field, and information is always expanding, scholars cannot ignore the literature at the start of their projects. She has endorsed some preliminary study and more reflective work on the part of the grounded theorist to integrate literature. Andrews (2006), in response to McCallin, wrote that some preliminary study is consistent with Glaser's model, but continuous remodeling of GTM has confused the role of literature. Martin (2006), in the same special issue, described the relationship between extant literature and an emerging theory as one of pacing. I proposed four phases –noncommittal, sampling, integration, and transcendence – to explain the relationship between an emerging theory and extant literature. In their contribution to this book, Thornberg and Dunne, conceive the pacing in three phases of initial, ongoing, and final literature review that flow through the theory construction process. They write, 'the literature review has to be understood as an open, non-committal, critical and pluralistic dialogue between the grounded theorist, the literature, the data and the "emerging" theory and its concepts and relationships' (pp. 206).

The pitfalls of preconceptions are evident in a range of information-gathering pursuits, such as journalism and law enforcement, where people have rushed to judgment because they could not let go of conventional wisdom or initial impressions. Reflexivity, constant critical thinking, and writing about data and decisions, can mitigate this very human tendency. As Thornberg and Dunne offer, grounded theory techniques such as memo-writing are opportunities for creative and critical thinking where the theorist can challenge theory construction at each stage.

Grounded theory methodology needs greater attention to the role of literature in theory development. Further, theorists should give more attention to the use of literature as data on a par with interviews and observations. Despite the grounded theory maxim of 'all is data,' the type of data utilized to build grounded theories is often limited. Interview data can be rich, but grounded theorists do not typically approach interviews with an appreciation of how utterances, accounts, and the way people narrate their lives shape that data. Moreover, the over reliance on interviews leaves other data possibilities unexamined. Heaton (2004), noting that Glaser wrote one of the first articles (1962) on the possibilities for the secondary analysis of data collected for other purposes, has advocated for the greater use of secondary analysis in qualitative inquiry. Such datasets come with challenges, particularly because the secondary analyst is removed from the context of the interviews, but are worth examining. Prior (2008) has taken the use of documents further, exploring the under-utilization of documents as data. His concern is not just with the content of documents; his interest has been in the function of documents, how people and institutions use them.

This chapter advances the use of literature as data, providing a rationale that, it is hoped, will help theorists seek different types of literature to build theory. Literature is broadly defined here, incorporating traditional academic literature, but also popular literature, particularly journalistic accounts, and published reports and proceedings by investigative bodies and commissions. To develop the concept of discounting awareness, I identified four dimensions of literature use which I will illustrate: *Scoping the literature* is the open-ended reconnaissance of the universe of possible extant literature across disciplines. Linguistic and epistemological connections are among the characteristics that are important in this phase. *Sampling the literature* is an iterative process through which theoretical sampling and selective sampling move the researcher toward greater densification and scale of the concepts she is developing and discovering. *Bridging the literature* describes how the theory is articulated with major related theories with which researchers must contend prior to bringing the theory into academic conversation. *Confirming the theory* is accomplished through the grounded theory techniques of sorting and resorting memos with the goal of writing a working paper of the emerging theory. The four dimensions of using literature are not extra procedures I have added to grounded theory methodology; rather, they are an expanded and more explicit accounting of how grounded theory development occurs.

FORMAL GROUNDED THEORY

What does a formal grounded theory say about knowledge? With a substantive grounded theory, we present a theory that addresses the way people deal with an ongoing concern or problem. Its test is how it works in the field, addressing the problem on which it theorizes. But what is a formal grounded theory for? What is its warrant? These questions need some attention as we work through the use of literature as data in formal theory.

Wuest's (2001) theory of precarious ordering, which theorizes women as caregivers across professional and familial settings, has many of the marks of a formal grounded theory. Wuest thought her work moved beyond substantive theory in its abstraction and discarding of substantive terms; yet she wrote of her reluctance to label her work a formal grounded theory.

> For this to be a formal theory of caring, further theoretical sampling would be needed to establish the influence of such factors as gender and compensation on the process. Although a more experienced grounded theorist might use what Glaser (1978) called

> 'anecdotal comparison' to check for theoretical fit with men and paid caregivers, I would be more confident with continued theoretical sampling and data collection using interviews and participant observation. My second reservation relates to the level of comparisons made. In my theoretical sampling and use of literature, I have, with a few exceptions, used comparative analysis among samples that appear to have something in common on the substantive level. Glaser (1978) indicated that in the development of formal theory, comparisons must be made among groups that may not appear to be comparable on the substantive level but are comparable on the conceptual level. Such comparisons raise the level of generality and abstractness to that of a formal theory. (Wuest, 2001, p. 171)

While admiring Wuest's rigor, one can also see how such concerns by highly regarded grounded theorists reflect the apprehension over generating formal grounded theory. Grounded theorists have come to talk of formal grounded theory as if it were a death-defying figure-skating move. In the above excerpt, Wuest appears to seek a level of detail, something especially descriptive, that is not as suited to a multidisciplinary formal theory as it would be for policymaking on women and caregiving. Her plans for future theory development raise questions about how complete or full formal grounded theories need to be. Wuest's precarious ordering has taken many turns, including hypothesis-testing studies in which she reconstituted some of the grounded theory concepts into survey language (Wuest & Hodgins, 2011).

Glaser (2006, 2007) continues to view extending a core concept in a substantive theory to multiple areas as the ideal formal grounded theory. He has criticized the syntheses of several studies situated in one area, such as those promoted by Kearney (1998a, 1998b, 2001, 2007), as 'QDA remodeling, dropping the level of generality to description' (Glaser, 2007, p. 103) rather than formal grounded theories. But he does not prescribe quotas for the number of different areas sampled for formal theory, describing the limit as one of time and resources (Glaser, 2006, 2007). It is also clear that much will depend on the content of the theory and the type of knowledge the theorist is creating. Glaser and Strauss's formal theory of status passage (1971), which they conceded was incomplete, is nonetheless useful as a theory that can inform practice – and simultaneously allow for comparisons in other substantive areas. Gibson, Sussex, Fitzgerald, and Thomson (2016) employed status passage to examine dental loss as more than just an individual life disruption, but rather in line with a social process that, they wrote, can be used to think about and treat other stigmatized illnesses.

The challenge for most grounded theorists, however, is just getting started on a formal grounded theory. Andrews (2011) began seriously considering a formal theory of visualizing worsening progressions after he completed his substantive theory. Colleagues suggested he had the potential for a theory about how people use soft signs to perceive deteriorating conditions in health and relationships, though he had challenges developing a plan for pursuing more data. In summarizing my formal theory, I address some decisions at the substantive level that support Gibson and Hartman's claim (2014) that the making of substantive and formal theory are implicated in one another. People would approach substantive theory differently if they anticipated doing a formal grounded theory. Yet one would not expect such prescience from the many graduate students working on their first grounded theory. (My dissertation, which eventually brought me to a formal theory, was my second time around with grounded theory. I grappled with the method and produced a 'grounded theory-informed' master's thesis on self-reconstruction in the midst of job loss.)

DISCOUNTING AWARENESS

Discounting awareness explains the processes through which people marginalize, dismiss, avoid, or seek to erase the uncomfortable. It addresses observable behavior – communicative actions – that people engage in when confronted with situations and information that trigger a sense of intrusion, guilt, shame, loss of agency, inconvenience, and other restrictions. Disattending has a practical use in everyday life as it allows people to triage much incoming stimuli so they might focus on what is most important in the moment. Some of this work is habitual. We must necessarily limit what we give attention to; in a world where stimuli are constant, we are always pushing something out of frame. Any number of people and phenomena swirl before us in a given day, but they do not come into frame because our attention has other priorities. Over time, we do not even know what we are not seeing. Discounting processes, a more intentional dimension of disattending awareness, become more heightened when unwelcome stimuli from the periphery move toward the center. Discounting awareness can be culturally learned and willful in instances where people do not want to know the truth about situations, and it can escalate into aggressive actions in which people wage war on the truth. More broadly, it is a theory about the social interaction of denial.

The formal theory grew out of the substantive theory of purposive attending (Martin, 2004, 2007, 2008), which focused on news-attending. The theory proposed that news-attending occurs in an awareness context in which the more awareness people have around a topic, the more they are likely to attribute relevance to it, and hence follow news on it. Attending recalibrates awareness, setting off the cycle again. This loop, however, may not complete itself in many instances. It takes a lot for incoming stimuli to penetrate social networks and other barriers. The eventual theory brought together a number of concepts and connected some previously disparate literature in communication and media studies. As I worked on the theory, it did not take long for me to see that news as a daily habit had many similarities with other daily regimens people manage, from religious practices to exercise, and that social networks and other orientations shaped these habits. However, when I went back to my substantive theory, I found I was more interested in the discounting awareness evident in the ways people deliberately avoided certain news they deemed too trivia or graphic, or disattended conversations around politically divisive issues in the news.

Glaser and Strauss used the concept of discounting awareness in *Awareness of Dying* (1965) to explain the observed process of medical professionals speaking openly in the presence of comatose patients, the senile and dying, and others whom they assumed to have no awareness of what was being said. In situations where professionals discounted awareness of patients, they made no effort to hide information and went about their usual routine. I began expanding the understanding of discounting awareness more broadly as a process working on intrapersonal, interpersonal, and structural levels (Martin, 2011, 2015). Diverse data came from numerous areas of life, observations and follow-up discussions, sets of essays from former anti-vaccination parents, comments on news websites, government commission reports on disasters and tragedies from 9/11 to Rwanda, court transcripts, extensive extant literature, journalistic and governmental, investigative reports, and trade literature.

Discounting awareness is a spectrum that moves from inadvertent disattending to willful denial, occurring in an awareness context in which some phenomena are central and hence the focus of attention. On the low end of the spectrum, people discount phenomena just to get through the day. It is distraction-proofing. They have attention- focus strategies that allow them to avoid distractions as they meet daily obligations. They know that turning on the radio or answering telephone calls will take them off task. The distinction between noncommittal and intentional disattending is not always easy to determine initially, but patterns become apparent through observation – and sometimes follow-up interviews. A few years beyond 9/11, a New Yorker visiting relatives left the room as a report on 9/11 started to air on the TV news. Asked about her behavior, the visitor explained that, having been in the city the day of the attacks, she avoided TV news reports and images of the day, which she found painful. Americans who travel have recalibrated the way they gauge reports of relative dangers of terrorist attacks, many of them discounting more extreme speculation in the media. These interactions are intentional though still far from some of the more aggressive incidents of discounting awareness that will be discussed.

The context for disattending can be organizational culture, a social network, or the routines and rituals of everyday life in interaction with emerging phenomena. Any number of situations, information, and people may be peripheral to the range of awareness but can begin to emerge inside the central sphere. The theory has several concepts. As an example, *the push-aside* is enacted in the early emergence of a disturbing phenomenon. People can become conditioned to discount because nothing in the environment suggests alternatives. Football players continue to play football despite pain. Initially, prior to the emerging awareness indicating that concussions led to a form of severe brain trauma, chronic traumatic encephalopathy (CTE), players lacked the knowledge that they should take concussions seriously. Sports journalists Mark Fainaru-Wada and Steve Fainaru (2014), authors of a book about the denial of the concussion problem in the NFL, one of a number of books I coded on this and related public problems, described a culture that evolved into outright willful denial. Initially players were 'programmed' to ignore pain. The authors quote one player who said, 'They'd drag your ass back to the huddle: "Shake it off man. We need your ass out here"' (Fainaru-Wada & Fainaru, 2014, p. 26). This form of *collaborative disattending* enables structures and cultures that can be maintained until an increasingly open awareness context disrupts it, though by then the dominant structures have moved on to more aggressive forms of organized denial.

People discount others with lesser status or position or whose proximity in likeness or distance differ from those doing the marginalizing. *Willful Ignorance* is present when people are in situations in which they have responsibility to know of wrongdoing or abuses but choose not to investigate. Willful ignorance can turn into a more aggressive *willful denial*, in which people and institutions wage war on the truth. People can choose to move toward greater awareness, but they do not typically seek out such opportunities unless confrontation with external events force awareness on them. This is easier for some issues than others.

FOLLOW THE CONCEPT

A grounded theory, according to Glaser, is a study about a concept (Glaser, 2010). Following the concept is the way to build grounded theories, generally. It is an especially important directive for formal theory as the theorist moves across a number of disciplines and specialties, making decisions about theoretical sampling, selective coding, and drawing boundaries around the concept. Glaser (2006, 2007) has advised that theorists should follow the general implications of the core concept of the substantive theory to create formal theory. Following the implications of the core means a theorist can spot pieces of it in popular or academic literature where it might be masked or on the run, yet also developing a sense, through constant comparison and memo-writing, of where the trail ends or moves off into processes not related to the concept.

Efforts to extend a concept start with assessing and evaluating its 'maturity' (Morse, Mitcham, Hupcey, & Tason, 1996). Morse, Mitcham, Hupcey, and Tason, among others (Penrod, 2001, 2007), argue that the analysis of a concept and its development are different phases of work. I came to understand the analysis and development of concepts involve incorporating different uses of the literature. For example, my reference to 'scoping the literature,' in which the theorist assesses the use of a concept across disciplines, aligns closely with the criteria of epistemological, pragmatic, and linguistic usages and logic of terms that Hupcey, Penrod, Morse, and Mitcham (2001) utilized for concept analysis on trust. They found usage of the concept ambiguous across several disciplines. The goal in the analysis phase is to interrogate the concept to determine what it does and does not address. The theorist should then proceed to develop the concept. Although it is important to treat concept analysis and concept development as separate activities analytically, the two are not so readily separated. Despite the need for an initial assessment of the strength of the concept, new data late in the process can affect the theorist's work. Too many strictures can hinder the process, which will need flexibility as it spreads outward.

Morse et al. (1996) have written that concepts newly introduced into scientific literature are vague and unclear, becoming more defined the more they are used. A concept might be in competition with other concepts to describe the same phenomenon. A concept that a theorist is moving from substantive to formal theory is in all likelihood not yet mature. We hope that our concepts have met theoretical saturation, the point where all theoretical questions and connections have been addressed, but this might not be possible given the limited amount of theoretical sensitivity often shaping such narrow discipline-bound studies. Moreover, core concepts that have been imported from extant theory may come with some of the limitations from the literature. As Morse et al., indicated, there could be a range of concepts competing to explain the phenomenon the theorist is studying. Writing in 1996, they cited five concepts in competition to explain receptivity.

Discounting awareness was not a robust concept at the start of my theory-building. Although I used disattending and discounting in my work on news-attending, I had not examined either concept in the same depth as I had the core concept of attending. But disattending is the flip side of attending, and I had accounted for it to some degree. Glaser and Strauss (1965) employed a narrow use of discounting awareness, though the implications were apparent. Goffman's *Framing Analysis* (1986 [1974]), which focused on the ways people leave elements of situations in or out of frame, quoted Glaser and Strauss (1964) in a discussion that invoked their use of discounting awareness and disattending. Zerubavel (2007, 2015), who was influenced by Goffman for his work on the way people ignore the elephant in the room and other ways of not seeing, also utilized the terms, but not in an operationalized sense. What I encountered, however, did suggest discounting awareness and disattending went far beyond my substantive area.

The awareness context, though more than 50 years old, has not been developed at the level Glaser and Strauss once envisioned (1965); it is still primarily used in nursing rather than other disciplines (Martin, 2015), with occasional departures (see Ekins, 1997, on male femaling). Discounting awareness occurs in certain types of contexts over others – trust often being low – and ultimately the variation in contexts needed attention. Awareness is both a word that is loosely employed in everyday parlance, and yet it is also what we might call a goal in any number of endeavors – public health awareness campaigns, language acquisition awareness, cross-culture awareness, situational awareness in aeronautics and the military, to name a few – though some have clearer definitions than others. Moreover, as an example of the conflation theorists must guard against, awareness and attention are not the same construct.

Following the concept requires the theorist to get creative about data. When I was working on the implications of purposive attending, and the awareness processes that fueled it, I wondered whether the court transcript of *voir dire* in the 2004 high-profile Martha Stewart insider trading trial, then in the news, might be a place to observe how awareness might be disattended or attended. Prospective jurors had varying levels of awareness of Martha Stewart, but some were barely able to identify her, or they had inadvertent awareness that she was famous but knew nothing else, not being interested enough to follow news reports or other traces of her that might move into their frame. They had a discounting awareness and disattended additional information. My theoretical sampling did not go beyond the first day or two of the transcripts; what I got from the exercise was enough to help me test court transcripts as a data source and develop some early thoughts on the spectrum of discounting awareness. These early 'tests' helped me think of places I might look for formal theory.

Scoping the literature initially involved searching for the state of discounting across disciplines. I also included disattending at this early stage, because it was clear the concepts are linked. This early sweep, which included all the key EBSCO social science, health, and general academic databases, produced little with which to work. Discounting is used in everyday parlance ('I don't mean to discount your idea'), and it is a financial term. In psychology, delay discounting is an indicator of risky behaviors by people who do not value the rewards gained by delaying gratification. The literature becomes more concerned with pathological behaviors. Transactional Analysis speaks of discounting as unsupportive and demeaning speech. In this literature there are traces of some of the ideas contained in discounting awareness, but the work is not concerned with processes. Discounting might appear as a descriptor, but never as an elaborated concept beyond the uses outlined here.

Disattending is even less of a realized concept than discounting. A literature sweep of the same databases using various lexical constructions – disattend, disattending, disattended – returned no more than 27, some overlapping. Researchers write of the inability of schizophrenics to disattend (detach) from strong meanings, but those few studies were not a line of inquiry to pursue beyond using it to establish the line between everyday disattending and psychopathology. Just one study, 'Conversation non-cooperation: An exploration of disattended complaints' (Mandelbaum, 1991/1992) used disattended in the way I conceived it. Importantly, the article had an affinity with some of the epistemological underpinnings of the ethnomethodological and other sociological works that have sensitized my theorizing.

The discovery of work drawing on similar traditions as the concept is important when developing formal theory. Grounded theorists who choose concepts without regard for epistemological foundations will find it difficult to draw linkages as they follow the concept through the literature. For example, experimental research and quantitative work have a different justification than qualitative inquiry. With different methodological justification come different questions, data and terminology. Attempting to reconcile the two can be like showing up to play golf with a basketball. Nevertheless, as I shall discuss in the section on bridging the literature, theoretical sensitivity does require the theorist to have a feel for how work from a different school or tradition delimits, operationalizes, and justifies the study of related phenomena.

SAMPLING THE LITERATURE

Glaser (2006) wrote that theorists need not draw on primary data for a formal theory. The ability to go to the literature has always been cited as one of the advantages of doing formal theory. I would argue that some areas are going to need primary data due to the limitations of secondary analysis (Heaton, 2004) and fresh theoretical questions that require more than the literature can provide. As I moved into sampling, I needed to draw on a combination of primary data from observation, some conversations, and the extant scholarly literature, as well as journalistic accounts and government reports. The sampling phase of theory-building is the most extensive as writing memos and reflection led to more questions. In this section I will address a few of the lines of query using different types of data to illustrate what is needed in this phase.

Governmental commission reports are particularly useful for secondary analysis. Such reports are often the result of extensive hearings, interviews, and examination of documents, with broad cooperation from the parties involved, albeit often under subpoena. There are often underlying political agendas, but that too is part of the data. Similar to journalistic articles and books, the commission studies and other government reports offer numerous incidents for coding, a sharp contrast to some academic literature, which have limited data from naturally occurring situations. Early in the project I became intrigued with the many questions raised by the 9/11 attacks and subsequent claims that the signs of an impending attack had been evident but ignored. I coded for discounting awareness, disattending, and awareness context issues in the 9/11 Commission Report, which I coded first as a 592-page book and later as a pdf file imported into computer software that facilitated data management. The 9/11 report documents extensive evidence of misread signals, failure to share information, lack of trust across agencies, weak leadership, and generally what has been described as a 'failure of imagination' to link available information (Martin, 2015). Structures of secrecy (Vaughan, 1997, on the Challenger Explosion, influences this concept) often rationed information from people within and across divisions. Both the Clinton and Bush administrations disattended information on the threat of Bin Laden, but as the report showed, the Bush administration treated with discounting awareness a series of memos and communications indicating a terrorist attack was imminent. As CIA Director George Tenet is quoted as saying in his interview with the commission, 'the system was blinking red' during the summer of 2001 prior to the attacks (9/11 report, National Commission on Terrorist Attacks on the United States, 2004, p. 277).

I found similar patterns when I examined the commission report in response to Hurricane Katrina, which destroyed sections of New Orleans and killed 1,100 people. As the authors of that report concluded, 'Many of the problems we have identified can be categorized as "information gaps" – or at least problems with information-related implications, or failures to act decisively because information was sketchy at best'

(Select Bipartisan Committee to Investigate the Preparation for and Response to Hurricane Katrina, 2006, p. 1). Incidents in the report helped me conceptualize awareness contexts in organizational culture.

As an aside, NVivo10's matrices, word trees, and cluster analysis with quantitative measures were useful for working with large data files such as these reports, despite my practice of coding on paper initially. I was able to identify all instances in which the word discount or variants of it were used in the documents. Discount is used just 47 times across four commission reports on disaster, with 9/11 and Katrina containing the bulk of those references. Synonyms – dismiss/dismissed –are sometimes used, but the terms do not always appear where actual incidents are discounted, possibly because of the heavy connotations of the term. Disattending is not used in any of the documents.

Some colleagues have asked why I did not collect more disasters for comparisons beyond the four I studied and the literature on the Challenger explosion. Remember the mission: follow the concept. My goal was not to study disasters, although the sociology of emergency disasters is an interesting field for which I coded concepts that could be developed. My interest, however, was in the spectrum of discounting awareness, a complex undertaking in its own right. It is important to have a sense, some of it more intuitive than measurable, of when enough is enough, using theoretical sampling to guide decisions. The broader issue to which this matter relates is the challenge of setting parameters for a concept.

I wrote several memos on how to distinguish between discounting and disattending awareness and related forms of dismissiveness or denial and legitimate debate. Some conversations are disrupted because one party seeks to inject legitimate corrections or clarification to errors of fact. Knowledge of studies about accounts, claims-making, and turn-taking as addressed in ethnomethodology and conversation analysis provided some sensitivity to the norms of everyday interactions and what occurs when they are breached. Swidler's notion of the 'cultural toolkit' (1986) informs my sense that people in cultures have a fairly patterned and limited repertoire that shapes how they talk about things both innocuous and contested. That understanding guided how I navigated boundaries. It is an example of how abduction, enhanced by theoretical sensitivity, facilitates inferences toward the best explanation.

Setting parameters for the concept invariably means the theorist must contend with concepts that overlap with the one she is developing. Denial was the concept that I met around a few corners. The mental gymnastics around issues from race – people upset when tours of former plantations turn to talk of the slaves who worked there – to political ideology often provoked knee-jerk claims of denial. Denial is both a psychoanalytic construct with which researchers have grappled for decades and a term widely used and abused in everyday conversation. The widespread use of the term makes it both suspect and in need of scrutiny.

> Could behaviors such as disattending uncomfortable media messages or conversations, or the initial ways in which people erase the unpleasant, all be viewed as denial? And how might that explain the nastiness in the public sphere as people confront opposing ideologies they quickly dismiss? How should we view situations where people and institutions discount and deny publicly even when, privately, they know there is a problem? That is the situation of tobacco, oil, and other corporations that have worked to hold onto their reputation and profits while waging war against the truth, 'organizing doubt' against those who would expose their wrongdoing. Would it be accurate to look at events such as the United States' failure to lead the international community in a fight to halt genocide in Rwanda as merely examples of denial? (Martin memo, 7/22/15)

What I was interested in, which became clearer through sampling, were the social processes that follow out of discounting awareness as a theory of social interaction. I was studying denial, but changing contexts created different dimensions, further suggesting a spectrum. Data that proved to be the most useful for working out the contours of denial were for the most part journalistic and scholarly books that narrated the story of various types of public crises in which public denials were prominent, from climate change to lead poisoning. Coding these works became especially useful because some, such as accounts of the NFL's denial of the emerging science linking concussions to dementia in football players, provide a timeline of events that allowed for coding of the earliest hints of discounting and the more extreme types of waging war on the truth by the league's leaders as damaging information became more public. Book accounts such as Oreskes and Conway's (2010) *Merchants of Doubt*, a study of scientists who helped corporations cover up the effects of tobacco, DDT, acid rain, and global warming, provided case studies indicating similar patterns of 'organized doubt,' an aggressive form of willful denial.

The abundance of available data means the theorist has to grapple with an issue raised earlier in this chapter: how many different areas should be sampled for a formal grounded theory? If we agree that the formal theories situated in a discipline do not fulfill the vision of formal grounded theory, what is the optimal number of disciplinary areas? I cannot answer this to complete satisfaction, but think the rule of thumb is something similar to what we would work toward in a substantive theory: answer theoretical possibilities and bring together concepts in a cohesive explanation. Even as we extend our core concept to new areas, the implications of the initial theory delimit the theory in some fairly obvious directions. Understanding what their theory is at heart will help theorists determine how close they are to closure. The implications of the core concept continue to set parameters. The theorist should be willing to stretch across enough areas to suggest further applications. Some of that work is in the writing and how the theorist demonstrates sociological imagination. I will now problematize the diversity of comparisons a little further to address how disciplinary responses to the issue might differ in the following section.

BRIDGING THE LITERATURE

The guidance for developing substantive grounded theory is that extant literature should be integrated only if it earns its way. Academia's gatekeeping apparatus pushes back when theorists, especially novices, propose new theories. That is perhaps why we see many studies that are billed as a 'grounded theory approach study' instead of bold claims of theory. Ideally, the theorist should make the theory the main focus and incorporate relevant literature as it fits – or at least explain why it does not. For formal theory, bridging is a little trickier. The theorist needs to articulate connections to the concept across disciplines as part of the final presentation of the theory. There is another wrinkle to this, however.

For all my advocacy of literature as data, I found that much extant quantitative literature could not be used in more than a summary fashion due to the sparse representation. Glaser and Strauss (1971) encountered a similar limitation when they developed their formal theory of status passage. Epistemological compatibility is at issue. In my early coding of data, I made notes of the many different communication theories that might be implicated in the data. Davison's (1983) Third Person Effect (TPE), for example, holds that people think others (third persons) are more affected by media than they, which can explain some support for restricting certain content. The people who think media are particularly hostile to their political orientations exhibit the hostile media effect (Perloff, 2015). Risk, uncertainty, and the discounting calculations people make; the sweeping misimpressions of confirmation bias; the suggestions of discounting in theories of social distance theory; and the psychological reactance, resistance, evoked when people feel pressure to change behavior, were all the subjects of memos indicating possible literature I might need to explore. A theory of discounting awareness helps move through the literature linking many of these ideas. But the literature is mainly comprised of experimental research, surveys, and multiple regression. And importantly, they do not address the same phenomenon directly. Qualitative theorists need to acknowledge the hypotheses-testing work that has some connection to what they are doing. They can accomplish this by treating the work as they would a selective, theme-oriented literature review. The use of quantitative data to analyze surveys and create indices similar to Glaser's work on comparative failure (1964) has promise for formal theory. But that is a differently designed project than what is discussed here.

CONFIRMING THE THEORY

Writing a working paper on an emerging theory is the best idea I got from Glaser during the first troubleshooting seminar I attended, in Paris, in 2002. The working paper is a test of sorts. The theorist can begin to see if she has something that works and answers all the theoretical questions, including alternatives. In this phase, the traditional sorting of memos precedes the writing, furthering connections and making gaps evident. It stops the enervating talk that makes it difficult to write.

As I moved deeper into the literature of denial I noticed that denial was being linked with inaction in works I coded. Sociologist Stanley Cohen (2001) linked the passivity amid human rights abuses and other tragedies to denial, arguing that even when people have knowledge of horrors, the apparatus of denial is more powerful than truth. Influenced by Cohen's theorizing, Norgaard (2011) identified similar problems surrounding inaction on climate change. The structures of apathy and other forces that suppress action are complex and not accounted for by a sociology of denial to date, however. Further, some sampling in the rather inconclusive area of bystander theory and whistleblowing gave me confidence as I determined that actions to halt wrongdoing did not need to be accounted for fully in my theory. Discounting awareness can explain instances where discounting patterns might be interrupted – network transfers, experiencing proximity – but systemic change is beyond the scope of the current theory even as it provides a path for further study through awareness processes.

The working paper is a springboard for presentations and smaller papers on the developing theory. The goal is a cohesive explanation of the core concept and its implications. The goal is not a Theory of Everything. A formal grounded theory, theorizing in general actually, is to provide tools for thinking about a phenomenon and thinking forward about related phenomena. (It should be clear by now that formal grounded theory requires theorists who are voracious readers on all types of issues.)

CONCLUSION

More than 50 years after it was first discussed, formal grounded theory remains elusive. Some theorists have attempted them; others have opted for more modified formal theories situated in one substantive area. This chapter is intended to advance the methodology, specifically by arguing that grounded theorists must take more seriously the maxim that 'all is data' and expand their engagement with literature both as a tool to expand their theoretical sensitivity and as data.

As part of greater attention to literature as data, grounded theorists must confront the limitations of inductive reasoning and better articulate the role of abduction in the development of grounded theory. Reichertz (2007) has written that abduction has long been a part of grounded theory despite the lack of explicit discussion. This chapter argues that greater elaboration of the use of literature as data highlights the abductive processes of grounded theory development, both substantive and formal. The successful application of the phases outlined in this chapter require that theorists are both aware enough to follow the implications of coding and sampling throughout the development of theory. The theorist needs to start with knowledge of theories, a sense of some of the dynamics in the field of study, and be open to the ever-evolving implications of the emerging theory.

A formal grounded theory is based on the general implications of the core concept of a substantive theory. Therefore, theorists looking to build a formal theory should follow the concept. Generally, the theorist can find data to build the theory from literature and other existing data. I do not rule out the possibility of collecting interviews and other primary data, but the general view (Glaser, 2006) is that most of the data from formal grounded theory is at hand. To demonstrate and discuss the use of academic and popular literature, I draw on the theory of defensive disattending and its core concept, discounting awareness, which addresses a series of processes as people interact with uncomfortable information and situations. I discuss the importance of analyzing the strength of a concept prior to its development. I then outlined four phases for using literature as data and building the theory. The phases are aligned with the stages of doing grounded theory. To summarize:

Scoping the literature: This is a data collection stage similar to going into the field to do interviews. Theorists should follow the concept through various disciplines. Linguistic and epistemological similarities are important, but the concept may be masked under other terms. This is a reconnaissance mission intended to get a sense of all the ways the concept might be utilized in extant scholarly literature, popular, and trade publications.

Sampling: Several iterations of sampling to address questions are necessary – and may be necessary throughout the study. It is very similar to theoretical sampling in substantive theory. Always keep the core concept in sight. Coding and memos help guide the work as it would with substantive theory. While theorists may worry about how many different areas they should sample, the fit for any particular study becomes apparent as the underlying theme of what the study is about connects the areas sampled.

Bridging the literature: In substantive theory it is important to engage with the relevant extant literature. Formal grounded theory has the same requirement. Theorists can integrate some literature as they would in a normal literature review, weaving their theory throughout. Quantitative data can be used for formal theory, but the theorist has more control if she is using original quantitative data rather than the experimental and other hypothesis-testing data so prominent in many disciplines. The concepts and phenomena utilized in quantitative work can differ significantly even when similar terms are used.

Confirming the theory: Sorting and writing are the same in formal grounded theory as they are in substantive theory. The working paper helps the theorist test the cohesiveness of her argument. Gaps become evident quickly, possibly sending the theorist back to sampling. The working paper allows for presentations and smaller papers, for which feedback will help the development of the theory.

Formal grounded theory remains the unfulfilled promise of grounded theory. Modifications, such as metasyntheses situated in one discipline, have been favored in nursing and other health studies. But formal grounded theory developed from a substantive theory and extended across multiple areas is still the ideal for some grounded theorists. This chapter attempts to demonstrate and make more explicit aspects of grounded theory methodology that need to be addressed before more theorists can begin to realize that vision.

REFERENCES

Andrews, T. (2006). The literature review in grounded theory: A response to McCallin (2003). *The Grounded Theory Review: An International Journal*, *5*(2/3), 29–41.

Andrews, T. (2011). Reflections on generating a formal grounded theory. In V. Martin & A. Gynnild (Eds.), *Grounded Theory: The Philosophy, Method, and Work of Barney Glaser* (pp. 277–292). Boca Raton, FL: BrownWalker.

Bendassolli, P. (2013). Theory building in qualitative research: Reconsidering the problem of induction. *Forum: Qualitative Social Research*, *14*(1). www.qualitative-research.net/index.php/fqs/article/view/1851/3497 (retrieved July 20, 2016).

Bruscaglioni, L. (2016). Theorizing in grounded theory and creative abduction. *Quality and Quantity*, *50*(5), 2009–2024. doi:10.1007/s11135-015-0248-3 (retrieved February 20, 2017).

Bryant, A. (2002). Re-grounding grounded theory. *Journal of Information Technology Theory and Application*, *41*(1), 25–42.

Bryant, A., Hughes, J., Myers, M. D., Trauth, E. M., & Urquhart, C. (2004). Twenty years of applying grounded theory to information systems: A coding method useful theory, generation method, or an orthodox positivist method of data analysis? In B. Kaplan, D. P. Truex, D. Wastell, A. T. Wood-Harper, & J. I. DeGross (Eds.), *Information Systems Research: Relevant Theory and Informed Practice* (pp. 646–650). Norwell, MA: Kluwer Academic. doi:10.1007/1-4020-8095-6_35 (retrieved January 14, 2017).

Bryant, A. & Charmaz, K. (2007). Grounded theory in historical perspective: An epistemological account. In A. Bryant & K. Charmaz (Eds.), *The Sage Handbook Of Grounded Theory* (pp. 31–57). Thousand Oaks, CA: Sage.

Charmaz, K. (2014). *Constructing Grounded Theory* (2nd ed.). London and Thousand Oaks, CA: Sage.

Chenail, R. J., George, S. St., Wulff, D., Duffy, M., Scott, K. W., & Tomm, K. (2012). Clients' relational conceptions of conjoint couple and family therapy quality: A grounded formal theory. *Journal of Marital and Family Therapy*, *38*, 241–264. doi:10.1111/j.1752-0606.2011.00246.x (retrieved August 10, 2016).

Cohen, S. (2001). States of Denial: Knowing about Atrocities and Suffering. London: Polity Press.

Davison, W. (1983). The third-person effect in communication. *Public Opinion Quarterly*, *47*(1), 1–15. doi:10.1086/268763 (retrieved February 12, 2015).

Denzin, N. K. (2010). *The Qualitative Manifesto: A Call to Arms.* Walnut Creek, CA: Left Coast Press.

Ekins, R. (1997). Male Femaling: A Grounded Theory Approach to Cross-dressing and Sex-changing. New York: Routledge.

Fainaru-Ward, M. & Fainaru, S. (2014). *League of Denial: The NFL, Concussions, and the Battle for Truth*. New York: Three Rivers Press.

Flick, U. (2015). Qualitative Inquiry – 2.0 at 20? *Developments, Trends, and Challenges for the Politics of Research*, *21*(7), 599–608. doi:10.1177/1077800415583296 (retrieved June 15, 2016).

Gibson, B. & Hartman, J. (2014). *Rediscovering Grounded Theory.* London: Sage.

Gibson, B. J., Sussex, P. V., Fitzgerald, R. P., & Thomson, W. M. (2016). Complete tooth loss as a status passage. *Sociology of Health and Illness, 39(3),* 412–427. doi:https://doi.org/10.1111/1467-9566.12492 (retrieved June 27, 2017).

Glaser, B. G. (1962). Secondary analysis: A strategy for the use of knowledge from research elsewhere. *Social Problems*, *10*(1), 70–74. doi:10.2307/799409 (retrieved May 5, 2015).

Glaser, B. G. (1964). Comparative failure in science. *Science*, *143*(3610), 1012. doi:0.1126/science.143.3610.1012 (retrieved January 6, 2017).

Glaser, B. G. (1978). Theoretical Sensitivity: Advances in the Methodology of Grounded Theory. Mill Valley, CA: Sociology Press.

Glaser, B. G. (1992). *Emergence vs. Forcing: Basis of Grounded Theory Analysis*. Mill Valley, CA: Sociology Press.

Glaser, B. G. (2007). Doing Formal Theory. In In A. Bryant & K. Charmaz (Eds.), *The Sage Handbook Of Grounded Theory* (pp. 97–113). Thousand Oaks, CA: Sage.

Glaser, B. G. (2006). *Doing Formal Grounded Theory: A Proposal*. Mill Valley, CA: Sociology Press.

Glaser, B. G. (2010). Grounded theory is the study of a concept. Retrieved from April 19, 2015, from www.youtube.com/watch?v=OcpxaLQDnLk

Glaser, B. G. & Strauss, A. L. (1964). Awareness contexts and social interaction. *American Sociological Review*, *29*, 669–679. doi:10.2307/2091417 (retrieved September 10, 2016).

Glaser, B. G. & Strauss, A. L. (1965). *Awareness of Dying.* Chicago, IL: Aldine.

Glaser, B. G. & Strauss, A. L. (1967). *The Discovery of Grounded Theory*. Chicago, IL: Aldine.

Glaser, B. G. & Strauss, A. L. (1971). *Status Passage*. London: Routledge & Kegan Paul.

Goffman, E. (1986 [1974]). *Framing Analysis*. Boston, MA: Northeastern University Press.

Haig, B. D. (1995). Grounded theory as scientific method. *Philosophy of Education Yearbook*, http://citeseerx.ist.psu.edu/viewdoc/summary?doi=10.1.1.483.3878 (retrieved December 12, 2017).

Hammersley, M. (2008). Questioning Qualitative Inquiry: Critical Essays. London: Sage.

Heaton, J. (2004). *Reworking Qualitative Data*. London: Sage.

Hupcey, J. E., Penrod, J., Morse, J. M., & Mitcham, C. (2001). An exploration and advancement of the concept of trust. *Journal of Advanced Nursing*, *36*, 282–293. doi:10.1046/j.1365-2648.2001.01970.x (retrieved February 12, 2017).

Kearney, M. H. (1998a). Truthful self-nurturing: A grounded formal theory of women's addiction recovery. *Qualitative Health Research*, *8*(4), 495–512. http://journals.sagepub.com/doi/10.1177/10497323980080040 (retrieved February 21, 2017).

Kearney, M. H. (1998b). Ready-to-wear: Discovering grounded formal theory. *Research in Nursing & Health*, *21*, 179–186. doi:10.1002/ (SICI) 1098-240X (199804)21:2<179: AID-NUR8>3.0.CO;2-G (retrieved February 13, 2017).

Kearney, M. H. (2001). Enduring love: A grounded formal theory of women's experience of domestic violence. *Research in Nursing & Health*, *24*, 270–282. doi:10.1002/nur.1029 (retrieved February 13, 2017).

Kearney, MH. (2007). From the Sublime to the Meticulous: The Evolution of Grounded Formal Theory. In A. Bryant & K. Charmaz (Eds.), *The Sage Handbook Of Grounded Theory* (pp. 127–150). Thousand Oaks, CA: Sage.

Mandelbaum, J. (1991/1992). Conversational non-cooperation: An exploration of disattended complaints. *Research on Language & Social Interaction*, *25*, 97–138.

Martin, V. B. (2004). Getting the news from the news: A grounded theory of purposive attending. PhD thesis, Union Institute and University, Dissertation Abstractions Internationals (UMI 3144535).

Martin, V. B. (2006). The relationship between an emerging grounded theory and the existing literature: Four phases for consideration. *The Grounded Theory Review: An International Journal*, *5*(2/3), 47–57.

Martin, VB. (2007). Purposive Attending: How people get the news from the news. In B.G. Glaser and J.A. Holton (Eds), *The Grounded Theory Seminar Reader* (chp. 11). Mill Valley, CA: Sociology Press.

Martin, V. B. (2008). Attending the news: A grounded theory about a daily regimen. *Journalism: Theory, Practice & Criticism*, *9*, 76–94. doi:10.1177/1464884907084341

Martin, V. B. (2011). The power of an enduring concept. In V. Martin & A. Gynnild (Eds.), *Grounded Theory: The Philosophy, Method, and Work of Barney Glaser* (pp. 297–308). Boca Raton, FL: Brown Walker Press.

Martin, V. B. (2015). The system was blinking red: Awareness contexts and disasters. *The Grounded Theory Review*, 2 December. Available at http://groundedtheoryreview.com/2015/12/19/the-system-was-blinking-red-awareness-contexts-and-disasters/

McCallin, A. M. (2006). Grappling with the literature in a grounded theory study. *Grounded Theory Review*, *5*, 11–27.

Morse, J. M., Mitcham, C., Hupcey, J. E., & Tason, N. (1996). Criteria for concept evaluation. *Journal of Advanced Nursing Practice*, *24*, 385–390.

National Commission on Terrorist Attacks on the United States. (2004). *The 9/11 Commission Report*. New York: W.W. Norton. Retrieved from www.9-11commission.gov/report/911Report.pdf

Norgaard, K. (2011). Living in Denial: Climate Change, Emotions, and Everyday Life. Cambridge, MA: MIT Press.

Oreskes, N. & Conway, E. M. (2010). Merchants of Doubt: How a Handful of Scientists Obscured the Truth on Issues from Tobacco Smoke to Global Warming. New York: Bloomsbury.

Penrod, J. (2001). Refinement of the concept of uncertainty. *Journal of Advanced Nursing*, *34*, 238–245. doi:10.1046/j.1365-2648.2001.01750.x (retrieved July 12, 2016).

Penrod, J. (2007). Living with uncertainty: Concept advancement. *Journal of Advanced Nursing*, *57*, 658–667. doi:10.1111/j.1365-2648.2006.04 (retrieved September 10, 2016).

Perloff, R. M. (2015). A Three-decade retrospective on the hostile media effect. *Mass Communication and Society*, *18*(6), 701–729. doi:10.1080/15205436.2015.1051234 (retrieved August 13, 2016).

Prior, L. (2008). Repositioning documents in social research. *Sociology*, *42*(5), 821–836. doi:10.1177/0038038508094564 (retrieved March 1, 2017).

Reichertz, J. (2007). Abduction: The logic of discovery of grounded theory. In A. Bryant & K. Charmaz (Eds.), *The SAGE Handbook of Grounded Theory* (pp. 214–228). Thousand Oaks, CA: Sage.

Seidel, S. & Urquhart, C. (2013). On emergence and forcing in information systems grounded theory studies: The case of Strauss and Corbin. *Journal of Information Technology*, *28*, 237. doi:10.1057/jit.2013.17

Select Bipartisan Committee to Investigate the Preparation for and Response to Hurricane Katrina (2006). A failure of initiative: The final report of the Select Bipartisan Committee to investigate the preparation for and response to Hurricane Katrina. Available at: http://katrina.house.gov/full_katrina_report.htm (retrieved April 12, 2015).

Shank, G. (1998). The extraordinary ordinary powers of abductive reasoning. *Theory & Psychology*, *8*(6), 841–860. doi:10.1177/0959354398086007 (retrieved January 17, 2017).

Strauss, A. & Corbin, J. (1990). Basics of Qualitative Research: Grounded Theory Procedures and Techniques. Newbury Park, CA: Sage.

Swidler, A. (1986). Culture in action: Symbols and strategies. *American Sociological Review*, *51*(2), 273–286. Available at: www.jstor.org/stable/2095521 (retrieved January 17, 2017).

Tavory, I. & Timmermans, S. (2014). *Abductive Analysis: Theorizing Qualitative Research*. Chicago, IL: University of Chicago Press.

Thornberg, R. & Dunne, C. (2019). The literature review in grounded theory. In Bryant, A. & Charmaz, K. (Eds.) *The SAGE Handbook of Current Developments in Grounded Theory*. London: Sage, pp. 206–221.

Thorne, S. (2017). Metasynthetic madness: What kind of monster have we created? *Qualitative Health Research*, *27*(1), 3–12. doi:10.1177/1049732316679370 (retrieved March 15, 2017).

Urquhart, C. (2007). The evolving nature of grounded theory method: The case of the information systems discipline. In A. Bryant & K. Charmaz (Eds.), *The Sage Handbook of Grounded Theory* (pp. 339–359). Thousand Oaks, CA: Sage.

Urquhart, C. & Fernandez, W. (2013). Using grounded theory method in information systems: The researcher as blank slate and other myths. *Journal of Information Technology*, *28*(3), 224–236. doi:10.1057/jit.2012.34 (retrieved May 10, 2016).

Urquhart, C., Lehmann, H., & Myers, M. D. (2010). Putting the 'theory' back into grounded theory: Guidelines for grounded theory studies in information systems. *Information Systems Journal*, *20*, 357–381. doi:10.1111/j.1365-2575.2009.00328.x (retrieved September 9, 2016).

Vaughan, D. (1997). The Challenger Launch Decision: Risky Technology, Culture, and Deviance at NASA. Chicago, IL: University of Chicago Press.

Ventura-Madangeng, J. & Wilson D. (2009). Workplace violence experienced by registered nurses: A concept analysis. *Australia Nursing Praxis*, *25*(3), 37–50.

Wuest, J. (2001). Precarious ordering: Toward a formal theory of women's caring. *Health Care for Women International*, *22*, 167–193. doi:10.1080/073993301300003144 (retrieved April 7, 2016).

Wuest, J. & Hodgins, M. J. (2011). Reflections on methodological approaches and conceptual contributions in a program of caregiving research: Development and testing of Wuest's theory of family caregiving. *Qualitative Health Research*, *21*(2), 151–161. doi: 10.1177/1049732310385010 (retrieved February 26, 2017).

Zerubavel, E. (2007). *The Elephant in the Middle of the Room*. New York: Oxford University Press.

Zerubavel, E. (2015). *Hidden in Plain Sight*. New York: Oxford University Press.

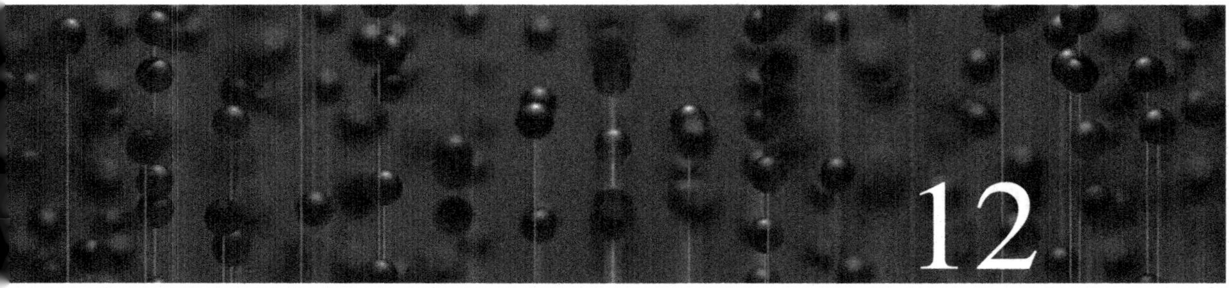

Rendering Analysis through Storyline

Melanie Birks and Jane Mills

INTRODUCTION

Stories are used in various research methodologies to both generate data and disseminate findings. Narrative can be powerful both as fodder for analysis and as a means of presenting research outcomes. In grounded theory studies, many researchers will use stories in various forms as data, yet the full potential of storyline as an analytical technique, particularly in the later stages of analysis, has yet to be realized. So, what is storyline? We define storyline as *an advanced analytical technique used in grounded theory research for the purpose of both integrating and articulating theory.*

This chapter will commence with a discussion of the roots of storyline in grounded theory. We will then explore the potential for storyline to aid analytical processes in grounded theory research. Storyline offers a means by which a grounded theory can be rendered and articulated, regardless of the approach to the methodology preferred by the researcher. The chapter incorporates guidelines for presenting a grounded theory as storyline. Keeping theory foremost, staying grounded, embracing variation and visually representing the theory will ensure that the storyline is a credible rendering of a grounded theory. The chapter then concludes with reflections on the use of storyline in practice. The value of storyline will be illustrated throughout this chapter by reference to the experiences of grounded theorists who have used storyline as a technique in their own research.

STORYLINE IN GROUNDED THEORY

Narrative analysis became more prominent in qualitative research in the early 1990s when there was a '...narrative turn ... remarkable in the intensity and enthusiasm with which it has shifted research methodological undertakings' (Clandinin, 2006, p. 45). At the heart of qualitative research that utilizes narratives is the analysis of stories. Clandinin and Connelly (2000) argue there are three dimensions to be considered in narrative inquiry: interaction, continuity and situation, each of which are pertinent for a grounded theory analysis.

In grounded theory research, data can take many forms and can come from various sources. In the context of 'all is data' (Glaser, 1998, p. 8), stories are no exception. Whether generated through direct engagement with research participants or sourced from existing work, narratives in the form of stories can be subjected to analytical techniques to generate theory. Glaser warns that there is a difference in the quality of what he terms descriptive capture, and participant interview transcripts generated with minimal input from the researcher (Glaser, 2002). This argument is premised on Glaser's entrenched positivist position and needs to be considered in this light. Consistent with our previous work, we prefer not to take an either/or approach to grounded theory design. It is enough to say, therefore, that traditional grounded theorists are less likely to use storyline in their research design if for no good reason other than to adhere to Glaser's position. It is important, however, to distinguish between stories as data, stories as product and storyline as a tool to facilitate and convey analytical processes.

While stories as data and product reflect their broad use in qualitative research, it is the value of storyline as an analytical tool that distinguishes its use in grounded theory. Grounded theory research emphasizes process, in the various ways that this concept may be defined (Birks & Mills, 2015). Social processes are dynamic rather than static. Stories are constructed through our engagement with others and this engagement is characterized through movement. Narrative has the potential to explicate the temporal and structural elements of actions and interactions (Dey, 2007) and thus make a grounded theory tangible. Indeed, the 'line' element is the inherent feature of storyline that characterizes the continuity of process. For a grounded theory to demonstrate the explanatory power that sets it apart from simple qualitative description, this process must be evident to the reader. Storyline forces the researcher's attention to the patterns of connectivity that convert analytical products into theory.

While Glaser and Strauss (1967) did not make specific reference to storyline in their seminal work, its relationship with grounded theory is not a recent development. The first and most extensive reference to storyline was made by Strauss and Corbin in their initial *Basics of Qualitative Research* text (Strauss & Corbin, 1990). In this text, storyline was defined as 'the conceptualization of the story' (p. 116) as part of the selective coding process. In developing the storyline, these authors assert that the researcher moves from descriptive to analytical telling of the story evident in the data. Through presenting the storyline as a mechanism for moving the research from description to conceptualization, Strauss and Corbin (1990) made a significant contribution to grounded theory.

Following Glaser's (1992) global rebuttal of Strauss and Corbin's 1990 text, reference to storyline was reduced significantly in subsequent versions of this work (Corbin & Strauss, 2008; Strauss & Corbin, 1990, 1998) and barely rates a mention in the most recent edition (Corbin & Strauss, 2015). In any event, Strauss and Corbin used storyline primarily as a tool to aid analysis. Conversely, Dey (2007, p. 183) argues convincingly, albeit briefly, for his use of storyline as an effective 'narrative framework ... for contextualizing and integrating the various elements ... which characterized the social process'. As we have argued previously (Birks & Mills, 2015; Birks, Mills, Francis, & Chapman, 2009), however, the potential of storyline as an analytical and rhetorical tool has remained largely untapped. In the discussion that follows we address this limitation of existing work and provide guidance and direction for the use of storyline to assist both novice and experienced researchers to use storyline to best effect in conducting grounded theory research.

STORYLINE AS AN ANALYTICAL TOOL

Storyline as an analytical technique enables the researcher to reach the highest level of abstraction while staying true to the data. As Cornelissen (2017, p. 370) states, 'all styles of theorizing are geared towards some form of explanation'. Storyline facilitates the articulation of a version of events (Vaismoradi, Jones, Turunen, & Snelgrove, 2016) that facilitates the explanatory power characteristic of theory grounded in data.

In grounded theory research, the initial coding process results in a fragmentation of each individual story (de Casterle, Gastmans, Bryon, & Denier, 2012). Even with careful attention to analytical processes, the potential for the researcher to be left with a pile of concrete codes and descriptive categories is great. Each of the vignettes in this chapter has been written by grounded theorists who used storyline as an analytical tool to move them beyond this morass to an elegant, abstract theoretical explanation of process. These stories are offered by the researchers in the spirit of empathy and hope that it is possible to move beyond description to a beautifully integrated grounded theory.

Researchers employ storyline as an analytical process as they progress to later stages of coding (Birks & Mills, 2015). At this time, feelings of being overwhelmed by the sheer quantity of analytical material generated by initial and intermediate coding are common, with many novice researchers becoming stressed as a result. Of course, the silver lining of being so immersed in the process of concurrent data collection and analysis is that for these same researchers, theoretical sensitivity has also been heightened. It is this nuanced understanding of context, participants, interactions and outcomes that comes to the fore in storyline to capture the action underlying process.

> During the data analysis phase, we are constantly told that the answers are in the data and to 'immerse' ourselves in the data. There came a point where I felt like I was floundering in the data and going around in circles. Writing the storyline gave me purpose and clarity, the feeling of gaining some traction. Storyline is the vehicle that draws you out of the data and lets you put the hundreds of concepts and thoughts from the data into a format that conveys it to the reader.
>
> Adele Baldwin

DEVELOPING THE STORYLINE

The final stages of analysis in grounded theory research aim to produce an integrated theory. This can often be the most challenging aspect of analysis for the researcher. Storyline aids this process by providing the researcher with a technique that enables them to fully synthesize and abstract the data. Indeed, it is the way in which a grounded theory takes data beyond simple description that sets it apart. It must be recognized, however, that higher levels of abstraction are dependent on the researcher having the necessary level of insight and being prepared to take conceptual leaps (Suddaby, 2006). Such insight will have been developed through the meticulous application of the essential grounded theory methods (Birks & Mills, 2015), in particular, memoing. The researcher will have been writing memos about 'what is going on' in the data (Glaser, 1978) from the early stages of their study. The use of memoing in this way is what moves the analysis from description to abstraction. Abstraction is the theoretical extraction of concepts that capture the essence of the substantive data. In developing the storyline, achieving the necessary level of abstraction can be aided through a number of practical techniques, including: stepping back, refining and evidencing.

Stepping Back

The first stage of writing the storyline involves moving away from the data to develop a storyline that is more conceptually abstract than stories told in any one participant's interview. While a high-quality grounded theory is dependent on staying grounded in the data, during the process of analysis it is necessary to stop focusing on each part of the developing theory in order to see the whole. Setting the data aside for a short while to engage in the highly abstract thinking required of storyline is one way of re-establishing a researcher's personal confidence and sense of control, yet at the same time moving the analytical process forward.

> Using storyline during my grounded theory PhD research study was challenging but above all it was rewarding. It was challenging because I was tied to the practice of describing research findings. 'Put aside the data and explain the story of your categories and sub-categories,' my supervisor said. But it was easy to describe the data – the data was tangible. Using storyline meant that I had to put the data aside and abstractly and creatively explain the broader story of my developing grounded theory. I remember feeling like I was free falling. The data was my safety net and I was being told to let go of it – temporarily at least.
>
> Jennifer Chamberlain-Salaun

Beginning with a blank page is an opportunity to write a theoretical story unfettered by participants' individual stories and experiences, forcing the writer to work at the necessary conceptual level. As a point of reference, the researcher may want to print a list of codes and categories. This list can be used to prompt thinking, although the aim of beginning with a blank page is not to cut and paste from existing analysis, much of which is contained in separate memos. Instead, the researcher needs to tell the story of the analysis as it exists at a particular point in time, with a focus on flow and integration. On a more practical note, beginning with a blank page also reduces the temptation to write around a particularly interesting or poignant data fragment. A temptation that has the potential to force the data (Glaser, 1992) in a particular direction to justify inclusion of a favoured quote. Instead of getting bogged down in a mire of data, the researcher instead steps up to render a storyline that explains the underlying process implicit in their analysis to date.

Moving away from the substantive data set may seem counter-intuitive in a grounded theory study. A researcher's early intense immersion in the minutiae of the data set does, however, create a personal safety net whereby they intuitively know where evidence is located. It is this intimate knowledge of the data that results in there being little risk of a 'flight of fancy' as a result of employing storyline that won't be easily corrected at a later date. Using storyline as a method of analysis is an iterative process that results in the researcher moving between writing multiple drafts of their storyline, revisiting memos, writing new memos, sorting and resorting data fragments. Storyline therefore becomes another method of analysis that sits alongside traditional methods in a researcher's analytical toolbox. Storyline is most powerful, however, when it comes to refining a grounded theory.

Refining

Because of the intellectual challenge that storyline provides, most grounded theorists will need to write many iterations before this goal of theoretical integration is achieved. Nurjannah, Mills, Park and Usher (2014) describe using storyline in the context of conducting grounded theory research in a language other than English, thus adding another layer of complexity to the process. In the following example (Box 12.1) there were 46 drafts of the storyline written over a six-month period with weekly meetings held to progress the developing theory. In the examples provided it is evident how the storyline developed over time.

Box 12.1 Refinement of a storyline

Extract from draft 1

Identifying and decision making related to the ability to provide care is a process in which stakeholders assess their competency, resources and willingness before they decide to take responsibility to provide care or to shift responsibility to other stakeholders.

Providing care is divided into two kinds: direct care or indirect care. Direct care means providing care for individual who is in a crisis, acute, maintenance and health promotion or individual/community who are at risk.

Indirect care means actions which is conducted to create a system in which the service available (mostly in community) and to create a link system between health care provider (mostly between hospital and community health centre/CHC).

Extract from draft 20

Decision making to share responsibility to provide care for individual living with a mental health issues is conducted by each stakeholder. There are three possible results of decision making which are: providing direct care, providing indirect care or transferring individual from one stakeholder to other stakeholders.

The decision made by one stakeholder will influence other stakeholders to also make a decision. This condition happens only if the decision made of one stakeholder is known or informed to other stakeholders. If the decisions made between two or more stakeholders involved are matched, there will be an appropriate share of responsibility and care will be connected. On the other hand, if there is unmatched decision making to share responsibility between two or more stakeholders involved then the care will be disconnected.

Both care connected or disconnected, the individual will be managed. The quality care however may turn [out] to be different. The competence and resources of stakeholders will influence the quality of care provided to individual. The quality of care will influence the individual condition and each stakeholder who are primary responsible will make a decision toward how to provide care for this individual at this time.

Extract from final draft

Decision making is a cognitive process used by stakeholders in order to respond to an individual's health status. The primary stakeholder will initiate the process of decision making and their decisions will in turn influence other stakeholders' decision-making processes. Stakeholders may then communicate with each other about their decisions and possibly negotiate about what kind of responsibility for the provision of care each should have. Although negotiations do not always happen, each stakeholder still makes decisions as a response to the individual living with mental health issues. Whether the decisions are matched or unmatched, there will be a shifting responsibility among stakeholders.

Three types of factors influence stakeholder's decision making: internal, external and the individual's health status. Stakeholders' internal factors include their levels of: knowledge, competency, willingness, motivation, altruism/humanity, insight, acceptance, awareness, expectancy, attention, enthusiasm or needs. External factors include: resources, institutional policy, work atmosphere and the existence of a linking system among stakeholders.

Matched decision making is defined by agreement on who has the appropriate level of competence, resources and willingness to take responsibility for the provision of care to an individual. A matched decision will lead to unforced acceptance of the need to provide care.

Unmatched decision making is defined by disagreement among stakeholders about who has the appropriate level of competence and resources to provide care. An unmatched decision results in forced acceptance to take responsibility to provide care as both parties have low levels of willingness.

As Nurjannah et al. refined their storyline over many iterations, it moved from defining and categorizing concepts, to beginning to explain the process that occurred when different stakeholders made decisions – including the potential outcomes, to fully explaining the process of connecting care for people living with a mental illness in Indonesia (Nurjannah, Mills, Park, & Usher, 2015).

Polkinghorne's (1995) seminal work on narrative configuration defines stories such as these as '...narratives that combine a succession of incidents into a unified episode' (p. 7). For Polkinghorne, stories unfold chronologically '...along a before-after continuum' (p. 16) around the narrative structure of plot. In grounded theory research, it is in the writing of the story told by the data that gaps and limitations in the narrative structure are exposed.

> Storyline allowed me to see the bigger picture, what was clear and what wasn't, the gaps and areas that required more attention. From that, I went back to the data, again and again, to confirm, consolidate or refute what I had written in the storyline. Where did I get that? In this way, it was a pivotal part of the higher order data analysis. Writing the storyline, seeing the gaps and returning to the data seemed logical, although on reflection, it was a key element in data analysis. It also allowed me to ensure that the findings were from the data, free from assumptions and preconceptions, which in turn added to the rigour of the research.
>
> Adele Baldwin

For a grounded theorist this process results in questioning the data, writing further memos and potentially returning to the field to generate more data as an outcome of theoretical sampling (Birks & Mills, 2015).

Evidencing

Evidencing the storyline is a particularly affirming step for researchers as they return to the data to choose fragments that really illustrate and support their analytical argument. Often at this point, the researcher is pleasantly surprised at how little of the mass of concrete codes and descriptive categories is left unaccounted for. The theoretical integration that is part of writing a storyline results in a refinement of thinking that pares away extraneous analytical ideas to leave the researcher with the key elements of the process at hand. However, because writing is always a method of analysis (Richardson, 2000), there remains a period of moving between the data and the storyline to account for the dimensions and variations apparent at every level of coding. As the storyline builds to a climactic conclusion, it is often the core category that is the last to be fully explained, a situation that may test a researcher's tolerance of ambiguity (Liu, 2015).

> If, when the data is added to support the story, there are evidence gaps, then saturation of data hasn't been achieved. Thinking about the storyline without the data excerpts forced me to use the process of abstraction.
>
> Karen Hoare

The examples presented to illustrate the stages of storyline development highlight the organic nature of the process. As the data are pulled together in a logical and understandable form, variations are accounted for and process is explicated. Ultimately, a well-developed storyline becomes greater than the sum of its parts.

PRESENTING THE STORYLINE

Beyond its function as an analytical tool, storyline facilitates the development of a digestible, readable expression of a grounded theory. At a time when qualitative research struggles to find a place in a publication environment dominated by a positivist paradigm, storyline functions as an abstract yet detailed and contextually-rich explanation of phenomena (Cornelissen, 2017).

Box 12.2 Guidelines for presenting a storyline

- Keep theory foremost
- Stay grounded
- Embrace variation
- Represent theory visually

Suddaby (2006) suggests that the rigid application of grounded theory methods can curb the creativity that is key to quality research. When presenting theory as a storyline, creativity is harnessed and the tacit, abstract interpretation of the researcher is brought to light. The purpose for which the storyline is produced will largely determine its format. In its briefest form it may be a synopsis of the grounded theory that serves as a summary for review by a funding body or conference committee. Researchers who wish to establish whether their research findings resonate with participants may produce a more substantial summary. For the purpose of publication, the storyline may be an extended version for which categories in the form of headings provide structure. In many cases, storyline may be used to present a grounded theory in its most detailed form in a thesis or dissertation. There are no limits to the form a storyline may take. The creative researcher may seek to bring a storyline to life through poetry, music or even video.

While producing a storyline is a creative endeavour, doing justice to a grounded theory by rendering it in this form can be challenging. The researcher must remain true to the data and the analytical processes that brought them to this point. They are required to make Suddaby's (2006) conceptual leaps of faith to convert their concrete, substantive segments of data into an abstract storyline through the process of rigorous analysis. Data becomes theory, and the storyline must represent an abstract summary of the experiences of those who experience the phenomenon.

We provide the following guidelines (Box 12.2) to assist the researcher to present a grounded theory as storyline and yield what Lips (2013) refers to as 'a realistic sequence of incidents and human responses' (p. VII).

Keep Theory Foremost

Throughout this chapter we emphasize that a key feature of storyline is how it provides for the researcher to render a grounded theory in a digestible form. We define theory as 'an explanatory scheme comprising a set of concepts related to each other through logical patterns of connectivity' (Birks & Mills, 2015, p. 108). Theory is thus characterized by the relationships between concepts as opposed to the presentation of a list of themed data in the form of categories which provides little value to the reader (Vaismoradi et al., 2016). Emphasis on integration in the service of explanation is paramount. Explication of process is key to highlighting the explanatory potential inherent in a theory grounded in data. Static description should be minimal and used only to provide a basis for exploring relationships, processes and movement. The example in Box 12.3 is drawn from a study of consumers' experiences of health care teams (Chamberlain-Salaun, 2015). Note how the extract from the storyline more effectively harnesses the explanatory potential of grounded theory when pushed to a more abstract level.

Box 12.3 Extract from a storyline

First draft:

> Consumers view the social world of health care as the 'professional' world of experts with the world beyond those parameters being the 'real' world. This infers that consumers view the social world of health care as a world into which experts enter and that in their 'personal/private' worlds, experts are a truer manifestation of themselves. The expert's profession is what they do not who they are. During interviews with experts most participants agree that this is how they consider their professional self, although most acknowledged that sometimes professional–personal boundaries become blurred.

Final draft:

> Consumers and experts each assume different roles within the world of health care. Unlike the experts, consumers do not have a position description; their role is unclear to them when they involuntarily arrive in the health care system. Although it may be argued that consumer rights charters and principles provide consumers with some indication as to their role, the focus of consumer rights is on what consumers can expect from experts and health systems more so than on what experts and health systems expect from consumers. Consumers enter the social world of health care unprepared for their roles, whereas experts are educated and qualified to assume established roles. Consumers are outsiders in a world dominated by experts who understand the machinations of the social world of health care.

This example highlights our previous assertion that writing the storyline is not divorced from analysis; analysis of the connections between codes and categories continues until the storyline is fully formed. The first storyline extract in Box 12.3 highlights consumers' and health professionals' differing perspectives of the social world of health care and their roles within that 'world'. Through the process of writing a storyline that became more conceptually abstract over time, the author moved away from only considering interview transcripts. By including artefacts such as consumer rights charters and policy documents to the data set, the researcher contextualized individuals' recounted experiences, which provided explanatory power to the theory of consumers as 'Outsiders in the experts' world'. As discussed previously, the process of writing is iterative, as the researcher moves between storyline and data to ensure that the final product reflects the colour and movement of the theory constructed through analysis. In this study, social worlds analysis added another dimension to the storyline, contextualized individuals' recounted experiences, and assisted the researcher to achieve their goal of linking and explaining concepts to explain process. This use of an extant theoretical framework is a form of theoretical coding, as discussed later in this chapter.

Stay Grounded

A grounded theory must be just that, grounded. While it may appear contradictory to our call for creativity, it is important to avoid poetic licence in producing the storyline. The balancing act that the researcher engages in involves ensuring that the storyline is sufficiently abstract, in that it extracts concepts to a theoretical level, while remaining true to the data. If the essential grounded theory methods are employed correctly, the generation of an abstract theory that is appropriately grounded should occur as a matter of course. There are, however, some strategies that can be employed to both ensure and demonstrate that the theory in the form of a storyline is grounded in the data.

As discussed previously, the initial writing of the storyline should be done without reliance on verbatim quotes or reference to raw material. In the final presentation, however, the use of quotes can illustrate abstract concepts and ground the storyline. The example in Box 12.4 is drawn from a study of women presenting to non-metropolitan emergency departments with possible miscarriage (Edwards, 2016). This study included the voices of the women, their partners and the nurses who provided their care. Note how this extract from the storyline is enhanced by the inclusion of verbatim statements made by a participant.

Similarly, category labels, particularly *in vivo* codes, can be integrated into the storyline. These data segments add a dynamic element to the storyline, further grounding and bringing it to life. Where gerunds (the noun form of a verb) have been used by the researcher, the added benefit is that the element of process is made more explicit (Charmaz, 2014). Observe in Box 12.4, that the bolded 'experiencing triage' is an example of using a gerund in this way. Where the storyline is by necessity lengthy, the use of these gerunds as sub-headings can enhance structure.

> When my grounded theory was sufficiently developed I returned to the data to select study participants' quotes to support and enrich the story being told. The story came to life in much the same way as dialogue enriches fictional stories. The difference being that the raw data of a grounded theory represents real peoples' stories. Using storyline enabled me to integrate participants' stories and my analysis and interpretation of their stories into a broader theory. During my early attempts at using the storyline method I could never have imagined that it would enable me to refine my data analysis and to present my grounded theory in a way that was coherent and engaging.
>
> Jennifer Chamberlain-Salaun

A danger during the interpretive process of producing the storyline is that the writer will drift beyond presenting findings into drawing conclusions about what they see. Again, the correct application of analytical procedures should help the grounded theorist to avoid adding commentary at the expense of progressing to abstraction. The researcher relies on their social and professional background to guide the interpretive process. If the potential

Box 12.4 Example of evidencing a storyline

The women felt anxious and exposed as all the patients waiting in line and those seated in the waiting room could hear what they were saying. During this time, the partners were **experiencing triage** in a different way, witnessing the care that was or was not provided to the women. The partners felt that the nursing staff were impersonal both through the language they used and the way the responded to the women and themselves.

I found that actually they were almost the same person … it was like they were reading from a script … um it didn't feel personal at all … honestly I don't know if they [the triage nurse] even looked up. (partner)

to editorialize is not kept in check, preconceived beliefs can take over from theoretical sensitivity and narrative can become narration. When this occurs, story can become commentary. The researcher will then need to reground the storyline by retracing assertions back through the analytical processes to the data.

> The storyline fostered reflexivity. While I believed I had acknowledged the presence of my professional background as an influence on my research, this lens became glaringly evident in the storyline. This was an unexpected, yet delightful reflection of the power of our life experiences and intellectual background in the qualitative research process.
>
> Jane Desborough

As this example shows, the researcher can take analytical risks in the grounded theory process while still staying grounded. Taking calculated analytical risks can be an essential element of the process; the key is to ensure that these are reflective of Suddaby's (2006) conceptual leaps of faith and not simply flights of fancy.

Embrace Variation

As a product of systematically applied research methods, a grounded theory is multidimensional, multifaceted and complex. It is not a linear, flat, lifeless account of events but rather a dynamic and variegated reflection of a phenomenon in abstract form. Development of the storyline involves the selection, sequencing and ordering of analytical artefacts to generate a valid account of the data (Vaismoradi et al., 2016). The challenge for the researcher is in rendering a storyline that does justice to the complexity inherent in the grounded theory. The easy option would be to present an ordered version of events, or to attempt to 'line up' categories to falsely imply the existence of a process. A grounded theory is rarely so simplistic, however, and attempting to present it as such will dilute the potential impact that a storyline can possess.

> For me, storyline is a way to solve a puzzle. Research data are puzzles; we find the different colours or shapes, then through coding and categorizing we find the patterns. The process is similar to the archaeologist searching for fossils, they may find many bones, these bones will eventually become something. Then the archaeologist may add more dimensions to this 'creature' such as how it behaves, how it eats and so on. The storyline brings this 'creature' to life.
>
> Intansari Nurjannah

The storyline is the narrative representation of a theory and the researcher must focus on ensuring that it has sufficient texture to reflect the multi-layered nature of the grounded theory that it seeks to exemplify. While the storyline is based on the 'whole of the data rather than isolated parts' (Vaismoradi et al., 2016, p. 107), the researcher must seek to ensure that any variation present in the data is evident. A concept has relevance because of what it brings to the theory qualitatively, regardless of how frequently it may have appeared quantitatively. A single event, incident or data segment may give a different dimension to an abstract storyline, ensuring that the research stays true to all accounts. The easy option is to present the storyline as a synthesis of homogeneous events. Doing so, however, reduces the validity of the theory, limits its reach and relevance and distances it from the data that it claims to represent.

> The use of storyline as a method turned the lights of my theory on by illuminating all the shadowy corners of the process I was endeavouring to explain. Seemingly dead or detached codes were brought to life with its light in an almost photosynthetic way, as each sentence unravelled another dimension or characteristic to the data and connected them in ways I hadn't noticed before. If software helped me to fracture the data, storyline healed it and allowed the body of data to be meaningfully connected.
>
> Nicholas Ralph

A grounded theory should do justice to the human experiences of phenomena that comprise it. Embracing variation in the presentation of a storyline fulfils this goal through breathing life into theory.

Represent Theory Visually

As mentioned previously, there are no rules that limit the way in which a storyline can be presented. As most data employed in grounded theory research is textual, often derived through interview (Ralph, Birks, & Chapman, 2014), the storyline is usually presented as a written narrative. Again, reflective of the non-linear nature of grounded theory development, diagramming and modelling are often used throughout the analytical processes to progress analysis and aid theoretical integration. While many grounded theories are modelled to provide a visual representation, often these are static figures that are not effective in expressing the element of process that is so effectively liberated by storyline. Using the storyline as the basis for designing illustrations can more fully portray the dynamic nature of a grounded theory and reinforce its explanatory capacity.

Figure 12.1 is an example of a diagram used in the study of the experiences of women experiencing possible miscarriage referred to above (Edwards, 2016). This diagram

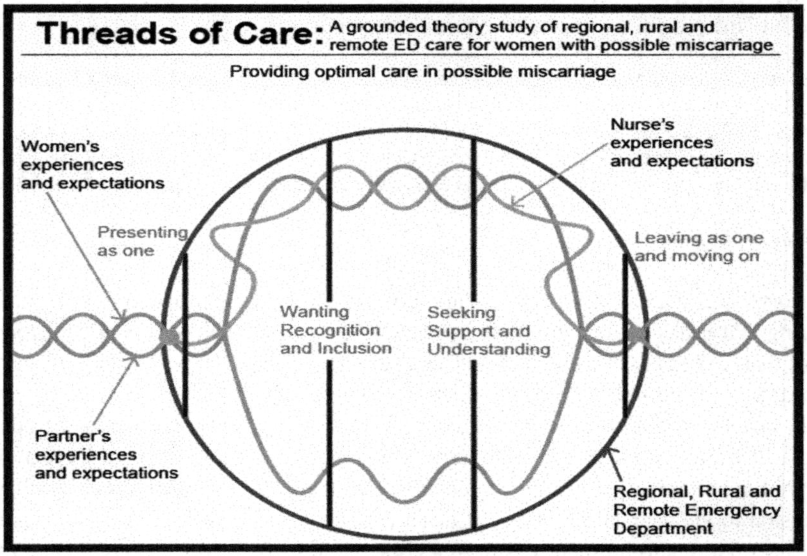

Figure 12.1 Example of a diagram used to illustrate a storyline

represents the theory of 'Threads of Care'. This theory describes the process that characterizes care of a woman and her partner when they present to an emergency department (ED) with first trimester miscarriage.

Figure 12.1 illustrates how the woman and her partner present as one to the ED but have distinct experiences as they move through this environment. They both want recognition, inclusion, support and understanding, but the care they receive is experienced in different ways. The nurses who provide care have some awareness of what is occurring yet are limited in what they can do about it. Ultimately, despite individual experiences, they leave the emergency department as one. The more detailed storyline generated from this study provides an explanation of how the process unfolds and each action and interaction contribute to the next.

Storyline aims to convey a grounded theory with clarity. Through the use of a diagram, such as the one presented as Figure 12.1, the researcher is able to visually reinforce what can often be complex processes that comprise a grounded theory.

STORYLINE AND THEORETICAL CODING

For researchers who struggle with moving their grounded theory beyond description, storyline is invaluable. As we have written elsewhere (Birks & Mills, 2015; Birks et al., 2009), storyline is also an important tool in assisting researchers as they grapple with the more advanced stages of grounded theory research. Often, researchers struggle with the final stages of integrating abstracted data into a grounded theory. Storyline provides a mechanism to support this process.

In particular, the theoretical coding that occurs during the final phases of developing a grounded theory can be difficult to grasp conceptually and apply practically. Theoretical coding is the process by which all categories and sub-categories become integrated into a final theory (Saldana, 2013). Glaser (2005) offers a number of potential theoretical codes for use in enhancing the abstraction of data to theory, but also indicates that others can be drawn from a number of disciplines.

Theoretical coding is a complex process and an important final phase in theory development. We have found that theoretical coding is less onerous when undertaken in conjunction with storyline. Glaser (2005) argues that theoretical codes should emerge during the process of sorting memos, while we suggest that these may become apparent to the researcher through a variety of analytical processes. Appropriate theoretical codes may become evident early in the analysis, but the process of theoretical coding should only occur in the final stages of theoretical integration.

Theoretical codes can be both generated and integrated into the storyline as it is developed, or a coding framework can be applied to a completed storyline. An example of the latter of these approaches was used in the study of women's experience of miscarriage referred to in the preceding examples. In that study, Swanson's Middle Range Theory of Caring (Swanson, 1991) was used to add explanatory power to the storyline. Application of that theory to the storyline enabled greater explanation and abstraction of concepts, while allowing the storyline to remain an accurate representation of the data from which it was generated.

REFLECTING ON STORYLINE IN PRACTICE

In our experience of using storyline in grounded theory research for more than a decade, we have come to appreciate its power as an analytical technique. Students and novice researchers with whom we have worked have benefited from using storyline in their grounded theory studies. We have observed that these researchers can initially struggle with the process, often stemming from the need to move from the structured mechanics of coding and category development to the more fluid and creative embodiment of the theory in narrative.

> I recall a shudder on first hearing the term 'storyline' in grounded theory as it conveyed all the wrong messages to a novice researcher wanting to be taken seriously. For a methodology that prides itself on systematically using hard-hitting methods such as constant comparative analysis, theoretical sampling and theoretical sensitivity, the notion of something as whimsical and unpredictable as a 'storyline' seemed entirely incongruent with the grounded theory I knew. In fact, the idea of how storyline could help, made about as much sense as the data in front of me. Despite me knowing 'what's going on' within a suite of categorized and codified data, no one else did. Something needed to be done to bring explanatory power to the data and storyline seemed like reasonable option.
>
> Nicholas Ralph

We seek to introduce students as early as possible to storyline. Some traditional grounded theory proponents may raise concerns that this is premature and risks the imposition of preconceptions. Rather, we have found that the opposite is true. Storyline is a powerful tool in the service of analysis and introducing it into the process at an early stage maintains the focus on theory as the endpoint of research. In so doing, its use heightens theoretical sensitivity while anchoring the storyline in the data.

> When I was told by my PhD supervisor to go and write the storyline of my theory without using any data excerpts, I was bemused and didn't understand the point she was trying to make. Once I got the point that the storyline needs to be true to the data, it all made sense.
>
> Karen Hoare

We propose that storyline is an evolutionary tool in grounded theory research. In our experience, it is key to taking grounded theory to the necessary level of abstraction. Storyline has an important place in the future of grounded theory and, in fact, in other forms of research and conceptual work more broadly.

CONCLUSION

For the novice researcher, storyline promotes analytical progress through the identification of subliminal relationships and gaps in the developing theory. For the experienced researcher, the ability to express findings through an analytical story raises the potential for the products of research to reach the reader in a meaningful way. This chapter has explored the potential that storyline offers the grounded theorist. Techniques to assist in the development of storyline have been discussed that will assist both novice and experience researchers to generating meaningful analysis of data to the point of producing an abstract theory. The chapter also described strategies for presenting credible theory that is relevant and applicable to those who are most likely to benefit from its articulation. Grounded theory is often considered the most challenging and difficult of the range of qualitative designs in a researcher's toolbox. The careful use of storyline at each stage of a grounded theory, however, will greatly assist in progressing a study to a successful and timely conclusion. With the growing popularity of using selected grounded theory methods in hybrid designs, it is important not to overlook the importance of storyline as a multi-purpose method that will allow researchers not only to integrate, but also to present a theorization of process with real-world application.

ACKNOWLEDGMENT

We would like to acknowledge the input of our former PhD candidates Dr Baldwin, Dr Chamberlain-Salaun, Dr Desborough, Dr Edwards, Associate Professor Hoare, Professor Nurjannah and Associate Professor Ralph who wrote about their experiences of using storyline. We appreciate their keen insights and thank them for their contributions to this chapter.

REFERENCES

Birks, M., & Mills, J. (2015). *Grounded theory: A practical guide* (2nd ed.). Los Angeles, CA: Sage.

Birks, M., Mills, J., Francis, K., & Chapman, Y. (2009). A thousand words paint a picture: The use of storyline in grounded theory research. *Journal of Research in Nursing*, *14*(5), 405–417.

Chamberlain-Salaun, J. (2015). *Consumers and the social world of health care: Outsiders in the expert's world: A grounded theory study*. (Dissertation/Thesis).

Charmaz, K. (2014). *Constructing grounded theory* (2nd ed.). London: Sage.

Clandinin, D.J. and Connelly, F.M. (2000). *Narrative Inquiry: Experience and Story in Qualitative Research*. Jossey-Bass, San Francisco.

Clandinin, D. J. (2006). Narrative inquiry: A methodology for studying lived experience. *Research Studies in Music Education*, *27*(1), 44–54. doi:10.1177/1321103X060270010301

Corbin, J. M., & Strauss, A. L. (2008). *Basics of qualitative research: Techniques and procedures for developing grounded theory* (3rd ed.). Los Angeles, CA: Sage.

Corbin, J. M., & Strauss, A. L. (2015). *Basics of qualitative research: Techniques and procedures for developing grounded theory* (4th ed.). Los Angeles, CA: Sage.

Cornelissen, J. P. (2017). Preserving theoretical divergence in management research: Why the explanatory potential of qualitative research should be harnessed rather than suppressed. *Journal of Management Studies*, *54*(3), 368–383.

de Casterle, B. D., Gastmans, C., Bryon, E., & Denier, Y. (2012). QUAGOL: A guide for qualitative data analysis. *International Journal of Nursing Studies*, *49*(3), 360–371.

Dey, I. (2007). Grounding categories. In A. Bryant & K. Charmaz (Eds.), *The SAGE Handbook of Grounded Theory* (pp. 167–190). Los Angeles, CA and London: Sage.

Edwards, S. (2016). Bringing together the 'threads of care' in possible miscarriage for women, their partners and nurses in non-metropolitan emergency departments (PhD thesis, James Cook University, Australia). Retrieved from https://researchonline.jcu.edu.au/48974/1/48974-edwards-2016-thesis.pdf.

Glaser, B. G. (1978). *Theoretical sensitivity: Advances in the methodology of grounded theory*. Mill Valley, CA: Sociology Press.
Glaser, B. G. (1992). *Emergence vs forcing: Basics of grounded theory analysis*. Mill Valley, CA: Sociology Press.
Glaser, B. G. (1998). *Doing grounded theory: Issues and discussions*. Mill Valley, CA: Sociology Press.
Glaser, B. G. (2002). Constructivist grounded theory? *Forum: Qualitative Social Research*, *3*(3), Art. 12.
Glaser, B. G. (2005). *The grounded theory perspective III: Theoretical coding*. Mill Valley, CA: Sociology Press.
Glaser, B. G., & Strauss, A. L. (1967). *The discovery of grounded theory: Strategies for qualitative research*. New York: Aldine.
Lips, N. (2013). Application of storylines for strategy development in flood risk management (FRM): A case study on the flooding of the island of Dordrecht (the Netherlands). Msc Thesis, Utrecht University, The Netherlands.
Liu, C. (2015). Relevant researches on tolerance of ambiguity. *Theory and Practice in Language Studies*, *5*, 1874+.
Nurjannah, I., Mills, J., Park, T., & Usher, K. (2014). Conducting a grounded theory study in a language other than English. *Sage Open*, *4*, 1–10.
Nurjannah, I., Mills, J., Park, T., & Usher, K. (2015). Human rights of the mentally ill in Indonesia. *International Nursing Review*, *62*, 153–161.
Polkinghorne, D. (1995). Narrative configuration in qualitative analysis. *International Journal of Qualitative Studies in Education*, *8*(1), 5–23. doi:10.1080/0951839950080103
Ralph, N., Birks, M., & Chapman, Y. (2014). Contextual positioning. *Sage Open*, *4*(3), 2158244014552425.
Richardson, L. (2000). Writing: A method of inquiry. In N. Denzin & Y. Lincoln (Eds.), *Handbook of Qualitative Research* (2nd ed., pp. 923–948). Thousand Oaks, CA: Sage.
Saldana, J. (2013). *The coding manual for qualitative researchers* (2nd ed.). Los Angeles, CA: Sage.
Strauss, A. L., & Corbin, J. M. (1990). *Basics of qualitative research: Grounded theory procedures and techniques*. Newbury Park, CA: Sage.
Strauss, A. L., & Corbin, J. M. (1998). *Basics of qualitative research: Techniques and procedures for developing grounded theory* (2nd ed.). Thousand Oaks, CA: Sage.
Suddaby, R. (2006). From the editors: What grounded theory is not. *Academy of Management Journal*, *49*(4), 633–642.
Swanson, K. (1991). Empirical development of middle range theory of caring. *Journal of Research Nursing*, *40*(3), 161–166.
Vaismoradi, M., Jones, J., Turunen, H., & Snelgrove, S. (2016). Theme development in qualitative content analysis and thematic analysis. *Journal of Nursing Education and Practice*, *6*(5), 100.

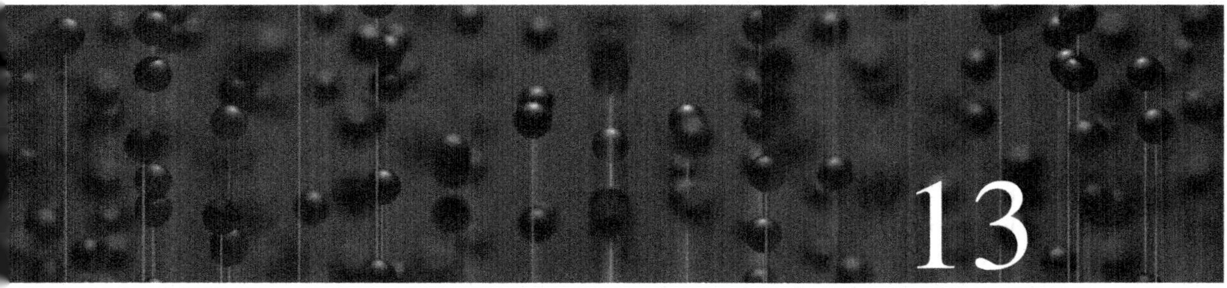

Abduction: The Logic of Discovery of Grounded Theory – An Updated Review

Jo Reichertz

> We decided to write a book about methods in the mid-1960s. We felt that changes were in the air and wanted to write for the new generation—the people over 30 were already too bound by convention. Barney was more positive about the project. I was more sceptical because I was older. The title indicates what was important to us *The Discovery of Grounded Theory* (1967): unlike the usual method books which are concerned with verification, we were more interested in the discovery of theory 'out of the data'. Grounded Theory is not a theory but a methodology to discover theories dormant in the data. (Legewie & Schervier-Legewie, 2004)[1]

Grounded theory (GT), which Anselm Strauss refers to here in an interview decades later, is one of the most successful methods ever developed and has added a more qualitative note to social research. This is, however, not a result of the clarity and simplicity of this method established by Barney Glaser and Anselm Strauss, but is rather due to the fact that it counteracts the common prejudice, which is to some extent entertained in science, that theories quasi emerge by themselves from the data (without any previous theoretical input). According to this belief, one only has to evoke the theory inherent in the data by means of suitable methods, the theory would then become apparent without the active actions of scientists. The theories are thus believed to emerge slowly in a process of gradual abstraction from the data. Therefore, one of the most famous quotations from *The Discovery of Grounded Theory* is the following: 'Clearly, a grounded theory that is faithful to the everyday realities of the substantive area is one that has been carefully induced from the data' (Glaser & Strauss 1967: 239).

Another reason for the enormous success of grounded theory appears to be that it does not include (or no longer includes[2]) a central reference text and a binding canonization. This structural openness of grounded theory is both a blessing and a curse: A blessing, because the users of the method are not bound to a specific form of working but just to general principles – which makes adaptation to the respective subject matter considerably easier. This openness is a curse because it allows anyone who does not know or does not want to know what their method of data collection exactly is but just want to perform a somehow 'open' and 'data-oriented' analysis to flag their respective practice as 'grounded theory'.

A second characteristic is closely linked to the openness of grounded theory: its '*diversity of species*'. Grounded theory has developed fast in the past few years and generated a number of variants and embodiments – and new phrases and accentuations can be found in each new edition of one of its central texts (by Glaser, Strauss, Corbin, Clarke, Charmaz) – which is why one should always read the latest versions of these books.[3] This makes it difficult to speak and assess grounded theory today. A candid reviewer will always have to specify the variant his or her assessment refers to.

Considering how grounded theory is put into practice internationally, one can currently observe at least *five* different varieties which are arranged consecutively, suggesting one may also talk about *various phases* of its development or about *different generations* of Grounded Theory (see Denzin 2007; Birks & Mills 2011, pp. 10ff.; Mey & Mruck 2011; Equit & Hohage 2016) or about a *family of methods* or *family resembles* (Bryant & Charmaz 2007a: 11).

1 *Inductively oriented* grounded theory by Barney Glaser and Anselm Strauss, advocating the idea that concepts and new theories emerge from the data without the researcher's interference (critical: Thornberg 2012). During this process of revealing a stable, hard truth, the researcher remains passive (critical: Dey 1999: 17, 35), which leads to the reasonable objection that this approach is ingrained with *Positivism* (Glaser & Strauss 1967; Glaser 2001, 2002, 2003; and Glaser & Holton 2004).
2 *Classic*[4] grounded theory by Anselm Strauss, which gradually reveals concepts and theories in a circular movement between the acquisition of theory, the gathering of data, and the interpretation of data – driven by constantly comparing each aspect to another (Strauss 1984, 1987, 1994; Strauss & Corbin 1990). This approach obviously is ingrained in American *Pragmatics* (Peirce, Dewey, Mead) and shows similarities to a *(non-reflective) sociology of knowledge* and to *social constructivism* (Berger & Luckmann 1966).
3 *Code-oriented* grounded theory by the late Anselm Strauss and Juliet Corbin[5] and mainly Juliet Corbin, the primary aim of which is to condense and categorize data by means of codes. This approach emphasizes precision, and strongly resembles *qualitative analysis of content*. This variety of Grounded Theory may most likely be linked to QDA-software, e.g., ATLAS.ti, MAXQDA (Strauss & Corbin 1998; Corbin & Strauss 2008 and 2015 – and especially Corbin 2011).
4 *Constructivist* grounded theory (Bryant 2002; Charmaz 2006, 2014; Bryant & Charmaz 2007a, 2007b; Charmaz & Keller 2016), which especially criticizes the inductive approach of the former grounded theory methodology and moreover critically scrutinizes the capability of code routines. This approach (referring to pragmatism and the concept of abduction) considers research work as a search of patterns and best explanations in making comparisons and interpretations – and hence as a process which is always bound to a perspective and which is communicative. This approach shows similarities to a *reflective sociology of knowledge* and the *communicative constructivism* (Reichertz 2004b; Keller, Knoblauch & Reichertz 2012).
5 *Postmodern, situative* grounded theory (Clarke 2005, 2007; Clarke & Keller 2014), which is explicitly not only concerned with people/social actors and their perspectives but also with artefacts, practices and discourses. It emphasizes that research is mainly a mutual *communicative* process of construction between researchers *and* the researched. This approach shows many

similarities with a *reflexive sociology of knowledge*, the *discourse analysis* and the communicative constructivism (Reichertz 2009; Keller et al. 2012).

In the past few years, a central question discussed in GT in addition to questions of theory development and the concrete coding practice of GT was whether GT is based on an abductive research logic (Charmaz 2006, 2014; Reichertz 2007; Tavory & Timmermans 2014; Atkinson 2015). It is indeed important to answer this question because it will depend on this answer if the results of GT can unveil anything new at all.

Therefore, the purpose of this chapter is to examine whether the logic of the various variants of GTM is actually abductive. This might contribute to a better understanding of the nature of empirical GT construction.

Thus, my thesis is that GT was to a very small extent abductive from the start and has become more and more abductive in its more recent stages. The controversy within GT can be characterized, at least in part, as one between induction and abduction.

ABDUCTION: A RULE-GOVERNED WAY TO NEW KNOWLEDGE

Social researchers who take an interest in the fluctuation of their own professional vocabulary have been able, for more than two decades, to witness the flourishing of a concept which is around 400 years old: it concerns the term *abduction*. The boom has been so significant that we sometimes hear talk of an 'abductive turn' (Reichertz 2004a, 2014). First introduced in 1597 by Julius Pacius to translate the Aristotelian concept *apagoge*, abduction remained quite unnoticed for almost three centuries. It was Charles Sanders Peirce (1839–1914) who first took it up and used it to denote the only truly *knowledge-extending* means of inferencing (so he claimed) that would be categorically distinct from the normal types of logical conclusion, namely *deduction* and *induction* (Peirce 1929, 1976, 1992). Several decades were to pass before Peirce's ideas were systematically received and adopted (Fann 1970; Anderson 1995; Reichertz 2004a, 2007, 2014; Chauviré 2005; Nubiola 2005; Paavola 2011; Plutynski 2011).

Today the term 'abduction' has become something of a catchword within social research (but not only there), although often even experienced researchers say they do not really understand what it means: educationists, linguists, psychologists, psychoanalysts, semioticians, theatre-scientists, theologians, criminologists, researchers in artificial intelligence, and sociologists announce in their research reports that their new discoveries are due to abduction. The great success of abduction, in my opinion, may be traced back to two particular features: first, to its indefiniteness and, second, to the misjudgement of the achievements of abduction that derive from this. Frequently, the use of the idea of abduction has led many of its users to one particular hope, that of a *rule-governed* and *replicable* production of new and *valid* knowledge. This hope is found, above all, in artificial intelligence research and in a number of variants of qualitative social research.

These approaches have in common that they stress both the *logical* and also the *innovative* character of abduction. For abduction is no longer treated as a traditional, classical means of drawing conclusions, but as a new method that is not yet incorporated into formal logic. However, it is, in every sense, a means of inferencing. It is precisely in this quality of being a 'means-of-inferencing' that we find the secret charm of abduction: it is a *logical* inference (and thereby reasonable and scientific), although it extends into the realm of profound insight (and therefore generates new knowledge). The secret charm of abduction lies straight in this kind of being a (logical) inference and extending to insight at the same time: abduction is sensible and scientific as a form of inference; however, it reaches to the sphere of deep insight and new knowledge. Abduction is intended to help social research, or rather social researchers, to be able to make new discoveries in a logically and methodologically ordered way – and without any doubt it leads to inventions and creations as well.

This hope, to be able to make new discoveries in a logically and methodologically ordered way, is directed against Reichenbach (1938) and Popper (1934/2002), who, by separating the logic of discovery from the logic of justification, 'drove' the first into the realm of psychology and allowed only the second into the realm of serious science. This separation should be reversed: the unfortunate disjunction of contexts of discovery and justification should be removed by means of abduction. A rethinking of this kind promises a great deal: liberation from the 'chance of a good idea' (Habermas 1973: 147), and (it is hoped) 'synthetic inferences *a posteriori*'. Kant still said that knowledge increasing conclusions (synthetic inferences) from experience (a posteriori) are *not* possible (Kant 2007). Abductive conclusions, however, promise exactly this: one must no longer wait for the lucky good idea, but one can, on the basis of experience, gain knowledge about the world – and this in a logically regulated way.

Because of this hope many social scientists have treated, and still do treat, abduction as a magic formula: always applicable when the cognitive basis of the process of scientific discovery is being investigated: 'The attempt to no longer characterize the act of hypothesis generation and subjective recognition only than arbitrary and not further analyzable, but capture it analytically in form of the abductive conclusion can perhaps point the way in a direction, which is in the humanities well-known as hermeneutic procedure for gaining knowledge' (Kreppner 1975: 69; see Reichertz 2004b). In my opinion, however, this hope is the result of a widespread misunderstanding of Peirce's position with regard to the differences between 'hypothesis' and 'abduction' as forms of inference. From the modern point of view, it is beyond question that, up to about 1898, Peirce combined two very different forms of inference under the name of 'hypothesis' (Peirce 1929). When he became aware of this unclear use of the term 'hypothesis', he elaborated a clear distinction in his later philosophy between the two procedures, and called the one operation 'qualitative induction' and the other 'abduction' (for more detail see Reichertz 2013, 2014; also Eco 1985). Many social scientists, with reference to the *achievements* of abduction, rely on Peirce's later work (in my view wrongly), but with reference to its *form* and *validity*, on his work on hypothesis. It is only on the basis of this 'hybrid meaning' that they succeed in designing a logical operation which produces new knowledge in a rule-governed way.

DEDUCTION, QUANTITATIVE AND QUALITATIVE INDUCTION, ABDUCTION

The social order around which humans (often but not always) orient themselves in their actions is constantly changing and is, moreover, 'sub-culturally fragmented' in the sense, that each sub-culture develops its own symbolic and social order. The different order(s) therefore possess only a localized validity and are continually and, since the advent of the 'modern', with increasing rapidity being changed by individuals who previously (up to a point) adhered to them (Eisenstadt 2003; Foucault 2004). Moreover, both the *form* and the *validity* of this order are bound to the meaning attributions and interpretations of the acting subjects. Social science explanations of actions aim at the (re)construction (and some aim at the deconstruction) of the order that is relevant to the acting subjects. Admittedly this kind of order can no longer be derived from proven grand theories, first, because these are, as a rule, not sufficiently 'local', and, second, because they have frequently already been overtaken by constant social change. Thus, suitable new views of the structure of social order must constantly be generated. For this reason, it is highly sensible to examine as closely as possible the everyday practical doings that is to be understood and (on the basis of these data) to (re-)construct the *new* orders. It is obvious that the examination must start from older views and so have some link to them.

If we are now to make a serious attempt in research to evaluate collected data, in other words, to *typologize* them according to particular features and orders of features, the question very soon arises of how we may bring a little order to the chaos of the data. This is only to a very small extent a matter of work organization (sorting of data) and much more a question of how the unmanageable variety of the data may be related to theories: either pre-existing or still to be discovered. In this undertaking (if one pursues the ideas of Peirce) we may, in ideal terms, distinguish *three* procedures and, in what follows, I shall subdivide the second procedure into two sub-groups; not because there are fundamental differences between the two, but rather because in this way the difference we have already spoken of between *abduction* and *hypothesis* or *qualitative induction* can be made clearer (for a fuller discussion of this, see Reichertz 2004a, 2013, 2014).

Subsumption

One type of data analysis consists of the procedure of *subsumption*. Subsumption proceeds from an already known context of features, that is from a familiar *rule* (e.g., all burglars who steal from a medicine chest are drug addicts), and seeks to find this general context in the data (e.g., the unknown burglar has robbed the medicine chest) in order to obtain knowledge about the individual case (e.g., the unknown burglar is a drug addict). The logical form of this intellectual operation is that of *deduction*: the single case in question is subjected to a known rule. Here a tried-and-trusted order is applied to the new case. New facts (concerning the order of the world) are not experienced in this way; we have deduced that the unknown burglar is a drug addict (knowledge that may be quite useful to the police, if the rule is true). Deductions are therefore *tautological*, they tell us nothing new. However, deductions are not only tautological but also *truth-conveying*: if the rule offered for application is valid, then the result of the application of the rule is also valid.

Generalizing

A second form of analysis consists of extending, or *generalizing*, into an order or rule the combinations of features that are found in the data material. Proceeding from the observation that 'in the case of burglaries a, b, and c the medicine chest was robbed'; and the case-knowledge that 'Mr Jones committed burglaries a, b, and c', the inference is drawn that 'Mr Jones always robs the medicine chest when he breaks in'. The logical form of this intellectual operation is that of *quantitative induction*. It transfers the quantitative properties of a *sample* to a totality, it 'extends' the single case into a rule. *Quantitative inductions*, therefore, are equally tautological but not truth-conveying. The results of this form of inferencing are merely *probable*.

One particular variant of the inductive processing of data consists of assembling certain qualitative features of the investigated sample in such a way that this combination of features resembles another (that is already available in the repertoire of knowledge of the interacting community) in essential points. In this case, one can use the term that already exists for this combination to characterize one's 'own' form. The logical form of this operation is that of *qualitative induction*. The existence of certain qualitative features in a *sample* implies the presence of other features (e.g., at the scene of a crime I see a particular set of clues. In very many respects these agree with the pattern of clues associated with Mr Jones. Conclusion: Jones is responsible for the clues). The observed case (*token*) is an instance of a known order (*type*). To summarize: if *quantitative induction* makes inferences about a totality from the quantitative properties of a *sample*, qualitative induction (in contrast) supplements the observed features of a sample with others that are not perceived. It is only in this sense that this form of induction transcends the borders of experience, that is, the experience of the sample in question. This inference only extends knowledge to the extent that it proceeds from a limited selection to a larger totality. *Qualitative induction* is not a valid but only a probable form of inference, although it does have the advantage of being capable of operationalization (albeit with difficulty). Qualitative induction is the basis of all scientific procedures that find, in collected data, only new versions of what is already known.

Abduction

The third type of data processing (apparently similar, but in fact totally different) consists of assembling or discovering, on the basis of an interpretation of collected data, such combinations of features for which there is no appropriate explanation or rule in the store of knowledge that already exists. This causes surprise. Real surprise causes a genuine shock (and not only in Peirce's opinion) and the search for the (new) explanation. Since no suitable 'type' can be found, a new one must be invented or discovered by means of a mental process. One may achieve a discovery of this sort as a result of an intellectual process and, if this happens, it takes place 'like lightning', and the thought process 'is very little hampered by logical rules' (Peirce 1931–1935, Vol. 5: 117). An order, or a rule, in this procedure must therefore first be discovered or invented, and this has to happen with the aid of intellectual effort. Something previously or initially unintelligible is discovered in the data and, on the basis of the mental design of a *new* rule, the rule is discovered or invented and, simultaneously, it becomes clear what the case is. The logical form of this operation is that of *abduction*. Here one has decided (with whatever degree of awareness and for whatever reason) no longer to adhere to the conventional view of things. This way of creating a new 'type' (the relationship of a typical new combination of features) is a creative outcome which engenders a new idea. This kind of association is not obligatory, and is indeed rather risky. *Abduction* 'proceeds', therefore, from a known quantity (= result) to *two* unknowns (= rule and case). Abduction is therefore a cerebral process, an intellectual act, a mental leap, that brings together things which one had never associated with one another: a cognitive logic of discovery.

TWO STRATEGIES FOR PRODUCING ABDUCTIONS

If one is to take seriously what has been outlined above, one would have to come to the conclusion (pessimistic though it might be for everyday scientific practice) that abductive discovery of new things is dependent either on pure chance, a benevolent God, a favorable evolution, or a particularly well-endowed brain. Science as a *systematic* endeavor would, according to this definition, seem doomed to failure. However, even if one cannot *force* lightning to strike in an algorithmically rule-governed way, could there perhaps be ways of proceeding and precautions that would make it easier for the (intellectual) lightning to strike? Even lightning is not entirely unexpected. To extend the metaphor, it happens only as a consequence of a particular meteorological situation. In a storm one can look for an oak tree or seek out the beeches or even go to the top of the church tower. None of these steps will make it certain that lightning will come and strike; but the likelihood is nonetheless very much greater than with someone who only loves the sunlight, who always takes refuge in a basement during a storm, and who (if he does happen to find himself in a storm) always tries to find out where the nearest lightning conductor is. In short, if discovery is truly related to accidents, then one can either give accidents a chance or deny or reduce the possibility.

Peirce himself cites two *macro-strategies* that are particularly well suited to 'enticing' abductive processes or at least to creating a favourable climate for their appearance. One can be derived from the story where Peirce talks retrospectively about his talents as an amateur detective (Peirce 1929). Peirce tells how, during a voyage at sea, his overcoat and a valuable watch were stolen. He was very alarmed, because the watch was not his own property. He therefore decided to recover the watch, by any means and as quickly as possible. He had all the crew called together and asked them to form up in a line. Then he walked along the line and addressed a few apparently inconsequential words to each of them.

> When I had gone through the row, I turned and walked from them, though not away, and said to myself: 'Not the least scintilla of light have I got to go upon'. But thereupon my other self (for our own communings are always in dialogues) said to me, 'but you simply *must* put your finger on the man. No matter if you have no reason, you must say whom you think to be the thief'. I made a little loop in my walk, which had not taken a minute, and I turned toward them, all shadow of doubt had vanished. (Peirce 1929: 271)

Peirce named one person as the culprit and subsequently, after a great deal of confusion (see Sebeok & Umiker-Sebeok 1979 for a full description), it emerged that the man suspected by Peirce was indeed the thief. The stimulus for this individual initiative in matters of 'detection' was therefore provided by *fear*: not the fear of losing the value of the watch, but the fear of a 'life-long professional disgrace' (Peirce 1929: 270). When, after his first conversations with the crew, he could not name a suspect, he increased, by an act of will, his pressure to do something. In this partially self-induced emergency situation, the abductive lightning struck.

Of course, abductions cannot be forced by a specific procedural program, but one can induce situations (and this is the moral of this episode) in which abductions fit. According to Peirce, the presence of *genuine doubt* or *uncertainty* or *fear* or *great pressure to act* is a favorable 'weather situation' for abductive lightning to strike. Peirce, however, develops another possible way of creating situations in which new knowledge may more frequently be obtained. For this to work the investigator, as Peirce advises, should let his mind wander with no specific goal. This mental game without rules he calls 'musement', a game of meditation, or daydreaming. How one achieves the condition of daydreaming may be seen in the following passage:

> Enter your skiff of musement, push off into the lake of thought, and leave the breath of heaven to swell your sail. With your eyes open, awake to what is about or within you, and open conversation with yourself: for such is all meditation! ... It is, however, not a conversation in words alone, but is illustrated, like a lecture, with diagrams and with experiments. (Peirce 1931–1935, Vol. 6: 315)

To do this requires leisure, that is to say, freedom from an immediate pressure to act is a fundamental condition without which the skiff will not be able to embark. This apparently contradicts quite vehemently the conditions for successful abductions which Peirce sets out in his detection example. Admittedly, the contradiction is resolved if one looks for what is typical in the two 'abduction-friendly' settings. In both cases the procedures mean that the *consciously working mind*, relying on logical rules, is outmaneuvered. Peirce-the-detective allows no time for the calculating mind to busy itself with the solution of his problem, and Peirce-the-daydreamer switches off his power of logical judgment by entrusting himself to the 'breath of heaven'.

All measures designed to create favorable conditions for abductions, therefore, always aim at one thing: the achievement of an *attitude* of preparedness to abandon old convictions and to seek new ones. Abductive inferencing is not, therefore, a *mode of reasoning* that delivers new knowledge, and neither is it an *exact* method that assists in the generation of *logically ordered* (and therefore operationalizable) hypotheses or some new theory. Abductive inferencing is, rather, an attitude towards data and towards one's own knowledge: data are to be taken seriously, and the validity of previously developed knowledge is to be questioned. It is a state of preparedness for being taken unprepared.

RESEARCH RESULTS: RECONSTRUCTION OR CONSTRUCTION?

Abductive efforts seek some (new) order, but they do not aim at the construction of *any* order, but at the discovery of an order which *fits* the surprising facts; or, more precisely, which solves the practical problems that arise from these. The justification for this selective attention (which targets a new order) is not the greatest possible closeness to reality or the highest possible rationality. The justification is, above all, the *usefulness* which the 'type' that is developed brings to the question of interest. It can bring order and the means of linguistic representation. However, these new 'types' are indispensable tools if one is to be able to make predictions about the future on the basis of a past that is hypothetically understood because it is ordered: they are indispensable when it is a matter of producing answers to the question of 'what to do next?' New orders, therefore, are also always oriented towards future action.

An abductive discovered order, therefore, is neither a (pure) reflection of reality, nor does it reduce reality to its most important components. Instead, the orders obtained are *mental constructs* with which one can live comfortably or less comfortably. Abduction is something we all do when there is a crisis or when we do not know what to do next. For many purposes, particular constructs are of use, and for other purposes, different constructs are helpful. For this reason, the search for order is never definitively complete and is always undertaken provisionally. So long as the new order is helpful in the completion of a task, it is allowed to remain in force: if its value is limited, distinctions must be made; if it shows itself to be useless, it is abandoned. In this sense, abductively discovered orders are neither (preferred) constructions nor (valid) reconstructions, but *usable* (re-)constructions.

When faced with surprising facts, abduction leads us to look for meaning-creating rules, for a possibly valid or fitting explanation that eliminates what is surprising about the facts. The endpoint of this search is a (verbal) hypothesis. Once this is found, a multistage process of checking begins. If the first step in the process of scientific discovery consists of finding a hypothesis by means of abduction, then the second step consists of *deriving predictions* from the hypothesis, which is deduction, and the third step consists of *searching for facts* that will 'verify' the assumptions, which is induction. If the facts cannot be found the process begins again, and this is repeated as often as necessary until 'fitting' facts are attained. With this definition Peirce designed a three-stage discovery procedure consisting of abduction, deduction, and induction.

Finding and checking are, in Peirce's opinion, *two* distinct parts of a *single* process of discovery or research. If the finding stage is largely a result of a conscious and systematic approach, checking takes place according to operationalizable and rule-governed standards that are controlled by reason. *Certainty* about the validity of abductive inferences, however, cannot be achieved even if one subjects an abductively developed hypothesis to extensive testing; that is to say, deduces it from its consequences, then seeks to determine these inductively, and then repeats these three steps many times. Verification in the strict sense of the word cannot be done in this way. All that one can achieve, using this procedure, is an intersubjectively constructed and shared 'truth'. In Peirce's opinion, even this is only reached if *all* members of a society have come to the same *conviction*. Since, in Peirce's work, 'all' includes even those who were born after us, the process of checking can in principle never be completed. For Peirce, certainty can never be achieved so: 'infallibility in scientific matters seems to me irresistibly comic' (Peirce 1931–1935, Vol. I: X).

Do the Terms 'Abduction' and 'Serendipity' Denote the Same Concept?

Some more recent publications liken 'abduction' to 'serendipity' (e.g., Bryant & Charmaz 2007a: 23). This is relevant in the context discussed here because Glaser and Strauss have made very early and clear statements on whether grounded theory has something in common with 'serendipity'. In a brief discussion of Merton's description of 'serendipity', they quite unambiguously say: 'Merton never reached the notion of the discovery of grounded theory in discussing the "theoretic functions of research". The closest he came was with "serendipity"; that is, unanticipated, anomalous, and strategic finding gives rise to a new hypothesis. This concept does not catch the idea of purposefully discovering theory through social research. It puts the discovery of a single hypothesis on a surprise basis' (Glaser & Strauss 1967: 2). The main distinctive feature therefore is 'purposefully'. This means that grounded theory does not lead to accidental discovery, but is intentional and systematic[6] – serendipity is not needed in grounded theory – though often also GTM researchers find surprising results in their work, quite unintentionally. Grounded theory, as Glaser and Strauss see it, is not an aimless endeavor, not an arrow shot into the blue, but a targeted and systematically acting, data-driven scientific search for a theory. The distinction Glaser and Strauss are making is the question if research findings come about by intent or by accident. But this is beside the point when it comes to the special nature of abductive thinking. The special nature of abductive thinking is to *find the novel*.

'Serendipity', in the meaning of the person who named it, Horace Walpole (1717–1797), who seeks to document the special feat by the three princes of Serendip in the discovery of a runaway camel (see Merton & Barber 2004), does not denote the systematic search for something as yet unknown, but finder's luck: Serendipity is a term for a situation in which you find something that you did not look for and did not expect, something that fell into your lap when you were not looking for anything, but when your mind is prepared to find anything. 'Serendipity', therefore, is not the kind of thinking that brings a novel idea into the world (like abduction) but the thinking that leads to find something valuable other than what you were looking for – which (as the history of scientific discoveries shows – e.g., the invention of Scotch tape, Velcro fastener, the tea bag, etc.) most frequently occurs in the sciences which look for concrete objects. The difference between 'serendipity' and abduction becomes particularly apparent here. As shown above, the special nature of abductive thinking is precisely not to find something by lucky coincidence (which can certainly happen) but that it brings *a novel idea* into the world. Serendipity owes its existence to lucky coincidence, Abduction, however, to hard work. And that is something completely different. This is why serendipity cannot be put on the same level with abduction.

THE DIFFERENCE BETWEEN AN INDUCTIVE AND AN ABDUCTIVE RESEARCH STRATEGY

What now is the difference between an inductive and an abductive approach to research? The difference between an inductive and an abductive research strategy is critical for research, not just because an abductive attitude is important for *discovering something new*. More importantly, the logic behind one's thinking makes a difference in theory development. Induction merely generalizes what has been found in the data (including what has been heard and seen), so it doubles the amount of data, although in a more abstract manner. Abductive inferencing does not double the amount of data but *construes* a concept, an idea, a theory which makes the action the data represent comprehensible and explains it. Research that takes an abductive approach makes action comprehensible by indicating the regularities this action is based on, making its motives apparent, to an extent far beyond what the acting individuals themselves are aware of.

Abductive research also uses interviews in this business. However, it does not condense interview statements into theories but uses the interviews to design theories which make actions and interview statements comprehensible: the path from data to a theory always involves a 'leap into the uncertain'. Abductions do not emerge on their own; they result from much analytical work and knowledge.

In addition, abductive research always considers the *situation* of the data collection in each data analysis, i.e., it takes into account that interviews are always justifications to an interviewer in specific situations, and that each statement in an interview is the result of a joint communicative construction of reality (Keller et al. 2012). Researchers, therefore, are always co-producers of the ideas of reality the respondents have.

A central and often unpronounced premise of inductive procedure is that the actors are willing and able to describe and explain their past actions and their motivation to the interviewer. Almost all components of this far-reaching premise can be doubted for good reasons, however. First, humans cannot accurately describe past actions even if they want to, since the human memory only stores what it likes or what fits to what has been stored before. Memorizing and forgetting are quite inventive in this respect. Second, humans typically do not want to disclose their actions, let alone their motives, to others. What they tell others always is a part of their image they present to others and with others. Scientists are not microphones that just record what they have heard; interviewers are always relevant people who take a position to what they have heard when they are silent or when they try to hide with all means that they interpret and evaluate in addition to listening.

Of decisive importance for the question whether any concept of GTM makes use of abductive thinking is therefore (a) whether it provides opportunities for the emergence of abductive conclusions at the level of single thinking acts, i.e., during concrete coding acts, or (b) whether the logic of research as a whole is abductive or not. Thus, the central issue is neither whether GT works abductively in all cases and in all fields (this would be nonsense), nor whether one is allowed to revert to knowledge apart from the data (this primarily pertains to qualitative induction), but whether GT systematically counts on the appearance of new codes or hypotheses. 'Abductive' here does not simply mean that the research data are taken seriously and that the findings have to fit the data (this must be accomplished by all serious research), but essentially that the research is laid out in such a way that new hypotheses can and do appear at every level, that the interpretation of the data is not finalized at an early stage but that new codes, categories, and theories can be developed and redeveloped if necessary.

THE GLASERIAN CONCEPT OF GT AND PEIRCE'S LOGIC OF RESEARCH

In early GTM there were two strands: an inductive one, which worked on the assumption that categories and even theories emerge out of the data if only one looks closely enough, and a theoretical strand, which banked on the fact that prior knowledge about the world and scientific theories (apart from the data) are useful (cf. Kelle 2005). In the later classic variant of GT by Strauss (1987) and Strauss and Corbin (1990 and 1998), one can find both strands, the inductive and the 'theoretical' one, but with reversed emphasis. In the inductive variant by Glaser and Strauss (1967) and especially later in the writings of Glaser himself, knowledge concepts or theories were officially and explicitly only founded on induction[7]: 'I wish to remind people, yet again, that classic GT is simply a set of integrated conceptual hypotheses systematically generated to produce an inductive theory about a substantive area' (Glaser & Holton 2004: [7]).

Glaser, who still insists on the exclusively inductive character of grounded theory, rejects any use of theory prior to analysis: 'To undertake an extensive review of literature before the emergence of a core category violates the basic premise of GT—that being, the theory emerges from the data not from extant theory' (Glaser & Holton 2004: [46]; see also Glaser 1992).

Barney Glaser maintains here that a researcher, if he or she does his or her research properly, that is in the way Glaser prescribes, is a type of induction machine. A researcher inductively condenses data, adds nothing to it in the process, only abstracts, filters out the unessential. So he or she by no means complements anything, e.g., something he or she has seen or known before; it is all just induction. Glaser apparently thinks that inductive thinking is a logical operation devoid of content that does not add anything to the data but only infers from the individual observation to the general concept. This idea of induction is not in line with the current state of discussion, and certainly not with the considerations on the various forms of induction which Peirce described in great detail and in ever new approaches at the beginning of the past century (Peirce 1992). According to these, induction does not just require a wealth of knowledge of the world, but also knowledge about which features of the phenomena observed are relevant and which are not.

When you hear a noise, it takes quite some knowledge of the world to determine by induction that this noise is the clopping of hooves. Even more such knowledge of the world is needed to be able to discern that the clopping hooves are those of horses rather than zebras. In short: each induction requires a wealth of knowledge to be able to infer. Straightforwardly put: someone who knows nothing about this world will not be able to say anything about the particularities of this world (Reichertz 2014). But whoever thinks that excluding explicit and scientific knowledge would result in interpretation without knowledge generally fails to see that such a position just leaves the individual to his or her unreflected common-sense knowledge, so the fundamentals of research are not obtained reflectively but left to chance or the individual's superficial knowledge of the world he or she lives in.

By demanding that, when practicing grounded theory, one must not add anything to the data, that one has to take the data as is, has to take the data seriously, and may just condense the data, Glaser (contrary to an abundance of his explicit statements[8]) re-introduces the concepts of reality, truth, and findings through the back door. One potential conclusion is: whoever does not add anything to the data (as Glaser wants it), will describe things the way they are, the way they really are. Only if something is added to the data (so Glaser), it becomes contaminated and you do not learn anything any more about the world but about the theories that are added to the data.

THE STRAUSS CONCEPT OF GT AND PEIRCE'S LOGIC OF RESEARCH

Anselm Strauss moved more and more clearly away from his inductive self-misunderstanding in his later works (Strauss 1984, 1987) and pointed out that any theory development without prior knowledge will be in vain. On the contrary, Strauss encouraged researchers to utilize any and all types of contextual knowledge:

> These experiential data should not be ignored because of the usual canons governing research (which regard personal experience and the data as likely to bias the research), for those canons lead to the squashing of valuable experiential data. We say, rather, 'Mine your

> experience, there is a potential gold there!' Experiential data are essential data, as we shall see, because they not only give added theoretical sensitivity but provide a wealth of provisional suggestions for making comparisons, finding variations, and sampling widely on theoretical grounds .... All of that helps the researcher eventually to formulate a conceptually dense and carefully ordered theory. (Strauss 1987: 11)

To observe and to theorize, in Strauss's grounded theory, means to turn towards, and have every sympathy for the institutions and organizations or the small social worlds within one's own culture to be examined. The position from which researchers view their subject matter is that of well-meaning contemporaries knowledgeable of, or close to, the respective culture; who look for meaning true to Max Weber's slogan that the actions of the people in their environments always have a meaning, the task is to find it. They observe the people's actions thoroughly and in detail to find that meaning. They focus in particular on small gestures and incidents and try to determine what the meaning is of all this for the people in the institutions and in the small social worlds. And because of this, Strauss's variant of grounded theory is understanding and reconstructive. The analysis of the researchers does not stop at statements by each of the respondents (and maybe just doubles them), and it does not just focus on their motives and wishes. Instead, it keeps trying to discover the social order, the trajectory and meaningfulness of the whole.

But Strauss is also expressly interested in finding the novel. If one takes a closer look at the work of Strauss (1987) and Strauss and Corbin (1990) to see whether there are methodical routines and practices within GT which favor the appearance of new hypotheses, much evidence can be found. In Strauss's work, one can find repeated references at the level of the research logic to a permanent testing of inferences that once are decided. Data elevation, coding, and the making of memos are related to each other in a three-step process: The consequences are derived from the hypotheses found by means of deduction; these have to be determined inductively in the data and by means of data analysis. This exactly corresponds to the logic of 'abductive' research:

> ...data collection leads quickly to coding, which in turn may lead equally quickly, or at least soon, to memoing. Either will then guide the searches for new data. Or they may lead directly to additional coding or memoing. Or—please note!—they may lead to inspecting and coding of already gathered (and perhaps already analysed) data. That latter kind of 'return to the old data' can occur at any phase of the research, right down to writing the last page of the final report of the theory. (Strauss 1984: Unit 1, 18)

Furthermore, recurring references to the necessity of not only relying on existing knowledge but of creating new codes, categories, and theories can also be found in the work of Strauss and Strauss and Corbin: 'Creativity is also a vital component of the grounded theory method. Its procedures force the researcher to break through assumptions and to create new order out of the old. Creativity manifests itself in the ability of the researcher to aptly name categories; and also to let the mind wander and make the free associations that are necessary for generating stimulating questions and for coming up with a comparison that leads to discovery' (Strauss & Corbin 1990: 27). The wording itself already reveals how close the ideas of Strauss and Peirce are.

In Strauss's GT one can find (in addition to the coding and the development of theories of a middle or long range) two intellectual operations: the finding of similarity (coding in known codes) and the development of the new (creating new codes). This kind of scientific work has its parallel in the distinction between *qualitative induction* and *abduction* as made by Peirce. The operation, the intellectual jump which 'states' things in common between acquaintance and data and codes in already known concepts is the first step: the qualitative induction (as executed above). This thinking act adds something to the data too. The second step is the intellectual jump which adds something very new to the data, something that they do not contain and that does not already exist as a concept or theory either. This is abduction.

The question whether GT (in the variant of Strauss and the early Strauss and Corbin) contains an abductive research logic can therefore be answered with a resounding 'yes'. Fortunately, however, it does not only contain the logic of abductive reasoning but also that of qualitative induction. The logic of Strauss's GT thus permits abductive reasoning, counts on it, enables it, grants it place. More is not necessary.

WHY DID STRAUSS NOT USE THE TERM 'ABDUCTION'?

One can, in conclusion, wonder why Strauss did not further develop the ideas of Peirce on abduction. Strauss undoubtedly knew the idea of abduction, because he mentioned it in his work at least once. In connection with the question where our knowledge for induction, deduction, and verification comes from, Strauss stated (and this is indeed an important but not the crucial determinant for his variant of GT) that this knowledge is nurtured by experience, but it can also derive from previous theoretical knowledge. 'They come from experience with this kind of phenomenon before—whether the experience is personal, or derives more 'professionally' from actual exploratory research into the phenomenon, from the previous research program, or from theoretical sensitivity because of the researcher's knowledge of technical literature' (Strauss 1987: 12). Strauss adds in a footnote here: 'See the writings of Charles Peirce, the American pragmatist, whose concept of abduction strongly emphasized the crucial role of experience in the first phase of research operations' (Strauss 1987: 12).

For Peirce, the fact that intellectual operations are nurtured by knowledge of every kind in the phase of discovery is not decisive for defining abduction. However, it is of crucial importance for him that new knowledge can be generated by means of this operation. The notion 'abduction' does not yet appear in 'Study Letters of the FernUniversität' in *Qualitative Analysis in Social Research: Grounded Theory Methodology* (Strauss 1984). In later documents, Strauss does without the explicit idea of abduction. Why did Strauss not use this term before? As a pragmatist, he would have had good reasons (and many opportunities) to see the parallels between his way of coding (particularly open and selective coding) as well as his type of generating theory by 'coherent perception' and the abductive reasoning of Peirce.

The following consideration might illuminate the sudden but brief appearance of the word 'abduction' in the work of Strauss (which, if correct, is explained by this surprising fact): Anselm Strauss became acquainted with pragmatism and its research logic via Blumer via Dewey[9]. Furthermore 'Strauss was introduced to the work of Dewey and James by Floyd House, his teacher while he was an undergraduate at the University of Virginia between 1935 and 1939' (Bryant 2017: 80). Strauss also mentions the influence of Peirce in some passages (see Reichertz & Wilz 2016; Bryant 2017: 80), but his notes are always very general. There is no evidence that Strauss has systematically studied the writings of Peirce, but Strauss's lack of reference to Peirce did not mean a lack of knowledge: Strauss primarily knew Peirce as an action theorist, a semiotician, and a logician, so that for him (Strauss) as an empiricist and 'working sociologist' in the tradition of the Chicago School there was no real need to look for notes in the work of Peirce as far as the logic of discovery is concerned. Strauss knew the concept of abduction from at least 1968[10] and when he got to know it, he saw the parallels to his form of coding and generating theories, but he did not further expound on these parallels. If he saw the chance to build a methodological basis (as a general theory) for his GT with the abductive research logic, he did not use it, possibly because (due to restricted time resources) he focused on convincing other researchers of the fertility of its methodology and methods, rather than on coordinating its procedure with the conceptualities of the dominant methodology and on consolidating it against criticism.

An insignificant, but nonetheless interesting, question is why Strauss used the term 'abduction' so many years later. My hypothesis (as a result of an abduction) is that *the explicit use* of the term 'abduction' (for a short time) found its way into grounded theory methodology via Germany. The following reasons support this hypothesis: A study visit of Anselm Strauss to Germany fell in the time between Study Letters (written in 1982/1983 and published in 1984) and the publication of *Qualitative Analysis for Social Scientists* (1987). During this study visit he exchanged thoughts with the research teams of Richard Grathoff (University of Bielefeld), Fritz Schütze (University of Kassel), and Hans-Georg Soeffner (FernUniversität Hagen). At that time, all of the above-mentioned researchers dealt with the features of abductive reasoning and my guess is, that the discussions in Germany sharpened his thinking about abduction.

THE CORBIN CONCEPT OF GT AND PEIRCE'S LOGIC OF RESEARCH

Juliet Corbin, who initially together with Strauss represented the classic variant of grounded theory (Strauss & Corbin 1990 and 1998), has modified it over the years and developed her own variant, which clearly differs from the initial approach. It is therefore correct that the third and fourth editions of *Basics of Qualitative Research* no longer listed Strauss and Corbin but instead Corbin and Strauss as authors. Her approach is most clearly shown in Corbin (2011).

It is important for Juliet Corbin's approach – she admitted in her later works that she 'has been influenced to some degree by the writings of contemporary feminists, constructivists, and postmodernists' (Corbin & Strauss 2008: 9) – that the researchers first and foremost take a research attitude that is open to the unexpected:

> Two of the most important characteristics we try to develop in our students are to be open to serendipity and flexible in their approach to data collection and analysis. ... They have to learn to live with a considerable amount of ambiguity regarding the meaning of data. ... We emphasize that constructing a theory is a deliberate and careful process and that researchers have to take the time to do it correctly. In addition they must be self-reflective about their role in the theory construction. Most of all, we teach our students to be skeptical of established theories, however enticing they seem, unless these are eventually grounded through active interplay with data. (Corbin & Strauss 2015: 9)

Although all data are allowed in general, she has a clear preference for interviews (unlike Strauss, who preferred field observations). 'This is because the methodology enjoins taking with great seriousness the word and the actions of the people studied' (Strauss & Corbin 2016: 130). This emphasis on the 'interview' data type results from Corbin's strong interest in the perspectives of her players[11] and their actions and in the interpretation of their actions.

In her notes on analyzing the interviews, Corbin provides very detailed instructions in her works on how to encode the interviews. This is why it is easy and correct to get the impression that the actual work of grounded theory consists in coding the data as exactly and comprehensively as possible, wherein Corbin systematically uses computer-aided data analysis methods (for details, see Corbin 2011; Corbin & Strauss 2015).

Although Corbin herself keeps emphasizing that such analysis software is just a tool that cannot and must not replace thinking, Corbin's variant of grounded theory, because of its pronounced interconnection of software and coding, has often been likened to the primarily descriptive *content analysis*,[12] and with reason in my view.

But since, despite her note, many users of Corbin's variant excessively and predominantly use analysis software and do not go beyond describing the contents of their data (which they think is grounded theory), Corbin keeps pointing out in her works that grounded theory should not stop at description but should always involve theory development as well.

> It is not always easy to differentiate description from theory especially when so many studies that purport to be grounded theory studies do not result in theory but in description. … Description tells a story. It provides insights and understanding into how persons experience significant events. … To become theory, major concepts or themes must be woven around a central or core category to form a highly integrated and abstract framework that explains who, what, where, when, and how of a phenomenon. (Corbin 2011: 29)

But these hints by Corbin are of little help in my view: Corbin's variant of grounded theory today is mostly represented by a type of predominantly descriptive approach which puts coding processes at the center and holds abductive theory development in lower esteem.

This variant of grounded theory is therefore probably the most misunderstood variant of grounded theory – which in part is the author's fault. Although she keeps emphasizing that her version of grounded theory is a direct successor of the classic version of grounded theory by Strauss, she has introduced considerable changes at the operative level of the analysis; first, the strong emphasis on exact coding and, second, the systematic use of QDA software for said coding. This strong emphasis on coding doubtlessly places abductive research logic on the back burner, but does not completely eliminate it.

THE CHARMAZ CONCEPT OF GT AND PEIRCE'S LOGIC OF RESEARCH

The special contribution to the further development of GT by Kathy Charmaz and Antony Bryant is that they have made GT theoretically viable. Where Glaser's variant and the classic variant of grounded theory by Strauss (as described) still come attached with a tinge of positivism and verification logic, Charmaz eliminates this by her criticism and her turn towards a constructivist position. 'I chose the term "constructivist" to acknowledge subjectivity of the researcher's involvement in the construction and interpretation of data and to signal the difference between my approach and conventional social constructivism of the 1980s and the early 1990s' (Charmaz 2014: 14).

In her dealing with social constructivism, Charmaz develops the position that the researchers always interact with the individuals studied in the research process and that both data and its interpretation result from such interaction with the individuals studied, that the researchers, as it were, are co-authors of the data and the theory and that interpretations of past practice of action therefore are not only interpretations of the individuals studied, but also joint communicative constructions that result from the research situation as a whole.

> Your grounded theory journey relies on interaction – emanating from your worldview, standpoints, and situations, arising in the research sites, developing between you and your data, emerging with your ideas, then returning back to the field or another field, and moving on to conversations with your discipline and your substantive fields. To interact at all, we make sense of our situations, appraise what occurs in them and draw on language and culture to create meanings and frame actions. (Charmaz 2014: 321)

Charmaz develops theory not just from the perspective of the subjects, i.e., their individual world; she opens the grounded theory for an analysis of the social sphere that systematically exceeds the individual perspective: 'A constructivist approach means more than looking at how individual view their situations. It not only theorizes the interpretive work that research participants do, but also acknowledges that the resulting theory is an interpretation .... The theory depends on the researcher's view; it does not and cannot stand outside of it' (Charmaz 2006: 130).

She abandons the idea that the world she studies, that is to be understood and explained, is consistent in itself and can be explained using a central core category. Instead, this social world is full of contradictions, disruptions, discontinuities, which make it impossible to find a core category and therefore a uniform explanation. 'Constructivism assumes the relativism of multiple social realities, recognizes the mutual creation of knowledge by the viewer and the viewed, and aims toward interpretive understanding of subjects' meanings' (Charmaz 2000: 510).

The destination of the grounded theory journey taken by Kathy Charmaz, therefore, is not a description of what is said about the individuals studied or what was observed in the field. Instead, she wants to develop theories that make social action comprehensible and explainable. She is looking for a latent pattern beyond the awareness of the respondents that can answer 'why' questions (Charmaz 2014: 228) (see also Clarke). This is why the researchers and not the respondents have the last word.

Theorizing is important, according to Charmaz, because description and induction alone cannot bring new ideas into the world. It is therefore essential to create an explanatory theory in addition to the description – creating to be understood as 'building', not 'inventing' a theory. Theories, therefore, cannot be found in the data; they must be created by the researchers with (much) knowledge and interpretation in dealing with the data. Therefore, this variant of grounded theory is explicitly designed as abductive reasoning.

'Why is grounded theory an abductive method? Because grounded theory involves reasoning about experience from making theoretical conjectures – inferences – and then checking them through further experience – empirical data' (Charmaz 2014: 201). Abductive reasoning, following the ideas of Peirce, is not just drafted as a type of creative thinking, but as the first step of a three-step research logic which provides justifiable theories in passing through the steps of abduction, deduction, and induction. 'Abduction provides an important path for interacting with your data and emerging analysis during your grounded theory journey. It means paying attention to data that do not fit under existing interpretive rules of earlier inductive generalizations' (Charmaz 2014: 201). This approach considers research work as a social manufacturing process – and hence as a process which is always bound to a perspective and which is communicative.

CLARKE'S CONCEPT OF GT AND PEIRCE'S LOGIC OF RESEARCH

The variant of grounded theory that differs most clearly from the early version of Glaser & Strauss as well as from the classic variant by Strauss is Situational Analysis by Adele Clarke. Taking up constructivist positions, she criticizes the strong orientation of grounded theory towards the actions of subjects and their views and clearly advocates going beyond the general limitation of grounded theory to the subjects' view and instead and in addition to study arenas, non-humans[13] and situations (in this respect continuing from Strauss). 'The major reason why I do not think the symbolic interactionist conceptual framework is sufficient today is that, in practice, interactionism does not usually go "beyond the knowing subject" to generate a conceptualization of discourse in the significant meso-level and historicized trans-institutional ways which Foucault did' (Clarke & Keller 2014: 57).

In addition, and (taking up Foucault and further developing the decentralization of the subject[14]), Clarke turns to discourses as important units of study: 'I should also say something about the unit of analysis here. In most quantitative research we think of the individual as the unit of analysis and there are opinions and comments and thoughts on an X, Y or Z topic. The speaking subject is centered. Instead, in the qualitative method of GTM, focus is on action, on social action or individual action' (Clarke & Keller 2014: 81).

Clarke supplements this theoretically substantiated reorientation of grounded theory by the systematic use of diagrams while at the same time reducing the importance of coding. This extensive use of diagrams is particularly favorable, from an epistemological perspective, for the advent of abductive reasoning. Without a doubt there is some use of diagrams by Strauss, Corbin and Charmaz as well, but they take center stage in theory development for Adele Clarke which makes an important difference.

According to Peirce, the use of diagrams and working out thoughts with the help of diagrammatic thinking allows fast configuration of presented facts and sequences of events and, more importantly: these configurations can be creatively redesigned with just a few pen strokes – regardless of the 'actual' nature of what is shown in the diagram (Houser 2010). One can create or visualize 'new' relations *in* the diagram and *with* the diagram and 'feed' intuition: 'Intuition is the regarding of the abstract in a concrete form, by the realistic hypostatization of relations; that is the one sole method of valuable thought' (see Peirce 1888). Thus, diagrams help discover the novel. In this respect, diagrams are, or can be, a good means of abductive thinking (Stjernfelt 2000). Since they allow easy rearrangement of lines and free experimenting, diagrams can help overcome old habits of thinking and create favorable conditions for abductive lightning – but they don't have to be used in this way (Reichertz 2014).

CONCLUSION

There is no easy telling which variants of grounded theory are based on an abductive research logic. It is safe to say that Glaser's variant is strictly inductive and expressly rejects any opening towards abductive thinking. It gets a little more difficult with the variant developed and represented by Juliet Corbin. When it comes to theoretical understanding and the obligation to self-reflection, all conditions for an abductive research logic are present – however, the practical analysis recommended by Corbin gives rise to the misunderstanding that the primary goal of grounded theory is the software-aided content-analytical breakdown of the data, which can easily remain stuck in description and is not at all abductive. The decision is simple for the concepts of Strauss, Charmaz, and Clarke. The theory and practice of these variants of grounded theory correspond to abductive research logic – even if Strauss does not use this concept systematically and rather pursues a verification strategy. Charmaz and Clarke have made abductive thinking in part explicitly the cornerstone of their grounded theory, which also results in them pursuing a research strategy that is primarily based on falsification theory. All in all, it is fair to say that the conviction of the pragmatist Charles Sanders Peirce that new insights come to humankind through abductive lightning alone is also a core belief of all essential variants of grounded theory.

Notes

1 Heiner Legewie and Barbara Schervier-Legewie led the 1974 interview with Anselm Strauss.
2 In the early days of Grounded Theory, *Discovery* was the central text – even though it has been quoted more than it has been read. Today, however, this is no longer true.
3 Or better, one should try always to read the latest version of each approach.
4 I use the term 'classic' knowing that Glaser claims this label for his variety of grounded theory (Glaser 2002). This decision can be justified in that the *core* of grounded theory was formulated before Glaser and Strauss (1967), as early as in Strauss et al. (1964), a book that has unjustly met with little attention so far and is now waiting for a wider reception.
5 It is difficult to say when the research logic of grounded theory by Strauss and Corbin changed. It presumably was a slow process, which in my view started with Strauss and Corbin (1998) and increased slowly until Corbin (2011). The change was marked in my view by changing the subtitle of the joint work: While in Strauss and Corbin (1990) it still was 'Grounded Theory Procedures and Techniques', in Strauss and Corbin (1998) it was 'Techniques and Procedures for Developing Grounded Theory'. This change of the subtitles indicates the new and different accentuation: now it is predominantly 'techniques and procedures' and somewhat less of 'grounded theory'.
6 At least Glaser has clearly changed his assessment of the significance of serendipity later on. He writes, for example: Grounded theory 'data collection and analysis procedures are explicit and the pacing of these procedures is, at once, simultaneous, sequential, subsequent, scheduled and serendipitous, forming an integrated methodological "whole" that enables the emergence of conceptual theory as distinct from the thematic analysis characteristic of QDA research' (Glaser & Holton 2004: [7]).
7 Because of the partly rhetorical purpose of that book and the authors' emphasis on the need for grounded theory, Glaser and Strauss overplayed the inductive aspects (Strauss & Corbin 1994: 277).
8 'It does not address the abstract nature of GT, which does not deal in facts or findings, but generates concepts that apply as explanations. The concepts are not facts, as I have reiterated over and over' (Glaser 2003: [3]).

9 'Contributing to its development were two streams of work and thought: first, the general thrust of American Pragmatism (especially the writings of John Dewey, but also those of George Mead and Charles Peirce) and including its emphases on action and the problematic situation, and the necessity for conceiving a method in the context of problem solving' (Strauss 1987: 5).

10 Kathy Charmaz recalls that Anselm Strauss in the early days (1968–1972) was talking about grounded theory as an abductive method several times (Charmaz 2014: 202). And in a footnote she remembers: 'On one foggy afternoon in 1969 I happened to meet Anselm on Parnassus Avenue near the Social and Behavioral Science Department office. We talked for a few minutes about grounded theory and then he asked with his eyes twinkling: 'Do you know what kind of method grounded theory is?' Before I could reply he pronounced: 'It's abductive!' and danced away, quite delighted to share this revelation. But I knew he would say that' (Charmaz 2014: 202). See also: Charmaz & Keller (2016: [49]).

11 Bryant and Charmaz voice justified criticism: 'Strauss was a theorist of action, not of individuals' (Bryant & Charmaz 2007b: 46).

12 The problem that computer assisted data analysis software (CADAS) are not neutral tools but suggest a specific type of content analysis is increasingly noticed in the relevant literature as well: CADAS 'tends to reinforce a linear and mechanistic process of data analysis that emphasizes the development of shared codes. The software also perpetuates a positivist understanding of "consensus" in conceptualizing validity by endorsing the use of inter-rater reliability' (Zhao et al. 2016 [46]; see also Glaser 2003).

13 'I poached the useful term "nonhuman" from ANT merely to underscore the importance of "things" because *adequate analyses of situations must include the nonhuman explicitly and in considerable detail*' (Clarke & Keller 2014: 52).

14 See also: 'I see the turn to discourse as a key part of the poststructuralist interpretive turn, in some ways a segue toward post-humanism. The social sciences have sorely needed to go beyond the speaking subject for well over a century. Literacy, newspapers and photography transformed the planet in the nineteenth century, and it was transformed again in the twentieth through television, silicon, the web, social media, etc. We are constantly awash in their seas of discourses – narrative, historical, visual' (Clarke & Keller 2014: 90).

REFERENCES

Anderson, D. (1995). *Strand of System: The Philosophy of Charles Peirce*. West Lafayette, LA: Purdue University Press.

Atkinson, P. (2015). *For Ethnography*. London: Sage.

Berger, P. L. & T. Luckmann (1966). *Social Construction of Reality*. New York: Free Press

Birks, M. & J. Mills (2011). *Grounded Theory: A Practical Guide*. London: Sage.

Bryant, A. (2002). Re-grounding grounded theory. *The Journal of Information Technology Theory and Application*, *4*, 25–42.

Bryant, A. (2017). *Grounded Theory and Grounded Theorizing*. New York: Oxford University Press.

Bryant, A. & K. Charmaz (2007a). Editors' introduction: Grounded theory research methods and practices. In A. Bryant & K. Charmaz (Eds.), *The Sage Handbook of Grounded Theory* (pp. 1–28). London: Sage.

Bryant, A. & K. Charmaz (2007b). Grounded theory in historical perspective: An epistemological account. In A. Bryant & K. Charmaz (Eds.), *The Sage Handbook of Grounded Theory* (pp. 31–57). London: Sage.

Charmaz, K. (2000). Grounded theory: Objectivist and constructivist methods. In N. K. Denzin & Y. S. Lincoln (Eds.), *Handbook of Qualitative Research* (2nd ed., pp. 509–535). Thousand Oaks, CA: Sage.

Charmaz, K. (2006). *Constructing Grounded Theory*. Thousand Oaks, CA: Sage.

Charmaz, K. (2014). *Constructing Grounded Theory* (2nd rev. and exp. ed.). Thousand Oaks, CA: Sage.

Charmaz, K. & R. Keller (2016). A personal journey with grounded theory methodology: Kathy Charmaz in conversation with Reiner Keller [60 paragraphs]. *Forum Qualitative Sozialforschung / Forum: Qualitative Social Research*, *17*(1), Art. 16, http://nbnresolving.de/urn:nbn:de:0114-fqs1601165 FQS http:// [accessed: 19.05.2016].

Chauviré, Ch. (2005). Peirce, Popper, abduction, and the idea of a logic of discovery. *Semiotica*, *153*, 209–222.

Clarke, A. E. (2005). *Situational Analysis: Grounded Theory after the Postmodern Turn*. Thousand Oaks, CA: Sage.

Clarke, A. E. (2007). Grounded theorizing using situational analysis. In A. Bryant & K. Charmaz (Eds.), *The Sage Handbook of Grounded Theory* (pp. 363–397). London: Sage.

Clarke, A. E. & R. Keller (2014). Engaging complexities: Working against simplification as an agenda for qualitative research today. Adele Clarke in conversation with Reiner Keller [137 paragraphs]. *Forum Qualitative Sozialforschung / Forum: Qualitative Social Research*, *15*(2), Art. 1, http://nbn-resolving.de/urn:nbn:de:0114-fqs140212.

Corbin, J. M. (2011). *Grounded Theory Methodology*. Studienbrief der FernUniversität Hagen.

Corbin, J. M. & A. L. Strauss (2008). *Basics of Qualitative Research: Techniques and Procedures for Developing Grounded Theory* (3rd ed.). Thousand Oaks, CA: Sage.

Corbin, J. M. & A. L. Strauss (2015). *Basics of Qualitative Research: Techniques and Procedures for Developing Grounded Theory* (4th ed.). Thousand Oaks, CA: Sage.

Denzin, N. K. (2007). Grounded theory and the politics of interpretation. In A. Bryant & K. Charmaz (Eds.), *Handbook of Grounded Theory* (pp. 454–472). London: Sage.

Dey, I. (1999). *Grounding Grounded Theory*. London: Academic Press.

Eco, U. (1985). Horns, hooves, insteps. In U. Eco & Th. Sebeok (Eds.), *The Sign of Three* (pp. 198–220). Bloomington, IN: Indiana University Press.

Eisenstadt, S. N. (2003). *Comparative Civilizations & Multiple Modernities*. Leiden: Brill.

Equit, C. & Ch. Hohage (Eds.) (2016). *Handbuch Grounded Theory*. Weinheim: Beltz.

Fann, K. T. (1970). *Peirce's Theory of Abduction*. The Hague, NL: Nijhoff.

Foucault, M. (2004). *Geschichte der Gouvernementalität*. Frankfurt am Main: Suhrkamp.

Glaser, B. G. (1992). *Emergence vs Forcing: Basics of Grounded Theory*. Mill Valley, CA: Sociology Press.

Glaser, B. G. (2001). *The Grounded Theory Perspective: Conceptualization Contrasted with Description.* Mill Valley, Ca.: Sociology Press.

Glaser, B. G. (2002): Constructivist grounded theory? In: *Forum: Qualitative Social Research*, *3*(3), Art. 12, http://nbn-resolving.de/urn:nbn:de:0114-fqs0203125 [Date of access: Oct. 15, 2014].

Glaser, B. G. (2003). Naturalist inquiry and grounded theory [68 paragraphs]. *Forum Qualitative Sozialforschung / Forum: Qualitative Social Research*, *5*(1), Art. 7, http://nbnresolving. de/urn:nbn:de: 0114-fqs040170.

Glaser, B. G. with the assistance of J. Holton (2004). Remodeling grounded theory [80 paragraphs]. *Forum Qualitative Sozialforschung / Forum: Qualitative Social Research*, *5*(2), Art. 4, http://nbn-resolving.de/urn:nbn:de:0114-fqs040245.

Glaser, B. G. & A. L. Strauss (1967). *The Discovery of Grounded Theory*. New York: de Gruyter.

Habermas, J. (1973). *Erkenntnis und Interesse.* Frankfurt am Main: Suhrkamp.

Houser, N. (2010). Introduction. In N. Houser (Ed.), *The Writings of Charles S. Peirce* (pp. xxv–xcv). Bloomington, IN: Indiana University Press.

Kant, I. (2007). *Critique of Pure Reason*. London: Penguin.

Kelle, U. (2005). 'Emergence' vs. 'Forcing' of Empirical Data? A Crucial Problem of 'Grounded Theory' Reconsidered. *Forum: Qualitative Social Research*, *6*(2). www.Qualitative-research.net/fqs/fqs-texte [accessed 09.2006].

Keller, R. & H. Knoblauch & J. Reichertz (Eds.) (2012). *Kommunikativer Konstruktivismus*. Wiesbaden. Springer.

Kreppner, K. (1975). *Zur Problematik des Messens in den Sozialwissenschaften*. Stuttgart: Klett.

Legewie, H. & B. Schervier-Legewie (2004). 'Research is hard work, it's always a bit suffering': Anselm Strauss in conversation with Heiner Legewie and Barbara Schervier-Legewie. *Forum Qualitative Sozialforschung / Forum: Qualitative Social Research*. Retrieved March 9, 2007 from www.qualitative-research.net/fqs-texte/3-04/04-3-22-e.htm

Merton, R. K. & E. Barber (2004). *The Travels and Adventures of Serendipity: A Study in Sociological Semantics and the Sociology of Science*. Princeton, NJ: Princeton University Press.

Mey, G. & K. Mruck (2011). Grounded-Theory-Methodology: Entwicklung, Stand, Perspektiven. In G. Mey & K. Mruck (Eds.), *Grounded Theory Reader* (2nd ed., pp. 11–50). Wiesbaden: VS Verlag.

Nubiola, J. (2005). Abduction or the Logic of Surprise. *Semiotica*, *153*, 117–130.

Paavola, S. (2011). Abductive cognition. *Transactions of the Charles S. Peirce Society*, *47*(2), 252–256.

Peirce, C. S. (1888). *A Guess at the Riddle*. MS 909. Available at: www.iupui.edu/~arisbe/menu/library/bycsp/guess/guess.htm.

Peirce, C. S. (1929). Guessing. *Hound and Horn*, *2*, 267–282.

Peirce, C. S. (1931–1935). *The Collected Papers of Charles S. Peirce* (8 Vols). Cambridge, MA: Harvard University Press.

Peirce, C. S. (1976). *The New Elements of Mathematics* (5 Vols). The Hague: Mouton.

Peirce, C. S. (1992). *Reasoning and the Logic of Things*. Edited by K. L. Ketner. Cambridge, MA: Harvard University Press.

Plutynski, A. (2011). Four problems of abduction. *Hopos: The Journal of the International Society for the History of Philosophy and Science*, *1*(2), 227–248.

Popper, K. R. (1934/2002). *The Logic of Scientific Discovery*. London/New York: Routledge.

Reichenbach, H. (1938). *Experience and Prediction*. Chicago, IL: Chicago Press.

Reichertz, J. (2004a). Abduction, deduction and induction in qualitative research. In U. Flick et al. (Eds.), *Companion to Qualitative Research* (pp. 159–165). London: Sage.

Reichertz, J. (2004b). Objective hermeneutics and hermeneutic sociology of knowledge. In U. Flick et al. (Eds.), *Companion to Qualitative Research* (pp. 290–296). London: Sage.

Reichertz, J. (2007, 2010). Abduction: The logic of discovery of grounded theory. In A. Bryant & K. Charmaz (Eds.), *The Sage Handbook of Grounded Theory* (pp. 214–229). London: Sage.

Reichertz, J. (2009). *Kommunikationsmacht: Was ist Kommunikation und was vermag sie? Und weshalb vermag sie das?* Wiesbaden: VS Verlag.

Reichertz, J. (2013). *Die Abduktion in der qualitativen Sozialforschung* (2nd rev. and exp. ed.). Wiesbaden: Springer.

Reichertz, J. (2014). Induction, deduction, abduction. In U. Flick (Ed.), *The Sage Handbook of Qualitative Data Analysis* (pp. 123–136). London: Sage.

Reichertz, J. & S. Wilz (2016). Welche Erkenntnistheorie liegt der Grounded Theory zugrunde? In C. Equit & C. Hohage (Eds.), *Handbuch Grounded Theory* (pp. 48–66). Weinheim: Beltz.

Sebeok, Th. & J. Umiker-Sebeok (1979). 'You know my method': A juxtaposition of Charles S. Peirce and Sherlock Holmes. *Semiotica*, *26*(2/3), 203–250.

Stjernfelt, Frederik (2000). Diagramms as centerpiece of a Peircean epistemology. *Transactions of the Charles S. Peirce Society*, *XXXVI*(3), 357–384.

Strauss, A. L. (1984). *Qualitative Analysis in Social Research: Grounded Theory Methodology*. Study Letter, University Hagen.

Strauss, A. L. (1987). *Qualitative Analysis for Social Scientists*. New York: Cambridge University Press.

Strauss, A.L./Schatzmann, L./Bucher, R./Ehrlich, D./Sabshin, M. (1964). *Psychiatric Ideologies and Institutions.* New York. Transaction Publishers.

Strauss, A. L. & J. Corbin (1990). *Basics of Qualitative Research: Grounded Theory Procedures and Techniques*. London: Sage.

Strauss, A. L. & J. Corbin (1994). Grounded theory methodology: An overview. In N. K. Denzin (Ed.), *Handbook of Qualitative Research* (pp. 273–285). London: Sage.

Strauss, A. L. & J. Corbin (1998). *Basics of Qualitative Research: Techniques and Procedures for Developing Grounded Theory* (2nd ed.). Thousand Oaks, CA: Sage.

Strauss, A.L. & J. Corbin (2016). Methodological Assumptions. In: C. Equit & C. Hohage (Eds.): *Handbuch Grounded Theory.* Weinheim: Beltz. S. 128–140.

Tavory, I. & S. Timmermans (2014). *Abductive Analysis. Theorizing Qualitative Research.* Chicago: University Press.

Thornberg, R. (2012). Informed Grounded Theory. In: *Scandinavian Journal of Educational Research.* June, 243–259.

Zhao, P., P. Li, K. Ross & Dennis, B. (2016). Methodological tool or methodology? Beyond instrumentality and efficiency with qualitative data analysis software [49 paragraphs]. *Forum Qualitative Sozialforschung / Forum: Qualitative Social Research*, *17*(2), Art. 16, http://nbn-resolving.de/urn:nbn:de:0114-fqs1602160.

14

Grounded Theory Analysis and CAQDAS: A Happy Pairing or Remodeling GT to QDA?

Susanne Friese

BACKGROUND

In contemporary books on qualitative methods one finds pointers and references to computer-assisted analysis, but little about how to translate manual ways of going about analysis to a computer-assisted way. Here are some examples: Remenyi (2014) dedicates half a page to the topic; Breuer (2018) two pages; Bryant and Charmaz (2007) four pages spread out across three chapters written by three different authors; Goulding (2002) three and a half pages; Charmaz (2014) zero pages; and Seale et al. (2004) a chapter written by Udo Kelle on the historical development, application and limitations of software. Again, nothing about implementation. A few exceptions can be found in journal articles, see for instance Hutchison et al. (2010) or Bringer et al. (2006). They explain how they have employed NVivo in the process of GT analysis. The fact that software is mentioned in qualitative method books does not necessarily mean that it is embraced. On the contrary, often the few sentences that have been added express dislike and rejection. Some authors even pride themselves on not using software:

> As a risk taker and a thrill seeker, I find hand coding and hand sorting exciting, and maybe a little dangerous; every time you present your research you risk your reputation, since someone in the audience may think you're a fool, and may say no. You have no statistics, no proofs; no software evidence that your take on a scene is meaningful. Fear of public shame may be the best impetus for making sense. (Stern 2007: 120)

Holton (2007) makes reference to Glaser (2003) to support her argument against the use of software. Glaser even dedicated two chapters to express his disapproval of software.

One of the arguments that he as well as Holton make is the inability of computers to replace human thinking. 'Experienced classic grounded theorists continue to await a "package" that can replicate the complex capabilities of the human brain for conceptualization of latent patterns of social behavior' (Holton 2007: 287). This statement is based on expectations some people had in the 1960s, expectations that have long been overcome. Even in the time of 'smart' phones, no one would expect computer software to perform such wonders. This has already been expressed by Strauss when he wrote in 1996 that the developer of ATLAS.ti, Thomas Muhr, made no claim to have produced a program that performs miracles (Strauss & Corbin 1996). Rather, he stated that it is still the researcher who 'will have to have the ideas and the gifts to do exceptional research' (Muhr 1997: 4).

Returning to Glaser, another reason he employs against the use of software is a quote from a PhD student who wrote: 'I wrote day and sometimes night. I got into the "drugless trip" and eventually the core variable of balancing came to me almost as a revelation. "Joy to the world the core has come"' (Glaser 2003: 36). Glaser appears to overlook that software provides many places for writing. The added advantage of software is that – if you want – you can attach your writing directly to the data segments you write about. And even if you decided not to use the editors provided by the software for writing, i.e., rather prefer to write in a text processor or on paper, software is not preventing the researcher from doing that.

Glaser, however, still has one more argument against using software. The final blow at the use of computer software, he states, is the process of sorting memos: 'SO WHY ON EARTH WOULD THE GT RESEARCHER WANT TO BLOCK THIS STAGE OF THE GT PACKAGE WITH A COMPUTERIZATION? The answer is there is no reason to. Computers would erode, block and remodel GT at the sorting stage' (Glaser 2003: 37, uppercase as in the original).

An immediate response to this could be: Every CAQDAS package has a button or a menu selection that allows users to print out memos. After printing one could go ahead to sort, re-arrange and reorder the paper versions of the memos as usual (in the old days). However, knowing how a computer-assisted analysis works, even this is no longer necessary. All of this can be done inside the digital environment. By attaching comments and memos to data segments that at some point are also coded, and by sorting and re-arranging the codes, one sorts memos all the time throughout the process of analysis. This will be shown in the sample case study. It is also no longer necessary to copy parts of the data onto the memo (cards) as done with manual analysis. Memos are digitally linked to the data. Thus, the data can always be accessed and do not have to be part of the memo content. Linked data segments can be exported (if desired) together with their memos.

IMPLICATIONS OF TERMINOLOGY

QDA or CAQDAS?

Glaser (2003) strongly emphasized the difference between classic GT and 'QDA' (Qualitative Data Analysis). Similarly, I have always placed value on using the term CAQDAS – Computer Aided Qualitative Data AnalysiS – as compared to QDA software (cf. Friese 2011). The term QDA software is easier on the lips, but it has been causing many misunderstandings. QDA software implies that the software is doing the analysis instead of being a tool aiding the researcher (who still must do the thinking). Automation is certainly an issue these days given the massive amounts of data available. But big data analysis is different from qualitative data analysis even if big data may consist of qualitative, i.e., non-numeric data (Friese 2016). Thus, we need to distinguish between the analysis of qualitative data and qualitative data analysis, whereby GT is a form of the latter.

Knowing only one of the available packages may also lead to false conclusions. If, for instance, one was to try a GT analysis with QDAMiner, which is more apt to support deductive approaches, one can easily become frustrated and might reject CAQDAS to be unsuitable for GT. Another common pitfall is the translation of methodological steps to software functionality. As will be shown later in this chapter, equating the GT coding process with the function to apply codes in a software package can already be troublesome.

Another issue might be that some researchers do not resist the temptation to use CAQDAS for a quick but dirty analysis. But this is no different from studies that were analyzed manually. Morse et al. (2009) wrote that there are many studies that refer to themselves as being GT-based but aren't true GT studies. This, however, is not a reason for rejecting GT as methodological approach, nor should quick and dirty computer-assisted studies be a reason against the use of software. As Strauss already said: Research is 'hard work', and without working hard, neither a manual nor a computer-assisted analysis will result in a good piece of academic writing. Not all GT researchers of the first and second generation, though, condemn the use of software. Corbin writes in the current issue of *Basics of Qualitative Data Analysis*: The computer has the ability '*to augment the human mind by doing a lot of the detailed and tedious work involved in many endeavors, thus freeing up the user to be creative and thoughtful. And this is what computer programs do for qualitative analysis*' (Corbin & Strauss 2015: 203).

Coding or Tagging?

Reflecting on the arguments put forward for not using software, it occurred to me that one reason for it could simply be a misunderstanding in terms of another commonly used term and its application. The use of the words 'code' and 'coding' in qualitative data analysis is probably a result of the widespread adoption of the Grounded Theory (GT) approach. It has also been embraced by almost all CAQDAS developers and those writing about software application for qualitative data analysis. But what does 'coding' mean in CAQDAS? It simply refers to the process of attaching a label to a data segment. Computer scientists call this 'tagging' – and this might be a much better term to use in order not to confuse it with the much more complex process of grounded theory coding.

Both Strauss (1987, 1998) and Corbin and Strauss (2015) mentioned that it is possible to write the concepts that they usually write on index cards as labels in the margin of a document. Strauss assumed that this was probably common practice but pointed out these 'codes' would then be less detailed and more difficult to sort (Strauss 1998: 114). Looking at the examples Strauss provides, the notes on his index cards often have quotes from the data, references to other related data segments, analytic reflections, pointers for theoretical sampling, and references to the coding paradigm. Further, there are notes about whether within a coded segment references to a condition, an interaction, or a consequence are contained, i.e., axial coding. This also applies to the examples given by Corbin and Strauss (2015). Thus, when using the word *coding* in the context of CAQDAS, it is not what Strauss and Corbin mean when they talk about coding in the GT sense. Grounded theory coding is more than just attaching a label to a data segment, it means writing a memo, or if you attach a label, writing about it. For Glaser, codes are something that 'just occur in the analyst's head as he immerses himself in the data by going from incident to incident' (Glaser 1992: 45). Labeling data with such premature ideas, according to Glaser, produces preconception. Applied in this way, Glaser's critique that CAQDAS remodels and erodes the grounded theory approach to QDA methodology is appropriate.

In the German edition of 1996, Strauss and Corbin define coding as 'the process of data analysis' (p. 43). In the 2015 edition, it is defined as delineating concepts to stand for interpreted meaning (Chapter 12). Applying this process to a computerized analysis, this means tagging and writing. Depending on the computer program you are using, the process of writing is supported in diverse ways. Most programs offer a memo function. The translation of writing notes and ideas on index cards, therefore could be to use memos in CAQDAS. In addition to memos, some programs offer more differentiated writing tools which allow users to better sort and structure the analytical writing process. When using CAQDAS, the first step is to understand the meaning and purpose of a specific analytic task in a methodological sense. Next, you need to be familiar with the various functions your preferred software package offers to find and use the suitable tool(s) for the task at hand (cf. Woolf & Silver 2017).

In the remainder of this chapter, I would like to offer a translation of the various methodological steps to computer mouse clicks based on a case study. I chose the CAQDAS ATLAS.ti as, based on my experience, it is the most suitable to support an interpretive approach like grounded theory. I am aware that it is a sensitive issue to suggest a specific software for a methodological approach as all programs claim that they support a wide range of approaches. Choosing one program over another is not to say that it is not possible to use, for instance, NVivo or MAXQDA to conduct a GT analysis, but, as I will show throughout the next section, the process of open coding is not supported as well and therefore researchers might be easily drawn into tagging rather than GT coding and thereby default to QDA, supporting Glaser's argument against the use of CAQDAS. I should add a note about GT coding, as it cannot be generalized across the various GT approaches that exist today. Strauss (1998) gives an example of openly coding about half a page of typed-out observational notes. The result is not a list of tags, but a memo of several pages in length that holds words that stand for categories, properties, or dimensions. Charmaz's initial coding process resembles much more what CAQDAS users normally do when tagging data. For her, the way of labeling makes the difference between grounded theory coding and general qualitative coding. Grounded theorists code for actions rather than topics. For instance, rather than 'Friends' support' or 'Hospitalization', a grounded theorist would use initial codes like 'Receiving friends' help in seeking care / Requesting regimen re-evaluation' or 'Gaining medical access / Being admitted to hospital' (Charmaz 2014: 122–123). And as mentioned above, Glaser would not even consider writing down those initial ideas.

ATLAS.ti offers a level of analysis below tagging that facilitates the various analytic steps by offering more than one technical entity to represent the different stages of the analysis process. A coded segment consists of what ATLAS.ti calls a quotation and a code linked to it. Thus, a quotation is an entity of its own and because of this in ATLAS.ti certain actions are possible that do not exist in other programs. A quotation can be named, commented, it can be linked to other quotations, and one or also multiple memos can be linked to it. Further, in terms of functionality, the ATLAS.ti margin area is an essential feature, especially when using an interpretive approach. It gives immediate feedback

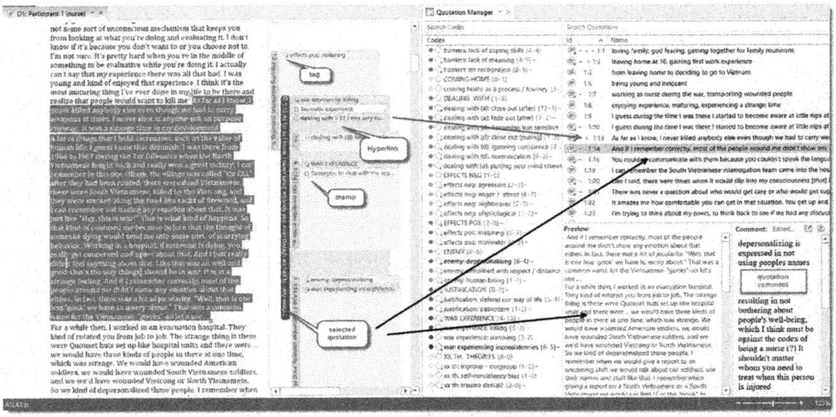

Figure 14.1 Interactive margin area in ATLAS.ti

throughout the analysis how a segment is tagged, whether it is linked to other segments, whether comments or memos have been written, or whether it is part of a network, which is a space for integrating analysis. This is illustrated in Figure 14.1.

One can certainly approximate this in other programs and I show below how this might be done based on the example of NVivo and MAXQDA.

CASE STUDY

The data of the sample project used here are the same that Juliet Corbin uses in the 2008 and 2015 editions of her book *Basics of Qualitative Data Analysis.* The data consist of an open interview carried out by Anselm Strauss in 1987 with a Vietnam veteran who worked in the medical corps; two others, one semi-structured with a US Marine who served in the Vietnam War, and an email conversation with a Panama, Saudi and Bosnia veteran, also US Marines, were conducted by Juliet Corbin in 2006. Initially, there are no detailed or fixed research questions. There is only a general broad interest in the experience of a soldier in the war.

The selected data material is used for demonstration purposes only and does not stand for the entire process of a GT study and it is also not enough to derive a full theory anchored in the data. Some ideas for further theoretical sampling are offered that highlight how one could extend this study to achieve saturation to build theory. Before I started the analytic process in the software, I did not read the analysis by Corbin. On an experimental level, I wanted to find out whether the software itself would have an impact on the analysis, or whether the data would speak for itself in line with the statements by Glaser and Corbin: ‘the data is never wrong’ (Glaser 2003:70), and: ‘*The data themselves do not lie*’ (Strauss & Corbin 1998: 44).

Open Coding – Identifying Concepts

This is how I translated the process of ‘open coding’ in ATLAS.ti:

During the first phase, I read through the data and recorded the ideas and thoughts that occurred to me using quotation comments. In addition, I tagged the data. My intention was to pre-structure the material to take advantage of the computer early, in that it allows me quick access to the material for further analysis via tags (called codes or nodes in most CAQDAS). If you look at Table 14.1, which compares the concepts (= words used by analysts to stand for interpreted meaning) that Corbin derived from her initial analysis and the tags I developed, it becomes clear that many of my tags tackle the same issues. In some instances, either Corbin or I chose a more abstract term, sometimes named a potential candidate for property or a sub-code.

Table 14.1: Results of open coding of interview 1

Concepts J.C.	*Tags in the software*
Locating the self: at time of entry	*family background professional background reasons to go into war attitude: patriotism attitude: war *war: preparation
Volunteering versus being drafted versus draft dodging	*about being drafted
Being a noncombatant versus being a combatant	
The enemy	*about the enemy
Zones of safety and zones of conflict or killing zones	
Military systems	military way
The war experience and strategies for blocking out minimizing inconsistencies	self-consistency bias
The war experience	War experience war experience: dealing with death death and war
The culture of war and its inconsistencies	Inconsistencies self-aware conscience
Psychological survival strategies	denial? dealing with: changing opinion to match facts dealing with: cleansing experience
The enemy and psychological survival strategies	Depersonalizing consequences of depersonalizing in-group / outgroup conditions: language issues
Letting down the emotional guard	War experience: dealing with death
Moral contradictions of war and psychological survival strategies	war experience: fade out / cut off war effect on attitude
Inconsistencies within the military system	military way

Table 14.1: Results of open coding of interview 1 (Continued)

Concepts J.C.	*Tags in the software*
Normalizing the situation: another survival strategy	war experience: normalization
Moral contradictions	nurse codex in action simple human feelings
Coming home and getting on with life	Dealing with war: effect on life war experience: fade out / cut off dealing with: dealing with: cleansing experience *feelings about Vietnam today
The American disillusionment: A new meaning of war	peace movement: explaining rejection peace movement: first reaction peace movement: retrospect dealing with: changing opinion to match facts Attitude: government
War as maturational stepping-stone: the changing self	War effect: maturation
The wall of silence	no exchange with others about experience
Breaking through the wall of silence	
Survival	
	*important incidences
	justifications

In ATLAS.ti initial tagging looks as shown in Figure 14.2. Tags are not yet sorted or colored. At this stage of analysis, I only created a list of terms, for the moment ignoring any possibility to sort tags for hierarchical structure. Please also note, even though I compare the list of tags with the concepts developed by Juliet Corbin, this first step of tagging is not the equivalent of open coding. Corbin extracted the list of concepts from her memos. Going through and tagging the data can be an initial step in software-supported analysis in order to make it easier to move through the data and find things, but in order to label it open coding according to the Strauss/Corbin approach, an essential step is missing – namely writing. When using ATLAS.ti this can be done by writing quotation comments.

The quotation level can also be used to translate the Charmaz approach to grounded theory. Instead of using the software entity 'code' for initial coding, I would recommend creating quotations at this first stage of analysis and rename the default name. The quotation name thus becomes the 'code'. The actual software entity 'code' comes into play later during the process of focused coding. This way it is possible to preserve all thoughts that went into initial coding and represent focused coding within a different software tool (Figure 14.3). When using 'codes' for the task of intitial coding, analysts may be tempted to leave them in the code list rather than to merge them, ending up with a very long list of codes resulting from different levels of analysis.

Continuing with the translation of the Corbin/Strauss approach based on the war experience data, I used code comments for the next level of abstraction. The purpose

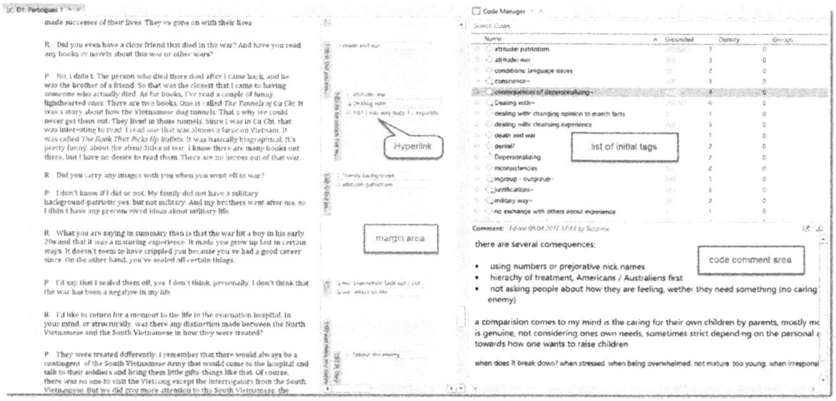

Figure 14.2 First phase of analysis in ATLAS.ti 8 – tagging, commenting, and linking data

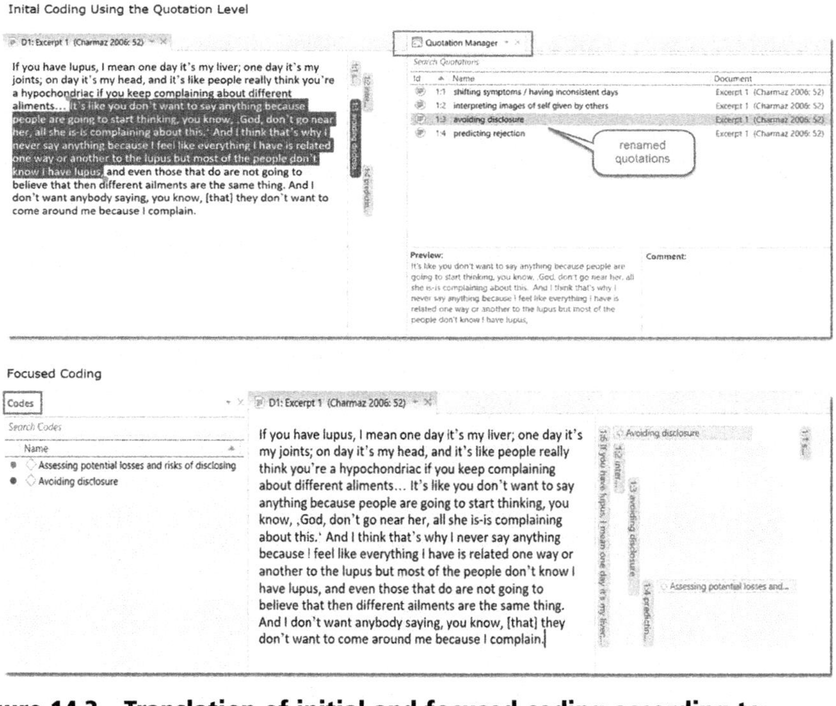

Figure 14.3 Translation of initial and focused coding according to Charmaz using ATLAS.ti

was to summarize the content of the tagged quotations as a step towards moving from a descriptive to the conceptual level. In addition, I wrote two memos. One was about background information on traumatic experience, as this is well researched. And the second one on Roger's congruence theory, as I was reminded of it while reading the

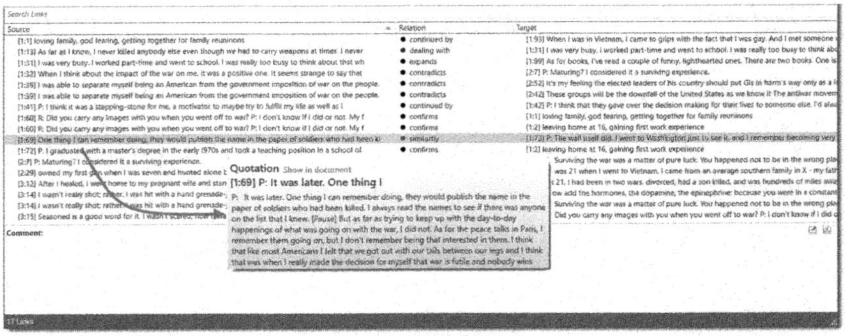

Figure 14.4 Link Manager in ATLAS.ti 8 with activated quotation content

data. If I had not prepared this data set as an exemplary case study, other memos of this type would have been written at earlier stages already, for instance to outline the project idea, to write down one's own thoughts and position about the topic at hand, etc. The availability of the quotation level and the comment function, plus having memos as containers for writing, allows me to better distinguish between various methodological activities.

Another ATLAS.ti feature that supports data level work is the ability to create named links between quotations called 'hyperlinks'. When creating a hyperlink in ATLAS.ti, i.e., linking two or more quotations to each other, the researcher specifies how the data segments relate to each other: A *explains* B, A *discusses* B, A *contradicts* B, A *is a supporting statement of* B, etc. Figure 14.4 shows the ATLAS.ti Hyperlink Manager and five links that were created while tagging the first interview. In the text itself, you can jump back and forth between hyperlinked quotations via double-click on a hyperlink, just as if you clicked a link on the Web. The link can be between two quotations only or continued to form a chain or star. It is not necessary to write down references on index cards as in manual analysis to search for them when needed – they are available instantaneously.

After tagging the first interview, I began with reviewing the code list, adding some structure to it. Next, I tagged interview two and three, continuing the interpretive process in writing quotation and code comments and linking quotations to each other as relations emerged. The changes to the tag list that resulted from this are shown in Figure 14.5, exemplifying the emerging category, 'dealing with'. The first two lists expand and clarify the open coding process as defined by Corbin & Strauss: open coding is the process of 'breaking apart data and delineating concepts to stand for blocks of raw data. At the same time, one is qualifying those concepts in terms of their properties and dimensions' (Corbin & Strauss 2008: 195). Thus, the initial tag list turns into a category system over time where tags receive methodological significance. The problem with all software packages is that they offer the researcher the technical entity 'code', 'node' or 'keyword'. Apart from offering a tree structure, CAQDAS does not offer tools for a methodological development of tags. Arranging tags in a tree structure is not synonymous with analytical differentiation of different concept levels. Especially novice researchers often have a challenging time with this initially (cf. Corbin & Strauss 2015; or Strauss 1998). The technical facility of simply shifting levels in a tree structure can lead to a false security that you have indeed created a proper higher order category or lower order sub-code.

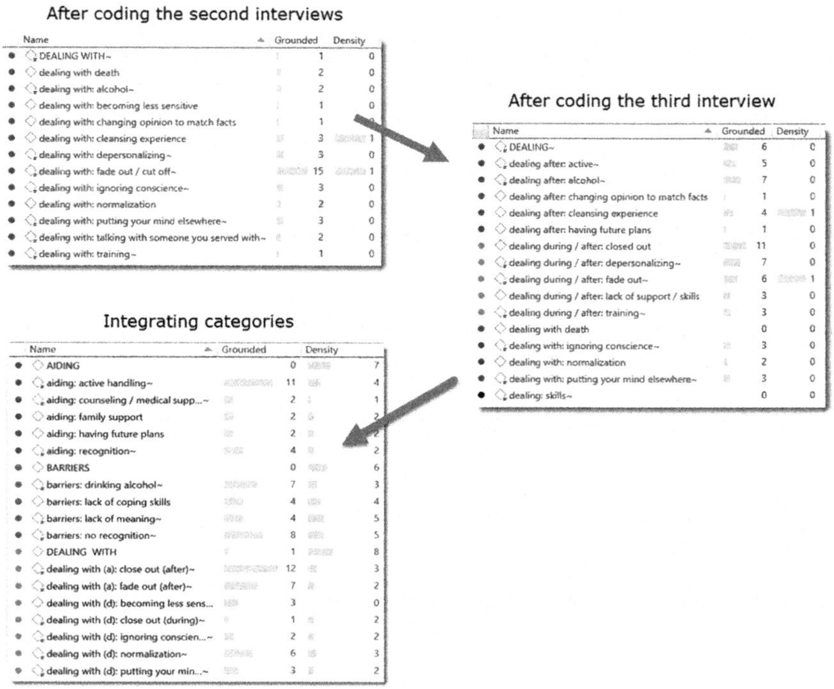

Figure 14.5 Ongoing changes in building the category DEALING WITH

No software will point out inconsistencies in parent and child codes. If you create 'Horse' as parent code and assign 'dog', 'animal', and 'cornflower' as sub-codes, the software will be indifferent about it. This may sound trivial, but unfortunately, I have seen too many coding schemes which were set up incorrectly or inefficiently. When using CAQDAS, there are certain rules to observe, already described by Richards and Richards (1995), and if those are not observed, you quickly end up in the 'back to Excel' or back to paper and pencil game. Errors of this kind in the methodological development of tag lists can of course also occur when using prefixes, as is common in ATLAS.ti.

Critics may argue that at this stage CAQDAS is remodeling GT to QDA because the software entity 'code' needs to serve two purposes for GT: initial tags are developed into categories, properties, or dimensions and thus takes on methodological meaning. Some 'codes', however, may never be methodological; they simply serve organizational purposes to support data retrieval. Further, the code system needs to be structured in a way to be able to use more advanced software tools later in the analysis. This is based on technical requirements of the software and might lead to the impression to remodel GT to QDA. The latter would only be the case if the analyst was only tagging the data without writing, and thus not translating the underlying methodology in the intended way. I assume that researchers working manually also have developed an organizational system for their memos. What I am presenting below is good practice advice that I have developed during more than 20 years of using CAQDAS. My coding schemas from 10 or 15 years ago looked different and over the years one finds out what works and what doesn't. I have summarized the lessons learned in what I call 'Notice-Collect-Think', or the NCT method of computer-assisted qualitative data analysis (Friese 2014 / 2019). I consider it the core of any computer-assisted analysis with necessary adaption for various methodological approaches like GT as presented here. Although not formulated as a method, similar good practice advice can be found by Richards and Morse (2013), Bazeley (2013), Richards (2009), Silver and Lewins (2014) or Silver and Woolf (2015).

For instance, to just give a few hints: if the list of sub-codes gets very long, this is a signal to take a closer look and to check whether some tags need to be aggregated, or whether they belong somewhere else (see Figure 14.5). During the process of integration, some of the tags in the category DEALING WITH were moved to two new categories AIDING and BARRIERS. Another pointer is the number of times a tag has been used. If the frequency gets quite large in comparison to other tags, it is likely that the researcher needs to further differentiate the tag. An example is the tag 'dealing with: fade out/cut off' – with a groundedness of 15 (= code frequency). I differentiated it into 'fade out' and 'closed out', obvious in this case as the label already indicated that two different things were collected here. However, it is not always this clear.

When differentiating, or aggregating, the contents of a tag, analysts need to revisit and reread the data and their notes and memos. The category DEALING WITH in Figure 14.5 is the result of the process of axial coding and concept integration, which I describe further below. It contains fewer codes than in the earlier lists as some of the sub-codes were moved into the categories 'barriers' and 'aiding', developed during the process of integrating data. See Figure 14.11. This exemplifies that the individual steps of coding are not necessarily consecutive but blend into one another (see Strauss 1998; Corbin & Strauss 2008).

NAMING CONVENTIONS WHEN DEVELOPING A CODE SYSTEM

As an attentive reader, you may have noticed in Figure 14.5 that I use uppercase for category names. Since there is no tree structure in ATLAS.ti, one uses prefixes for sub-code, e.g., for the properties of a class. Dimensions can be part of code names, or you separate out dimensions to form a category of their own and code twice, i.e., once with the sub-code, and once with the dimension. This can be helpful for further analysis, if you want to relate dimensions to properties in the form of a table. This rule is not ATLAS.ti-specific and should be considered also when using other programs.

For all the tags that have not yet become a category or do not belong to one, I use an *asterisk* as a prefix. If a program offers a tree structure to organize tags, these can be collected under a branch UNSORTED. All attribute tags, such as family background, professional biography, etc., I prefix with a *hashtag* (#). As ATLAS.ti sorts the tag list in the following order: special characters, numbers, letter, those types of codes are listed first. In a tree structure, those codes could be sorted under a branch BACKGROUND. Table 14.2 summarizes the naming conventions that I use in ATLAS.ti to turn a list of tags into a code system that differentiates between different levels and types of codes.

Glaser (1978) and also Charmaz (2014) advise to code with gerunds because it helps researchers to detect processes and to stick to the data. In a computer-assisted analysis, given the multiple functions of tags that also need to serve as codes in a methodological sense, there is no straight-forward general translation for it. When starting to sort tags in ATLAS.ti, it is best to work with prefixes. In addition, the alphabetic order needs to be observed. This makes it difficult to start all code labels with a gerund. A gerund might occur as part of the label or can be used when describing the code in the code comment.

Table 14.2: Syntax for the meanings of tags on the various levels

Meaning	*in ATLAS.ti*	*Examples*
Concept	Small letters, black	Depersonalizing Conscience In group – outgroup
Category	Capital letters, colored	WAR EXPERIENCE
Sub-code	Small letters, colored like all other codes in the category	War experience: inconsistencies War experience: killing War experience: survival
Concepts in developing a code schema	Small letters, prefixed by special character (*), black	*about the enemy *about being drafted
Dimension	Small letters, prefixed by special character, colored	/TIME /time: during /time: after
Socio demographics, i.e., if you code attribute of actors, group interviews / focus group data / comments of different people on a blog, comments on YouTube videos	Small letters, prefixed by # or any other special character, grey	#background: personal #background: professional #gender: male #gender: female

Further, in a computer-assisted analysis you may also tag for occurrences of certain actors, background context information, etc. This is done to quickly finding something again, or because of the query logic used by CAQDAS; queries that a researcher working manually is unlikely to consider as it would not be feasible, or a lot of work. These could be queries like: find all occurrences in the data set where actor x is doing y, or all contexts where respondents are receiving help from friends.

Axial Coding

Axial coding, which is coding along the axis of a category, is not visible at once in the tag list. In the third edition, Corbin defined axial coding as 'crosscutting or relating concepts to each other' (Corbin & Strauss 2008: 195). And in more detail in the fourth edition (Corbin & Strauss 2015):

> When researchers are coding for context, they are doing what Strauss (1987: 156) called 'axial coding'. They are locating and linking action-interaction within the framework of sub concepts that give it meaning and enable it to explain what interactions are occurring, and why and what consequences real or anticipated are happening because of action-interaction.

While tagging is no solution here, creating linkages is. Yet, easy as it is to create links in the software, you first must work out exactly where and how to link something meaningfully. This is only possible if you start to think about your data and in writing. Axial coding therefore takes place in notes primarily, not during 'tagging' raw data. In addition, first diagrams might be drawn, using, for instance, the network feature in ATLAS.ti. Figure 14.6 shows an example of the axial coding process. I started with the personal biographies of

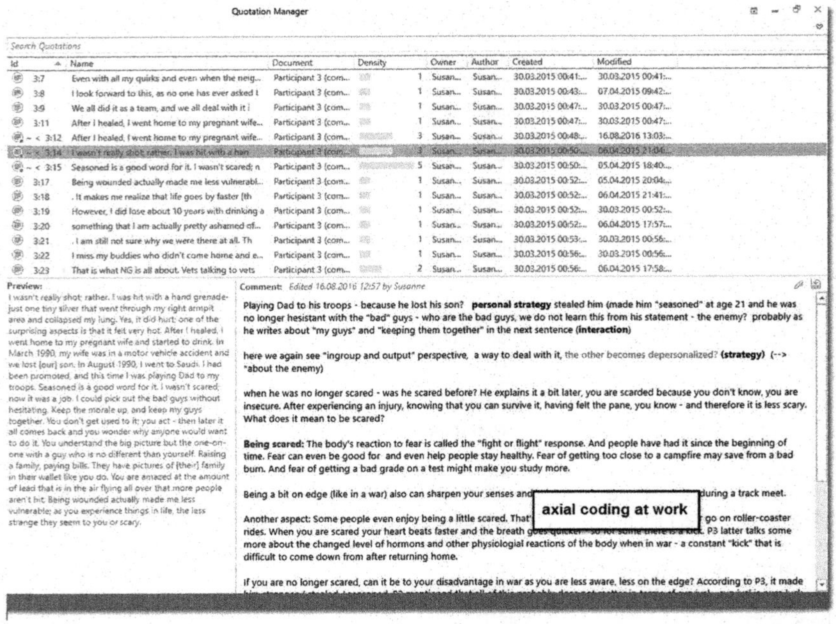

Figure 14.6 Using the comment field in the Quotation Manager for axial coding

the veterans reading the quotations of the category*: #background*, their motivations for going to war, their war experiences, and how these were perceived, described, and processed (category: *war experience*, with sub-codes *effects* and *dealing with*). The advantage of tagging the data in the software now becomes clear, as the tags offer quick and reliable access to data and allow the researcher to move smoothly within the data.

So far, all analytical notes in ATLAS.ti up to this point were written in the comment field for each quote. Figure 14.6 shows the Quotation Manager. Quotation 3:14 is selected, and the detailed analysis of this quote appears in the lower right-hand part of the window as comment. The quotation itself is shown in the Preview field. In this quotation, it was possible to identify various strategies used by the respondent, interactions and a consequence. Other quotations may also hold information about the various types of conditions or other combinations of the paradigmatic elements suggested by Corbin and Strauss (2008).

The commentary also holds references to other tags in the form of '—> code name', as a note for a connection to consider. Cross-connections to other quotations that came to mind while reflecting on and writing about the axis of a category were implemented by creating a hyperlink. In addition to the Link Manager, hyperlinks can also be accessed and visualized using the network function. Figure 14.7 shows three quotes with their codes and document source, and one commented link.

Along with writing during the axial coding phase, the list of tags continuously changed. I proceeded topic by topic: war experience, strategies for coping with the experiences during and after the war, explanations or justifications for the war, public response to the Vietnam War from the perspective of veterans, etc. This makes it possible to see connections within and across categories. The tags make it very simple to find specific segments. The descriptions become more focused and the connections obvious. While doing this, the researcher

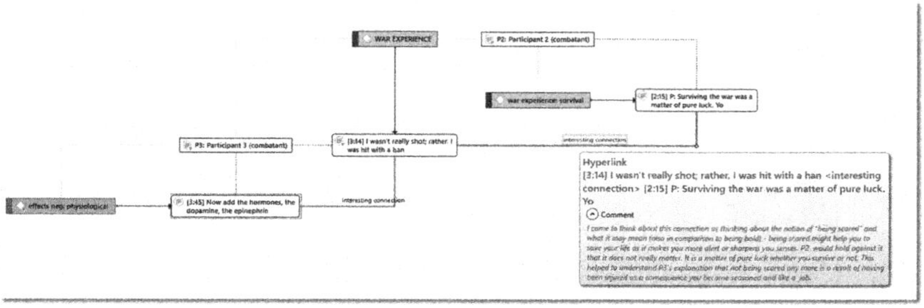

Figure 14.7 Diagramming using the ATLAS.ti network function

sorts and renames tags and builds categories. With the reordering of tags, everything that I had written about the data is also reordered. The need for sorting memos, as highlighted by Glaser (2003), thus is eliminated. It is not a separate step but happens organically. If desired, one can output any written texts (i.e., comments or memos), with or without the raw data. If your computer screen is big enough, or if you work with multiple monitors, actual printing may be unnecessary. A mere reordering of tags, without dealing more closely with the data behind it, would not have this effect and would indeed remodel GT to QDA.

Integration and Visualization

In the analysis presented by Juliet Corbin, the concept 'survival' was developed into a core category. As I was only working with the three sample files, for me it was the concept of 'coming home' that caught my attention. It would, however, be too early to call it a core category based on the small data set, and with more data at hand and further immersion into the topic, this might have been different.

At the time, I had several ideas on how 'coming home' connects to other developed concepts and categories in the data. I therefore called up a network and dragged my 'coming home' tag in the center. To build the connection, I approached the data with several questions in mind: For a soldier who had been in the war, what makes him feel that he has fully arrived back home? What might inhibit a successful homecoming? What strategies counteract the impact of war? Are there differences between those who fought on the front lines and those who served behind the lines as paramedics? What type of experiences did the respondents report and what effects did they have? What coping strategies were employed during the war? What impact the original attitude toward the war had, and was the experience altered by it? In other words, I worked backwards in time from the present to the past. I looked for evidence in the data and dragged all applicable tags into the network. Since a representation of the entire network would need a larger format, I present only two partial aspects that, step by step, interrelate all the aspects that lead to 'coming home' with one another.

Figure 14.8 shows the relational context of the category 'war experience' in an ATLAS.ti network. This includes aspects of the war experience, the consequences of these experiences, and coping strategies with these experiences, as well as the perception of the enemy, broken down by group of persons (combatants / non-combatants). For writing the summary analysis, I made use of ATLAS.ti memos (see Figure 14.10).

Figure 14.9 illustrates another partial aspect; it examines the question of whether the attitude towards war changed over time.

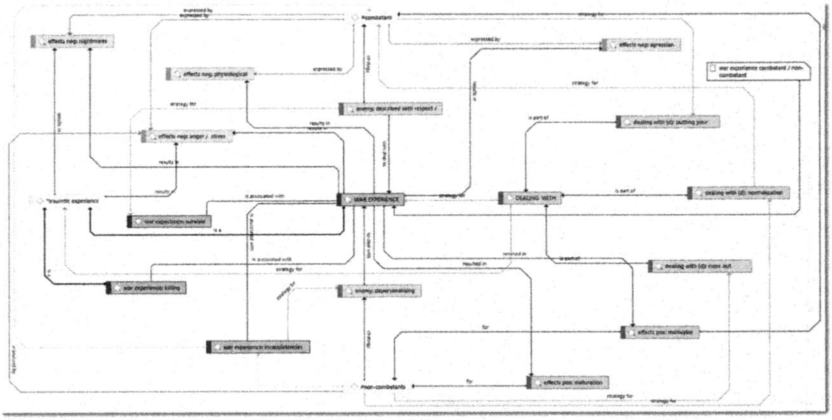

Figure 14.8 Network 'War Experience'

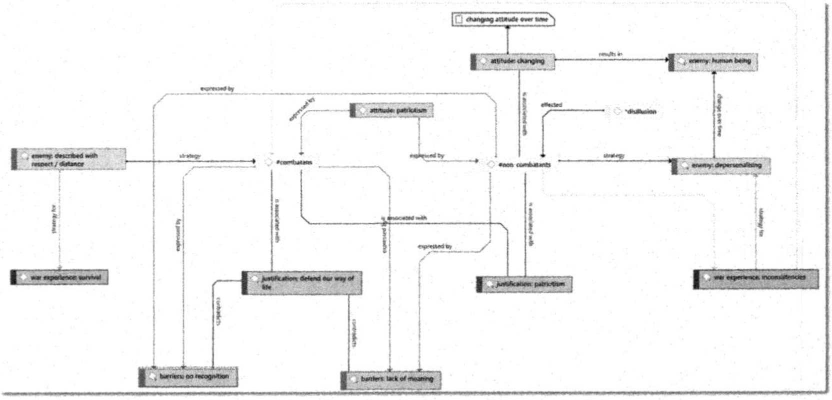

Figure 14.9 Network on changing attitude towards the military and war over time

In Figure 14.10, you see the ATLAS.ti memos I have started to write in the process of integration. I created a memo for each partial aspect, which may be helpful when focusing the analysis with respect to the core category. It is also possible to write comments for memos like a brief note where the memo might fit into the theory, or when working in a team, a comment written by another analyst. While writing the analysis, I linked memos to quotations, e.g., because I would like to use them later in the final report (see column: Grounded). This makes them easily searchable and retrievable. The 'density' column specifies the number of items the memo is linked to.

Emerging Code System

In Figure 14.11 and Figure 14.12, you see the code system for this sample study. I would not call it a 'final' code system yet as it would certainly change if I were to add further

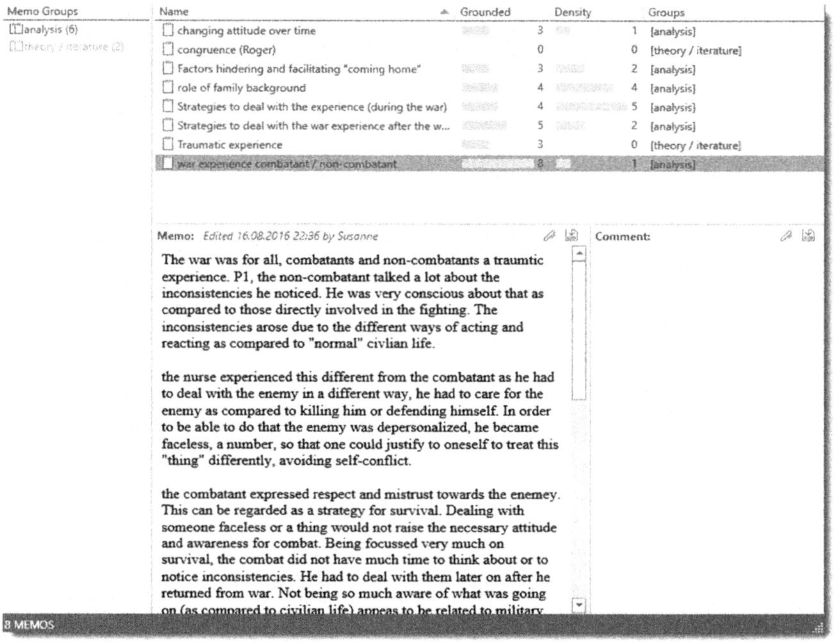

Figure 14.10 ATLAS.ti Memo Manager

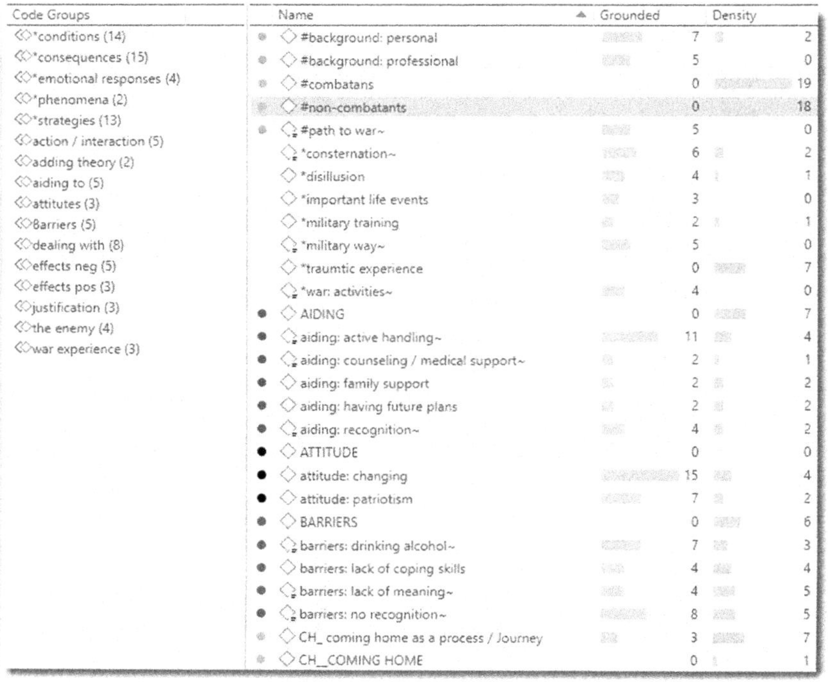

Figure 14.11 Sample study code system page 1

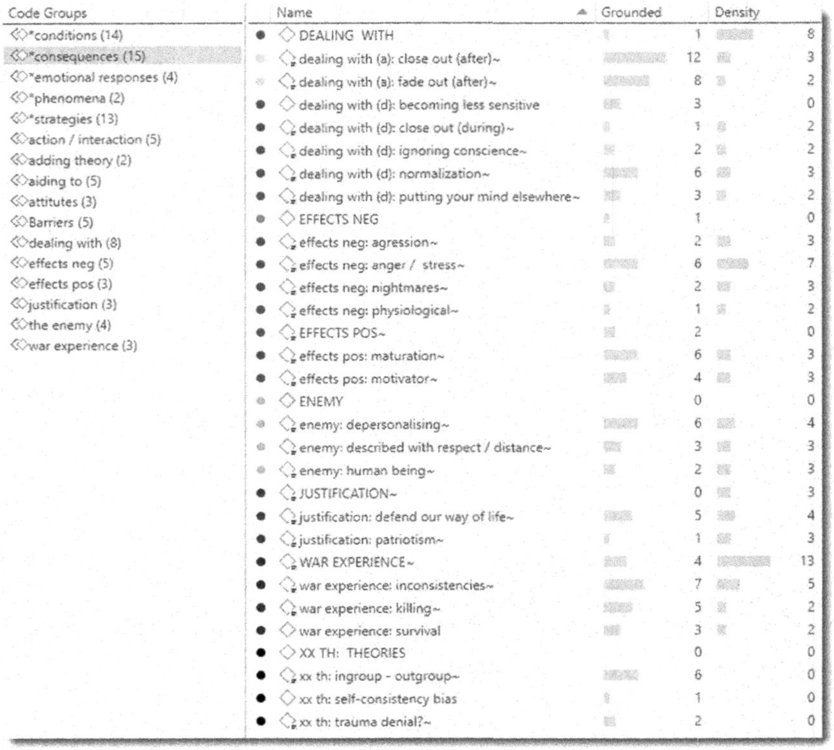

Figure 14.12 Sample study code system page 2

data material to continue the analysis. Comparing it to the first tag list shown in Table 14.1, it illustrates the progressing analysis where tags acquire methodological meaning.

There are seven tags that do not yet belong to any category (those beginning with an *). With more data being tagged, these might become a property of a category, or they might lead to building a new category. Based on the current state of the analysis, this is not obvious yet. Depending on how much would change with more data coming in, this is an indicator of how stable a code system is already – given an open mind. If only a few changes and adjustments need to be made, i.e., you mostly apply already existing tags, no new properties are emerging, and the existing ones are filling with content, you approach theoretical saturation.

In the process of developing categories, all tags belonging to a category were colored and added to code groups. Code groups in ATLAS.ti are useful for filtering, sorting and organizing tags and for use in advanced analysis tools. Code groups were created for categories and for the different aspects of the coding paradigm. As ATLAS.ti codes can be sorted into multiple code groups, I added the codes to a category group plus the fitting coding paradigm group.

Continuing Analysis

The process described above can now be continued with more material through theoretical sampling until saturation is reached. Software can help you retain ideas for further theoretical sampling, e.g., by writing them down at once when they occur in a comment or memo. This can be implemented via easily searchable and retrievable *abbreviations*. I used the abbreviation *TS when writing a note regarding theoretical sampling (see Figure 14.13) and used it as search term in the project-wide text search to retrieve all notes on further data collection.

The procedures for further analysis after adding more data stay the same: tag the data, develop categories, expand axial coding while writing quotation comments, take note of interesting connections through hyperlinks, and use the network diagrams for drawing and visualizing relationships. The nodes in a network are always directly linked to the actual data. This means you are not just juggling empty labels, but you can look at the underlying data at any time, reread and redevelop their comments as well as your summary memos. This is a stage where you can fall into the trap of remodeling GT to QDA, if you stop writing comments and memos and only apply tags.

Based on Corbin's ideas (Corbin & Strauss 2015), Figure 14.14 shows where more data could still be collected for the further development of a theory. The left column shows the existing as well as desirable document groups. There are no data yet for all document groups that show zero (0) members.

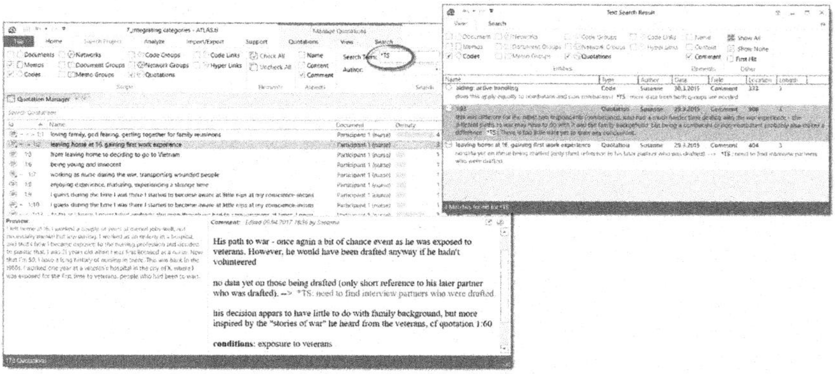

Figure 14.13 Using the Project Search function to find notes on theoretical sampling

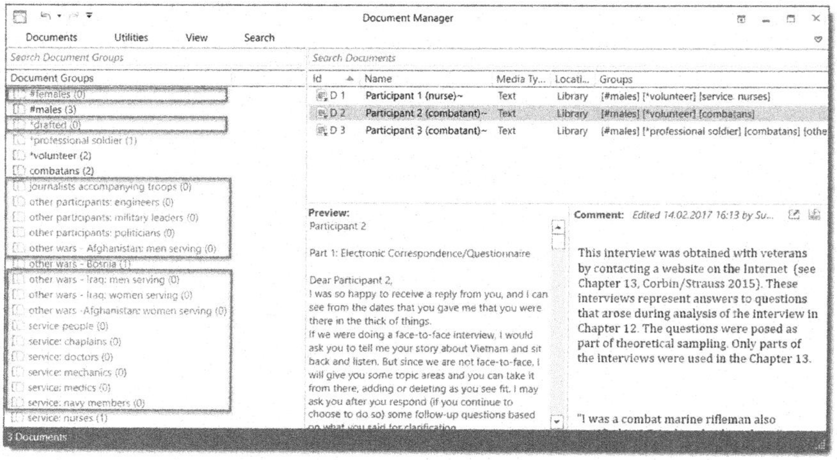

Figure 14.14 Ideas for further data collection (theoretical sampling)

Based on my personal history starting to work with CAQDAS over 20 years ago, I can hardly imagine how one would handle the expected data material manually, and how to keep track of it. Using ATLAS.ti or similar software, I cannot only manage the entire data material, but I can also ask important questions. Continuous comparison is a fundamental principle of grounded theory. CAQDAS enables me to compare statements on specific issues across diverse groups, e.g., do the testimonies of soldiers who served in Vietnam, in Iraq, or in Afghanistan differ from one another? I can ask whether women report different things from men? Are there similarities? Are different or similar coping strategies employed? How is 'homecoming' experienced depending on the context? These are all questions to which software can offer the data with a few clicks. The tools in ATLAS.ti that a researcher can use for this type of analysis are the query tool, the code co-occurrence tools, and the code-document table. These tools present common functionality across CAQDAS packages.

The code-co-occurrence tools perform a cross-tabulation of codes that are applied to the same or overlapping data segments. Figure 14.16 shows the cross-tabulation of the barrier with the 'negative effects' category. As the sample is very small, the frequency of occurrence is not very high yet. The purpose of showing the table is to show the potential of this type of analysis. The insights gained from such tables are not the numbers *per se*, but the data that is behind the numbers. At the bottom of the table you see the list of quotations for the column and the row codes. Based on this, the researcher can access the data and continue to develop the analysis paying attention to potential

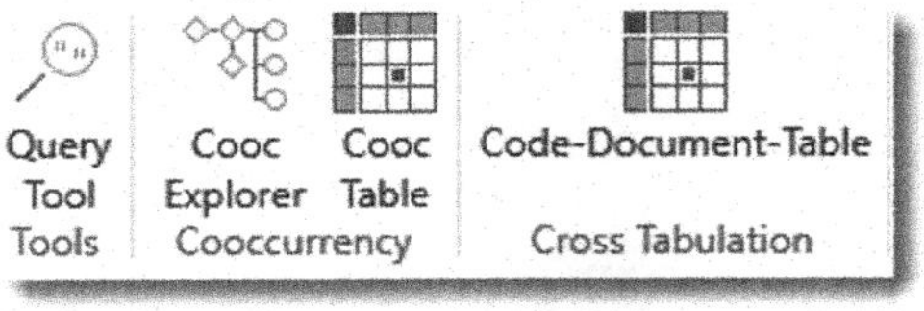

Figure 14.15 Advanced analysis tools

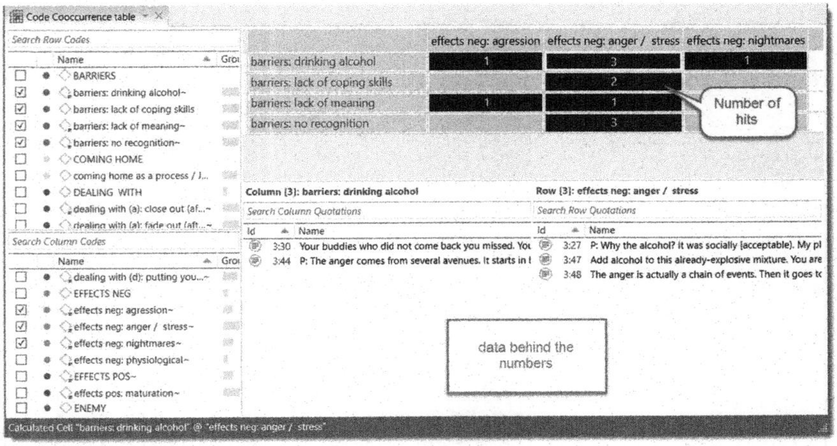

Figure 14.16 Code-occurrence Table

relations between certain types of barriers resulting in certain types of consequences, and so on.

The code-document table (Figure 14.17) is a cross-tabulation of codes or code groups by documents or documents groups that the analyst can use to compare combatants and non-combatants, respondents that served in different wars, male and female respondents, or as illustrated below for a case-by-case comparison. I already find this interesting given the current data set. Based on looking at the code frequency distribution, ideas for further sampling might arise, and issues are pin-pointed that are worthwhile to pay attention to. This type of analysis simply cannot be performed manually with growing amounts of data; it would be too time-consuming.

Reflecting on the application of such tools, the reaction could be that this is no longer GT but QDA. Based on research publications using CAQDAS for a GT analysis, it is often difficult to assess whether indeed a grounded theory analysis was carried out, or whether only the label was used as it is much easier to explain the application of tools rather than the thinking process that took place in writing memos, comments, annotations, etc. (e.g., Hutchison et al. 2010).

Theorizing itself happens throughout and cannot be linked to any specific software tool. It is taking place during all activities: when you create first tags, when you later build categories, when you link data, when you relate data to each other using various tools, and most obviously when you write. What you need to keep in mind is when using CAQDAS is that there will always be elements of description as you also use the software to organize and manage your data, in addition to analyzing them. Not all tags will end up being a part of the developed theory. Some categories might look different when compared to a manual analysis, because you built them in ways to allow running more advanced analyses that have become possible because you are using software. For example, I use the hashtag (#) prefix for codes that refer to sociodemographic characteristics, time, various actors, etc., that occur within a document to compare and contrast data across various characteristics. However, this does not mean that you remodel GT to QDA. The translation of the methodological activities just looks a bit different because you are using a different tool. An indicator for not having moved beyond content analysis is if you only have applied tags and have not made use of the writing tools. Writing comments, annotations and memos, of course, does not necessarily by itself lead to the development of theory. As yet another technique, I recommend checking your final memos against the criteria for Grounded Theory Studies

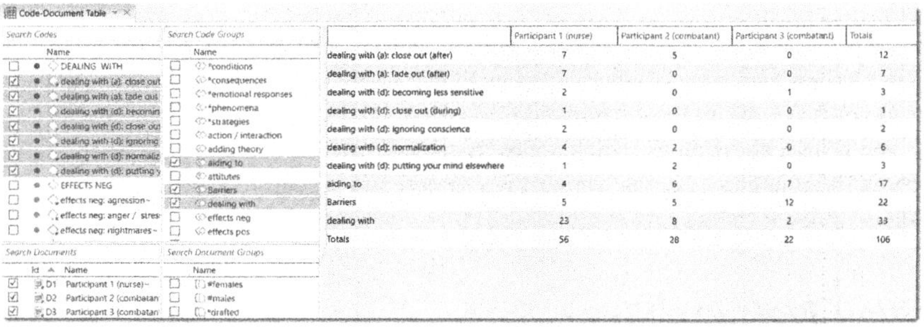

	Participant 1 (nurse)	Participant 2 (combatant)	Participant 3 (combatant)	Totals
dealing with (a): close out (after)	7	5	0	12
dealing with (a): fade out (after)	7	0	0	7
dealing with (d): becoming less sensitive	2	0	1	3
dealing with (d): close out (during)	1	0	0	1
dealing with (d): ignoring conscience	2	0	0	2
dealing with (d): normalization	4	2	0	6
dealing with (d): putting your mind elsewhere	1	2	0	3
aiding to	4	6	7	17
Barriers	5	5	12	22
dealing with	23	8	2	33
Totals	56	28	22	106

Figure 14.17 Code-Document Table

listed by Charmaz (2014: 336–337) to evaluate whether you indeed have developed a grounded theory.

TRANSLATING GT USING OTHER SOFTWARE TOOLS

In the following section I offer some ideas how the process described above might be translated using NVivo and MAXQDA.

Tagging and Data Level Work in NVivo

NVivo offers the possibility to organize tags in a hierarchical tree system, and it is also possible to have more than one tag list. For initial tagging, my advice is to 'code along the stem', which means to resist the temptation to begin organizing tags into higher and lower order tags too soon, just because it is easy to do. Based on my experience in teaching software, learners often want to know after 5 or 10 minutes into a coding exercise how to organize codes into trees and sub-trees. For the sample study presented here, I began to sort and order tags after having gone through the first interview.

The open coding process explained above as 'tagging + writing' needs to be translated differently in NVivo than in ATLAS.ti. If you want to write comments on selected data segments, you can do this using annotations. Annotations, however, cannot be longer than 1024 characters. If you want to write longer comments, the workaround is to attach two annotations to the same segment (Figure 14.18).

If you want to link data segments to each other, you can use 'See Also Links' (available in the pro and plus version, see Figure 14.18). Different from ATLAS.ti hyperlinks, where you can specify that statement A *explains / discusses / contradicts / supports* etc. statement B, the researcher in NVivo cannot specify *how* data segments relate to each other when using 'See Also Links'.

Figure 14.19 shows how list of tags can be organized in NVivo. Higher and lower order codes can be sorted into a hierarchical tree structure. Thereby it is possible to have multiple lists. In Figure 14.19 you see three lists, one containing the list of nodes after the step of integrating, one for all nodes referring to already existing theories, and one for yet unsorted tags.

In translating the Charmaz approach in NVivo, you could have a folder for all initial codes and one for nodes that you keep or add during the process of focused coding (Figure 14.20).

If you compare the NVivo interface with the ATLAS.ti interface (Figure 14.1), NVivo does not have a margin area where all tags, linked memos, or hyperlinks (= see also links) are shown. It is possible to display coding stripes, but this feature has a different function. The researcher decides which codes to display and the display is used for analytical purposes to compare 'codings' rather than to give immediate feedback of what happens during the process of tagging (Figure 14.21).

Writing Tools in NVivo

In ATLAS.ti one can write comments for every entity. This is different in NVivo. The researcher can describe a node in the node properties. This description can be shown as a

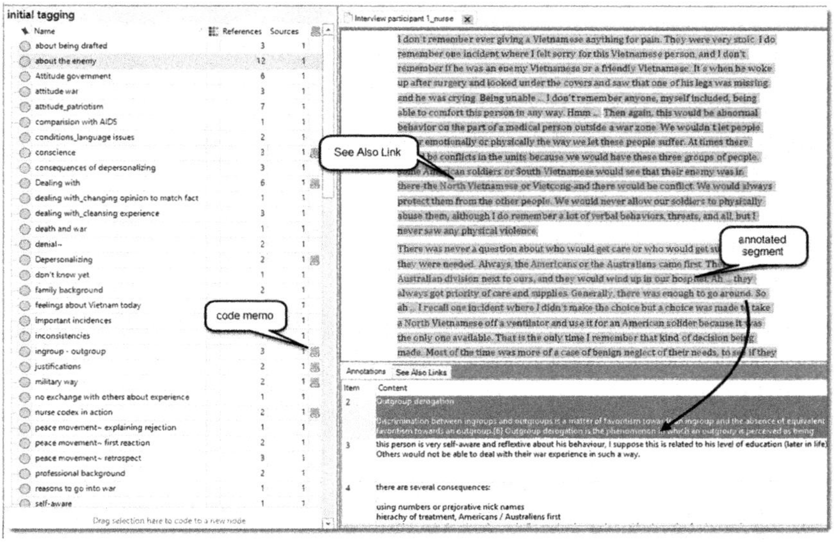

Figure 14.18 Initial tagging in NVivo

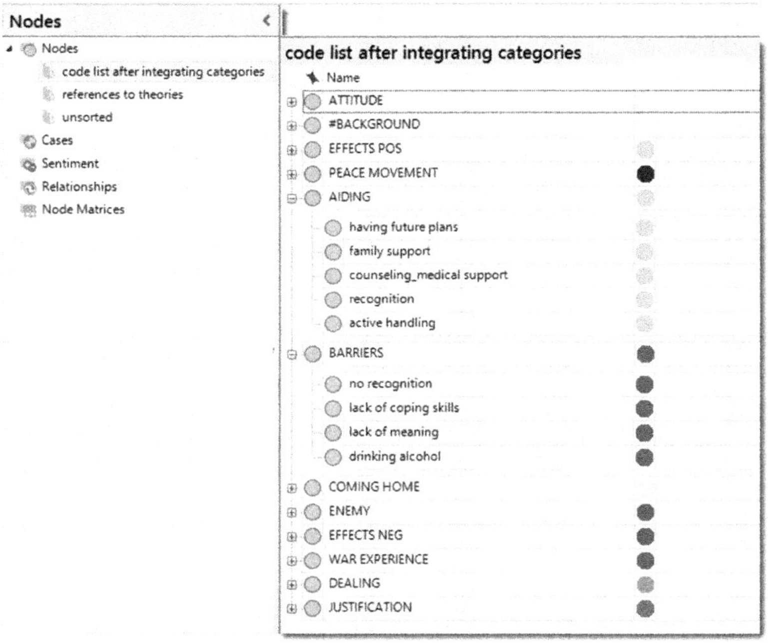

Figure 14.19 Ways of sorting tags in NVivo

one-liner in the code list. Therefore, the node description should be short, not containing further analysis. For this, a memo can be used. Figure 14.22 shows an example. Whether a code node has a memo is visible by the memo icon in the column to the right. The content of the code memo can be viewed via the context menu or a keyboard short-cut.

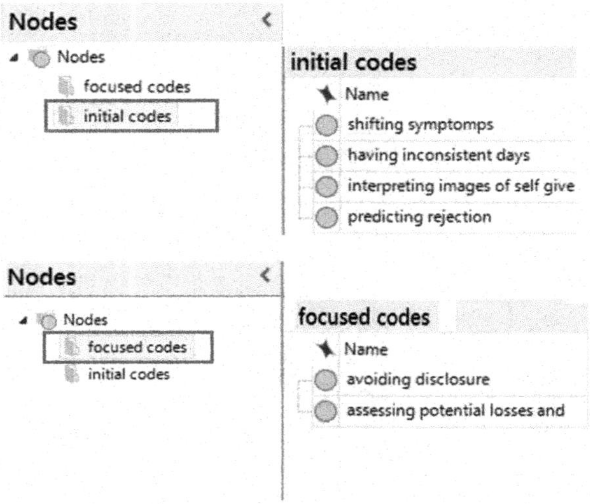

Figure 14.20 Translating the Charmaz approach of GT using the example provided by Charmaz (2014)

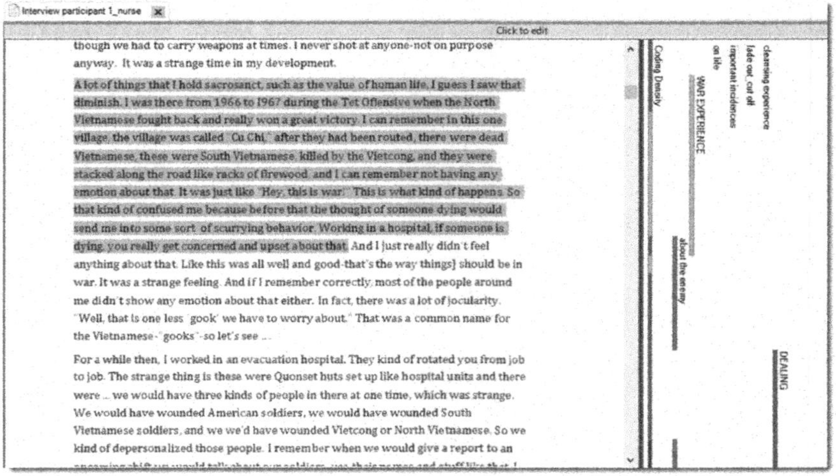

Figure 14.21 Coding stripes in NVivo

In addition to writing a memo for a code, the researcher can also write memos for document selections, or free memos that are not linked to anything. Memos can also be coded to facilitate later retrieval. Like code nodes, memos can also be organized in folders.

When comparing the translation given for ATLAS.ti with the functionality offered by NVivo, for quotation comments one could use annotations or memos linked to document selections. As shown in Figure 14.23, one could, for example, create a folder for all document memos per participant. For analytic thoughts related to multiple data segments coded with the same node, one can add a folder 'code memos' and add all memos linked to code

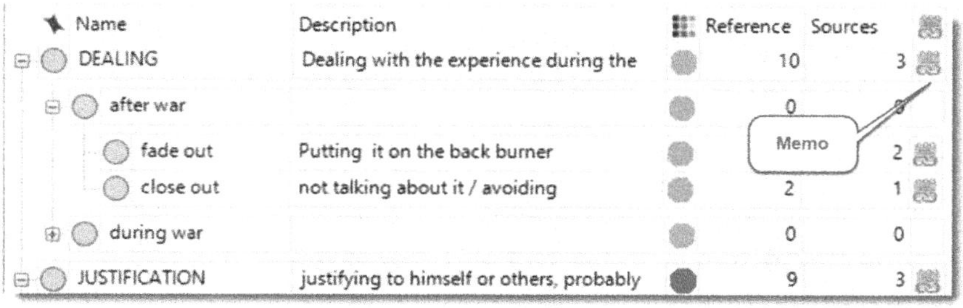

Figure 14.22 List of code nodes with description and code memo

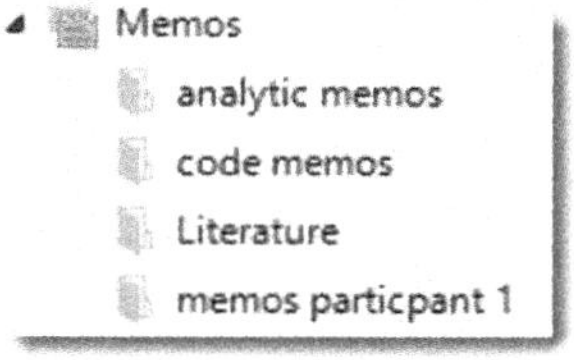

Figure 14.23 Memo folders in NVivo

nodes to this folder. In ATLAS.ti, I used the code comment field for this task. For memos on overlapping or overarching topics, I created free memos and grouped them in a folder called 'analytic memos' (Figure 14.23). This is where, in ATLAS.ti, I also used memos.

Applying the coding paradigm during axial coding: In ATLAS.ti, I utilized quotation and code comments for this analytic step; in NVivo *code memos* and memos linked to document selections could be used in a similar way. Note that you do not find 'code memos' in NVivo; this is my translation for memos that I create for nodes. Bringer et al. (2006) explained how the conditional matrix supported them in translating axial coding. They used the matrix as a heuristic diagram to assist with identifying conditions and consequences of the core category.

Integration and Visualization in NVivo

Based on the earlier sections, you may already guess that the way I integrated data in ATLAS.ti in relation to the core category needs to be realized differently in NVivo. Networks in ATLAS.ti are an interactive tool where I can drag-and-drop any item that I want to link into a visual space. While I link them to each other, I can think about the type of relation I want to use. I can comment on each link, view the data that is behind each node in a network, or have a memo opened alongside and write. NVivo offers mind maps and concepts maps for brainstorming and theorizing. Bringer et al. (2006), for example, used concepts maps for early conceptual development in building their hierarchical code structure. Depending on your preference, you may also want to use a piece of paper, or sticky notes on a board to translate this process of data integration. Once you have an idea how the various concepts, actors, contexts, etc. relate to each other, you can define relations and apply them like code nodes. These can be visualized using project maps (Figure 14.24).

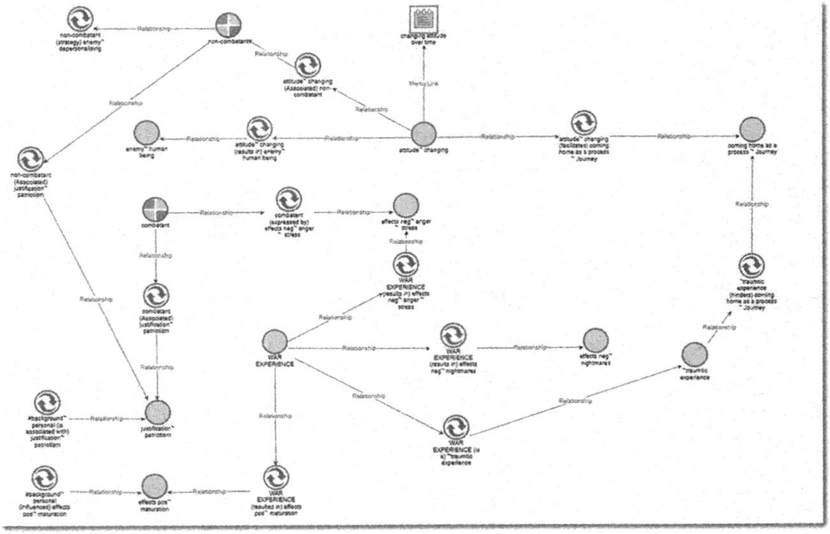

Figure 14.24 Project Map on 'changing attitudes' in NVivo

Tagging and Data Level Work in MAXQDA

MAXQDA, like NVivo, offers a hierarchical code list. Thus, what I wrote above on organizing initial tags and building a code system also applies here. Translating the process of open coding, one needs to consider the options MAXQDA offers for writing at the data level. One choice is to comment tagged data segments; however, such a comment can only be 127 characters long. A further possibility, and likely the better translation for this task, is to write 'in-document memos' (Figure 14.25). These show up like post-it notes alongside the document. Each memo has a title and you can link a 'code' to it. I recommend changing the default memo title, which just adds a consecutive number to each memo: memo 1, memo 2, memo 3, etc., so that later you can find your way around in the list of all memos.

MAXQDA, like many other programs, use the term 'code' to tag data. If you want to apply the Strauss and Corbin approach to grounded theory, the recommendation is to use them initially as tags and to write memos for the process of open coding, as it was described above for ATLAS.ti. Trying to implement the open coding process by just applying what MAXQDA calls codes is likely to result in an extensive list of terms that quickly becomes difficult to manage and leads to frustration and often abandonment of the software (Weber 2014).

When following a constructive grounded theory approach, initial codes can be created along the stem of the code tree. When comparing the MAXQDA Code System to the node structure using folders in NVivo, an idea that might occur is to create sub-trees for initial and focused codes. I would recommend not using the Code System for this as it interferes with later analysis possibilities like the ones explained in the section 'Continuing Analysis'. For instance, when you want to relate codes to each other using the Code Relation Browser, it is unlikely that you want to relate initial and focused codes to each

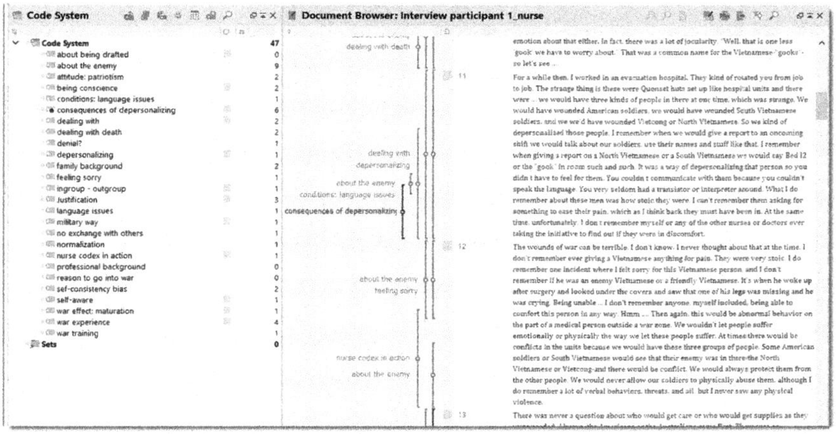

Figure 14.25 Translating open coding in MAXQDA: Tagging + writing in-document memos

other as they present phases in your analysis rather than categories resulting from analysis. More generally, it is not very useful for the analysis to use organizational codes as main branches of the code tree. If you wanted to keep track of the tags developed during various phases of the analysis, a possibility is to use code sets.

Writing Tools in MAXQDA

As already mentioned, MAXQDA offers memos for writing. You can write a memo for each document, e.g., to write down context information; you can write a memo for document groups and document sets to describe the group or set; you can write a memo for each code; you can attach memos to a section within a document, the so called in-document memos; and you can write free memos.

As explained, I recommend using in-document memos to support the process of open coding. Code memos can be used in the same way as explained for NVivo and ATLAS.ti, for describing what is meant by a code label and how to apply it, and for further analysis on all data segments coded with what MAXQDA calls code. Also, in MAXQDA, codes should be understood as tags in the beginning phases of the analysis, which might turn into a category, property or dimension during the course of the analysis. If you want to implement axial coding and the coding paradigm, the analytic writing for this phase can be done in in-document and code memos. Figure 14.26 shows the Overview of Memos table. As MAXQDA only offers one type of entity for writing, use memo titles carefully and create a branch in the code system for codes linked to memos, so that you can easily retrieve what you are looking for and do not get lost in an extensive list of memos.

Another function for writing is the summary grid (Figure 14.27). It offers a per-document overview of which code has been applied and how often. When clicking on a cell, the coded segments for the selected code per document, e.g., an interview participant, are retrieved in the column 'Coded segments'. The column 'Summary' is initially an empty space that the analyst can use to write. This tool is useful if one wants to concentrate on a per-case analysis.

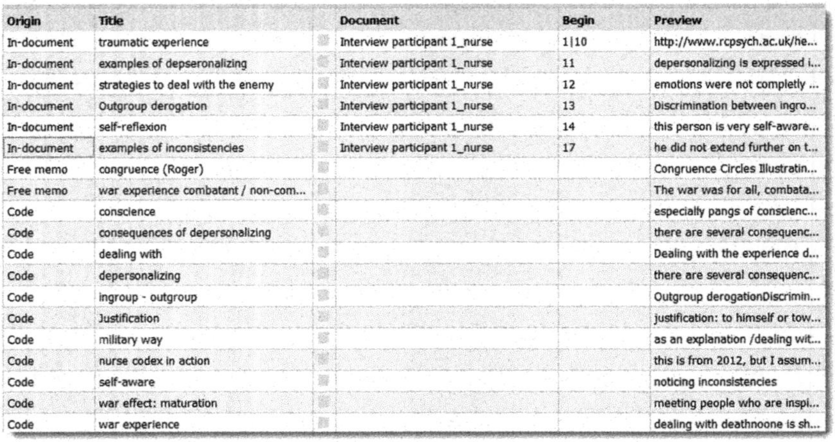

Origin	Title	Document	Begin	Preview
In-document	traumatic experience	Interview participant 1_nurse	1|10	http://www.rcpsych.ac.uk/he...
In-document	examples of depseronalizing	Interview participant 1_nurse	11	depersonalizing is expressed i...
In-document	strategies to deal with the enemy	Interview participant 1_nurse	12	emotions were not completly ...
In-document	Outgroup derogation	Interview participant 1_nurse	13	Discrimination between ingro...
In-document	self-reflexion	Interview participant 1_nurse	14	this person is very self-aware...
In-document	examples of inconsistencies	Interview participant 1_nurse	17	he did not extend further on t...
Free memo	congruence (Roger)			Congruence Circles Illustratin...
Free memo	war experience combatant / non-com...			The war was for all, combata...
Code	conscience			especially pangs of conscienc...
Code	consequences of depersonalizing			there are several consequenc...
Code	dealing with			Dealing with the experience d...
Code	depersonalizing			there are several consequenc...
Code	ingroup - outgroup			Outgroup derogationDiscrimin...
Code	Justification			justification: to himself or tow...
Code	military way			as an explanation /dealing wit...
Code	nurse codex in action			this is from 2012, but I assum...
Code	self-aware			noticing inconsistencies
Code	war effect: maturation			meeting people who are inspi...
Code	war experience			dealing with deathnoone is sh...

Figure 14.26 Overview of memos in MAXQDA

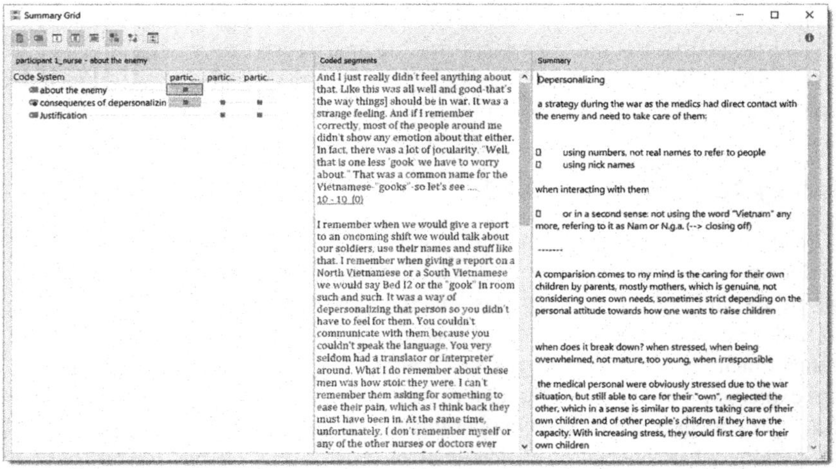

Figure 14.27 Summary Grid for a case-based analysis in MAXQDA

Linking Data, Integration, and Visualization in MAXQDA

In MAXQDA data segments can be linked to each other without being able to name the link, the same as in NVivo. Like in ATLAS.ti, these are called hyperlinks. However, you need to be careful when engaging in translation across different programs. NVivo also has hyperlinks. They can be created in documents or memos to link to webpages or external sources. In MAXQDA, hyperlinks are links between two data segments within a document or between documents; or you can use them to create links to webpages and external sources. In ATLAS.ti, hyperlinks create a link between two or more quotations. These links can be named and commented. Therefore, the use of hyperlinks in all three programs is different. MAXQDA hyperlinks can be used in similar fashion to 'See Also Links' in NVivo (see above).

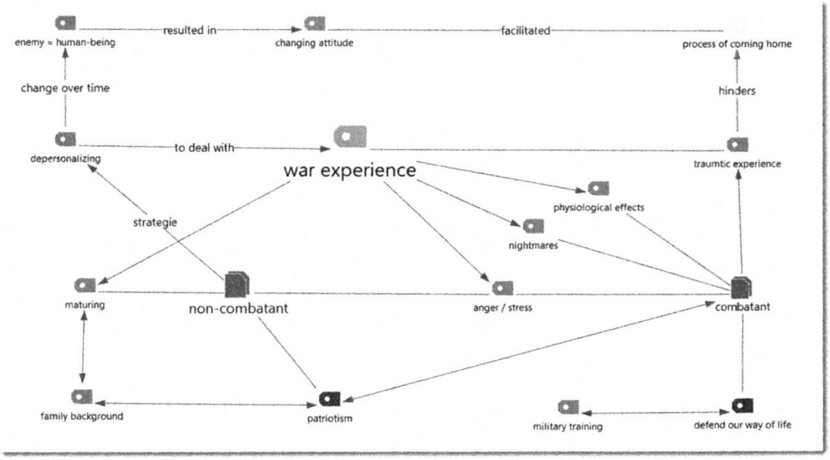

Figure 14.28 Linking data, integrating analysis: maps in MAXQDA

When you want to link data during the process of axial coding or during the process of integration, you can use MAXQDA maps. Like ATLAS.ti, you can drag and drop all items that you want to link, or want to think about, into a map. You can name the relation between two nodes in the map. Different from ATLAS.ti, there is no set of relations to choose from. Figure 14.28 shows a MAXQDA map, comparable to the ATLAS.ti network show in Figure 14.9.

SUMMARY

I started this chapter reflecting on why some researchers outright reject the use of software for a grounded theory analysis. As a person using CAQDAS for 25 years, I would not want to do without it, also not for a grounded theory analysis. While I was pondering about the debate, it occurred to me that one issue could be the different usages and applications of the same terms by grounded theory analysts and CAQDAS. An important practice in grounded theory analysis is coding and it is exactly here where lots of translation errors and misunderstandings happen. This results in some researchers not wanting to use software at all, or in others thinking that they do a grounded theory analysis because they are coding, but never do more than thematic analysis. Yet, another outcome is frustrated researchers who drown in too many codes, get stuck with their analysis, and end up blaming the software for it (cf. Woolf & Silver, 2017).

I continued the chapter by walking the reader through a case study and explained how I translated each methodological step in the software ATLAS.ti. As different researchers use different tools, I also showed how the translation can be done using NVivo or MAXQDA. There is thus no blue-print as to how a grounded theory analysis can be accomplished using CAQDAS, but there is one common rule that you should keep in mind, no matter which software package you are using: First, reflect on what you want to achieve from a methodological point of view, then think about how you can translate this into software functions and tools. In this chapter, I offered a translation of the Strauss and Corbin approach and some ideas about how to translate initial and focused coding based on Charmaz. Depending on the approach you want to choose, the translation is likely to be a bit different. It can, however, also be the case that it is not possible to translate a methodological task directly, or that you feel more comfortable doing it on paper or using sticky notes on a big wall. If you want to sort your memos like in the old days, just print them out. You are the master; the software is the tool.

Because of the translation process you need to engage in, it is not a promising idea to begin learning to use a software tool because you have some data and now want to analyze them. A probable outcome is that the software will drive your analysis, rather than you overseeing the process. My recommendation is that your first software-assisted analysis should be a simple content or thematic analysis. This will allow you to become familiar with the various tools and you will learn about the process of tagging data and how to build a code system that works. The code system in CAQDAS for a grounded theory analysis does not only need to fit the methodological requirements of the chosen grounded theory approach. To harness the full functionality and power of the software, the researcher also needs to be mindful of some housekeeping tasks and how to best manage and organize the list of tags. This is a matter of experience that you gain over time, and, if possible, learning the use of software from a methodological aware teacher.

Rather than condemning CAQDAS, I would like to suggest the use of CAQDAS as a way forward into the future of grounded theory. When GT first was developed, personal computers were not yet available and only in recent years, electronic devices have become daily companions for all kinds of research tasks. Also, GT itself has been developed further, most notably by the mentoring efforts of Glaser and Strauss themselves (Morse et al. 2009: 10). Today there is not only one approach, there are several. A third-generation development could be a computer-aided grounded theory analysis, which stays true to core principles but extends the approach, encompassing new analysis options that are possible today due to technical advancement.

USEFUL LINKS AND RESOURCES

List of available CAQDAS: www.surrey.ac.uk/sociology/research/researchcentres/caqdas/support/choosing/

ATLAS.ti research blog: http://atlasti.com/topic/blog/

NVivo research blog: www.qsrinternational.com/blog

MAXQDA research blog: www.maxqda.com/blog

Quirkos research blog: www.quirkos.com/blog/

Five-level QDA blog: www.fivelevelqda.com/blog

Bazeley, Patricia and Jackson, Kristi (2013). *Qualitative Data Analysis with NVivo*. London: Sage.

Bourdon, Sylvain (2002). The integration of qualitative data analysis software in research strategies: resistances and possibilities [30 paragraphs]. *Forum Qualitative Sozialforschung / Forum: Qualitative Social Research*, 3(2), Art. 11, http://nbn-resolving.de/urn:nbn:de:0114-fqs0202118

Carvajal, Diógenes (2002). The artisan's tools: Critical issues when teaching and learning CAQDAS [47 paragraphs]. *Forum Qualitative Sozialforschung / Forum: Qualitative Social Research*, 3(2), Art. 14, http://nbn-resolving.de/urn:nbn:de:0114-fqs0202147.

Friese, Susanne: Building an efficient coding system: Do's and Don'ts. Prezi presentation: https://prezi.com/qane-q4ax16z/?utm_campaign=share&utm_medium=copy&rc=ex0share

Friese, Susanne: Qualitative data analysis with ATLAS.ti: Book summary. YouTube Video: www.youtube.com/watch?v=Qpzc7__5e_k

Woolf, Nick (2014). Analytic strategies and analytic tactics. In Friese, Susanne and Ringmayr, Thomas (Eds.), *ATLAS.ti User Conference 2013: Fostering Dialog on Qualitative Methods*. Berlin: University Press, Technical University Berlin. http://nbn-resolving.de/urn:nbn:de:kobv:83-opus4-44159

REFERENCES

Bazeley, Pat (2013). *Qualitative Data Analysis: Practical Strategies*. London: Sage.

Breuer, Franz (2018). *Reflexive Grounded Theory: An Introduction for Research Practice*. Wiesbaden: VS Verlag.

Bringer, Joy D., Johnston, L. H., & Brackenridge, C. H. (2006). Using computer-assisted qualitative data analysis software to develop a grounded theory project. *Field Methods*, *18*(3), 245–266.

Bryant, Antony & Charmaz, Kathy (Eds.) (2007). *The SAGE Handbook of Grounded Theory*. London: Sage.

Charmaz, Kathy (2014). *Constructing Grounded Theory* (2nd edition). London: Sage.

Corbin, Juliet & Strauss, Anselm L. (2008/2015). *Basics of Qualitative Research: Techniques and Procedures for Developing Grounded Theory* (3rd and 4th editions). London: Sage.

Friese, Susanne (2011). Using ATLAS.ti for analyzing the financial crisis data [67 Paragraphs]. *Forum Qualitative Sozialforschung / Forum: Qualitative Social Research*, *12*(1), Article 39, http://nbn-resolving.de/urn:nbn:de:0114-fqs1101397 (Polling: 04/07/2015).

Friese, Susanne (2014). *Qualitative Data Analysis with ATLAS.ti* (2nd edition). London: Sage.

Friese, Susanne (2016). Qualitative data analysis software: The state of the art. *Special Issue: Qualitative Research in the Digital Humanities*, Bosch, Reinoud (Ed.), KWALON, *61*, *21*(1), 34–45.

Glaser, Barney G. (1978). *Theoretical Sensitivity: Advances in the Methodology of Grounded Theory*. Mill Valley, CA: Sociology Press.

Glaser, Barney G. (1992). *Emergence vs Forcing: Basics of Grounded Theory*. Mill Valley, CA: Sociology Press.

Glaser, Barney G. (1992). *Emergence vs Forcing: Basics of Grounded Theory*. Mill Valley, CA: Sociology Press.

Glaser, Barney G. (2003). *The Grounded Theory Perspective II: Description's Remodeling of Grounded Theory Methodology*. Mill Valley, CA: Sociology Press.

Goulding, Christina (2002). *Grounded Theory: A Practical Guide for Management, Business and Market Researchers*. London: Sage.

Holton, Judith A. (2007). The coding process and its challenges. In A. Bryant & K. Charmaz (Eds.), *The SAGE Handbook of Grounded Theory*. London: Sage, pp. 265–290.

Hutchison, Andrew J., Johnston, Lynne H., & Breckon, Jeff D. (2010). Using QSR-NVivo to facilitate the development of a grounded theory project: An account of a worked example. *International Journal of Social Research Methodology*, *13*(4), 283–302.

Kelle, Udo (2007). The development of categories: Different approaches in grounded theory. In A. Bryant & K. Charmaz (Eds.), *The SAGE Handbook of Grounded Theory*. London: Sage, pp. 191–213.

Morse, J., Stern, P. N., Corbin, J., Bowers, B., Charmaz, K., & Clarke, A. E. (2009). *Developing Grounded Theory: The Second Generation*. London: Routledge.

Muhr, Thomas (1997). *ATLAS.ti: Visual Qualitative Data Analysis, User's Manual and Reference Guide. Version 4.1*. Berlin Scientific Software Development.

Remenyi, Dan (2014). *Ground Theory: A Reader for Researchers, Students, Faculty and Others*. Reading: ACPI.

Richards, Lyn (2009). *Handling Qualitative Data: A Practical Guide*. London: Sage.

Richards, Lyn & Morse, Janice M. (2013). *Qualitative Methods*. Thousand Oaks, CA: Sage.

Richards, Lyn & Richards, Tom (1995). Using hierarchical categories in qualitative research. In U. Trowel, (Ed.) (1998), *Computer-Aided Qualitative Data Analysis: Theory, Methods and Practice*. London: Sage.

Seale, Clive, Gobo, Giampietro, Gubrium, Jaber F., & Silverman, David (2004). *Qualitative Research Practice*. London: Sage.

Silver, Christina & Lewins, Ann (2014). *Using Software in Qualitative Research: A Step-By-Step Guide*. London: Sage.

Silver, Christina & Woolf, Nickolas (2015). From guided-instruction to facilitation of learning: The development of Five-level QDA as CAQDAS pedagogy that explicates the practices of expert users. *International Journal of Social Science Research Methodology*, *18*(5), 527–543, http://dx.doi.org/10.1080/13645579.2015.1062626

Stern, Phyllis N. (2007). On solid ground: Essential properties for growing grounded theory. In A. Bryant & K. Charmaz (Eds.), *The SAGE Handbook of Grounded Theory*. London: Sage, pp. 114–126.

Strauss, Anselm L. (1987). *Qualitative Analysis for Social Scientists*. Cambridge: Cambridge University Press.

Strauss, Anselm L. (1998). *Grundlagen Qualitativer Sozialforschung* (2nd edition). Paderborn: UTB.

Strauss, Anselm L. & Corbin, Juliet (1990/1998). *Basics of Qualitative Research: Grounded Theory Procedures and Techniques* (1st and 2nd editions). London: Sage.

Strauss, Anselm & Corbin, Juliet (1996). *Grundlagen Qualitative Sozialforschung*. Weinheim: Beltz.

Weber, Kristina Maria (2014). Computergestützte Datenauswertung: Entwicklung der Software qintexA. In Jan Kruse (Ed.), *Qualitative Interviewforschung: Ein integrativer Ansatz*. Weinheim und Basel: Beltz Juventa, pp. 604–614.

Woolf, Nickolas H. & Silver, Christina (2017). *Qualitative Analysis Using ATLAS.ti / MAXQDA / NVivo: The Five Level QDA Method*. Oxford: Routledge.

APPENDIX

The following table gives an overview how to apply software functions in a GT analysis.

Table 14.3: Software functions and their application in GT

Software functions	*Application*
code (tag) node (NVivo)	• Initial structuring of the data • concepts • categories • sub codes • dimensions
Quotation comment (ATLAS.ti) Annotations (NVivo) In-document memos (MAXQDA)	• open and axial coding • code notes • notes on theoretical sampling
Code comment (ATLAS.ti) Code Memo (NVivo, MAXQDA)	• first thoughts that serve concept building • Description of properties • Summaries and interpretation of data segments tagged with a code (Summary Grid (MAXQDA)
Hyperlinks (ATLAS.ti) Approximation: See Also Links (NVivo); Hyperlinks (MAXQDA)	• References to other data segments, which would be noted on a record card when analyzing data manually • The type of link can be named like: confirms / explains / is consequence of / is strategy for / contradicts, etc. • The linked data segment can be retrieved in context; one can directly jump to it via a mouse click • Hyperlinks can also be created and displayed in network views
Memos	• Research diary • Notes on theoretical concepts that might be helpful in interpreting the data • Writing up answers to research questions based on queries • Writing up the various parts that will later form the theory • Summaries of existing theories, models, research finding
Networks (ATLAS.ti) Maps (NVivo and MAXQDA)	• Recommended when working on the conceptual level • Supports the process of integration • Presentation of core category and its connections • Concept and mind maps for project planning and brainstorming (NVivo)

15

Keep your Data Moving: Operationalization of Abduction with Technology

Andrea Gorra

INTRODUCTION

The purpose of this chapter is to contribute to the ongoing debate about software use for the analysis of qualitative data using the Grounded Theory Method. I want to shed light on the ways in which grounded theorists use their method and make more explicit the process of moving from data to a grounded theory – with a focus on technology and techniques that are actually used by today's researchers, since I agree with Bryant and Charmaz (2007) in that this is not always transparent.

This aim is achieved in three ways. First, by conducting a Grounded Theory (GT) study and sharing how I have used the method. I share some of the categories developed as well as some quotes to provide an insight into my participants' way of thinking. Due to the brevity of the chapter, I only briefly cover sampling and have not included any lists of codes (for a much better explanation on how to use the method, see e.g., Charmaz, 2014). I share one Memo and demonstrate how this has helped me clarify my thinking and bring my findings together in relation to the literature, with the result being the basis of a substantive Grounded Theory.

The second and more theoretical contribution to the ongoing CAQDAS (Computer-Aided Qualitative Data AnalysiS) debate is the substantive Grounded Theory which I began building based on my Core Category 'Moving', which subsumes the other smaller categories. My initial intention was to interview researchers and predominantly focus on CAQDAS software, but the more I spoke to researchers and coded their interview data, the more it became clear to me that GT researchers use a whole range of technologies and different strategies to make sense of their collected qualitative data. I noticed that none of the researchers I spoke to actually stayed within the boundaries of one software program, and it seemed that the journey was the destination, i.e., the more researchers interacted with the data – sometimes in creative, other times in more repetitive ways – the more successful they became in making sense of it. This is not a new or surprising finding, but what I believe has changed is the way in which technology can support this process of interacting with the data.

The third contribution concludes my chapter and consists of the development of some tangible recommendations for novice researchers based on my findings. These are, in essence: Keep *moving* your data; make use technology to be efficient and organized; use software – not just CAQDAS – as *you* see fit to 'find your own way' (in vivo code) of interacting with the data to help make sense of it.

CHANGING LANDSCAPES: TECHNOLOGY, METHOD, DATA AND RESEARCHERS

Since the publication of Glaser and Strauss's first books about the Grounded Theory Method (GTM) 50 years ago, many changes to the wider research environment have taken place. Technology has changed at an unprecedented pace, the GTM has developed, the nature of research data and perhaps even researchers themselves have changed. These four factors impact on how GTM is actually used by researchers, and I will explore this in the following sections, as well as points commonly made about the use of CAQDAS software.

Specialist software to help with the analysis of qualitative data has been around for many years and various established programs, both commercial and open-source, exist. The CAQDAS Networking Project at the University of Surrey (2017) offers a good overview of available software, and states that the term 'CAQDAS' (Computer-Aided Qualitative Data AnalysiS) software was coined at one of their Research Methods conferences in the 1980s. Others use the term QDA, which I choose not to utilize here as, for some, it has different connotations in the context of GTM (see the debate about QDA and GTM in Glaser and Holton, 2004). Some software has been claimed to have been created specifically for GTM, such as Atlas.Ti as part of the ATLAS project (1989–1992) at the Technical University of Berlin. However, at the time some contested this and suggested that various manufacturers simply chose to jump on the 'GT bandwagon' and used an 'established brand name in qualitative research' to promote their product (Kelle, 1997, p. 20).

Today a plethora of the other software and technology is available to researchers, and, in addition to specialist qualitative data analysis software, the internet offers generalist advice on GTM: Youtube video lectures (e.g., by Bryant 2009; Charmaz, 2012) and tutorials by scholars (e.g., Gibbs, 2010). Also, very popular with researchers are Office applications, such as Microsoft Word, Excel and their open-source counterparts, but also other software, such as Mind Mapping software for tablets or computers to help visualize ideas. Using these technological capabilities, it is entirely possible to 'do research' and write a research report or a thesis *without* using pen and paper. Computers are used for typing, the smart phone is a good device to record interviews, visualizing of ideas is done with a tablet, reading and annotating journal papers can be easily done on tablet or laptop.

Some believe that members of the younger generation, sometimes referred to as Generation X, Millennials or Digital Natives (Prensky, 2001), process information differently.

Already two decades ago, Tapscott (1998) described the learning activities of the 'millennial generation' as substantially different from that of previous generations. Some argue that their use and understanding of digital technologies, such as computers, mobile phones and video consoles, from a young age has modified how they perceive and interact with the environment, both physically and socially (Prensky, 2001). Of course, over the last 50 years the Grounded Theory Method also has evolved, split into different schools or variants (Apramian et al., 2016) and 'taken on a life of its own' (see Bryant and Charmaz, 2007, p. 6). It seems that the digital revolution, and with it the proliferation of computers, may also have impacted on the nature of qualitative data of interest to GT researchers. Nowadays, not only written text can be analyzed, but also videos, audio, photos, music and so on can be captured, coded and analyzed (Gibbs et al., 2002; see also Chapter 17 in this volume by Krzysztof Konecki). In this sense, the well-known dictum expressed by Glaser 'All is data' certainly holds true. As he explains: 'It means that exactly what is going on in the research scene is the data, whatever the source, whether interview, observation, documents' (Glaser, 2007, p. 1).

CAQDAS Software versus *Method?*

Much has been written about the pros and cons of CAQDAS software use, and novice researchers are exposed to many types of advice that may guide – or confuse – them in making decisions about their technology-supported research strategies. Welsh (2002, para 9) sees qualitative researchers divided into two camps – for some the use of software is central to the analysis process, while others feel that software use is unimportant and could result in the 'wrong kind of analysis taking place'.

Woods and Wickham (2006) offer a more helpful categorization of the interplay between research methods and software functionality, by identifying three ways in which this interaction can take place. First, method-behaviour *dominates* software-behaviour: use of CAQDAS to perform familiar techniques, e.g., use of the computer to code and make notes about those codes. Second, software *complements* method: use of new techniques, possibly through technology, which are included in the data analysis repertoire. For example, 'query' or 'auto coding', execute search and retrieval functions are not possible using manual methods, resulting in new forms of data interrogation. Third, software-behaviour could *dominate* method-behaviour by influencing analytical output: e.g., creation of overly elaborate coding schemes, including hierarchical categories which are comprehensive but not useful, and do not support the sense-making and interpretative process. Miles et al. (2014) offer the advice to consider the type of study. They suggest that a specialist CAQDAS program might not be needed if the research project is small but they also strongly recommend using software when it comes to studies that include photographs and video.

Focusing on Grounded Theory, some of its eminent scholars seem rather sceptical regarding the use of CAQDAS software; they appear to be either vehemently opposed to using CAQDAS (Glaser & Holton, 2004), show wariness (Bryant & Charmaz, 2007, p. 24) or show 'concern' (Corbin & Strauss, 2008, p. 310). Glaser specifically refers to the problems of using CAQDAS software as wasting time and effort. This view is widely recognized in the literature and was also expressed by some of the researchers I interviewed. In addition, Kathy Charmaz (2016, para 40) cautions against using CAQDAS as a 'counting tool'. Indeed, software makes it very easy to set up exact or approximate keyword searches and put an emphasis on coding and technical aspects, which may distract the researcher from focusing on interpretation and instead encourage the 'quantification of qualitative data'. The disadvantages of extending the coding beyond any real benefit, which may not help understanding, are widely acknowledged (see Welsh, 2002; and Chapter 14 in this volume by Friese). Indeed, researchers have debated since the widespread use of personal computers whether technology is 'Configuring the User', as the title of Woolgar's (1990) paper suggests, i.e., whether technology *determines* how users interact with a particular piece of technology. Similar concerns are still being raised today in relation to the widespread use of opaque algorithms impacting on what internet search results and social media content users are being presented with (Willson, 2016). Following on from this, some see parallels between the delegation of filtering the news to Google's search algorithms or the selection of the best holiday snaps by software, and trusting the capacity of technology to determine a researcher's decisions when making analytical choices.

However, much has changed since Woolgar's (1990) paper on the division between IT developers and users, and many CAQDAS software packages have improved their functionalities over the years.

Indeed, according to Gilbert et al. (2014), the particular choice of program has become less critical due to the maturing of the technology. However, they also emphasize the importance of the researcher's expertise in understanding both their chosen method *and* the software tool.

A recent example of CAQDAS software developers working together with researchers is the KWALON Experiment and related conference. Using different CAQDAS software packages, teams worked together to analyze the same set of data. The aim of the experiment was to investigate whether CAQDAS packages were comparable, to further the development of software to analyze qualitative data and to contribute to the limited discussion between the relationship between theory, method and software (Evers et al., 2011).

Despite some cautious views on the use of software to analyze qualitative data, unsurprisingly specialist software for CADQAS can also provide many advantages to the qualitative researcher. This is particularly so when reading Weitzman's (1999) paper, where he reflects back to the 1980s when qualitative researchers had to conduct their data analysis by typing and photocopying notes, using paper, index cards and highlighter pens. Among the many benefits of using CAQDAS software for GTM is the single-location access that enables the researcher to access large amounts of data through one central repository. Some even use the software to support and code their review of the literature. The systematic nature and speed of text retrieval based on a particular code is an essential feature of 'Code Retrieve Programs', which is one of Weitzman's five software type families already identified in 1999. Another common feature of CAQDAS programs is their ability to make linkages between concepts and the graphical display of findings (see Chapter 14 in this volume by Friese for an example), which has evolved with technology advances such as touch screens. Silver and Lewins (2014) believe that using software for qualitative data analysis can demystify the process, which can be perceived as a 'craft' by some, and, according to Kelle and Laurie (1995), can help with validity and reliability in qualitative research.

There have been many calls for researchers to share their qualitative data analysis journey (see, e.g., Bringer et al., 2004; Odena, 2013), but also warnings of the apparent 'gloss of rigour' by including in some proposals the promise to analyze the data with a CAQDAS program (Gibbs et al., 2002, para 21).

Paulus et al. (2017) have identified different levels of reporting the use of CAQDAS software in research studies and make recommendations on effective practice when writing about CAQDAS use. For example, they advise researchers to not just 'name drop', but also to include the version number of the CAQDAS software used, to reference the sources consulted when learning the software and, most importantly, to include a reflection on the limitations and merits of the CAQDAS software used for the study.

In order to contribute to this sharing of the technology-supported data analysis journey and the ways in which grounded theorists use their method, the next sections focus on my own qualitative data which I collected for this chapter and its analysis.

GROUNDED THEORY ABOUT USING GROUNDED THEORY: COLLECTING DATA AND DEVELOPING CATEGORIES

My own experience of using CAQDAS software has been a chequered one. After having studied for a computer science BSc, and a technology-related Master's degree, it seemed a good idea to utilize CAQDAS software to analyze the qualitative data collected for my PhD research. However, this strategy did not quite work out, and I conceded to using post-it notes instead of CAQDAS software (for an account and visualization of my coding process, see Birks & Mills, 2015, pp. 99–101; and Gorra, 2008). Technological developments have moved on since completing my PhD a decade ago, and devices such as mobile phones and tablets have now become ubiquitous and are literally in everybody's pocket. Hence, I wondered whether this might influence how researchers use technology to support their data analysis. Following Charmaz's variant of GT, I decided to interview researchers about their experiences of analyzing their data and their software choices. To analyze the interview data, I chose to give CAQDAS software NVivo (Version 11) another go, which helped me to reflect on the technology-supported analysis process and brought me closer to the qualitative researchers I talked to.

My primary focus was on software use for coding and analysis; less on other elements of grounded theory, such as memoing, the place of literature review, or differences between the different strands of the method. Using a common approach in GTM, I followed a purposive and snowball sampling approach to find my interview participants, initially using some of my connections and networks from my time as a PhD student and researcher, followed by some referrals. Some of the PhD students I spoke to referred to CAQDAS software as a 'tool of the trade'. Being at the beginning of their PhD journey, they explicitly expressed the expectation of using specialized software to analyze their data. By talking to GT researchers, I wanted to find out whether computer support was seen as strictly necessary or even desirable when it came to collecting and analyzing data, and whether the two camps of researchers referred to by Welsh (2002) – those in favour of CAQDAS software and those against – would still exist.

The first interviews I coded were with two women who had completed their PhDs using GTM a few years ago, followed by six interviews with current PhD students. All interviewees are referred to by pseudonyms. The researchers I spoke with used a range of technologies to make sense of their data, with some having decided against using specialist CAQDAS software, seemingly following Glaser's advice of avoiding the loss of 'precious time and effort'. Instead, they jumped straight into the data analysis with tools they were familiar with, such as Microsoft Word or Excel. After the first few interviews, I used theoretical sampling to 'fill out' my initial categories and embarked on a second round of interviews. This time I purposefully sought to talk with people who made use of specialist

CAQDAS software. This meant that I chose to talk with some who were not exclusively using GTM as their methodology but were, for example, using thematic analysis and other methodologies that required coding. However, this 'variety' seemed to be a suitable solution to help me fill in my categories and help me understand how researchers utilized technology to do the 'theorizing part'.

In the following, I provide a succinct insight into the categories I developed, including the Core Category 'Moving', which subsumes the other four categories. Due to the brevity of the chapter, I have decided not to share any codes, but have included some quotes to provide an insight into my participants' ways of thinking. The only memo I share is my Cookbook Memo. I wrote it to summarize what my participants told me about their *successful* ways of working, and it sums up the paths they chose to get from codes to theory. At the same time, this memo helped me to relate what I heard to the literature. By identifying common steps in their ways of working, including a creative, often technology-supported analysis phase, I realized that this related to a concept I had come across in the literature: Peirce's idea of abduction. Moving the researcher's steps into a table, side-by-side with what I found in the literature, helped me to formulate the beginning of my own theory, which is based on my core category.

I use the final section of this chapter to explicate those links to the literature and finish off by formulating some practical advice for those new to GTM, which is also distilled in each of the category synopses in the following section.

Categories

Based on my interviews, I developed a small number of categories and provide a brief overview of these in the following. After some deliberation, I split my Category 1 into two separate ones (1a and 1b) to signify that they were still hanging together and both were related to the concept of time, particularly time efficiencies and time pressures, which were mentioned so frequently by those PhD students I spoke with.

In essence, three aspects of time were of importance to the researchers I interviewed: first, the limited *length of time available* to do their study, which caused anxiety at times; second, making a decision about whether to *invest time* to learn how to use a CAQDAS software package to gain potential time savings later on (Category 1a); and, third, the time required for the actual *data analysis* (see Category 1b, below).

Category 1a: 'Finding My Way' – Time waits for no one

The researchers I spoke to not only had to decide which 'School of GTM' they wanted to belong to, but particularly the interviews with novice researchers were about having to explore and to develop *their own way* of doing their grounded theory. I got the impression that this stage of the GT journey was all about 'muddling through' and one respondent explained about the need to '*find my way*' (in vivo code) of dealing with the data. It was intriguing to learn about the very different ways researchers used to organize, structure and make sense of their data, utilizing a host of different software packages, including CAQDAS and non-CAQDAS. I was reminded of Kelle's (2004) reference to the 'frequently very idiosyncratic' ways in which individual researchers work and think. Respondents were painfully aware of the passing of time, of submission deadlines and other sources of time pressure, which may have impacted on their choices of data analysis. Some preferred developing their own ways of working with the data using software familiar to them, instead of investing time to learn how to use a CAQDAS software package. As Schuhmann (2011) points out, it takes time to develop literacy for different software and the researchers I spoke to were very much aware of this.

Category 1a: Synopsis

Researchers having to make careful and time-pressured choices about their use of software to help analyze their data

Category 1b: Using software to be efficient and organized – a helpful time saver ('a filing cabinet')

Researchers appreciated the support of software in organizing their data, but some stressed that *they* wanted to stay in charge and did not want to be guided by the analysis software: 'The human still needs to do the thinking' (Interview Tina). And as another researcher explained:

> I recognized as I said, from very early on that *I only wanted the minimum functionality out of it* [NVivo]. Partly because of the stage I was researching. ... And I was kind of fearful of that as I didn't understand the software. And I didn't want to do anything to the data that I couldn't explain in a conversation, you know. Where you go from the data to some abstract point and without knowing how that's been arrived at. I wouldn't have any confidence in that. ... I used it as a filing system, as a filing cabinet. Just with a lot of data, and well organised. (Interview Ted)

Ted refers here to the common fears and concerns expressed in relation to CAQDAS software, in a similar vein to what Weitzman (1999) has already argued – that software programs cannot, 'nor would you want them to, build theory for you' (p. 1248). Kelle (2004) supports this when he points out that even though the term CAQDAS has become established, this abbreviation is partly misleading, with the second 'A' standing for 'Analysis'. However, Qualitative Data Analysis (QDA) programs cannot do analysis *per se* as they work in a different way from statistics programs. They can merely support the researcher, and some of those I spoke with reflected on this conundrum.

Category 1b: Synopsis

CAQDAS software makes a great filing cabinet – 'but the human still needs to do the thinking' [In vivo Code Tina])

Category 2: 'SEEing Data'

'Not being able to see the wood for the trees' when looking at data on the computer screen was an issue perceived by some when using CAQDAS software. To overcome this challenge, some displayed their data, coding chunks and notes in different media and at times simultaneously, using printouts, tables, flip charts, or laptop, tablet or mobile phone screens. Researchers stated that they '*could not get to their data*' (Interview Birgit) when using CAQDAS software, as the screen acted as a barrier and would not allow them direct access to its meaning. When experiencing that they could not express thoughts or ideas in an immediate fashion through the software, some questioned *their knowledge* of the software (Interview Dorothy), while others criticized the computer for not being fast enough (Interview Tina).

Category 2: Synopsis

Looking at data in different media (at times simultaneously) helps with making sense of it

Category 3: 'Thinking Fast, Drawing Fast (by Hand)'

Researchers talked about the amount of time it took them to do the data analysis and their analytical thinking, after some data collection had taken place. They weighed up the options of working with software on the computer screen as opposed to writing or drawing by hand, as the latter was perceived to be faster and more immediate. Interacting physically with their data, e.g., by drawing or doodling by hand, but also at times with electronic means such as a touch screen tablet, helped my participants to interact with their data in a more immediate and creative way. It seemed they used this approach to 'Let the mind wander' – a quote by Peirce (1931–1935) (quoted in Reichertz, 2010). Charmaz, as well as Glaser, refer to the benefits of physically or kinesthetically (Charmaz, 2012) interacting with their data: sorting by hand 'releases the creativity necessary to see a theoretical code in memos' (Glaser, 2005, cited in Bryant and Charmaz, 2007, p. 611). And it seems that with technological advances this physical interaction with qualitative data need not be done exclusively with paper and pen, but instead touch screen and different hand-held devices may hold the same usefulness for some.

Category 3: Synopsis

Drawing by hand is an immediate and creative way to interact with data – this immediate manipulation can be accomplished using pen and paper or touch screen

Cookbook Memo: A Recipe for Good Practice?

I chose the latter category as a basis for my Core Category 'Moving', i.e., the key category that has helped me to distil my participants' experiences about their technology-assisted grounded theory journey. I decided to write the very pragmatic 'Cookbook Recipe Memo' (Figure 15.1) to capture the best practice of my participants' interactions with their data. This Memo should not be seen a set of instructions, as I agree with Kathy Charmaz (2006a) that GTM is 'a way of thinking about data' and hence cannot be standardized. Instead, the Memo helped me to understand the different phases of analysis the interviewees went through and acted as a useful springboard to develop my Core Category.

CORE CATEGORY 'MOVEMENT: KEEP MOVING (SELF, MIND AND DATA) – THE JOURNEY IS THE DESTINATION'

None of the researchers I spoke to actually stayed within the boundaries of one software program. It seemed that in order to *do* grounded theorizing and to undertake data analysis

Cookbook Memo:
'The Doing' of a Grounded Theory – *How* to get from codes to GT

A cookbook recipe for coming up with *your* Grounded Theory

Ingredients:
- Having read literature about GT and being familiar with coding procedures
- Dictaphone or other voice recorder
- Having some interviews as a starting point
- Having a computer and some sort of CAQDAS and/or (Open) office software

Optional
- Having Mind mapping or similar software
- Having coloured pens, flipchart paper, post-it notes
- A tablet, mobile phone
- Use Dictaphone to record thoughts
- Walking or running shoes

Recipe

0. Have trust in GT process
1. Transcribe the interview (yourself)
2. Code the data in Ms Word or straight in CAQDAS software e.g. NVivo (or in Ms Word and possibly move to specialised software later)
3. MOVE! Step away from that first piece of software used: doodle on paper, move your own body and think (walk, run), do a couple of drawings, move data into tables, move data into different formats
4. Try mind mapping software or creating models in NVivo
5. Reflect on it, look at data simultaneously on different screens and paper
6. Write memos, and even more memos. Write some more memos
7. Optional: Print out, look at it
8. Connect 'data with data, codes with codes', finalise your categories
9. Apply codes to more interviews, revise; repeat steps 3-8 if necessary
10. Arrive at *your* GT

Figure 15.1 'Cookbook Recipe Memo': Capturing participants' best practice in interacting with their data

and theory construction, it was necessary to move the data about. The researchers spoke about trying out different ways of interacting with the data in order to find an approach that they were happy and confident with (see Category 1a: 'Finding my Way'). I learned that all of those I spoke to embedded some form of *movement* in their steps of GT data analysis. Of course, this is nothing new since the interaction with data is recommended by all schools of GT: Charmaz (2006a, p. 178) stresses that using the Grounded Theory Method 'depends on using constant comparative methods *and* YOUR engagement'. Kelle (2007) reminds us, that the *constant comparison* of data, codes and emerging categories is one of the substantial building blocks for developing categories. And we are aware that GT is about developing theories, 'whilst moving to and fro between collection of data, coding and memoing' (Reichertz, 2010, para 29).

Based on the analysis of my interviews with GT researchers, I believe that the many changes in the wider research environment, as discussed in the introduction, have had an impact on the actual practice of grounded theorizing. Researchers' interactions with data seem to have changed as a result of the plethora of technologies available, including software to manipulate the increasingly wide array of types of data, along with methodological developments.

I therefore argue that it is vital to alert novice GTM researchers to the importance of *interacting* with their data with whatever means suit them, which is the essence of my Core Category *Movement*. My participants were largely aware of the possibilities that technology offered, although at times they seemed hesitant to utilize technology to support them to look at the data in different Gestalts, in different shapes, forms or guises. But exactly this is what should be encouraged and made explicit, to help especially novice researchers arrive at *their* grounded theory using their own personal strategies. The purpose of this chapter is exactly this, making explicit 'the tricks of the trade', the sharing of good strategies to get from quotes to codes to a grounded theory.

The researchers I talked to perceived pen, paper and voice recorder as 'immediate', fast mediums to record their thoughts and ideas. But they also made use of the technology available to them, and used their mobile phones for note taking, or their iPads or tablets for Mind Mapping (Category 3: 'Think Fast, Draw Fast'). Regardless of the specific tools used, the crucial step was that the data, codes and ideas were transferred from one way of displaying them to another. *Moving* their data enabled researchers to interact with it more deeply, and it forced them to see the data anew when they transferred it from one medium to the next (Category 2: 'SEEing Data'). It seemed that with every movement the data could evolve, develop, change and become something different, and the following quote provides a snapshot of this process of Movement:

> Again, so I used the computer in the initial stage, the NVivo, and then I came out of that and just did some sketches and wrote notes next to them and that really helped me think things through. (Interview Dorothy)

My researchers used a combination of the following Movements to help them harness their creativity and ability to make sense of the data – to move away from descriptions or summaries to a more conceptual picture of their research findings:

a. Drawing by hand on paper OR moving graphics on a (touch) screen (= moving body parts for ideas – kinesthetics: Charmaz, 2012)
b. Moving the data across different media (from tables, to paper, to post-its)
c. Moving the body physically for ideas (going for a walk, running)

Some of my novice researchers expressed frustration at this non-linear process of doing things and perceived it to be a waste of time. However, this was a necessary step in a researcher's journey of making sense of data, as I learned by talking to researchers who were 'stuck' in their data analysis and others who reflected back on their GT journey, as well as my own at times frustrating data dealing strategies for this study.

Core Category Synopsis

Keep moving – yourself, your mind and your data; the Journey is the Destination

RELATING MY CORE CATEGORY TO THE LITERATURE – FILING CABINET VERSUS CREATIVITY

The interview findings from my small-scale study correspond to what Karen Locke (2007, p. 565) described as 'Rational control' versus 'irrational free-play'. She persuasively justifies these two thinking modes as a necessary tension in grounded theorizing, which others have identified in a very similar way before her:

> Our important ideas are not 'in' the data, and however hard we work, we will not find these ideas simply by scrutinizing our data ever more obsessively. We need to work at analysis and theorizing, and we need to do the intellectual, imaginative work of ideas in parallel to the other tasks of data management. (Coffey & Atkinson, 1996, pp. 154–155)

I would equate Coffey and Atkinson's 'hard working' and 'scrutinizing our data ever more obsessively' to Locke's concept of 'rational control', and my observations of using the CAQDAS software as an efficient way to hold and manipulate data (Category 1b: 'Filing Cabinet'). This phase is necessary to 'deal' with the data, to organize and crunch it. Precise field notes and 'tedious and time-consuming sequences' can help check against faulty memory (Timmermans & Tavory, 2012, p. 175). Using (specialist) software to organize data can provide numerous benefits for this phase in the grounded theory journey, as referred to earlier in this chapter.

The counterpart to this 'rational control phase' of data management is 'the intellectual, imaginative work of ideas' (Coffey & Atkinson, 1996), the moving of data or moving one's body either by diagramming or going for a walk (Core Category Moving). As explained above, this phase is about researchers using technology in a smart way to support *their* data analysis in a way that suits them (Category 1a: 'Finding my way'). The action or process of moving data with the help of different technologies – such as laptop/PC, tablet, mobile phone, software – helped my participants with their 'imaginative work'. Using a host of different media and technologies, including specialized coding software, was perceived by researchers as beneficial to help them interact with their data and support their analysis. This reinforces the argument that the computer is needed nowadays to 'do' research – it is a necessary tool, as already suggested in the introduction. However, as one of my interviewees rightly explained, 'the human is still doing the thinking'. Even though I can personally understand Glaser, Charmaz, Bryant and others' wariness of the use of CAQDAS software for GT, I think one needs to go beyond general caution and differentiate between these two different purposes for software use: first, the use of software to help organize data and, second, to interact with data creatively in order to help understand what's going on in the area of investigation.

Welsh's (2002) categorization of the two camps of qualitative researchers – those who favour software to aid the analysis process and those who do not – is not quite fitting any more. I believe this is an out-dated premise due to the technological advances in hardware, such as touch screens, tablets, mobile phones, as well as recent developments in software programs, many of which are available free of charge to today's researchers. The question is not any more *whether* to use technology, but *in what ways* we can make use of it to help us do grounded theorizing. At no point must it be forgotten that the method should stand in the foreground since software certainly is not a replacement for methodological training (my interview participants; Weitzman, 1999; Gibbs et al., 2002), but instead there are different ways in which these two spheres of technology and method can interact (see Woods & Wickham, 2006, in section 2).

OPERATIONALIZING ABDUCTION THROUGH CREATIVE SOFTWARE USE

I wrote many notes and memos while trying to make sense of my data – often writing by hand and disregarding the technology available to me. The Cookbook Recipe Memo in particular (see previous section) helped me to identify the different phases of analysis my researchers experienced. The diverse ways in which my participants made use of software reminded me strongly of the concept of Abduction. Steps 3–7 in my GT Cookbook Recipe Memo (Figure 15.1) are nothing new, as terms such as 'doodling', 'letting your imagination run free', 'day-dreaming' have been mentioned by Charles Peirce in his work in terms of abduction (Peirce, 1931–1935; Reichertz, 2010). 'A mental game without rules he calls "musement", a game of meditation, or daydreaming', which Peirce describes as one of the two ways to enable 'for abductive lightning to strike' (Peirce, 1931–1935, Vol. 6, p. 315; Reichertz, 2010, para 20). Charmaz (2006b, p. 15) poignantly explains the concept of abduction as follows: 'So, the notion of "theoretical agnosticism" is quite good, because you go in with that doubt, and you look for some kind of interesting category or finding, which is consistent with abduction, or abductive reasoning. Then you explore, and re-check how that category holds up.'

Many authors eloquently and, in my view, convincingly have connected the concept of abduction to GTM (see Charmaz, 2006a; Richardson & Kramer, 2006; Locke, 2007; Reichertz, 2007; Strubing, 2007; and Timmermans & Tavory, 2012, who provide a list of references to abduction and GT on p. 168). The more I read about this concept, the more certain I became that my Core Category Moving related to abduction. In order to understand what was going on in my data, I mapped the data analysis phases my participants experienced with the phases illustrated in the literature (see Table 15.1).

According to Reichertz (2010), Peirce described the three-stage discovery procedure consisting of abduction, deduction, induction. However, what my GT researchers described fitted this but in a slightly different order: induction, abduction, deduction. This may be a result of the nature of GTM, as, in my view, the first phase of dealing with data resembles inductive thinking.

What this mapping exercise helped me with was to understand the different phases the GT researchers went through, but it also highlighted the role that technology played in helping them with their GT journey, using the same principles as many researchers before them, including Peirce nearly a century ago.

After coding the collected data and looking for patterns (Stage 1 – Induction), Stage 2 (Abduction) is about moving from one medium, such as computer, paper, tablet or mobile phone, to the next. The key to creativity and being able to make sense of data is to actively interact with the data by putting it through the different media, in order to then to go back to previously or newly collected data to 'test' the concepts (Stage 3 – Deduction).

The following quote illustrates the process undergone for Stage 2 – Abduction:

> I started off with ... about, at most ... one interview of line by line coding. And then I went to NVivo ... erm... for a few interviews. And then I felt like I was getting too many codes, and it wasn't ... it was kind of losing its focus.

Table 15.1 Mapping of participants' data analysis phases with literature concepts

My Participants' Actions *(8 interviews with GT and qualitative researchers)*	***Memo: Cookbook Recipe – Steps in Developing a GT*** *(For a detailed version see Memo)*	***Peirce's Stages*** *(Peirce, 1931–1935; Reichertz, 2010)*	***Locke's Interpretation of GT*** *(Locke, 2007)*
Step 1 – Induction Start coding data by using CAQDAS or other type of software. Start making sense of codes and data.	**Cookbook Recipe Memo Steps 0–2** 0. Have trust in GT process. 1. Transcribe the interview. 2. Code the data.	**Induction Stage** Look for patterns and meaning in the codes generated	**Rational Control** 'we draw on our controlled mode to systematically carry out our analytic practices such as the micro level naming that helps us to become intimately acquainted with our data or those that help us to articulate and specify the defining elements of a conceptualization' (Locke, 2007, p. 578).
Step 2 – Abduction Move Data between different Media, Doodle; Move Body & Mind (i.e., go for a walk or a run); Refine Codes & Thinking.	**Cookbook Recipe Memo Steps 3–7** 3. MOVE! (data, body, mind) 4. Try using visualizing software or post-it notes 5. Look at data simultaneously on different screens and paper. 6. Write Memos, Notes and even more memos. 7. Optional: Print out and review.	**Abduction Stage** 'Discovering, on the basis of an interpretation of collected data, such combinations of features for which there is no appropriate explanation or rule in the store of knowledge that already exists. This causes surprise.' 'Abduction is therefore a cerebral process, an intellectual act, a mental leap, that brings together things which one had never associated with one another' (Reichertz, 2010, para 16).	**Creative Free-play** 'we are then free to putter around with the various feelings and attitudes evoked, the associations and memories aroused, the ideas, and the stream of images that pass through, to see how they may connect to our data and our emerging conjectures and to consider where they may lead us in our thinking' (Locke, 2007, p. 575).

Table 15.1 (Continued)

Step 3 – Deduction	Cookbook Recipe Memo Steps 8–10:	Deduction Stage
Go back to computer (possibly to the CAQDAS software) and explain codes and concepts, solidify them. Try applying codes to more interviews and evolve codes.	8. Connect 'data with data, codes with codes', finalize your categories. 9. Apply codes to more interviews, revise; repeat steps 3-8 if necessary. 10. Arrive at your GT.	'Derivation of predictions from the hypothesis' (Reichertz, 2007, p. 222).

> So I came out of NVivo again [laughs] and did some more ... erm yeah... by hand ... erm... and started to diagram a little bit, to kind of, um... clarify my ideas and then I went back into NVivo and used the ideas I had kind of drawn from that to try and structure the codes that I developed... erm in line with, I guess, how my thinking had changed. (Interview Dorothy)

Birks and Mills (2015, p. 100) suggest that 'diagramming is *the* creative tool to use when operationalizing the logic of abduction'. I would expand on this and say that it is not just about the process of diagramming, of drawing, and so on. Instead, this 'operationalizing of abduction' is partly fostered by the 'immediacy' of diagramming (hand-brain connection) (Category 3: 'Think Fast, Draw Fast'), partly by SEEing data in a different medium (Category 2: 'SEEing Data'). What I learned from my research participants was that the *Moving* of data from one medium to another brought out the most fruitful and creative thoughts in terms of GT conceptualizing. And it it is this process of interacting with the data, seeing the data in different forms or guises, that helps with the sense-making. As explained above, this moving of data – codes, thoughts, memos, diagrams – was executed by some with pen and paper, but with tablet or computer by others (Core Category Moving). In an interview, Kathy Charmaz also refers to this concept of interacting with the data as she believes 'something *kinesthetic* occurs when we are coding; we are mentally and physically active in the process' (Charmaz 2012, p. 5). However, this action of 'sorting' and interacting with the data (see also Glaser, 2005; Bryant and Charmaz, 2007, p. 611) does not have to be executed manually, but instead can be done as efficiently, if not more so, with help of the technologies that have become so ubiquitous.

CONCLUSION AND ADVICE OR HOW TO GET FROM CODES TO THEORY? MOVE TO SOLVE YOUR GT PUZZLE!

I set out to provide an insight into how specialist CAQDAS software is utilized by researchers to support them in their GTM journey. Based on coding and analyzing interviews with qualitative researchers, I arrived at four categories which helped me to develop one core category. At this point, I could now go back into the field to do some more interviews in order to 'fill in' and saturate my categories, in order to add more detail to my emerging theory.[1] My findings at this point highlight two things, which are noteworthy, particularly for novice GTM researchers:

First, the need to be aware of two different ways in which software can and should be used: (a) using specialist CAQDAS or other software to help with organizing the data, and (b) making use of technologies – in the wider sense – for the creative development of ideas.

Second, the sense-making of data needed for grounded theorizing can be supported and perhaps even coaxed by *Moving your Data* consciously between different media with the help of technology, and hence seeing data in different guises, shapes and formats. This creative phase, together with a concomitant set of techniques, is needed to help researchers make sense of data to create a grounded theory, and this aspect of grounded theorizing can be understood as an operationalization of abduction. It is important here to relate back to Peirce's principle of abduction, which is about being able to consciously nurture one's creativity and one's ability to come up with something new. Timmermans and Tavory (2012) refer to Charmaz (2009, pp. 137–138), where she writes 'we adopt abductive logic when we engage in imaginative thinking about intriguing findings and then return to the field to check our conjectures'. This is exactly what my participants did with their interplay of technology, pen and paper. In my view, GT theory construction is indeed a 'pragmatic process of puzzling out' (Timmermans & Tavory, 2012) and it is the process of *Movement* that helps to 'solve the puzzle', or at least helps with speeding up the process of making sense of the data. As a result of the process of moving data, thoughts and codes, the data are being reworked and changed with every iteration. This is what I observed my participants were doing with their theory construction. This is what they did at times with software, other times without, in order to construct meaning from their data, using a host of different technologies and media available to them.

Novice researchers need to be aware of the value of the Movement Process. They need to keep in mind that the 'journey is the destination' and it is not wasted time to 'play with the data' and put it through different media in order to tease out its meaning.

Bryant and Charmaz (2007, p. 23) refer to Reichertz and point out that the concept of Serendipity has gained 'renewed importance'. And I would add that serendipity can be elicited by using different media and doing plenty of *Moving* – of data, of oneself, of data between media – perhaps by following my GT Cookbook Recipe Memo. One needs to make sure to leave time and space for 'Movement' and creativity when undertaking a GT-guided research project. Some see software as being 'just a supportive tool' (Schuhmann, 2011), but it needs to be acknowledged that technology in the wider sense, i.e., software and hardware such as touch screens, can play a central role in supporting the sense-making process.

Serendipity can be encouraged by careful preparation, through the meticulous management of data – often supported by technology – but in addition what is also needed is the 'creative free-play' consisting of moving data and body. The old adage 'the harder I work the luckier I get' or Pasteur's saying about chance favouring the prepared mind (for a discussion, see Bryant, 2017, p. 385) may hold true. In other words, one is better at recognizing luck and seizing it when one has made some effort to get ready for 'chance' to happen. In terms of grounded theory, this may mean: the more purposefully I interact with data, the more smoothly I am going to arrive at my GT – even under time pressures.

Note

1 I am planning to complete my emerging grounded theory in future.

REFERENCES

Apramian, Tavis, Cristancho, Sayra, Watling, Chris, & Lingard, Lorelei (2016) (Re)Grounding grounded theory: A close reading of theory in four schools. *Qualitative Research*, *1*, 2016.

Birks, M. & Mills, J. (2015) *Grounded Theory: A Practical Guide* (2nd ed.). London: Sage.

Bringer, Joy, Johnston, Lynne H., & Brackenridge, Celia H. (2004) Maximizing transparency in a doctoral thesis1: The complexities of writing about the use of QSR*NVIVO within a grounded theory study. *Qualitative Research*, *4*. First published online 1 August. doi.org/10.1177/1468794104044434

Bryant, A. (2017) *Grounded Theory and Grounded Theorizing: Pragmatism in Research Practice*. Oxford: Oxford University Press.

Bryant, A. & Charmaz, K. (Eds.) (2007) *The SAGE Handbook of Grounded Theory*. Los Angeles, CA: Sage.

Bryant, T. (2009) Research Training two-day Workshop: Grounded Theory Method. Professor Tony Bryant, September 2015. Available from: www.youtube.com/watch?v=fmWKf5L0mfA [accessed 4 April 2017].

CAQDAS Networking Project (2017) Available from the University of Surrey at: www.surrey.ac.uk/sociology/research/researchcentres/caqdas/support/choosing/ [accessed 4 May 2017].

Charmaz, K. (2006a). *Constructing grounded theory: A practical guide through qualitative analysis*. London: Sage Publications.

Charmaz, K. (2006b) Special: An Interview with Kathy Charmaz: On Constructing Grounded Theory by Antony J. Puddephatt. *Qualitative Sociology Review*, *Vol. II* Issue 3, December 2006. Available from: www.qualitativesociologyreview.org/ENG/Volume5/QSR_2_3_Interview.pdf.

Charmaz, K. (2009) Shifting the grounds: *Constructivist Grounded Theory Methods*. In J. M. Morse, P. N. Stern, J. Corbin, B. Bowers, K. Charmaz, & A. Clarke (Eds.), *Developing Grounded Theory: The Second Generation* (pp. 127–154). Walnut Creek, CA: Left Coast Press.

Charmaz, K. (2012) The power and potential of grounded theory. *Medical Sociology Online*, *6*(3). Available from: www.medicalsociologyonline.org/resources/Vol6Iss3/MSo-600x_The-Power-and-Potential-Grounded-Theory_Charmaz.pdf and at www.youtube.com/watch?v=zY1h3387txo.

Charmaz, K. (2014) *Constructing Grounded Theory* (2nd ed.). London: Sage.

Charmaz (2016) A personal journey with grounded theory methodology, Kathy Charmaz in conversation with Reiner Keller. *Forum Qualitative Sozialforschung / Forum: Qualitative Social Research*, *17*(1), Art. 16. Available from: www.qualitative-research.net/index.php/fqs/rt/printerFriendly/2541/3936 [accessed 4 April 2017].

Coffey, A. & Atkinson, P. (1996) *Making Sense of Qualitative Data: Complementary Research Strategies*. Thousand Oaks, CA: Sage.

Corbin, J. M. & Strauss, A. L. (2008) *Basics of Qualitative Research: Techniques and Procedures for Developing Grounded Theory* (3rd ed.). Thousand Oaks, CA: Sage.

Evers, Jeanine C., Silver, Christina, Mruck, Katja, & Peeters, Bart (2011) Introduction to the KWALON experiment: Discussions on Qualitative Data Analysis software by developers and users. *Forum Qualitative Sozialforschung / Forum: Qualitative Social Research*, *12*(1), Available from: www.qualitative-research.net/index.php/fqs/article/view/1637 [accessed 4 June 2016].

Gibbs, Graham R. (2010) *Grounded Theory: Open Coding*. Available from: www.youtube.com/watch?v=gn7Pr8M_Gu8 [accessed 4 April 2017].

Gibbs, G. R., Friese, S., & Mangabeira, W. C. (2002) The use of new technology in qualitative research. *Forum Qualitative Sozialforschung / Forum: Qualitative Social Research*, *3*(2), 1–16. Available from: www.qualitative-research.net/index.php/fqs/article/view/847.

Gilbert, L., Jackson, K., & di Gregorio, S. (2014). Tools for analyzing qualitative data: The history and relevance of qualitative data analysis software. In J. M. Spector, M. D. Merrill, J. Elen, & M. J. Bishop (Eds.), *Handbook for Research on Educational Communications and Technology* (4th ed., pp. 221–236). London: Routledge.

Glaser, B. G. (2005) *The Grounded Theory Perspective: Theoretical Coding*. Mill Valley, CA: Sociology Press.

Glaser, B. G. (2007) All is data. *The Grounded Theory Review: An International Journal*, *6*(2), 1–22.

Glaser, B. G. & Holton, J. (2004) Remodeling grounded theory. *Forum Qualitative Sozialforschung/ Forum: Qualitative Social Research*, *6*(2), 1–21.

Gorra, A. (2008). An Analysis of the Relationship between Individuals' Perceptions of Privacy and Mobile Phone Location Data - a Grounded Theory Study (Doctoral thesis), Leeds Metropolitan University, UK. Available from: http://eprints.leedsbeckett.ac.uk/1554/.

Kelle, U. (1997) Theory building in qualitative research and computer programs for the management of textual data. *Sociological Research Online*, *2*(2). Available from: www.socresonline.org.uk/2/2/1.html.

Kelle, U. (2004) Computer-assisted analysis of qualitative data. In U. Flick, E. von Kardoff, & I. Steinke (Eds.), *A Companion to Qualitative Research* (pp. 276–283). London: Sage.

Kelle, U. (2007) The Development of Categories: Different Approaches in Grounded Theory. In A. Bryant & K. Charmaz (Eds.), *The SAGE Handbook of Grounded Theory*. Los Angeles, CA: Sage.

Kelle, U. & Laurie, H. (1995) Computer use in qualitative research and issues of validity. In Udo Kelle (Ed.), *Computer-Aided Qualitative Data Analysis: Theory, Methods and Practice* (pp. 19–28). London: Sage.

Locke, K. (2007) Rational Control and Irrational Free-play: Dual-thinking Modes as Necessary Tension in Grounded Theorizing. In A. Bryant & K. Charmaz (Eds.), *The SAGE Handbook of Grounded Theory*. Los Angeles, CA: Sage.

Miles, M. B., Huberman, A. M., & Saldana, J. (2014) *Qualitative Data Analysis: A Methods Sourcebook*. Thousand Oaks, CA: Sage.

Odena, O. (2013) Using software to tell a trustworthy, convincing and useful story. *International Journal of Social Research Methodology*, *16*(5), 355–372. doi: 10.1080/13645579.2012.706019.

Paulus, Trena, Woods, Megan, Atkins, David, & Macklin, Rob (2017) The discourse of QDAS: Reporting practices of ATLAS.ti and NVivo users with implications for best practices. *International Journal of Social Research Methodology*, *20*(1), 35–47. Available from: www.tandfonline.com/doi/full/10.1080/13645579.2015.1102454.

Peirce, Charles Sanders (1931–1935) *The Collected Papers of Charles S. Peirce* (*8 Vols*). Cambridge, MA: Harvard University Press.

Prensky, M. (2001) *Digital Natives, Digital Immigrants*. Available from: www.marcprensky.com/writing/Prensky%20-%20Digital%20Natives,%20Digital%20Immigrants%20-%20Part1.pdf.

Reichertz, J. (2007) Abduction: The Logic of Discovery of Grounded Theory. In A. Bryant & K. Charmaz (Eds.), *The SAGE Handbook of Grounded Theory*. Los Angeles, CA: Sage.

Reichertz, J. (2010) Abduction: *The Logic of Discovery of Grounded Theory*. *Forum: Qualitative Social Research*, *10*(1).

Richardson, R. & Kramer, E. H. (2006) Abduction as the type of inference that characterizes the development of a grounded theory (NL). *Qualitative Research*, *6*(4), 497–513.

Schuhmann, C. (2011) Computer technology and qualitative research: A rendezvous between exactness and ambiguity. *Forum Qualitative Sozialforschung / Forum: Qualitative Social Research*, *12*(1).

Silver, C. & Lewins, A. (2014) *Using Software in Qualitative Research: A Step-By-Step Guide* (2nd ed.). London: Sage.

Strübing, J. (2007) Research as pragmatic problem-solving: the pragmatist roots of empirically-grounded theorizing. In A. Bryant, & K. Charmaz. *The SAGE handbook of grounded theory*:. Los Angeles, CA: SAGE.

Tapscott, D. (1998). Growing up digital: The rise of the net generation, New York: McGraw Hill.

Timmermans, S. & Tavory, I. (2012) Theory construction in Qualitative Research: From Grounded Theory to Abductive Analysis. *Sociological Theory*, *30*(3), 167–186.

Weitzman, E.A. (1999) Analyzing qualitative data with computer software. *Health Services Research*, *34*(5), 1241–1263.

Welsh, E. (2002) Dealing with data: Using NVivo in the qualitative data analysis process. *Forum Qualitative Sozialforschung / Forum: Qualitative Social Research*, *3*(2).

Willson, M. (2016) *Algorithms (and the) Everyday. Information, Communication & Society*. London: Routledge.

Woolgar, S. (1990) Configuring the User: The Case of Usability Trials. The Sociological Review, *38*(1_suppl), 58–99. https://doi.org/10.1111/j.1467-954X.1990.tb03349.x

Woods, M. & Wickham, M. (2006) Methodological implications of software use: An empirical investigation of software programs on literature analysis using N6 and Nvivo, in Ruth, A. (Ed) Quality and Impact of Qualitative Research. 3rd annual QualIT Conference, Brisbane: Institute for Integrated and Intelligent Systems, Griffith University pp 163–172.

16

Grounded Text Mining Approach: A Synergy between Grounded Theory and Text Mining Approaches

Mitsuyuki Inaba and Hisako Kakai

INTRODUCTION

The knowledge frames we construct never become independent of the methodology[1] that we adopt to construct them. That is, the methodology that we select to construct knowledge frames never becomes independent of how we view the nature of knowledge. The methods that we use are determined by the chosen methodology. Thus, social inquiry is always influenced by how researchers view the world. Furthermore, context, such as the new ideas and discussions (including their limitations) that result from the development of science and technologies, historical events, institutional changes (e.g., allocation of research funds), etc., affects researchers' world view. These cyclical relations among methods, methodology, and the larger social context show the dynamic nature of knowledge construction (see Figure 16.1). These observations explain the evolution of the grounded theory method (GTM) since its introduction in the 1960s.[2]

In the 1960s, Barney G. Glaser, a quantitatively trained sociologist at Columbia University, and Anselm L. Strauss, a qualitative researcher with an ethnographic background from the Chicago School, challenged and attempted to overcome the shortcomings of the quantitatively driven approach to social science inquiry, which was dominant at the time. Glaser and Strauss developed grounded theory at the University of California, San Francisco (UCSF) in the 1960s and early 1970s. When their seminal methodological book on grounded theory (Glaser & Strauss, 1967) was published in the late 1960s, qualitative research was not considered a legitimate approach to social science inquiry because of its lack of discernible, explicit and replicable processes and procedures. Because Glaser and Strauss's grounded theory used complex and explicit guidelines for data collection and analysis, it was a breakthrough for

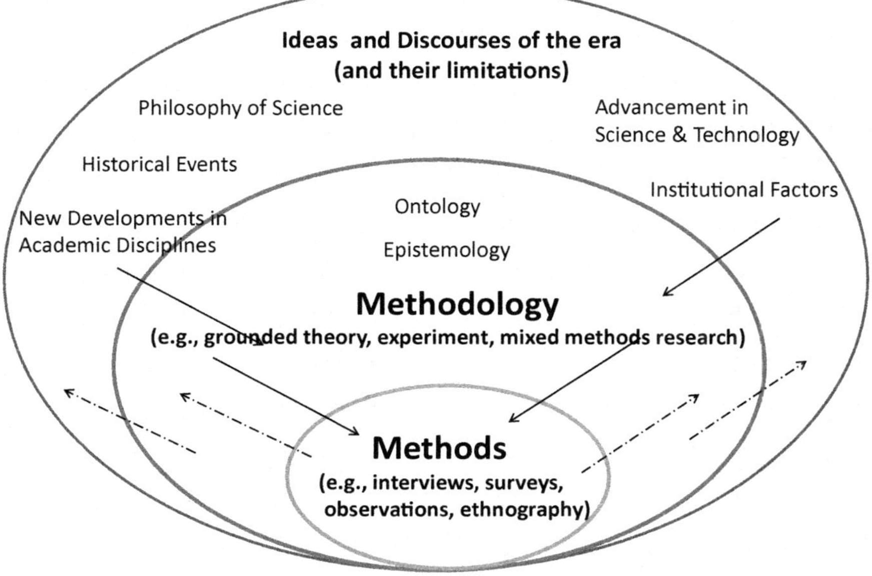

Figure 16.1 Cyclical relations among methods, methodology, and the larger social context

qualitative research during an era dominated by quantitatively driven research. Grounded theory created an opportunity for qualitative research, which was considered 'second-rate, a poor relation (if related at all) to rigorous statistically based research' (Bryant & Charmaz, 2007b, p. 35), to be accepted as a legitimate approach to social science investigation. Glaser and Strauss used grounded theory not to describe a social phenomenon, which is the case for many qualitative research methods, but to conceptualize a social phenomenon to develop a theory; a significant expansion in qualitative research has been produced by grounded theory (Bryant & Charmaz, 2007a; Charmaz, 2006, 2014).

Despite the contribution that grounded theory has made to improve the status and credibility of qualitative research, the method still incorporates positivistic views, although grounded theory arose from dissatisfaction with these views. According to Bryant and Charmaz (2007b, p. 33), 'the key weaknesses of Glaser and Strauss's statement of the GTM resided in the positivist, objectivist direction they gave grounded theory'. The positivistic assumptions embedded in Glaser and Strauss's original GTM reflected the epistemological perspective of many qualitative researchers in the 1960s.

At the turn of this century, Charmaz had an interpretivist epistemological position and used a different approach to grounded theory. Then, other scholars, such as Antony Bryant (2002) and Adele Clarke (2003, 2005), began to use her approach (Charmaz, 2006). Charmaz's seminal book (2006) on the constructivist approach to the GTM was published a decade ago. Connecting constructivist epistemology with the GTM was controversial, and yet this connection rapidly gained acceptance from qualitative researchers whose interpretive epistemological position reflects Charmaz's.[3]

Second-generation grounded theorists, many of whom learned directly from Glaser and Strauss at UCSF, followed Charmaz and began to develop their own variations of the grounded theory approach (GTA) (Morse et al., 2009).[4] These authors responded to an invitation from Glaser and Strauss 'to use grounded theory strategies flexibly in their own way'. Because of this invitation, Charmaz modified the original GTM to emphasize 'examining processes, making the study of action central, and creating abstract interpretive understandings of the data' (Charmaz, 2006, p. 9). Charmaz's constructivist GTM was another addition to the diverse variations of it, which included Glaserian GTM and Straussian GTM (Morse, 2009; Stern, 1995).[5]

Many articles, books, and book chapters on Charmaz's constructivist grounded theory have been published (e.g., Charmaz, 2000, 2006, 2014). These writings show that what makes her constructivist GTM unique is her epistemological position in approaching grounded theory construction. Because of her constructivist assumption, Charmaz's views regarding the nature of data, the relationship between the researcher and the participants who are researched, the data analysis procedures, and the nature of the resulting theories are very different from the original GTM (Glaser & Strauss, 1967).

OBJECTIVIST COMPARED WITH CONSTRUCTIVIST GROUNDED THEORY

In this section, we summarize the differences between the original grounded theory and Charmaz's constructivist grounded theory (2000, 2006, 2014). To emphasize the uniqueness of her constructivist grounded theory, Charmaz often contrasts it with what she calls 'objectivist grounded theory', which is represented by the original grounded theory (Glaser & Strauss, 1967) and Glaser's (1978, 1998, 2013) version. The differences in the goals and procedures of data analysis of the two approaches arise from their epistemological positions.

According to Charmaz (2000, 2006, 2014), objectivist grounded theory still has elements of positivistic quantitative research, even though it was developed to address the problems inherent in this type of scientific inquiry. Ontologically, objectivist grounded theory assumes the existence of an objective reality. Therefore, the key concepts are always found in the data. This view leads to an epistemological position that emphasizes objectivity in data collection and analysis. Consequently, the method of objective grounded theory assumes that the inquirer is a neutral observer and that the collected data reflect social reality. Thus, the goal of objectivist grounded theory research is to provide causal explanations and predictions concerning phenomena in the external world. As discussed above, the theories that are produced by using objectivist grounded theory are causal explanations described with identified variables. Therefore, these theories are proposed as objective descriptions of causes, conditions, results, predictions, or problem solutions. Thus, the writing style used for objectivist grounded theory is highly objective and scientific.

In contrast, constructivist grounded theory reflects the views of social constructivism. Ontologically, social constructivism assumes the existence of multiple realities. Epistemologically, social constructivism emphasizes the role of the researcher by acknowledging the interactive and interpretive nature of data construction. Therefore, key concepts are considered to originate from the interaction between a researcher and research participants rather than solely from the data. Thus, the purpose of a study based on constructivist grounded theory is to explore the meaning of participants' actions and the meanings implied in their narratives. In addition, the writing style of constructivist grounded theory is more creative than the precise scientific writing style used by objectivist grounded theorists. An interpretive analysis used by constructivist grounded theory 'invites the reader's imaginative participation in related experiences through the theoretical rendering of the category' (Charmaz, 2006, p. 147). Heavily influenced by the perspectives of the pragmatist tradition of the Chicago School, constructivist grounded theory encourages us to 'construct an interpretive rendering of the worlds we study rather than an external reporting of events and statements' (Charmaz, 2006, p. 184).

We assert that both the objectivist and constructivist grounded theory approaches have strengths and weaknesses. Depending on the research purpose, a pragmatic researcher may choose one approach over the other by adopting the perspective of philosophical pragmatism, in which 'facts and values are linked rather than separate and scientific truth is relative, provisional, and assessed through what works in empirical practice' (Charmaz, 2014, p. 263). For the pragmatic researcher, the research question determines which version of the GTM to use. Such methodological flexibility may be appreciated in applied fields, such as health, education, social work, and policy development, which prioritize solving future problems over other concerns.

GROUNDED TEXT MINING APPROACH

The grounded text mining approach (GTxA) that we propose in this chapter uses text mining techniques to aid in the construction of grounded theory. Before discussing the details of the GTxA, let us provide a definition of grounded theory and a definition of text mining. Grounded theory is 'a rigorous method of conducting research in which researchers construct conceptual frameworks or theories through building inductive theoretical analyses from data and subsequently checking their theoretical interpretations' (Charmaz, 2014, p. 343). Text mining is a new method for achieving 'the discovery by computer of new, previously unknown information, by automatically extracting information from different written resources' (Gupta & Lehal, 2009). Text mining software provides (semi) automatic analyses that rely on natural language processing technology that originated from research on artificial intelligence. Accordingly, the GTxA allows researchers to creatively and subjectively analyze data while ensuring that their analyses are fully grounded in the data. This method is possible because it uses automatic language processing and a visualization of the emerging codes.

The GTxA lies in the middle of the epistemological continuum between the objectivist and constructivist grounded theories. That is, a researcher who uses the GTxA believes that theories can be either plausible causal explanations or interpretations of the meanings and actions of the study participants. Our research questions determine the type of theory to develop.

A researcher who uses the GTxA can use text mining techniques to approach data construction and analysis automatically by continually validating that her interpretation of the data is grounded in the data and by addressing any gaps that are found. The GTxA embraces the pluralism of the Chicago School, which uses diverse methods to gather data, such as interviews, participant observation, document analysis, etc. With the GTxA, the researcher analyzes text data quantitatively and interpretively. In this sense, the GTxA is a qualitatively driven, mixed methods approach (Hesse-Biber, 2010; Hesse-Biber, Rodriguez, & Frost, 2015; Johnson, Onwuegbuzie, & Turner, 2007).

Coding Strategies of the GTxA

Because of the flexibility of the GTM, the GTxA uses the same coding strategies. The coding strategies of the constructivist GTM are simpler than the coding strategies of the objectivist GTM. Coding tools used by the Glaserian GTM (e.g., 18 theoretical codes) and Straussian GTM (e.g., axial coding, paradigm, and condition/consequences matrix) were originally developed to facilitate data analysis by encouraging the researcher to examine the data from multiple perspectives. However, the complexity of these tools may prevent a researcher from immersing herself in the data. As a result, Charmaz (2000) proposes using only two types of coding, namely, initial coding and focused coding, to allow researchers to pay closer attention to the data rather than to the coding tools.

In the first coding stage, the researcher closely examines the data and labels each word, line, or segment. In this phase, the researcher considers all possible theory constructions. The focused coding phase is next. During this phase, the researcher selects the most meaningful or frequently observed codes and then sorts and consolidates them according to their meanings to organize a larger amount of data.

Importantly, Charmaz (2014) also argues for the role of language in constructing codes. She states that '...we know the empirical world through language and the actions we take towards it. In this sense, no researcher is neutral because language confers form and meaning on observed realities' (p. 114). Her statement demonstrates her social constructivist perspective. Similar to the constructivist GTM, language is also central to the analysis of data in using the GTxA. Different words are used by research participants to convey similar meanings. To utilize an automatic coding, or autocoding function, which will be discussed in the following section, researchers first interpret the meanings of words and phrases in a specific context and then define the coding rules for the text mining software based on their interpretations. Failing to provide accurate definitions of the coding rules for the text mining software will result in irrelevant and confusing categories. As a result, researchers must meticulously read the data and refine the coding rules. By repeating this process, researchers can deepen their understanding of the voices included in the text. Although GTxA stands in the middle of the epistemological continuum between the objectivist and constructivist grounded theories, the GTxA's meaning-oriented approach to data analysis is more compatible with constructivist grounded theory than with objectivist grounded theory.

Locating the GTxA in the Current Literature

Recently, there has been an increase in the use of Computer Assisted Qualitative Data Analysis Software (CAQDAS) for qualitative inquiries that include the practices of the GTM. CAQDAS provides tools to construct theories based on qualitative data such as text, audio, image, and video. The tools improve the efficiency of coding and the retrieval of data (Gibbs, 2013). However, many concerns have been expressed regarding an analysis using CAQDAS (e.g., Charmaz, 2011; Fielding & Lee, 1998; Weitzman, 2000). Two concerns are that it puts distance between the researchers and the data, and the analysis is constrained by the software design. However, it is important to remember that the researcher, not CAQDAS, conducts the analysis.

CAQDAS is a set of tools that assists researchers' analytical work. For example, CAQDAS makes it easy for researchers to create and retrieve links between the data and the codes that researchers input. Using CAQDAS, researchers can also evaluate how a word or phrase is used in different contexts by retrieving a list of sentences that contain the expression. Charmaz (2011) notes that CAQDAS 'may fit general qualitative coding for topics and themes more than coding for processes and engaging in comparative analysis' (p. 370). In other words, although CAQDAS has succeeded in streamlining part of the coding work in the constructivist GTM, it can be said that it has not reached the stage of supporting the overall process of the GTM.

Another trend in computer-based text analysis is the use of text mining software. This software provides automatic or semi-automatic analyses that rely on natural language processing technology that originated from research on artificial intelligence. Text mining is a data mining technique aimed at extracting information from big data. The goal of text mining is to gather information from a specific set of text data (Hearst, 1999). Text mining software has the ability to lemmatize (determining the lemma of a word or dictionary form in the inputted text), parse (structuring the text based on linguistic features), and visualize (representing the frequency and co-occurrence of words and phrases graphically). By using these functions, researchers can gain an overall view of a large amount of text data. Thus, the text mining techniques enable a 'breadth' of vision for the text data.

CAQDAS and text mining software offer the researcher different ways to analyze text data. These approaches also have many similarities. Yu, Jannasch-Pennell, and DiGangi (2011) assert that both text mining and qualitative analysis using CAQDAS are compatible with the constructivist epistemology. In both approaches, researchers are encouraged to be open-minded regarding the iterative process of coding and building categories and are discouraged from having preconceptions. In addition, Bryant and Raja (2014) evaluate the similarities and differences between Knowledge Discovery from Data (KDD), a synonym of data mining, and the GTM practices with CAQDAS. They argue regarding the possibility that KDD analysts may conduct mining to obtain objective and quantified results that reflect the entire spectrum of the target big data source using certain algorithms based on their preconceptions. At the same time, they assume that KDD and the GTM are similar with respect to the spiral interpretive process of the data. They note that 'the aim of both the GTM and KDD is best thought of not as a circle but rather as a spiral moving from an origin focused on the data towards ever higher levels of abstraction and conceptual reach'. They also mention that 'both approaches can be seen as instantiations of hermeneutics'(p.327).

To put it another way, researchers of both the GTM with CAQDAS and text mining aim to understand the text data with open-mindedness, to extract the important themes, and to build a theory from the bottom-up. The approaches differ in the perspectives that they provide. By using the GTM with CAQDAS, researchers can gain an in-depth understanding of the text data. In contrast, text mining allows researchers to gain a broader understanding of the text data. Researchers may be able to construct holistic theories by using both methods to analyze text data.

Based on this discussion, the authors propose the use of the GTxA to analyze both the depth and breadth of data. The GTM allows researchers to interpret text data at a deep level via the interpretation of words or phrases based on a specific context. In addition, researchers interpret the characteristics of the whole text data based on the result of quantifying and visualizing the words and phrases via text mining. By checking the results of both rather than conducting each analysis independently, researchers can obtain a deep and comprehensible understanding.

The following section outlines the GTxA by using a transcript that the second author collected in her previous studies (Kakai, 2013).

Illustrating a GTxA Analysis

In this section, we demonstrate how the GTxA is used for grounded theory analysis. We use a section of data obtained by the second author from cancer patients/survivors, caregivers, medical professionals, and complementary and alternative medicine providers. All of these individuals were participating in a community-based integrative medicine practice at a cancer clinic on the west coast of the United States.[6]

Integrative medicine is a medical practice that incorporates both conventional medicine and complementary and alternative medicine (CAM). The integrative approach at this clinic was unique because it was operated by a group of volunteers under the leadership and supervision of medical professionals. Community cancer patients and caregivers of cancer patients/survivors received CAM for free, regardless of their affiliation with the clinic. CAM volunteers included, but were not limited to, specialists in mind and body practices such as massage, qigong, yoga, reiki, acupuncture, and biofeedback, as well as modalities involving natural products, such as homeopathy.[7] The clinic also offered opportunities for cancer survivors to share their stories and to use their experiences to help other cancer patients who were being treated. In one case, a post-treatment cancer survivor became a licensed hypnotherapist and volunteered his hypnotherapy skills at the clinic.

In the following section, we provide an example of the GTxA analysis. We attempt to answer the question, 'How have cancer experiences changed perspectives about life and living among cancer patients/survivors who are participating in the clinic's integrative medicine program?' Because of our focus on cancer patients/survivors, we will not include the data from medical professionals and CAM providers.

Overview of the GTxA procedure

The GTxA is an integrative, reflective, and cyclical process that obtains an overview of the text data (Step 1), completes a qualitative data analysis (Step 2), creates visualization and performs an analysis with text mining (Step 3), and then develops a meta-inference (Step 4). By cyclically repeating these steps, researchers obtain a deeper understanding of the text data (Figure 16.2).

It is important for researchers who use the GTxA not only to follow the steps in order but also to repeat part or all of the analysis if there are any discrepancies or uncertainties during the meta-inference stage. For example, codes and categories may be redefined to resolve an inconsistency in the meta-inference. In Step 3, the parameters for searching or autocoding may be modified to create a more relevant visualization of the text data. During the meta-inference in Step 4, researchers confirm the consistency and inconsistency of the interpretation of Steps 1 to 3 and estimate the cause of contradiction. Furthermore, by repeating Steps 1 to 3, the researchers' interpretation in each stage is updated and refined. By using these reflective and cyclical processes until all inconsistencies or gaps are eliminated, researchers can obtain a deeper understanding of the specific voices and overall tendencies included in text data.

The most important feature of this approach is that it provides a holistic view of the data by integrating the researchers' qualitative analysis of the text data with the autocoding/

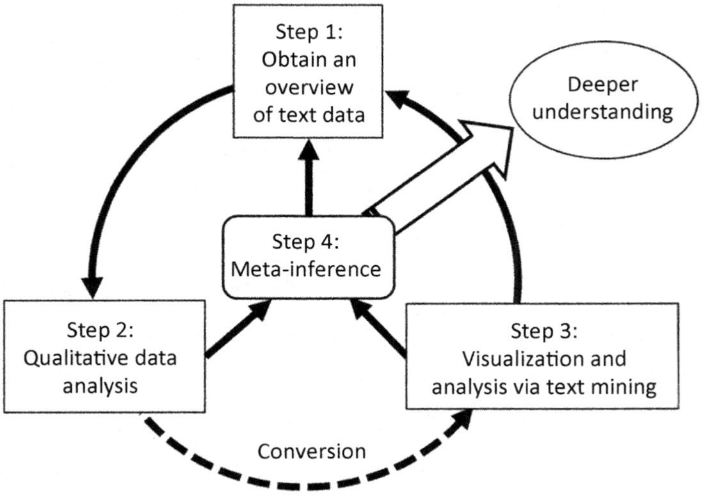

Figure 16.2 Framework and cyclic process of the GTxA

visualization of a computer. First, researchers identify qualitative features of the text data by reading and interpreting them. Then, they compare their results with the quantified outcomes of the text data. By repeating this work, researchers can understand the text data from both subjective and objective perspectives. In addition, the approach is based on a conversion mixing design, which integrates quantitative and qualitative data by transforming one type to another (Teddlie & Tashakkori, 2009).

Computer-supported process of the GTxA

The GTxA assumes the use of a computer during all stages of the analysis to increase efficiency. The method is useful to researchers who use WordCloud[8] or other graphs to obtain a big picture of the data in addition to reading the text data in Step 1. As mentioned above, the use of CAQDAS in Step 2 is a convenient way to manage the links between the codes and the original texts. In Step 3, the autocoding function of text mining software can be a powerful tool to determine the accuracy of human-defined codes.

In general, there are two types of autocoding: simple automatic coding using text mining software and semi-automatic coding in which researchers define the coding rules. The former is a method in which the software automatically extracts codes based on the frequency or grammatical structure of words. The latter is a method in which researchers first define a coding rule and then the software performs coding based on it. For example, if researchers define a rule in which the phrase ‘changed my perception’ relates to the code ‘1_Learning’, the software can perform semi-automatic coding based on the rule. The GTxA emphasizes the comparison between the results of the semi-automatic coding and the results of the GTM conducted by researchers because researchers can easily find missing coding or codes that involve unnatural leaps by considering both results.

There are many types of CAQDAS (e.g., NVivo, MaxQDA, or Atlas.ti) and text mining software that support both types of autocoding (e.g., WordStat or KH Coder). Recently, it has become possible to perform both qualitative data analysis and text mining with one

CAQDAS package. For example, NVivo 11 Plus and beyond support not only autocoding and text visualization functions (such as WordCloud) but also the conventional CAQDAS capabilities. Therefore, in this chapter, we illustrate an example of the GTxA in practice using NVivo 11 Plus.

Example of the GTxA procedure

In the following, we illustrate an example of GTxA analysis. The transcript used here was originally collected by the second author through semi-structured interviews of cancer patients/cancer survivors (P1–P9) and their families/caregivers (C5–C6) who had participated in a community-based integrated medical practice at a cancer clinic in United States. As discussed previously, the research question is 'How have cancer experiences changed perspectives about life and living among cancer patients/survivors who are involved in the integrative medicine program at the clinic?'

Step 1: Obtaining an overview of text data The researchers who use the GTxA first read the text data to understand the topics, impressions, or issues concerning the cancer experience and practice of CAM as described in the transcript. These researchers also explore the similarities and differences among participants. At this stage, it is also useful for researchers to refer to the visualization of word and phrase frequency by using text mining software as an auxiliary means.

Figure 16.3 shows a screenshot of NVivo including the transcript and a memo window. While they read the transcript, it is useful for researchers to use memos to record their impressions, feelings, and responses.

Some CAQDAS tools can display how a specific word is used in a specific context. Figure 16.4 shows the results of the *Text Search* function in NVivo, which provides a visualization of the context of the word 'cancer'. Figure 16.4 also shows that some participants indicated that cancer was a positive experience. This type of observation may be used to

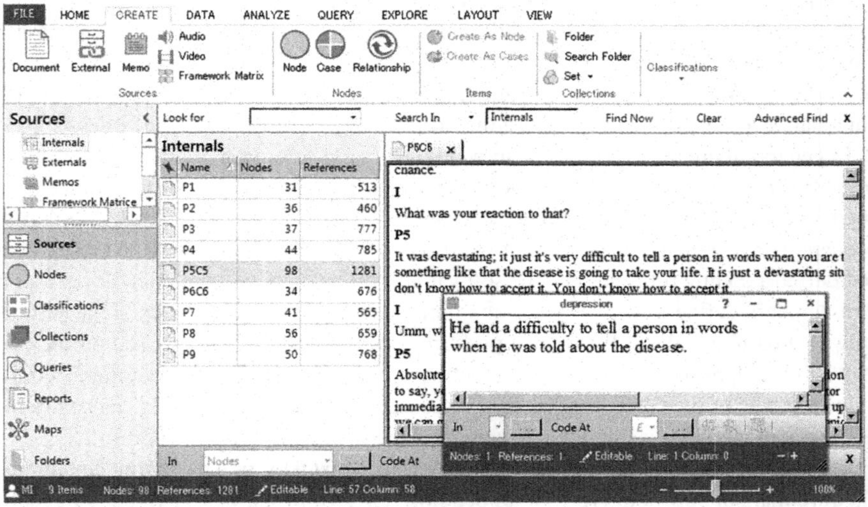

Figure 16.3 Screenshot of NVivo

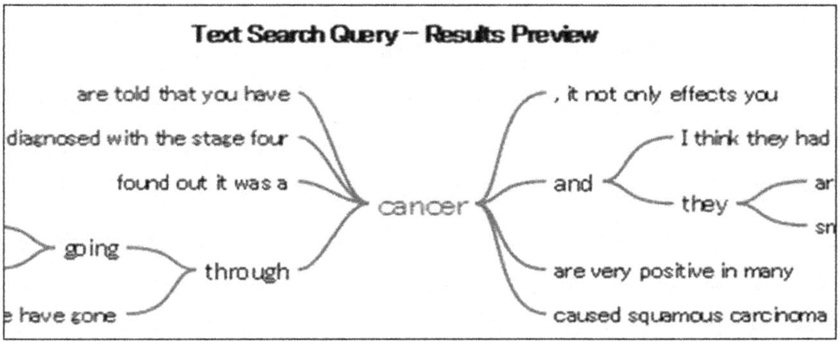

Figure 16.4 Results of a *Text Search* of the word 'cancer'

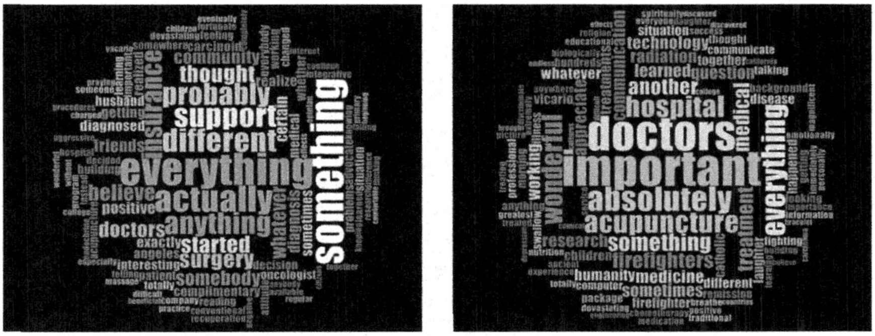

Figure 16.5 *WordCloud* generated based on word frequency (Left: P3, Right: P5)

gain an overview of the text data. In addition, the visualization function of CAQDAS can provide an easily understood overview of the differences among participants. For example, Figure 16.5 uses the WordCloud function of NVivo to show these differences.

Many advanced text-processing functions and visualization capabilities are currently available in CAQDAS. Therefore, researchers may use these functions as a way to enhance their understanding of text data, in addition to reading the text and interpreting the participant's meaning.

Step 2: Qualitative data analysis based on constructivist GTM The GTxA relied on a constructivist GTM (Charmaz, 2006) to gain a deeper understanding of the text data. The constructivist GTM uses initial coding, focused coding, and categorizing. To avoid an illogical coding of the text data, initial coding is performed in two steps, namely, word-by-word coding and sentence-based coding. Then, focused coding is used. According to Charmaz (2014, p. 138), focused coding 'means using the most significant and/or frequent earlier codes to sift through and analyze large amounts of data. Focused coding requires decisions about which initial codes make the most analytic sense to categorize your data incisively and completely.' The step that follows is to categorize focused codes in order to generate a theory.

Figure 16.6 is an example of a coding task with the constructivist GTM by using NVivo. In the first step of the initial coding, researchers conduct in vivo coding. In vivo coding is a

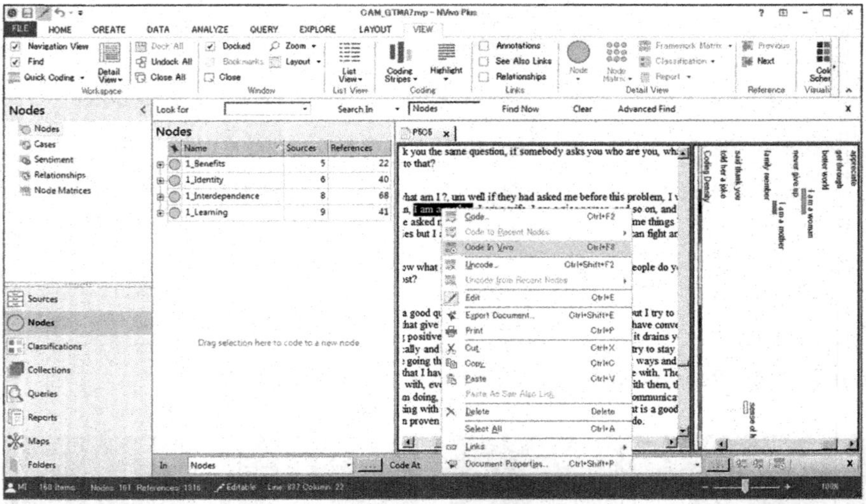

Figure 16.6 Coding process in NVivo

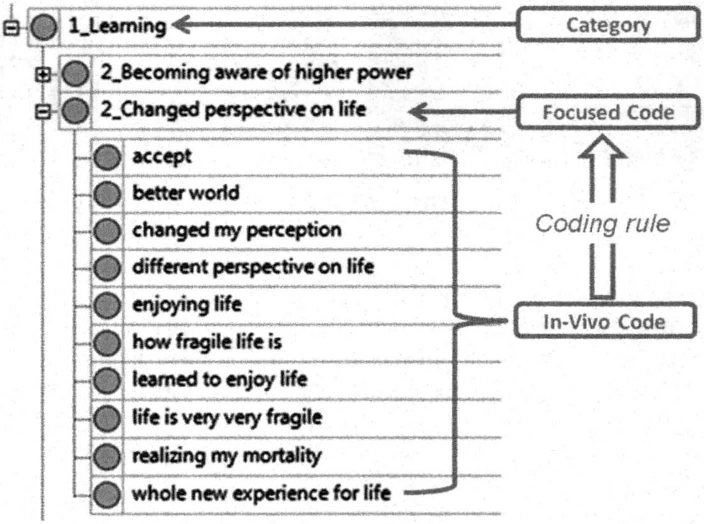

Figure 16.7 Hierarchy of codes and categories in NVivo

way of assigning a word or short phrase in the original text to an in vivo code. They select the text content, right-click to display the shortcut menu, and choose 'Code In-Vivo'. After all necessary in vivo codes are defined, focused coding is performed. A focused code is a collection of in vivo codes grouped into a more abstract label. Furthermore, a procedure for collecting a set of focused codes into categories is conducted.

Figure 16.7 shows the hierarchy of categories, focused codes, and in vivo codes. To improve the ease of interpretation, '1_' is added to the names of categories (e.g., '1_Learning') and '2_' is added to the names of focused codes (e.g., '2_Changed perspective on life').

The codes without numbers are in vivo codes directly extracted from the original transcript. Similar to other CAQDAS, NVivo allows users to define a hierarchy of codes.

As Charmaz (2006) discussed, the analytical processes in the constructivist GTM are not linear. When new ideas or questions arise during analysis, researchers should review the coding process and restructure the coding hierarchy if necessary.

Step 3: Visualization and analysis by text mining In this step, text mining is used to re-examine the manually generated codes and hierarchies. First, the code hierarchy is exported to a plain text file. Then, researchers define coding rules for the text mining software by combining in vivo codes and focused codes. The vertical arrow on the right side of Figure 16.7 shows the information that is the basis for defining the coding rules. The coding rule here is that if a string in the in vivo codes appears in a certain text data, it is assumed that a focused code appears in the data. A set of these rules, defined based on the code hierarchy, is used in the autocoding of the text mining software.

Next, we explain how to perform autocoding by using the *Text Search* function of NVivo.[9] First, the code hierarchy (Figure 16.7) is exported as plain text. Then, the query pattern for the *Text Search* function is defined by using the plain text file. In Figure 16.8, the query pattern that was extracted from the text file is shown under the field 'Search for'. The program searches for the text data related to the focused code '2_Changed perspective on life'. The query pattern includes words and phrases in in vivo codes that are separated by the 'OR' condition. By saving the query results as 'Results Node' in NVivo with code labels such as '2_Changed perspective on life', researchers can retrieve the search results in various graph formats, such as three-dimensional matrixes (as shown in Figures 16.9–16.11).

Step 4: Meta-inference In Step 4, researchers compare the manual coding in Step 2 with the autocoding in Step 3. In general, text mining software is better than human coders at detecting words and phrases based on coding rules. However, it is possible that text mining software selects incorrect codes because it cannot recognize the meaning of words and phrases in a specific context. Therefore, researchers should review the results to determine whether they missed necessary codes or whether the computer program selected incorrect codes. While exploring the cause of this inconsistency by referring to the original text and refining codes, researchers can obtain the viewpoints of the computer, which processes the entire text data all at once, and of humans, who understand words at a deep level within a specific context. In other words, these processes allow researchers to improve the depth and breadth of their understanding of the text data.

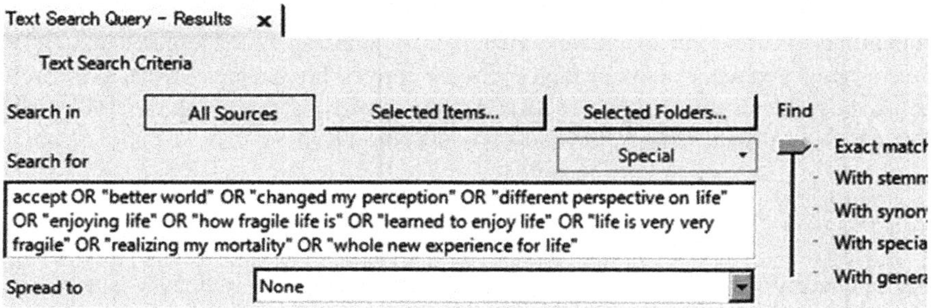

Figure 16.8 Text Search Query (for '2_Changed perspective on life')

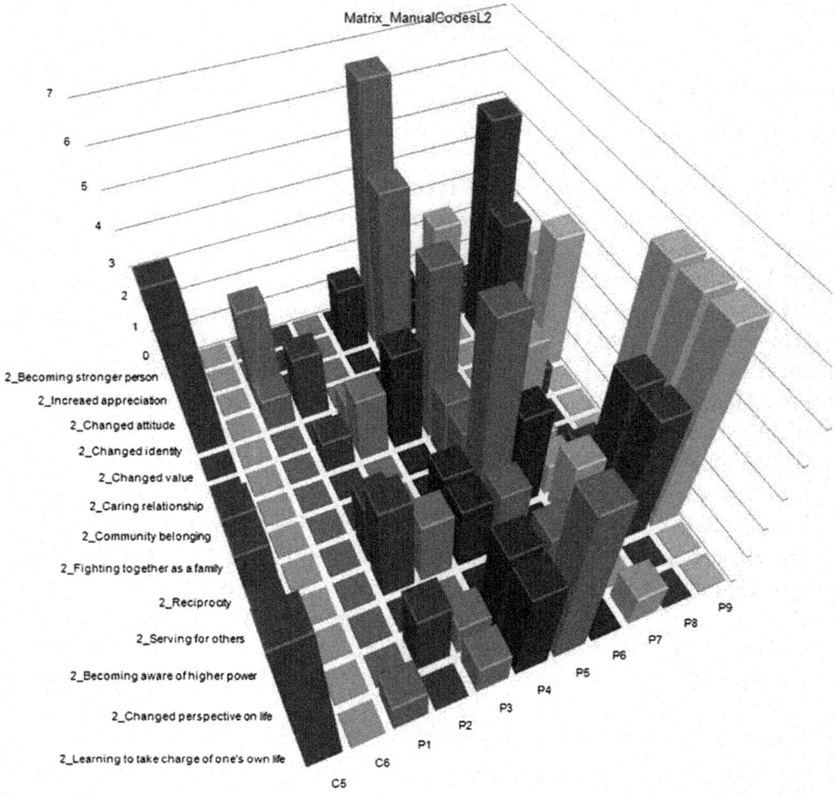

Figure 16.9 Matrix of participants and codes defined in Step 2

Meta-inference based on the comparison of codes frequency

Figure 16.9 is a matrix that shows the relations between the research participants and the focused codes defined by researchers. In contrast, Figure 16.10 shows a matrix of the focused codes and research participants that were found by using the *Text Search* function in NVivo. The height of the bars in the matrix correlates with the number of codes.

The similarities and differences between human coding and computer coding are shown in Figures 16.10 and 16.11. Although both figures have a similar shape, some vertical bars have slightly different heights. This difference in height indicates that researchers may fail to code some of the text. Therefore, it is necessary for researchers to return to the original text and examine which codes are correct. For example, when a researcher obtains the result shown in Figure 16.10 and clicks the vertical bar in column 'P3' and row 'ID2_Changed attitude', the following sentence is displayed.

> … most *positive* was just the loving and caring support of everybody that I knew before and I got to know …

This sentence does not mention a change of attitude of the participants. Therefore, it should not be coded as '2_Change_attitude'. In contrast, the following sentence is related to a change of attitude.

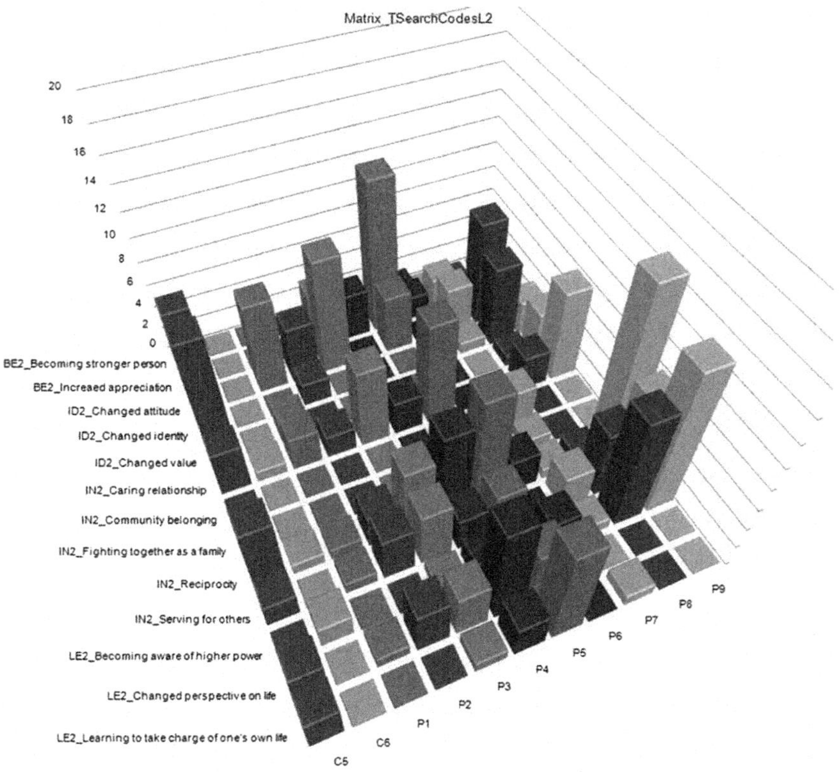

Figure 16.10 Matrix of participants and codes defined in Step 3

> … I realized that *positive* attitude and uh, having faith really makes a difference in, in how you get through things and how you recuperate.

Although the sentence above was not manually coded by the researchers, it should be added to the focused code '2_Changed attitude' because it indicates the change of attitude after P3 experienced cancer. This example demonstrates that text mining techniques can help researchers to improve their coding by finding the text data that they overlooked. Figure 16.11 shows the outcome of the modification that uses the comparison of manual coding with autocoding.

Meta-inference on the relationship between categories and participants

At the end of the meta-inference, the researchers conduct theory construction from the viewpoint of the research question. For this process, it is useful to draw diagrams that visualize the links between the codes and participants. The *Project Map* function of NVivo is a tool that retrieves a set of related codes and participants and generates a diagram that consists of these nodes. Figure 16.12 is a diagram created by the *Project Map* function,[10] and it shows all codes that are linked to participant P3. Figure 16.12 can be interpreted as follows. P3 had a change of 'Identity' through her cancer experience. More specifically, her change included 'changed value', 'changed perspective on life',

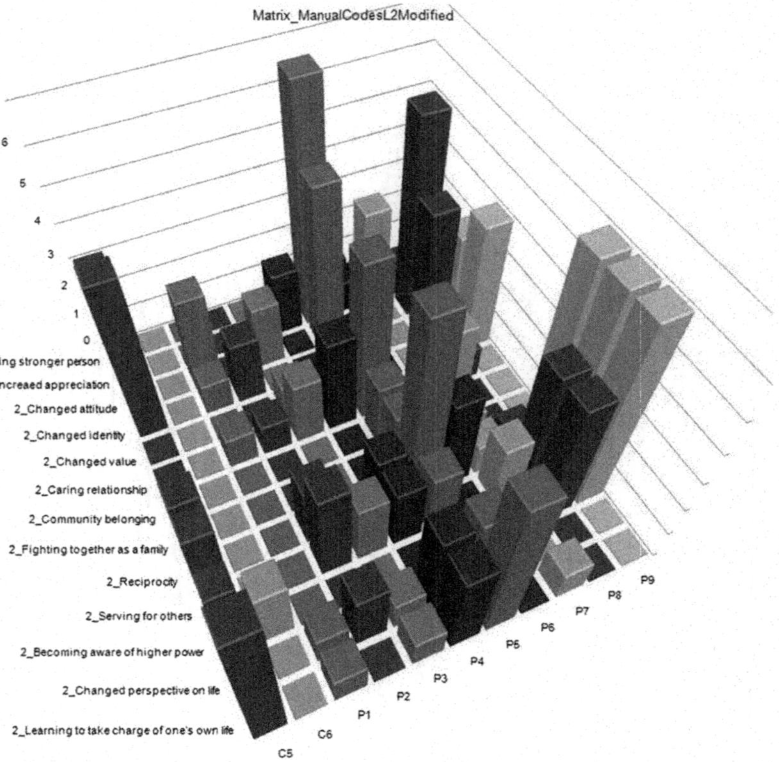

Figure 16.11 Modified matrix of participants and codes

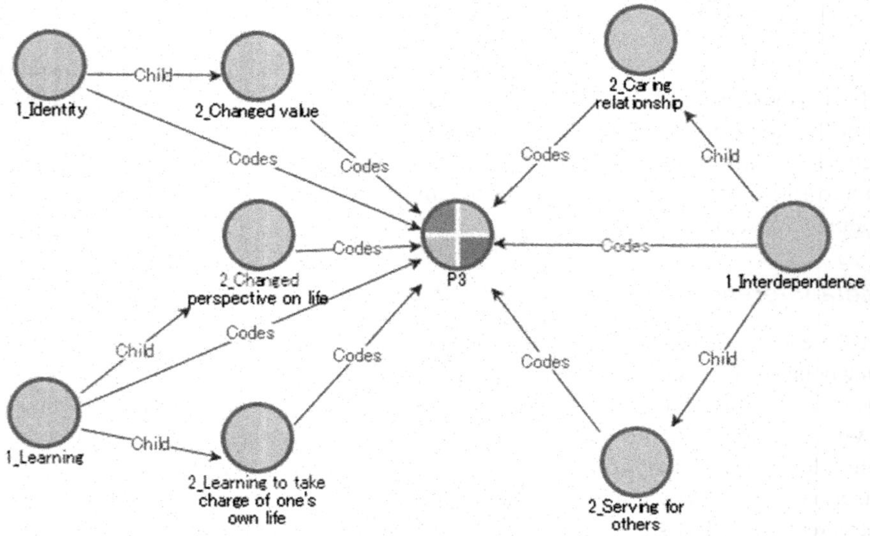

Figure 16.12 Changes in the viewpoints of P3 due to her cancer experience

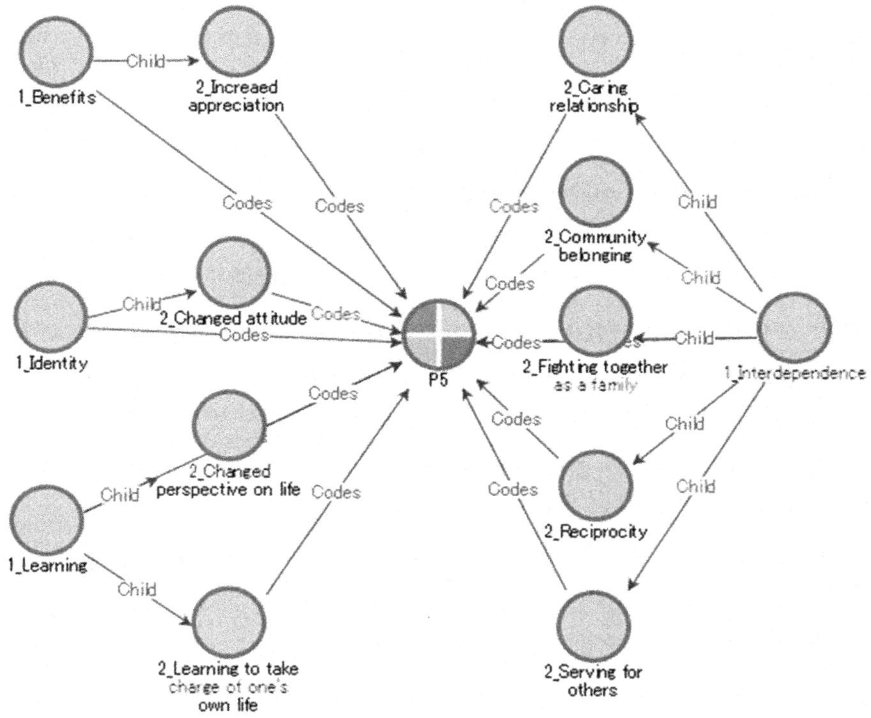

Figure 16.13 Changes in the viewpoints of P5 due to his experience with cancer

and 'learning to take charge of her own life'. As a result, she enhanced her sense of 'Interdependence', which included a 'caring relationship' and 'serving for others'.

Figure 16.13 is another *Project Map* diagram that shows the codes related to participant P5. This diagram outlines the following story of P5. Through his cancer experience, he felt 'Benefits', especially 'increased appreciation' of nature or life. He also experienced a change of 'Identity', which included a 'changed attitude' towards his illness. Another change was 'Learning'. He had a 'changed perspective on life' and experienced 'learning to take charge of his own life'. As a result, he developed a stronger sense of 'Interdependence'. More specifically, he experienced feeling a 'caring relationship' and 'community belonging'. He was also encouraged to work towards 'fighting together as a family' and paying more attention to 'reciprocity', and he started having a sense of 'serving for others'.

Although the changes among the participants were diverse, we argue that many of them experienced constructive changes because of cancer.

CONCLUSIONS

In this chapter, we introduced the GTxA as a qualitatively-driven mixed methods research that integrates qualitative data analysis based on the constructivist GTM and text mining techniques. With the GTxA, it is possible for researchers to integrate their subjective judgment with the objectivity provided by a computer through the process of meta-inference. We also provided an example of the GTxA by using a transcript of the interviews of cancer survivors. NVivo 11 Plus was used to perform both the constructivist GTM and text mining. Through the cyclical analysis of the GTxA, a theory on the process of the transformation of cancer survivors has been constructed.

Based on the information in this discussion, the advantages of the GTxA are as follows.

1 Balancing viewpoints in theory construction
The GTxA provides a balance between the two perspectives of depth and breadth in understanding text data by combining the GTM, which is based on the constructivist paradigm, and the visualization of text resources via text mining. Researchers first apply the GTM-based analysis to the target text resource to obtain a deep level of understanding based on the concrete context. Next, researchers quantify and visualize the text data via text mining, thereby obtaining an understanding of the characteristics of the entire text data. By comparing the results of both rather than implementing the GTM and text mining independently, it is possible for researchers to obtain a deep and comprehensive understanding of the text data, that is, a balance between depth and breadth.
2 Enhancing transparency in the data analysis process
In the GTxA, researchers use autocoding rules for text mining software. Although the final code is modified based on researchers' subjective judgment, the coding process is more transparent than conventional qualitative data analysis. This coding procedure makes it possible for a third party to check the data analysis process.
3 Reducing the cognitive load of a researcher
When the GTM researchers have large amounts of text data or a large number of cases, it requires a great deal of attention not only to code but also to check the coding results of the text data. The GTxA aids researchers by providing an exhaustive check of the coding through text mining in addition to searching and retrieving codes with CAQDAS. Therefore, this approach will reduce the cognitive load of researchers.

The current framework of the GTxA has several limitations. First, because the GTxA assumes that researchers conduct GTM, there is a limit to the amount of text data that can be analyzed. Second, to use the GTxA, researchers must learn how to use both CAQDAS and text mining tools. Finally, because the GTxA uses the methods of both the GTM and text mining, more time is required to obtain the final result compared with conducting each analysis independently.

Despite these limitations, researchers can gain many benefits by using the GTxA. It allows researchers to obtain well-balanced results from a large data set that contains many cases that may be difficult to manage without assistance from CAQDAS and text mining tools. By taking advantage of the computer-assisted and computer-based analyses, researchers can process a large data set with less cognitive load. Additionally, in qualitative data analysis, researchers usually require much time to check the appropriateness of coding for text data. Researchers using the GTxA are able to quickly compare the differences between performing the coding themselves and performing autocoding using a computer. As a result, researchers can reduce their cognitive loads to find missed coding or codes that involve unnatural leaps.

Furthermore, rapid progress is being made in the field of natural language processing technology such as new statistical methods for language analysis, the visualization of textual information, and automatic classification based on machine learning. Therefore, the GTxA has the potential to improve with new technology while still adhering to the concepts of the GTM.

Notes

1 Borrowing from Teddlie & Tashakkori (2009, p. 21), we define methodology as 'a broad approach to scientific inquiry specifying how research questions should be asked and answered' and methods as 'specific strategies and procedures for implementing research design, including sampling, data collection, data analysis and interpretation of the findings'.
2 See Bryant and Charmaz (2007b) for a discussion of the epistemological shift in the GTM.
3 Thus far, Charmaz's constructivist grounded theory has been introduced in numerous qualitative research handbooks. Several examples of the books in which her version of the GTM is introduced include, but are not limited to, *The Sage Handbook of Qualitative Research* (2nd ed.), edited by N. Denzin and Y. Lincoln; *The Sage Handbook of Grounded Theory* (1st ed.), edited by A. Bryant and K. Charmaz; and *Handbook of Feminist Research Methods* (2nd ed.), edited by S. Hesse-Biber.
4 Examples of grounded theory approaches developed by the second-generation scholars include dimensional analysis by Schatzman (1991), situational analysis by Clarke (2003, 2005), the constructivist approach by Charmaz (2000, 2006, 2014), the expansion of Glaserian GTM by Stern (1995) and Straussian GTM by Strauss and Corbin (Strauss & Corbin, 1990, 1998; Corbin & Strauss, 2008). In Japan, the modified grounded theory approach (M-GTA) was developed by Kinoshita (2003, 2007), a PhD graduate of UCSF.
5 Glaser's *Theoretical Sensitivity* (Glaser, 1978) and Strauss's *Basics of Qualitative Research: Grounded Theory Procedures and Techniques* (Strauss & Corbin, 1990), along with *Qualitive Analysis for Social Scientists* (Strauss, 1987), marked the beginning of Glaserian GTM and Straussian GTM, respectively. See Bryant and Charmaz (2007b) and Clarke (Chapter 1 in this volume) for details regarding the historical development of the GTM.
6 Kakai (2013) is an empirical article published from this field research project. The GTxA was not used in the analysis of this paper.
7 For a detailed description of CAM modalities, please refer to the following site: https://nccih.nih.gov/health/integrative-health
8 WordCloud allows the display of words with varying font sizes based on the frequency of words in the text data.
9 In a search with a default setting, NVivo filters out stop words, or the most common words (e.g., 'a', 'an', or 'the'). Therefore, the stop words list must be cleared in *Project Properties* before starting the search.
10 In this diagram, the label 'Child' on the arrow line shows the hierarchical relationship between the codes. For example, '1_Identity' is a category code, and '2_Changed value' is a focused code, which is a subordinate level of the category code. The label 'Code' on the arrow line indicates that the codes are found in the transcript of P3.

REFERENCES

Bryant, A. (2002). Re-grounding grounded theory. *Journal of Information Technology Theory and Application*, *4*, 25–42.

Bryant, A. (2017). *Grounded theory and grounded theorizing: pragmatism in research practice*. NY: Oxford University Press.

Bryant, A. & Charmaz, K. (2007a). Introduction: Grounded theory research – Methods and practices. In A. Bryant & K. Charmaz (Eds.), *The Sage handbook of grounded theory* (pp. 1–28). London: Sage.

Bryant, A. & Charmaz, K. (2007b). Grounded theory in historical perspective: An epistemological account. In A. Bryant & K. Charmaz (Eds.), *The Sage handbook of grounded theory* (pp. 31–57). London: Sage.

Bryant, A. & Charmaz K. (Eds.) (2007c). *The Sage handbook of grounded theory*. London: Sage.

Bryant, A. & Raja, U. (2014). In the realm of Big Data. *First Monday, 19*. Retrieved May 1, 2016 from http://firstmonday.org/article/view/4991/3822

Charmaz, K. (2000). Grounded theory: Objectivist and constructivist methods. In N. K. Denzin & Y. S. Lincoln (Eds.), *The Sage handbook of qualitative research* (2nd ed., pp. 509–535). Thousand Oaks, CA: Sage.

Charmaz, K. (2006). Constructing grounded theory: A practical guide through qualitative analysis. London: Sage.

Charmaz, K. (2011). Grounded theory methods in social justice research. In N. K. Denzin & Y. S. Lincoln (Eds.), *The Sage handbook of qualitative research* (4th ed., pp. 359–380). Thousand Oaks, CA: Sage.

Charmaz, K. (2014). *Constructing grounded theory* (2nd ed.). London: Sage.

Clarke, A. E. (2003). Situational analyses: Grounded theory mapping after the postmodern turn. *Symbolic Interaction*, *26*, 553–576. doi:10.1525/si.2003.26.4.553.

Clarke, A. E. (2005). Situational analysis: Grounded theory after the postmodern turn. Thousand Oaks, CA: Sage.

Corbin, J. & A. Strauss (2008). *Basics of Qualitative Research: Grounded Theory Procedures and Techniques* (3rd ed.). Thousand Oaks, CA: Sage.

Denzin, N. K. & Lincoln, Y. S. (Eds.) (2000). *The Sage handbook of qualitative research* (2nd ed.). Thousand Oaks, CA: Sage.

Fielding, N. G. & Lee, Raymond M. (1998). *Computer analysis and qualitative research*. London: Sage.

Gibbs, G. R. (2013). Using software in qualitative analysis. In U. Flick (ed.) *The Sage handbook of qualitative data analysis* (pp. 277–295). London: Sage.

Glaser, B. G. (1978). *Theoretical sensitivity*. Mill Valley, CA: Sociology Press.

Glaser, B. G. (1998). *Doing grounded theory: Issues & discussion.* Mill Valley, CA: Sociology Press.

Glaser, B. G. (2013). *No preconceptions: The grounded theory dictum*. Mill Valley, CA: Sociology Press.

Glaser, B. G. & Strauss, A. L. (1967). The discovery of grounded theory: Strategies for qualitative research. New York: Aldine.

Gupta, V. & Lehal, G. S. (2009). A survey of text mining techniques and applications. *Journal of Emerging Technologies in Web Intelligence*, *1*(1), 17.

Hearst, M. A. (1999). Untangling text data mining. In *Proceedings of the 37th Annual Meeting of the Association for Computational Linguistics on Computational Linguistics* (pp. 3–10). Morristown, NJ: Association for Computational Linguistics.

Hesse-Biber, S. N. (2010). *Mixed methods research: Merging theory with practice*. New York: Guilford Press.

Hesse-Biber, S. N. (Ed.) (2012). *Handbook of feminist research methods* (2nd ed.). Thousand Oaks, CA: Sage.

Hesse-Biber, S. N., Rodriguez, D., & Frost, N. A. (2015). A qualitatively driven approach to multimethod and mixed methods research. In S. N. Hesse-Biber & R. B. Johnson (Eds.), *The Oxford handbook of multimethod and mixed methods research inquiry* (pp. 3–20). New York: Oxford University Press.

Johnson, R. B., Onwuegbuzie, A. J., & Turner, L. A. (2007). Toward a definition mixed methods research. *Journal of Mixed Methods Research*, *1*(2), 112-133. doi.org/10.1177/1558689806298224

Kakai, H. (2013). A community of healing: Psychosocial functions of integrative medicine perceived by oncology patients/survivors, healthcare professionals, and CAM providers. *Explore: The Journal of Science and Healing*, *9*, 365–371. doi:10.1016/j.explore.2013.08.002.

Kinoshita, Y. (2003). *Practice of grounded theory approach*. Tokyo: Koubundou Publishers (in Japanese).

Kinoshita, Y. (2007). *Modified grounded theory approach*. Tokyo: Kobundo Publishers (in Japanese).

Morse, J. M., Stern, P. N., Corbin, J., Bowers, B. Charmaz, K., & Clarke, A. E. (2009). *Developing grounded theory: The second generation*. Walnut Creek, CA: Left Coast Press.

Schatzman, L. (1991). Dimensional analysis: Notes on an alternative approach to the grounding of theory in qualitative research. In D. Maines (Ed.), *Social organization and social process: Essays in honor of Anselm Strauss* (pp. 303–314). Hawthorne, NY: Aldine de Gruyter.

Stern, P. N. (1995). Eroding grounded theory. In J. M. Morse (Ed.), *Critical issues in qualitative research methods* (pp. 212–223). Thousand Oaks, CA: Sage.

Strauss, A. L. (1987). *Qualitive analysis for social scientists*. New York: Cambridge University Press.
Strauss, A. L. & Corbin, J. (1990). Basics of qualitative research: Grounded theory procedures and techniques. Newbury Park, CA: Sage.
Strauss, A. L. & Corbin, J. (1998). Basics of qualitative research: Techniques and procedures for developing grounded theory (2nd ed.). Thousand Oaks, CA: Sage.
Teddlie, C. & Tashakkori, A. (2009). Foundations of mixed methods research: Integrating quantitative and qualitative approaches in the social and behavioral sciences. Thousand Oaks, CA: Sage.
Weitzman, E. A. (2000). Software and qualitative research. In N. K. Denzin & Y. S. Lincoln (Eds.), *The Sage handbook of qualitative research* (2nd ed., pp. 803–820). Thousand Oaks, CA: Sage.
Yu, C. H., Jannasch-Pennell, A., & DiGangi, S. (2011). Compatibility between text mining and qualitative research in the perspectives of grounded theory, content analysis, and reliability. *The Qualitative Report*, *16*, 730.

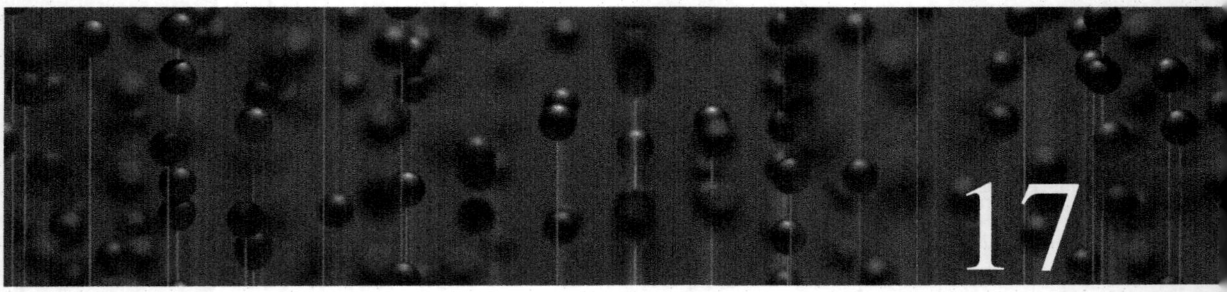

Visual Images and Grounded Theory Methodology

Krzysztof T. Konecki

'Seeing is not natural, however much we might think it to be.' (Banks 2001: 7)

Images, such as photographs, videos, drawings, etc., are increasingly employed in sociological, anthropological, psychological, social work, historical, geographical, mental health and nursing studies, although not as often as other types of qualitative data (such as interview transcripts). Grounded theory analysis of visual data can add order and offer more applicability than text alone when creating models of visual processes. Thus, visual grounded theory combines the analysis of visual and textual data. Generally, textual data still dominate, both those produced by the investigator, as well as in extant texts. The same goes for grounded theory methodology (GTM), in which textual data are most common.

To change this emphasis, I introduce a procedure, multislice imagining, for analyzing visual images and to show the potentiality of using visual analysis in GTM. Multislice imagining consists of identifying the layers of image that should be analyzed (levels of creation, structure, presentation and reception of image). To provide the background for this procedure, I begin by introducing contexts for interpreting images. Next, I present grounded theory applications for using visual analysis to lay the foundation for formulating the principles of visual grounded theory. Later, I introduce how to conduct multislice imagining, the basic procedure of visual grounded theory. This procedure is described together with the grounded theory procedures that should be used in each GTM study: coding (open and selective), constant comparative method, theoretical sampling and saturation. At the end of chapter, I discuss other uses of GTM with visual data analysis. Not all visual researchers follow every grounded theory procedure and not all aim for or achieve the main goal of this methodology: the creation of a conceptual-theoretical framework of the analyzed empirical area. However, we can see the potentiality of GTM analysis, for example, as used together with photovoice participatory research, to create the context for applying grounded theories in real-life and work situations.

INTERPRETATIONS AND DIMENSIONS OF VISUAL DATA

The tradition of using photographs as both documents for 'validating' certain conclusions as well as for analytical materials has been present since the 'visual turn' that took place in the 19th and 20th century. Taking sociology into consideration as an example, 31 articles making use of photographs as illustrations or evidence of sociological theses were published between 1896 and 1916 in a prestigious journal, *The American Journal of Sociology*. Since 1914, with a change of the editor, the policy of the journal changed as well – from publishing papers employing photographs to promoting more 'objective' statistical reports (Holliday 2000: 504; see also Dowdall & Golden 1989: 184). Despite this radical policy change in this influential sociological journal, sociological theses were still illustrated with photo visualizations of presented problems and hypotheses elsewhere but without a clear purpose for their inclusion.

Photography has been used as both empirical and analytical material from almost the beginning of academic sociology. However, visual representation methods and archiving of data, as well as data analysis were used in cultural anthropology (Jacknis 1988). Photographs have been used as an instrument of presenting data and even theoretical findings in this field (Henley 2013), and also in engaged reformist sociology (see Becker 1974: 3). We live in a visual culture that requires more research methods to make use of 'images'. Consequently, we need more scientific methods for the presentation and interpretation of data, as well as technical research applications, in which 'visualization' of concepts and hypotheses play a more significant role in research reports.

Interpretation

A photograph, as well as other images, requires 'reading'. Reading, like seeing an image, then becomes an interpretation (Magala 2000; Banks 2001: 5; see also Harper 1988, 1994: 407–408), which can take place on many levels/dimensions (Ferrarotti 1993: 88). The first one is the aesthetic dimension – exemplifying certain artistic conventions that may be applied to represent a subject. Although this aspect rarely is at the heart of sociological interests, it can become appropriate when analyzing the social and historical conditions of photography styles, or when historians or sociologists deal with photography as an art (see Becker 1982, 2002: 341–343; Mey & Dietrich 2016: 19, 34–35). It is also likely that the compositional analysis of an image is of utmost importance. 'This includes planimetrics (the reconstruction of the overall composition of the image), perspectivity (e.g., central perspective), and scenic choreography (how groups of persons or objects are related to one another or separated from one another' (Bohnsack 2009: 58–72, quoted in Mey & Dietrich 2016: 36).

The esthetics can also refer to the situation when photography is a part of a solemnization ritual that consecrates the family and other groups by picturing important moments of the life (Bourdieu 1990). The second dimension is the socio-psychological aspect, which concerns the level of subjective and interpersonal interpretations, if a researcher is interested in the motives of human actions, as well as their definitions of the situation. Participating in family rituals may elicit different motives for different members of the family. Rituals can be perceived as boring ceremonies or as social obligations or as opportunities, for example, to express love towards parents or grandparents. The third dimension refers to historical contextuality, where an individual is located within a historical process and where the researcher synthesizes idiographic and nomothetic elements of this process (Ferrarotti 1993: 88; see also Mey & Dietrich 2016: 18–19). In my opinion, the fourth dimension that should be included here is the cultural dimension, where certain idioms of representation of specific subjects are reflected, not always deliberately, in the photographs under study (cf. Goffman 1979; Ven Den Berg 2004). The fifth dimension is, I propose, a purely social one, where any interpretation of the photographed people, the attributes of their social positions, the social meanings of the photographed objects, or images relating to the interpretation of a group become the centre of not merely sociological (see Becker 1982) but any socio-anthropological analysis (Bourdieu 1990).

Temporality

If we reflect upon images, we should take into consideration their temporal dimension, such as the function of private photographs. These pictures constitute the extension of memory or the 'memory prosthesis'. They allow keeping in mind a certain point in time in a specific situation. Photographing creates a certain image – for the future – of something in the present time, which will soon become the past. Amateur photography of the 20th century was focused on the individual or family time, some historical continuations, predictions about the future, and duration – generally, on what Henri Bergson referred to as *durée* (Walker & Moulton 1989: 158). Temporality of social or cultural phenomena can be presented by picturing the phenomena and presenting it in a sequence that the researcher created. This kind of presentation is what Douglas Harper calls '*narrative mode*' (Harper 1988: 63–66). This point applies to a series of photographs and thus differs from what is gained from a single image.

Historical Context

Clear signs of a broader historical context can also be observed in the 21st century. War posters represent a testimony of the propaganda techniques and the intentions their initiators had in the past. Such posters vividly reflect the historical past. But at the same time, these posters reflect more universal mechanisms of propaganda and their impact on the targeted audiences due to the use of symbols, pictures, and short captions picturing the war in an expressive way. In short, such posters convey meanings and their socio-historical context. The poster images can be an active agent of the activities in everyday life that are embedded in the historical and temporal context of their presentation (Bird & Rubenstein 1998).

Interactions

Thus, what can GTM using photographs, images, or video recordings, or other visual and electronic forms of gathering data, offer as a research method? And, as a result, how does the application of such research techniques impact visual studies? In general, due to its strong ties with the symbolic interactionist tradition and social constructionism (see

Charmaz 2006), GT is well adapted to uncovering the understandings of how various individuals and groups interpret visual ideas within their socio-cultural locations and contexts and how they interact (Gold 1997: 3; Clarke 2005; Clarke & Keller 2014). Qualitatively-oriented GTM can use images as data for further theoretical interpretations. Visual research seems particularly suitable to investigate activities, interactions, and processes of communication and interpretation. Its application within the context of the so-called interpretive and symbolic interactionist traditions thus seems to be a logical consequence. If we assume that social worlds are constructed on the interactional level – as a result of defining situations and agreeing on these by those partaking in the world at hand – its context and directions, co-existence and embodiment seem easy to visualize.

Common definitions of a given situation, as well as motives for interaction can be read and interpreted through gestures, glances, how one locates oneself in a physical space, 'stage props', and objects present within the physical environment of the photographed (or video-recorded) people. A field researcher usually focuses his/her direct attention on people, groups, and situations. Thus, observation as a method, as well as images analyzed therein, seems necessary. The analysis of visual images gives way to interpreting both the context and details of any activity and interactions (Konecki 2008). In addition, immortalizing a given situation in a picture allows for the later (re)conceptualization of data. As three basic concepts of interpretative research, interpretation, interaction, and action can be read through visual representation, embracing both the context and meaning of these, e.g., as perpetuated in photography or video recording.

Yet another way of analyzing data can be used with visual data (e.g., news in TV) as an object of scrutiny (Figueroa 2008). One can analyze the context of producing/creating images that illustrate some phenomena or social reality. One can also pay attention to the social and power relations included in the context and content of visual images. Both of these styles can be combined in the so-called visual GT, where the context of image production is analyzed along with any phenomena visualized and represented in specific situations (see next paragraph).

TOWARDS VISUAL GROUNDED THEORY

GTM focuses on generating/constructing theories from empirical data through empirical research understood as a reiterative process – with a researcher cruising between field data deposits (e.g., libraries, online resources, researcher collection files) and his/her analytical work.[1] Having analyzed a batch of data, the researcher returns to the field for more data, traced with the insights provided by previous analyses. Data are coded, conceptual labels honed, and theoretical categories constructed. As the point of 'saturation' of categories is approached, data collection gives way to defining and conceptual refinement (Glaser & Strauss 1967; Glaser 1978; Strauss 1987; Strauss & Corbin 1990; Charmaz 2006; Bryant & Charmaz 2007). GTM is very popular among qualitative researchers. It allows the possibility to create theoretical statements during empirical investigation. Researchers become more courageous in formulating generalizations based on qualitative data. GTM also provides tools for researchers to subject qualitative data to rigorous analysis while giving them some freedom to direct their analyses.

Some GTM procedures have penetrated and become part of the general field of qualitative inquiry. Researchers today often do not recognize the origin of the procedures they use, e.g., theoretical saturation and/or theoretical sampling in ethnography. The popularity of GTM does not go hand in hand with the popularity of visual studies. GTM researchers rarely use visual data to generate generalizations. I hope to compensate for this lack by showing the benefit of connecting GTM with the analysis of visual data.

Examples of Visual Data Analysis and Grounded Theory[2]

I next describe examples of using grounded theory model of analysis with visual data. I depict how some procedures of GTM have been used and identify which have been not used (as constant comparative method) through analyzing visual data. In addition, some innovations in GTM employ visual images, e.g., the procedure of *locating images* and creating the *big picture* of them (Clarke 2005). Another innovation is projecting '*shooting scripts*' for theoretical sampling (Suchar 1997). Shooting scripts are lists of research topics or questions which can be examined and answered through collecting and analyzing photographic information within the framework of a photo-documentary project (Suchar 1997: 33). Generally, a tendency in GTM research using visual data accents the ethnographical part of the research but reveals less analytical work in creating theoretical frameworks of the investigated substantive areas. Researchers stress descriptions of situations and create codes and categories for the classification of these phenomena rather than concentrate on creating an integrated and dense synthesis of hypotheses.

Visual data have been quietly but consistently neglected as both potential primary and secondary sources for generating/constructing GT. Given the 'visual turn' in social communications at the end of the 20th century, it is difficult to explain why so little theoretical attention has been paid to visual data in GT studies. Maybe the reason is that social research has, in general, been based upon the analysis of textual data, mainly supported by statistical methods, and more recently, narrative methods (Riessman 2008; Lal, Suto & Ungar 2012). The interpretation of pictures and visual data has been difficult to elaborate quantitatively. Only the last two decades of strong growth of visual research in the social sciences has influenced launching visual analysis using GTM. But still, mere seeds of visual data analysis have consistently and rigorously used GTM procedures. We think about using the procedures of theoretical sampling, coding, and theoretical memo writing. These procedures provide the possibility of reaching generalized conclusions from empirical studies. Pictures become more than the tool for representations of the researched topic or proof of facts. Instead, pictures become the basis of codes and categories.

Whatever works to help a researcher in generating theory can acquire the status of 'data' (Glaser 2002). One can rely on interviews or observations, movies or newspapers, archival documents, popular fiction, and the Internet to generate categories and list their properties. Charmaz points out that researchers' activities and the context of their respective research projects influence their data. Thus, data are emergent phenomena and so are the researchers' theoretical knowledge and the perspectives they choose to adopt (Charmaz 2006; see interview with Charmaz in Puddephatt 2006; Bryant & Charmaz 2007).

Among those few examples of combining GT with visual data research that merit attention as notable exceptions, Suchar's (1997) study of grounding visual research in shooting scripts stands out. His research strategy follows the interrogatory principle: a researcher attempts to answer research questions by photographing particular objects

(Suchar 1997: 34) and analyzing these photographic data in order to find patterns and start conceptualizing. Granted, Suchar's approach seems to belong more to ethnography or qualitative data analysis (QDA) than to GT (cf. Glaser 2004). Suchar is concerned about 'worrisome accuracy' (if the descriptions of phenomena are adequate and trustworthy: Glaser 2002; see also critique of the concept by Bryant 2003):

> The process of interrogating images and examining field notes provides a means of intellectually interacting with documented observations. This is a creative and thought-provoking process. We can also 'check' our interpretations against other data, including our observed subject's interpretations, to reduce script-based bias. (Suchar 1997: 39)

Suchar's research seems to be closer to photographic fieldwork and an exercise in ethnography and qualitative data analysis (QDA) than to a GT approach because he is concerned about 'worrisome accuracy' (Glaser 2002). However, Suchar provides an interesting example of the use of conceptualized visual data. Grounded theorists can profit from following Suchar's approach in order to sensitize their concepts:

> I also argue that the grounding of conceptualization in specific visual referents qualitatively enhances the grounding process itself. I have found that reference to very detailed visual documents, and the information they contain, allows for a closer link between the abstractive process of conceptualizing and experientially derived observations. (Suchar 1997: 52)

Suchar finishes his analysis on the conceptualization stage. We do not see the theoretical framework emerging from his scrutiny. The analysis at hand is not immersed enough in comparing the objects and concepts to create the dense and coherent theory or theoretical statements. Suchar provides some qualitative data analysis and theoretical descriptions, but mainly to explain the ethnographic findings. Using the constant comparative method surely would increase the power of his conceptualization and provide the basis for the creating the hypothetical construction of the phenomena.

A more direct attempt to match visual data and GT inspirations has been made by Adele Clarke (2005), who announced her departure from the basics of GT and instead proposed concentration on situational analysis using visual materials. Clarke wishes to combine critical and empirical paradigms in visual research. She is interested in gender-related gazes, the process of othering, and the orientalization of gaze with imperial connotations. Her intention is to trace the gazes of power.[3] She recommends four steps before the analysis begins: deciding, locating, collecting, and tracking the materials best suited to the researched situation (Clarke 2005: 223). Next, she proposes to analyze the images and to write analytic memos about these. Clarke (2005: 229) distinguishes three kinds of memos, which can subsequently serve as narrative data to be coded:

- *locating* (who produces an image, for what audiences, from which social world),
- *the big picture* (first impressions, writing the narrative description of the image, dividing the picture into smaller parts to describe details),[4]
- *specification* (deconstruction of the image by observing it in different ways and getting outside the frame through which one is supposed to view the image). (Clarke 2005: 224–228)

Clarke suggests creating situational maps of visual materials: '*Your situational map should include all analytically pertinent human and non-human, material, and symbolic/discursive elements of a particular image*' (Clarke 2005: 229, italics in original). She suggests enriching the maps with elements not directly visible in actual photographs, but detected by the researcher in the studied situation. These may include different implicated actors, actants, and institutions.

Clarke presents a case study of research on visual discourse. She follows some procedures of GTM, such as theoretical sampling and comparative method. She is interested in the 'medical gaze' by historical reconstruction of anatomy atlases used in medical education. She uses external theoretical inspirations, so does not follow the principle of limited pre-conceptualization. She treats anatomy as a discipline in Foucault's sense, i.e., as the way of subjecting seeing and gazing to discipline. Positional maps of pictures in atlases show that the presentation of anatomy at the beginning of the 20th century emphasized reproduction (not sexuality) and that some parts of body presentation were deliberately left unclear. Clarke carries out theoretical sampling and looks for contemporary presentations of anatomy atlases (CD versions edited for educational purposes) to make comparisons. Her analysis demonstrates that these are more sex education-oriented and that sexuality is stressed in positional maps.

Visual discourse analysis of the anatomic presentation shows that genital size is a synonym for the physical superiority of men. A female may or may not have a clitoris, while a male always has a penis, and the penis is in the centre of narration. Heterosexuality is always assumed and the presentation is always connected with two sexes, erasing such sex variations as hermaphrodisms, intersexuality, transsexuality. 'Males are largely visualized as sexual, while females are reproductive' (Clarke 2005: 255).

Clarke used some procedures of GT (coding, theoretical sampling, theoretical memoing) in her visual discourse analysis. However, she also engaged in a situational analysis of visual materials and 'grounded theorizing,' as she calls it, stopping short of the construction of a GT. Nevertheless, she clearly demonstrates that the theory of a visual process of the 'construction of disciplined gazing' is feasible. It can be built, if one engages more in theoretical sampling and performs a more systematic comparative analysis, and ultimately obtains more data from fieldwork on constructing images. Clarke's technical suggestions and the style of her detailed analysis can be very useful and instructive for grounded theoreticians, although her analysis is not a classical GT, nor a constructivist one. She concentrates mainly on a situation, which is always complex and fuzzy, and she does *theorizing* about the situation rather than construct a theory.

Another case of a quite successful combination of visual studies with GTM can be found in Cornelius Schubert's (2006) GT approach to a 'videographic' field study in the hospital setting (see also Dietrich & Mey 2018: 7, 17, 20). I believe that Schubert has made a significant contribution to visual GT. He analyzed video recordings of anesthetic work during surgical operations using the GT approach and applied the procedure of theoretical sampling by 'selecting comparison groups'. His comparative entities were interactions in mixed teams (between humans and between humans and a medical apparatus) in numerous operation theatres. Schubert attempted to organize the data from the fieldwork by writing *content logs* of video recordings. Content logs are 'rough descriptions of the filmed situations and may contain references to analytical concepts' (Schubert 2006: 120). Theoretical saturation is achieved through sampling and identifying of ethnographic 'chunks' of described processes and through the content logs coding the data. Later on in his research, video-based interviews were carried out in order to describe the social, technical, and medical perspectives of medical doctors. All of these materials were 'slices' of data allowing the researcher to refine theoretical categories (Schubert 2006: 123; for audio-visual analysis with the use of GTM see also Konecki 2008).

The method of analyzing audio-visual texts by Silvana Figueroa (2008) represents another a very interesting contribution to the development of visual GT. The author, while analyzing the TV audio-visual materials, distinguished two levels of analysis.

- The analysis of social problems through the prism of the analysis of audio-visual data – audio-visual material as a medium (a lens) through which a phenomenon is viewed (*AVM – audio-visual material as a medium to analyze other social phenomena*). In this perspective, the investigator assumes that the phenomena reflect the entire reality.
- *Audio-visual data analysis as an object of the analysis, AVO* – audio-visual data are purposely constructed messages about certain phenomena and these should be analyzed as a valuable material in itself (Figueroa 2008: 3, 6). Figueroa (2008: 6) stresses that audio-visual data are not neutral but 'fictitious' since every narrative is a structure, and, given the latter, the way (the manner) in which reality is being represented or reinvented through purposely constructed images is of great importance. The author therefore emphasizes the *AVO* analysis type, i.e., the reconstruction of a manner in which certain phenomena are represented in audio-visual materials. Figueroa stresses that a picture of the whole message, e.g., a whole TV news programme, should be analyzed from the beginning, since the sequence of individual messages, as well as the structure of the programme at hand, may influence one's interpretation of individual messages regarding certain and separate phenomenon. Interpretations are often implied, not openly expressed, in a visual message. Individual messages can therefore be understood through the prism of embracing an overall picture, as with hidden messages, e.g., ones regarding political corruption in censored countries. So, in the analysis of audio-visual texts, one should (1) acknowledge the overall picture by watching the whole audio-visual material – to get the first impression of the programme at hand (and write impressionistic notes; Figueroa 2008: 8, 11); (2) reconstruct the main topic(s) in order to get the impression of the whole programme; here, one can make certain assumptions or initial hypotheses; and (3) move on to a detailed analysis of the data, searching for data maintaining or contradicting one's earlier assumptions and hypotheses.

The analysis at hand is thus the opposite of how it should proceed within the frames of the classical GTM, i.e., instead of moving from 'the particular to the general' (e.g., open coding and later axial coding), one goes here from 'the general to the particular'. One also uses all known procedures of GTM (theoretical sampling, theoretical saturation, constant comparison method, searching for the core category, and finally integrating categories into a theory).

Figueroa argues that the proposed method of research and analysis is similar to the concept of Herbert Blumer – her method exemplifying Blumer's exploration aimed at reaching a large image of the area of research, as well as further inspection as a detailed conceptual analysis of the phenomena under study. She also proposes to focus more on the review of scientific literature while analyzing the visual data than has been suggested by classic statements of GTM (Figueroa 2008: 9–10). Scientific and technical literature from a particular field (*AVO*, on the construction of materials presenting visual phenomena) should be compared with one's hypotheses. It is also important that such theory be capable of offering an explanation of the phenomenon under scrutiny, i.e., different ways in which an audio-visual presentation of social phenomena can be created (e.g., corruption or poverty).

An interesting project dealing with the use of visual images in GT research and analysis has been launched due to the efforts of Liebenberg, Didkowsky, and Ungar (2012), who internationally investigated the process of negotiating resilience among marginalized youth. The report is very well methodologically documented and we know how the data were collected and analyzed (open coding, focused coding, memo writing, and theory generation). The authors used participatory methods to give voice to local discourses. They also compared their data interpretation cross-nationally. The researchers used the constructivist GTM, according to Kathy Charmaz's concept. The participants, the youth, received disposable cameras and took photographs that were later used in auto-driven photo-elicitation interviews (Liebenberg et al. 2012: 62). The authors also video-recorded the youth they followed – during their trips to the city. A video compilation of how they were spending their day was shown to each participant of the study group for comments, and also used in the interviews. A voice was also given to the participants during the analysis of raw data (transcripts), i.e., in open coding. They were allowed to challenge the researchers' interpretations. The researchers were mindful and reflective about the knowledge they brought to the research situation (Liebenberg et al. 2012: 63), what seems to be very important in the constructivist GT.

The researchers analyzed photographs that were grouped and regrouped to construct the patterns. What was absent in the photographs was also important, and participants were able to comment on these (cf. Clarke 2005: 176, who also is interested in analyzing the elements absent from certain domains of the research situation). Narratives from photo-elicitation were contrasted with the video compilations. Participants' interpretations of the data were of utmost importance to the researchers. Multiple perspectives (of researchers and participants) were taken into consideration to generate theory and to better understand their social environment, the agency of the youth, and their power to shape the environment they live in, as well as to understand the research context. The collaborative GT kind of research and analysis seems to be a new approach that gives more opportunities for interventional use of GT theories (see also later the paragraph on photovoice and GTM).

The Basics of Visual Grounded Theory

In the article on which this chapter draws (Konecki 2011), I proposed the concept of visual grounded theory. This approach is a methodology of collecting and analyzing visual data to reconstruct visual processes and to create the conceptual framework of them based on the multislice imagining. Visual grounded theory is inspired by the above-mentioned concepts of GTM (e.g., Suchar 1997; Schubert 2006; Figueroa 2008), as well as Adele Clark's situational analysis and constructivist GT (Charmaz 2006) and my own visual studies. In Konecki (2011) I proposed using visual data as the main source of empirical evidence, collected in order to generate a visual GT.

What do we do when we visualize something about our life or work? First, we are always busy visualizing 'something'. We may visualize identity, homelessness (Konecki 2009), individualizing our body through impression management (Jacobs 2003), gentrification of an urban environment (Suchar 1997), also sports practice (Curry 2008), scientific achievements, a stylization of the body (make-up, piercing, body-building: Hicks 2005), persuasion (as in marketing, PR, or commercial advertising: Messaris 1997), 'construction of disciplined gazing' (as in 'scientific discourse on sex': Clarke 2005), a representation of a city (Pink 2008), physical and intellectual disability (Bates 2011), family integrity (Bourdieu 1990), etc. The latter is linked to the social practices of photographing, presenting the photographs, categorizing, and sorting them. The solemnization of family rituals is visualized, and we should study this kind of imagining of family life since it is a part of it (see Bourdieu 1990: 26, 29–30). Thus, a visualization process can be an object of a study (cf. Figueroa 2008), not only a medium through which a researched phenomenon is observed.

Data emerge from the scaffolding of one's theoretical questions, suppositions, and assumptions, and often from *implicit* everyday life assumptions (see Emmison & Smith 2000; Clarke 2005). We can see the objects in many slices. Observation, at face value, can be enriched by the slow and careful description of a picture and coding. What is important in analyzing visual data is this reconstruction of the multislice imagining of reality in visual representations and their contexts. Slices of data are different sources of data on the same phenomenon, after they have been conceptually elaborated:

> In theoretical sampling, no one kind of data on a category, nor technique for data collection, is necessarily appropriate. Different kinds of data give the analyst different views or vantage points from which to understand a category and to develop its properties; these different views we have called *slices of data*. (Glaser & Strauss, 1967: 65)

The approach that I take, multislice imagining, is different. I perform 'multislice imagining' assuming that visual data are multilayered. All layers should be analyzed in order to fully conceptualize visual processes. This assumption is a projection of my vision of multilayered reality and echoes the claim that reconstructing multilayered phenomena is the main goal of qualitatively generated theory. According to Glaser and Strauss, different kinds of data are layers delivering to any researcher different points of view. However, it is not enough to analyze the visualization processes. The processes are too complicated and not always verbalized. Understanding the visual process is possible only by the full description of the multilayered context of visualization. Multislice imagining is the methodological device for making this multilayered context accessible. It is based, of course, on the theoretical meta-perspective of symbolic interactionism and especially the theory of social worlds (Strauss 1978; Becker 1982; Clarke 2005). The visualization of something as it happens in social worlds, or social gatherings/interactions, or social institutions, or even in cities, or any social space (and place) involves:

a. An act of creating pictures and images (the analysis of context of creation). The inner context of the image ('how' it was created) is connected with the outer context of the image ('how' it will be perceived). The outer context includes stylistic conventions and clues to visual presentations (visual cultures and subcultures [Pink 2007: 31–33], local visual representations [Pink 2008]). The pictures are embedded in the social and cultural conventions of representing social objects (Bourdieu 1990; Banks 2007). Many of these conventions clash or compete among themselves in the same image or in an act of imagining. An act of creating an image (whether it is created by investigated subjects or by a researcher) needs to be observed and described by the researcher. Detecting motives and cooperation strategies can help explain why and how the actors build visual worlds (cf. Becker 1982). The analysis of the method, of how the picture creator, i.e., the photographer, worked, also plays an important role in the analysis at hand. How a certain situation is being experienced by the photographer can impact on his/her way of working: preferring one exposure over another, narrowing down the story to visualize his/her perception of the situation (Guzzo & Noordebos 2017: 181). The 'producer' of the images uses a certain strategy of taking pictures, including,for example, formation of topic, reflecting on the visual strategy that he/she is going to use, sharpening the series of pictures and doing a final selection (ibid.: 182). Preparation to making images is quite often very detailed and similar to scientific methods:

   > Bringing statistics, news, stories, observations, scholarly articles, images, reflections, experiments, works of other photographers and other works related to the theme is very important

step in grounding abstractions and subjective analysis in reality. The material is reviewed to list what is important and what and how the information can be used in the series. (ibid.: 184)

b. Participation in demonstrating/communicating visual images (presentation). This slice of imagining helps focus on the emergent structure of social communications as a process. If we cannot reconstruct these acts by ethnographic methods, we should reconstruct them in any available way (e.g., by historical methods, comparative analogy, deduction based on the empirical evidence, and testimony provided by experts, etc.). Photographs, as any other visual images, acquire their meaning in a specific context of their presentation (Becker 1995). A meaning of a photograph depends on where it is presented, e.g., in a museum or in a daily newspaper, how it is captioned, and what has thus far been written about it, as well as what other visual objects, besides the one being presented, are visible and what people think and feel about the visual image at hand (Becker 1995).[5]
c. The visual product communicated – its content and stylistic – aesthetic structure (perceived differently by different recipients, who are active co-creators of visual images). Once in the possession of the image, we should perform, at the beginning of the research, 'replicative transcription'. First, we should describe pictures that we want to analyze in detail. We need such transcription to extract from the picture every detail that could be salient in later analysis, including the formal structure of the picture (how its elements are related, central focus, and peripheral elements, etc.) Transcription (the verbal description of a picture) sensitizes us to details and helps us to search for structural aspects, also revealing a certain aesthetical domain which is dominant in a particular historical epoch (Konecki 2009: 75–76).[6] Later on, having chosen core and auxiliary categories for fuller elaboration of their properties and connections with other categories and properties (selective coding), we code visual images directly.
d. The reception of an 'image' and visual aspects of presenting/representing something ('slices' of the visual dimension of the psycho-social processes). This slice is also connected with the reconstruction of the aesthetic, social, and broad cultural conventions among the factual and potential recipients (audiences: Van Den Berg 2004), but it is also connected with individual experiencing of the whole image or of a specific part of the image. In photographers' work, viewers' awareness is important in making the final selection of the images. Moreover, their methods of working are connected with the image of the audience, as well as with the space wherein these are to be displayed: '***Choosing an opening image*** should seduce the viewer to enter the series. … In addition, the concept of exhibition and presentation of the material should help that concept and how and where people will come in contact with the series' (Guzzo & Noordenbos 2017: 187–188).

Coding outer context and how the image is being experienced (e.g., feelings) is essential to meet the requirements of GT, to generate a broader understanding of the visual image creation, presentation, content, and contextual reception in a given culture, subculture, or social world, but also an individual level of reception of the images in the research.

Procedures of Analysis

Specific examples of how multislice imagining can be applied are presented in Konecki (2011). I start by thinking abstractly about data and constructing basic categories conceptualizing them, which means that I begin with open coding. Open coding is a procedure of labelling parts of the transcribed text to move the analysts' mode of thinking from the concrete description to the conceptual level. We code four slices of data to better understand contexts and actions/interactions, displays of image/visual artifacts, and contents of visual artifacts (see Konecki 2011: 143–146).

After open coding and writing memos on the codes and coded images, a researcher decides which category should be theoretically elaborated (it could become one of the core categories in a future theoretical scheme). This is selective coding. There are many visualization processes that could be chosen. In one of my research projects, the process of visualization of hatha-yoga practice was chosen (Konecki 2016a: 141–174). The context of yoga visualization by photographs, movies, and drawings indicates that in order to explain the meaning of yoga, it is necessary to show its exact practice (poses; see Photo 4). Due to visualizing how the body moves during yoga practice, it is possible to bring memories of feelings to the surface, which could thus be verbally presented to others. The embodiment of practice is not verbal, but verbal accounts of the practice could be elicited by the visualization of yoga poses (e.g., by photos or video recordings in movie-elicited interviews: see Konecki 2016a; see Photos 1 and 4). So, first, the context of the presentation of pictures (visualization) is one of the layers of an understanding of meanings of yoga and interpretations of it; second, the context of reception is strictly connected with it (who and where, when and how one sees the presented images). Theoretical memos on the advanced and not advanced practitioners explain the process of visualization of yoga practice that is inherently included in teaching, practising, explaining, justifying, criticizing, and advertising of hatha-yoga. Within the Western cultural context, there is no yoga practice without visualizing it (Konecki 2011: 141–145).

Another procedure consists of comparing the pictures (constant comparative method). By comparing different images of contexts of practising yoga (training halls, parks, private spaces, retreats houses), we may see many social situations of practising yoga. What can be observed is practice in groups, interventions of teachers, observing other practitioners to compare oneself with them, participation in collective retreats, and, finally, we can

Photo 1. Yoga in the park. *Ashwa Sanchalanasana* pose. Importance of details in the body movement (photo by Kamil Głowacki)

Photo 2. Following the teacher in *Trikonasana* pose. Importance of interactions and instructions; practice in group; instructor in the center of the picture. 'Meditation for managers' class for Erasmus Students in University of Lodz (photo by Kamil Głowacki)

Photo 3. Making corrections. *Uttanasana* pose. Importance of direct physical contact in instruction; touching; practice in group setting; instructor in the center and he dominates the picture. 'Meditation for managers' class for Erasmus Students in University of Lodz (photo by Kamil Głowacki)

Photo 4. Visualization of asana for teaching students; importance of details; the use of arrows to explain importance of moves and position of body parts to each other; necessity of visualization. *Utthita parsvokonasana* pose. 'Meditation for managers' class for Erasmus Students in University of Lodz (photo by Kamil Głowacki)

propound one of many theses in our theoretical memos on visual images: Yoga is a collective practice, although it is generally considered by the instructors and yoga gurus as a very individual one (Konecki 2016a; see also Photo 2).

Another important procedure is theoretical sampling. Theoretical sampling answers to the researcher's questions generated by the analysis of empirical data. While writing theoretical memos, we become more aware of the direction of the research and analysis. The initial sampling is necessary to start the research, and the researcher should select criteria for choosing empirical data: places, structures, groups, physical artifacts, etc. However, it is not the sampling itself that has a theoretical character. The theoretical sampling emerges later during the analysis while coding and writing memos (Charmaz 2006), although we should remember that the theoretical sampling occurs all the time together with data collecting, coding, and theoretical memos writing.

Theoretical sampling is the precursor for saturating categories, when we elaborate conceptual properties of the category by looking for more contexts of the activities that could be conceptually covered by it. If we choose diverse contexts for visualization of yoga practice, we can see the phenomenon of hatha-yoga as a visual one, and the visualization work is done in business world, educational system, medical world, academia world, climbing world, pop-culture world, pornography, etc., and finally in hatha-yoga social world. Visualization work is done differently by professionals and amateurs. Its perception also depends on the degree of advancement in yoga practice of the perceiver. Experts of hatha-yoga evaluate what is correct in the presentation of practice and what is not. Thus, the visualization of hatha-yoga practice is a process that is distributed to many social worlds and is given evaluative descriptions, and there is no one correct visualization of yoga. Many ongoing disputes (arenas) regarding the correctness of practice and the meaning of hatha-yoga are based on images of it (see the movie and comments on it: 'B.K.S. Iyengar 1938 newsreel Part1 (SILENT)' on YouTube). Comparing visual data offers theoretical inspirations and allows for theoretical conclusions. However, we should remember (1) when the image was created, (2) in what historical and social contexts, (3) where and how it was presented, and (4) in which historical and social context it was received and interpreted (Konecki 2016a: 53–55, 59).

OTHER INSTRUMENTAL USAGES OF GMT

Some instrumental usages of GTM are applied for the sake of justifying the use of qualitative methods and/or data. These kinds of studies and data analyses do not produce theory; however, some strategies of GTM are somehow applied. Instrumental usage of GTM means that the methodology (some set of procedures of analyzing data) is used for doing qualitative research and classifications of the phenomena with the creation of descriptive codes but without building a theoretical set of propositions to explain or/and to interpret the course of the phenomena. I have encountered several examples of such research on visual images, wherein the term GTM has been introduced in methodological paragraphs of the papers, but generally the authors did not produce theory or a set of theoretical statements.

Hence, GTM can be used for other purposes (not only creating middle-range theories) and it has been adapted, e.g., for geographical research. This adaptation creates a hybrid of geographical visualization and GT. Knigge and Cope (2006) propose a 'grounded visualization' approach combining Geographic Information System (GIS) and GTM. Geographical visual images of demographic and physical changes in different locations are used to facilitate the interpretation of qualitative data in the iterative process. And, inversely, the qualitative data help to interpret quantitative data visualized in maps, and fill the gaps visualized by the former.[7] The grounded visualization is, according to the authors, exploratory, iterative, pays attention to the particular and the general at the same time, and represents multiple interpretations of the world (Knigge & Cope 2006).

GTM was also used to interpret the data from experimental research on the perception of manipulated and unmanipulated visual images (Caldwell, Gedeon, Jones & Copeland 2015). The researchers used eye tracker to follow the concentration spots (eye gaze fixation) and gaze duration while participants were watching images. Both the fixation and duration of eye gaze concentrated on the manipulated area of photographs are, in statistical terms, significantly associated with the accuracy of deciding whether the pictures at hand are manipulated. The GTM type of analyses and qualitative research helped to interpret the data – although the majority of investigated persons were uncertain about which images were manipulated, those who perceived manipulation referred to logical operations and they were informed by pre-existing knowledge and beliefs. Additionally, the context reference images were important in correctly interpreting the images (Caldwell et al. 2015: 308). So, GTM can also be used as a support tool for the interpretation of an experimental research project on visual perception.

Another study which refers to GTM and visual images is about using visual language in teaching English as a second language (ESL) (Petrie 2003). In this research, interviews as well as observations during these interviews (observational notes were taken) were applied. The analysis was done according to GTM, as described by Anselm Strauss (1987), but only of the textual data, based on teachers' opinions. Loosely connected categories of the visual language in the teaching process were reconstructed. Although the analysis did not result in the construction of a theory, it was a study of the use of visual images without analyzing the images themselves. So, there are two dimensions of the analysis: 'the use of visual images' (although it is based on interviews only, not on the observation method) and one group's (teachers, not children) reception of the image. No analysis of the context of creation is given, nor of the image content. Subsequently, the GTM analysis is limited regarding the scope of dimensions, as well as depth concerning the images. However, due to qualitative research and analysis, the phenomenon of changing opinion about using e-texts in teaching was discovered, and this change showed a more favourable opinion on teachers using e-texts. This change was a reflective response to the researcher's questions (Strauss 1987: 157).

All of these studies attempted to use GTM to analyze data. However, based on the reports included in these papers, one cannot reconstruct how the researchers employed the method. No analysis of literacy and visual culture in the educational system was included (see Banks 2001: 9) in the latter study, and of local visual cultures in the former studies. Nevertheless, we should take these efforts into consideration as possible ways of applying GTM to the analyses of data on using visual images in daily interactions and work in many fields. However, when undertaking research on visual processes, we should be more detailed and procedural in any analysis of visualization as a domain to study social reality. Visual processes can be analyzed by multislice imagining and use of other GTM procedures.

Photovoice Studies and Grounded Theory

Some worthwhile studies have been conducted by using photovoice combined with GTM. Photovoice is 'a process by which people can identify, represent and enhance their community through a specific photographic technique' (Wang & Burris 1997: 369). The photographs give insight into people's often marginalized lived experiences (Schell, Ferguson, Hamoline, Shea & Thomas-Maclean 2009). Photovoice is a research strategy that usually has a goal of impacting groups, systems, and policy. It can help to assess community needs and empower research participants, as well as inform policy-makers, for example, in matters of mental health issues in a community (Becker, Reiser, Lambert & Covello 2014: 190). People participating in the photovoice projects often belong to marginalized groups, such as those with intellectual disabilities (Akkerman, Janssen, Sabina & Meininger 2014: 544). In these projects, each participant receives a camera to record daily life, work, and problems related to his or her needs. By using photographs, the participants visualize their personal story. They also create and bring up the images to the analysts that inform community consciousness and programme changes. Researchers using the photovoice method sometimes apply grounded theory procedures to analyze the data.

Moreover, what is of importance here is that the approach of community-based participatory research (CBPR) stresses collaboration with the participants who are active actors in data collection, analysis, and interpretation. This approach stresses empowerment, shared decision-making, and supports the social change, as was the case in the research on individuals with mental health needs (Becker et al. 2014: 189). The participants could even become social activists or leaders of the mental health community who could inform and educate the community members through photography exhibitions and presentations of stories of the lives and needs of the marginalized participants (Becker et al. 2014: 203). The combination of grounded theory with CBPR and photovoice changes the established paradigm of grounded theory. The participants become legitimate collaborators of professional researchers as they can impact decisions regarding what kind of data will be gathered next (such as occurs in theoretical sampling) and the interpretation of data (coding and glossing on data). Becker et al. (2014: 204) state, 'Participants, in their role as coresearchers, help to identify the meanings and themes that are expressed within the photographs and stories'. These authors contend that photographs should be separated from narratives and analyzed first. The participants' stories are analyzed by using the constant comparative method. Experiences, perceptions, and feelings are being compared. First, open coding of gathered materials is done. Next, through comparing the resultant themes, the authors grouped them in broader themes and created categories. Finally, theoretical relations between categories are constructed and these are integrated into the summary of the researched phenomenon (Becker et al. 2014: 205). The themes derived from analyzing the photographs are also involved in focused and theoretical coding. The participants/co-researchers discuss the data and coding with the researchers, indicating the most important descriptors of their experiences, which are covered by the photographs and stories, so that all crucial themes are included.

The goal of the GTM analysis – to create a theory – is, in the above approaches, subsumed into presenting the voices of people in an ordered way to ascertain a full coverage of the most important topics. Thus, this GTM analysis only becomes an additional tool of ordering and controlling the integration of codes. The most important thing here is to enable the active participation and to give insight – without interference by the researchers – into how the situation is perceived, what gives a sense of pride and empowers the participants (e.g., persons with intellectual disabilities in their work environment [Akkerman et al. 2014: 551]). Generally, although they constitute a very important step in applying GTM in photovoice studies in collaborative research, such studies are explorative in nature and are not used for constructing grounded theory (see Akkerman et al. 2014: 552).

One of the most interesting and promising studies combining GTM and photovoice method has been conducted by López, Eng, Randall-David and Robinson (2005) on African American women – breast cancer survivors in rural North Carolina. The research goal was to develop the conceptual framework of survivorship of Quality of Life (QOL). The project was also aimed at reconstructing how the social context influences the perception of QOL and at developing the conceptual scheme that would inform potential interventions on this social context. The photovoice method was used to enable the survivors to visually reflect on their concerns and promote critical discussions and knowledge on the issues at hand, as well as to reach the policy-makers (López et al. 2005: 101).

Twelve women took part in the photo assignments and participated in three-hour photo discussion sessions. They discussed what was on the photographs, how it was related to their lives, why such issues existed, and how they could be empowered by a new understanding of the issues at hand. The next photo assignments were chosen during the sessions – to ensure that the participants influenced the theoretical sampling. After five sessions, the participants decided that no new information emerged to further illuminate properties of the categories. In this way, they also influenced the saturation of categories. So we have the iterative process of GTM associated with the analysis of data and data collection using the photovoice method (López et al. 2005: 105). The academic researchers constructed the analysis, coded the data, used the comparative methods across different transcripts, and grouped the codes into categories. The conceptual framework was created to unify all categories around the main concepts represented in the data.

> Although the women did not choose to be involved in reading and coding the transcripts, our process of reviewing preliminary findings at each of our photo discussion sessions provided survivors with the opportunity to discuss and clarify emerging concepts, themes, and conceptual linkages. Furthermore, we held a series of 'final' findings meetings, during which the women reviewed the final themes and conceptual framework. We conducted these meetings until the women felt the findings credibly depicted what they wanted others to understand about their survivorship experiences. (López et al. 2005: 104)

Theoretical results show a connection between social forces (stigmatizing beliefs about the cancer, racial discrimination, cultural beliefs about African American women) impacting upon personal strategies of surviving and achieving a certain quality of life (concerns of seeking for safe sources, role adjustment, feeling comfortable with the future, serving community as role models). From the concerns about creating personal strategies, two primary and general strategies emerge: relying on faith and spirituality (religion is important for the participants, and sometimes the religious leaders support their faith as the only way of dealing with the cancer) and maintaining social standing (fulfilling the roles of women and their obligations).

The created theoretical model of QOL shows the community and policy-makers what issues are important and/or difficult for the cancer survivors in their lives – so they can support them and offer an arena where the survivors can exchange information and get support (from religious leaders, families, male partners, and peers). Now, along with the development of photovoice method, grounded theory can be applied in practice, as propounded by its founders (Glaser & Strauss 1965: chapter 14).

CONCLUSIONS

Visual images can be valuable data for analysis in constructing a GT. These can be used as an additional kind of data to get more slices of data for further interpretation of the studied phenomenon and theoretical coding (Konecki 2011: 141; Mey & Dietrich 2016: 61). However, we can use the images to reconstruct visual processes and analyze the visual data as an object of our study (an example of this type of analysis is called *AVO*: Figueroa 2008; Dietrich & Mey 2018). If we assume that visual processes are the lenses through which one can see the socio-psychological phenomena, it seems necessary to understand how these lenses are constructed, and by what means and with what kind of motivations such a construction was made. Multislice imagining is a tool to deconstruct the images and later build a visual GT on socio-visual processes. It helps in understanding the context of creation, in addition to learning how the images were presented and received. We can thus embrace the whole picture of a situation and of a visual process embedded therein. The question is: Should we, as researchers, proceed with the investigation and analytical process by ourselves alone, not including the participants of our research/analysis, or should we include people whose activities we observe and analyze? What is interesting about these new developments of GTM that make use of visual data for analysis is including the subjects under scrutiny in the investigation process and data analysis (Liebenberg et al. 2012; Freedman et al., 2014). The photovice method used with GTM in collaborative research (López et al. 2005; Ackerman et al. 2014; Becker et al. 2014) and transformational GT, i.e., inductive and participatory GT, can offer some new pragmatic inspirations for data analysis: 'By discussing and adapting the developing grounded theory with coresearchers, who had experienced the phenomenon being studied, the final grounded theory had greater fit, grab, relevance, and modifiability than if the theory had been generated by the researcher alone' (Redman-MacLaren & Mills 2015: 5). In this kind of GT, the co-researchers decide who will be next for interviewing or being observed – they participate in theoretical sampling. This kind of methodology is focused on creating a decolonized context for social justice in relation to the situation being researched and also on creating a reformist context for marginalized groups and communities.

If we take the constructivist approach as a basic view of social 'reality', it is also very important to analyze the position of the researcher/analysts. The situation of the research, as well as the relations a researcher has with the research participants, should also be analyzed and taken into account (Knigge & Cope 2006; see also the concept of holistic ethnography by Davis & Breede 2015; Pink 2008). New analytical perspectives can enrich visual GT in this aspect, as, for example, the feminist approaches that facilitate an understanding of difference, context, and power relations (Clarke 2006; Knigge & Cope 2006) or reflexive approaches that help to understand how the researcher's mind and self construct the picture of the social world (Konecki 2016b). Visual GT inspired by the constructivist approach should take into account new epistemological considerations on the situation of the research in a broader socio-cultural context, as well as consider the position of the researcher in relation to his or her collaborators and intellectual biography.

FUNDING

This work was supported by the National Science Center in Poland [grant number 2018/29/B/HS6/00513].

Notes

1 Various proponents of GT disagree about whether it is an inductive (one can generate theory) or abductive methodology (abduction involves reformulating our previous knowledge and subsequently constructing theories). GT can therefore be treated as an abductive methodology because it includes rational reasoning on empirical data to formulate a theoretical argument, which continues to be tested experimentally. This idea combines the methodology of GT with abduction, and is presented in the later work of Anselm Strauss, in which he refers to Charles Peirce's abduction. Although it is only a reference to the inductive part of the abductive reasoning, i.e., Strauss indicates the great importance of *a priori* experience of the investigator in creating a theory (cf. Strauss, 1987: 12). When

a new and unique empirical observation cannot be explained on the basis of existing knowledge and categories or assumptions, the existing knowledge must be reformulated, resorted for an explanation of a new fact. Abduction is the process of innovation by modifying the emerging theory and recognizing new elements of present knowledge. Scientific discovery always requires the integration of previous knowledge with new experiences. Reconstruction of existing knowledge in new ways with the addition of new observations builds abductive inference. This new scheme should undergo modification and does not allow for artificially matching empirical data to existing concepts and theoretical schemes. From this point of view, we can call GTM abductive methodology (Kelle, 2005: 31; cf. Strübing, 2004, 2007; Bryant, 2009; Reichertz, 2009).

2 Some examples presented in the paper by Konecki (2011) have been used in this paragraph.

3 Gazing, with consideration of the aesthetics of power imbedded in it, could also be traced in many interactions and/or in parades, holidays, spectacular celebrations, and even in embodied gestures such as Roman salute in the Fascist period in Italy that has been a sign of loyalty, dynamism, and efficiency of the regime (Griswold, 2008: 175).

4 Notes on the whole image are extremely important to later grasp the details therein. The whole image often determines the meaning of smaller parts, and without taking into account the whole, it is difficult to understand a part of it (Figueroa, 2008: 7). GTM most often begins with open coding, which is the analytical concentration on detail and not on the whole text. The breakdown of text data to small pieces is often too early to get a deeper understanding of what is going on in the text and/or what is going on in the study area. The atomistic perspective of analysis often does not allow us to see the whole that determines the meaning of parts (Figueroa, 2008: 7). Dewey (1931: 98) explains the necessity of viewing part of the whole as follows: 'A work of art provides an apter illustration. In it, as we have already noted, the quality of the whole permeates, affects, and controls every detail. There are paintings, buildings, novels, arguments, in which an observer notes an inability of the author to sustain a unified attention throughout. The details fall to pieces; they are not distinctions of one subject-matter, because there is no qualitative unity underlying them.'

The main theme is essential in understanding single, seemingly scattered, elements. What we, as analysts, can do is to understand certain phenomena and mindfully 'decipher' the existence of *unifying qualitativeness*. For example, a meaning of a particular emotion can only be understood in the aftermath of revealing its 'unifying quality'. Anger exists in everyday life, and can be experienced and perceived in reference to the situation in which it occurs. However, sometimes the individual cannot perceive certain emotion as it appears. This brings us to another universe of discourse, where the accuracy of our reasoning depends upon direct perception of 'overall quality' of a previous situation (Dewey, 1931: 99).

5 Then, the same photograph can be seen in a museum as a work of art, in a newspaper as a journalistic photograph, and in a published album a photograph can be seen as a documentary photography. Images on Facebook can be private or presented to the general public, or to the registered friends only. Places of presentation are 'direct contexts', which means everything that concerns a dialogue on a situation, plus the direct interaction with physical environment in which such dialogue is conducted (Scheff, 1990: 199); in this case, we think about an internal or external dialogue which represents an interpretation of the visual images. The context of presentation determines the meaning of any individual image, and if it is poorly specified, the same observers, based on their experience, construct both the context and meaning of the visual image. Observers build a so-called 'extended context,' which is all that has thus far happened, could be happening, or may happen in the future. Thus, internal and subjective dimension of consciousness (also experiences) and external physical environment of the context of interaction are extremely important in working out a specific definition of the situation (Scheff, 1990: 199), as well as an interpretation of the visual image. In this case, it concerns meaning supposedly *inherent* in the visual image. However, the effect of the context of presentation is the interpretation of what we see and what the image socially represents.

6 We can go deeper into the analysis of the image. What is vital, I would say, is that this is very important part of the analysis of the image at this stage of VGT procedure. 'Images depicting a main character, for example, can be segmented easily by the compositional analysis following the documentary method

(planimetrics, scenic choreography, perspectivity)' (May & Dietrich, 2016: 49). There is a focus on the image itself with no reference to external knowledge. The extracted element of the picture should be analyzed as separate from the visual context. Next, various contexts are considered to fully interpret the image and contexts. 'By including ever more image elements into an interpretative context, the plausibility of the reading can be assessed' (ibid.: 38–39). We agree that the plausibility of the reading could be assessed; however, the plausibility of the interpretation of the whole image in the real social context could be lost. The interpretation deriving from created artificial horizons, with no reference to the receiver's experiences in specific social context, could be misleading and force some interpretation beyond the context at hand. Thus, the reference to the context of creation, especially the methodology of creating video images or photos (Guzzo & Noordenbos, 2017), esthetic conventions, and the reception of the image *in situ* seems to be a vital part of reading the image without pre-conceptualization coming from far-reached contexts. This far-reached context could be created by theoretical, methodological, epistemological, and ontological perspectives/assumptions of the researcher.

7 'Other techniques such as linking of maps with other forms or sources of data such as charts, graphs, or ethnographic data including digital photographs, text, or sounds can provide rich, contextual data for consideration in analysis. Additional features, including interactive legends, data-exploration tools, user-controlled animation, virtual environments, real-time 3D modeling, wearable computing devices, semi-immersible environments, and 3D flybys, greatly enhance the visual, iterative exploration of data, allow simultaneous attention to both the particular and the general, the concrete and the abstract, at multiple scales, and accommodate multiple interpretations of the world and diverse views of reality' (Knigge & Cope, 2006: 2027).

REFERENCES

Akkerman, A., Janssen, C. G. C., Sabina, K. P., & Meininger, H. P. (2014) Perspectives of Employees with Intellectual Disabilities on Themes Relevant to Their Job Satisfaction: An Explorative Study using Photovoice. *Journal of Applied Research in Intellectual Disabilities*, *27*, 542–554.

Banks, M. (2001) *Visual Methods in Social Research*. London: Sage.

Banks, M. (2007) *Using Visual Qualitative Data*. London: Sage.

Bates, Ch. (2011) *Vital Bodies: A Visual Sociology of Health and Illness in Everyday Life*. Doctoral thesis, Goldsmiths, University of London. Retrieved 10 October 2010 from http://research.gold.ac.uk/6373/1/SOC_thesis_Bates_2011.pdf

Becker, H. S. (1974) Photography and Sociology. *Studies in the Anthropology of Visual Communication*, *1*, 3–26.

Becker, H. S. (1982) *Art Worlds*. Berkeley, CA: University of California Press.

Becker, H. S. (1995) Visual Sociology, Documentary Photography, and Photojournalism: It's (Almost) All a Matter of Context. *Visual Studies*, *10*(1), 5–14.

Becker, H. S. (2002) Studying the New Media. *Qualitative Sociology*, *25*(3), 337–343.

Becker, K., Reiser, M., Lambert, S., & Covello, Ch. (2014) Photovoice: Conducting Community-Based Participatory Research and Advocacy in Mental Health. *Journal of Creativity in Mental Health*, *9*, 188–209.

Bird, William L., Jr. & Rubenstein, Harry R. (1998) *Design for Victory: World War II Posters on the American Home Front*. New York: Princeton Architectural Press.

Bohnsack, Ralf (2009) *Qualitative Bild- und Videointerpretation. Die dokumentarische Methode*. Opladen: Budrich.

Bourdieu, P. (1990) *Photography: A Middle-Brow Art*. Stanford, CA: Stanford University Press.

Bryant, A. (2003, January). A Constructive/ist Response to Glaser [25 paragraphs]. *Forum Qualitative Sozialforschung / Forum: Qualitative Social Research* [Online], *4*(1). Retrieved 10 October 2010 from www.qualitative-research.net/fqs-texte/1-03/1-03bryant-e.htm

Bryant, A. (2009) Grounded Theory and Pragmatism: The Curious Case of Anselm Strauss. *Forum Qualitative Sozialforschung / Forum: Qualitative Social Research*, *10*(3), Art. 2. Retrieved 10 October 2010 from http://nbn-resolving.de/urn:nbn:de:0114-fqs090325.

Bryant, A. & Charmaz, K. (2007) Grounded Theory in Historical Perspective: An Epistemological Account. In A. Bryant & K. Charmaz (Eds.), *The Sage Handbook of Grounded Theory*. London: Sage.

Caldwell, S., Gedeon, T., Jones, R., & Copeland, L. (2015) Imperfect Understandings: A Grounded Theory and Eye Gaze Investigation of Human Perceptions of Manipulated and Unmanipulated Digital Images. *Proceedings of the World Congress on Electrical Engineering and Computer Systems and Science (EECSS 2015)*, Barcelona, Spain, 13–14 July 2015, paper no. 308.

Charmaz, K. (2006) *Constructing Grounded Theory: A Practical Guide Through Qualitative Analysis*. London: Sage.

Clarke, A. (2005) *Situational Analysis: Grounded Theory after the Postmodern Turn*. Thousand Oaks, CA: Sage.

Clarke, A. (2006) Feminisms, Grounded Theory and Situational Analysis. In S. Hesse-Biber (Ed.), *Handbook of Feminist Research: Theory and Praxis* (pp. 345–370). Thousand Oaks, CA: Sage.

Clarke, A. & Keller, R. (2014) Engaging Complexities: Working against Simplification as an Agenda for Qualitative Research Today. Adele Clarke in Conversation with Reiner Keller. *Forum Qualitative Sozialforschung / Forum: Qualitative Social Research*, *15*(2), Art. 1. Retrieved 15 October 2015 from www.qualitative-research.net/index.php/fqs/article/view/2186/3667.

Curry, T. (2008) Where the Action Is: Visual Sociology and Sport. *Social Psychology Quarterly*, *71*(2), 107–108.

Davis, Ch. S. & Breede, D. C. (2015) Holistic Ethnography: Embodiment, Emotion, Contemplation, and Dialogue in Ethnographic Fieldwork. *The Journal of Contemplative Inquiry*, *2*(1). Retrieved 14 July 2016 from http://journal.contemplativeinquiry.org/index.php/joci/article/view/34

Dewey, J. (1931) Qualitative Thought. In J. Dewey (Ed.), *Philosophy and Civilization* (pp. 93–116). New York: Minton, Balch and Company.

Dietrich, Marc & Mey, Günter (2018). Grounding Visuals: Annotationen zur Analyse audiovisueller Daten mit der Grounded- Theory-Methodologie. In Christine Moritz & Michael Corsten (Eds.), *Handbuch Videoanalysen*. Wiesbaden: Springer VS.

Dowdall, G. W. & Golden, J. (1989) Photographs as Data: An Analysis of Images from a Mental Hospital. *Qualitative Sociology*, *12*(2), 183–213.

Emmison, M. & Smith, P. (2000) *Researching the Visual: Images, Objects, Contexts, and Interactions in Social and Cultural Inquiry*. London: Sage.

Ferrarotti, F. (1993) Culture and Photography: Reading Sociology Through a Lens. *International Journal of Politics, Culture, and Society*, *7*(1), 75–95.

Figueroa, S. K. (2008) The Grounded Theory and the Analysis of Audio-Visual Texts. *International Journal of Social Research Methodology*, *11*(3), 1–12.

Freedman D. A., R. O. Pitner, M. C.F. Powers, T. P. Anderson (2014) Using Photovoice to Develop a Grounded Theory of Socio-Environmental Attributes Influencing the Health of Community Environments, *The British Journal of Social Work*, *Volume 44*(5), 1301–1321, https://doi.org/10.1093/bjsw/bcs173

Glaser, B. G. (1978) *Theoretical Sensitivity*. Mill Valley, CA: Sociology Press.

Glaser, B. G. (2002) Constructivist Grounded Theory? *Forum Qualitative Sozialforschung / Forum: Qualitative Social Research*, *3*(3), Art. 12. Retrieved 30 November 2007 from www.qualitative-research.net/index.php/fqs/article/view/825/1793.

Glaser, B. G. (2004) Naturalist Inquiry and Grounded Theory. *Forum Qualitative Sozialforschung / Forum: Qualitative Social Research*, *5*(1), Art. 7. Retrieved 27 May 2011 from http://nbn-resolving.de/urn:nbn:de:0114-fqs040170.

Glaser, B. G. & Strauss A. L. (1965) *Awareness of Dying.* Chicago, IL: Aldine.

Glaser, B. G. & Strauss, A. L. (1967) *Discovery of Grounded Theory: Strategies for Qualitative Research*. Chicago, IL: Aldine.

Goffman, E. (1979) *Gender Advertisements*. New York: Harper Colophon.

Gold, S. (1997) Introduction. *Qualitative Sociology*, *20*(1), 3–6.

Griswold, W. (2008) *Cultures and Societies in a Changing World*. Thousand Oaks, CA: Sage.

Guzzo, M. S. L. & Noordenbos, C. (2017) Considering Apparitions: Towards a Conceptual Documentary Photography Methodology. *Trama Interdisciplinar*, São Paulo, *8*(1), 176–194.

Harper, D. (1988) Visual Sociology: Expanding Sociological Vision. *The American Sociologist*, *19*(1), 54–70.

Harper, D. (1994) On the Authority of the Image: Visual Methods at the Crossroads. In N. Denzin & Y. S. Lincoln (Eds.), *Handbook of Qualitative Research* (pp. 403–412). Thousand Oaks, CA: Sage.

Henley P. (2013) From Documentation to Representation: Recovering the Films of Margaret Mead and Gregory Bateson, *Visual Anthropology*, *26*(2), 75-108, DOI: 10.1080/08949468.2013.751857

Hicks, L. (2005) Explorations of Visual Culture: Written on the Body. *Culture Work. A Periodic Broadside for Arts and Culture Workers*, *9*(3). Retrieved 10 October 2010 from http://pages.uoregon.edu/culturwk/march05hicks.html#author

Holliday, R. (2000) We've Been Framed: Visualizing Methodology. *The Sociological Review*, *48*(4), 503–521.

Jacknis, I. (1988) Margaret Mead and Gregory Bateson in Bali: Their Use of Photography and Film. *Cultural Anthropology*, *3*(2), 160–177.

Jacobs, M. B. (2003) Obsessed with Impression Management: A Critical Sociology of Body Image in Capitalist Society. *Human Architecture: Journal of the Sociology of Self-Knowledge*, *2*(2), 66–73.

Kelle, U. (2005) 'Emergence' vs. 'Forcing' of Empirical Data? A Crucial Problem of 'Grounded Theory' Reconsidered. *Forum Qualitative Sozialforschung / Forum: Qualitative Social Research*, *6*(2), Art. 27. Retrieved 26 January 2008 from www.qualitative-research.net/fqs-texte/2-05/05-2-27-e.htm.

Knigge, L. & Cope, M. (2006) Grounded Visualization: Integrating the Analysis of Qualitative and Quantitative Data Through Grounded Theory and Visualization. *Environment and Planning A*, *38*, 2021–2037.

Konecki, K. T. (2008) Touching and Gesture Exchange as an Element of Emotional Bond Construction: Application of Visual Sociology in the Research on Interaction between Humans and Animals [93 paragraphs]. *Forum Qualitative*

Sozialforschung / Forum: Qualitative Social Research, *9*(3), Art. 33. Retrieved 1 September 2017 from http://nbn-resolving.de/urn:nbn:de:0114-fqs0803337

Konecki, K. T. (2009) Teaching Visual Grounded Theory. *Qualitative Sociology Review*, *5*(3), Retrieved 1 December 2009 from www.qualitativesociologyreview.org/ENG/Volume14/QSR_5_3_Konecki.pdf.

Konecki, K. T. (2011) Visual Grounded Theory: A Methodological Outline and Examples from Empirical Work. *Revija za sociologiju*, *41*(2), 131–160.

Konecki, K. T. (2016a) *Is the Body the Temple of the Soul? Modern Yoga Practice as a Psychosocial Phenomenon*. Cracow: Jagiellonian University Press.

Konecki, K. T. (2016b) Meditation as Epistemology: How Can Social Scientists Profit from Meditation? In Valerie M. Bentz & Vincenzo M. B. Giorgino (Eds.), *Contemplative Social Research: Caring for Self, Being, and Lifeworld*. Santa Barbara, CA: Fielding University Press.

Lal, S., Suto, M., & Ungar, M. (2012) Examining the Potential of Combining the Methods of Grounded Theory and Narrative Inquiry: A Comparative Analysis. e Qualitative Report, *17*(21), 1–22. Retrieved 30 December 2015 from http://nsuworks.nova.edu/tqr/vol17/iss21/1

Liebenberg, L., Didkowsky, N., & Ungar M. (2012) Analysing Image-Based Data Using Grounded Theory: The Negotiating Resilience Project. *Visual Studies*, *27*(1), 59–74.

López, E. D. S., Eng, E., Randall-David, E., & Robinson, N. (2005). Quality-of-Life Concerns of African American Breast Cancer Survivors within Rural North Carolina: Blending the Techniques of Photovoice and Grounded Theory. *Qualitative Health Research*, *15*(1), 99–115.

Magala, S. (2000) *Szkoła widzenia, czyli świat w subiektywie aparatu fotograficznego* (*School of Seeing, or the World in the Subject of the Camera*). (In Polish). Wroclaw: Biblioteka Format-u.

Mey, Günter & Dietrich, Marc (2016) From Text to Image: Shaping a Visual Grounded Theory Methodology. *Forum Qualitative Sozialforschung / Forum: Qualitative Social Research*, *17*(2), Art. 2. Retrieved 14 July 2016 from http://dx.doi.org/10.17169/fqs-17.2.2535.

Messaris, P. (1997) *Visual Persuasion: The role of Images in Advertising*. London: Sage.

Petrie, G. M. (2003) ESL Teachers' Views on Visual Language: A Grounded Theory. *The Reading Matrix*, *3*(3), 137–168.

Pink, S. (2007) *Doing Visual Ethnography*. London: Sage.

Pink, S. (2008) Mobilising Visual Ethnography: Making Routes, Making Place, and Making Images. *Forum Qualitative Sozialforschung / Forum: Qualitative Social Research*, *9*(3), Art. 36. Retrieved 14 July 2016 from http://nbn-resolving.de/urn:nbn:de:0114-fqs0803362.

Puddephatt, A. J. (2006) An Interview with Kathy Charmaz: On Constructing Grounded Theory. *Qualitative Sociology Review*, *2*(3), 5–20. Retrieved 20 December 2009 from www.qualitativesociologyreview.org/ENG/archive_eng.php.

Redman-MacLaren, M. & Mills, J. (2015) Transformational Grounded Theory: Theory, Voice, and Action. *International Journal of Qualitative Methods*, *14*(3), 1–12.

Reichertz, J. (2009) Abduction: The Logic of Discovery of Grounded Theory. *Forum Qualitative Sozialforschung / Forum: Qualitative Social Research*, *11*(1), Art. 13. Retrieved 25 May 2011 from http://nbn-resolving.de/urn:nbn:de:0114-fqs1001135.

Riessman, C. K. (2008) *Narrative Methods for the Human Sciences.* London: Sage.

Scheff, T. (1990) *Microsociology. Discourse, Emotion, and Social Structure*. Chicago, IL: University of Chicago Press.

Schell, K., Ferguson, A., Hamoline, R., Shea, J., & Thomas-Maclean, R. (2009) Photovoice as a Teaching Tool: Learning by Doing with Visual Methods. *International Journal of Teaching and Learning in Higher Education*, *21*(3), 340–352. Retrieved 28 October 2012 from www.isetl.org/ijtlhe/.

Schubert, C. (2006) Video Analysis of Practice and Practice of Video Analysis: Selecting Field and Focus in Videography. In H. Knoblauch, B. Schnettler, J. Raab, & H. Soeffner (Eds.), *Video-Analysis: Methodology and Methods. Qualitative Audiovisual Data Analysis in Sociology* (pp. 115–126). Frankfurt am Main: Peter Lang.

Strauss, A. L. (1978) A Social World Perspective. In N. Denzin (Ed.), *Studies in Symbolic Interaction* (pp. 119–128). Greenwich, CT: JAI Press.

Strauss, A. L. (1987) *Qualitative Analysis for Social Scientists*. Cambridge: Cambridge University Press.

Strauss, A. L. & Corbin, J. (1990) *Basics of Qualitative Research*. London: Sage.

Strübing, J. (2004) *Grounded Theory: Zur sozialtheoretischen und epistemologischen Fundierung des Verfahrens der empirisch begründeten Theoriebildung*. Wiesbaden: VS Verlag für Sozialwissenschaften,

Strübing, J. (2007) *Anselm Strauss*. Konstanz: Uvk Verlags GmbH.

Suchar, Ch. S. (1997) Grounding Visual Sociology Research in Shooting Scripts. *Qualitative Sociology*, *20*(1), 33–55.

Van Den Berg, Dirk J. (2004) What is an Image and What is Image Power? *Image [and] Narrative: Online Magazine of the Visual Narrative*, *8*. Retrieved 26 January 2015 from www.imageandnarrative.be/inarchive/issue08/dirkvandenbergh.htm.

Walker, A. L. & Moulton, K. R. (1989) Photo Albums: Images of Time and Reflections of Self. *Qualitative Sociology*, *12*(2), 155–218.

Wang, C. C. & Burris, M. (1997) Photovoice: Concept, Methodology, and use for Participatory needs Assessment. *Health Education & Behavior*, *24(3)*, 369–387.

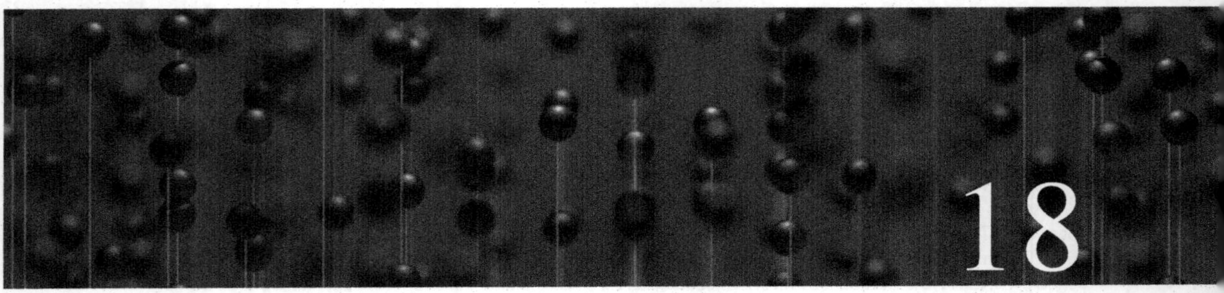

Grounded Theory Methods in the Context of Masculinity and Violence

Katherine Irwin

When Charmaz (2006) published *Constructing Grounded Theory: A Practical Guide through Qualitative Analysis*, I breathed a sigh of relief. As an ethnographer with approximately 20 years of qualitative data gathering and analysis experience,[1] I have a deep respect for the history of grounded theory (GT) and grounded theory methods (GTMs). However, I never developed a particularly orthodox approach to either. I picked and chose what I liked from GTMs, especially from Glaser and Strauss's (1967) original statement, but my culling of techniques did not seem in step with pure GTM. For many years, I felt like a GTM imposter.

I covered my imposter status well. When it was time to give a written account of my data analysis approaches, I became fairly cagey, arguing that I 'borrowed from' Glaser and Strauss's (1967) classic work. If pressed to explain more, I argued that I coded my data and used Glaser and Strauss's (1967) constant comparative approach, writing that my system of 'mixing analysis and data collection closely resembled the constant comparative and theoretical sampling procedures articulated by Glaser and Strauss (1967)' (Irwin 2001, p. 54). I was lucky in my early publishing days. Editors and peer reviewers rarely asked for more analysis details, and my articles were eventually published, allowing me to continue masquerading as a researcher who used some GTM techniques.

Thanks to Charmaz's (2006) constructivist approach, my GTM pretender persona fell away. Poring over her statements, I realized that others were probably grappling with the same constraints within the various GTM statements (Glaser 1978, 1992; Glaser and Strauss 1967; Strauss and Corbin 1990, 1998) that troubled me. For example, I never particularly favored the effort to discover a unitary, basic social process encompassing all individuals' experiences in a setting, nor did I enjoy attempting to use the conditional matrix (Strauss and Corbin 1990, 1998).

Charmaz's (2006, p. xi) 'flexible approach' invited skeptical researchers like me to 'enter the methodological fray' and 'messy' debates about methods. She (Charmaz 2006, p. xi) also allowed us to view GTM as more than a precise 'recipe' or set of 'rigid methodological procedures' (Charmaz 2014, p. 239) to follow, but rather as a collection of guidelines about which multiple 'interpretation[s] and reconstruction[s]' exist. Methodological journeys are what Charmaz (2006) encouraged researchers to take as they traveled from engagement with data to conceptual and theoretical analysis, and back to engagement with the data. The creative back and forth movement between and among data, concepts, and theories is what I had always done, and now, it had a legitimate source and a name: constructivist GTM (Charmaz 2006, 2014).

Playing on Charmaz's (2006, 2014) imagery of GTM as a journey, I use this chapter to outline my passage through building a GT of masculinity and violence. On the surface, this is a story about the self-transformation of a researcher who went from being a GTM imposter to an enthusiast of a hybrid GTM, which combined critical methodologies (Fine 1994; Fine and Weis 2005; Foley and Valenzuela 2005; Smith 2012; Tengan 2008), feminist GTM (Keddy, Sims, and Stern 1996; Kushner and Morrow 2003; Rickards and Wuest 2006; Wuest 1995), and constructivist GTM (Charmaz 2006, 2014). Something deeper and more scholarly rests beneath this personal account. Underneath my evolution from a GTM borrower to an advocate of a hybrid GTM is a tale about how theoretical and epistemological shifts in the late 20th and early 21st centuries have enabled particular GTM innovations. Because my epistemological adventure follows feminist advances, especially feminist standpoint and multiracial feminist perspectives, this chapter is about how constructivist and critical paradigms (Guba and Lincoln 2004) can co-mingle and create a GTM that crosses epistemological boundaries sometimes thought to be fairly impassable.

DISCOVERING A GROUNDED THEORY OF MASCULINITY AND VIOLENCE

My discovery of a GT explanation of masculinity and violence included numerous transformations, oscillations, and moves. One salient shift was when I went from being a graduate student to an assistant professor, which simultaneously uprooted me from the University of Colorado at Boulder and planted me in Honolulu, Hawai'i and my new position at the University of Hawai'i, Manoa (UHM). While in Colorado, I was trained by symbolic interactionists (Adler and Adler 1987) who also encouraged me to be fluent in the social psychology field. I happily studied Blumer's (1969, p. 2) methodological understandings, and I especially embraced the premise that 'human beings act toward things on the basis of the meanings that the things have for them.' The methodological trick during data collection, which I learned at that time, seemed to be rather simple – ask people to explain what things (e.g., physical objects, other humans, social categories, institutions, activities, and other everyday life encounters) mean to them and give them the opportunity to describe their lives using their own terms and definitions.

To the degree that I was concerned in graduate school about social justice and social change, symbolic interactionism and the history of the first and second Chicago School of Sociology (Fine 1995) provided a viable strategy. Becker's (1967) article 'Whose Side are We On?' was especially instructive and became the logical bridge between my social justice consciousness and social constructionism. Like Snow and Morrill (1993), I also believed that social justice goals were best met when sociologists rigorously adhered to principles of high-quality data gathering and analysis (see also Corte and Irwin 2017).

My relocation to Honolulu, Hawai'i was displacing in many ways. Hawai'i was described by some early Chicago School sociologists as an assimilation success story. For example, Lind (1938, p. vi) wrote, 'Island conditions have thus far prevented the establishment of a racial caste system,' and Robert Park (1938, p. xiv), Lind's dissertation chair, saw the Hawaiian Islands as 'the most notable instance of a melting-pot of the modern world.' Thirty years later, Lind (1969, p. 100) saw racial tensions in Hawai'i emerging – which is unsurprising given the racial upheavals and civil rights activism throughout the US at the time – and he argued, 'One might say that in Hawaii, as well as other areas of racial contacts, prejudice is part of the price that must be paid for desired change,' with modernization and statehood as the desired changes in Lind's (1969) view.[2] Importantly, Lind (1969) noted that such racial tensions might subside because of the high rates of interracial marriage in Hawai'i.

Where Chicago School sociologists saw a cosmopolitan melting-pot and interracial merging in Hawai'i, I discovered a different reality. During my first days in Honolulu, I began to see dozens (if not hundreds) of everyday examples of racism, economic exploitation, and American imperialism at work. One memorable illustration of tensions was the way by which university staff tended to explain language use in Hawai'i. Below, I outline an example of the stigmatization of indigenous languages in Hawai'i.

Seeing Agency and Structure in Hawai'i: Questioning the Chicago School of Sociology

When I first came to UHM in 2001, I was told by many university staff that Hawaiian Creole English – often referred to as Pidgin and is a unique language that mixes sentence structures from Hawaiian with words from Hawaiian, Standard American English, Portuguese, and other languages spoken by plantation workers – is spoken by the poor and working classes in Hawai'i. Another professor told me that public high school teachers were encouraging their students to be illiterate by speaking Pidgin in the classroom.

Although the use of languages is not the topic of my research, the everyday politics of languages in K-12[3] schools is exemplary of the many conflicts, inequalities, and competitions to define situations in Hawai'i that I witnessed. Specifically, I saw three processes underscoring public school teachers' Pidgin speaking, and these are (1) facilitating students' language skills, (2) providing a bridge to Hawaiian fluency, and (3) resisting American colonialism.

Regarding facilitating language skills, speaking Hawaiian Creole English was the way by which teachers encouraged students to be multilingual. Students who spoke Standard American English and Hawaiian Creole English were bilingual, and teachers assumed this ability would help students pick up a third language, such as Japanese, Spanish, or French, in high school. In terms of bridging language systems, some high school staff avoided taking overt political stances, such as openly discussing Native Hawaiian sovereignty.[4] If Standard American English was the official language of the state of Hawai'i, and Hawaiian was the indigenous language suppressed by American colonizers, then Hawaiian Creole English, some educators explained, was a link allowing high school students access to the indigenous language of the land. Remember that Hawaiian Creole English contains some Hawaiian words and sentence structures. A benefit of bridging languages was that students could be prepared to learn Hawaiian at a later date in Hawaiian language immersion high schools or at UHM.

In terms of resisting colonial control, a few teachers explained that as a part of the history of colonial occupation in Hawai'i, teachers were prohibited from speaking Hawaiian in schools and were, instead, instructed to teach students Standard American English. In the early 2000s, few public school students whom I met could speak or understand Hawaiian, but a number of students in areas where I conducted research spoke Pidgin fluently. Therefore, speaking an unofficial language in school was sometimes framed as resisting a history of American prohibitions against indigenous languages in Hawai'i.

The processes underlying university staff's constructions of Hawaiian Creole English speaking revealed the connections between structural constraints (i.e., the historic systems of domination associated with colonial occupation in Hawai'i) and individuals' collective negotiations and agency that I saw. Assimilation in Hawai'i, I came to believe, was an early Chicago School of Sociology misunderstanding of what was occurring in Hawai'i. Within the first few years of living and working in Honolulu, I learned to bracket many previous assumptions and keep an open mind (Dey 1993) to understanding the multiple conflicts, contestations, negotiated orders, and acts of resistance that individuals in Hawai'i were experiencing and openly discussing. These insights into language speaking in Hawai'i as a process imbued with structural constraints and human agency also provide the background to understand how I used GTM to theorize masculinity and violence.

Developing a Grounded Theory of Masculinity and Violence

As noted, upon moving to Hawai'i, I found myself let down by pragmatist-inspired writings regarding ethnic assimilation in Hawai'i. A new path needed to be taken for me to make sense of and develop theories from what I was seeing on the ground. This sense making and theorizing would spotlight youth violence and the everyday construction of gender identities, the focus of my research program.

During my first year at UHM, I was recruited to work with community members and other UHM researchers on a collection of youth violence prevention initiatives, many of which were based in public schools. In 2005, the violence prevention grant initiatives expanded, and I became a participating investigator in one large study funded by the Department of Health and Human Services. My responsibility in this study was to conduct focus groups in two high schools (one urban and one rural) in Oahu, and I designed these groups to allow students and parents, first, to describe what they thought were the most pressing concerns within their self-defined geographic and ethnic communities. Second, because the goal of the entire grant was to develop violence prevention programs, I thought that researchers and stakeholders should allow students and parents the chance to define youth violence for themselves.[5]

My time completing focus groups and developing violence prevention programs in high schools was parlayed into an ethnographic study of youth violence in 2007, when a group of high school counselors invited me and my colleague, Karen Umemoto, to develop, participate in, and observe weekly group counseling meetings for high school teens, which were called the 'lunch bunch.' If one uses the common parlance of youth development researchers, the students in the lunch bunch program could be viewed as 'at risk' for violence, dropping out of school, and other problem behaviors. Using less stigmatizing terms than the expression 'at risk students,' many considered these teens as individuals who needed extra support in school for a number of reasons. Importantly, while the lunch bunch was not explicitly labeled as a counseling group for violent students, many of the lunch bunch teens acted violently in school and/or had experienced violence in their families and communities. One group was for boys, and another was for girls, although the groups sometimes combined for special events (e.g., end-of-the-year celebrations, field trips, camping trips). Leading up to my work on masculinity and violence, I tried to spend equal time with the boys' and the girls' groups.

From 2007 to 2017, I conducted an ethnographic study with high school teens by intensively interviewing teens and school staff, observing teens by sitting in on weekly lunch bunch sessions, and participating in a number of field trips, camping excursions, assemblies, and other events with the teens, teachers, and counselors.

Students', school staff members', parents', and community organizers' definitions and meanings, worldviews, and experiences with youth violence (not to mention other violent expressions) provided me with extensive data (interviews, focus groups, and observations of 80 teens and 52 adults) to start my theorizing on violence and masculinity, and, in fact, I started to see processes related to masculinity and violence in the early days of the ethnography. I sat down to formalize my analysis in 2010 and published my theoretical understandings in co-authored journal articles and chapters (Irwin and Adler 2012; Irwin and King forthcoming; Irwin and Umemoto 2012), as well as in a book (Irwin and Umemoto 2016).

Because of my disagreement with Chicago School of Sociology-trained researchers' (Lind 1938, 1969; Park 1938) depictions of Hawai'i, I was in search of a GTM that would allow me to add nuanced understandings of the histories of structural inequalities in Hawai'i, including historic systems of racialization under colonialism, to equally nuanced conceptions of how individuals defined situations and acted toward things according to the meanings that these things had for them. Advances in feminist GTM (Keddy, Sims, and Stern 1996; Kushner and Morrow 2003; Rickards and Wuest 2006; Wuest 1995) were especially helpful (see also Hesse-Biber's chapter in this volume), although my colleagues and I also drew from other critical methodologies (Fine 1994; Fine and Weis 2005; Foley and Valenzuela 2005; Smith 2012; Tengan 2008).

Regardless of whether we progressed with a critical, feminist, or a more traditional GTM, the analytical steps we took were somewhat generic to GTM. We used initial coding, focused coding, and memo writing, as well as made constant comparisons that allowed us to interact with the data while also asking 'what is going on?' in each piece of data and for each individual in the study (Charmaz and Mitchell 2010, p. 163).

During the initial coding phase, the boys in the study clearly described many challenges to their masculine identities. I offered codes, such as 'being a man,' 'proving masculinity,' and 'distancing from femininity.' Some initial codes did not seem to relate to masculine identity construction explicitly. I offered other codes, such as 'establishing a reputation,' 'confronting disrespect,' 'reflecting on injustice,' 'righting wrongs,' and 'evaluating stereotypes.'

While generating the initial codes, I began to write analytic memos, first, to tease out what concepts, such as 'being a man,' 'proving masculinity,' and 'distancing from femininity,' meant in the context of the study and to identify variations within the data tagged with these codes. The second analytic task during my early memo writing was to compare the initial codes developed from the boys' data with those developed from the girls' data. This comparison added considerable depth to my analysis. For example, the girls were articulate about boys' masculine efforts to prove themselves, and they often discussed the boys' everyday strategies to 'win' battles and place themselves on top of male status hierarchies at school; the girls usually explained the boys' status maneuvers as these boys' attempts to prove their physical prowess. I sensed that the girls framed the boys' efforts mostly through a lens of competition that put the most physically dominating boys at the top of peer hierarchies.

When comparing the boys' accounts with my initial set of codes and with the girls' insights, I discovered some important nuances underscoring the boys' claims about what 'proving masculinity,' 'establishing a reputation,' and 'confronting disrespect' meant. The boys seemed to be evoking and responding to a sense of racial and ethnic identities along with their efforts to construct masculine toughness. For example, here are two sections of text that I initially coded as confronting disrespect.[6]

> Koa: Disrespect leads to fights. People don't back down; they usually try to make others 'awk' (act like a chicken) and back down. What really causes problems is that people come, and they boss you around—'do this, do that'—and guys take it personally. Then, they have one problem. All the freshmen, the youngest punks, they try to fight everybody. Freshmen always try to make a name for themselves. Sooner or later, the upperclassmen will take care of them. That's what I did my freshman year that got me into all kinds of troubles. I tried to make a name for myself and show people that I can scrap (fight) and that I'm not scared.

> Chad: There's a fight every day. Maybe it will go a month where there is not a fight, but then there will be a huge one. Last month, there was one whole week there was straight fighting every day. In intermediate [school], I remember it used to be the base [military] kids and the locals [individuals born and raised in Hawai'i]. 'Cause they started calling all the locals pineapple pickers. There was a riot basically—all of the locals on one side of the school and all the base kids on the other side. Every single day after school, there will be four cops outside of the school. I guess the base kids think they are better than us.

Complicated status hierarchies among teens emerged in each of these narratives labeled as confronting disrespect, and being considered 'fearful' seemed to be tied to disrespect for some boys. Koa, for example, mentioned not wanting to be a 'chicken' by 'backing down' from a fight, suggesting that avoiding fights can lead to spoiled identities in the form of appearing afraid. Interestingly, in his next sentence, Koa argued that being bossed around and told to 'do this, do that' was also problematic. In this scheme, those on top of status hierarchies appeared to be leaders who could dominate others. Correspondingly, being dominated and bossed around was a sign of disrespect. In the remainder of the quote, Koa pointed to the idea that cycles of fights could unfold when younger students wanted to make names for themselves, often by standing up to anyone who was older and had a leadership or dominant status in school in terms of age and seniority.

If an explicitly stated sense of masculine identity construction existed in Koa's narrative, it was limited to his mention that 'guys take it personally,' indicating that he was probably discussing boys when he talked about occasions when 'people don't back down,' 'people come, and they boss you around,' and 'all the youngest punks, they try to fight everybody.' When comparing the boys' and the girls' data, I found that it was only the boys who discussed establishing a reputation by not showing fear and standing up to those who tried to dominate them. Masculinity, it seemed, was a theme woven underneath the boys' accounts of confronting disrespect, leading me to note that disrespect was gendered (Irwin and Adler 2012).

Narratives similar to Chad's excerpt added an important insight that confronting disrespect was not only an effort to avoid being bossed around but was also about confronting racist slurs, such as the term 'pineapple pickers,' an expression alluding to the fact that in the history of Hawai'i, pineapple plantation workers (among other types of plantation workers) held a lowly position in Hawai'i, and their hard labor was a sign of their discredited status. During the initial phases of coding, disrespect for boys seemed to be multidimensional, with racist attacks comprising one form of disrespect and being bossed around and dominated connoting another. After looking at all my initial codes, deciphering the dimensions of and variations within each, and asking the important question, 'What is going on?' (Charmaz and Mitchell 2010, p. 163), with all segments of the data, I reached more abstract levels in my analysis. It was then that I began to develop focused codes and articulate the overarching framework about masculinity and violence that I saw emerging.

The first glimmer of a larger conceptual frame came when I noticed that the boys' status hierarchies were not just about who is tougher and more dominating in terms of physical power – traits that are traditionally associated with masculinity. Racism and race-based systems of injustice were also salient markers of the boys' status, with the boys fighting to oppose racist stereotypes according to their interpretation of the histories of racial demoralization confronting them. For example, the boys' interpretation that the term 'pineapple pickers' was, first, racist and, second, tied to a history of the demoralization of plantation workers in Hawai'i indicated that the boys saw racism in the present as being linked with racist demoralization in the past.

Being seen as afraid and dominated, I eventually understood, was also related to teens' impressions of racialization in Hawaiian history. Looking at the data that I coded as 'reflecting on injustice,' 'righting wrongs,' and 'evaluating stereotypes,' I saw the teens explaining a particular history of their racial and/or ethnic group in Hawai'i. For example, many teens explained the history of Hawai'i as one in which powerful foreigners came and 'took land,' 'overthrew the Queen [Queen Lili'oukalani],' 'dominated,' and 'looked down' on Native Hawaiians. Examining all the data, I noticed that the mentions of disrespect in the form of domination, being called 'chicken,' and being told 'to do this, do that' were the types of disrespect mentioned by the boys who identified themselves as Native Hawaiian. The concepts of being dominated, controlled by others, and constructed as afraid, weak, and easily taken advantage of seemed to me and my colleagues to be connected to a shared consciousness among Native Hawaiian boys about the history of American colonial power in Hawai'i.

Being fearless became the larger theoretical category to capture the way by which many Native Hawaiian boys[7] viewed severe disrespect against a backdrop of the history of American colonial control in Hawai'i, which included the racialization of Native Hawaiians. When we used the term 'backdrop of Hawaiian history,' we were not pointing to an objective or realist reading of history; rather, we were connoting a process of collective sense making about past injustices in the present. For example, a layer of youthful interpretation of Hawaiian history existed, and the sources of teens' knowledge about colonial occupation and past colonial injustices came from their everyday experiences;

teens were indeed keen observers of the world around them. What adult family members recounted to the youth, how other young people spoke about Hawaiian history, and what teens learned in school combined with adolescents' observations to form the foundation or youth's consciousness about the history of their racial and/or ethnic groups in Hawai'i. Placed in Charmaz's (2014, p. 241) framework, the teens' 'meanings and actions' were located 'in larger social structures and discourses of which they [individuals in a study] may be unaware,' although in our case, the teens seemed to be very much aware of and articulate about larger power arrangements.

Using symbolic interactionism (Blumer 1969) to explain the youth's consciousness of Hawaiian history, such 'things' as Americans' taking of land, the overthrow of Queen Lili'oukalani (the last reigning monarch of the sovereign Hawaiian nation), and the suppression of language and other cultural traditions were meaningful to all youth, with those of Native Hawaiian ancestry having a particular set of interactions, meanings, and relationships with these abstract ideas and moral principles related to justice and exploitation (Blumer 1969, pp. 10–11).

What eventually emerged after my memo writing and focused coding was a story about structure and agency. The meanings associated with histories of injustice and racial demoralization were shared, constructed, and reconstructed through young people's interactions, such that teens often expressed a collective understanding of historic conflicts and injustices, a process that we called developing a critical consciousness. Violence was often a part of boys' efforts to present themselves as fearless and was an everyday identity maneuver. Moreover, how boys negotiated being fearless was often in response to the formation of their critical understandings of the history of their self and other defined racial and ethnic groups.

Importantly, boys who identified themselves as coming from parts of the Pacific outside of Hawai'i tended to have a different shared consciousness and definitions of disrespect. For example, those who considered themselves to be Samoan (usually from American Samoa) discussed facing stereotypes that Samoan boys and men are big, brawny, good at sports, and prone to violence. Consequently, few Samoan boys discussed feeling particularly disrespected if they were called 'chicken' or were told to 'do this, do that.' In other words, fearfulness and domination were not often brought up as degrading scenarios among the boys who self-identified as Samoan. Using the same techniques to derive the focused code of being fearless, we found that many boys who traced their ancestry to Samoa manipulated rather than resisted the racist stereotypes of the physically dominating Samoan male as a way to portray fearsome reputations. In the end, our conceptualization highlighted two processes, namely, being fearless and being fearsome, as masculinity maneuvers attuned to varying ethnic and racial stereotypes and histories of conflict that the boys came to understand through their contextual interactions.

Theorizing Masculinity and Violence

Explaining the links between boys, young men, and violence in sociology has a rather long tradition, making the process of locating an explicit GT tradition in the context of masculinity and violence difficult. In fact, if readers want to follow the theoretical developments related to this field, they will find themselves traveling to a time before the establishment of GT. The first stop for inquisitive readers might be the Chicago School of Sociology during the mid-20th century, the time and place for the production of classic statements about boys' violence. They will move from Thrasher's (1927) early writings about male gang members, to Shaw and McKay's (1942) examinations of boys' violence in disorganized communities, and eventually to Cloward and Ohlin's (1960) thoughts about boys who live in neighborhoods where violent gangs and thus violent opportunities exist.

One might stop off at Harvard and discover the intellectual foundations for Merton's (1957), Cohen's (1955), and Miller's (1958) theories. Merton (1957) argued that violence (and delinquency, in general) was an adaptation to structural constraints (i.e., strain), whereas Cohen (1955) was especially concerned with status frustration among lower-class boys, and he advanced the notion that toughness among working-class males is a type of subcultural resistance to middle-class norms and morality. Miller (1958) argued that lower-class cultural values, which included an emphasis on physical strength and prowess for boys, was the source of some boys' penchant for violence (see also Harding 2010).

While these theories about boys and violence continue to influence our thinking, some important contemporary innovations have been offered. One set of developments focused on the topic of masculinity, with scholars noting that maleness and masculinity are not natural and biological states, but are socially constructed identities achieved 'through interactional and micropolitical activities' (West and Zimmerman 1987, p. 126). Another group of masculinity scholars has drawn from theories of hegemony (Gramsci 1971) to argue that power, ideology, and domination are tied to masculinity as a concept and social process. Although masculinity as a source of structure and product of social practices has some variations (Connell 2005), in the end, masculinity is seen as a coercive social phenomenon that reinforces numerous inequalities, especially systems of male domination.

Another group of scholars has advanced a political economy thesis about boys, men, and violence. In this vein, researchers have argued that the rise of neoliberal systems of governance in the US and the deindustrialization of American cities have gutted inner-city areas, creating a particularly crushing form of economic, political, and social exclusion for inner-city dwellers, which some call the state of advanced marginalization (Wacquant 2010). If structural vulnerabilities encourage male violence, then the contemporary conditions confronting poor and working-class boys are ripe for the rise of a hyper-violent form of masculinity.

Regardless of the developments in theories explicating masculinity and violence, my colleagues and I (Irwin and Umemoto 2016) argue that current male violence theories have largely stayed true to the early frameworks. Violence is still seen by many as working- and lower-class boys' reactions to blocked opportunities to gain middle-class status and success. Summarizing the links between contemporary and past theories, my colleague and I (Irwin and Adler 2012, pp. 350–351) wrote the following:

> For decades, marginalized males have been seen in similar ways: as emphasizing trouble, toughness, and autonomy (Miller 1958); projecting a 'tough guy' or 'street' image (Oliver 1984; Wilkinson 2001); cleaving to a 'compulsive masculinity' (Oliver 1984); striving to become 'badasses' (Katz 1988); and using violence to display their 'nerve' or 'juice,' and to seek retaliation against those who harm them (Anderson 1999). In essence, violence has historically been seen as a resource for men to accomplish their masculinity (Messerschmidt 1993, 1997) in locations ravaged by poverty, race-based segregation and stigma, and the rampant failure and under-funding of civic institutions meant to serve inner-city residents.

However, what is the relationship between GT and explanations of masculinity and violence? The answer is muddy. Currently, many qualitative researchers examining male violence do not explain their analysis techniques (for an exception, see Oselin 2016). Furthermore, ethnographers who offer rich depictions of male violence in their books (Anderson 1999; Black 2010; Contreras 2013; Fader 2013; Goffman 2015; Rios 2011) sometimes relegate their discussions of data collection methods to the appendixes where, more often than not, full accounts of the data analysis techniques used by the authors are missing. Many of the contemporary theories about masculinity and violence may have been generated through GTM techniques, but knowing this is difficult.

DISCOVERING FEMINIST GROUNDED THEORY METHODS

To tell a story about structure and agency, I found myself drawing from critical methodologies, including feminist research traditions (Reinharz 1992). Importantly, the move toward critical methods and feminist GTM was not a fully conscious choice, but it occurred through a series of personal ideological and identity negotiations, with becoming a scholar and activist as one of the most salient identities for me. Moreover, this identity construction occurred within specific places, times, and social networks, similar to how many other Generation X researchers and I were exposed from young ages to collections of ideas, social trends, and philosophical currents in North America during our early lives. I argue that it is this exposure of a generation of researchers to theoretical and epistemological developments in the late 20th and early 21st centuries that accounts for why and how GTM is currently being used to develop theories linking structure and agency.

Looking at my case as an example of a larger pattern underlying the emergence of a hybrid GTM, the place associated with my development as a scholar and activist was inner-city San Francisco, and the decades were the 1970s and 1980s. I was one among a number of children in the 1970s and 1980s raised within middle-class, unconventional family arrangements and also by a set of progressive and social justice-oriented parents. Consequently, feminism was never in my wildest imagination an 'F' word (Beck 1998), nor was the term '*feminist*' a problem among my peers who were growing up in families similar to my own.

I attended an all-women's college (Smith College), where feminist perspectives and gender studies concepts were woven throughout the college curriculum. While in graduate school, I gravitated toward feminist perspectives, especially feminist research methods (Acker, Barry, and Esseveld 1983; DeVault 1990; Fonow and Cook 1991; Harding 1987; Oakley 1981; Reinharz 1992; Stacey 1988; Stanley and Wise 1990) and gender studies classes. I was not alone in this intellectual journey, as sociology departments across North America are currently filled with Generation X faculty members who were born during the second wave of feminism and became young adults enamored with third-wave feminist ideas (see Collins 1990; Davis 1981; hooks 1981; Moraga and Anzaldua 1981; Zinn et al. 1986).

For many years, my activist and feminist leanings unfolded side by side with my symbolic interactionist and social psychology training. What seemed to keep these epistemological and methodological interests apart was that they carried tensions and contradictions, making the merging of third-wave feminist ideas with GT and GTM seem unlikely. At best, what appeared possible was the generation of a women's centered GT that could explicate women's agency, experiences, and voices (Olesen 2010).

When formal articulations of a feminist GTM (Keddy, Sims, and Stern 1996; Kushner and Morrow 2003; Rickards and Wuest 2006; Wuest 1995)[8] were published, scholars saw a way to combine pragmatist, symbolic interactionist, and feminist-inspired work. More specifically, researchers, such as Wuest (1995) and Kushner and Morrow (2003), allowed a feminist GTM because they resolved some of the inherent tensions that kept feminist methodologies and GTM apart.

One tension between feminist methods and GTM, which needed to be resolved, related to feminists' call for reflexivity (see Mruck and Mey 2010 for a review of reflexivity in qualitative research). For many feminists, reflexivity means that researchers recognize and give accounts of their own subjectivity, assumptions, and ideological leanings. Furthermore, feminist reflexivity acknowledges that all individuals (including researchers) are situated within complex relations of ruling (Smith 1974, 1987) and multiple vectors of oppression (Collins 1990; Collins and Bilge 2016), as well as occupy particular standpoints and positions within histories of oppression. More to the point, feminist researchers often note how their subjectivity and positionality influence their research processes, products, and relationships with study members.

The traditional GTM notion that an individual's interpretation of her own life was something to be cross-checked, triangulated, and constantly compared with emerging concepts and frameworks conflicted with feminist researchers' goals to shed light on the mutual subjectivity of researchers and research participants as co-creators of knowledge. Additionally, the implication that research participants' lives, narratives, and actions should be thoroughly scrutinized, triangulated, and questioned – all while researchers were raised above the fray of being second-guessed and cross-checked – seemed to be a way of privileging researchers and disempowering research participants.

Feminist GTM enthusiasts (Keddy, Sims, and Stern 1996; Kushner and Morrow 2003; Rickards and Wuest 2006; Wuest 1995), as well as Charmaz (2006, 2014), resolved the reflexivity tension by encouraging researchers to lean away from the objectivist strains within GTM and embrace GT as a co-created, situated, and inherently subjective enterprise. Notably, Charmaz's (2014, p. 240) constructionist vision also moves GTM closer to feminist traditions and standpoint epistemologies when she wrote the following:

> Constructivist grounded theorists take a reflexive stance toward the research process and products. ... Constructivist grounded theorists assume that both data and analysis are social constructions that reflect the conditions of their production. ... In this view, we construct research processes and products, but these constructions occur under pre-existing structural conditions, arise in emergent situations, and are influenced by the researcher's perspectives privileges, positions, interactions, and geographical locations.

A second tension between feminist methods and GTM, which required a resolution, was that GTM was accused by some of offering mid-range explanations of social life rather than theories about structural, historical, and global processes, such as sexism, racism, nationalism, and ageism, to name a few. Glaser's (1978) emphasis on the six Cs (i.e., cause, context, contingency, condition, consequence, and covariance) and Strauss and Corbin's (1990, 1998) conditional matrix certainly encouraged theories that could explain the interplay between the everyday world and large-scale structural arrangements. Feminist methodologists wondered why such GTM tools were not used for large-scale theorizing. Kuchner and Morrow (2003, p. 37) wrote, 'although grounded theory formally introduced the notion of a conditional matrix as a way of getting at the larger social structural factors that impinge on local settings, these concerns largely drop out of site in actual research.'

Kuscher and Morrow (2003) outlined the solution to the mid-range versus macro theory conflict by arguing that GTM has the capacity to offer theories about patriarchy and other interlocking inequalities. For example, Wuest (1995, p. 127) wrote, 'in discovering the core variable through the constant comparative methods of a grounded theory study, questions are raised about existing social structures.' It follows that GTM researchers had the necessary tools to build theories linking micro and macro processes, but had yet to use these approaches to implicate social structures.

The above-mentioned statements gave feminist and critical leaning researchers pathways to move forward. First, as students of feminist theory in the 1980s, 1990s, and early 2000s, we clearly learned that multiple feminisms and multiple feminist methodologies existed instead of one brand of feminism. Also important to our intellectual development was the insight that gender is one among many vectors of oppression, such that woman, womanhood, and femininity are never unitary experiences and expressions. Racism, histories of racialization, nationalism, classism, ableism, heterosexism, and ageism (to name a few oppressions) also create multiple dimensions of difference that impinge on everyday life. In the early 2000s, researchers attuned to these developments began to coin terms for this type of approach by calling it multiracial feminism, intersectional feminisms, or intersectionality (Collins and Bilge 2016; Crenshaw 1991).

For many who took up the quest for intersectional theories in the 1990s and early 2000s, our work became a matter of acknowledging and reflecting on inter-subjectivity and the co-creation of knowledge as one engages in research. It also entailed looking simultaneously at individual, interpersonal, community, state, and even global processes, meanings, constructions, and contexts.

When looking at masculinity and violence, my colleagues and I traced the ways by which power and privilege moved and flowed along several dimensions of difference structuring social life. Because of the histories of conflict in Hawai'i – colonial occupation by the American government, historic systems of racialization, and histories of struggles for indigenous rights in Hawai'i – we wanted to acknowledge the methodological advances made by feminist researchers, as well as the work of critical and indigenous researchers who, similar to third-wave feminists, were searching for approaches with the potential to empower study members and allow social justice on many fronts. We (Irwin and Umemoto 2012, p. 12) eventually distilled all of these complex epistemological, theoretical, and methodological frameworks into the following account:

> To analyze the data, we borrowed aspects of grounded theory techniques (Charmaz 2006; Glaser and Strauss 1967; Strauss 1987; Strauss and Corbin 1990). Given recent developments in urban (Anderson 1999; Burawoy 1991; Jones 2010; Wacquant 2004), feminist (Wuest 1995), critical (Fine 1994; Fine and Weis 2005; Foley and Valenzuela 2005), and indigenous ethnography (Tengan 2008), we also wanted to stay attuned to the ways in which relations of power impinged on the everyday experiences of study members. Therefore, we also borrowed analysis techniques of critical ethnographers to link situational social processes with larger structural forces surrounding these two communities and schools.

Karen Umemoto and I were not the only scholars attempting to combine critical methodologies and feminist research methods with GTM. Since the early 2000s, a score of researchers has been fleshing out the links between and among structure, interactions, and individuals' subjectivity and meaning making. Using GTM, Rafalovich (2006) explained how heavy metal music in the 1990s reinforced traditional ideologies about masculine domination (see Smith 1990), and he specifically explained how the lyrics of popular music can reinforce ruling ideologies, especially ideologies supporting male domination. While studying the violence of male sex workers, Oselin (2016, p. 219) used GTM to derive a concept of pacifist masculinity, which is a hybrid masculine identity. He (Oselin 2016, p. 219) acknowledged that masculinity is 'a flexible and adaptable performance' and that enacting gender in ways that counter hegemonic expectations can 'be a catalyst to disrupt entrenched gender regimes within a given context' (Oselin 2016, p. 220). Roschelle and Kaufman (2004, p. 23) investigated the 'gap between the rich and the poor' by highlighting the experiences of homeless youth. They (Roschelle and Kaufman 2004, p. 40) saw the stigma attached to homelessness 'not as an individual attribute but as a relationship to the social structure,' and they noted that the youth's behaviors were shaped and interpreted according to homeless youth's locations in structural hierarchies, such as age, race, and class.

Summarizing how contemporary theorists have linked the everyday experiences of women to systems of inequalities without acknowledging Richie's (1996, 2012) work would be difficult. Her (Richie 1996, 2012) research offers an explicit Black feminist theory of social control in the US that is focused closely on the ways in which Black women resist and confront a violence-producing nation. For future researchers looking to uncover what researchers mean by the term 'context,' Richie's (1996, 2012) work is foundational. The core contextual arrangements for her (Richie 2012) include Black women's shared and intimate living spaces (e.g., domestic spheres), the community surrounding Black women's intimate lives, and the state, including its governing ideologies (e.g., neoliberalism), discourses, and institutions (e.g., welfare and criminal justice systems) that often impinge on Black women's intimate and community contexts.

The above-mentioned research examples provide a snapshot of how contemporary researchers are exploring the everyday world by using GTM and other methods designed to highlight the subjectivity and experiences of individuals in interactional contexts, while also linking these interaction-based meanings and actions to structural arrangements. Looking at landmark journals publishing GTM work (*Qualitative Research*, *Qualitative Inquiry*, *Qualitative Sociology*, *Qualitative Health Research*, *Symbolic Interaction*), one will see that GTM has a place among researchers hoping to explain the interplay of structure and agency.

CONCLUDING THOUGHTS

In their introduction to *The Sage Handbook of Grounded Theory*, Bryant and Charmaz (2010) celebrate GTM innovations and claim that a sign of developmental maturity for a methodology is tolerance to new ways of approaching and applying methodological tools. The end result, they note (Bryant and Charmaz 2010), is the formation of a variety of approaches, many of which may not resemble the original statements. Despite welcoming new approaches, Bryant and Charmaz (2010) warn that not every GTM innovation will be welcomed. The question is 'whether or not some new or hybrid form of the method is actually a valid or legitimate variation rather than an anathema' (Bryant and Charmaz 2010, p. 9).

Feminist GTM (Keddy, Sims, and Stern 1996; Kushner and Morrow 2003; Rickards and Wuest 2006; Wuest 1995) is certainly an approach that has gained traction since the 1990s. The formal articulations and applications of the approach suggest that feminist GTM will be seen as a legitimate extension. My colleagues and I certainly find feminist GTM to be a useful tool that helps us uncover the ways by which everyday masculine identity maneuvers are linked with colonial histories of conflict and inequalities. Importantly, our reliance on this feminist innovation was inspired by third-wave feminism, which specifically acknowledges the multiple inequalities at work in any one setting and the many dimensions of difference (e.g., race, class, age, sexuality, cognitive and physical functioning, and nationality) that need to be addressed.

Benchmark journals for qualitative research are increasingly publishing work that uses GTM to generate explanations of how structure and agency intertwine, and upcoming additions to the GTM family are plausible. For example, scholars who have had a similar intellectual and personal trajectory as some Generation X researchers may be moved to coin a term for their structure and agency version of GTM. In reference to me and my colleagues' work (Irwin and Adler 2012; Irwin and King forthcoming; Irwin and Umemoto 2012, 2016), the term 'critical GTM' or 'intersectional GTM' come to mind (see also Hadley's contribution in this volume). In what directions future GTM researchers decide to travel and what names they choose to apply to their developments is wide open and fairly unpredictable, though. Whether a critical GTM will be a welcomed contribution or if it will be seen as threatening the integrity of GTM remains unclear as well.

Notes

1 While in college and for a few years afterward, I was employed as a research assistant by University of California at San Francisco-trained sociologists, Marsha Rosenbaum and Sheigla Murphy, to examine the experiences of heroin and crack users as they negotiated drug treatment, parenting, criminality, and legal employment (Kearney, Murphy, and Rosenbaum 1994; Rosenbaum and Murphy 1998). These researchers were well trained in and relied heavily on GTM in their National Institute on Drug Abuse-funded studies. Much of the work on the grant included coding, memo writing, and attending analysis meetings to derive a GT explanation of the processes at work in the data. In a quest for reflexivity, I must disclose that Marsha Rosenbaum is my stepmother, and her long-time friend, Sheigla Murphy, has been a second mother to me and my siblings. Thus, UCSF-inspired GTM was a central part of my childhood.

2 Lind (1969: 100) offered his own explanation of racial prejudice and tension in Hawai'i, noting that 'overt expressions of uncritical sentiments of derogation or hostility towards other groups, was unquestionably least evident in Hawai'i during the period of plantation dominance,' which was a time when racial distinctions were seen 'as a natural and essential part of the established order.' Many scholars of Hawaiian history do not agree with this vision and see the era of plantation dominance as a time of rigid racist segregation and oppressive racialization.

3 K-12 in the US means kindergarten (the grade before 1st grade) through the 12th grade, and these are the school years that are publicly funded and provide free education for US citizens, generally speaking. In most cases, parents are allowed to enroll their child in kindergarten when their child is five years old, although compulsory education laws in many US states require children to begin their education by age six (the equivalent of the 1st grade).

4 Looking at news articles, letters, and petitions written in Hawaiian, Silva (2004) found that 95% of the population in Hawai'i who were Native Hawaiian signed a petition against the annexation of Hawai'i to the US in 1897, although Hawai'i was annexed a year later. In 1959, Hawai'i became a US state. Many in Hawai'i decry the illegal overthrow of the Hawaiian Kingdom, and there are lasting sentiments to re-establish Hawai'i as a sovereign nation.

5 A third motivation was that I wanted to allow open discussions of community-based strengths to emerge, thus avoiding a tendency of researchers to focus on community problems and pathologies (Jones 2010).
6 A part of Koa's narrative, it should be noted, was also coded as establishing a reputation and fighting cycles. Furthermore, aspects of Chad's narrative were also initially coded as fighting cycles.
7 Not to essentialize the experiences of Native Hawaiian youth is important. The teens who were involved in my study were not representative of all Pacific Islander young people in Hawai'i; they were teens who were referred to counseling services because they were having trouble in school, and their life histories were similar to those of teens around North America who have experienced many types of trauma and whose families have been targets of systematic structural violence (Richie 2012). I also do not want to paint the teens as victims. These youth possessed resilience and expressed resistance to oppression in multiple ways. For example, the critical awareness of the teens in this study was often more sophisticated than the sociological analysis offered by students in my undergraduate courses, suggesting that the teens were turning the hardships in their lives into opportunities to hone their analytical skills. I often found myself relying on interviews with teens in my college classes to demonstrate ways for college students to develop their own highly nuanced social critiques.
8 I did not discover Wuest's (1995) statement about feminist GTM until the 2000s because I was rather narrowly focused in graduate school. It is when I started searching for a feminist model of GTM that I found Wuest's (1995) seminal work published in the area of health and medicine.

REFERENCES

Acker, Joan, Kate Barry, and Johanna Esseveld. 1983. Objectivity and Truth: Problems in Doing Feminist Research. *Women's Studies International Forum 6*: 423–435.

Adler, Patricia A. and Peter Adler. 1987. *Membership Roles in Field Research*. Newbury Park, CA: Sage.

Anderson, Elijah. 1999. *Code of the Street: Decency, Violence, and the Moral Life of the Inner City*. New York: Norton.

Beck, Debra Baker. 1998. The 'F' Word: How the Media Frame Feminism. *NWSA Journal 10*(1): 139–153.

Becker, Howard S. 1967. Whose Side Are We On? *Whose Side Are We On?" is Social Problems.14*: 239–247.

Black, Timothy. 2010. *When a Heart Turns Rock Solid: The Lives of Three Puerto Rican Brothers on and off the Streets*. New York: Vintage Books.

Blumer, Herbert. 1969. *Symbolic Interactionism: Perspective and Method*. Berkeley, CA: University of California Press.

Bryant, Anthony and Kathy Charmaz. 2010. Introduction. Grounded Theory Research: Methods and Practices. In *The Sage Handbook of Grounded Theory*, edited by A. Bryant and K. Charmaz, pp. 1–28. Los Angeles, CA: Sage.

Burawoy, Michael, ed. 1991. *Ethnography Unbound: Power and Resistance in the Modern Metropolis*. Berkeley, CA: University of California Press.

Charmaz, Kathy. 2006. *Constructing Grounded Theory: A Practical Guide through Qualitative Analysis*. Thousand Oaks, CA: Sage.

Charmaz, Kathy. 2014. *Constructing Grounded Theory*. Second Edition. Thousand Oaks, CA: Sage.

Charmaz, Kathy and Richard G. Mitchell. 2010. Grounded Theory in Ethnography. In *Handbook of Ethnography*, edited by P. Atkinson, A. Coffey, S. Delamont, J. Lofland, and L. Lofland, pp. 160–74. Los Angeles, CA: Sage.

Cloward, Richard A. and Lloyd E. Ohlin. 1960. *Delinquency and Opportunity: A Theory of Delinquent Gangs*. Glencoe, IL: Free Press.

Cohen, Albert K. 1955. *Delinquent Boys: The Culture of the Gang*. Glencoe, IL: Free Press.

Collins, Patricia Hill. 1990. *Black Feminist Thought: Knowledge, Consciousness, and the Politics of Empowerment*. Boston, MA: Unwin Hyman.

Collins, Patricia Hill and Sirma Bilge. 2016. *Intersectionality*. Malden, MA: Polity Press.
Connell, R. W. 2005. *Masculinities*. Second Edition. Berkeley, CA: University of California Press.
Contreras, Randol. 2013. *The Stickup Kids: Race, Drugs, Violence, and the American Dream*. Berkeley, CA: University of California Press.
Corte, Ugo and Katherine Irwin. 2017. The Form and Flow of Teaching Ethnographic Knowledge: Hands-on Approaches for Learning Epistemology. *Teaching Sociology*. Retrieved May 1, 2017 (http://journals.sagepub.com/doi/abs/10.1177/0092055X17697771)
Crenshaw, Kimberle. 1991. Mapping the Margins: Intersectionality, Identity Politics, and Violence against Women of Color. *Stanford Law Review 43*(6): 1241–1299.
Davis, Angela. 1981. *Women, Race, and Class*. New York: Random House.
DeVault, Marjorie L. 1990. Talking and Listening from Women's Standpoint: Feminist Strategies for Interviewing and Analysis. *Social Problems 37*(1): 96–116.
Dey, Ian. 1993. *Qualitative Data Analysis: A User-Friendly Guide*. New York: Sage.
Fader, Jamie J. 2013. *Falling Back: Incarceration and Transitions to Adulthood among Urban Youth*. New Brunswick, NJ: Rutgers University Press.
Fine, Gary Alan, ed. 1995. *A Second Chicago School?: The Development of a Postwar American Sociology*. Chicago, IL: University of Chicago Press.
Fine, Michelle. 1994. Working the Hyphens: Reinventing Self and the Other in Qualitative Research. In *The Handbook of Qualitative Research*, edited by N. K. Denzin and Y. S. Lincoln, pp. 70–82. Thousand Oaks, CA: Sage.
Fine, Michelle and Lois Weis. 2005. Compositional Studies, in Two Parts: Critical Theorizing and Analysis on Social (In)justice. In *The Handbook of Qualitative Research*. Third Edition, edited by N. K. Denzin and Y. S. Lincoln, pp. 65–84. Thousand Oaks, CA: Sage.
Foley, Douglas and Angela Valenzuela. 2005. Critical Ethnography: The Politics of Collaboration. In *The Sage Handbook of Qualitative Research*. Third Edition, edited by N. K. Denzin and Y. S. Lincoln, pp. 217–34. Thousand Oaks, CA: Sage.
Fonow, Mary M. and Judith A. Cook. 1991. *Beyond Methodology: Feminist Scholarship as Lived Research*. Bloomington, IN: Indiana University Press.
Glaser, Barney G. 1978. *Theoretical Sensitivity*. Mill Valley, CA: Sociology Press.
Glaser, Barney G. 1992. *Basics of Grounded Theory Analysis: Emergence vs Forcing*. Mill Valley, CA: Sociology Press.
Glaser, Barney G. and Anselm Strauss. 1967. *Discovery of Grounded Theory: Strategies for Qualitative Research*. Chicago, IL: Aldine.
Goffman, Alice. 2015. *On the Run: Fugitive Life in an American City*. New York: Picador.
Gramsci, Antonio. 1971. *Selections from the Prison Notebooks of Antonio Gramsci*. New York: International Publications.
Guba, Egon G. and Yvonna S. Lincoln. 2004. Competing Paradigms in Qualitative Research: Theories and Issues. In *Approaches to Qualitative Research: A Reader on Theory and Practice*, edited by S. N. Hesse-Biber and P. Leavy, pp. 17–38. New York: Oxford University Press.
Harding, David J. 2010. *Living the Drama: Community, Conflict, and Culture among Inner-City Boys*. Chicago, IL: University of Chicago Press.
Harding, Sandra. 1987. The Method Question. *Hypatia 2*(3): 19–35.
hooks, bell. 1981. *Ain't I a Woman: Black Women and Feminism*. Boston, MA: South End.
Irwin, Katherine. 2001. Legitimating the First Tattoo: Moral Passage through Informal Interaction. *Symbolic Interaction 24*(1): 49–73.
Irwin, Katherine and Corey Adler. 2012. Fighting for Her Honor: Girls' Violence in Distressed Communities. *Feminist Criminology 7*(4): 350–380.
Irwin, Katherine and Sanna King. Forthcoming. A Critical View of Female Bullying and Aggression: Pacific Islander Girls Confront Patriachy, Racialization, and Imperialism. In *Female Aggression and Intersectionality: Transforming the Discourse of 'Mean Girls'*, edited by K. McQueeny and A. A. Girgenti-Malone. New York: Routledge.

Irwin, Katherine and Karen Umemoto. 2012. Being Fearless and Fearsome: Colonial Legacies, Racial Constructions, and Male Adolescent Violence. *Race and Justice 2*(1): 3–21.

Irwin, Katherine and Karen Umemoto. 2016. *Jacked Up and Unjust: Pacific Islander Teens Confront Violent Legacies*. Berkeley, CA: University of California Press.

Jones, Nikki. 2010. *Between Good and Ghetto: African American Girls and Inner-City Violence*. New Brunswick, NJ: Rutgers University Press.

Katz, Jack. 1988. *Seductions of Crime: Moral and Sensual Attractions in Doing Evil*. New York: Basic Books.

Kearney, Margaret, Sheigla Murphy, and Marsha Rosenbaum. 1994. Mothering on Crack Cocaine: A Grounded Theory Analysis. *Social Science and Medicine 38*(2): 351–361.

Keddy, Barbara, Sharon L. Sims, and Phyllis Noerager Stern. 1996. Grounded Theory as Feminist Research Methodology. *Journal of Advanced Nursing 23*(3): 448–453.

Kushner, Kaysi Eastlick and Raymond Morrow. 2003. Grounded Theory, Feminist Theory, Critical Theory: Toward Theoretical Triangulation. *Advances in Nursing Science 26*(1): 30–43.

Lind, Andrew W. 1938. *An Island Community: Ecological Succession in Hawaii*. Chicago, IL: University of Chicago Press.

Lind, Andrew W. 1969. *Hawaii: The Last of the Magic Isles*. New York: Oxford University Press.

Merton, Robert K. 1957. *Social Theory and Social Structure*. Glencoe, IL: Free Press.

Messerschmidt, James. 1993. *Masculnities and Crime: Critique and Reconceptualization of Theory*. Lanham, MD: Rowman and Littlefield.

Messerschmidt, James. 1997. *Crime as Structured Action: Gender, Race, Class, and Crime in the Making*. Thousand Oaks, CA: Sage.

Miller, Walter. 1958. Lower Class Culture as a Generating a Milieu of Gange Delinquency. *Journal of Social Issues 14*: 5–19.

Moraga, Cherrie and Gloria Anzaldua, eds. 1981. *This Bridge Called My Back: Writings by Radical Women of Color*. Watertown, MA: Persephone.

Mruck, Katja and Gunter Mey. 2010. Grounded Theory and Reflexivity. In *The Sage Handbook of Grounded Theory*, edited by A. Bryant and K. Charmaz, pp. 515–538. Los Angeles, CA: Sage.

Oakley, Ann. 1981. Interviewing Women: A Contradiction in Terms. In *Doing Feminist Research*, edited by H. Roberts, pp. 30–61. Boston, MA: Routledge & Kegan Paul.

Olesen, Virginia L. 2010. Feminist Qualitative Research and Grounded Theory: Complexities, Criticisms, and Opportunities. In *The Sage Handbook of Grounded Theory*, edited by A. Bryant and K. Charmaz, pp. 417–435. Los Angeles, CA: Sage.

Oliver, William. 1984. Black Males and Tough Guy Image: A Dysfunctional Compensatory Adaptation. *The Western Journal of Black Studies 8*(4): 199–203.

Oselin, Sharon S. 2016. You Catch More Flies with Honey: Sex Work, Violence, and Masculinity on the Streets. *Sociological Forum 31*(1): 203–222.

Park, Robert E. 1938. Introduction. In *An Island Community: Ecological Succession in Hawaii*, by A. Lind, pp. ix–xvi. Chicago, IL: University of Chicago Press.

Rafalovich, Adam. 2006. Broken and Becoming God-Sized: Contemporary Metal Music and Masculine Individualism. *Symbolic Interaction 29*(1): 19–32.

Reinharz, Shulamit. 1992. *Feminist Methods in Social Research*. New York: Oxford University Press.

Richie, Beth. 1996. *Compelled to Crime: The Gender Entrapment of Battered Black Women*. New York: Routledge.

Richie, Beth. 2012. *Arrested Justice: Black Women, Violence, and America's Prison Nation*. New York: New York University Press.

Rickards, Tracey and Judith Wuest. 2006. The Process of Losing and Regaining Credibility When Coming-Out at Midlife. *Health Care for Women International 27*(6): 530–547.

Rios, Victor M. 2011. *Punished: Policing the Lives of Black and Latino Boys*. New York: New York University Press.

Roschelle, Anne R. and Peter Kaufman. 2004. Fitting in and Fighting Back: Stigma Management Strategies among Homeless Kids. *Symbolic Interaction 27*(1): 23–46.

Rosenbaum, Marsha and Sheigla Murphy. 1998. *Pregnant Women on Drugs: Combating Stereotypes and Stigma*. New Brunswick, NJ: Rutgers University Press.
Shaw, Clifford and Henry D. McKay. 1942. *Juvenile Delinquency in Urban Areas*. Chicago, IL: University of Chicago Press.
Silva, Noenoe K. 2004. *Aloha Betrayed: Native Hawaiian Resistance to American Colonialism*. Durham, NC: Duke University Press.
Smith, Dorothy E. 1974. Women's Perspective as a Radical Critique of Sociology. *Sociological Inquiry 44*(1): 7–13.
Smith, Dorothy E. 1987. *The Everyday World as Problematic: A Feminist Sociology*. Boston, MA: Northeastern University Press.
Smith, Dorothy E. 1990. *The Conceptual Practices of Power: A Feminist Sociology of Knowledge*. Toronto: University of Toronto Press.
Smith, Linda Tuhiwai. 2012. *Decolonizing Methodologies: Research and Indigenous Peoples*. Second Edition. London: Zed Books.
Snow, David and Calvin Morrill. 1993. Reflections on Anthropology's Ethnographic Crisis of Faith. *Contemporary Sociology 22*(1): 8–11.
Stacey, Judith. 1988. Can There Be a Feminist Ethnography? *Women's Studies International Forum 11*(1): 21–27.
Stanley, Liz and Sue Wise. 1990. Method, Methodology and Epistemology in Feminist Research Processes. In *Feminist Praxis. Research, Theory, and Epistemology in Feminist Sociology*, edited by L. Stanley, pp. 20–59. New York: Routledge.
Strauss, Anselm L. 1987. *Qualitative Analysis for Social Scientists*. Cambridge: Cambridge University Press.
Strauss, Anselm L. and Juliet M. Corbin. 1990. *Basics of Qualitative Research: Grounded Theory Procedures and Techniques*. Newbury Park, CA: Sage.
Strauss, Anselm L. and Juliet M. Corbin. 1998. *Basics of Qualitative Research: Techniques and Procedures for Developing Grounded Theory*. Second Edition. Thousand Oaks, CA: Sage.
Tengan, Ty P. Kāwika. 2008. *Native Men Remade: Gender and Nation in Contemporary Hawai'i*. Durham, NC: Duke University Press.
Thrasher, Frederic M. 1927. *The Gang*. Chicago, IL: University of Chicago Press.
Wacquant, Loïc. 2004. *Body & Soul: Notebooks of an Apprentice Boxer*. New York: Oxford University Press.
Wacquant, Loïc. 2010. *Urban Outcasts: A Comparative Sociology of Advanced Marginality*. Cambridge, MA: Polity Press.
West, Candace and Don H. Zimmerman. 1987. Doing Gender. *Gender & Society 1*(2): 125–151.
Wilkinson, Deanna L. 2001. Violent Events and Social Identity: Specifying the Relationships between Respect and Masculinity in Inner-City Violent Youth. *Sociological Studies of Children and Youth 8*: 235–269.
Wuest, Judith. 1995. Feminist Grounded Theory: An Exploration of the Congruency and Tensions between Two Traditions in Knowledge Discovery. *Qualitative Health Research 5*(1): 125–137.
Zinn, Maxine Baca, Lynn Weber Cannon, Elizabeth Higginbotham, and Bonnie Thornton Dill. 1986. The Costs of Exclusionary Practices in Women's Studies. *Signs: Journal of Women in Culture and Society 11*: 290–303.

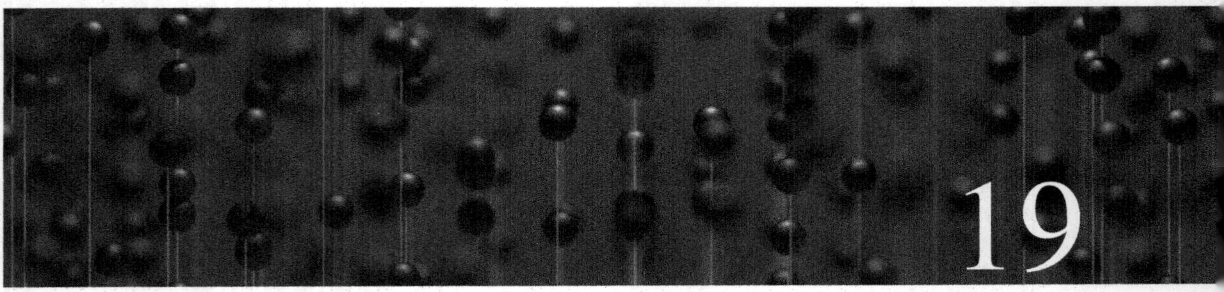

Using Constructivist Grounded Theory Methodology: Studying Suffering and Healing as a Case Example

Kumar Ravi Priya

Gham-e-hasti ka Asad kis se ho juzmarg Ilaaj
Shama har rang me jalti hai sahar hone tak
[What is going to remedy suffering of existence?
The flame glows in every hue until dawn descends.]

-Mirza Ghalib, an Urdu poet

While *The Discovery of Grounded Theory*, authored by Barney G. Glaser and Anselm L. Strauss (1967), has been considered by scholars such as Denzin and Lincoln (1994, p. ix), as a 'revolution' in the history of qualitative social science, as it provided a huge impetus for the use of qualitative methodology to be considered as legitimate rather than 'impressionistic and unsystematic' (Charmaz, 2014, p. 8), Kathy Charmaz's social constructivist version of the methodology has brought this research tradition much closer to realizing the goals of reaching out to or recovering voices of human beings. As Charmaz (1990, 1995, 2000, 2014) noted, these goals remained at the margins of inquiry in the entire research process (from generating research problems through data analysis and report writing) within the traditional grounded theory approaches (GT) by Glaser and Strauss (1967) and Strauss and Corbin (1998) as they considered the objectivist and universalistic goals of positivist and post-positivist paradigms of science to be paramount in developing 'scientific' knowledge. Dwelling on the critique of GT from grounded theorist as well as other qualitative researchers, Charmaz (2000) has pointed out that the major criticisms of GT have been that it '(a) limits entry into subjects' worlds, and thus reduces understanding of their experience; (b) curtails representation of both social world and subjective experience; (c) relies upon viewer's authority as expert observer; and (d) posits a set of objectivist procedures on which analysis rests' (p. 521). However, as I have elaborated elsewhere, Charmaz's constructivist grounded theory approach (CGT) has had an overall 'humanizing' impact on the methodology, as CGT and all its procedures remain closely concerned with providing space for the experiences or worldview of the human beings being studied (Priya, 2015a).

Rather than claiming value-neutrality and rushing into generalizable abstractions, CGT allows the researcher to be reflexive and open about ontological assumptions that help reach closer to people's social, political and experiential realities. Unlike GT, where the researcher claims to detach him/herself from the process of data collection, the epistemological stance in CGT considers research interactions to be a site for co-construction that may help bring to the fore an in-depth understanding of experiences from the participant's standpoint through a more flexible procedure of negotiations of meanings or interpretations of shared experience. Finally, the realist or reified images of human or social world in GT may unknowingly contribute to legitimizing of social hierarchies that stifle the human voice, but in applying CGT, where the concerns about recovering silenced voices or experiences are important, researchers can choose research problems that address the major goals of recovering silenced or marginalized voices (Charmaz, 2000, 2017a, 2017b).

How does this paradigm shift in grounded theory methodology towards a CGT approach open up inquiry into various aspects of human and social world? What does it mean to be reflexive while collecting data and analyzing the same? Do empathy and compassion play a role in the process of data collection and analysis? Can the same data be viewed again from a different vantage point that might help further our insights into the studied phenomenon? Building on the developments in the social studies of health towards a paradigm shift from focusing merely on the symptoms of a disease or disorder to the expressed and inarticulable experiences of suffering and healing, in this chapter, I choose to address these pivotal questions in understanding and applying CGT with the help of illustrations from the studies that have applied CGT to explore the experiences of suffering and healing. This chapter is focused on how constructivist grounded theory (CGT) methodology contributes to the understanding of the experience and expressions of suffering and healing shaped within diverse relational, cultural and socio-political contexts. The specific focus is on (1) the types of research problems concerning human suffering and healing that necessitate adopting this methodology, (2) the nature of the research space that may make the interviews or research interactions a humanizing experience for the participants, and (3) the process of analysis (particularly focused coding and the use of abductive reasoning) that may help develop insights about such experiences.

To pursue a systematic inquiry of the above-mentioned goals, I have made use of the details of and reflections on the methodological procedures (ambiguities, questions and insights related to formulating research problems, data collection and analysis) of my CGT studies[1] of the experiences of suffering and healing among the survivors affected by an earthquake that hit Kachchh district in Gujarat in 2001, communal violence that occurred near Godhra, Gujarat, in 2002, and political violence that affected the villagers of Nandigram from 2007 to 2009, who were non-violently resisting their eviction from their own land forced upon them by the state of West Bengal (Priya, 2004, 2010, 2011, 2012a, 2015b; Viswambharan & Priya, 2016). Besides, such methodological details or reflections from other CGT studies on suffering and healing were also reviewed. These studies primarily utilized CGT methodology as per some basic texts on the methodology, such as the ones authored by Charmaz (1995, 2006, 2014). Some studies combined the use of CGT as laid out by Charmaz with the methodological procedures found in the works of other grounded theory scholars, such as Chamberlain (1999), Clarke (2005), Glaser and Strauss (1967), Henwood and Pidgeon (2003) or Strauss and Corbin (1998). These studies were included on the premise as per Charmaz (2008a) that:

> Effective use of the grounded theory method depends on adopting several of Glaser and Strauss's (1967; Glaser, 1978; Strauss, 1987) early grounded theory guidelines—with 21st-century caveats. Adopting comparative, interactive analytic strategies in coding, memo-writing, theoretical sampling, sorting, and integrating the analysis is only part of the grounded theorist's task. In keeping with constructivist premises, researchers must also (1) entertain a range of theoretical possibilities and (2) examine their own epistemological premises and research principles and practices. (p. 163)

For example, in a CGT study conducted by Mabhala (2013) to explore the pedagogical knowledge of nurse educators in order to better address health inequalities in the UK, the author combined the use of methodologies by Charmaz (2000, 2006) with Glaser and Strauss (1967), Strauss and Corbin (1990, 1998) for data collection and analysis, but the overall design of the study was guided by CGT premises about the methodology. The reason the author gives is as follows:

> One aspect of this research consistent with constructivist grounded theory was its fundamental ontological assumption of multiple realities…, constructed through the experience and understanding of different participants' perspectives, and generated from their different academic, social, cultural and political backgrounds. Another was its epistemological belief that public health knowledge is shaped by the cultural, historical, political and social norms that operate within that context and time. (Mabhala, 2013, p. 2)

Based on the review of methodological assumptions and procedures in these CGT studies, as well as my reflections on the use of CGT in my own research on disaster survivors, I have organized this chapter in sections highlighting (a) the kind of research problems pertaining to suffering and healing that would entail the use of CGT, (b) data collection as a co-construction (of meanings) through a research relationship based on care and compassion, and (c) data analysis as a reflexive, systematic and creative process. However, let us begin with a pertinent and broad question about the suitability of CGT for the study of suffering and healing in the domain of social studies of health.

WHY A CONSTRUCTIVIST GROUNDED THEORY APPROACH TO SUFFERING AND HEALING?

A paradigm shift in the social studies of health entails not only focusing on the symptoms of a disease or a disorder, but an exploration of the experiences of suffering and healing. As suffering (intense distress arising out of a threat to the coherence of selfhood) and healing (reformulation of selfhood by developing an enabling meaning in life through cultural beliefs or symbols and having space for one's voice) situate the person's experience within prevailing cultural and socio-political context, it demands that a researcher adopts a new paradigm, such as social constructionism (Cassell, 2004, 2013; Charmaz, 1999, 2002, Kleinman, Das, & Locke, 1998a, 1998b). This position allows a researcher to learn from the participants about their experiences or worldview as shaped within their relational, cultural or socio-political context. For example, in my CGT study of the survivors or political violence in Nandigram, India, rather than being distressed due to the symptoms of post-traumatic stress disorder or PTSD (such as re-experiencing and numbness, which constitute a major psychiatric disorder after one is exposed to traumatic events like violence), survivors' intense distress or suffering was related to a serious disruption in the relational and political aspects of their everyday life (Priya, 2015b). One category of such suffering was 'betrayed self'. Its definition and sub-categories were as follows:

> *Betrayed self*: Feeling extremely distressed about the breaking of trust and harm caused by people who were trusted by the sufferer.
>
> a *An intense feeling of being betrayed by fellow villagers*: Distress associated with trust broken by and harm caused by the fellow villagers.
>
> b *An intense feeling of being betrayed by the state government*: Distress associated with the trust broken by the state government that had promised to listen to the villagers' voice. (Priya, 2015b, p. 425)

A 24-year-old participant, Ramesh, whose father had gone 'missing' in violence, shared his experiences related to his sense of betrayal:

> Betrayed Self
> He shared his anguish over the betrayal of trust by the state government,
> 'The biggest cheating was done by the state government as it proclaimed that it cared for farmers but it began to kill us.'
> He also narrated how he suffered as his own villagers broke the trust and the relationship shared with the community,
> 'The people who were threatening me of abduction are still living in this village. They have not left their homes. After my father was abducted, they were telling me, "We will abduct you too. We will cut you into pieces, pack you in a box and throw it in the river".' (Priya, 2015b, p. 436)

CGT AS A 'NEW' PARADIGM INQUIRY FOR SUFFERING AND HEALING

What follows from the above is that for the study of suffering and healing, a critical understanding of the prevailing socio-political context, the process of interviewing (in which the researcher is a trustworthy and compassionate or empathic listener) and data analysis (where the researcher is critically aware of and is open to modify the extant theory associated with the phenomenon under study) is warranted. It entails that the researcher be reflexive about his or her experiential as well as theoretical standpoints, rather than claiming objectivity and value-neutrality. This paradigm shift in the approach to inquiry constitutes a 'new' paradigm of inquiry.

A 'new' paradigm of inquiry, according to Guba and Lincoln (2005), includes critical theory and participatory inquiry paradigms, besides social constructionism. As Lincoln (1995) has elaborated, new paradigms are committed: 'first, to new and emergent relations with respondents; second, to a set of stances – professional, personal, and political – toward the uses of inquiry and toward its ability to foster action; and finally, to a vision of research that enables and promotes social justice, community, diversity, civic discourse, and caring' (pp. 277–278). Based on the readings of the scholars who have made seminal contributions in advancing the knowledge of social constructionist paradigm (Cisneros-Puebla, 2008; Gergen, 1973, 1985, 1994, 1997, 2009; Misra & Gergen, 1993; Sampson, 1993), I have outlined its basic postulates as:

1 questioning or deconstructing the realist ontological claims that reality exists independent of the observer and universal and decontextualized theories represent its discovery through induction,
2 reality is constructed through socio-historically situated interchanges amongst people,
3 the primary function of a talk or social interaction is to initiate or regulate some social action rather than to represent a discourse-independent reality, and
4 understanding about human experiences may be co-constructed through dialogic partnership between a researcher and a participant where the worldview of none is privileged over the other. (Priya, 2012b, p. 213)

As I have noted, the social constructionist paradigm could provide meaningful conceptual windows to explore suffering and healing by considering: 'deconstructing realist ontological claims of biomedicine and analyzing how such claims may enhance human suffering', 'human suffering and healing as socio-historically contextualized phenomena', 'suffering and healing as a performance constituted in the interactions of healers, doctors or researchers with the sufferer', and 'research on suffering and healing through dialogic partnership between a researcher and a participant' (Priya, 2012b). A dialogic partnership entails that the standpoints or stories of neither the researcher nor the participant is privileged over the other as the research dialogue is taken as a site of co-construction of meanings (Sampson, 1993).[2]

Although it is beyond the scope of this chapter to deliberate in detail on the conceptualization of suffering and healing in health sciences, a brief description of the differences between the experiences and expressions of suffering is necessitated to appreciate how CGT can be applied to explore these aspects of human experience.

SUFFERING AND HEALING: PERSPECTIVES ON EXPERIENCING AND EXPRESSING

Cassell's (2004) depiction of the following cancer patient presents an example of the *expression* of lived experience of suffering a threat to a sense of coherent meaning about herself:

> A thirty-five-year-old sculptor with cancer of the breast that had spread widely was treated by competent physicians employing advanced knowledge and technology and acting out of kindness and true concern. ... After her ovaries were removed and a regimen of medications that were masculinizing, she became obese, grew facial and body hair of a male type, and her libido disappeared. When tumor invaded the nerves near her shoulder, she lost strength in the hand she used in sculpting and became profoundly depressed. ... Each tomorrow was seen as worse than today, as heralding increased sickness, pain, or disability—never as the beginning of better times. Despite the distress caused by such thoughts, she could not think otherwise. She felt isolated because she was not like other people and could not do what other people did. She feared that her friends would stop visiting her. (pp. 29–30)

Clearly, she not only suffered due to physical pain of having the disease and the treatment for that, but her suffering was also about the potential disruptions that could be caused to various aspects of her life 'that were social and others that were personal and private' (p. 30). In a similar vein, Bracken, Giller and Summerfield (1995), in their study of civil war in Uganda in the 1980s, often found the presence of symptoms of PTSD among the survivors; however, the authors found them to be more concerned about potential disruptions to their relational world. For example, they interviewed a female survivor of sexual assault during the civil war whose intense distress was related to the denial of a dignified life or the right to nurture her children due to the patriarchal norms:

> A 34-year-old woman with five children had been rejected by her husband because of the fact that she had been raped by two soldiers five years prior to her interview with us. He had turned her off the small holding which she had cultivated. ... Five years later she was still suffering terrible grief over the loss of her children and had had no other relationship during that period. The lack of support because of social attitudes towards rape and the political position of women at that time in Uganda prevented her from asserting any rights she may have had regarding the custody of her younger children. (Bracken, Giller, & Summerfield, 1995, p. 1079)

In both examples given above, the disruptions to social, personal and private aspects of the person's life led to intense distress, whether it emerges from a disease and its treatment or a socio-politically induced assault on one's body and self.

Unarticulated Experience of Suffering

In their decades' long engagement in the study of human suffering, social scientists, such as Charmaz (1999, 2002), Radley (2004), and Frank (2001) have realized and strongly advocated the need to distinguish between the memories of suffering and the lived experiences of suffering in the current time. Charmaz (1999) posits, 'Talking about events that indicate past suffering is one thing; identifying self as continually suffering is quite another' (p. 366). While going through intensely distressing life events, as Radley (2004) reflects, people's suffering may not have any 'intrinsic form' (p. 35), as they 'may find it impossible to convey what engulfs them' (p. 34). Charmaz (2002) cautions researchers of suffering against being in a hurry to get the person's lived experience of distress communicated to them,

> Imposing a narrative frame on research participants' experience may mask rather than illuminate its meanings, particularly those of suffering. From a participant's perspective, the raw experience of suffering may fit neither narrative logic nor the comprehensible content of a story.[3] (p. 303)

These authors indicate that it may take a considerable time before a person may want to share the memories of experiences of suffering, provided he or she has developed trust in the listener. However, they also contend that even when the person is overwhelmed with suffering, there is a possibility of making sense of what he or she might be going through with the help of the empathy or compassion. Radley (2004) posits that suffering may be

> ...mute but need not be silent, and that compassionate responses (even if they do not issue in action) involve acts of imagination that depend upon being able to empathise in ways that are not always under rational control. (p. 39)

The challenge before social scientists has been to explore (through listening to and empathizing with) human distress resulting from disruptions to aspects of selfhood that may not always be verbalized as it may remain unarticulated owing to the overwhelming intensity of suffering. As Charmaz (2005, 2017a, 2017b,) has indicated, qualitative research approaches, such as CGT, may help develop a meaningful understanding of such experiences, which are apparently elusive yet important for a sufferer's sense of wellbeing as well as social justice.

As this chapter aims to provide a detailed and nuanced understanding of how the CGT approach forms a suitable framework for research on suffering and healing, let us begin with the nature of research problems that may suit this approach.

FORMULATING RESEARCH PROBLEMS: THE CENTRALITY OF CONTEXT

A researcher's sensitivity towards the paradigmatic assumptions about his or her research as well as the aforementioned conception of suffering and healing may help him or her recognize the relational, cultural and socio-political contexts that are pivotal in shaping such experiences. Let us first look at how adopting the ontological position of the social constructionist paradigm (that informs CGT) facilitates the researcher's critical awareness of the socio-political context within which the experiences of the sufferer need to be located.

Discerning the Socio-political Context of Experience

In CGT studies, as the researcher is sensitized about the social and political hierarchies or the conditions of inequality and injustice that often shape human experiences such as suffering, he or she faces the question of how to be aware of and incorporate such a context. There are two major ways in which a CGT researcher discerns the socio-political settings that shape human life: (a) analyzing the information from available literature on the subject, and (b) being reflexive about the extent to which both the researcher himself or herself as well as participants experience the everyday realities (e.g., the neighbourhood, community, institutions, local or national/state governance of which they are stakeholders) to be safe or unsafe, comforting or discomforting, and fairly predictable or uncertain. The former (i.e., analyzing) usually begins before entering into the field, while the latter (reflecting) is a continual process throughout the duration of research.

In my CGT studies of violence in India, I have utilized the information available in reports based on surveys or interviews conducted by NGOs, researchers, or a tribunal (Priya, 2012b, 2015b; Viswambharan & Priya, 2016). For example, in my study of the post-Godhra riots in Gujarat, I utilized the report by a researcher from an NGO about the living conditions of the survivors, thousands of whom have been displaced from their native place, besides the state's inadequate response to ensure their safety and security (Priya, 2012b). Also, in my study of political violence in Nandigram, West Bengal state, the killing or torture inflicted on the villagers by the state police or the cadres of the ruling political party was reported in a book based on a tribunal hearing the atrocities faced by the survivors. More importantly, however, it was my reflections on fear about my own safety and life that made me aware of, and relate to, survivors' narratives about the hostile political climate, uncertainties about the safety and security of the villagers and the 'community' divide on ideological grounds that had surfaced during the years of political violence (Priya, 2015b):

> During the fieldwork, I often feared the loss of my own life and being tortured as I thought that I too could be the target of the perpetrators of violence for being seen as a sympathizer of villagers' movement. These feelings were coming to me when the village was relatively 'quiet' after the Panchayat and Lok Sabha polls of May 2008 and April 2009, respectively, in which CPI(M) lost most of its seats in Nandigram. This was my first clue about the trauma people at the village or in Nandigram, in general, might have undergone since January 2007. The positive contribution of my fear was that it could help me empathize to some extent with farmers' consistent fear and agony of constant threat to life and dignity that they had been [sic] going through for months together. (pp. 432–433)

Similarly, Kruger and Lourens (2016) formulated the major research problem in their CGT study, that is, to explore the subjective experience of 'emotional distress' of those non-White South African women of lower socio-economic strata who were diagnosed with major depressive disorder (p. 124). The rationale to explore emotional distress stemmed from their previous study on the same population, which suggested that their inability to prevent their children from starving was an important factor that led to their depressed state, and a review of literature, which highlighted that 'the mechanisms by which the cycle of poverty and mental health is maintained are complex and multi-dimensional and should be further investigated' (p. 125). They also noted that the semi-rural community of Western Cape Province to which these women belonged was a hub of several 'social problems including poverty, violence, crime, substance abuse, occupational hazards, accidents, health problems, and relationship problems' (p. 127). Some basic questions (related to the socio-economic and political context of these women) that formed the foundation of their research problem were:

- Did the symptoms of major depressive disorders alone constitute the women's lived experience of emotional distress?
- If not, what were other aspects of such an experience?
- Was their experience of emotional distress merely a pathological individual condition or was it a psychological manifestation of the affliction caused by poverty and gender roles in the context of the neoliberal economic context of South Africa?
- Did the diagnostic category serve as a tool for the state to conceal the ill effects of neoliberal economic policy on the impoverished women?

These basic probes about the socio-political context of emotional distress of women informed their CGT inquiry and helped discern how it is 'the powerful gender and neo-liberal discourses within which mothers are interpellated to care for children, and more specifically, to ensure that children are not hungry. If mothers fail at doing this, they are thought not to be fulfilling their responsibility' (Kruger & Lourens, 2016, p. 138).[4]

Incorporating the Cultural Context of Experience

The two important ways in which cultural context has been incorporated in the research problems pertaining to suffering and healing have been to develop an understanding of (a) shared meanings of health, illness and recovery within the community that the participants are members of, and (b) nature of participants' socio-moral roles (prescribed within their cultural group) that are associated with suffering and healing.

An example of the former is my study (Priya, 2010, 2011) in which, before gaining some insights about an earthquake survivors' experiences of suffering and healing in rural Kachchh, India, I interviewed the local priests, social activists and journalists of the region to understand the culturally shared meanings of health, natural calamity and recovery. The shared belief[5] in *karma* (carrying out one's internalized duty towards self, family, community and nature) came up as a central theme that was associated with survivors' suffering and healing (Priya, 2010, p. 485). One of the highly respected priests in the village shared the following:

> According to me, the earthquake occurs because gases get accumulated inside the earth and it has to come out due to pressure. But the gases get accumulated inside the earth due to the result of our *karma* [one's duty towards oneself, family, community and nature]. Tell me, who saved us [pointing towards himself and Amrit Bhai, the interpreter] from the earthquake? It was nothing but our *karma*. If people lead their lives according to *dharma* [principals of virtue] – and by *dharma*, I mean *mānava dharma* [humane religion], which is above all caste, religion and community – they will achieve *ānand* [joy]. If they don't do it, they will suffer. (Priya, 2011, p. 214)

These narratives about the cultural belief in *karma* clearly indicate its linkage with fostering certain socio-moral roles of adhering to righteous or humanitarian values in the rural setting of Kachchh. Recent studies have incorporated the critical understanding of the cultural context in their research focus while studying suffering and healing by primarily examining the socio-moral roles one is generally expected to carry out (towards oneself and others) by virtue of being brought up or socialized into a cultural group. Such a focus has been part of studies on survivors of disasters, besides the patients with physical ailments and psychiatric disorders (Allen, Oyebode & Allen, 2009; Bocchieri, Meana, & Fisher, 2002; Brown et al., 2012; Eastwood, Kemp, & Jalaluddin, 2015; Galvin, 2004; Hackett, Godfrey, & Bennett, 2016; Kehler et al., 2008; Priya, 2010, 2012b, 2015, 2018; Ravindran, Rempel, & Ogilvie, 2013a, 2013b; Takai, Yamamoto-Mitani, & Chiba, 2016).

As noted above, the understating of such socio-political and cultural contexts of experience are gathered through a review of relevant literature besides research interactions with participants. Let us now explore how the research interaction that is comprised of negotiations of shared meanings or co-construction facilitates understanding the phenomenon of suffering and healing within their socio-political and cultural contexts.

CO-CONSTRUCTING QUALITATIVE DATA: INTERVIEWING AS A CREATION OF HUMANIZING SPACE

While considering a qualitative inquiry on the experiences of suffering, Frank (2000) and Ellingson (1998) have accentuated that the primary need of a sufferer is to find a voice or an empathic listener in the research space rather than interacting with a researcher, who has the primary task of just *completing* data collection. Again, CGT, taking a departure from traditional approaches to GT, lays emphasis on reaching closer to human experience by entering into the experiential world of the participants through compassion and negotiations of shared meanings. Elaborating on the process of interviewing in the social constructionist paradigm, Charmaz (2014) highlights the need for such a paradigm shift in the study of human experiences:

> What participants do not say can be as telling as what they do say. A constructivist perspective differs from conceptions of the interview as either a mirror of reality or a mere account served up to answer a question. A constructivist approach views interviews as emergent interactions in which social bonds may develop. Hence this approach attends to mutuality during the course of interview and ways to build that mutuality. … [I]t is a site of exploration, emergent understandings, legitimation of identity, and validation of experience. (p. 91)

What are the challenges in creating such a research space for the researcher–participant dyad in a CGT study of suffering and healing? Does the researcher go through a feeling of guilt that the participant's painful memories have been touched? Does he or she face the ethical dilemma of whether to continue with research when the participant feels overwhelmed while narrating distressing moments of life? Like any other researcher of suffering, these questions were real for me during the study of suffering and healing of survivors of an earthquake that struck Kachchh, India, in 2001. In a specific interview setting with Nirmala Ben, a widow whose husband died in the earthquake, I faced a tough situation when she choked while interacting with me. Sitting before her while she was overpowered by emotions relating to the loss of her husband, I was clueless as several thoughts surrounded me:

> These minutes of silence posed to me some serious questions about my role as a researcher. Was it ethical to interact with her when there was a risk of her feeling disturbed about the traumatic incident? My gut feeling told me to just be existentially with the person (Kleinman, 1988a) and hope for some more communication that might help her feel better, but the minutes of silence did not seem to be coming to an end. (Priya, 2010, p. 485)

Fortunately, the fieldwork allowed me to meet Nirmala Ben multiple times, and I could derive a sense of satisfaction over the fact that in my subsequent meetings and interviews with her, she was more comfortable about talking to me. Since I conducted three phases of fieldwork with about a one-year gap between two sequential phases, I could also observe the changes over time in her healing process. One of the reasons for her 'moving on' with life was her resolve to live her life through her belief in *karma*, that is, to carry out her duties towards self, family, community and nature. I could observe this change in her in Phase II of the fieldwork: 'She had become more active and social as she called us to a *satsang* (collective activity in which a priest delivers sermons) organized by her at her residence' (Priya, 2010, p. 486). Upon asking her about this positive approach to life, Nirmala Ben said:

> My two nephews stay with me. Sending them to school, looking after them, offering my services at the ashram of Mansingh Das Baba [a Hindu priest of the village], and doing satsang there keeps me engaged the entire day. My work, satsang, and devotion to God are everything for me. (Priya, 2010, p. 486)

As this positive research relationship was unfolding over a period of time, my guilt about scratching her emotional wound in our first meeting started to diminish. However, out of my concern for not re-evoking the emotional pain, I could not ask Nirmala Ben whether she felt distressed due to my initiating an interaction with her (about her then life condition) in our first meeting, until I had reached the end of my final phase of fieldwork. She replied:

> '*Tame prem thi puchu chho, tyare bikh nathi laagto*' ('You interact with compassion; therefore, I do not feel sad talking to you about the incident'). ... While taking leave from her when I said that I wished to come back to the village again and meet the villagers, she answered back with a smile and energy in her voice, '*Tamne avavuj padshe*' ('You shall have to come'). This, to me, was an indication of a genuine relationship I had been able to develop with her. I did meet her in an informal visit in January 2005, and Sudhakar Bhai continued telling me over the telephone about her welfare. (Priya, 2010, p. 486)

As Kleinman (1988a), Radley (2004), Frank (2000) and Charmaz (2014) have noted, in a social constructionist approach to research, our attempts to be compassionate with the sufferer and being reflexive about the interview processes often make the research space a humanizing experience for the participant. In a CGT study, creating such a research space facilitates further exploration of context and experiences of the participant.

ANALYZING QUALITATIVE DATA OF SUFFERING AND HEALING

Charmaz (1995, 2000, 2006, 2014) has illustrated how, by adopting a constructivist approach to grounded theory, a researcher may use the processes of coding, constant comparison, memo writing, and theoretical sampling and theoretical saturation to unravel the nuances of human experiences or worldviews within their relational, cultural and socio-political contexts. Since the experiences of suffering and healing can be intense for the participants (often not articulable or verbally expressible) and a study of that necessitates a research relationship based on compassion and trust, the analysis or coding process needs to foreground the role of empathy (besides checking or reflexively handling researcher's bias) and creative explorations of insights intuitively arrived at. Therefore, two aspects of CGT procedures may require greater attention: focused coding and use of abductive reasoning. As Charmaz (2006, 2014) has illustrated, these procedures require the researcher to pay attention to implicit data (pauses, silences or emphasis through detailed description or a surprising turn in the plot of storytelling) as well the explicit data in the form of expressed experiences. Also, as Priya (2010, 2015b) has pointed out, CGT researchers may get 'affected' by the shared experiences of the participants, and also have intuitions about an aspect of the lived but unexplored realities of participants' lives. Being reflexive as well as memo writing help the CGT researchers to explore such intuitions further.

Focused Coding

Focused coding undertakes the question about 'which initial codes make the most analytic sense to categorize your data incisively and completely' (Charmaz, 2006, p. 58). The published CGT research on suffering and healing indicate that the following processes may help researchers decide which initial codes can be raised to focused codes (these may not be exclusive or exhaustive of the processes and may often be overlapping or combined together in decision making):

- Empathic connection with the participant
- Participant's verbal or non-verbal emphasis
- Experience related to critical life events.

Empathic connection with the participant

For the researcher, the research interaction with the participant often involves a relationship of trust and compassion. Reflexivity may help the researcher not only become critically aware of his or her theoretical and personal bias or standpoints, but also realize the empathic connection with the participant. As I could observe in my study of the survivors of disasters (Priya, 2010, 2015b), my empathizing with the participant could help in the process of focused coding.

In my study of the earthquake survivors of Kachchh, India, during an interview with a widow, Nirmala Ben (her husband died in the earthquake and they had no children), I observed that it was difficult for her to share much about her experiences as she was overpowered by the sense of loss:

> I remember sitting in Nirmala Ben's house along with her brother-in-law and Sudhakar Bhai [key informant]. I tried to initiate interaction with her by asking about her general daily routine at the current time. After a silence of about 2 minutes, she slowly uttered a sentence, '*kain … kain karun chhun*' ('Something … I do something'). Then tears came to her eyes and neither she nor I spoke for about 10 minutes. (Priya, 2010, p. 485)

While grappling with the ethical question of whether or not I should go to meet her again during the fieldwork (as I was guilty of making her reflect on her life and feel the agony of loss), I reflected:

> The intensity and nature of pain contained in that one sentence from Nirmala Ben was much greater than any intensity of pain I have ever faced. I confess that it was extremely difficult for me to empathize with the agony she was undergoing. Her sorrow and silence made me once again feel the sorrow and loneliness that I had felt when my mother was seriously ill (and had to be hospitalized in a different town) after the death of my eldest brother in 1982. I was 5 or 6 years old then. I, along with my elder brother and sister, was sent to my maternal grandmother's house. Every now and then, we used to be horrified by the news that my mother's condition was critical. We were told that she might not stay alive. It was strange and difficult to even imagine it. It took my mother almost a year to recover from meningitis, and another year to completely recover from the partial loss of memory resulting from the disease and its treatment. I do not remember myself crying at that time, but I can still feel the loneliness and peculiar sense of meaninglessness associated with that time. … This interaction with Nirmala Ben made me realize the 'littleness' of my suffering in life. (Priya, 2010, p. 492)

I could connect with Nirmala Ben's sense of loss and how that could overpower her while narrating it before anyone. This empathic connection gave me more confidence in raising the initial code, '*Getting overwhelmed while verbalizing suffering*' as a focused code with the definition: Getting overpowered by intense and incomprehensible feelings while attempting to narrate them before a listener (Priya, 2010, p. 484).

Participant's verbal or non-verbal emphasis

As Charmaz (2006) observed, interviews in the constructivist mode facilitate the process of participants taking the interaction in directions that may be relevant for their current life situation. Also, participants' sharing about suffering and healing may be marked by the emphasis they give to certain experience of theirs. The intonation, pause, silence and the *intensity* of voice matter. For example, while analyzing a documentary on violence to study survivors' suffering, Visambharan and Priya (2016) observed how a mother, whose son and daughter died in the post-Godhra communal riots in India, felt overwhelmed and marked by a sense of meaninglessness and helplessness:

> That's my son as a kid and that's Tara [her daughter; indicating towards a family photograph]. My son's pants were taken off before Bhanu and his son hurled him into the fire. They stabbed me but the dagger fell off. My son said, 'Mummy, run away before they kill you.' He was burning ... still he was thinking of me, not himself [sobs]. *Only I know how I live.* ... My heart is filled with despair. Women who tried to escape the fire were raped. Some clamped their mouth, some took off their clothes. Shanu, standing next to me was pregnant. Her womb was split open. The fetus impaled on a sword! (Visambharan & Priya, 2016, p. 52, emphasis added)

The relevance of this narrative as an experience of suffering in the context of the untimely death of a family member in the communal violence assumed more value in the light of the emphasis given by the participant. This helped us raise the initial code 'overwhelmed by losses' as a focused code with this definition: sharing the experiences of meaninglessness in current life because of losses and of helplessness when faced with barbaric acts (often accompanied by emotional expressions of sobbing or crying) (Visambharan & Priya, 2016, p. 51).

Experience related to critical life events

The study by Kruger and Lourens (2016) on 'emotional distress' of non-White South African women of lower socio-economic strata who were diagnosed with major depressive disorder indicated a pattern in the narratives. For some of the participants, there came a phase in their lives when the burden of responsibility (solely on themselves and not their husband) for feeding the hungry children as a parent brought them to an emotional breaking point. Such patterns in the CGT study of suffering and healing may be indicative of the fact that an initial code denoting such a change in the experience of participants would help explain aspects of suffering. Such a focused code and final category in their study was 'Anomie: "I Don't Know What to do Anymore"'. They pointed out about this category:

> Feeling despondent about their unbearable circumstances was also a prominent emotional response to children's hunger:
> Leila: And these are things that I cannot handle ... but unfortunately I am just a human being, and I can't carry everybody's things {sobbing} (...) I sometimes don't know whatto, I don't know what to do anymore. {sobbing} (...) With my situation, my circumstances. (Kruger & Lourens, 2016, p. 135)

As the authors indicate, the women's experience of entering a phase of life due to cumulative distress out of the burden of responsibility owing to asymmetrical gender roles in the household assumed importance as an experience related to a critical phase in life. This apparently facilitated focused coding for the authors.

Use of Abductive Reasoning

Charmaz (2014, 2017a) has pointed out the role of re-examining intuitions about data with possible explanations. The researcher begins with certain research objectives that pivotally guide the process of data collection and analysis. However, during this process, the researcher may come across some questions or intuitions related to the area of research or the experiences of participants (but apparently beyond the scope of current research problems). The researcher can return to an analysis of the same data to address these questions and intuitions. This is referred to as the use of abductive reasoning in CGT. The subjective experiences of suffering and healing shared by the participants often become open to meaningful interpretation to address the emerging intuitions and questions. For example, as I noted during my study of the experiences of suffering and healing among the survivors of an earthquake in India (Priya, 2010), the nature of participants' narratives as well as the process of interview were giving rise to some intuition about the healing process:

> As the work progressed I became aware that my research relationship with participants was providing an experiential space for their remoralization. Therefore, for the purpose of the present study, I decided to interrogate data for insights into the nature of my role and relationship over the 3-year course of the research, and to specifically explore how empathic witnessing by a researcher might create within the researcher–participant relationship a space for remoralization of the participants. (Priya, 2010, p. 481)

This new direction in analyzing the already collected data led to some meaningful insights into the process of healing of the participant (and of the researcher, possibly) facilitated by the research relationship. Some important categories that I could develop using abductive reasoning were: 'getting overwhelmed while verbalizing suffering, search for the cultural meaning of the research relationship, piecing together of self, reaffirmation of moral status, and continuing bond revalidating the self' (Priya, 2010, pp. 484–485).

CONCLUDING COMMENTS

In this chapter, I have attempted to illustrate how the constructionist version of grounded theory practised and popularized by Kathy Charmaz has offered a qualitative researcher, who adopt this methodology, meaningful and systematic ways to provide space for, and reach out to participants' experiences or voice within their relational, cultural or socio-political context. This contrasts with earlier positivist and post-positivist versions of GT that, rather than engaging with the participants in co-construction of meanings or their lived realities, hastens the researcher into abstractions that often mutes participants' perspectives due to the guiding principles of objectivity. As this chapter has indicated through an illustration of the application of CGT in the study of the experiences and expressions of suffering and healing, it may help researchers develop a critical understanding of the socio-political and cultural context of the experience, negotiations or co-construction of meanings in research interactions, and the analysis process that includes abductive reasoning. However, what becomes amply clear from the constructivist turn in grounded theory is the much-needed re-emphasis in the process of data collection and analysis on compassion and empathy for the research participant, particularly those who have been denied voice or dignity owing to either illness or challenging circumstances in life.

There seems to be an upsurge among social science researchers as far as realizing the suitability of the CGT approach in conducting studies that may stimulate academic and social action towards social justice. Getting inspired by the works of Charmaz (2003, 2008b), Mathews and Salazar (2014) affirmed,

> Social justice inquiry seeks to further justice and ameliorate injustice by studying hierarchies and inequities in relationships … [A] constructivist, social justice, grounded theory approach helps to determine how participants have constructed their world, along with considering hierarchies and relationships within that world… (p. 190)

As Charmaz (2017a, 2017b) posits, the contructivist turn in grounded theory is not just about the new ontological, epistemological and methodological orientation, but, most importantly, the axiological (the purpose the research serves towards welfare or growth of the research participants) and ideological shifts. She reminds the researchers that this shift must make us critically aware of the potential of social justice that our CGT studies carry for the research participants and the general populace. More than a decade ago, Charmaz (2004) had made a similar appeal to qualitative researchers:

> Choose topics that ignite your passion. If need be, dispute negative decisions from your institutional committees. Do something that makes a difference in the world. Then enter the phenomenon and open yourself to the research experience. Face the inevitable ambiguities. Flow with the existential dislocation of bewilderment. Bring passion, curiosity, and care to your work. In the end, you will transform our images of studied life, and your research journey will transform you. (p. 991)

In today's world, when capitalist forces have become perhaps the strongest and the most divisive ever in the guise of neoliberal discourse, Charmaz (2017a) re-emphasizes the need for compassion and empathy (besides critical thinking and reflexivity for furthuring the social justice agenda of research) that 'our lives blend with those of our participants' (p. 41). As she explicates, 'Constructivist grounded theory propels our thinking forward in unanticipated ways and subsequently sparks new understandings of *experiencing* and *redressing* injustice' (p. 42, emphasis added).

Notes

1 In all these studies (excluding Viswambharan & Priya, 2016), I used a combination of ethnographic and CGT approaches. Such a combination helps getting sensitized about the context of study, as Charmaz (2006) posits, 'concentrating on a basic social process can help you to gain a more complete picture of the *whole* setting' rather than describing the setting that is taken up in the traditional ethnography (p. 23). Also, a CGT approach that focuses on exploring experiences within a cultural and socio-political context also provides constructivist ontological and epistemological orientation to the ethnographic fieldwork (Charmaz, 2006, 2014). This combination of methodologies facilitated generating field notes and narratives of the survivors that depicted their everyday life within the post-disaster socio-political context.

2 Several eminent researchers in the fields of medicine and social science have recognized, adopted and advocated the salience of social constructionist paradigm, with its methodology rooted in such a dialogic partnership, in the study of suffering and healing processes. Eric J. Cassell (2004, 2013) in the field of medicine, Arthur Kleinman (1973, 1987, 1988a, 1988b) and Laurence J. Kirmayer (1989, 2004) in the field of cross-cultural psychiatry, and Kathy Charmaz (1999, 2002), Alan Radley (2004) and Arthur Frank (2000, 2001) among other scholars in the field of interdisciplinary social science

have contributed to the progress in the study of suffering and healing experiences using social constructionist paradigm.

3 While in the phase of being overwhelmed by the impact of the event (illness or other debilitating life events), the meaning of their experiences may not only be silenced, but also paradoxically eulogized. As Charmaz (2002) puts it, in contrast with the experience of the sufferer, 'lay persons and scholars alike valorize stories and storytellers' (p. 303). Citing Levinas (1988) and Charmaz (1999), Radley (2004) also observed the tendency of the lay persons or social scientists to legitimize 'the moral demands that are made upon the sick to bear up in the face of illness' (p. 36). More realistically, as Levinas (1988) and Radley (2004) have maintained for such experiences of being overwhelmed that 'intrinsically, suffering is 'for nothing'; it is useless' (p. 36).

4 Similar to the study by Kruger and Lourens (2016), other researchers adopting CGT approach in their research on suffering and healing have carefully incorporated the socio-political context in their research problems featuring professional or community-based care for illness (Brüggenmann & Swahnberg, 2013; Dastjerdi, Olson, & Ogilvie, 2012; Eastwood, Kemp, & Jalaluddin, 2015; Festen et al., 2014; O'Brien, Davis, Strike, Young, & Bayoumi, 2009; Patel, Wittkowsky, Fox, & Wieck, 2013; Pitaloke & Hsieh, 2015; Thurston et al., 2014; Wolf et al., 2014). In these studies, the context of hierarchy (that may often lead to exclusion, ridicule, stigmatization and discrimination) within institutionalized care and community care settings is centred on how the beliefs, values and practices of the patients or family caregivers are subjugated by those of either the medical professionals (and policies governing institutionalized care) or community or family members (often through the patriarchal norms). Importantly, in the domain of the institutionalized care, studies have been inclusive of the context of justice and empowerment too. The context of justice and empowerment in these settings has been focused on the extent to which participants narratives denote health professionals' concern to provide space for the end-users' values and beliefs about seeking and utilizing health care (Bennett, Reyes-Roudriguez, Altamar, & Soulsby, 2016; Mabhala, 2013; McCalman, 2013).

5 Such efforts to develop a close understanding of the cultural beliefs or values that aid the process of healing have been evident in the CGT studies by Meeker, Waldrop, Schneider and Case (2014), Pitaloka and Hsieh (2015), Kodwo-Nyameazea and Nguyen (2008), Takai, Yamamoto-Mitani and Chiba (2016), and Bentur, Stark, Resnizky and Symon (2014).

REFERENCES

Allen, J., Oyebode, J. R., & Allen, J. (2009). Having a father with young onset of dementia. *Dementia*, *8*(4), 455–480. doi: 10.1177/1471301209349106

Bennett, K. M., Reyes-Roudriguez, M. F., Altamar, P., & Soulsby, L. K. (2016). Resilience amongst older Columbians living in poverty: An ecological approach. *Journal of Cross-Cultural Gerontology*, *31*, 385–407. doi: 10.1007/s10823-016-9303-3

Bentur, N., Stark, D. Y., Resnizky, S., & Symon, Z. (2014). Coping strategies for existential and spiritual suffering in Israeli patients with advanced cancer. *Israel Journal of Health Policy Research*, *3*, 21. Retrieved from www.ijhpr.org/content/3/1/21

Bocchieri, L. E., Meana, M., & Fisher, B. L. (2002). Perceived psychosocial outcomes of gastric bypass surgery: A qualitative study. *Obesity Surgery*, *12*, 781–788.

Bracken, P., Giller, J. E., & Summerfield, D. (1995). Psychological responses to war and atrocity: The limitations of current concepts. *Social Science and Medicine*, *40*, 1073–1082.

Brown, A., Scales, U., Beever, W., Rickards, B., Rowly, K., & O'Dea, K. (2012). Exploring the expression of depression and distress in aboriginal men in Central Australia: A qualitative study. *BMC Psychiatry*, *12*, 97. Retrieved from www.biomedcentral.com/1471-224X/12/97

Brüggenmann, A. J., & Swahnberg, K. (2013). What contributes to abuse in health care? A grounded theory of female patients' stories. *International Journal of Nursing Studies*, *50*, 404–412.

Cassell, E. J. (2004). *The nature of suffering and the goals of medicine* (2nd ed.). New York: Oxford University Press.

Cassell, E. J. (2013). *The nature of healing: The modern practice of medicine*. New York: Oxford University Press.

Chamberlain, K. (1999). Using grounded theory in health psychology: Practices, premises, and potential. In M. Murray & K. Chamberlain (Eds.), *Qualitative health psychology* (pp. 183–201). London: Sage.

Charmaz, K. (1990). 'Discovering' chronic illness: Using grounded theory. *Social Science and Medicine*, *30*(11), 1161–1172.

Charmaz, K. (1995). Grounded theory. In J. A. Smith, R. Harré, & L. Van Langenhove (Eds.), *Rethinking methods in psychology* (pp. 27–49). London: Sage.

Charmaz, K. (1999). Stories of suffering: Subjective tales and research narratives. *Qualitative Health Research*, *9*, 362–382.

Charmaz, K. (2000). Grounded theory: Objectivist and constructivist methods. In N. K. Denzin and Y. S. Lincoln (Eds.), *Handbook of Qualitative Research* (2nd ed., pp. 509–536). Los Angeles, CA: Sage.

Charmaz, K. (2002). Stories and silences: Disclosures and self in chronic illness. *Qualitative Inquiry*, *8*, 302–328.

Charmaz, K. (2003). Grounded theory: Objectivist and constructivist methods. In N. K. Denzin & Y. S. Lincoln (Eds.), *Strategies of qualitative inquiry* (pp. 249–291). Thousand Oaks, CA: Sage.

Charmaz, K. (2004). Premises, Principles, and Practices in Qualitative Research: Revisiting the Foundations. *Qualitative Health Research*, *14*(7): 976–993.

Charmaz, K. (2005). Grounded Theory in the 21st century: Applications for advancing social justice studies. In N. Denzin & Y. Lincoln (Eds.). *The Sage Handbook of Qualitative Research* (pp. 507–537). (3rd ed.). Thousand Oaks, CA: Sage.

Charmaz, K. (2006). *Constructing grounded theory: A practical guide through qualitative analysis.* Thousand Oaks, CA: Sage.

Charmaz, K. (2008a). Grounded theory as an emergent method. In S. N. Hesse-Biber & P. Leavy (Eds.), *Handbook of emergent methods* (pp. 155–172). New York: Guilford Press.

Charmaz, K. (2008b). Grounded theory in the 21st century: Applications for advancing social justice studies. In N. K. Denzin & Y. S. Lincoln (Eds.), *Strategies of qualitative inquiry* (pp. 203–241). Thousand Oaks, CA: Sage.

Charmaz, K. (2014). *Constructing grounded theory.* Thousand Oaks, CA: Sage.

Charmaz, K. (2017a). The power of constructivist grounded theory for critical inquiry. *Qualitative Inquiry*, *23*, 34–45. doi:10.1177/1077800416657105

Charmaz, K. (2017b). Special Invited Paper: Continuities, contradictions, and critical inquiry in grounded theory. *International Journal of Qualitative Methods*, *16*, 1–8. doi: 10.1177/1609406917719350

Cisneros-Puebla, César A. (2008). The deconstructive and reconstructive faces of social construction. Kenneth Gergen in conversation with César A. Cisneros-Puebla, with an introduction by Robert B. Faux [83 paragraphs]. *Forum Qualitative Sozialforschung / Forum: Qualitative Social Research*, *9*(1), Art. 20, http://nbn-resolving.de/urn:nbn:de:0114-fqs0801204

Clarke, A. E. (2005). *Situational analysis: Grounded theory after the post-modern turn*. Thousand Oaks, CA: Sage.

Dastjerdi, M., Olson, K., & Ogilvie, L. (2012). A study of Iranian immigrants' experiences of accessing Canadian health care services: A grounded theory. *International Journal for Equity in Health*, *11*, 55. Retrieved from www.equityhealthj.com/content/11/1/55

Denzin, N. K. & Lincoln, Y. S. (Eds.) (1994). *Handbook of qualitative research.* Thousand Oaks, CA: Sage.

Eastwood, J. G., Kemp, L. A., & Jalaludin, B. B. (2015). Being alone and expectations lost: A critical realist study of maternal depression in South Western Sydney. *Springer Plus*, *4*, 700. doi: 10.1186/s40064-015-1492-7

Ellingson, L. L. (1998). 'Then you know how I feel': Empathy, identification, and reflexivity in fieldwork. *Qualitative Inquiry*, *4*, 492–514.

Festen, H., Schipper, K., de Vries, S. O., Reichart, C. G., Abma, T. A., & Nauta, M. H. (2014). Parents' perceptions on offspring risk and prevention of anxiety and depression: A qualitative study. *BMC Psychology*, *2*, 17. Retrieved from www.biomedcentral.com/2050-7283/2/17

Frank, A. W. (2000). The standpoint of storyteller. *Qualitative Health Research*, *10*, 354–365.

Frank, A. W. (2001). Can we research suffering? *Qualitative Health Research*, *11*, 353–362.

Galvin, R. (2004). Challenging the need for gratitude: Comparisons between pain and unpaid care for disabled people. *Journal of Sociology*, *40*(2), 137–155. doi: 10.1177/1440783304043453

Gergen, K. J. (1973). Social psychology as history. *Journal of Personality and Social Psychology*, *26*, 309–320.

Gergen, K. J. (1985). The social constructionist movement in modern psychology. *American Psychologist*, *40*, 266–275.

Gergen, K. J. (1994). *Realities and relationships: Soundings in social construction.* Cambridge, MA: Harvard University Press.

Gergen, K. J. (1997). Social psychology as social construction: The emerging vision. In C. McGarty & S. A. Haslam (Eds.), *The message of social psychology* (pp. 113–128). Oxford: Blackwell.

Gergen, K. J. (2009). *An invitation to social construction* (2nd ed.). London: Sage.

Glaser, B. G. (1978). *Theoretical sensitivity.* Mill Valley, CA: Sociology Press.

Glaser, B. G. & Strauss, A. L. (1967). *The discovery of grounded theory*. New York: Aldine.

Guba, E. G. & Lincoln, Y. S. (2005). Paradigmatic controversies, contradictions, and emerging confluences. In N. K. Denzin & Y. S. Lincoln (Eds.), *The Sage handbook of qualitative research* (3rd ed., pp. 191–215). Thousand Oaks, CA: Sage.

Hackett, J., Godfrey, M., & Bennett, M. I. (2016). Patient and caregiver perspectives on managing pain in advanced cancer: A qualitative longitudinal study. *Palliative Medicine*, *30*(8), 711–719. doi: 10.1177/0269216316628407

Henwood, K. & Pidgeon, N. (2003). Grounded theory in psychological research. In M. Paul, J. E. Rhodes, & L. Yardley (Eds.), *Qualitative research in psychology: Expanding perspectives in methodology and design* (pp. 131–155). Washington, DC: American Psychological Association.

Kehler, D., Christensen, B., Lauritzen, T., Christensen, M. B., Edwards, A., & Risor, B. (2008). Ambivalence related to potential lifestyle changes following preventive cardiovascular consultations in general practice: A qualitative study. *BMC Family Practice*, *9*, 50. Retrieved from www.biomedcentral.com/1471-2296-9-50

Kirmayer, L. J. (1989). Cultural variation in the response to psychiatric disorders and mental distress. *Social Science and Medicine*, *29*, 327–329.

Kirmayer, L. J. (2004). The cultural diversity of healing: Meaning, metaphor and mechanism. *British Medical Bulletin*, *69*, 33–48.

Kleinman, A. (1973). Some issues for a comparative study of medical healing. *International Journal of Social Psychiatry*, *19*, 159–165.

Kleinman, A. (1987). Anthropology and psychiatry: The role of culture in cross-cultural research on illness. *British Journal of Psychiatry*, *151*, 447–454.

Kleinman, A. (1988a). *The illness narratives: Suffering, healing and human condition*. New York: Basic Books.

Kleinman, A. (1988b). *Rethinking psychiatry: From cultural category to personal experience*. New York: The Free Press.

Kleinman, A., Das, V., & Lock, M. (Eds.). (1998a). *Social suffering.* New Delhi: Oxford University Press.

Kleinman, A., Das, V., & Lock, M. (1998b). Introduction. In A. Kleinman, V. Das, & M. Lock (Eds.), *Social suffering* (pp. ix–xxvii). New Delhi: Oxford University Press.

Kodwo-Nyameazea, Y. & Nguyen, P. V. (2008). Immigrants and long-distance elder care: An exploratory study. *Ageing International*, *32*, 279–297. doi: 10.1007/s12126-008-9013-4

Kruger, L. & Lourens, M. (2016). Motherhood and the 'madness of hunger': '...*Want Almal Vra vir My vir 'n Stukkie Brood*' ('...Because everyone asks me for a little piece of bread'. *Culture, Medicine and Psychiatry*, *40*, 124–143. doi: 10.1007/s11013-015-9480-5

Levinas, E. (1988). Useless suffering. In R. Bernasconi & D. Woods (Eds.), *The provocation of Levinas: Rethinking the other* (pp. 156–167). New York: Routledge.

Lincoln, Y. S. (1995). Emerging criteria for quality in qualitative and interpretive research. *Quality Inquiry, 1*(3), 275–289.

Mabhala, M. A. (2013). Health inequalities as a foundation for embodying knowledge within public health teaching: A qualitative study. *International Journal for Equity in Health, 12*, 46. Retrieved from www.equityhealthj.com/content/12/1/46

Matthews, C. H. & Salazar, C. F. (2014). Second-generation adult former cult group members' recovery experiences: Implications for Counseling. *International Journal for Advancement of Counselling, 36*, 188–203

McCalman, J. R. (2013). The transfer and implementation of an Aboriginal Australian wellbeing program: A grounded theory study. *Implementation Science, 8*, 129. Retrieved from www.implementation-science.com/content/8/1/129

Meeker, M. A., Waldrop, D. P., Schneider, J., & Case, A. A. (2014). Contending with advanced illness: Patient and caregiver perspectives. *Journal of Pain and Symptom Management, 47*(5), 887–895.

Misra, G. & Gergen, K. J. (1993). On the place of culture in psychological science. *International Journal of Psychology, 28*, 225–243.

O'Brien, K. K., Davis, A. M., Strike, C., Young, N. L., & Bayoumi, A. M. (2009). Putting episodic disability into context: A qualitative study exploring factors that influence disability experienced by adults living with HIV/AIDS. *Journal of the International AIDS Society, 12*, 30. doi: 10.1186/1758-2652-12-30

Patel, S., Wittkowski, A., Fox, J. R. E., & Wieck, A. (2013). An exploration of illness beliefs in mothers with postnatal depression. *Midwifery, 29*, 682–689.

Pitaloka, D. & Hsieh, E. (2015). Health as submission and social responsibility: Embodied experiences of Javanese women with Type II diabetes. *Qualitative Health Research, 25*(8), 1155–1165. doi: 10.1177/1049732315577607

Priya, K. R. (2004). Post-quake recovery in urban Kachchh. *Economic and Political Weekly, 39*(38), 4229–4231.

Priya, K. R. (2010). Research relationship as a facilitator of remoralization and self-growth: Postearthquake suffering and healing. *Qualitative Health Research, 20*, 479–495.

Priya, K. R. (2011). Broadening of consciousness: A healing process among the survivors of Kachchh earthquake. In R. M. M. Cornelissen, G. Misra, & S. Varma (Eds.), *Foundations of Indian psychology, Vol. II: Practical applications* (pp. 209–224). New Delhi: Pearson.

Priya, K. R. (2012a). Social constructionist approach to suffering and healing: Juxtaposing Cassell, Gergen and Kleinman. *Psychological Studies, 57*, 211–223.

Priya, K. R. (2012b). Trauma reactions, suffering and healing among riot-affected internally displaced children of Gujarat: A qualitative inquiry. *Qualitative Research in Psychology, 9*, 189–209.

Priya K. R. (2015a). *Humanizing grounded theory: A journey lived by Kathy Charmaz.* Paper presented at the Eleventh International Congress of Qualitative Inquiry, University of Illinois, Urbana-Champaign, USA.

Priya, K. R. (2015b). On the social constructionist approach to traumatized selves in post-disaster settings: State-induced violence in Nandigram, India. *Culture, Medicine and Psychiatry, 39*(3), 428–448. doi: 10.1007/s11013-014-9423-6

Priya, K. R. (2018) Well-being and mental health in the aftermath of disasters: A social constructionist approach. In G. Misra (Ed.), *Psychosocial interventions for health and well-being* (pp. 355–368). New Delhi: Springer.

Radley, A. (2004). Suffering. In M. Murray (Ed.), *Critical health psychology* (pp. 31–43). Basingstoke, UK: Palgrave Macmillan.

Ravindran, V., Rempel, G. R., & Ogilvie, L. (2013a). Parenting burn-injured children in India: A grounded theory study. *International Journal of Nursing Studies, 50*, 786–796.

Ravindran, V., Rempel, G. R., & Ogilvie, L. (2013b). Embracing survival: A grounded theory study of parenting children who have sustained burns. *Burns, 39*, 589–598.

Sampson, E. E. (1993). Identity politics: Challenges to psychology's understanding. *American Psychologist*, *48*, 1219–1230.
Strauss, A. L. (1987). *Qualitative analysis for social scientists*. New York: Cambridge University Press.
Strauss, A. L. & Corbin, J. (1990). *Basics of qualitative research: Grounded theory procedures and techniques*. Newbury Park, CA: Sage.
Strauss, A. L. & Corbin, J. (1998). *Basics of qualitative research: Grounded theory procedures and techniques* (2nd ed.). Thousand Oaks, CA: Sage.
Takai, Y., Yamamoto-Mitani, N., & Chiba, I. (2016). The process of motivating oneself to resist being controlled by chronic pain: A qualitative study of Japanese older people living in the community. *Pain Management Nursing*, *18*(1), doi: 10.1016/j.pmn.2016.10.004
Thurston, W. E., Coupal, S., Jones, C. A., Crowshoe, L. F. J., Marshall, D. A., Homik, J., & Barnabe, C. (2014). Discordant indigenous and provider frames explain challenges in improving access to arthritis care: A qualitative study using constructivist grounded theory. *International Journal for Equity in Health*, *13*, 46. Retrieved from www.equityhealthj.com/content/13/1/46
Viswambharan, A. P., & Priya, K. R. (2016). Documentary analysis as a qualitative methodology to explore disaster mental health: Insights from analyzing a documentary on communal riots. *Qualitative Research*, *16*(1), 43–59. doi: 10.1177/1468794114567494
Wolf, H. T., Halpern-Felsher, B. L., Bukusi, E. A., Agot, K. E., Cohen, C. R., & Auerswald, C. L. (2014). 'It is all about the fear of being discriminated [against] the person suffering from HIV will not be accepted': A qualitative study exploring the reasons for loss to follow-up among HIV-positive youth in Kisumu, Kenya. *BMC Public Health*, *14*, 1154. Retrieved from www.biomedcentral.com/1471-2458/14/1154

PART IV

Reflections on Using and Teaching Grounded Theory

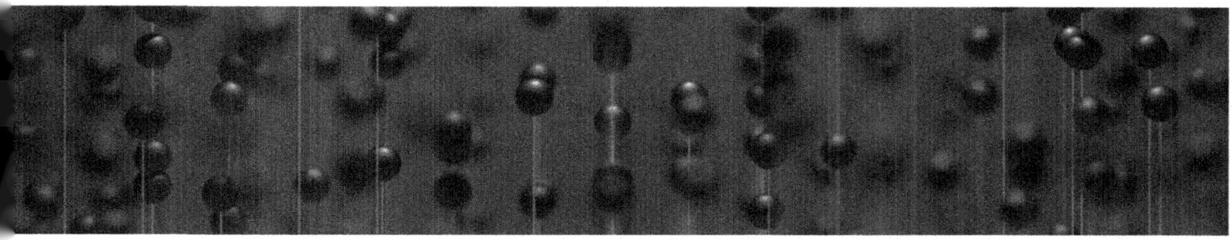

20

Teaching and Learning Grounded Theory Methodology: The Seminar Approach

Judith A. Holton

Barney Glaser has referred to learning grounded theory as 'development driven' (Glaser, 1998, pp. 56–60); a 'delayed action learning process' (1978, p. 6, 1998, p. 220, 2001, p. 1, 2003, p. 78) where the experiential is essential to truly understanding and effecting the methodology. Having worked for several years with graduate students at University of California San Francisco (UCSF), he recognized the limitations of *Discovery* (Glaser & Strauss, 1967) as a methodological guide. Indeed, this was a primary motivation for his authoring of *Theoretical Sensitivity* (Glaser, 1978), in which he offers guidance in applying the 'full package' of classic grounded theory methodology. The guidance offered was grounded in his years of teaching at UCSF, from which he concluded that learning together in a seminar format was the optimum way of teaching or learning grounded theory.

Glaser's early seminars adopted what he called a 'revolving collaboration' model with 'committed full time participants' (Glaser, 1978, p. 33). The intention was to encourage openness to ideas, to 'de-contain' participants' preconceptions and often strongly defended perspectives, replacing defensiveness with 'the right to be wrong' (p. 33), all in aid of advancing the conceptual analysis of the data as presented. As Charmaz (2011) explains, Glaser's approach was unconventional at a time when the typical graduate seminar was focused on exploring and critiquing extant literature. She suggests, '...Barney's innovative method of engaging students in theory construction in class sessions turned the conventional sociology graduate seminar inside out and, simultaneously, encouraged students' analytic thinking' (p. 181). Over the years, Glaser has continued to employ a seminar approach in his teaching and mentoring of grounded theory. While the intention and focus of his seminars have remained consistent over the ensuing decades, the structure has changed to a 'fly-in, fly-out' (Gynnild, 2011, p. 38) intensive three-day format that enables students from all corners of the globe to attend. Glaser has also effectively embraced both virtual technologies and a growing cadre of experienced classic grounded theorists to extend the reach of his work and to help in overcoming the 'minus mentoring' challenge (Glaser, 1998), a term Glaser has used to describe those students who do not have access to local expertise in grounded theory, whether through supervisors or collegial networks.

My own experience of Glaser's troubleshooting seminars began in 2003. Like many new to GT, I had encountered confusion in working my way through the various GT perspectives offered in texts and journal papers. The more I read, the more confusing I found the advice being offered. My wish was to do GT as it was originally presented in *Discovery* (Glaser & Strauss, 1967). I had tried using strategies and advice offered in Strauss and Corbin's (1990) text but I found the advice took me through repetitive cycles of analysis that resulted in what seemed to me to be rather predictable descriptive outcomes. Where was the creativity that *Discovery* has promised? Where were the eureka insights (Glaser, 1978)?

An internet search in March 2003 led me to Sociology Press and the Grounded Theory Institute. Glaser's several books pointed me in the right direction, but it was the notice of face-to-face seminars with Glaser that truly excited my learning. The April 2003 seminar in London was already fully subscribed but I was advised to keep watching the website for future seminars. What truly amazed me, however, was that Barney Glaser emailed me to ask about my research! Thus began a most memorable mentoring relationship; further solidified when I was able to attend a GT seminar in Malmo, Sweden, in September 2003. The seminar experience was exhilarating. To begin with, here was the man himself! The symbiosis between Glaser as author and Glaser as seminar leader was evident in his tone, his theoretical sensitivity as evidenced in his ability to conceptualize data from whatever source, and his passion for just doing it!

The composition of the seminar was, however, unexpected. As participants introduced themselves, the range of disciplines around the table was impressive if somewhat intimidating. I was a PhD student in management. What did I have in common with these students of medicine, nursing, occupational therapy, education, social work? Would I be able to understand their research? Would they understand mine? Was this seminar going to help me unravel my confusion? As the first day progressed, I found myself engrossed in the troubleshooting process regardless of the study focus. It was the data and its conceptualization that focused our attention. Following that first seminar, I was fortunate to attend additional seminars in New York, London, Mill Valley and Stockholm. With each seminar, not only did my own research progress but I continued to develop my understanding of the GT process through participating in the troubleshooting of over 50 other GT studies in progress. My initial hesitation regarding the disciplinary range of seminar participants had been replaced with enthusiasm for discovering concepts and theories in any data and for seeing how GT can be applied to any and all kinds of data.

Through the seminars, I also developed collaborative relationships with fellow grounded theorists from around the globe; a network of connections that continues to inform my research and understanding of GT. Indeed, this fluctuating support network is a living example of my grounded theory of rehumanizing knowledge work (Holton, 2006, 2007). Seminar attendance certainly rehumanized the PhD trajectory for many of those who attended! In 2006, I began to offer my own seminars; many in collaboration with my GT colleagues. These seminars have been offered in Canada, the USA, the UK, Hong Kong, Sweden and France. Through seminars, my editorship of *The Grounded Theory Review* (2004–2011) and email connections facilitated via the Grounded Theory Institute,

I have also served as a mentor to many novice grounded theorists, offering me additional experience as a teacher of the methodology.

This chapter explores the evolution of Glaser's troubleshooting seminar approach through first-hand experiences of his students (e.g., Charmaz, 2011; Gynnild, 2011; Simmons, 2011), to which I will add my own experiences as both a participant and as a facilitator of several international troubleshooting seminars. The chapter begins by offering some thoughts on the reasons for choosing GT and the challenges frequently faced by novice grounded theorists in getting started, in tolerating attendant confusion, and in achieving autonomy as a grounded theorist. Next, I will elaborate on the seminar approach, its structure and process, as well as offering additional suggestions for extending the troubleshooting approach in the teaching and mentoring of grounded theory through exampling, group work, mentoring and solo learning processes.

WHY CHOOSE GROUNDED THEORY?

The motivations for choosing GT are, of course, varied, but it is worth noting both its *utility* and *fit* attraction for many students, particularly for those in the practice professions, such as nursing, medicine, various allied therapies, social work, education, and management. Students speak of the practical value in turning their professional experiences into theories that explain and provide 'access variables' (Glaser & Strauss, 1967, pp. 248–249), enabling more effective interventions and treatments. In doing so, students not only seek to achieve a contribution to knowledge in their discipline but also to effectively offer a social value through enhanced practice, echoing Zetterberg's (1962) call for practical value in social theory. Simmons (2011) notes a strong personal motivation to use emergent theory to bring about change, while Wu and Beaunae (2014) suggest that GT methods have been growing in popularity for doctoral researchers because they offer a type of rigour that can often be challenged in qualitative studies (p. 249), i.e., that qualitative studies can be accused of being unsystematic and lacking in rigour. Charmaz (2014) suggests that GT has helped to rebalance these 'taken-for-granted hierarchies' (p. 1074) in academia that had previously privileged the positivistic emphasis on theory verification over theory generation, and that disregarded qualitative methods as holding little value, possibly even being unscientific (Brinkmann Jacobsen, & Kristiansen, 2014, p. 17) and lacking scholarly rigour (Gioia, Corley, & Hamilton, 2013, p. 15). Wu and Beaume (2014) note GT's inherent quality of 'thinking beyond the current body of literature in their disciplines … [and] … its meticulous attention to systematic data collection and analysis as well as coding and subsequent theory development' (p. 251) as offering the novice researcher confidence in a research outcome worthy of a degree.

Glaser (2010) speaks of the importance of *fit* between the researcher and the approach, noting the relevance of experience, stage of career development and, to a lesser degree, chronological age of the researcher. He asserts that GT is not a fit for every researcher, that a GT researcher requires three characteristics: 'an ability to conceptualize data, an ability to tolerate some confusion, and an ability to tolerate confusion's attendant regression [which are necessary to] … enable the researcher to wait for the conceptual sense making to emerge from the data' (p. 4). Glaser (2014) quotes GT Fellow, Hans Thulesius, as suggesting this fit entails 'the promise of being able to develop, by discovery, theory directly from the data and not having to deal with existing theoretical assumptions in a field. … The researcher reads about the CGT [Classic Grounded Theory] method and recognizes a fit with his/her way of thinking about how to work scientifically' (p. 7). This notion of fit extends as well to the researcher's philosophical stance. Wu and Beaunae (2014) suggest that the growing popularity of GT is due in part to 'its ability to be congruent with multiple epistemological frameworks' (p. 250). Glaser (2014) asserts that it is GT's grab, the excitement of discovery and the desire to work autonomously (p. 29) that motivates choosing GT. While the fit may be tentative at first, and the firmness of the choice 'var[ying] with the learning curve of the researcher [the choice] usually increases with the conceptualizing experience when doing CGT [Classic GT] productively' (p. 6).

The mature student may also be attracted to GT as offering a new challenge, one where their creative autonomy (Holton, 2011) is encouraged. Gynnild (2011) notes the 'youthifying' effect of GT as commonly evidenced in GT seminars where the average age of participants may well be in the fifties. She quotes Glaser as saying:

> Grounded theory is youthifying. If you look around the table you'll see that people who attempt to do grounded theories tend to be older – they have come to a stage in life where they know it's OK to wonder and that you don't know everything constantly. Did I tell you about Tara? She was 80 when she started and ran around like a 30 year old when she found her core category. (Gynnild, 2011, p. 44)

Hesse-Biber (2007) has acknowledged the challenge of teaching GT to undergraduate students. Her experience resonates with Glaser's (1998) comments that GT is a methodology for mature students, that semester-bound undergrads are too time-compressed, grade-sensitive and insufficiently life-experienced, all of which undermine their ability to be open (Glaser, 1998, pp. 228–229). Glaser, however, has also often commented at his seminars that novice researchers readily grasp the essence of GT as it is something we all do naturally in our efforts to make sense of what may be happening around us. GT simply provides a rigorous and systematic approach to fully developing that explanation at a conceptual level.

CHALLENGES FACING THE NOVICE

While acknowledging the maturity requirement of undertaking a GT study, Glaser sees advantages in the novice researcher's enthusiasm and their openness to learning unconstrained by previous training in other methodologies. As such, they are more likely to see fresh patterns in the data rather than falling back on accepted ideas grounded in preconceived professional interests or established practice and are perhaps more willing to trust what emerges through the creativity of constant comparative analysis. 'The novice need only have an ability to conceptualize, to organize, to tolerate confusion with some incident depression, to make abstract connections, to remain open, to be a bit visual, to thinking multivariately and most of all to trust to preconscious processing and to emergence' (Glaser, 2003, p. 62).

Wu and Beaunae (2014), however, describe their experiences of choosing GT as '...a long walk through a dark forest [with] ... issues such as the changing nature of grounded theory, time constraints, theses advisors, doctoral committee procedures and Institutional Review Board regulations creat[ing] challenges for doctoral candidates (researchers) who choose to use GT' (p. 249). Nagel, Burns, Tilley and Aubin's (2015) experience of navigating the GT process was 'time intensive and require[d] stamina, tenacity, and personal nourishment – it is a long haul' (p. 380). These experiences are unfortunately all too common to those who must work without experienced guidance in classic GT methodology. Gynnild (2016) suggests that:

> Classic grounded theory might be scary simply because it prompts researchers to get out of their personal and professional comfort zone when hunting inductively for data to explain human patterns of behaviour. Taking on the responsibility of doing a grounded theory is possible only if a researcher is willing to invest in individual growth and experience while simultaneously engaging with data. (p. 1)

So, whether the researcher is a novice setting out on their first project, or a more mature researcher entering the domain of grounded theory, it is important to recognize that a level of commitment to learning new skills and new perspectives will be part of the journey. A willingness to stay open (Glaser, 2013) is the requisite dictum. For those who can, the journey promises freedom, empowerment and excitement in generating new concepts to explain the world around us (Glaser, 1998, Chapter 4).

Getting Started

Knowing how to get started, and in particular what to read, is a challenge for most novices, especially those who do not have an experienced grounded theorist to advise them. Many academics who supervise doctoral students continue to view GT as a qualitative research method which leads to much procedural divergence and novice confusion. Glaser notes that issues with coding, resolving confusions due to the jargonized use of GT terminology, and the search for experienced mentors, are the most frequent cries for help that he receives from novice researchers (Glaser, 2016). Certainly, the decision to choose CGT can place the novice researcher outside the norm in many academic departments where

> ...novice researchers are trained in theory-testing, theory-to-theory comparisons or problem-solving methods, but seldom in theory generation. An argument often used is that a theorizing approach might be too challenging. ... GT troubleshooting seminars are therefore one of few face-to-face arenas where novice researchers are trained in specified procedures for generating new theory. (Gynnild, 2011, p. 31)

Reading the seminal text, *Discovery of Grounded Theory* (Glaser & Strauss, 1967), is an obvious strategy. However, *Discovery* is more an introduction than a 'how to' guide (Holton & Walsh, 2017; Walsh, Holton, Bailyn, Fernandez, Levina & Glaser, 2015). As Glaser (1978) notes, those who rely solely on this text '...tend to become stuck and then to leave out various stages of the process, such as sorting to integrate, or memoing or reworking or not coding enough [producing] ... thin theory' (p. 33). Supervisor recommendations for further reading can then lead to a muddling of methods (Stern, 1994). Those who attend GT troubleshooting seminars are advised to read – as a minimum – *Discovery* (Glaser & Strauss, 1967) and *Doing Grounded Theory* (Glaser, 1998) with his *Perspectives* series (Glaser, 2001, 2003, 2005) also highly recommended reading as seminar preparation. Returning to these texts repeatedly throughout a GT study also helps to alleviate momentary regression and the accompanying loss of confidence.

Glaser is often critical of supervisors who attempt to 'rescue' students who encounter the inevitable confusions of working through a GT study. 'Unfortunately, many supervisors … cannot stand student confusion and suggest preconceived concepts and dropping the research level to full description' (Glaser, 2011, p. 44). This is a significant loss for the student in terms of both their achieving autonomy as a researcher and making a valuable contribution to knowledge in their chosen field. It also places the novice in a bind as satisfying their supervisory team can be essential to their successful achievement of the coveted degree. Glaser advocates supervisor patience as the novice researcher struggles initially to find a level of comfort and confidence in the methodology. 'The supervisor should learn patience with his student and should support him and refrain him from feeling lost and impatient' (Glaser, 2011, pp. 43–44). While what is in the data may seem obvious to a busy supervisor, the rush to prescribe not only risks short-circuiting the student's confidence in their skill development, but equally important it risks shutting down the student's creative engagement in conceptual ideation, with the subsequent loss of any new and exciting theoretical discovery.

Given the global reach of GT, we must also acknowledge that ways of knowing and doing can differ across various cultures. To date, not enough attention has been given to the challenges that novice grounded theorists face in different cultures. Chen (2016) has offered some insight into teaching GT in the Chinese context. It is worth attending to some of the issues he has raised. For example, he notes the strong positivistic preferences in the Chinese academy where research using qualitative data is not widely embraced as it is 'considered too "subjective", "impressionistic" and "unsystematic"' (p. 73). He suggests as well that while in Chinese cultural traditions '[e]verything is inter-related' (p. 78), which should facilitate GT's latent pattern recognition, students are resistant to fracturing the data for conceptualization, finding it difficult to transcend their natural inclination for imagery of the whole and concluding that a significant challenge in teaching GT is 'to keep a balance between imagery thinking and conceptual thinking' (p. 80). He notes as well that the Chinese have a natural inclination for concrete thinking and that '[i]n data analysis, however, we have to push our students further to transcend their concrete thinking … [b]y integrating their concrete thinking with abstract thinking' (p. 80).

This challenge in transcending the concrete detail necessary for conceptualization of data is, of course, not unique to the Chinese culture. Many novice grounded theorists find it difficult to 'let go' of the rich descriptive detail of qualitative data in service to abstract conceptual theorizing. There are a number of reasons for this hesitancy. First, their personal philosophical stance (i.e., what they believe to be truth and how truth can be discovered) may be incompatible with GT's conceptual abstraction. Second, those who have been trained in qualitative methods, where rich descriptive detail is valued, will find it hard to unlearn such training, especially if this perspective is reinforced by supervisors and departmental perspectives on what 'good' research entails. Here the researcher's autonomy becomes essential to achieving skill development as a grounded theorist.

Tolerating Confusion

Glaser has dealt extensively with the importance of tolerating confusion in doing GT (Glaser, 1978, 1998, 2012, 2013). He views it as a form of regression whereby the researcher is left scrambled without feeling desperate. This can be a disconcerting outcome not only for the novice but also for the supervisor! Those unable to tolerate this sense of confusion may revert to preconceived ideas about the data, what it should reveal and how the resultant work should sit in relation to extant theory. Without having fostered some level of autonomy, the novice will invariably seek to be reassured or rescued through consultation with colleagues or supervisors.

As novice grounded theorists, Nagel et al. (2015) recall '...weaving through a myriad of paths in a landscape of varied and divergent perspectives ... differences of opinion ... differing paradigmatic inclinations or lack of agreement amongst established GT methods and procedures' (p. 366). Among the challenges they faced in transcending confusion were: 'distinguishing the paradigmatic attributes of main GT approaches, lack of clear articulation of methods and procedures (e.g., coding and analysis), the necessity ... to familiarize other individuals involved in our dissertation work, such as supervisors and committee members' (p. 369) and '...confidently tak[ing] a stance on paradigmatic and research design issues with mentors when discordance in viewpoints occurs and there is perceived or real imbalance in power' (p. 373). They also cite challenges in the 'lack of respect for alternate approaches within [the] GT community, terminology varied and fluid, slurring of methods between approaches' and '...biases inherent to the institution and program of study ... selection of supervisor(s) and committee ... depth of literature review required ... imposition of a priori theoretical framework ... forcing of concepts in analysis' (p. 369) and 'divergent views on basic GT methods ... meanings and importance of concepts like emergence, reflexivity and verification' (p. 374). Wu and Beaunae (2014) similarly note a number of novice challenges that created considerable initial confusion, including confusion among the various 'renditions' of GT around coding (open, selective, theoretical), (open, axial, selective), (open, focused...); lack of clear explanations or direction for coding procedures; lack of familiarity with GT among doctoral committees and thesis advisors or differing perspectives as to the 'correct' approach; and conflict between GT's 'openness' in relation to the expected level of specificity required by supervisors, committees and institutional review boards. Finally, one of the authors recounts her supervisor's confusing GT with other approaches to qualitative research as a major source of confusion to be resolved: '...one of her committee members told her to do a *thematic analysis* rather than a GT analysis...' (p. 255) '...because the theory that emerged from her data was unfamiliar to committee members, she was encouraged to superimpose a previously established theory on her data to explain the findings of her study. This was problematic since [her] findings and theory development were beyond the scope of the established theory and some of her most important findings were eliminated from her dissertation' (p. 255).

Achieving Autonomy

Glaser (2014) emphasizes the importance of researcher autonomy in choosing GT but suggests that few young novice researchers possess this level of maturity. The requirement to suspend preconceptions with its inherent initial confusion so as to enable preconscious processing through constant comparative coding and memoing of data can be challenging for the uncertain, who may revert to seeking reassurance – what Glaser has termed the cry for help:

> Claiming autonomy when doing research within a structure of control by superiors can be highly problematic for the novice. Level of success varies from losing all control thus failure to get autonomy to achieving a high level of autonomy and being sometimes quite alone

> with no help. ... Though autonomy is a big draw to choosing GT for a dissertation it can become very frightening about doing it right. 'Am I using the GT procedures correctly?' ... 'Am I doing it right?' is their constant question. So they seek help, if only a constant OK. (Glaser, 2016, p. 11)

Hence, for those supervising novice grounded theorists, it is important to foster autonomous engagement (Gynnild, 2011, p. 37). 'Too much accessibility to others, too many interruptions, over commitments, overloads, being spread thin – all block the generating process. ... The best way for the analyst to frustrate or to abort his creativity is to start criticizing himself for what he is accomplishing' (Glaser, 1978, pp. 21–22). At the same time, Glaser acknowledges that autonomy seeking can be a 'mixed bag' (Glaser, 2016, p. 12) as some who select GT soon discover that they cannot tolerate the requisite autonomy and instead seek constant assurance that they are following the methodology as intended. This need for reassurance can effectively paralyze (Glaser, 2016, p. 12) as assurance-seeking becomes a slippery slope into supervisor rescue to a remodelled version of GT (Glaser, 2003).

Glaser (2016) asserts that only a well-trained, experienced GT mentor will know how to help without taking away the novice's autonomy with preconceptions from a departmental perspective (p. 13). Guthrie and Lowe (2011) press the importance of a supervisor or mentor being an experienced grounded theorist. They advocate that a student should actually conduct a background check on their prospective mentor or supervisor (p. 57). With regard to formal supervisors, they suggest contacting the home academic library of the individual to view PhDs completed under their supervision and then contacting the thesis authors (i.e., the students) to inquire about their supervisory experience – questions such as how long the PhD process took; how often they met with their supervisor; what happened during meetings; how productive they found the relationship to be; would they recommend the individual as a supervisor (pp. 58–59). In choosing to add a GT mentor to the formal PhD process, a critical requirement is the comfort level of the formal supervisor(s) with such an arrangement. Some supervisors are quite happy to have the expertise on board while others may view it as an intrusion or an erosion of their formal role and responsibilities. A frank conversation between the student and the supervisor(s) will be important in surfacing and addressing questions or concerns about the respective roles. Should the student detect discomfort on the part of the formal supervisor, an alternative may be to seek the support of a mentor informally. Students frequently contact the Grounded Theory Institute (www.groundedtheory.com) or Grounded Theory Online (www.groundedtheoryonline.com) as a means of networking with experienced grounded theorists who are willing to serve in a mentoring capacity. Here, the mentoring role is intended to support the novice's developing autonomy as a researcher and theorist.

An important aspect of developing autonomy is finding the rhythm and personal pacing fit between the researcher and the method – what Glaser (1978) refers to as theoretical pacing. This experiential aspect of learning GT is highly individual and requires developing a pace and rhythm in research and analysis that accommodates the temperament of the researcher, the nature of the area under study, and the important cycling through the nonlinear, iterative stages of data collection, coding and memoing, so as to sustain the researcher's energy and creativity throughout the full theory generation process. Here he speaks of GT as a delayed action phenomenon:

> Little increments in coding, analysing and collection data cook and mature then to blossom later into theoretical memos. Significant theoretical realizations come with growth and maturity in the data, and much of this is outside the analyst's awareness until it happened. (Glaser, 1978, p. 18)

Those who pursue autonomy find the rewards in their growing methodological understanding and confidence:

> Autonomy helps the novice decide on his own many vital procedural issues when doing CGT. Some are: how to vet the participants without preconceiving their thoughts, when to theoretically sample, when are memos mature enough to sort, when is enough interchangeable indicators enough for generating a concept so data collection can stop, is a main concern with a core category 'OK' and many more issues to decide which materially affect the resulting generated theory. (Glaser, 2016, p. 16)

Nagel et al. (2015) echo Glaser's assessment in their own experiences as novice grounded theorists, '...having to rely on our own innovations, motivation, and, at times, sheer tenacity ... the less travelled path we chose has afforded us a great opportunity to evolve our own thinking' (p. 376). However, for many novices it does take some initial confidence and courage to trust one's autonomy.

The troubleshooting seminar approach that Glaser has refined over time has proven to be an effective way of fostering researcher autonomy. For many PhD students, periodic participation in GT troubleshooting seminars over the course of their research trajectory can provide important methodological clarification, motivational inspiration and sufficient mentoring support to sustain energy and move their work ahead:

> The main purpose of grounded theory seminars is to support and accelerate each participant's development of conceptual research skills and successive research autonomy ... to bring each participant one step further, wherever they are in their research ... [with] the overall goal ... to help people get their PhD degrees. (Gynnild, 2011, p. 36)

THE SEMINAR APPROACH

Glaser recognized early on the importance of appropriate methodological training, having developed his seminar model while at University of California at San Francisco (UCSF). *Theoretical Sensitivity* (Glaser, 1978) was written based on his experiences in developing and leading seminars with graduate students as a means of accelerating the learning process. He recognized that students could 'stagnate' if they focused exclusively on their own study; that there was much to be said for breaking up attention to their own data and flexing their conceptualization skills on data from the studies of other students, by hearing what others saw in the data and by working to 'one up' each other's conceptual level. In his seminars, students shared challenges that they were encountering and problem-solved together in a mutually supportive learning exchange. Gynnild (2011) relates Glaser's seminar approach to Carl Rogers' person-centred theory (Rogers, 1969) wherein significant learning is fostered in environments of minimal threat and maximal differentiated perceptions (Gynnild, 2011, p. 46). She suggests, '... both Glaser and Rogers are concerned with opening up to, and theorizing from, experience ... [t]he strength in both approaches lies in the focus on presence and relational qualities in a learning situation, and the supervisor or facilitator's function as a role model [offering] genuineness … non-possessive caring … empathetic understanding' (Gynnild, 2011, pp. 46–47).

Glaser (1996) acknowledges the seminars as intended mutual support:

> These seminars were a support group encouraging theoretical sampling in different directions, looking at different slices of data, and a constant source of 'running by' their latest ideas. These seminars did away with the 'put downs' of normal discourse with many colleagues, and the energy draining nature of colleagues who just listen and say little more than an 'OK' for quick closure, instead of fiery feedback which keeps the researcher active, thinking and generating. In short, it is important to have this positive discussion if available, but just as important not to talk to the wrong people and give away the energy for putting down in writing what was just said. (p. xiii)

While Glaser's seminars at UCSF would run over the course of a full semester, he has since devised a condensed three-day troubleshooting seminar approach that continues the ethos of experiential, collaborative learning:

> I designed the troubleshooting seminars to help candidates complete their dissertations. Candidates have many questions that need answering when doing a GT dissertation to get it moving and finished. The seminar focuses on exactly where the candidate is and tries to move him/her to the next step. Problem coverage is achieved by participant-candidates listening to the troubles of eleven other participant-candidates, and after listening, then engaging in an extensive free and open discussion of all the participants' views of what to do within the GT procedural framework. (Glaser & Holton, 2007, p. vii)

Gynnild (2011) suggests that designing a time-intensive seminar posed a dilemma for Glaser in that learning the basics of GT usually takes about eighteen months of intensive work (Glaser, 1998), given the delayed action learning nature of the methodology. Here both the atmosphere of collaborative support and the temperament of the seminar leader are important. Gynnild (2011) suggests that '… in order to encourage researchers to have confidence in [their] data, [the seminar leader] needs to ensure that they trust the method … which implicitly challenges the leader to demonstrate expertise skills in the field. Being relaxed, flexible, and in control of the situation is part of building confidence' (p. 42).

> A participant presents at exactly where he is, not where he should be, in the process … the goal is to systematically put each member through each stage of generating theory so they can learn it … the prime purpose of the seminar is training and then secondarily it is to produce a paper for publication. … Without this eventual airing to the outside, the seminar becomes an ingrown self-satisfied group that can easily lose touch with the worth of its product for the larger enterprise…. (Glaser, 1978, pp. 34–35)

Over the past twenty years, Glaser has regularly offered troubleshooting seminars in both Europe and America. Each seminar is fully subscribed with highly motivated PhD students at various stages of the GT process, and generally from all corners of the globe. Participants are highly motivated to attend and learn: '…candidates worry whether or not they can truly accomplish a GT dissertation. They are highly motivated to find answers to their GT questions' (Glaser & Holton, 2007, p. vii). Many come seeking to push past a specific stumbling block to advance their theorizing; others come full of confusion as to how to sort through the various approaches labelled GT in the literature. The range of issues and levels of expertise present at each seminar may create some initial confusion for the first-time attendee but the relaxed and open atmosphere soon stimulates engagement and accelerated learning for all: '…a few days of intense coding of several people's data goes a long way in teaching coding to all seminar students' (Glaser, 2011, p. 46). Gynnild (2011) has explored the importance of the atmosphere that Glaser intentionally promotes at the outset of each seminar. She quotes from his opening remarks at a GT seminar:

> We're going to do perspectives on perspectives. People will see data and I'll expect you all to chime in with a potential concept, for the data. I want you to start getting abstract. So leave the data and get on a conceptual level which is abstract of time, place and people, and start talking about the general patterns of life. The one thing I can't stand is tiny topics. (pp. 42–43)

The expectations are clear and the learning intense, as one first-time attendee confesses: 'I'm listening so hard that I'm afraid others can hear it' (p. 42). The learning value is clear. Seminar participation stimulates energy and a desire to share. Many participants return a second, even third time for more troubleshooting participation as their dissertation research advances. Having achieved the PhD, some will return to share their success and continue their learning through troubleshooting new issues all the while experiencing again the mutual support and stimulating learning exchanges. After attending a number of seminars, some will become 'local experts' at their home universities, mentoring other students or offering their own seminars (Glaser & Holton, 2007, p. viii). As one seasoned seminar attendee commented: 'People bring different backgrounds and different experiences with theory and research. But for the two to three days [of the seminar] I always got a sense of renewal with my work' (personal communication, August 10, 2015).

Glaser begins each seminar by emphasizing its pedagogy, which is grounded in the principles of:

- *Cognitive stripping* as mindset disruption to dislodge preconceptions and enable emergence (i.e., realization). At seminars, participants 'can take conceptual flyers (ideational chances) with no fear of being wrong as they try to fit concepts to data or generate theoretical memos' (Glaser, 1978, p. 34).
- *Seed planting* for later emergent realization as participants offer perspectives on a perspective dislodging the researcher's assumptions about what is in the data and thereby raising the potential for originality in emergent grounded theories.
- *Preconscious processing* whereby Glaser emphasizes the importance of allowing ideas to 'cook' as conscious deliberations are too slow to make important conceptual leaps. Preconscious processing is much faster in processing the input from coding and analyzing of data, but it produces 'conscious confusion'; hence, mindset disruption and potential regression. The grounded theorist must be able to tolerate this cognitive stripping to allow the creative intuition of realization to emerge – those eureka moments.
- *Realization* occasionally occurs during the seminar itself but more likely is a delayed action phenomenon, a consequence of the participant's openness to discovery, aided by the seminar's cognitive stripping and seed planting. Realization cannot be pressured by external deadlines. The analyst must develop a pacing and cycling pattern that keeps the work moving but that alternates conscious periods of analysis and writing with periods of respite and relaxation so as to support preconscious processing. This cycling pattern begins during the seminar as participants feel free to alternate between active and vocal engagement in the troubleshooting of others' work with periods of reflective silence.

The Process

Glaser (1978) offers us a snapshot of the troubleshooting process:

> The general stance of the seminar is to leave citizen type issues outside the door and become objective analysts, no matter where it takes them. ... The right to be wrong is vital since wrong tracks lead to right ways. The objective is to de-contain oneself which being correct inhibits ... there is no need to defend. They can one-up each other conceptually, with no fear of implicitly putting each other down, since the job of all is to raise the conceptual level of the analysis. ... Fracturing [the data] should be done with no fear of hurting or violating the person who might cherish the story because of collecting it or for other personal reasons. (p. 34)

At each seminar, one individual – usually a returning attendee – offers to take notes for the session so that the remaining participants can fully engage in thinking and talking without the worry of capturing extensive notes. As each person presents their data or memos, the rest of the group thinks, analyzes and suggests what concepts or patterns they are seeing and gradually they begin to recognize methodologically what is going on as the analysis proceeds.

The atmosphere created during each seminar is essential to facilitating openness to learning and to discovery. Gynnild (2011) describes it as 'a holistic, experiential, exploratory, and yet grounded mentoring approach' (p. 32) and a '...safe psychological space' (p. 37) that facilitates '[a] process of building trust through a feeling of authentic communication' (p. 33), whereby '[i]mplicitly, properties of outspoken curiosity and active problem-solving are encouraged' (p. 34). Young (2016) echoes Gynnild in asserting that, 'Teachers need to create safe environments as threat often hinders learning. Conversely, a challenging classroom enhances learning' (p. 139).

While the format of the seminars has evolved, Glaser's basic rules of engagement haven't. In *Theoretical Sensitivity* (Glaser, 1978), he set out the following conditions for participation: no sharing of experiences – stick to the data; no logical elaboration – stick to the data; no need for apologies or preambles before offering ideas; interrupting is OK if it is in service to generating ideas; and humility not ego, cooperation not competition (p. 34). Appendix 20.A offers further insight into the intentional structure and process of the troubleshooting seminar.

The seminar process places no pressure on any participant to compete in demonstrating their expertise, but rather to be open to learning and to accepting suggestions and advice. This 'deliberate detachment of personal, emotional, political as well as other presuppositions in the situation ... implies training in non-judgmental attitudes' (Gynnild, 2011, p. 43) – a skill that can challenge those who have been trained to know. In an effort to balance the potential regression that first-time attendees may experience, Glaser makes skilful use of humour and playfulness to encourage participants to detach in service to learning. Gynnild (2011) sees additional value in the role of humour: 'Humour helps keep energy up, and it is a generous way of telling people to keep on track. Moreover, playfulness helps create psychological space for exploration and for breaking out within a group ... fosters risk-taking ... might take the edge off otherwise embarrassing situations' (p. 44). While the first-time attendee may find that they leave feeling somewhat overwhelmed and even deflated, Glaser's anthem to trust in emergence often provides the longed-for reward:

> After my seminar I felt a bit down, everybody seemed to have found the core category after a real experience of epiphany. ... Barney told me to go back to my data because he suggested I was forcing, and this is what I did. I went home and restarted the analysis from zero and bosh ... there it was – my wonderful core category. (Email from PhD Student, March 14, 2016)

Gynnild (2011) suggests that atmosphering fosters psychosocial properties of 'authentic presence, explicitness, full acceptance, and playfulness' (p. 34) and emphasizes that it is '... a conscious teaching act aimed at escalating participants' learning curve as much as possible within the given time frame [and] ... where the structuring of seminars conditions [both] the emergent individual and collective learning processes' (p. 31). Gynnild conceptualizes the atmosphering process around five distinct framing principles:

- *Across-ism* whereby the mix of research disciplines, substantive areas and GT skill levels 'takes the edge off unproductive competition between participants in favour of productive, collaborative sharing' (p. 38),
- *Fly-in, fly-out* as a temporary physical relocation and decontextualization whereby 'participants literally have to let go of their everyday life routines and environment ... going global ... accelerates the process of opening up for new discoveries' (pp. 38–39),
- *Sense orchestrating* through informality to reduce anxiety and 'purposive ambiance' (p. 39) through careful selection of seminar locations (i.e., inspiring global settings) and facilities that excite and inspire through an 'aura of distinction' (p. 39). No dreary university classrooms!
- *Dressing down* as Glaser himself invariably does in blue jeans and sweaters – no suits or tweedy jackets! Dressing down is a sociological leveller 'signal[ling] a peer-to-peer approach' (p. 40) intended to further reduce performance anxiety.
- *Group individualism* whereby seminars are designed to accommodate binary needs for both plenary and individual sessions and supports the idea of 'multiple experientiality' (p. 40) as participants are offered an intensive burst of learning by 'conceptualizing across disciplines and stages of theory development' (p. 40).

The overall aim is to set the stage for collaborative support, both during the intensive engagement of the three-day seminar and potentially extending this support in follow-up interactions with seminar leaders as well as among participants themselves: '...a future set of intimate, collaborative colleagues in research ... with a depth of understanding of what the analyst is doing in generating grounded theory. ... Eventually such collaboration becomes an internal dialogue and the participant is trained to go it alone' (Gynnild, 2011, pp. 34–35). The seminar process '...empowers its participants by building confidence in doing grounded theory ... experientially grounding the method ... networking ... planting seeds for further strategies and methods ... clarifying the method jargon ... ok-ing the tolerance for confusion and regression' (Glaser, 1998, p. 232). Appendix 20.B offers a range of comments from seminar attendees demonstrating both the experiential nature of the methodology and the value in connecting with others seeking to advance understanding and skill.

The Structure

Glaser (1998) explains that the seminar structure that he used at UCSF extended over a semester or two, with four to eight students working on a grounded theory for journal publication. Students would meet weekly for three of the four weeks per month, with the fourth week open to provide a necessary break so as to allow the various works in progress to 'cook'. Meeting weekly on the other three weeks per month was necessary to sustain momentum. He explains that everyone worked on everyone's study in progress. As such, 'each participant will end up doing some measure of 4 to 8 studies' (p. 218).

He elaborates the division of labour as consisting of four positions: a presenter, two note takers (one substantive-focused and one methodology-focused), with the remaining participants as analysts. 'No teachers are needed as people help each other, but a mentor is always helpful … no lectures of more than a few minutes, just lots of discussion' (p. 219). The first session was devoted to coding and memoing an 'intuitive sampling' (p. 226) of field notes (10 to 15 pages) from across a participant's data. The sampling would not be taken from one interview transcript or one long field note but would be 'a sampling of many in order to get the patterns over many incidents' (p. 226). 'One goal of the first session is to firm up a choice for core category as best as possible to use as selective coding for session two' (p. 227). This second session is then devoted to coding and memoing a second 'intuitive sample' of field notes that appear to relate to the selected core category, the goal here being to 'sufficiently confirm the core category by its relations to other categories and to write many memos on these categories, other properties and their relationships' (p. 227). During the third session, the group works on hand sorting all of the memos that have been written by the researcher and other group members so as to 'try to firm up an overall emergent integration of the memos into a beginning theory' (p. 227). The researcher then takes this sort home and continues to sort and prepare a working paper as a first draft. The fourth session is devoted to reworking and editing the full draft in anticipation of its submission for journal publication.

Of course, these sessions are spread over several months in tandem with the studies of the other participants. Overall, the process takes months, thus facilitating GT's delayed action learning curve. Participation was limited to those actually engaged in a GT study and seeking to publish their work. No 'auditors' or 'observers' were allowed as Glaser felt they constrained the robust engagement of those with a firm stake in the seminar outcome (Glaser, 1978, p. 33). Also important was the rule of no late entries into the group. Glaser believed that unless they were there from the outset, 'they would never be able to experientially catch up to the assumptive buildup [*sic*] to which the seminar tacitly refers as they analyse each others [*sic*] data' (p. 33).

While the seminar approach has evolved over time, the basic structure of collaborative support in service to conceptual emergence remains but in a more intensive learning climate. Day 1 of the three-day intensive seminar begins with an opening 'lecture' intended to set the atmosphere, where participants are asked to set aside emotions and anxieties around their participation and to expect and indeed embrace confusion as a necessary step to discovering theory from data. The seminar proceeds with each participant briefly introducing themselves, stating their name, affiliation and one or two sentences about their study. Doing so breaks the tension as everyone has spoken and has an idea about who else is attending. Participants are usually awed by the geographic scope and disciplinary range represented around the table; it is a new experience as most are accustomed to disciplinary-specific seminars.

Following the round of introductions, the first participant is invited to present their study, state where they are in the GT process and what they would like help with from the seminar. The order of presentations is important to give participants a sense of where they 'sit' in relation to others' studies and problems, offering both confirmation that others may be facing problems similar to theirs and reassurance that others have been able to successfully solve similar issues and progress their studies. In listening to others presenting their challenges, everyone learns by actively engaging in the troubleshooting discussions and suggestions. Presentations and troubleshooting continue throughout the day. A leisurely lunch break offers another opportunity for networking among participants, thus further building a sense of collaborative support that often carries forward into an evening of informal dining and sharing of experiences.

Day 2 begins with a short debrief of the first day, offering an opportunity for participants to raise any thoughts or questions that may have emerged over night. The remainder of the day is devoted to troubleshooting. A celebratory dinner and presentation of certificates often caps the second day. The agenda for Day 3 is more relaxed and informal, with a series of one-on-one or small group meetings with the seminar leader for those who wish to have this opportunity to explore what has emerged for them over the course of the two days and what to do next. It is also an opportunity for some to be more open and candid than they may have felt comfortable doing in the full seminar. The day often includes an informal Q&A session that runs in parallel with the one-on-one sessions. Here, more experienced grounded theorists offer responses to questions from novices and seek to resolve concerns or misunderstandings that may not have been fully addressed in the first two days. The more relaxed and intimate approach on Day 3 also responds to a range of learning dispositions ensuring that those who are more reserved still have an opportunity to air their questions and concerns. Apart from this basic structure, the seminars remain largely emergent, offering help just where each individual participant is in the process and what they are having difficulty with. 'This approach brings the workshop right to the edge of current problems of participants in the workshop which is their most meaningful next increment of learning. Its details are planned on the spot according to the ability level of participants as they emerge' (Glaser, 1998, p. 231).

TEACHING CLASSIC GT METHODOLOGY

Young (2016) suggests that '[t]eaching is not about ultimate control. It is about affecting learners with the least possible influence, and most positive outcomes' (p. 140). He likens teaching to a complex adaptive system cautioning that '...learning environments can suffer from reductionist beliefs resulting in linear teaching models and frameworks ... the zone between order and chaos – this is where the intense learning occurs' (p. 132). He asserts that, as such, '...the role of the teacher is to create opportunities for emergence. The teacher is required to assume a decentralized role in learning ... if the teacher assumes the central role, the student is limited by the knowledge of the teacher' (p. 136) and that '[t]eachable moments, or emergence, are the direct result of creating a classroom collective – a place where student learning occurs in relation to other students, ideas, and experiences' (p. 137). So what are some achievable methods for fostering moments of learning emergence along the GT learning curve?

Schreiber (2001) has raised a very practical challenge in teaching GT: '... it is difficult to capture fully in writing the 'how to' of the method without sacrificing its more intuitive aspects. Part of the difficulty is that getting a handle on the method involves process learning: you learn as you do' (p. 109). Hesse-Biber (2007) reminds us of the reality in academia today where GT is so frequently conflated with qualitative methods and the '...importance of relaying to students the idea that grounded theory is a "craft" ... that students need to hone their skills over a period of time ... that instructors are often strapped for time, and many are teaching grounded theory as only a small section of a larger methods course' (p. 334). Glaser (1998) reminds us that those who try to teach GT are often also in want of training as '...their training is usually partial compared to the full package ... usually focuses on only some, not all stages and dimensions of grounded theory' (p. 216). And as Gynnild and Martin (2011) note, 'When the novice scholars and their supervisors are uninformed, they rewrite the method with their own misunderstandings' (p. 4). McCallin, Nathaniel and Andrews (2011) advise that '...novices seldom appreciate the fine distinctions of the method until they engage in the research process. If a researcher is under supervision from a qualitative researcher who is not familiar with grounded theory at all, the learner is exposed to qualitative generalizations that are at odds with what is a specialist methodology' (p. 71).

Glaser has written extensively about the power of exampling (Glaser, 1996; Glaser & Holton, 2007) as a means of instilling in students what a good GT might look like: 'Reading dissertations is a modeling phenomenon on many dimensions. ... It is a grounded support at those heavy moments of what to do next. ... It breeds a beginning autonomy for the student' (Glaser, 1996, pp. ix–x). He has also advised that reading theory from other disciples is an excellent way to cultivate a student's theoretical sensitivity to how theory is written (i.e., style) and to various theoretical codes that may have relevant emergence in their own work (Glaser, 1978, 2005). His advice is to 'skip and dip' through a wide range of books and papers:

> ...to get an overview of the theory being presented – what is the main concern, how does the core category explain the resolution of this concern, what are the categories related to the core, how has the author theoretically sampled in developing the theory, what data were used. We can study the conceptual integration of the theory – how the theorist has used theoretical coding to organize and model the theory, to produce a theory that is empirically grounded yet abstract of empirical detail, a theory that grabs with conceptual imagery and yet balances parsimony and scope. (Glaser & Holton, 2007, p. xiv)

In *Doing Grounded Theory* (1998), Glaser offers additional practical exercises that a GT teacher or mentor might wish to consider as part of their pedagogical approach: monography construction reading; five properties; and class analysis.

Monograph Construction Reading

Here he suggests having the student take 45 minutes to look for construction techniques and the general idea of the monograph. His recommended methodology is to start with the table of contents and then the last chapter which often offers a synopsis; i.e., the 'little logic [of the text] ... the goal or purpose of the book ... the main hypothesis' (Glaser, 1998, p. 211) followed by the preface, introductory chapter and appendices. He advises to '... read backwards. Look for sentence construction, paragraph construction, section construction. ... How are the chapters related or tied together?' (p. 212). Doing so allows the reader to discover 'construction and meaning' (p. 213), all the while honing their GT skill for pattern recognition.

Five Properties

Here, the class is offered a topic familiar to everyone (e.g., friendship, inheritance, celebrities, neighbours) and everyone writes a memo suggesting five properties of the concept.

Glaser suggests that this exercise '...increases confidence in the ability to conceptualize ... shows how easily people can generate categories and properties ... [but also] ... a cautionary exercise for being aware of how easy it is to yield to conjecture, preconception and forcing' (pp. 213–214) when not using GT methods.

Class Analysis

As in the exercise above, the class is offered a topic that all know about and each student offers an experience of the topic (i.e., an incident). The incidents are compared with each other as they are shared within the group and students start to generate categories and properties. One student writes memos on the emergent categories and properties. Another student takes methodological notes (i.e., how the analysis is unfolding, what underlying pattern is emerging). Memos are then sorted within the class and more memos are written and sorted. The class then discusses the emergent integration, arguing for the best fit of all memos. The sort is then written up (pp. 214–215).

MENTORING FOR SOLO LEARNING

Despite the growing availability of GT seminars offered by Glaser and experienced grounded theorists, many who wish to learn how to do GT will have to do so without experienced guidance – i.e., they will be minus-mentored (Stern, 1994) '...in the sense that their professors do not know the method or ways of teaching it' (Gynnild & Martin, 2011, p. 1). Morse (1997) emphasizes the experiential importance of mentorship by likening the attempt to learn a methodology from reading methodological texts to learning to drive by reading a manual about driving. She asserts: 'The fastest way, the most efficient way, and the most painless way is to find a mentor, even if distant' (p. 182). Gynnild and Martin (2011) assert that: 'Mentoring not only concerns methodological support; it also socializes and informs new researchers into a community of scholars' (p. 4); that the '...psychosocial aspects of mentoring tends to be just as important as the strictly skill-dependent aspects' (p. 5).

While it is possible to develop the necessary skill in doing GT while minus-mentored, Glaser (1998) cautions that the minus-mentored researcher '...should not expect conscious results too fast ... [should] always take respites from coding and memoing to let the patterns germinate in the preconscious, and then try days later to one-up oneself conceptually ... should try and trigger memos and codes by writing a lot. Once it is preconsciously processed, writing allows the conceptual material to pour out' (p. 217). Curbing anxiety and the pressure to know in advance by tolerating the consequent confusion is a necessary part of respecting the integral role of preconscious cognitive processing in emergent theorizing. Theoretical pacing is an integral aspect of GT's iterative nature. It is essential to the creative nurturing of ideas into conscious realization:

> built into each stage of the method are techniques which ensure some level of creativity ... memos allow creative theoretical forays with the data and concepts; sorting forces creative integration of the theory; reworking of initial drafts can be highly creative as the theoretical perspective becomes sharpened; and the inductive logic leans heavily on the analyst's creative boost, which comes from concepts and ideas emerging from the data ... creativity is not

> the gift of some privileged person, rather, it is a matter of developing one's personal recipe for pacing himself through the grounded theory process … creativity can both be learned and turned on when desired. (Glaser, 1978, pp. 20–22)

Each grounded theorist must find his or her own pacing rhythm, fitting it into individual life patterns by cycling periods of intense engagement with data analysis, memoing, sorting and writing with respites for relaxation, other work and professional commitments as well as time with family and friends. Doing so allows ideas to grow with the data and the theorist's increasing theoretical sensitivity. Glaser (2001) quotes one student's experience of pacing:

> 'There were periods of intensity interspersed with respites designed to allow me to step back from the all-encompassing effects of being in the thick of the action.' The interstices indicated are important. Their function is to enable the researcher to fragment the data, giving some distance in order to allow a more conceptual view to prevail. These are breathing spaces that prevent the researcher from suffocating in the intoxicating atmosphere surround[ing] captivating data. (p. 119)

The cycling pattern becomes a personal pacing recipe that aligns naturally with the theorist's temperament, commitments and obligations and keeps the theorist energized and the ideas emerging through to the writing-up stage. However, the pacing pattern may differ from one research project to another. Over time, a grounded theorist may develop several different pacing patterns as (s)he cycles through various GT studies adapting different patterns to meet varying conditions and commitments.

CONCLUDING REMARKS

In this chapter, I have set out some aspects of teaching and learning GT based on my own experience of the GT learning curve, my experience of participating in and leading a number of GT troubleshooting seminars and of mentoring a number of PhD students to the successful completion of their degree requirements. I have as well drawn upon the experience and advice of others who have also travelled this path, including, of course, the man who pioneered this learning journey. While these experiences share much in common and can offer valuable insights to those tasked with teaching GT as a research methodology, each learning and teaching journey is unique and has its own delayed action learning curve wherein much can be learned from the experiences of those who have been taught and those who have had to teach themselves! It is hoped that the ideas set forth in this chapter will offer some encouragement and support to those who journey the path in grounded theory methodology.

REFERENCES

Brinkmann, S., Jacobsen, M. H., & Kristiansen, S. (2014). Historical overview of qualitative research in the social sciences. In P. Leavy (Ed.), *The Oxford Handbook of Qualitative Research* (pp. 17–42). Oxford: Oxford University Press.

Charmaz, K. (2011). Lessons for a lifetime: Learning grounded theory from Barney Glaser. In A. Gynnild & V. Martin (Eds.), *Grounded Theory: The Philosophy, Method and Work of Barney Glaser* (pp. 177–187). Boca Raton, FL: BrownWalker Press.

Charmaz, K. (2014). Grounded theory in global perspective reviews by international researchers, *Qualitative Inquiry*, 20(9), 1074–1084.

Chen, X. (2016). Challenges and strategies of teaching qualitative research in China. *Qualitative Inquiry*, 22(2), 72–86.

Gioia, D. A., Corley, K. G., & Hamilton, A. L. (2013). Seeking qualitative rigor in inductive research notes on the Gioia methodology, *Organizational Research Methods*, 16(1), 15–31.

Glaser, B. G. (1978). *Theoretical Sensitivity: Advances in the Methodology of Grounded Theory*. Mill Valley, CA: Sociology Press.

Glaser, B. G. (1996). *Gerund Grounded Theory: The Basic Social Process Dissertation*. Mill Valley, CA: Sociology Press.

Glaser, B. G. (1998). *Doing Grounded Theory: Issues and Discussions*. Mill Valley, CA: Sociology Press.

Glaser, B. G. (2001). *The Grounded Theory Perspective: Conceptualization Contrasted with Description*. Mill Valley, CA: Sociology Press.

Glaser, B. G. (2003). *The Grounded Theory Perspective II: Description's Remodeling of Grounded Theory Methodology*. Mill Valley, CA: Sociology Press.

Glaser, B. G. (2005). *The Grounded Theory Perspective III: Theoretical Coding*. Mill Valley, CA: Sociology Press.

Glaser, B. G. (2010). The roots of grounded theory, *The Grounded Theory Review*, 9(2), 1–14.

Glaser, B. G. (2011). *Getting Out of the Data: Grounded Theory Conceptualization*. Mill Valley, CA: Sociology Press.

Glaser, B. G. (2012). *Stop, Write: Writing Grounded Theory*. Mill Valley, CA: Sociology Press.

Glaser, B. G. (2013). *No Preconceptions: The Grounded Theory Dictum*. Mill Valley, CA: Sociology Press.

Glaser, B. G. (2014). *Choosing Classic Grounded Theory: A Grounded Theory Reader of Expert Advice*. Mill Valley, CA: Sociology Press.

Glaser, B. G. (2016). *The Cry for Help: Preserving Autonomy Doing GT Research*. Mill Valley, CA: Sociology Press.

Glaser, B. G. & Holton, J. A. (Eds.) (2007). *The Grounded Theory Seminar Reader*. Mill Valley, CA: Sociology Press.

Glaser, B. G. & Strauss, A. L. (1967). *The Discovery of Grounded Theory: Strategies for Qualitative Research*. New York: Aldine de Gruyter.

Guthrie, W. & Lowe, A. (2011). Getting through the PhD process using GT: A supervisor–researcher perspective. In V. B. Martin & A. Gynnild (Eds.), *Grounded Theory: The Philosophy, Method, and Work of Barney Glaser* (pp. 51–68). Boca Raton, FL: BrownWalker Press.

Gynnild, A. (2011). Atmosphering for conceptual discovery. In V. B. Martin & A. Gynnild (Eds.), *Grounded Theory: The Philosophy, Method, and Work of Barney Glaser* (pp. 31–50). Boca Raton, FL: BrownWalker Press.

Gynnild, A. (2016). Editorial: New perspectives on conceptual growth through GT. *The Grounded Theory Review*, 15(1), 1–3.

Gynnild, A. & Martin, V. (2011). Mentoring a method. In V. B. Martin & A. Gynnild (Eds.), *Grounded Theory: The Philosophy, Method, and Work of Barney Glaser* (pp. 1–11). Boca Raton, FL: BrownWalker Press.

Hesse-Biber, S. N. (2007). Teaching grounded theory. In A. Bryant & K. C. Charmaz (Eds.), *The SAGE Handbook of Grounded Theory* (pp. 311–338). London: Sage.

Holton, J. A. (2006). *Rehumanising Knowledge Work through Fluctuating Support Networks: A Grounded Theory*. Unpublished doctoral thesis, University of Northampton, UK.

Holton, J. A. (2007). Rehumanising knowledge work through fluctuating support networks: A grounded theory. *The Grounded Theory Review*, 6(2), 23–46.

Holton, J.A. (2011). The autonomous creativity of Barney G. Glaser: Early influences in the emergence of classic grounded theory methodology, In Gynnild, A. & Martin, V.B. (Eds.), *Grounded Theory: The Philosophy, Method and Work of Barney Glaser* (pp.201-223), Boca Raton, Florida: Brown Walker Press.

Holton, J. A. & Walsh, I. (2017). *Classic Grounded Theory: Applications with Qualitative and Quantitative Data*. Thousand Oaks, CA: Sage.

McCallin, A., Nathaniel, A., & Andrews, T. (2011). Learning methodology minus mentorship. In V. B. Martin & A. Gynnild (Eds.), *Grounded Theory: The Philosophy, Method, and Work of Barney Glaser* (pp. 69–84). Boca Raton, FL: BrownWalker Press.

Morse, J. E. (1997). Learning to drive from a manual? *Qualitative Health Research*, 7(2), 181–183.

Nagel, D. A., Burns, V. F., Tilley, C., & Aubin, D. (2015). When novice researchers adopt constructivist grounded theory: Navigating less travelled paradigmatic and methodological paths in PhD dissertation work. *International Journal of Doctoral Studies*, 10, 365–383.

Rogers, C. (1969). *Freedom to Learn: A View of What Education Might Become*. Columbus, OH: Charles Merrill.

Schreiber, R. S. (2001). The grounded theory club, or who needs an expert mentor. In R. S. Schreiber & P. N. Stern (Eds.), *Using Grounded Theory in Nursing* (pp. 97–111). New York: Springer.

Simmons, O. E. (2011). Why classic grounded theory. In V. B. Martin & A. Gynnild (Eds.), *Grounded Theory: The Philosophy, Method, and Work of Barney Glaser* (pp. 15–30). Boca Raton, FL: BrownWalker Press.

Stern, P. N. (1994). Eroding grounded theory. In J. Morse (Ed.), *Critical Issues in Qualitative Research Methods* (pp. 212–223). Thousand Oaks, CA: Sage.

Strauss, A. L. & Corbin, J. M. (1990). *Basics of Qualitative Research: Grounded Theory Procedures and Techniques.* Newbury Park, CA: Sage.

Walsh, I., Holton, J. A., Bailyn, L., Fernandez, W., Levina, N., & Glaser, B. G. (2015) What grounded theory is … A critically reflective conversation among scholars. *Organizational Research Methods*, 18(4), 581–599.

Wu, C.-H. V. & Beaunae, C. (2014). Personal reflections on cautions and considerations for navigating the path of grounded theory doctoral theses and dissertations: A long walk through a dark forest. *International Journal of Social Research Methodology*, 17(3), 249–265.

Young, C. (2016). Assuming an epistemology of emergence: Classrooms as complex adaptive systems. In S. S. Ercetin (Ed.), *Chaos, Complexity and Leadership* (pp. 131–141). Dordrecht, NL: Springer International.

Zetterberg, H. L. (1962). *Social Theory and Social Practice*. Edison, NJ: Transaction.

Appendix 20.A The GT Troubleshooting Seminar: Structure and approach

Pre-Seminar Troubleshootee Selection and Preparation	Applicants are expected to read *Theoretical Sensitivity* (Glaser, 1978) and *Doing Grounded Theory* (Glaser, 1998) and to forward a brief overview of their research problem to the seminar coordinator by answering the following questions: – *What is the area/focus of your research?* – *Where are you in the GT process?* – *Have you identified your core category? If so, please elaborate.* – *What would you like help/feedback on from the seminar?* The goal is to select a range of participants at various stages of the GT process but all should have some data and/or memos to be shared and 'worked' during the seminar.
Meeting and Greeting	The networking and collaborative support begins on the evening prior to the seminar with an informal Meet and Greet reception. This informal social time establishes 'connects' among participants, renews connections made at previous seminars or through virtual mentoring relationships. It also provides time with Barney Glaser – important for both novices and repeat attendees. The atmosphering here establishes an initial toning for the seminar proceedings, allows opportunity for any questions or concerns to be addressed with either the seminar coordinator (logistics, etc.) or Barney (troubleshooting presentations, etc.).
The overall approach in the seminar is to coach rather than to lecture	
Atmosphering	Glaser begins the seminar by *toning* the group through: 1. open sharing and generosity (sharing of resources, books, info on Sociology Press, etc.) 2. connecting and drawing participants in by addressing them individually by name 3. informality, humbleness and humour to reduce anxiety and 'presentation nerves'
Expectationing	1. Setting realistic yet aspiring goals for seminar participation – 'getting your PhD, getting publications' 2. Negotiating the rules of engagement for seminar participation – engaging through choice – 'Breaking up mindsets', participating as 'analysts rather than citizens'
Sensitizing	Raising level of theoretical sensitivity by: 1. using conceptual language in toning and sharing 2. illustrating with concepts, e.g., *desisting residual selves*, *binary retreat*, *status accumulation*, *status passage* 3. emphasizing earned relevance by discussing eroding impact of preconception 4. introducing GT concepts of preconscious processing, delayed action learning, confusion, depression, regression, interchangeability of indicators, etc. 5. reviewing 'all is data' – types of data – vague, properline, interpreted, baseline 6. emphasizing GT's 'memo centrality' – the focus on writing rather than talking

(Continued)

Appendix 20.A (Continued)

Participants who have done the pre-seminar readings begin to relax and open up to what is ahead	
Structuring	The teaching approach is *unordered thinking*. The strategy is to overload through *seed planting* with resultant confusion and later preconscious processing for *realization*. Glaser sets out the functions of the seminar: 1. *embodiment* (through live interaction with the methodology's originator and other practitioners) 2. *inspiration* (through hearing others' experiences and successes) 3. *jumpstarting progress* (through help in getting to the next step as concerns and needs are addressed) 4. *empowerment* (through personal autonomy, contribution, originality) 5. *networking* (to foster collaborative support) 6. *seed planting* (for delayed action learning) 7. *jargoning* (by learning the correct use of the terminology) 8. *confidence building* (in a safe environment that enables learning) 9. *experiential* (by interaction and doing) 10. *youthifying* (by energizing both novices and mature GT researchers) 11. *realization* (by fostering assurance of emergence through Eureka after months of confusion) 12. *credentializing* (by legitimating participant's GT knowledge and expertise)
Setting up the Interaction	The rules of engagement: Participants are analysts, not citizens of the world, i.e., no identity, just data (empirical objectivity) 1. Need to suspend assumptions, social sensitivities, ideologies and 'rescuing urges' in service to conceptualization of data 2. Openness, norm breaking, taking chances, permitting, emotion sharing in a safe environment 3. Necessary to break down mindsets to open up to what is really going on in the data 4. All questions are valid as they feed associative thinking and pattern building that facilitates preconscious processing 5. Interruptions (one-upping) are welcomed to get on the conceptual level; to get beyond description to the concept 6. Stop 'story talk' and get to the point – what's the concept? 7. Encourage optimal contradictions ('what you're really saying is this…') to clarify the concept, properties, and dimensions 8. Overcome fear of identity loss when interrupted or challenged
Relieving Concerns	Addressing questions from participants about: 1. epistemology and ontology of GT 2. description vs conceptualization 3. QDA's worrisome accuracy overriding GT's ready modifiability 4. Symbolic interactionism and constructivism 5. dealing with professional colleagues and supervisors who lack GT understanding 6. limitations of statistical data – going beyond the 'facts' to what's really going on – conceptualizing underlying patterns

The Opening Lecture	Reviewing the roots of Grounded Theory – rather than summing up indices (neutralization), GT compares indices to develop conceptual properties (constant comparative method) – comparing incident to incident to get the real meaning of the concept – rather than developing hypotheses to be verified, GT inductively analyses to see what emerges – latent patterns – latent structure analysis – running the core against everything else to look for latent patterns – interchangeability of indicators – with 20 indicators, use any four to get same result – comparing incident to incident, then incident to concept to get properties – elaboration analysis – patterns are constantly modifiable whereas description is quickly stale-dated – GT not an argument against qualitative data analysis but an extension of traditional quantitative data analysis – research gets legitimating power through a theoretical perspective (epistemology) but is at same time restricted by this – in contrast, GT is philosophically flexible and can use any data – symbolic interactionism/constructivism are merely theoretical perspectives on a descriptive level but not on a conceptual level – symbolic interaction offers theoretical codes to GT but these are not the only theoretical codes used in GT – GT is abstraction that gets applied; a theory that offers explanation and access variables for intervention
The Troubleshooting Process	Addressing in turn each participant's immediate issue and getting them to the next step in the GT process. Important to work with their data (i.e., field notes and memos). Data provide different views/perspectives/vantage points. Troubleshooting helps to get perspectives on perspectives through: – interrupting descriptions to jumpstart and raise the conceptual level – one-upping to abstract conceptualizations – cognitive stripping/mindset destruction to rebuild conceptually – atmosphering/opening up/mutual conferring/toning through reversal humour

(*Continued*)

Appendix 20.A (Continued)

Capitalizing on Teachable Moments	Various misunderstandings that emerge through troubleshooting interactions provide additional opportunities for learning that: 1. GT is a methodology not just a method. 2. It is 'just theory' – probability that gets modified BUT it is theory grounded in data not conjectured by a brilliant mind. 3. 'Instilling the spill' important in data collection while being careful not to collect duplicate data (wasteful effort). Remember the interchangeability of conceptual indicators. 4. Many professionals are like 'walking surveys' of data collected from accumulated experience …'I've seen a lot of these cases…' Latent patterns are intuited but this data is not analyzed. 5. Empty generating of concepts without data is simply spinning off into conjecture. 6. Constant comparative method constantly corrects for researcher and interviewee bias. 7. In coding and in naming core category need to keep the language neutral (i.e., open) to conceptualize the pattern rather than describe the incident. 8. Theoretical codes must emerge if they are not to preconceive or force theory. 9. Knowing when to cease sampling – when the core is clear – 'you can't do it all' – you've done enough – GT is always a slice, not full capture. Need to stop and write up to bring your readers up to your slice. You will always know more than your reader will. 10. Writing up first, then integrating extant literature/theory if required – use research data rather than conjectured theory. Instead, correct conjectured theory with your grounded theory. 11. Drafts are OK – don't worry about 'perfect'; it's the ideas that matter. 12. Beware of the competitive barriers of supervisors and write for a wider audience – the people who matter – get the professional critique not just the individual perspective. 13. Acknowledge your exposure anxiety but claim your autonomy over theoretical capitalists and your admiration for senior academics. 14. Use an appeal to future research to address issues not elaborated in your GT data. 15. Be careful in how you use software. Do not be fooled into thinking it can do the real work of coding and analyzing your data. Too mechanical and without the elegance and sophistication of human cognition.

Appendix 20.B GT Seminar participant reflections

On the Seminar Experience	– Learning atmosphere created in the seminar was casual, flexible, yet with constantly sharpening focus – Open climate for discussions was inviting, nurturing, no pressure to be wise and perfect – Everyone being so friendly, interesting, inspirational, dedicated, generous and brilliant – Listening to those at later stages of GT study as it helps me envisage where I am going – Barney's 'skill spill' and teachable moments. His willingness to respond to individual questions no matter how basic. I learn better from a verbal explanation – Listening to others' problems even though at different stages provides more insight into the process – Discussions regarding academic requirements versus the essence of GT – Barney was tough enough to push new learning without being overly critical – Self-sufficiency and the ability to keep learning with some sense of confidence that I was on the right track. A new inner energyl took so much away from the seminar. Particularly the importance of memoing. Without them, there isn't a GT. I have gone back to my data and found so much more in it and am writing many more memos

(*Continued*)

Appendix 20.B (Continued)

Most Powerful Learning	– How to use theoretical codes – Lecture on roots of GT (many times mentioned!) – Troubleshooting with so many research projects in different fields being presented and seeing how we can learn from others' work from totally different fields of research – Seeing how we can start to recognize the general aspects of GT in others' work and make the connective points to our own work – That it's OK to be where I am in my GT skill development and that coming away from the seminar, I have improved my ability to write more conceptually – Getting a real sense of abstraction and moving the theory beyond the descriptive level – That the theory when discovered is abstract of the data (i.e., that data are dead as soon as they are collected) – The preconscious processing that follows each seminar during which something new emerges – Opening up to new learning and feeling motivated to get back into research – Gaining a better understanding of the principles of GT – I took so much away from the seminar; particularly the importance of memo writing. Without them there isn't a GT. I have gone back to my data and found so much more in it and am writing many more memos – A reinforced belief in myself that I understand GT and can do it. Hearing from others about how they have dealt with PhD committee resistance and lack of knowledge – Barney's comments that I had related concept to concept were re-assuring and confidence building for me. My lack of assuredness had stalled my writing up of the theory and this gave me the boost I needed. The seminar also broadened my understanding of grounded theory. Each exposure and discussion sheds new light on how concepts are generated and articulated. I also feel privileged to consider myself part of the growing community of classic grounded theorists. The connection with others is an important part of the support network. Addressing the committee concerns on grounded theory is a very real issue for some and it was good to discuss this even if it is a rhetorical wrestle – The importance of conceptualization, how Barney would also ask, 'how would you conceptualize that?' – It was important for me to hear over and over again: Just do it! It was important to see how the other participants made progress, it was important to feel the inspiring atmosphere, it was important to meet Barney, it was important to meet people from different countries and different fields sharing their ideas, it was important to get the feeling of being part of something special. So, for me it was the encouragement I got from the seminar that affected my research process most

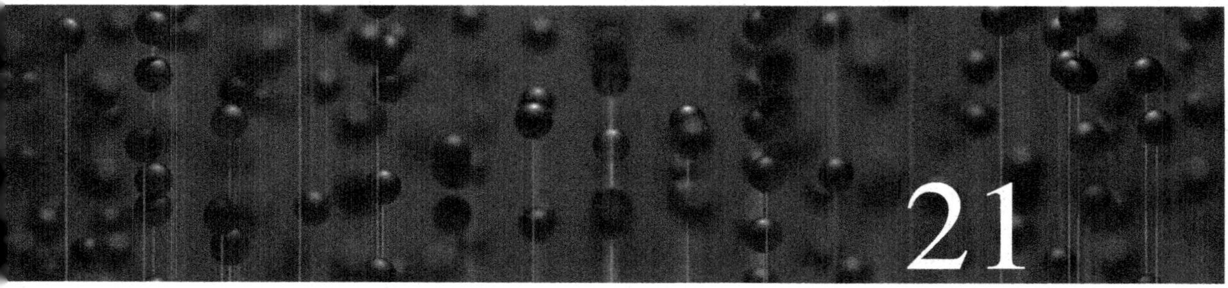

Grounded Description: No No

Barney G. Glaser

Grounded description is on the increase with the increase of grounded theory throughout the world. Much grounded description is jargonized as GT and it is not GT. Grounded description is trying to describe the population studied, like a qualitative data analysis (QDA) study requires, by describing all the interchangeable indicators that grounded the concept. In contrast, GT is not to describe the population. GT is the relation between concepts which emerged from the population by constant comparing and then are related to each other by a theoretical code. The GT theory then becomes general and abstract of the study population by time, place and people. The GT stands on its own, and the data on which it is grounded is often forgotten for the grab and general implications of the theory. For example, rooting from here to there is based on basic mobility resources (BMRs) (e.g., planning basic mobility resources for a trip).

Why is this happening? There are several reasons. Description is frequently demanded by an academic department perspective and professor demands since research is traditionally descriptive nearly 100% of the time. Being abstract of time, place and people is not the normal quest of academic research. Accurate description is the quest. The generated concepts used for normal description can be very discreet and its indicators also. They prove relevance and fit for population data. The abstract nature and its general implications of a GT core concept and its potential for generating a GT are ignored or lightly referred to while describing takes over.

Grounded description is a step toward discovery of a GT, not a GT. But many new to the GT methodology do not realize this. They become thrilled with generating a grabby concept and think that it is the final step to generating a GT and then describe it at length to prove its accurate existence. This approach, of course, suits the descriptive perspective of most academic research.

Grounded description is further supported by the simple fact that most people, including academics, cannot conceptualize. It is best, if at all, if they can come up with one generated concept. Or if not, they can use a conjectured – usually ungrounded – concept, taken from their field literature. That is fine, since description, proven accurate, runs the world, with conjectured concepts based on no facts a close second. A distant third is conceptualizing concepts, however powerful they may actually be.

There are many books written now on GT that are actually about grounded description. They confuse the definition and methodology of GT with lofty academic scholarship backed by high-level positions in a university department. They bring GT back to description. Mixed writing on QDA and GT often tend to regress GT to description procedures, such as taping preformed interviews.

In this chapter I will discuss many of the differences between GT and conceptual description, so the reader can spot the latter being termed the former. Conceptual description easily results in data overload in the quest of full coverage. For a GT concept, why keep collecting interchangeable indicators as required by full accurate description once you have a concept? Five or six indicators can be enough, as opposed to dissertation requirements to get data from all respondents on a concept for descriptive generality that will soon become 'stale dated' anyway. Full coverage of data collection is a waste of research resources for generating a GT once a core concept pattern is discovered and theoretically sampled for.

Since concepts are abstract of time, place and people, accuracy is not an issue. Concepts are ranges varying from none to a strong presence, as told by other conceptual properties of the core concept that give the core concept a value on the range. And the properties can come from other data. For example, rooting (getting from here to there) is a core concept with many general implications, depending on the BMRs involved. I will not tell you the data that this theory was generated from. It is not necessary as its generality is so clear and applies so easily. We all root every day to work, to meetings, etc. with planning and budgets.

Coopting GT's conceptual power, popularity etc. for certifying a paper, a meeting, a program occurs frequently by authors, professors etc. Certifying by reference to GT core variables is easily described at length since core variable general implications are so rich in description. Then GT is lost to its being treated as grounded description. It's called the reversibility of interchangeable indicators. It is hard to stop the flow of indictors for a concept.

GT's goal is to provide conceptual explanation of general patterns of behavior. It is not for verifying hypotheses like descriptive data is. Thus, if GT is used to verify facts it easily becomes conceptual description and the GT power is lost to its descriptive use. And a GT has many indicators that can vary the GT conceptually. Some indicators may support the hypothesis and some disprove it. The loss of the GT goal and its power is great when a GT is reduced to descriptive verification.

Many novices and supervisors wish a double goal which is a grabby concept for a GT with lots of illustration. Conceptual theory suffers usually and description dominates. Lots of description easily crowds out conceptual theory with its rich empirical story talk about the general implications of a single rich core concept like super normalizing. Wanting credit for the rich full description wins, by giving many interchangeable indicators. Wanting full descriptive coverage is typical in rich, qualitative research that many colleagues want. Good grounded theory, concepts related to concepts, takes a minimum of illustration if at all. Often a good core concept is self-illustrating. No matter how rich conceptual description may emerge, it is not grounded theory. GT does not require full coverage. Indeed, often the data is forgotten for the emergent GT, which is abstract of the data and applies to many different substantive data. GT is not description, especially not full coverage.

In fact, many a novice is never told about conceptual description not being GT, and they pursue the former as the latter. They may discover later in the dissertation process that it is only conceptual description. Or they never discover it and firmly believer they did a GT thesis. Supervisors have a similar problem when they have spent a long career doing conceptual description, do not know GT and simply call conceptual description GT. They feel the jargon fits. They give up nothing methodologically, since a highly illustrated paper, whether conceptual, or just description without concepts, is the way to do it. In short, combining concept with heavy description is the way to success. And it is a perspective that is often departmentally required for the dissertation as the OK perspective. Indeed, many students who have done a GT (interrelated concepts) have been forced by their committee or supervisor to add much description to the theory to get their dissertation approved.

Conceptual description is forced as descriptive coverage of a topic or group of participants. It is ignored or forgotten or not known that with GT the data from which the GT was generated can easily be forgotten for its general implications for many other data. That GT is abstract of time, place and people is forgotten in favor of descriptive coverage.

Conceptual theory (a GT) can be confused with another type of description and then related to conceptual description, thereby weakening the GT. A supervisor wrote me after reading this paper, 'I just read a paper and this is exactly what the authors were doing. Even when they come up with concepts they just do not get the difference between empirically describing the findings from their study for a GT. A theory to them is not abstract of their full descriptive coverage that they considered the basis of their full data coverage that was the basis of their study.' It is hard for novices and supervisors to give up traditional QDA. And of course many cannot conceptualize. The individualized autonomy, provided by GT methodology, is required of researchers for doing GT fully conceptualized plus the ability to conceptualize new concepts. This confusion is usually and often supported by departmental social structures, especially for the PhD process.

Both GT and description are products of different methodologies that get confused to conceptual description. This occurs often during a collaboration of two or more researchers trained in different methodologies, GT methodology being one and a QDA descriptive methodology another. It is hard to give up one's training and its vision and a departmental structure of which there are many structures supporting QDA methods. The researcher sees the way of his methodology, his department perspective and his colleagues. The QDA perspective, as conceptual description, wins for its simplicity compared to GT and for its simple methodology that has been in use many years before GT. The same applies to journals: papers are often returned with the request for more description.

Both products are generated from a methodology, conceptual description being far simpler and requiring less ability to conceptualize. And most people, including researchers, live on descriptive accuracy with little or no abstraction. Few individuals and researchers live conceptually. Thus, learning to conceptualize and then using the concepts is highly individualized and requires autonomy. Not many researchers can hold the conceptual level according to GT methodology. Slipping down to conceptual description occurs easily and automatically as normal.

To be sure, GT and description with a concept or two are both generated by a different methodology. Slipping to description is a slipping from the GT methodology to a descriptive methodology that to most researchers is known. The difference between the particularistic, routine normative data we all garner in our everyday lives and scientific data is that the latter is generated using a methodology. The method makes the product scientific. This may sound trite, but it is just the beginning of many complex research methodology issues. Whatever methodology may be chosen to make a research scientific has many implicit and explicit varying types of data collections. That is, what respondents, what pacing and timing for data collection, what type of analysis, etc. and what type of product (book, paper and/or lecture) is the goal. In the case of description or conceptual description, the explicit research goal must be decided. Is full coverage wanted, how to achieve worrisome accuracy, how to interpret the findings etc., etc., how to give the actual generality of the data, what procedures to use? These issues and many more are debated at length in the QDA literature. Thus, slipping from GT into conceptual description puts a non-GT claim of many issues on the ensuing analysis. GT is lost to another method with its own issues and problems. GT procedures are passed over and regaining them is doubtful.

There is doubtful correcting of the loss and of slipping away of conceptualization theory (GT) and its procedures. It is a growing problem for GT with still little recognition of the problem in the literature. Given the natural, automatic aspects of conceptual description and its integration into departmental structure and journal requirements, corrections back to GT are apt to come slow and hard to explain, however necessary.

GT is itself a grounded theory with conceptualization being the core category. We all know or have an idea what conceptualization is in general. It comes naturally to most of us, yet GT has procedures for generating emergent, discovered GT concepts. They must be followed for secured grounding. I discussed at length in *Doing Grounded Theory* (Glaser 1998), the conceptual license offered by GT methodology to the researcher. In exchange, the GT researcher is supposed to use his procedurally generated, emergent, discovered concepts from his data, as opposed to using the reified concepts of conjecture offered by theoretical capitalists. Discovering one's own concept from the research data with fit and relevance is usually very exciting for the researcher. Only four or five concepts are usually necessary for a GT. New concepts are one of the original contributions of GT.

Unfortunately, this is where generating GT often stops by slipping into extensive description of the general implications of the core concept that was discovered. Further steps of generating a GT for the core concern are ignored for and in favor of description procedures. The GT perspective is lost. The freedom, autonomy and license required to generate and write conceptual theory that explains the continual resolving of a main concern is lost. GT methodology is very different from conceptual description which uses a QDA methodology. The GT methodology goal is the multivariate integration of concepts, that is of patterns named as concepts and their properties, generated by the constant comparative method. Conceptual description is full of accurate descriptive coverage. Interchangeability of conceptual indicators is ignored and used as description. GT methods abstractly transcend all description methods and are never stale dated as descriptions soon are. Worrisome accuracy for GT is not an issue as with conceptual description. Most GT is generated from qualitative data since it is easier to obtain and less expensive than other data, but it can be generated from quantitative data. And qualitative data easily becomes descriptive.

These are but a few of the vast differences in the GT and conceptual descriptive methodologies. The reader who knows GT methodology can probably think of many more differences. The reader who does not know GT methods will just have to believe me. He/she will pursue descriptive methods to generate conceptual description with no conflict and not realizing the great loss to GT. As GT spreads slowly throughout the world, the methodological conflict between concepts and description grows and is being resolved in favor of GT conceptualization. It is social and psychological scientists who are mandated to conceptualize a theory and thus learn the rigorous GT procedures of concept generation so they can generate a GT.

The two most important properties of conceptualization that attract researchers are that they are abstract of time, people and place, and the naming of the concept usually has much grab. Thus, concepts can live with us forever. One grounded concept can attract much delightful description. Like supernormalizing.

The GT concepts must be generated from data: from a series of interchangeable indicators (see my book *Getting Out of the Data*; Glaser 2011). Concepts based on a single impression do not work, they must be based on the constant comparative method. That is comparing interchangeable indicators showing a pattern of behavior. Forcing a pattern on behavior to surmise a pattern does not work as grounded GT is a form of discovered latent structure analysis grounded in systematically collected data. Conceptual description is accurate description.

In sum, the researcher should guard against letting a GT research slip into routine extensive description of one grounded concept.

REFERENCES

Glaser, B. G. (1998). *Doing Grounded Theory: Issues and Discussions*. Mill Valley, CA: Sociology Press.

Glaser, B. G. (2011). *Getting Out of the Data: Grounded Theory Conceptualization*. Mill Valley, CA: Sociology Press.

PART V

GTM and Qualitative Research Practice

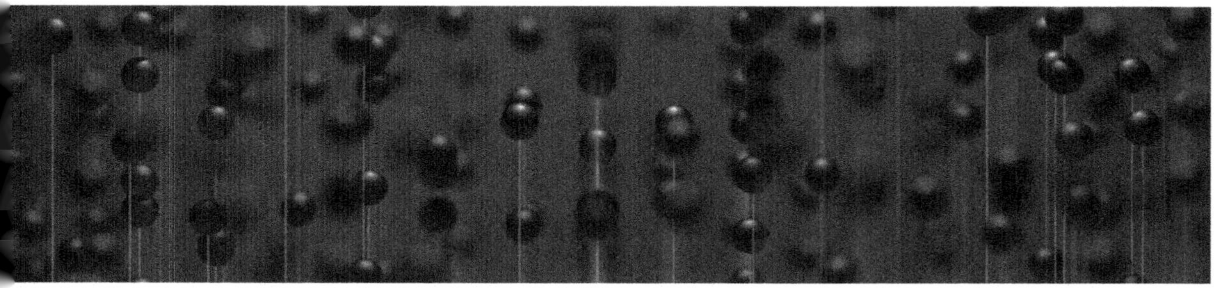

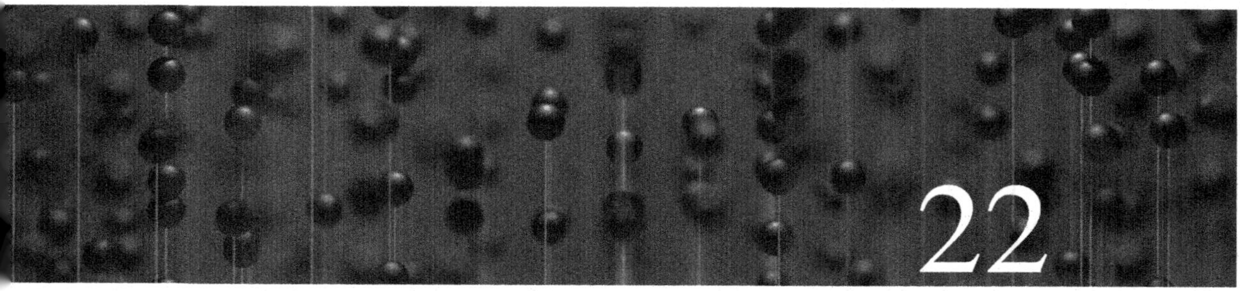

Grounded Theory and the Politics of Interpretation, Redux

Norman K. Denzin

Critics and fans of grounded theory observe:

> If theory is dead and if data are dead, then why do we need grounded theory? I mean what does a grounded theory look like anyway (anonymous critic)?

The writing is direct, and immediate, subversive, no big words. To wit:

> The grounded theorist has a tool kit which includes: inductive and abductive logic, emergent strategies, comparative methods, critical, analytic thinking.
>
> Theory is the basis for social action; for social justice inquiry (Charmaz, 2011, pp. 359–361; Charmaz, Thornberg & Keane, 2017).
>
> Grounded theory is a powerful method for social justice inquiry. It is a theory/methods package that incorporates symbolic interactionism and Pragmatist philosophy (Clarke, Friese & Washburn, 2015, p. 12). It can be used to connect C. Wright Mills' notion of personal troubles to public issues, and inform interpretive analyses of these connections. It can help expose ideological biases in social practices, reveal social injustices, and identify new lines of action (Mills, 1959; Charmaz, Thornberg & Keane, 2017).

Who could disagree? Aren't we all grounded theorists? Don't we all believe that our understandings of the world need to be anchored in concrete interpretive materials? And subversive: there is no grand or middle or formal theory here, no formal propositions, no testable hypotheses. No wonder grounded theory is so popular.

It is all grounded. It is two things at the same time, a verb, a method of inquiry, and a noun, a product of inquiry (Charmaz, 2005, p. 507, 2011, p. 360). It is intuitive, interpretive.

You let the obdurate empirical world speak to you, you listen, take notes, write memos to yourself, form writing groups. No hierarchy, the social theorists are not privileged. In the world of GT, anybody can be a theorist, and should be. What could be more democratic?

Grounded theory (GT) is not a unified framework. As this *Handbook* evidences, there are multiple versions, and they move up against and flow into one another: Glaserian, Straussian, Strauss and Corbin, dimensional analysis, positivist, post-positivist, classic, informed, constructivist, critical, critical realism feminist, objectivist, postmodern, situational, computer-assisted (Charmaz, Thornberg & Keane, 2017; Clarke, 2005, 2015a; Clarke, Friese & Washburn, 2015). Traditional positivist grounded theory stresses the importance of correspondence theories of truth, of objective inquirers, and processes of discovery (Corbin & Strauss, 2015). In contrast, Charmaz's constructivist version privileges reflexivity, symbolic interactionism, a John Dewey version of Pragmatism, and a social justice focus.

Like Charmaz, Clarke's postmodern, situational analysis (SA), deploys constructivist models of truth, and rejects objectivist views of the inquirer. Compared to traditional GT, Clarke's social arena framework privileges poststructural feminism, Foucault over the study of analytic maps, systems of discourse, and the effect of nonhuman (buildings, technology) elements on situations of inquiry (Clarke, 2005: 32, 291, 2015b; Clarke, Friese & Washburn, 2015).

Yet underneath, these differences, there are commonalities: flexible guidelines for data collection (and analysis), including interviewing, archival analysis, observation, and participant observation. Most importantly, the commitment is to remain close to the world being studied, while developing integrated theoretical concepts grounded in data that show process, relationship, and social world connectedness (Charmaz, 2005: 508; Clarke, 2005: 292, 2015a).[1]

WHERE IS THE THEORY IN GROUNDED THEORY?

So where is the theory in grounded theory? The short answer is, there is no formal or classical theory. GT and SA are performances, strategies for analyzing empirical research materials. Analysis is the goal, grounded theory refers to data-grounded theorizing (Clarke, 2015a, p. 121). GT and SA represent complex ways of creating interpretations that move back and forth between empirical materials and ways of thinking about them. As with any system of discourse, it is a language unto itself: sensitizing concepts, memo writing, abductive reasoning, theoretical sampling, analytic codes, initial, and focused coding, situational analysis, social worlds, positional maps, conditional and situational matrix, structural conditions, constant comparison, arenas, processes, categories, grounded theory versus grounded theories explain? (Charmaz, Thornberg & Keane, 2017; Clarke, 2015b, p. 99).

Perhaps theory is a misnomer, a better word might be interpretation, grounded interpretation (GI). But there are drawbacks with GI in so far as a set of categories come between the observer and the observed. Granted GT and SA theorists talk about letting the data speak, but data are only heard or seen through a set of interpretive practices: the codes, memos, matrices, maps. The world is made visible through an a priori interpretive scheme. In classic hermeneutic-interpretive theory, the scholar embraces the phenomenon free of prejudice, understanding that this is an impossible goal. GT brings its own framework to the empirical world. Glaser's GT has a heavy frame, Strauss and Corbin, a prescriptive frame, and Charmaz less so.

THE APPEAL OF GROUNDED THEORY

Negative comments aside, grounded theory's appeals, in its constructivist and situational forms are many. It provides a set of steps and procedures any researcher can follow in the construction of an interpretation fitted to a particular problem. For some, in its postmodern turn, it offers a situational, cartographic approach to the study of social structure, social action, and infrastructure. (Clarke, 2005: xxii). GT offers guidelines for doing fieldwork, for doing interviewing, and for the analysis of qualitative materials, including ethnographic, interview, 'narrative, visual and historical discourse materials' (Clarke, 2005: xxiii). It offers a way of addressing issues of voice, discourse, texts, the materiality of power, thick analyses of complex social processes (Clarke, 2005: xxiii). Its goals clearly resonate with the postpositivist program in the human disciplines, especially the emphasis on the importance of induction and deduction, generalizability, comparisons between cases, and the systematic relating of concepts grounded in data.

At the same time its theory of interaction celebrates Pragmatism's unique contribution to American social psychology, a linguistically based theory of mind, self, and action. This can be seen in Clarke's (2005, 2015b) and Charmaz's (2005, 2011) focus on postmodern deconstructions, on interconnecting social worlds, on arenas, matrices of structure, trajectories of action, resources, hierarchies of power and influence, social policies, hierarchies of suffering, situated, and local readings of ordinary people and their lives (Charmaz, 2005: 524–528; Charmaz, Thornberg & Keane, 2017).

MOVING FORWARD

Now, a new generation seeks to 'reclaim the tools of the method, to form a revised, more open-ended practice ... that stresses its emergent, constructivist elements' (Clarke, 2015b), 'for advancing social justice studies' (Charmaz, Thornberg & Keane, 2017).

I want to extend this project, by aligning it with the critical performance-based turn in the human disciplines. For at least two decades rhetoric and performance studies scholars, ethnodramatists, critical interpretive ethnographers, community theatre activists, and autoethnographers have been staging performance events. These performances create spaces for a merger of praxis, ethnography, rhetoric, and activism in public (and private) life (Conquergood, 2006; Madison, 2012; Saldana, 2011). We are in the eighth moment, a post-experimental, open-ended phase, critiquing culture as we write and perform it.[2]

It is time to take stock.[3] Time to revise and critique where we have come. Where does grounded theory fit in this space? It is time to rethink our key terms, including theory, interpretation, analysis, qualitative inquiry, ethnography, and performance. We researchers need to recommit to a reflexive performance [auto] ethnography [and grounded theory][4] that will engage a postcolonial, post-civil-rights, post-cold war, postfeminist, post-racial and postmodern world (Madison, 2006, pp. 347–348, paraphrase). Time to start over. I seek a new genealogy, in Foucault's sense. But where to begin? I seek leverage for those who use moral inquiry for social justice ends.

Indigenous participatory theatre, which nurtures a critical self-consciousness, and privileges indigenous voices, is central to my argument. An indigenous participatory theatre is central to this performance discourse. Indigenous performance is a means of political representation, a form of resistance and critique, and a way of addressing issues of equity, healing, and social justice.

GROUNDED THEORY AND INDIGENOUS DISCOURSE

We are mid-way through the United Nations Second Decade of the World's Indigenous Peoples. There is a great desire by indigenous scholars to decolonize Western epistemologies, to open up the academy to non-Western forms of wisdom, knowing, knowledge, and knowledge production (Bishop, 2005; Smith, 2005, 2012). Grounded theory, because of its commitment to critical, open-ended inquiry, can be a decolonizing tool for indigenous and non-indigenous scholars alike. A performance-based grounded theory using indigenous epistemologies and methodologies is one way to do this.

In proposing a conversation between critical grounded theory and indigenous discourses I am mindful of several difficulties. First, the legacy of helping Western colonizing of the other must be resisted. As Linda Smith observes (1999, p. 80): 'They came, They saw, They named, They claimed.' This means, as Bishop argues (2005), that indigenous persons are excluded from discussions concerning who has control over the initiation, the methodologies, evaluations, assessments, representations, and distribution of the newly defined knowledge. The decolonization project challenges these practices.

Second, critical theory, and grounded theory, without modification, will not work within indigenous settings. The criticisms of G. Smith (2000), L. Smith (1999, 2000, 2005), Bishop (1994, 1998, 2005), and others make this very clear. There must be a commitment to transforming the institutions and practices of research. GT concerns for data, basic underlying social processes, and causal narratives may not accord with the pressing social justice concerns of indigenous persons. Critical theory's criteria for self-determination and empowerment may perpetuate neo-colonial sentiments, while turning the indigenous person into an essentialized 'other' who is spoken for (Bishop, 2005). Taking a lesson from grounded theory, critical theory must be localized, grounded in the specific meanings, traditions, customs, and community relations that operate in each indigenous setting. Localized, grounded critical theory can work if the goals of critique, resistance, struggle, and emancipation are not treated as if they have 'universal characteristics that are independent of history, context, and agency' (L. Smith, 2000, p. 229). So this resonates with the idea of a substantive GT?

Third, there is a pressing need to decolonize and deconstruct those structures within the Western academy that privilege Western knowledge systems and their epistemologies (Mutua & Swadner, 2004, p. 10; see also Kovach, 2009; Semaili & Kincheloe, 1999). Indigenous knowledge systems are too frequently turned into objects of study, treated as if they were instances of quaint folk theory held by the members of a primitive culture.

The decolonizing project reverses this equation, making Western systems of knowledge the object of inquiry. And perhaps sets up a dialogue between different systems/discourses?

Fourth, and paraphrasing Smith (2005), the spaces between decolonizing research practices and indigenous communities must be carefully and cautiously articulated. They are fraught with uncertainty. Neo-liberal and neo-conservative political economies turn knowledge about indigenous peoples into a commodity. There are conflicts between competing epistemological and ethical frameworks, including institutional human subject research regulations. Research is regulated by positivist epistemologies. Indigenous scholars and native intellectuals are pressed to produce technical knowledge that conforms to Western standards of truth and validity. Conflicts over who initiates and who benefits from such research are especially problematic (Bishop, 2005). Culturally responsive research practices must be developed. Such practices locate power within the indigenous community. What is acceptable and not acceptable research is determined and defined from within the community. Such work encourages self-determination and empowerment (Bishop, 2005).

Fifth, in arguing for a dialogue between grounded, critical, and indigenous theories, I recognize that I am an outsider to the indigenous colonized experience. I write as a privileged Westerner. At the same time, I seek to be an 'allied other' (Kaomea, 2004, p. 32), a fellow-traveler, of sorts, an anti-positivist, an insider who wishes to deconstruct from within the Western academy and its positivist epistemologies.

CRITICAL INDIGENOUS PEDAGOGY

I seek a productive dialogue between grounded theory, critical pedagogy, and indigenous and critical [race] scholars. This involves a re-visioning of Paulo Freire's pedagogy of the oppressed (2000, see also Freire 1996) in local, indigenous contexts (see Diversi & Moreira, 2009; Kovach, 2009). I call this merger of grounded, indigenous and critical methodologies, *critical indigenous pedagogy* (Denzin & Lincoln, 2008, p. 2). It understands that all inquiry is political and moral. It confronts the tension between the Western critical theory paradigm and indigenous knowledge, theory and praxis (Grande, 2008a, p. 238, 2008b).[5] It uses methods critically, for explicit social justice purposes. It values the transformative power of indigenous, subjugated knowledges. It values the local pedagogical practices that produce these knowledges. At the same time, it studies the political, ethical and aesthetic technologies that transform the practices of indigeneity into marketable commodities and performances.[6] Critical indigenous pedagogy seeks forms of praxis and inquiry that are emancipatory, collaborative and empowering. The critical scholar should be an allied other (Kaomea, 2004, p. 32). Building on this framework, I attempt to chart a performance-based critical discourse modeled in part after the arguments of Madison (2010, 2012), Saldana (2011), Giroux (2014a, 2014b), and Conquergood (2013). A single, yet complex thesis organizes my argument. Centred around the characterization of indigenous grounded theory?

Indigenous grounded theory inquiry is performative. It connects research to struggles for liberation, to struggles which empower, which challenge the status quo, rebuild leadership, restore environments, and revitalize language, culture, and community

(Smith, 2005, p. 89). 'Indigenous grounded theory research is performative research carried out by indigenous scholars, in and for indigenous communities, using the principles of indigenous grounded theory inquiry' (Smith, 2005, p. 89). This form of inquiry is collaborative and participatory and is characterized by the absence of a need to be in control, by a desire to be connected to and to be a part of a moral community where a primary goal is the compassionate understanding of another's moral position (Bishop, 1998, p. 203). The indigenist researcher wants to participate in a collaborative, altruistic relationship, where nothing 'is desired for the self' (Bishop, 1998, p. 207), where research is evaluated by participant-driven criteria, by the cultural values and practices that circulate, for example, in indigenist culture, including metaphors stressing self-determination, the sacredness of relationships, embodied understanding, and the priority of community over self.

Researchers are led to develop new storylines and criteria of evaluation reflecting these understandings. These participant-driven criteria function as resources for resisting positivist and neo-conservative desires to 'establish and maintain control of the criteria for evaluating indigenous experience' (Bishop, 1998, p. 212). They privilege a spoken, indigenous epistemology which emphasizes indigenous knowledge, and indigenous, traditional ways of knowing. The earth is regarded as the spiritual center of the universe. There is a commitment to dismantle and resist global capitalism. Positivist forms of knowing, educating, and of doing science and research are contested (Grande, 2000; Meyer, 2003; Rains, Archibald & Deyhle, 2000, p. 337).

Indigenist pedagogy moves epistemology out of a methodological framework, into the spaces of indigenous culture. Akin to grounded theory, specific indigenist ways of knowing and being in the world are emphasized. For Meyer (2003, p. 193) this epistemology is organized around the themes, of spirituality, physical space, the cultural nature of the senses, relational knowing, practical knowing, language as being, and the unity of mind and body. This framework stresses the performative place of morality in knowledge production. Knowing is always moral and political. Culture restores culture. Culture is sacred. Culture is performed, culture is pedagogy. Spirituality is basic to culture. It is sensuous and embodied, involving the senses: taste, sight, smell, hearing, and touch. Knowledge is experienced and expressed in sensuous terms, in stories and critical personal narratives focusing on the importance of practice and repetition. Knowledge is a process. It is relational, it locates the person in a moral relation with the other. This involves harmony, balance, being generous, responsible, being a good listener, and being kind.

GROUNDED THEORY ON TRICKY GROUND

Paraphrasing Linda Tuhiwai Smith (2005, p. 85), the ground on which grounded theory stands is tricky. It is tricky because it is 'complicated, and changeable, and it is tricky also because it can play tricks on research and on the researcher' (Smith, 2005, p. 85). Grounded theory's ground, and the spaces it encompasses, are always constructed, never bedrock solid, always nuanced, and potentially dangerous. The ground itself is a function of the researcher's shifting relationship to the world. And always 'lurking around the corners are countervailing conservative forces that seek to disrupt any agenda of social justice that may form on such tricky ground' (Smith, 2005, p. 85). These forces may seek to derail the project. They may have little tolerance for public debate, for alternative views, for grounded theory methodology, and even disdain for projects espousing social justice (Smith, 2005, p. 85). Under such circumstances, interpretive grounded theory is stripped of its radical politics. It is returned 'to a positivist research paradigm that, like life in general, should be simple' (Smith, 2005, p. 85).

Interpretation is always performative, a performance event involving actors, purposes, scripts, stories, stages, and interactions. Performance is an act of intervention, a method of resistance, a form of criticism, and a way of revealing agency and presence in the world. Performances foreground the intersection of politics, institutional sites, and embodied experience. The performative is always (or perhaps intended to be?) pedagogical, and the pedagogical is always political. A politics of representation shapes the interpretive process. The practices of interpretation involve story-telling, different ways of organizing and representing the world, and different ways of making the world appear real.

Grounded theory is a performance, a set of performative and interpretive practices and ways of making the world visible. This commitment to visibility is anchored in the belief that the world, at some level, is orderly, and patterned. The world of social interaction and social experience can be theoretically sampled, saturated, located in situational social world, arena mapped, coded, fitted into conceptual categories, diagramed, placed in conditional and consequential matrices, and represented in narrative, visual, and historical discourses. These discourses, in turn, can be analyzed in terms of social relationships, identities, and intersecting arenas and social worlds.

In contrast, the performance ethnographer is a troublemaker. The practices of ethnography are not tools for creating order out of chaos. Instead ethnographies are for creating chaos, ways of disrupting the world and its representations. Performance ethnographers see disorder in the world, reading orderliness as a dramaturgical production (Goffman, 1959; Kincheloe & McLaren, 2000). Politics of representation suggest that the world's orderliness is imposed through a political, pedagogical, and interpretive process. These pedagogies of order reinforce the belief and the appearance that the world is in fact orderly. But order is an ideological concept, a fiction, a sometimes-shameless concept that justifies the interpretive practices of science and grounded theory. Order may be partial, provisional, and temporary, even a performance, or presentation in Goffman's sense.

The differences between GT and ethnography here are foundational; they are about more than causing trouble. They are about how the world is represented so that social justice interventions can be produced. They are about not seeing the world in terms of disciplinary conceptual categories. Taken to its logical extension, GT is not about seeing the world in these ways either. These differences are about writing the world in this historical moment where the personal and the political intersect, in this space which is already deeply moral, critical, and interpretive. Grounded, indigenous inquiry, folded into performance, [auto]ethnography searches for ways of disrupting the smooth structures of everyday colonial and postcolonial life. Performance grounded theory sees disorder and unruliness where others see patterns, processes, and interconnections. This focus on disorder and illusion is intended to illuminate the arbitrary and unjust, the unfair practices that operate in daily life. But don't the unfair practices constitute a pattern?

DECOLONIZING, DISRUPTIVE PERFORMANCES

> Critical indigenous pedagogy interrogates the repressive residues of the ideological practices that came before, during and after colonization. The decolonizing indigenizing project moves back and forth across these spaces and discourses (Smith, 2012, p. 25). However, 'naming the word as "post-colonial" is, from indigenous perspectives, to name colonialism as finished business' (Smith, 2012, p. 25). The past is never post, never free from history, never free from the disgraces of the Indigenous-relationship. (Kovach, 2009, p. 76)

The word 'decolonization', as Tuck and Yang (2012) argue, must be used carefully. It should not only be a metaphor for change, or a way of addressing white guilt, or a call to improve our schools and eradicate racism, as in decolonize our schools, or decolonize our methods. In radical form, decolonization is a chaotic contradictory often violent process. Ideally, it is nothing short of a call for the repatriation of indigenous land and life. It is a demand for indigenous sovereignty. It is a recognition that decolonization involves more than just a call for social justice, more than the application of critical indigenous pedagogy to the problems of colonialism. Decolonization signals an end to innocence, an opening to an elsewhere that is yet unnamed (Tuck & Yang, 2012, pp. 1, 38, paraphrase). Yet it is always utopic, a 'call to work toward healing, unity, and cooperation' (Diversi, 2015).

Moreira elaborates on the legacies of borders, bodies, and decolonization:

> Can these borders, legacies, and injustices be
> transgressed?
> Can my body be transgressive as a form of scholarship?
> I have the duty
> To manipulate and transform
> The tale of colonization
> Using my life as source to show
> With a political propose
> An experience
> To expand the sacredness of life.
> Amen (Diversi & Moreia 2009, p. 223)

The insertion of indigenous voices, epistemologies, ethics and ways of knowing into Western colonial discourse is transformative. The process changes the nature of the discourse itself (Kovach, 2009, p. 12). It creates a racialized, gendered performative space where Indigenous knowledges and tribal-based methodologies – stories, oral histories, performances, rituals, art – can live, be staged, be disruptive, empowering and community-affirming (Kovach, 2009, p. 12).

Listen to Kovach describe being in such a space, but not knowing the language:

> I am taking Cree, it is my first class today. Walking into the First Nations University there are Indians everywhere with shiny hair flying as both instructors and students race down the hall to class. The instructor is Plains Cree, he was raised with the language. He asks who is Cree. We put up our hands. He asks why we do not know our language. He points to me. I say adopted. He nods. (Kovach, 2009, p. 113)

Let the healing begin.

Kovach's performance text brings a painful memory alive, Canada's 'Baby Scoop Era' (1945–1990). High numbers of Native babies and young children were taken from their Native mothers and placed for adoption in non-Native homes. In most cases their native heritage was denied by the adoption parents. The system prevented new mothers from accessing their own infants. This is why Kovach did not learn how to speak Cree.

The public performance stage of the classroom (primary, secondary, higher, post-secondary) is a constant battleground for decolonizing praxis. The struggle moves from memory to counter-memory, to new memories of resistance (and oppression). Co-performers bear witness to new acts of resistance. Together they watch oppressed marked bodies perform their own utopian possibilities of barely imagined, uncharted futures (Diversi & Moreira, 2009, p. 208). Maggie Kovach and her Cree classmates are learning how to take hold of their Cree heritage. In order for the voices of the oppressed to be heard, they must be made visible, through performance.

First Nation, Native American, Maori, Aboriginal indigenous scholars extend the argument by articulating a performative, spoken, indigenous epistemology 'developed over thousands of years of sustained living on this Land' (Rains, Archibald & Deyhle, 2000, p. 337,). The indigenous methodology embedded in a performative Red Pedagogy has these characteristics, which are not necessarily pan-indigenous (Grande, 2008a, pp. 250; Kovach, 2009, p. 37): (1) It is inherently political, cultural, spiritual and intellectual. It honors tribal culture and ancestral relationships grounded in the land; (2) It is dialogical, ethical, rooted in tribal knowledge, epistemologies, and praxis; (3) It is informed by critical theory, finding victories in small struggles (Kovach, 2009, p. 80); (4) It is focused on indigenizing education for decolonization; (5) It interrogates the meanings of democracy and sovereignty; (6) It cultivates a praxis of collective agency; (7) It is based on a belief in hope, in survivance, of going beyond survival to an active repudiation through performance of oppression and tragedy (Vizenor, 1993, 2008; Grande, 2008, p. 250; Kovach, 2009, p. 102); (8) Red Pedagogy is grounded in sacred rituals, in performance, in storytelling. It is anchored in a search for sovereignty, for Grande in *Indianismo*, the New Indian (Grande, 2008a, p. 241; see also Grande, 2008b).

The performance of sacred tribal rituals, the telling of oral histories, and the performance of sacred identities validates traditional ways of life. The performances embody the ritual. They are the ritual. In this sense the performance becomes a form of public pedagogy. It uses a performative aesthetic to foreground cultural meaning, and to teach these meanings to performers and audience members alike.

Such inquiry, to summarize, should stress self-determination, dialogue, healing, the sacredness of relationships, embodied understanding, and the priority of community. It must meet peoples' perceived needs. It must resist efforts to confine inquiry to a single paradigm or interpretive strategy. It should be unruly, disruptive, critical and committed to the goals of justice and equity. Such an alliance will 'further advance the decolonizing project of making indigenous ways of knowing, being, and representing central to our version of inclusive social justice' (Diversi & Henhawk, 2012, p. 70).

The goal is to undo official racial history and to create a space for marginalized voices, alternative histories, new ways of writing and performing the past so new futures can be imagined. This performative discourse imagines a politics of resistance, a new politics of possibility, new ways of re-imagining the future and the past. Madison, after Dolan (2005), calls these re-imaginings utopian performatives. They are akin to Freire's pedagogies of hope (Freire, 1999; see also Dolan, 2005, p. 5; Madison, 2010, p. 26, 2012, p. 182). Freire reminds us that without hope there is tragic despair, hopelessness (Freire, 1999, pp. 8–9).

HOPE AND ACTS OF ACTIVISM[7]

Performances of possibility create spaces 'where unjust systems ... can be identified and interrogated' (Madison, 2010, p. 159). Persons can become radicalized when confronted with such performances. As Madison notes. 'One performance may or may not change someone's world ... but one performance can be revoutionary in enlightening citizens as to the possibilities that grate against injusstice' (Madison, 2010, p. 159).

Munoz (2005, pp. 9–10) asks, how do we stage utopian performatives? How do we enact utopia? How do we realize performances of possibility? The utopic stages itself. It pushes and pulls us forward. It incites the imagination. It offers blueprints for hope, bare 'outlines of a world not quite here, a horion of possibility, not a fixed scheme' (Munoz, 2005, p. 9). Utopia is flux, change, stasis, chaos, and disorganization all jumpled together, a fluid 'moment when the here and now is transcended by a then, and a there that could be and indeed should be' (Munoz, 2005, p. 9). Utopia is always a critique of the here and now. It involves a politics of emotion, an insistance that something is missing from the present, a hope, a dream, freedom. It involves the belief that things can be different, better, there can be social justice in a place called utopia where hope dwells.

A performative, pedagogical politics of hope imagines a radically free democratic society, a society where ideals of the ableist, ageist, indigenist, feminist, queer, environmental, green, civil rights, and labor movements are realized. In their utopian forms these movements, offer 'alternative models of radical democratic culture rooted in social relations that take seriously the democratic ideals of freedom, liberty, and the pursuit of happiness' (Giroux, 2014b, p. 9).

Madison is quite explicit: critical, performative autoethography begins:

> With a duty and ethical responsibility to address suffering, unfairness and injustice within a particular historical moment. There is a commitment to perform acts of activism that advance the causes of human rights. (Madison, 2012, p. 5; 2010, p. 1, paraphrase)

Accordingly, a radical performative discourse revolves around specific acts of resistance and activism, performances were persons put their bodies on the line, staged re-enactments which incite resistance. These acts are public interventions. That is performance is used subversively, as a strategy for awakening critical consciousness and moving persons to take human, democratic actions in the face of injustice, efforts that serve social justice, and that are expected to bring net gains in the lives of people (Madison, 2010, p. 1; see also Cohen-Cruz, 2005, p. 4). These explicit acts of activism imply an embodied epistemology, a poetic reflexive performing body moving through space, an ethical body taking responsibility for its action.

Corey (2015) observes that the use of performance

> to initiate social change predates the theatres of Greece, where, by way of example, in *Lysistrata*, Aristophanes created a lead character who corals her friends to withhold sex from their husbands in order to stop the wars. Contemporary examples include Brecht's Epic Theatre, Boal's Theatre of the Oppressed, agit prop, and guerilla theatre. (p. 1, paraphrase)[8]

Gloria Anzaldua's (1987, pp. 2–3) writing performs its own acts of resistance. She speaks of border crossing, crossing the borders:

I walk through the hole in the fence
To the other side
Beneath the iron sky
Mexican children kick the soccer ball across,
run after it, entering the U. S.
1,950-mile-long open wound …
staking fence rods in my flesh …
This is my home
this thin edge of barbwire.
This land was Indian always and is
And will be again.

GROUNDED THEORY AND THE WORK OF ADVOCACY

In moving from fieldwork and inquiry to page and then to stage and performance, researchers as advocates resist speaking for the other (Spry, 2011). Rather they assist in the struggles of others, staging performance events, screening and re-presenting history, offering new versions of official history, performing counter-memories, exposing contradictions in official ideology, reflexively interrogating their own place in the performance thereby taking ethical responsibility for the consequences of their own acts and performances (Madison, 2010, p. 11).

In these ways staged ethnography, ethnodramas and performance autoethnographies do the work of advocacy (see Saldana, 2011). The performance is not a mirror, it is, as Madison argues, after Bertolt Brecht, the hammer that breaks the mirror, shatters the glass and builds a new reality (Madison, 2010, p. 12). In their performances autoethnographers incite transformations, cause trouble, act in unruly ways. They self-consciously become part of the performance itself, the instrument of change. Performance now becomes a moral, reflexive act, more than a method, an ethical act of advocacy.

Radical performances are acts of activism; that is, they are radical acts that confront root problems, not just surface manifestations of social injustice. Beneath the sources of daily injustices lies a deeper level of overriding root causes. Madison is explicit concerning these underlying causes or sources: 'troubling local human rights and social justice activism are *the machinations of neoconservatism [and neoliberalism] and a corporate global political economy* that affects small stories everywhere' (Madison, 2010, p. 19, italics in original). Radical performances are located in these small stories. Trapped in the same small and large spaces, we struggle to get free.

Acts of activism use performance as the vehicle for getting free, as the way of contesting official history and the status quo. A double reflexivity is at work. The performance text uses performativity as a method for making a slice of contested reality visible. The performance is intended to bring the audience and/or Spec-Actors into a state of critical reflexivity concerning the events under discussion. The act of witnessing (and performing) utopian performatives is itself a performative, interpretive act, somehow the world can be a better place (Dolan, 2005, p. 5). The coyote trickster leads us into this new space (Conquergood, 2013). The intent is to create a counter-memory, an alternative history of the present.

Excerpts from Mary Weems's (2002) poem 'This evolution will not be televised' clarify the project.

> 'This evolution will not be televised'
> Our image, our braids, our music, our mistakes,
> our asses, our rhythms are played on TV
> like a long 78 album in commercial after commercial.
> The Colonel in plantation-dress raps and moonwalks
> selling a black woman's stolen fried chicken, black kids
> snap their fingers, think that's so cool, bug their mamas
> for extra-crispy
> This is a never-ending story, that won't be televised
> (Weems, 2002, p. 4)

The ways in which the world is not a stage are not easy to specify. Today everything is already performative, staged, commodified, and dramaturgical. The dividing line between performer and actor, stage and setting, script and text, performance and reality, disappears. As this disappearance occurs, illusion and make-believe prevail. In this space, where the hyperreal appears more real than the real. Pragmatists and cultural critics require apparatuses of resistance and critique, methodologies and pedagogies of truth, ways of making real realities that envision and enact pedagogies of hope.

CRITICAL PEDAGOGY, ETHICS AND PROPHETIC PRAGMATISM

When the divisions between reality and its appearances disappear, critical indigenous grounded theory inquiry necessarily becomes disruptive, explicitly pedagogical, and radically democratic. We need a new politics of truth. We must embrace the justice of our rage. June Jordan and Patricia Hill Collins remind us (paraphrase):

> We must reclaim the neglected legacy of the Sixties, an unabashed moral certainty, an incredible outgoing energy of righteous rage. We cannot restore and expand the forms of justice that our lives require until and unless we change the language of current political and methodological discourse. If we do not reintroduce our concepts of Right and Wrong, of Truth and Evidence, then how shall we finally argue for our cause. (Collins, 1998, p. 250; Jordan, 1998, p. 178)

I answer the call of Jordan and Collins by turning to the post-pragmatists and the social justice based grounded theorists (see Denzin, 1996, for a review; see also Charmaz, 2005; Seigfried, 1996). For the post-pragmatist grounded theorist there is no neutral standpoint, no objective God's eye view of the world. The meaning of a concept, or line of action, or a representation, lies in the practical, political, moral, and social consequences it produces for an actor or collectivity. The meanings of these consequences are not objectively given. They are established through social interaction and the politics of representation. All representations are historically situated, shaped by the intersecting contingencies of power, gender, race, and class (Collins, 2000; Seigfried, 1996, p. 269). Representations are performance events.

Shaped by the sociological imagination, building on George Herbert Mead's discursive, performative model of the act, critical pragmatic qualitative research imagines and explores the multiple ways in which performance can be understood, including: as imitation, or *mimesis*; as *poiesis*, or construction; as *kinesis*, or movement, gendered bodies in motion (Conquergood, 1998, p. 31). The researcher-as-performer moves from a view of performance as imitation, or dramaturgical staging, to an emphasis on performance as liminality, construction, to a view of performance as embodied struggle, as an intervention, as breaking and remaking, as kinesis, and as a socio-political act. Viewed as struggles and interventions, performances and performance events become gendered transgressive achievements, political accomplishments which break through 'sedimented meanings and normative traditions' (Conquergood, 1998, p. 32). This model presumes a performative politics of resistance. Extending indigenous initiatives, this model is committed to a form of revolutionary, catalytic political theatre, a project that provokes and enacts pedagogies of dissent for the new millennium.

GROUNDED CRITICAL THEORY AND EPISTEMOLOGIES OF RESISTANCE

Indigenist pedagogies resist the positivist and post-positivist methodologies of Western science because these formations; for example, standardized achievement tests are too frequently used to validate colonizing knowledge about indigenous peoples. Indigenists deploy, instead, interpretive strategies and skills fitted to and grounded in the needs, language, and traditions of their respective indigenous community (Bishop, 2005). These strategies emphasize personal performance narratives, collaborative research relationships, compassionate understanding, self-determination, and the sacredness of community relationships. Researchers develop participant-driven criteria of evaluation reflecting these understandings. Grounded critical pedagogy respects indigenous epistemologies, and encourages interpretive, first-person methodologies. It honors different versions of science and empirical activity, and values cultural criticism in the name of social justice. It seeks models of human subject research that are not constrained by bio-medical positivist assumptions. It turns the academy and its classrooms into sacred spaces where indigenous and non-indigenous scholars interact, share experiences, take risks, explore alternative modes of interpretation, participate in a shared agenda, and come together in a spirit of hope, love, and shared community.

Theory, method, and epistemology are aligned in this project, anchored in the moral philosophies that are taken for granted in indigenous cultures and language communities (L. Smith, 2000, p. 225). A pedagogy of emancipation and empowerment is endorsed, a pedagogy that encourages struggles for autonomy, cultural well-being, cooperation, and collective responsibility. This pedagogy demands that indigenous groups own the research process. It speaks the truth 'to people about the reality of their lives' (Collins, 1998, p. 198). It equips them with the tools to resist oppression, and it moves them to struggle, to search for justice (Collins, 1998, pp. 198–199). This truth, sometimes unwelcome, is situated in the indigenous life-world. Some individuals or groups, for example, may not wish to affirm the oppression that researchers may define and oppose.

INDIGENOUS RESEARCH AS LOCALIZED CRITICAL THEORY

In these commitments, indigenous epistemologies overlap with critical grounded theory. Indeed, Linda Smith (2000) connects her version of indigenous inquiry, Kaupapa Maori research, with critical theory, suggesting, with G. Smith (2000), that Kaupapa Maori research is a 'local theoretical position that is the modality through which the emancipatory goal of critical theory, in a specific historical, political and social context is practised' (L. Smith, 2000, p. 229; see also Bishop, 2005). Critical theory, like Pragmatism, presumes that individuals are influenced by social and historical forces. Educational and everyday realities 'are constructed in and through people's linguistic, cultural, social, and behavioral interactions which both shape and are shaped by social, political, economic, and cultural forces' (Fishman & McLaren, 2005, p. 1). It is not enough to understand any given reality. There is a need to 'transform it with the goal of radically democratizing educational sites and societies' (Fishman & McLaren, 2005, p. 1). Critical scholars as transformative intellectuals actively shape and lead this project.

Critical pedagogy disrupts those hegemonic cultural and educational practices that reproduce the logics of neo-liberal conservatism (Giroux & Giroux, 2006). Critical pedagogy subjects structures of power, knowledge, and practice to grounded theory inquiry, demanding that they be evaluated 'in terms of how they might open up or close down democratic experiences' (Giroux & Giroux, 2006, p. 1). Critical pedagogy holds systems of authority accountable through the critical reading of texts, the creation of radical educational practices, and the promotion of critical literacy (Giroux & Giroux, 2006, p. 2). Concretely, these practices help to implement the goals of critical pedagogy. In a grounded theory context, they anchor lofty goals to specific actions, patterns, arenas, and meanings.

In turn, critical pedagogy encourages resistance to the 'discourses of privatization, consumerism, the methodologies of standardization and accountability, and the new disciplinary techniques of surveillance' (Giroux & Giroux, 2006, p. 3). Resistance takes many interpretive forms, including calling for fair labor and non-destructive environmental practices, and endorsing organic or green consumer ideologies. Critical pedagogy provides the tools, linking discourses to practices, for understanding how cultural and educational practices contribute to the construction of neo-liberal conceptions of identity, citizenship, and agency. Critical pedagogy, as critical discourse, operates in the classrooms of daily life, in the media, in schools, in offices, and in the workplace. Informed citizens model for one another alternative ways of responding to the meanings that circulate in daily life. Critical understanding is achieved when citizens understand that things are not, nor do they need to be, as they appear in the media.

Critical, pedagogical grounded theory offers the scholar a set of interpretive procedures for locating analysis in the worlds of social experience. It encourages processual thinking, requires a comparative focus, examines *how*, not *why* questions, demands intimate familiarity with a setting, values observations that challenge current ideas, draws links between the local and the institutional, and, using strategies of saturation and situational maps and analyses, suggests avenues for pursuing social justice concerns (Charmaz, 2005, p. 528; Clarke, 2005, p. 289).

Grounded theory thus merges with critical pedagogy. The local which localizes and grounds indigenous critical grounded theory is always historically specific. The local is grounded in the politics, circumstances, and economies of a particular moment, a particular time and place, and a particular set of problems, struggles, and desires. A politics of resistance and possibility (Madison, 1998; Pollock, 1998) is embedded in the local. This is a politics that confronts and breaks through local structures of resistance and oppression. This is a politics that asks 'Who writes for whom? Who is representing indigenous peoples, how, for what purposes, for which audiences, who is doing science for whom?' (Smith, 1999, p. 37).

A critical politics of interpretation leads the indigenous scholar to ask eight questions about any research project, including those projects guided by grounded critical theory:

1 What research do we want done?
2 Who is it for?
3 What difference will it make?
4 Who will carry it out?
5 How do we want the research done?
6 How will we know it is worthwhile?
7 Who will own the research?
8 Who will benefit? (L. Smith, 2000, p. 239).

These questions are addressed to indigenous and non-indigenous scholars alike. They must be answered in the affirmative; that is, indigenists must conduct, own, and benefit from any research that is done on or for them.

CRITERIA FOR GROUNDED THEORY STUDIES IN SOCIAL JUSTICE INQUIRY

Charmaz outlines four criteria which merge grounded theory studies with social justice inquiry. Her terms include credibility, originality, resonance, and usefulness. Inquiry has credibility when it is anchored in the languages, values, and politics of the local. Inquiry must resonate with the local. It should be shaped by local needs. It should make a positive difference in that world. Findings should be owned by the local community. Her interpretive criteria can be read back through Smith's eight questions; that is, we want locally grounded critical inquiry that advances social justice issues for persons in indigenous communities.

These eight questions and four criteria serve to interpret critical theory through a moral lens. They shape the moral space that aligns indigenous research with grounded critical theory. Thus, both formations are situated within the antipositivist debate. They both rest on antifoundational epistemologies. Each privileges performative issues of gender, race, class, equity, and social justice. Each develops its own understandings of community, critique, resistance, struggle, and emancipation (L. Smith, 2000, p. 228). Each understands that the outcome of a struggle can never be predicted in advance, and that struggle is always local and contingent. It is never final (L. Smith, 2000, p. 229).

By localizing discourses of resistance, and by connecting these discourses to performance ethnography and critical pedagogy, indigenous research enacts what grounded critical theory 'actually offers to oppressed, marginalized and silenced groups … [that is] through emancipation groups such as the Maori would take greater control of their own lives and humanity' (L. Smith, 2000, p. 229). This requires that indigenous groups 'take hold of the project of emancipation and attempt to make it a reality on their own terms' (L. Smith, 2000, p. 229). This means that inquiry is always political and moral, grounded in principles centered on autonomy, home, family, kinship, on a collective community vision that requires that research not be a 'purchased product … owned by the state' (L. Smith, 2000, p. 231). Localized critical indigenous theory, folded into grounded theory, encourages indigenists and non-indigenists to confront key challenges connected to the meanings of science, community, and democracy. In proactively framing participatory views of science, empirical research, democracy, and community, persons take control of their own fate. They refuse to be sidetracked into always responding to the attempts by the state to define their life situations (G. Smith, 2000, p. 210). This means that persons and communities craft their own version of science and empirical activity. They are challenged to develop a participatory model of democracy that goes beyond the 'Westminster "one person, one vote, majority rule"' (G. Smith, 2000, p. 212). They learn how to use grounded critical theory proactively as an agent of change. They learn how to act in ways that are accountable to the indigenous and non-indigenous community, and not just the academy and its scholarly standards.

Patricia Hill Collins (2000) offers four criteria – primacy of lived experience, dialogue, an ethics of care, an ethics of responsibility – for interpreting truth and knowledge claims. This framework privileges lived experience, emotion, empathy, and values rooted in personal expressiveness (Edwards & Mauthner, 2002, p. 25). The moral inquirer – whether a politician or a social scientist – builds a collaborative, reciprocal, trusting, mutually accountable relationship with those studied. This feminist ethical framework is care- and justice-based. It seeks to contextualize shared values and norms. It privileges the sacredness of life, human dignity, nonviolence, care, solidarity, love, community, empowerment, and civic transformation. It demands of any action that it positively contribute to a politics of resistance, hope, and freedom (Denzin, 2003, p. 258).

For the prophetic post-pragmatists there are no absolute truths, no absolute principles, no faith-based beliefs in what is true or false. At the level of politics and ideology, the post-pragmatist, following Cornel West (1989, p. 234, 1991, p. 36) acts as a critical moral agent, one whose political goal is the creation of greater individual freedom in the broader social order. Paraphrasing West (1991, pp. 35–36), prophetic Pragmatists as moral agents understand that the consequences of their interventions into the world are exclusively political, judged always in terms their contributions to a politics of liberation, love, caring, and freedom. Following Collins (2000), Pelias (2004, p. 163), and Freire (1999), the moral inquirer enacts a politics of love and care, an ethic of hope and forgiveness. Love, here, to borrow from Darder and Mirón (2006, p. 150):

> means to comprehend that the moral and the material are inextricably linked. And, as such, [we] must recognize love as an essential ingredient of a just society. Eagleton (2003) defines this concept of love as a political principle through which we struggle to create mutually life-enhancing opportunities for all people. It is grounded in the mutuality and interdependence of our human existence—that which we share, as much as that which we do not. This is a love nurtured by the act of relationship itself. It cultivates relationships with the freedom to be at one's best without undue fear. Such an emancipatory love allows us to realize our nature in a way that allows others to do so as well. Inherent in such a love is the understanding that we are not at liberty to be violent, authoritarian, or self-seeking.

Materially, actions are thus judged in terms of moral consequences and the meanings people bring to them. Consequences are not self-evident. They are socially constructed through the politics of representation. The concept of truth is thus replaced with a consequential theory of meaning. Experience, folded through what Stuart Hall (1996, p. 473) calls the politics of representation, becomes the site of meaning and truth. Facts about the world are treated as 'facticities,' as lived experiences. The Pragmatist examines the effects, or consequences, of any line of action on existing structures of domination. The Pragmatist asks, what are the moral and ethical consequences of these effects for lived human experience? Do they contribute to an ethical self-consciousness that is critical and reflexive, empowering people with a language and a set of pedagogical practices that turn oppression into freedom, despair into hope, hatred into love, and doubt into trust? Do they engender a critical racial self-awareness that contributes to utopian dreams of racial equality and racial justice? If people are being oppressed, denied freedom, or dying because of these effects, then the action, of course, is morally indefensible.

I am calling for an engagement with and a promotion of a grounded theory research paradigm that imagines creative and critical responses to the feminist, indigenous, and post-pragmatic efforts outlined above. This paradigm is forthright in its belief that the personal is political, and that the political is pedagogical. It shares in experiences, problems, and hopes concerning the conduct of critical, qualitative inquiry in this time of global uncertainty. The values of progressive democracy must be at the forefront when scientific advice is used for policy-making decisions. The pragmatic consequences for a radical democracy must be taken into account when scientific recommendations for social action are implemented.

This is a gendered project, a project where feminist, postcolonial, queer, and indigenous theorists question the logic of the heterosexual ethnographic narrative. It is a moral, allegorical, and therapeutic project, one in which the researcher's own self is inscribed in the text as a prop to help men and women endure and prevail in the opening years of the twenty-first century. And it is avowed in its commitment to a project of social justice and radical progressive democracy. But there are no absolute truths, no absolute principles. The moral inquirer enacts a politics of love and care, an ethic of hope and forgiveness. As Ron Pelias suggests (paraphrase):

> The heart learns that stories are truths that won't keep still. The heart learns that facts are the possibilities we pretend we trust. The heart's method of pumping, loving and forgiving encourages us to proceed with our hearts first. What matters most is that we learn how to use our rage in positive ways, to love, to struggle to forgive. We have little other choice. (Pelias, 2004, pp. 162–163, 171)

Cornel West is instructive (1989, p. 234, 1991, p. 36, paraphrased):

> At the level of politics and ideology, the post-pragmatist acts as a critical moral agent, one whose political goal is the creation of greater individual freedom in the broader social order. Prophetic Pragmatists as moral agents understand that the consequences of their interventions into the world are exclusively political, judged always in terms their contributions to a politics of liberation, love, caring and freedom.

A critically, grounded Pragmatism embraces an ethics of truth, love, care, hope, and forgiveness. Patricia Hill Collins provides direction (2000, p. 251, paraphrase):

> This moral vision relies on a righteous rage to spur us on, to keep us headed in the right direction, to point the way, to move people toward justice. If it does this then it has made a very important difference in the lives of people.

We demand that history's actors use models of evidence that answer to these moral truths. An indigenous, performative, grounded theory inquiry helps us get to these truths and these spaces.

Notes

1 Other critical qualitative theoretical frameworks aligned with GT, include: participatory action and policy research, feminist, indigenist, critical race, postcolonial, LGBT/queer approaches (Clarke, Friese & Washburn, 2015, pp. 16–22).
2 Denzin and Lincoln (2011, p. 3) define the eight moments of inquiry, all of which operate in the present, as: the traditional (l900–l950), the modernist (l950–l970), blurred genres (l970–l986), the crisis of representation (l986–l990), postmodern or experimental (l990–1995), post-experimental (1995–2000), and the methodologically contested present (2000–2010), the future (2010–) which is now. For a review of the criticisms of this model, see Denzin and Lincoln (2011, p. 7).
3 As such, this chapter builds on and extends the arguments in *Interpretive Ethnography* (Denzin, 1997, pp. 90–125), and *Interpretive Autoethnography* (2nd ed., 2014).
4 Throughout I will connect reflexive ethnography with autoethnography using both terms to reference the most recent developments in performance. I will locate those arguments in first person, mutli-layered texts that work outward from the writer's life. Thus understood, the researcher becomes the research subject. This is the topic of reflexive performance autoethnography. Researchers stage and perform ethnographies of their own experience.
5 These tensions turn on differing models of the individual, subjectivity, spirituality, property, the land and sovereignty (Grande, 2008a, p. 238).
6 See www.indigeneity.net/ – *Indigeneity in the Contemporary World: Performance, Politics, Belonging* is a five-year research initiative funded by the European Research Council and based at Royal Holloway, University of London.
7 I steal the phrase acts of activism from Madison (2010, 2012).
8 Cohen-Cruz (2005, p. 1) expands Corey's examples to include such community-based performances as public protests, skits at union halls, rallies, ritual, dance, music making and public theatre.

ACKNOWLEDGEMENTS

I thank Kathy Charmaz and Tony Bryant for their insightful and critical comments on earlier versions of this chapter, sections of which draw from arguments in Denzin (2003, Denzin and Lincoln (2005), Denzin, and Giardina (2006), Denzin, Lincoln and Giardina (2006), and Denzin (2014).

REFERENCES

Anzaldua, Gloria. 1987. *Borderlands/La Frontera: The New Mestiza.* San Francisco, CA: aunt lute books.

Bishop, Russell. 1994. Initiating empowering research. *New Zealand Journal of Educational Studies, 29*(1): 175–188.

Bishop, Russell. 1998. Freeing ourselves from neo-colonial domination in research: A Maori approach to creating knowledge. *International Journal of Qualitative Studies in Education, 11*: 199–219.

Bishop, Russell. 2005. Freeing ourselves from neocolonial domination in research: A Kaupapa Maori approach to creating knowledge. In N. K. Denzin & Y. S. Lincoln (Eds.), *Handbook of Qualitative Research* (4th ed., pp. 109–138). Thousand Oaks, CA: Sage.

Charmaz, Kathy. 2005. Grounded theory in the 21st century: A qualitative method for advancing social justice research. In N. K. Denzin & Y. S. Lincoln (Eds.), *Handbook of Qualitative Research* (3rd ed., pp. 507–535). Thousand Oaks, CA: Sage.

Charmaz, Kathy. 2011. Grounded theory methods in social justice research. In N. K. Denzin & Y. S. Lincoln (Eds.), *Handbook of Qualitative Research* (4th ed., pp. 359–380). Thousand Oaks, CA: Sage.

Charmaz, Kathy, Robert Thornberg & Elaine Keane. 2017. Grounded theory methods and social justice inquiry. In N. K. Denzin & Y. S. Lincoln (Eds.), *Handbook of Qualitative Research* (5 th ed., pp. 720–776. Thousand Oaks, CA: Sage.

Clarke, Adele E. 2005. *Situational Analysis: Grounded Theory after the Postmodern Turn*. Thousand Oaks, CA: Sage.

Clarke, Adele E. 2015a. Feminisms, grounded theory, and situational analysis revisited. In Adele E. Clarke, Carrie Friese & Rachel Washburn (Eds.), *Situational Analysis in Practice: Mapping Research with Grounded Theory* (pp. 119–154). Walnut Creek, CA: Left Coast Press

Clarke, Adele E. 2015b. From grounded theory to situational analysis: What's new? Why? How? In Adele E. Clarke, Carrie Friese & Rachel Washburn (Eds.), *Situational Analysis in Practice: Mapping Research* with Grounded Theory (pp. 84–118). Walnut Creek, CA: Left Coast Press.

Clarke, Adele E., Carrie Friese & Rachel Washburn. 2015. Introducting situational analysis. In Adele E. Clarke, Carrie Friese & Rachel Wshburn (Eds.), *Situational Analysis in Practice: Mapping Research with Grounded Theory* (pp. 11–75). Walnut Creek, CA: Left Coast Press.

Cohen-Cruz, J. *Local Acts: Community-Based Performance in the United States,* Rutgers University Press.

Collins, Patricia Hill. 1998. *Fighting Words: Black Women and the Search for Justice*. Minneapolis, MN: University of Minnesota Press.

Collins, Patricia Hill. 2000. *Black Feminist Thought* (2nd ed.). New York: Routledge.

Conquergood, Dwight. 1998. Beyond the text: Toward a performative cultural politics. In Sheron J. Dailey (Ed.), *The Future of Performance Studies: Visions and Revisions* (pp. 25–36). Annadale, VA: National Communication Association.

Conquergood, Dwight. 2006. Rethinking ethnography: Towards a critical cultural politics. In D. Soyini Madison & Judith Hamera (Eds.), *The Sage Handbook of Performance Studies* (pp. 351–365). Thousand Oaks, CA: Sage. Reprinted in Patrick Johnson (Ed.) (2012), *Cultural Struggles: Performance, Ethnography, Praxis: Dwight Conquergood* (pp. 81–103). Ann Arbor, MI: University of Michigan Press.

Conquergood, Dwight. 2013. Performance studies: Interventions and radical research. In Patrick Johnson (Ed.), *Cultural Struggles: Performance, Ethnography, Praxis: Dwight Conquergood* (pp. 32–46). Ann Arbor, MI: University of Michigan Press (originally published 2002).

Corbin, Juliet & Anselm Strauss. 2015. *Basics of Qualitative Research* (4th ed.). Thousand Oaks, CA: Sage.

Corey, Frederick C. 2015. Editor's introduction: Performance and social change. *Text and Performance Quarterly*, *35*(1), January: 1–3.

Darder, A. & Mirón, L. F. 2006. Critical pedagogy in a time of uncertainty: A call to action. In N. K. Denzin & M. D. Giardina (Eds.), *Contesting Empire/Globalizing Dissent: Cultural Studies after 9/11* (pp. 136–151). Boulder, CO: Westview Press.

Denzin 1997 *Interpretive ethnography.* Thousand Oaks, CA: Sage.

Denzin, Norman K. 1996. Post-pragmatism. *Symbolic Interaction*, *19*(1): 61–75.

Denzin, Norman K. 2003. *Performance Ethnography: Critical Pedagogy and the Politics of Culture*. Thousand Oaks, CA: Sage.

Denzin, Norman K. 2014. *Interpretive Autoethnography* (2nd ed.). Thousand Oaks, CA: Sage.

Denzin, Norman K. & Michael Giardina. 2006. Introduction: Qualitative inquiry and the conservative challenge. In N. K. Denzin & M. Giardina (Eds.), *Qualitative Inquiry and the Conservative Challenge* (pp. ix–xxxi). Walnut Creek, CA: Left Coast Press.

Denzin, Norman K. & Yvonna S. Lincoln. 2005. Introduction: The discipline and practice of qualitative research. In Norman K. Denzin & Yvonna S. Lincoln (Eds.), *The Handbook of Qualitative Research* (3rd ed., pp. 1–32). Thousand Oaks, CA: Sage.

Denzin, Norman K. & Yvonna S. Lincoln. 2008. Introduction: Critical methodologies and indigenous inquiry. In N. K. Denzin, Y. S. Lincoln & L. T. Smith (Eds.), *Handbook of Critical and Indigenous Methodologies* (pp. 1–20). Thousand Oaks, CA: Sage.

Denzin, Norman K., Yvonna S. Lincoln & Michael Giardina. 2006. Disciplining qualitative research. *Qualitative Studies in Education*, *6*: 122–144.

Denzin, N. & Lincoln, Y. '*The Discipline and practice of Qualitative Research*', Editors' Introduction to Sage Handbook of Qualitative Research 4th edition pp.1–18

Diversi, Marcelo, 2015. On decolonizing: E-mail. 9 April.

Diversi, Marcelo & Dan Henhawk. 2012. (Re)Awakening, together, from a long colonizing slumber. *International Review of Qualitative Research*, *5*(1), Spring: 51–72.

Diversi, Marcelo & Claudio Moreira. 2009. *Betweener Talk: Decolonizing Knowledge Production, Pedagogy, and Praxis*. Walnut Creek, CA: Left Coast Press.

Diversi, Marcelo & Claudio Moreira. 2012. Decolonizing constructions of childhood and history: Interrupting narratives of avoidance to children's questions about social justice. *International Journal of Qualitative Studies in Education*, *25*(2), (January–February): 189–203.

Dolan, Jill. 2005. *Utopia in Performance: Finding Hope in the Theater.* Ann Arbor, MI: University of Michigan Press.

Eagleton, T. 2003. *After Theory*. New York: Basic Books

Edwards, Rosalind & Melanie Mauthner. 2002. Ethics and feminist research: Theory and practice. In Melanie Mauthner, Maxine Birch, Julie Jessop & Tina Miller (Eds.), *Ethics in Qualitative Research* (pp. 14–31). London: Sage.

Fishman, Gustavo E. & Peter McLaren. 2005. Rethinking critical pedagogy and the Gramscian legacy: From organic to committed intellectuals. *Cultural Studies – Critical Methodologies*, *5*(1):

Freire, Paulo. 1996. *Letters to Cristina: Reflections on My Life and Work*. Translated by Donaldo Macedo with Quilda Macedo and Alexandre Oliveira. London: Routledge.

Freire, Paulo. 1999. *Pedagogy of Hope*. Translated by Robert R. Barr. New York: Continuum (originally published 1992).

Freire, Paulo. 2000. *Pedagogy of the Oppressed* (30th Anniversary edition, with an introduction by Donaldo Macedo). New York: Continuum (originally published, 1970; fifth reprinting, 2015).

Giroux. Henry. 2014a. *Neoliberalism's War on Higher Education*. Chicago, IL: Haymarket Books.

Giroux. Henry. 2014b. *The Violence of Organized Forgetting*. San Francisco, CA: City Lights Bookstore.

Giroux, Henry & Susan Searls Giroux. 2006. Challenging neoliberalism's new world order: The promise of critical pedagogy. *Cultural Studies – Critical Methodologies*, *6*(1): 21–32.

Glaser, Barney G. & Anselm L. Strauss. 1967. *The Discovery of Grounded Theory: Strategies for Qualitative Research*. Chicago, IL: Aldine.

Goffman, Erving. 1959. *The Presentation of Self in Everyday Life*. New York: Doubleday.

Grande, Sandy. 2000. American Indian identity and intellectualism: The quest for a new Red Pedagogy. *Qualitative Studies in Education*, *13*: 343–360.

Grande, Sandy. 2008a. Red Pedagogy: The uni-methodology. In N. K. Denzin, Y. S. Lincoln & L. T. Smith (Eds.), *Handbook of Critical and Indigenous Methodologies* (pp. 233–254). Thousand Oaks, CA: Sage.

Grande, Sandy. 2008b. *Red Pedagogy: Native American Social and Political Thought*. Lanham, MD: Rowman & Littlefield.

Hall, Stuart. 1996. What is this 'Black' in Black popular culture? In David Morley & Kuan-Hsing Chen (Eds.), *Stuart Hall: Critical Dialogues in Cultural Studies* (pp. 465–475). London: Routledge.

Jackson, Alecia Y. & Lisa A. Mazzei. 2012. *Thinking with Theory in Qualitative Research*. New York: Routledge.

Jordan, June. 1998. *Affirmative Acts.* New York: Anchor.

Kaomea, Julie. 2004. Dilemmas of an Indigenous academic: A native Hawaiian story. In Kagendo Mutua & Beth Blue Swadener (Eds.), *Decolonizing Research in Cross-Cultural Contexts: Critical Personal Narratives* (pp. 27–44). Albany, NY: State University of New York Press.

Kincheloe, Joe L. & Peter McLaren. 2000. Rethinking critical theory and qualitative research. In Norman K. Denzin & Yvonna S. Lincoln (Eds.), *Handbook of Qualitative Research* (2nd ed., pp. 279–314). Thousand Oaks, CA: Sage.

Kovach, Margaret. 2009. *Indigenous Methodologies*. Toronto: University of Toronto Press.

Madison, D. Soyini. 1998. Performances, personal narratives, and the politics of possibility. In Sheron J. Dailey (Ed.), *The Future of Performance Studies: Visions and Revisions* (pp. 276–286). Annadale, VA: National Communication Association.

Madison, D. Soyini. 2006. Dwight Conquergood's 'Rethinking Eethnography'. In D. Soyini Madison & Judith Hamera (Eds.), *The Sage Handbook of Performance Studies* (pp. 347–350). Thousand Oaks, CA: Sage.

Madison, D. Soyini. 2010. *Acts of Activism: Human Rights as Radical Performance*. Cambridge: Cambridge University Press.

Madison, D. Soyini. 2012. *Critical Ethnography* (2nd ed.). Thousand Oaks, CA: Sage.

Meyer, Manulani Aluli. 2003. *Ho'oulu: Our Time of Becoming: Hawaiian Epistemology and Early Writings*. Honolulu: 'Ai Pohaku Press Native Books.

Mills, C.W. 1959. *The Sociological Imagination*. Oxford University Press: Oxford.

Munoz, Jose Esteban. 2005. Stages: Queers, Punks, and the Utopian Performative. In D. Soyini Madison & Judith Hamera (Eds.), *The Sage Handbook of Performance Studies* (pp. 9–20). Thousand Oaks, CA: Sage.

Mutua, Kagendoo & Beth Blue Swadner, 2004. Introduction. In Kagendo Mutua & Beth Blue Swadener (Eds.), *Decolonizing Research in Cross-Cultural Contexts: Critical Personal Narratives*. (pp. 1–23). Albany, NY: State University of New York Press.

Pelias, Ronald J. 2004. *A Methodology of the Heart: Evoking Academic and Daily Life*. Walnut Creek, CA: AltaMira.

Pollock, Della. 1998. A response to Dwight Conquergood's Essay: 'Beyond the Text: Towards a Performative Cultural Politics'. In Sheron J. Dailey (Ed.), *The Future of Performance Studies: Visions and Revisions* (pp. 37–46). Annadale, VA: National Communication Association.

Rains, F. V., J. A. Archibald, & D. Deyhle. 2000. Through our eyes and in our words – the voices of indigenous scholars. Special Issue. *International Journal of Qualitative Studies in Education*, *13*(4): 337–342.

Saldana, J. 2011. *Ethnotheatre: Research from Page to Stage*. Walnut Creek, CA: Left Coast Press.

Seigfried, Charlene Haddock. 1996. *Pragmatism and Feminism: Reweaving the Social Fabric*. Chicago, IL: University of Chicago Press.

Semaili, Ladislaus, M. & Joe L. Kincheloe. 1999. Introduction: What is Indigenous Knowledge and why should we study it? In Ladislaus M. Semaili & Joe L. Kincheloe (Eds.), *What is Indigenous Knowledge? Voices from the Academy* (pp. 3–57). New York: Falmer Press.

Smith, Graham. 2000. Protecting and respecting Indigenous Knowledge. In Marie Battiste (Ed.), *Reclaiming Indigenous Voice and Vision* (pp. 209–224). Vancouver: UBC Press.

Smith, Linda Tuhiwai. 1999. *Decolonizing Methodologies: Research and Indigenous Peoples*. London: Zed Books.

Smith, Linda Tuhiwai. 2000. Kupapa Maori research. In Marie Battiste (Ed.), *Reclaiming Indigenous Voice and Vision* (pp. 225–247). Vancouver: UBC Press.

Smith, Linda Tuhiwai. 2005. On tricky ground: Researching the native in the age of uncertainty. In N. K. Denzin & Y. S. Lincoln (Eds.), *Handbook of Qualitative Research* (3rd ed., pp. 85–108). Thousand Oaks, CA: Sage.

Smith, Linda Tuhiwai. 2012. *Decolonizing Methodologies: Research and Indigenous Peoples* (2nd ed.). London: Zed Books.

Spry, Tami. 2011. *Body, Paper, Stage: Writing and Performing Autoethnography*. Walnut Creek, CA: Left Coast Press.

Strauss, Anselm. 1987. *Qualitative Analysis for Social Scientists*. New York: Cambridge University Press.

Strauss, Anselm & Juliet Corbin. 1998. *Basics of Qualitative Research: Techniques and Procedures for Developing Grounded Theory* (2nd ed.). Thousand Oaks, CA: Sage.

Tuck, E. & Yang, K. Wayne. 2013. Decolonization is not a metaphor. Retrieved from http://www.buddhistpeacefellowship.org/eve-tuck-and-k-wayne-yang-decolonization-is-not-a-metaphor/

Vizenor, G. (1993). The Ruins of Representation: Shadow Survivance and the Literature of Dominance. *American Indian Quarterly*, *17*(1): 7–30.

Weems, Mary. 2002. *I Speak from the Wound that is my Mouth*. New York: Peter Lang.

West, Cornel. 1989. *The American Evasion of Philosophy: A Genealogy of Pragmatism*. Madison, WI: University of Wisconsin Press.

West, Cornel. 1991. Theory, pragmatisms and politics. In Jonathan Arac & Barbara Johnson (Eds.), *Consequences of Theory* (pp. 22–38). Baltimore, MD: Johns Hopkins University Press.

23

Grounded Theory Methodology and Self-Reflexivity in the Qualitative Research Process

Katja Mruck and Günter Mey

INTRODUCTION

Fifty years after Barney Glaser and Anselm Strauss published their groundbreaking book *The Discovery of Grounded Theory* (1967), we are facing a rather heterogeneous area of approaches. In some regards it makes sense to talk about grounded theory in the plural: after the *Discovery* book was published, Glaser and Strauss did not develop grounded theory methodology (GTM[1]) together. Coming from different research backgrounds – Glaser, a student of Paul Lazarsfeld at Columbia University and familiar with quantitative research;[2] and Strauss from the University of Chicago, a student of Herbert Blumer and socialized within a tradition of pragmatism and social interactionism – their understanding of (doing) GTM gradually drifted apart and led to separate elaborations. Additionally, a 'second generation' (Morse et al., 2009) of grounded theorists appeared on the scene. Most prominent were: Juliet Corbin, who co-authored *Basics of Qualitative Research* (1990) with Strauss, providing a fundamentally revised version after Strauss's death (Corbin & Strauss, 2015); Kathy Charmaz, who developed a *Constructing Grounded Theory* approach (2006, fundamentally revised in 2014); and Adele Clarke (2005) with *Situational Analysis*.

Within these approaches, not only do the methods vary (for a systematization of different coding procedures, see e.g., Mey & Mruck, 2011; Ruppel & Mey, 2017), but so do background epistemologies and theories referred to (e.g., pragmatism, symbolic interactionism, social constructionism/constructivism,[3] and discourse theory, see Bryant & Charmaz in this volume). Others tried to combine GTM with additional methods, for example, applying action research procedures within a 'grounded action' approach

(Olson, 2007; Simmons & Gregory, 2003); developing how to combine GTM with narrative analysis (Lal, Suto & Ungar, 2012; Ruppel & Mey, 2015); or elaborating a 'visual' GTM (Konecki, 2011, and his chapter in this volume; Mey & Dietrich, 2017). The first edition of this *Handbook* has already demonstrated the plurality of what is called GTM, which becomes even more apparent with this second edition.

From plurality and heterogeneity many challenges arise for those interested in doing grounded theory research – not only but especially for novice researchers, those 'kids' Glaser and Strauss were interested in empowering with their *Discovery of Grounded Theory* book.[4] Which is the 'best' GTM? Which one best fits a specific research topic one is interested in, which one offers the amount of guidance versus freedom a researcher needs? Is it actually possible to follow one GTM approach step by step the way the respective creator(s) intended?

To deal with such questions, decisions are unavoidable, and this points to the central issue we are dealing with in this chapter – namely the necessity of (self)reflection in any empirical research. That research and its results depend on time, place, and the context a researcher belongs to is what Kuhn (1962) referred to as the psychology or sociology of research, in contrast to the 'logic of research' (Popper, 1934/1992). Kuhn, in his work, learned from a still rather neglected microbiologist, Ludwik Fleck. Fleck used his own research on syphilis to demonstrate the 'genesis and development of a scientific fact' (Fleck, 1935a/1979) and its historical and socio-psychological grounding in 'thought collectives'. According to Fleck, analyzing data – and more fundamentally any scientific observation – is not best understood in terms of the fit between a fact and a theory which should be tested, but instead in terms of 'style-locked re-interpretations' within preferred epistemologies and 'thought systems' (including accessible concepts, routines, sanctions, etc.). He writes: 'There is no isolated researcher, no ahistoric, no style-free observation possible at all', and within the respective style the 'mental past and presence of the thought collective's … real and mental fathers' (1935b/1983: 81, our translation) have an essential impact. For Fleck, this affiliation is unavoidable, and it leads not to *one* truth, but to relative, style-locked truths, dependent on the respective systems of reference.

Kuhn's and others' work influenced science and technology studies; well-known examples of 'science as it happens' are those of Knorr-Cetina (1981), Latour and Woolgar (1979), and Lynch (1985). And it led to a critical appraisal of scientific practices and a 'crisis of representation' during the 'writing culture' debate in anthropology (Clifford & Marcus, 1986; for a summary, see Tedlock, 2000). Clifford Geertz (1988), for example, analyzed from the perspective of the 'anthropologist as author' how researchers – situated in specific historio-political contexts – created their objects in a distancing way, which 'leads to an exclusive focus on the Other as primitive, bizarre, and exotic' (p. 14). This turn to historical Othering practices resulted in the subsequent call for a reflexive stance towards culturally constructed academic discourses and writing practices in the social sciences in general and qualitative research in particular, fields already attentive to Kuhn's work in the 1960s and 1970s. To a first critical re-examination on 'subjectivity and reflexivity in qualitative research', more than 120 proposals were submitted, with more than 50 articles ultimately published (Mruck, Roth & Breuer, 2002; Roth, Breuer & Mruck, 2003). Taking a closer look at them, it is apparent that 'reflexivity' is interpreted in many different ways. What these variations share is what Steier (1991: 2) called a recursive 'turning back on one's own experience', but how and why this should be done mostly differs.

A new attempt to deal with what might be called 'reflexivity in the plural' has been proposed by Kühner, Ploder, and Langer (2016), differentiating 'weak' from 'strong reflexivity'. While the former's interest is to 'reveal and *control* the influence of researchers and their environment on the research process' (p. 2, our italics), strong reflexivity stresses the researcher's professional background and personal involvement, his/her 'sympathies, prejudices, fears, emotional, mental, and physical reactions' (ibid.) as decisive resources during the research process.[5] For Kühner et al., the use of strong reflexivity means giving up 'the authoritative position of the sovereign researcher' (p. 3), that often still leads to undermining one's own position in academic discourse. Or, in the words of Finlay (2002: 212): 'The process of engaging in reflexivity is perilous, full of muddy ambiguity and multiple trails.' Nevertheless, successive elaborations had been generated within GTM, negotiating the difficult path between weak and strong reflexivity and allowing a first shaping of a reflexive GTM.

SHAPING A REFLEXIVE GROUNDED THEORY METHODOLOGY

In GTM, reflexivity started to become a more explicit topic of concern since the beginning of the twenty-first century (Glaser, 2001, 2002; Hall & Callery, 2001; see Cutcliffe, 2000, for an early review of 'creativity and reflexivity in grounded theory' at that time), and especially within a constructionist/constructivist framework (Bryant, 2003; Charmaz, 2000, 2014; Mills, Bonner & Francis, 2006a, 2006b). More recent discussions on including reflexivity in GTM are provided, for example, by Engward and Davis (2015), or Gentles, Jack, Nicholas, and McKibbon (2014).

Bearing in mind the theoretical foundations of symbolic interactionism and pragmatism, one would expect reflection on the interaction between researchers and research participants to be a constitutive element of GTM from the very beginning. But at least in the Glaserian tradition, the concept of 'emergence' of theory from the data led to a strong rejection of 'forcing GTM' (Glaser, 1992) (with 'forcing' referring to the impact of the researcher in this perspective). While Glaser explicitly polemicizes against reflexivity as 'paralysing' and 'self-destructive' (Neill, 2006), Strauss (1987: 9) advocates 'a highly self-conscious approach to the work of research'. According to Strauss and Corbin, researchers need to build on professional and personal life experiences: 'We know that our perspectives and belief systems influence how we view and work with data. We want our readers to understand why it is important to look at experiences, feelings, [and] action/interaction, to denote the structure or context in which these are located' (Corbin, in Cisneros-Puebla, 2004: §21). At the same time, Strauss and Corbin continued to rely 'on terms such as recognising bias and maintaining objectivity when describing the position the researcher should assume in relation to the participants and the data. … This has led some researchers to remark that "people can find support in it [Strauss and Corbin's GTM approach] for any ontology that they wish"' (Mills et al., 2006a: 3–4).

A 'reflexive stance' is explicitly recommended by Kathy Charmaz in her book *Constructing Grounded Theory* (2006, 2014). She explicitly turns away from positivist and objectivist positions not only within Glaserian GTM, but also underpinning at least the earlier versions of the work of Strauss and Corbin (see also Corbin, 2009, on her 'analytic journey'). Leaning on pragmatism, Charmaz (2017) acknowledges reflexivity to be a basic ingredient of doing research within co-constructed social realities. Researchers are no longer regarded as neutral and passive (Bryant, 2003), but actively involved – their positioning, beliefs, and values do play a central role in shaping the research process. 'Situating grounded theories in their social, historical, local, and interactional contexts strengthens them and supports making nuanced comparisons between data and among different studies' (Charmaz, 2014: 322).

The involvement and positionality of researchers is even more stressed by Adele Clarke (2005; Clarke & Keller, 2014). According to her, researchers should not only reflect on the use of pre-existing (scientific) knowledge and research contexts systematically, but also on their own personal interests in doing research. This is not limited to conducting research, but should also be part of writing up results, i.e., part of the grounded theories developed.

Differing from Charmaz, who refers to social constructivist epistemologies, and from Clarke's post-structuralist foundation, Franz Breuer developed his reflexive grounded theory approach (2010) mainly leaning on the ethno-psychoanalyst Georges Devereux. In his book *From Anxiety to Method in the Behavioral Sciences* (1967), like Glaser and Strauss's *Discovery of Grounded Theory* published in 1967, Devereux turned prominently against traditional methodological concepts. For him, researchers and research participants act within a symmetric relation, observing and influencing each other: data in social sciences result from (1) the behaviour of the research participant; (2) disturbances produced by the existence and observational activities of the observer during interaction; and (3) the behaviour of the observer, i.e., the researcher (Devereux 1967: xix). Researchers should therefore reflect on their own 'stimulus value' for the respective Other continuously (p. 28).

Breuer situates his approach within 'strong reflexivity', an ascription most GTM researchers would probably not support. On the contrary, maintaining the 'positivist adherence to objectivity and rigour' (Kennedy & Lingard, 2006: 102) may also be true for studies explicitly settled within a constructivist GTM approach. Nagel et al. (2016), for example, did research on the delivery of care by nurses in virtual environments, and there is only a short paragraph on 'reflexivity and qualitative rigour' (p. 5). Doyle and Goldinggay (2012: 42) just mention that 'the use of reflexivity supported data gathering' (see also, for example, De Bie & De Poot, 2016; Martin, 2016; or Niebieszczanski, Dent & McGowan, 2015). At the same time, Glaser's harsh rejection of reflexivity does not mean that research using his approach ignores the necessity of a reflexive stance. Alvinius, Starrin, and Larsson (2016), for example, describe step by step how they developed the concept of 'reflexive serendipity', exploring the role of the researcher while doing research on disaster management and military operations. And Neill (2006) carves out the contribution of reflexivity for theoretical sampling in Glaserian GTM.

On the one hand, the phenomenon described above may partly be due to the fact that today, 'grounded theory' as well as 'reflexivity' are used as legitimizing labels: deciding for a specific GTM approach as well as whether to mention reflexivity or not depends on the context a researcher belongs to – or would like to belong to (see Greckhamer & Koro-Ljungberg, 2005; and O'Reilly, Paper & Marx, 2012, for the use of GTM as an authoritative hallmark; and Pillow, 2003, for the uses of reflexivity as 'methodological power'). On the other hand, this phenomenon leads us back to a question previously raised: Is it actually possible to follow any GTM approach step by step the way the respective creator(s) intended? Our answer is no: within language- and meaning-based qualitative research, the use of methods always entails interpretation. The process of co-constructing data is accompanied by the process of co-constructing methods: 'Methods do not operate in a vacuum but are discursively and epistemologically constructed' (Greckhamer & Koro-Ljungberg, 2005: 745).

Neglecting the co-constructive character of research results in an unquestioned mix of the impact of researchers and research participants on the research process – or, in the words of Weston La Barre (1967: viii) in his preface to Devereux's *From Anxiety to Method* – in 'a species of autobiography'. Therefore, researchers should not only critically self-reflect on how their 'background, assumptions, positioning and behaviour impact on the research process' (Finlay & Gough, 2003: ix), but they should also strive to preserve the contexts and voices of the research participants for each stage of the research process (Charmaz & Keller, 2016).

Taking into account and systematizing the above-mentioned groundwork, examining the impact of reflexivity on the research process and its results concerns:

1 *General schemata and processes of knowledge construction*. Generating knowledge always implies 'Othering': naming/defining any phenomenon means not just representing something existing inside or outside but constructing an object by the conceptual means of the researcher. Such human ways of perceiving, conceptualizing, re-structuring, and communicating, shape any (research) endeavour, while being simultaneously subject to (historical) development and its creators.[6]
2 *Epistemologies, theories, methods, and routines within a scientific community*. 'Style-locked re-interpretations' and practices should be subjected to analysis, but in 'normal science' concepts existing in a specific time and within specific disciplines are usually taken for granted. Only in times of crisis do scientific efforts turn reflexively to their own foundations (Kuhn, 1962). The difficulty in overcoming taken-for-granted routines and concepts is obvious when trying to imagine radical shifts in time or place. Thus, living (and conducting research) 200 years ago meant using completely different terminologies as well as completely different access to and ideas about 'reality' and its adequate 'representation' in (social) science. Or in some cases, the same terms are used but with different meanings.
3 *The closer institutional context in which a researcher is involved*. The immediate academic background, the team he/she is a part of, sponsors, funding institutions, etc. will influence decisions during the full research process, shaping what might be accepted or not accepted terms, knowledge, methods, outcomes, etc.
4 *The researcher's social, historical, and cultural positionality*. Belonging to a different class, gender, race, or nationality means different access to resources; different ways to act, feel, and behave in different lifeworlds; and different concepts and experiences, while conducting research as an insider or outsider of a field, etc.
5 *The researcher's personal characteristics*, acquired and continuously developed during his/her biography while interacting with significant others. What a person has learned to like or dislike, to love or fear, to look for or avoid, is of essential importance even when just deciding for or against a research topic. The way he/she dresses, looks like, smells – his/her stimulus value for different others – shape every move and interaction in the research field as well as within academic contexts.
6 *Interactions within the field of research/with research participants*. The characteristics mentioned above will serve as a complex background while interacting with research participants, keeping in mind that both 'researchers and research participants make assumptions about what is real, possess stocks of knowledge, occupy social statuses, and pursue purposes that influence their respective views and actions in the presence of each other' (Charmaz, 2014: 27).

Co-construction characterizes each step of the research process. The researcher (a person, biographically socialized and situated within a historically and culturally-specific community and institution) identifies (i.e., creates) a research topic and field; decides on (and thus interprets) what seem to be appropriate (scientifically and institutionally available and accepted) methods for data collection; interacts with a research participant (a person, biographically socialized and situated within a historically and cultural specific [professional] background) to collect (i.e., co-construct) data; applies (again, interprets scientifically and institutionally available and accepted) methods for data analysis; successively develops a (co-constructed) grounded theory, shedding light on those parts of the field that are accessible, visible, and interpreted within specifically situated (inter)actions for specific audiences.

In the following, we will highlight how researchers, their interaction with research participants, and the contexts all act to influence the research process from an initial, pre-research stage, through to data collection and analysis, and up to the writing and publishing stages. We will then provide an overview of strategies that support reflexivity while doing research. By engaging in this endeavour, we do not intend to convince (post-) positivist GTM researchers to give up realist or objectivist ideals, nor to bring 'bricoleur-researchers' back to the path of ensuring scientific rigour in traditional ways. We also do not aim to provide prescriptive rules on 'how to do' reflexivity, but we wish to sensitize readers to the decisions, choices, alternatives, and limitations of the research process.

RESEARCH AS AN ITERATIVE DECISION PROCESS, REQUIRING CONTINUAL REFLECTION

Initial Stage: Posing a Research Question and Determining the Design of a Study

GTM research starts with a researcher or a research group interested in learning something new about a topic and developing a theory. As a potentially unlimited number of research questions and ways to work on them exist, preferences for theories and methods, as well as personal interests, skills, prejudices, sensibilities, etc., already influence this initial process. Researchers are not only co-constructively involved while interacting bodily in the field but are also already defining/addressing it. Their perspectives represent specific ways of Othering, which are important for the field and worth careful reflexive analysis.

As research usually is not just a private endeavour but exists within a specific disciplinary and institutional context as part of professional career aspirations, researchers have to be aware of what is accepted within the academic area to which they refer or belong. This already concerns epistemological predefinitions, underpinning terms used to secure understanding and acceptance as an expert and a scientist within a community. Such preconceptions structure in a very fundamental way what later on are assigned as characteristics to an object/field/topic to be researched. Nilson (2016), for example, describes her 'journey' in dealing reflexively with concepts and worldviews shaping her 'attitudes, behaviours, values, beliefs' (p. 123); see also Greenbank (2002) on the role of values, and Berger (2015) on positioning and reflexivity in qualitative research.

Theories also play a crucial role right from the initial stages of any research. *Tabula rasa* is a fiction, as experienced researchers may previously have worked for some time on an area of interest and are familiar with the available stock of knowledge. Novice researchers usually do not start independently, but are part of institutions and are supervised by experienced researchers. In the case of external funding, reports on the state of the art of research within a certain domain are required. So, on the one hand, a degree of familiarity with extant theories is unavoidable; on the other hand, the acquisition of theoretical knowledge at a very early stage is also a necessary precondition to deciding whether to use GTM at all, as methodologically, GTM makes sense if an appropriate theory has not yet been developed. Therefore, researchers should know what already exists and what does not (for a short summary of the 'disputed literature review', see Charmaz, 2014: 305f; McGhee, Marland, & Atkinson, 2007; Ramalho, Adams, Huggard, & Hoare, 2015; and see also Thornberg and Dunne, and Martin in this volume).

As not one but many GTMs exist, researchers additionally need to be aware of the different GTM approaches, of the epistemologies they refer to, the methods (coding procedures, etc.) they suggest, and so on. Thus, for Glaserian GTM, what 'is important is to use the complete package of GT procedures as an integrated methodological whole' (Glaser & Holton, 2004: §41). While Glaser turns against any 'method slurring' (Baker, Wuest & Stern, 1992) – i.e., mixing methods, mislabelling, etc. – Strauss advises adjusting the method to different contexts and purposes (in Legewie & Schervier-Legewie, 2004: Track 7). Charmaz and Bryant (2010: 411) explicitly welcome 'the usefulness of combining grounded theory with other approaches'. Researchers should know about these different positions and what happens when transferring 'methods from one epistemological realm and theoretical stance to another one' (Greckhamer & Koro-Ljungberg, 2005: 729), as this will shape the following research process. Howard-Payne (2016), for example, describes how she decided whether to follow Glaser or Strauss using examples from research on HIV prevention in South Africa. Evans (2013) presents the 'confusing world of grounded theory' from his perspective as a novice researcher close to a Glaserian approach (see also Piantanida, Tananis & Grubs, 2004, for an example of a reflexive 'journey' into GTM).

Even the aim of generating theory may be asking too much of PhD students, and preferences for one GTM approach or for combining one approach with other (GTM) methods may be 'strategical[ly] or intuitive[ly]' chosen (Greckhamer & Koro-Ljungberg, 2005: 741) in the beginning. Especially those who are new to the field and overwhelmed by the vagueness of methodological concepts in qualitative research compared to quantitative research may end up searching for 'recipes' or use methods as if such 'secure recipes' exist. Furthermore, the context of application, time, and financial restrictions may lead to the usage of more standardized methods or of 'ad hoc standardizations'. The problem is not that researchers need to adjust to external conditions – what we are asking for is thorough reflection on the continual decisions necessary from the very beginning, as they will shape the way in which the research project will be methodically constructed and finally fixed in a grounded theory.

Certainly, researchers differ in their willingness and ability to navigate the complex challenges arising from the impact of style-locked reinterpretations and (sub-)disciplinary or institutional routines, of their own positionality and subjectivity, prior to entering the field and any personal encounter with research participants. But the decision to expose oneself to the endeavour of reflexivity may be rewarded with two major benefits: the more researchers are familiar with their own preconceptions, preferences, etc., the better they will be prepared and curious to try to take a look at the Other. And they will enter the field with an instructive package of data, as reflexive accounts from this initial stage will shed a first light and provide first heuristic options for generating theory during the following stages.

Entering the Field/data Collection

Collecting data entails several decisions on the part of the researcher before any personal encounter. He/she must opt for the kind of data to include and for the data collection methods to use. Also, cases need to be defined, i.e., where to start in a field or with whom. Data may result from participant observation during ethnographical research; may be collected during interviews, group discussions, or within online research; may include existing documents such as newspapers; and may also arise from quantitative research. The data may be visual, material, or textual; may be collected personally by the researcher or by external assistants; or the researcher may refer to data available from previous research for secondary consideration and re-analysis.

However, which data to include and which data collection methods to use should depend on the question a researcher poses, although 'pet methods', personal preferences, and disciplinary routines do play an important role at this stage. Grounded theorists such as Bryant (2017) continuously stress the impact of critically reflecting on one's own decisions on the research process to provide a clearer basis for judging validity. Nevertheless, notions of 'naturalistic' versus more or less 'contaminated' data persist: the more the researcher's constructing effort is visible, the less validly the data are regarded. Thus, observation protocols and field notes seem to be less reliable than interviews, and videotaped interviews closer to 'reality' than interview transcripts. Ashmore and Reed (2000) criticize this attitude, addressing tapes as 'found objects' and 'concerned with what can be done with a recording, not with the activity of recording itself' (§9). This is even truer for the corpus of data created during reflexive GTM: diaries, memos dealing with the researcher's emotional feedback, protocols from research supervisions, etc. are often handled as mere tools to become aware of and avoid the researcher's impact – as opposed to data subject to analysis like any other data. But *all* data included, and each data collection method used, depend on active choices and are 'contaminated': 'Each encounter or interview, even if it is concerned with the same topic and conducted with the same participants, will produce different data, since it is a product of the unique circumstances operating at the time' (Gardner, 2006: 261). The more the researcher tries to act as a 'witness' who should 'fix' the world(views) of the research participants, the more he/she is in danger of ignoring the co-constructiveness of research encounters. There is no way to get rid of the 'mess' of co-construction and individual choices. What researchers can and should do is make them as visible, transparent and open for further debate and research as possible.

Interviews[7] play the most prominent role within GTM research (e.g., Charmaz, 2014, included two chapters on interviewing in the new edition of *Constructing Grounded Theory*). While deciding which interview method to use, disciplinary and national habits come into the play. In Germany, for example, different interview methods exist that are thoroughly grounded epistemologically and theoretically (e.g., Schütze, 1983, for the narrative interview; and Muylaert et al., 2014, for an English summary of Schütze's approach). In contrast, within Anglo-American contexts, so-called 'intensive interviews' or 'in-depth interviews' are often used. Neither are methods in any strict sense, but techniques: they are defined by the aim to generate 'rich data', openness to the voice, and meanings of the research participants (e.g., Charmaz, 2014: 56), and are accompanied by some how-to guidelines. As epistemological and theoretical preconceptions play a crucial role not only in choosing a GTM approach but also in selecting data collection methods, researchers are left alone with basic reflexive work if the introduction of interviews in literature is limited to pure tools.

Both familiarity and being unfamilar influence the decision for cases to start with. Still, there is a dominant notion that researchers need to be unfamiliar/strangers to avoid possible biases and problems of validity. The more researchers and participants belong to similar cultures, the more interviewers may presuppose concepts and values as shared, and therefore fail to attend to elaboration during the interview; even central topics will be obscured or lost. Conversely, intimate knowledge will hardly be given to strangers, so familiarity will provide other insights than in the case of a researcher unfamiliar with a person or issue. So far, both being familiar and being unfamiliar point to complementary perspectives, each of them helpful in understanding different facets of the phenomenon addressed. Dwyer and Buckle (2009) use the insider status of one and the outsider status of the other author to reflect on interviewing different parent groups. Neill (2006) provides an example of reflecting on process, context, and self during sampling within a Glaserian GTM.

The first encounter means anticipating and recognizing the respective other – his/her interests, motives, etc. – and influences the interviewee's (un-)willingness to participate: 'Each touches and impacts on the other, and that affects how the research unfolds' (Finlay, 2009: 2). The interview setting and location themselves shape what happens during the research encounter. Mills et al. (2006b: 10) recommend 'scheduling interviews at a time and location of the participant's choice' as one component 'to establish[ing] a more non-hierarchical relationship'. Though the idea of empowering research participants is certainly creditable, this implies that they do need empowerment and that, sufficiently empowered, their 'true voices' will be visible. But interviewees and their voices and choices are visible anyway, though always perceived through the lens of the interviewer, and unfolding in a mutually constructed unique interaction. In some cases, interviewees may be inclined to use interviewers as a 'megaphone' to communicate (at least tacitly) expectations of what others should know or acknowledge. If adult researchers interested in youth cultures interview adolescents, they may remind the latter of former experiences with social workers, and their stories will probably be 'designed' accordingly, mentioning those aspects they think of interest to social workers; their story would be completely different if told to a friend or in a peer group. McCartan, Schubotz, and Murphy (2012) thus worked (and published) together as young and adult co-researchers. Sultana (2007), drawing from international fieldwork, describes how he 'was also "othered" by those observing and studying [him] in the field … [and] positioned [him] with ties to not only (privileged) educational institutions, but also with the US and its global hegemony' (p. 379f; see also Bourke, 2014). Gentles et al. (2014), referring to examples from a GTM study on 'how parents with children with autism navigate intervention' (p. 1), discuss their use of reflexivity during the different research stages, and how they handled issues of positioning or dealt with sensitive topics within 'co-constructive interaction' (p. 9).

Conversely, interviewers may be sensitive to some topics volunteered by the interviewees and ignore or avoid others. This is partly due to the fact that, besides those directly involved in an interview, 'invisible others' are present and influential in the results obtained – namely, those who will hear the interview tapes, read the transcripts, or evaluate the work, and who may play a crucial role already when determining interview questions, the way they should be asked, and what interviewers should or should not mention.

Contrary to the still dominant opinion that researchers should be as invisible as possible to elicit interviewees' narrations and perspectives, Mills et al. (2006b) recommend 'sharing the researcher's understanding of the key issues ... as well as ... personal details and answering questions asked both during the interview and afterward ... to establish a more non-hierarchical relationship' (p. 9f). In contrast, novices in particular tend to work through extensive interview schedules in a rather 'bureaucratic' and mechanistic manner. From a traditional point of view, both may be regarded as so-called 'interview errors'. But in which way does the researcher act: research participants do not merely *re*-act but *act* in *their* own way, and it is those subtle interactions and dynamics between the persons involved in a unique situation that will shed specific light onto the scene, subject to further analysis.

Data Analysis

Data derived and available for analysis are 'in principle interactive, social, sub/cultural, situated, and contextual constructions by all persons involved' (Mruck & Breuer, 2003: §9). However, while the co-constructive character of (generating) data is always present (though not necessarily reflected) during interviewing or while in the field, many researchers try to ignore it during subsequent analysis. That a particular research participant told a specific story to an individual researcher at a specific point in time and a specific place is lost in an approach to analysis that is solely trying to lean on the 'responses' of interviewees. Usually these responses are fixed in transcripts and regarded as 'realistic objects'. Similarly, 'the use of technology confers an air of scientific objectivity onto what remains a fundamentally subjective, interpretative process' (Mauthner & Doucet, 1998: 122). Against naturalizing approaches, Ochs already in 1979 critically examined transcribing as a selective and theory-laden process; see Davidson (2009) for a review of three decades of literature on transcription in qualitative research, and Chadwick (2016) for reflecting on an example of turning talk into text within an ethnopoetic transcribing effort. Woods, Macklin, and Lewis (2015), reviewing three decades of literature on computer-assisted qualitative data analysis software, discuss how its use may support or undermine reflexivity. Konopásek (2008), leaning on sociology of science and using the metaphor of a 'textual laboratory', sheds light on what researchers do *practically* while using software for data analysis (in his case, ATLAS.ti within a GTM approach) (see chapters by Friese and Gorra in this volume).

Like transcription and technology, data analysis methods are not just neutral techniques, but are imbued with epistemological and theoretical assumptions: besides more general aspects relevant to selecting an appropriate GTM approach, as mentioned above, one has to keep in mind those pre-existing sociological theories implicitly underlying key instruments of analysis, for example Glaser's 'coding families' (1978, 1998: 170ff), or Strauss and Corbin's 'paradigm model' (1990: Part II). Additionally, a researcher's a priori knowledge and experiences are indispensable in making sense of data, recognizing patterns, etc. This is even truer as coding 'initially requires the researcher to fracture the data through open coding and then put it back together again in a more abstract and conceptual theoretical form' (Mills et al., 2006b: 12; Ruppel & Mey, 2015). Here, varying capacities for abstraction (from data to codes to categories to theory) become evident. Novices in particular often stick to description, as they are afraid of making 'unscientific' interpretations. Some tend to avoid a feeling of being inundated by data by looking for 'authorities' and concealing their own involvement in the analysis process. Others may lean unwittingly on some 'pet concepts' while accessing and analyzing data.

The challenging task during analysis is to be as aware as possible of the co-constructiveness of data and methods on the one hand, i.e., focusing on the researcher's continuous impact on every single decision during the data analysis process. On the other hand, in traditional research,[8] this stage is most important for preserving the voices of research participants in theory construction in any possible way. But each encounter with the Other, each single word heard during the interview or written in a text, has to pass the bodily, cognitive, and emotional filters of the analyst, and leads to specific embodied resonances – there is no way to not (re)act personally. Researchers should not ignore this in the hope that, if they pretend 'long enough that it does not exist, it should just quietly go away' (Devereux, 1967: xviii). Instead, the researcher's anxieties and 'warding-off manoeuvres', quite as much as his/her 'research strategy, perception of data, and decision making … can shed light' (ibid.) on the topic under interest, and enrich data analysis and theory development in two different ways:

1 As researchers are not neutral observers but part of the field, their responses are responses to the performance and narrations of the Other, the interviewee, be it as insiders sharing parts of his/her lifeworld, or as outsiders reacting to him/her, for example, in a friendly or aversive manner. This may help to get in touch with issues not explicitly mentioned during the interview but which are important for analysis. For example, while we worked on a study on theatre performance in a research group we supervised, different group members continuously reported feelings of severe time pressure while reading interview texts and preparing the sessions. Even though until that point 'time' had not been mentioned explicitly by the interviewees, this observation led to taking into account the role of 'limited time' slipping in as a new actor alongside the existing ones, and as an important aspect of further theory development (Mruck & Mey, 1998).
2 Trying to see the world as strictly as possible through the interviewee's eyes, researchers need to 'bracket' one's own experiences, involvement, etc. Without reflexive strategies, 'perspective slurring' is unavoidable. This means that different perceptions and interpretations (of interviewees, field members, the researcher, members of research groups) need to be taken seriously and subjected to constant comparison (Glaser, 1965). Trying to understand interviewees' perspectives is especially difficult in cases, far away from interviewers' everyday life. In another research group we supervised, group members were asked to work individually on an interview with a sexual offender to prepare a group session. In the beginning of the session, a group member started by describing in detail the slaughtering of an animal he had witnessed some time ago. Other group members contributed their own 'bloody' everyday experiences, partly giggling and expressing feelings of disgust in a rather pleasurable way. In this way, the group in a way re-enacted bodily (and in this way got a first glimpse of) the offender's trivialization of his actions during the interview, and at the same time tried to get closer to what the members (not the interviewee!) felt to be the monstrosity of murders (Mey & Mruck, 1998: 298f).

According to Glaser's 'all is data' dictum, 'exactly what is going on in the research scene is the data, whatever the source, whether interviews, observations, or documents, in whatever combination. It is not only what is being told, how it is being told, and the conditions of its being told, but also all the data surrounding what is being told' (Glaser, 2001: 145). Taken this seriously, within an expanded data concept, reflexive accounts like those mentioned above also gain the dignity of data and should be explicated, documented, and analyzed for their heuristic options of generating theory (Breuer, 2010).

Writing and Publishing

Due to the iterative character of GTM, data collection, data analysis, and writing are intertwined: writing takes place from the very beginning. Developing through research diaries, and while writing and ordering codes and memos, the grounded theory takes shape until it is finally fixed and ready to publish.

We prefer to reflect early on possible ways of writing, as several invisible and partly also visible Others (supervisors, publishers, etc.) are at least implicitly addressed during this process. 'Secret audiences' need to be convinced, proven wrong, etc.: 'Will the research participants accept my results?' and 'Will my research be evaluated positively by my supervisor, funding organization, reference community, and the journal to which I will submit my article?' Both types of questions already influence the data analysis, as some interpretations may be avoided or may be coloured by the respective recipients in mind. This leads researchers to eliminate possible indicators of the communicative and contextual character of their research, and to report 'facts'. Novices, in particular, are often fearful of reporting 'mistakes' and of possible negative consequences for the evaluation of their work, or more generally, of damaging their reputation in the community. Reflecting on their doctoral studies, Mauthner and Doucet (2003) discuss how their respective academic and personal biographies as well as their institutional and (inter)personal contexts influenced data analysis. According to them, 'the security of a job, and a position within academia … undoubtedly make it easier to admit and articulate the confusions and tensions we felt' (p. 415). But as published work is crucial for all academic careers, experienced researchers may also resort to actions of eliminating reflexive accounts when preparing drafts for submission and publication.

A commonly employed strategy of being invisible and gaining reputation is to rely on traditional ways of structuring and presenting results. Some even use a narrative based on the hypothetico-deductive model, i.e., first the state of research is reported, then methods, followed by empirical findings, and then the theory is developed. Suddaby (2006), leaning on his experience as peer reviewer of articles submitted to the *Academy of Management Journal*, complains that 'though grounded theory research is conducted iteratively, by analysing and collecting data simultaneously, it is usually presented sequentially. … Doing so has the unfortunate consequence of creating the impression of methodological slurring', following positivist 'norms of presentation' (p. 637), while GTM exactly opposes the underlying deductive model.

Even if writing acknowledges the iterative character of GTM, empirical reports may nevertheless be presented in traditional, representational ways without explicitly addressing 'the question of the researcher's voice in the text' (Mills et al., 2006b: 11). Thus, 'the researcher – inter-acting, choosing, pre-supposing, sympathetic – becomes invisible in favour of mirroring "the other", the object, the phenomenon' (Mruck & Breuer, 2003: §9).

In these cases, writing strategies dominate, which Macbeth (2001) called 'positional reflexivity': examining positional effects of self, (professional) biography, etc. during data analysis, but abandoning them from written texts. Against this, 'textual reflexivity' invites 'readers to muse about the construction of the writing and representation' (Harris, 2016: 118). For the latter, 'confessional tales' differ from endeavours of 'textual radicalism' (Seale, 1999). Confessional tales explicitly deal with ethical and methodological dilemmas experienced during research, trying to provide a kind of 'natural' (though highly subjective) story. They do not depart 'from realist assumptions' but constitute 'a claim to authenticity' (p. 161). Instead, textual radicalism implies a rejection of realism and of objectivist ideals, of pure representational and monologic ways of writing. It challenges the researcher's privileged position, stressing that there is 'not one "voice" but polyvocality; not one story but many tales, dramas, pieces of fiction' (Lincoln & Denzin, 1994: 584).

There are different ways to handle the dilemma between positional and textual reflexivity, between confessional tales and textual radicalism. In some cases, exhibiting personal involvement is limited to anecdotes about personal encounters during after-work hours. Other researchers shed light on the interdependence of person and work (sometimes after retirement) in autobiographies or during interviews (e.g., Becker & Keller, 2016). Some authors mention the importance of their own involvement without elaborating further. Glaser and Strauss (1965), for example, in their study on 'awareness of dying', report their own personal and familial experiences only in the appendix of the book without any systematic reflection, though these predetermined the central concept of 'awareness contexts'. Charmaz (2014) stresses that 'completed grounded theories need not be voiceless, objective recordings. We can weave our points of view into the text and portray a sense of wonder, imagery, and drama' (p. 318), while at the same time encouraging 'writing apart from typical scientific format without transforming it into fiction, drama, or poetry' (p. 314). She herself prefers to 'remain in the background as an interpreter of scenes and situations' (p. 317), hoping that her 'voice pervades the passages and persuades the reader' (ibid.). Though this is an important step in comparison to the beginning of GTM, it nevertheless indicates the difficult path towards fully acknowledging co-constructedness. Ruppel and Mey (2015: 182) state:

> The idea of a narratively-constructed GT which is founded on co-constructed data is not only a narrative by, but also partially a narrative about, ourselves as researchers. Such a view offers the opportunity to reflectively integrate one's own entanglement into the GT (narrative) that is to be developed.

Awareness of possible audiences, writing styles, and genres, along with ethical issues of authority and responsibility, are most prominent in endeavours of textual reflexivity or textual radicalism. Multiple voices and perspectives play a crucial role, for example, within social constructionism (Gergen & Gergen, 1991). Autoethnography stands for both a process and a product, using personal experiences for cultural understanding (Ellis, Adams, & Bochner, 2010; Holman Jones, 2005). Performative social science approaches deal with employing a variety of 'postmodern' presentations and writing strategies (Jones et al., 2008). In cooperative inquiry, participants are treated as co-researchers, and researchers as co-participants: both are engaged in cycles of shared reflection and practice (Reason & Heron, 1995).

For many researchers, leaning on approaches like those mentioned above still means crossing an unpleasant and precarious border, as they feel in danger of getting their fingers burnt, of losing reputation, and fading away into marginality, or even of being personally hurt and violated (Ploder & Stadlbauer, 2016). Nevertheless, several grounded theorists have worked against 'the usually sanitised research report' (Freshwater, 2005: 314). Kennedy (2009), for example, builds on experimental writing traditions for infusing participants' voices into grounded theory research. Böhm, Legewie, and Dienel (2008) introduce the concept of the 'citizens' exhibition', combining a GTM approach with participative and performative methods. And Sharp and Durham DeCesaro (2013) searched for ways to integrate the social scientist's perspective using constructionist GTM with those of a dance choreographer, relying on kinaesthetic analysis.

REFLEXIVE STRATEGIES

There are various strategies to scrutinize the impact of the researcher's own biographical, academic, and cultural background and involvement in doing research – some of them have been used for a long time, for example, in anthropology or (ethno-) psychoanalysis. Those reflexive practices do not end in themselves but should be used systematically for theory development. They will help the researcher to step by step gain knowledge about their own characteristics, positioning, and perspective (schemata, preconceptions, values, attitudes, attractions, aversions, etc.), and how they shape the understanding of research participants and the conceptualization of the research topic (Breuer, Mey, & Mruck, 2011).

Two kinds of activities do play a central role in the reflexive process: (1) various ways of reflective *writing in the first person* help to express one's own involvement and to develop an understanding of the movement of thoughts beyond isolated events and towards 'making connections and facilitating creativity' (Jasper, 2005: 253; see also Richardson, 2000, on writing as a method of inquiry; and Kaufman, 2013, on 'writing as thinking'); and (2) as researchers are hardly able to reflect on their own implicitness and assumptions without others, continuous *communicative exchange* (with colleagues, in research teams, with external supervisors) supports decentring one's own perspective and gaining insights into contrasting understandings.

Reflexive methods such as writing research diaries and self-reflexive memos, '"time out" relaxation techniques, [and] debriefing and counselling strategies should be … carefully considered before, during, and after fieldwork experiences' (Arber, 2006: 156). They at the same time serve as 'self-care strategies' (Rager, 2005), as well as provide important data for GTM research (for a differentiation of research diaries, memos, and field notes, see Gibbs, 2010).

Writing a Research Diary

Research diaries are self-reflexive resources to record whatever may make an impression on the researcher: initial ideas for research, preconceptions, values and prejudices, knowledge from extant literature, and design outlines. But they also record personal interests and motives, involvement with the topic of interest during their (professional) career, and later on emotional responses, uncertainties, and stagnation during the research process, as well as feedback from personal or academic contexts and any issues with supervisors. The research diary serves as a companion to manage the difficult 'boundary between closeness and distance' (Arber, 2006: 147) during research and in the academic field.

To avoid any fear and confusion about possible responses from others, it seems clear that the research diary, as any diary, should be an intimate refuge, and not something accessed or used by anyone else without explicitly being invited to by the author. The act of writing should be unhindered from having to ask oneself how to use entries from the diary and how useful they may be later on in the research. Sometimes it will only be possible to retrospectively understand the importance of astonishing episodes, communicative flops, disorientation, and breakthroughs for theory development. Especially in the beginning, entries could be fragmentary and unsystematic, with the intention of coming back to them later on to elaborate and explicate characteristics of the field under research. The diary then helps to reconstruct the process of theory development from first personal and (sub)cultural preconcepts to structured theoretical accounts.

Another important benefit of keeping a diary, especially for novice researchers, is that it helps the researcher become familiar with elaborating thoughts in written accounts without psychological barriers. Learning to express one's own emotional and bodily involvement is especially challenging against enduring academic constraints. Here, work from researchers such as Ellingson (2006) is helpful. From a feminist perspective, Ellingham provides suggestions for incorporating bodily details and experiences into research accounts, showing how her 'impaired body' (misshapen leg and knee) 'shaped how people understood and responded to [her]' (p. 306). Sharma, Reimer-Kirkham, and Cochrane (2009) report ways of reflecting bodily, emotional, and positional effects in research participants' encounters, and how to make use of them for data analysis. Leaning on diary entries, psychoanalytic strategies like countertransference analysis (e.g., Marks & Mönnich-Marks, 2003), dream analysis, or fantasy analysis are helpful in becoming aware of one's own 'response patterns' and in using them for theory generation (Brown, 2006).

The research diary is the first place for 'wading into the embodied messiness of qualitative research' (Sharma et al., 2009: 1649). Decisions about disclosing this content in written accounts later on should be done separately, as disclosure in the final text is certainly not obligatory, especially if the costs of making an invisible 'disability' explicit would be too high. Rinaldi (2013), critically discussing the expectation to disclosure in feminist research and disclosing her own eating and obsessive-compulsive disorders, gives reasons for 'reflexivity without publicly taking a position, to conduct responsible research … working quietly', as she is 'unconvinced that we have enough safe spaces' (n.p.). Laws (2004) provides insights into the process of writing, moving 'the process of reflexivity between the reading, the doing, the thinking, the writing' (p. 113) from 'private writing' in her diary to a more public space.

Memo-Writing

Memo-writing is a central activity within all GTM approaches: Glaser (1978: 83) understands memos as 'the theorizing write-up of ideas about codes and their relationships as they strike the analyst by coding'. Besides theoretical memos, there are also memos on the use of literature, memos on procedural aspects of the research process, etc. (see Strauss, 1987: ch. 5 on different memo types; Corbin & Strauss, 2015: ch. 6 on memos and diagrams; Charmaz, 2014: ch.7, and 2015: 1617ff on ways of memo-writing). Reflective memo-writing tries to make 'clear the multiplicity of influences' (Mills et al., 2006b: 11) during theory construction. It may be initiated by an event or experience while collecting or analyzing data, during a discussion with colleagues, or while thinking by oneself about a (theoretical) idea and its possible relevance. Bryant (2017: ch.10) provides detailed information on 'memoing and reflective research', giving examples for the use of memos 'from informal and exploratory' (p. 200) to descriptively detailed and conceptualizing. Though memos serve 'a variety of purposes' at different stages of the research process, they 'have in common the role of integrating the processes of abstraction and conceptualization that move the research from data gathering to articulation of a theory or model' (p. 198). Munkejord (2009), in an insider account on the impact of emotions in fieldwork during organizational research, shows how he used 'spontaneous memoing' (p. 163). He more systematically tries to integrate the concept of 'methodological emotional reflexivity' in GTM memoing.

'Conscious-raising questions' (Mills et al., 2006b: 10) are central through all research stages to bring presumptions and limitations to the surface and for thinking about data and memoing analytically. These may be 'standard questions' to establish a 'consistent format of coding' already in traditional GTM: Chiovitti and Piran (2003: 429), leaning on Glaser (1978), Strauss (1987), and Strauss and Corbin (1990), mention questions like 'What is happening in the data?' 'What does the action in the data represent?' 'Is the conceptual label or code part of the participant's vocabulary?' 'In what context is the code/action used?' 'Is the code related to another code?' 'Is the code encompassed by a broader code?' or 'Are there codes that reflect similar patterns?'

Especially in the beginning stages of research, we additionally encourage introspection, including questions such as: 'What understanding am I aiming for?' 'What kind of knowledge can I possibly gain?' and 'How do I understand the role of the researcher?' (Finlay, 2006: 18ff). During data collection and analysis, researchers should ask: 'Which emotional responses are initiated while contacting research participants/interviewing?' 'What might be my "stimulus value" for different Others while interacting in the research and academic field?' 'In what way do my position and role change over time (concerning, for example, trust, expertise, affiliation, intimacy, and partisanship), and how does this influence the kind of information I get?' Petrovic, Lordly, Brigham, and Delaney (2015: 3), leaning on the listening guide developed by Brown and Gilligan (1992), additionally recommend questions like: 'In what ways do I "identify with or distance" from others?' 'In what ways are our experiences different or the same?' 'Where am I confused or puzzled?' or 'Where am I certain, upset or delighted, amused or pleased, disturbed or angered?'

Elaborating these accounts may help to reflect on how one's own responses interlink with 'external data' and the research problem one tries to solve. As for 'awareness contexts' in the case of Glaser and Strauss (1965), innovative concepts may already come from antecedent experiences. Working on memos analytically over time will help to explicate the concepts' heuristic potency while systematically comparing them to other data and sources. Continuously updated, memos allow us to follow the development of preconcepts and attitudes during the research process. To support this, researchers should think about dating and referencing memos from the very beginning in such a way that they are easily retrievable whenever needed.

Using Collaborative Tools

Single researchers are hardly able to reflect on their own biographical and professional pre-assumptions, on 'thought systems' and 'style-locked re-interpretations' without external support and disturbance. Only while comparing one's own associations, responses, and interpretations to those of others, do blind spots and idiosyncratic patterns become visible: Others' feedback will open up a multifaceted picture to be systematically integrated into the developing theory. Besides traditional colloquia or (individual) supervision, collaboration might be organized in different ways.

In our own work, we use *research interviews*, i.e., ask team members to interview each other as a starting point for research projects, to report their emotions and (theoretical) pre-assumptions, to reflect on the topic they decided for and its possible personal importance, and in this way to try to help them to get a first overview and first insights in sometimes overwhelming differences of experiences and perspectives (Mruck & Mey, 1998). Within qualitative health research, Bolam, Gleeson and Murphy (2003) use 'reflexive interviews', whereby the researchers turn the tables and become interviewees, enabling them to examine their roles 'as both lay person and health expert, insider and outsider' (§30; more generally on researcher interviewing, see Bryman & Cassell, 2006). Others, such as Rolls and Relf (2006), recommend 'bracketing interviews' on how the researcher's personal and professional background influences data collection and analysis. Tufford and Newmann (2012) additionally define some characteristics of 'experienced bracketers' beyond usual academic and personal supervision and make suggestions for integrating bracketing into qualitative methodologies.

Research teams help to plan and conduct research collaboratively. Arber (2006) describes how – besides journals and research diaries documenting her thoughts and feelings – 'good support' by colleagues and a peer group helped her during 'emotional labour to fit into the research setting, manage relationships, and deal with untoward situations' (p. 156). Hall et al. (2005) elaborate strategies for working with multidisciplinary teams while relying on a GTM example, focusing on, among others, the development of reflexivity and theoretical sensitivity in the team while analyzing data. According to them, sharing 'information, articulating project goals and elements, acknowledging variation in individual goals, and engaging in reciprocity and respectful collaboration are key elements of mutual adjustment' (p. 394). Barry et al. (1999) report on the sharing of reflexive writing and on using group discussions in the team; see also Conlon, Carney, Timonen, and Scharf (2015) on 'constructing grounded theory as a team process' (p. 43). Nevertheless, it should be noted that, especially in teams structured hierarchically or collaborating for a long time, specific blind spots are unavoidable, making reflexive work without external feedback – and ideally external supervision – hardly possible.

Teams may consist of researchers working together on one topic or working on different topics, banded together in a collective organized by a peer-to-peer-approach or supervised by experienced researchers. In Germany, *Forschungswerkstätten* have a long tradition in the influential work of Anselm Strauss and his cooperation with different German research groups. Here, researchers collaborate face to face or via the Internet to share any issues gaining importance during the research process. Besides methodical support and exchange, these collectives also provide emotional and social support for the individual research endeavours. In our own work, we lean on 'theme-centred interaction'

(TCI) (Cohn, 1969, 1991) as a heuristic framework to clarify and discuss factors influencing the research process, and to establish a supportive atmosphere essential to reflecting on personal involvement. TCI's four-factor model helps to organize what happens in the group on the side of the individual researcher ('I'), within group processes ('WE'), or towards the respective topic that the group is working on ('IT'). This triangle is placed within the 'GLOBE', i.e., the academic, political, physical, etc. surroundings both influencing and being influenced by teamwork (Mruck & Mey, 1998).

Teaching and Learning Reflexivity

Knowledge about and practice in reflexive strategies needs to be acquired. Thus, videotaped interview training and role play may be useful for both students and experienced researchers in becoming aware of their specific ways of perceiving, anticipating, acting, and talking. In the case of sensitive topics, it may be difficult to approach interviewees in an open and respectful manner, and here supervising is a must, especially for novice researchers, 'to recognise and negotiate complex ethical and professional issues' (Smith, 2011: 211). Smith (pp. 218ff.) discusses 'assessing and monitoring critical reflection in learning' and 'teaching critical reflection' in healthcare higher education, while Landy et al. (2016) provide an extensive literature review on 'educational strategies to enhance reflexivity among clinicians and health professional students' (see also Wright & Cochrane, 2000, on research training for supervisors; Roche, Guta, & Flicker, 2010, for the training of field members as co-researchers; and see Holton's chapter in this volume). Charmaz (2015) provides an excellent introduction to teaching and learning GTM, especially helpful for supervisors of doctoral students. Using various examples and focusing on interviewing, coding, and memoing, she describes the steps she uses to make students familiar with GTM and to achieve three main goals: to 'involve students in "active learning"', to help them to 'raise the level of conceptual development of their research' (p. 1611), and to continuously support their ability to reflect on their own involvement in doing research. And teaching is certainly not a one-way street: 'All my life I have used teaching as a stimulant—to my own thinking [...] So I turn the teaching into a learning experience for myself. And a creative experience' (Strauss, in Riemann, 2011: 405).

CONCLUSION

Thinking about GTM and reflexivity is a difficult task. GTM asks for groundedness, for 'being there', but even a few minutes of (interview) conversation appear far too complex for modest interpretative (and reflexive) procedures to be fully comprehended. And GTM is interested in generating new knowledge instead of just testing what is already known. But the paradigms, epistemologies, and methodologies that a researcher leans on, as well as his/her personality, limit which kinds of (reflexive) analysis are accepted or rejected. And relying on different approaches means viewing the world differently. Keeping this in mind, the old scientific dream to represent 'what really has been' is doomed to failure or deficiency.

'Reflexivity' means to subject oneself to a personally and professionally challenging endeavour. From Thomas Kuhn we know that taken-for-granted knowledge is only threatened in times of crisis. And indeed, reflexive work requires a researcher's willingness and ability to continuously initiate and manage crisis. Doing this is not rewarded by 'true knowledge', as, undeniably, all sorts of insights (as well as new ones) are subject to epistemological and methodological limitations, and this also affects reflexive analysis. Thinking about the analysis of an interview extract, Bishop and Shepherd (2011: 1283) state that 'despite our best efforts of "doing reflexivity" ... there are influential factors that escape our gaze'. Mauthner and Doucet (2003: 425) also point to the 'limits to reflexivity, and to the extent to which [the authors] can be aware of the influences on [their] research both at the time of conducting it and in the years that follow'. Reflexivity needs reflection.

So why should we engage in reflexive GTM? Just reflecting on one's own perspectivity and positionality helps decentring and fosters being as open as possible in order to recognize and acknowledge otherness. Taking one's own perspective and worldview for granted ultimately leads to scientifically polished autobiography: researchers 'discover' in the data what they already knew but attribute it as characteristics of the Other, with at times trivial and partly irresponsible outcomes published in research reports. Some readers will follow what has been declared to be 'the truth' and experience harm, while others will be frustrated by researchers claiming to provide what is true, while a look at the work of different researchers makes it clear that different truths are presented – an important loss of credibility of science at all might be a possible consequence. To fight against this, we have 'to improve our research skills and ... continue to be reflexive; to throw as much light as possible onto our research practices and processes' (Bishop & Shepherd, 2011: 1290). Only by being as transparent as possible will others – research participants, co-researchers, readers, practitioners, laypersons – be able to get an idea of (the situatedness of) our knowledge, to evaluate it, and, hopefully, find it useful for their practice and/or further research. Instead of 'what has really been', we should accept and make apparent that all knowledge is fragile and preliminary, something Glaser and Strauss already conceded 50 years ago:

> When generation of theory is the aim, however, one is constantly alert to emergent perspectives that will change and help develop his [and for sure: her] theory. These perspectives can easily occur even on the final day of study or when the manuscript is reviewed in page proof: so the published word is not the final one, but only a pause in the never-ending process of generating theory. (1967: 40)

ACKNOWLEDGEMENT

We would like to cordially thank the editors for their helpful comments. Special thanks to our colleague Franz Breuer for his initial input and the shared thoughts on reflexivity in GTM (e.g., Breuer et al., 2011). And we are very grateful to Myriam Birch for her language copy-editing.

Notes

1 We use the term GTM to distinguish the methodology from the result of research – grounded theory (GT).
2 It should be noted that Lazarsfeld has not only been one of the founders of American sociology, developing statistical methods for survey research, but he also co-authored the ground-breaking

Marienthal study: Jahoda, Lazarsfeld, and Zeisel (1933/1971) examined the social and psychological impact of unemployment in a small Austrian community during the Great Depression, using a to-this-day impressive mixed-methods approach.

3 In the 2014 edition of *Constructing Grounded Theory*, Charmaz uses 'social constructivism' instead of 'social constructionism', while stating that her 'position is consistent with the form it [social constructionism] takes today' (p. 14). For several reasons, which cannot be explained further due to space restrictions, we are using both terms (see Reichertz & Zielke, 2008, for some main characteristics of social constructionism).

4 See Legewie and Schervier-Legewie (2004: Track 7). In this interview from 1994, Anselm Strauss talked about his becoming a social scientist and the development and use of GTM.

5 The term 'strong reflexivity' was coined by Harding (1993), who closely linked it to 'strong objectivity', i.e., the aim to generate general knowledge beyond the 'old notion of objectivity as requiring value-neutrality' (p. 72). While 'strong reflexivity' in Kühner et al.'s sense is influenced by the 'crisis of representation' in anthropology, 'weak reflexivity' follows Bourdieu's concept of 'epistemic reflexivity', aiming at an objectification of sociological practice (see Maton, 2003, for 'epistemic' versus 'narcissistic reflexivity' in Bourdieu's work; and Langenohl, 2009, for critical 'remarks on an absent debate' between the two approaches).

6 An impressive example of the culturalization of senses is provided by Wolfgang Schivelbusch (1979), who describes how long it took before train travel became an everyday experience (at least within some cultures), basically reshaping human awareness and senses.

7 Due to space restrictions, we limit ourselves to interviews.

8 Most GTM research is traditional, as research participants do not act as co-researchers and co-authors, although some exceptions already exist. For example, Teram, Schachter, and Stalker (2005) provide an example of integrating GTM and participatory action research. And Redman-MacLaren and Mills (2015: 1) use the term 'transformational' GTM, leaning on participatory action research, with an interest in 'decolonizing research methodologies'.

REFERENCES

Alvinius, Aida, Starrin, Bengt, and Larsson, Gerry (2016) Reflexive serendipity: Grounded theory and serendipity in disaster management and military research. *Qualitative Sociology Review*, *12*(3): 28–42.

Arber, Anne (2006) Reflexivity: A challenge for the researcher as practitioner? *Journal of Research in Nursing*, *11*(2): 147–157.

Ashmore, Malcolm and Reed, Darren (2000) Innocence and nostalgia in conversation analysis: The dynamic relations of tape and transcript. *Forum Qualitative Sozialforschung/Forum: Qualitative Social Research*, *1*(3): Art. 3. Retrieved from: http://dx.doi.org/10.17169/fqs-1.3.1020

Baker, Cynthia, Wuest, Judith, and Stern, Phyllis (1992) Method slurring: The grounded theory/phenomenology example. *Journal of Advanced Nursing*, *17*: 1355–1360.

Barry, Christine A., Britten, Nicky, Barber, Nick, Bradley, Colin, and Stevenson, Fiona (1999) Using reflexivity to optimize teamwork in qualitative research. *Qualitative Health Research*, *9*(1): 26–44.

Becker, Howard S. and Keller, Reiner (2016) Ways of telling about society. Howard S. Becker in conversation with Reiner Keller. *Forum Qualitative Sozialforschung/Forum: Qualitative Social Research*, *17*(2): Art. 12. Retrieved from: http://dx.doi.org/10.17169/fqs-17.2.2607

Berger, Roni (2015) Now I see it, now I don't: Researcher's position and reflexivity in qualitative research. *Qualitative Research*, *15*(2): 219–234.

Bishop, Emily C. and Shepherd, Marie L. (2011) Ethical reflections: Examining reflexivity through the narrative paradigm. *Qualitative Health Research*, *21*(9): 1283–94.

Böhm, Birgit, Legewie, Heiner, and Dienel, Hans-Liudger (2008) The citizens' exhibition: A combination of socio-scientific, participative and artistic elements. *Forum Qualitative Sozialforschung/Forum: Qualitative Social Research*, *9*(2): Art. 33. Retrieved from: http://dx.doi.org/10.17169/fqs-9.2.380

Bolam, Bruce, Gleeson, Kate, and Murphy, Simon (2003) 'Lay person' or 'health expert'? Exploring theoretical and practical aspects of reflexivity in qualitative health research. *Forum Qualitative Sozialforschung/Forum: Qualitative Social Research*, *4*(2): Art. 26. Retrieved from: http://dx.doi.org/10.17169/fqs-4.2.699

Bourke, Brian (2014) Positionality: Reflecting on the research process. *The Qualitative Report*, *19*: Art. 18. Retrieved from: www.nova.edu/ssss/QR/QR19/bourke18.pdf

Breuer, Franz (2010) *Reflexive Grounded Theory: Eine Einführung für die Forschungspraxis*. Wiesbaden: Springer VS.

Breuer, Franz, Mey, Günter, and Mruck, Katja (2011) Subjektivität und Selbst-/Reflexivität in der Grounded-Theory-Methodologie. In Günter Mey and Katja Mruck (Eds.), *Grounded Theory Reader* (pp. 427–448). Wiesbaden: Springer VS.

Brown, Joanne (2006) Reflexivity in the research process: Psychoanalytic observations. *International Journal of Social Research Methodology*, *9*(3): 181–197.

Brown, Lyn Mikel and Gilligan, Carol (1992) *Meeting at the Crossroads: Women's Psychology and Girls' Development*. Cambridge, MA: Harvard University Press.

Bryant, Antony (2003) A constructive/ist response to Glaser. *Forum Qualitative Sozialforschung/Forum: Qualitative Social Research*, *4*(1): Art. 15. Retrieved from: http://dx.doi.org/10.17169/fqs-4.1.757

Bryant, Antony (2017) *Grounded Theory and Grounded Theorizing: Pragmatism in Research Practice*. Oxford: Oxford University Press.

Bryman, Alan and Cassell, Catherine (2006) The researcher interview: A reflexive perspective. *Qualitative Research in Organizations and Management: An International Journal*, *1*(1): 41–55.

Chadwick, Rachelle (2016) Embodied methodologies: Challenges, reflections and strategies. *Qualitative Research*, *17*(1): 54–74.

Charmaz, Kathy (2000) Grounded theory: Objectivist and constructivist methods. In Norman K. Denzin and Yvonna S. Lincoln (Eds.), *Handbook of Qualitative Research* (2nd ed., pp. 509–536). London: Sage.

Charmaz, Kathy (2006) *Constructing Grounded Theory: A Practical Guide Through Qualitative Analysis*. London: Sage.

Charmaz, Kathy (2014) *Constructing Grounded Theory* (2nd ed.). London: Sage.

Charmaz, Kathy (2015) Teaching theory construction with initial grounded theory tools: A reflection on lessons and learning. *Qualitative Health Research*, *25*(12): 1610–1622.

Charmaz, Kathy (2017) The power of constructivist grounded theory for critical inquiry. *Qualitative Inquiry*, *23*(1): 33–45.

Charmaz, Kathy and Bryant, Antony (2010) Grounded theory. In Penelope Peterson, Eva Baker, and Barry McGaw (Eds.), *International Encyclopedia of Education* (3rd ed., pp. 406–412). Oxford: Elsevier.

Charmaz, Kathy and Keller, Reiner (2016) A personal journey with grounded theory methodology. Kathy Charmaz in conversation With Reiner Keller. *Forum Qualitative Sozialforschung/Forum: Qualitative Social Research*, *17*(1): Art. 16. Retrieved from: http://dx.doi.org/10.17169/fqs-17.1.2541

Chiovitti, Rosalina F. and Piran, Niva (2003) Rigour and grounded theory research. *Journal of Advanced Nursing*, *44*(4): 427–435.

Cisneros-Puebla, Cesar A. (2004) To learn to think conceptually. Juliet Corbin in conversation with Cesar A. Cisneros-Puebla. *Forum Qualitative Sozialforschung/Forum: Qualitative Social Research*, *5*(3): Art. 32. Retrieved from: http://dx.doi.org/10.17169/fqs-5.3.550

Clarke, Adele E. (2005) *Situational Analysis: Grounded Theory after the Postmodern Turn*. London: Sage.

Clarke, Adele E. and Keller, Reiner (2014) Engaging complexities: Working against simplification as an agenda for qualitative research today. Adele Clarke in conversation with Reiner Keller. *Forum Qualitative Sozialforschung/Forum: Qualitative Social Research*, *15*(2): Art. 1. Retrieved from: http://dx.doi.org/10.17169/fqs-15.2.2186

Clifford, James and Marcus, George E. (1986) *Writing Culture: The Poetics and Politics of Ethnography*. Berkeley, CA: University of California Press.

Cohn, Ruth C. (1969) The theme-centered interactional method: Group therapists as group educators. *Journal of Group Psychoanalysis and Process [now Group Process]*, *2*(2): 19–36.

Cohn, Ruth C. (1991) *Von der Psychoanalyse zur themenzentrierten Interaktion. Von der Behandlung einzelner zu einer Pädagogik für alle* (10th ed.). Stuttgart: Klett-Cotta.

Conlon, Catherine, Carney, Gemma, Timonen, Virpi, and Scharf, Thomas (2015) 'Emergent reconstruction' in grounded theory: Learning from team-based interview research. *Qualitative Research*, *15*(1): 39–56.

Corbin, Juliet (2009) Taking an analytic journey. In Janice M. Morse, Phyllis Noerager Stern, Juliet Corbin, Barbara Bowers, Kathy Charmaz and Adele E. Clarke (Eds.), *Developing Grounded Theory: The Second Generation* (pp. 35–53). Walnut Creek, CA: Left Coast Press.

Corbin, Juliet and Strauss, Anselm L. (2015) *Basics of Qualitative Research: Techniques and Procedures for Developing Grounded Theory* (4th ed.). Los Angeles, CA: Sage.

Cutcliffe, John R. (2000) Methodological issues in grounded theory. *Journal of Advanced Nursing*, *31*: 1476–1484.

Davidson, Christina (2009) Transcription: Imperatives for qualitative research. *International Journal of Qualitative Methods*, *8*(2): 35–52. Retrieved from: https://ejournals.library.ualberta.ca/index.php/IJQM/article/viewFile/4205/5401

De Bie, Jasper L. and De Poot, Christianne J. (2016) Studying police files with grounded theory methods to understand Jihadist networks. *Studies in Conflict and Terrorism*, *39*(7–8): 580–601.

Devereux, Georges (1967) *From Anxiety to Method in the Behavioral Sciences*. Paris/The Hague: Mouton.

Doyle, Christina and Goldingay, Sophie Jennifer (2012) The rise of the 'silver surfer': Online social networking and social inclusion for older adults. *Journal of Social Inclusion*, *3*(2): 40–54.

Dwyer, Sonya Corbin and Buckle, Jennifer L. (2009). The space between: On being an insider-outsider in qualitative research. *International Journal of Qualitative Methods*, *8*(1). Retrieved from: https://journals.library.ualberta.ca/ijqm/index.php/IJQM/article/view/2981

Ellingson, Laura L. (2006) Embodied knowledge: writing researchers' bodies into qualitative health research. *Qualitative Health Research*, *16*(2): 298–310.

Ellis, Carolyn, Adams, Tony E., and Bochner, Arthur P. (2010) Autoethnography: An overview. *Forum Qualitative Sozialforschung/Forum: Qualitative Social Research*, *12*(1): Art. 10. Retrieved from: http://dx.doi.org/10.17169/fqs-12.1.1589

Engward, Hilary and Davis, Geraldine (2015) Being reflexive in qualitative grounded theory: Discussion and application of a model of reflexivity. *Journal of Advanced Nursing*, *71*(7): 1530–1538.

Evans, Gary L. (2013) A novice researcher's first walk through the maze of grounded theory. *Grounded Theory Review*, *1*. Retrieved from: http://groundedtheoryreview.com/2013/06/22/a-novice-researchers-first-walk-through-the-maze-of-grounded-theory-rationalization-for-classical-grounded-theory/

Finlay, Linda (2002) Negotiating the swamp: The opportunity and challenge of reflexivity in research practice. *Qualitative Research*, *2*(2): 209–230.

Finlay, Linda (2006) Mapping methodology. In Linda Finlay and Claire Ballinger (Eds.), *Qualitative Research for Allied Health Professionals: Challenging Choices* (pp. 9–29). Chichester: Wiley.

Finlay, Linda (2009) Ambiguous encounters: A relational approach to phenomenological research. *Indo-Pacific Journal of Phenomenology*, *9*(1): 1–17.

Finlay, Linda and Gough, Brendan (2003) Prologue. In Linda Finlay and Brendan Gough (Eds.), *Reflexivity: A Practical Guide for Researchers in Health and Social Sciences* (pp. xiii–ix). Oxford: Blackwell Science.

Fleck, Ludwik (1935a/1979) *The Genesis and Development of a Scientific Fact*. Edited by Thaddeus J. Trenn and Robert K. Merton. Chicago, IL: University of Chicago Press.

Fleck, Ludwik (1935b/1983) Über die wissenschaftliche Beobachtung und die Wahrnehmung im allgemeinen. In L. Schäfer and T. Schnelle (Eds.), *Erfahrung und Tatsache. Gesammelte Aufsätz* (pp. 59–83). Frankfurt/Main: Suhrkamp.

Freshwater, Dawn (2005) Commentary: Writing, rigour and reflexivity in nursing research. *Journal of Research in Nursing*, *10*(3): 311–315.

Gardner, Lyn (2006) Review: Grounded theory sampling. The contribution of reflexivity. *Journal of Research in Nursing*, *11*(3): 261–262.

Geertz, Clifford (1988) *Works and Lives: The Anthropologist as Author*. Stanford, CA: Stanford University Press.

Gentles, Stephen J., Jack, Susan M., Nicholas, David B., and McKibbon, K. Ann (2014) Critical approach to reflexivity in grounded theory. *The Qualitative Report*, *19*(44): 1–14. Retrieved from: http://nsuworks.nova.edu/tqr/vol19/iss44/3/

Gergen, K. J. and Gergen, Mary (1991) Towards reflexive methodologies. In Frederick Steier (Ed.), *Research and Reflexivity* (pp. 21–38). London: Sage.

Gibbs, Graham R. (2010) Writing as analysis. *Online QDA: Learning Qualitative Data Analysis on the Web.* Retrieved from: http://onlineqda.hud.ac.uk/Intro_QDA/writing_analysis.php

Glaser, Barney G. (1965) The constant comparative method of qualitative analysis. *Social Problems*, *12*: 436–445.

Glaser, Barney G. (1978) *Theoretical Sensitivity: Advances in the Methodology of Grounded Theory*. Mill Valley, CA: Sociology Press.

Glaser, Barney G. (1992) *Emergence vs Forcing: Basics of Grounded Theory Analysis*. Mill Valley, CA: Sociology Press.

Glaser, Barney G. (1998) *Doing Grounded Theory: Issues and Discussions*. Mill Valley, CA: Sociology Press.

Glaser, Barney G. (2001) *The Grounded Theory Perspective: Conceptualization Contrasted with Description*. Mill Valley, CA: Sociology Press.

Glaser, Barney G. (2002) Constructivist grounded theory? *Forum Qualitative Sozialforschung/Forum: Qualitative Social Research*, *3*(3): Art. 12. Retrieved from: http://dx.doi.org/10.17169/fqs-3.3.825

Glaser, Barney G. and Holton, Judith (2004) Remodeling grounded theory. *Forum Qualitative Sozialforschung/Forum: Qualitative Social Research*, *5*(2): Art. 4. Retrieved from: http://dx.doi.org/10.17169/fqs-5.2.607

Glaser, Barney G. and Strauss, Anselm L. (1965) *Awareness of Dying*. Chicago, IL: Aldine.

Glaser, Barney G. and Strauss, Anselm L. (1967) *The Discovery of Grounded Theory: Strategies for Qualitative Research*. New York: Aldine de Gruyter.

Greckhamer, Thomas and Koro-Ljungberg, Mirka (2005) The erosion of a method: Examples from grounded theory. *International Journal of Qualitative Studies in Education*, *18*(6): 729–750.

Greenbank, Paul (2002) The role of values in educational research: the case for reflexivity. *British Educational Research Journal*, *29*(6): 791–801.

Hall, Wendy A. and Callery, Peter (2001) Pearls, pith, and provocation. Enhancing the rigor of grounded theory: Incorporating reflexivity and relationality. *Qualitative Health Research*, *11*(2): 257–272.

Hall, Wendy A., Long, Bonita, Bermbach, Nicole, Jordan, Sharalyn, and Patterson, Kathryn (2005) Qualitative teamwork issues and strategies: Coordination through mutual adjustment. *Qualitative Health Research*, *15*(3): 394–410.

Harding, Sandra (1993) Rethinking standpoint epistemology: What is strong objectivity? In Linda Alcoff and Elizabeth Potter (Eds.), *Feminist Epistemologies* (pp. 49–82). New York: Routledge.

Harris, Kate Lockwood (2016) Reflexive voicing: A communicative approach to intersectional writing. *Qualitative Research*, *16*(1): 111–127.

Holman Jones, Stacy (2005) Autoethnography: Making the personal political. In Norman K. Denzin and Yvonna S. Lincoln (Eds.), *The Sage Handbook of Qualitative Research* (3rd ed., pp. 763–792). Thousand Oaks, CA: Sage.

Howard-Payne, Lynlee (2016) Glaser or Strauss? Considerations for selecting a grounded theory study. *South African Journal of Psychology*, *46*(1), 50–62.

Jahoda, Marie, Lazarsfeld, Paul F., and Zeisel, Hans (1933/1971) *Marienthal: The Sociography of an Unemployed Community*. Chicago, IL: Aldine.

Jasper, Melanie A. (2005) Using reflective writing within research. *Journal of Research in Nursing*, *10*(3): 247–260.

Jones, Kip, Gergen, Mary, Yallop, J. Guiney, Lopez de Vallejo, Irene, Roberts, Brian, and Wright, Peter (Eds.) (2008) Performative social sciences. *Forum Qualitative Sozialforschung/Forum: Qualitative Social Research*, *9*(2). Retrieved from: www.qualitative-research.net/index.php/fqs/issue/view/10

Kaufman, Peter (2013) Scribo ergo cogito: Reflexivity through writing. *Teaching Sociology*, *41*(1): 70–81.

Kennedy, Brianna L. (2009) Infusing participants' voices into grounded theory research. *Qualitative Inquiry*, *15*(8): 1416–1433.

Kennedy, Tara J. and Lingard, Lorelei A (2006) Making sense of grounded theory in medical education. *Medical Education*, *40*(2): 101–108.

Knorr-Cetina, Karin D. (1981) *The Manufacture of Knowledge: An Essay on the Constructivist and Contextual Nature of Science*. Oxford: Pergamon Press.

Konecki, Krzysztof (2011) Visual grounded theory: A methodological outline and examples from empirical work. *Revija za Sociologiju*, *41*(2): 131–160.

Konopásek, Zdeněk (2008) Making thinking visible with Atlas.ti: Computer assisted qualitative analysis as textual practices. *Forum Qualitative Sozialforschung/Forum: Qualitative Social Research*, *9*(2): Art. 12. Retrieved from: http://dx.doi.org/10.17169/fqs-9.2.420

Kuhn, Thomas S. (1962) *The Structure of Scientific Revolutions*. Chicago, IL: University of Chicago Press.

Kühner, Angela, Ploder, Andrea, and Langer, Phil C. (2016) Introduction to the Special Issue: European contributions to strong reflexivity. *Qualitative Inquiry*, *22*(9), published online before print.

La Barre, Weston (1967) Preface. In Georges Devereux (1967) *From Anxiety to Method in the Behavioral Sciences* (pp. vii–xii). Paris/The Hague: Mouton.

Lal, Shalina, Suto, Melina, and Ungar, Michael (2012) Examining the potential of combining the methods of grounded theory and narrative inquiry: A comparative analysis. *The Qualitative Report*, *17*(21): 1–22. Retrieved from: http://nsuworks.nova.edu/tqr/vol17/iss21/1

Landy, Rachel, Cameron, Cathy, Au, Anson, Cameron, Debra, O'Brien, Kelly K., Robrigado, Katherine, Baxter, Larry, Cockburn, Lynn, O'Hearn, Shawna, Oliver, Brent, and Nixon, Stephanie A. (2016) Educational strategies to enhance reflexivity among clinicians and health professional students: A scoping study. *Forum Qualitative Sozialforschung/Forum: Qualitative Social Research*, *17*(3): Art. 14. Retrieved from: http://dx.doi.org/10.17169/fqs-17.3.2573

Langenohl, Andreas (2009) Zweimal Reflexivität in der gegenwärtigen Sozialwissenschaft: Anmerkungen zu einer nicht geführten Debatte. *Forum Qualitative Sozialforschung/Forum: Qualitative Social Research*, *10*(2): Art. 9. Retrieved from: http://dx.doi.org/10.17169/fqs-10.2.1207

Latour, Bruno and Woolgar, Steve (1979) *Laboratory Life: The Social Construction of Scientific Facts*. Beverly Hills, CA: Sage.

Laws, Catherine (2004) Poststructuralist writing at work. *International Journal of Qualitative Studies in Education*, *17*(1): 113–127.

Legewie, Heiner and Schervier-Legewie, Barbara (2004) Research is hard work, it's always a bit suffering. Therefore, on the other side research should be fun. Anselm Strauss in conversation with Heiner Legewie and Barbara Schervier-Legewie. *Forum Qualitative Sozialforschung/Forum: Qualitative Social Research*, *5*(3): Art. 22. Retrieved from: http://dx.doi.org/10.17169/fqs-5.3.562

Lincoln, Yvonna S. and Denzin, Norman K. (1994) The fifth moment. In Norman K. Denzin and Yvonna S. (Eds.), *Handbook of Qualitative Research* (pp. 575–586). London: Sage.

Lynch, Michael (1985) *Art and Artifact in Laboratory Science: A Study of Shop Work and Shop Talk in a Research Laboratory*. London: Routledge and Kegan Paul.

Macbeth, Douglas (2001) On 'reflexivity' in qualitative research: Two readings, and a third. *Qualitative Inquiry*, *7*(1): 35–68.

Marks, Stephan and Mönnich-Marks, Heidi (2003) The analysis of counter-transference reactions is a means to discern latent interview-contents. *Forum Qualitative Sozialforschung/Forum: Qualitative Social Research*, *4*(2): Art. 36. Retrieved from: http://dx.doi.org/10.17169/fqs-4.2.709

Martin, Jennifer (2016) Child sexual abuse images online: Implications for social work training and practice. *The British Journal of Social Work*, *46*: 372–388.

Maton, Karl (2003) Reflexivity, relationism, and research: Pierre Bourdieu and the epistemic conditions of social scientific knowledge. *Space and Culture*, *6*(1): 52–65.

Mauthner, Natasha S. and Doucet, Andrea (1998) Reflections on a voice-centred relational method: Analysing maternal and domestic voices. In Jane Ribbens and Rosalind Edwards (Eds.), *Feminist Dilemmas in Qualitative Research: Public Knowledge and Private Lives* (pp. 119–144). London: Sage.

Mauthner, Natasha S. and Doucet, Andrea (2003) Reflexive accounts and accounts of reflexivity in qualitative data analysis. *Sociology*, *37*(3): 413–431.

McCartan, Claire, Schubotz, Dirk, and Murphy, Jonathan (2012) The self-conscious researcher: Post-modern perspectives of participatory research with young people. *Forum Qualitative Sozialforschung/Forum: Qualitative Social Research*, *13*(1): Art. 9. Retrieved from: http://dx.doi.org/10.17169/fqs-13.1.1798

McGhee, Gerry, Marland, Glen, and Atkinson, Jacqueline (2007) Grounded theory research: Literature reviewing and reflexivity. *Journal of Advanced Nursing*, *60*(3): 334–342.

Mey, Günter and Dietrich, Marc (2017) From text to image: Shaping a visual grounded-theory-methodology. *Forum Qualitative Sozialforschung/Forum: Qualitative Social Research*, *17*(2): Art. 2. Retrieved from: http://dx.doi.org/10.17169/fqs-17.2.2535

Mey, Günter and Mruck, Katja (2011) Grounded-Theory-Methodologie: Entwicklung, Stand, Perspektiven. In Günter Mey and Katja Mruck (Eds.), *Grounded Theory Reader* (pp. 11–48). Wiesbaden: Springer VS.

Mills, Jane, Bonner, Ann, and Francis, Karen (2006a) The development of constructivist grounded theory. *International Journal of Qualitative Methods*, *5*(1): Retrieved from www.ualberta.ca/~iiqm/backissues/5_1/HTML/mills.htm

Mills, Jane, Bonner, Ann, and Francis, Karen (2006b) Adopting a constructivist approach to grounded theory: Implications for research design. *International Journal of Nursing Practice*, *12*: 8–13.

Morse, Janice M., Stern, Phyllis Noerager, Corbin, Juliet, Bowers, Barbara, Charmaz, Kathy and Clarke, Adele E. (2009) *Developing Grounded Theory: The Second Generation*. Walnut Creek, CA: Left Coast Press.

Mruck, Katja and Breuer, Franz (2003) Subjectivity and reflexivity in qualitative research: The FQS issues. *Forum Qualitative Sozialforschung/Forum: Qualitative Social Research*, *4*(2): Art. 23. Retrieved from http://dx.doi.org/10.17169/fqs-4.2.696

Mruck, Katja and Mey, Günter (1998) Selbstreflexivität und Subjektivität im Auswertungsprozeß biographischer Materialien—zum Konzept einer 'Projektwerkstatt qualitativen Arbeitens' zwischen Colloquium, Supervision und Interpretationsgemeinschaft. In Gerd Jüttemann and Hans Thomae (Eds.), *Biographische Methoden in den Humanwissenschaften* (pp. 284–306). Weinheim: Beltz/PVU. Retrieved from: www.ssoar.info/ssoar/handle/document/120

Mruck, Katja, Roth, Wolff-Michael, and Breuer, Franz (Eds.) (2002) Subjectivity and reflexivity in qualitative research I. *Forum Qualitative Sozialforschung/Forum: Qualitative Social Research*, *3*(3). Retrieved from: www.qualitative-research.net/index.php/fqs/issue/view/21

Munkejord, Keith (2009) Methodological emotional reflexivity: The role of researcher emotions in grounded theory research. *Qualitative Research in Organizations and Management: An International Journal*, *4*(2): 151–167.

Muylaert, Camila Junqueira, Sarubbi Jr., Vicente, Gallo, Paulo Rogério, Neto, Modesto Leite Rolim, and Reis, Alberto Olavo Advincula (2014) Narrative interviews: An important resource in qualitative research. *Revista da Escola de Enfermagem da USP*, *48*(2): 184–189. Retrieved from: www.scielo.br/pdf/reeusp/v48nspe2/0080-6234-reeusp-48-nspe2-00184.pdf

Nagel, Daniel A., Stacey, Dawn, Momtahan, Kathryn, Gifford, Wendy, Doucet, Shelley, and Etowa, Josephine B. (2016) Getting a picture: A grounded theory of nurses knowing the person in a virtual environment. *Journal of Holistic Nursing*, Online first. Retrieved from: http://journals.sagepub.com/doi/pdf/10.1177/0898010116645422

Neill, Sarah J. (2006) Grounded theory sampling. The contribution of reflexivity. *Journal of Research in Nursing*, *11*(3): 253–260.

Niebieszczanski, Rebecca J., Dent, Helen, and McGowan, Amanda (2015) 'Your personality is the intervention': A grounded theory of mental health nurses' beliefs about hope and experiences of fostering hope within a secure setting. *The Journal of Forensic Psychiatry and Psychology*, *27*(3): 419–442.

Nilson, Caroline (2016) A journey toward cultural competence: The role of researcher reflexivity in indigenous research. *Journal of Transcultural Nursing*, *28*(2): 119–127. Retrieved from: http://journals.sagepub.com/doi/pdf/10.1177/1043659616642825

O'Reilly, Kelley, Paper, David, and Marx, Sherry (2012) Demystifying grounded theory for business research. *Organizational Research Methods*, *15*(2): 247–262.

Ochs, Elinor (1979) Transcription as theory. In Elinor Ochs and Bambi B. Schieffelin (Eds.), *Developmental Pragmatics* (pp. 43–72). New York: Academic Press.
Olson, Mitchell M. (2007) Using grounded action methodology for student intervention – Driven succeeding: A grounded action study in adult education. *Forum Qualitative Sozialforschung/Forum: Qualitative Social Research*, *9*(1): Art. 9. Retrieved from: http://dx.doi.org/10.17169/fqs-9.1.340
Petrovic, Sanja, Lordly, Daphne, Brigham, Susan, and Delaney, Mary (2015) Learning to listen: An analysis of applying the listening guide to reflection papers. *International Journal of Qualitative Methods*, *14*(5). Retrieved from: http://ijq.sagepub.com/content/14/5/1609406915621402.full.pdf+html
Piantanida, Maria, Tananis, Cynthia A., and Grubs, Robin E. (2004) Generating grounded theory of/for educational practice: The journey of three epistemorphs. *International Journal of Qualitative Studies in Education*, *17*(3): 325–346.
Pillow, Wanda (2003) Confession, catharsis, or cure? Rethinking the uses of reflexivity as methodological power in qualitative research. *International Journal of Qualitative Studies in Education*, *16*(2): 175–196.
Ploder, Andrea and Stadlbauer, Johanna (2016) Strong reflexivity and its critics: Responses to autoethnography in the German-speaking cultural and social sciences. *Qualitative Inquiry*, *22*(9): 753–765.
Popper, Karl R. (1934/1992) *The Logic of Scientific Discovery: On the Epistemology of Modern Natural Science*. New York: Routledge.
Rager, Kathleen B. (2005) Self-care and the qualitative researcher: When collecting data can break your heart. *Educational Researcher*, *34*(4): 23–27.
Ramalho, Rodrigo, Adams, Peter, Huggard, Peter, and Hoare, Karen (2015) Literature review and constructivist grounded theory methodology. *Forum Qualitative Sozialforschung/Forum: Qualitative Social Research*, *16*(3): Art. 19. Retrieved from: http://dx.doi.org/10.17169/fqs-16.3.2313
Reason, Peter and Heron, John (1995) Co-operative inquiry. In Jonathan A. Smith, Rome Harré and Luk von Langenhove (Eds.), *Rethinking Methods in Psychology* (pp. 122–142). London: Sage.
Redman-MacLaren, Michelle Louise, and Mills, Jane (2015) Transformational grounded theory: Theory, voice and action. *International Journal of Qualitative Methods*, *14*(3). Retrieved from: https://ejournals.library.ualberta.ca/index.php/IJQM/article/view/21771
Reichertz, Jo and Zielke, Barbara (2008) Editorial: Theories that matter: On some pragmatic aspects of social constructionism. *Forum Qualitative Sozialforschung/Forum: Qualitative Social Research*, *9*(1). Retrieved from: http://dx.doi.org/10.17169/fqs-9.1.346
Richardson, Laurel (2000) Writing: A method of inquiry. In Norman Denzin and Yvonna S. Lincoln (Eds.), *Handbook of Qualitative Research* (pp. 923–948). Thousand Oaks, CA: Sage.
Riemann, Gerhard (2011) Grounded theorizing als Gespräch – Anmerkungen zu Anselm Strauss, der frühen Chicagoer Soziologie und der Arbeit in Forschungswerkstätten. In Günter Mey and Katja Mruck (Eds.), *Grounded Theory Reader* (pp. 405–426). Wiesbaden: Springer VS.
Rinaldi, Jen (2013) Reflexivity in research: Disability between the lines. *Disability Studies Quarterly*, *33*(2). Retrieved from: http://dsq-sds.org/article/view/3711/3227
Roche, Brenda, Guta, Adrian, and Flicker, Sarah (2010) *Peer Research in Action I: Models of Practice*. Community Based Research Working Paper Series. Toronto: The Wellesley Institute. Retrieved from: www.wellesleyinstitute.com/wp-content/uploads/2011/02/Models_of_Practice_WEB.pdf
Rolls, Liz and Relf, Marilyn (2006) Bracketing interviews: Addressing methodological challenges in qualitative interviewing in bereavement and palliative care. *Mortality*, *11*(3): 286–305.
Roth, Wolff-Michael, Breuer, Franz, and Mruck, Katja (Eds.) (2003) Subjectivity and reflexivity in qualitative research II. *Forum Qualitative Sozialforschung/Forum: Qualitative Social Research*, *4*(2). Retrieved from: www.qualitative-research.net/index.php/fqs/issue/view/18
Ruppel, Paul Sebastian and Mey, Günter (2015) Grounded theory methodology: Narrativity revisited. *Integrative Psychological and Behavioral Science*, *49*(2): 174–186.
Ruppel, Paul Sebastian and Mey, Günter (2017) Grounded theory methodology. In Roxanne Parrott (Ed.), *Encyclopedia of Health and Risk Message Design and Processing* (4 volume-set; Oxford Research Encyclopedia of Communication). New York: Oxford University Press.

Schivelbusch, Wolfgang (1979) *Geschichte der Eisenbahnreise. Zur Industrialisierung von Raum und Zeit im 19. Jahrhundert*. Frankfurt/Main: Ullstein.

Schütze, Fritz (1983) Biographieforschung und narratives Interview. *Neue Praxis*, *13*: 283–293.

Seale, Clive (1999) *The Quality of Qualitative Research*. London: Sage.

Sharma, Sonya, Reimer-Kirkham, Sheryl, and Cochrane, Marie (2009) Practicing the awareness of embodiment in qualitative health research: Methodological reflections. *Qualitative Health Research*, *19*(11): 1642–1650.

Sharp, Elizabeth A. and Durham DeCesaro, Genevieve (2013) What does rejection have to do with it? Toward an innovative, kinesthetic analysis of qualitative data. *Forum Qualitative Sozialforschung/Forum: Qualitative Social Research*, *14*(2): Art. 4. Retrieved from: http://dx.doi.org/10.17169/fqs-14.2.1897

Simmons, Odis E. and Gregory, Toni A. (2003) Grounded action: Achieving optimal and sustainable change. *Forum Qualitative Sozialforschung/Forum: Qualitative Social Research*, *4*(3): Art. 27. Retrieved from: http://dx.doi.org/10.17169/fqs-4.3.677

Smith, Elizabeth (2011) Teaching critical reflection. *Teaching in Higher Education*, *16*(2): 211–223.

Steier, Frederick (1991) Introduction: Research as self-reflexivity, self-reflexivity as social process. In Frederick Steier (Ed.), *Research and Reflexivity* (pp. 1–11). London: Sage.

Strauss, Anselm L. (1987) *Qualitative Analysis for Social Scientists*. New York: Cambridge University Press.

Strauss, Anselm L. and Corbin, Juliet M. (1990) *Basics of Qualitative Research: Grounded Theory, Procedures and Techniques*. London: Sage.

Suddaby, Roy (2006) From the editors: What grounded theory is not. *Academy of Management Journal*, *49*(4): 633–642.

Sultana, Farhana (2007) Reflexivity, positionality and participatory ethics: Negotiating fieldwork dilemmas in international research. *ACME: An International E-Journal for Critical Geographies*, *6*(3): 374–385.

Tedlock, Barbara (2000) Ethnography and ethnographic representation. In Norman K. Denzin and Yvonna S. Lincoln (Eds.), *Handbook of Qualitative Research* (2nd ed., pp. 455–486). Thousand Oaks, CA: Sage.

Teram, Eli, Schachter, Candice L., and Stalker, Carol A. (2005) The case for integrating grounded theory and participatory action research: Empowering clients to inform professional practice. *Qualitative Health Research*, *15*(8): 1129–1140.

Tufford, Lea and Newman, Peter (2012) Bracketing in qualitative research. *Qualitative Social Work*, *11*(1): 80–96.

Woods, Megan, Macklin, Rob, and Lewis, Gemma K. (2015) Researcher reflexivity: Exploring the impacts of CAQDAS use. *International Journal of Social Research Methodology*, *19*(4): 385–403.

Wright, Toni and Cochrane, Ray (2000) Factors influencing successful submission of PhD theses. *Studies in Higher Education*, *25*(2): 181–195.

24

Using a Feminist Grounded Theory Approach in Mixed Methods Research

Sharlene Hesse-Biber and Hilary Flowers

INTRODUCTION

Feminist research seeks to support social change and unearth subjugated knowledge by placing the lives of women and other marginalized groups at the center of research inquiry. One of feminist research's guiding principles – privileging the voices of the research participants – finds reinforcement in grounded theory analysis. This chapter focuses on the value that joint feminist grounded theoretical approaches can bring to mixed methods research designs.

We begin with an overview of feminist research goals and practices before proceeding to a discussion of grounded theoretical approaches and mixed methods research. Next, we demonstrate these practices in action by highlighting five mixed methods case studies that apply grounded theoretical approaches to very different research designs. Each case study is oriented toward social justice and policy change, and each demonstrates the various ways in which grounded theory can support feminist research goals. These case studies also provide examples of how feminist principles can stretch and expand grounded theory praxis. We conclude by revisiting the basic tenets of grounded theory analysis in the context of the case studies, emphasizing the many ways in which feminist research, mixed methods, and grounded theoretical approaches can productively coexist within the same study.

FEMINIST RESEARCH

Feminist researchers hail from many different theoretical perspectives, ask a variety of questions, and utilize a wide spectrum of methodologies and methods. Some use quantitative methods; others use qualitative methods; and still others combine these methods or invent emergent methods in the service of their research goals. What draws these strands of feminist inquiry together is their common pursuit of knowledge building that centers on women's lives and those of other oppressed or marginalized groups.

Research is 'feminist' when one applies theoretical perspectives that focus on women's lives – in particular, their concerns and experiences. A feminist perspective expands understanding of gender differences on social problems by including gender as a distinct category of analysis. In addition, feminist research resists the assumption that all women are the same, and feminists seek to understand how socially constructed, gendered categories interact with other individual characteristics that also comprise social identities, such as race, ethnicity, socioeconomic class, sexual preference, disability, nationality, and so on.

A feminist approach to research is 'connected in principle to feminist struggle' (Sprague & Zimmerman, 1993, p. 266), often with the intent of changing the basic structures of oppression. By pursuing research problems that expose power, discrimination, silence, and oppression, feminist researchers seek to promote social justice by moving toward a more just society for women and other oppressed groups. Patti Lather (1991) notes that in the practice of feminist research, feminists 'consciously use [their] research to help participants understand and change their situations' (p. 226).

GROUNDED THEORY AND FEMINIST RESEARCH

Grounded theory has been a critical analytical tool and a perspective that has adopted a broad spectrum of meanings and research practices for more than forty years. Barney Glaser and Anselm Strauss's *The Discovery of Grounded Theory* (1967) initially detailed grounded theory's research praxis; several different forms of grounded theory subsequently emerged following this initial account. Research that utilizes grounded theory may use only some of the tenets, such as the constant comparative method, or may use a wider spectrum of grounded methods, such as the analytical techniques proposed by Barney Glaser (1978); Kathy Charmaz (1983, 2014); Anselm Strauss and Juliet Corbin (1990); and Antony Bryant and Kathy Charmaz (2010). How a researcher conducts their research depends upon which methodological approach to grounded theory they subscribe to. This chapter considers 'grounded theory' as an umbrella term that includes an entire spectrum of analytical methods. Fundamentally, grounded theory explores social reality through an inductively driven systematic analytical praxis. Its goal, which is emergent in nature, seeks to develop new knowledge by collecting and analyzing research data to generate a range of theoretical ideas that remain closely tied to real-world social processes. By grounding analytical processes in raw data, researchers enable the emergence of new understandings and perspectives that often resist, enhance, or add greater depth to existing theoretical frameworks.

Grounded theory praxis, while inductively driven, nevertheless maintains its investigative rigor by seeking out new insights and negative instances within the data. Working hypotheses are subject to deductive testing when new data is obtained, and the analytical process is therefore dynamic, iterative, and open to changes in meaning. In this sense, grounded theory is an abductive process wherein the researcher infers a hypothesis (explanation) given the relevant analytical findings from the data gathered thus far. Grounded theory praxis is a critical analytical technique that also reflects and complements the principles of feminist research approaches. Because feminist research is aimed at exploring subjugated knowledge, grounded theory serves to elucidate women's concerns and those of other oppressed groups in order to promote social transformation and social change. Grounded theory aligns with feminist research in its attention to raw data (the voices of marginalized populations), commitment to iterative praxis, which allows for the constant reexamination of existing data, and ability to empower research subjects.

DEFINING FEMINIST RESEARCH PRAXIS

Feminists dig into the knowledge landscape in order to listen to previously unheard voices and perspectives relating to pre-existing research problems and issues. A researcher's awareness of his or her research standpoint is an important characteristic of a feminist approach to research and requires careful attention to axiological practice. Axiology refers to being cognizant of one's values, attitudes, and biases, and acknowledging how these might affect one's research praxis in terms of (l) what research questions are asked or not asked; (2) what types of data are or are not collected; and (3) the type of methods, measurements, analyses, and interpretations that shape the research process. This relationship can be explored with a helpful model (Figure 24.1). The research question implies a worldview or theoretical paradigm that is based in one's ontology, epistemological standpoint that can be conscious (the solid arrow), unconscious (the broken arrow) or somewhere in between.

Feminist praxis maintains a tight link between the elements of the research process – epistemology, methodology, and method – and shapes research work that is greater than the sum of its parts. This synergy can be found in feminist researchers' engagement with the research process, from the research questions they ask to their use of research methods to the ways they address issues of power, authority, reflexivity, ethics, and difference. In the hands of feminist researchers, methods take on a new context of practice. For instance, feminists practice survey methods by interrogating the androcentric bias of survey questions or the power differentials between researcher and researched in a survey interview. Feminist researchers question whether a survey's sampling frame is responsive to issues of difference in order to ensure that survey findings are inclusive of the experiences of

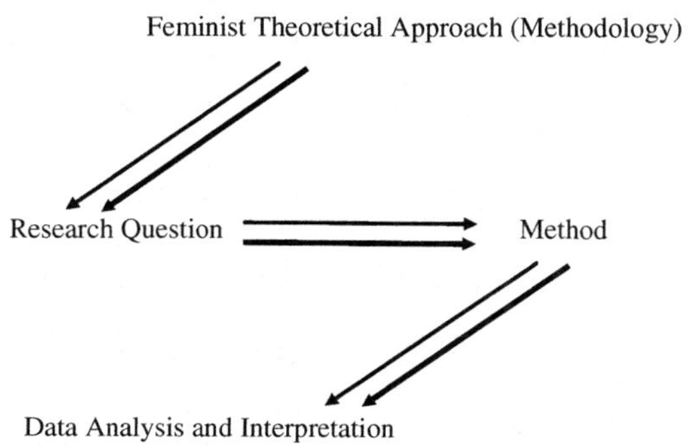

Figure 24.1 Feminist research praxis's axiological perspective

marginalized populations. Increasingly, feminist researchers are tweaking old methods and inventing new ones to uncover marginalized knowledge (see Hesse-Biber, 2007, 2014, 2017; Hesse-Biber & Leavy, 2008).

Qualitative methods are more often associated with feminist research than quantitative methods; however, feminist researchers have debated the appropriateness of using different methods to study women's lives (Roberts, 1981; Bowles & Duelli Klein, 1983). Some feminist researchers argue that only qualitative methods can capture the subtleties and nuances of women's lived experiences and that qualitative methods are 'better' and 'more feminist' than quantitative approaches (see Miner-Rubino & Jayaratne, 2007, p. 300). Those who advocate a 'qualitative methods-only' approach see quantitative methods as tools that reinforce the 'status quo'; in the words of Audre Lorde, 'the master's tools will never dismantle the master's house' (1984, p. 13). Indeed, some feminist researchers claim that quantitative methods are patriarchal tools that only serve to undermine steps toward social change on behalf of women's issues and concerns (see Reinharz, 1985).

Quantitative research methods *per se* are not antithetical to feminist inquiry, but, just as with any research inquiry, careful attention needs to be paid to the types of questions researchers ask and the types of subjects researchers recruit; the ways in which researchers practice their methods; and the extent to which researchers' data analysis, findings, and interpretations reinforce the status quo or promote social change and social justice goals (for examples of positivist research working toward feminist ends, see Chafetz, 2004). Feminist sociologist Shulamit Reinharz notes in *Feminist Methods in Social Research* (1992) that 'feminism supplies the perspective, and the disciplines supply the method. The feminist researcher exists at their intersection' (p. 243).

During the 1970s and 1980s, feminist researchers worked to 'deconstruct' what they perceived as errors within their disciplines. Feminist researchers' insights into male bias in science cascaded across disciplines including psychology, philosophy, history, sociology, education, anthropology, and the fields of language and communications, with the goal of eradicating sexist research. These feminist empiricist researchers argued that women were 'left out' of existing knowledge and that women's issues, needs, and concerns needed to be included in the research process. Feminist empiricists, as they were described, embraced a positivist methodology but were mindful of not simply 'adding and stirring' women into positivist research projects (Hundleby, 2007; Naples & Gurr, 2015). Margrit Eichler and Jeanne Lapointe's classic research primer, *On the Treatment of the Sexes in Research* (1985), critiques the lack of inclusion of gender in traditional empirical research and provides a checklist for integrating gender as a category of analysis in social research. Their most profound suggestions include advice concerning what not to do when women are included in a research project, such as:

- Treat Western sex roles as universal
- Transform statistical differences into innate differences
- Fail to recognize that difference does not mean inferiority (p. 9)

Further, feminist researchers challenged the viability of generally accepted positivist concepts like objectivity (Bhavnani, 1993). By questioning this traditional tenet of scientific knowledge building by unpacking positivism's claim to being scientifically objective, feminist philosopher Donna Haraway (1991) posited instead the concept of 'situated knowledge' to counter positivism's claim of a value-free science, which referred to the idea that all knowledge and truth claims are partial, situated, subjective, power-imbued, and relational. With this understanding, denying the existence of values, biases, and politics in academia and research is futile. Instead, many suggest that knowledge is 'achieved' by acknowledging the specificity and unique aspects of women's experiences. Feminist philosopher Sandra Harding (1993) introduced the concept of 'strong objectivity' that locates the origin of all knowledge in a particular 'point of view.' Objectivity is gained once we acknowledge our situated location and become reflexive of our positions within it:

> Maximizing the objectivity of our accounts requires that the conceptual frameworks within which we work—the assumed and/or chosen ones of our discipline, culture, and historical moment—be subjected to the same critical examination that we bring to bear on whatever else we are studying. (Harding, 1993, p. 59)

Strong objectivity requires an axiological awareness. Feminist researchers often reflect on their values, attitudes, agendas, personal histories, positionalities, and so on. By reflecting on how their value systems and sociocultural contexts affect the research process, feminist researchers maintain axiological awareness (Harding, 1993).

FEMINIST STANDPOINT THEORIES

Feminist research is rooted in women's lives and designates women's everyday experiences as primary sites of inquiry. One way of approaching these experiences is through feminist standpoint theory (Hartsock, 1997 Harding, 1993; Haraway, 2003). Dorothy Smith (1987), an early pioneer of feminist standpoint perspectives, located research's starting point in women's lives, and recommended that researchers pay attention to women's everyday experiences. Smith argued that sociocultural gaps should be a point of focus. For example, what happens when women try to fit their lives into the dominant culture's way of conceptualizing women's situations? By investigating the gaps between women's experiences and the dominant culture's narratives about those experiences, the researcher gains a more accurate and theoretically richer set of explanations about the dynamic between the oppressors and the oppressed.

Early feminist empiricists and early feminist standpoint theorists advocated for the development of new questions that could unearth women's subjugated knowledge outside of a positivist lens:

> [S]tandpoint epistemologies and methodologies were constructed in opposition to the all-powerful dictates of rationalist/empiricist epistemologies and methodologies ('positivism') in the natural and social sciences and in public institutions such as the law, medicine, state economic policy, and ... the 'interpretationist' oppositions to them imagined by most philosophers and social theories to be the only possible such alternatives. (Harding, 1997, p. 383)

Both feminist approaches understood sex as a universal and historical category of analysis (this was also replicated in studying other differences, such as race; for example, see Harding, 1991; Mohanty, 1988). However, this view of difference obviates the interconnections between categories of difference (see Zinn, Hondagneu-Sotelo & Messner,

2008, p. 6–7). While early feminist standpoint theorists collapsed all women's experiences into one defining experience, more recent iterations of standpoint theory accommodate the interlocking relationships between racism, sexism, heterosexism, and class oppression as additional starting points for understanding social reality (see Harding, 2007; Naples, 2007; Wylie, 2012). Feminist standpoint theory today is sensitive to differences between women and recognizes that an individual woman's standpoint is just that: individual, and therefore dependent upon her specific set of social positionalities (for example, age, race, socioeconomic status, etc.).

FEMINIST DIFFERENCE AND GLOBALIZATION RESEARCH

Standpoint theory acknowledges difference in part because feminist research underwent a shift toward globalization when feminists of color criticized early feminist researchers for perpetuating essentialist thinking about gendered experience. Gender, they argued, is not universal, but inflected by categories of difference such as ethnicity, race, and class (see hooks, 1984; Mohanty, 1988; Anzaldúa, 1990; Collins, 1990; Hirsch & Keller, 1990). As these categories were increasingly integrated into analyses of difference, some differences remained excluded, such as women's particular geographical and cultural placements across the globe. Today, there is also a growing awareness among feminist researchers that taking women's experiences in a globalized context into consideration with respect to issues of imperialism, colonialism, and national identity is a key factor to understanding social phenomena (see Mohanty, 1988; Bhavnani, 2007; Kim, 2007; Mendez & Wolf, 2007; Biccom, 2009). Colonialism has been taken up by feminist researchers because it is a power structure that has the authority to simultaneously define legitimate knowledge and dismiss the knowledge base of marginalized populations. Linda Smith's discussion of decolonizing methodologies describes the influence of colonialism in research that is unaware of global systems of oppression:

> It is research which is imbued with an 'attitude' and a 'spirit' which assumes a certain ownership of the entire world, and which has established systems and forms of governance which embed that attitude in institutional practices. These practices determine what counts as legitimate research and who counts as legitimate researchers. (1999, p. 56)

Feminist researchers involved in broad discussions about these issues raise questions such as: How do we study these differences? What models allow for an understanding of women's experiences within a global context that serves to empower and promote social change? One model frames women's differences as locations or roads taken; women's experiences intersect when their differences 'cross' or match. Kum-Kum Bhavnani (2007) argues that this metaphor empowers women and implies a crossroads, although it also does not provide a way for new roads to be charted, as all the 'roads' are fixed. Bhavnani notes:

> A discourse of intersectionality that draws on a crossroads metaphor … directs the gaze to the intersections of the roads and the directions in which they travel and meet. … This matters because if we are not only to analyze the world but also to change it, then the easiest way to imagine the shifts in the relationships between race/ethnicity and gender is to imagine the roads being moved to form new intersections. (p. 640)

Bhavnani offers another level to this metaphor when she posits the idea of interconnections that connote 'more movement and fluidity than lies in the metaphor of intersection' (p. 641).

Interconnections offer feminists a way of conceptualizing differences beyond race and gender as interacting with each other. For example, difference categories such as nationality, sexuality, and socioeconomic status can interconnect and reshape each other as well as race and gender. Global critical race feminism similarly focuses on interconnections, and feminists working in this tradition work to create a new feminism of difference drawing on postmodern conceptualizations of power and knowledge in a global and increasingly interconnected context. Adrien Katherine Wing (2000) explains that global critical race feminists must contextualize the nature and impact of intersectionality – the standpoint based on a combination of locations such as race, class, gender, etc., within the social structure – within global, postmodern forms of power. Intersectionality as a research paradigm, according to Ange-Marie Hancock (2007):

> [Joins] with other constructivist efforts in asserting first and foremost that reality is historically and socially constructed. In this way intersectionality represents an emerging paradigm from critical theory and ... acknowledge[s] and incorporate[s] the historical context in which contemporary power relations operate ... [and] serves as an important corrective for imprudent overemphasis on generalizability that overlooks the priority of producing valid knowledge claims. (p. 74)

Research subjects' intersectionalities, or existence at different locations along the dimensions of these categories of difference, mean that they may be simultaneously constrained and enabled by the social structure of inequalities. Feminist researchers work to link different ways of knowledge building together to obtain a nuanced understanding of the dynamics of racism, imperialism, and neocolonialism that account for multiple categories of difference.

WHAT CAN MIXED AND MULTI-METHOD RESEARCHERS LEARN FROM FEMINIST GROUNDED THEORY APPROACHES?

Mixed methods practitioners can benefit from iteratively incorporating a range of methods innovations instead of utilizing pre-existing templates for mixed methods designs that may assume that either quantitative or qualitative methods are more useful in answering any given research question. Feminist researchers seek tools that are flexible and fluid, and there is a movement to rehabilitate and reclaim methods with histories of patriarchal use.

Mixed methods researchers might recognize the importance of the dialogue between the researcher and researched; for researchers working from feminist and grounded theoretical approaches, this dialogue is central to the research project, as it indicates an awareness of researcher reflexivity, power structures within the research project, and research participant positionalities. A mixed methods researcher may foster this dialogue by enhancing his or her listening skills. The case studies in this chapter will demonstrate how important it is to dialogue with participants by carefully listening across researcher–researched differences with the primary goal of promoting understanding rather than furthering one's own research agenda (DeVault, 1990):

> [It] can be [difficult] to hear things said in unfamiliar forms, and ... damaging when respondents are not heard. But ... the critical point is that feminist researchers can be conscious of listening as a process, and can work on learning to listen in ways that are personal, disciplined, and sensitive to differences. (p. 105)

Dialoguing is essential to confront our assumptions (especially the traditional assumptions concerning the role of women in society), suspend judgment, accept and embrace differences, and internally listen as a means toward building a set of shared understandings.

FEMINIST APPROACHES TO MIXED METHODS RESEARCH

Mixed methods research, defined as having at least one qualitative and one quantitative method used in the same research project, provides feminist researchers with an important set of knowledge excavation tools. Methods are not inherently feminist or non-feminist; they are tools or techniques researchers employ to answer specific research questions.

While qualitative methods and the use of multiple qualitative methods are an important part of feminist research praxis, mixed methods (qualitative and quantitative) research designs can lend themselves to the following feminist research goals:

- Exploring women's subjugated knowledge by giving voice to women's experiences
- Being attentive to knowledge ignored by traditional research approaches that neglect gender as a category of inquiry
- Exploring multiple understandings of the nature of social reality that pertain to women's issues and standpoints
- Studying across differences such as race, class, gender, and so on
- Fostering social justice and social change on behalf of women and other oppressed groups.

There are often multiple objectives contained within any given feminist research project, and, as the case studies will demonstrate, feminist researchers use a variety of mixed methods designs. This chapter explores how feminist researchers tackle some of the major dimensions of feminist research and specifically how mixed methods can serve to further feminist research problems and perspectives.

CASE STUDIES: FEMINIST APPROACHES TO MIXED METHODS RESEARCH UTILIZING GROUNDED THEORY

In the following section, we will explore five case studies as a means of understanding feminist approaches that utilize mixed methods designs and grounded theory analytical techniques. As you approach each of these case studies, there are sensitizing questions you might apply to each, namely:

- What particular research problems lend themselves to a feminist approach to mixed methods?
- How does a feminist approach to mixed methods research begin to take on a new context of research praxis?
- How do feminist researchers tend to issues of power, authority, reflexivity, ethics, and difference in their mixed methods research designs?
- How and why do feminist researchers deploy mixed methods research designs that utilize a grounded theory analysis?

Case 1: Grounded Theory in a Randomized Controlled Trial (RCT)

Catallo et al.'s (2013) study demonstrates how a grounded theory approach can enrich and deepen the interpretation of collected data. Catallo et al. described their mixed methods project as a two-phase explanatory design wherein a quantitative approach (a randomized controlled trial [RCT] phase) is complemented by a qualitative component (a grounded theory phase). In this case, the qualitative component was added to an ongoing RCT focusing on women's disclosure of intimate partner violence (IPV) in urban emergency department settings. While the quantitative phase preceded the qualitative phase, both data types were nevertheless connected and embedded in the project's trajectory. The quantitative results shaped the initial interview questions and supported the analysis and interpretation of the qualitative data by providing participant comparison groupings for identifying codes and categories, while the qualitative results further explained, nuanced, and contextualized the quantitative results.

In order for this mixed methods design to yield rich results, neither the quantitative nor the qualitative could be treated as a secondary component; that is, both methods held equal weight and importance across the entirety of the project. While the RCT evaluated the intervention, the grounded theoretical approach explored the meaning that participants attributed to the intervention, thereby opening up an additional layer of evaluation based on intervention feasibility from participant perspectives. For Catallo et al., the quantitative findings from the RCT sub-analysis were enhanced by the qualitative findings, which offered a more comprehensive and expansive account of abused women's decision-making processes. To be more specific, the qualitative portion of the research sought to address issues in the data that could not be addressed by the RCT alone, such as reasons why women chose not to disclose IPV and descriptions of the disadvantages women associate with disclosure. In order to adhere to a grounded theory approach, the researchers first interviewed a small sample (N=4) from the RCT sub-analysis, and then used the insights from these interviews to guide future interviews. This iterative process meant that codes were generated from initial data before being refined by later data in the theoretical sampling phase (in total, analysis consisted of three levels of coding: in vivo, substantive, and theoretical):

> Continuous comparison is an essential feature of grounded theory where comparisons are made between the developing theory and the raw data until no new findings or views emerge regarding a concept or category—a key feature of saturation. (p. 3)

Catallo et al. emphasize the grounded nature of their qualitative inquiry by pointing to their steps to ensure that their theories were grounded in the data: drawing constant comparisons between interview data; seeking saturation and conceptual density in their sample; moving through emerging levels of theoretical hypotheses toward higher levels of theoretical abstraction; and aiming to build a substantive theory that identifies the central characteristics of and contributing factors to a social problem and its attendant strategies.

The introduction of a grounded theory method into a pre-existing RCT project aligns the overall project with feminist research goals in a few different ways. For one, grounded theory shares a goal with feminist research – the outcome of research should take into account multiple perspectives and truths – that is different from positivist RCT goals geared toward discovering a single empirical truth by using deductive methods. A second alignment considers the participant type: in this study, grounded theory opens up the space for the voices of abused women, which are often unheard or marginalized, to be heard. Because grounded theory centers on understanding participant perspectives, the daily lives of the women experiencing IPV not only become significant to the interpretation of the intervention, but also form the basis of that interpretation. A third alignment can be found in the intersection between grounded theory's tolerance for multiple truths and feminist theory's commitment to underscoring participant individuality. Given their positionalities, not all participants had similar experiences with the intervention, and both grounded and feminist theory embrace the complex, multifaceted explanations of social behavior that arise from studying a heterogeneous group of individuals. Overall, grounded theory in this case advanced feminist research goals by accounting for multiple perspectives, centering the lived experiences of individuals marginalized by patriarchal systems, and embracing complexities emerging from individual stories.

Catallo et al.'s study shows how grounded theory can successfully be incorporated into an RCT project to reveal new information that deepens our understanding of a social phenomenon. Discovering why and how women make decisions about disclosing IPV to healthcare providers could not have been accomplished with the RCT sub-analysis data alone, and mixed methods allowed for an integration of data and results that ultimately led to a multidimensional understanding of abused women's social behavior regarding disclosure in medical settings. Because Catallo et al. recognized the benefit of a high number of opportunities for mixing RCT and interview data, the authors recommended planning mixed methods from the beginning of a project, as this aids in participant recruitment, engagement, and retention, while enabling multiple layers of measurement as different data types interact at different stages of the research project.

Case 2: A Mixed Methods Literature Review

Eijzenga et al.'s (2014) literature review of cancer-related psychosocial issues utilized three components of grounded theory: inductive reasoning, bottom-up exploration, and iterative analyses. In order to identify specific psychosocial issues encountered by individuals undergoing genetic counseling for cancer, Eijzenga et al. deployed a two-phase mixed methods study. The first phase consisted of a literature search, and the second phase featured a meta-analysis of the selected articles through a seven-step model meta-ethnography. By mixing methods – a literature search and a meta-analysis – Eijzenga et al. elevated a review of articles that identifies common themes to a high-level analysis that involved the interpretation and explication of identified issues as they relate to their research subjects, the counselees.

The grounded theoretical approach in this study emerges throughout the research process, and is particularly visible in the ways in which the authors sorted through the selected articles (N = 25). As the authors progressed through reading the selected articles, their strategy was inductive: they determined how the articles related to each other, translated the articles into each other, and synthesized those translations, leaving the definition of overarching themes open and flexible until all articles had been processed. In this way, they resisted a conclusion about overall trends by putting individual themes from individual articles in dialogue. This bottom-up strategy is based in grounded theory and is in opposition to a top-down approach that might posit overarching themes first and then find evidence of them in the articles. Further, the iterative nature of this analysis is a demonstration of grounded theory's valuation of raw data. By maintaining an iterative procedure, the authors ensured that all articles remained active sources of theme generation while simultaneously ensuring that no articles become sites of passive evidence provision.

While not explicitly framed by a feminist research agenda, this meta-analysis did adhere to and uphold fundamental feminist research values that grounded theory served to support. Grounded theory views each individual source as the key to inductive knowledge building, and feminist research is attentive to the power structure interactions between the individual source and its surrounding hierarchies. Eijzenga et al. (2014) examine both the individual and surrounding hierarchies by paying attention to the individual source: the counselees, those respondents within the articles who report their experiences of psychosocial issues during genetic counseling. Feminist research seeks to give voice to those who are underprivileged, and the feminist goal here was to listen to those who were undergoing the intervention – the counselees, who are not necessarily experts like the doctors, nurses, genetic counselors, and other healthcare professionals involved with the genetic testing process. Eijzenga et al. (2014) excluded several articles during the selection process because 'they did not focus on the content of the specific issues experienced by the counselees,' thereby adhering to the feminist research goal of listening to those whose stories have historically been left out of conversations about medical treatment (p. 136). Because research on genetic counseling for cancer at this time more prominently features cancers that affect women through hereditary breast and ovarian cancer (HBOC), the majority of analyzed articles sampled women exclusively (N = 13), and some of the overarching themes used gender as an important consideration in evaluating psychosocial issues counselees may face (for example, when discussing child-related problems, counselees at times directed their concerns toward their daughters; p. 141).

By conducting a mixed methods literature review, Eijzenga et al. (2014) were able to explore not only what the literature discusses, but how the literature can be understood from a counselee's perspective of what matters during the genetic testing process. Had this study been solely comprised of a literature search, the final description of themes may not have fully considered what matters to those who undergo genetic testing for cancer. Here, grounded theory combined with a feminist research approach results in the discovery of new knowledge that can help counselees navigate the genetic testing process and help researchers in the field identify points of saturation and avenues for future inquiry.

Case 3: A Feminist Grounded Theoretical Approach

Based on a questionnaire and semi-structured qualitative interviews with girls from two high schools in the English Midlands, Wetton et al.'s (2013) exploration of extracurricular team sports and physical activity uncovered the impact of four barriers on girls' participation levels. This mixed methods study is an example of a feminist approach to grounded theory, as the research subject – gender inequality manifested in girls' participation in a perceived male-dominated sphere – falls within the scope of feminist studies, and the method displays an adherence to the tenets of grounded theory. Through this specific research methodology, Wetton et al. were able to identify four barriers (internal factors, existing stereotypes, other hobbies, teachers) that contributed to the gendered imbalance of physical activity levels in adolescents.

Central to a grounded theoretical approach is the close connection to the voices from which the data originated. In this case, 60 research participants filled out a questionnaire, and then one of the researchers conducted face-to-face interviews with a sub-sample. The girls who were interviewed stated in the survey that they did not participate in extracurricular team sports and were given a chance to describe this in further detail during the interviews. Wetton et al.'s incorporation of a qualitative element constituted a 'more sensitive approach' to collecting data, as participants could 'express their true feelings in more detail following on from the questionnaires' (p. 2). Using mixed methods was an opportunity for the research team to enrich their quantitative findings by hearing about the phenomenon in question directly from the research participants, and grounded theory opens up the study to re-examine its foundations. Although the questionnaire was based on previous research findings, the interviews functioned as an opportunity for the participants themselves to adjust or nuance the researchers' understandings of previous findings by contributing their own personal experiences, which added layers of meaning to the interpretation of results. This was an important addition to the data, especially because some of the questionnaire data were inconsistent.

In this study, as in the next case study, the selection of participants was in strategic alignment with feminist research goals. As there are many others involved in girls' participation in extracurricular team sports, we will note that Wetton et al. could have selected a range of other potential participants to explore this gendered imbalance: parents, teachers, school administrators, policy makers, coaches, etc. However, Wetton et al. only surveyed and interviewed girl students in order to obtain information about the physical activity imbalance from not just those who experience it, but those whom it negatively affects. For example, the girls' stories reveal information that may not have been found had Wetton et al. pursued other participants:

> The lack of enthusiasm and motivation from PE teachers was noted by the majority, who agreed that their teachers focused on the better players. Similarly, 70% felt that girls' sports teams are not treated equally by their teachers, compared to the boys' sports teams. (p. 2)

The girls describe their marginalization in sports activities which they perceive their teachers, peers, and wider society (represented through the media) understand as primarily for boys (and men). One respondent believed that for sports, the 'stereotype will be that boys will always be better than girls because that's what people think' (p. 3). Without selecting girls as research participants, this perspective may not have emerged in the data, and a significant explanation for why girls do not participate in team sports at the same level that boys do may have gone unnoticed. For Wetton et al., a mixed methods design provided data enrichment, as qualitative and quantitative results together create an understanding of a multi-layered issue; feminist research goals guided the forming of a research question and the selection of appropriate participants; and a grounded theoretical approach promoted the location of the explanation of the research subject in the stories of the participants.

Case Study 4: Social Constructionism and Grounded Theory

Pomrenke's (2007) study of child resiliency in the context of interparental conflict identified factors that contributed to the development of children's resilient attributes. A total of twelve families participated in this research, and the methods of data collection included semi-structured interviews with parents, children, and collateral informants; fieldwork observations; case-study documentation; family and/or court file review; and focus groups. Grounded theory informed all phases of the research project, perhaps most visibly during the data analysis stage of the research trajectory. Questions regarding resiliency were posed in three major areas at the beginning of the research process: the promotion of children's resilient behaviors in family and community interactions; children's perceptions of ongoing parental conflict and surrounding mediation attempts; and barriers to resiliency and methods of overcoming such barriers.

Social constructionism was infused in this research via the assumption that meaning and knowledge are located in the fluid, constantly changing, socially derived narratives. To the extent that this understanding of social reality prompts close attention to the social experience as voiced by participants in the research context, this additional theoretical framework fits well with grounded theory. The 'stories told by the children represented their ideas of resilience,' meaning that the narratives shared by the research participants are primary data sources; grounded theory, too, privileges participant data at this initial level (p. 357). Pomrenke explicitly stated 'this study starts from understanding the experience of the research participants (i.e., how they construct their worlds)' (p. 358). The data analysis phase maintained the importance of the participants' narration by focusing on themes in the data before refining a theory based on those themes. In this way, Pomrenke argued that the social, psychological, and structural processes in motion in the phenomenon at hand emerged naturally from the raw data. This organic emergence of processes and themes is underscored by the way in which Pomrenke approached the data collection methods. Because grounded theory expects topics to be fully explored and theoretical categories be saturated, Pomrenke at times adapted the interview questions to better understand the main social mechanism of interest, resilience. As social constructionism views meaning as fluid, the grounded theory interview process similarly remained fluid, allowing different or related questions to be posed to participants so that a richer understanding could be reached.

While a feminist approach was not described as a guiding component of the research, nevertheless there were features of this research that advanced feminist research goals. For example, the participant pool consisted of a group of individuals (children) whose voices are typically left out of scholarship. Beyond this exclusion, children were also partially excluded from the phenomenon at hand that affects them; children in this study explained their confusion regarding their parents' conflict and their inability to ameliorate the situation. Pomrenke stressed the inclusion of children (and parents and collateral contacts) in the co-creative process of knowledge building; by returning to the participants after coding and categorizing the data, Pomrenke verified that 'the information adequately states what they had intended' (p. 361). Participants were involved in the analytic stage and contributed directly to the study's theoretical conclusions.

Grounded theory added a richness and depth to the study's findings, and feminist research praxis allowed children's voices to be heard and incorporated into narratives about parental conflict. Because children are 'active players in their own identity,' they should also play active roles in the research surrounding this topic; Pomrenke argued 'as a way of respecting the child's knowledge and interdependence, the child should be consulted with respect to what external resources they could best utilize' (p. 372). The study found that children's external support systems, such as step-parents, extended family members, and peers, augmented children's resilient characteristics. These findings emphasized the need for involved parties, such as clinicians or social workers, to listen to the needs of children who navigate interparental conflict.

Case Study 5: Feminist Geography and Mixed Methods

Maureen G. Reed, a feminist and social activist geographer, employed a mixed methods research design to explore women's experiences working in male-dominated occupations in Canadian rural forestry communities. At the time of study, government forestry policies and related research neglected women's work and community contributions, which were understood as peripheral to forestry work. Government policy reinforced popular conceptions of forestry work by defining men as the primary workers who are able to tolerate an occupation characterized by hard physical labor, danger, and a rough-and-tumble lifestyle. According to government policy:

> [Women] were considered part of forestry communities only when they were attached as partners to male workers who were considered the dominant breadwinners. In 1994, the Commission on Resources and Environment (CORE) reported that 'on Vancouver Island about 95% of resource workers are male, and about 80% of them are married. ... In this statement, CORE only considered women by their conjugal status and recognised only one possible status. Furthermore, CORE neglected that women themselves might be forestry workers with insights and experiences relevant to the changing employment conditions for forestry workers. (Reed, 2003a, p. 373)

During the mid-1990s, Canada's forestry industry was undergoing structural changes in land management: transitioning from old growth to second growth of timber; struggling with over-cutting and inadequate tree-renewal policies; and shifting to new governmental forestry protection policies. Further, the Canadian forestry industry was also facing land allocation issues, especially regarding the rights of Aboriginal First Nations. Governmental policies were changing in response to the changing nature of forest work; logging decreased while forest management positions increased due to a new demand for forest cultivation and planning. Reed began her research journey here, as forestry's transition from heavy labor to management opened the door for women's further employment in forestry.

Reed sought to unearth the subjugated experiences of women in transitioning forestry communities:

> I believe that the voices of women have been muted within the institutions that shape public policy making and that their stories are legitimate ones. My interest in activism is strategic.

> I deliberately go beyond the front lines of political protest and enter the communities, the homes, and the personal lives of forestry-town women whose stories have yet to be told. (Reed, 2003b, p. x)

By choosing 'women whose stories have yet to be told' as her research subjects, Reed demonstrated how feminist research goals drove the formation of her research question: 'How do women experience life in forestry communities undergoing transition?'

Reed conducted 37 in-depth interviews with women employed in the forestry industry, as well as three focus groups with women who lived and worked in the nine forestry communities. Reed extended the focus group segment by training ten women as community researchers. These women, who participated in the focus groups, conducted additional in-depth interviews with women in the studied communities and shaped Reed's analysis by 'corroborating and refining emerging themes and social categories' (2003b, p. 21). This participatory action research model also featured community workshops, which functioned as additional opportunities to refine the analysis of the data. Reed also collected quantitative data that consisted of a content analysis of public policy documents and examined census data to obtain a demographic profile of women's employment in forestry occupations in the nine forestry communities of Vancouver, British Columbia. These quantitative data allow Reed to compare the extent to which she can generalize the findings from her convenience in-depth interview sample and focus group data comparing her sample to the demographic statistics of women employed in the forestry industry regionally.

Overall, Reed's mixed methods research design was iterative: she collected data, analyzed the data, collected more data, and so on. There did not appear to be a specific sequencing of qualitative and quantitative methods, nor was there any stress on the importance of ordering methods in a specific sequential or concurrent manner. Similarly, neither quantitative nor qualitative method was designated as primary. Instead of supplying an order or hierarchy of methods, this study emphasized the purpose of the methods – to answer questions about women's marginalized experiences working in an industry that renders them invisible to policy makers, academics, and government agencies.

Reed's iterative mixed methods used a grounded approach that enabled her to weave her findings together in a back-and-forth analytical motion that resisted categorization within traditional mixed methods design templates. For example, respondents were able to 'talk back' to the qualitative analytical component of her study through focus group and workshop feedback, and this feedback prompted Reed to revisit her analysis. Reed noticed that the census's occupational categories reflected male-dominated cultures and led to an undercount of women's actual contributions, and the in-depth interview and focus group data allowed her to argue for the refinement of these categories in order to reflect women's occupational lives. One purpose of feminist research is to 'seek methods that empower ... respondents and participants' (Hesse-Biber & Yaiser, 2004, p. 277). Through the qualitative findings, grounded in the lived experience of women, Reed raised issues with the androcentrist census categories, thereby opening up the possibility for a more accurate measurement of women's labor force activity within the forestry industry.

The data gathered from both quantitative and qualitative methods dramatically impacted Reed's initial theories about women's roles in male-dominated occupations. Reed found a dramatic paradox contained within her data: employed women both supported and challenged patriarchal cultural practices in their workplace and community.

The concept of 'social embeddedness' was central to understanding the women's contradictory behaviors:

> Women's choices and perspectives about employment are located within systems of social relations and cultural norms that fix their work in particular social and geographic locations. In short, the discourses and practices of women in forestry were socially embedded within local and societal norms and values. Rather, contradictory ideas about inclusion and exclusion, and appropriate feminine and masculine behaviours ran simultaneously within individual interviews and across the discussions with women of differing employment, age and life-stage status. Women's adoption of cultural norms and values associated with forestry reflected and reinforced their own marginality. Women are both social activists against patriarchal norms and at the same time compliant with some aspects of these norms. (2003a, p. 387)

Women were dually embedded socially and occupationally within their communities. They simultaneously participated in their own subjugation while actively challenging their oppressed position. The interaction of these two forces kept them at the margins of the forestry industry. Such insights were made possible through a grounded approach:

> The binary of victim/victor does not grant sufficient attention to the complexity and contradiction that characterize women's lives and perspectives. Rather, I suggest that through discourse and practice, women are co-creators of the forestry culture and communities that provide openings and closures for women in the paid work of forestry. Greater attention to women's participation in forestry—in practice and in discourse—provides more nuanced theoretical explanations and more accurate empirical descriptions to inform policy choices about forestry employment. (2003a, p. 387)

Through Reed's integration of mixed methods both at the data collection and data analysis stages of her research, women's work contributions to forestry became 'visible,' which has implications for women's opportunities to be included in government policy initiatives and shape community-specific policy debates. By paying close attention to the lived experiences of marginalized women, Reed uncovered male bias not only within the communities she studied, but also in the very tools that she used to approach her research question (census categories). The iterative nature of her research maintained its flexibility and resulted in findings that were grounded in participants' voices.

CONCLUSION: SOCIAL POLICY AND SOCIAL CHANGE IMPLICATIONS OF A FEMINIST GROUNDED THEORY APPROACH TO MIXED METHODS INQUIRY

Feminist researchers employ both qualitative and quantitative methods. What is striking to note in these case studies is the process of mixing a range of qualitative and quantitative methods, such as in-depth interviews, focus groups, content analyses, literature reviews, meta-analyses, and field observations, among others. These case study researchers also mixed a range of different analytical methods, including a grounded theory approach through which researchers could iteratively go 'back and forth' from different forms of data collection and analysis. The deployment of grounded theory as an analytical tool allows researchers to get at subjugated knowledge. For example, Reed's use of grounded theory allowed her to uncover a paradox regarding women's experiences in forestry employment. She uncovered how the range of different types of women's jobs in forestry work is often not counted in official statistics. In addition, she also unearthed how women at times may contribute to their marginal place in this industry through 'adherence to discourses and practices that reinforce stereotypes about the industry' (Reed, 2003a p. 373).

Mixed methods research praxis can generate knowledge that empowers women and other oppressed populations by opening avenues for social justice and transformation and traversing diverse macro- and micro-layered understandings of lived experiences. By allowing for multi-layered analyses of lived experiences in a wider social context, mixed methods projects generate sophisticated and divergent meanings. The combination of quantitative and qualitative data is powerful, especially in its ability to relay information to social policy decision makers who expect the researcher to make generalizations regarding their qualitative findings while presenting the situation as experienced by the population of interest. In order to achieve the 'synergistic promise' of mixed methods social transformation, researchers must place their dual findings in dialogue with one another – quantitative and qualitative findings must 'speak' to each other.

The case studies in this chapter demonstrate a range of possibilities for feminists employing a mixed methods approach to inquiry. Both mixed-methods and multi-methods designs can serve feminist research goals by uncovering subjugated knowledge and focusing on difference, empowerment, and social change. Feminist researchers are cognizant of the power that relationships inherent in any given research project hold, and are mindful, through their practices of reflexivity, of how their roles as researchers and the methods they utilize can either disempower or empower their research participants. For example, Reed's inclusion of a participatory component in her data gathering and analysis addresses some of the inequalities between her own research position and those of her respondents. To further extend the role of the respondent population, Reed selected respondents to interview their peers in a participatory action research model.

In each of these case studies, the research problem sets the agenda for each study; there is no prior set of fixed mixed or multi-methods designs that feminists choose from. Instead, the design process itself is iterative, with researchers selecting methods of an analytical style that will best answer their research questions as new findings arise and will keep data findings from different methods in conversation with the research goals and ongoing findings. Catallo et al.'s (2013) study exemplifies the flexibility of an iterative design process, wherein a qualitative component was added to an ongoing RCT. A helpful way to conceptualize this research process is by using Deleuze and Guattari's (1987) patchwork metaphor: feminist researchers draw on multiple data sources (patches) and designs (quilt designs), and create space for contradictions, tensions, and transformations within their research findings.

Feminists' practice of mixed and multiple methods responds to findings that crop up during the research process and lead to new questions. Sprague and Zimmerman (1993) comment that when feminist researchers, in efforts to integrate qualitative and quantitative research methods, 'encounter apparently different findings from each method … [they] need not immediately assume that one should be refuted and the other accepted' (p. 272). Pomrenke's study displays an awareness of this tension by including the voices of children alongside data sources that may propose alternative perspectives (for example, case study documentation, court files).

Accommodating opposing research findings within the same study allows feminist researchers to clarify disparate results and add complex meaning to their research. It is in this sense that the process of designing a mixed methods project is iterative; the decision to employ mixed methods design depends on prior research findings and on whether or not new questions require the use of a new method or methods. This is not to say, however, that feminist research approaches to mixed and multi-methods research cannot employ fixed methods designs. Some research questions demand an a priori mixed methods design at the outset, while other projects may be more serendipitous in their deployment of additional methods. Either way, the researcher's questions always guide the use of a mixed methods research design.

Feminist researchers' use of mixed methods designs outlined in this chapter is not exhaustive. This chapter addresses characteristics of feminist research that lend themselves to mixed methods designs and grounded theory approaches. By employing grounded theory, feminist research can understand and address the neglected concerns of women and other oppressed groups with an emphasis on the lived experiences of the research participants. Grounded theory, therefore, can serve feminist research in its goals of social transformation, social change, and challenging the status quo of scientific knowledge building.

REFERENCES

Anzaldúa, G. E. (1990). *Making face, making soul/haciendo caras: Creative and critical perspectives by feminists of color*. San Francisco, CA: Aunt Lute Books.

Bhavnani, K. (1993). Tracing the contours: Feminist research and feminist objectivity. *Women's Studies International Forum*, *16*, 95–104.

Bhavnani, K. (2007). Interconnections and configurations: Toward a global feminist ethnography. In S. Hesse-Biber (Ed.), *Handbook of feminist research: Theory and praxis* (p. 639–649). Thousand Oaks, CA: Sage.

Biccom, A. (2009). *Global citizenship and the legacy of empire: Marketing development*. New York: Routledge.

Bowles, G. & Duelli Klein, R. (1983). *Theories of women's studies*. London: Routledge & Kegan Paul.

Bryant, A. & Charmaz, K. (Eds.) (2010). *The SAGE handbook of grounded theory*. Thousand Oaks, CA: Sage.

Catallo, C., Jack, S. M., Ciliska, D., & MacMillan, H. L. (2013). Mixing a grounded theory approach with a randomized controlled trial related to intimate partner violence: What challenges arise for mixed methods research? *Nursing Research and Practice*, Article ID 798213, 12 pages, doi:10.1155/2013/798213

Chafetz, J. S. (2004). Some thoughts by an unrepentant 'positivist' who considers herself a feminist nonetheless. In S. Hesse-Biber & M. L. Yaiser (Eds.), *Feminist perspectives on social research* (pp. 302–329). New York: Oxford University Press.

Charmaz, K. (1983). The grounded theory method: An explication and interpretation. In R. M. Emerson (Ed.), *Contemporary field research: A collection of readings* (pp. 109–126). Prospect Heights, IL: Waveland Press.

Charmaz, K. (2014). *Constructing grounded theory* (2nd ed.). Thousand Oaks, CA: Sage.

Collins, P. H. (1990). *Black feminist thought: Knowledge, consciousness, and the politics of empowerment*. New York: Routledge.

Deleuze, G. & Guattari, F. (1987). *A thousand plateaus: Capitalism and schizophrenia*. Minneapolis, MN: University of Minnesota Press.

DeVault, M. (1990) Talking and listening from women's standpoint: Feminist strategies for interviewing and analysis. *Social Problems*, *37*(1), 96–116.

Eichler, M. & Lapointe, J. (1985). *On the treatment of the sexes in research*. Ottawa: Social Sciences and Humanities Research Council of Canada.

Eijzenga, W., Hahn, D. E., Aaronson, N. K., Kluijt, I., & Bleiker, E. M. (2014). Specific psychosocial issues of individuals undergoing genetic counseling for cancer: A literature review. *Journal of Genetic Counseling*, *23*(2), 133–146.

Glaser, B. G. (1978). *Theoretical Sensitivity*. Mill Valley, CA: Sociology Press.

Glaser, B. G. & Strauss, A. L. (1967). *The discovery of grounded theory: Strategies for qualitative research*. Chicago, IL: Aldine.

Hancock, A. M. (2007). When multiplication doesn't equal quick addition: Examining intersectionality as a research paradigm. *Perspectives on Politics*, *5*(1), 63–79.

Haraway, D. (1991). *Simians, cyborgs, and women*. New York: Routledge.

Haraway, D. (2003). Situated knowledges: The science question in feminism and the privilege of partial perspective. In Y. S. Lincoln & N. K. Denzin (Eds.), *Turning points in qualitative research: Tying knots in a handkerchief* (pp. 21–46). Walnut Creek, CA: AltaMira Press.

Harding, S. (1991). *Whose science? Whose knowledge?* Ithaca, NY: Cornell University Press.

Harding, S. (1993). Rethinking standpoint epistemology: What is 'strong objectivity'? In L. Alcoff & E. Potter (Eds.), *Feminist epistemologies* (pp. 49–82). New York: Routledge.

Harding S, (1997). Comment on Hekman's "Truth and Method: Feminist Standpoint Theory Revisited": Whose Standpoint Needs the Regimes of Truth and Reality?," *Signs: Journal of Women in Culture and Society 22*, no. 2 (Winter, 1997): 382-391.

Harding, S. (2007). Feminist standpoints. In S. Hesse-Biber (Ed.), *Handbook of feminist research: Theory and praxis* (pp. 45–69). Thousand Oaks, CA: Sage.

Hartsock, N. C. M. (1997). "Comment on Hekman's "Truth and Method: Feminist Standpoint Theory Revisited": Truth or Justice?," *Signs: Journal of Women in Culture and Society 22*, no. 2 (Winter, 1997): 367-374

Hesse-Biber, S. (Ed.) (2007). *Handbook of feminist research: Theory and praxis*. Thousand Oaks, CA: Sage.

Hesse-Biber, S. (Ed.) (2014). *Feminist research practice: A primer*. Thousand Oaks, CA: Sage.

Hesse-Biber, S. (2017). *The practice of qualitative research: Engaging students in the research process*. Thousand Oaks, CA: Sage.

Hesse-Biber, S. N. & Yaiser, M. L. (Eds.). (2004). *Feminist perspectives on social research*. New York: Oxford: Oxford University Press.

Hesse-Biber, S. N. & Leavy, P. (2008). *Handbook of emergent methods in social research*. New York: Guilford Press.

Hirsch, M. & Keller, E. F. (1990). *Conflicts in feminism*. New York: Routledge.

hooks, b. (1984). *Feminist theory from margin to center*. Boston, MA: South End Press.

Hundleby, C. (2007). Feminist empiricism. In S. Hesse-Biber (Ed.), *Handbook of feminist research: Theory and praxis* (pp. 29–44). Thousand Oaks, CA: Sage.

Kim, H. S. (2007). The politics of border crossings: Black, postcolonial, and transnational feminist perspectives. In S. Hesse-Biber (Ed.), *Handbook of feminist research: Theory and praxis* (pp. 107–122). Thousand Oaks, CA: Sage.

Lather, P. (1991). *Getting smart: Feminist research and pedagogy with/in the postmodern*. New York: Routledge.

Lorde, A. (1984). *Sister outsider: Essays and speeches*. Berkeley, CA: The Crossing Press.

Mendez, J. B. & Wolf, D. L. (2007). Feminizing global research/globalizing feminist research: Methods and practice under globalization. In S. Hesse-Biber (Ed.), *Handbook of feminist research: Theory and praxis* (pp. 651–659). Thousand Oaks, CA: Sage.

Miner-Rubino, K. & Jayaratne, T. E. (2007). Feminist survey research. In S. Hesse-Biber (Ed.), *Feminist research practice: A primer* (pp. 293–325). Thousand Oaks, CA: Sage.

Mohanty, C. T. (1988). Under Western eyes: Feminist scholarship and colonial discourses. *Feminist Review*, *30*, 61–88.

Naples, N. (2007). Standpoint epistemology and beyond. In S. Hesse-Biber (Ed.), *Handbook of feminist research: Theory and praxis* (pp. 579–589). Thousand Oaks, CA: Sage.

Naples, N. & Gurr, B. (2015). Feminist empiricism and standpoint theory: Approaches to understanding the social world. In S. Hesse-Biber (Ed.), *Feminist research practice: A primer* (pp. 14–72). Thousand Oaks, CA: Sage.

Pomrenke, M. (2007). Using grounded theory to understand resiliency in pre-teen children of high-conflict families. *The Qualitative Report*, *12*(3), 356–374.

Reed, M. G. (2003a). Marginality and gender at work in forestry communities in British Columbia, Canada. *Journal of Rural Studies*, *19*, 373–389.

Reed, M. G. (2003b). *Taking stands: Gender and the sustainability of rural communities.* Vancouver: University of British Columbia Press.

Reinharz, S. (1985). Feminist distrust: Problems of context and content in sociological work. In D. Berg & K. Smith (Eds.), *Exploring clinical methods for social research* (pp. 63–84). New York: Wiley.

Reinharz, S. (1992). *Feminist methods in social research*. New York: Oxford University Press.

Roberts, H. (1981). *Doing feminist research*. Boston, MA: Routledge & Kegan Paul.

Smith, D. (1987). *The everyday world as problematic: A feminist sociology*. Boston, MA: Northeastern University Press.

Smith, L. T. (1999). *Decolonizing methodologies: Research and indigenous peoples*. New York: St Martin's Press.

Sprague, J. & Zimmerman, M. (1993). Overcoming dualisms: A feminist agenda for sociological methodology. In P. England (Ed.), *Theory on gender/feminism on theory* (pp. 255–280). New York: Aldine DeGruyter.

Strauss, A. L. & Corbin, J. (1990). *Basics of grounded theory methods*. Thousand Oaks, CA: Sage.

Wetton, A. R., Radley, R., Jones, A. R., & Pearce, M. S. (2013). What are the barriers which discourage 15–16-year-old girls from participating in team sports and how can we overcome them? *BioMed Research International*. Article ID 738705 ref.44. doi: 10.1155/2013/738705.

Wing, A. K. (2000). *Global critical race feminism: An international reader*. New York: New York University Press.

Wylie, A. (2012). The feminism question in science: What does it mean to 'do science as a feminist'? In S. Hesse-Biber (Ed.), *Handbook of feminist research: Theory and praxis* (2nd ed., pp. 567–578). Thousand Oaks, CA: Sage.

Zinn, M. B., Hondagneu-Sotelo, P., & Messner, M. A. (2008). *Gender through the prism of difference*. New York: Allyn & Bacon.

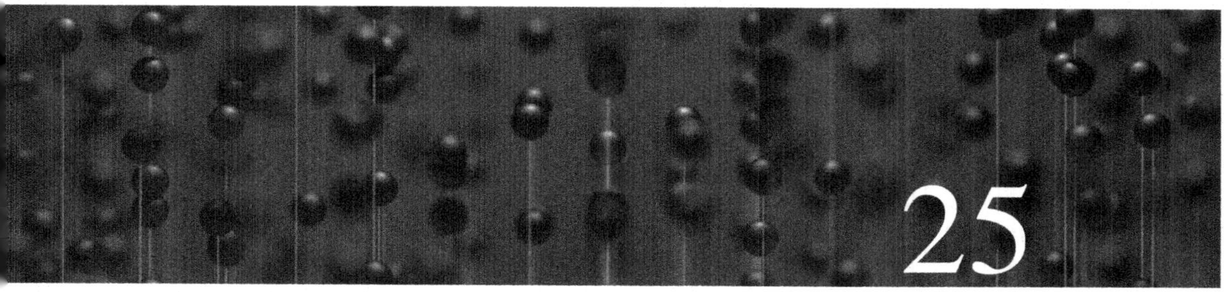

Mixed Grounded Theory: Merging Grounded Theory with Mixed Methods and Multimethod Research

R. Burke Johnson and Isabelle Walsh

The purpose of this chapter is to show how careful and thoughtful combining of grounded theory and mixed methods research can result in an exciting methodology that we call mixed grounded theory (MGT). MGT is an approach to research that relies on ideas found in grounded theory and mixed methods research (it is formally defined in the third section of the chapter). In this chapter, we review each of the component parts of mixed grounded theory (i.e., grounded theory concepts and mixed methods research concepts). Then we formally define MGT, including its features and characteristics. Last, we develop a useful notational system for MGT and provide empirical examples of MGT.

GROUNDED THEORY

The purpose of this very brief summary of the history of grounded theory is not to compare or evaluate the various possible visions and interpretations of grounded theory (Barney Glaser names them 'remodeling' of grounded theory) that have emerged over the years from different philosophical perspectives, but rather to acknowledge the source of their differences and their common denominators.

A Living and Dynamic Tradition

According to Barney Glaser, grounded theory (GT) is a 'search for patterns' (Walsh et al., 2015a) and 'the systematic generation of theory from data that has itself been systematically obtained' (Glaser, 1978, p. 2). Glaser's contribution emerged through an approach to quantitative data that he used during his doctoral studies at Columbia University. Following the dominant research paradigm, which acknowledged solely hypothetical-deductive quantitative research at the time, the logic of research was one of confirmation and not discovery: empirical quantitative data were used to verify hypotheses; qualitative research had very bad press as it was considered by many as 'unscientific'. Meanwhile, through the work of Paul Lazarsfeld in Columbia, whose interest was to identify unobserved variables through latent structure analysis, Glaser was initiated into elaboration analysis and 'qualitative mathematics' (Glaser, 1998). Thus, in his doctoral work, Glaser used quantitative data in an exploratory stance to discover unanticipated patterns (Holton & Walsh, 2016).

Glaser believed that this originally quantitative analytic approach could also be applied to qualitative data and, hence, help provide qualitative research with a more systematic approach, whose roots were found in 'hard' sciences. His meeting with Anselm Strauss, who was trained in Chicago School symbolic interactionism and worked with qualitative data, proved him right, allowed Glaser and Strauss to combine their methodological ideas into GT, and led to them co-authoring their famous study about the awareness of dying (Glaser & Strauss, 1965). Both were then asked to detail the methodology they used for this study, which in turn led to the seminal book about GT they co-authored in 1967. In this book, and despite its title, which highlights qualitative data, the use of both qualitative and quantitative data is proposed (a full chapter of the 1967 book is dedicated to quantitative data), even though only secondary quantitative data were considered by Glaser at the time. GT has become the dominant qualitative approach since the late 1980s in many disciplines (Bryant & Charmaz, 2007).

The original 1967 work was subsequently built upon by both Glaser (see for instance Glaser, 1978) and Strauss (see for instance Strauss & Corbin, 1990) separately, through their own diverging philosophical perspectives (postpositivism for Glaser and symbolic interactionism for Strauss), as well as by other authors through still different philosophical perspectives, such as constructivism for Charmaz (see for instance Charmaz, 2009). However, all these authors (except Glaser) mostly used qualitative data. Since GT was first described in 1967 through the epochal collaboration of Glaser and Strauss, GT has been understood by various authors as a technique, a method, a methodology, a framework, a paradigm, or as a meta-theory of inductive research design (Walsh et al., 2015a). It is only in very recent years that a renewed interest in its application with primary quantitative data and mixed qualitative and quantitative data has emerged (Walsh, 2015a, 2017; Walsh et al., 2015a, 2015b).

Whatever the philosophical perspective adopted by the researcher, and whatever the data that are used, one has to understand that the term 'grounded theory', and the corresponding acronym 'GT' that we use, refer both to a process through which a research study may be conducted and also an output, specifically a theory, a 'grounded theory', a theory grounded in data, which results from this process. The resulting theory, and its possible form, scope, and reach, will depend on the philosophical perspective adopted by the researcher, ranging from *nomothetic* (basic assumption: reality is governed by universal laws) to *idiographic* (basic assumption: reality is multiple, individually and socially constructed, and context-dependent), including all possible alternative philosophical positions in between these two extreme positions (Walsh et al., 2015b).

The Process of Doing GT

Whatever the philosophical perspective, and resulting GT remodeling, which is adopted by a researcher, the GT process has four foundational pillars: all is data, emergence (of categories, relationships, theory, and research design), constant comparative analysis, and theoretical sampling. Any data, numerical data, textual data, images, music, films, etc. may be used when doing GT: any element that informs and helps develop the emerging theory may be used as data. A GT emerges directly from the data, with the aspirational goal that it emerges independently of the researcher's preconceptions. The researcher must adopt and maintain an exploratory stance. All slices of data are constantly compared and interpreted as they are collected, together with all previously collected data. Sampling is not statistically representative; it is theoretically driven, that is the emerging theory helps the researcher choose where to sample next.

The purpose of induction is to add new beliefs and deduction to draw implications from what is already believed (Evans & Over, 2013). The overall movement of a GT is inductive, that is, it adds new beliefs and theory to the repertoire of social science knowledge. Whatever the philosophical perspective and resulting GT remodeling, which are adopted by a researcher, and the type of theory aimed at, the overall research approach of a grounded theorist is inductive (Amsteus, 2014; Dey, 1999). However, if along the way, and to build their theories, grounded theorists have to use some deductive arguments, this does not automatically disqualify their resulting theory as being grounded. Glaser himself indicated: "to be sure, grounded theory is an inductive methodology, but there is some deduction in grounded theory" (Glaser, 1978, p. 43).

According to mixed and multimethod approaches to research, discussed in the next section, the scientific process includes induction, deduction, and abduction, i.e., respectively, discovering patterns and theories, testing theories, and relying on the best explanation to understand obtained results. Where researchers begin, or how they begin, should not be considered as an issue to qualify a theory as grounded. When induction, deduction, and abduction are put together, they lead to modifiable, self-correcting theories (Holton, 2011).

The End-result of a GT Study: A Theory (Grounded in Data)

There are many different ways of defining a theory that range from general, etic (nomothetic) or particular, local, emic (idiographic) perspectives. For instance, a positivist or postpositivist view of a theory could be 'a system of constructs and variables in which the constructs are related to each other by propositions and the variables are related to each other by hypotheses' (Bacharach, 1989, p. 498). A more constructivist or interpretive view of a theory could be an 'approximation' of a complex reality (Weick, 1995). In 2006, Gregor proposed a broad, all-encompassing definition of a theory as an abstract entity that aims 'to describe, explain, and enhance understanding of the world and, in some cases, to provide predictions of what will happen in the future and to give a basis for intervention and action' (Gregor, 2006, p. 616). Even though different theories may have different structures and may take many different forms, Gregor (2006) argues that the primary goals of any theory are analysis and description, explanation, prediction, and/or prescription, which lead to five types of theories that are interrelated: analytic, explanatory, predictive, explanatory and predictive, and theory for design and action. Depending on the researcher's philosophical assumptions, different types of theories will be acceptable. Traditional hypothetical-deductive research will mostly lead to 'incremental' theorizing, i.e., theorizing while using existing concepts or constructs. Incremental theorizing, although essential to help a research field mature and grow, represents additional information and gradual developments on existing concepts/constructs. However, one ultimate purpose of any grounded theory, greatly facilitated by the exploratory stance adopted by the researcher, is to propose a theory 'in rupture' with existing literature, either because no theory exists on the investigated phenomenon or because it provides a new perspective on a phenomenon that was previously explored. Rupture theorizing uses nascent concepts/constructs, which were previously unrevealed and unstudied in the literature, or which were previously applied in, and adapted to, completely different domains. Rupture theorizing may involve defining and specifying these new concepts/constructs and/or investigating relationships between these and other, previously established and studied, concepts/constructs (Walsh, 2015a).

MIXED METHODS RESEARCH, MULTIMETHOD RESEARCH, AND MIXED RESEARCH

The purpose of the following brief summary of the history of mixed methods research (MMR) and multimethod research is to show their recent origins over the past 40 years. Although MMR and multimethod research were occasionally practiced on a small scale during the early and mid-20th century (Johnson & Gray, 2010; Maxwell, 2016), the earlier 'proto-MMR' was typically framed and presented in a way acceptable to the dominant quantitative research paradigm. For example, the famous work of the psychologist Stanley Milgram on obedience to authority included significant qualitative data collection that was omitted from his journal publications, and his qualitative work is little known in mainstream psychology (Milgram, 1974). Against the quantitative scientific milieu during the first 75 years of the 20th century, during the last 25 years of the century qualitative research mounted a powerful attack on quantitative research and produced the second major research approach called 'qualitative research' that relied on the philosophical paradigm of constructivism (e.g., Guba, 1990). The first SAGE Handbook of Qualitative Research was an important material outcome of the qualitative movement (Denzin & Lincoln, 1994). This handbook is currently in its fifth edition (Denzin & Lincoln, 2018).

It is out of the clash between quantitative and qualitative research that both MMR and multimethod research were born, especially during the 1980s and 1990s (e.g., Brannen, 1992; Brewer & Hunter, 1989; Bryman, 1988; Creswell, 1994; Fielding & Fielding, 1986; Greene, Caracelli, & Graham, 1989; Jick, 1979; Kelle & Erzberger, 1999; Morse, 1991; Reichardt & Cook, 1979; Rossman & Wilson, 1985; Tashakkori & Teddlie, 1998). In contrast to MMR, multimethod research continued to rely on a positivist/postpositivist philosophy of science (Brewer & Hunter, 1989, 2015). Although the ideas of using both qualitative and quantitative data and their related epistemologies appeared in the 1980s, MMR and multimethod research would not become powerful research movements until approximately two decades later. An epochal moment in the history of MMR was the publication of its first handbook in 2003 (Tashakkori & Teddlie, 2003).

Briefly, *mixed methods research* or MMR advocates the collection and integration of qualitative and quantitative data, logics, and philosophies, and *multimethod research* encourages the collection of data using any thoughtful combination of methods/methodologies (e.g., qualitative and qualitative, quantitative and quantitative, and/or qualitative and quantitative). In a sense, MMR might be viewed as a subset of multimethod research, although leaders in the MMR movement disagree (e.g., Greene, 2015). MMR is usually seen as the outgrowth of the qualitative–quantitative paradigm war, whereas multimethod research simply took the stance that it is usually helpful to use multiple methods in a research study. The concept of triangulation (i.e., the convergence of findings across methods) is more popular in multimethod research than in MMR because in MMR interest is equally focused on epistemological and empirical *divergence* and obtaining knowledge of different perspectives of the social/natural world. Although it appears that the MMR movement is somewhat larger than the multimethod research movement, both movements are important and both contribute important ideas and approaches for studying the human world.

Defining Mixed Methods and Multimethod Research

In this section, brief definitions of MMR and multimethod research are given. First, MMR (Johnson, 2018; also see Johnson & Onwuegbuzie, 2004; and Johnson, Onwuegbuzie, & Turner, 2007) is the type of research in which a researcher or team of researchers mixes or combines qualitative and quantitative research philosophies/paradigms, methodologies, methods, techniques, approaches, concepts, and/or language into a single research study or a set of closely related studies. The use of multiple disciplines is also integral to MMR.

According to the latest thinking about MMR, Greene (2015) adds an important twist to traditional definitions of MMR. She points out that mixed methods research encourages an interactive combination or mixing at three levels (or more), including (a) *method* (or method of data collection), (b) *methodology* (or what is sometimes called 'research method' in quantitative research and 'theoretical framework' in qualitative research), and (c) *paradigm* (i.e., a philosophical worldview, which includes shared assumptions regarding ontology, epistemology, axiology, and methodology). Greene's point is important because sometimes it has been assumed that MMR is *only* about methods. In fact, we mentioned above that MMR was born out of the paradigm wars, making it about much more than just methods. It is important to understand that MMR encourages mixing at multiple "levels". Mixing at the level of methods might rely on *intra*method or within-method mixing (e.g., using a mixed questionnaire that includes open-ended and close-ended items) or *inter*-method or between-method mixing (e.g., the use of a structured quantitative questionnaire and in-depth qualitative interviews) (Johnson & Turner, 2003).The concepts of intramethod and intermethod mixing also apply at the levels of methodology and paradigm. Mixing at the level of methodology might include a mixed methods case study (Onghena, Maes, & Heyvaert, 2018), a mixed methods phenomenology (Mayoh & Onwuegbuzie, 2015), or a mixed methods experiment (Johnson & Schoonenboom, 2016). Mixing at the level of paradigms might include the use of pragmatism and critical theory.

Second, multimethod research is research that uses multiple methods and/or methodologies, and '[i]ts fundamental strategy is to *attack a research problem with an arsenal of methods that have nonoverlapping weaknesses in addition to their complementary strengths*' (Brewer & Hunter, 2006, p. 4, emphasis in original). Its early development (Brewer & Hunter, 1989) was heavily influenced by Campbell and Fiske's (1959) work on the multitrait-multimethod approach to measurement. Brewer and Hunter emphasized the concept of triangulation, validation, and the importance of using multiple methods in a research study. They warned against the use of any single research method, and they recommended the systematic combining of different kinds of methods/methodologies.

Combining Mixed Methods Research and Multimethod Research into 'Mixed Research'

The label and concept of 'multimethod research' seems to be more popular in sociology (Brewer & Hunter, 2006) and political science (Seawright, 2016), and the label and concept of 'mixed methods research' seems to be more popular in education, psychology, program evaluation, and the health sciences. Some authors have called for the mixed and multimethod movements to merge into a larger, more diverse and expansive whole (Hesse-Biber & Johnson, 2013, 2015). One purpose of Hesse-Biber and Johnson's *Oxford Handbook of Multimethod and Mixed Methods Research Inquiry* (2015) was to promote increased recognition and communication between the MMR and multimethod research communities. Another, broader purpose was suggesting that all research disciplines and sub-disciplines that are interested in learning from differences should communicate and learn from each other.

One workable name for the larger combined movement is *mixed research*. The word 'mixed' suggests the mixing or interplay of differing perspectives, methods, methodologies, paradigms, and so forth. Currently, MMR does not recognize the mixing or use of multiple methods, methodologies, and/or paradigms within qualitative research or within quantitative research, despite the fact that those differences can also be powerful and drive new, creative syntheses. For example, in qualitative research, we sometimes see realism and qualitative methods used together (Maxwell, 2012), or postmodernism and traditional ethnography joined (Fontana & McGinnis, 2003; Kuhn & Woog, 2005).

For a philosophy of social science for dialoging with differences, see Johnson's *dialectical pluralism* (DP) (Johnson, 2017). DP combines a pluralist ontology with a dialectical/dialogical/hermeneutical epistemology for social science research (and beyond). DP provides users with a philosophy and theory for dialoging and learning from differences (e.g., different results, interpretations, ontologies, epistemologies, methodologies, methods, theories, disciplines, etc.). A key idea in DP is to produce new wholes, and to work toward 'win-win' solutions. In addition to using the dialectical logic of thesis-antithesis-synthesis, DP recommends the use of a 'both-and' logic, in contrast to a traditional 'either-or' (binary) logic because an either-or logic often results in dualisms, false choices, and impasses (such as paradigm wars).

The key strategy in DP is to construct heterogeneous groups (representative of multiple voices, paradigms, stakeholders, social classes) to produce new *syntheses* of different/divergent ideas using intellectual and empirically supported group-process strategies (Johnson, Onwuegbuzie, Tucker, & Icenogle, 2014). In MMR, DP supports and justifies the use of different methods, methodologies, and paradigms that provide different 'lenses' to view our ontological research 'objects' in different ways and to see different aspects of the objects of inquiry. There are three major kinds of MMR, including qualitatively driven MMR (i.e., MMR where the qualitative component and epistemology, as well as a rather idiographic or local stance, are emphasized), quantitatively driven MMR (i.e., MMR where the quantitative component and epistemology, as well as a rather nomothetic or general stance, are emphasized), and equal-status or 'interactive' MMR (where the different approaches are put into full interplay to construct highly creative syntheses that are acceptable to different stakeholders and to different sides of issues) (Johnson, Onwuegbuzie, & Turner, 2007).

DP is especially good in interacting with difficult differences appearing in equal-status MMR (e.g., that must dialogue with constructivist and postpositivist viewpoints). Here are a few more differences that might arise in heterogeneous research teams and in mixed research of all types: similarity and difference; quantity and quality; induction, deduction, abduction, dialectic, hermeneutics, and criticism; natural science and human science; objectivity and subjectivity; etic and emic perspectives; structure and agency; explanation and understanding; reason and emotions; facts and values; nomological and idiographic causation; exploration and confirmation; open-ended and closed-ended data; and knowledge and wisdom. DP and the type of research we are articulating here (i.e., mixed research) are specifically aimed at learning from both poles of these and many more dualisms that arise in our research. DP is open to many sources and kinds of knowledge and producing new and creative syntheses.

In sum, mixed research offers a broad form of research upon which mixed grounded theory (MGT) can be built. Mixed research is an approach to research that looks at our research objects in multiple ways to better understand them. Mixed research is teamed with the philosophical theory of dialectical pluralism to help researchers effectively incorporate differences into new syntheses of interpretations, results, and wider practical applications. The bringing of mixed research logic to grounded theory can be used to produce many excellent MGT designs. The use of MGT offers many new opportunities for researchers desiring to construct new forms of GT in the study of the world in which we live.

DEFINING MIXED GROUNDED THEORY (MGT)

It is time to formally define mixed grounded theory (MGT). MGT is a research approach that includes the development of a grounded theory using qualitative and/or quantitative data and it uses elements, logics, and strategies from both GT and mixed research traditions. It results from the creative and strategic merging of these traditions on a study-by-study basis. There are perhaps an infinite number of versions of MGT to be explored and 'invented' by practicing researchers in the production of new knowledge. Analogous to the terms 'grounded theory' and 'ethnography,' 'mixed grounded theory' (MGT) can refer to both a process (just defined) and a product. Therefore, mixed grounded theory is an approach to research, and the outcome of its use is a mixed grounded theory.

Here are a few ways for producing an MGT. First, although GT has traditionally emphasized induction, mixed research justifies and promotes the use of multiple logics, such as inductive, deductive, abductive, dialectical, critical, and any additional logic that helps facilitate theory and knowledge production (Johnson & Gray, 2010). The 'opening up' of GT to multiple logics is one important way to produce an MGT. A second way to produce an MGT is to attempt to understand both nomothetic/general and idiographic/local levels of reality; this is important because it offers a strategy for producing a 'practical theory' (Lewin, 1951). A practical theory is a somewhat general (e.g., middle range) theory that works in practice (i.e., in particular, local contexts and situations, with particular people). A strategy for obtaining a practical theory is to construct a GT that takes into account the local environment and allows contextualization.

Third, quantitative research tends to focus on type/generic/nomothetic/group-level causation (e.g., 'proximity leads to decreased prejudice and discrimination'); qualitative research tends to focus on token/singular/single-case/local/idiographic causation (e.g., 'That particular iceberg caused the Titanic to sink'); MGT allows one to examine both and interrelate these different kinds of causation to obtain a more informative causal theory (see Johnson, Russo, & Schoonenboom, 2017; Johnson & Schoonenboom, 2016). Fourth, although traditional GT focused on exploration, one can conduct both exploration and confirmation in an MGT. Fifth, in mixed research one often mixes methodologies (e.g., an experiment followed by interviews, a survey followed by subset ethnographies); the same sort of methodological/methods mixing is allowable in MGT (e.g., developing a GT followed by a confirmatory experiment). There are many additional ways to produce an MGT. We encourage readers to use MGT in new and creative ways, aiming to discover new possibilities in the production of warranted theory and knowledge.

ILLUSTRATION OF SOME MGT RESEARCH DESIGNS FOUND IN THE EMPIRICAL LITERATURE

In a grounded theory research, the design is not supposed to be planned but rather to emerge through constant comparative analysis and theoretical sampling. As such, MGT research cannot be fully 'designed' a priori. As often highlighted by Barney Glaser, GT is a grounded theory in itself, that is, a methodological approach that keeps evolving and being enriched as it is applied in specific research projects. So is MGT. Therefore, and rather than trying to 'invent' some unexplored designs, in the present work we used as data and investigated existing published works that used qualitative and quantitative data and a grounded theory approach for at least part of each individual work. In order to guide researchers and feed their creativity, we propose in this section to illustrate some possible MGT designs that we found in existing literature and to summarize these designs. In the examples that we provide, we do not describe the GTs in detail as this can be achieved by reading the cited works themselves. We rather highlight the striking and unusual features.

A popular strategy in mixed methods research is to begin by assuming three possible 'basic' designs that include one qualitative and one quantitative component and then oftentimes *constructing* more advanced designs (Schoonenboom & Johnson, 2017). We actually found in existing literature the same three basic mixed designs applied with GT: (a) the parallel/concurrent/convergent design (QUAL+QUAN), (b) the exploratory sequential design (QUAL→QUAN), and (c) the explanatory sequential design (QUAN→QUAL) (Note that QUAN is short for research with quantitative data and using quantitative research techniques and QUAL is short for research with qualitative data and using qualitative research techniques; a + sign refers to concurrent data collection and an → sign refers to sequential data collection). We found that the three basic mixed methods research designs subdivide into six basic MGT designs. These basic designs, focusing just on the two dimensions of (a) type of data and techniques applied, and (b) type of data analysis, are summarized in Table 25.1 and are discussed below. One should note that many

Table 25.1 illustrations of basic designs of mixed grounded theory studies found in the literature*

Data collection	*MMR basic designs*	*MGT basic designs*	*Description*	*Stance*	*Qualitative and quantitative data analyzed…*	*Constant comparative analysis performed…*	*Illustrations*
Concurrent/ Parallel	QUAL + QUAN	QUAL GT + QUAN	Qualitative GT study and quantitative non-GT study conducted in parallel	Exploratory QUAL and confirmatory QUAN	Separately	Only during QUAL phase with QUAL data	Kaplan & Duchon (1988)
		(QUAL + QUAN) GT	GT study involving qualitative and quantitative data and methods	Exploratory QUAL and QUAN	Together	All through the research process	Walsh (2014)
Sequential	QUAL → QUAN Exploratory sequential	QUAL GT → QUAN GT	Qualitative GT study followed by a quantitative GT study	Exploratory QUAL followed by exploratory QUAN	Together	All through the research process	Ågerfalk & Fitzgerald (2008)
		QUAL GT → QUAN	Qualitative GT study followed by a non-GT quantitative study	Exploratory QUAL followed by confirmatory QUAN	Separately	Only during QUAL phase with QUAL data	Spears & Barki (2010)
	QUAN→ QUAL Explanatory sequential	QUAN GT → QUAL GT	Quantitative GT study followed by a qualitative GT study	Exploratory QUAN followed by exploratory QUAL	Together	All through the research process	Renaud et al., 2016
		QUAN → QUAL GT	Non-GT quantitative study followed by a qualitative GT study	Descriptive QUAN followed by exploratory QUAL	Separately	Only during QUAL phase	Forrest et al. (2013)

**Notation:* QUAL denotes qualitative data collection/analysis, and QUAN denotes quantitative data collection/analysis. An arrow (→) denotes a sequential design, and a plus sign (+) denotes a concurrent/parallel design. The components of the concurrent/parallel design are often placed in parentheses, e.g., (QUAL+QUAN). Note that you can construct more complex designs through the joint use of parentheses and arrows, e.g., (QUAL+QUAN)→QUAN.

additional and creative design dimensions (e.g., methodologies, sampling methods, logics of inquiry, levels of reality, approaches to validity, etc.) can be used in constructing more complex and nuanced designs. Also, the following *basic* designs have only one QUAL component (use of qualitative techniques applied to a qualitative data slice) and one QUAN component (use of quantitative techniques applied to a quantitative data slice); in practice, complex designs can and often do have more than two components.

First, there are two basic QUAL + QUAN MGT designs In this type of basic design, the two sets of data are collected in parallel. However, the GT approach and the constant comparative analysis might be restricted to the QUAL data [resulting in a QUAL GT + QUAN design] or applied with both QUAL and QUAN data [resulting in a (QUAL + QUAN) GT design]. In the first case, the two sets of data are analyzed separately with an exploratory stance mostly maintained when analyzing/constantly comparing the qualitative data and a confirmatory stance (based on prior knowledge obtained from the literature) when analyzing the quantitative data. In the second case, all data sets are analyzed together as they are collected and with an exploratory stance. Hence, the constant comparative analysis is applied all through the research process to all collected data.

A good example of QUAL GT + QUAN is Kaplan and Duchon (1988). These two authors came from different philosophical backgrounds and approached the different data sets in different ways and independently of each other. The GT approach was applied only to the qualitative data set. Results were then compared and analyzed further. In this study, the authors investigated interrelationships between perceptions of work and a computer information system. Based on statistical analyses of the quantitative data, Duchon first considered the research not worth pursuing. However, based on her qualitative GT approach, Kaplan found interesting new patterns to investigate. Subsequently, Duchon reanalyzed the quantitative data as proposed by Kaplan which eventually supported her qualitative analyses. This led the authors to propose new measures for job-related responses to computer systems and to highlight 'the need to move beyond outcome evaluations to investigating how a computer system affects processes' (Kaplan & Duchon, 1988, p. 582).

An example of the (QUAL + QUAN) GT is Walsh (2014). Using a critical realist philosophical perspective, qualitative and quantitative data were collected in parallel when needed (theoretical sampling), and constantly compared and analyzed all through the research process. The GT approach was applied with all data slices. The author investigated what leads to people actually using information technologies and aimed to reach beyond the traditional models established in the Information Systems (IS) literature. Mixing qualitative and quantitative data and techniques, while remaining in an exploratory stance with both types of data and analyzing all data together as one set, allowed her to reach and understand a counter-intuitive result: how and why highly IT-acculturated users may hinder (rather than facilitate, as one might have expected) new-IT acceptance if their situational IT needs are ignored.

Second, there are two basic QUAL → QUAN MGT designs. In this type of basic design, qualitative data are first collected, then quantitative data. The GT approach can be applied only with the qualitative data [QUAL GT → QUAN] or with both the qualitative and quantitative data [QUAL GT → QUAN GT]. In the first case, the qualitative data are first analyzed using an exploratory stance and findings are then tested/confirmed with the help of the newly collected quantitative data; the process of constant comparative analysis is applied only with the qualitative data. In the second case, the first slice of qualitative data is investigated using an exploratory stance; then, when the second slice of quantitative data is added, the exploratory stance is maintained and the constant comparative analysis process proceeds all through the research process with all collected data treated as one set.

An example of QUAL GT → QUAN is Spears and Barki (2010). To complement the existing literature, the authors first conducted an exploratory GT phase with qualitative data. Hypotheses were then highlighted, based on the qualitative results. The proposed hypotheses were then tested with quantitative data using a confirmatory stance. Spears and Barki investigated 'user participation in information systems security risk management and its influence in the context of regulatory compliance' (2010, p. 503). As they did not find in the literature all they needed to lay down hypotheses and conduct a confirmatory quantitative study, they first collected qualitative data to understand the types of activities and security controls in which users participated. Using also the literature as data, their qualitative findings allowed them to propose the 'buy-in theory of user participation' that included a number of hypotheses that they then subsequently verified with quantitative data.

An example of QUAL GT → QUAN GT is Ågerfalk and Fitzgerald (2008). A qualitative phase with a GT approach was first conducted; then a second slice of quantitative data was added to the data set, while maintaining a GT stance and undertaking constant comparative analysis of all data as they were collected. Ågerfalk and Fitzgerald investigated the development of open source software, what leads organizations to adopt this approach, their strategy, and their business model. When Ågerfalk and Fitzgerald conducted their research in 2008, the open source movement was a completely new phenomenon with no pre-existing solid research base. Hence, they first started with the collection of qualitative data from a small number of cases. Then, they did not aim at statistical validity when sampling their quantitative data but rather used 'theoretical sampling' (Glaser & Strauss, 1967), aiming to use information-rich cases and 'real world operational examples of the phenomenon of interest' (Ågerfalk & Fitzgerald, 2008, p. 398). As they remained in an exploratory stance, and analyzed all data as one set, this allowed them to readjust their qualitative findings. Their mixed GT approach allowed them to develop an open source strategy model that may be considered as generalizable to many firms.

Third, there are two basic QUAN → QUAL MGT designs. In this type of basic design, quantitative data are first collected, then qualitative data. The GT approach can be applied only with qualitative data [QUAN → QUAL GT] or with both quantitative and qualitative data [QUAN GT → QUAL GT]. The exploratory stance is maintained only during the qualitative phase in the first instance or during both the qualitative and quantitative phases in the second instance.

An example of QUAN → QUAL GT is Forrest et al. (2013), where the authors first used quantitative data using a quantitative descriptive stance and then conducted a qualitative GT study with an exploratory stance. These authors investigated faculty behaviors in doctoral training programs, especially when dealing with trainee competence issues. Using mixed GT allowed them to understand better the survey responses, and hence faculty behaviors.

An example of QUAN GT → QUAL GT is Renaud, Walsh and Kalika (2016). The authors first used bibliometric quantitative data and statistical methods using an exploratory stance. They then added to their various exploratory statistical analyses the qualitative content of the texts highlighted in the first quantitative phase of their work. They constantly compared their full data set all through the research process as the data, qualitative and quantitative, were collected. Renaud et al. applied bibliometric quantitative techniques to a big set of references that cited Henderson and Venkatraman (1993), which is a seminal text in the strategic alignment literature. By adding a slice of qualitative data, and coding them through 'open', 'selective', and 'theoretical coding' (Glaser, 1978), they were able to highlight the three basic assumptions that are implicitly applied by researchers of this field and that need to be re-assessed.

One can, of course, find in the literature more complex MGT designs, which can be described using the notation system we have used (inspired by Morse, 1991). For example, Shim, Johnson, Gasson, Goodill, Jermyn, and Bract (2017) used a QUAL GT → (QUAN + QUAL) design. These researchers were interested in the following research question: What theoretical model, grounded in qualitative and quantitative data, explains the therapeutic factors and mechanisms of DMT for resilience building in people living with chronic pain? Phase one was exploratory, including an exploratory analysis of the literature and the independent conduct of a traditional qualitative grounded theory using in-depth interviews. Phase two was the model testing or confirmation stage, and it was conducted using a mixed methods experiment (i.e., an experiment that collected quantitative and qualitative data). Following phase two, the "final" and stronger theoretical model was produced.

Another example of a complex design is a (QUAL + QUAN) GT → QUAN design, where an exploratory-concurrent (QUAL + QUAN) GT phase described above is followed by a confirmatory QUAN phase or study. An illustration of this is Walsh, Gettler-Summa and Kalika (2016).

A label we recommend for researchers to apply to the more advanced designs is the 'hybrid design'. The reader can construct many additional hybrid designs using the notation we have shown in this chapter (see footnote to Table 1). We expect to see many hybrid designs used in practice.

SUMMARY AND CONCLUSIONS

In this chapter we provide a history of GT, pointing out that GT has always included the possibility for the use of qualitative and quantitative data, and this combined use was justified in Glaser and Strauss's original 1967 book *The Discovery of Grounded Theory*. We also provide a brief history and explanation of mixed methods research and multimethod research that produces what we call mixed research. That subsection shows many and diverse ways for mixing (e.g., data types, methods of data collection, methods of analysis, methodologies, paradigms, etc.) and design construction. Next, we defined mixed grounded theory or MGT, which essentially creatively merges GT with mixed research. Last, we provided a set of six 'basic' MGT designs to help beginning researchers get started in their conduct of MGT.

We have emphasized that MGT research design involves multiple dimensions, including, for example, types of data, methods of data collection, general methodologies, techniques applied to help analyze data, logics of inquiry, methods of sampling, methods of analysis, timing of research phases, and much more. We encourage researchers to build upon and extend the basic designs we have provided in this chapter. We look forward to seeing these MGT designs and hybrid MGT designs in future research!

REFERENCES

Ågerfalk, P. J., & Fitzgerald, B. (2008). Outsourcing to an unknown workforce: Exploring opensourcing as a global sourcing strategy. *MIS Quarterly*, *32*(2), 385–409.

Amsteus, M. N. (2014). The validity of divergent grounded theory method. *International Journal of Qualitative Methods*, *13*, 71–87. doi.org/10.1177/160940691401300133

Bacharach, S. (1989). Organizational theories: Some criteria for evaluation. *Academy of Management Review*, *14*, 496–515. doi.org/10.5465/amr.1989.4308374

Brannen, J. (1992). *Mixing methods: Quantitative and qualitative research*. Aldershot, UK: Avebury.

Brewer, J., & Hunter, A. (1989). *Multimethod research: A synthesis of styles*. Newbury Park, CA: Sage.

Brewer, J., & Hunter, A. (2006). *Foundations of multimethod research: Synthesizing styles*. Newbury Park, CA: Sage.

Bryant, A., & Charmaz, K. (Eds.) (2007). *The SAGE handbook of grounded theory*. London, England: Sage.

Bryman, A. (1988). *Quantity and quality in social research*. London, England: Unwin Hyman.

Campbell, D. T., & Fisk, D. W. (1959). Convergent and discriminate validation by the multitrait-multimethod matrix. *American Psychologist*, *24*, 409–429. doi.org/10.1037/h0046016

Charmaz, K. (2009). Shifting the grounds: Constructivist grounded theory methods. In J. M. Morse et al. (Eds.), *Developing grounded theory: The second generation* (pp. 127–154). Walnut Creek, CA: Left Coast Press.

Creswell, J. W. (1994). *Research design: Qualitative and quantitative approaches*. Thousand Oaks, CA: Sage.

Denzin, N. K., & Lincoln, Y. S. (Eds.) (1994). *The SAGE handbook of qualitative research* (1st ed.). Thousand Oaks, CA: Sage.

Denzin, N. K., & Lincoln, Y. S. (Eds.) (2018). *The SAGE handbook of qualitative research* (5th ed.). Thousand Oaks, CA: Sage.

Dey, I. (1999). *Grounding grounded theory: Guidelines for qualitative inquiry.* San Diego, CA: Academic Press.

Evans, J. S. B., & Over, D. E. (2013). Reasoning to and from belief: Deduction and induction are still distinct. *Thinking & Reasoning*, *19*(3–4), 267–283. doi.org/10.1080/13546783.2012.745450

Fielding, N. G., & Fielding, J. L. (1986). *Linking data* (Qualitative Research Methods 4). London: Sage.

Fontana, A., & McGinnis, R. A. (2003). Ethnography since postmodernism. *Studies in Symbolic Interaction*, *26*, 215–234.

Forrest, L., Elman, N. S., Huprich, S. K., Veilleux, J. C., Jacobs, S. C., & Kaslow, N. J. (2013). Training directors' perceptions of faculty behaviors when dealing with trainee competence problems: A mixed method pilot study. *Training and Education in Professional Psychology*, *7*(1), 23. doi.org/10.1037/a0032068

Glaser, B. G. (1978). *Theoretical sensitivity: Advances in the methodology of grounded theory.* Mill Valley, CA: Sociology Press.

Glaser, B. G. (1998). *Doing grounded theory: Issues and discussions*. Mill Valley, CA: Sociology Press.

Glaser, B. G., & Strauss, A. L. (1965). *Awareness of dying*. Chicago, IL: Aldine.

Glaser, B. G., & Strauss, A. L. (1967). *The discovery of grounded theory: Strategies for qualitative research.* New York: Aldine.

Greene, J. C. (2015). Preserving distinctions within the multimethod and mixed methods research merger. In S. Hesse-Biber & R. B. Johnson (Eds.), *The Oxford handbook of multimethod and mixed methods research inquiry* (pp. 606–615). New York, NY: Oxford University Press.

Greene, J. C., Caracelli, V. J., & Graham, W. F. (1989). Toward a conceptual framework for mixed-method evaluation designs. *Educational Evaluation and Policy Analysis*, *11*, 255–274. doi.org/10.3102/01623737011003255

Gregor, S. (2006). The nature of theory in information Systems. *MIS Quarterly*, *30*(3), 611–642.

Guba, E. G. (1990). The alternative paradigm dialog. In E. G. Guba (Ed.), *The paradigm dialog* (pp. 17–27). Newbury Park, CA: Sage.

Henderson, J.C., Venkatraman, N., 1993. Strategic alignment: leveraging information technology for transforming organizations. IBM Syst. J. *32* (1), 4–16.

Hesse-Biber, S., & Johnson, R. B. (2013). Coming at things differently: Future directions of possible engagement with mixed methods research. *Journal of Mixed Methods Research*, *7*, 103–109. doi.org/10.1177/1558689813483987

Hesse-Biber, S. N., & Johnson, R. B. (Eds.) (2015). *The Oxford handbook of multimethod and mixed methods research inquiry*. New York, NY: Oxford University Press.

Holton, J. A. (2011). The autonomous creativity of Barney Glaser: Early influences in the emergence of classic grounded theory. In V. B. Martin & A. Gynnild (Eds.), *Grounded theory: The philosophy, method and work of Barney Glaser* (pp. 201–223). Boca Raton, FL: Brown Walker Press.

Holton, J. A., & Walsh, I. (2016). *Classic grounded theory: Applications with qualitative and quantitative Data*. Los Angeles, CA: Sage.

Hunter, A., & Brewer, J. (2015). Designing multimethod research. In S. Hesse-Biber & R. B. Johnson (Eds.), *The Oxford handbook of multimethod and mixed methods research inquiry* (pp. 185–205). New York, NY: Oxford University Press.

Jick, T. D. (1979). Mixing qualitative and quantitative methods: Triangulation in action. *Administrative Science Quarterly*, *24*, 602–611. doi.org/10.2307/2392366

Johnson, R. B. (2018). *Mixed methods research design and analysis with validity: A primer, Version 4.4.* Department of Counseling and Instructional Sciences, University of South Alabama, USA.

Johnson, R. B. (2017). Dialectical pluralism: A metaparadigm whose time has come. *Journal of Mixed Methods Research*, *11*(2), 156–173. doi:10.1177/1558689815607692

Johnson, R. B., & Gray, R. (2010). A history of philosophical and theoretical issues for mixed methods research. In A. Tashakkori & C. Teddlie (Eds.), *Handbook of mixed methods in social and behavioral research* (2nd ed., pp. 69–94). Thousand Oaks, CA: Sage.

Johnson, R. B., & Onwuegbuzie, A. J. (2004). Mixed methods research: A research paradigm whose time has come. *Educational Researcher*, *33*(7), 14–26. doi.org/10.3102/0013189x033007014

Johnson, R. B., Onwuegbuzie, A. J., & Turner, L. A. (2007). Toward a definition mixed methods research. *Journal of Mixed Methods Research*, *1*, 112–133. doi.org/10.1177/1558689806298224

Johnson, R. B., Onwuegbuzie, A. J., Tucker, S., & Icenogle, M. L. (2014). Conducting mixed methods research using dialectical pluralism and social psychological strategies. In P. Leavy (Ed.), *The Oxford handbook of qualitative research* (pp. 557–578). New York: Oxford University Press.

Johnson, R. B., Russo, F., & Schoonenboom, J. (2017). Causation in mixed methods research: The meeting of philosophy, science, and practice. *Journal of Mixed Methods Research*, *11*, 156-173 doi:10.1177/1558689817719610

Johnson, R. B., & Schoonenboom, J. (2016). Adding qualitative and mixed methods research to health intervention studies: Interacting with differences. *Qualitative Health Research*, *26*, 587-602. doi:10.1177/1049732315617479

Johnson, R. B., & Turner, L. A. (2003). Data collection strategies in mixed methods research. In A. Tashakkori & C. Teddlie (Eds.), *Handbook of Mixed Methods in Social and Behavioral Research* (pp. 297-319). Newbury Park, CA: Sage.

Kaplan, B., & Duchon, D. (1988). Combining qualitative and quantitative methods in information systems research: a case study. *MIS Quarterly*, *12*(4), 571–586. doi.org/10.2307/249133

Kelle, U., & Erzberger, C. (1999). Integration qualitativer und quantitativer methoden: Methodologische modelle und ihre bedeutung für die forschungspraxis. *Kölner Zeitschrift für Soziologie und Sozialpsychologie*, *51*(3), 509–531.

Kuhn, L., & Woog, R. (2005). Vortical postmodern ethnography: Introducing a complexity approach to systemic social theorizing. *Systems Research and Behavioral Science*, *22*, 139–150.

Lewin, K. (1951). *Field theory in social science: Selected theoretical papers* (edited by Dorwin Cartwright.). Oxford, UK: Harpers

Mayoh, J., & Onwuegbuzie, A. J. (2015). Toward a conceptualization of mixed methods phenomenological research. *Journal of Mixed Methods Research*, *9*, 91-107. doi:10.1177/1558689813505358

Maxwell, J. A. (2012). *A realist approach for qualitative research*. Los Angeles, CA: Sage.

Maxwell, J. A. (2016). Extending the history and range of mixed methods research. *Journal of Mixed Methods Research*, *10*, 12–27. doi.org/10.1177/1558689815571132

Milgram, S. (1974). *Obedience to authority: An experimental view*. New York: Harper & Row.

Morse, J. M. (1991). Approaches to qualitative-quantitative methodological triangulation. *Nursing Research*, *40*, 120–123. doi.org/10.1097/00006199-199103000-00014

Onghena, P., Maes, B., & Heyvaert, M. (2018). Mixed methods single case research: State of the art and future directions. *Journal of Mixed Methods Research*. Advance online publication. doi:10.1177/1558689818789530

Reichardt, C. S., & Cook, T. D. (1979). Beyond qualitative *versus* quantitative methods. In T. D. Cook and C. S. Reichardt (eds.) Qualitative and quantitative methods in evaluation research. Beverly Hills, CA: Sage.

Renaud, A., Walsh, I., & Kalika, M. (2016). Is SAM still alive? A bibliometric and interpretive mapping of the strategic alignment research field. *The Journal of Strategic Information Systems*, *25*(2), 75–103. doi.org/10.1016/j.jsis.2016.01.002

Rossman, G. B., & Wilson, B. (1985). Numbers and words: Combining quantitative and qualitative methods in a single large-scale evaluation study. *Evaluation Review*, *9*, 627–643. doi.org/10.1177/0193841x8500900505

Schoonenboom, J., & Johnson, R. B. (2017). How to construct a mixed methods research design. *Kölner Zeitschrift für Soziologie und Sozialpsychologie (Cologne Journal for Sociology and Social Psychology)*, *69*(2), 107-131. Link: http://rdcu.be/tXiS

Seawright, J. (2016). *Multi-method social science: Combining qualitative and quantitative tools*. Cambridge: Cambridge University Press.

Shim, M, Johnson, R. B., Gasson, S., Goodill, S, Jermyn, R., & Bract, J. (2017). A Model of Dance/Movement Therapy for Resilience-Building in People Living with Chronic Pain. *European Journal of Integrative Medicine*, *9*, 27-40.

Spears, J. L., & Barki, H. (2010). User participation in information systems security risk management. *MIS Quarterly*, *34*(3), 503–522.

Strauss, A., & Corbin, J. (1990). *Basics of qualitative research: Grounded theory, procedures and techniques*. Newbury Park, CA: Sage.

Tashakkori, A., & Teddlie, C. (1998). *Mixed methodology: Combining qualitative and quantitative approaches*. Thousand Oaks, CA: Sage.

Tashakkori, A., & Teddlie, C. (Eds.). (2003). *Handbook of mixed methods in social & behavioral research*. Thousand Oaks, CA: Sage.

Walsh, I. (2014). A strategic path to study IT use through users' IT culture and IT needs: A mixed-method grounded theory. *The Journal of Strategic Information Systems*, *23*(2), 146–173. doi.org/10.1016/j.jsis.2013.06.001

Walsh, I. (2015a). Using quantitative data in mixed-design grounded theory studies: An enhanced path to formal grounded theory in information systems. *European Journal of Information Systems*, *24*(5), 531–557. doi.org/10.1057/ejis.2014.23

Walsh, I. (2017). *Discovering new theories*. EMS Editions: Cormelles-le-Royal, France.

Walsh, I., Gettler-Summa, M., & Kalika, M. (2016). Expectable use: An important facet of IT usage. *The Journal of Strategic Information Systems*, *25*(3), 177-210.

Walsh, I., Holton, J. A., Bailyn, L., Fernandez, W., Levina, N., & Glaser, B. (2015a). What grounded theory is… a critically reflective conversation among scholars. *Organizational Research Methods*, *18*(4), 581–599. doi.org/10.1177/1094428114565028

Walsh, I., Holton, J. A., Bailyn, L., Fernandez, W., Levina, N., & Glaser, B. (2015b). Rejoinder: Moving the management field forward. *Organizational Research Methods*, *18*(4), 620–628. doi.org/10.1177/1094428115589189

Weick, K. E. (1995). What theory is not, theorizing is. *Administrative Science Quarterly*, *40*(3), 385–390. doi.org/10.2307/2393789

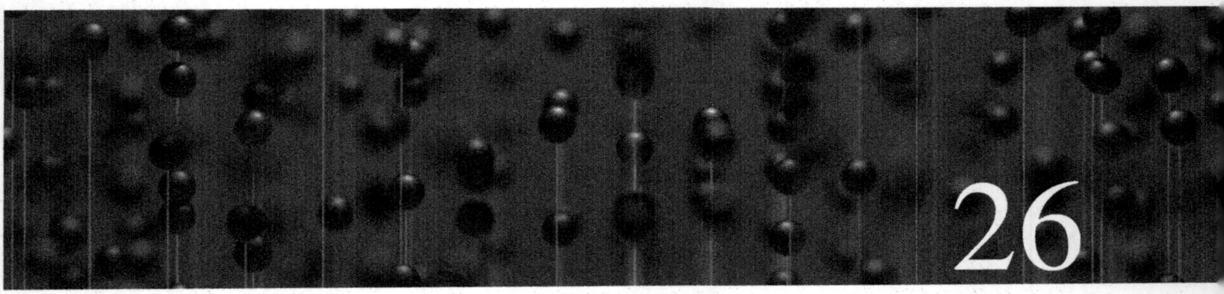

Abductive Analysis and Grounded Theory

Iddo Tavory and Stefan Timmermans

This chapter outlines the difference between starting from an inductive and an abductive logic of research – between grounded theory and abductive analysis epistemologies. We argue that the changed status of qualitative research within the disciplinary ecology over the past 50 years has given rise to different challenges and opportunities for data analysis. Grounded theory methodology acted as a powerful way to legitimize qualitative research as scientific, discipline-relevant work in an era marked by the search for universal covering laws of sociology and an increasingly quantitative takeover of sociological methodology. Abductive analysis and other current methodological approaches emerge instead in an era in which the challenge of legitimization has been put to rest: few people currently question the legitimacy of qualitative research approaches. Instead, the challenge that abductive analysis has been designed to think through is the question asked of all good research beyond the question of evidence – What is this a case of?

The difference between grounded theory and abductive analysis is thus between a research strategy that is best used to outline the ways in which people make sense of their world together, and codifying these 'ethno-narratives' (Tavory and Timmermans 2009) into general themes, thus answering the question '*what is going on here*?' and one that is geared – from its inception – to the question of theoretical relevance. And while, under the best circumstances, grounded theory ends up asking about the theoretical relevance of cases, and abductive analysis necessarily ends up providing a thematic story of empirical materials, the differences are more than a matter of slight emphasis. Instead, they emerge from different epistemological underpinnings, produce different ways of approaching the research act, and generate ways of both practically working with empirical observations and engaging in our disciplinary, theoretical, worlds (see also Swedberg 2012). Ultimately, although we still draw heavily on grounded theory's emphasis on forms of coding and memo-writing, we must go beyond it if we are to meaningfully engage with our communities of inquiry.

DIFFERENT HISTORICAL MOMENTS

The emergence of both grounded theory and abductive analysis cannot be understood apart from the wider sociological research landscape in the United States. Grounded theory methodology emerged precisely when it seemed that covering law forms of theorizing promoted by theorists such as Talcott Parsons, and positivist quantitative research emanating from the Columbia school of survey research were poised to take over sociology. In this context of a shifting discipline, *The Discovery of Grounded Theory* (Glaser and Strauss 1967) must be read alongside other major treatises of the late 1960s: Herbert Blumer's *Symbolic Interactionism* (1969), Berger and Luckmann's (1966) *The Social Construction of Reality* and Harold Garfinkel's (1967) *Studies in Ethnomethodology*. For all these works, despite their deep differences, shared a diagnosis of the ills of the discipline, and bucked the twin trends of armchair grand theorizing and quantitative work in favor of accounts that were more tightly situated in actors' understandings and processes of meaning-making.

The Discovery of Grounded Theory is a peculiar historical articulation of this countermovement. Glaser and Strauss implicitly predicated their book on an interactionist vision of the world, and a modest 'middle range' sense of what theorizing is about. Although the grounded theory program aspired to stimulate theorizing, it was not written as a theoretical book in the same way as Strauss's earlier *Mirrors and Masks* (1959) or later book *Permutations of Action* (1993). Despite its name, the approach was strongest as a methodology for qualitative data analysis. And yet, *Discovery* was groundbreaking. It promised not only an epistemological alternative – something that was achieved by others as well – but also practical reassurance and guidance. The angst of qualitative research, the moments of doubt and hope when qualitative researchers aren't completely sure what they are doing, and they question whether any sociology would ever emerge from their research endeavors, were suddenly valorized as both inevitable and necessary moments in the craft of sociology. Especially since the accompanying work to *The Discovery* book – Glaser and Strauss's *Awareness of Dying* (1965) – was so impressive and influential as a work of symbolic interactionist-inspired sociology, aspiring researchers not only had methodological guidance but a substantive exemplar. The methodological precepts of *The Discovery* book then served as a form of legitimization. Researchers could not only assuage their doubts and use the book as a roadmap for qualitative data analysis, but also could use it to convince colleagues that their research conformed to state-of-the-art standards of qualitative research. Citing grounded theory signaled disciplinary expertise in the methods section of an article or PhD thesis.

Thus, although coding and memo-writing, as well as the later distinction between open-, axial-, and selective-coding were important in themselves (e.g., Strauss and Corbin 1990), the success of grounded theory owes to its timely intervention in debates within the larger discipline. The incredible number of citations to *The Discovery* are explained, at least partially, by this legitimizing effect. Grounded theory methods allowed researchers – some of whom have only cursory knowledge of what grounded theory actually means – to claim in their methods section that their work constitutes legitimate social research.

At the same time, the fact that grounded theory allowed researchers to argue that the fact that they didn't come into the field knowing what they would find should be viewed as an asset for theory construction, was helpful in another important way. Doing so, grounded theory also legitimized early-career researchers and students to enter the fray more confidently. By turning theoretical agnosticism into a methodological virtue, grounded theory lowered the entrance costs for conducting qualitative research.

But half a century after *The Discovery*, the shape of American sociology has changed. Qualitative research is far more prestigious today than it was 50 years ago. Although the flagship journals of American sociology are still dominated by quantitative research, qualitative work – and especially interview-driven research and ethnography – is enjoying unprecedented prestige. Any one of the top 20 American sociology departments boasts at least one avowed ethnographer and some qualitative interviewers; American Sociological Association presidents are as likely to have made their name in qualitative as in quantitative research; qualitative research is more visible than it has ever been (but see Culyba, Heimer, and Petty 2004).

This isn't to say that sociology has finally achieved post-paradigmatic bliss, and that qualitative researchers don't periodically have to justify the size of their 'Ns,' but the kinds of anxieties faced by qualitative sociologists are fundamentally different than they were in the 1960s or even in the 1980s. Instead of a fear of increased marginalization, the kind of questions that qualitative researchers get today are the 'normal science' questions that sociologists anticipate when they present their work. They are asked 'how do you know?' referring to the evidentiary grounds of their claims and how their claims and arguments compare to what others have found; and, especially, 'what is this a case of?' or how does their research contribute and move beyond the known status of a field. It is this challenge, we think, that structures researchers' contemporary drive for continued methodological innovation.

Meta-theoretical approaches that emerged in the 1990s and 2000s, including Burawoy's retooling of the extended case method and Jack Katz's and Howard Becker's revival of analytic induction (Becker 1998; Katz 2001), have all reacted to this sea change. Thus, despite taking a very different tack, it is quite striking how similar some of the motivating factors between the extended case method (e.g., Burawoy 1998), analytic induction, and abductive analysis are. In all these approaches, the central question is explicitly about connecting observations with existing bodies of theory. And although the starting place of abductive analysis with its focus on multiple areas of theory differs from extended case method's favorite theorization of the social world and understanding of what is an 'anomalous' case for theoretical reasons, both are geared towards a historical challenge that is different than the one Glaser and Strauss needed to react to in their work. Furthermore, these methodological innovations are in response to grounded theory's hegemony of qualitative research and its distancing of existing theories: Burawoy, for example, explicitly developed the extended case method as an alternative to grounded theory by deeply immersing research in a current theory.

In order to see how different the contemporary situation of qualitative research is, we can focus on an interesting epistemic marker – the way that ethnographers critique each other. Thus, the debates about theorization and evidence in the field have become visible in both Wacquant's (2002) critique of Anderson, Duneier, and Newman as well as Duneier's (2004) subsequent critique of Klinenberg. Although these exchanges may have been unnecessarily adversarial, we would like to point out that a sub-discipline needs to be quite confident about its place to go after its own. This happens regularly in quantitative research without raising an eyebrow (for a recent example, see Luo et al. 2016). Theoretical and empirically driven attacks can be a sign of maturity, not simply a fracturing of the field. But perhaps more importantly, these debates revolved around the relationship between evidence and theorization. For Wacquant, it was the uneasy relationship between urban ethnography and the construction of a morally-upright bourgeois subject; for Duneier it was the movement from neighborhood-level data to individual-level theorization of Klinenberg's work. When ethnographers debate each other, it is the relationship between theorization and observations that is often at stake.

In short, given the shifting location of qualitative work in the discipline, it is no surprise that abductive analysis, like extended case method or analytic induction, focuses on the relationship between theorization and observations. And yet, the differences between abductive analysis and grounded theory go deeper than the historical challenges that structured their emergence. They are, instead, a matter of the basic meta-methodological position we begin with, and how this position percolates into the practice of research.

GROUNDED THEORY AND ABDUCTIVE ANALYSIS, INDUCTION AND ABDUCTION

Beyond their therapeutic and pedagogic qualities, grounded theory and abductive analysis are also arguments about how the production of knowledge occurs: about the relationship between scientific discovery and justification, and about how and where theory is infused in the research process. As readers of this volume will appreciate, grounded theory has dramatically shifted the methodological and theoretical conversation in the social sciences. Rejecting a logico-deductive model that sociology still too often aspires to, grounded theory posited a more inductive approach to the social world. Thus, rather than beginning with theory and going to the field, Glaser and Strauss provocatively asked researchers to go the field first, and theorize later by letting theoretical and conceptual insights emerge from working with empirical materials. In an era in which qualitative research seemed to play a minor supportive role in the deductive syllogism (where the researcher goes to the field to 'test' the general rule thought up by the "real" theorists), grounded theory reinserted and legitimized the thrill of theorizing that makes social research an exciting place to dwell. In emphasizing the emergence of theory 'from the ground up' and providing a set of methodological guidelines for how to accomplish theorization, Glaser and Strauss problematized a Popperian philosophy for which science happens when hypothesis-generation ends.

At the same time, the move from deduction to induction was a fraught one. If the goal of grounded theory is theory *generation*, then induction is a poor choice. To understand this, it is useful to dwell for a moment on the formal properties of induction and deduction. Deduction begins with a 'major premise,' moving to an observation, and culminating in an assertion:

All A are B. (e.g., all swans are white)

C is A. (e.g., this bird is a swan)

Thus, C is B. (Thus, this bird is white)

In deduction, no room for the creative crafting of theory in the process of research exists. This mode of inquiry relies on a philosophy of science that separates the context of discovery from the context of justification, so that 'The initial stage, the act of conceiving or inventing a theory, seems to me neither to call for logical analysis nor to be susceptible of it' (Popper 1959: 31). In this view, the process of theorizing is not amenable to codification, and not part of science proper. It is the realm of dreams, hunches, and psychology. And while, according to Popper, this is something that all 'serious' scientists may have to rely on, it is a scaffold best discarded after it is used.

Induction, in contrast, starts with a bundle of observations and examines their implied results:

All observed A are C (e.g., all observed swans are white)

Thus, all A are C. (Thus, all swans are white)

In moving from deduction to induction, one of the most important moves grounded theory has made has been the rejection of the focus on justification at the expense of discovery. Thus, the emphasis on *discovery* in the title of the grounded theory book is telling. Grounded theory squarely addressed the part of scientific inquiry conveniently ignored by positivist philosophers of science: how theories come into being. But, as the formalization of induction in later qualitative data analysis computer programs brought into sharp relief, this rejection came at a high price. Although induction attends to details, it does not, in fact, allow us to propose a theory. It cannot tell us what to attend to (swans, for example), or what qualities to look at (why their color? Why not beaks, mating rituals, or webbed feet? There is an endless number of things that make swans unique creatures). In other words, it tells us very little about what an *interesting* problem might look like. That is, how the generalization from specific cases contributes to a larger set of ongoing conversations. While induction may tell us something about a common theme, it does not tell us why this theme matters. The creative act of figuring out the world requires us to think of a different form of logic.

Moving beyond the straightjacket of induction and deduction, Charles S. Peirce, the founder of American pragmatism, pointed out a third scientific logic characteristic of the creative process of scientific discovery. His approach rested upon what he termed *abduction*, a term he derived from the Latin etymology (and that has its basis in Aristotle and later in the scholastics) suggesting a 'leading away.' As Peirce defined it, abduction was a 'process of forming an explanatory hypothesis' when confronted with a surprise. If we follow Peirce's position, abduction is the only logical mechanism that introduces new ideas into a scientific body of knowledge:

The surprising fact C is observed.

But if A were true, C would be a matter of course.

Hence, there is a reason to suspect that A is true. (CP 5.189; Hartshorne et al. 1931–1958)

In other words, abduction is the form of reasoning through which we relate a surprising, unexpected, or anomalous observation to other observations by specifying the grounds of a plausible relationship. Being 'related' could mean different things – it could be the assumption of a cause and effect, or, alternatively, that the observation is similar to others already experienced and explained. For abduction, the nature of the relationship is the puzzle to be solved. As opposed to both induction and deduction, the proposition 'A' is neither assumed before the fact (as it is in deduction) nor directly observed (as it ideally is in induction). Rather, the proposition is guessed at, presumed after the fact to explain observations we cannot easily account for. Abduction is an inference to the best explanation. It's our most promising guess.

Abduction, of course, does *not replace* induction and deduction. In his later writings, Peirce considered abductive logic as the first step in a methodological process of scientific inquiry. Once a hypothesis has been abductively formed, deduction helps work out the hypothesis by providing a plausible set of predictions about what should also happen (or what should have happened). Induction then constitutes the evaluation of these hypotheses as it provides the data that should conform to the deductively delineated premises. As a 'guess,' abduction is the weakest of the three modes of inference. It seeks a situational fit between observed facts and untested generalizations without recourse to an explanatory proposition to begin with. Abduction, as Peirce noted, thus provided less certainty than induction, and both were less secure than deduction. And yet, abduction is the only form of inference that has any innovative potential: where deduction tests a rule, and 'induction seeks for facts,' 'Abduction seeks a theory' (EP 2: 106; Hartshorne et al. 1931–1958).

Peirce, however, was no social scientist, and to translate his writings into a qualitative data analysis approach we need to further elaborate his writings. This, then, is the key gambit of *abductive analysis*: abduction should be located at the center of social science research. But why would this matter? Are we not engaging in lengthy epistemological debates, where instead we should be focusing on the actual work of social science research? Moreover, the call to move from induction to abduction arose precisely in grounded theory circles. As anyone reading either the last edition of the *Handbook of Grounded Theory* (Bryant and Charmaz 2007) or the present volume can clearly see, abduction is prominently displayed as a more accurate depiction of the epistemology undergirding grounded theory than induction. Thus, writers like Karen Locke, Jörg Strübing, Jo Reichertz, Kathy Charmaz, and Adele Clarke all take abduction to be paramount to grounded theory. In fact, given that these excellent pieces are precisely those that woke us from our inductive slumber, why would we think that anything more than a friendly amendment to grounded theory is necessary? In other words, the question is the following: given that grounded theory clearly requires a process of abduction, couldn't we simply take our favorite grounded theory books, find and replace the word 'induction' with 'abduction' and call it a day?

FROM 'WHAT IS GOING ON HERE?' TO 'WHAT IS THIS A CASE OF?'

Rather than amending grounded theory, we argue that a more radical rethinking of qualitative data analysis is necessary. Whether or not grounded theory is 'really' rooted in abduction or 'really' induction, and even whether Anselm Strauss mentioned abduction in a footnote (Strausss 1987, 1993), or in a conversation in 1969 (Charmaz 2014) does not change the fact that the logic of inquiry developed in grounded theory assumes induction. Beyond all the disputes between the founders and protagonists of grounded theory, the popularity of this approach has been due to the fact that it tuned into two important insights – that in order to do decent qualitative research one needs to go to the field without already assuming all that one would find, and that the researcher needs to be attentive to patterns emerging in the field as people construct their world. As grounded theory practitioners followed these marching orders, they needed to be attentive to the ways in which people bound their actions and their world, the way that they themselves narrated and coordinated their action. It is in this sense that grounded theory has become the key methodological guide that focuses on actors' 'ethno-narratives,' the way actors make sense of their world has always been the first-order analytic work. These ethno-narratives are then generalized further using social-scientific language.

The entire coding and memo-writing armamentarium of grounded theory methodology is geared towards the identification of emerging themes in actors' actions, discourses, and personal narratives based on a process of abstracting ethno-narratives. Through line-by-line, interview-by-interview, observation-by-observation coding following a coding scheme of who-does-what-when-where-with-what–kind-of-consequences the researcher looks for the story in the empirical materials. Once settled upon some themes, the researcher next goes across observations and interviews to explore similarities and differences with axial coding. Then, the researcher explores the most promising theme at a higher abstract level using selective coding. Throughout the process, the grounded theorist develops memos on potential codes and their relationships. This process buttresses the emerging theme-generalization. It is for this reason that 'in-vivo codes' (analytical categories articulated by research subjects) have been relatively popular in grounded theory circles.

This modus operandi leads to a distinct form of writing and publication experience. In spite of complaints that there is much variation and dilution in grounded theory analysis, journals receive remarkably similar grounded theory articles. They highlight a set of themes found in a body of empirical materials. Thus, a statement such as 'Using grounded theory, we distinguished between four emergent themes in the data' is typical of such articles' abstract. Often, the analysis consists of little more than an illustration of these themes, with a hesitant overture to the literature appearing at the end of the article. Thus, grounded theory's strength is in providing the contours of a story of interest in the research process. It tells us 'what is going on here?' in generalized terms. Much of the contemporary elaboration of grounded theory provides further heuristic help to distinguish what is going on with maps of situations, positions, and social worlds (Clarke 2005). While eschewing a narrative analysis, these maps nevertheless visually alert researchers to the main actors – present and invisible – and their actions. And yet, articles that simply delineate major themes in the empirical materials face a difficult peer review process because while the researchers, following inductive thinking, may have a good grasp on what is happening in their observations, they have less insight into why and how these themes matter for others in the field. They tend to leave the 'so what?' question unanswered.

Of course, grounded theory practitioners are well aware of the danger of descending from theory to description. In a number of powerful texts, leading authors distinguish between 'qualitative description' and the production of grounded theory (e.g., Charmaz

2014; Glaser 1978). And yet, the focus on induction has suffused the entire research process so that such a theoretical move is increasingly hard. As we were writing this chapter, we found the following cry for help on a bulletin board aimed at qualitative researchers:

> I have been utilising in-vivo codes on various established definitions in two fields of study in order to determine if theories derived from the code analysis can be grouped into the two fields of studies. What has emerged is 141 codes that have been grouped into 11 logical categories.
>
> These categories can be linked to some prominent theories such as (…) but others cannot.
>
> I need assistance with:
>
> 1. Are there any principles in linking coding outputs to established theories?
>
> 2. Are there any principles in handling code categories that do not logically link to established theories?

As the responses to this slightly lost grounded theory-soul noted, description is not enough. But the danger of turning grounded theory into a kind of 'butterfly collection' of themes and sub-themes is an ongoing and predictable risk. Even as grounded theory practitioners attempt to extricate novices from such problems and stress the role of theoretical sensitivity, they do so by asking them to link their typology to existing bodies of theory at the *end* of inquiry. Theory matters only once themes have been identified.

In other words, the danger is that the basic architecture of grounded theory often stands in the way of meaningful interaction with one's community of inquiry. While we agree that focusing on actors' ethno-narratives is crucial, the problem inherent in this approach is that it assumes that we know which ethno-narratives are of interest to the broader scholarly community. We are constantly enmeshed in a multitude of ways of doing and seeing the world together. Although slightly narrowing the scope of the great blooming buzzing confusion of social life, such an approach is still too wide to lead us to meaningful interventions in the field.

Indeed, although grounded theorists made some substantive contributions to specific bodies of theory, such theoretical innovations have been all too rare. Students of grounded theory still often harken to the early work produced by Glaser and Strauss, and while there have been great elaborations of these works in other grounded theory works on medical institutions and the sociology of death and dying (Charmaz, 1991; Mamo 1999; Star and Strauss 1999; Timmermans 1994), the scope of theorizing from a grounded theory platform remains limited. Moreover, the fact that it is in these specific areas where elaborations are most pronounced – areas that any beginning reader of the grounded theory canons ends up knowing about theoretically as well as methodologically – unexpectedly points to the importance of being enmeshed in a theoretically driven community of inquiry.

In short, thematizing ethno-narratives, while good as a descriptive strategy, and as a useful heuristic at certain points of the research, fails as an analytic strategy geared towards the development of theory. But if themes do not emerge inductively from observations, nor emerge deductively from pre-conceived notions that leave little room for discovery, how do they emerge?

As we argued in earlier work (Tavory and Timmermans 2014; Timmermans and Tavory 2012), abductive analysis relies on a different approach to the relationship among theory, observations, and method. Rather than beginning with as little theory as possible (or, on the other side of the spectrum, a singular 'favorite theory'), researchers need to approach the field with a wide array of theorizations. In this, researchers actually model their approach on that of mundane actors. For, when we face everyday surprises, we always have more than one way to puzzle them out. A loved one fails to call, and we go through different scenarios that would 'normalize' this failure. Perhaps their cellphone battery died; perhaps we said something that offended them; perhaps they met their fate in a horrible car accident; perhaps they had an allergic reaction to shellfish; perhaps they forgot; perhaps they don't love us after all. Abduction is common in everyday life and results in many hunches that could render the situation understandable.

Likewise, instead of trying to keep ignorant regarding the field of study, researchers should read as much as they can, both within the field and around it before they enter the field and while they are doing research. While this may sound onerous, or even make it seem out of reach to beginning researchers, a broad familiarity with various literatures is required to make contributions to a scholarly body. After all, if our approach is geared towards contributing to intellectual work, why would anyone think that researchers would be able to make a contribution to a discipline they are not immersed in? Armed with a wide array of theories, researchers are then encouraged to code their observations in light of various theorizations, constantly asking not only 'what is going on here?' but also how the observations fit with the bodies of theory we are embedded in, and – importantly – whether the explanation provided by the theorization we land upon would seem theoretically plausible to the audiences we are talking to, or whether we have to rule out other possibilities before we can confidently put forth our own (Tavory and Timmermans 2013).

Moreover, it is within the context of previous literature that observations stand out as *surprising*. If researchers lack familiarity with what others have written about how the world works, prevailing power relationships, interactional dynamics, conventional vocabularies of motive, etc., they will be unable to appreciate their empirical materials. Familiarity with various theoretical literatures then not only hones the researchers' analytical sensibilities but also cultivates the need for abductive inferences, the recognition of moments of surprise. Where grounded theory presumes that empirical observations are inherently sociologically relevant, abductive analysis sifts through these observations based on how they relate to existing theories. As such, abductive analysis privileges theory construction as the purpose of qualitative research. The corollary is that the most widely read researchers are positioned to make the strongest theoretical contributions, which could be daunting for novices but should actually be reassuring since it suggests that theorizing is an acquired skill that one cultivates through practice and exposure to peer feedback.

This approach to the role of theories in the act of research is complemented by our approach to observations and method. Here, abductive analysis is more closely inspired by grounded theory. Like grounded theory, abductive analysis focuses on the role of memo-writing and coding, if for slightly different reasons. For grounded theory, coding and memo-writing is where theory organically emerges through a process of increased abstraction. If we find a theme emerging in open coding, then keep finding similar themes in other cases compared through axial coding, and hone these insights through selective coding, we end up with the generalization we aim at. For abductive analysis, the goal of coding and memo-writing is different. Based on the work of Shklovsky (1965 [1917]), we focus on the role of note-taking, transcription, coding and memo-writing as moments of de-familiarization. Thus, much like poetry allows us to see the world of prose anew through line breaks, contrived grammatical structures, and unfamiliar metaphors, activities such as transcription or coding allow us to take a poetic distance from our everyday way of seeing the world – and thus the taken-for-granted inferences we usually fall upon. In other words, the practice is designed as a way to problematize the world anew.

Again, this intensive work with empirical materials is purposeful for abductive reasoning. De-familiarization of empirical materials through coding and comparative analysis allows researchers to question the taken for granted and zoom in on what is distinct in the empirical materials. Through carefully working with the data, certain patterns and their exceptions may come to stand out. These emergent puzzles will then require reconciliation, either through additional research to get a fuller picture or through tinkering with received theoretical wisdom.

Grounded theory correctly warned against researchers imposing stock theoretical ideas on their research materials. That danger is real. However, coding without constantly referring to theoretical anticipations may have created the opposite problem: a collection of thinly abstracted analyses unmoored from our community of inquiry – the reviewers, readers, interlocutors, and subjects of our work. Researchers then tend to stay too close to their own case, or make somewhat labored leaps of faith to the literature, leaps that are usually separate from the thematized ethno-narratives and appear at the end of an article.

Abductive analysis as an alternative qualitative data analysis epistemology aims to avoid both problems: working methodologically with data creates resistance against the unwarranted imposition of preconceived theoretical ideas. Here, abductive analysis has a distinct realist dimension: not anything goes, the researcher cannot wish analytical categories into existence. The empirical materials resist, facilitate, and shape some theorizations but not others. Resistance becomes apparent through the coding process: when codes that were preliminarily assigned to a data point hold up or require reformulation in light of subsequent observations and feedback to the original theorizations that motivated these codes in the first place. At the same time, abductive analysis renders the process purposeful. Research is – from the outset and through every step of the research act – aimed at developing or challenging existing theories and it is only within the context of existing theories that surprising findings requiring abductive inferences occur. The process of working with empirical materials while immersed in contemporary scholarship, then, is geared towards cultivating abductive inferences, requiring further data gathering and theorizing to make an original and innovative scholarly contribution.

Taken together, abductive analysis constitutes an alternative data analysis approach to grounded theory aimed explicitly at theorizing. Abductive analysis works towards the cultivation of surprises in qualitative observations based on a sustained dialogue between coding/memoing and a broad array of existing literatures and then abductively works out explanations for these surprises to modify existing theories or develop innovative and creative novel theorizations.

TWO EXAMPLES

We use the work of two sets of scholars who have used an abductive approach in their work. First, the work of Anna Mueller and Seth Abrutyn about suicide is a mixed method study resulting in an ongoing stream of publications (Abrutyn and Mueller 2014, 2016; Mueller and Abrutyn 2015, 2016) that engages with some of the most cherished Durkheimian building blocks of sociology. Second, Eliasoph's work on the fraught dynamics of youth volunteering and 'empowerment' projects provides a novel theorization of organizational action. These examples are presented both because the authors explicitly used an abductive analytic approach, and because they show two ways in which themes emerge in abductive analysis, as opposed to the logic of emergence in grounded theory.

Coming from a background in social networks (Mueller) and social psychology (Abrutyn), and with extensive familiarity with a wide range of theories, Mueller and Abrutyn first envisioned their work a little too deductively. It was conceived as a study of the role of emotions and dyadic ties in suicide clusters in communities in which a number of suicides takes place in close proximity in time and place. They intended their study as a social psychological elaboration of Durkheim. To study this phenomenon, they settled on the 'Poplar Grove' community, an affluent neighborhood that had an ongoing cluster of teenage suicides. And yet, as Abrutyn tells it, as they started conducting focus groups with Poplar Grove residents they realized that the stories they kept hearing didn't fit a focus on 'dyadic ties' and the emotional dynamics of such ties: 'By the mid-afternoon, Anna and I had both, independently, become aware of (a) a massive awareness of a suicide problem within the community, and not just some dyadic dynamics, (b) the level of solidarity was quite high and, like a small rural town, everyone was in everyone's business.'[1] This constituted an unanticipated puzzle, out of line with what would have been expected from a Durkheimian perspective.

Of course, in retrospective accounts the surprises are somewhat too neatly drawn, but, *in relation to the theory*, something didn't quite work in the narratives they kept hearing. Turning to Durkheim's work, both 'Altruistic' and 'Fatalistic' suicide seemed to miss the kinds of narratives of intense shame and the desperate attempt to 'fit in' that they encountered repeatedly in their research. There was nothing either fatalistic or altruistic in the suicide cluster they saw, even if the cultural and social cohesion of the community was substantial. They also found little assistance in the epidemiological literature, as it tended to be too descriptive, and spoke of correlations rather than processes. Fascinated by this puzzle, and as opposed to grounded theory precepts, the themes could not emerge untainted by theory, and *then* be connected to theory, but emerged precisely because of their uneasy and puzzling relation to theory. Consequently, the authors increasingly crafted a meso-level ecologically and culturally sensitive rethinking of Durkheimian suicide.

What is the added value of abductive analysis versus grounded theory in this study? Abrutyn and Mueller remained quite close to members' own ethno-narratives, their perspectives of why and how a teenage suicide cluster was possible in this affluent community. Thus, a grounded theory practitioner would have heard the same narratives told by community members, and perhaps even coded for them in their analysis. And yet, and this is, we believe, the crucial point, constantly attending to the bodies of theory within which they were engaged in a dialogue helped the authors decide where they could make a contribution. This is not because the grounded theory practitioners would not hear these themes, but rather because they would hear too many other themes. A grounded theorist risks being inundated by multiple themes, which then may lead more readily to a typology of themes than it would to an engagement with theory during the analytical process.

Our second example comes from Nina Eliasoph's work (2011, 2016). Based on years of ethnographic research, Eliasoph developed a theorization of volunteer projects, and the internal dynamics of new 'empowerment' schemes. At the center of Eliasoph's work are the ways in which structural tensions in empowerment projects persist and become the defining feature of the 'organizational styles' of these projects. Thus, relying on her earlier theorization of culture in interaction (Eliasoph and Lichterman 2003), and the literature on volunteering and on the new 'regime of the project' (Boltanski and Chiapello 2007), Eliasoph produces a new way to think about organizational life – one that is based on the continued production and navigation of intractable tensions.

However, and much like in her earlier work (Eliasoph 1998), Eliasoph focuses not only on the themes that actors themselves bring up, but often on the themes they either are only 'half aware' of, or that they take pains not to talk about. Thus, for example, in one of the most powerful parts of her book, Eliasoph describes paradoxes of temporality that she witnessed in the volunteer program. Youth needed to be empowered and freely choose their projects based on their own proclivities, but the timing of requests for program funding were such that adult organizers needed to decide in advance what the youth will 'spontaneously' choose. In another temporal tension, many youth volunteer groups were comprised of both 'at risk' youth from working-class backgrounds who were encouraged to volunteer as a way to 'get off the streets,' and middle-class and even upper-middle-class youth who were there (partly) to pad their CVs in preparation for their college applications. These groups, as Eliasoph describes, are located on different temporal trajectories (Tavory and Eliasoph 2013), which affect the way they act within the youth volunteering groups.

These mismatches, importantly, are seldom talked of, and often not explicitly noted in interaction, even as they structure the activities the volunteers pursue, and even as they cause 'glitches' in the smooth interaction of the group. The upshot of this form of theorization, is that instead of theorizing empowerment as a narrative, or even as an organizational goal, Eliasoph theorizes empowerment precisely as a set of intractable dilemmas that define a certain organizational environment. Rather than an ideal type built through what an institution *is*, she constructs her ideal type through the problems it can never fully solve.

Why is this, then, an example of an abductive analysis research design? After all, as we noted above, grounded theory was developed following, and as a methodological explication of, *Awareness of Dying* (Glaser 1965), a work that is predicated precisely on 'what is not said' rather than on what stays explicit. And yet, the search for themes through coding, and the emphasis on in-vivo codes came to mean that there are extremely few examples of grounded theory work in which the themes are those that actors enact but do not thematize. The sociological audacity to break actors' ethno-narratives and present alternative thematic narrative is made far more feasible – and less mysterious – when one starts coding always-already in light of alternative theories.

CONCLUSIONS

After half a century, grounded theory finds itself in a peculiar place. Once a radical epistemological position and a powerful legitimization tool in the struggle against covering laws and quantitative domination, it is now the mainstream approach to qualitative data analysis. *The Discovery of Grounded Theory* is better cited than the core texts of the sociological canon: *The Protestant Ethic*, *Das Kapital*, or *Suicide*. Qualitative research is no longer on the defensive.

Grounded theory, however, promised from the outset the nirvana of formal theories, growing out of substantive theories. And here, we believe, the approach fell short. After 50 years, we have very few influential formal theoretical innovations that came out of grounded theory research projects. We argued that this is due to the bargain grounded-theory founders struck when it embraced induction as the primary logic of scientific inquiry. Epistemologically and logically induction does not construct theories, it collects more facts, or more themes. Indeed, to the degree that sociologists have an adverse reaction to grounded theory today, it is because they either have problems with the logic of induction as an 'epistemological fairytale,' (Wacquant 2002) or because they see it as an excuse to present generalized themes without needing to deeply engage with current sociological theory, a nod towards rigor rather than an engagement with the field.

Grounded theory is good at answering the question: *what is the story here?* It tells us what is going on in a research project and opens up analytical possibilities. It does not tell us, however, why these themes matter sociologically, substantively, or theoretically. Grounded theory does not have an answer to the question: '*what is this a case of?*' Although it promises to lead researchers in this direction, its formalization had often stood in the way of such a move. It has trouble telling us why the opened-up themes and ethno-narratives affect our theoretical understanding of the world.

In order to increase the chance of a research project ending in innovative theories, we need to recognize a different mode of inquiry: abduction. And we need to appropriate the prevailing methodological strengths of grounded theory for the purpose of abductive reasoning. Finally, abductive analysis is an attempt to answer the contemporary challenge of theorizing qualitative data, a challenge made possible by the success of grounded theory.

Note

1 Quotes are from personal correspondence.

REFERENCES

Abrutyn, Seth and Anna S. Mueller. 2014. Are Suicidal Behaviors Contagious in Adolescence? Using Longitudinal Data to Examine Suicide Suggestion. *American Sociological Review*, *79*(2): 211–227.

Abrutyn, Seth and Anna S. Mueller. 2016. When Too Much Integration and Regulation Hurts: Re-Envisioning Durkheim's Altruistic Suicide. *Society and Mental Health*, *6*(1): 56–71.

Becker, Howard S. 1998. *Tricks of the Trade: How to Think about Your Research while You're Doing it*. Chicago, IL: University of Chicago Press.

Berger, Peter L. and Thomas Luckmann. 1966. *The Social Construction of Reality: A Treatise in the Sociology of Knowledge*. New York: Doubleday.
Blumer, Herbert. 1969. *Symbolic Interactionism: Perspective and Method*. Englewood Cliffs, NJ: Prentice-Hall.
Boltanski, Luc and Eve Chiapello. 2007. *The New Spirit of Capitalism*. London: Verso.
Bryant, Antony and Kathy Charmaz. Eds. 2007. *The SAGE Handbook of Grounded Theory*. Los Angeles, CA: Sage.
Burawoy, Michael. 1998. The Extended Case Method. *Sociological Theory*, *16*(1): 4–34.
Charmaz, Kathy. 1991. *Good Days, Bad Days: The Self in Chronic Illness and Time*. New Brunswick, NJ: Rutgers University Press.
Charmaz, Kathy. 2014. *Constructing Grounded Theory*. Thousand Oaks, CA: Sage.
Clarke, Adele. 2005. *Situational Analysis: Grounded theory after the Postmodern Turn*. Thousand Oaks, CA: Sage.
Culyba, R. J., C. A. Heimer, and J. C. Petty. 2004. The Ethnographic Turn: Fact, Fashion or Fiction. *Qualitative Sociology*, *27*(4): 365–389.
Duneier, Mitchel. 2004. Scrutinizing the Heat: On Ethnic Myths and the Importance of Shoe Leather. *Contemporary Sociology*, *33*(2): 139–150.
Eliasoph, Nina. 1998. *Avoiding Politics: How Americans Produce Apathy in Everyday Life*. Cambridge: Cambridge University Press.
Eliasoph, Nina. 2011. *Making Volunteers: Civic Life after Welfare's End*. Princeton, NJ: Princeton University Press.
Eliasoph, Nina. 2016. The Mantra of Empowerment Talk. *Journal of Civil Society*, *12*(3): 247–265.
Eliasoph, Nina and Lichterman Paul. 2003. Culture in Interaction. *American Journal of Sociology*, *108*(4): 735–794.
Garfinkel, Harold. 1967. *Studies in Ethnomethodology*. Oxford: Blackwell.
Glaser, Barney. 1978. *Theoretical Sensitivity*. San Francisco, CA: Sociology Press.
Glaser, Barney G. and Anselm L. Strauss. 1965. *Awareness of Dying*. Chicago, IL: Aldine.
Glaser, Barney G. and Anselm L. Strauss. 1967. *The Discovery of Grounded Theory*. New York: Aldine.
Hartshorne, Charles, Paul Weiss, and Arthur Burks. Eds. 1931–1958. *Collected Papers of Charles Sanders Peirce* (*8 vols*). Cambridge, MA: Harvard University Press.
Katz, Jack. 2001. Analytical Induction. In N. J. Smelser and P. B. Baltes (Eds.), *International Encyclopedia of the Social and Behavioral Sciences* (*vol. 1*, pp. 480–484). Oxford: Elsevier.
Luo, Liying, James Hodges, Christopher Winship, and Daniel Powers. 2016. The Sensitivity of the Intrinsic Estimator to Coding Schemes: Comment on Yang, Schulhofer-Wohl, Fu, and Land. *American Journal of Sociology*, *122*(3): 930–961.
Mamo, Laura 1999. Death and Dying: Confluences of Emotion and Awareness. *Sociology of Health and Illness*, *21*(1): 13–39.
Mueller, Anna S. and Seth Abrutyn. 2015. Suicidal Disclosures among Friends: Using Social Network Data to Understand Suicide Suggestion. *Journal of Health and Social Behavior*, *56*(1): 131–148.
Mueller, Anna S. and Seth Abrutyn. 2016. Adolescents under Pressure: A New Durkheimian Framework for Understanding Adolescent Suicide in a Cohesive Community. *American Sociological Review*, *81*(5): 877–899.
Popper, Karl. 1959. *The Logic of Scientific Discovery*. New York: Harper.
Shklovsky, Victor. 1965 [1917]. Art as Technique. In L. T. Lemon and M. Reiss (Eds.), *Russian Formalist Criticism* (pp. 3–25). Lincoln, NB: University of Nebraska Press.
Star, S. Leigh and Anselm Strauss. 1999. Layers of Silence, Arenas of Voice: The Ecology of Visible and Invisible Work. *Computer Supported Cooperative Work*, *8*(1): 9–30.
Strauss, Anselm L. 1959. *Mirrors and Masks: The Search for Identity.* Glencoe, Ill: Free Press.
Strauss, Anselm L. 1987. *Qualitative Analysis for Social Scientists*. Cambridge: Cambridge University Press.
Strauss, Anselm L. 1993. *Continual Permutations of Action*. New York: Aldine de Gruyter.

Strauss, Anselm L. and Juliet Corbin. 1990. *Basics of Qualitative Research*. Newbury Park, CA: Sage.

Swedberg, Richard. 2012. Theorizing in Sociology and Social Science: Turning to the Context of Discovery. *Theory and Society*, *41*(1): 1–40.

Tavory, Iddo and Nina Eliasoph. 2013. Coordinating Futures: Towards a Theory of Anticipation. *American Journal of Sociology*, *118*(4): 908–942.

Tavory, Iddo and Stefan Timmermans. 2009. Two Cases of Ethnography: Grounded Theory and the Extended Case Method. *Ethnography*, *10*: 1–21.

Tavory, Iddo and Stefan Timmermans. 2013. A Pragmatist Approach to Causality in Ethnography. *American Journal of Sociology*, *119*(3): 682–714.

Tavory, Iddo and Stefan Timmermans. 2014. *Abductive Analysis: Theorizing Qualitative Research*. Chicago, IL: University of Chicago Press.

Timmermans, Stefan. 1994. Dying of Awareness: The Theory of Awareness Contexts Revisited. *Sociology of Health and Illness*, *16*(3), 322–336.

Timmermans, Stefan, and Iddo Tavory. 2012. Theory Construction in Qualitative Research: From Grounded theory to Abductive Analysis. *Sociological Theory*, *30*(3): 167–186.

Wacquant, Loic. 2002. Scrutinizing the Street: Poverty, Morality, and the Pitfalls of Urban Ethnography. *American Journal of Sociology*, *107*(6): 1468–1532.

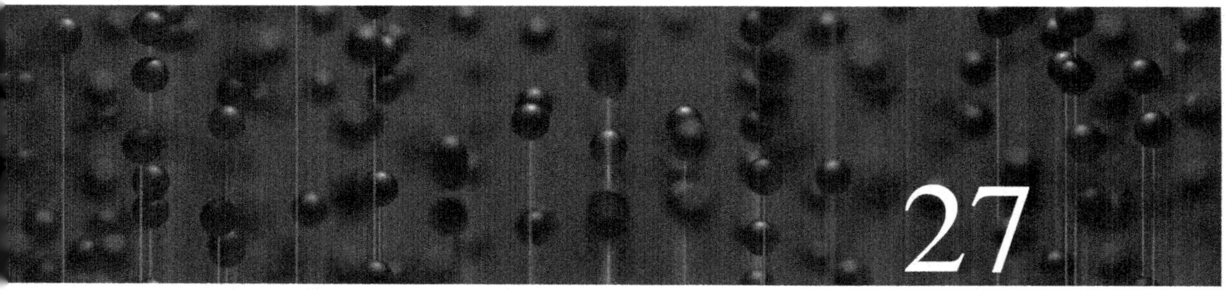

27

Grounded Theory and Empirical Ethics

Stacy M. Carter

An activist critiques the valorization of men who join the Violence Against Women Movement (Charmaz 2014: 126). A young person believes she is worthless as a result of relentless bullying at school (Charmaz 2014: 143). An employee with a disability protests that it is unfair that she should not be allowed to lie down in the office in her lunchbreak (Charmaz 2014: 145). These are all examples taken from grounded theory studies, examples that focus on the moral dimensions of social life, the everyday judgements we make about whether things are right or wrong. In this chapter I will consider how grounded theory approaches and moral considerations might be explicitly married in the doing of social research.

I will argue that explicit attention to normativity can enhance grounded theory research, but also that grounded theory, and the symbolic interactionist and pragmatist commitments that animate it, have much to offer normative theorizing. Before we proceed, some definitions. Throughout I will be referring to normativity, and normative statements, reasoning or judgements. When I use 'normative' as an adjective in this way, I am indicating a particular quality: that of expressing a prescription about how things ought to be, or an evaluation of whether actions or states of affairs are good or bad, right or wrong, laudable or blameworthy. The issues I consider in this chapter relate to an old debate about the place of normativity in social research: the degree to which social research should not only describe things or explain how they come to be, but also examine moral judgements, and perhaps even make moral prescriptions.

To illustrate the broad difference between descriptive or explanatory work, and normative work, consider the dairy industry. The former type of study could provide a detailed explanation of how the industry works: a typical day in the life of a dairy farmer or a farming family, how cows are acquired and looked after, what happens when they get sick, what happens to calves when they are born, how much farmers are paid for their milk, how it is distributed. But a study focused on the normative dimensions of dairy farming would also ask whether the treatment of the humans and the animals involved is justifiable, indeed whether the industry itself is justifiable, and on what grounds we might argue for or against that conclusion, weighing up considerations such as benefits and harms to humans and other animals, and what freedoms may be either considered absolute, or reasonably restricted.

Notice here a critical difference. The more descriptive a claim, the more it can be verified by examining evidence (*Do dairy farmers get up at 4am? Do they express a strong sense of vocation?*). The more normative a claim, the more contestable it becomes: rather than being verified using evidence, it needs to be supported with good arguments, and good arguments may be available on both sides of a question (*Is the way calves and cows are treated in this industry morally justifiable? Why or why not?*). It's useful to keep this distinction in mind. However, I will take the position throughout that the descriptive (or explanatory) and the normative are interleaved rather than dichotomous. If we don't pay attention to normative issues such as animal welfare, we may not collect adequate empirical data about them, and conversely if we don't do good empirical work, we might make moral judgements that don't adequately reflect the social process under study.

The academic discipline that traditionally concerns itself with theories of good and bad, right and wrong, is moral philosophy or ethics; a person who works in this discipline would usually be called a moral philosopher or an ethicist. For a long time, ethicists have put most of their attention into making good arguments and haven't seemed too concerned with whether those arguments related much to the world as it exists. Indeed, some ethicists seem deliberately to make their case studies unlike the social world, 'cleaning them up' in an effort to make their philosophical points more strongly (e.g., see Fried, 2012, for a critique of one such tradition). More recently, however, a rapprochement between social science and ethics has seen a greater acceptance that ethics isn't much use unless it is informed by rigorous research about the social world (De Vries 2004; Scully 2016). This is how the practice referred to as empirical ethics or empirical bioethics was born, on the border between social science and ethics, and attempting – usually – to make best use of the methods of each discipline.

My purpose here is to argue that grounded theory can benefit from engagement with empirical ethics, and that the reverse is also true. Explicit attention to ethical reasoning and values encourages normative theoretical sensitivity, presentation of counterfactuals and elicitation of moral reasoning in data collection, attention to values as significant components of most social and psychological processes, and a sophisticated approach to the problem of epistemic authority. Grounded theory can offer empirical ethicists a path to epistemological sophistication, a systematic set of empirical methods, connection to social science traditions and theories, and attention to valuing as a dynamic process. Any grounded theorist who advocates social change based on her findings takes a position on what people or institutions *ought* to do. Here I seek to make a case that the synergy between empirical ethics and grounded theory can expand both approaches, and can provide a better basis for making the *ought* statements that often arise – implicitly or explicitly – from social research.

EXISTING THEORY AND GROUNDED THEORIZING – AN UNEASY RELATIONSHIP

As the questions I'm considering here turn on the relationship between existing theory and the creation and interpretation of qualitative data, I begin briefly with this issue in the fractured grounded theory tradition. I will assume that most readers are familiar with the various forms of grounded theory and the tensions between them (e.g., Glaser and Strauss 1967; Glaser 1978, Morse et al. 2009; Corbin and Strauss 2015). I locate myself in the later, 'constructivist' traditions led by Kathy Charmaz, Antony Bryant and others (Bryant 2002; Bryant and Charmaz 2007b; Charmaz 2014). These authors explicitly developed grounded theory methodology and methods in several ways, including recognizing that data, concepts and eventual theory were co-constructions between the researcher and the participants. Theories were no longer absolute truths that somehow 'emerged' *de novo* from the data; they were active interpretations in which the analyst connected data with existing concepts and theories to create new knowledge, knowledge which may resonate with, or challenge, previous conceptualizations (Charmaz 2014). A common but somewhat naïve critique of grounded theory is that grounded theorists believe themselves to begin from nowhere, and thus fail to take advantage of centuries of theoretical development. Although a small proportion of grounded theorists may believe that they enter a new study as a blank slate and create completely original codes and categories, there is little in contemporary grounded theory methodology to support this view. As Dey has noticed in relation to grounded theory analysis, 'there is a difference between an open mind and an empty head' (Dey 1999, cited in Charmaz 2014: 48), and none of us have truly empty heads.

If this position is accepted, the important question is not whether existing theory should be used in grounded theorizing (as doing so is unavoidable), but rather which existing theory should be used, and how. It also seems reasonable to expect an analyst to be aware of and reflexive about the concepts she employs, concepts that will reflect what she thinks is worth paying attention to in the social world. I hope to make a case that values and normative reasoning are central enough to the social world to be worth our explicit analytic attention.

FACTS, VALUES AND SOCIAL RESEARCH

There is a considerable literature regarding whether social science researchers should attend to values at all. This prompts me to consider two issues: first, what I mean when I talk about values, and second, how scholars have (dis)connected facts and values.

Defining Values

What are values? To provide a starting point, I will draw on just two of the scholars who have written extensively on this question: the legal, moral and political philosopher Joseph Raz, and the critical realist social scientist Andrew Sayer. Raz defines value in this way:

> Any property which (necessarily) makes anything which possesses it good (or bad) at least to a degree is an evaluative property, standing for some value. ... We could also say that every property whose presence in an item (action, person, institution, or anything else) can in itself make an action, a choice, or a positive or negative appreciation or preference, intelligible or justified, is an evaluative property. (Raz 2001: 43–44)

Sayer defines values as follows:

> I suggest that we should think of values as 'sedimented' valuations that have become attitudes or dispositions, which we come to regard as justified. They merge into emotional dispositions and evaluations we make of particular things, as part of our conceptual and affective apparatus. They are more abstract than the particular concrete evaluations from which they derive and which they in turn influence. The relation between value and particular valuations is thus recursive. (Sayer 2011: 26)

Bringing Raz and Sayer together suggests that the value of something (to a person or a group of people) makes sense of people's positive or negative attitudes towards it; in addition, people hold values – more abstract 'sedimented' attitudes or dispositions – which inform their everyday evaluative judgements in different situations. This establishes a connection between the values people hold and the making of evaluative, or normative, judgements. Sayer's reading also draws our attention to the agency of people in the process of valuing, an inflection that will become important later in the chapter.

The Fact/Value Dichotomy and Social Research

Traditionally, a hard line has been drawn in social science and philosophy between facts and values, description and normativity, is and ought, with science (including social science) on the 'is' side, and moral judgements and prescriptions on the 'ought' side. For those committed to the hard line, discovering facts is the work of science and making prescriptions is the work of moral and political philosophy. Despite much criticism (e.g., Sayer 2011: 49–54; see also Hedgecoe 2004) this view persists in some methodological writing. There are two interconnected assumptions embedded in this way of thinking: (1) that values and facts come apart cleanly; and (2) that social researchers should focus on facts (empirically grounded description or explanation) rather than values, in their research questions, analyses and outcomes. Gewirtz and Cribb (2006) refer to this as the 'value-neutral' model of social research, and note that it can lead to different kinds of errors. On the one hand, in assuming that their research can be value-neutral, researchers may fail to recognize that there are inevitable policy and ethical implications of their work. Conversely (often in the critical tradition), researchers may leap to normative conclusions without the careful work required to justify them, demanding that 'things ought to be done differently, with insufficient attention being given either to clarifying or defending the evaluative judgements made or ... working through the feasibility of, and practical dilemmas associated with, implied alternatives' (Gewirtz and Cribb 2006: 149).

People who defend a strong fact/value distinction often connect it back to David Hume, the 18th-century Scottish enlightenment philosopher, via 'Hume's Law' or 'Hume's

Guillotine'. Hume's Law is often simplified to 'you cannot derive ought from is', and people take this to mean that it is not possible to draw normative conclusions (about what ought to be done) from empirical findings.[1] In my view, and that of others (see McMillan 2016), this is not the best interpretation. Hume seems to me simply to ask that we clearly distinguish two different types of statement – descriptive statements of fact on the one hand, and normative statements about what one ought to do on the other – and to be thoughtful about the relation between them. Hume doesn't condemn authors for making 'ought' statements: rather, he says that he often observes that people leap from a statement about how things are to a statement about how things ought to be, as though the second follows automatically from the first. Against this, he says: '…as this ought, or ought not, expresses some new relation or affirmation, it is necessary that it should be observed and explained; and at the same time that a reason should be given'. That is, researchers shouldn't just sneak the 'ought' in, but should move from is to ought mindfully and explicitly and set out clear reasons to explain how they connect the two.[2]

Hilary Putnam, the eminent late 20th-century American philosopher in the pragmatist tradition,[3] argued both against dichotomizing facts versus values, and against using this dichotomy as a trump. 'The worst thing about the fact/value dichotomy' he argued, 'is that in practice it functions as a discussion-stopper, and not just a discussion-stopper but a thought stopper' (Putnam 2002: 44). Putnam saw the fact/value dichotomy and similar binaries as modernist dogma and argued that genuine 'post-modernism' requires their abandonment, and opens up 'a whole new field of intellectual possibilities in every important area of culture' (Putnam 2002: 9). Consistent with this, most writers who reject the fact/value dichotomy see values as problematic in social research only when they are held dogmatically and without insight (Gewirtz and Cribb 2006; Sayer 2011).

So far, our focus has been on the values held by researchers, and the evaluative implications of research. Some methodologists propose another way in which values matter: that researchers should form questions, collect data, and do analysis with particular attention to the values held by the social actors they are studying. Values, this argument goes, are an intrinsic part of social life, so if researchers want to understand social life, they need to pay attention to values. Sayer, for example, argues that social science has traditionally privileged 'bloodless' analysis, in which 'macho' interests (power, discourse and structure) are privileged, while morality, values, ethics and emotions are neglected (Sayer 2011: 14–15). Turning away from this bloodlessness requires paying attention to aspects of human existence that it can be too easy to ignore: our embodiment, our relations with others, the effect of these relations on the development and maintenance of our sense of self, our caring, neediness and vulnerability, our concern and empathy for others, our attachments and commitments, our judgments about virtues, vices, good and 'evil', the things people are ashamed of and the way they allocate responsibility and blame, and our conceptions of human wellbeing (Sayer 2011: Chapters 4 and 5). Grounded theorists, perhaps especially those in the constructivist tradition, will immediately recognize these latter concerns as central to our work, suggesting a natural affinity with the project of foregrounding values.

Sayer goes further to contend not only that values are central to the social world, but that the objects of social research cannot be understood without their normative valence. To illustrate, he suggests that if a researcher or reader did not understand that suffering was bad, she could not fully understand suffering, or research about suffering. Suffering is one of those concepts – like oppression, racism, humiliation, cruelty, respect, vulnerability and many others – that require both conceptual depth and empirical detail to be fully understood. They are 'thick' ethical concepts, which, after Iris Murdoch, Sayer contrasts with labels such as good, bad or duty, thinner and more abstracted evaluative words that may lack the same depth and force (Sayer 2011: 42–43). As McMillan (2016: 27) has argued, thick ethical concepts belie any fact/value dichotomy: they are both factual, in that we can determine whether or not they are occurring, and evaluative or normative, in that they give us a reason to act. I am not suggesting a hard line between thin and thick concepts here, rather I am suggesting that engaging with the moral detail of everyday life is likely to land us in 'thicker' territory than simply theorizing in the abstract.

Thicker ethical concepts and the processes by which they are enacted, I contend, are the natural subject matter of grounded theory research, and provide an immediate point of connection between grounded theory traditions and normative work. The grounded theory tradition of focusing on concepts and exploring what they mean to people in the contexts of their lives can thus contribute significantly to ethical conceptual development. However, in my view, grounded theorists often have limited resources with which to engage these values, because they are not often the focus of social science disciplines. It is here that the ethics literature can help. Say, for example, that it becomes apparent that feelings of vulnerability or invulnerability are important to the way people evaluate a certain problem. These feelings can be interrogated by a researcher in an interview, and again in analysis. But if the researcher is aware of the way in which vulnerability is constructed in the ethics literature, they are likely to be in a better position to ask insightful questions and test the boundaries of the concept (Carter et al. 2010; Rogers, Mackenzie, and Dodds 2012). I am arguing here about concepts from the ethics literature but note the resonance with those grounded theorists who have made similar arguments that researchers need to understand the existing social science literature on a problem before they set out to create a new theory about it (Lempert 2007: 254).

For the remainder of this chapter I will take the position of contemporary scholars who see normativity as more or less inevitable in social science, and advocate its deliberate inclusion, with reflexivity and care. Gewirtz and Cribb (2006), for example, advocate ethical reflexivity in social research, which in their view entails:

1. Being explicit about the evaluative commitments and judgements that inform the research;
2. Being able to defend these;
3. Taking the values and moral dilemmas of participants seriously;
4. Acknowledging and responding to tensions between values; and
5. Taking responsibility for the moral and political implications of one's research. (Gewirtz and Cribb 2006: 147–148)

This list provides some sense of what is required to work explicitly with normativity, and takes us to the question of how to integrate the methods of grounded theory with a normative theoretical sensitivity.

WAYS OF WORKING WITH IS AND OUGHT

I have already introduced empirical ethics, which has used social science methods to address normative questions since around the turn of the millennium. Researchers in this new form of practice have generated both methodology (e.g., Molewijk et al. 2003; De Vries 2004; Solomon 2005; Leget, Borry, and De Vries 2009; Rehmann-Sutter, Porz, and Scully 2012; Davies, Ives, and Dunn 2015) and practical research work (e.g., Ives et al. 2008; Molewijk et al. 2008; Scully et al. 2012; Brosnan et al. 2013; Haire and Jordens 2015; Williams, Carter, and Rychetnik 2017) that is likely to be of interest to grounded theorists.

Ethics is the reference discipline for empirical ethicists. While the majority of social scientists may have agreed to put the caricatured form of Hume's Law out of its misery some time ago, for many ethicists it is not only alive and well but standing in the middle of the room shouting and making rude hand gestures. Thus, much empirical ethics methodology is focused on placating those within ethics and philosophy who continue to take the 'no ought from is' position seriously. Philosophers accustomed to having only to think for a living have reacted in a range of ways to the 'empirical turn' (Hurst 2010), as it is known, ranging from embracing its power and novelty to expressing outright hostility and disdain. And while many social researchers probably remain unaware of this nascent movement, some – perhaps those with prior training in ethics, or with a particular moral sensibility, or those who happen to be professionally co-located with ethicists – have embraced the opportunity to examine the ethical dimensions of the social worlds they are studying more explicitly.

The 'empirical turn' was inspired in part by the work of sociologists including Charles Bosk (1992, 2003, 2010), Renée Fox (Fox, Swazey, and Watkins 2008) and Barry Hoffmaster (1992), medical sociologists who tended to be critical of bioethicists (De Vries 2004). This history means that the empirical turn in bioethics is in part a dialogue between the discipline of sociology (or social science more broadly) and the discipline of bioethics. De Vries, for example, typologizes empirical bioethics research on a spectrum from 'sociology in bioethics' to 'sociology of bioethics' (De Vries 2004). Sociology in bioethics, in De Vries' typology, captures social science work that serves bioethics, for example studying how ethics interventions such as Institutional Review Boards work in practice. De Vries notes that this work can be done while still assuming a clear separation between facts and values: the philosophers remain in charge of the moral reasoning; the purpose of social science is to discover facts. At the 'sociology of bioethics' end of the spectrum, in contrast, facts and values are inseparable. Studies of the implicit normativity in medical work, for example (often in the Social Studies of Science tradition), or openly critical empirical study of the discipline of bioethics itself (such as the work of Bosk, Fox, and Hoffmaster referred to earlier), problematize the instantiation of values and the moral authority of bioethicists.

Hedgecoe characterizes the critique arising from such sociological analyses of bioethics as follows: that bioethics over-emphasizes rational and idealized modes of thinking; that bioethics over-individualizes, neglecting social and cultural influences on action; and that bioethics assumes that the theoretical categories defined in moral philosophy are all that is needed to understand the social world (that 'social reality cleaves down neat philosophical lines'), which leads bioethicists to miss much of what is important in everyday moral judgements and actions (Hedgecoe 2004). Astute readers will notice some parallels between this sociological critique of bioethics and the original grounded theory critique of deductive quantitative sociology (Glaser and Strauss 1967). In particular, *Discovery* was a rhetorical statement against over-reliance on deductive inquiry constrained by commitment to a particular sociological theory, on the grounds that such deductively-driven work was likely to miss the meanings that explained people's actions from their perspectives. This parallel suggests that the five decades of work done in launching and then refining grounded theory could be informative for the development of empirical bioethics (Bryant and Charmaz 2007a). Grounded theorists have wrestled, for example, with issues including how to connect existing theory to the analysis of empirical data (Lempert 2007; Reichertz 2007), how to think about particularity and generality (Carter 2009; Charmaz 2014), and more generally how to make a case for finely-grained empirical work in the face of a discipline dominated by the exegesis and reproduction of existing grand theory: all of these conversations seem to have relevance for empirical ethics.

Later developments in empirical ethics have tended to focus on how to achieve a practical and productive enmeshing of philosophy and social science in such a way that neither partner is subservient to the other (Hedgecoe 2004). Various proposals for how to achieve this are currently in play in the developing methodological literature. Methodological principles again resonate with grounded theory traditions. Hedgecoe (2004), for example, proposes that this new discipline should be empirically grounded, theory-challenging as well as theory-informed, sceptical of authority and received ways of knowing, and reflexive, all values familiar to grounded theorists. A number of typologies have been proposed for empirical ethics. Molewijk and colleagues (2004), for example, contrasted five approaches, the distinction between them hinging on: (1) the relationship between moral theory and data; (2) the use of inductive, deductive or case-based reasoning with data; and (3) the degree to which moral authority is located in social practice or existing moral theory. They advocate an integrated empirical ethics, in which theorizing is seen as a social practice, moral authority is grounded in experience, and there is a strong interaction and co-constitution between moral theorizing and empirical work. A decade later, Davies and colleagues (2015) extended Molewijk's analysis by conducting a systematic review of integrated empirical ethics work. They found 32 distinct methodologies in use, which they arranged in a spectrum between dialogical approaches and consultative approaches. In dialogic approaches, stakeholders and researchers enter into dialogue to reach a shared understanding and pursue analysis and a conclusion together: the value of these methodologies is argued via something like democratic legitimacy.[4] Qualitative approaches, such as action research and community-based participatory research, and deliberative democratic methods, such as community or citizens juries, are examples. In consultative approaches, an external 'thinker' undertakes data collection and then independently analyses that data and draws normative conclusions from it. The work practices in these latter consultative approaches are closer to the work practices traditional in grounded theory.[5]

How might grounded theory meet this much newer tradition of empirical bioethics? It is my contention that grounded theory has a lot to offer empirical bioethics, and that empirical bioethics can extend grounded theory research to more explicitly consider the important moral dimensions of social life. In the remaining sections, I make three points to support this view. The first is that, whether or not it is acknowledged, grounded theory arises from a philosophical and social tradition that is heavily normatively inflected. The second is that grounded theory researchers could learn to more explicitly attend to the normative dimensions of social life, and include these in our conceptual analyses. Finally, I will suggest that the relatively young empirical ethics movement could be enriched by a greater awareness of grounded theory traditions.

GROUNDED THEORY ARISES FROM A NORMATIVELY-INFLECTED THEORETICAL TRADITION

In this section I will take as given the common view that grounded theory is, at least in part, a way of putting symbolic interactionism into research practice: that grounded theory offers, in the words of Charmaz, Clarke, and others, a 'theory methods package' with symbolic interactionism and pragmatism (Clarke 2005; Star 2007; Bryant 2009; Charmaz 2014: Chapter 10). The focus in making this link tends to be two-fold. The first is epistemological, refuting 'view from nowhere' or 'spectator' views of knowledge, and instead – in keeping with pragmatist epistemologies – taking knowledge to be a fallible tool actively created for the practical purpose of coping with the world (Bryant 2009). The second focus is to introduce a particular social ontology, creating, in Blumer's terms, 'lines along which to look' in data collection and analysis (Blumer 1954). Interactionist theory, for example, might lead a researcher to: (1) see actions, interactions and relationality as central to human life; (2) see the social world as dynamic and processual, rather than as being deterministically caused by static traits or conditions; (3) understand all human action in the context of the situations in which it occurs; (4) see people as active, thinking, interpreting, meaning-making beings; and (5) understand actions and interactions as both constituting and being shaped by the meanings humans ascribe to objects (Blumer 1969; Charon 2010; Charmaz 2014). On the interactionist view, social reality is obdurate, but can be understood only through our interpretations and perspectives. Social groups share perspectives that shape individual group members' definitions of situations, and thus their actions; a recursive relationship exists between individual interpretations and actions and these shared perspectives. The symbolic objects animating our actions include our selves: we are simultaneously subject and object, acting on our self as an object, with an eye to the way we are viewed by others (Blumer 1969; Charon 2010; Charmaz 2014). Whether or not they are aware of their theoretical origins, grounded theorists (at least in the constructivist tradition) are likely to absorb these commitments via the methodology and method. Grounded theory will, for example, encourage them to approach the social world with curiosity about and openness to participants' meanings and perspectives, focus on action and process, and expect and study change (Charmaz 2014: 263–265).

What is often missed in this attention to the pragmatist and interactionist roots of grounded theory is the extent to which these are normatively inflected. American pragmatists, such as William James and John Dewey, provided the bedrock of interactionism. They were as likely to be theorizing ethics as epistemology, and saw the two as linked. Ruth Anna Putnam argues that 'James and Dewey developed their philosophies precisely in response to the passionate desire to make sense of our moral lives, of the importance of moral values as well as the anguish caused by moral conflict'. In her view, this moral impulse 'explains their metaphysical and epistemological positions as well as their account of value inquiry' (R. A. Putnam 2009: 279). Dewey advocated the application of an 'active, fallibilistic, experimental inquiry in moral questions', and held that understandings of the good needed to both respond to people's experience of particular consequences in situations and provide intelligent critique or evaluation of these, without dogmatism or appeals to authority (H. Putnam 2009: 270–272). Thus, a pragmatist philosophy relies on empirical work: its claims, including its moral claims, should be subjected to empirical examination. These strong moral-empirical threads in pragmatism suggest the possibility of a normative inflected grounded theory.

So too does the problem-orientation of pragmatism. As both pragmatist philosophers (R. A. Putnam 2009) and grounded theory methodologists (Strübing 2007) have noted, inquiry in pragmatism – particularly Dewey's pragmatism – was prompted by problems that interrupted habitual forms of action. This was carried forward into Mead's interactionism (Strübing 2007). On this view, inquiry of any kind 'is prompted when one finds oneself in a problematic or indeterminate situation … when, for one reason or another, we cannot go on in habitual ways' (R. A. Putnam 2009: 286). It is commonly observed that grounded theory is centrally concerned with problems and their resolution, and this can be traced back to these pragmatist roots: moral inquiry in pragmatism and social inquiry in grounded theory respectively become most necessary when such problems arise (R. A. Putnam 2009; Charmaz 2014). Charmaz's methodological writing gestures to this problem-orientation and its moral dimensions in grounded theory. Drawing on Shibutani, she notes that problems arise when people find themselves conflicted because of irreconcilable desires, demands or directions, their current practices cannot resolve this conflict, and 'the problem lies outside of their existing normative framework': it is in these problematic situations that Blumer's active, inquiring self is most likely to emerge (Charmaz 2014: 271).

These normative inflections can be observed not only in contemporary grounded theory studies, as observed at the outset of this chapter, but also in the roots and establishment of grounded theory. Chicago School teachers such as Everett C. Hughes and Robert Park encouraged their students to engage not only with the powerful but also with those socially constructed as deviant, and to demonstrate the ways in which, from their shared perspective, these peoples' social worlds made sense. Park famously exhorted his students to 'go sit on the lounges of the luxury hotels and on the doorsteps of the flophouses; sit on the gold coast settees and the slum shakedowns; sit in the orchestra hall and in the Star and Garter burlesque … get the seat of your pants dirty in real research (McKinney 1966: 71)'.[6] And Hughes is perhaps best-known for his maxim 'humble the proud and elevate the humble' (Bosk 1992: x). These snippets of the past show a fundamental ethical impulse in Chicago-inspired traditions: to pay respectful attention to those whom society might systematically shun or oppress. Chicago School urban ethnography was a morally-inflected project mapping the ways in which the rapidly changing city became geographically and socially patterned, and the effect this had on the least well-off (Bulmer 1984). Many iconic interactionist studies (think here of *Boys in White*, or *Stigma*) dealt with subjects of direct relevance to bioethics (Becker et al. 1961; Goffman 1963; De Vries 2004). And as is well known, grounded theory itself began with an in-depth study of the process of dying, a theme that remains central in bioethics (Glaser and Strauss 1968; McMillan 2016). All of this suggests that issues of normative significance fall within the everyday territory of the grounded theorist, practically and theoretically.

EXPLICITLY INCORPORATING VALUES AND NORMATIVITY INTO GROUNDED THEORIZING

However, grounded theory studies, like much of social science (Sayer 2011), tend not to confront this normativity directly, preferring to focus on explaining how things happen and what things mean without explicitly theorizing the moral and values-oriented aspects of social life. In this section I want to argue that empirical ethics and value-rich social science can offer three things to grounded theory. The first is an additional depth to data collection, retaining openness but encouraging the presentation of counterfactuals and elicitation of moral reasoning. The second is a new kind of theoretical sensitivity: to normative concepts and questions, which will encourage greater attention to values as significant components in most social and psychological processes. The final benefit is to strengthen the sophisticated approach to the problem of epistemic authority already available in pragmatist traditions.

How can a normatively inflected grounded theory add depth to data collection? By encouraging active elicitation of moral reasoning. Much like the previously mentioned confusion of open minds with empty heads, in data collection it is easy to confuse openness with blankness. Being a sensitive and supportive interviewer does not require being a silent sponge. I find it helpful to ask explicitly about people's moral experience with questions such as: 'Who is the person you most admire [in this situation]? Tell me about them.' 'What are you most proud of in this program? What is it about that that makes you proud?' 'Think about a time when you were asked to do something at work that you thought was wrong. Tell me about that.' Counterfactuals, a strong part of the philosophical tradition, can also be useful in qualitative data collection, as observed by Ives (2008), and can be introduced in a non-confrontational way that does not undermine the interviewing relationship. If an interviewee puts one of several possible conflicting moral positions, for example, the interviewer can recount a conflicting view that 'some people' take and invite a response to that view. This takes us to my second point: an interviewer can only put counterfactuals if they are theoretically sensitized to normative concepts and questions. It is impossible to do with an out-dated 'empty head' version of grounded theory, in which the literature is largely unknown. As Lempert suggests: 'in order to participate in the current theoretical conversation, [the researcher] needs to understand it' (2007: 254). I would contend that a values-oriented grounded theorist needs to be familiar enough both with ethical theories and with empirical findings on the substantive topic under study that they can make and interrogate important connections, ideally during the initial interview, or alternatively during follow up interviews.[7]

Recall Davies and colleagues' contrast between consultative and dialogic methods in empirical bioethics (2015). The third benefit of normativity in grounded theory may be to foreground the strong connection between ethics and epistemology in the pragmatist tradition (H. Putnam 2009), and thus to begin to connect the consultative and dialogic. I contend that good grounded theory research will have elements of both: it will be dialogic enough that the final theory is credible to the community of practice it pertains to, but consultative in that a researcher or small team of researchers are likely to produce a theoretical 'whole' that is larger, and possibly more abstract, than the sum of the individual data sources that are its parts. It's possible that normative theorizing – perhaps more than social theorizing – does not allow the theorist to slip between the cracks of epistemic authority. A normative argument is an argument about what ought to be. Arguments about what ought to be – perhaps more than arguments about how the social world works – are part of everyday discourse. A reasonable and common response to such an argument is thus 'according to whom?' or 'on whose authority?' Rehmann-Sutter and colleagues, considering this problem for empirical bioethics, observed:

> ...it would be a shortcoming in the argument if we (as researchers) were to conclude that an argument Q is valid just because people in the interviews said so. If we make a validity claim about a moral argument, we need to argue for it. In other words, as researchers who have learned what might be valid excuses and arguments for the participants, we then need to reconstruct the argument in our own terms. We need to present it to ourselves and then to our readers in papers or talks in a form that is generally accessible to criticism. Here, then, the credibility of a normative conclusion depends on the quality of the ethical argument of the bioethicist. To be very clear: it is the researcher/bioethicist who explicitly produces the ethical argument. The information provided by qualitative empirical studies contributes to the conditions that make it possible to evaluate these arguments and the conclusions drawn from them, but as ethical researchers making normative claims, we cannot hide behind the interviewees or what they have said. We need to be clear that it is our normative argument, in the end. (Rehmann-Sutter, Porz, and Scully 2012: 440)

This echoes Putnam's account of Dewey on 'warranted valuation' (Putnam 2002: 103–109). The fact that something is valued, Dewey argued, did not make it valuable. Only criticism, intelligent reflection, can determine whether something we value is indeed valuable. This will be done on the background of all of the facts we know and the values we already hold, draws on all forms of knowledge (lay knowledge, scientific knowledge and philosophical knowledge), will be open to all possible hypotheses, and will be able to be responsibly defended, whether through empirical testing or close analysis. We should employ fallibilism, be willing to test different ways of resolving problems, and democratize inquiry as best we can by observing something similar to discourse ethics, which was presaged by the pragmatist G. H. Mead, and most famously developed by the political philosopher Jürgen Habermas (Bohman and Rehg 2014). A values-oriented grounded theory, then, asks about values, interrogates value positions, resists suppression of competing value positions in developing an understanding. However, to return to our earlier discussion of the difference between criteria for evaluating grounded and normative theories respectively: as Rehmann-Sutter and colleagues argue above, the researcher herself is eventually required to arrive at a defensible normative position. And this position needs to have those qualities earlier described such as coherence and recourse to good reasons. A plurality of values may be relevant, and should be empirically described, but empirical ethics generally resists relativism. Values and valuations are taken to require justification: it accepted that some reasons and values may be better than others.

EXPLICITLY INCORPORATING GROUNDED THEORY METHODOLOGY INTO EMPIRICAL ETHICS

So far we have considered what empirical ethics can offer grounded theory. Grounded theory and its theoretical roots also have much to offer empirical bioethics. Many empirical ethicists are new to empirical work, and grounded theory offers them a flexible, systematic method with sound methodological underpinnings and considerable analytic power. Grounded theory, in its attention to agency and action, can also highlight the processual and situational nature of valuing and evaluating. Recall the two definitions of 'values' with which I began this chapter. Sayer (2011), the social scientist, emphasizes the place of the agent in valuing. Raz (2001), the philosopher, defines a value as an attribute of an entity. Pragmatic and interactionist theory guides us towards the more situated and processual version: towards valuing as a human activity. This helpfully orients us away from excessively deductive approaches to empirical ethics, and towards understanding how and why valuing varies in human reasoning and action, informed by intensive data collection and analysis.

This leads us to a considerable contribution that I believe grounded theory and its antecedents can make to empirical ethics. As discussed earlier, empirical ethics researchers – because of our disciplinary location – worry at length about deriving ought from is. Let us assume that social research can usefully inform normative reasoning. Bioethicists have strong and differing opinions, and endless debates, over the soundness and applicability of competing moral theories. Interestingly, though, they do not often trouble the social ontology underpinning their work, despite the fact that their research questions are questions about how valuing and moral judgement operates *in the social world*. Thus, their work frequently contains implicit social ontologies: conceptions of the self, of institutions, of relationships, and so on. To choose an easy target, much normative theorizing assumes the same vision of the self that qualitative researchers have railed against for decades: the independent, rational, implicitly male agent, uninhibited by the messiness of relationships and affect, always analytic and acting only on principle. It is not necessary to rehearse the arguments against this impoverished view here; suffice to say that interactionist notions of the self resonate with, and have much to add to, more contemporary views within bioethics, including those that emphasize that autonomy exists only in a network of conditions that arise from our social, institutional and relational positioning (Mackenzie 2014).

Just as empirical ethics can perhaps teach grounded theorists to be explicitly rather than implicitly normative, grounded theory could bring to empirical ethics a more reflexive and detailed view of the workings of the social world. And grounded theory, in its attention to detail, situations and meanings, is well placed to fulfil the many promises of empirical work for bioethics: to make bioethics more effective by connecting it to practice, to test the claims of moral theory (such as whether consequences occur, and whether formal moral principles are relevant to situated actors), and to reveal previously undetected moral problems (Solomon 2005).

CONCLUSIONS

My goal in this chapter was to demonstrate that a relationship between empirical ethics and grounded theory could be mutually beneficial. Grounded theories often implicitly incorporate processes of moral evaluation; empirical ethics often implicitly incorporates a view of the social world. By thoughtfully connecting the two, a more complete and powerful analysis is possible. Any grounded theorist who advocates social change based on her findings takes a position on what ought to be done. Through collaboration or self-expansion, the application of grounded theory methodology to empirical ethics research can provide both a foundation for and enrichment of our understanding of the moral dimensions of social life, and, in my view, can benefit grounded theorists, empirical ethicists, and those for whom their research has relevance.

Notes

1 Hume's Law was not expressed by Hume as a law – it is an almost throwaway remark in his *A Treatise of Human Nature: Being an Attempt to Introduce the Experimental Method of Reasoning*

into Moral Subjects, published (anonymously) in 1739. In full, the 'law' reads as follows: *I cannot forbear adding to these reasonings an observation, which may, perhaps, be found of some importance. In every system of morality, which I have hitherto met with, I have always remarked, that the author proceeds for some time in the ordinary way of reasoning, and establishes the being of a God, or makes observations concerning human affairs; when of a sudden I am surprized to find, that instead of the usual copulations of propositions, is, and is not, I meet with no proposition that is not connected with an ought, or an ought not. This change is imperceptible; but is, however, of the last consequence. For as this ought, or ought not, expresses some new relation or affirmation, it is necessary that it should be observed and explained; and at the same time that a reason should be given, for what seems altogether inconceivable, how this new relation can be a deduction from others, which are entirely different from it. But as authors do not commonly use this precaution, I shall presume to recommend it to the readers; and am persuaded, that this small attention would subvert all the vulgar systems of morality, and let us see, that the distinction of vice and virtue is not founded merely on the relations of objects, nor is perceived by reason* (Hume 1739, Book III Section I Part I).

2 See McMillan (2016) for a more detailed argument about Hume's body of work, particularly that Hume's radical epistemology may remove any basis for making moral claims, and as such should be employed with caution.

3 Although Putnam made significant contributions to pragmatist thought, he refused to call himself a pragmatist. He was notable for his non-dogmatism, regularly changing his views on important matters and remaining open to challenge until the end of his career.

4 Legitimacy generally requires that certain ideal conditions be met that satisfy the requirements for due process: for example, that a wide range of – or even all – relevant stakeholders have been included and had a chance to participate, and that the conclusions are based on reasons that would be recognized by most or all stakeholders as relevant.

5 Importantly, although the work practices of consultative empirical ethics and usual grounded theory research look similar prima facie in that they involve the researcher taking responsibility for the analysis and conclusions, the criteria for evaluating the knowledge produced are different. An ethical argument is evaluated by the criteria common in the discipline of philosophy: for example, whether the argument provides a reasonable fit with considered moral intuitions, whether it is supported by a plausible rationale, whether it is coherent. It may be possible to produce sound ethical arguments on either side of the same question. A grounded theory, on the other hand, is evaluated according to its usefulness, completeness, reflection of variation in the social world and other such criteria. Although the theoretical and personal resources available to the researcher will always shape the theory produced, one would hope that two grounded theories about the same problem would not reach radically different conclusions.

6 Quotation unpublished by Park, recorded by Howard Becker while a graduate student at Chicago in the 1920s.

7 See Charmaz (2014: 210–212) for some examples of grounded theorists taking a more active or even challenging role in interviewing.

REFERENCES

Becker, H., B. Geer, E. C. Hughes, and A. Strauss. 1961. *Boys in White: Student Culture in Medical School*. Chicago, IL: University of Chicago Press.

Blumer, H. 1954. What is wrong with social theory? *American Sociological Review 19*(1): 3–10. doi: 10.2307/2088165.

Blumer, H. 1969. *Symbolic Interactionism: Perspective and Method*. Berkeley, CA: University of California Press.

Bohman, J., and W. Rehg. 2014. Jürgen Habermas. In E. N. Zalta (Ed.), *The Stanford Encyclopedia of Philosophy*. https://plato.stanford.edu/archives/fall2014/entries/habermas/.

Bosk, C. L. 1992. *All God's Mistakes: Genetic Counseling in a Pediatric Hospital*. Chicago, IL: University of Chicago Press.

Bosk, C. L. 2003. *Forgive and Remember: Managing Medical Failure* (2nd ed.). Chicago, IL: University of Chicago Press.

Bosk, C. L. 2010. Bioethics, raw and cooked. *Journal of Health and Social Behavior 51*(1 suppl.): S133.

Brosnan, C., A. Cribb, S. P. Wainwright, and C. Williams. 2013. Neuroscientists' everyday experiences of ethics: The interplay of regulatory, professional, personal and tangible ethical spheres. *Sociology of Health & Illness 35*(8): 1133–1148.

Bryant, A. 2002. Re-grounding grounded theory. *The Journal of Information Technology Theory and Application 4*: 25–42.

Bryant, A. 2009. Grounded theory and pragmatism: The curious case of Anselm Strauss. *Forum: Qualitative Social Research*, *10*(3), July. Available at: www.qualitative-research.net/index.php/fqs/article/view/1358. Date accessed: 21 September 2017.

Bryant, A., and K. Charmaz. 2007a. Grounded theory in historical perspective: An epistemological account. In A. Bryant and K. Charmaz (Eds.), *The SAGE Handbook of Grounded Theory* (pp. 31–57). London and Thousand Oaks, CA: Sage.

Bryant, A., and K. Charmaz. 2007b. Grounded theory research: Methods and practices. In A. Bryant and K. Charmaz (Eds.), *The SAGE Handbook of Grounded Theory* (pp. 1–28). London and Thousand Oaks, CA: Sage.

Bulmer, M. 1984. *The Chicago School of Sociology: Institutionalization, Diversity, and the Rise of Sociological Research*. Chicago, IL: University of Chicago Press.

Carter, S. M. 2009. Beware dichotomies and grand abstractions: Attending to particularity and practice in empirical bioethics. *American Journal of Bioethics 9*(6–7): 76–77.

Carter, S. M., G. N. Samuel, I. Kerridge, R. Day, R. A. Ankeny, C. F. C. Jordens, and P. Komesaroff. 2010. Beyond rhetoric in debates about the ethics of marketing prescription medicines to consumers: The importance of vulnerability in people, situations, and relationships. *AJOB Primary Research 1*(1): 11–21.

Charmaz, K. 2014. *Constructing Grounded Theory* (2nd ed.). London: Sage.

Charon, J. M. 2010. *Symbolic Interationsim: An Introduction, an Interpretation, an Integration* (10th ed.). Upper Saddle River, NJ: Prentice-Hall.

Clarke, A. E. 2005. *Situational Analysis: Grounded Theory after the Postmodern Turn*. Thousand Oaks, CA: Sage.

Corbin, J. M., and A. L. Strauss. 2015. *Basics of Qualitative Research: Techniques and Procedures for Developing Grounded Theory* (4th ed.). Thousand Oaks, CA: Sage.

Davies, R., J. Ives, and M. Dunn. 2015. A systematic review of empirical bioethics methodologies. *BMC Medical Ethics 16*: 15.

De Vries, R. 2004. How can we help? From 'sociology in' to 'sociology of' bioethics. *The Journal of Law, Medicine & Ethics 32*(2): 279–292.

Dey, I. 1999. *Grounding Grounded Theory*. San Diego, CA: Academic Press.

Fox, R. C., J. P. Swazey, and J. C. Watkins. 2008. *Observing Bioethics*. Oxford & New York: Oxford University Press.

Fried, B. H. 2012. What does matter? The case for killing the trolley problem (or letting it die). *The Philosophical Quarterly 62*(248): 505–529.

Gewirtz, S., and A. Cribb. 2006. What to do about values in social research: The case for ethical reflexivity in the sociology of education. *British Journal of Sociology of Education 27*(2): 141–155.

Glaser, B. G. 1978. *Theoretical Sensitivity*. Mill Valley: CA: Sociology Press.

Glaser, B. G., and A. L. Strauss. 1967. *The Discovery of Grounded Theory*. Chicago, IL: Aldine.

Glaser, B. G., and A. L. Strauss. 1968. *Time for Dying*. Chicago, IL: Aldine.

Goffman, E. 1963. *Stigma: Notes on the Management of Spoiled Identity*. New York: Simon & Schuster.

Haire, B., and C. Jordens. 2015. Mind the gap: An empirical study of post-trial access in HIV biomedical prevention trials. *Developing World Bioethics 15*(2): 85–97.

Hedgecoe, A. M. 2004. Critical bioethics: Beyond the social science critique of applied ethics. *Bioethics 18*(2): 120–143.

Hoffmaster, B. 1992. Can ethnography save the life of medical ethics? *Social Science and Medicine 35*(12): 1421–1431.

Hume, D. 1739. *A Treatise of Human Nature: Being an Attempt to Introduce the Experimental Method of Reasoning into Moral Subjects*. Available at: http://ebooks.adelaide.edu.au/h/hume/david/h92t/index.html: eBooks@Adelaide.

Hurst, S. 2010. What 'empirical turn in bioethics'? *Bioethics 24*(8): 439–444.

Ives, J. 2008. 'Encounters with experience': Empirical bioethics and the future. *Health Care Analysis 16*(1): 1–6.

Ives, J., H. Draper, H. Pattison, and C. Williams. 2008. Becoming a father/refusing fatherhood: An empirical bioethics approach to paternal responsibilities and rights. *Clinical Ethics 3*(2): 75–84.

Leget, C., P. Borry, and R. De Vries. 2009. 'Nobody tosses a dwarf!': The relation between the empirical and the normative re-examined. *Bioethics 23*(4): 226–235.

Lempert, L. B. 2007. Asking questions of the data: Memo writing in the grounded theory tradition. In A. Bryant and K. Charmaz (Eds.), *The SAGE Handbook of Grounded Theory* (pp. 243–264). London and Thousand Oaks, CA: Sage.

Mackenzie, C. 2014. Three dimensions of autonomy: A relational analysis. In A. Veltman and M. Piper (Eds.), *Autonomy, Oppression, and Gender* (pp. 15–41). New York and Oxford: Oxford University Press.

McKinney, John C. 1966. *Constructive Typology and Social Theory*. New York: Appleton-Century-Crofts.

McMillan, J. 2016. Empirical bioethics and the fact/value distinction. In A. Cribb, J. Ives, and M. Dunn (Eds.), *Empirical Bioethics: Theoretical and Practical Perspectives* (pp. 17–32). Cambridge: Cambridge University Press.

Molewijk, A. C., A. M. Stiggelbout, W. Otten, H. M. Dupuis, and J. Kievit. 2003. Implicit normativity in evidence-based medicine: A plea for integrated empirical ethics research. *Health Care Analysis 11*(1): 69–92.

Molewijk, B., A. M. Stiggelbout, W. Otten, H. M. Dupuis, and J. Kievit. 2004. Empirical data and moral theory. A plea for integrated empirical ethics. *Medicine, Health Care and Philosophy 7*(1): 55–69.

Molewijk, B., A. M. Stiggelbout, W. Otten, H. M. Dupuis, and J. Kievit. 2008. First the facts, then the values? Implicit normativity in evidence-based decision aids for shared decision-making. *Zeitschrift fur Evidenz Fortbildung und Qualitat im Gesundheitswesen 102*(7): 415–420.

Morse, J. M., P. N. Stern, J. Corbin, B. Bowers, K. Charmaz, and A. E. Clarke. 2009. *Developing Grounded Theory: The Second Generation*. Walnut Creek, CA: Left Coast Press.

Putnam, H. 2002. *The Collapse of the Fact/Value Dictotomy and Other Essays*. Cambridge, MA: Harvard University Press.

Putnam, H. 2009. Intelligence and ethics. In John R. Shook and Joseph Margolis (Eds.), *A Companion to Pragmatism* (pp. 267–277). Chichester: John Wiley & Sons.

Putnam, R. A. 2009. Democracy and value inquiry. In John R. Shook and Joseph Margolis (Eds.), *A Companion to Pragmatism* (pp. 278–289). Chichester: John Wiley & Sons.

Raz, J. 2001. *Value, Respect and Attachment*. Cambridge: Cambridge University Press.

Rehmann-Sutter, C., R. Porz, and J. L. Scully. 2012. How to relate the empirical to the normative: Toward a phenomenologically informed hermeneutic approach to bioethics. *Cambridge Quarterly of Healthcare Ethics 21*(4): 436–447.

Reichertz, J. 2007. Abduction: the logic of discovery in grounded theory. In A. Bryant and K. Charmaz (Eds.), *The SAGE Handbook of Grounded Theory* (pp. 214–228). London and Thousand Oaks, CA: Sage.

Rogers, W., C. Mackenzie, and S. Dodds. 2012. Why bioethics needs a concept of vulnerability. *IJFAB: International Journal of Feminist Approaches to Bioethics 5*(2): 11–38.

Sayer, A. 2011. *Why Things Matter to People: Social Science, Values and Ethical Life*. Cambridge: Cambridge University Press.

Scully, J. L. 2016. Feminist empirical bioethics. In A. Cribb, J. Ives and M. Dunn (Eds.), *Empirical Bioethics: Theoretical and Practical Perspectives* (pp. 177–194). Cambridge: Cambridge University Press.

Scully, J. L., E. Haimes, A. Mitzkat, R. Porz, and C. Rehmann-Sutter. 2012. Donating embryos to stem cell research. *Journal of Bioethical Inquiry 9*(1): 19–28.

Solomon, M. Z. 2005. Realizing bioethics' goals in practice: Ten ways 'is' can help 'ought'. *Hastings Center Report 35*(4): 40–47.

Star, S. L. 2007. Living grounded theory: cognitive and emotional forms of pragmatism. In A. Bryant and K. Charmaz (Eds.), *The SAGE Handbook of Grounded Theory* (pp. 75–94). London and Thousand Oaks, CA: Sage.

Strübing, J. 2007. Research as pragmatic problem-solving: The pragmatist roots of empirically-grounded theorising. In A. Bryant and K. Charmaz (Eds.), *The SAGE Handbook of Grounded Theory* (pp. 580–602). London and Thousand Oaks, CA: Sage.

Williams, J., S. Carter, and L. Rychetnik. 2017. Contested guideline development in Australia's cervical screening program: Values drive different views of the purpose and implementation of organized screening. *Public Health Ethics 10*(1): 5–18.

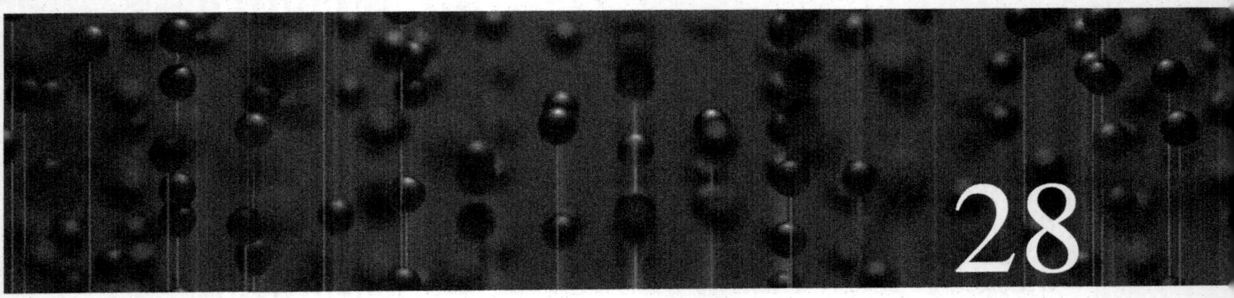

28

Critical Grounded Theory

Gregory Hadley

INTRODUCTION

The Grounded Theory Methodology (GTM) operates as a dynamic 'family of methods' (Bryant & Charmaz 2007, pp. 11–12), with empiricist (Glaser 1978, 1992), constructivist (Charmaz 2014), and postmodernist versions (Clarke 2005). Beginning in 1995, with Wuest's (1995) appeal for greater attention to gender-based concerns, and further punctuated by Charmaz's (2005) call for grounded theories of social processes related to injustice, inequality, and economic disparity, there has been a small but steady stream of books and papers appearing under the banner of Critical Grounded Theory (CGT) (e.g., Abrahams 2009; Postma et al. 2013; Hadley 2015).

However, scholars have only recently started to consider the deeper implications of what it means to engage in critical grounded theorization (Belfrage & Hauf 2016; Hense & McFerran 2016). Many questions still remain: How should one define CGT? What sources of scholarly discourse and philosophical beliefs support a critical version of Grounded Theory? How should Critical Grounded Theorists respond to those who might see their work in terms of forcing empirical data into preconceived categories? Where would CGT fit within the current Grounded Theory family of methods? What are the dispositions and methodological practices of CGT?

This chapter considers these and related questions. After proposing a definition for CGT, schools of philosophical thought that support its development and methodological practices will be reviewed. Diverse streams of scholarly discourse, such as Critical Social Theory, Autopoietic Theory, and lesser-known methodological practices, such as Personal Construct Repertory Grids, will be discussed in order to construct a more nuanced view of Critical Grounded Theory. By the end of this chapter, it is hoped that readers will have a deeper understanding of CGT and a greater appreciation for its potential in highlighting injustice and inequality in specific social arenas.

DEFINING CRITICAL GROUNDED THEORY

If, as Wittgenstein has postulated, the meaning of a word is derived from its use, then *critical* has been difficult to define due to the myriad of ways it has been used by scholars and researchers. Moore's (2013) investigation found that meanings range from that of assessing diverse perspectives in a fair manner, maintaining a sceptical attitude towards assumptions, thinking logically, being sensitive to the unspoken implications in the data, interpreting events in an original manner and practising self-reflexivity, to that of positing research as an ethical, socially transformative activity. These notions are certainly intertwined within the fabric of CGT, but viewing criticality in this way leaves us with a somewhat hazy and efferent picture. A clearer definition is needed, one that is rooted in a scholarly discourse community, linked to notable methodological processes, and focused on a particular theoretical output.

Critical Grounded Theory is defined here as an abductively retrodactive methodology that systematically constructs small-scale to mid-range social theories from empirical data. Analysis is carried out through recurring stages of Open Exploration, Focused Investigation, Theoretical Construction, and Transformative Dissemination. Critical Grounded Theory highlights social processes and phenomena pertaining to the problems of power, inequality, and discrimination in all its varied manifestations. Both the theoretical product and methodological processes of CGT engage in transformative discourse that seeks to stimulate positive action towards the creation of more enlightened societies. The terminology underpinning this definition will be further discussed during the course of this chapter, but for now, let us shift our attention to CGT's supporting schools of thought.

CGT is supported by Critical Social Theory (CST), a school of thought which Kincheloe and McLaren (2000, p. 281) define as 'concerned in particular with issues of power and justice in the ways that economy, matters of race, class, and gender, ideologies, discourses, education, religion and other social institutions, and cultural dynamics interact to construct a social system'. CST owes its beginnings to a group of German social philosophers in the 1930s who came to be known as The Frankfurt School. Representative scholars from this school were Max Horkheimer, Herbert Marcuse, and Theodor Adorno (Carr 2000). Drawing from the philosophical works of Marx, Hegel, Kant, and others, they offered an insightful critique on the corrosive effects of western capitalism. To their chagrin, after the Second World War, the West opted to further develop their societies around a free market model (Kincheloe 2008, p. 60). Instead of completely withering away, however, Lincoln (1998, p. 318) explains that during the subsequent decades other scholars began to graft the concerns of the Frankfurt School onto:

> ...the highly fruitful trees of feminist theory, theories of social justice grounded in Jeffersonian ideals of democracy, American philosophical pragmatism ... emerging race and persons-of-color epistemologies, theories of social valuation ... emancipatory models of evaluation ... theories of social and political power, organizational theory, and cultural studies.

CST today also makes use of Foucauldian, neo-Marxist, Poststructuralist, and even Postmodern critique (Agger 1991; Manias & Street 2000). Despite this diversity, however, the core concerns of Critical Social Theorists have remained steady for over 80 years, and have influenced the viewpoint of many researchers, even some who might not identify themselves as having a CST perspective.

Examples of CST's influence in grounded theory can be observed in the introduction of Foucauldian concepts (Hook 2002, 2007), feminist concerns (Wuest 1995, 2000), neo-Marxist musings (Hadley 2015), an interest in social equality (Charmaz 2005, 2011), misgivings about the socially-damaging processes of financial organizations (Belfrage & Hauf 2016), and calls for social transformation (Redman-MacLaren & Mills 2015; Redman-MacLaren et al. 2017). At this point in the development of CGT, only some, such as Belfrage and Hauf (2016) or Hook (2007), clearly link their work to Critical Social Theorists. Others highlight critical concerns without a discussion of CST (Wuest 1995, 2000). A few have positioned their work as CGT, but fail to demonstrate sufficient evidence in support of this claim (Abrahams 2009). There are also those who might initially baulk at being linked to a CST tradition, since they have already stated their preference for other traditions (Duckles et al., Chapter 31 in this volume). This should be seen as neither surprising nor negating the influence of CST on the development of CGT. Just as Critical Social Theorists coalesced to form a group out of diverse philosophical perspectives, so too are grounded theorists coming from disparate backgrounds to form a new community of research practice. Each theorist contributes their part to the critical study of social process and human interaction. CGT is still evolving, but I would argue that it has already emerged as a new, distinctive member of the GTM family of methods. In light of these familial ties, let us now survey points of consonance and dissonance between CST and the beliefs that have supported the more established methodologies of grounded theory.

Identifying Complementary Features

We have seen that CST has as one of its goals the idea of transformational awareness (Ulrich 2007, p. 1109). Interaction with the theorist transforms the way that participants view their social arenas, and in an act of co-construction, the understanding of the researcher is also transformed by the informants. This transformational element is a strong feature of Constructivist versions of GTM. Another feature that CST shares with GTM is its reliance on abductive inference for theory generation (Kushner & Morrow 2003, pp. 33–34).

CST and GTM have common philosophical roots in American Pragmatism (Ulrich 2007; Bohman 2008; Bryant 2017). Grounded and Critical Theorists both work towards practical, useful outcomes for people in specific situations, and create theories 'embodied in cognition, speech and action' (Habermas 1984, p. 10). Like American Pragmatists, Critical Social Theorists view sociological inquiry within the flux and flow of paradoxical human discourse. They seek to understand restive social dynamics so as to make provisional sense of the chaos, and to locate it within a wider historic and cultural milieu. Straussian GT shares a similar interest (Strauss 1987; Strauss & Corbin 1990, 1997; Corbin & Strauss 2008, 2015) and attempts to contextualize social phenomena within their historic, political, social, economic and national settings. The focus in CST on paradox, chaos, and provisional sense-making is also a kindred concern of Situational Analysis (Clarke 2005).

Addressing Questions of Compatibility

Despite these reciprocal points, interest in integrating CST within the methodology of Grounded Theory has been largely muted, partially because of doubts among some regarding its compatibility with the key methodological tenets of GTM. Chief among these is whether a critical perspective, with its interest in emancipation, transformation, and challenging the status quo, forces empirical data into preconceived categories: 'In CGT the choice of research problem is explicitly driven by moral and social concerns in an ambition to produce critical knowledge to enable social emancipation' (Belfrage & Hauf 2016, p. 9). Classic Grounded Theorists would take issue with the idea of an investigation being 'explicitly driven by moral and social concerns' and 'produc[ing] critical knowledge' for the purposes of emancipation. Glaser would find this not only explicitly forceful, but running counter to the core mission of Grounded Theory, which 'is about *what is*, not what should, could, or ought to be' (Glaser 1999, p. 840). Choosing a research problem based on one's moral and social concerns opens the door to biased theorization. Positioning one's work as emancipatory 'partisanship in the struggle for a better world' (Kincheloe & McLaren 2000, p. 291) would be viewed by Glaser as a clear case of data torture, one in which the data has been prevented from speaking for itself (Glaser 1992, p. 123).

These concerns are bound up within debates about the degree of objectivity and neutrality that theorists can exercise when interacting with the data and the research informants. Viewed historically, it can be seen that objective neutrality is a socially and epistemologically contested concept. Gibson (2007) notes that questions of this sort were first seen during the middle of the 20th century during Theodor Adorno's critique of the sociologist Paul Lazarsfeld. Lazarsfeld was a mentor of Glaser, and arguably the progenitor of Glaser's primary philosophical and methodological beliefs. From a CST perspective, Adorno denounced Lazarsfeld's preference for describing 'life as it is' as nothing more than 'a bourgeois sociology reinforcing the domination inherent in society' (Gibson 2007, p. 438). Similar criticisms were levelled against Symbolic Interactionism, an early methodological forerunner of the Grounded Theory Methodology (Fine 1993). Layder (1993) and Burawoy (1991) have echoed comparable concerns about GTM, stating that Grounded Theorists who claim to be letting the data speak for itself are, in fact, only serving to strengthen the status quo. As Kincheloe and McLaren (2000, p. 284) explain, theoretical descriptions of this sort 'are not simply about the world but serve to construct it ... language in the form of discourses serves as a form of regulation and domination'.

To illustrate this argument, consider the purely hypothetical example of a grounded theorist who has gained access to an organization dedicated to the proliferation of conspiracy theories and prejudiced news stories designed for social media. If one were taking a Glaserian approach to GTM, some of the social processes emerging from informants within this substantive area might be those such as *Spinning the Content*, *Gaming the Internet*, *Google-busting*, or *Firewalling the Feds*. Informant data would likely tell a story of entrepreneurs on the cutting-edge of a new market who, while providing for underserved customers, struggle to protect their rights to free speech against dangerous liberals and authoritarian government agencies. All of this would make for a theory that would be both interesting and transferrable, but it would entirely miss the point of how the people working in such organizations were fomenting political instability, supporting the rise of racist public discourse, and contributing to a social climate where untold thousands have become unable to distinguish between empirical facts and wishful thinking.

The theory would also overlook, among other things, the social processes revealing how rich, well-educated managers and their company shareholders profit off poor, often less-educated people through the purposeful fabrication of fiction packaged as fact. The point being made here is that even if one does not actively take sides, focusing on social processes without considering the wider context, historical factors, and deeper social implications runs the risk of *passively* taking the side of those with the power both to influence the theorists and shape subsequent theoretical explanations, which in turn will have social ramifications.

Charmaz (2000) has persuasively problematized the question of objectivity, arguing that our sensitivity to what we perceive in the field is shaped by our mental constructs. Scholars such as Blumer, James, Lazarsfeld, and Merton influenced the theoretical perspectives of Glaser and Strauss. It would be rather arbitrary if one were to preclude those whose sensitivity has been enhanced by Marcuse, Marx, or Hegel. Critical or otherwise, it is through embracing rather than repressing one's perspective that complements the original position of Glaser and Strauss (1967/1999, p. 253), who stated that Grounded Theory allows analysts to study substantive social arenas from their own theoretical perspectives, so long as they strive to be fair and honest with others as to how they generated their theory. Therefore, Critical Grounded Theorists should not be cynical grounded theorists; within the grounded theory context, it is vital that Critical Grounded Theorists remain open to alternative possibilities. Charmaz explains:

> Any extant concept must earn its way into the analysis. Thus, we cannot import a set of concepts such as hegemony and domination and paste them on the realities of the field. Instead, we can treat them as sensitizing concepts, to be explored in the field settings. (2005, p. 512)

Theoretical concepts such as hegemony, power, and injustice are sensitizing in nature, but at the onset they can only offer possibilities for inquiry. They cannot be soldered on without rigorous study. The aptness of concepts drawn from a critical perspective should be evaluated in terms of how well they fit the scene. Critical Grounded Theorists must carry out their investigation in an honest, reflexive, and fair manner. If issues of power, inequality, economic domination, or other forms of exploitation do manifest themselves as prominent within the substantive area of study, then a CST perspective will enhance the explanatory and transformative power of the theory.

LOCATING CRITICAL GROUNDED THEORY: AN AUTOPOIETIC MODEL

Different philosophies of science lead scholars to different forms of theorization. This section will argue, however, that the variety of approaches to GTM need not be construed as contradictory, but rather, as part of an interactive and interdependent network. Autopoietic Theory will be used to explain how this works.

The Theory of Autopoiesis studies how communication, discourse, and social organizations act as self-producing and self-constructing systems (Mingers 1995; Arnoldi 2001). It maintains that social interactions, human discourse groups, research communities and philosophical systems of thought operate in a manner similar to that of living organisms, in that component functions, interactions, and distinct sets of activities lead to the creation of other supporting functions. In the process, all work to re-create each other. Autopoiesis, which is a Greek word that means 'self-generating', has as a theoretical concept been quite influential in some circles. It is the cornerstone of Luhmann's (1995) social theory, and Mitchell (2007) has been among those who have considered applications of Autopoietic Theory to the methodology of Grounded Theory.

As with Glaser and Strauss (1967/1999), the originators of Autopoietic Theory used unique terminology and made little effort to link their theory to the wider body of scholarly literature sharing similar philosophical concerns (Mingers 1995). In order to explain the autopoieticity of Grounded Theory's methodological family, therefore, it is necessary to briefly survey its perspective and unique nomenclature.

Overview of Autopoietic Theory

In the mid-1970s, philosophers of Biology, Humberto Maturana and Francisco Varela, developed the Theory of Autopoiesis as a means of describing the self-producing, self-constructing systems that result in life (Maturana 1975; Maturana & Varela 1987; Cuff, Sharrock & Francis 2006, p. 108). Autopoiesis was later extended to explain the self-generating systems of human cognition, discourse, and social interaction (Maturana & Varela 1980). Maturana explains that an autopoietic system is:

> A composite unity whose organization can be described as a closed network of productions of components that through their interactions constitute the network of productions that produce them, and specify its extension by constituting its boundaries in their domain of existence. (Maturana 1987, p. 349, in Mingers 2002, p. 294)

Autopoiesis has a strong affinity with Systems Theory, in that both interpret the emergence of complex entities and their social processes as emanating from smaller interactions (Larsen-Freeman 2007). Autopoietic Theory entered the social sciences through multiple avenues, where it has been applied to understanding social systems, policies, and discourse (Luhmann 1994, 2001; Brans & Rossbach 1997; Arnoldi 2001; Cuff, Sharrock & Francis 2006, p. 107). Framing social, organizational and academic discourse as autopoietic systems has been particularly helpful, and according to Mingers (2002), this theoretical perspective has worked in tandem with social constructivism and other contemporary theories on communication.

Further advances in Autopoietic Theory came from the physicist, systems theorist, and philosopher Frijof Capra (1996, pp. 162–168), who postulated that the concepts of Structure, Pattern and Process operated interactively to generate and maintain biological life. Capra (1996, p. 172) believed his version of Autopoietic Theory could also be applied metaphorically towards a better understanding of the formation of human cognition, how knowledge is produced within research disciplines, and how the beliefs of scholarly discourse communities contribute to a preference for certain forms of research.

British researchers Sid Lowe, Adrian Carr, and Michael Thomas then built upon Capra's ideas to propose the 'paradigmapping' of scholarly research approaches within this triadic matrix of structure, pattern and process (Lowe & Carr 2003; Lowe, Carr & Thomas 2004). Let us now consider autopoietic paradigmapping more deeply, as this has particular applications to understanding the dynamic nature of grounded theorizing.

A Framework for Paradigmapping

My use of the term 'paradigm' follows Guba and Lincoln (1998, p. 200), who define it 'as a set of *basic beliefs* (or metaphysics) that deals with the ultimates or first principles. It represents a *worldview* that defines, for its holder, the nature of the "world," the individual's place in it, and the range of possible relationships to that world and its parts, as, for example, cosmologies and theologies do.' In metaphorical terms, the notion of a cosmology is particularly helpful, because much in the manner of, for example, the early formation of our solar system, the particulate matter of discourse, ideas, and beliefs crash into each other, break apart, and recoalesce while whirling around in distinctive bands of ontology, epistemology, and preferred methodologies.

This view of research paradigms of Structure, Pattern, and Process as the result of heated discourse orbiting philosophical concepts and practical issues has been added to the paradigmapping matrix found in Figure 28.1. Research paradigms, as swirling centres of discourse, represent the 'worded world' (Richardson 2000, p. 923) – a place where certain ontologies, epistemologies, and methodological preferences are discussed, debated, named, and renamed over time. This complements Strauss (1987, pp. 146, 231–245) and Clarke (2005), who both understand ways of knowing and ways of understanding as 'constantly awash in seas of discourses that are constitutive of life itself' (Clarke 2005, p. xxx). I will further unpack the meaning of these paradigm labels shortly, but before doing so, Lowe et al. (2005, p. 189) describe the relationship between these research paradigms as interdependent: 'Structure ... is merely a manifestation of the "process" of embodiment of the "pattern" of organization of a system. As a result, "structure" is not ontologically "real" as such, because it is always a reification of process and pattern.' For these reasons, I have further enhanced the paradigmapping matrix to include an element of cyclical flow, one moving from structure to pattern, pattern to process, and then back to structure.

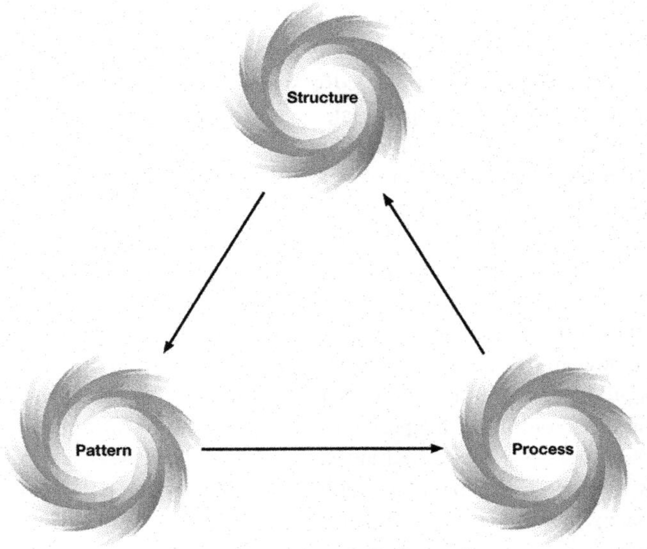

Figure 28.1 Paradigmapping matrix (adapted from Lowe et al. 2004)

An Autopoietic Understanding of Research Paradigms

Framing research paradigms autopoietically disposes with the plethora of terms that are a common feature of such philosophical discussions. Instead, we now work with three functional clusters of basic beliefs. The Paradigm of Structure relates to what is often referred to as positivism. The ontology associated with this paradigm is a form of realism, which in its most naïve or empirical form, states that both a natural and social world is 'out there' separate and independent of us, whether we know it or not. Through the right methods, this reality can be discovered (Lincoln & Guba 2000, p. 165) The epistemology is objectivist, meaning that truth exists, and that knowledge of the truth can be discovered empirically. The role of the researcher is to transmit knowledge of the truth free of any value statements (Hutchinson 1988, p. 124). Research seeks either to prove or disprove hypotheses, thereby validating the generation of truthful theories. The methodology of social research often preferred by those who believe in the Paradigm of Structure is usually quantitative in nature. Interviews or observational data are considered unquantifiable and unreliable, unless they can be placed in a replicable matrix where discreet items can be counted or otherwise validated (Babbie 2004, p. 396). Hard data emerges from removing variables through structured sets of widely accepted methods, such as statistical studies or cross-sectional surveys. Truth is often found in quantity, and for that reason, discovering the overall trends of large populations is seen as more valid than what can be learned from studies with smaller samples (Bryman 2001, pp. 284–285).

The Paradigm of Pattern studies the manifestations of repeated human activities and discourse. The ontology of this paradigm tends towards the philosophical belief stating that an external reality, apart from a mind to perceive it, does not exist. The world is 'in there', that is, in the mind of the one who sees and thinks about what is happening. The mind is not the only source of reality-construction: certainly there is something 'out there', but ultimately, it cannot be perceived by observation alone (Guelke 1976, p. 170). Shared reality takes place through the creation of socially constructed symbols, which as Locke explains:

> is built up over time through shared history, experience and communication so that what is taken for 'reality' is what is shared and taken for granted as to the way the world is to be perceived and understood. (2005, p. 9)

Epistemologically, this paradigm is interpretivist in nature. Knowledge is believed to be shaped by the values and worldviews of like-minded groups of individuals (Michell 2003, p. 17). Knowledge is intersubjective and created through the ever-evolving consensus of many participants, including that of the researcher (Lincoln & Guba 2000, p. 165). Instead of deductively testing pre-existing theories, interpretivist researchers reflexively induce new theoretical concepts that occur during their interaction with the data. They attempt to reconstruct new understandings into a narrative discussing the possible 'whys' and 'hows' of the phenomenon being studied (Ritchie 2004, pp. 28–29).

Research methodologies tend to be more flexible in their procedures, since social realities are viewed as emergent (Bryman 2001). Denzin and Lincoln (2000, p. 3) describe the researcher within this paradigm as a *bricoleur*, one who tinkers about and 'uses the tools of his or her methodological trade, deploying whatever strategies, methods or empirical materials as are at hand'. The focus of the research project is less predetermined in the beginning, but over time, researchers explore various avenues of inquiry while abandoning others as dead ends. Various methods are used to investigate social phenomena, and the researcher can change directions if serendipitous events uncover issues that are core to understanding the study. Methodologies, as explained by Potter (1996), are also usually qualitative or those that use a combination of qualitative and quantitative, and there is a preference for open, unstructured interviews, reflective journalling and observational techniques.

Researchers and theorists working within the Paradigm of Process constantly question and deconstruct the established knowledge, theories, and assumptions formed from structuring and patterning. Those who locate themselves within the maelstrom of this discourse community – and it is a disparate and wilfully paradoxical group – advocate deconstructionism, the transgression of traditional academic conventions, anti-establishmentarianism and call for plurality. They raise awareness of the chaos of human interaction, and focus upon the immediacy of the present without seeking to impose their interpretations of what it might mean:

> The world is characterized by uncertain dynamic process rather than such certain structures. Process does not involve certainty or foundations and discourse is characterized by paradox, contradiction and indeterminate meaning. Language, as the principle vehicle of the cultural process, is uncertain and indeterminate because it is a process that reflexively contains its own antithesis and upon which meaning is politically imposed. The 'active' world is thus a chameleonic process without structure or certainty. (Lowe 2001, p. 326)

Ontological questions treat reality as neither 'in there' nor 'out there', but instead, *nowhere*, until created by a particular group, and even this is historically inconclusive, highly contextualized, and culturally limited (Grenz 1996, p. 7; Scheurich 2001, p. 33). Multiple realities are layered one on top of another, each with something important to add. However, those occupying a space further away between process and structure (see again Figure 28.1), and discourse communities on the periphery of this paradigm, such as Critical Theory, often ascribe to a critical realist (sometimes called transcendental realist) ontology. This states that an empirical reality exists, but our ability to perceive it is limited by our social constructs and historical perspectives (Archer 1998). Accepting aspects of constructivism without denying the existence of an empirical reality allows one to maintain the 'hard sciences' while approaching the study of social realities as 'open-ended with multiple mechanisms co-determining events, overlapping, reinforcing or counteracting one another [and] impossible to close the system experimentally in order to isolate a single mechanism as in the natural sciences' (Belfrage & Hauf 2016, p. 4).

Researchers tend towards epistemological relativism, which in relation to social inquiry, relates to multiple ways of knowing and doing. These manifold ways do not entail, as opponents claim, that illogicality or unbridled eclecticism are acceptable (Guba 1992, pp. 18–20). Instead a relativist epistemology enables researchers:

> to know 'something' without claiming to know everything. Having a partial, local, historical knowledge is still knowing. In some ways, 'knowing' is easier, however, because postmodernism recognizes the situational limitations of the knower. (Richardson 2000, p. 928)

For those who move further from process towards structure, the epistemological view of researchers will be more in line with American Pragmatism, which states that while people will certainly have different ways of knowing, doing, and seeing, in the final analysis, some viewpoints are more useful than others. Accepting that people will have different perspectives and understandings shaped by their background does not mean that 'alternative facts' are acceptable. Through the process of what Bhaskar (2009) has called *retrodaction*, informant perspectives are assessed through asking *what must be true for a certain perspective to be actually possible*. This line of questioning opens the door for discovering empirical conditions and causes behind why some persist in beliefs or actions that are either untrue or harmful to society. The goal is to go beyond the description of social patterns, to find the causes for pressing problems, and to produce critical knowledge of the type that will lead to positive social transformation (Belfrage & Hauf 2016, p. 4; Blunt 2016).

While those informed by this paradigm avoid the creation of grand, overarching theories, localized theories are possible so long as readers know as much as possible about the theorist and how the theory was created. Theorists from this paradigm 'are not concerned about the "truth" of their research but rather the pragmatic applicability of their results' (Annells 1996, p. 391). Furthermore, the preference is for the process of *theorizing* than that of *theory* as a product. This perspective deepens the sense of immediacy and highlights restive, chaotic dynamics constantly at work within the socio-historical milieu.

Kilduff and Mehra (1997) note that researchers guided by more of a postmodern process perspective often use the same methodologies associated with the paradigms of pattern, especially ethnographic or phenomenological methods. However, Blunt (2016) has observed that those taking a critical stance often have not relied on systematic ways of carrying out empirical research, and has suggested that GT might be an ideal platform for systematically developing retrodactive social processes.

Researchers of process tend to avoid quantitative methods, though some are confident that nothing prevents their use (Guba 1992, p. 18; Reinharz 1992, pp. 92–94). The difference would be in how they are implemented and how the data would be interpreted. While structure-based research seeks the verification and/or falsification of theories, and of prediction and control, research from the paradigms of pattern focus on understanding the experiences of informants in order to challenge oppressive social structures.

Despite their respective ontologies, epistemologies and inspired methodologies, they are not at odds with each other, and these paradigms should not be treated, as Lincoln and Guba (2000) have claimed, like separate religions competing for converts. Rather, the Paradigms of Structure, Pattern and Process are an autopoietic network; each makes a vital contribution to a fuller understanding of our complex, multilayered social reality.

The Autopoietic Interplay of Grounded Theorization

Portraying the family of GTMs as an autopoietic system has already been envisaged *in potentia* by other grounded theorists, such as Hallberg (2006, p. 144), who describes the emergence of distinctive forms of GTM as arising out of 'differing basic underlying assumptions concerning ontological and epistemological standpoints'. Mills, Bonner and Francis (2006) concur:

> If we envisage Grounded Theory methodology as a spiral that starts with the traditional form, we can see that such adaptations are reflective of the various moments of philosophical thought that have guided qualitative research and that it is the researcher's ontological and epistemological position that determines the form of Grounded Theory they undertake. (p. 9)

Certainly, Urquhart and Fernández (2013) argue that GTM, in and of itself, is devoid of paradigmatic positions, but this may be a question of semantics, and I have not sought to

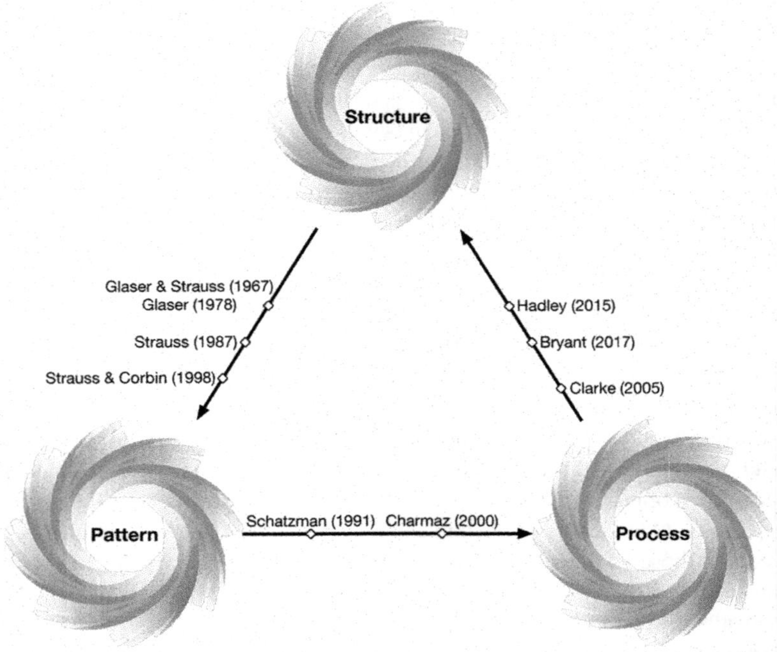

Figure 28.2 Autopoietic interpretation of grounded theory methodologies

separate the methodology from the theorists who have wielded it, because as Bryant (2017) has argued, approaches to GTM are always idiosyncratic. Notwithstanding these points of distinction, the spiral envisaged by Mills, Bonner and Francis is represented autopoietically in Figure 28.2.

By focusing primarily on the seminal works of GTM, we can see that in the beginning, the methodology of Grounded Theory was rooted in Paradigms of Structure, even as it was moving away from the more inflexible canons of positivist practice and thought (Glaser & Strauss 1967/1999; Glaser 1978). Glaser still holds to many of the ontological and epistemological beliefs of the Paradigms of Structure, but the ways that GTM has been used by subsequent theorists have steadily taken it to the Paradigms of Pattern, Process, and back again towards Structure.

This helps to shed light on some of the underlying reasons for Glaser's (1992) intense critique of Strauss. Far more than Strauss, Glaser's writings reveal beliefs related to the Paradigm of Structure, with a realist ontology and epistemology (Charmaz 2000). This has implications for coding. Coding is intimately connected to ontology and epistemology. One cannot code something that does not exist. I feel Glaser and Strauss focused on the methodology of coding to the point of obsession because at some level they sensed that important paradigmatic issues were at stake. For example, if one subscribes to a realist ontology, as Glaser does, it follows that researchers should be rigorously trained in techniques that will make them more objective and detached, so that whatever is going on 'out there' can be discovered and reported accurately. From the late 1980s onward Strauss and Corbin provided methodological guidance underwritten by the paradigms of pattern (Strauss 1987; Strauss & Corbin 1997, 1998). This has been something of an enigma, since Strauss's other major works, *Mirrors and Masks* (Strauss 1959/1969) and *Continual Permutations of Action* (Strauss 1993) reveal greater affinity with the paradigms of process. It is possible that Strauss, a prolific writer, was able to discern the zeitgeist of sociological inquiry and flexibly craft his message accordingly. At the time of his methodological publications with Corbin, their books were certainly within the epistemological mainstream.

Schatzman (Schatzman & Strauss 1973; Schatzman 1991) worked from an interpretive perspective, and saw rigid methodologies as a barrier to the natural human ability to analyze social phenomenon. His Dimensional Analysis, which by his own admission operates only as a partial form of GTM (Gilgun 2010), nevertheless anticipated the next turn that took place in GT, which was to understand social reality as something more elastic. In the case of Charmaz (2006), social reality and ways of knowing it are seen as a co-construction between the researcher and the informants. Therefore, coding is less a question of scientific technique and more of an intuitive art developed according to the researcher's individual talents, worldview, and temperament. A postmodern, relativist Grounded Theory, similar to Charmaz, highlights the process of *theorizing* over the product of theory (Clarke 2005, pp. 88–90). Situational Analysis rejects the idea of framing the resulting theory into basic social processes and instils within readers an awareness of the chaos of our imagined order. For Clarke, definitions about what is real are in a constant state of flux, and the methodology reflects this chaos. Coding is deconstructive and similar to postmodern art, in that it is constantly being transformed and reinterpreted by each individual. Bryant's methodological work is rooted in American Pragmatism, and challenges approaches to GTM that are taught in a restrictive, authoritarian manner, in order to liberate GTM as a transformative force in the lives of researchers. My work is less focused on methodology as it is on critical issues in higher education, and has been described as having strong links with neo-Marxist thought (Holobrow, personal communication).

Charmaz (2006, pp. 134–135) has noted that past Grounded Theorists expressed little interest in issues related to power and inequality, but this, she argues, has been an oversight of the *theorists*, not the *methodology*. Gibson (2007) was one of the first to forecast that critical grounded theories regarding power and injustice would be the next developmental phase of Grounded Theory, and we have seen in this chapter that Critical Grounded Theorists are now indeed coming to the fore. The critical realist perspective of those taking a CGT approach does not deny the notion of social reality as constructions out of chaos, but there is also a corollary of commonality (Kelly 1955/1991, pp. 63–65) that both transcends and connects our dimly perceived human conceptions of existence. There are things that are real, apart from a mind to perceive it, but multiple ways of understanding are necessary; theorization takes place from not only those people and groups who, so to speak, have the power to keep the light on their own narratives, but also among those with less power, and who have been relegated to obscurity (Kempster & Parry 2011). Coding is omnivorous in choice, rigorous in practice, but not onerous to the point of stifling theoretical thinking. Critical Grounded Theory, when it is deemed to be appropriate for the analysis of a certain substantive area, deconstructs oppressive power structures and questions reified social processes, in light of their historical backgrounds, trajectories and implications. The hope is to reconstruct more civilized solutions to social problems, and to challenge those who will listen to consider new ways of peaceful, pragmatic action.

To further aid readers in locating their paradigmatic positions, and to help in applying this framework to their theoretical concerns, an inventory (see Appendix 28.1 at the end of the chapter) has been provided. First-time practitioners and graduate students will find suggested Grounded Theory methodological texts that roughly correspond to their deeply-held beliefs. For new researchers, the inventory can facilitate their choice of methodological guide as they theorize about issues affecting participants in specific social arenas.

Autopoiesis fosters rapprochement in the debate on whether GT should be viewed as a product or a process. Referring earlier to my definition of CGT, in which a grounded theory is described both as a process and product, an autopoietic view can ameliorate distracting debates of the type found in Strübing (Chapter 2 in this volume), who in favouring methodology of Grounded Theory as itself representing the ongoing process of Grounded Theorizing, questions Bryant's use of GTM as a means of distinguishing it from Grounded Theory as product.

An autopoietic perspective of grounded theorization frames is both a structured product and an ongoing process. Metaphorically, it is similar to how two aunts might describe their nephew as 'a growing boy'. There is a boy (product) who is a structured entity, and a boy who is steadily growing (process). In like manner, Grounded Theories are constructions emerging from and supporting the process of ongoing theorization. Each form of theorization energizes the other along the lines of autopoiesis. All share the same genetic code. The value of such diversity in the way GTM has been construed means that theorists have greater freedom in determining which procedures fit best for their paradigmatic, theoretical, and methodological perspective. In the process, theories will be generated, constructed, deconstructed, and reconstructed within a system of dynamic intellectual activity.

METHODOLOGICAL OVERVIEW OF CRITICAL GROUNDED THEORY

Because a critical approach should be employed only after issues of power, gender, injustice, and similar concerns become apparent, the methodology of CGT, Hense and McFerran (2016) argue, could readily be framed as simply an extension of Constructivist GT. While epistemological proximity need not always result in similar procedures for knowledge construction, their assertion is nevertheless largely borne out in the way that I have formulated the methodology of CGT (Hadley 2017b). Coding, memo-writing, when to start accessing the scholarly literature, and the recursive movement from description to theory, bear many similarities to GTM as approached by Charmaz and Glaser, with aspects of Strauss and Corbin during later stages of Theoretical Construction. However, even though CGT shares many familial similarities to other approaches to GTM, differences do exist. I will devote more attention to these points, and enhance this discussion with examples from my recent Theory of Professional Disarticulation (Hadley 2015). After briefly explaining the meaning of this term, and the substantive area within which it was incubated, unique methodological approaches during the stages of Open Exploration, Focused Investigation, Theory Construction, and Transformative Dissemination (Figure 28.3), will be presented.

Concepts in Context

Professional Disarticulation is a social process within work environments where long-established ideological beliefs and vocational identities have become progressively deconstructed and replaced by the beliefs of a new caste of powerbrokers. A person or

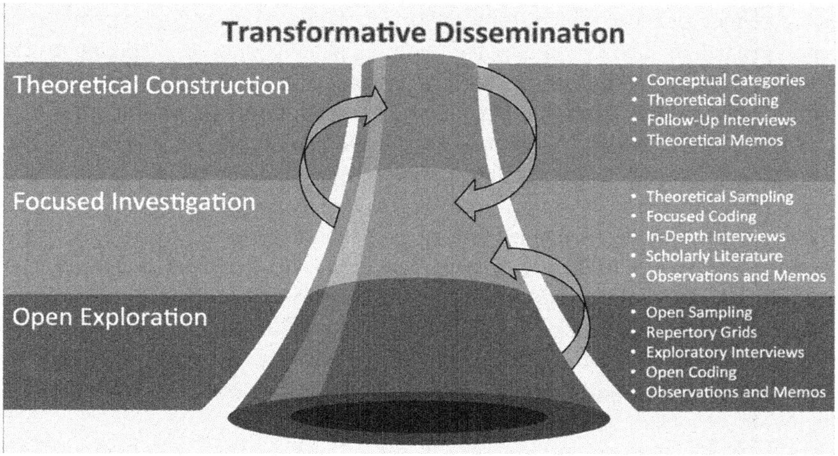

Figure 28.3 Methodological stages of Critical Grounded Theory

group of people with special skills in an organization are, through various organizational and conditional changes, suddenly pulled out of their spaces of normative activity, and twisted from their earlier sense of vocational calling. They are then left hanging in a powerless state until willing to be rehabilitated by the new management. Job titles often stay the same, but formerly respected skills become subsumed under new, more pressing expectations from above. Workers experiencing Professional Disarticulation are often transferred to isolated organizational 'third spaces', where employment conditions become increasingly precarious.

This theory was developed from a study of university English for Academic Purpose (EAP) programs (often called Intensive English Programs (IEP) or English as a Second Language (ESL) programs in the US and Canada). EAP was among the first disciplines to experience changes of the type now affecting university academics around the world. From the 1990s to the mid-2000s, EAP teachers were jettisoned from Humanities and Language Departments, often because they were seen as related more to training than to scholarly pursuits. They were then put into either administrative programs or outsourced to corporate management. Ironically, this move served as a precedent for many of the professional challenges currently experienced by academics in the liberal arts and social sciences.

The substantive study of Professional Disarticulation at it relates to EAP is critically important not only for those directly involved in the task of teaching English for Academic Purposes, but also to scholars in other disciplines, since the conditions of EAP units in universities act as a social barometer for understanding the aspirations of university management and for predicting the likely future of other academics within the institution.

Open Exploration

Open Exploration begins in curiosity. It starts when a theorist encounters something that makes them stop in puzzlement and ask, 'What's going on here?' Before going out into the field, however, it is important for theorists to reflect upon what they may already know (or think they know) about their area of curiosity. Criticality begins with reflexivity.

Critical Grounded Theorists therefore must first look inward in order to externalize their assumptions, beliefs, and hypotheses about the social arena they are preparing to study.

The way I encourage doing this is through either writing an essay or a transcript of an imaginary interview with oneself. This allows a theorist to articulate what they believe they know about the substantive area, and the document becomes a sounding board for constant comparison during later coding, memo-writing, or when asking questions during interviews, because theorists can periodically compare their codes and musings with their preconceived notions and challenge themselves to look for opposite cases.

As noted earlier in this chapter, however, the paradox is that even though one can go through the effort of honing one's reflexivity in order to maintain an open stance to the research informants' perspective, it is still difficult not to impose one's worldview on the participants, especially during Open Exploration. Interview questions and observation notes still tend to generate answers to the researchers' concerns, and can miss hidden problems and processes important to the informants.

To address this problem, for a number of years I have used a research tool known as Personal Construct Repertory Grids, or repertory grids. Repertory grids were developed over 50 years ago by George Kelly (Kelly 1955, 1963), a pioneer in the field of psychology, whose Personal Construct Theory (PCT) anticipated many of the ideas put forth later by cognitivists and social constructionists (Berger & Luckmann 1967). Greatly expanding upon Werkmeister's (1948, p. 95) use of 'construct' and 'knowledge construction', Kelly's coinage of the term *personal construct* has so permeated the English lexicon that laypeople and scholars alike effortlessly use this conceptual metaphor to describe the unique, yet interconnected way that people perceive and pragmatically respond to their social worlds. Similar to Schatzman's (1991) notion of Natural Analysis, Kelly posited people as 'incipient scientists' (Kelly 1955, p. 4), who make predictive theories about the social reality based upon the beliefs they have formed from previous experiences. Kelly's perspective, which was heavily influenced by American Pragmatism, complements CGT and Constructivist Grounded Theory:

> [T]he scientist of PCT is not a positivist, collecting nuggets of truth that are then put together in a representation of the world 'as it really is'. Science is not only a matter of discovery, but also of construction. And constructions are to be judged not in terms of their truth, but of their usefulness. ... All events in the world are open to differing perspectives and constructions. (Butt & Parton 2005, p. 798)

Kelly designed the repertory grid technique in order to gain a better understanding of these differing perspectives. Jankowicz (2004, pp. 14–15) describes it as 'a form of structured interviewing, with ratings or without, which arrives at a precise description uncontaminated by the interviewer's own viewpoint', and adds that is especially useful during the beginning of the research process, since it helps research participants to describe events and social interactions as they see them, and in their own words. Figure 28.4 shows a completed repertory grid from a university teacher.

The key features are *elements*, *bipolar constructs*, and usually a rating system. Elements are located at the top of the grid, and feature 'people, events, objects, ideas, institutions and so on' (Cohen, Manion & Morrison 2003, p. 338). These are empirical, observable phenomena that are 'well-known and personally meaningful' to research informants (Shaw 1980, p. 10). Easterby-Smith (1981, p. 11) explains that it is helpful 'to think of elements as being the objects of people's thoughts, and constructs as the qualities

1	2	3	4	5
Dealing with administrative Demands	Experiencing Frequent microaggressions	International Travel for University	Being Required to Recruit Students	Helping others through Teaching and Research

1	1	2	3	4	5	5
Creating Spaces for authentic Student Learning	5	x 5	x 1	3	x 1	Dealing with Barriers to Innovative Teaching
Making a Lasting Educational Contribution	x 5	4	x 1	4	x 1	Wasting Time in Senseless meetings
Isolated in a Sea of Pouty & Disinterested Students	1	x 1	4	x 1	x 5	Connected to a Dynamic Community of Scholars
Forced to Become a "Salesperson" for the university	x 1	2	x 5	x 1	4	Escaping the "mental Prison"
Scorned as Incompetent for Duties outside my Educational Training	x 1	x 1	4	1	x 5	Confidently Happy as I use my Creative Talents

Figure 28.4 Completed repertory grid

that people attribute to these objects'. Kelly (1963) believed that there was a bipolar aspect to personal constructs. In order to discover how someone understands value-laden constructs such as *innovative*, *dynamic*, or *incompetent*, the analyst needs to know about the contrasting limits within which such values are framed (Kelly 1963, pp. 105–108). In Figure 28.4, the bipolar constructs are written on the left and right sides of the grid. The numbers in the middle represents a rating scale of one to five, one being most like the construct on the left-hand side, and five being most like the construct on the right-hand side. Each element at the top of grid has been rated in relation to the constructs.

There have been numerous modifications to Kelly's original procedure, but all variations share the common goal of studying how individuals and groups see the world around them in their own terms (Fransella, Bell & Bannister 2004). The approach which I take is based on Shaw and McKnight (1981) and Jankowicz (2004).

The research participant and I arrange to meet in a place that is comfortable and free from distractions. I provide the participant with an empty grid sheet, five cards numbered on one side from one to five (which corresponds to the elements numbered one to five at the top of the grid), and a pen. I ask research participants to write as elements a list of routine problems, pressing issues, and aspirations within the context of their social arena. The reason I start here is because I believe that, within the tension of such social dynamics lies a crucible from which one can forge a theory. The restive discourse that bubbles up from the passions of talking about problems and aspirations, once amalgamated with the perspectives of more participants from the same social sphere, can suggest critical concerns (if any exist), which can then be used to construct the later theory.

In Figure 28.4, the interest was in such dynamics taking place within the informant's university setting. From one to five on the top row, we see the answers to the questions of (1) In your work environment, what activity takes up most of your day?, (2) What is the most common problem you often experience in your workplace?, (3) What is a workplace activity that you really enjoy?, (4) What is an activity at work that you really dislike?, and (5) What do you wish you could be doing more of? When eliciting elements, the activities should focus on observable activities, not the research participant's feelings about those activities. The participant then shuffles the cards, places them face down on the table, and chooses three at random. A small 'X' is placed in the rating boxes to indicate which were chosen. The participant is then asked which two of these elements have something in common. This quality, value, emotion, or actions are written on the left side of the grid. Then the participant is asked what was it that made the third element different from the other two. This is written on the right side. Then the participant would rate all of the elements on a scale from 1 to 5 according to how they corresponded with the bipolar construct. This process is then repeated with different element combinations until they either fill the grid or run out of ideas.

A grid of five elements and five bipolar constructs should be seen as the smallest possible sample. If the research participant has more time, a grid of eight elements and eight constructs often yields a richer sample. What results from repertory grid analysis is a 'cognitive snapshot' of informant beliefs around a certain area of research interest. The data derived from repertory grids can be then analyzed by using either an interpretive study of what the informant has written or through specialist software packages (Shaw & Gaines 2009; Fromm & Bacher 2014). Sitting with the research participant and continuing with the interview, one can ladder both up and down the grid to explore issues in more detail. For those wanting even more detail, the rating system allows for the use of Principle Components Analysis, by which one can map the constructs with clusters of multiple correlations. If it is possible to carry out these analyses and then return for a follow-up interview, sitting together with the informant while looking at the graph will often result in a more focused conversation and an excellent beginning to Open Exploration.

Because the repertory grid interview takes time and it is less wieldy than simply talking to research participants, I only use grids with the first few people I encounter in the field. However, the elicited elements and constructs have enormous value as *in vivo* codes. Created by the informants, not the theorist, the elements and constructs help the theorist to become more deeply embedded into the beliefs and social interactions of the informants early on. Such data also serve to guide them later on during unstructured interviews with other informants. If conducted carefully, repertory grids can literally shave weeks off of the investigation process by saving theorists from having to fumble around in their struggle to understand the perspectives of their informants.

After repertory grids, the line of questioning during subsequent exploratory interviews, together with memo-writing and open coding, will be largely indistinguishable from Classic or Constructivist methodologies (Figure 28.5).

Similar to Glaser (1998, pp. 107–113), I write summaries of interviews or observations first. However, while he has convincing reasons for not working with transcripts, the demands of modern academia require these when possible, so I will transcribe interviews, and apply earlier codes to the transcripts, as well as new codes to anything I missed while

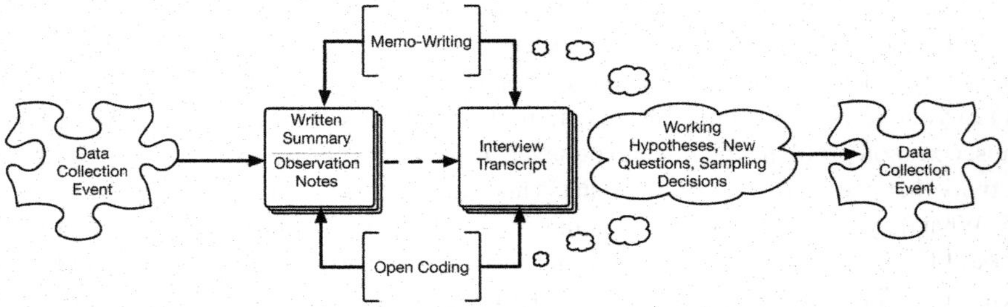

Figure 28.5 Open Exploration procedures

writing the summary. During coding, in addition to asking the question 'What is going on here?' (Glaser 1978, p. 57), I also interrogate the data with a question that is also of interest to Charmaz (2008, p. 408): '*Why* is this going on here?' Finding the answers will require further investigations into the background issues, contexts, and causes. If there is an indication of recurring problems and social interactions intimately linked to power, inequality, gender, class stratification, or related critical concerns, further questions are then used to guide later memo-writing and coding:

- How is dominance being maintained here?
- What strategy is being used to privilege one group's narrative over another?
- How are things of value being gained here?
- How are things of value are being lost here?
- What tactic is being used to gain an advantage over others here?
- What are the marginalizing interactions here?
- What are the resistance strategies of those who are disempowered?
- How is gender/age/class affecting the dynamics discussed here?
- Who has been excluded from the established narrative?
- What activities are the 'invisible ones' engaging in while the dominant group seeks to carry out their plans?
- What are the problems that arise as a result of the social processes of dominant and disenfranchised groups?

Questions such as these are certain to generate further codes and ideas, which will soon require a shift towards Focused Investigation.

Focused Investigation

Techniques used for grouping open codes into interpretive focused codes follow the same procedures as found in the works of Glaser and Charmaz. This is also the stage when theorists should begin accessing any scholarly literature pertinent to the data which have been collected and analyzed. Examples of how theory construction can take the 'critical turn' will be considered.

It is sometimes the case that research informants are unaware of the critical concerns affecting them. It may be the theorist who, due to their broader perspective gained from purposeful observation and multiple interviews of other research informants, identifies such issues. Often, due to the interaction between the theorist and the research participants, over time both will have developed a heightened awareness of critical questions in their social sphere.

Such dynamics could be seen in my study of EAP programs situated in universities that are following a 'neoliberal model' (Hadley 2017a). International students, especially those from Asia, tended to trust the institution to fulfil a protective, parental role. Many were blissfully unaware of the predatory practices of third-party groups, departments, and university administrative units, who charged them for goods and services that they were either unable to use, or due to language issues, unable to access. Students on short-term study programs were especially susceptible to tuition increases that far exceeded the rate of inflation at these universities. EAP teachers, however, were often more aware of how their students are being taken advantage of on campus, and often referred to the practice using terms such as *squeezing*, *milking*, *extracting*, or *juicing*. Some connected these practices to the way that other service corporations essentially deceive customers by hiding important details in the fine print or through later service fees, as seen in this interview excerpt:

Hadley: They're juicing the students then?
Informant: In my opinion yes. So they're saying we're not raising tuition, but actually they're just doing it in other fees. It's just kind of like everything in the US right now, all the utility companies, 'we're not raising our rates' but they stick extra taxes on the end but those aren't raising our rates – we're calling them user fees and they just add them on the end.
Hadley: What, you mean since coming here they've got to pay these extra fees now?
Informant: Well I mean just it's kind of the way the US whole system is turning, so like our telephone is that way, our cable, our electricity, everything is going to ... I mean 'it's not bad, we're not raising it' but if you notice on the bottom, you say, well you're not raising it, like my cell phone is $40 a month, I'm up to $55 now – $15 of extra fees they just add on the bottom. And that's kind of the way our whole...
Hadley: (exasperated) Well that's just lying.
Informant: That's the way ... (long pause) It's the trend I think in all of those things. (Interview, October 26, 2009).

EAP program managers, and mid-level administrators were also aware of the practice, and referred to international students as *slices of cake*, *herds*, and on occasion, *cash cows*. The open codes and memos surrounding this language of exploitation, and the positing of international students first as livestock, and then as food by which the neoliberal university seeks sustenance in the form of additional monetary resources, was eventually constructed into the focused code of 'Cash Cow Milking'. Later on, together with other focused codes, this supported the creation of a conceptual category expressed as 'Hunting and Gathering'. This encompassed many activities that were valued and rewarded by university elites in neoliberal universities, and was a significant factor in determining whether one would survive the experience of Professional Disarticulation.

Theoretical Construction

Theoretical coding of conceptual categories tends to be the most challenging and abstract aspect of grounded theorization. What I have done is to try to reconstruct what I think took place during the early years when Glaser and Strauss worked together. My theoretical coding matrix draws from Glaser's theoretical coding families and Strauss and Corbin's various forms of axial coding. The structure of the matrix was influenced in part by Ajzen's Theory of Planned Behavior (Ajzen 1991). I do not limit the use of codes to only one family, but sometimes mix different theoretical codes from different lists in order to tease out new properties and dimensions of the categories. An example of this is in Figure 28.6, where a selection of theoretical codes drawn from different families has been placed around the concept. Naturally, not every choice or combination yields new insights, but this structured procedure often helps to shed light on new facets about the conceptual categories, which can then lead to additional theoretical sampling and higher levels of conceptualization.

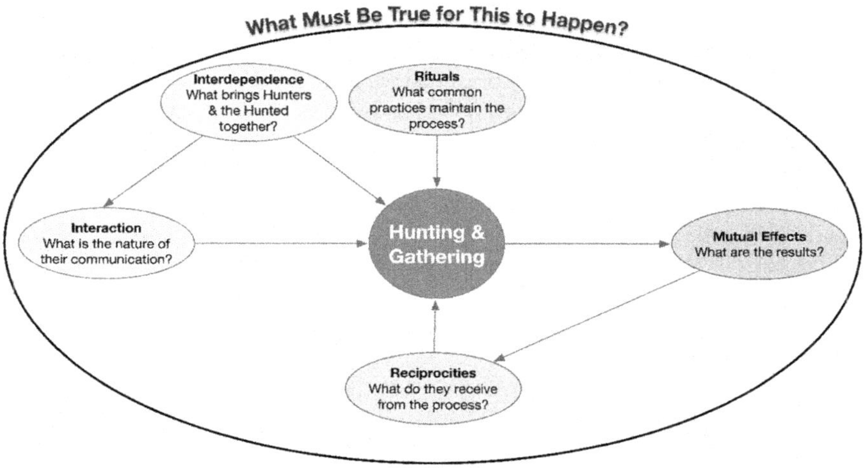

Figure 28.6 Retrodactive theoretical coding matrix

Retrodactive inquiry continues with the theorist exploring what must be taking place in order for the theoretical coding and dimensions surrounding the concept to be true. Doing this will also draw one closer to possible causes and contextual issues, and enable the theorist to critically consider whether the social processes are desirable, and what should be done in order to address any social problems. However, this matrix should simply be one of several items to keep in one's methodological toolbox. Bryant's caveat is especially pertinent here: 'if used in an indiscriminate or mechanistic manner, the outcome is unlikely to constitute a substantive grounded theory' (Bryant 2017, p. 233).

Transformative Dissemination

The writing-up stage of Critical Grounded Theory begins almost immediately through the writing of memos. Those memos that eventually earn their place in the theory, due to their apparent fit with the data, are saved. Later categories formed from substantive and theoretical coding also become the structure for later chapters. Scholarly literature, accessed during the focused and theoretical generation stages, becomes the literature review for explaining social, historical, economic, and political issues that contextualize the theory. Critical Grounded Theorists should include something about their own background and perspective so that readers will understand the basic stance of the work. They should not shrink from commenting upon oppressive social processes and offer, as appropriate, possible solutions. Similar to what is seen in almost all forms of GTM, the theory is crafted into a narrative that attempts to be fair and relevant as a small mid-range critical analysis of a substantive area of sociological interest.

Assessment of the theory's successful utility will depend on whether it transforms, empowers, and motivates people towards peaceful discourse and cooperative action. Evidence of this for the Theory of Vocational Disarticulation can be seen partly in that it has become part of the ongoing scholarly discussion urging EAP educators to think more deeply about the critical issues affecting their profession (Holborow 2015; Ding & Bruce 2017;

Pearson 2017). Implications of the theory have been considered by presenters in conferences Europe, Asia, and North America. The strongest evidence for me came in May 2017 during a symposium at the University of Durham in the UK, where I had been invited as a featured speaker. During the later workshop sessions, I encountered several EAP teachers who were members of reading circles at several British universities. They were studying my book, incorporating the theoretical concepts into their work vocabulary, and discussing ways of reclaiming their vocational identities. Interesting conversations ensued about how to restore their collective agency and seek positive, proactive ways of addressing those who would reshape their work as educators into that of linguistic service providers.

CONCLUSION

This chapter has drawn from a number of interrelated perspectives, theories, and methods in order to present a fuller picture of what constitutes the process and product of Critical Grounded Theory. A definition of the methodology, its autopoietic relationship to other members of the GTM family, and distinct practices have been considered.

CGT is in a state of becoming: other theorists will further add to or subtract from what has been presented here. Even so, our work as Critical Grounded Theorists will continue to support and flow into the theoretical work of others as we seek to foster a deeper, wider understanding of social processes affecting our world.

This is of even greater urgency today, as the 21st century has become increasingly scarred by the rise of authoritarianism and crude populism. Social stratification along economic, ethnic, and educational lines are widening. Within the realm of Higher Education, the research activities of academics are effectively being censored under the guise of 'ethics'. Educational discourse in the classroom touching upon unpopular topics are being purged and sanitized as a result of managerial guidelines aimed at ensuring student satisfaction. This has allowed the proliferation of blurred narratives, half-truths, and outright lies to wreak havoc on the hitherto informed liberal societies. 'Post-truth' has become a dark watchword for describing the toxic nature of public discourse around the world.

In times such as these, theories that expose oppressive social processes, and which question the injustices taking place within our societies, are desperately needed. Descriptive theories on 'life as it is' run the risk of supporting a status quo that currently rewards those who both prey on and profit off of the weakest members of society. The time has come for Critical Grounded Theory.

REFERENCES

Abrahams, F. (2009). Examining the Preservice Practicum Experience of Undergraduate Music Education Majors: Exploring Connections and Dispositions through Multiple Perspectives: A Critical Grounded Theory. *Journal of Music Teacher Education*, *19*(1), 80–92.

Agger, B. (1991). Critical Theory, Poststructuralism, Postmodernism: Their Sociological Relevance. *Annual Review of Sociology*, *17*, 105–131.

Ajzen, I. (1991). The Theory of Planned Behavior. *Organizational Behavior and Human Decision Processes*, *50*(2), 179–211.

Annells, M. (1996). Grounded Theory Method: Philosophical Perspectives, Paradigm of Inquiry, and Postmodernism. *Qualitative Health Research*, *6*(3), 379–393.
Archer, M. (1998). Introduction: Realism in the Social Sciences. In M. Archer, T. Lawson, A. Collier, A. Norrie & R. Bhaskar (Eds.), *Critical Realism: Essential Readings* (pp. 189–205). London: Routledge.
Arnoldi, J. (2001). Niklas Luhmann: An Introduction. *Theory Culture Society*, *18*(1), 1–13.
Babbie, E. (2004). *The Practice of Social Research* (10th ed.). Belmont, CA: Thomson-Wadsworth.
Belfrage, C. & Hauf, F. (2016). The Gentle Art of Retroduction: Critical Realism, Cultural Political Economy and Critical Grounded Theory. *Organization Studies*, Online First, 31 August, pp. 1–21.
Berger, P. & Luckmann, T. (1967). *The Social Construction of Reality* (3rd ed.). London: Penguin.
Bhaskar, R. (2009). *Scientific Realism and Human Emancipation*. London: Routledge.
Birks, M. & Mills, J. (2011). *Grounded Theory: A Practical Guide*. London: Sage.
Blunt, S. (2016). Critical Realism and Grounded Theory: Analysing the Adoption of Outcomes for Disabled Children Using the Retroduction Framework. *Qualitative Social Work*, Online First, 21 September, pp. 1–19.
Bohman, J. (2008). Critical Theory. *The Stanford Encyclopedia of Philosophy* (Fall 2008 Edition), Stanford, CA: Stanford University Press. Retrieved 26 January, from http://plato.stanford.edu/archives/fall2008/entries/critical-theory/
Brans, M. & Rossbach, S. (1997). The Autopoeisis of Administrative Systems: Niklas Luhmann on Public Administration and Public Policy. *Public Administration*, *75*, 417–439.
Bryant, A. (2017). *Grounded Theory and Grounded Theorizing: Pragmatism in Research Practice*. Oxford and New York Oxford University Press.
Bryant, A. & Charmaz, K. (2007). Grounded Theory Research: Methods and Practices. In A. Bryant & K. Charmaz (Eds.), *The Sage Handbook of Grounded Theory* (pp. 1–28). London: Sage.
Bryman, A. (2001). *Social Research Methods*. Oxford: Oxford University Press.
Burawoy, M. (1991). The Extended Case Method. In M. Burawoy, A. Burton, A. Ferguson, K. Fox, J. Gamson, N. Gartrell, L. Hurst, C. Kurzman, L. Salzinger, J. Schiffman & S. Ui (Eds.), *Ethnography Unbound: Power and Resistance in the Modern Metropolis* (pp. 271–287). Berkeley & Los Angeles, CA: University of California Press.
Butt, T. & Parton, N. (2005). Constructive Social Work and Personal Construct Theory: The Case of Psychological Trauma. *British Journal of Social Work*, *35*, 793–806.
Capra, F. (1996). *The Web of Life*. New York: Anchor Books.
Carr, A. (2000). Critical Theory and the Management of Change in Organizations. *Journal of Organizational Change Management*, *13*(3), 208–220.
Charmaz, K. (2000). Grounded Theory: Objectivist and Constructivist Methods. In N. Denzin & Y. Lincoln (Eds.), *Sage Handbook of Qualitative Research* (2nd ed., pp. 509–535). Thousand Oaks, CA: Sage.
Charmaz, K. (2005). Grounded Theory in the 21st Century: Applications for Advancing Social Justice Studies. In N. Denzin & Y. Lincoln (Eds.), *Sage Handbook of Qualitative Research* (3rd ed., pp. 507–536). Thousand Oaks, CA: Sage.
Charmaz, K. (2006). *Constructing Grounded Theory*. London: Sage.
Charmaz, K. (2008). Constructionism and the Grounded Theory Method. In J. Holstein & J. Gubrium (Eds.), *Handbook of Constructionist Research* (pp. 397–412). New York: Guilford Press.
Charmaz, K. (2011). Grounded Theory Methods in Social Justice Research. In N. Denzin & Y. Lincoln (Eds.), *The Sage Handbook of Qualitative Research* (4th ed., pp. 359–380). Thousand Oaks, CA: Sage.
Charmaz, K. (2014). *Constructing Grounded Theory*. Thousand Oaks, CA: Sage.
Clarke, A. (2005). *Situational Analysis: Grounded Theory after the Postmodern Turn*. Thousand Oaks, CA: Sage.
Clarke, A. (2015). From Grounded Theory to Situational Analysis: What's New? Why? How? In A. Clarke, C. Friese & R. Washburn (Eds.), *Situational Analysis in Practice: Mapping Research with Grounded Theory* (1st ed., pp. 84–118). Walnut Creek, CA: Left Coast Press/Routledge.
Cohen, L., Manion, L. & Morrison, K. (2003). *Research Methods in Education* (5th ed.). London & New York: RoutledgeFalmer.
Corbin, J. & Strauss, A. (2008). *Basics of Qualitative Research: Techniques and Procedures for Developing Grounded Theory* (3rd ed.). Thousand Oaks, CA: Sage.

Corbin, J. & Strauss, A. (2015). *Basics of Qualitative Research: Techniques and Procedures for Developing Grounded Theory* (4th ed.). Thousand Oaks, CA: Sage.

Cuff, E., Sharrock, W. & Francis, D. (2006). *Perspectives in Sociology* (5th ed.). London: Routledge.

Denzin, N. & Lincoln, Y. (2000). Introduction: The Discipline and Practice of Qualitative Research. In N. Denzin & Y. Lincoln (Eds.), *Handbook of Qualitative Research* (2nd ed., pp. 1–29). Thousand Oaks, CA: Sage.

Ding, A. & Bruce, I. (2017). *The English for Academic Purposes Practitioner: Operating on the Edge of Academia*. Cham, Switzerland: Springer International.

Easterby-Smith, M. (1981). The Design, Analysis and Interpretation of Repertory Grids. In M. L. G. Shaw (Ed.), *Recent Advances in Personal Construct Technology* (pp. 9–30). London: Academic Press.

Fine, G. (1993). The Sad Demise, Mysterious Disappearance and Glorious Triumph of Symbolic Interactionism. *Annual Review of Sociology*, *19*, 61–87.

Fransella, F., Bell, R. & Bannister, D. (2004). *A Manual for Repertory Grid Technique* (2nd ed.). Chichester, UK: John Wiley & Sons.

Fromm, M. & Bacher, A. (2014). *GridSuite 4*. University of Stuttgart, Stuttgart, Germany.

Gibson, B. (2007). Accommodating Critical Theory. In A. Bryant & K. Charmaz (Eds.), *The Sage Handbook of Grounded Theory* (pp. 436–453). London: Sage.

Gibson, B. & Hartman, J. (2013). *Rediscovering Grounded Theory*. London: Sage.

Gilgun, J. (2010). An Oral History of Grounded Theory: Transcript of an Interview with Leonard Schatzman. *Current Issues in Qualitative Research: An Occasional Publication for Field Researchers from a Variety of Disciplines*, *1* (10), (Online) https://janegilgun.wordpress.com/2012/03/06/transcript-of-an-interview-with-leonard-schatzman/ (accessed 18 June 2015).

Glaser, B. (1978). *Theoretical Sensitivity: Advances in the Methodology of Grounded Theory*. Mill Valley, CA: Sociology Press.

Glaser, B. (1992). *Basics of Grounded Theory Analysis*. Mill Valley, CA: Sociology Press.

Glaser, B. (1998). *Doing Grounded Theory: Issues and Discussions*. Mill Valley, CA: Sociology Press.

Glaser, B. (1999). The Future of Grounded Theory. *Qualitative Health Research*, *9*(6), 836–845.

Glaser, B. (2008). *Doing Quantitative Grounded Theory*. Mill Valley, CA: Sociology Press.

Glaser, B. & Strauss, A. (1967/1999). *The Discovery of Grounded Theory: Strategies for Qualitative Research*. New York: Aldine de Gruyter.

Grenz, S. (1996). *A Primer on Postmodernism*. Grand Rapids, MI: William P. Eerdmans.

Guba, E. (1992). Relativism. *Curriculum Inquiry*, *22*(1), 17–23.

Guba, E. & Lincoln, Y. (1998). Competing Paradigms in Qualitative Research. In N. Denzin & Y. Lincoln (Eds.), *The Landscape of Qualitative Research* (pp. 195–220). Thousand Oaks, CA: Sage.

Guelke, L. (1976). The Philosophy of Idealism. *Annals of the Association of American Geographers*, *66*(1), 168–173.

Habermas, J. (1984). *The Theory of Communicative Action*. London: Heinemann.

Hadley, G. (2015). *English for Academic Purposes in Neoliberal Universities: A Critical Grounded Theory*. New York & London: Springer.

Hadley, G. (2017a). The Games People Play: A Critical Study of 'Resource Leeching' among 'Blended' English for Academic Purpose Professionals in Neoliberal Universities. In M. Flubacher & A. Del Percio (Eds.), *Language, Education, and Neoliberalism: Critical Studies in Sociolinguistics* (pp. 184–203). Bristol, UK: Multilingual Matters.

Hadley, G. (2017b). *Grounded Theory in Applied Linguistics Research: A Practical Guide*. London & New York: Routledge.

Hallberg, L. (2006). The 'Core Category' of Grounded Theory: Making Constant Comparisons. *International Journal of Qualitative Studies on Health and Well-Being*, *1*, 141–148.

Hense, C. & McFerran, K. (2016). Toward a Critical Grounded Theory. *Qualitative Research Journal*, *16*(4), 402–416.

Holborow, M. (2015). Neoliberalism. In *The Encyclopedia of Applied Linguistics* (pp. 1–6). Hoboken, NJ: John Wiley & Sons.

Hook, D. (2002). Psychotherapy, Discourse, and the Production of Psychopathology. In D. Hook & G. Eagle (Eds.), *Psychopathology and Social Prejudice* (pp. 20–54). Cape Town, SA: University of Cape Town Press.

Hook, D. (2007). *Foucault, Psychology and the Analytics of Power*. Basingstoke, UK & New York: Palgrave Macmillan.
Hutchinson, S. (1988). Education and Grounded Theory. In R. Sherman & R. Webb (Eds.), *Qualitative Research in Education: Focus and Methods* (pp. 123–140). London: Falmer.
Jankowicz, D. (2004). *The Easy Guide to Repertory Grids*. Chichester, UK: Wiley.
Kelly, G. A. (1955). *A Theory of Personality*. New York: Norton.
Kelly, G. A. (1955/1991). *The Psychology of Personal Constructs: A Theory of Personality*. London & New York: Routledge.
Kelly, G. A. (1963). *A Theory of Personality: The Psychology of Personal Constructs*. New York: Norton.
Kempster, S. & Parry, K. (2011). Grounded Theory and Leadership Research: A Critical Realist Perspective. *The Leadership Quarterly*, *22*(1), 106–120.
Kilduff, M. & Mehra, A. (1997). Postmodernism and Organizational Research. *Academy of Management Review*, *22*(2), 453–481.
Kincheloe, J. (2008). *Knowledge and Critical Pedagogy: An Introduction*. New York: Springer Science and Business Media.
Kincheloe, J. & McLaren, P. (2000). Rethinking Critical Theory and Qualitative Research. In N. Denzin & Y. Lincoln (Eds.), *Handbook of Qualitative Research* (2nd ed., pp. 279–313). Thousand Oaks, CA: Sage.
Kushner, K. & Morrow, R. (2003). Grounded Theory, Feminist Theory, Critical Theory: Toward Theoretical Triangulation. *Advances in Nursing Science Critical & Postmodern Perspectives*, *26*(1), 30–43.
Larsen-Freeman, D. (2007). On the Complementarity of Chaos/Complexity Theory and Dynamic Systems Theory in Understanding the Second Language Acquisition Process. *Bilingualism: Language and Cognition*, *10*(1), 35–37.
Layder, D. (1993). *New Strategies in Social Research: An Introduction and Guide*. Cambridge, UK: Polity Press.
Lincoln, Y. (1998). The Ethics of Teaching in Qualitative Research. *Qualitative Inquiry*, *4*(3), 315–327.
Lincoln, Y. & Guba, E. (2000). Paradigmatic Controversies, Contradictions, and Emerging Confluences. In N. Denzin & Y. Lincoln (Eds.), *Handbook of Qualitative Research* (2nd ed., pp. 163–188). Thousand Oaks, CA: Sage.
Locke, K. (2005). *Grounded Theory in Management Research*. London: Sage.
Lowe, S. (2001). In the Kingdom of the Blind, the One-Eyed Man is King. *International Journal of Cross-Cultural Management*, *1*(3), 313–332.
Lowe, S. & Carr, A. (2003). Paradigmapping and Management as a Moral Art: Clearing a Path through the Incommensurability Debate in Organisation and Management Studies. In J. Biberman & A. Alkhafaji (Eds.), *Business Research Yearbook: Global Business Perspectives* (*Vol. 10*, pp. 778–782). Saline, MI: McNaughton & Gunn.
Lowe, S., Carr, A. & Thomas, M. (2004). Paradigmapping Marketing Theory. *European Journal of Marketing*, *38*(9/10), 1057–1064.
Lowe, S., Carr, A., Thomas, M. & Watkins-Mathys, L. (2005). The Fourth Hermeneutic in Marketing Theory. *Marketing Theory*, *5*(2), 185–203.
Luhmann, N. (1994). Speaking and Silence. *New German Critique*, *61*, 25–37.
Luhmann, N. (1995). *Social Systems*. Stanford, CA: Stanford University Press.
Luhmann, N. (2001). Notes on the Project 'Poetry and Social Theory'. *Theory, Culture & Society*, *18*(1), 15–27.
Manias, E. & Street, A. (2000). Possibilities for Critical Social Theory and Foucault's Work: A Toolbox Approach. *Nursing Inquiry*, *7*(1), 50–60.
Maturana, H. (1975). The Organization of the Living: A Theory of the Living Organization. *International Journal of Man Machine Studies*, *7*, 313–332.
Maturana, H. (1987). The Biological Foundations of Self-Consciousness and the Physical Domain of Existence. In E. Caianiello (Ed.), *Physics of Cognitive Processes* (pp. 324–379). Singapore: World Scientific.
Maturana, H. & Varela, F. (1980). *Autopoiesis and Cognition: The Realization of the Living*. Dordrecht, NL: Reidel.

Maturana, H. & Varela, F. (1987). *The Tree of Knowledge*. Boston, MA: Shambhala Press.

Michell, J. (2003). The Quantitative Imperative: Positivism, Naive Realism and the Place of Qualitative Methods in Psychology. *Theory and Psychology*, *13*(1), 5–31.

Mills, J., Bonner, A. & Francis, K. (2006). The Development of Constructivist Grounded Theory. *International Journal of Qualitative Methods*, *5*(1), 1–10, (Online) www.ualberta.ca/~iiqm/backissues/5_1/pdf/mills.pdf (accessed 23 October 2006).

Mingers, J. (1995). *Self-Producing System: Implications and Applications of Autopoiesis*. New York: Springer Science+Business Media.

Mingers, J. (2002). Can Social Systems be Autopoietic? Assessing Luhmann's Social Theory. *Sociological Review*, *50*(2), 278–299.

Mitchell, R. C. (2007). Grounded Theory and Autopoietic Social Systems: Are They Methodologically Compatible? *Qualitative Sociology Review*, *3*(2), 105–118, (Online) www.qualitativesociologyreview.org/ENG/archive_eng.php (accessed July 4, 2008).

Monk, M. & Dillon, J. (Eds.). (1995). *Learning to Teach Science: Activities for Student Teachers and Mentors*. London: Falmer.

Moore, T. (2013). Critical Thinking: Seven Definitions in Search of a Concept. *Studies in Higher Education*, *38*(4), 506–522.

Pearson, J. (2017). Processfolio: Uniting Academic Literacies and Critical Emancipatory Action Research for Practitioner-Led Inquiry into EAP Writing Assessment. *Critical Inquiry in Language Studies*, *14*(2–3), 158–181.

Postma, L., Blignaut, S., Swan, K. & Sutinen, E. (2013). Reflections on the Use of Grounded Theory to Uncover Patterns of Exclusion in an Online Discussion Forum at an Institution of Higher Education. *International Journal of Qualitative Methods*, *12*(1), 529–550.

Potter, W. (1996). *An Analysis of Thinking and Research About Qualitative Methods*. Mahwah, NJ: Lawrence Erlbaum Associates.

Redman-MacLaren, M. & Mills, J. (2015). Transformational Grounded Theory: Theory, Voice, and Action. *International Journal of Qualitative Methods*, *14*(3), 1–12.

Redman-MacLaren, M., Mills, J., Tommbe, R., MacLaren, D., Speare, R. & McBride, W. (2017). Implications of Male Circumcision for Women in Papua New Guinea: A Transformational Grounded Theory Study. *BMC Women's Health*, *17*(53), 1–10. PMC database.

Reinharz, S. (1992). *Feminist Methods in Social Research*. New York: Oxford University Press.

Richardson, L. (2000). Writing: A Method of Inquiry. In N. Denzin & Y. Lincoln (Eds.), *Handbook of Qualitative Research* (pp. 923–948). Thousand Oaks, CA: Sage.

Ritchie, J. (2004). The Applications of Qualitative Methods to Social Research. In J. Ritchie & J. Lewis (Eds.), *Qualitative Research Practice* (pp. 24–46). London: Sage.

Schatzman, L. (1991). Dimensional Analysis: Notes on an Alternative Approach to the Grounding of Theory in Qualitative Research. In D. Maines (Ed.), *Social Organization and Social Process: Essays in Honor of Anselm Strauss* (pp. 303–314). New York: Aldine de Gruyter.

Schatzman, L. & Strauss, A. (1973). *Field Research: Strategies for a Natural Sociology*. Englewood Cliffs, NJ: Prentice-Hall.

Scheurich, J. (2001). *Research Method in the Postmodern*. London: RoutledgeFalmer.

Shaw, M. L. G. (1980). *On Becoming a Personal Scientist: Interactive Computer Elicitation of Personal Models of the World*. London: Academic Press.

Shaw, M. L. G. & Gaines, B. (2009). *Rep 5*, Centre for Person-Computer Studies, Cobble Hill, British Columbia, Canada.

Shaw, M. L. G. & McKnight, C. (1981). *Think Again: Personal Problem-Solving and Decision-Making*. Englewood Cliffs, NJ: Prentice-Hall.

Strauss, A. (1959/1969). *Mirrors and Masks*. Mill Valley, CA: Sociology Press.

Strauss, A. (1987). *Qualitative Analysis for Social Scientists*. New York: Cambridge University Press.

Strauss, A. (1993). *Continual Permutations of Action*. New York: Walter de Gruyter.

Strauss, A. & Corbin, J. (1990). *Basics of Qualitative Research*. Newbury Park, CA: Sage.

Strauss, A. & Corbin, J. (Eds.) (1997). *Grounded Theory in Practice*. Thousand Oaks, CA: Sage.

Strauss, A. & Corbin, J. (1998). *Basics of Qualitative Research: Techniques and Procedures for Developing Grounded Theory* (2nd ed.). Thousand Oaks, CA: Sage.

Ulrich, W. (2007). Philosophy for Professionals: Towards Critical Pragmatism. *The Journal of the Operational Research Society*, *58*(8), 1109–1113.

Urquhart, C. & Fernández, W. (2013). Using Grounded Theory Method in Information Systems: The Researcher as Blank Slate and Other Myths. *Journal of Information Technology*, *28*(3), 224–236.

Werkmeister, W. (1948). *The Basis and Structure of Knowledge*. New York: Harper & Brothers.

Wuest, J. (1995). Feminist Grounded Theory: An Exploration of the Congruency and Tensions between Two Traditions in Knowledge Discovery. *Qualitative Health Research*, *5*(1), 125–137.

Wuest, J. (2000). Negotiating with Helping Systems: An Example of Grounded Theory Evolving Through Emergent Fit. *Qualitative Health Research*, *10*(1), 51–70.

APPENDIX

Research Philosophy Inventory

This inventory will help you to position your philosophy of science with complementary version of the Grounded Theory Methodology. Aspects of this questionnaire have been adapted from Monk, M. & Dillon, J. (Eds.) (1995). *Learning to Teach Science: Activities for Student Teachers and Mentors.* London: Falmer, and Hadley, G. (2017). *Grounded Theory in Applied Linguistics Research: A Practical Guide.* London and New York: Routledge.

Step One: Expressing Your Beliefs

Within the context of conducting your own research, which of the statements below would you feel most comfortable with? Circle a number on the scale that most closely represents your position. Remember that there are no right or wrong answers in this inventory, and that number values are simply used to help you to locate some possible features that form part of your research philosophy.

1. Both a social and empirical reality exist out there, regardless of our ability to perceive them. | Neither a social nor empirical reality can exist without a human mind to perceive them. | An empirical reality exists out there, but our perceptions differ with regard to the social reality.

0	1	2	3	4	5	6	7	8	9	10

2. Valid and replicable findings about language learning are best derived from numerical data. | When studying issues related to language learning, attending to the words and statements of research informants provides a better quality of data. | Words and numbers are simply symbols for exploring language learning. Either, both, or neither might be useful, depending on the situation.

0	1	2	3	4	5	6	7	8	9	10

3. Research methods should follow clearly set procedures in order to produce reliable data. | Research methods should be flexible enough to uncover frequent patterns of human behavior. | Research methods should be mixed strategically in order to create a fuller picture of the issues being investigated.

0	1	2	3	4	5	6	7	8	9	10

4. Theories should be produced from knowable, empirical events. Intuition, imagination, and challenging the status quo are all distractions. Theories should help people to assess their situation and make necessary adjustments. | Theories should fit with empirical events, but should also allow for intuition, inference, and the use of one's 'sociological imagination' in order to provide a fuller, richer understanding of issues taking place in the social world. | Theorization both should challenge and transform the status quo. Continuous theorization, rather than 'theory' as a static product, should be the goal, because the social world is dynamic and constantly changing.

0	1	2	3	4	5	6	7	8	9	10

5. Truth is an external concept that can be discovered, in part, through rational means. Real truth is not a matter of personal opinion. | 'Truth' is an internal construct that must be understood within the context of the community within which it was formed. What is true for one group or person may not be true for others. | There are many perspectives regarding what is true, but not all of them are equally useful.

0	1	2	3	4	5	6	7	8	9	10

6\. Researchers should discover factors that will enable others to predict potential issues and take action before they happen.

Researchers should seek for greater insight into the experiences of research participants, thereby helping them and others to better understand important issues that are affecting them.

Researchers should critically deconstruct current thinking and beliefs in order to create the impetus for building better social systems and structures.

0	**1**	**2**	**3**	**4**	**5**	**6**	**7**	**8**	**9**	**10**

7\. Successful researchers have personal endurance, focus, as well as specialist knowledge and skills.

Successful researchers build rapport with research informants while also developing supportive communities of expertise and wisdom.

Successful researchers engage in compassionate, interactive discourse that encourages research participants to embrace positive change.

0	**1**	**2**	**3**	**4**	**5**	**6**	**7**	**8**	**9**	**10**

8\. The most useful research results are valid, reliable, and replicable.

The most useful research results are believable, insightful, and original.

The most useful research results are pragmatically applicable and revolutionary.

0	**1**	**2**	**3**	**4**	**5**	**6**	**7**	**8**	**9**	**10**

9\. The researcher must strive to be distinct and separate from the research subjects. This is in order to protect the data from becoming contaminated.

The worldview of the researcher will inevitably become intertwined with the worldview of the informants. This results in new, more nuanced knowledge constructions.

The researcher works together with the research participants in order to change and improve the issues being studied.

0	**1**	**2**	**3**	**4**	**5**	**6**	**7**	**8**	**9**	**10**

10\. When conducting research, you should have some idea about what you want to investigate and the answers that you are looking for.

When conducting research, you never know where it will take you and what you might find. It is important to discover new perspectives.

When conducting research, it is important to develop results that have pragmatic value to the research participants.

0	**1**	**2**	**3**	**4**	**5**	**6**	**7**	**8**	**9**	**10**

Step Two: Plotting Your Position

In the table below, add up all of the numbers from each of the ten statements. You will have a total score somewhere between '0' and '100'.

1.	2.	3.	=
4.	5.	6.	=
7.	8.	9.	=
		10.	=
		Total:	

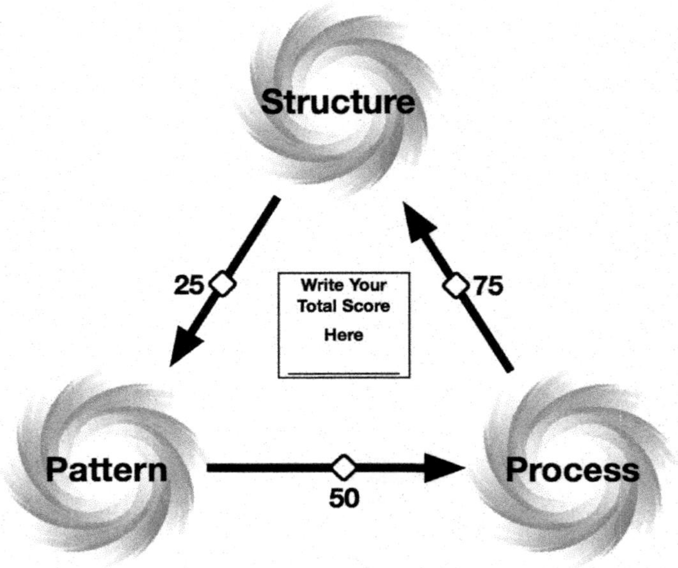

Step Three: Interpreting the Results

Few researchers are completely within one paradigm or another. The interconnected nature of our beliefs about knowledge, existence, and methodology suggests that many of us work in blended spaces. For that reason, this assessment can only point to tendencies. The following is a list of suggestions as to where you might want to explore more as you use the Grounded Theory Methodology in your upcoming research project.

0 - 25: You might feel more comfortable working with quantitative data, and finding out how large groups of people deal with certain issues. Consult Barney Glaser's *Doing Quantitative Grounded Theory* (2008, Sociology Press) for methodological advice. If you are comfortable with qualitative data, Barry Gibson and Jan Hartman's *Rediscovering Grounded Theory* (Sage, 2013) is another very accessible presentation of Classic Grounded Theory. Your resultant theory will likely represent a discussion of empirically observable social processes, and center on problems which can be predicted, thereby giving people greater control over difficult situations.

26 - 45: You may be most interested in understanding regularly occurring patterns of social interaction, and will need clearcut procedures for understanding these frequent transactions and the conditions which give them meaning. There are many methodological guides by Juliet Corbin and Anselm Strauss, that you might find helpful. The most current is *Basics of Qualitative Research, 4th Edition* (Sage, 2015). Those with scores from the high 30s may also wish to consult Melanie Birks and Jane Mills' *Grounded Theory: A Practical Guide* (2011, Sage).

46 - 65: It is likely that you view reality as a social construction, and that you would enjoy collaborating with research informants in order to create an ever-developing theory on problematic social phenomena. You need procedures that are flexible enough to be adapted according to co-constructed social sphere. Kathy Charmaz's *Constructing Grounded Theory* (Sage, 2014) is recommended for your methodological and theoretical concerns.

66 - 99: It is likely that you see social realities and knowledge as multilayered and with many valid interpretations. Those with scores up to the low 70s will likely seek for novel, creative theorizing about the shared experiences of specific discourse communities. Charmaz's book, together with Adele Clarke's books on Situational Analysis (2005, Sage; 2015, Routledge), would likely be helpful. Those with scores from the mid 70s upward will see theory as an ongoing process of reconstructing social chaos into pragmatic frameworks that challenge common assumptions. Seeking positive, pragmatic solutions to social issues might underpin your research motivations. Bryant's *Grounded Theory and Grounded Theorizing* (Oxford, 2017) should be able to complement these concerns. Critical Grounded Theory might also complement your research perspective.

PART VI

GT Researchers and Methods in Local and Global Worlds

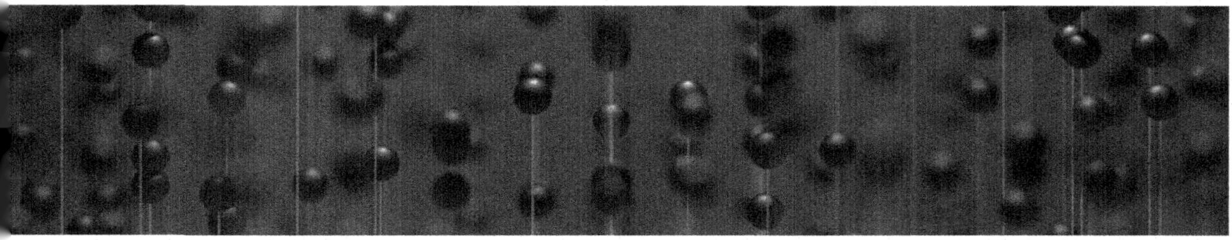

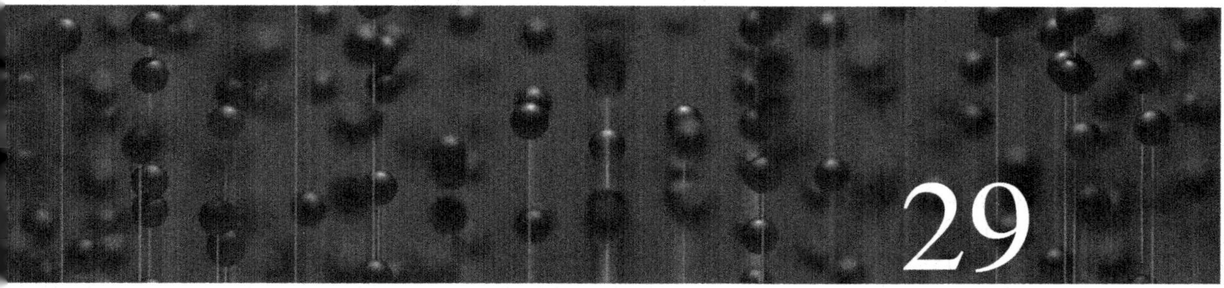

The Implications of Internationalization for Teaching, Learning and Practising Grounded Theory

Joanna Crossman and Hiroko Noma

CONCEPTUALIZING INTERNATIONALIZATION AND GROUNDED THEORY AND THE RELATIONSHIP BETWEEN THE TWO

The purpose of this chapter is to argue that the internationalization of universities around the world has fostered the exportation of grounded theory, now learned and practised by many researchers who are neither North American nor western. It explores the implications of internationalization for teaching, learning, practising and developing grounded theory. We argue that the paradigmatic and operational nature of internationalization has the potential to influence these processes profoundly. Much of the discussion will focus on culture, language and meaning, as key elements embedded within internationalization in higher education that are relevant to how grounded theorists learn, practise and develop their craft.

In the second edition of Charmaz's, *Constructing Grounded Theory* (2014a), the author explored the implications of internationalization for research education and practice with respect to grounded theory. With characteristic insight, she brought the voices of practising grounded theorists and research educators working in a variety of cultural contexts, to address the subject. As Charmaz (2014a) remarked, further scholarly and empirical work on the topic is timely.

In order to appreciate the implications of grounded theory being used around the world, it is useful to consider how prevailing conditions at the time of its development have contributed to its nature. Charmaz (2014b) has argued that the cultural, economic, historical, political and geographic conditions of the United States have determined the logic, values, epistemological assumptions and worldview that influence the kinds of problems investigated and the research questions posed within grounded theory.

Two pertinent lines of enquiry have yet to be explored in any depth. First, and somewhat ironically, Charmaz observed that despite the widespread exportation of grounded theory to study phenomena in a variety of cultures, few scholars have explored the cultural assumptions that underpin the methodology itself (Charmaz, 2014b). Second, little is known about the implications of globalization and more specifically, internationalization, for the teaching, learning, practice and development of grounded theory. Thirty years after the publication of *The Discovery of Grounded Theory* (Glaser & Strauss, 1967), Glaser declared, '...grounded theory has gone global, seriously global' (Glaser, 1999, p. 837). However, Glaser did not pursue the implications of his observation, beyond a cursory reference to the utility of the methodology for exploring diversity in a variety of professional settings and suggesting that grounded theorists were somehow less vulnerable to overlooking realities inconsistent with their own cultural preconceptions (Glaser, 1999, p. 837).

The widespread and sometimes indiscriminate use of the term 'internationalization' has given rise to criticisms that the concept is at risk of losing its meaning, and the field its direction (Knight, 2012, p. 22). Compounding the problem, 'globalization' and 'internationalization' are sometimes used synonymously despite extensive discussion and debate on how the terms can be defined and differentiated (see Altback & Knight, 2007; Beerkens, 2003; Crossman, 2003; Crossman & Clarke, 2010; Knight, 2004, 2012; Lumby & Foskett, 2016).

Few would gainsay Daly's (1999) observation that globalization is associated with global, economic integration. Curiously, perhaps, as its meaning has become increasingly sophisticated, given the varied contexts to which it is applied, that sophistication has come with a certain obfuscation. Given this state of affairs, Giddens' (1999) assessment of the contested nature of globalization is not difficult to understand. Georgantzas, Katsamakas and Solowiej (2010, p. 622) have also noted a 'divisive public discourse' where one can witness at once, both derision and affirmation. One reason for the complexity of this concept, lies in the context of a transforming world (Georgantzas et al., 2010; Giddens, 1999). Globalization, as Giddens sees it, influences 'everything' and to this end, his work has highlighted the meaning and implications of this dynamic process in the contexts of politics, society, technology and economies, with consideration to its impact on the movement of labour and access to welfare, for example (Georgantzas et al., 2010; Giddens, 1999, 2001; Giddens, Diamond, & Liddle, 2006).

Globalization has contributed to the internationalization of higher education that manages the operationalization of practices, in terms of goals, academic systems and functions, such as policies and delivery of programmes, orchestrated at institutional and national levels (Altbach & Knight, 2007; Knight, 2004). Internationalizing strategies in western universities are evident in the increasing enrollments of international students (mostly from Asia) (González & Lincoln, 2006; Park & Lunt, 2015; Singh & Guihua, 2011), staff mobility, exchanges and transnational partnerships (Feng, 2013; Mamiseishvili, 2013; Park & Lunt, 2015). Against this backdrop, the impact of internationalization on research practices, at all levels, has been described as transformational (Frølich, 2006).

Discussions with respect to globalization and internationalization, as concepts, help to frame perspectives on how grounded theory relates to them. One way to do this is to consider the globalization and internationalization through an emic and etic lens.

Emic perspectives are grounded in 'knowledge informed by the culture of those under study' (Buckley, Chapman, Clegg, & Gajewska-De Mattos, 2014) necessitating, fostering and celebrating the role of *insider* and a particularist way of knowing (Zhu & Bargiela-Chiappini, 2013). Etic perspectives are associated with those of the *outsider*, where concepts are derived from the culture of the researcher and applied to interpret other cultures (Zhu & Bargiela-Chiappini, 2013). Despite this somewhat polarizing presentation of emic and etic perspectives, a grounded theory study of nursing practice in New Zealand (Hoare, Buetow, Mills, & Francis, 2012) illustrates how theoretical sensitivity can be heightened by drawing on both at different points in the research process. The authors posit that emic and etic approaches are not in fact, binary constructs but fall on a continuum, depending upon the relationships, experiences and role of the researcher plays during the research process (Hoare et al., 2012).

Returning to the context of distinctions between globalization and internationalization, a globalized lens would tend to view higher research education, in etic ways, based on assumptions around being 'culture free' and emphasizing consistencies across national boundaries. Nerad (2010, p. 2), for example, conceives globalization as a force that drives greater commonality across the world in the practices and trends of research education. Gobo (2011) advocates monocultural research methods developed in Europe and the USA, suggesting less emphasis upon the needs, interests and voice of local contexts. An etic perspective is distinct from an internationalized and emic approach that tends to value and celebrate any differences in national and local cultural identities (Crossman, 2003). However, it is the emic promotion of cultural distinctiveness and equality that Lumby and Foskett (2016, p. 96) believe presents a real challenge for the champions of internationalization.

An emic perspective aligns well with grounded theory, first, because it is focused on participant daily experiences that encompass multiple and complex perspectives of individuals and communities (Elliott & Higgins, 2012). Second, like grounded theory, it tends to value local, cultural identities that rest on relativist, subjectivist, pluralist epistemologies, allowing for the co-creation of perspectives between researcher and participants (Denzin & Lincoln, 2005; Schreiber & Tomm-Bonde, 2015, p. 659). As proponents of grounded theory no longer necessarily take the view that the researcher is a 'neutral knower' (Lempert, 2007, p. 247), and since constructivist grounded theory has developed as a widely used variant of the methodology, it seems likely that the co-creation of perspectives in international spaces has highlighted the theoretical assumptions internationalization and grounded theory appear to share.

The relationship of grounded theory to internationalization is revealing from a paradigmatic perspective. The concept of the paradigm has been highly influential over the last half-century, but interpretations of its meanings have evolved from being concerned with patterns, methods and recipes, to definitions encompassing values, belief systems and actions (Kuhn, 1962; Vogel, 2012, p. 34). On a simplistic level, internationalization constitutes a paradigm in that it has changed the way we view and experience the world and engage with cultural elements in human activity in contexts such as education. Thus, it has the capacity to bring about social and cultural change that in turn influence grounded theorists as students and academics, shaping their epistemological and ontological perspectives.

According to Gringeri, Barusch and Cambron (2013, p. 762), paradigms such as post-positivism, constructivism, critical theory and participatory action frameworks structure assumptions about knowledge. They influence how we view reality and are implicit in the research process and consequent publications. While paradigms have been distinguished from perspectives (such as feminism, ethnicity and cultural perspectives) (see Denzin, 2009, p. 89), the impact of internationalization on social and academic discourse, its acknowledgement of multiple perspectives being brought to political, economic and social issues, suggests a pervasive influence in how we think about problems and solutions on a range of issues and levels.

If a researcher's epistemological and ontological premises constitute a paradigm (Denzin & Lincoln, 2005, p. 22), then what we begin to see are multiple paradigms interacting in dynamic ways with one another. Another synergy between grounded theory and internationalization is that as paradigms, they tend to be focused on actions as well as beliefs and are taught through skills and techniques (Vogel, 2012). Just as learning is required in order to practise grounded theory, internationalization involves learning and the acquisition of intercultural skills, thinking in new ways as an embedded aspect of the curriculum (Brewer & Leask, 2012). Observing some synergies between grounded theory and internationalization does not suggest that they are conceptually one and the same, however. The paradigmatic synergies between internationalization and grounded theory are complex and ambiguous, as is common, according to Kuhn (1962), in relationships between similar paradigms.

The relationship between the two may also be understood in terms of Ludwig Fleck's work on thought collectives, where communities exchange their thoughts and ideas in an intellectual interaction (Sak & Pawlikowski, 2012). No doubt, it is premature to suggest such an exchange exists between grounded theorists and internationalization experts, or is discussed much in the literature, but Fleck's thought collectives help us to envision the potential for future intellectual interaction. In the present time, nevertheless, the process of paradigmatic comparisons between the two does suggest that grounded theory is an appropriate research methodology to explore internationalization given its capacity for cultural sensitivity and its potential to operationalize internationalization by illuminating the processes, actions, relationships and concepts that underpin it.

As a paradigm, internationalization constitutes a social shift, creating changes that, as Ralph, Birks and Chapman (2015) suggest, serve to bring about innovation in grounded theory, facilitated by a capacity for methodological dynamism. They argue that a contemporaneous interpretation of grounded theory is dependent upon prevailing forces that shape societal views about the world and, ultimately, the ontological and epistemological assumptions of the researcher. Over time, changing circumstances and the responsiveness of grounded theorists to them, affect methodological consumerism or, more specifically, the extent to which communities become receptive to variants of grounded theory (Ralph et al., 2015). Essentially, this process is the thesis of what Denzin and Lincoln (2005) referred to as moments, moments we suggest, that may be influenced by internationalization. Thus, while grounded theory, as a methodology has been described as a 'family' of similar methods (Bryant & Charmaz, 2007, p. 11), a focus on epistemological and ontological dissimilarities (Ralph et al., 2015) may in some way provide the flexibility required to engage with the social change internationalization brings, and, as Denzin (2009, p. 85) suggests, make sense of what has been discovered (Denzin, 2009, p. 85).

However, internationalization not only alters researcher interpretation, but also generates innovation in research methods, education (Nerad, 2010) practice and, ultimately, society, in a cycle of adjustment and renewal. Paradigms, such as internationalization, arise from societal change and innovation but with time may become assimilated into thoughts, values and beliefs about the world in mainstream society and, eventually, when they are no longer able to provide adequate explanations, they are usurped by others that do. Paradigms, as Kuhn (1962) pointed out, only exist 'for a time' (p. viii) because when they fail to address 'anomalies' they become modified (p. ix) until the anomalous becomes the expected (p. 53) and explainable within the paradigm. At the point when paradigms become widely accepted ways to explain the world, Wolgemuth et al. (2015) caution that conforming to them does not take precedence over remaining flexible, responsive and focused upon participants – a defining perspective of grounded theorists.

TEACHING AND LEARNING GROUNDED THEORY

Many grounded theorists learn their craft as higher-degree research students in mentored relationships with other qualitative researchers and, in the best of circumstances, with seasoned grounded theorists. The cultural backgrounds of researchers and the research settings they explore are becoming increasingly complex (Park & Lunt, 2015). Internationalization has changed the cultural profiles of university academics and research students at a fundamental level and, in consequence, the teaching and learning experience, including research education. Eclectic cultural profiles can bring strengths to designing and conducting grounded theory studies. For example, international research supervisors can capitalize upon their 'foreignness' for the benefit of a domestic research students (Mamiseishvili, 2013, p. 97) by bringing personal, linguistic, cultural perspectives to the research process that might otherwise be overlooked. One way to do this is by posing questions about taken-for-granted assumptions. The intercultural relationship that ensues between an international higher-degree student and a supervisor can be rich and rewarding with implications for learning about and conducting grounded theory. It can involve intercultural contexts that draw on the cultural capital of both research student and supervisor, as a ghostly co-constructor, guiding, in the questions (s)he asks, the things (s)he notices, the suggestions (s)he makes. Thus, interactions between grounded theory supervisors and students, in this way, can contribute to cultural sensitivity and reflexivity (see Evans, 2013; McCreaddie & Payne, 2010; Thornberg, 2012) and respond to a call for reflexivity in culturally co-constructed research work (Mruck & Mey, 2007, p. 515).

International grounded theory students enrolled in western universities do not always conduct cross-cultural or intercultural research, but many do, often capitalizing upon their own cultural identity to provide insights arising from an insider's heightened theoretical sensitivity. That sensitivity can be critical to counter the curious experience of some educated cultural insiders who find it difficult to engage with studies that explore their own local contexts through a western lens, managed through authors, editors and reviewers, as gatekeepers (see Noma, 2009). The cultural capital of a grounded theory student is an asset warranting a supervisor's careful attention and encouragement. Doing so may involve becoming a critical listener with the humility to become, at times, a learner, taken by the hand of a cultural insider in order to appreciate the research context through the eyes of the student and participants. Critical listening, questioning and learning with (and not simply, *from*) a grounded theory supervisor can thus empower an international student and honour, in emic ways, their own and their participants' cultural perspectives.

The observation that action researchers rarely acknowledge when they veer from standard practice in their qualitative studies (Zhang et al., 2014) is unlikely to be one peculiar to that methodology. Engaging with seminal texts in grounded theory is one way to appreciate what constitutes 'standard' practice and is an important means of developing an ontological and epistemological sense of self-awareness (Ralph et al., 2015) that serves as a methodological rudder for the grounded theorist. Without an in-depth appreciation for its principles and practices and any developed variants to them, it is hard to make good judgements in the field about where boundaries might lie, in thinking through the rationales entailed in any modifications that seem necessary in a certain cultural context. A tension can arise, however, in conforming to 'standard' practice on the one hand, and the empowerment of a researcher to innovate and appreciate the possibilities for flexibility that grounded theory presents on the other. Indications of that flexibility lie in the opportunities available to grounded theorists and qualitative researchers more broadly, to be more than one thing at a time (Denzin, 2009), by drawing on a portfolio of methods and methodologies to explore issues. It is the spirit of this kind of flexibility that is complemented by the concept of the researcher as a bricoleur, who utilizes any tool at hand in order to fashion meaning and interpretation (Denzin, 2009; Lévi-Strauss, 1966) and essentially extends permission for invention.

If intercultural teaching and learning research relationships arising from internationalization are capable of creating rich insights to inform decision making in grounded theory studies, the social and cultural power relations inherent in the supervisor/student relationship may present some risks. Power and expertise are cogent persuaders that can invite conformity to standardized practice. Perhaps this is particularly likely where a research student is influenced by Confucian and collectivist values that tend to respect status and hierarchy relatively more than individualist cultures (Smith, Peterson, & Schwartz, 2002). There is nothing inherently wrong in a grounded theory research supervisor insisting on a thorough understanding of principles that characterize the methodology. However, power relationships between student and supervisor have the potential to become problematic when conformity or deference stifles opportunities to take advantage of the flexibility inherent in grounded theory. Flexibility supplies the necessary oxygen for independent thought, so it is necessary for innovation.

For the international grounded theory student, navigating the respective realities of localized cultures and western academic expectations can create tensions and dilemmas when the two do not seem to align well. Without confidence and much experience, coupled with a perception of guiding cultures that appear to insist on compliance to strict rules in the practice of grounded theory, a student can assume a certain furtiveness about what actually occurs in the field. Furtiveness, where it exists, may arise from confusion about the extent to which the adoption of a responsive modification arising from sensitivity to a local context may or may not compromise grounded theory principles. For this reason, encouraging transparency, questions and developing rationales for diverging from planned practices is critical, especially when a student is entering the field for the first time. As Denzin (2009, p. 321) pointed out, qualitative and interpretive researchers, as a global community, need to share problems and experiences that showcase, celebrate and honour paradigmatic and methodological diversity and scholarship.

Working through dilemmas like these enables grounded theorists to learn and develop tolerance for ambiguous contexts (Nicolaidas, 2015) or what Glaser (1999) refers to as confusion – a capacity that is particularly necessary when working with multiple cultures

(Harman, Stevens, Bird, Mendenhall, & Oddou, 2010) and internationalized contexts that tend to invite creative engagement with methods (Ralph et al., 2015). Ambiguity inherent in many grounded theory studies can trigger 'unexpected insights' (Charmaz, 2014b, p. 1080) and at the same time may suggest modifications to known practices. Determining whether modifying any practices runs counter to expectations about what constitutes grounded theory is itself a process swathed in ambiguity, given the varied perspectives of grounded theorists who may more or less interpret procedures and methods in prescriptive ways or, in contrast, view them as heuristics or guidelines (Bryant & Charmaz, 2007, p. 10).

For example, when participants refuse to be recorded during interviews, for fear of being identified, the neophyte researcher may feel uncertain about how a lack of verbatim transcription may suggest poorer research. In addressing these kinds of issues during interviews, when expectations about how data are collected in grounded theory appear to conflict with the cultural values of participants, Charmaz (2014b, p. 1077) advises researchers to modify their approaches so that they are consistent with or 'fit' with the cultural values and norms of participants. The confident grounded theorist knows that by acknowledging apparently problematic aspects of the cultural context, participant reluctance to trust others can result in an interpretive richness that strengthens a study and is made possible by the flexibility of grounded theory. Its focus on the living world of participants should therefore empower early career grounded theorists to expect the unexpected in the life worlds they study, where 'ideal' conditions rarely seem to present themselves.

Supporting an evolving confidence in a grounded theory student's ability to develop, modify, invent and innovate, in ways that are transparently rationalized and sensitive to cultural contexts, can be a delicate business. However, some empirical evidence suggests that research students do explore ways to be creative – a process Elizondo-Schmelkes (2011, p. 3) refers to as *authenticizing*. When practice in the field forces us to probe the implications for methodological integrity in our research decisions, the process constitutes the life blood of developing reflection about what it means to be a grounded theorist.

NAVIGATING CULTURAL ASSUMPTIONS AND RESEARCH EXPECTATIONS

How students of grounded theory navigate the tricky spaces of their research is an underdeveloped area in grounded theory publications. If properly appreciated, flexible responses to them, particularly perhaps in international contexts, should enrich the research process and sharpen insights. Supervisors can assist students in simultaneously negotiating local, non-western research contexts and methodological expectations, emphasizing the value of memoing as part of an audit trail to enhance transparency. Memoing presents one means to critically deliberate over appropriate responses and rationales to support research decisions. The cultural complexity that internationalization presents tests notions of methodological purity and intensifies the now clichéd metaphor of *messiness* in qualitative research. It is only through understanding grounded theory and appreciating the blurry boundaries of methodological orthodoxy and unorthodoxy that research decisions can become part of a calculated and reasoned strategy. Encouraging critical and reflective discussions assists international research students navigating local realities, conventions and expectations in non-western cultural research sites, on the one hand, and those of western examiners, universities, journal editors and reviewers in the west, on the other.

We know very little about the experience of international research students in learning their craft in a western setting or about those who return home to conduct grounded theory research in their native lands. However, if, as Singh and Guihua (2011) argue, a western university education tends to promote western knowledge via monolingual English pedagogies that privilege western researchers, the western-trained international grounded theorist on returning home may need, if not to 'unlearn' some practices, then at least to adapt them, when local, cultural communication protocols and conventions are based on entirely different assumptions. Precisely how this unlearning plays out specifically and in practical terms will depend very much upon what and how a new researcher has learned about grounded theory, and how a particular research context presents a dilemma that draws that learning into question.

The literature addressing transnational or transcultural research often assumes that researchers have a cultural and linguistic background that differs from that of the research participants (Hennink, 2008; Irvine, Roberts, & Bradbury-Jones, 2008; Laverack & Brown, 2003). The assumption that cross-cultural qualitative research generally involves westerners exploring cultures other than their own probably arises from a heritage of, arguably, imperialist, objectivist, western, ethnographic researchers who investigated *The Other* as a studied stranger – alien and foreign. The period has been described by Denzin and Lincoln (2005) as the traditionalist twentieth-century moment in qualitative research. A residual and historical assumption from that period has probably given rise to what González and Lincoln (2006) have suggested is an assumption that qualitative researchers publish the outcomes of cross-cultural research to inform western end-users rather than non-western audiences, even when studies have been undertaken in non-western cultural contexts. For this reason, international grounded theorists operate as cultural brokers (a term borrowed from the work of Park and Lunt (2015)). In other words, they are called upon to navigate between local worlds and the expectations of the western academe that are premised upon quite different criteria.

The rising number of dissertations published by non-western and international research students arguably augurs well for the honouring of non-western cultural traditions in research practice (González & Lincoln, 2006) and calls for a transition from monocultural methods to those that are more culturally flexible (Gobo, 2011). Contemporaneously, internationalization now means that it is more common to read studies conducted by researchers as insiders of non-western cultural contexts. Their participants, too, are no longer the apparently passive and compliant subjects of research but are increasingly informed and knowledgeable activists with insights, views and sometimes resistance to western hegemony in cultural research (Smith, 2005, p. 87). Such shifts are undoubtedly rooted in what has been termed 'the triple crisis' (Smith, 2005, p. 20) of the fifth moment, which is characterized by struggles to represent *The Other* in different ways, the emergence of epistemologies capturing the worlds of marginalized groups and a focus upon small-scale theories about particular situations (Denzin & Lincoln, 2005). In consequence, Denzin (2009, p. 113) envisaged an ongoing future of proliferous epistemological variations arising from research *by* and about marginalized groups and individuals. Grounded theory, like other qualitative methodologies, can hardly fail to be immune to these shifting trends, fostered by internationalization.

The pressure upon international research students to publish well and gain tenured positions before and after they return home (Kwan, 2010) may not be conducive to risk-taking methodologically (or at least admitting it) in the face of challenges. Western approaches to research methodologies continue to represent the dominant paradigm (Park & Lunt, 2015) and qualitative studies that enable insights into cultural contexts around the world are arguably under a renewed attack (Denzin, 2009). Too much may be at stake financially, and in terms of future career aspirations, despite the need for reasoned risks in grounded theory to be acknowledged more widely than they are currently (Charmaz, 2014b, p. 1081). Many international grounded theory students and academics are operating in universities that are internationalizing to remain globally competitive (Mamiseishvili, 2013), jostling for favourable rankings (Elizondo-Schmelkes, 2011) and often prioritizing research publication in the process. Whether by international enrollment, or recruitment, membership in both aspirational and elite universities comes with a *quid pro quo* of publishing in highly ranked and western journals.

When cultural products are borrowed and incorporated into a host culture, they are invariably altered in order to maximize their usefulness in the new context (Ferraro & Briody, 2013). In other words, when grounded theory, as a western cultural product, is selected to try to understand the world of participants in a non-western setting, some accommodations are likely to be required. The observation that ideas lose some of their original meaning when they cross borders was made with regard to paradigms by Vogel (2012, p. 34), and again resonates with respect to internationalization as a process that changes how people see, how they believe things are, and how they value those things.

As Park and Lunt (2015) observed, each cultural context will call for its own assumptions, traditions and techniques that suggest necessary modifications to research methods, perhaps in terms of transcription or conventions around how interviews are arranged and scheduled. Those assumptions are part of the terrain for the researcher in the field and may well be at odds with not only expectations about how grounded theory is undertaken, but also with the cultural practices of the western university as a social institution shaped by pervasive cultural practices (Otten, Allwood, Aneas, & Busch, 2009).

As a cultural insider operating in a non-western setting, the international student of grounded theory understands the cultural assumptions, processes and protocols necessary to gain access to participants. These insights are invaluable but may not always fit neatly with the research conventions and expectations of western institutions and can be problematic and stressful to navigate. For example, Japanese cultural norms with respect to communication between a researcher and a business person are based on quite different social assumptions from western ones. Social relationships that are culturally constructed are relevant to the tone of written documents, often generated from standardized western university templates developed by their research departments to ensure consistency in discourse, no doubt with the intention to ensure adherence to ethical standards. In judging the university formulaic communications inviting participants to take part to be disrespectful in their tone, a Japanese administrative assistant employed in a target organization admonished Noma for not displaying appropriate humility in addressing Japanese HR managers, given the hierarchical power distance between a researcher and a manager in Japanese culture.

Documents that are designed to provide information about a research study in order to recruit western participants or organizations can be framed in ways that are perceived by a Japanese participant as prescriptive and offensive. Given the hierarchical structure described previously, and the nature of communication in high-context cultures, concise, direct, written communication is perceived through a Japanese lens as impolite, lacking the tentative and apologetic genre expected, as compared to western conventions. As an international grounded theory researcher operating within the requirements of an Australian university, conducting research involving Japanese participants, Noma felt stressed, embarrassed and conflicted in this regard. Experiencing intra-personal conflict as an outcome of navigating cultures is perhaps not wholly unexpected, if one accepts that intercultural qualitative studies tend to generate these kinds of experiences (González & Lincoln, 2006; Park & Lunt, 2015). Some flexibility in designing culturally appropriate recruitment documents may assist international grounded theory students in attracting participation, rather than annoyance, among non-western stakeholders.

The example above describes how western universities, in insisting upon certain practices, can run counter not only to the flexibility required for the internationalization of research practices, but also in terms of the values and conditions championed in grounded theory. Tone in research documents matters in grounded theory because humility in relating to participants is encouraged, perhaps particularly in internationalized cultural contexts (see, for example, Schreiber & Tomm-Bonde, 2015, p. 657). Internationalization is not, however, the only factor at play where formal documents can present a challenge in participant recruitment. Charmaz (2014a), for example, recounts her own experiences of how consent forms can give rise to feelings of participant reluctance within the United States. Noma's account also illustrates how, as Kusow (2003) observed, insider status, by virtue of a shared national culture, is no guarantee that the research process or participant cooperation will proceed smoothly.

Etic assumptions about what is appropriate in all research contexts may do little to reduce conflict when western research processes insist upon generic tools and protocols for intercultural contexts. Western universities would be well advised to collaborate with international grounded theorists when functioning as cultural insiders to ensure that the spirit and intention of protocols are achieved without damaging intercultural research relationships that can only be founded on principles of respect and trust.

LANGUAGE, CULTURE AND GROUNDED THEORY

Embedded, unspoken meanings that can be interpreted, but not directly translated, pose a challenge for grounded theory students in international contexts. The international student of grounded theory, as an insider, may recognize, for example, the cultural reasons why a participant may appear unresponsive and the meaning in what is not said. In a personal communication (January 18, 2016), Dr Jessica Leong reflected on this issue as a Singaporean grounded theorist collecting data from nurses and preceptors in that cultural context. Monosyllabic responses and general reluctance to engage on certain issues or to provide much detail could easily be understood by Leong, who is aware that, in general terms, Singaporeans and those who live in neighbouring Asian countries do not like to share sensitive information readily (see Lindquist, 2004; Takeno, 2010). In Singapore, criticizing those from within the same community, especially to an outsider, is discouraged and metaphorically described by Ganapathy (2006) as 'washing one's dirty linen in public'. Refraining from emotional expression, or remaining unresponsive or silent to preserve harmony and avoid loss of face and shame (Ganapathy, 2006; Lindquist, 2004; Smith & Bond, 1993, p. 147; Takeno, 2010), is a common strategy to signal discontent or disapproval directed towards the subject matter in a conversation, and it cannot be captured in a transcript alone.

The structure and content of languages influences how research is undertaken, and tensions between English and any other language used in a study can become apparent in coding (Charmaz, 2014b, p. 1078). Inspired by the work of Charmaz (2006) and trained as a researcher in a western university, Noma began coding interview transcripts using gerunds to reflect action. However, she quickly encountered difficulty, in that the sentence structure of English is dissimilar from Japanese, as are communication styles. For example, subjects are often omitted because interlocutors assume that the subject is so obvious that it need not be explicitly stated, and, as a result, important points are simply only suggested. Noma needed to add or explain the suggested points using brackets in the process of translating the texts and findings into English. In order to make sure these points were addressed correctly, the Japanese text translated by Noma was back-translated by another bilingual Japanese person who specialized in English.

Where ambiguity exists about the nature of an action, the western grounded theory researcher may seek clarification by asking the participant what he or she did or felt or will repeat the sentence with a suggested verb. A difficulty arises in that a Japanese participant is likely to become somewhat annoyed with these questions because Japanese people tend to expect their counterpart to understand their thoughts and feelings without having to be explicit. Requests for clarification during an interview would suggest to the participant that they were not perceived as effective communicators of their own deep thoughts or feelings. In the Japanese context, it is assumed that the recipient has a greater responsibility than might be expected in English, to interpret intended meaning, verbally and nonverbally. Thus, in some ways, seeking clarification may be perceived as a sign of poor effort on the part of the interviewer by the participant.

Noma understood, as a cultural and linguistic insider, that her continued strategies for seeking clarification for the purpose of transcription, which is essential to analysis in English, would serve to irritate or frustrate a Japanese participant. Clarifying can become an important strategy for grounded theory data collection and analysis, but also, ironically, in non-western contexts, ultimately it can prove a risk to trust development, compromising the creation of conducive conditions for disclosure, which are so important to the interview process. Yet, at the same time, the process of analysis requires that participants do communicate their perceptions and experiences in ways that can be understood by western end-users, and for the same reason, categories and properties are constructed through coding in English, enabling an audit trail to become accessible to them.

Language has a crucial role in grounded theory in shaping meaning, revealing or concealing its connection with action and influencing data collection and analysis (Charmaz, 2014b, p. 1078), but concepts do not always translate in conceptually synonymous ways. The richness of the data enhanced through metaphors, *in vivo* codes and other concepts are often only truly appreciated through the lens of the culture that constructs them. Unfortunately, the translation process may even serve to diminish analytical richness. At the same time, for the international and multilingual grounded theory researcher, interpreting leads to a meshing of the two languages and cultures in ways that, for Noma at least, meant that it was difficult to define, in any clear-cut way, what language was used at certain points in the analytical process of her research on trust in Japanese multinationals.

From her own perspective, the co-mingling of language and cultural concepts serves to intensify the intuitive nature of processes, yet at the same time leads to ambiguities because of the difficulty of communicating precisely how some categories and properties come into being. Noma's experience of using data from interviews that were not conducted in English, but coded from a translated, transcribed text, seemed to compromise the richness of the data because nuances that are communicated through shared cultural knowledge during interviews are not easily explainable or apparent when translated into English for the benefit of non-Japanese. Therefore, Noma embedded data in both English (back-translated from Japanese) and the Japanese text, taken from the original transcripts, to retain the integrity of those nuances of meanings for those who could understand them. Nevertheless, back-translation may never truly resolve the issue of capturing Japanese meaning from the data in English because it cannot address the problem of incongruity of language systems and how we categorize concepts because even apparent sameness are compromised by 'the different structure of the surrounding categories' (Buckley et al., 2014, p. 311).

The experiences of grounded theorists described in this section – Leong, in Singapore, exploring new nurse experiences in transitioning to professional practices, and Noma, studying intercultural trust between Japanese and Australian employees – highlight how it can be challenging to capture unspoken cultural meanings in ways that are easily communicated in transcripts. Such situations draw attention to the critical role of memoing because it encourages transparent communication and strengthens interpretive meanings in intercultural research. Using memos to explore the unspoken essentially creates an allied form of data. Viewing memos in this way, however, is in itself likely to be contested. Lempert (2007), for example, recommends treating memos as narratives, *like* data but clearly not *as* data, being useful for discovery and theory development rather than application. Whatever the status of memos, few would dispute their usefulness in capturing the intertwining of the reflexive role of the researcher with participant perspectives, which is a distinguishing focus of constructivist grounded theory (Charmaz, 2014a).

The issues raised by Leong and Noma, in reflecting upon their experiences as international students of grounded theory, may not constitute methodological 'deal breakers'. As Charmaz (2014a) remarked, with respect to interviewing, the traditions and situations of participants need to be approached with respect. Acknowledgment and respect are indeed hallmark values throughout the grounded theory research process. If internationalization sometimes seems to challenge an interpretation of methodological conventions, it can call for critical reflection about what values and assumptions underpin our perceptions of tensions between research practices and prioritizing respect for the cultural mores of participants and the context. Repeated questioning of those assumptions is the basis of rigorous decision making. Explaining them contributes to transparency, and creatively addressing them characterizes our research in original and innovative ways.

CONCLUDING REMARKS

Individuals with multiple national affiliations are becoming increasingly common as human emigrant populations move around the world in search of work, education, business (Ho, 2011) and, indeed, safety. Whether widespread diaspora is as a result of strategic emigration or fleeing from disruptive and dangerous circumstances, the world, our communities and our identities are changing, and societies will need to absorb the consequent transitions by trying to understand them and create positive opportunities from them. At a time when, as Denzin (2009) points out, so much global uncertainty exists, the capacity for grounded theory to respond sensitively to new realities of culturally complex societies will no doubt continue to attract some scrutiny and discussion.

In this chapter, we have focused on how the internationalization of higher research education in universities has influenced the teaching, learning, practice and development of grounded theory and we have discussed its appropriateness in terms of methodology and methods for examining research settings where cultural capital and identity of both the researcher and participants are relevant to that activity. As O'Neil Green, Creswell, Shope and Plano Clark (2007) emphasize in the broader discussion of using grounded theory in diversity studies, acknowledging researcher positionality is crucial.

We have argued that grounded theory and internationalization are sympathetic to one another on a paradigmatic level, in terms of embracing inclusive, emic and relativist worldviews with the potential to create new and alternative ways of doing and knowing and inherently inviting a questioning of predominant western perspectives. This occurs not by observing, translating and interpreting one culture for the consumption of another, but through a much more complex and dynamic interplay where the cultural identities of researcher, participants and the worlds they respectively inhabit are co-created in unique ways that somehow help us to make sense of what is occurring and why in that serendipitous moment. The dynamic nature of this process is quite a different phenomenon from the so-called objective ethnographer in a foreign territory or from earlier grounded theory cross-cultural studies, because the influence of internationalization on grounded theory enables a sensitivity to the *inter-space* of cultural co-mingling in ways that abandon convenient but perhaps illusory and misleading boundary markers of culture.

Internationalization, as a paradigm, is in its ascendancy as one way to understand events such as the human diaspora and how people can live together. It is a way of explaining the world and suggests how we need to conceptualize changing relationships within it. It seems likely that internationalization has altered how grounded theory is learned and practised and how the methodology itself is developed. Simultaneously, the inherent flexibility of grounded theory and its capacity to engage with ambiguity suggests that, in turn, it also provides a means to operationalize internationalization.

In the first instance, however, a call for empirical research into the implications of internationalization in, and for, grounded theory research is warranted as a way to begin conversations about the relevance and implications of the relationship between the two. Knowing how internationalization influences grounded theory in conducting and adapting to non-western cultures to ensure relevance to local (as opposed to western) interests and imperatives may contribute to the development of the methodology in transformative and innovative ways, benefiting the very broad church of grounded theorists internationally. As Knight (2012, p. 20) noted, internationalization is a powerful force for change. We conclude that grounded theory is both the object of that force and its enabler.

REFERENCES

Altbach, P. G., & Knight, J. (2007). The internationalisation of higher education: Motivations and realities. *Journal of Studies in International Education*, Fall/Winter, 290–305.

Beerkens, E. (2003). Globalisation and higher education research. *Journal of Studies in International Education*, *7*(2), 128–148.

Brewer, E., & Leask, B. (2012). Internationalization of the curriculum. In D. K. Deardorff, H. Wit, & J. D. Heyl (Eds.), *The Sage handbook of international higher education (pp. 245–267)*, Thousand Oaks, CA: Sage.

Bryant, A., & Charmaz, K. (2007). Introduction: Grounded theory research: Methods and practices. In A. Bryant, & C. Charmaz (Eds.), *The Sage handbook of grounded theory* (pp. 1–29). London: Sage.

Buckley, P., Chapman, M., Clegg, J., & Gajewska-De Mattos, H. (2014). A linguistic and philosophical analysis of emic and etic and their use in international business research. *Management International Review*, *54*, 307–324.

Charmaz, K. (2006). *Constructing grounded theory: A practical guide through qualitative analysis*. London: Sage.

Charmaz, K. (2014a). *Constructing grounded theory* (2nd ed.). Thousand Oaks, CA: Sage.

Charmaz, K. (2014b). Grounded theory in global perspective: Reviews by international researchers, *Qualitative Inquiry*, *20*(9), 1074–1084.

Crossman, J. (2003). Secular spiritual development in education from international and global perspectives. *Oxford Review of Education*, *29*(4), 503–520.

Crossman, J. (2005). Work and learning: The implications of Thai transnational distance learners. *International Education Journal*, *6*(1), 18–29.

Crossman, J., & Clarke, M. (2010). International experience and graduate employability: Stakeholder perceptions on the connection. *Higher Education*, *59*(5), 599–613.

Daly, H. (1999) Globalization versus internationalization implication: Some implications. *Ecological Economics*, *31*, 31–37.

Denzin, N. (2009). *Qualitative inquiry under fire: Toward a new paradigm dialogue*. Walnut Creek, CA: Left Coast Press.

Denzin, N., & Lincoln, Y. (Eds.). (2005). *The Sage handbook of qualitative research* (3rd ed.), Thousand Oaks, CA: Sage.

Elizondo-Schmelkes, N. (2011). Authenticizing the research process. *The Grounded Theory Review*, *10*(2), 1–20.

Elliott, N., & Higgins, A. (2012). Surviving grounded theory research method in an academic world: Proposal writing and theoretical frameworks. *The Grounded Theory Review*, *11*(2), 1–12.

Evans, G. L. (2013). A novice researcher's first walk through the maze of grounded theory: rationalization for classical grounded theory. *The Grounded Theory Review*, *12*(1), 37–55.

Feng, Y. (2013). University of Nottingham Ningbo China and Xián Jiaotong-Liverpool University: Globalization of higher education in China. *Higher Education*, *65*(4), 471–485.

Ferraro, G., & Briody, E. (2013). *The cultural dimension of global business* (7th ed.). New York: Routledge/Taylor & Francis.

Frølich, N. (2006). Still academic and national: Internationalisation in Norwegian research and higher education. *Higher Education*, *52*, 405–420.

Ganapathy, N. (2006). The operational policing of domestic violence in Singapore: An exploratory study. *International Criminal Justice Review*, *16*(3), 179–198. doi: 10.1177/1057567706295489

Georgantzas, N., Katsamakas, E., & Solowiej, D. (2010). Exploring dynamics of Giddens' globalization. *Systems Research and Behavioural Science*, *27*(6), 622–638.

Giddens, A. (1999). *Runaway world: Business online network*. London: Profile Books.

Giddens, A. (2001). The third way: Where we have got to? *Korea Observer*, *32*(3), 431–452.

Giddens, A., Diamond, P., & Liddle, R. (Eds.). (2006). *Global Europe, social Europe*. Cambridge, UK: Polity Press.

Glaser, B. G. (1999). The future of grounded theory. *Qualitative Health Research*, *9*(6), 836–845.

Glaser, B. G., & Strauss, A. L. (1967). *The discovery of grounded theory: Strategies for qualitative research*. Chicago, IL: Aldine.

Gobo, G. (2011). Globalizing methodology? The encounter between local methodologies. *International Journal of Social Research Methodology*, *14*(6), 417–437.

González, E., & Lincoln, Y. (2006). Decolonizing qualitative research: Non-traditional reporting forms in the academy. *Forum: Qualitative Social Research*, *7*(4). Retrieved from: www.qualitative-research.net/index.php/fqs/article/view/162/359

Gringeri, C., Barusch, A., & Cambron, C. (2013). Examining foundations of qualitative research: A review of social work dissertations, 2008–2010, *Journal of Social Work Education*, *49*(4), 760–773.

Harman, J., Stevens, M., Bird, A., Mendenhall, M., & Oddou, G. (2010). The tolerance for ambiguity scale: Towards a more refined measure for international management. *International Journal of Intercultural Relations*, *34*(1), 58–64.

Hennink, M. (2008). Language and communication in cross-cultural qualitative research In P. Liamputtong (Ed.), *Doing cross-cultural research: Ethical and methodological perspectives* (pp. 21–23). London: Springer.

Ho, E. (2011). 'Claiming' the diaspora: Elite mobility, sending state strategies and the spatialities of citizenship. *Progress in Human Geography*, *35*(6), 757–772.

Hoare, K., Buetow, S., Mills, J., & Francis, K. (2012). Using an emic and etic ethnographic technique in a grounded theory study of information use by practice nurses in New Zealand. *Journal of Research in Nursing*, *18*(8), 720–731.

Irvine, F., Roberts, G., & Bradbury-Jones, C. (2008). The researcher as insider versus the researcher as outsider: Enhancing rigour through language and cultural sensitivity. In P. Liamputtong (Ed.), *Doing cross-cultural research: Ethical and methodological perspectives* (pp. 35–38). London: Springer.

Knight, J. (2004). Internationalisation Remodeled: Rationales, strategies and approaches. *Journal of Studies in International Education*, *8*(1), 5–31.

Knight, J. (2012). Student mobility and internationalisation: Trends and tribulations. *Research in Comparative and International Education*, *7*(1), 20–33.

Kuhn, T. (1962). *The structure of scientific revolutions* (2nd ed.). Chicago, IL: University of Chicago Press.

Kusow, A. (2003). Beyond indigenous authenticity: Reflections on the insider/outside debate on immigration research. *Symbolic Interaction*, *26*(4), 591–599.

Kwan, B. (2010). An investigation of instruction in research publishing offered in doctoral programs: The Hong Kong case. Higher Education, *59*(1), 55–68.

Laverack, G. R., & Brown, K. (2003). Qualitative research in a cross-cultural context: Fijian experiences. *Qualitative Health Research*, *13*(3), 333–342.

Lempert, L. (2007). Asking questions of the data: Memo writing in the grounded theory tradition. In A. Bryant & K. Charmaz (Eds.), The Sage handbook of grounded theory (pp. 245–265). Thousand Oaks, CA: Sage.

Lévi-Strauss, C. (1966). The savage mind. Chicago, IL: University of Chicago Press.

Lindquist, J. (2004). Veils and ecstasy: Negotiating shame in the Indonesian borderlands. *Ethnos*, *69*(4), 487–508.

Lumby, J., & Foskett, N. (2016). Internationalisation and culture in higher education. *Educational Management Administration and Leadership*, *44*(1), 95–111.

Mamiseishvili, K. (2013). Contributions of foreign-born faculty to doctoral education and research. *New Directions for Higher Education*, *163*(Fall). doi: 10.1002/he.20068.

McCreaddie, M., & Payne, S. (2010). Evolving grounded theory methodology: Towards a discursive approach. *International Journal of Nursing Studies*, *47*, 781–793.

Mruck, K., & Mey, G. (2007). Grounded theory and reflexivity. In A. Bryant & K. Charmaz (Eds.), The Sage handbook of grounded theory (pp. 515–539). Thousand Oaks, CA: Sage.

Nerad, M. (2010). Globalization and internationalisation of graduate education: A macro and micro view. *Canadian Journal of Higher Education Revue*, *40*(1), 1–12.

Nicolaides, A. (2015). Generative learning: Adults learning within ambiguity. *Adult Education Quarterly*, *65*(3), 179–195.

Noma, H. (2009). How unique is Japanese culture? A critical review of the discourse in intercultural communication literature. *Journal of International Education in Business*, *2*(2), 1–13.

O'Neil Green, D., Creswell, J. W., Shope, R. J., & Plano Clark, V. L. (2007). Grounded theory and racial/ethnic diversity. In A. Bryant & K. Charmaz (Eds.), *The Sage handbook of grounded theory* (pp. 472–492). Thousand Oaks, CA: Sage.

Otten, M., Allwood, J., Aneas, M., & Busch, D. (2009). Editorial: Qualitative research and intercultural communication. *Forum: Qualitative Social Research*, *10*(1). Retrieved from: www.qualitative-research.net/index.php/fqs/article/view/1252/2710

Park, S., & Lunt, N. (2015). Confucianism and Qualitative interviewing: Working Seoul to Soul. *Forum: Qualitative Social Research*, *16*(2). Retrieved from: www.qualitative-research.net/index.php/fqs/article/view/2166/3792

Ralph, N., Birks, M., & Chapman, Y. (2015). The methodological dynamism of grounded theory. *International Journal of Qualitative Methods*, (Online). First published 20 November. doi: 10.1177?1609406915611576.

Sak, J., & Pawlikowski, J. (2012). Medicine and thought styles: On the 50th anniversary of the death of Ludwik Fleck (1896–1961). *The Israel Medical Association Journal: IMAJ*, *14*(4), 214–218.

Schreiber, R., & Tomm-Bonde, L. (2015). Ubuntu and constructivist grounded theory: An African methodology package. *Journal of Research in Nursing*, *20*(8), 655–664.

Singh, M., & Guihua, C. (2011). Internationalising western doctoral education through bilingual research literacy. *Pertanika Journal of Social Science and Humanities*, *19*(2), 535–545.

Smith, L. Tuhiwai (2005). On tricky ground: Researching the native in the age of uncertainty. In N. Denzin & Y. Lincoln (Eds.), *The Sage handbook of qualitative research* (3rd ed., pp. 85–108). Thousand Oaks, CA: Sage.

Smith, P. B., & Bond, M. (1993). *Social psychology across cultures: Analysis and perspectives*. Boston, MA: Allyn & Bacon.

Smith, P. B., Peterson, M. F., & Schwartz, S. (2002). Cultural values, sources of guidance, and their relevance to managerial behavior a 47-nation study. *Journal of Cross-Cultural Psychology*, *33*(2), 188–208.

Takeno, Y. (2010). Facilitating the transition of Asian nurses to work in Australia. *Journal of Nursing Management*, *18*(2), 215–224.

Thornberg, R. (2012). Informed grounded theory. *Scandinavian Journal of Educational Research*, *56*(3), 243–259.

Vogel, R. (2012). Paradigms revisited: Towards a practice-based approach. *Review of Contemporary Philosophy*, *11*, 34–41.

Wolgemuth, J., Erdil-Moody, Z., Opsal, T., Cross, J., Kaanta, T., Dickmann, E., & Colomer, S. (2015). Participants' experiences of the qualitative interview: Considering the importance of research paradigms. *Qualitative Research*, *15*(3), 351–372.

Zhang, Z., Fyn, D., Langelotz, L., Lonngren, J., McCorquodale, L., & Nehez, J. (2014). Our way(s) to action research: Doctoral students' international and interdisciplinary collective memory work. *Action Work*, *12*(3), 293–314.

Zhu, Y., & Bargiela-Chiappini, F. (2013). Balancing emic and etic: Situated learning and ethnography of communication in cross-cultural management education. *Academy of Management Learning and Education*, *12*(3), 380–395.

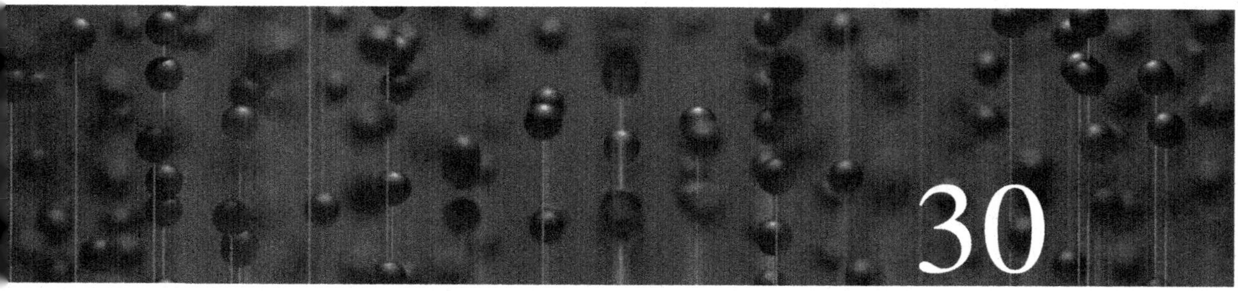

Grounded Theory as Systems Science: Working with Indigenous Nations for Social Justice

Roxanne Bainbridge, Janya McCalman, Michelle Redman-MacLaren and Mary Whiteside

INTRODUCTION

Twenty-seventeen marks the 50th anniversary of Glaser and Strauss's seminal text on *The Discovery of Grounded Theory* (1967). Grounded theory has stood the test of time as an inductive, interactive, emergent method with purposeful explanatory intent in the field of qualitative research (Charmaz, 2008b). Its various iterations, such as Charmaz's constructivist grounded theory and Clarke's postmodern situational analysis, attest to its epistemological flexibility (Clarke, 2005; Charmaz, 2006). Our phronetic grounded theory approach and transformational grounded theory contributed a decolonizing variation of grounded theory methods and demonstrated its use in the Indigenous Australian and Pacific contexts (Bainbridge, Whiteside, & McCalman, 2013; Redman-MacLaren & Mills, 2015). In a phronetic grounded theory approach, reflective practice informs morally-oriented action that leads to change (Flyvberg, 2001; Bainbridge, Whiteside, & McCalman, 2013). With the exception of Charmaz (2017a), for instance, few theorists have explicitly taken up the proposition and utility of grounded theory as decolonizing tool in research. Yet, grounded theory's pragmatist roots and its commitment to social justice suggest that it can be used purposefully in its intent as a decolonizing method (Charmaz, 2017a). Indeed, grounded theory methods respond to many of the discrete critiques of Western research that Indigenous researchers have proffered in recent decades. We contemplate how the utility of grounded theory methods can provide a fresh perspective and maximize the value of research for Indigenous nations.

There is a moral imperative for methodological change agendas across all research endeavours and that impact and benefit are prioritized. Methodological innovation and greater research accountability are needed to meet the inherent opportunities and challenges of our increasingly complex and dynamic society. Contemporaneously, innovation in research is widespread. But, while there is general acceptance of multi-methodological approaches to research, and a profusion of novel methods, methodological innovations that specifically counter reductionist analyses and are sensitive to culture, context and diversity still appear troublesome to many researchers – particularly in terms of their amalgamation, implementation and producing societal change.

Grounded theory as a systems science analytic method has much to offer in thinking about decolonizing research methodologies to maximize impact and benefit for Indigenous nations. A failure of many current research approaches is to treat research phenomena in isolation of the broader socio-economic, cultural and political environments in which they occur. A systems science approach using grounded theory as a method of data generation and specifically as analytical tools can connect these domains and explain the situation under study. In this chapter, we unpack how the values, expectations and cultures of Indigenous communities can be integrated into Western ways of researching for increased research impact and benefit in ways that address Indigenous critiques of Western research approaches. We suggest that grounded theory methods as an analytic tool provide an avenue for achieving this goal. Our premise is that complex problems require complex solutions and must be context-dependent – accounting for individuals' attributes, cultural, social, environmental and historical contexts in which they developed and exist – and ascribe significance to ethics and a power analysis as a context-sensitive point of departure.

We propose a methodological-methods package – a principles-based research approach and methods for enacting it – through which to generate grounded theory to meet the contemporary needs of Indigenous research inquiry. It is strengths-based, ecological, action-oriented, emancipatory and contextually responsive, and it speaks to Indigenous aspirations, self-determination, values and nation-building. A strengths-based approach inherently focuses on the strengths of a situation and produces a counter-narrative that feeds a decolonizing agenda. We aim to balance rigour and innovation in developing the approach, which has universal application and is based on our reflective models of working with Indigenous populations over many years (Bainbridge, McCalman, Tsey, & Brown, 2011; Bainbridge, Whiteside & McCalman, 2013; McCalman et al., 2013). Our collective expertise and practice as Australian-based Indigenous and non-Indigenous researchers working with Indigenous nations throughout Australia and the Pacific spans almost a century. We have a goal of supporting health equity and social justice for Indigenous nations, the broad aim of which is to ensure that research is ethical, responsive, has impact and is relevant to community-identified priorities, their daily lives, needs and aspirations. We explicate a framework embedded in the philosophical foundations of systems science and phronetic social science (Bainbridge, Whiteside & McCalman, 2013) and integrated in a participatory action design and continuous quality improvement processes. Few analytic methods have the capacity to work alongside such approaches. The iterative, interactive and systemic nature of ground theory methods avails all kinds of methodological innovation. Claiming grounded theory as a critical methodology-method in the tradition of systems sciences, we commend grounded theory to explicate and map context and action, including all constituent elements of the research phenomena and the interrelationships inherent in situations at multiple levels.

WHY DO WE NEED FRESH PERSPECTIVES TO MEET DECOLONIZING AGENDAS?

The multiplicity of research practices in both quantitative and qualitative traditions reveals the empirical world in various ways to different researchers. Methodological fit to researchers' ways of being in the world saturates research endeavours. However, 'the locations of both researchers and participants matter' (Charmaz, 2017a, p. 36). This notion of an epistemological partnership often remains unaccounted for in research and the resulting research directions and findings are more meaningful to researchers than participants. Making research relevant to individual lives and society should also be an imperative for all researchers. As researchers, we must question the value of research in which we engage with our research partners, particularly in terms of accomplishing impact and benefits to society. We need to ensure ethical practice, the integrity of the evidence produced, and that research leads to better decision-making (Bainbridge et al., 2015; Tsey et al., 2016). It must be useful and directly relevant to the advancement of knowledge for societal progress, human health and flourishing, and designed to produce innovations that have impact in such contexts (Bainbridge et al., 2015). Yet globally, colonized Indigenous nations still proclaim that in the over-abundance of research conducted *on* issues concerning Indigenous populations there is little evidence of a corresponding translation into raising their health, social and economic prosperity (Bainbridge et al., 2015; Tsey et al., 2016). This proclamation continues despite considerable methodological reform. Poor translation is unequivocally evidenced by the health and socio-economic status of colonized Indigenous nations around the world, which registers as poorer on almost every indicator relative to benchmark populations (Anderson et al., 2016).

Global movements of Indigenous research scholars are producing new research regimes; counter-narratives and research practices that lie at the confluence of Indigenous and Western knowledge and value systems (Smith, 1999; Bainbridge et al., 2015). Decolonizing research methodologies have been at the forefront of Indigenous research priorities for decades (Semali & Kincheloe, 1999; Smith, 1999, 2005; National Health and Medical Research Council, 2003; Bishop, 2005). Linda Tuhawai Smith's seminal text on decolonizing methodologies was published in 1999 at the height of the movement (Smith, 1999). To be clear, from the outset of this chapter, our determination of decolonizing or anti-colonial research approaches are not about 'rejecting all theory or research or Western knowledge. Rather, they are about centering our [Indigenous] concerns and world views and then coming to know and understand theory and research from our own perspectives and for our own purposes' (Smith, 1999, p. 39). This emancipatory movement advocates building a coalition of knowledge that has relevance, practical application and vision for Indigenous nations. However, while principles of decolonizing processes are clear, the implementation of such remains tenuous at best, and clear research methodologies and methods to manage implementation are suboptimal (Bainbridge, Tsey, Andrews, & McCalman, 2013a; Bainbridge et al., 2015; Kinchin et al., 2017).

Persistent ethical and pragmatic issues stand in the way of progress. A legacy of mistrust between Indigenous communities and researchers remains. Over time, the exploitive nature of Western research initially focused on the fascination with the 'exotic other'. This was quickly followed by documentation of a 'dying race', protecting the health, wealth and status of Western societies (Thomas, Bainbridge, & Tsey, 2014). Researchers were more interested in progressing their careers, and were 'responsible for the extraction, storage, and control over Indigenous knowledges' (Irabinna Rigney, 1999, p. 109) and policy directions that were detrimental to Indigenous nations. Increasingly, Indigenous researchers, communities and organizations are controlling and decolonizing research to better meet their needs – sensitive to their distinctive epistemologies and ontologies, identities, values and history. Indigenous scholars and communities have submitted critiques of research practices and outcomes for decades, yet researchers continue to fail to address these criticisms in any substantive way (Bainbridge et al., 2015). The key reason for the limited gains from research for Indigenous people is because, in large measure, research is mainly controlled by non-Indigenous people; conducted 'on' Indigenous people; been strongly biased towards the incentives of colonizing societies; mirrors the exploitive nature of colonial power relations; focuses on describing the 'Indigenous problem'; imposes a Western cultural framework of meaning and interpretation to the findings; is not sensitive to context or culture; is narrowly-focused; and is generally of poor methodological quality (Smith, 1999; Sanson-Fisher et al., 2006; Bainbridge, Whiteside, & McCalman, 2013; Thomas, Bainbridge, & Tsey, 2014; Bainbridge et al., 2015). The significant issue here is the nature of the evidence produced and its usefulness in informing particular decision-making processes.

Decolonizing research methodologies requires more than good intentions and a simple shift in the conceptualization of the research process (Bainbridge, Whiteside, & McCalman, 2013). Such paradigmatic shifts often lead to innovative approaches and repertoires of social science methods (Bainbridge, Whiteside, & McCalman, 2013). With the development of new paradigms comes a need for new ways of perceiving reality, fresh perspectives, thinking about what is possible, and new ways of doing – changing business as usual. Grounded theory methods were borne from the need for innovation and critiques of the grand traditions of social inquiry (Gibson, 2007). Its many iterations and longevity pay credence to its flexibility and usefulness in the social sciences.

We propose the utility of grounded theory as an analytic decolonizing tool. Its deep immersion in data forces context-dependent research; reductionist views are expanded in systematic systemic examination, explication and explanation of all constituent elements and their interrelationships in given social situations relevant to the phenomenon under study; and an 'all is data' (Glaser, 1978, p. 2) approach enables accountability for population diversity and culturally-specific ways of knowing, being and doing in the world through an acknowledgement of different knowledge forms and thus the production of different kinds of evidence.

ANTI-COLONIAL RESEARCH FOR SOCIAL JUSTICE AND EQUITY

Indigenous research reform agendas are still emerging in scope. In the past, they focused predominantly on process issues such as ethics and collaboration. In more recent years, research translation to maximize benefits became a priority.

Thomas, Bainbridge, and Tsey (2014, p. S18) suggested that for change to occur, 'improved research processes and ethical frameworks to guide and keep accountable researchers and research organizations, alongside the development of methods to assess research impact and benefit for Indigenous people' are critical. Others raised concerns about research implementation fidelity (McCalman et al., 2012); and Humphrey (2001) raised questions about the extent of Indigenous research transformation and its potential to bring 'about fundamental change in research practice' *vis-à-vis* 'being sidelined into too great a reliance on written guidelines and positive rhetoric' (p. 201). More innovation in the ways we identify and perceive Indigenous research priorities, engage and collaborate with Indigenous partners, set agendas for impact and benefit, and assess and evaluate specific pieces of research are essential (Bainbridge et al., 2015; Tsey et al., 2016; Ramanathan et al., 2017).

Indigenous methodologies align with aspirations of empowerment and self-determination, have a liberatory agenda, and incorporate sustainable benefit. In the past, participatory and collaborative research processes led the agenda in methodological reform for Indigenous people. While one critical component of any reform package in Indigenous research, engagement alone does not necessarily produce change. We need new participatory frameworks that are transformational (Redman-MacLaren & Mills, 2015): a decolonizing approach that is underpinned by critical theories and 'effective in analyzing power differences between groups; provides hope for transformation; and has a role for structural change and personal agency in resistance' (Kovach, 2009, p. 80). For instance, grounded theory in the constructivist tradition provides a way of sharing power arrangements in the research process, researcher engagement in critical reflexivity, and 'locates the research process and product in historical, social, and situational conditions (Charmaz, 2017a, p. 34). We also need to enable actionable findings and to identify intervention points for current and future change efforts in a shared humanity that is not contingent upon any particular standpoint. That is, there is fluidity in the approach whereby various standpoints can be incorporated through a shared position. And, we need new ways to use research as decision-making tools that account for the complexity of entire rapidly-changing social worlds and systems, and the historical and contemporary situations in which they are embedded. In producing such a framework, we must further ensure that there are continuous quality improvement processes embedded, and that the integrity of feedback loops is closed.

Anti-colonial research is fundamentally about social justice. Social justice inquiry, according to Charmaz (2011), attends to 'inequities and inequalities, barriers and access, poverty and privilege, individual rights and collective good, and their implications for suffering [and flourishing]' (p. 359). Power struggles saturate Indigenous spaces, and historically and contemporaneously both enable and constrain Indigenous people's capacity for agency and human flourishing. More sophisticated ecological approaches in social justice inquiry that respond to the nature of complex problems, particularly those manifesting in colonized spaces, must be recognized and understood for what they are. In doing so, any approach must align with amenable philosophical underpinnings and research methodologies and methods. Conventional, narrowly-focused research approaches have unproductively tackled complex so-called 'wicked' problems and, in some instances, exacerbated situations by implementing solutions that generated further problems. For example, in Indigenous policy in Australia, alcohol management plans implemented in Aboriginal and Torres Strait Islander communities have made changes to accessing alcohol but have also brought a range of other unintended consequences to the fore, such as sly grogging (alcohol sold illicitly), home-brew, binge drinking and increased incarceration rates.

We offer a methodological-methods package, an approach and tools, embedded in a broader framework of systems sciences, as a collaborative, holistic knowledge-building process for action. We duly note that 'no single method can grasp all the subtle variations in ongoing human experience' (Denzin & Lincoln, 2000, p. 19). In our practice, we thus respond to complex problems by combining the strengths of several coherent, complementary methodologies and methods that hinge on the analytic power of grounded theory methods. The methodological-methods package uses research inquiry as a tool to ameliorate persistent challenges faced by Indigenous nations. We claim constructivist grounded theory methods as a systems science analytic that is valuable in the pursuit of social justice agendas with decolonizing nation-building goals, and able to uncover points of intervention and change for stakeholders alongside advocacy. We reflect on our own work to demonstrate that broadening constructivist grounded theory enables it to:

- be ethically-situated and embedded in an explicit moral process philosophy/value position;
- be directly relevant to the lives of the people with whom we work;
- be culturally-sensitive and responsive to people, their priorities and context;
- be reflective and action-oriented;
- work from the strengths of given situations and Indigenous agency;
- be situated as a two-way learning process, explicitly incorporating mutual capacity development;
- value Indigenous knowledge and centre Indigenous voices and experiences;
- explicitly acknowledge and address power dynamics and discourse;
- involve authentic collaboration and trust in the co-creation of knowledge and action;
- integrate Indigenous and Western knowledges;
- study and explicate processes, including why, how and for what purpose;
- capture and explicate in detail a 'big picture' view of research phenomenon that is temporally situated;
- explain what works for whom, under what conditions, through what mechanisms and with what consequences;
- identify points for action, change and intervention.

In the following sections, we discuss the relevance of grounded theory methods as a systems science analytic in attending to the current impasse in which researchers find themselves in their attempts to address 'wicked' problems that often characterize Indigenous issues. We then consider the ways in which grounded theory as a systems science can work to ameliorate some of the critiques that Indigenous people have about conventional research processes and their continuing failure to deliver benefits. We demonstrate the value of the approach in response to six key critiques that Indigenous nations have made of conventional research approaches: (1) narrowly-focused, reductionist thinking; (2) a preponderance of deficit-focused descriptive research that is of generally suboptimal methodological quality; (3) issues of power and control; (4) devaluing of Indigenous knowledge systems; (5) onerous amounts of research without corresponding impact; and (6) context-independent and culturally-insensitive research. We specifically account for how the seemingly disparate methodologies of phronetic social sciences and participatory action research approaches can be integrated with constructivist grounded theory methods to make issues of social justice explicit in the research endeavour.

We note that a full, detailed explication of grounded theory's relevance to all the issues listed above is not feasible in one chapter. However, a solid understanding of the rationale behind these issues will prompt and enable further reflexivity and exploration in which individual researchers can engage to improve their practice.

COMPLEX QUESTIONS NEED ECOLOGICAL RESPONSES: COUNTERING REDUCTIONIST THINKING AND DISPERSING POWER

Grounded theorists purposively develop theory grounded from the data generated about a specific phenomenon – *vis-à-vis* testing theory or describing the problem under view. Explicitly aligning the self as researcher with a constructivist view of grounded theory enables the study of action, process and meaning *alongside* research partners while seeking multiple perspectives (see Charmaz, 2017a, for more detail). Constructivist grounded theory methods provide an avenue for generating data that captures the 'bigger picture', including all its constituent parts and actors. Most researchers, however, account for their very small part in the bigger picture of multiple social worlds and actors, and many rely on thick description and/or descriptive statistics. Yet, almost all pressing contemporaneous challenges faced by Indigenous people globally relate to the colonial legacies of their exploitation and domination, and are partially the result of historical actions implemented to alleviate them. For many Indigenous populations, these legacies give rise to multilayered dynamic and complex problems that resist resolutions – the so-called 'wicked' problems (Rittel & Webber, 1973).

The very issues that many researchers and others are attempting to resolve *for* Indigenous people are the products of imposing Western systems and knowledge. Paradoxically, proposed solutions often derive from and are implemented through the same power dynamics and reductionist thinking that precipitated the concerns in the first instance. These impositions both reinforce Western authority as *the* knowers, disparage Indigenous knowledges, embed ethnocentric assumptions and practices and enact parochial solutions that further entrench social problems and impede cultural survival and flourishing.

Dealing with complex problems in dynamically complex environments require ecological solutions, particularly those that are historically embedded and dependant on factors and actors outside the immediate environment. For instance, while colonial legacies positively and negatively impact the lives of Indigenous nations, so too do many other determinants of health – many of which are distinct to their life positions. Proximal (health behaviours, physical environments, employment and income, education, food security), intermediate (healthcare systems, educational systems, community infrastructure, resources and capacities, environmental stewardship, cultural continuity) and distal determinants (colonization, racism, social exclusion, self-determination) that shape the conditions of daily living for Indigenous people have considerable influence on their health and social status, but are rarely captured or even acknowledged in analyses (Reading & Wien, 2009). Accounting for these determinants is imperative in transformational inquiry that aims to alleviate health and social inequalities, oppression, poverty and other injustices.

THE ROLE OF SYSTEMS SCIENCES TO ADDRESS WICKED PROBLEMS

Conceptually, systems thinking is concerned with accounting for all aspects of a situation with specific focus on interactions between different parts in the situation and their relationship to the functioning whole. The approach concentrates on the ways in which the phenomenon under study interact with the constituent elements of a whole system – a set of elements that interact to produce behaviour – of which it is a part. It expands its view to take into account larger and larger numbers of interactions as an issue being studied (Arnold & Wade, 2015). A systems science approach, in which grounded theory is firmly embedded, offers a better way to think about researching complex issues – as an effective approach to interpret even the most difficult problems, ascertain causal relationships more accurately, think of new possibilities and solutions, and identify intervention points for change and action. It takes a very different perspective on the conventional standards of Western research methodologies and responds to several Indigenous critiques of Eurocentric research practices.

Grounded theory as a systems science analytic method resonates with ecologically-focused and contextually-responsive research. Its epistemological elasticity can account for epistemological plurality in practice and its iterative and interactive nature enables an easy fit with a number of other methods. Current reductionist approaches that often typify Indigenous research, fail to capture context and the complex causal pathways. That is, the specific ways in which historical, socio-cultural, economic and environmental elements of systems give rise to Indigenous people's opportunities and challenges in life. Reductionist analytic processes 'focus on reliably estimating in great detail the makeup of each component of a system' (Lich, Ginexi & Mabry, 2013, p. 280), but do not illuminate the complex dynamic relationships between them. Reductionist thinking and methods are foundational in modern sciences and have indisputably served society well, particularly in the 'hard' sciences. Such processes demonstrate linear causality that is common in Western thinking. While useful in some disciplines, simple models of causality are often inadequate for social science research and are totally insufficient in attempting to resolve complex phenomena. The circumstances of Indigenous people's lives are complex and embedded in multiple layers of historical, social and environmental contexts that cut across the life course. Reductionist models cannot fully explicate or understand in any depth complex and dynamic situations (Dominici, 2012). Relying entirely on reductionist approaches to respond to these complexities has detrimental implications, the least of which enable the maintenance of the status quo in power relations between Indigenous and non-Indigenous people and perpetuate 'victim blaming'. It makes comprehensive understandings of broader system behaviours influencing the pressing problems experienced by Indigenous nations impossible (Lich, Ginexi & Mabry, 2013). A systems approach, on the other hand, stresses the need to understand dynamic interrelations between its various components and how these work together as a whole.

In thinking about systems science, we need a complementary suite of methodologies and methods through which we can engage in critical interpretative inquiry and that are capable of addressing the types of questions that come about as a result – with particular attention paid to questions of power, inequality and injustice. Grounded theory as a systems method is one way of tackling the kind of 'wicked' problems that often characterize

Indigenous fields of research – systems defined as a 'set of things working together as parts of a mechanism or an interconnecting network' (Oxford, 2006). A systems approach recognizes that people's situations arise from the functioning of systems – that individuals are embedded within social, cultural, political and economic systems that shape behaviours and access to resources necessary for human flourishing (Israel, Schulz, Parker, & Becker, 1998; Diez Roux, 2011). It works from the proposition that 'because the effect of any given input depends on other conditions in a system, emphasis shifts from isolating the causal effect of a single factor to comprehending the functioning of the system as a whole' (Diez Roux, 2011, p. 1627). A key aim of systems approaches is to identify and fully understand systems, and to predict their behaviours so that adaptations can be made to produce desired effects (Arnold & Wade, 2015). Take, for instance, a project that aims to develop resilience for Indigenous students attending boarding schools. Working to develop student resilience in isolation of other factors and conditions would hold little value when their complicated social and environmental contexts includes multiple systems of peers, families, communities, schools, health and education systems, policies, and so forth. Further, these systems are combined with individual students' discrete genetic, biological and psychosocial capabilities. Instead, what is needed is understanding how these seemingly discrete components interact and come to bear on students' situations prior to intervening for change. Having identified those components, their interrelationships and the strength of influence in the situation across time and space, appropriate work towards change lies in the engagement of several key arenas, such as students' individual strengths; school leadership; school and boarding staff; families, elders and communities; government agencies; policy-makers; and health services, including mental health (see Figure 30.1). When so many intervening factors are at play, there is obviously little value in conducting siloed research.

As in the example, what is critical is that 'the behavior and characteristics of the system as a whole cannot be anticipated from – and are typically far different from – the behavior and characteristics of any one element of that system or the sum of the behavior and characteristics of those components when considered separately'

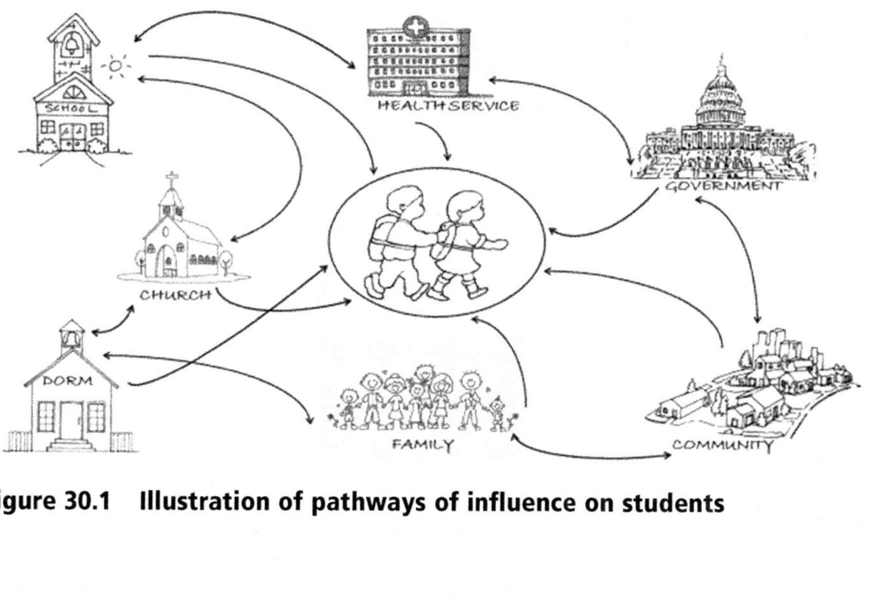

Figure 30.1 Illustration of pathways of influence on students

(Gallagher & Appenzeller, 1999, p. 79), as in reductionist approaches. By extension, systems thinking requires 'a set of synergistic analytic skills used to improve the capability of identifying and understanding systems, predicting their behaviors, and devising modifications to them in order to produce desired effects. These skills work together as a system' (Arnold & Wade, 2015, p. 675). In the anti-colonial space, a systems approach avoids duplicating the over-abundance of descriptive research that perpetuates Indigenous people as the 'problem' to be solved, and, as such, opens up possibilities for meaningful determinations and innovative and active responses to persistent problems. The approach also fits well with the relational understandings of Indigenous life and living – their ways of knowing, being and doing (Bainbridge, Whiteside, & McCalman, 2013).

GROUNDED THEORY METHODS AS A DECOLONIZING TOOL

Grounded theory is a systems science and grounded theorists are systems thinkers. Grounded theory methods clearly bring to the fore the value of using systems approaches to see the bigger picture. Grounded theorists 'think systemically as they explain relationships between incidents, concepts, categories, and properties. They think systemically as they look at processes and stages of change. They recognize the interrelationships that are central to systems thinking, and think systemically as they invite the generation of universal concepts and models' (Stillman, 2006, p. 499). Along with others, such as social network analysis and computational techniques that typically create quantitative models (Frerichs, 2016), we claim grounded theory methods as one of the analytical skills of systems thinking in the qualitative tradition. Grounded theorists speak back to Indigenous critiques of conventional research in several ways.

First, as systems thinkers, they shift from a deficit model to solutions-based research propositions and avoid 'victim-blaming' – seeing Indigenous people as the problem. For instance, taking a systems approach using grounded theory methods enables more innovation in the analysis of actions that relate to the agency of individuals. Importantly, it also moves the analysis beyond Indigenous individuals. It accounts for how the entire system and the actions of other agents play a role in the situation under study. It accounts for what is working and what is not. In turn, we can identify intervention points for building on strengths that already exist and remedial action where change is needed. Reductionist approaches yield limited insights in the context of dynamic systems because this approach limits opportunities to see 'the big picture'. This way of thinking about the world maintains the status quo, particularly in terms of power. Holistic ways of thinking feed a general sense of humanity – and to think differently for those who persist with reductionist thinking means relinquishing value systems and sharing power. On the other hand, systems thinking expands this view and can target multi-level issues. When looking for impact and opportunities for change, complex systems approaches can make the most difference. To maximize possibilities, feedback loops must be closed: for instance, feedback between behavioural and environmental elements – healthy food availability promotes healthier food consumption and thus greater demand for healthy food. The feedback between the health and social arena shows that health affects income and income affects health (Diez Roux, 2011). Ground theory as an analytic tool can help identify such relationships, and explain how and why they work, under what conditions and with what consequences. It can additionally determine points of intervention. However, other methods that encourage participation and action are needed for real-time translation of this knowledge. Undertaking priority-setting with research partners must be emphasized throughout the research process to ensure that we raise the most critical questions in the lives of participants. Facilitating such processes requires a broadening of grounded theory methods.

Grounded theorists have the critical skillsets to counter reductionist thinking and provide explanations that shift away from entrenched simplistic causal models that lead to policy failure and misguided interventions for Indigenous people. What is significant here is that such action can happen as the research progresses because grounded theorists engage in constant interaction with people and data. By extension, this participatory process ensures corresponding impact and that benefit flows to participants in time-oriented ways. Working from a strengths-based approach maximizes participation, investment and ownership, and the likelihood of translation, action and change on the ground. We suggest 'focusing on the population's own resolves in life and attending carefully to the voice of the research population by promoting them as experts in their own lives...' (Bainbridge, Whiteside, & McCalman, 2013, p. 277). The approach invests in a phenomenon that already works and logically serves as the foundation for realistic growth and change.

Second, using grounded theory methods means avoiding descriptive research that reduces the complexity of life and meaning to a catalogue of themes, and instead developing a theory about the research phenomenon under review. As Charmaz (2008a) attests, grounded theory embeds analysis of latent action. She suggests that unlike most qualitative researchers who code for themes, grounded theorists code 'actions and analytic possibilities' (Charmaz, 2008). As a qualitative research method, grounded theory 'uses a systematized set of procedures to develop and inductively derive grounded theory about a phenomenon' (Strauss & Corbin, 1990, p. 24). Grounded theory methods, like systems approaches are used to explicate the behaviour of complex systems and inform directions for change directly relevant to the issue under study. They were specifically developed as a systems analytic technique to capture the dynamic nature of complex multidimensional systems and constantly changing social worlds across time. Its purpose is 'to generate a theory that accounts for a pattern of behavior which is relevant and problematic for those involved' (Glaser, 1978, p. 93).

Grounded theory was designed to explore the nature of complex social phenomena, particularly phenomena about which little is known (Strauss & Corbin, 1998). It is ideally suited to the task of conducting exploratory research, particularly in areas like Indigenous research, where a solid evidence-base is lacking. Much of the research conducted *on* Indigenous issues is descriptive, commonly of low methodological quality, and problem-saturated. The latter points are a distinctive finding of any number of systematic reviews conducted across time, on different subject matter and with various colonized Indigenous nations (e.g., Sanson-Fisher et al., 2006; McCalman et al., 2012; Bainbridge, Tsey, McCalman, & Towle, 2014; Jongen, McCalman, Bainbridge, & Tsey, 2014; Clifford, McCalman, Bainbridge, & Tsey, 2015; McCalman, Bainbridge, Percival, & Tsey, 2016; Kinchin et al., 2017). Descriptive studies do little more than persistently reiterate the problem under investigation. Historically, reductionist methods are not strengths-based or solutions-focused – the problem was constructed as always laying with Indigenous people, with no thought given to how the many other circumstances of living impact on their capacity to flourish.

Third, grounded theory methods limit the burden of research for Indigenous populations – this is a significant criticism reiterated by Indigenous people over time. Grounded theory streamlines data collection processes. While we need appropriate levels of evidence to guide decision-making, the value in a grounded theory approach is that it rationalizes data generation and avoids replication of the same data. That is, as Charmaz (2003) explains, the simultaneous collection and analysis of data streamlines the research process and 'avoids being overwhelmed by volumes of general, unfocused data that do not lead to anything new' (p. 86). While Charmaz references researchers in this point, the upside for participants is that it also limits their data burden without sacrificing quality.

Fourth, a central tenet of grounded theory is the claim that 'all is data' (Glaser, 1998). This means that different knowledges and their various artefacts can be integrated into the analysis. Thus, in applying grounded theory methods, theorists readily accept that the different products, representations and textual materials that can come about when working in oral cultures, for instance, or where language barriers exist. Theorists also become more intimately engaged with their research partners, data and analysis. Further, the research practices and their creations can truly represent the dispersal of power in the research relationship, appropriate valuing and centring of Indigenous voices, the explicit integration of Western and Indigenous knowledges, and evades interpretation from a Western lens.

Last, grounded theorists are engaged researchers and aim to explicate patterns, interrelationships, properties and processes inherent in particular situations through investigations of the dynamic interrelationships of system components across multiple levels of analysis. In this way, the research analysis integrates context as we partake in constant sampling and analyzing of the particular situation under study. Grounded theory was developed with the express intent of developing a theory with great 'explanatory power' (Glaser & Strauss, 1967, p. 247) and which demonstrates fit and relevance to the research stakeholders' realities and aspirations. This aim has all the hallmarks of deconstructing power relationships, placing importance on context and valuing Indigenous knowledge by centring the voices of participant populations in the research.

DISMANTLING THE MASTERS' HOUSE WITH THE MASTERS' TOOLS

There are strong correlations between a constructivist grounded theory approach as a social justice tool in critical inquiry and its utility as a tool for decolonizing methodologies (Charmaz, 2011, 2017a). Critical inquiry is 'embedded in a transformative paradigm that seeks to expose, oppose, and redress forms of oppression, inequality, and injustice' (Charmaz, 2017b, p. 35). Charmaz (2017b) encourages the expansion of the practice of critical inquiry 'by including an emergent approach with inductive qualitative research' (p. 35), as, for example, constructivist grounded theory. However, constructivist grounded theory depends on engaging 'methodological self-consciousness' (p. 35). Charmaz defines the latter as 'detecting and dissecting our worldviews, language, and meanings … being aware of unearned and taken-for-granted privileges … and defining intersecting relationships with power, identity, subjectivity and marginality for both the researcher and research participants' (p. 36). Strong reflexive actions, however, require practical processes through which they can be facilitated both individually and collectively.

DISCERNING PHILOSOPHICAL POSITIONS IN GROUNDED SOCIAL JUSTICE INQUIRY

Glaser denied allegiance to any specific philosophical position (Glaser, 2005). However, more contemporary proponents of grounded theory have privileged various philosophies that mirror their underlying ontologies (Birks & Mills, 2015). We claim integration of constructivist and phronetic epistemologies. We share epistemological consistency with the grounded theory methods reclaimed by Charmaz in the constructivist tradition (2006, 2011) – although it should be noted that Mills, Bonner, and Francis (2006) found a 'discernible thread of constructivism in their [Strauss & Corbin's] approach to inquiry' (p. 25). A constructivist paradigm proposes the existence of 'multiple, socially constructed realities that are influenced by social, cultural, and historical contexts; the inquirer and participant are connected in such a way that the findings are inseparable from their relationship; and the methods used emphasize a continual dialectic of iteration, analysis, assessment, reiteration, and reanalysis' (Israel, Schulz, Parker, & Becker, 1998, p. 176). The researcher must be actively acknowledged as author in the 'reconstruction of experience and meaning' (Mills, Bonner, & Francis, 2006, p. 26). Adopting a constructivist grounded theory approach propositionally legitimizes the experiences of Indigenous people as a valid source of knowledge; facilitates the development of theory directly interpreted from the words expressed by them; considers the influence of contextual social processes and structures; recognizes the diversity of experience; and assumes a regard for the relational aspects of the research enterprise – things that fall under what one might term critical inquiry.

Discerning a philosophical position has implications for how research is conceptualized and conducted.

Standards of ethical practice for working with Indigenous nations can best be determined by the epistemological and methodological stance of researchers and their fit with those of their Indigenous partners. In anti-colonial inquiry, claiming an explicit value position is vital, even more so in cross-cultural endeavours. Yet, as Charmaz (2011) suggests, 'some [social justice] researchers remain silent about their value commitments and instead choose to frame their studies in conceptual terms, rather than social justice concerns' to avoid having their work contested (p. 360). Nevertheless, a process philosophy is important because researchers and research partners can bring their ontological and epistemological accounts to the fore, including their assumptions about the situation under study. It is important that the approach accounts for 'the constraints that historical, social, and situational contexts exert on these actions and acknowledges the researcher's role in shaping the data and analysis' (Charmaz, 2011, p. 360). Being explicit about researcher's and participants' perceptions is what counts here. In making our assumptions vulnerable to broader deliberation, their validity can be tested through examination and critique. Points of difference and congruence can be identified and negotiated as the research develops and unfolds. Having a shared values-base is not the only goal in this interaction; rather, the aim is to ensure a process through which we can understand and work together – a matter of great significance, but which is difficult to achieve in reality.

ARISTOTELIAN VIRTUES: A PHRONETIC SOCIAL SCIENCE FOR SHARED HUMANITY

Explicit recognition of the complex power dynamics facing Indigenous populations is an essential aspect of any emancipatory work. A phronetic research approach is useful in surfacing value positions and evoking 'methodological self-consciousness' (Charmaz, 2017b). The notion of a phronetic social science rests on the Aristotelian philosophy that well-functioning societies rely on the concurrent interaction and functioning of three knowledge systems or intellectual virtues: *phronesis* (practical wisdom, ethics and values); *techne* (arts and craft); and *episteme* (scientific knowledge). Flyvberg (2001) proposed that the interaction between the different schools of knowledge provides a holistic and contextual orientation towards gaining knowledge of the social world. Phronesis, or practical wisdom, concerns how one should act ethically in certain situations and whereby importance is also placed upon experience of its application. The integration of the three Aristotelian virtues are critical in contemplating a systems approach, developing a shared values orientation with diverse stakeholders, seeking ways of dispersing power differentials and integrating Indigenous and non-Indigenous knowledge systems. Flyvberg's way of refocusing the notion of phronetic social science for research foregrounds the concept of praxis. He contends that phronesis is best achieved by the analysis of values and power 'as a point of departure for action' (Flyvberg, 2001, p. 57). Thus, while phronetic research focuses on values, ethics and action, it importantly places power at the centre of the analysis. As guidance, Flyvbjerg proposed five value-rational questions for working in a phronetic framework: (1) Where are we going? (2) Who gains and who loses? (3) By which mechanisms of power? (4) Is this desirable? (5) What, if anything, should be done?

PARTICIPATORY REFLECTION AND ACTION: A FRAMEWORK FOR PRAXIS

Phronetic inquiry, like grounded theory, does not seek to test theory or claim epistemic dominance. It aims to 'clarify and deliberate about the problems and risks we face and to outline how things may be done differently' (Flyvberg, 2001, p. 140). Thus, it does not fixate on particular paradigms and is not wedded to any specific methodological privilege. A phronetic social science orientation enables movement beyond epistemologies that centre the privileges, beliefs and experience of dominant others and thus more equitably distribute power to those who seek action to deliver social change for the common good (Bainbridge, Whiteside, & McCalman, 2013). Like constructivist grounded theory, phronetic social inquiry strives for pragmatically governed interpretation (Flyvberg, 2001). It further hones one of the inherent strengths in grounded theory; that is, it closely attends to context by 'turning away from acontextual description' (Charmaz, 2006, p. 271).

In a phronetic grounded theory approach, values and assumptions are made explicit, power and privilege are addressed, contextually-responsive research is undertaken, and pragmatism and the integration of diverse knowledge systems and standpoints are well managed. These are consistent with the hallmarks of a constructivist grounded approach. Phronetic practice, however, advocates a combination of methods that values praxis, and ensures that actions are embedded in philosophies of common humanity, working for the common good and thus pre-empt flourishing societies. The phronetic researcher aims for pragmatism (a workable ethical course of action) that focuses on context (localized Indigenous knowledge) and responds to the variable or particular, as opposed to the universal and context-independent (Flyvbjerg, 2001). Phronesis involves the reflective capacity of individuals to inform morally-oriented action that leads to change (Flyvberg, 2001). The latter is critical in decolonizing research practices.

Authentic engagement and collaboration are critical to how we conduct the business of doing research with a social change agenda. Translating a phronetic approach requires a workable framework that can interpret power and practice in everyday situations, and through which it can function in real-world situations. Despite advocacy by international development and aid communities in recent decades for supporting ecological bottom-up solutions to promote health and sustainable social development and change, in reality the approach represents a major challenge to implement. In a decolonizing approach, we suggest 'focusing on the population's own resolves in life and attending carefully to the voice of the research population by promoting them as experts in their own lives...' (Bainbridge, Whiteside, & McCalman, 2013, p. 277). The approach invests in a phenomenon that already works and logically serves as the foundation for realistic growth and change. We propose five reflexive, action-oriented questions to generate data: (1) What is the situation; (2) What do we want to change? (3) What is already happening? (4) What's working, what's not, and who is missing out? (5) How can we improve the situation?

The phronetic nature of the two sets of value-rational questions provides a departure point for reflective practice, interaction, discussion, planning and action – a reflexive model of praxis. An organic, collaborative and iterative research process enables continuous quality improvement in the research situation. But to happen, understanding and interpreting how the relationships between the everyday experiences of our research partners and the contexts in which they function is needed. It means unpacking the assumptions that we make about how the interrelationships embedded in the research phenomenon, including what works for whom and under what conditions; the opportunities and constraints inherent in the situation; the mechanisms through which they are addressed; and the consequences and outcomes of these actions.

Participatory action research processes and grounded theory as a systems analytic method are ideally suited to this assignment. Many researchers have amended their approaches to emancipatory research by nurturing closer partnerships with Indigenous research stakeholders and reorienting to participatory action research methodologies to increase the appropriate application of research evidence in policy and practice (Bainbridge et al., 2015). Dick (2007) outlines the differences and parallels between participatory action research approaches and grounded theory. Their complementarity, however, is noted (see Dick, 2007, for further reading). But what is important in making them both an easy fit is that they are both emergent, interactive, reflective and cyclic in nature and thus feed into each other in terms of facilitating data generation, analysis and theory building.

CONCLUSION

Flourishing societies depend on the capacity of researchers to implement practical wisdom in their activities. We posed the question of whether researchers also have the prudence to seek evidence that is relevant to Indigenous priorities. Critiquing conventional epistemologies and understanding how to achieve decolonizing propositions in reality is inherently difficult for many researchers. Our mission in this chapter was to stimulate fresh perspectives in thinking about potential resolutions to 'wicked' problems when partnering with Indigenous people in research, in ways that are meaningful to them. We suggested that using grounded theory methods provides flexible opportunities to implement and produce anti-colonial research. We tried not to be prescriptive about how best to tackle these 'wicked' problems. Rather, we provided a rationale for adopting innovation in research. We offered a suite of approaches and methods: decolonizing methodologies as critical precursors to thinking about doing research; innovative ways of perceiving issues; and ways of working that related the value of grounded theory methods in responding to complex problems.

Systems science and analytics such as grounded theory methods, phronetic inquiry and participatory approaches all have their foundations in pragmatism and responses that move away from reductionist positivist approaches to alternative critical inquiry paradigms. However, there is a persistent practice among the research community to engage in reductionist thinking and to seek universal, objective solutions to dynamic complex and situated social problems. Thus, we submitted a conceptual and methodological-methods framework for thinking about how to make research more relevant to the lives and aspirations of Indigenous nations. The framework broadens the current proliferation of descriptive research to incorporate theorizing of the determinants of the particular situations under study. This systems approach maximizes translation and impact for Indigenous nations by identifying the amalgamations and interactions of individual, social, policy, and environmental variations and relationships inherent in the situation. The framework is embedded in research practice in real-world settings reflexively drawn from our own practice of working with the Indigenous nations of Australia and the Pacific. A systems science approach incorporating several converging trends in the social sciences can reveal culturally- and contextually-relevant evidence for better decision-making. However, to engage such a framework means conducting more engaged research with research partners and fostering stronger hybrid partnerships, including interdisciplinary teams of researchers, to bring together and address the ecology of multi-levelled elements that are the root causes of issues we seek to resolve.

REFERENCES

Anderson, I., Robson, B., Connolly, M., Al-Yaman, F., Bjertness, E., King, A., ... Yap, L. (2016). Indigenous and tribal peoples' health (*The Lancet*–2013; Lowitja Institute Global Collaboration): a population study. *The Lancet*, *388*(10040), 131-157. doi:10.1016/S0140-6736(16)00345-7

Arnold, R. D., & Wade, J. P. (2015). A definition of systems thinking: A systems approach. *Procedia Computer Science*, *44*, 669–678. doi: 10.1016/j.procs.2015.03.050

Bainbridge, R., Tsey, K., Andrews, R., & McCalman, J. (2013). A partnership approach to transitioning policy change in Aboriginal Australian communities. Journal of Australian Indigenous Issues, *16*(1), 55.

Bainbridge, R., McCalman, J., Tsey, K., & Brown, C. (2011). Inside-out approaches to promoting Aboriginal Australian wellbeing: Evidence from a decade of community-based participatory research. *The International Journal of Health, Wellness and Society*, *1*(2).

Bainbridge, R., Whiteside, M., & McCalman, J. (2013). Being, knowing, and doing: A phronetic approach to constructing grounded theory with Aboriginal Australian partners. *Qualitative Health Research*, *23*(2), 275–288.

Bainbridge, R., Tsey, K., McCalman, J., Kinchin, I., Saunders, V., Watkin Lui, F., … Lawson, K. (2015). No one's discussing the elephant in the room: Contemplating questions of research impact and benefit in Aboriginal and Torres Strait Islander Australian health research. *BMC Public Health*, *15*(1), 696. doi:10.1186/s12889-015-2052-3

Bainbridge, R., Tsey, K., McCalman, J., & Towle, S. (2014). The quantity, quality and characteristics of Indigenous Australian mentoring: A systematic review. *BMC Public Health*, *14*, 1263. doi: 10.1186/1471-2458-14-1263

Birks, M., & Mills, J. (2015). *Grounded theory: A practical guide*. Los Angeles, CA: Sage.

Bishop, R. 2005. "Freeing ourselves from neocolonial domination in research". In *The handbook of qualitative research*, 3rd ed., Edited by: Denzin, N.K. and Lincoln, Y.S. 109–138. Thousand Oaks, CA: Sage.

Charmaz, K. (2003). Charmaz, K. (2003). Grounded theory. In J. A. Smith (Ed.), *Qualitative psychology: a practical guide to research methods* (pp. 81–110). London, Thousand Oaks, New Delhi: SAGE Publications.

Charmaz, K. (2006). *Constructing grounded theory: A practical guide through qualitative analysis*. London: Sage.

Charmaz, K. (2008a). Constructionism and the grounded theory method. In J. Holstein & J. Gubrium (Eds.), *Handbook of constructionist research* (pp. 397–412). New York: Guilford Press.

Charmaz, K. (2008b). Grounded Theory as an Emergent Method. In S. N. Hesse-Biber & P. Leavy (Eds), *Handbook of Emergent Methods* (pp. 155-172. New York: The Guilford Press.

Charmaz, K. (2011). Grounded theory methods in social justice. In N. Denzin & Y. Lincoln (Eds.), *The SAGE handbook of qualitative research* (pp. 359–380). Thousand Oaks, CA: Sage.

Charmaz, K. (2017a). The power of constructivist grounded theory for critical inquiry. *Qualitative Inquiry*, *23*(1), 34–45. doi: 10.1177/1077800416657105

Charmaz, K. (2017b). Special Invited Paper: Continuities, contradictions, and critical inquiry in grounded theory. *International Journal of Qualitative Methods*, *16*(1). doi:10.1177/1609406917719350

Clarke, A. E. (2005). *Situational analysis: Grounded theory after the postmodern turn*. Thousand Oaks, CA: Sage.

Clifford, A., McCalman, J., Bainbridge, R., & Tsey, K. (2015). Interventions to improve cultural competency in healthcare for Indigenous peoples of Australia, New Zealand, Canada and the United States: A systematic review. *International Journal for Quality in Health Care*, *27*(2), 1–10, doi: 10.1093/intqhc/mzv010

Denzin, N. K., & Lincoln, Y. S. (2000). *Handbook of qualitative research* (2nd ed.). Thousand Oaks, CA: Sage.

Dick, B. (2007). What can grounded theorists and action researchers learn from each other? In A. Bryant & K. Charmaz (Eds.), *The SAGE handbook of grounded theory* (pp. 398–416). Los Angeles, CA: Sage.

Diez Roux, A. V. (2011). Complex systems thinking and current impasses in health disparities research. *American Journal of Public Health*, *101*(9), 1627–1634. doi: 10.2105/AJPH.2011.300149

Dominici, Gandolfo, Why Does Systems Thinking Matter? (May 1, 2012). Business Systems Review, *Vol. 1*, No. 1, pp.1-2, 2012. Available at SSRN: https://ssrn.com/abstract=2046736

Flyvbjerg, B. (2001). *Making social science matter: Why social inquiry fails and how it can succeed again*. Cambridge, UK: Cambridge University Press.

Frerichs, L., Lich, K. H., Dave, G., & Corbie-Smith, G. (2016). Integrating systems science and community-based participatory research to achieve health equity. *American Journal of Public Health*, *106*(2), 215–222. doi:10.2105/ajph.2015.302944

Gallagher, R., & Appenzeller, T. (1999). Beyond Reductionism. *Science*, *284*(5411): 79.

Gibson, B. (2007). Accommodating critical theory. In A. Bryant & K. Charmaz (Eds.), *The SAGE handbook of grounded theory* (pp. 436–453). London: Sage.

Glaser, B. G. (1978). *Theoretical sensitivity: Advances in the methodology of grounded theory*. Mill Valley, CA: Sociology Press.

Glaser, B. G. (1998). *Doing grounded theory: Issues and discussions*. Mill Valley, CA: Sociology Press.

Glaser, B. G. (2005). *The grounded theory perspective III: Theoretical coding*. Mill Valley, CA: Sociology Press.

Glaser, B. G., & Strauss, A. L. (1967). *The discovery or grounded theory*. New York: Aldine.

Humphery K. (2001). Dirty questions: Indigenous health and 'Western research'. *Australian and New Zealand Journal of Public Health*, *25*(3), 197–202.

Irabinna Rigney, L. (1999). Internationalization of an indigenous anticolonial cultural critique of research methodologies: a guide to indigenist research methodology and its principles [Electronic Version]. *Wicazo Sa Review*, *14*, 109-113. Retrieved 28 August, 2006, from http:/www.links.jstor.org/sici=07496427%28199923%2914%3A2%3C109%3AIOAIAC%3E2.0.CO%3B2-1.

Israel, B. A., Schulz, A. J., Parker, E. A., & Becker, A. B. (1998). Review of community-based research: Assessing partnership approaches to improve public health. *Annual Review of Public Health*, *19*, 173–202. doi:org/10.1146/annurev.publhealth.19.1.173

Jongen, C. S., McCalman, J., & Bainbridge, R. G. (2017). The implementation and evaluation of health promotion services and programs to improve cultural competency: A systematic scoping review. *Frontiers in Public Health*, *5*(24). doi:10.3389/fpubh.2017.00024

Jongen, C., McCalman, J., Bainbridge, R., & Tsey, K. (2014). Aboriginal and Torres Strait Islander maternal and infant health and wellbeing: A systematic search of programs and services in Australian primary health care settings. *BMC Pregnancy and Childbirth*. *14*(251). DOI: 10.1186/1471-2393-14-251

Kinchin, I., McCalman, J., Bainbridge, R., Watkin, F., Tsey, K. (2017). Does Indigenous health research have impact? A systematic review of reviews. *International Journal for Equity in Health*, *16*(52). doi: 10.1186/s12939-017-0548-4

Kovach, M. 2009. *Indigenous Methodologies: Characteristics, Conversations and Contexts,* Toronto, Canada, University of Toronto Press.

Lich, K. H., Ginexi, E. M., & Mabry, P. L. (2013). A call to address complexity in prevention science research. *Prevention Science*, *14*(3), 279–289. doi:10.1007/s11121-012-0285-2

McCalman, J., Bainbridge, R., Percival, N., & Tsey, K. (2016). The effectiveness of implementation in Indigenous Australian healthcare: An overview of literature reviews. *International Journal for Equity in Health*, *15*, 47. doi: 10.1186/s12939-016-0337-5

McCalman, J., Tsey, K., Bainbridge, R., Shakeshaft, A., Singleton, M., & Doran, C. (2013). Tailoring a response to youth binge drinking in an Aboriginal Australian community: A grounded theory study. *BMC Public Health*, *13*, 726. doi:10.1186/1471-2458-13-726

McCalman, J., Tsey, K., Clifford, A., Earles, W., Shakeshaft, A., & Bainbridge, R. (2012). Applying what works: A systematic review of the transfer and implementation of promising services and programs. *BMC Public Health*, *1*(2), 600.

Mills, J., Bonner, A., & Francis, K. (2006). The development of constructivist grounded theory. *International Journal of Qualitative Methods*, *5*(1), 25–35.

National Health and Medical Research Council. Values and ethics: guidelines for ethical conduct in Aboriginal and Torres Strait Islander health research. Canberra: Commonwealth of Australia, 2003. http://www.nhmrc.gov.au/_fi les_nhmrc/publications/attachments/e52.pdf (accessed Jan 2014).

Ramanathan S, Reeves P, Deeming S, et al. Encouraging translation and assessing impact of the Centre for Research Excellence in Integrated Quality Improvement: rationale and protocol for a research impact assessment. BMJ Open 2017;7:e018572. doi: 10.1136/bmjopen-2017-018572

Reading, C. L., & Wien, F. (2009). *Health inequalities and social determinants of Aboriginal peoples' health*. Prince George, BC: National Collaborating Centre for Aboriginal Health.

Redman-MacLaren, M., & Mills, J. (2015). Transformational grounded theory: Theory, voice, and action. *International Journal of Qualitative Methods*, *14*(3).

Rittel, H., & Webber, M. (1973). Dilemmas in a general theory of planning. Policy Sciences, *4*, 155–169. doi:10.1007/BF01405730

Sanson-Fisher, R. W., Campbell, E. M., Perkins, J. J., Blunden, S. V., & Davis, B. B. (2006). Indigenous health research: A critical review of outputs over time. *Medical Journal of Australia*, 184.

Semali, L. M., & Kincheloe, J. L. (1999). Introduction: What is indigenous knowledge and why should we study it. *What is indigenous knowledge*, 3-57.

Smith, L. T. (1999). *Decolonizing methodologies: Research and Indigenous peoples*. London: Zed Books.

Smith, L. T. (2005). On tricky ground: Researching the native in the age of uncertainty. In N. K. Denzin & Y. S. Lincoln (Eds.), *Handbook of qualitative research* (3rd ed., pp. 85–108). Thousand Oaks, CA: Sage.

Stillman, S. (2006). Grounded theory and grounded action: Rooted in systems theory. *World Futures*, *62*(7), 498–504.

Strauss, A. L., & Corbin, J. (1990). *The basics of qualitative analysis: Grounded theory procedures and techniques*. Newbury Park, CA: Sage.

Strauss, A. L., & Corbin, J. (1998). *The basics of qualitative analysis: Grounded theory procedures and techniques* (2nd ed.). Newbury Park, CA: Sage.

Thomas, D. P., Bainbridge, R., & Tsey, K. (2014). A brief history of Aboriginal and Torres Strait Islander health research, 1914–2013. *Medical Journal of Australia*, *201*(1), S15–18.

Tsey, K., Lawson, K., Kinchin, I., Bainbridge, R., McCalman, J., Watkin, F., Cadet-James, Y., & Rossetto, A. (2016). Evaluating research impact: The development of a 'research for impact' tool. *Frontiers in Public Health*, *4*(1), August. doi: 10.3389/fpubh.2016.00160

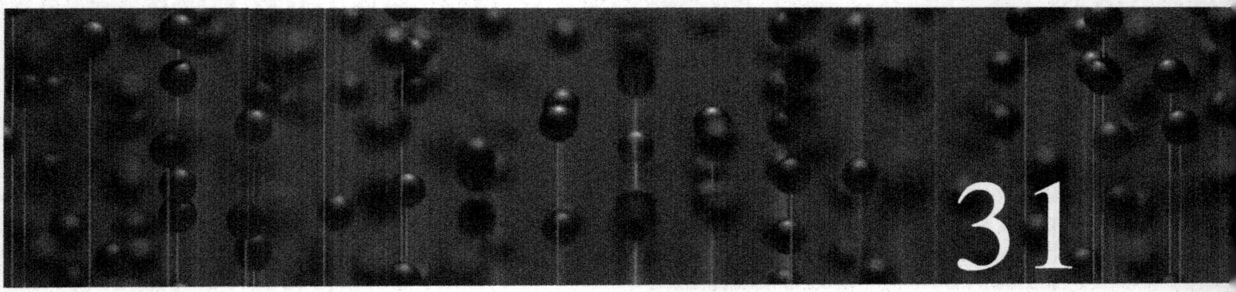

31

Community-based Participatory Research and Constructivist Grounded Theory: Aligning Transformative Research with Local Ways of Being and Knowing

Joyce M. Duckles, George Moses and Robert Moses

Stemming from symbolic interactionist and pragmatic theoretical foundations, the cycles of inductive and abductive reasoning of Constructivist Grounded Theory (CGT) encourage researchers to attend to the practical and local activities of community building and adopt pluralistic and participatory processes that reach into multiple perspectives. These practices align with community-based participatory research (CBPR) and participatory action research (PAR) goals and methodologies. The pragmatic foundations also lead us to embrace the provisional nature of inquiry. The resulting praxis, the 'oscillation' between the practical and propositional (Hense & McFerran, 2015), has increasingly shaped critical inquiry, particularly in CGT. As Hense and McFerran (2015) propose, CGT is a strategy for engaging in iterative cycles in praxis, working with tension and doubt, engaging in democratic collaborations, and ensuring rigor. They conclude that these tensions have the potential to foster and support more robust and inclusive research directed at meaningful social action and change.

As a team of community–university researchers and activists, we find these tensions generative and foundational in our practices of critical ethnographic inquiry. Over the past six years, we have engaged in an ethnographic study of the transformation of the Cedarwood neighborhood, an urban community with a rich history of activism and innovation that continues to face the challenges of concentrated poverty. Within our community-based participatory research orientation, we actively work together as co-researchers, co-authors and co-implementers bridging theory, praxis and dissemination. As a diverse research team, we have learned that collaborative research and critical inquiry focused on sustainable change must align with local understandings of being and knowing (ontologies and epistemologies) and values (axiologies). As Charmaz (2016) maintains, 'Our methods do not stand outside the structures in which we live' (p. 47).

We propose that the methodological and epistemological pluralism we intentionally adopt has created the tools and dialogic spaces to bring local theories, knowledge and values into our analysis and praxis. With goals of urban transformation, we reach across traditional and emerging research methodologies to develop a nuanced approach to inquiry and practice directed at sustainable change. We build on traditions of action research (AR), participatory action research (PAR), and community-based participatory research (CBPR) that focus on co-learning, creating local knowledge, and adopting iterative cycles of research and action to address both local issues and systemic change (Dick, Stringer, & Huxham, 2009; Israel, Eng, Schultz, & Parker, 2005; Minkler & Wallerstein, 2011). Across disciplines, in the fields of nursing (e.g., Schrieber & Tomm-Bonde, 2015), health and health disparities (e.g., Minkler & Wallerstein, 2011), youth activism (e.g., Ginwright & Cammarota, 2007), and indigenous and African-centered research (e.g., Akom, 2011; King & Swartz, 2015), researchers are conducting critical inquiry through CBPR and BEAR (Black Emancipatory Action Research). Many of these researchers have integrated grounded theory methods and approaches with collaborative practices, demonstrating how grounded theory can provide the methodological rigor that PAR and CBPR studies often trade in exchange for generating evidence to inform local, practice-based processes.

Similarly, our work emerges from the constructivist grounded theory (CGT) iterative cycles of data collection-analysis-implementation-sharing-reflection-collection. These processes also bring value to local, community-generated knowledge and evidence within goals of relevant action for social change. In this chapter, we begin by exploring the theoretical traditions of symbolic interactionism and pragmatism that frame CGT and argue for their place in both community-based participatory research and practices of community development. We explore the literature across diverse fields that is bringing attention to the potential power of CGT for critical inquiry. Through examples from our collaborative research, we demonstrate how, through inductive and abductive reasoning and assiduous theoretical sampling, we build local analytic concepts as we co-construct emergent situated findings and questions. We pay special attention here to our processes of abduction, reaching into the deep situated and historical knowledge of our research team and to the literature across multiple fields of study. As such, we align with others (Charmaz, 2017; Gibson, 2007; Locke, Golden-Biddle, & Feldman, 2008) who situate abductive reasoning, doubt and tensions at the root of collaborative and critical inquiry.

These processes have led us to recognize the foundations of Afrocentric philosophies to the ways of knowing and being in this community. We demonstrate how these philosophies align with and inform our collaborative and CGT research processes, and how we adopt them as sensitizing concepts to keep us grounded in local values and goals. In our research, these processes have led us to current threads of analysis, including creating and defining selves through 'pushing back' and 'naming ourselves.' As we navigate the diverse histories, cultures and perspectives of our team, these threads were recognized and named within our group as embodying and enacting the Nguzo Saba principle of Kujichagulia or Self-Determination ('to define ourselves, name ourselves, create for ourselves and speak for ourselves' (Karenga, 1988, p. 52)). This concept, along with other Nguzo Saba principles, have entered our cycles of inductive and abductive reasoning, shaping and informing our analysis and practices.

Collaborative research in urban contexts presents many challenges. One persistent challenge is the pull back toward methodological and theoretical individualism because of the Eurocentric research practices and Anglo-North American epistemologies framing much research, as well as the university paradigms of research and publishing. In addition, we construct and stay within contentious and contested spaces; spaces of doubt, tensions and negotiating multiple identities. We stay here because we recognize the generative potential of these spaces. As one community member reminded us, in transformative work 'Stagnation is not an option.'

Stagnation is also not an option because as community activists we share goals of meaningful local action for social change. In this chapter, we explore how integrating CGT and CBPR methodologies provide the philosophies, principles and practices to move beyond Eurocentric framings, bridge multiple identities and epistemologies while embracing the nuances of differences, and place local axiological ideologies at the center of critical and rigorous work. We propose that bringing together the ways of being and knowing that emerge through our epistemological, theoretical and methodological pluralism, and grounded firmly in values of activism and change, frames a valuable way of engaging with one another as researchers and practitioners and with our multiple communities.

THEORETICAL FOUNDATIONS FRAMING COLLABORATIVE RESEARCH: SYMBOLIC INTERACTIONISM, PRAGMATISM, AND ABDUCTION

In the urban neighborhood in which we work and live, community members experience disparities in education, health, housing and economics. Our schools are graduating less than 50% of our youth (www.nydatabases.com, [NYSED] 2017), the life expectancy of residents is eight years less than in surrounding suburbs (Finger Lakes Health Systems Agency, 2014), and access to food is limited by the overabundance of corner stores (26 at last count) and one small supermarket. Our practices of critical inquiry naturally emerge from constant reminders of structural racism and inequities that background and foreground our practices and research. At the same time, this community is actively engaged in development, activism and change. A primary focus of our research has been to explore how interactions within our community are shifting from transactional to transformational, while always acknowledging and challenging the broader structures that shape these interactions. Charmaz (2017) views critical inquiry as 'embedded in a transformative paradigm that seeks to expose, oppose, and redress forms of oppression, inequality, and injustice' (p. 35), but she also frames (and encourages us to reframe) these abstract processes of justice, injustice, power, and privilege as '*enacted processes*, made real through actions performed again and again' (p. 35, italics in original). She proposes that CGT provides the framework and tools to keep our attention as researchers on the constructed, contested and situated nature of these processes.

The power of constructivist grounded theory for critical inquiry stems from its theoretical foundations. This begins with symbolic interactionism and its core emphasis on meaning-making through interactions, human agency, language and interpretation. Beginning with Glaser and Strauss (1967), symbolic interactionism has provided a philosophical foundation for grounded theory research. Aldiabat and Le Navenec (2011) summarized how the assumptions of grounded theory and symbolic interactionism align: symbolic interactionism (SI) provides a guiding framework to explore the meaning of actions and interactions of actors, 'the contextual sources of such meanings, and how they change in and through social and physical time and space,' while grounded theory 'affords a systematic approach to generate a theory' that provides insights into meaning-making, social processes and their interactional contexts (p. 1068). In her book *Constructing Grounded Theory*, Charmaz (2014) demonstrates how SI brings attention to processes and meaning-making at the micro level of interactions but can also address macro processes of change, emergence, agency and negotiated order. She highlights these tensions between structure and processes:

> ...symbolic interactionists assume process and explain stability. Thus symbolic interactionism offers an alternative to other social scientific perspectives that assume stability and attempt to explain change. (Charmaz, 2014, p. 266)

Challenging the stable nature of social structures is also a central tenet of pragmatism. To extend our practices of social justice inquiry, we reach into the pragmatist traditions of Strauss and Peirce (Charmaz, 2016, 2017), and, in particular, the pragmatic goals of social reform. Several comprehensive reviews explore the potential of adopting pragmatism and CGT (Charmaz, 2017; Lincoln & Guba, 2013) and pragmatism and community inquiry (Bruce & Bloch, 2013). They highlight key assumptions of pragmatism that align with practices of CGT, with principles of CBPR, and with research for social change. Bruce and Bloch (2013) proposed four salient features of pragmatism: 'its emphasis on the *practical* dimensions of inquiry, the *pluralistic* nature of the tools that are used to study phenomena, the *participatory* role of individuals with different perspectives, and the *provisional* nature of inquiry' (p. 28, italics added). Charmaz (2017) speaks to the pragmatic assumptions of processes, the problematic views of stability, the emergent nature of meanings and actions, and the fluid and indeterminate nature of reality.

As we look across the traditions of pragmatism, we find they provide a foundation for our CBPR practices. We begin with the focus on the *practical* approach to exploring concepts and experiences as situated in particular social contexts, with local understandings and consequences. The *pluralistic* perspective touches on the multiple realities and perspectives at the core of CBPR. We adopt the principle of distributed expertise in our team, recognizing the strength of this pluralism. Bruce and Bloch propose that *participatory* processes highlight the 'active nature of inquiry,' building on Peirce's belief that 'the most robust inquiry must involve full participation of all who may have knowledge of the situation' (p. 30). Gibson (2007) argued that pluralism is associated with the democratic principles underlying pragmatism. Rather than seeing contradicting views as barriers, they are 'recast as productive tensions around which social inquiry can begin' (Gibson, 2007, p. 443). Within CBPR, this begins with the pragmatic assumption of all research participants as agentic actors (Charmaz, 2017), which is supported by adopting grounded theory as a form of social inquiry that includes engaging as equal participants in the research process (Gibson, 2007).

Both pluralism and participatory processes lead to the final tenet of pragmatism: the provisional nature of inquiry. A pluralistic perspective embracing contradictory views assumes that our grounded theories can always look different. Embracing this attitude of 'radical doubt' (Gibson, 2007) (addressed within grounded theory through iterative theoretical sampling) pushes us to diverse and local sensitizing concepts and, thus, becomes generative. Charmaz (2017) maintains that constructivist grounded theory and pragmatism involve doubt, and along with others (Bajc, 2012; Locke et al., 2008; Paavola, 2014; Timmermans & Tavory, 2012) encourages us to explore this generative potential of doubt. She leads us to Peirce's associated notion of abduction.

'Abduction involves pursuing doubt rather than dismissing it' (Charmaz, 2017, p. 38). It encompasses fluid views of 'truth,' directing us to move back and forth between theoretical explanations (academic, historical and local). Locke et al. (2008) situated doubt, and abductive reasoning, at the root of research practices: '…doubt is an essential, not aberrant, part of the research process: The question is not whether, but *how*, to engage doubt' (p. 908). Timmermans and Tavory (2012) proposed that abduction in grounded theory can address the challenges of generating new theory, arguing that we should privilege abduction as an analytic approach to move us toward novel theoretical insights. They concluded that the process of abduction 'contains an irreducible social component of exchanging theoretical ideas in a network of researchers' (p. 181). Theorizing is not new to our community researchers – community philosophies and values, cultural and spiritual understandings, and the problem solving of everyday life have always been woven into analytic practices. We have learned together how to both capitalize on these local, social and situated understandings while also pulling from theories from the multiple fields of study of research team members.

As such, the concept of abduction captures essential characteristics and current practices of our collaborative and diverse research team. In CBPR, abduction leads us to expand our theoretical repertoires across academic and local ways of knowing and being, philosophical traditions, and values. For example, as we uncovered the interdependent connections across multiple hubs in our community, we employed the concepts of rhizomatic structures of interdependence and generativity (Deleuze & Guattari, 1987) along with rich understandings of grassroots organizing practices as we sought sensitizing concepts to uncover and understand the interdependent hubs emerging across the neighborhood (Larson, Hanny, Duckles, Pham, Moses, & Moses, 2017). With similar botanical structures, 'grassroots' and rhizomes are adopted as conceptual metaphors of web-like open systems with multiple connections, contrasting with tree-like hierarchical models that reduce relations to one core or foundation (Colombat, 1991; Malins, 2004). These metaphors captured the nature of the interdependent relationships emerging from our data. When we grappled with writing together, with how to re-present our multiple voices, we recognized that we were 'working the hyphen' between researchers and informants (Fine, 1994), creating dialogic and polyvocal spaces (e.g., Bakhtin, 1981; Marcová, 2003) as we navigated the diverse histories, cultures and perspectives of our team. As these spaces and processes became intentionally co-constructed to value multiple voices, they were recognized and named within our group as enacting the Nguzo Saba principle of Kujichagulia or Self-Determination. Our conceptual repertoires continue to expand through the Nguzo Saba principles that frame our community's philosophies and practices.

Across the literature, we have found theoretical threads connecting CBPR and CGT. By making these threads explicit, we have uncovered a foundation for our work that stretches across symbolic interactionism, pragmatism and abduction. We adopt CBPR methods and CGT approaches because they provide the framings and tools to engage in research together (as a team with multiple perspectives), to bring our research directly into practice and activism (iterative cycles), to critically explore relations between structures and processes (adopting a critical lens), and to embrace the generative potential of doubt (using abductive reasoning) to expand our repertoire of theoretical possibilities to inform our research and praxis.

CBPR AND CGT: THE CHALLENGES AND POTENTIAL OF INTEGRATING METHODOLOGIES

To situate our work, we begin with a brief review of the literature on collaborative research (e.g., AR, PAR and CBPR) and constructivist grounded theory (CGT) and, in particular, address recent attention to the potential power of these methodologies for critical inquiry. As Charmaz (2017) concluded, 'Pragmatism offers ways of thinking about critical inquiry, constructivist grounded theory offers ways of doing it' (p. 34). Across the fields of nursing (Schreiber & Tomm-Bonde, 2015), health and health disparities (Teram, Schachter, & Stalker, 2005), youth activism (Ginwright & Cammarota, 2007), social work (Oliver, 2011), and mental health (Hense & McFerran, 2015), we find evidence of collaborative and constructivist methodologies being adopted to intentionally explore intersecting relationships with power and identities with diverse research teams across varied contexts. However, integrating these methodologies has presented some challenges, and researchers have made trade-offs. We explore these trade-offs and then present two examples of collaborative research that have adopted pragmatic principles and abductive reasoning by exploring the potential of local, indigenous and Afrocentric principles to inform methods, analysis, interpretations, and practices.

Community-based participatory research provides an orientation to research that 'emphasizes issues of trust, power, dialogue, community capacity building, and collaborative inquiry toward the goal of social change' (Minkler & Wallerstein, 2011, p. 7). Core characteristics of this approach include its focus on co-learning and the balance between research and action (Israel et al., 2005) as well as creating local knowledge and promoting systems change (Minkler & Wallerstein, 2011). Charmaz (2016, 2017) argues that CGT provides a valuable 'toolkit' for social justice studies through the ways it systematically leads us to define and develop emergent critical questions. When used together, researchers argue that CGT provides the methodological rigor that PAR and CBPR studies often give up in exchange for generating evidence directed at authentic, local, and practice-based processes of transformation (Kemmis & McTaggart, 2000).

Within the fields of health and health disparities, researchers are integrating these approaches in ways that take into account the conflicting and nuanced needs and demands of participants and co-researchers, clinicians and practitioners, and academia. Teram et al.

(2005) described the choices they made as they adopted PAR and grounded theory methods to explore the experiences of female sexual abuse survivors taking part in physical therapy. With a goal of 'amplifying the voices of clients in a way that is acceptable to health professionals' (p. 1130), these researchers made explicit methodological choices. They adopted traditional grounded theory to address perceived requirements for rigor and validity of the physical therapists. However, they did not engage their participants in design or analysis because of concerns over rekindling issues of trauma. Such trade-offs are not uncommon, and they point to the challenges of integrating these approaches.

Other health researchers adopting CBPR have examined how to more effectively engage community members in data analysis and interpretation. In their review of 60 public health studies adopting CBPR approaches, Cashman et al. (2008) found engagement in recruitment, design and implementation, but less frequently in data analysis and interpretation of findings. They argue for increasing levels of engagement, concluding that it increases face and content validity, adds to insights by integrating multiple perspectives and voices, and ensures that interpretations have authentic meanings for communities. However, they also pointed to challenges stemming from the time required to train and engage actively with a team in the iterative processes of data analysis and building consensus around interpretations. They presented only one case that adopted grounded theory methods, recognizing the value of adopting inductive reasoning in systematic multi-stage processes with participants as team members. In this study on improving Latino men's health (Parker, Eng, Laraia, Ammerman, Margolis, & Cross, 1998), the iterative processes of analysis created space for participants' cultural knowledge to inform theme development. A participant described the inductive and abductive processes: 'What we are doing is comparing what we think and know to what others think and know. We [then] walk away knowing more' (Parker et al., 1998, as cited in Cashman et al., 2008, p. 1413).

Across fields of health and nursing, there is much attention to CBPR designs and increased levels of engagement of participants, but less detailed exploration of methods of data analysis. Reaching across methods of participatory research and CGT, Hense and McFerran (2016) proposed a critical grounded theory to overcome differences and tensions between these approaches in research design and analysis. They highlight the current principles of PAR approaches in participation, social change and praxis that situate the locus of control with the collective research group as co-researchers while 'attuning' to issues and outcomes that benefit the community of researchers (p. 404). Their description of praxis expands our Peircian pragmatic principle of provisional knowledge, pointing to the tensions and balance between the practical and the propositional:

> ...propositional knowing carries little value without application to the real world. Yet the critical tradition also indicates that practical knowing without any conscious awareness or critique offers little opportunity for change. Critical theorists such as Freire (2014) refer to praxis as the oscillation between these forms of practical and propositional knowing in which people engage in forms of critical inquiry and informed action. (Hense & McFerran, 2016, p. 405)

They present constructivist grounded theory as a way of engaging with cycles of practical and propositional knowing in participatory research as a 'strategy for engaging in praxis' (p. 409) and propose critical grounded theory as an overarching methodology to ensure rigor in analysis, to provide opportunities to engage participants in democratic collaborations, and to embrace critical inquiry.

In some ways, the iterative cycles of action and reflection in action research (AR) are similar. AR prioritizes a strong commitment to engaging participants as equal partners and to using evidence to foster their well-being. However, it has often been criticized for a preoccupation with local theories for practical problems. Dick, Stringer and Huxham (2009) argue that action research has always been about merging practice and theory, and specifically about theories for social change. They encourage researchers to more explicitly examine how these theories are constructed and their relationships to the research process. If theory is, as proposed, 'a grand word for these everyday activities of knowing, understanding and sense-making' (p. 7), then how is it uncovered and used to inform methods and practice? They propose that we honor the theories of the communities we work with, both to clarify and understand the issues guiding our action research, and to strengthen processes of inquiry.

We argue that CGT, when integrated with CBPR, can provide rigor as well as tools for participant engagement, voice, and meaning-making in participatory and collaborative research. This becomes most evident in critical inquiry and emancipatory research when abductive reasoning reaches into community knowledge and understandings. As we consider ways to value different ways of knowing, different local realities, and reach across the practical and the propositional, we find insights from non-Western paradigms of research. Several studies provide valuable insights into ways Afrocentric, indigenous, and local principles are informing research across different communities. Akom (2011) introduced a Black emancipatory action research (BEAR) framework to challenge researchers to engage in 'rigorous collaborations' to 'move beyond theories of social production/reproduction toward other methodological approaches and levels of analysis' (p. 114). BEAR reaches into Afrocentric principles such as self-determination, healing, love and social justice to achieve a 'more grounded analysis' as part of critical and collaborative ethnography, especially when working with people of African descent across the Diaspora. Collaboration includes meaningful participation in identifying problems, designing studies, conducting analysis, civic engagement, and writing together with goals of authentic action for social change.

We identified one study that captured the potential of integrating CGT and CBPR to reach into local philosophies to inform social justice research. Schreiber and Tomm-Bonde (2015) explored how the African philosophies of Ubuntu (encompassing the interrelated principles of solidarity, spirituality and harmony) provided epistemologies and ontologies to guide their research in nursing, and then demonstrated the congruence between these Afrocentric principles and the theories and practices of constructivist grounded theory. They stated their intention as showing 'how the marriage of this local philosophy with a Western methodology can be a starting point for anti-oppressive research' (p. 657). Beginning their research with an atheoretical stance, and adopting constant comparative and abductive processes, Schreiber and Tomm-Bonde uncovered the principles of Ubuntu as sensitizing concepts. Both Ubuntu and CGT adopt relativist ontologies, honoring the co-creation of knowledge through negotiated meaning-making (p. 659). They share axiologies as well, such as humility and social justice, honoring the expertise of participants, and working together to explore issues such as poverty and privilege. They concluded that 'future researchers can benefit by using local wisdom to frame and underpin their methodologies if they are to engage in a culturally-safe way and produce culturally appropriate findings' (p. 662).

Newman (2012) proposed that the epistemologies of people of African ancestry are expanding to new ways of identifying with their 'African-centerdness' (p. 208). He sees these ways of knowing extending beyond fragmented theories of race or class toward overarching theories of culture. King and Swartz (2015) have also outlined an Afrocentric worldview, or cultural framework, with concepts, values and assumptions that are shared among many in the African Diaspora. They frame this worldview with five elements, including the ontologies of collectivity, interdependence and harmony; epistemologies of relational knowing, empathy and intuition; axiologies of community-mindedness and service to others; and virtues of truth, reciprocity and justice (pp. 2–3). Their fifth element encompasses the principles shaping family and community and are expressed in the Nguzo Saba (or Kwanzaa Principles) and include unity, collective work and responsibility, self-determination, cooperative economics, purpose, creativity and faith (p. 4).

In our work, our inductive and abductive processes, emerging from our integration of CBPR and CGT, have led us to the principles and philosophies of Nguzo Saba as sensitizing concepts to keep us grounded in the values and goals of our community. We first discuss the CGT methods of analysis and interpretation we have adopted, and then demonstrate through our own evidence how our research practices, analysis and interpretation have become embedded in these local ways of knowing and being.

GROUNDED THEORY IN CBPR: ANALYTIC PROCESSES AND METHODS

As a team of community activist-researchers and university faculty and students, we have adopted constructivist grounded theory methods of data collection and analysis to guide our research on urban transformation and inform our practices in community development. We meet weekly, and these collaborative team meetings have emerged as an essential space for our research, for getting the work done, for working across differences with one another, for negotiating understandings, and for debriefing and coming back together. In addition to our observations (recorded as fieldnotes) from our neighborhood corner store, community and family gatherings, youth programs, and home visits, and our interviews from across these spaces, our team meetings are also recorded and transcribed and have become a valuable part of our corpus of data. Just as Conlon, Carney, Timonen, and Scharf (2015) propose that interviews are sites of 'emergent reconstruction' of meaning, we have created an interactional and dialogic space in which knowledge and meaning are co-constructed and emerge through negotiated interpretation and concept building while remaining always grounded in our data. Our meetings are active and participatory endeavors, however, as our research team has noted, 'participatory endeavors do not equate to shared meanings, and the assumptions that participants are on the same page can work against collaborative efforts (Hanny & O'Connor, 2013; Larson, Webster, & Hopper, 2011)' (Larson et al., 2017, p. 8). In this section, we briefly discuss how CGT and CPBR methods align with our participatory, dialogic, and activist goals while also creating tools and spaces for nurturing the generative potentials of tension and doubt.

Charmaz (2016) describes grounded theory as 'a systematic method of inquiry that begins with inductive data, moves back and forth between collecting and analyzing data, relies on comparative methods, builds checks into the research process, and aims to construct theory' (Charmaz, 2016, p. 47).

Our constructivist grounded theory methods include reviewing fieldnotes, reading through transcripts of interviews and past team meetings, and coding our data. We code both individually and as a team, develop consensus categories, review our data to saturate the categories and build themes. We reach into academic research literature, but also into local literature, stories and knowledge as part of our constant comparative methods and processes of abduction, as we challenge, revise, and enrich our analysis (Larson et al., 2017).

The methods of CGT align with both the participatory and dialogic nature of our work and our activist and social justice goals. As Charmaz (2016) points out (citing from Saldaña, 2014), coding, by nature, is a democratic process. It is also active and kinesthetic. As we fracture our fieldnotes and transcripts, we 'break data open to view it anew' (Charmaz, 2016, p. 49). Through these iterative processes of analysis, we build analytic momentum. Through the collaborative processes, as we navigate the multiple perspectives of our team, we link researchers to the stories that are emerging. Thus, the enactment of our analysis is also consistent with our CBPR orientations to research, collaboration and distributed expertise. CGT provides us with the tools to ensure rigor in our research, to keep us grounded in our data even as we are distracted by the daily tasks of community development. Through our integration of these methodologies, we believe our research is adding to the evidence that 'CBPR can be both community driven and scientifically sound' (Minkler & Wallerstein, 2011, p. 6).

The inductive, indeterminate, and abductive processes of CGT also 'systematically bring doubt into the analytic process' (Charmaz, 2016, p. 35). We have learned to recognize the generative potential of this doubt to make room for our multiple positionalities and social locations and our diverse ways of knowing. We argue that the methodological and epistemological pluralism we intentionally adopt has created the tools and the space to reach across our multiple framings and perspectives.

REACHING INTO LOCAL WAYS OF KNOWING AND BEING: KUJICHAGULIA

In this section, we present evidence from our collaborative research of the inductive and abductive processes that have led to the co-construction of current threads of analysis. In our work, this often means reaching into local ways of knowing and being. Many of our themes have been explicitly informed by the collective and diverse stories, histories and knowledge of our team. The community in which we work is predominantly African American, and the community-based organization (CBO) where many of our research team members work has a 51-year history of activism in this neighborhood. These community-researchers emerged from the civil rights movement, the settlement house history of our city, and the ongoing fight against poverty and structural racism that shapes many of the issues facing our youth and neighborhoods. In 2012, the CBO purchased a corner store across the street from their main office. The Liberty Market became one of the only corner stores in this area owned and operated by African American residents (most of the other 25 stores are run by mid-Eastern families who do not live in this community). During the month that the Liberty Market was formed, the team at the CBO reached out to the local university to partner with them in documenting how a corner store can become a corner stone of a community as it shifts from being solely transactional to being transformational. This hub became the nexus of our research for the first two years of our collaboration. And, this collaboration emerged from the determination of the community members to become co-researchers and create a diverse research team to collect, analyze and present their own evidence.

This project is thus rooted in a philosophy that embodies self-determination. From the start, we have evidence of how this principle weaves through our data and drives our practices. Our community-researchers recognized and named this as Kujichagulia, Self-Determination, one of the seven Nguzo Saba principles that form the foundation of their philosophies as African American activists. It means 'to define ourselves, name ourselves, create for ourselves, and speak for ourselves instead of being defined, named, created for and spoken for by others' (Karenga, 1988, p. 52). As we have more actively named and come to understand Kujichagulia and made it more explicit as part of our analysis and writing, we are finding evidence of the power of this process, as well as the tensions that shape it in our city and in our collaborative work across community and university. Although we have evidence of many of the Nguzo Saba principles across our research, we focus here on self-determination to illustrate how this has emerged as a sensitizing concept to drive our analysis, interpretations, and our praxis. We present two examples that demonstrate how our analysis leads us back to this principle to inform our work, and how it enriches the principle by providing evidence of the complex and contested ways it takes shape within our group and within our society. Through these examples, we illustrate our processes of abductive reasoning, the potential strengths of CBPR when co-researchers engage in analysis together, and the value of integrating CGT and CBPR to iteratively and reflexively inform our practices as researchers and members of multiple communities.

DEFINING AND CREATING SELVES: PUSHING BACK

As part of our community development work, we have created an alternative program at the Liberty School, another hub in our community, for 17–21 year-olds who have been labeled in the school as 'over-age, under-credit.' Fifteen young adults have chosen to attend the satellite program at the Liberty School, working on their equivalency diplomas 'and beyond' as we craft alternative pathways to adulthood with and for these young scholars. Our city is graduating less than 50% of our youth (NYSED, 2017), although numbers as low as 21% for black males have been reported ('Black Lives Matter,' 2015). The Schott Foundation addressed the perceptions that allow us to accept these graduation rates, arguing that the 'persistent systemic disparity in opportunity creates a climate and perception of a population that is less valued' ('Black Lives Matter,' 2015). Over the past two years, as part of our research we have been documenting how young men and women in our community have been positioned as 'less valued' and some of the ways we are working with youth to push back and create spaces for novel identities and pathways to emerge. The words of youth, community activists and university co-researchers spoken during team meetings illustrate how these young adults are coming to define themselves, to create for themselves, and speak for themselves.

An incident occurred when several of our students went to the traditional high school one afternoon to pick up some papers for sports, and were asked to leave. Although it was reported that they were 'causing havoc,' they left without any reported incidents. As the day progressed, the situation escalated when one Liberty School youth returned. He was asked to leave; he exchanged words with the school resource officer (SRO). A Liberty teacher was called, but it quickly moved from havoc to handcuffs. In our research meeting the next day, when emotions were still raw and the issues for the youth were still unresolved, the teacher recounted the events:

> So I'm talking to him [the student] on Main Street ... not even 30 seconds later three cop cars swarm. So I'm getting in my car ready to leave ... I hear him – 'Yo, Mr. S,' so I'm like, 'Oh God' and I get out of the car. The cop at the high school took it upon himself to say, 'Like oh yeah, he wants to be a tough guy, we're going to arrest him, we're going to arrest him.'

He was arrested for disorderly conduct. They put him in handcuffs. The teacher continued:

> So I am just confused about why they are so eager to put him in handcuffs. And I said to the cop ... putting him in handcuffs, that transpires down the road. Five, ten years from now that may psychologically be on him, that you know that maybe handcuffs is what I need to be in. [Team meeting, Spring 2017]

The boy was charged and arraigned. This was viewed by community members as pathways being formed: 'They start it there ... once you get the paper it's setting a series of actions in place ... they start it there, it's like how do you do.'

The youth in our program had dis-engaged from the traditional high school. In fact, many of them told us that they had stopped going to school or to classes. However, they were not disengaged from their futures or their families. In fact, being at Liberty School was part of their pathway to engagement. We have much evidence of the youth actively pushing back against the deviant and deficit positioning and dominant discourses that positioned them as criminals, as trespassers, as dis-engaged. At the Liberty School, 'showing up' was valued and recognized as complex for young adults with inconsistent housing, jobs, and for many, children of their own. They challenged the boundaries being constructed and being labeled as trespassers or 'over-age' at the high school. Belonging was broadened to include taking care of family and helping to build their community. They did not accept being 'less valued.' When asked about their goals at the end of the year, they spoke of becoming entrepreneurs, architects, and engineers.

We found evidence of youth co-constructing and re-framing identities as engaged scholars and valued community members. In the dialogic spaces of the alternative program and research team meetings, these young scholars were actively resisting being positioned, being named. They often joined our weekly community–university research team meetings; they read through transcripts with us, coded with us, and wrote memos. They were engaging in processes of self-determination, of Kujichagulia, as they were defining themselves and creating pathways for themselves. Our data also demonstrates the contested nature of this process, the ways that it is situated and constrained by forces and discourses within our society, and the individual determination and community support it takes to push back. As they engaged in team meetings, taking part in our collaborative research and our CGT methods of data collection and analysis, the youth not only led us to and confirmed our interests in self-determination, they extended and enriched this concept.

WRITING TOGETHER: 'NAMING OURSELVES'

The resistance to being named, the attention to self-determination, weaves through our data. As we write together, we also find Kujichagulia at the center of our work across community and university. Over the past year we have been writing a book as a team. Our experiences co-writing have embodied the processes of abduction, as situated in the dialogic and generative spaces we have constructed over six years of working together. We describe our processes to illustrate the complex and potentially contested nature of determining sensitizing concepts and theories to bring to our work and inform our analysis.

One chapter, '*When theory met practice: Methodology in the versus*,' explores the evolution of our community–university partnership and the challenges we have faced with the ways we were re-presenting events, analytic insights, and one another. In the chapter, we present the 'versus' as 'those points of turning together and against that reflect and perpetuate generative frictions in a space of dissensus' (Hanny, Larson, Duckles, Pham, Moses, & Moses, in press). We recounted the frictions we had experienced early in our research between feminism and fatherhood. As we analyzed data from our first two years at the Liberty Market, the university researchers found patterns suggesting that the store felt like a masculine space. We also recognized that many of the university researchers identified as feminists and critical theorists, and thus often viewed interactions as gendered. However, when this perspective was raised in our team meeting, several of our community partners were offended that we assumed that they were allowing for 'chauvinistic' practices in the store. As we worked on the chapter in our writing groups, the energy behind this resistance to being named, being fit into a category of feminist or chauvinist, was clearly articulated by the team. It was the process of being named, of being labeled, that was offensive:

> There is a problem when others try to name us, or tell us who we are. Every person has a right to name and define themselves. The problem is when others try to come in and try to name or define you, off their experience. People's past experiences, positive or negative, they try to impose them on you. And we reject it. The principle of Kujichagulia, we have named self-determination. Historically, when you're coming to a group of men [in our community] it is very intentional. We believe in a living God. We pray every morning. From the experience of Black men – you know Black men did not have names. The men here know that history, we thought that by coming here you would come to understand the history. We study American history to see how we fit into it. So, if you've only understood American history, you're going to miss a whole part of it. So, you have to fit the research into where do I fit in history? So, we are not going to let others name. Words matter. Words enslaved people. [Team meeting, March 2017]

We thought that we had identified a tension around gender and feminism, but we learned that it was more about the powerful meanings embedded in 'naming others.' The process of abduction of CGT can remind us that we must keep our analysis provisional to create the space for alternative and multiple interpretations to emerge. This process leads us to relevant theories, to bodies of literature, to key principles that we need to bring light to our analysis. In collaborative research, abduction can also lead us to histories and principles that are embedded in our data and yet often hidden to outsiders. Spaces of trust can be constructed in which abduction, in teams with multiple perspectives and understandings, naturally occurs. In our work, the histories and philosophies that are indexed through our analysis together are central to our understandings of the transformation of this neighborhood, and to our praxis as co-implementers and co-authors with one another.

BRINGING TOGETHER WAYS OF BEING AND KNOWING: CHALLENGES AND STRATEGIES FOR CO-RESEARCHING, CO-IMPLEMENTING, AND CO-AUTHORING

Critical inquiry and collaborative research focused on sustainable transformation is strengthened when it aligns with local epistemologies, values and goals. We argue that CGT provides a theoretical foundation, with symbolic interactionist and pragmatic principles and processes of inductive and abductive reasoning, that can uncover local ways of being and knowing to inform and guide iterative cycles of research and implementation. However, there are many challenges inherent in collaborative work (co-researching), in working toward change in urban communities (co-implementing), and in writing together (co-authoring). We briefly discuss these challenges here and the strategies our team is adopting to address them.

Co-researching

Becoming co-researchers has required that we remain reflexive about our practices, our positionalities and biases, and the multiple identities and voices we bring to our work. In our team, we are working across races, classes, and histories, as well as navigating different contexts. As researchers, we are aware that, at times, we can be drawn toward a tacit methodological and theoretical individualism. This threat partially emerges from the university paradigms of research and publishing that often privilege certain notions of expertise and singular voices. In addition, we recognize the individualism that underlies many Anglo-American cultures. Instead, we work toward explicitly integrating multiple methodologies, adopting diverse theoretical traditions to guide our work and embracing abductive reasoning to reach into local ways of understanding. Our goal, however, is not to adopt this integration as another singular process, or to find and bring exclusive sensitizing concepts to our analysis. Instead, we heed Lincoln and Guba's (2013) caution against developing an 'epistemological or theoretical 'melting pot' in which researchers come to share lenses or standpoints (which have primarily been Eurocentric) and instead, to adopt approaches that bring attention and understanding to the nuances of difference' (p. 10).

To counter the pull toward individualism, and to keep us situated in the spaces of difference and polyvocality, we adopt several strategies and mindsets. First, we integrate CBPR and CGT to strengthen our critical lens. Adopting practices of critical inquiry, we actively engage in 'untangling and re-doing nested relations of power' (Denzin & Giardina, 2016, p. 7), including race, gender and poverty. As Akom (2011) points out, our critical perspective, our attention to issues of power and structural racism and inequalities, is especially essential in collaborative qualitative work:

> If universities and communities do not continue to rethink the role of race and intersectionality in the research process then the fragile and often hostile relationship between schools,

> universities and communities remain in the balance ... and the ongoing development of CBPR will take place outside of institutional structures rather than working with each other in a collaborative process of mutual engagement. (Akom, 2011, p. 126)

Constructivist grounded theory provides the tools to ensure rigor, to actively engage in processes of analysis together as co-researchers, and to honor community knowledge and histories.

In addition, we intentionally construct and stay within contentious and contested spaces, spaces of doubt and tensions. We stay here because we recognize and value the generative potential of these spaces. As one community member reminded us, in transformative work, 'Stagnation is not an option.' However, studying spaces and movement and transformation presents additional challenges. The radical democratic construct of dissensus (Ziarek, 2001) has directed us to explore spaces where practices are in the process of being mutually constituted both in the community and in our research team. This means creating spaces to speak across difference and respectfully challenge diverse perspectives. This is most evident in the daily interactions of our research team, where we 'resist the temptation to insist upon consensus and allow our mutually respected differences to inform authentic debate to energize our research and practices' (Duckles, Moses, & Van Alstyne, in press). We practice dissensus to challenge stagnation and to work toward building relationships across differences based on trust and our shared passion for social justice.

Co-implementing

Stagnation is also not an option because as community activists, there is always work to get done. Gergen and Gergen (2000), referencing the work of Robin McTaggart (1997), proposed that, in participatory action research, validity should be 'reconceptualized in terms of the efficacy of research in changing relevant social practice' (p. 1034). As co-implementers, from the start our goal has been to uncover what was working in the practices of this community, to bring them to the surface and wrap theory around them to make them more explicit and intentional. Many initiatives and programs, particularly from outsiders (including the university), had come and gone with few positive outcomes. We believe that we are addressing the call of researchers (Denzin & Giardina, 2016) to move beyond adopting practices that 'foreclose possibilities for the new' (p. 6). They are encouraging us to create spaces where 'theory turns back on itself, re-reading itself through the biographical, the historical, and the ideological' (p. 7). Through the CGT and abductive processes that we have embedded in our research practices, we reach into community theories, ideologies, and values to create the foundation for the unique space that we have created. In this space, as we embrace dissensus, disagreement and doubt, we are doing the work of theory building that researchers call for and that community activists require to drive change in intentional and local ways.

Co-authoring

As we bring this chapter to a close, we raise the issues and challenges of writing together. Our sensitizing concept of self-determination provides insights into our current writing struggles and practices. When recently working on a written draft, we believed that we were moving toward shared narratives. However, we were reminded of the tacit individualism that could creep into our texts and lead us to name others, rather than providing space for us all to name ourselves. As Michelle Fine (1994) reminds us, we need to enter 'negotiated relations of whose story is being told, why, to whom, with what interpretation, and whose story is being shadowed, why, for whom, and with what consequence' (p. 72). In our practice, the university researchers often write an outline or a first draft. We then speak around it, edit together, make room for telling stories and for bringing in histories, and engage in iterative cycles of rewriting. As we engaged in this process with this chapter, a community researcher reminded us that, 'He who has the pen owns the history.' Within our dialogic spaces of dissensus and doubt, we are finding ways to keep passing around the pen.

Through our processes of researching, implementing and writing together, we are uncovering strategies and creating spaces to address calls for creating novel research orientations and methods that move beyond Eurocentric practices; bridge multiple identities, voices and epistemologies while embracing the nuances of difference; and place explicit, local values of activism and change at the center of our critical and rigorous work. For community and university researchers and activists undertaking collaborative inquiry, we conclude with our insights about spaces, doubt and praxis. In our weekly research team meetings, we have worked to create interactive and dialogic spaces in which knowledge and meaning are co-constructed and emerge through negotiated interpretations and analysis. Building on the participatory and pluralistic processes at the foundation of CBPR, we intentionally embrace contradictory views as we speak across difference and respectfully challenge diverse perspectives. We adopt the radical democratic construct of dissensus (Ziarek, 2001) as we explore and create spaces where practices are in the process of being mutually constituted both in our research team and in the community. This means that our grounded theories can always look different, and that tensions and doubt become an integral part of engaging in democratic collaborations.

CGT provides us with the theoretical foundation and strategies for pursuing doubt rather than dismissing it. Embracing the provisional nature of analysis, we find that tensions encourage our abductive and reflective processes and support our critical inquiry goals. As Lincoln and Guba (2013) point out, with increased attention to abductive reasoning in grounded theory (Charmaz, 2017), there is an increased recognition of 'constructivist inquiry as a means to open up the hidden social life and thereby begin to extend the possibilities for an extended social justice' (p. 10). As such, we align with others (Charmaz, 2017; Gibson, 2007; Locke et al., 2008) who situate abductive reasoning, doubt and tensions at the root of collaborative and critical inquiry. We argue that tensions are generative, leading us to more robust, rigorous and inclusive research and to discursive spaces to reach into local theories and knowledge.

As Hense and McFerran (2016) argue, 'propositional knowing carries little value without application to the real world' (p. 405). We agree, and our processes of abduction and reflection in our iterative cycles of data collection and analysis have led us to the rich local ways of knowing and being of our diverse research team. They also remind us that practical knowing must be coupled with critique. It is this praxis, the 'oscillation between the practical and propositional' (p. 405) that shapes our critical inquiry and activism.

In this chapter, we have pointed to the local theory of Kujichagulia that has been named and recognized as weaving through our practices, informing our collaborative research.

As a sensitizing concept, this conceptualization of self-determination has informed our analysis but also helped us see the complex and contested ways defining, naming and creating for ourselves is being negotiated within our research team, our neighborhoods, and our society. It humbles and strengthens us as we reflect on the power of our words, where we fit in history and where our research fits in history, and inspires us as we work toward co-constructing spaces and transformational practices for sustainable change. And, it keeps us mindful of ways that others continue to try to define, name, create and speak for us, informing and guiding our critical inquiry and praxis as co-researchers, co-implementers, and co-authors with one another.

REFERENCES

Akom, A. A. (2011). Black emancipatory action research: Integrating a theory of structural racialization into ethnographic and participatory action research methods. *Ethnography and Education*, *6*(1), 113–131. http://dx.doi.org/10.1080/17457823.2011.553083

Aldiabat, K. M., & Le Navenec, C.-L. (2011). Philosophical roots of classical grounded theory: Its foundations in symbolic interactionism. *The Qualitative Report*, *16*(4), 1063–1080.

Bajc, V. (2012). Abductive ethnography of practice in highly uncertain conditions. *The Annals of the American Academy of Political and Social Science*, *642*(1), 72–85. http://dx.doi.org/10.1177/0002716212438197

Bakhtin, M. (1981). *The dialogic imagination: Four essays by M.M. Bakhtin*. Ed. M. Holquist and Trans. C. Emerson & M. Holquist). Austin, TX: University of Texas Press.

Black Lives Matter (2015). *The Schott 50 State report on public education and black males*. Retrieved from: http://blackboysmatter.org

Bruce, B. C., & Bloch, N. (2013). Pragmatism and community inquiry: A case study of community-based learning. *Education and Culture*, *29*(1), 27–45. http://dx.doi.org/10.1353/eac.2013.0004

Cashman, S. B., Adeky, S., Allen, A. J., Corburn, J., Israel, B. A., Montaño, J., … Rafelito, A. (2008). The power and the promise: Working with communities to analyze data, interpret findings, and get to outcomes. *American Journal of Public Health*, *98*(5), 1407–1417. http://dx.doi.org/10.2105/AJPH.2007.113571

Charmaz, K. (2014). *Constructing grounded theory* (2nd ed.). Thousand Oaks, CA: Sage.

Charmaz, K. (2016). The power of stories and the potential of theorizing for social justice. In N. K. Denzin & M. D. Giardinia (Eds.), *Qualitative inquiry through a critical lens* (pp. 41–56). New York: Routledge.

Charmaz, K. (2017). The power of constructivist grounded theory for critical inquiry. *Qualitative Inquiry*, *23*(1), 34–45. http://dx.doi.org/10.1177/1077800416657105

Colombat, A. P. (1991). A thousand trails to work with Deleuze. *SubStance*, *20*(3), 10–23.

Conlon, C., Carney, G., Timonen, V., & Scharf, T. (2015). 'Emergent reconstruction' in grounded theory: Learning from team-based interview research. *Qualitative Research*, *15*(1), 39–56.

Deleuze, G., & Guattari, F. (1987). *A thousand plateaus: Capitalism and schizophrenia*. Minneapolis, MN: University of Minnesota Press.

Denzin, N. K., & Giardina, M. D. (2016). Introduction: Qualitative inquiry through a critical lens. In N. K. Denzin & M. D. Giardinia (Eds.), *Qualitative inquiry through a critical lens* (pp. 1–16). New York: Routledge.

Dick, B., Stringer, E., & Huxham, C. (2009). Theory in action. *Action Research*, *7*(1), 5–12.

Duckles, J., Moses, G., & Van Alstyne, R. (2018). Doing Double Dutch: Rhythms of transformation within and across community. In J. Larson & G. Moses (Eds.), *Community literacies as shared resources for transformation*. New York: Routledge.

Fine, M. (1994). Working the hyphens: Reinventing self and other in qualitative research. In N. K. Denzin & Y. S. Lincoln (Eds.), *Handbook of qualitative research* (pp. 70–82). Thousand Oaks, CA: Sage.

Finger Lakes Health Systems Agency. (2014). 'What's goin' on?' Report on local health disparities commissioned by the African American Health Coalition. Figure 1. Years of potential life lost by Monroe County zip code: Five-year average (2006–2010; p. 3). Rochester, NY: Author.

Freire, P. (2014). *Pedagogy of the oppressed, 30th Anniversary edition*. London: Bloomsbury.

Gergen, M. M., & Gergen, K. J. (2000). Qualitative inquiry: Tensions and transformations. In N. K. Denzin & Y. S. Lincoln (Eds.), *Handbook of qualitative research*, (2nd ed., pp. 1025–1046. Thousand Oaks, California: Sage.

Gibson, B. (2007). Accommodating critical theory. In A. Bryant & K. Charmaz (Eds.), *The Sage handbook of grounded theory* (pp. 436–453). Thousand Oaks, CA: Sage. http://dx.doi.org/10.4135/9781848607941

Ginwright, S., & Cammarota, J. (2007). Youth activism in the urban community: Learning critical civic praxis within community organizations. *International Journal of Qualitative Studies in Education*, *20*(6), 693–710. http://dx.doi.org/10.1080/09518390701630833

Glaser, B. G., & Strauss, A. L. (1967). The discovery of grounded theory: Strategies for qualitative research. Chicago, IL: Aldine.

Hanny, C., & O'Connor, K. (2013). A dialogical approach to conceptualizing resident participation in community organizing. *Mind, Culture, and Activity*, *20*(4), 338–357.

Hanny, C., Larson, J., Duckles, J., Pham, H., Moses, R., & Moses, G. (2018). When theory met practice: Methodology in the versus. In J. Larson & G. Moses (Eds.), *Community literacies as shared resources for transformation*. New York: Routledge.

Hense, C., & McFerran, K. S. (2016). Toward a critical grounded theory. *Qualitative Research Journal*, *16*(4), 402–416. Doi: 10.1108/QRJ-08-2015-0073

Israel, B. A., Eng, E., Schultz, A. J., & Parker, E. A. (2005). *Methods in community-based participatory research for health*. San Francisco, CA: Jossey-Bass.

Karenga, M. (1988). The African American holiday of Kwanzaa: A celebration of family, community and culture. Los Angeles, CA: University of Sankore Press.

Kemmis, S., & McTaggart, R. (2000). Participatory action research. In N. K. Denzin & Y. S. Lincoln (Eds.), *Handbook of qualitative research* (2nd ed., pp. 567–605). Thousand Oaks, CA: Sage.

King, J. E., & Swartz, E. E. (2015). The Afrocentric praxis of teaching for freedom: Connecting culture to learning. New York: Routledge.

Larson, J., Webster, S., & Hopper, M. (2011). Community coauthoring: whose voice remains?. *Anthropology & Education Quarterly*, *42*(2), 134–153.

Larson, J., Hanny, C., Duckles, J., Pham, H., Moses, R., & Moses, G. (2017). Expressing community through freedom market and visual connections. *Pedagogies: An International Journal*, *12*(1), 4–20. doi:10.1080/1554480X.2017.128300

Lincoln, Y. S., & Guba, E. G. (2013). *The constructivist credo*. Walnut Creek, CA: Left Coast Press.

Locke, K., Golden-Biddle, K., & Feldman, M. S. (2008). Making doubt generative: Rethinking the role of doubt in the research process. *Organization Science*, *19*(6), Nov.–Dec., 907–918. doi.org/10.1287/orsc.1080.0398

Malins, P. (2004). Machinic assemblages: Deleuze, Guattari and an ethico-aesthetics of drug use. *Janus Head*, *7*(1), 84–104.

Marková, I. (2003). *Dialogicality and self-representations: The dynamics of mind*. Cambridge, UK: Cambridge University Press.

McTaggart, R. (1997). *Participatory action research: International contexts and consequences*. Albany, New York: State University of New York Press.

Minkler, M., & Wallerstein, N. (2011). Introduction to community-based participatory research: New issues and emphases. In M. Minkler & N. Wallerstein (Eds.), *Community-based participatory research for health: From processes to outcomes* (pp. 5–23). Hoboken, NJ: John Wiley.

Newman, L. M. (2012, January). Using the Nguzo Saba to determine the worldview of people of African Ancestry. In *NAAAS Conference Proceedings* (pp. 201–217). National Association of African American Studies. Solving social issues through multicultural experiences, San Diego, CA, September–October 2011.

NYSED (2017). *New York high school graduation rates*. Retrieved from New York Databases at: http://rochester.nydatabases.com/database/new-york-high-school-graduation-rates

Oliver, C. (2011). Critical realist grounded theory: A new approach for social work research. *British Journal of Social Work*, *42*(2), 1–17.

Paavola, S. (2014). From steps and phases to dynamically evolving abduction. Paper presented at the Charles S. Peirce International Centennial Congress 2014. Invigorating Philosophy for the 21st Century, Lowell, USA, 16–19 July.

Parker, E. A., Eng, E., Laraia, B., Ammerman, A., Margolis, L., & Cross, A. (1998). Coalition building for prevention: Lessons learned from the North Carolina Community-Based Public Health Initiative. *Journal of Public Health Management Practice*, *4*, 25–36.

Saldaña, J. (2014). Blue-collar qualitative research: A rant. *Qualitative Inquiry*, *20*(8), 976-980.

Schreiber, R., & Tomm-Bonde, L. (2015). Ubuntu and constructivist grounded theory: An African methodology package. *Journal of Research in Nursing*, *20*(8), 655–664. http://dx.doi.org/10.1177/1744987115619207

Teram, E., Schachter, C. L., & Stalker, C. A. (2005). The case for integrating grounded theory and participatory action research: Empowering clients to inform professional practice. *Qualitative Health Research*, *15*(8), 1129–1140. http://dx.doi.org/10.1177/1049732305275882

Timmermans, S., & Tavory, I. (2012). Theory construction in qualitative research: From grounded theory to abductive analysis. *Sociological Theory*, *30*(3), 167–186. http://dx.doi.org/10.1177/0735275112457914

Ziarek, E. P. (2001). An ethics of dissensus: Postmodernity, feminism, and the politics of radical democracy. Stanford, CA: Stanford University Press.

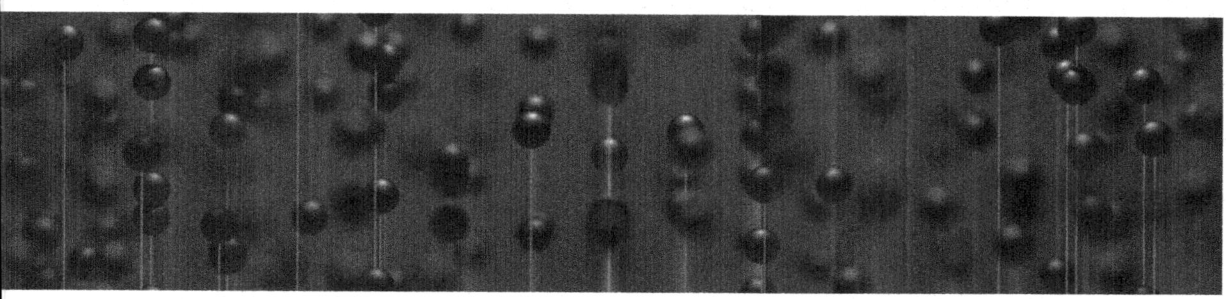

Discursive Glossary of Terms

The terminology used with regard to GTM can be confusing, and any effort to produce a single authoritative and definitive set of definitions is certain to be contentious and self-defeating. Different authors refer to different exemplars, and sometimes even the same author will use or imply different definitions of a single term central to GTM. Kathy Charmaz's book Constructing Grounded Theory (2006, 2014) offers a clear and concise set of definitions, and many of these have been incorporated below as part of this Discursive Glossary.

The purpose of this glossary is to illustrate how some of the contributors, both to this edition and the one from 2007, have characterized key GTM terms and ideas. As such it is meant to serve as an indicator and guide, prompting readers to refer to the specific chapters and to other sources. The text in italics is taken from either the 2007 edition or this companion volume of the Handbook (as are some of the headings).[1] All non-italicized text is taken verbatim from Charmaz's book, unless stated otherwise.[2]

Abduction: A type of reasoning that begins with the researcher examining inductive data and observing a surprising or puzzling finding that cannot be explained with conventional theoretical accounts. After scrutiny of these data, the researcher entertains all possible explanations for the observed data, and then forms hypotheses and tests to confirm or disconfirm each explanation until he or she arrives at the most plausible theoretical interpretation of the observed data. Hence, abduction begins but does not end with induction. Rather, the search for a theoretical explanation involves an imaginative leap to achieve a plausible theoretical explanation. At this point, the research may create a new theory or put extant theories together in a novel way. Thus, abduction brings creativity into inquiry and takes the iterative process of grounded theory further into theory construction.

> *...it is a logical inference (and thereby reasonable and scientific), however it extends into the realm of profound insight (and therefore generates new knowledge). The secret charm of*

abduction lies straight in this kind of being a (logical) inference and extending to insight at the same time: abduction is sensible and scientific as a form of inference, however it reaches to the sphere of deep insight and new knowledge – Reichertz (2007)

Something unintelligible is discovered in the data, and on the basis of the mental design of a new rule the rule is discovered or invented and, at the same time, it also becomes clear what the case is. The logical form of this operation is that of abduction. Here one has decided (with whatever degree of awareness and for whatever reasons) no longer to adhere to the conventional view of things – Reichertz (2007)

Grounded theorists construct fresh concepts from inductive data and check and develop them through abduction… – Charmaz (2014: 342)

Abductive inferencing: *Does not double the amount of data but construes a concept, an idea, a theory which makes the action the data represent comprehensible and explains it. Research that takes an abductive approach makes action comprehensible by indicating the regularities this action is based on, making its motives apparent, to an extent far beyond what the acting individuals themselves are aware of – Reichertz (2019)*

Analytic induction: *Analytic induction was concerned with generating and proving an integrated, limited, precise, universally applicable theory of causes accounting for a specific behavior (e.g., drug addiction, embezzlement). … it tests a limited number of hypotheses with all available data, consisting of members of clearly defined and carefully selected cases of the phenomena – Hammersley, quoted by Kelle (2019)*

Axial coding: A type of coding that treats a category as an axis around which the analyst delineates relationships and specifies the dimensions of this category. A major purpose of axial coding is to bring the data back together again into a coherent whole after the researcher has fractured them through line-by-line coding. Axial coding is a procedure applied to data, rather than emerging from them.

Axial coding, the next step, is used to pull one's data back together by relating categories to subcategories, using a coding paradigm – Belgrave and Seide (2019)

While she does not use Strauss and Corbin's axial coding herself, Charmaz (2006, 2014) argues that the availability of this framework will be valuable to some, helping them to extend their analytic reach, but at the risk of being limited or restricted if it is applied mechanically – Belgrave and Seide (2019)

The coding paradigm comes into play during 'axial coding', an advanced stage of open coding. Whereas open coding starts by 'scrutinizing the fieldnote, interview, or other document very closely; line by line, or even word by word. The aim is to produce concepts that seem to fit the data' (Strauss 1987: 28), axial coding 'consists of intense analysis done around one category at time in terms of the paradigm items' (Strauss 1987: 32). This category forms the 'axis' around which further coding and category building is done and may eventually become the core category of the emerging theory – Kelle (2007 and 2019)

Charmaz (2006) points to axial coding as a further type of coding introduced by Strauss in 1987 (that of relating categories to subcategories); this is a most helpful way of describing axial coding – Urquhart (2007)

the purpose of this element of axial coding is to 'hypothesise about conditions, consequences, interactions, strategies and consequences' – Urquhart (2019)

open codes were grouped into categories as per the axial coding stage (following Strauss and Corbin) – Urquhart (2019)

'When researchers are coding for context, they are doing what Strauss (1987) called "axial coding". They are locating and linking action-interaction within the framework of

sub-concepts that give it meaning and enable it to explain what interactions are occurring, and why and what consequences real or anticipated are happening because of action-interaction.' (Chapter 8, position 4126). – Corbin and Strauss, 2015, quoted by Friese (2019)

This phase requires more conceptual analysis because it will give a 'big picture' or 'paradigm' through the integration of 'structure and process'. This is in terms of looking at the relationship among the categories to their sub-categories which provide 'more precise and complete explanations about the phenomena' (Strauss & Corbin 1998)

CAQDAS: Computer Aided/Assisted Qualitative Data Analysis Software

Categorizing: *The analytic step in grounded theory of selecting certain codes as having overriding significance or abstracting common themes and patterns in several codes into an analytic concept. As the researcher categorizes, he or she raises the conceptual level of the analysis from description to a more abstract, theoretical level. The researcher then tries to define the properties of the category, the conditions under which it is operative, the conditions under which it changes, and its relation to other categories. Grounded theorists make their most significant theoretical categories into the concepts of their theory.*

Categorizing – selecting codes; raising codes to higher levels of abstraction – Bryant, 2017

***NB** Charmaz offers a definition of 'categorizing' that seems to encompass 'conceptualizing' in all but name. See Conceptualizing/Conceptualization*

Category: *Glaser (1978) presents the meaning of categories in terms of the indicators through which they are observed. Thus the category social loss is not to be defined abstractly but in terms of particular ways in which nurses respond to patients. However, indicators are used not to substantiate a category empirically through description but rather to elaborate the category through exploring its different dimensions (Glaser 1978: 43) – Dey (2007)*

Nevertheless, categories play a dual role in grounded theory which transcends the classical definition of concepts in terms of indicators. They can be both 'analytic' and 'sensitizing'. They allow us to conceptualize the key analytic features of phenomena, but also to communicate a meaningful picture of those phenomena in everyday terms. They allow us to classify phenomena, but also to construct relationships among the different elements of a theory – Dey (2007)

'A category is, simply, a range of discriminably different events that are treated "as if" equivalent' (Bruner et al. 1986: 231) – Dey (2007)

The most basic challenge in grounded category building is to reconcile the need of letting categories emerge from the material of research (instead of forcing preconceived theoretical terms on the data) with the impossibility of abandoning previous theoretical knowledge – Kelle (2007)

From the early days of grounded theory, many users of the method found it difficult to understand the notions 'category' and 'property' and to utilize them in research practice, since these terms were only vaguely defined in The Discovery of Grounded Theory – Kelle (2007)

... the crucial difference between Glaserian and Straussian category building lies in the fact that Strauss suggests the utilization of a specified theoretical framework based on a certain understanding of human action, whereas Glaser emphasizes that coding is a process of combining 'the analyst's scholarly knowledge and his research knowledge of the substantive field' (Glaser 1978: 70) and has to be realized in the ongoing coding process, which often

means that it has to be conducted on the basis of a broad theoretical background knowledge which cannot be made fully explicit in the beginning of analysis – Kelle (2007)

Glaser and Strauss described categories as 'conceptual elements of a theory' (1967: 36). Categories emerge initially from a close engagement with data, but can achieve a higher level of abstraction through a process of 'constant comparison' which allows their theoretical elaboration and integration – Dey (2007)

In Glaser and Strauss's understanding of what a theory is and what it consists of the concept of 'category' played a crucial role: categories are not only the building blocks and basic elements of theories, they are also important tools used throughout the whole research process to develop full-fledged theories. Theoretical statements (or in other words, 'hypotheses') are basically formed by connecting categories. Thus, the first and most important question for non-deductive, data-based construction of theories would be: how can researchers ensure the 'grounding' of categories in empirical data? In the Discovery-book, two basic rules are given:

- *Categories must not be forced on data, they should 'emerge' instead in an ongoing process of data collection and analysis.*
- *While developing categories the sociologist should employ 'theoretical sensitivity', which means the ability to 'see relevant data' and to reflect upon empirical data material with the help of theoretical terms – Kelle (2019)*

Chicago school sociology: A tradition in sociology that arose at the University of Chicago during the early decades of the twentieth century. Pragmatist philosophy, life history analysis, and field research formed the respective intellectual foundations and methodological principles of this tradition. Chicago school sociologists were not as homogeneous as textbooks portray them and not all members of the Sociology Department at the University of Chicago at that time had any affinity towards the Chicago school. However, the designation of a 'school' stuck. Its adherents spawned a rich tradition of symbolic interactionist social psychology and of ethnographic and qualitative research. Chicago school sociology assumes dynamic, reciprocal relationships between interpretation and action. Social life is interactive, emergent, and somewhat indeterminate. Chicago school ethnography fosters openness to the world and curiosity about it, and symbolic interactionism fosters developing an empathetic understanding of research participants and their worlds.

Code: *What is a code? A code sets up a relationship with your data, and with your respondents – Star (2007)*

Codes in grounded theory are such transitional objects. They allow us to know more about the field we study, yet carry the abstraction of the new – Star (2007)

Codes capture patterns and themes and cluster them under an evocative title – Lempert (2007)

Essential relationship between data and theory is a conceptual code – Holton (2007)

***NB** In the context of CAQDAS, some 'codes', however, may never be methodological; they simply serve organizational purposes to support data retrieval – Friese (2019)*

Coding: The process of taking data apart, defining and labelling what these data are about. Unlike quantitative researchers, who apply preconceived categories or codes to data, a grounded theorist creates qualitative codes by defining what he or she sees in the data. Thus, grounded theory codes are emergent. Researchers develop codes as they study and interact with their data. The coding process may take the researcher to unforeseen areas and research questions. Grounded theory proponents follow such leads; they do not pursue previously designed research problems that lead to dead-ends.

> *The most basic operations which provide the basis for category building are 'coding' and the constant comparison of data, codes, and the emerging categories – Kelle (2007)*
>
> *In the first edition of this Handbook, Bryant and Charmaz offer perhaps the most straightforward definition of coding: 'the process of defining what the data is about' (2007: 605). They also take on emergence, incorporating their constructivist approach, by explaining that 'codes are emergent', developing as researchers study their data; codes are not in the data but are developed through researchers' work. Anselm Strauss and Juliet Corbin point to the centrality of coding when they define it as 'the process of analyzing data' (1990: 61); a clearer definition is offered in Corbin and Strauss (2015: 57) — 'denoting concepts to stand for meaning'. Note that Strauss and Corbin (1990) provide additional definitions of coding for each element of their approach. Similarly, Charmaz tells us that 'coding means that we attach labels to segments of data that depict what each segment is about' (2006: 3) and that 'through coding, we raise analytic questions about our data from the very beginning of data collection' (2014: 5). Note that these latter definitions make clear that codes, even modest or in-vivo codes, are conceptual, not simple labels – Belgrave and Seide (2019)*

Coding families: *Given Glaser's talk of 'coding families' and the 'coding paradigm' of Strauss and Corbin it is not surprising that coding has become a central analytic procedure in grounded theory – Dey (2007)*

> *In 1978 (more than one decade after the publication of The Discovery of Grounded Theory), Barney Glaser tried to clarify the concept of theoretical sensitivity in his own monograph of that title. In doing so, he coined the terms 'theoretical codes', 'theoretical coding', and 'coding families' to describe a process whereby analysts have a great variety of theoretical concepts at their disposal to structure the developing categories and the emerging theory – Kelle (2007)*
>
> *The diverse coding families can obviously serve as a fund of concepts which may guide researchers in developing their ability to think about empirical observations in theoretical terms. However, their utility for the development of theoretical relations between the 'substantive codes' is limited – Kelle (2007)*
>
> *It was thus usually Glaser who defined concepts such as properties, dimensions, basic social processes, or cutting points, illustrating them using data supplied by students in his seminar – Covan (2007)*
>
> *Identify a basic social process that accounts for most of the observed behavior that is relevant and problematic for those involved – Wiener (2007)*
>
> *Glaser introduces 18 coding families, an analytic tool that can be used to stimulate, broaden and strengthen the theoretical sensitivity the researcher brings to theoretical coding. ... Glaser discusses potential pitfalls of depending on some of these 'families', rather than grounding them and notes that his coding families are not exhaustive, that other authors will introduce additional families. ... Charmaz (2006, 2014) argues that some of Glaser's coding families reflect positivist concepts, that important families are missing (e.g., agency, power, and narrative) while others, such as inequality, are either buried or presented in a conceptually biased way – Belgrave and Seide (2019)*

Coding paradigm: The coding paradigm fulfils the same function as a Glaserian coding family; it represents a group of abstract theoretical terms which are used to develop categories from the data and to find relations between them. Similar to Glaser´s coding families, the coding paradigm takes into account that the development of categories requires either a previously defined theoretical framework or at least the possibility to draw on a selection of such frameworks if one wants to avoid being flooded by the data – Kelle (2007 and 2019)

Concept: *Glaser and Strauss started The Discovery of Grounded Theory by criticizing the 'overemphasis in current sociology on the verification of theory, and a resultant de-emphasis on the prior step of discovering what concepts and hypotheses are relevant for the area that one wishes to research' (Glaser & Strauss 1967: 1f) – Kelle (2007)*

> *Often these researchers translate the instruction to let categories emerge from the data into a demand to transform every idea or concept which comes into their minds when reading the textual data into a category – Kelle (2007)*
>
> *In the inductive variant by Glaser & Strauss, knowledge concepts or theories were officially and explicitly founded on induction – Reichertz (2007)*
>
> *What are the boundaries and attributes of the concept? And then we sample further by seeking participants with those characteristics or experiences in situations in which humility is required. Similarly, we may also investigate what it is, or what is meant by 'losing a piece of yourself'. In this way, the project moves forward by sampling using the concepts in the interviews to guide the sampling frame – Morse (2007)*
>
> *The skill of the grounded theorist is to abstract concepts by leaving the detail of the data behind, lifting the concepts above the data and integrating them into a theory that explains the latent social pattern underlying the behaviour in a substantive area (Locke, 2001) – Holton (2007)*
>
> *We are now moving toward a more 'focused coding' procedure that consists of building and clarifying concepts. Focused coding employed in grounded theory starts to examine all the data in a category, by comparing each segment of data with every other segment working up to a clear definition of each concept. Such concepts are then named and become 'codes' – Hesse-Biber (2007)*
>
> *researchers commonly use grounded theory method to generate concepts, as opposed to generating theory – Urquhart (2007)*
>
> *It is through the production of concepts that the subjects of a grounded theory study are transformed into theoretical objects – Gibson (2007)*

Concept-indicator model: A method of theory construction in which the researcher constructs concepts that account for relationships defined in the empirical data and each concept rests on empirical indicators. Thus, the concept is 'grounded' in data.

Conceptualizing/Conceptualization*: The term conceptualizing is not defined in many GTM texts, including The Handbook of Grounded Theory (Bryant & Charmaz 2007). Yet Strauss and Corbin clearly noticed its relevance and argued that it was the 'first step in theory building' (1998: 103), a form of abstracting. This implies that it comes into force in the middle and later stages of GTM-oriented research, after some form of preliminary or open coding of initial data has been performed (Bryant 2017).* ***NB*** *See entry for categorizing.*

Conditional/consequential matrix: A coding device created by Strauss and Corbin (1990, 1998) to show the intersections of micro and macro conditions/consequences on actions and to clarify the connections between them. The matrix is *applied* to the data rather than emerging from them.

> *Conditional matrix denotes a context of social frames, within which social interactions evolve. The main purpose of the conditional matrix is 'to help researchers to think beyond*

> *micro social structures and immediate interactions to larger social conditions and consequences' (Charmaz 2006: 118) – Hildenbrand (2007)*

Constant comparative method: A method of analysis that generates successively more abstract concepts and theories through inductive processes of comparing data with data, data with code, code with category, category with category, and category with concept. In the last stage of analysis, researchers compare each stage of analytic development. Grounded theorists use this method to reveal the properties and range of the emergent categories and to raise the level of abstraction of their developing analyses.

> *The constant comparison technique is used to tease out similarities and differences and thereby refine concepts – Wiener (2007)*
>
> *Glaser and Strauss agree that comparisons can be used to establish facts and to verify theories (1967: 23–27). Indeed, they explained that all general methods of data analysis including grounded theory, experimental designs and statistical analysis rely on the logic of comparison (Glaser and Strauss 1967: 21) – Covan (2007)*
>
> *One virtue of 'constant comparison' as a method in grounded theory is that it protects against the tendency to overinterpret data and find connections where there are none. The inclination to focus on positive evidence as confirmatory can be challenged through the systematic use of constant comparison – Dey (2007)*
>
> *The most basic operations which provide the basis for category building are 'coding' and the constant comparison of data, codes and the emerging categories – Kelle (2007)*
>
> *Three types of comparison: incident to incident to generate concepts; concept to further incidents; concept to concept – Holton paraphrase (2007)*
>
> *If memos are the skeleton of the grounded theory method, use of the constant comparison is the full body – Wiener (2007)*

Constructivism: A social scientific perspective that addresses how realities are made. This perspective assumes that people, including researchers, construct the realities in which they participate. Constructivist inquiry starts with the experience and asks how members construct it. To the best of their ability, constructivists enter the phenomenon, gain multiple views of it, and locate it in its web of connections and constraints. Constructivists acknowledge that their interpretation of the studied phenomenon is itself a construction.

Constructivist GT: A contemporary version of grounded theory that adopts methodological strategies such as coding, memo-writing, and theoretical sampling of the original statement of the method but shifts its epistemological foundations and takes into account methodological developments in qualitative inquiry occurring over the past 50 years. Thus, constructivist grounded theorists attend to the production, quality, and use of data, research relationships, the research situation, and the subjectivity and social actions of the researcher. Constructivist grounded theorists aim for abstract understanding of studied life and view their analyses as located in time, place, and the situation of inquiry.

Data: *For me, the beauty of the method lies in its everything-is-data characteristic; that is to say, everything I see, hear, smell, and feel about the target, as well as what I already know from my studies and my life experience, are data. I act as interpreter of the scene I observe, and as such I make it come to life for the reader. I grow it – Stern (2007)*

> *flexible guidelines for data collection and data analysis, commitments to remain close to the world being studied, the development of integrated theoretical concepts grounded in data that show process, relationship, and social world connectedness – Denzin (2007)*
>
> *Problem of staying too close to the data: codes simply summarize the data, and we then produce far too many codes – Locke (2007)*
>
> *The assumption that data exist is common to Durkheim and Glaser & Strauss – Covan (2007)*

Deduction: A type of reasoning that starts with the general or abstract concept and reasons to specific instances.

Deductive Qualitative Analysis (DQA): *DQA is an updating of analytic induction … an approach older than GT. Unlike GTM, DQA and its predecessor – analytic induction – 'allows for qualitative hypothesis testing and theory testing as well as concept-guided descriptive research – Gilgun (2019)*

Dimensional Analysis: *Leonard Schatzman's method, presented to students at UCSF prior to the course on GTM – a partial form of GTM – Bryant (2019)*

Emergence: *Emergence is a notorious philosophical term of art. A variety of theorists have appropriated it for their purposes ever since George Henry Lewes gave it a philosophical sense in his 1875* Problems of Life and Mind. *We might roughly characterize the shared meaning thus: emergent entities (properties or substances) 'arise' out of more fundamental entities and yet are 'novel' or 'irreducible' with respect to them – Stanford Encyclopedia of Philosophy – quoted by Bryant (2019)*

> *The emergence of theoretical codes or categories from the data is dependent on the ability to grasp empirical phenomena in theoretical terms, or, in other words, on 'theoretical sensitivity', a competence that demands training and background in sociological theory (which also Glaser still conceded, see Glaser 1992: 28) – Kelle (2007)*

Formal grounded theory: A theoretical rendering of a generic issue or process that cuts across several substantive areas of study. The concepts in a formal theory are abstract and general, and the theory specifies the links between these concepts. Theories that deal with identity formation or loss, the construction of culture, or the development of ideologies can help us understand behaviour in diverse areas such as juvenile gangs, the socialization of professionals, and the experience of immigration.

> *FGT's abstraction allows its application over a wide range of empirical areas virtually forever, as opposed to descriptive generalizations which are rooted in one empirical area and soon stale dated – Glaser (2007)*
>
> *Formal theories exacerbate the tension between our need to create rules of thumb to get things done and our postmodern awareness that the complexity of life can never be fairly captured in any theory – Kearney (2007)*

Grounded theory: A rigorous method of conducting research in which researchers construct conceptual frameworks or theories through building inductive theoretical analyses from data and subsequently checking their theoretical interpretations. Thus, researchers' analytic categories are directly 'grounded' in the data. The method favours the following: (1) analysis over description, (2) fresh categories over preconceived ideas and extant theories, and (3) systematically focused sequential data collection over large initial samples. This method involves the researcher in data analysis while collecting data. Data analysis and collection inform and shape each other in an iterative process. Thus, sharp distinctions between data collection and analysis phases of traditional research are intentionally blurred in grounded theory studies.

Induction: A type of reasoning that begins with study of a range of individual cases and extrapolates patterns from them to form a conceptual category.

Memo-writing: The pivotal intermediate step in grounded theory between data collection and writing drafts of papers. When grounded theorists write memos, they stop and analyse their ideas about their codes and emerging categories in whatever way that occurs to them (see also Glaser 1998). Memo-writing is a crucial method in grounded theory because it prompts researchers to analyse their data and to develop their codes into categories early in the research process. Writing successive memos keeps researchers involved in the analysis and helps them to increase the level of abstraction of their ideas.

> *If data are the building blocks of the developing theory, memos are the mortar – Stern (2007)*
>
> *Memos are uniquely complex research tools. They are both a methodological practice and a simultaneous exploration of processes in the social worlds of the research site. Memos are not intended to describe the social worlds of the researcher's data; instead, they conceptualize the data in narrative form. Remaining firmly grounded in the data, researchers use memos 'to create social reality' (Richardson 1998: 349) by discursively organizing and interpreting the social worlds of their respondents – Lempert (2007)*
>
> *When memoing a topic analytically, the researcher generates a set of categories, contrasts, comparisons, questions, and avenues for further consideration which are more abstract than the original topic – Lempert (2007)*

Methodological sensitivity: Methodological sensitivity might be defined as the skill or aptitude required by researchers in selecting, combining, and employing methods, techniques, and tools in actual research situations. Researchers can and need to develop this skill as a result of a combination of guidance from and working with other researchers; insightful study of available research methods, techniques, and tools; and learning from their own experience (Bryant 2017).

Methodologizing: The ways in which researchers link their actual approach to other methods – in the context of GTM-oriented research it involves … discussion of the scope of GTM; reference to philosophical issues such as induction, deduction; and concern with ontological and epistemological topics (Bryant 2017).

Mixed methods: *Briefly, mixed methods research or MMR requires the collection and integration of qualitative and quantitative data, logics, and philosophies, and multimethod research or MR encourages the collection of data using any two methods (e.g., qualitative and qualitative, quantitative and quantitative, or qualitative and quantitative). In a sense, MMR might be viewed as a subset of MR; however, leaders in the MMR movement disagree (e.g., Greene 2015) – Johnson and Walsh (2019)*

Multi-slice imaginings: *A process that involves identifying the layers of image that should be analyzed (levels of creation, structure, presentation and reception of image) – Konecki (2019)*

Objectivist grounded theory: A grounded theory approach in which the researcher takes the role of a neutral observer who remains separate from the research participants, analyses their world as an outside expert, and pursue theory construction. Although individual followers may examine their data collection practices, current leading proponents concentrate on emergent theory construction without preconception from data-gathering guidelines, research literature, and earlier theories. Most adhere to Glaser's ruling principles, 'All is data' (2001: 145) and 'trust in emergence' (2001: 1). Objectivist grounded theorists distinguish their approach from other approaches to qualitative research, which they often explicitly oppose. Objectivist grounded theorists seldom include the following concerns in their discussions of specific research projects and methodological approaches: the research situation, research relationships, representation of research participants, and the standpoints and subjectivity of the researcher. Objectivist grounded theory is a form of positivist qualitative research and thus subscribes to many of logic of the positivist tradition and to its central tenets concerning empiricism, generalizability, universality, abstraction, and parsimony.

Open coding: *Open coding is 'the process of breaking down, examining, comparing, conceptualizing, and categorizing data' (1990: 61) – Strauss and Corbin, quoted by Belgrave and Seide (2019)*

Positivism: An epistemology that subscribes to a unitary scientific method consisting of objective systematic observation and experimentation in an external world. Positivism relies on empiricism as the source of generalizations. The goal of positivistic inquiry is to discover and to establish generalizations that explain the studied phenomena and from which predictions can be made. Subsequently, experimentation and prediction can lead to scientific control over the studied phenomena.

Postmodernism: A theoretical turn that challenges the foundational assumptions of the Enlightenment with its beliefs in human reason, science, and progress through science. Postmodernists range from those who wish to acknowledge intuitive forms of knowing to those who call for nihilistic rejection of modern ways of knowing and of being in the world and their foundation in Enlightenment values.

Pragmatism: A North American philosophical tradition that views reality as characterized by indeterminacy and fluidity, and as open to multiple interpretations. Pragmatism assumes that people are active and creative. In pragmatist philosophy, meanings emerge through practical actions to solve problems, and through actions people come to know the world. Pragmatists see facts and values as linked rather than separate and truth as relativistic and provisional.

Rashomon effect: *There is never just one version of the narrative. The term itself is taken from the film in which a murder is described by four witnesses in four entirely contradictory ways. It is best encapsulated in this extract from* The Simpsons:

> **Marge:** *Come on, Homer. Japan will be fun! You liked* Rashomon.
>
> **Homer:** *That's not how I remember it Bryant (2019)*

Reflexivity: The researcher's scrutiny of the research experience, decisions, and interpretations in ways that bring the researcher into the process. Reflexivity includes examining how the researcher's interests, positions, and assumptions influence his or her inquiry. A reflexive stance informs how the researcher conducts his or her research, relates to the research participants, and represents them in written reports.

Research design: *Research design is a plan for collecting and analyzing evidence that will make it possible for the investigator to answer whatever questions he or she has posed. The design of an investigation touches almost all aspects of the research, from the minute details of data collection to the selection of the techniques of data analysis (Ragin, 1994: 191) – quoted by Flick (2019)*

Sampling: *We argue that sampling is not a procedure that is delegated for locating subjects who represent the population at the beginning of the study, as it is in quantitative inquiry. Rather, in qualitative inquiry, the goal of sampling is to represent the phenomenon. In grounded theory, it is a procedural tool that is integral to the entire research process, with the goal of attaining excellent data that enables to development and verification of an abstract and generalizable theory – Morse and Clark (2019)*

Sensitizing concept: *A sensitizing concept 'lacks such specification of attributes or bench marks and consequently it does not enable the user to move directly to the instance and its relevant content. Instead, it gives the user a general sense of reference and guidance in approaching empirical instances.' – Blumer, quoted by Bryant (2019)*

> *Sensitizing concepts do not obstruct our studies and insights, but on the contrary afford 'a general sense of reference and guidance in approaching empirical instances' – Blumer, quoted by Bryant (2019)*
>
> *'hundreds of our concepts – like culture, institutions, social structure, mores, and personality – are not definitive concepts but are sensitizing in nature. They lack precise reference and have no benchmarks which allow a clean-cut identification of a specific instance and of its content. Instead, they rest on a general sense of what is relevant.' – Blumer, quoted by Bryant (2019)*
>
> *Examples include feminism, culture, social injustice, indigeneity, domination, hegemony and emancipation – Bryant (2019)*
>
> *In some senses the term 'theory' was used largely as a sensitizing concept in the early GTM writings, but since then the term has been taken up and discussed in more substantive terms – Bryant (2019)*

Serendipity: *Glaser (1998: 15) describes the 'subsequent, sequential, simultaneous, serendipitous and scheduled' nature of grounded theory – Holton (2007)*

> *Reading widely opens a researcher to serendipitous discovery of new theoretical codes from other disciplines – Holton (2007)*
>
> *This procedure of theoretical sampling in no way interferes with a salient aspect of qualitative research: being ready for the serendipitous opportunity – Wiener (2007)*

Social constructionism: A theoretical perspective that assumes that people create social reality or realities through individual and collective actions. Rather than seeing the world as given, constructionists ask, how is it accomplished. Thus, instead of assuming realities in an external world – including global structures and local cultures – social constructionists study what people at a particular time and place take as real, how they construct their views and actions, when different constructions arise, whose constructions become taken as definitive, and how that process ensues. Symbolic interactionism is a constructionist perspective because it assumes that meanings and obdurate realities are the product of collective processes.

Storyline: *as an advanced analytical technique used in grounded theory research for the purpose of both integrating and articulating theory – Birks and Mills (2019)*

> *[T]he first and most extensive reference to storyline was made by Strauss and Corbin in their initial* Basics of Qualitative Research *text (Strauss & Corbin 1990). In this book, storyline was defined as 'the conceptualization of the story' (p. 116) as part of the selective coding process. In developing the storyline, these authors assert that the researcher moves from descriptive to analytical telling of the story evident in the data. Through presenting the storyline as a mechanism for moving the research from description to conceptualisation, Strauss and Corbin (1990) make a significant contribution to grounded theory – Birks and Mills (2019)*

Substantive grounded theory: A theoretical interpretation or explanation of a delimited problem in a particular area, such as family relationships, formal organizations, or education.

> *[SGT] not only provides a stimulus to a 'good idea', but it also gives an initial direction in developing relevant categories and properties and possible modes of integration [theoretical codes] (Glaser & Strauss 1967: 79)*
>
> *By substantive theory we mean theory developed for a substantive or empirical area of sociological inquiry, such as patient care, geriatric life styles, etc. … By formal theory we mean theory developed for a formal or conceptual area of sociological area such as status passage, stigma, deviant behavior, etc. (Glaser & Strauss, 1967: 177)*

Symbolic interactionism: A theoretical perspective derived from pragmatism that assumes that people construct selves, society, and reality through interaction. Because this perspective focuses on dynamic relationships between meaning and actions, it addresses the active processes through which people create and mediate meanings. Meanings arise out of actions, and in turn influence actions. This perspective assumes that individuals are active, creative, and reflective and that social life consists of processes.

Theoretical codes/coding: *Theoretical codes are tools for looking at a variable in an abstract rather than a substantive way – Stern (2007)*

> *According to Charmaz (2006), 'theoretical codes specify possible relationships between categories you have developed in your focused [substantive] coding' (p. 63) – Stern (2007)*
>
> *If one sets aside Glaser's inductivist rhetoric, his concepts of 'theoretical codes' and 'coding families' represent a way systematically to introduce theoretical knowledge into the coding process without 'forcing' preconceived categories on the data – Kelle (2007)*
>
> *However, Glaser makes clear elsewhere that theoretical concepts do not simply arise from the data alone but require careful 'theoretical coding' (that means: the categorizing of empirical data on the basis of previous theoretical knowledge) – Kelle (2007)*
>
> *Theoretical codes are terms which describe possible relations between substantive codes and thereby help to form theoretical models – Kelle (2007)*
>
> *theoretical codes 'weave the fractured story back together again' (Glaser 1978: 72) into 'an organized whole theory (Glaser 1998: 163)' – Hernandez, quoted by Bryant (2019)*

[T]he emergence of theoretical codes or categories from the data is dependent on the ability to grasp empirical phenomena in theoretical terms, or, in other words, on 'theoretical sensitivity', a competence that demands training and background in sociological theory (which also Glaser still conceded) – Kelle (2019)

At later stages of GTM-oriented research, the researcher(s) need to substantiate their categories and concepts by taking the findings back to the literature – this is in part what GTM writers refer to as Theoretical Coding (Bryant 2017).

Theoretical sampling: A type of grounded theory sampling in which the researcher aims to develop the properties of his or her developing categories or theory, not to sample randomly selected populations or to sample representative distributions of a particular population. To engage in theoretical sampling, the researcher must have already developed a tentative theoretical category from the data. When engaging in theoretical sampling, the researcher seeks people, events, or information to illuminate and define the properties, boundaries, and relevance of this category or set of categories. Because the purpose of theoretical sampling is to sample in order to develop the theoretical categories, conducting it can take the researcher across substantive areas.

Theoretical sampling is the process of data collection for generating theory whereby the analyst jointly collects, codes, and analyses his data and decides what data to collect next and where to find them, in order to develop his theory as it emerges (Glaser & Strauss 1967: 45).

theoretical sampling; that is, directing the data search to advance the developing theory – Stern (2007)

The main principle of theoretical sampling is that the emerging categories, and the researcher's increasing understanding of the developing theory, now direct the sampling – Morse (2007)

Theoretical saturation: Refers to the point at which gathering more data about a theoretical category reveals no new properties nor yields any further theoretical insights about the emerging grounded theory.

GTM specifies the point at which data gathering and analysis can be ended. This is when the researcher(s) can justify their view that there is sufficient data to substantiate their model – i.e., that the categories in their model are borne out by the data, and that further data drawn from their research context adds no further detail to the categories and concepts already articulated. Theoretical Saturation can be seen as a basis for claiming validation of a research project. This is not to claim that some definitive end- point has been reached (Bryant 2017).

Theoretical sensitivity: *In developing categories the sociologist should employ 'theoretical sensitivity', which means the ability to 'see relevant data' and to reflect upon empirical data material with the help of theoretical terms – Kelle (2007)*

Theoretical sorting: *Sorting helps the analyst integrate the theory – Stern (2007)*

According to Glaser (2005) sorting is a creative activity:

Tempting one's creativity is actuated by this process. Fear that one does not have creativity stops this type of sorting and causes the fleeing to computer retrieval of data on each category, resulting in full conceptual description [Glaser's term for research that fails to reach the theoretical level]. Hand sorting releases the creativity necessary to see a TC [theoretical code] in the memos, as the analyst constantly compares and asks where each memo goes for the best fit (p. 36) – quoted by Stern (2007)

Theory: *A famous metaphor of Hempel, a theory is a network of terms (following our terminology we would say 'categories') which 'floats, as it were, above the plane of observation and is anchored to it by rules of interpretation'. These rules of interpretation link certain points of the network 'with specific places in the plane of observation (…): From certain observational data, we may ascend, via an interpretive string, to some point in the theoretical network, thence proceed, via definitions and hypotheses, to other points, from which another interpretive string permits a descent to the plane of observation' – quoted by Kelle (2019)*

> *an abstract entity that aims 'to describe, explain, and enhance understanding of the world and, in some cases, to provide predictions of what will happen in the future and to give a basis for intervention and action' (Gregor 2006: 616) – quoted by Johnson and Walsh, and Urquhart (2019)*
>
> *there are 'different ways of defining "theory". These range from "general, etic (nomothetic) or particular, local, emic (idiographic) perspectives". The differences are largely derived from differing positions with regard to epistemology and ontology, so from a "positivist or post-positivist view" … a theory could be "a system of constructs and variables in which the constructs are related to each other by propositions and the variables are related to each other by hypotheses" (Bacharach 1989: 498).' For constructivists or interpretivists a 'theory could be an "approximation" of a complex reality (Weick 1995)' – Johnson and Walsh (2019)*

Theory of the Middle Range: *In* Discovery, *Glaser and Strauss drew on Merton's work (Merton 1949), in which he argued for 'theories of the middle range' – i.e., Theories that lie between the minor but necessary working hypotheses that evolve in abundance during day-to-day research and the all-inclusive systematic efforts to develop a unified theory that will explain all the observed uniformities of social behaviour, social organization and social change. (Merton, quoted by Glaser & Strauss 1967: 39) – quoted in Bryant (2019)*

Triangulation: *The main idea of triangulation is to extend the research by using several methods, differing theories or multiple researchers. The resulting extension of data and interpretations in the process is seen as a contribution to make research and results more credible and fruitfu. – Flick (2019)*

Notes

1 Indicated by either 2007 or 2019
2 The extracts from Charmaz's book are all taken from the second edition.

REFERENCES

Bruner, J. S., Goodnow, J. J. and Austin, G. A. (1986). *A Study of Thinking.* 2nd edition. New Brunswick, NJ: Transaction.

Bryant, A. (2017). *Grounded Theory and Grounded Theorizing: Pragmatism in Research Practice*. New York: Oxford University Press.

Bryant, A. & Charmaz, K. (Eds.) (2007). *The Sage Handbook of Grounded Theory.* London: Sage.

Charmaz, K. (2006 & 2014). *Constructing Grounded Theory* (1st and 2nd ed.). Thousand Oaks, CA: Sage.

Corbin, J., & Strauss, A. L. (2015). *Basics of Qualitative Research: Techniques and Procedures for Developing Grounded Theory (4th edition).* London: Sage.
Covan, E. K. (2007). The discovery of grounded theory in practice: The legacy of multiple mentors. In A. Bryant & K. Charmaz (Eds.), *The Sage Handbook of Grounded Theory* (pp. 58–74). London: Sage.
Denzin, N. (2007). Grounded theory and the politics of interpretation. In A. Bryant & K. Charmaz (Eds.), *The Sage Handbook of Grounded Theory* (pp. 454–471). London: Sage.
Dey, I. (2007). Grounding categories. In A. Bryant & K. Charmaz (Eds.), *The Sage Handbook of Grounded Theory* (pp. 167–190). London: Sage.
Gibson, B. (2007). Accommodating grounded theory. In A. Bryant & K. Charmaz (Eds.), *The Sage Handbook of Grounded Theory* (pp. 436–453). London: Sage.
Glaser, B. (1978). *Theoretical Sensitivity.* Mill Valley, CA: Sociology Press.
Glaser, B. (1992). *Emergence vs. Forcing: Basics of Grounded Theory Analysis.* Mill Valley, Ca: Sociology Press.
Glaser, B. (1998). *Doing Grounded Theory: Issues and discussions.* Mill Valley, Ca: Sociology Press.
Glaser, B. (2005). *The Grounded Theory Perspective III.* Mill Valley, Ca: Sociology Press.
Glaser, B. (2007). Doing Formal Theory. In A. Bryant & K. Charmaz (Eds.), *The Sage Handbook of Grounded Theory* (pp. 97–113). London: Sage.
Glaser, B., & Strauss, A. L. (1967). *The Discovery of Grounded Theory: Strategies for Qualitative Research.* Chicago, IL: Aldine.
Greene, J. C., (2015). Preserving distinctions within the multimethod and mixed methods research merger. In S. Hesse-Biber & R. B. Johnson (eds.) *Oxford handbook of multimethod and mixed methods research inquiry* (pp. 606-615). New York, NY: Oxford University Press.
Gregor, S. (2006). *The Nature of Theory in information Systems.* MIS Quarterly 30(3), 611–642
Hildenbrand, B. (2007). Mediating structure and interaction in Grounded Theory. In A. Bryant & K. Charmaz (Eds.), *The Sage Handbook of Grounded Theory* (pp. 539–564). London: Sage.
Hesse-Biber, S. (2007). Teaching Grounded Theory. In A. Bryant & K. Charmaz (Eds.), *The Sage Handbook of Grounded Theory* (pp. 311–338). London, Sage.
Holton, J. (2007). The coding process and its challenges. In A. Bryant & K. Charmaz (Eds.), *The Sage Handbook of Grounded Theory* (pp. 265–289). London: Sage.
Kearney, M. (2007). From the sublime to the meticulous. In A. Bryant & K. Charmaz (Eds.), *The Sage Handbook of Grounded Theory* (pp. 127–150). London: Sage.
Kelle, U. (2007). The development of categories: Different approaches in Grounded Theory. In A. Bryant & K. Charmaz (Eds.), *The Sage Handbook of Grounded Theory* (pp. 191–213). London: Sage.
Lempert, L. (2007). Asking questions of the data. In A. Bryant & K. Charmaz (Eds.), *The Sage Handbook of Grounded Theory* (pp. 245–264). London: Sage.
Locke, K. (2001). *Grounded Theory in Management Research.* London: Sage.
Locke, K. (2007). Rational control and irrational free-play. In A. Bryant & K. Charmaz (Eds.), *The Sage Handbook of Grounded Theory* (pp. 565–579). London: Sage.
Merton, R. K. (1949). *Social Theory and Social Structure*. New York: Free Press.
Morse, J. (2007). Sampling in Grounded Theory. In A. Bryant & K. Charmaz (Eds.), *The Sage Handbook of Grounded Theory* (pp. 229–244). London: Sage.
Ragin, C. C. (1994). *Constructing Social Research.* Thousand Oaks, CA: Pine Forge Press
Reichertz, J. (2007). Abduction: The logic of discovery in grounded theory. In A. Bryant & K. Charmaz (Eds.), *The Sage Handbook of Grounded Theory* (pp. 214–228). London: Sage.
Richardson, L. (1998). Writing: A Method of Inquiry. In Norman K. Denzin and Yvonna S. Lincoln (Eds.), *Collecting and Interpreting Qualitative Materials*. Thousand Oaks, CA: Sage, 345-371.
Star, S. L. (2007). Living Grounded Theory: Cognitive and emotional forms of pragmatism. In A. Bryant & K. Charmaz (Eds.), *The Sage Handbook of Grounded Theory* (pp. 75–93). London: Sage.
Stern, P. (2007). On solid ground: Essential properties for growing Grounded Theory. In A. Bryant & K. Charmaz (Eds.), *The Sage Handbook of Grounded Theory* (pp. 114–126). London: Sage.

Strauss A. L. (1987). *Qualitative Analysis for Social Scientists.* Cambridge: CUP.
Strauss A. L., & Corbin, J. (1990 & 1998). *Basics of Qualitative Research* (1st and 2nd ed.). Thousand Oaks, CA: Sage.
Urquhart, C. (2007). The evolving nature of Grounded Theory method. In A. Bryant & K. Charmaz (Eds.), *The Sage Handbook of Grounded Theory* (pp. 339–359). London: Sage.
Wiener, C. (2007). Making teams work in conducting Grounded Theory. In A. Bryant & K. Charmaz (Eds.), *The Sage Handbook of Grounded Theory* (pp. 293–310). London: Sage.

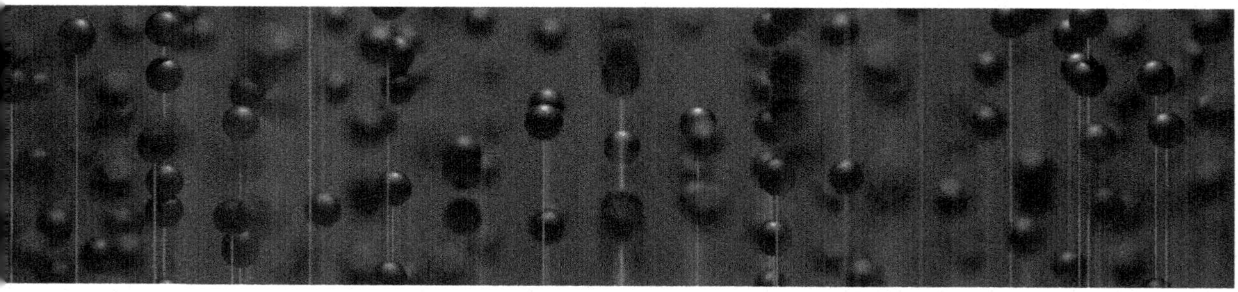

Index